EGON RONAY'S

CELLNET GUIDE

HOTELS &
RESTAURANTS
1988

**HOTELS, RESTAURANTS
AND INNS
GREAT BRITAIN AND
IRELAND**

*NEW HALL —
Q2*

EGON
RONAY'S
GUIDE

■ Establishment research is conducted by a team of full-time professional inspectors, who are trained to achieve common standards of judgement with as much objectivity as this field allows. Their professional identities are not disclosed until they seek information from the management after paying their bills. The Guide is independent in its editorial selection and does not accept advertising, payment or hospitality from establishments covered.

Egon Ronay's Guides
Second Floor, Greencoat House
Francis Street, London SW1P 1DH

EDITORIAL CONCEPT
Moyra Fraser
CHIEF COPY EDITOR
Michèle Roche
CHIEF COPYWRITER
Peter Long
RESEARCH EDITOR
Coreen Williams
EDITORIAL CONTRIBUTORS
Joy Langridge
Roy Johnstone
BARGAIN BREAKS RESEARCHER
John Vocking
DESIGN
David Warner/Augustine Studios
COVER DESIGN
Spero Communications Design Ltd
MARKETING AND SPONSORSHIP CONSULTANTS
Spero Marketing Consultancy Ltd
HEAD OF EDITORIAL
Barbara Littlewood
PUBLISHER
William Halden

Cartography revised by Intermap PS Ltd
All road maps are based on the Ordnance Survey Maps, with the permission of the Controller of HM Stationery Office. Crown copyright reserved. All town plans are based on aerial photographs.

The contents of this book are believed correct at the time of printing. Nevertheless, the publisher can accept no responsibility for errors or omissions or changes in the details given.

Distributed in the United Kingdom by the Publishing Division of The Automobile Association, Fanum House, Basingstoke, Hampshire RG21 2EA and overseas by the British Tourist Authority, Thames Tower, Black's Road, London W6 9EL.

ISBN 0 86145 627 0

AA Ref 50911

Typeset in Great Britain by William Clowes Limited, Beccles and London

Printed in Great Britain by Jarrold and Sons Ltd, Norwich

CONTENTS

Upper crust.

Wedgwood

Presentation is everything. Especially when you present your guests with Candlelight in fine bone china.

PLEASE WRITE TO JOSIAH WEDGWOOD & SONS LTD., BARLASTON, STOKE-ON-TRENT, STAFFORDSHIRE ST12 9ES OR 32–34 WIGMORE ST., LONDON W1H 0HU.

Town plans including sights and establishments

Summary of Coverage

This Guide includes the following number of establishments:

Hotels	1552
Inns	100
Restaurants	982
Total	2634

With a portable cellphone, you need never be away from your work.

(Even if you are out to lunch)

With a portable cellphone in your pocket or a transportable by your side, you are always able to get that urgent message, or make that vital call.

It means always being in touch – even when you are away from your desk. And being on hand to make the key decisions when they need to be made.

If your work takes you out of the office, you need to find out more about how Cellnet can help you.

For further information or a free demonstration, call 0800 400 433 today.

Cellnet
THE CELLPHONE NETWORK

HOW TO USE THIS GUIDE

ORDER OF LISTINGS

London and London Airports appear first and are in alphabetical order by establishment name. Listings outside London are in alphabetical order by location within divisions of England, Scotland, Wales, Channel Islands, Isle of Man, Northern Ireland and the Republic.

MAP REFERENCES

Map references are to the map section at the back of the book or to a town plan printed with the entries.

SYMBOLS

HOTELS

Percentage Ratings

According to their percentage rating, hotels are classified as

De luxe 85–100%
Grade 1 70–84%
Grade 2 50–69%

Some entries are ungraded because of major construction or refurbishment programmes.

■ The percentage shown on a hotel entry is an individual rating arrived at after careful testing, inspection and calculation according to our unique grading system.

■ We assess hotels on 19 factors, which include the quality of service and the public rooms – their cleanliness, comfort, state of repair and general impression.

Bedrooms are looked at for size, comfort, cleanliness and decor. The exterior of the building, efficiency of reception, conduct and appearance of the staff and room service are among other factors. The percentage is arrived at by comparing the total marks given for the 19 factors with the maximum the hotel could have achieved.

■ The size of the hotels and the prices charged are not considered in the grading, nor is the food. If we recommend meals in a hotel or inn, a separate entry is made for its dining room.

Price Categories

These are based on the current price, including VAT (also service if applicable), for a double room for two occupants with private bath and cooked breakfast.

£A	over £120
£B	£90–£120
£C	£70–£90
£D	£55–£70
£E	£38–£55
£F	under £38
H	Hotel entries are identified by the letter 'H' printed before the establishment name.
HR	Hotels with restaurants that have a separate entry are identified by the letters 'HR'.
I	Inns are identified by the letter 'I', and are not graded. We distinguish them from hotels by their more modest nature, usually with respect to the day rooms. For our purposes, an inn is normally either a pub with hotel-style accommodation or a small hotel with a bar and the atmosphere of a pub.
R	Restaurants are identified by the letter 'R' or, if they also have accommodation, by the letters '**RR**' (see also p. 111).

E

We print the letter 'E' after the percentage to denote an Executive Hotel. This applies to establishments graded 70% or more that combine luxury with the facilities required by business executives. See also p. 86.

Where possible we print the name of an owner-manager, or a manager who has been in charge for at least five years.

Room service

If an establishment provides no room service, we print *None. All day* and *24 hours* give the hours during which room service is available. The exact nature of the service – whether you can get a sandwich or a full meal, whether at any time or only at mealtimes – will vary from one place to another.

   Considered by the management as suitable for wheelchairs.

Credit

Credit cards accepted by the establishment.

RESTAURANTS

★
★★
★★★

We award one to three stars for excellence of cooking. One star represents cooking much above average, two outstanding cooking, and three the best in the land.

■ We only include restaurants where the cooking comes up to our minimum standards, however attractive the place may be in other respects. We take into account how well the restaurant achieves what it sets out to do as reflected in the menu, decor, prices, publicity, atmosphere – factors that add up to some sort of expectation.

ẅ
ẅ ẅ
ẅ ẅ ẅ

These refer to the degree of luxury in a restaurant and have nothing to do with the quality of the cooking.

This shows that the cooking is done by the owner or a member of the family.

Ꭹ

We use the wine glass symbol to indicate a house wine that is judged well chosen by our inspectors.

▭

This symbol represents a wine list that is outstanding – the only grading we award this year. Also see page 36.

LVs

Indicates an establishment where Luncheon Vouchers are welcomed.

☺

Indicates a restaurant with a good cheeseboard

About £..... for two

The approximate cost (except in the Budget Section) of a three-course meal including wine, coffee, service and VAT. This is based on a choice from average-priced dishes on the menu and includes one of the least expensive bottles of wine.

Parties

The maximum number for a meal in a separate room.

CELLNET AND EGON RONAY'S GUIDE

Cellnet and the Egon Ronay's Guide to Hotels, Restaurants and Inns are now entering the second year of partnership together. We have already proved over the past year that the combination of the UK's premier mobile communications system and the UK's premier reference listing of the best in accommodation and cuisine can provide innumerable benefits to the busy traveller.

As someone who has cause to use both, I can vouch for the high quality that is maintained through hard work on the part of Cellnet's engineers and the Guide's Inspectors whose recommendations fill this book. I believe that this is because the philosophy behind the efforts of both groups of experts is precisely the same - to provide the best and most useful service possible to our customers and readers.

Cellnet is proud to be involved with the Guide and to have been able to suggest some specific sections which will be of use to people on the move. We are continuing with the Off-the-Motorway Guide to Hotels and Restaurants and the Cellnet Theatre Guide which proved so popular in 1987. This means that within one volume, which can easily be kept in the glove compartment of your car, you have all the information you need to plan a complete night out whether for business entertaining or purely for pleasure.

I know that there are many Cellnet customers who already find this Guide a useful addition to their 'mobile' reference library. To those readers who do not yet have a cellphone can I offer my sympathies for those occasions when you find one of the excellent Restaurants listed within these covers is full - perhaps because you were unable to phone ahead and book a table. To prevent this may I recommend to you the Cellnet section of the Guide (pages 24 - 30) which will provide you with all the details of how Cellnet can keep you ahead of the crowd.

Colin Davis

Colin Davis
Managing Director
Cellnet

WHEN PLASTIC MAKES A POOR IMPRESSION . . .

It's as though your best friend has turned round and hit you.

First the surprise, then the pain and then: Why? For a Guide inspector, credit and charge cards are our best friends. No bundle of notes – even £50 ones – can pay our sort of bills. Try finding the cash to meet a bill of £290 for an overnight bed, breakfast and dinner for one at a London hotel or £160 for a restrained dinner for two at a Mayfair restaurant – just two of the bills which have brought tears even to our eyes recently.

When you need that sort of money once or even twice a day then you have to rely on, and trust, plastic cards. You quickly realise that 'our flexible friend' is not just one of a variety of advertising slogans.

This year that friendship has gone sour. The rift has occurred because we have been victims of a growing conspiracy between hotels and restaurants and the card companies to cut corners on the way transactions are handled.

Take booking in at an hotel for instance. We have all become used to handing in a credit card at the check-in so that an impression can be taken and the slip signed as you check out. This is sensible, and at least it protects the hotel from a moonlight flit through the fire exit. However, hotels are becoming more aggressive. Time and again on checking in we have had demands not only to hand our card over for an impression to be taken, but also to sign a blank slip.

One inspector, like most of us, has a totally justified aversion to this under any circumstances. Taking an impression of his card is one thing, leaving the total blank is another.

He faced the situation when booking into one of the most famous luxury hotels in the North. In this case the inspector signed his slip but only when a room rate total had been filled in. Then came the problem of charges. The hotel refused to open up a phone line until a deposit was paid. The inspector had to produce a £10 note.

Unknown to the hotel, the inspector was in fact making a special visit because the management had complained bitterly about its entry in the Guide. It claimed that the £6 million it spent on improvements deserved an increased rating. It didn't get it. What point is there in 158 redecorated bathrooms when guests are treated like this?

The card companies are becoming equally careless with our cash. The Chief Inspector paid by card for a stay at New York's most famous hotel. When he returned to London from his world-wide trip, he found a letter from the hotel saying that two orange juices, price $16, had been omitted from his bill. The credit card slip, the hotel announced, had been altered above his signature to include the charge.

Naturally, the now-angry Chief Inspector wrote to the card company asking why they had accepted an altered slip. They promptly adjusted his account – without any apology.

It could not happen here, I hear you say.

But it does. The inspector, who was still smarting from his experience in the North, was staying in a Belgravia hotel. He paid the £200 for his one-night single with his credit card. Six weeks later when his account arrived there was not just one slip but two. The second showed £7 for 'room service' and instead of a signature, the hotel had simply written on it 'signature on file'.

Again it required an angry letter to the credit card company reminding them of their responsibilities before the charge was withdrawn and an apology received. Needless to say, in not one of these cases did the hotel ever present a claim – or an apology.

Restaurants are also getting the taste for hiding behind the card companies. We recently discovered that a country restaurant we rate highly now demands a credit card number when you ring to make a booking. They also ask for a deposit. What they conveniently forget to say is that they make out a separate slip for the amount of the deposit and present it immediately to the card company, even if you're arriving the next day.

The money spent on hotels and restaurants through credit cards is now measured in £billions. Is it really too much to ask that, with this amount of spending at stake, much of it on impulse, we should be treated as valued guests by hotels and restaurants even if we are clutching plastic rather than pounds? And that the cards companies should protect much more closely what is, after all, our money? They overwhelm us with slogans but at this rate can they really claim: That will do nicely, thank you?

Behind the smokescreen

You will have noticed that more and more hotels are offering 'Non-smoking bedrooms'. As there is nothing worse for non-smokers than checking into a room with a still-lingering presence of tobacco, this move is overdue.

Cynically, as the year progressed, we wondered: What happens if a smoker arrives at reception and the only rooms left are 'non-smokers'? What prompted this was the claim by one hotel chain that 15 per cent of its rooms were non-smoking. Yet whenever we made a booking over the phone we were not asked whether we required a smoking or non-smoking room.

So how is it possible for the allocation of rooms to be left until guests arrive at the reception desk? For three months we researched this puzzle. To every hotel we visited that boasted non-smoking bedrooms we posed the question: 'What happens if . . . ?'

All but one admitted that, if this situation arose, they would let a non-smoking room to a smoker.

Since some of our inspectors are smokers and the majority are not, we were able to research both sides of the question. The result: every member of the team found himself (or herself) in a non-smoking room at some time this year – without any request to refrain from smoking. And non-smokers are still wondering why it is that the non-smoking rooms are always furthest away from reception.

Taking care . . .

Encouraging signs of increased awareness of the need for hygiene have been observed in hotels and restaurants this year. The AIDS scare may have led to extreme measures –

closures of jacuzzis, free condoms on pillows instead of good-night chocolates and so on – but it has also led to much greater care and more stringent controls by owners and managers.

One serious shortcoming still needs to be eradicated, however. It is the habit that chambermaids have of washing up the bedroom crockery in the washbasin and then drying it with used guest towels. All of us have seen this time and time again and it really must be stamped out.

Eau dear . . .

Overcharging by hotels and restaurants, particularly in London, has been another problem this year. Nowhere is it more marked than in the price charged for Perrier water. We have found that £1.50 for a 330 ml bottle is almost standard (mark-up 400 per cent) and the top charge for a 1 litre bottle, in an Indian restaurant, was £3.50 (mark-up 500 per cent).

. . . what can . . .

Last year we detailed our search for fresh orange juice.

This actually happened:

Chief Inspector: 'Do you have freshly squeezed orange juice?'

Waiter: 'Yes, sir.'

Chief Inspector: 'How fresh?'

Waiter: 'Fresh out of the packet.'

. . . the matter be!

Finally, an award for Customer of the Year. He was a particularly nasty and difficult overseas visitor who had dined far too well. At the end of the meal he called over the wine waiter and asked him to recommend a good port.

The waiter respectfully suggested he try Southampton.

WILLIAM HALDEN
PUBLISHER

Good Morning, Britain . . .

It should be the perfect start to a day: a traditional breakfast served amid the grandeur of a British hotel dining room.

For most of us, at home clutching our bowls of muesli, it's an experience that only happens on holidays or business trips.

For the Guide's inspectors, it is how they start every working day. And, they report, it is a depressing experience. This, they say, is typical.

On entering the dining room, the first challenge is to find a table that is clean and cleared – the best tables are those by the window but they are still laid for the previous night's dinner. When staff finally reach you, they are grumpy and barely awake. You start by ordering coffee – if it's real, you find it is warmed up from the night before or, if it is frothy and piping hot, it's instant.

You then realise that the hotel has changed from service to buffet style. If the display is still intact, then the selection of cereals, rolls and juices begins to lift your spirits. But when you return for the main course your hopes are dashed – fried eggs, still cooking under overhead lights and stuck to the plate; scrambled eggs merged into one solid lump; rashers of bacon glued to one another. Even the toast is unevenly cooked and left to go cold.

And when you complain, management say: 'You should have come down when it looked nice.'

AN EGON RONAY'S GUIDE ONLY INCLUDES THE BEST.

AWARDS FOR EXCELLENCE

Each year the Guide selects a Hotel and a Restaurant of the Year, chosen on the basis of consistent excellence and/or outstanding enterprise. There are three finalists for each award, and the winners for 1988 will be announced in early December at the Guide's celebrity launch, where they will be presented with unique Wedgwood plaques which will be theirs to keep. Made of Queensware, these plaques will feature, as pictured here, a handpainted view of each winning establishment.

The most recent winners, starting with 1987, have been:

HOTEL OF THE YEAR

Homewood Park
Freshford

Inn on the Park
London W1

Hambleton Hall
Oakham

Cromlix House
Dunblane

Ston Easton Park
Ston Easton

RESTAURANT OF THE YEAR

Walnut Tree Inn
Abergavenny

Le Manoir aux Quat' Saisons
Great Milton

Chez Nico
London SW8

Dorchester Grill Room
London W1

La Tante Claire
London SW3

HOTEL OF THE YEAR 1988

Our finalists for 1988 are as follows, listed alphabetically:

THE GORING HOTEL
London SW1

One of London's few family-run luxury hotels, probably the best, offering outstanding standards of personal service in relaxed surroundings. The hotel has long been a favourite meeting place for those in S.W.1, and the comfortable lounge and bar (the latter overlooking a delightful garden) are havens of rest and peace. Bedrooms, too, are splendidly appointed.

PARK HOTEL KENMARE
Co. Kerry, Republic of Ireland

Unashamedly, we shortlist this elegant hotel again, simply because it is one of the best. Francis Brennan is a genial host, and together with his marvellous staff offers Irish hospitality at its most delightful in magnificent surroundings. Rooms and public areas are models of good taste and style, whilst housekeeping standards throughout are exemplary.

SUMMER LODGE
Evershot, Dorset

Margaret and Nigel Corbett run a really homely country house hotel in well-tended gardens on the edge of a Dorset village. Apart from their fine collection of cheese dishes (to be found in every room), furnishings throughout create a lovely atmosphere, and the personal touches are all complemented by the excellent staff. Not least amongst the hotel's attractions are the superb breakfasts.

RESTAURANT OF THE YEAR 1988

EGON RONAY'S GUIDE

Our finalists for 1988 are as follows, listed alphabetically:

GAY HUSSAR
London W1

For 35 years, septuagenarian Victor Sassie (a lovable rascal with the ladies!) has been presiding over his Soho restaurant, famous not only for its illustrious clientele, but also, and quite rightly, for its satisfying food. You need a good appetite to make the most of the robust Hungarian specialities, and if in doubt ask the wise and worldly staff for recommendations as to what to choose.

MORELS
Haslemere, Surrey

Consistency is the keynote at Mary-Anne and Jean-Yves Morel's pretty restaurant tucked away in stockbroker belt. As befits a husband and wife partnership, teamwork is of the essence – Jean's interesting and ambitious menu, though not overlong, offers ample variety at reasonable prices while Mary-Anne provides exactly the right sort of service with the help of young French waiters.

RESTAURANT NINETEEN
Bradford, West Yorkshire

Self-taught chef Stephen Smith and his front-of-house partner Robert Barbour are quietly dedicated in running this candlelit restaurant situated in a Victorian house. Bradford, a city not previously known for its gastronomic excellence, is in debt to them for being able to boast such a fine restaurant. Meals are memorable, from the nibbles and home-baked bread to subtly seasoned, delicately sauced main dishes and some wonderful puddings.

STARRED RESTAURANTS

THREE STAR RESTAURANTS

LONDON

La Tante Claire, SW3

ENGLAND

Great Milton: Le Manoir aux Quat' Saisons
  Restaurant

TWO STAR RESTAURANTS

LONDON

L'Arlequin, SW8
The Dorchester, The Terrace, W1
Le Gavroche, W1
Inigo Jones, WC2
Inter-Continental Hotel, Le Soufflé, W1
Simply Nico, SW1

ENGLAND

Bray-on-Thames: Waterside Inn
Staddle Bridge: McCoy's Restaurant
Storrington: Manleys

SCOTLAND

Peat Inn: The Peat Inn

ONE STAR RESTAURANTS

LONDON

Alastair Little, W1
The Connaught Restaurant, W1
The Dorchester, Grill Room, W1
Gay Hussar, W1
Harveys, SW17

Moycullen ●

● Shanagarry

Ahakista ●

Guernsey

France

CHANNEL ISLANDS Jersey

GREAT MILTON ● Best cooking in the British Isles ★★★
Storrington ● ★★ Outstanding Cooking
Canterbury ● ★ Cooking much above average

Ullapool

Port Appin
Kilchrenan
Crinan
Dunblane
Linlithgow
Peat Inn
Gullane

Portrush

Dunderry

Bray

Ullswater
Grasmere
Staddle Bridge

Ilkley
Pool-in-Wharfedale
Bradford
Huddersfield

Wilmslow
Bakewell
Nantwich

Oakham

Wymondham
Bramp
Fressingfield
Stonham

Hockley Heath
Leamington Spa
Malvern
Corse Lawn
Northleach
Abergavenny
Stroud
Oxford
Cricklade
Streatley-
on-Thames
Yattendon
Bristol
Bath
Shinfield
Freshford
Stockbridge
Taunton
Gillingham
Stuckton
Lymington
Chagford
Gulworthy
New Milton
Dartmouth
Broxted
Old Hatfield
GREAT
MILTON
Maidenhead
Bray-on-
Thames
LONDON
Windsor
Ascot
Canterbury
Haslemere
Romsey
Tunbridge Wells
East Grinstead
Storrington

21

© 1987 Egon Ronay's Guides
Crown Copyright Reserved

Inn on the Park, Four Seasons Restaurant, W1
Ken Lo's Memories of China, SW1
Le Mazarin, SW1
Le Meridien Piccadilly, Oak Room, W1
Odins, W1
Le Poulbot, EC2
Rue St Jacques, W1

ENGLAND

Ascot: Royal Berkshire Restaurant
Bakewell: Fischer's
Bath: Priory Hotel Restaurant
Bath: Royal Crescent Hotel Restaurant
Bradford: Restaurant Nineteen
Brampton: Old Rectory
Bristol: Les Semailles
Broxted: Whitehall Hotel Restaurant
Canterbury: Restaurant Seventy Four
Chagford: Gidleigh Park Hotel Restaurant
Corse Lawn: Corse Lawn House Hotel
   Restaurant
Cricklade: Whites
Dartmouth: Bistro 33
Dartmouth: Carved Angel
East Grinstead: Gravetye Manor Restaurant
Freshford: Homewood Park Restaurant
Fressingfield: Fox & Goose
Gillingham: Stock Hill House Restaurant
Grasmere: White Moss House Restaurant
Gulworthy: Horn of Plenty
Haslemere: Morels
Hockley Heath: Nuthurst Grange Restaurant
Huddersfield: Weavers Shed
Ilkley: Box Tree Restaurant
Leamington Spa: Mallory Court Restaurant
Lymington: Provence
Maidenhead: Fredrick's Hotel Restaurant
Malvern: Croque-en-Bouche
Nantwich: Rookery Hall Restaurant
New Milton: Chewton Glen Hotel, Marryat Room
Northleach: Old Woolhouse
Oakham: Hambleton Hall Restaurant
Old Hatfield: Salisbury

Oxford: Le Petit Blanc
Pool-in-Wharfedale: Pool Court
Romsey: Old Manor House
Shinfield: L'Ortolan
Stockbridge: Sheriff House
Stonham: Mr Underhill's
Streatley-on-Thames: Swan Hotel Restaurant
Stroud: Oakes
Stuckton: The Three Lions
Taunton: Castle Hotel Restaurant
Tunbridge Wells: Thackeray's House
Ullswater: Sharrow Bay Hotel Restaurant
Wilmslow: Stanneylands Hotel Restaurant
Windsor: Oakley Court Hotel, Oak Leaf Room
Wymondham: Adlard's
Yattendon: Royal Oak Hotel Restaurant

SCOTLAND

Crinan: Crinan Hotel, Lock 16 Restaurant
Dunblane: Cromlix House Restaurant
Gullane: La Potinière
Kilchrenan: Ardanaiseig Restaurant
Linlithgow: Champany Inn Restaurant
Port Appin: Airds Hotel Restaurant
Ullapool: Altnaharrie Inn

WALES

Abergavenny: Walnut Tree Inn

NORTHERN IRELAND

Portrush: Ramore

REPUBLIC OF IRELAND

Ahakista: Shiro
Bray: Tree of Idleness
Dunderry: Dunderry Lodge Restaurant
Moycullen: Drimcong House
Shanagarry: Ballymaloe House Restaurant

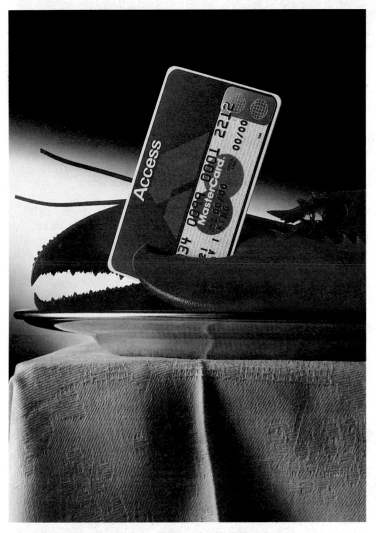

Do you really hold the best card?

More restaurants and hotels throughout Britain accept Access than any other credit, charge or dining card. Surprising isn't it?

So if you really want the best choice of the best food, perhaps you should find out more about Britain's leading credit card.

For further details write to us at Access, Southend-on-Sea, SS99 0BB.

Access puts you in control.

ABOUT CELLNET

In this guide we hope to provide some of the answers to questions you may have about cellular mobile communications – what it is, how it works and how it can benefit *you* as a user.

Cellular Mobile Communications is a remarkable development in communications technology that enables you to make or receive telephone calls to or from a phone in your car, briefcase or pocket. You are directly connected with almost any other telephone in the world – it's as easy to use as your home or office phone.

Telecommunications have become an essential feature of modern business – and of modern life in general. Now advanced cellular technology provides the means for you to keep in constant touch with clients, business contacts or colleagues wherever you may be – with the ease of an ordinary telephone.

Cellular telephones (cellphones) using the Cellnet system are already essential tools of modern business.

Just how essential is clear whenever you are away from the office. Being out of touch, even for a few hours, can pose real problems. It means delay, wasted time, wasted journeys and wasted effort – which all means wasted money and lost profits.

So mobile cellphones using the Cellnet system can be as valuable to you as the phone on your desk. Who needs mobile communications? In short – you do.

Proposed Cellnet coverage at mid 1988

Cellnet now covers most of the country. The Cellnet system is continuing to grow month by month and is already the largest integrated cellular system in the world.

In the London area – which carries the heaviest number of calls – Cellnet has the highest capacity cellular system in the world which is specially designed to give top quality service to all cellphones, including hand portables.

How does it work?

The system is called 'cellular' because the country has been divided up into small areas known as 'cells', each one equipped with its own radio transmitter/receiver. Careful planning of the use and re-use of radio frequencies has ensured that a cellphone user, moving from cell to cell, can continue a call without any perceptible interruption. The design allows Cellnet to provide hundreds of channels across the country so that thousands of business people are able to enjoy the benefits of comprehensive calls.

The cellular system uses a network of base stations (cell sites) which have their own dedicated radio channels. These cells are spread across the country (see map). Wherever you are on the network, you are close to a cell site – so your cellphone, large or small, will give high-quality service.

When a call is made it is transmitted to the cell in which you are travelling, which in turn links into a digital exchange connected directly into the worldwide telephone system – allowing you to talk to almost every telephone in the world – including other cellphones.

System Features

A cellphone can do many things which a conventional phone cannot yet achieve.

The following are all available as **standard** features with every cellphone:

- Call Forwarding ● No Answer Transfer ● Divert on Busy ● Call Waiting
- Three Party Conference ● Selective Call Barring

What Types of Cellphone are Available?

Car Mounted Cellphones

These are permanently installed in vehicles. All new types offer hands-free operation enabling the driver to keep both hands on the wheel, and eyes on the road, even while talking. Car cellphones operate from the vehicle battery and offer the best possible coverage on the Cellnet System.

Transportable Cellphones

Transportable cellphones with long-lasting battery packs are ideal for on site use as temporary 'fixed' phones. For anyone whose work involves travelling from site to site: photographers, film crews, haulage contractors, farmers, engineers, surveyors, plumbers, having an on site phone is vital for ordering supplies and arranging visits. A transportable will fit the bill.

Portable Cellphones

Portable cellphones, small enough to fit into a briefcase, are ideal for travellers who work away from their cars, particularly in an urban context. The portable fits into your pocket or briefcase and a simple adaptor can be fitted to the car to make it an in-car cellphone also.

Can Cellnet Make a Computer Mobile?

Being away from your office means being away from your computer database. If this is an important part of your business it can be essential that you have ready access to your computer. Cellnet have developed Celldata which allows all kinds of data transmission over the Cellnet system. With the appropriate modem and a portable terminal, Celldata enables the transmission of Telex and Facsimile, interface with mainframe or portable computers or access to Prestel and other public services.

Private Wire

Private Wire has been developed by Cellnet to cater for the needs of customers using a large number of cellphones who would wish to integrate their mobile communications system with their office switchboard. Private Wire makes the cellphones extensions of the switchboard; and for large users can save a considerable amount of time and money.

Cellnet 600 Messaging and Messaging **Plus** are services designed to give our customers even more control over their personal communications and increase efficiency to the point at which **all** calls received can be dealt with within minutes. 600 Messaging linked to a cellphone completes a total voice communications package which gives absolute freedom of movement to you. Not only can you be released from the bond of your office phone but with 600 Messaging you can also leave your cellphone and still receive messages from colleagues deposited in your voice mailbox – making you contactable at any time, in any place.

Cellnet 600 Messaging incorporates these Key Features:

Combination of Cellular communications, Voice Mail and Alerting services to provide an integrated personal communications package.

Distributed messaging network ensuring a resilient system catering for all eventualities.

Flexible service which can link into existing communications packages, including cellphones and pagers, or provide a complete system with Cellnet's personal alerter.

How it works – Simply

Messages can be deposited on your voice mailbox by callers diverted automatically to your unique 600 Mailbox number from your cellphone, ensuring that unanswered calls are routed to your messaging system. Calls can also be made direct to your mailbox if the caller knows its number. Messages can then be retrieved using your high security PIN code from a cellphone or normal telephone.

Not Only – But Also

This then, in essence, is the Cellnet 600 Messaging service, a 24 hour personal answering service which is totally automatic and completely under your direct supervision and control. This, however, is by no means the end of the story. The 600 Messaging Service allows you:

● 48 Message storage space ● 60-second message length ● 72 hour message storage ● Record and forward messages to another mailbox ● Message editing ● 'Timed Delivery' and 'Limited Life' Messages to be delivered at a pre-programmed time and lasting a preset duration. ● Extensive help throughout operation through voice menu at every stage providing instructions and guidance. ● High security Personal Identification Numbers ensuring total privacy. ● Optional retrieve only number.

Further Information

For further information about Cellnet and details of prices and products available or a demonstration contact your local Cellnet Dealer or call free on 0800 400433.

Cellnet
THE CELLPHONE NETWORK

Free Guide Updates

To be sure of receiving free updates of Egon Ronay's Cellnet Guide recommendations, together with information about Cellnet, please complete and return the
coupon below or, if you prefer, ring 0800 400 433 giving the necessary details.

The updates are published exclusively in Cellnet's customer magazine Selection and
your name will be added to our distribution list for future issues.

Please cut along the perforation and send to:

Cellnet
Freepost BS3333
Bristol
BS1 4YP

Please tick the appropriate box:

☐ Please send me information about Cellnet and future copies
of Selection

☐ I am an existing Cellnet user but do not receive copies of
Selection. Please add my name to your distribution list. My
cellphone number is 0860 ☐☐☐☐☐☐

Name_____

Position/Title_____

Company_____

Nature of Business_____

Address_____

_____

Postcode_____Business Tel_____

THEY APPRECIATE THE CHOICE

–TAKE IT AS RED

The secret of **Nescafé Gold Blend** decaffeinated is that the caffeine is extracted naturally <u>before</u> the beans are golden roasted – no more than 0.3% caffeine remains. The coffee is then ground, filtered and freeze dried, just the rich taste and aromas of our selection of the finest coffees including superb mild arabicas are left to be enjoyed. Available in 500g resealable catering cans, 100g jars and individual one cup sachets.

Nescafé and **Gold Blend** are registered trade marks to designate Nestlé's instant coffees.

The Nestlé Company Ltd, Foodservice Division, St. George's House, Croydon, Surrey CR9 1NR Telephone 01-686 3333

SHARE OUR SECRET.

CELLAR OF THE YEAR

The perfect wine list is a notional ideal, but we look for something pretty near it in those we grade *outstanding*.

Such a list should offer a fine selection of exciting wines: if you were to close your eyes, stick a pin in the list at random, you should find a wine that is a good example of its type. The overriding criterion of an outstanding cellar is the inherent excellence of each selected wine: a Bourgogne Pinot Noir, ready to drink, from a first-rate grower is infinitely preferable to an immature Nuits St Georges from an average *négociant*.

A serious list should offer a well-balanced selection of fairly priced wines from the correct, though not necessarily the most fashionable, vintages for current drinking. Clarets and Rhônes should be sufficiently mature, but wines like Muscadet, Beaujolais and Dolcetto should be young and fresh.

A comprehensive coverage of wines from around the world is desirable, but it is less important than the imaginative shaping of the list to suit the restaurant's style of cooking – the admirable Bahn Thai restaurants in London, for example, currently have a fine range of Gewürztraminers, ideal partners for spicy food.

The restaurateur also has a responsibility to change and update his list regularly, in particular, weeding out dud bottles and those which are past their best.

Our wine experts nosed their way through hundreds of lists to select the final candidates for Cellar of the Year. Past winners of the award have been disbarred but it must be said that outstanding wine lists such as those of the White Horse Inn in Sussex and Gidleigh Park in Devon, still set standards by which others are judged.

EGON RONAY'S NOILLY PRAT
Cellar of the Year

THE PANEL IN VINTAGE FORM
From left to right
William Halden: Publisher, Egon
Ronay's Guides; David Rutherford,
OBE: Deputy Chairman, Wine and
Spirit Association; Michael Edwards:
Wine Writer, Egon Ronay's Guides;
Mark Elliott: Product Group Manager,
Noilly Prat; Andrew Eliel: Chief
Inspector, Egon Ronay's Guides.

Here is the list of the regional winners:

LONDON
Pollyanna's
London SW11
A memorable list with a sure eye for real quality and value, not transient fashion. Very strong in fine Bordeaux with eight vintages of Château Gruaud-Larose, St Julien including 1964, 1966 and 1970.

SOUTH OF ENGLAND
Gravetye Manor
East Grinstead, Sussex
An exemplary classic list, meticulously annotated as to provenance and grower. Particularly fine 1976 German wines. Go now before limited stocks are exhausted: Maximin Grünhäuser Abtsberg Auslese (von Schubert), Wehlener Sonnenuhr Auslese Lange Goldkapsel (J.J. Prüm).

WEST COUNTRY
Castle Hotel
Taunton, Somerset
An extensive, impressively chosen list of classic and New World wines, impeccably annotated. Particular gems include Acacia Chardonnay, Carneros 1985, Penfold's Grange Hermitage 1976, Château Latour 1961 and Hermitage 'La Chapelle' 1961.

HEART OF ENGLAND
Bell Inn
Aston Clinton, Buckinghamshire
A fine very well-balanced cellar with a powerful showing of fine clarets. Such classics as Châteaux Beychevelle 66, la Mission-Haut-Brion 66, Grand-Puy-Lacoste 61 and Lafite 53 are reasonably priced.

MIDLANDS
Old Beams
Waterhouses, Staffordshire
A keenly priced, concise list, remarkable for the excellent flair of selection. Clarets range from Château Pichon Baron 1979

(a steal at £16.85) to the magnificent Château Ausone 1976, and the Zind-Humbrecht Alsace wines are also exceptionally good.

EAST OF ENGLAND
The Starr
Great Dunmow, Essex
An impeccably presented list with helpful, informative comments. Bordeaux and burgundy offer real value: Château Chasse-Spleen 1979 (£15.45) Château Talbot 1975 (£25.50) Les Forts de Latour 1970 (£36.00) Château Léoville-Las Cases 1970 (£49.00) Morey-St Denis, Dujac 1976 (£25.10).

NORTH OF ENGLAND
Porthole Eating House
Bowness-on-Windermere, Cumbria
A rambling but fascinating cellar, the collection of a passionate enthusiast, Gianni Berton. Note the superb (and rarely seen) Venegazzu Black Label 1982 (a mere £11·50), two vintages of Sassicaia and four of Brunello di Montalcino (Biondi Santi).

SCOTLAND
Champany Inn
Linlithgow, Lothian
A beautifully set out list, perfectly shaped to the style of food, simply the best steaks in Britain. What sets it apart is the in-depth magnificence of the red burgundy selection (listed under each Côte d'Or Commune) back to Richebourg Domaine de la Romanée-Conti 1969. Very serious listing of Rhône, South African, Californian and Australian wines, too.

WALES
Walnut Tree Inn
Abergavenny, Gwent
A universally splendid list, Franco Taruschio's love of wine shining out of every page. The wine comments are a model of helpful brevity, and older wines include some marvellous bottles.

REPUBLIC OF IRELAND
Tree of Idleness
Bray, Co. Wicklow
An outstanding wine list with an especially powerful showing of Château-bottled clarets back to Château Cos d'Estournel 1945. Remarkably reasonable prices for an Irish restaurant.

NOILLY PRAT
French, Dry, Different

Every year in September the village of Marseillan on the Mediterranean coast sees the arrival of the wines from the surrounding hills which go to make Noilly Prat, the unique French vermouth.

As with all good wines, extraordinary care goes into making Noilly Prat. Quality is strictly controlled, and there can be no short cuts – blending and maturation takes a full three years to complete.

The recipe, invented by Monsieur Noilly, has remained unchanged since the early 1800's. Fine wines from the Picpoul and Clairette grapes are fortified, and then flavoured with fruits and a secret blend of more than 20 herbs.

The vermouth is then allowed to rest in huge oak vats for at least a year before being transferred into smaller barrels to rest under the hot sun and sea air for a further 12 months. It is this ageing process which changes the character of the wine, turning it almost amber in colour and making it full-bodied and dry in flavour. A further year of maturation is required and only then is it bottled as Noilly Prat – French, Dry and Different.

OUTSTANDING WINE LISTS

LONDON

Au Jardin des Gourmets, W1
Boulestin, WC2
Dorchester Grill Room & Terrace, W1
Le Gavroche, W1
Hilaire, SW7
Inigo Jones, WC2
Inn on the Park, Four Seasons & Lanes
    Restaurants, W1
Inter-Continental Hotel, Le Soufflé, W1
Maxim's de Paris, SW1
Ménage à Trois, SW3
Mijanou, SW1
Ninety Park Lane, W1
Pavilion, EC2
Pollyanna's, SW11
Rue St Jacques, W1
Scotts, W1
La Tante Claire, SW3

ENGLAND

Alfriston: Moonrakers Restaurant
Aston Clinton: Bell Inn Restaurant
Bath: Popjoy's
Bath: Priory Hotel Restaurant
Bath: Royal Crescent Hotel Restaurant
Beanacre: Beechfield House Restaurant
Bowness on Windermere: Porthole Eating
    House
Bray-on-Thames: Waterside Inn
Bristol: Harveys
Buckland: Buckland Manor Restaurant
Burghfield: Knights Farm
Chagford: Gidleigh Park Hotel Restaurant
Chedington: Chedington Court Restaurant
Chilgrove: White Horse Inn
Coggeshall: White Hart Hotel Restaurant
Cuckfield: Ockendon Manor Hotel
Dartmouth: Carved Angel
East Grinstead: Gravetye Manor Restaurant
Faversham: Read's
Great Dunmow: Starr
Great Milton: Le Manoir aux Quat' Saisons
    Restaurant
Herstmonceux: Sundial
Hungerford: Bear at Hungerford Restaurant
Hunstrete: Hunstrete House Restaurant
Ilkley: Box Tree Restaurant
Kilve: Meadow House Restaurant
Kintbury: Dundas Arms
Ledbury: Hope End Hotel Restaurant

Malvern: Croque-en-Bouche
Nantwich: Rookery Hall Restaurant
New Milton: Chewton Glen Hotel, Marryat Room
North Huish: Brookdale House
Oakham: Hambleton Hall Restaurant
Oxford: Cherwell Boathouse
Oxford: Restaurant Elizabeth
Pool-in-Wharfedale: Pool Court
Shepton Mallet: Bowlish House Restaurant
Southwold: Crown Restaurant
Speldhurst: George & Dragon, Oak Room
Stamford: George of Stamford
Ston Easton: Ston Easton Park Restaurant
Taplow: Cliveden Dining Room
Taunton: Castle Hotel
Thornbury: Thornbury Castle Restaurant
Waterhouses: Old Beams

SCOTLAND

Dunblane: Cromlix House Restaurant
Fort William: Inverlochy Castle Restaurant
Gullane: La Potinière
Linlithgow: Champany Inn Restaurant
Peat Inn: The Peat Inn
Port Appin: Airds Hotel Restaurant
Uphall: Houstoun House

WALES

Abergavenny: Walnut Tree Inn
Llanrwst: Meadowsweet Hotel Restaurant

REPUBLIC OF IRELAND

Bray: Tree of Idleness
Cork: Arbutus Lodge Hotel Restaurant
Dublin: Le Coq Hardi
Dun Laoghaire: Restaurant Mirabeau
Kenmare: Park Hotel Kenmare Restaurant

*THE ULTIMATE TEMPTATION.

5. GLUTTONY.

A TASTE OF
TWENTY OF THE BEST

This year, for the first time ever, the Egon Ronay Cellnet Guide picks out 'Twenty of the Best' wines to enjoy in 1988.

Now, instead of being confused by over-elaborate wine lists, you can look out for these selected vintages. MICHAEL EDWARDS, one of our senior inspectors, whose background and training has been in the wine trade, has chosen wines, not from the usual supermarket or off-licence chains, but from specialist shippers, until now known generally only to restaurateurs.

Also, having tasted these wines in a restaurant, you can enjoy them over your own dining table because Michael gives you the shippers' addresses and tells you how to order a case and have it delivered to your door.

You don't have to pay a fortune to drink well in restaurants. True, most restaurateurs tend to mark up their cheaper wines by 100 per cent on cost, but the profit margin on finer wines should be much less.

The 20 selected wines (plus some 'house wines' and sherries) are of the type you will regularly see on a wine list – and a very decided cut above the quality found in a supermarket or off-licence. Each is a fine example of its kind, from an excellent grower, directly imported by a leading specialist wine merchant who will sell direct to the public for a minimum order of a dozen bottles. A case price is therefore quoted for each wine, including VAT.

Particular care has been devoted to red and white burgundies because these are the most difficult wines to buy. It is far more important to buy from the right grower in Burgundy than to choose a famous *appellation* such as Clos Vougeot where there are over 70 different growers; one vigneron's wine may be sublime, another's intensely disappointing.

Most people, when ordering a better wine in a restaurant, need to look for a price from around £10 to £20 a bottle. In this range, the Rhône Valley offers probably the best quality/price ratio for red wine, Alsace for white. Dry Loire wines are popular and fashionable, though many have too high a level of acidity to make them happy partners for food, apart from fish: the Muscadet and Sancerre recommended are both exceptional, with the true balance of fine wine. Good claret *which is ready for drinking* is not forgotten: the focus here is on the excellent and under-rated 1981 vintage, the best buy from Bordeaux today.

Much is written about New World wines from California, Australia and New Zealand. But as they are not yet widely appreciated in this country, I have not included many. I have, however, recommended an excellent New Zealand Sauvignon and a California Chardonnay of reasonable price.

In the age of the carefully budgeted expense account, no one can afford to choose expensive wines in a restaurant every day. A most encouraging trend in better restaurants this year has been the careful selection of house wines – often as many as three or four – which go way beyond *vin de table* quality and which any business host can order without embarrassment. My own pick of House Wines highlights some outstanding values from Italy and Portugal as well as France.

HOUSE WINES

I have selected four wines for everyday drinking from three very different countries – France, Italy (including Sardinia) and Portugal. Each has real character and stands comparison with much grander appellation wines costing 50 per cent more.

White Wines

Blanguy Vin de Table 12° Guilbaud Frères Mouzillon Loire Atlantique.
A crisp dry wine with delicate fruit, clean as a whistle. From one of Muscadet's best producers. £28·30 per case from Anthony Beccle.*

1985 Vermentino di Sardegna

Cantina Sociale di Dolianova.
A great bargain. Exotic herby spiciness balanced by excellent acidity and a salty character. Remarkably fresh for a wine so far south. It costs about £27·60 per case. Enquiries to the UK agents Eurowines (Southern).

Red Wines

1985 Chianti Putto Doc Fattoria del Ugo (Amici Grossi).
For easy early drinking, the Putto zone of Chianti offers the most immediately attractive Tuscan reds – of fine purple colour with a warmth of flavour balanced by a pleasant tart 'bite'. Better than many straight Beaujolais. About £37·50 per case from Turl Wine Vaults.

1981 Quinta da Folgorosa

Vinho Tinto, Carvalho Ribeira Ferreiro.
A lot of class for about £3 a bottle. Excellent limpid burgundy colour. Soft tannins dominate the bouquet which nonetheless has the true vinosity of a fine red wine. Savoury, complex, yet clean on the palate. At this price, shows most Rioja the door. £37·47 per case from Turl Wine Vaults.

* Suppliers' addresses are given at the end of this article.

DRY WHITE LOIRE

With the very high prices of classic white burgundy, the dry white wines of the Loire – particularly Muscadet and Sancerre – are popular choices in the restaurant. But success has brought some very indifferent wines, acid and characterless. These two are excellent examples of their kind, with the true balance of fine wine.

1985 Muscadet de Sèvre-et-Maine
Château du Cléray.
The 1985 vintage in Muscadet saw generous round flavours and ripe fruit, typified in this wine from a leading property. Considerable length of flavour. £47·40 per case from Le Nez Rouge Wine Club.*

*Suppliers' addresses are given at the end of this article. Prices were correct at the time of going to press, but may have altered.

1986 Sancerre Domaine Daulny.
A lovely wine – gentle, perfumed and elegant. The grapes come from four of Sancerre's communes and both main types of soil, the terres blanches and caillottes. Exceptional balance. £67·70 per case from Haynes, Hanson & Clark.

NEW ZEALAND SAUVIGNON

1986 Sauvignon Blanc 'Rothesay Bay' Collard Brothers, Henderson.
From a cool-climate area, a remarkable wine of great intensity yet with a classy refined smoky character. Like a powerful Pouilly-Fumé. £71·30 per case from Green's.

ALSACE

Alsace is the Cinderella of the great white wines of France, grossly underrated with a standard of winemaking that is impressively high. Great years like 1983 and 1985 match fine white burgundy for quality. Rolly Gassmann and the Domaine Zind-Humbrecht are two very highly regarded estates producing wines of concentration and complexity.

1985 Pinot Blanc Rolly Gassmann.
Impressive combination of tight fruit, excellent acidity and deep 'goût de terroir' flavour. £52·90 per case from Green's.

1984 Gewürztraminer Rolly Gassmann.
Text-book Gewürz. Great spice on nose and palate with a long, totally dry finish. £58·54 per case from Bibendum.

1986 Muscat Grand Cru Goldert
Domaine Zind-Humbrecht.
Incredible perfume of spring flowers. A model of its kind. Although the smell is exotic, the wine is totally dry. £80·50 per case from Pavilion Wine Company.

1983 Tokay, Rangen Clos St Urbain Vendange Tardive Domaine Zind-Humbrecht.
A glorious wine of mind-blowing complexity, rated among the ten greatest white wines in the world by the authoritative magazine *Cuisine et Vins de France* in November, 1986. Very expensive but worth every penny. £195·50 per case from Pavilion Wine Company.

WHITE BURGUNDY

It's a great pleasure to report that, following the large and successful 1986 vintage, prices of white burgundy are beginning to come down. For best current value look to the excellent, deliciously fresh 1986 Mâconnais wines: in the opinion of experienced tasters they will be more elegant and longer lived than the 1985s. In Chablis, however, 1985 *is* splendid, the Premier Crus of Monsieur Durup, for example, suddenly looking good value against, say, horrendously priced Meursault of variable quality. Do not overlook the unfairly slated 1984 Côte d'Or whites: the best growers have produced wines of elegance and clean fruit, with good keeping qualities.

1986 Mâcon Clessé 'Le Château'
Gilbert Mondrand.
From the best situated vineyard in Clessé. Beautifully made, tightly knit wine, freshness enhanced by complexity of flavour. £71·40 per case from Pugsons Food & Wine.

1984 Auxey-Duresses Blanc
Domaine Duc de Magenta.
A model of what a good grower can do in a difficult year. Very pretty Chardonnay nose, rounding out nicely on the palate, the clean fruit winning over the acid. £98·90 per case from Heyman Brothers.

1985 Chablis Premier Cru Vau de Vey
Domaine Jean Durup.
A new premier cru appellation coinciding with a marvellous vintage. Chablis at its modern, oak-free best: steely restraint but with lovely fruit and latent power; will develop splendidly in bottle. Ace. £113·30 per case from Haynes, Hanson & Clark.

1984 Chassagne Montrachet Premier Cru les Caillerets
Domaines Albert Morey et Fils.
Classic white burgundy from one of the very best wine makers. £157·80 per case from Le Nez Rouge Wine Club.

CALIFORNIA CHARDONNAY

1984 North Coast Chardonnay
Guenoc Winery, Lake County.
This gentle, refined Chardonnay is included in the selection because it has a subtle 'European' style akin to white burgundy. Lake County is to the north of Napa with cooler nights. The estate once belonged to Lillie Langtry, girlfriend of Edward VII. Real value at £81·40 per case from Anthony Beccle.

RED BURGUNDY

Good red burgundy is notoriously difficult to buy. But when weather conditions allow the Pinot Noir grape to ripen fully, the results can be among the most exciting red wines in the world. 1983, *when carefully selected*, is a very great vintage which will last into the next century. 1985s are marvellous wines, uniformly delicious and problem-free. Drink them before the 1983s.

1985 Bourgogne Rouge Clos de la Fortune A. & P. de Villaine.
A simple appellation but an immensely attractive wine which captures all the charm of the Pinot Noir grape. It may look expensive but it is the equal of pretentious burgundy at twice the price. £78·20 per case from Pavilion Wine Company.

1983 Auxey-Duresses Premier Cru Les Duresses Jean-Pierre Diconne.
A chance to buy first-rate classic red burgundy at a relatively reasonable price. Soft tannins mask a fine-drawn structure and considerable style. You could broach a bottle at the end of 1988. £117·20 per case from Haynes, Hanson & Clark.

1983 Volnay Michel Lafarge.
Monsieur Lafarge is arguably the greatest winemaker in Volnay, a village of outstanding domaines. This straight Volnay is a stunner, putting some premier crus to shame. £118·20 per case from Le Nez Rouge Wine Club.

RED BORDEAUX

Very little has been written about the excellent 1981 clarets. They have stood in the shadow of the great 1982s which need to be kept for another 10 years. 1981s are beginning to drink nicely, displaying qualities of fruit, balance and elegance. This trio is available from Haynes, Hanson & Clark. Perfect restaurant wines.

1981 Château Le Bosq Médoc, Cru Bourgeois.
A subtle light claret, typically Médoc, gentle smell of cedar, savoury Cabernet character on palate. Ready to drink. £63·25 per case.

1981 Château Fourcas-Hosten Listrac-Médoc, Bourgeois Superieur.
Wines from this commune are very full-bodied with a strapping four-square character. Deep plum colour (no brown), assertive bouquet; weight, roundness and length on the palate. The 1981 style gives a welcome elegance. £92·00 per case.

1981 Château Branaire Ducru St Julien, Cru Classé.
One of the most successful Médocs of the vintage. Intense colour, classic blackcurrant bouquet, packed with fruit. £146·90 per case.

RHÔNE

The northern Rhône produces some of the most serious red wines in the world. Unfortunately the best wines – Hermitage in particular – are becoming expensive. Real value is found in neighbouring appellations such as Crozes-Hermitage and St Joseph. 1985 is a very attractive vintage, perfectly ripe Syrah fruit the dominant characteristic.

1985 Crozes-Hermitage Domaine des Entre Faux Médaille d'Or Mâcon.
An immediately appealing wine made in an intelligently modern manner. Fruit, masses of it, will make it ready to drink in 1988, but it will improve for five years. £56·05 per case from Bibendum.

1985 St Joseph Rouge Forestier Frères.
Huge cqlour. Lovely bouquet of soft fruits (mulberries?). Another ready-to-drink wine, but also a keeper. A bargain at £52·90 per case from Pavilion Wine Company.

Wine suppliers mentioned above:
(We give only the telephone number because it is advisable to check that stocks are available before sending an order.)
Prestige Vintners Ltd, London (01-485 5895); Anthony Beccle, London (01-794 2158); Eurowines (Southern), London (01-994 7658); Turl Wine Vaults, Oxford (0865-247966); Le Nez Rouge Wine Club, London (01-609 4711); Haynes, Hanson & Clark, London (01-736 7878); Green's, London (01-236 7077); Bibendum, London (01-586 9761); Pavilion Wine Company, London (01-628 8224); Pugsons Food & Wine, London (01-736 6145); Heyman Brothers, London (01-730 0324).

■ *The case prices given were correct at the time of going to press but may have changed since then.*

SHERRY

Sherry is the classic aperitif – a little out of fashion these days, which explains why wonderful old wines can be bought for very little money. The 500-year-old house of A. R. Valdespino and their sherries are remarkable by any standards. The wines listed are made in rigorously old-fashioned manner – that is, fermented in wood and racked by hand. Exceptional quality. Shipped by Prestige Vintners Ltd. (address given at the end of this article). Expect to pay £2·50 per generous glass at the bar.

Manzanilla MONTANO
Fine light colour, true salty smell of its provenance (San Lucar), fresh as a daisy, bone-dry but with fruit and roundness. £46·58 per case.

Fino INOCENTE
A rare single vineyard wine. Splendid brilliant colour, exquisitely elegant bouquet, magnificent balance on the palate with a long, long finish. The best fino I have ever tasted. £53·08 per case.

Oloroso SOLERA 1842
Light amber, medium-sweet but so well made that there's no cloying fault. A winter sherry, great class. £65·50 per case.

VINTAGE CHART

Ratings in red indicate that the lesser wines may be fading, but the great ones may be at their best. These ratings are a rough 'rule of thumb' with many exceptions. Where we print a dash, you are unlikely to find this particular vintage available.

■ 0 = No good　　　7 = The best

RED WINES

Vintage	Beaujolais	Burgundy	Bordeaux	Rhône	California	Rioja	Port
1945	–	6	7	5	–	–	7
1947	–	5	5	5	–	–	5
1948	–	3	5	–	–	–	7
1949	–	6	7	4	–	–	–
1952	–	5	5	5	–	–	–
1953	–	3	6	4	–	–	–
1955	–	3	6	5	–	–	6
1957	–	3	2	5	–	–	–
1959	–	6	6	6	–	5	–
1960	–	–	1	3	–	–	6
1961	–	5	7	6	–	–	–
1962	–	5	5	5	–	4	–
1963	–	1	0	–	–	4	6–7
1964	–	3	3–6	6	–	7	–
1966	–	5	6	5	–	–	5
1967	–	6	4	6	–	–	5
1968	–	2	0	–	7	5	–
1969	–	7	2	6	5	–	–
1970	–	4	6	5	7	6	5
1971	–	6	3–5	6	2	2	–
1972	–	5	1	4–6	3	1	4
1973	–	4	4	4	5	5	–
1974	–	2	3	3	7	3	–
1975	–	0	3–6	1	6	·4	3
1976	5	1–5	4–5	5–6	–	4	–
1977	0	3	3	3	6	1	7
1978	6	6	5	7	5	6	–
1979	·4	5	4–6	5	4	3	–
1980	2	2–5	3	4	6	3	4
1981	5	1–4	4	1–5	2	5	–
1982	3	4	6	4	3–4	–	3
1983	5	2–6	4–6	4–6	3	4	4–5
1984	2	3	3	3–4	4	2	–
1985	7	6	5	4–6	6	3	6

VINTAGE CHART

WHITE WINES

Vintage	Burgundy	Alsace	Sweet Bordeaux	Dry Loire	Germany	California	Champagne
1945	–	–	6	–	6	–	6
1947	–	–	5	–	5	–	6
1948	–	–	4	–	–	–	–
1949	–	–	5	–	5	–	6
1952	–	–	4	–	–	–	4
1953	–	–	5	–	3	–	5
1955	–	–	6	–	–	–	5
1957	–	–	3	–	–	–	–
1959	–	–	4	–	5	–	5
1960	–	–	–	–	–	–	–
1961	2	–	4	–	2	–	6
1962	5	–	6	–	–	–	5
1963	–	–	–	–	–	–	–
1964	2	–	0	–	5	–	5
1966	4	–	3	–	2	–	6
1967	4	6	7	–	4	–	–
1968	–	–	–	–	–	6	–
1969	5	–	3	–	3	3	5
1970	4	–	6	–	2	5	5
1971	5	6	6	–	6	6	5
1972	2	–	0	–	–	4	–
1973	3	3	4	–	3	6	6
1974	2	–	1	–	1	6	–
1975	2	5	6	–	4–6	6	5
1976	4	7	6	–	7	5	5
1977	2	2	0	–	3	6	–
1978	7	4	4	–	2	5	4
1979	5	5	2	–	5	5	4
1980	3	3	2	–	3	5	–
1981	4	4	4	–	4	5	–
1982	4	4	3	–	4	5	6
1983	3–5	7	6–7	3	6	2–4	–
1984	4	4	3	4	–	2–4	–
1985	5	6	4	5	3	6	–

Oh, to be in England!

There's nothing like purely English 'Ashbourne' Water.
Rising from a source in the Derbyshire hills above the ancient
town of Ashbourne, it's cool, refreshing, natural,
deliciously versatile—and clearly the best.

Sparkling 'Ashbourne' Natural Water— the perfect complement to fine food.

Anonymous Celebrity

It isn't often that our inspectors have time to chat or linger over a meal. On duty, they are solitary folk, to be found (and usually *un*discovered) eating quietly and quickly, picking their way through a menu with professional skill. It isn't that they're unsociable – far from it, but there's a great deal of ground to be covered in the course of a year: reports to be filed, copy dates to be met, itineraries planned, maps to be read, in-service training sessions to attend and new information to be digested. It isn't always a piece of cake, this eating for a living. Not every establishment visited is worthy of inclusion. Each year brings its out-takes, its crop of Menu Unpleasant Surprises.

A cast-iron constitution helps, of course, a sense of dedication, a sprinkling of enthusiasm and a pinch of humour. These were some of the qualities we hoped to find – along with a genuine liking for food – in this year's guest inspectors. We were not disappointed, and for once, our inspectors enjoyed having someone on the spot with whom to compare notes.

And there was much to discuss. Ken Livingstone first picked a restaurant in the Islington area of London – a regular Guide entry – but a place to which he had not been for some time. Neither food nor service was up to scratch, we had a forty-minute wait between starter and main course – and this at lunchtime. Any longer, and Ken would have missed his plane to Australia.

Patrick Lichfield's first choice of hotel restaurant was closed for a month for redecoration. When we arrived at his second, Ninety Park Lane, a little ahead of our guest, we were told there was no table booked in our (anonymous) name. A moment of panic, then we decided to pull rank just this once: there was a lot at stake. A whisper of the name of our distinguished guest – and a choice of three tables was instantly made available with the greatest courtesy. (We don't advise you to do this if you are *not* actually accompanying His Lordship.)

Jenny Pitman very nearly turned the tables on us. We met in the bar, by the one-arm bandit. 'How can we mention that bar snacks are not the order of the day?' we wondered. Then to our relief, we spotted the entrance to the restaurant neatly concealed in a corner. Jenny knew full well, of course. The joke was on us. . . .

'Where are the amusing *gueules*?' asked Ned Sherrin as he entered Harvey's Restaurant in Wandsworth. 'I'm told they're the best in town.' They may have been, but the chef had decided no longer to serve them – we forgave him, though, and you will see why.

All our guests entered into the spirit of the task with gusto. At least one would make a first-class professional, though we didn't know it at the time. So, for their choices and opinions, read on. . . .

JOY LANGRIDGE

THE TERRACE ROOM
at the Dorchester Hotel,
Park Lane, London W1

'It was not as I remembered – the green and gold of *The Terrace* has lost some of its elegance in the redecoration, and certainly something very strange had happened to the lighting: dim rather than atmospheric. (Even supposing I could crane my neck round the giant freesias and eye-level table-lamp, there was no guarantee I would clearly see the person opposite.) Our glass of house champagne was served quickly and courteously, if perhaps not quite cold enough, and we settled on the Menu Surprise: 'six light courses chosen from produce available today at the Market'. (How does the considerate host order appropriate wine for a surprise menu?)

We were presented with a delicious but minuscule circle of steak tartare on toast. I panicked . . . was this the first of our surprises? Were we a sixth of the way already? 'Just an appetiser madame,' soothed the waiter reassuringly. A wonderful first course followed: chopped wild salmon, a quail's egg, some winter leaves and a couple of great sauces. Next: a good chicken consommé with wild mushrooms, and as the meal was by now being washed down with a fabulous Chassagne-Montrachet 1984, I minded less the intrusive strains of the live band. On to No. 3 – very disappointingly tasteless turbot – had this really been bought fresh from the market the day after a Bank Holiday? Moving quickly along . . . a cleansing, refreshing granité of citrus fruits – or grapefruit 'Slush Puppy' as my children would see it – then No. 4, the saving grace of the meal: one of the best plates of lamb I have ever eaten. Pink, tender little slices of best end arranged neatly in a circle; plenty of it – none of your 'minceur' here –

and quite, quite delicious. This was hugely enjoyed by all, and helped by a good Cabernet Sauvignon (Robert Mondavi, 1982). The cheese trolley – I can't call something so magnificent a 'board' – is a triumph, although I would have liked to see England better represented. Course No. 6 was a feuilleté of pear with a sabayon sauce. The service was terrific and although the meal was expensive, the lamb made up for my disappointment in the ambience . . . and the turbot. '

JANE ASHER

When asked to write about food for this year's Hotel and Restaurant Guide, Jane Asher's response was refreshingly direct. She is utterly unspoilt by a lifetime's success as an actress and is no mean cook. Three of her books: *Party Cakes*, *Quick Party Cakes* and *Easy Entertaining* are bestsellers and there are more on the horizon. She is married to Gerald Scarfe, political satirist, artist and stage designer, and they have three growing children. They both enjoy eating out, though 'to no set pattern', often sample their local restaurants and admit to 'happily catholic tastes in food'. Jane can eat whatever she likes without ever putting on an ounce, but Gerald has to ration his puddings. . . .

On this occasion, they chose to pay a return visit to the Terrace.

Diners offer you a second Card. Free. What you do with it is your business.

This is an offer of two Diners Club cards for you.

One has Business Account marked on it. And that's exactly what it's for. The second card is for your personal expenses.

You get a two-part statement each month. One cheque settles both bills.

The second card doesn't cost you any extra.

Needless to say, your Diners Club Cards are acceptable at over 850,000 establishments around the World, wherever you do business.

Diners Club are the first and only card to offer two cards. If you'd like to know how two cards are better than one, telephone 0252 513 500.

Diners means business (and pleasure)

THE BELL INN
**East Langton,
near Market Harborough**

'This restaurant is small, relaxed and informal; though it's slightly off the beaten track, it's popular and the food is always good. There's a fair choice of interesting dishes (five starters, seven or so main courses) and the menu changes according to the time of year (and sometimes according to the time of evening). The dishes are freshly cooked and well presented without being 'finicky'. You can relax over your meal (no whipping away of plates before you've finished. I like to feel the 'patron' has reasonable consideration for his diners!). I can always overlook minor problems if the atmosphere's right. My starter of Moules Marinière tasted good but was a shade gritty, Vicki's Prawn and Langoustine Salad was delicious, and the Queen Scallops in Curry Sauce with Fresh Marjoram were delicately cooked. My Loin of Veal with Fresh Tomatoes, Tarragon and White Wine was excellent – a bit different from the usual veal chop – and the seasonal vegetables were tasty and crisp. Vicki's Tournedos with Wild Fresh Mushrooms was, she says, lovely – and tender (I didn't get a taste). We chose pudding instead of cheese. My Mango Parfait with Fruit Salad was, quite simply, 'parfait'. The Lemon and Orange Mousse was light and smooth – as was the Château Cissac '81 which accompanied our main courses. We both enjoyed a port after the meal – well-balanced, well chosen and quite enough to eat . . .'

DAVID GOWER

Blessed with a sound constitution and a healthy appetite, it's no surprise to hear that David Gower loves his 'grub'. He spent a year at London University making a thorough study of 'kebab houses and the

A-Z street atlas' before cricket took over his life. Characteristically modest about his achievements, David would probably deny that he is one of England's finest ever cricketers. He first played for Leicestershire in 1975, made his Test debut for England in 1978, and has since captained both teams. He set himself a cracking pace by scoring centuries against New Zealand, Australia and India in his first year of Test cricket. As England's leading scorer in one-day international matches, he is one of only six Englishmen to have scored over 6,000 Test runs – so far. Not fussy about food 'as long as it's good', he'll tackle anything 'within reason', has no set routine – due to his erratic professional lifestyle – but says 'If there's any meal I miss – it's breakfast.' On the England Test circuit, 'the best food is at Lord's, which may explain why Middlesex cricketers are often a touch overweight'. Abroad, David Gower enjoys ethnic dishes, loves India, and appreciates 'the variety and generally high standard of food and wines' in Australia. He isn't in the habit of sending dishes back ('I'm usually too hungry!'), but will quietly let it be known if the food is badly cooked. In a restaurant, he prefers a relaxed atmosphere, friendly staff and a menu which shows some imagination. He has happy memories of Hambleton Hall, but on a quietish weekend, he and his girlfriend Vicki Stewart chose the Bell Inn.

NINETY PARK LANE
at the Grosvenor House,
London W1

'The lighting is discreet, the décor rich but predictable, the ambience reassuring yet impersonal with its soft tones of brown and green. The service is very professional and I'm relieved to find I can smoke if I choose. The menu looks inviting – if rather ambitious – and the wine list I leave to my host (we drank a smooth St Julien, Château Ducru Beaucaillou – 2ème Cru). Two of us chose the Menu Gourmet (five courses) and two the Menu Surprise (eight light courses created by Maître Louis Outhier of L'Oasis in La Napoule). I gave eight out of ten to my first course of Marjolaine de Foie Gras et son Consommé au Vin de Paille, rather less to my taste of Terrine de Foie Gras with a truffle sauce from the 'Surprise'. After that, I'm afraid we stopped counting. An avalanche of rich dishes followed, some very good (an imaginative Consommé de Fenouil, a Salade de Langoustines and an excellent Brie aux Truffes with Mascarpone), but everything was very smooth – no change of pace or texture. On my Menu Gourmet there was nothing to cleanse and sharpen the palate (I longed for a cool slice of watermelon!); we all found the sauces repetitive and rather too heavy, and why is it suddenly fashionable to serve all food lukewarm? I'm told the desserts from the Caravane were disappointing. Though I appreciate the efforts made by the kitchen, I feel they set themselves high standards which they don't necessarily achieve. The potential is great; maybe they try too hard. Perhaps if the Maître is there, it's a different story.'

PATRICK LICHFIELD

Initially, Lord Lichfield was a trifle hard to pin down. A professional photographer with assignments literally all over the world, he's in Mexico one minute, Australia the next and 'just off to the West Indies, but back by Friday'. A self-confessed workaholic who's lucky enough to exist on five hours' sleep a night, he relaxes at Shugborough (his country seat) at weekends 'by helping plant trees'. Being a man of his word, though, once the arrangement was made, we had no fears. Patrick Lichfield was brought up on 'very good food', with spells in Paris and Libya (his stepfather was a diplomat). He is constantly surprised that the British don't make more of food: in other lands, as he observes, 'it is woven into their culture'. He is also saddened by the fact that 'there are no *treats* any more. Once you could bring home a really good Brie from the Ile-de-France; now it's everywhere.' He enjoys entertaining, and reveals that as a child, he was 'made to understudy all the house roles – from waiting at table to cleaning the boots'. This makes him a very formidable guest inspector indeed. Lord Lichfield enjoys oxtail (and wishes more restaurants would feature offal on their menus), appreciates a good consommé, loves Oriental food and vegetable purées – especially parsnip and swede . . . . He spends around 250 nights a year in hotels, so has written his own *Book of the Best*, as well as his books on photography. He feels that the best hotel food is to be had in Hong Kong and London. Perhaps that is why he chose a hotel restaurant in London, bringing with him a fellow gourmet and restaurateur, Eddie Lim, from Singapore.

INIGO JONES
**Garrick Street,
London WC2**

❛Ideally placed (for an opera-loving actor) between Covent Garden and the Garrick Club, Inigo Jones is quiet, comfortable, very expensive, and offers exceptionally interesting food in quantities that leave you satisfied but not bloated. My Sauté of Snails (encased in the flimsiest ravioli-sized envelopes of celery with oyster mushrooms) was delicious in its lightly anise-flavoured sauce – more fun, I think, than my wife's Cream of Langoustine Soup, which was perfectly all right but could have been hotter. She was then seduced from her almost-vegetarianism by some Veal Kidneys and Sweetbreads with Truffles and Madeira (the aroma was gorgeous) and they vanished without strain. My young Guinea Fowl in a tarragon sauce was simply and straightforwardly done, the breast left plain in neat little slices and the leg encased in breadcrumbs like a miniature Chicken Kiev. We both felt we would have liked to choose our own vegetables, rather than have the chef dictate to us; that said, however, the vegetables *were* well chosen and beautifully prepared. The wines (a Santenay and a Brouilly) were quite outstanding, and a luscious Madeira accompanied my dessert of citrus fruits in a chocolate shell. Stella's Poire Glacée Belle Hélène was pronounced 'divine'.

The service is impeccable, the china exquisite, the arrangment of the food is pretty in the 'nouvelle' style – verging on the precious. No, I wouldn't want to eat here every day, but it is lovely for a special night out.❜

DENIS QUILLEY

As luck would have it, Denis Quilley was leafing through last year's Hotel and Restaurant Guide when we contacted him – so he knew what was in store when he agreed to report on a restaurant for us. However, we had to be fitted in between filming in Nottingham, rehearsals for a special performance at The National Theatre, his wife Stella's commitments and a quick trip to Spain. All this simply shows that Denis Quilley is a very busy actor indeed. His roles have been many and varied since his days in the Birmingham Rep. Recently, he's won two SWET (Society of West End Theatre) Awards for *Privates on Parade* and *Sweeney Todd* (at Drury Lane). He played Molokov in *Chess* at The Barbican, Antony in *Antony and Cleopatra* at the Chichester Festival Theatre and most of 1986 was taken up with his leading role in the glittering *Cage aux Folles* at the London Palladium. His films include *Life at the Top* and *Murder on the Orient Express* and he has been in several television series. A natural musician, he plays the piano, cello and flute – and loves to sing. Cheerfully 'omnivorous', he's as happy with a simple omelette as with more elaborate food. He recently gave up smoking, believes his palate has improved – though his weight has not, and suggests (jokingly) that 'foodie' restaurants should give a discount if the chef's away and the food's not up to scratch. He sent in his report on the back of two pages of a script. (We had very little to go on, but the would-be thespians among us identified it as that classic *Dear Octopus*.) There was, however, no squid on the menu when he and Stella went to Inigo Jones.

Dine
à la carte!

The Bank of Scotland AA Visa Card is the one friend you *must* take to dinner, to the shops, out motoring, in fact – anywhere!

Over 450,000 AA Members have already discovered the card's many benefits (too many to mention here) so phone Chester (0244) 311891 for written details and you too can go à la carte!

First choice card
for AA Members.

THE OLD BAKERY
Tatsfield, near Westerham, Kent

'**A** fellow-trainer brought me here (we had a few hours to spare before flying off from Gatwick) and I think it's good value. The food is plain enough for David, but 'different' enough for me and they serve generous portions. The food is freshly cooked, well seasoned and there's a nice choice of dishes. Their service is courteous and efficient and I feel I can relax. My grilled Lobster Tails in Garlic were very good, and David's Avocado with Prawns was fresh and ripe. The Fried Scallops in Bacon looked sizzling and juicy. The evening was warm, so we both chose fish. I had Skagerak Scampi, cooked in white wine with oregano and garlic, served with aubergines and peppers, while David chose Sole-wrapped Jumbo Scampi with white sauce, crab and 'caviar'. Our neighbour's Steak Diane was seasoned as it should be – and enormous! You can have Crêpes Suzette or Banana Flambé if you're feeling dramatic, but we chose more modest sweets from the well-stocked trolley; there's a generous cheeseboard, too. The white house wine was light and pleasant (I don't drink red, but was told it was in the 'full, rich and fruity' category). And full marks for serving tea after a meal without making you feel a freak. '

JENNY PITMAN

'Well,' said Jenny Pitman, when asked how she came to be running a racing stable, 'it was the only thing I knew how to do.' Brought up on a Leicestershire farm, she has worked with horses all her life, now has sixty, 'and they all get five-star hotel treatment, believe you me!' With a little luck and a jockey's skill, they repay her by bringing home a string of winners. Corbière won the Grand National at Aintree in 1983, Burrough Hill Lad won the Welsh National in the same year, then went on in 1984 to collect the Cheltenham Gold Cup, the King George VI Steeplechase and the Hennessy Gold Cup. In 1983–4, Jenny Pitman was named Trainer of the Year; the title of her autobiography, *Glorious Uncertainty*, says it all. 'But I wouldn't live any other life.' One son is a jockey, the other an accountant, and with David Staite, her assistant trainer, it's a very well-organised concern. Warm, outgoing, forthright, Jenny Pitman definitely loves her food. Her day starts very early – with bacon and eggs – and she loves meat. 'With two brothers both butchers – are you surprised?' Jenny dislikes 'being ripped off, restaurant service that's so formal it's a pain' and can't abide rising from the table feeling there wasn't enough to eat. She doesn't understand why 'the sandwiches on British racecourses are so appalling – and the tea's not much better'. She enjoys seafood, jellied eels, ('What's happened to that nice stall at Wincanton?') and recommends the Seafood Platter at the seafood bar at Kempton Park. She takes her caviar neat, 'none of your chopped egg and onion', and introduced us to the Old Bakery.

HARVEY'S RESTAURANT
**Wandsworth Common,
London SW17**

❝ I had read a lot about Marco-Pierre White, the 25-year-old chef-proprietor; survivor and graduate of the kitchens of Roux, Koffmann, Ladenis and Blanc, celebrated both for cooking and 'caractère' (which can mean temper as well . . .). But no knives flew, no screams accompanied the delicious procession of dishes from the kitchen to the cool, elegant dining room which overlooks Wandsworth Common – though Mr White (at six-foot-three a difficult man to hide) could at times be seen casting his beady eye and designer-stubbled chin over his clientèle. He is an absolute wiz. with pasta and three of our starters proclaimed his skills: succulent Tortolini of Fresh Lobster with Basil, Tagliatelle of Oysters with Cucumber and Chives and a Ravioli of Crab and Fresh Ginger. (I'm told the Nage of Fresh Fishes with Coriander was marvellous, too.) I went for the baby (milk-fed) pigeon in red wine on a bed of Rösti, because pigeon is usually hard and dry when I get it (and *always* when I cook it). This one was succulent and tender, as were the bites of sweetbreads in a light Madeira sauce and the lamb which I stole from my neighbours' plates. Mr White's 'coup de grace', however, is his puddings. I don't eat puddings, but a generous sampling of three – the silkiest Chocolate Marquise, the creamiest Bisquit Glacé and a delectable Honey Ice Cream with a trellis of caramelised orange biscuits – slipped gracefully down and I feel not a wisp of guilt. The wine list produced a very pleasant Australian Chardonnay 1984 and no-one could manage the petits fours. This was, for me, a first visit. Not, I trust, a last! ❞

NED SHERRIN

'I'm afraid he's still at lunch,' said his producer when we rang the BBC studio to speak to Ned Sherrin, presenter of the award-winning Saturday morning talk-show *Loose Ends* on Radio 4. He was limbering up for his stint as an Egon Ronay inspector, for every assignment he undertakes is meticulously researched. His long and varied career as producer, director, writer, collaborator and occasional performer has introduced him to many a restaurant, bar and café on both sides of the Atlantic, and he is always assured of a good table at Sardi's, the famous showbiz restaurant off Broadway. Among the films he has produced are *The Virgin Soldiers*, *Up Pompeii* and *The National Health.* He arranged, produced and appeared in the long-running success *Side by Side by Sondheim* and more recently, his *Ratepayers' Iolanthe* won him an Olivier Award. His wit, unerring instinct for 'le mot juste' and inherent good manners make him a perfect dinner guest. He cooks 'with great confidence', and taught himself in New York one season, from 'Pierre Franey's excellent cooking course *The 60-Minute Gourmet*'. His favourite food? Ned's face assumes a faraway expression: 'Ah! The prisoner's last meal . . . It would have to be very British – tender young asparagus with butter sauce – and lightly poached wild salmon.' He has been spotted dining at Lou Pescadou, favours the Caprice and enjoys his local – La Famiglia. For after the theatre, he prefers somewhere 'with no noise and clatter' and will sidle off to Orso's. He asks me to point out that he's equally happy to eat at humbler establishments.

HOIZIN
**72 Wilton Road,
London SW1**

'This is one of the best Chinese restaurants I've eaten in; I've been here several times now and there isn't a dish that has not been up to standard. It specialises in seafood cuisine, but not exclusively so – and it's not *grippingly expensive*. The service is good without being unduly deferential (I hate obsequious waiters) and there's space to talk. We checked the monosodium glutamate content of the oyster sauce before ordering! We had lightly poached scallops so fresh they were still attached to the shells, crisply delicious seaweed and really good spring rolls. The Sesame Prawn Fingers were succulent, not dry, and the Clear Steamed Fish with ginger and spring onions was followed by an admirably crispy duck. They grow their own Chinese vegetables, so you know these are always fresh and varied, and our noodles arrived 'al dente' and not – as so often – overcooked. It was very hot indeed on the day we turned up for lunch, so we didn't reach dessert (I must confess to a sweet tooth: the *nouvelle cuisine* has been my saviour weight-wise as I can never send anything back!). I enjoyed the subtle tastes and combination of flavours which good Chinese food can bring; the tea was refreshing – but I must admit we managed a bottle of good Chablis with the meal as well.'

KEN LIVINGSTONE

A formidable politician, Ken Livingstone shot to media fame as controversial left-wing Leader of The Greater London Council in 1981 and still reduces political opponents to impotent fury with his sweet reasonableness. He holds the singular distinction of being runner-up to the Pope in a BBC 'Man of the Year' Poll and has a rare ability for making – and keeping – friends. These days, Ken avoids 'noisy wine bars and pubs where you can't move'; even in his local he tends to get 'lobbied'. He prefers to relax over his food. He loves good fish and chips, is near-vegetarian at home, likes to cook but has no time to shop, and admits there are weeks when 'we exist on takeaways'. He loves Indian vegetarian food (but wouldn't turn down a good Beef Wellington), admires the Italians for 'being able to whip up an imaginative pasta dish out of next to nothing' and, if running his own restaurant, 'would have to construct a politically acceptable menu – no red meat . . . no liqueurs . . .' It would have to be a co-operative, of course, run on purely democratic lines. 'We'd spend so much time *discussing* that no-one would get served . . .' Ken Livingstone's lifetime hobby has been the study of amphibians, he has an over-riding concern for the future of this planet, and concedes that 'there wouldn't be much meat on a newt'. Ambitions? 'Well, I'd like to see the Great Chinese Newt at London Zoo actually *move* again (it does so about once every five years . . .) and perhaps it's time I learnt to drive.' He particularly likes the Gay Hussar, admits to an allergy to excessive amounts of monosodium glutamate, but loves good Chinese food.

Cellnet

15 MINUTES OFF THE MOTORWAY

Eating in the motorway service areas may cut out extra travelling time, but it also cuts out any possibility of pleasing the discerning palate.

Yet throughout the land outstanding eating is available just a short drive from the motorway network, and the map and list that follow pinpoint starred restaurants that need no more than a 15-minute detour. And if you're looking for somewhere to spend the night in style, we also feature de luxe and grade 1 hotels within a similar range.

So even when time is important, you don't have to leave out the good things—just leave the motorway!

For further details of these establishments, see individual entries in the main section of the Guide.

ENGLAND

■ **M1**
Junction 7
St Albans, Noke Thistle Hotel
Junction 12
Flitwick, Flitwick Manor
Junction 16
Northampton, Swallow Hotel
Junction 22
Leicester, Holiday Inn
Junction 23
Quorn, Quorn Country Hotel
Junction 25
Nottingham, Albany Hotel
Nottingham, Royal Moat House International Hotel
Junction 28
South Normanton, Swallow Hotel
Junction 34
Rotherham, Rotherham Moat House

■ **M2**
Junction 7
Canterbury, County Hotel
Canterbury, Howfield Manor
Canterbury, Restaurant Seventy Four

■ M3
Junction 2
Egham, Great Fosters
Egham, Runnymede Hotel
Junction 3
Ascot, Royal Berkshire Hotel & Restaurant
Bagshot, Pennyhill Park Hotel
Junction 5
Rotherwick, Tylney Hall
Junction 8
Winchester, Lainston House

■ M4
Junction 4
Heathrow Airport (West Drayton), Excelsior
    Hotel
Heathrow Airport (West Drayton), Holiday Inn
Heathrow Airport, Sheraton-Heathrow
Heathrow Airport (Hayes), Sheraton Skyline
Junction 6
Slough, Holiday Inn
Windsor, Oakley Court Hotel & Oak Leaf Room
Junction 8/9
Bray-on-Thames, Waterside Inn
Maidenhead, Fredrick's Hotel & Restaurant
Taplow, Cliveden
Junction 11
Reading, Ramada Hotel
Shinfield, l'Ortolan
Junction 13
Yattendon, Royal Oak Hotel Restaurant
Junction 15
Swindon, Blunsdon House Hotel
Junction 17
Beanacre, Beechfield House
Castle Combe, Manor House
Easton Grey, Whatley Manor Hotel
Junction 19
Bristol, Grand Hotel
Bristol, Holiday Inn
Bristol, Ladbroke Dragonara Hotel
Bristol, Les Semailles

■ M5
Junction 4
Bromsgrove, Grafton Manor
Junction 5
Abberley, Elms Hotel
Droitwich Spa, Château Impney Hotel
Junction 8
Malvern, Croque-en-Bouche
Junction 9
Corse Lawn, Corse Lawn House

Junction 10
Cheltenham, The Greenway
Junction 11
Gloucester, Hatton Court
Junction 13
Stroud, Oakes
Junction 14
Thornbury, Thornbury Castle
Junction 25
Taunton, Castle Hotel & Restaurant
Junction 29
Whimple, Woodhayes

■ M6
Junction 2/3
Coventry, De Vere Hotel
Junction 4
Solihull, Regency Hotel
Wishaw, Belfry Hotel
Junction 6
Birmingham, Albany Hotel
Birmingham, Copthorne Hotel
Birmingham, Holiday Inn
Birmingham, Metropole & Warwick Hotel
Birmingham, Plough & Harrow Hotel
Junction 17
Congleton, Great Moreton Hall Hotel
Nantwich, Rookery Hall & Restaurant
Junction 40
Penrith, North Lake Gateway Hotel
Ullswater, Leeming House Hotel
Ullswater, Sharrow Bay Hotel & Restaurant
Junction 43
Brampton, Farlam Hall Hotel

■ M11
Junction 7
Ware, Briggens House Hotel
Junction 8
Broxted, Whitehall Hotel & Restaurant

■ M20
Junction 3
Wrotham Heath, Post House Hotel
Junction 8
Hollingbourne, Great Danes Hotel
Lenham, Chilston Park
Junction 9
Ashford, Eastwell Manor
Junction 11
Hythe, Hythe Imperial Hotel
Junction 13
Dover, Dover Moat House

■ M23
Junction 10
East Grinstead, Gravetye Manor & Restaurant
Gatwick Airport (Copthorne), Copthorne Hotel
Gatwick Airport, Gatwick Hilton International
Gatwick Airport (Horley), Gatwick Penta Hotel
Junction 11
Cuckfield, Ockenden Manor Hotel
Lower Beeding, South Lodge
Rusper, Ghyll Manor

■ M25
Junction 7
Croydon, Holiday Inn
Junction 9
Dorking, Burford Bridge Hotel
Junction 23
Old Hatfield, Salisbury

■ M27
Junction 1
Brockenhurst, Rhinefield House Hotel
Junction 2/3
Romsey, Old Manor House
Junction 12
Portsmouth, Holiday Inn

■ M40
Junction 4
Marlow, Compleat Angler Hotel
Junction 7
Great Milton, Le Manoir aux Quat' Saisons &
    Restaurant
Oxford, Le Petit Blanc
Oxford, Randolph Hotel

■ M53
Junction 12
Chester, Chester Grosvenor
Chester, Crabwall Manor

■ M54
Junction 4
Shifnal, Park House Hotel

■ M56
Junction 5
Manchester Airport, Ladbroke International
Junction 6
Wilmslow, Stanneylands Hotel & Restaurant

■ M62
Junction 4
Liverpool, Atlantic Tower Thistle Hotel
Junction 23
Huddersfield, Weavers Shed
Junction 26
Halifax, Holdsworth House Hotel

■ M63
Junction 9
Manchester, Britannia Hotel
Manchester, Hotel Piccadilly
Manchester, Portland Thistle Hotel

■ A1(M) Northern Section
Junction A
Kirkby Fleetham, Kirkby Fleetham Hall
Junction E
Stockton on Tees, Swallow Hotel
Junction N
Newcastle upon Tyne, County Thistle Hotel
Newcastle upon Tyne, Gosforth Park Thistle
    Hotel
Newcastle upon Tyne, Holiday Inn

SCOTLAND

■ M8
Junction 2
Edinburgh, Caledonian Hotel
Edinburgh, Carlton Highland Hotel
Edinburgh, Edinburgh Sheraton
Edinburgh, George Hotel
Edinburgh, King James Thistle Hotel
Edinburgh, Ladbroke Dragonara
Junction 3
Uphall, Houstoun House
Junction 16
Glasgow, Hospitality Inn
Junction 17
Glasgow, One Devonshire Gardens
Glasgow, Stakis Grosvenor Hotel
Junction 17/18
Glasgow, Albany Hotel
Junction 18
Glasgow, Holiday Inn
Junction 31
Langbank, Gleddoch House Hotel

■ M9
Junction 3
Linlithgow, Champany Inn Restaurant
Junction 9
Dunblane, Cromlix House & Restaurant

WALES

■ M4
Junction 25
Llangybi, Cwrt Bleddyn Hotel
Junction 26
Newport, Celtic Manor Hotel
Junction 32
Cardiff, Holiday Inn
Cardiff, Park Hotel
Junction 34
Miskin, Miskin Manor

NORTHERN IRELAND

■ M1
Junction 1
Belfast, Europa Hotel

■ M2
Junction 1
Holywood, Culloden Hotel

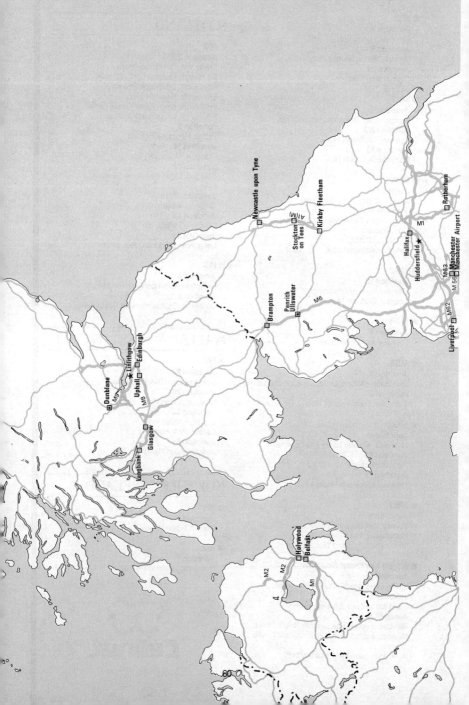

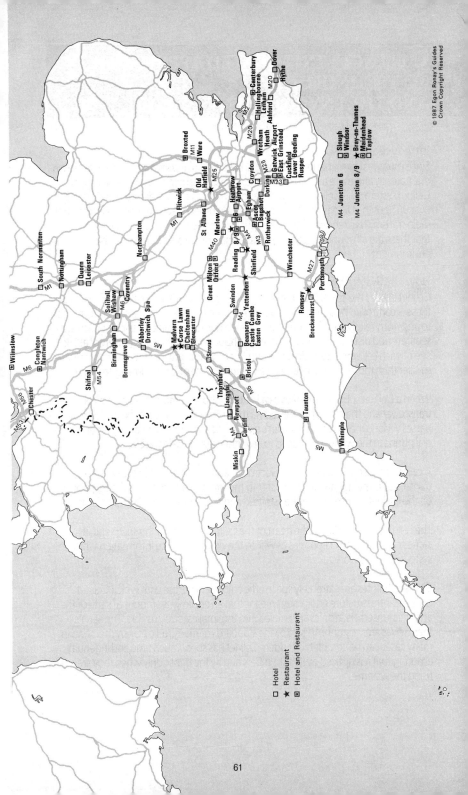

Hotel □
Restaurant ★
Hotel and Restaurant ⊡

M4 Junction 6
Slough □
Windsor ⊡

M4 Junction 8/9
Bray-on-Thames ★
Maidenhead ⊡
Taplow □

Dover ⊡
Hythe □
Canterbury ⊡
Hollingbourne □
Lenham □
Ashford ⊡
M20

Broxted ⊡
Ware □
M11

Wrotham □
Heath
Gatwick Airport ⊡
East Grinstead □
Cuckfield □
Lower Beeding
Rusper □

Old Hatfield ⊡
M25
Croydon ⊡
Dorking M23

Flitwick ⊡
Heathrow Airport ★

St Albans ⊡
Marlow □
M40
Egham □
Ascot ⊡
Bagshot □
Rotherwick □
Reading 8/9 ⊡
M4
M3
Shinfield ★

Northampton □
Great Milton ⊡
Oxford ⊡
Winchester □

South Normanton □
Nottingham ⊡
Quorn □
Leicester ⊡
M1
Swindon □
Yattendon ★
M27
Portsmouth ⊡

Solihull ⊡
Wishaw
Coventry □
M6
Romsey □
Brockenhurst □

Droitwich Spa □
Abberley □
Malvern ★
Corse Lawn ⊡
Cheltenham ⊡
Gloucester □
Beanacre □
Castle Combe
Easton Grey

Birmingham □
Bromsgrove □
M5
Stroud □
Bristol □

Willmslow ⊡
Congleton ⊡
Nantwich □
M6
Shifnal □
M54
Thornbury ⊡

Chester □
M53
M56
Llangybi □
Newport □
Taunton ⊡

Miskin □
M4
Cardiff □
Whimple ⊡
M5

CELLNET'S INTEGRATED APPROACH TO TECHNOLOGY AND THE ENVIRONMENT

Introduction

Since it was first available in 1985 the market for cellular communications has grown dramatically and there are now thousands of businessmen and women using the Cellnet system. The Cellnet network has grown to match this demand and already over 90% of the UK has access to the system. In order to achieve this more than 350 radio transmitters/receivers have been put in place but Cellnet have taken great care that these are all as unobtrusive as possible and will not adversely affect the environment.

How The System Works

Cellnet divides the country up into a large number of small units called cells. Each of these is controlled by a cell transceiver which both transmits and receives information to and from cellphones. The transceiver uses a number of radio channels which are separate and distinct from those in the neighbouring cell to avoid interference. The size of each cell varies according to a number of factors but in general urban cells are smaller than those in rural areas with a variance in size of 2km diameter to 20 km.

When a Cellnet subscriber makes a call, the cellphone contacts the nearest cell transceiver and the call is transmitted via the radio waves. Once at the cell, the call passes via landlines to one of Cellnet's exchanges and from there to any other direct dial phone in the world. Or, indeed to any other cellphone in the UK.

A cellsite consists of sophisticated electronics and aerials by which the calls are transmitted. The signals which constantly monitor the position of all the cellphones on the Cellnet system are also transmitted and received via the cellsite and its aerials.

The cellsite therefore lies at the heart of the Cellnet system. At the sharp end, it carries calls made on cellphones as well as the vital monitoring information which the system needs to work.

Cellnet's cellsites are extremely space efficient. The expertise with which Cellnet chose its infrastructure equipment means that an enormous amount of state of the art miniaturised electronics are packed into the smallest size possible. The aerials themselves are very unobtrusive by the standards of many radio transmitters and in many cases can be completely hidden. Cellnet has spent much time and ingenuity ensuring that it is noticed by its subscribers and by the public only when they are using the system.

Again, we did not want obtrusive aerials marring the famous profile of buildings such as Ely Cathedral, so we have subtly disguised our aerials, or hidden them behind turrets, protecting the environment and providing the best possible service to our subscribers.

Ely Cathedral
The Cellnet transmitter/receiver equipment is housed in the great tower of one of Britain's most beautiful cathedrals. It was hauled up through the trap door in the painted ceiling of the nave. The aerials are on top, hidden inside the flagpole and behind the four corner turrets of the tower.

Leith Hill

This lovely eighteenth century folly is situated on one of the highest points in the south east of England with beautiful views across the surrounding countryside. Cellnet have helped to preserve this countryside by using this building as the site for its transmitter/receiver.

Gorey Castle, Jersey

This picturesque medieval castle houses one of the cellsites which serve the Channel Islands where Cellnet was chosen to be the sole cellular system.

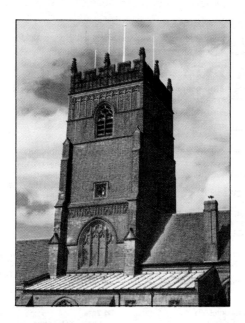

Holy Cross Church, Knutsford
Cellnet's aerials are disguised as flagpoles on the roof of this beautiful Victorian church.

Cellnet – caring for the customer and the environment
Cellnet's achievement is unparalleled. Not only have we brought the first real, high quality mobile voice and data communications to subscribers in the UK after only two and a half years, a figure that is expected to grow to six figures by the third anniversary of the system. We have rolled the network out across the country to cover 90% of the population – more than two years before the government licence's deadline.

Providing this coverage took some doing. Cellnet had to find literally hundreds of sites for the transmitter/receivers which relay cellphone calls to the Cellnet exchange and on into the public telephone network. In urban centres where Cellnet was introduced initially, the problem was not so great as there are many high buildings on which to mount aerials.

However, as the network rapidly spread out of the cities and into more remote sites, the task became more difficult. The easy solution would have been to erect radio masts in the middle of the countryside. Cellnet did not do that. We used imagination and ingenuity to protect the countryside and the environment by selecting sites in existing buildings many of which are historic and picturesque sites.

For further information see the Cellnet section, pages 24-30.

DE LUXE AND GRADE 1 HOTELS

LONDON

■ **91%**
The Connaught, W1
■ **90%**
The Berkeley, SW1
Claridge's, W1
The Dorchester, W1
Inn on the Park, W1
The Savoy, WC2

■ **89%**
Hyatt Carlton Tower, SW1
■ **87%**
Howard Hotel, WC2
The Ritz, W1
■ **86%**
Inter-Continental Hotel, W1
Le Meridien Piccadilly, W1
■ **85%**
Grosvenor House, W1
Hyde Park Hotel, SW1
London Hilton on Park Lane, W1
London Marriott Hotel, W1
Londonderry Hotel, W1
May Fair Inter-Continental Hotel, W1
Sheraton Park Tower, SW1
■ **81%**
Capital Hotel, SW3
Dukes Hotel, SW1
Royal Garden Hotel, W8
Royal Lancaster Hotel, W2
■ **80%**
Athenaeum Hotel, W1
Hotel Britannia Inter-Continental, W1
Churchill Hotel, W1
The Halcyon, W11
Park Lane Hotel, W1
The Selfridge, W1

■ **79%**
Holiday Inn (Swiss Cottage), NW3
Lowndes Thistle Hotel, SW1
Portman Inter-Continental Hotel, W1
■ **78%**
Belgravia-Sheraton, SW1
The Gloucester, SW7
The Montcalm, W1
Westbury Hotel, W1
■ **77%**
Brown's Hotel, W1
Goring Hotel, SW1
Stafford Hotel, SW1
The Waldorf, WC2

■ **76%**
Blakes Hotel, SW7
Dorset Square Hotel, NW1
The Fenja, SW3
Holiday Inn (Mayfair), W1
St James Court Hotel, SW1
Tower Thistle Hotel, E1
■ **75%**
Chesterfield Hotel, W1
Whites Hotel, W2
■ **74%**
Chelsea Hotel, SW1
Holiday Inn (Marble Arch), W1
Mountbatten Hotel, WC2
Stakis St Ermin's Hotel, SW1
■ **73%**
Marlborough Crest, WC1
White House, NW1
■ **72%**
Ladbroke Westmoreland Hotel, NW8
Royal Horseguards Thistle Hotel, SW1
■ **71%**
Cadogan Thistle Hotel, SW1
Kensington Palace Thistle, W8
Ladbroke at Park Lane, W1
Ramada Hotel London, W1
■ **70%**
Cavendish Hotel, SW1
The Clifton-Ford, W1
Hilton International Kensington, W11
Royal Westminster Thistle Hotel, SW1

LONDON AIRPORTS

Gatwick
■ **76%**
Gatwick Hilton International
■ **71%**
Copthorne Hotel
Gatwick Penta Hotel

Heathrow
■ **77%**
Sheraton Skyline
■ **73%**
Holiday Inn
■ **72%**
Excelsior Hotel
■ **70%**
Sheraton-Heathrow Hotel

ENGLAND

■ **89%**
Taplow: Cliveden
■ **88%**
Bath: Royal Crescent Hotel
Ston Easton: Ston Easton Park
■ **87%**
New Milton: Chewton Glen Hotel
Warminster: Bishopstrow House
■ **86%**
Eastbourne: Grand Hotel
■ **85%**
Great Milton: Le Manoir aux Quat' Saisons
Nantwich: Rookery Hall
Stratford-upon-Avon: Ettington Park Hotel
■ **84%**
Torquay: Imperial Hotel
■ **83%**
Buckland: Buckland Manor
Hunstrete: Hunstrete House
■ **82%**
Ashford: Eastwell Manor
Bath: Priory Hotel
Chester: Chester Grosvenor
Oakham: Hambleton Hall
Thornbury: Thornbury Castle Hotel
Windsor: Oakley Court Hotel
■ **81%**
Birmingham: Metropole & Warwick Hotel
Chagford: Gidleigh Park Hotel
East Grinstead: Gravetye Manor
Leamington Spa: Mallory Court
Longhorsley: Linden Hall Hotel
Rotherwick: Tylney Hall
■ **80%**
Brighton: The Grand
Freshford: Homewood Park
Hintlesham: Hintlesham Hall
Taunton: Castle Hotel
Ullswater: Sharrow Bay Hotel
Winchester: Lainston House
■ **79%**
Birmingham: Plough & Harrow Hotel
Broadway: Lygon Arms
Cheltenham: The Greenway
Dedham: Maison Talbooth
Grasmere: Michael's Nook
Grimston: Congham Hall
Maidenhead: Fredrick's Hotel
■ **78%**
Bagshot: Pennyhill Park Hotel
Lower Beeding: South Lodge
Reading: Ramada Hotel
York: Middlethorpe Hall
■ **77%**
Ascot: Royal Berkshire
Bakewell: Hassop Hall Hotel
Battle: Netherfield Place
Beanacre: Beechfield House
Bilbrough: Bilbrough Manor Hotel
Borrowdale: Lodore Swiss Hotel
Marlow: Compleat Angler Hotel
Newcastle upon Tyne: Gosforth Park Thistle Hotel

Portsmouth: Holiday Inn
Stratford-upon-Avon: Billesley Manor
Uckfield: Horsted Place
■ **76%**
Bath: Apsley House Hotel
Bournemouth: Carlton Hotel
Broxted: Whitehall Hotel
Chaddesley Corbett: Brockencote Hall
Kirkby Fleetham: Kirkby Fleetham Hall
Manchester: Portland Thistle Hotel
North Stoke: Springs Hotel
Six Mile Bottom: Swynford Paddocks
Slough: Holiday Inn
Storrington: Little Thakeham
■ **75%**
Bolton Abbey: Devonshire Arms
Bournemouth: Royal Bath Hotel
Bristol: Ladbroke Dragonara Hotel
Chester: Crabwall Manor
Climping: Bailiffscourt
Droitwich Spa: Château Impney Hotel
Easton Grey: Whatley Manor
Gittisham: Combe House Hotel
Gloucester: Hatton Court
Hurstbourne Tarrant: Esseborne Manor
Lenham: Chilston Park
Manchester: Hotel Piccadilly
Newcastle upon Tyne: Holiday Inn
St Albans: Noke Thistle Hotel
Shifnal: Park House Hotel
Tetbury: Calcot Manor
Ullswater: Leeming House Hotel
Woodstock: Feathers Hotel
■ **74%**
Abberley: Elms Hotel
Aston Clinton: Bell Inn
Baslow: Cavendish Hotel
Birmingham: Copthorne Hotel
Flitwick: Flitwick Manor
Great Ayton: Ayton Hall
Hockley Heath: Nuthurst Grange
Langdale: Langdale Hotel
Liskeard: The Well House
Northampton: Swallow Hotel
Poole: Mansion House
Quorn: Quorn Country Hotel
Stow-on-the-Wold: Wyck Hill House
Stratford-upon-Avon: Welcombe Hotel
Whimple: Woodhayes
Wishaw: Belfry Hotel
Wrotham Heath: Post House Hotel
■ **73%**
Castle Donington: Donington Thistle Hotel
Crathorne: Crathorne Hall Hotel
Eastbourne: Cavendish Hotel
Holbeton: Alston Hall Hotel
Hythe: Hythe Imperial Hotel
Leicester: Holiday Inn
Lower Slaughter: Lower Slaughter Manor
Maiden Newton: Maiden Newton House
Rotherham: Rotherham Moat House
Wareham: Priory Hotel
Windermere: Miller Howe Hotel
Woodstock: Bear Hotel
■ **72%**
Bampton: Huntsham Court

DE LUXE AND GRADE 1 HOTELS

Bedford: Woodlands Manor Hotel
Birmingham: Albany Hotel
Birmingham: Holiday Inn
Brampton: Farlam Hall Hotel
Brockenhurst: Rhinefield House Hotel
Canterbury: County Hotel
Castle Combe: Manor House Hotel
Chelmsford: Pontlands Park
Congleton: Great Moreton Hall Hotel
Dedham: Dedham Vale Hotel
Dover: Dover Moat House
Grasmere: Wordsworth Hotel
Harrogate: Majestic
Henley in Arden: Yew Trees Hotel
Manchester Airport: Ladbroke International Hotel
Penrith: North Lakes Gateway Hotel
Salcombe: Tides Reach Hotel
Scarborough: Royal Hotel
Solihull: Regency Hotel
Tunbridge Wells: Spa Hotel

■ **71%**
Ambleside: Rothay Manor
Bristol: Grand Hotel
Bristol: Holiday Inn
Broadway: Dormy House
Bury St Edmunds: Angel Hotel
Croydon: Holiday Inn
Cuckfield: Ockenden Manor Hotel
Doncaster: Doncaster Moat House
Eastbourne: Queen's Hotel
Evershot: Summer Lodge
Halifax: Holdsworth House
Handforth: Belfry Hotel
Jervaulx: Jervaulx Hall Hotel
Leeds: Ladbroke Dragonara Hotel
Ludlow: Feathers Hotel
Markington: Hob Green Hotel
Matlock: Riber Hall
Moreton-in-Marsh: Manor House Hotel
Newcastle upon Tyne: County Thistle Hotel
North Huish: Brookdale House
Nottingham: Albany Hotel
Nottingham: Royal Moat House International
Rusper: Ghyll Manor
South Normanton: Swallow Hotel
Stamford: George of Stamford
Stratford-upon-Avon: Moat House International
Woodbridge: Seckford Hall Hotel
York: Viking Hotel

■ **70%**
Bournemouth: Highcliff Hotel
Brighton: Brighton Metropole Hotel
Brighton: Old Ship Hotel
Bromsgrove: Grafton Manor
Canterbury: Howfield Manor
Clanfield: Plough at Clanfield
Coventry: De Vere Hotel
Dorking: Burford Bridge Hotel
Egham: Great Fosters
Egham: Runnymede Hotel
Felixstowe: Orwell Moat House
Ferndown: Dormy Hotel
Gillingham: Stock Hill House Hotel

Hatch Beauchamp: Farthings Country House Hotel
Helmsley: Black Swan Hotel
Hollingbourne: Great Danes Hotel
Huntingdon: Old Bridge Hotel
Ipswich: Belstead Brook Hotel
Kilve: Meadow House
Liverpool: Atlantic Tower Hotel
Lymington: Passford House Hotel
Manchester: Britannia Hotel
Oxford: Randolph Hotel
Plymouth: Copthorne Hotel
Plymouth: Holiday Inn
Poole: Hospitality Inn, The Quay
Staddle Bridge: McCoy's at the Tontine
Stockton on Tees: Swallow Hotel
Storrington: Abingworth Hall
Stratford-upon-Avon: Shakespeare Hotel
Swindon: Blunsdon House Hotel
Tetbury: Snooty Fox Hotel
Upper Slaughter: Lords of the Manor Hotel
Ware: Briggens House Hotel
Warwick: Ladbroke Hotel
Wilmslow: Stanneylands Hotel

SCOTLAND

■ **91%**
Fort William: Inverlochy Castle

■ **88%**
Auchterarder: Gleneagles Hotel

■ **82%**
Advie: Tulchan Lodge
Dunblane: Cromlix House

■ **81%**
Turnberry: Turnberry Hotel

■ **78%**
Edinburgh: Caledonian Hotel
Edinburgh: Edinburgh Sheraton
Glasgow: Holiday Inn

■ **77%**
Edinburgh: George Hotel
Gullane: Greywalls
St Andrews: Old Course Golf & Country Club
St Andrew's: The Rusack's

■ **76%**
Glasgow: One Devonshire Gardens
Inverness: Culloden House

■ **75%**
Aberdeen: Holiday Inn
Arisaig: Arisaig House
Glasgow: Albany Hotel
Knipoch: Knipoch Hotel
Newton Stewart: Kirroughtree Hotel

■ **74%**
Edinburgh: Ladbroke Dragonara Hotel
Humbie: Johnstounburn House Hotel
Kelso: Sunlaws House Hotel
Kilwinning: Montgreenan Mansion House
Old Meldrum: Meldrum House Hotel
Stewarton: Chapeltoun House

■ **73%**
Aberdeen: Bucksburn Moat House
Aviemore: Stakis Four Seasons Hotel

Eriska: Isle of Eriska
Kilchrenan: Ardanaiseig
■ **72%**
Auchterarder: Auchterarder House
Bonnyrigg: Dalhousie Castle Hotel
Callander: Roman Camp Hotel
Glasgow: Stakis Grosvenor Hotel
■ **71%**
Aberdeen: Copthorne Hotel
Banchory: Raemoir House Hotel
Edinburgh: Carlton Highland Hotel
Edinburgh: King James Thistle Hotel
Kildrummy: Kildrummy Castle Hotel
Nairn: Clifton Hotel
Peebles: Peebles Hotel Hydro
Portpatrick: Knockinaam Lodge Hotel
■ **70%**
Ballater: Tullich Lodge
Crinan: Crinan Hotel
Glasgow: Hospitality Inn
Langbank: Gleddoch House Hotel
Uphall: Houstoun House

WALES

■ **78%**
Newport: Celtic Manor Hotel
■ **75%**
Cardiff: Holiday Inn
Llandudno: Bodysgallen Hall
■ **74%**
Llandderfel: Palé Hall
Llangybi: Cwrt Bleddyn Hotel
■ **71%**
Cardiff: Park Hotel
Miskin: Miskin Manor

CHANNEL ISLANDS

■ **81%**
St.Saviour, Jersey: Longueville Manor Hotel

■ **77%**
St Peter Port, Guernsey: St Pierre Park Hotel
■ **76%**
St Brelade's Bay, Jersey: Hotel l'Horizon
■ **75%**
St Brelade, Jersey: Atlantic Hotel
■ **71%**
St Lawrence, Jersey: Little Grove Hotel

■ **70%**
Bouley Bay, Jersey: Water's Edge Hotel
St Brelade's Bay, Jersey: St Brelade's Bay Hotel

NORTHERN IRELAND

■ **74%**
Holywood: Culloden Hotel
■ **70%**
Belfast: Europa Hotel

REPUBLIC OF IRELAND

■ **88%**
Kenmare: Park Hotel Kenmare
■ **87%**
Cong: Ashford Castle
■ **80%**
Dublin: Shelbourne Hotel

■ **79%**
Dublin: Berkeley Court
Gorey: Marlfield House
■ **77%**
Dublin: Jurys Hotel
Dublin: Westbury Hotel
Maynooth: Moyglare Manor
■ **76%**
Cashel: Cashel Palace Hotel
Newmarket-on-Fergus: Dromoland Castle
Parknasilla: Parknasilla Great Southern Hotel
■ **74%**
Dromahair: Drumlease Glebe House
Dublin: Burlington Hotel
Newmarket-on-Fergus: Clare Inn
■ **73%**
Cashel: Cashel House Hotel
Killarney: Hotel Europe
■ **72%**
Ballynahinch: Ballynahinch Castle
Beaufort: Hotel Dunloe Castle
Mallow: Longueville House
■ **71%**
Killiney: Fitzpatrick's Castle Hotel
■ **70%**
Ballyvaughan: Gregans Castle Hotel
Cork: Imperial Hotel
Rathnew: Tinakilly House Hotel

S cotch whisky is the world's leading drink. It outsells every other spirit. But it has taken hundreds of years rich in history for Scotch to conquer the world.

The art of distilling was first attempted in Asia in 800 BC and found its way to Europe via Egypt. There is some evidence that the art could have been brought to Scotland by Christian monks. But it has never been proved that Highland farmers did not discover for themselves how to distil spirits from their surplus barley.

The term 'whisky' comes originally from the Gaelic 'uisge beatha' or aqua vitae meaning water of life. The first actual recorded mention of distilling in Scotland was not until 1494 — an entry in the Exchequer Rolls list, 'Eight bolls of malt to Friar John wherewith to make aqua vitae'.

In 1578 an Act of Parliament prohibited distilling by everyone except 'Lords' and 'gentlemen'. The government were not concerned about drunkenness in the labouring classes. They were in fact worried that grain supplies for food were running short.

The first excise tax was introduced by the Scottish Parliament in 1644. Dodging the revenue became a national pastime and the 18th century became the age of the smuggler. The authorities were openly flouted and far more whisky was being distilled illegally than through stills licensed by the government. It is estimated that in Edinburgh in 1777 there were only eight licensed stills compared with 400 being run illegally.

THE
OF

WILLIAM GRANT

ELIZABETH GRANT

HISTORY
SCOTCH

CHARLES GORDON IN INDIA

THE GLENFIDDICH DISTILLERY 10TH ANNIVERSARY

Local dignitaries and sometimes the excise officers themselves were involved in smuggling. Rewards were offered for information on illegal stills, but often the ones uncovered were in fact recently abandoned or worn out. The person who got the reward was the still's former owner who would use the money to buy a new still.

In 1823 the duty was reduced and the illicit trade began to die out, clearing the way for Scotland's great distilling families like William Grant & Sons to take over.

It was in July 1886 that the company's founder, William Grant, bought the equipment for his first distillery for the princely sum of £119 19s 10d. A year later, on Christmas Day, the first Glenfiddich ran from the stills just in time to celebrate Queen Victoria's Jubilee.

Today, 100 years on, the company is still independent, and owned and managed by the direct descendants of William Grant. The history of the Grant family reveals an unrivalled

»—→

THE HISTORY OF SCOTCH

dedication to quality and craftsmanship and respect for heritage and tradition...

William Grant was born in December 1839, the son of a Waterloo veteran, and became an apprentice shoemaker in the Highland village of Dufftown.

For a while he served at the Limeworks of Crachie where his early ambition was to quarry his own limestone. But his plans foundered. At the last moment, the laird refused him the concession for fear of the kilns setting fire to his game woods.

Undeterred, at 27 William Grant became book-keeper, and later manager, at Mortlach Distillery. He then set his sights on producing the finest malt whisky in the world.

It took 20 years for William Grant to save enough money to start the family business. He had nine children to clothe and educate on less than £100 a year. Yet he managed to send five of his sons to university.

In the summer of 1886 William Grant bought stills from the old Cardow distillery. Within a year he and his children, with the help of a stonemason, had built the Glenfiddich distillery.

The distillery is blessed with an abundant and pure source of water —the mountain spring known as

the Robbie Dubh (pronounced doo). It is said that an old Catholic priest "imparted the secret of these magical waters" whilst William was prospecting in the Conval hills around Dufftown. He told William how the Robbie Dubh (Gaelic for Black Robert) was known by the ancient whisky smugglers of Mortlach for the excellent illicit whisky its waters produced.

In 1892 William Grant built his second distillery, Balvenie, a mere stone's throw from Glenfiddich and converted from the new Balvenie Castle, abandoned by the Duff family some 200 years earlier.

In 1898, faced by the failure of Pattisons, his largest customer, William Grant decided to market his own blended whisky, and

OPEN ALL YEAR ROUND
WEEKDAYS
9.30 AM–4.30 PM
FROM MAY-OCTOBER
SATURDAYS
9.30 AM–4.30 PM
SUNDAY
12 NOON–4.30 PM

OLD PHOTOGRAPH OF
GLENFIDDICH DISTILLERY

the Grant's brand was born.

The expansion into overseas markets began in 1905. William Grant's son, John, established agencies in Canada and the United States and son-in-law, Charles Gordon travelled the Far East including India, China and Japan. Glenfiddich and William Grant's, were now available on every continent.

When William Grant died in 1923, at the age of 83, he had laid the foundation of a whisky business whose wares would soon be of worldwide reputation.

Today, William Grant & Sons is Scotland's largest independent distiller, with markets in over 190 countries. Glenfiddich is the world's favourite malt whisky and there have been no sacrifices in the quality of the original.

Glenfiddich is the only distillery in the Scottish Highlands where malt whisky is distilled, matured and bottled on the premises — so ensuring the continued purity of taste that Glenfiddich is renowned for the world over.

William Grant's has become one of the major blended whiskies in the world today, and the fastest growing in the UK in recent years.

∴ THE GLENFIDDICH DISTILLERY ∴
DUFFTOWN BANFFSHIRE
TEL: (0340) 20373

TOWN HOUSE HOTELS

This exclusive category highlights a small number of hotels of distinctive personality. Most are conversions of town residences which retain not only their period facades but also interior character and, to some extent, the feel of a private house. None of them has more than 50 bedrooms, and very few are owned by groups. Excellent personal service is another attribute.

Brighton: Granville Hotel
Brighton: Topps Hotel
Bury St Edmunds: Angel Hotel
Harrogate: Russell Hotel
Harrogate: Studley Hotel
Ipswich: Marlborough Hotel
Poole: Mansion House
Sherborne: Eastbury Hotel
Shifnal: Park House Hotel
Stratford-upon-Avon: Stratford House Hotel
Wareham: Priory Hotel
Wickham: Old House Hotel
Woodstock: Feathers Hotel
York: Judges Lodging
York: Mount Royale Hotel

LONDON

Alexander Hotel, SW7
Dorset Square Hotel, NW1
Drury Lane Moat House Hotel, WC2
Dukes Hotel, SW1
The Fenja, SW3
The Halcyon, W11
Portobello Hotel, W11

ENGLAND

Bath: Priory Hotel
Bath: Royal Crescent Hotel
Birmingham: Plough & Harrow Hotel

SCOTLAND

Edinburgh: Howard Hotel
Glasgow: One Devonshire Gardens
Glasgow: White House
Nairn: Clifton Hotel

WALES

Llandudno: St Tudno Hotel

REPUBLIC OF IRELAND

Cashel (Co. Tipperary): Cashel Palace Hotel

JUST DESSERTS

When you are entertaining family or friends to a special meal, there is nothing nicer than a really spectacular dessert to round off the occasion in style. With this in mind, we asked several of the chefs from our starred restaurants to send us a favourite recipe for an interesting and unusual dessert.

These are health-conscious days for many of us, so most of our desserts are based on fruit. They are all, of course, sweetened with sugar, but unless you are following a sugar-free diet because of a medical condition, this should not be a problem. Sugar is a perfectly natural food derived either from sugar-cane or sugar beet, and has for centuries been recognized not only as a sweetener but as a valuable preservative for all kinds of foods. And remember, each teaspoonful contains only 16 calories!

BRUNO LOUBET
Le Petit Blanc
Oxford

MILLE-FEUILLE OF CITRUS FRUITS
WITH A PASSION FRUIT SORBET AND COULIS

INGREDIENTS (for 8 portions)

200 gr puff pastry
125 gr natural yoghourt
125 ml double cream
1 tablespoon Grand Marnier
50 gr sugar
6 oranges
4 grapefruit
100 gr icing sugar
15 passion fruits
$\frac{1}{2}$ mango
100 gr caster sugar
1$\frac{1}{2}$ dcl of sugar syrup to make:
300 gr passion fruit sorbet
2 dcl passion fruit coulis

METHOD

Segment all the citrus fruits and remove skin and pips. Make a light sugar syrup with 50 gr of sugar and a little boiling water and pour over the segments. Whip cream and yoghourt until it forms a ribbon, perfume with Grand Marnier and refrigerate. Make the sorbet and the coulis of passion fruits (see method below).

Pre-heat the oven to 220 degrees C. Meanwhile, roll out the pastry until very thin ($\frac{1}{2}$ mm) on a board dusted with icing sugar. Allow to rest for 15 mins, then put on a greased baking tray and cook for about 4 mins. Using a pastry cutter, cut out 24 circles.

For the coulis and sorbet you will need a sorbet machine. Halve the passion fruits and scoop out the pulp. Put pulp in a pan with the caster sugar and bring to the boil, stirring constantly. Remove from the heat and put the mixture through a moulinette, then pass through a fine hair sieve. Chill until needed.

Scoop the flesh from the half-mango and liquidise ready for the sorbet. Take 1 dcl of the passion fruit coulis, the mango flesh and mix with the sugar syrup, then turn into the sorbet machine to make the sorbet.

On a plate, put a circle of puff pastry, topped with a spoon of cream, then a layer of orange and grapefruit segments; top with another circle of pastry, cream and fruit, then finish with a pastry circle and dust with icing sugar.

Arrange more fruit segments around the mille feuille, with the passion fruit coulis and two small spoonfuls of the sorbet. Serve.

CINNAMON SOUFFLÉ
WITH DRAMBUIE CREAM

INGREDIENTS (for 4 portions)

1 lb 6 oz pears
1 pt water
1 level tspn cornflour
1 tblspn water
3 tblspn cinnamon
3 oz caster sugar
5 egg whites
½ pt whipping cream (plus caster sugar to taste)
½ measure Drambuie
½ oz icing sugar

METHOD

For the panade:

Roughly chop and core pears, place in saucepan, barely cover with water and cook until soft, then liquidize and rub through a sieve. Return to heat in a clean pan and simmer till thick, stirring occasionally (approx. 10 mins).

Mix cornflour and water to a smooth paste, then whisk into the pears and leave on a low heat for approx. 10 mins. Add cinnamon powder and whisk. (If prepared in advance, store in the fridge).

For the cream:

Whisk cream until it forms peaks, then sweeten and flavour with Drambuie.

For the soufflé:

Pre-heat oven to gas mark 7. Warm the panade in a bain Marie. Whisk egg whites until they peak. Add caster sugar a little at a time. Mix one spoonful of the egg whites into the panade, then fold in the rest.

Butter and sugar individual ramekins and spoon in the soufflé mixture until 1 in above the rim. Shape the edges at a 35 degree angle, leaving the top flat.

Place on a baking sheet in the oven for about 10–12 mins.

Dust with icing sugar and serve immediately, with a saucer of cream.

NORWEGIAN CREAM CAKE
(BLØTKAKE MED MARSIPANLOKK)

INGREDIENTS FOR SPONGE

4 eggs
130 gr sugar
125 gr plain flour
½ tspn baking powder

INGREDIENTS FOR MARZIPAN

100 gr ground almonds
100 gr icing sugar
white of an egg

INGREDIENTS FOR FILLING

1·2 ltr whipping cream
150 gr cloudberries
2 tblspns brown sugar
2 tblspns ground hazelnuts

METHOD

Whisk eggs and sugar until white and fluffy. To ensure good results, introduce lots of air into the mixture by holding the whisk partly out of the mixture. Sieve flour and baking powder and carefully blend into the eggs and sugar.

Grease a loose-bottomed tin (10 in) and shake flour all round the inside. Pour mixture in and cook at 150 degrees C for 1 hour. Test with skewer to ensure middle has cooked. Free from tin and place on rack till cool, then cut horizontally into three layers. If you wish, the cake can be moistened with a little suitable liqueur.

Whip cream until fairly stiff, but not dry. Use half the cream to mix with the cloudberries. Put the bottom layer of cake onto a plate, then spread with half the cloudberry cream, and top with half the hazelnuts and sugar. Place the second layer of cake on top and repeat the cream, hazelnut and sugar layers. Put the last layer of the cake in place, then use the remaining half of the cream to spread all over the top and sides of the cake.

Roll out the marzipan thinly into a big enough circle to cover the entire cake – the marzipan should be about 2 mm thick.

Finally, decorate with small blobs of cream and fresh flowers (violets look particularly lovely).

DAVID ADLARD
Adlard's Restaurant
Wymondham, Norfolk

WARM WINTER TART
WITH SPICED APPLE AND A CALVADOS SABAYON

INGREDIENTS (serves 6; use an 8 in ring mould)

The Pastry
8½ oz plain flour
2¼ oz ground almonds
6 oz butter
1 beaten egg
vanilla essence
5 oz caster sugar

Almond Covering
3 oz softened butter
5 oz granulated sugar
½ vanilla pod
¾ tsp cinnamon
4 oz chopped almonds
4 dessert apples

Calvados Sabayon
3 egg yolks
1 level tablespoon caster sugar
1 tblspn calvados
4 tblspn white wine

METHOD

Pastry
In a bowl place the flour, almonds, and butter. Work the ingredients in as for short-crust pastry. In another bowl beat the egg, sugar and vanilla essence until the mixture is very pale. Add the egg mixture to the flour mixture and rapidly combine. Finish on the table by kneading gently until the pastry is uniform. Wrap in cling film and rest in the fridge for two hours. Roll the pastry out ⅛" thick and line the ring mould (the pastry may be too hard after being in the fridge so leave it at room temperature for 15 mins).

Almond Covering
To make the almond covering, cream the sugar and butter, add the vanilla seeds and beat in cinnamon and chopped almonds to make the mixture uniform. Peel and core apples and cut into dice. Almost fill the pastry case. Press out a circle of almond paste to cover the apples. Fill in spaces to form a solid layer. Bake at 400 degrees F (gas mark 6) when the top should be golden brown and the pastry cooked (about 40 minutes). Before serving, warm the tart and then portion it. Make the sabayon.

Sabayon
Put the sabayon ingredients in an ample, heat-proof, round bowl. Whisk to blend. Put the bowl over a saucepan of simmering water. Whisk vigorously for 3–4 mins. until the mixture is light and white, forming a thick mousse. Don't overcook and make scrambled egg! Put the sabayon round/on top of the tart.

COUNTRY HOUSE HOTELS

This is a select category of small hotels offering civilised comfort, good service and fine food in an attractive and peaceful rural setting. Most of them are imposing country mansions, converted and run with loving care by dedicated owners, often a husband-and-wife team. Generally they have no more than 35 bedrooms; all have recommended in-house restaurants, many of star standard.

ENGLAND

Ashford: Eastwell Manor
Bampton: Huntsham Court
Battle: Netherfield Place
Beanacre: Beechfield House
Bedford: Woodlands Manor Hotel
Bilbrough: Bilbrough Manor
Brampton: Farlam Hall Hotel
Broxted: Whitehall Hotel
Buckland: Buckland Manor
Chaddesley Corbett: Brockencote Hall
Chagford: Gidleigh Park Hotel
Cheltenham: The Greenway
Chester: Crabwall Manor
Corse Lawn: Corse Lawn House Hotel
Dedham: Dedham Vale Hotel
East Grinstead: Gravetye Manor
Ettington: Chase Hotel
Evershot: Summer Lodge
Flitwick: Flitwick Manor
Freshford: Homewood Park
Gillingham: Stock Hill House Hotel
Gittisham: Combe House Hotel
Grasmere: Michael's Nook
Great Milton: Le Manoir aux Quat' Saisons
Grimston: Congham Hall
Hintlesham: Hintlesham Hall
Hockley Heath: Nuthurst Grange
Hunstrete: Hunstrete House
Hurstbourne Tarrant: Esseborne Manor
Kildwick: Kildwick Hall
Kilve: Meadow House
Kingsbridge: Buckland-Tout-Saints Hotel
Kirkby Fleetham: Kirkby Fleetham Hall
Leamington Spa: Mallory Court

Liskeard: The Well House
Maiden Newton: Maiden Newton House
Matlock: Riber Hall
Nantwich: Rookery Hall
New Milton: Chewton Glen Hotel
North Huish: Brookdale House
Oakham: Hambleton Hall
Ston Easton: Ston Easton Park
Storrington: Abingworth Hall
Storrington: Little Thakeham
Taplow: Cliveden
Tetbury: Calcot Manor
Thornbury: Thornbury Castle Hotel
Uckfield: Horsted Place
Ullswater: Leeming House Hotel
Ullswater: Sharrow Bay Hotel
Warminster: Bishopstrow House
Whimple: Woodhayes
Windermere: Miller Howe Hotel
Worfield: Old Vicarage Hotel
York: Middlethorpe Hall

SCOTLAND

Arisaig: Arisaig House
Auchterarder: Auchterarder House
Ballater: Tullich Lodge
Drumnadrochit: Polmaily House Hotel
Dunblane: Cromlix House
Eriska: Isle of Eriska
Fort William: Inverlochy Castle
Gullane: Greywalls
Inverness: Culloden House
Kentallen of Appin: Ardsheal House
Kilchrenan: Ardanaiseig
Knipoch: Knipoch Hotel
Newton Stewart: Kirroughtree Hotel
Old Meldrum: Meldrum House Hotel
Portpatrick: Knockinaam Lodge Hotel
Scarista: Scarista House
Sleat: Kinloch Lodge
Uphall: Houstoun House

WALES

Llandudno: Bodysgallen Hall

CHANNEL ISLANDS

St Saviour, Jersey: Longueville Manor Hotel

REPUBLIC OF IRELAND

Ballyvaughan: Gregans Castle Hotel
Cashel (Co. Galway): Cashel House Hotel
Dromahair: Drumlease Glebe House
Gorey: Marlfield House
Kenmare: Park Hotel Kenmare
Maynooth: Moyglare Manor

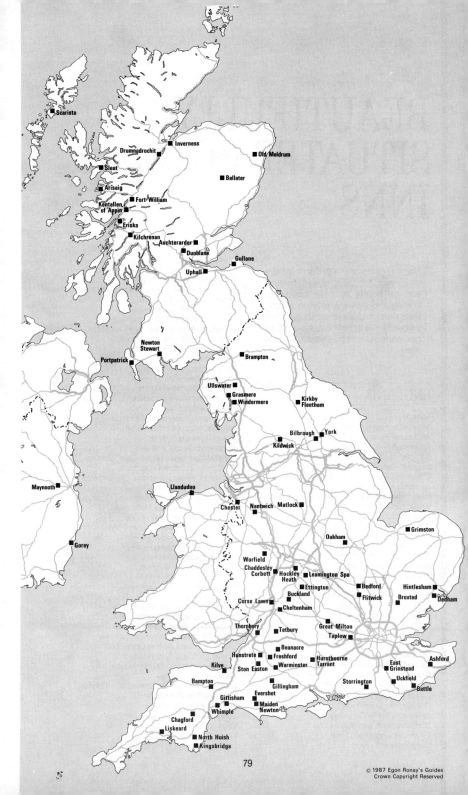

Scarista

Inverness
Drumnadrochit
Sleat   Old Meldrum
Arisaig   Ballater
Fort William
Kentallen
of Appin
Eriska
Kilchrenan
Auchterarder
Dunblane   Gullane
Uphall

Newton
Stewart   Brampton
Portpatrick

                   Ullswater
                   Grasmere   Kirkby
                   Windermere   Fleetham

                        Bilbrough   York
Maynooth   Kildwick

        Llandudno
Gorey   Chester Nantwich Matlock

                                Grimston

                        Oakham

                Worfield
                Chaddesley
                Corbett   Hockley
                           Heath Leamington Spa
                              Ettington   Bedford   Hintlesham
                        Buckland   Flitwick Broxted
                Corse Lawn   Dedham
                        Cheltenham

        Thornbury   Great Milton
                Tetbury   Taplow
                    Beanacre
        Hunstrete Freshford Hursthourne
        Kilve   Ston Easton Warminster Tarrant   Ashford
                                          East
Bampton   Grinstead
                                          Uckfield
                        Gillingham   Storrington   Battle
                Gittisham Evershot
        Whimple   Maiden
        Chagford   Newton
        Liskeard
            North Huish
            Kingsbridge

79

© 1987 Egon Ronay's Guides
Crown Copyright Reserved

BEAUTIFULLY SITUATED HOTELS & INNS

Many regions of the British Isles are renowned for their scenic beauty, and for hotels in these areas the setting and views are often among their most important attributes. The following is a list of hotels judged by our inspectors to be beautifully situated.

ENGLAND

Abberley: Elms Hotel
Ambleside: Nanny Brow
Ambleside: Rothay Manor
Applethwaite: Underscar Hotel
Ashford: Eastwell Manor
Bagshot: Pennyhill Park Hotel
Bakewell: Hassop Hall Hotel
Bampton: Huntsham Court
Bassenthwaite: Armathwaite Hall
Battle: Netherfield Place
Bibury: Bibury Court Hotel
Bilbrough: Bilbrough Manor
Bonchurch: Winterbourne Hotel
Borrowdale: Borrowdale Hotel
Borrowdale: Lodore Swiss Hotel
Boughton Monchelsea: Tanyard Hotel
Brampton: Farlam Hall Hotel
Branscombe: Masons Arms
Brockenhurst: Rhinefield House Hotel
Buckland: Buckland Manor
Burley: Burley Manor Hotel
Calstock: Danescombe Valley Hotel
Carlyon Bay: Carlyon Bay Hotel
Carlyon Bay: Porth Avallen Hotel
Cartmel: Aynsome Manor Hotel
Castle Combe: Manor House Hotel
Chaddesley Corbett: Brockencote Hall
Chagford: Gidleigh Park Hotel
Chagford: Teignworthy
Chedington: Chedington Court
Cheltenham: The Greenway
Chittlehamholt: Highbullen Hotel
Churt: Frensham Pond Hotel
Climping: Bailiffscourt

Congleton: Great Moreton Hall Hotel
Cornhill-on-Tweed: Tillmouth Park Hotel
Crathorne: Crathorne Hall Hotel
Crosby-on-Eden: Crosby Lodge Hotel
Dedham: Maison Talbooth
Dovedale: Izaak Walton Hotel
Dovedale: Peveril of the Peak Hotel
Dulverton: Ashwick Country House Hotel
East Grinstead: Gravetye Manor
Easton Grey: Whatley Manor
Egham: Great Fosters
Fairy Cross: Portledge Hotel
Flitwick: Flitwick Manor
Freshford: Homewood Park
Freshwater: Farringford Hotel
Frome: Selwood Manor
Gillingham: Stock Hill House Hotel
Gittisham: Combe House Hotel
Golant: Cormorant Hotel
Grasmere: Michael's Nook
Great Milton: Le Manoir aux Quat' Saisons
Grizedale: Grizedale Lodge Hotel
Hackness: Hackness Grange Country Hotel
Harrow Weald: Mansion House at Grim's Dyke
Haslemere: Lythe Hill Hotel
Hawkchurch: Fairwater Head Hotel
Hawkshead: Field Head House
Haytor: Bel Alp House Country Hotel
Helland Bridge: Tredethy Country Hotel
Hintlesham: Hintlesham Hall
Hockley Heath: Nuthurst Grange
Holbeton: Alston Hall Hotel
Hope Cove: Cottage Hotel
Hope Cove: Lantern Lodge Hotel
Horton-cum-Studley: Studley Priory Hotel
Hunstrete: Hunstrete House
Jervaulx: Jervaulx Hall Hotel
Kingsbridge: Buckland-Tout-Saints Hotel
Kirkby Fleetham: Kirkby Fleetham Hall
Lamorna Cove: Lamorna Cove Hotel
Leamington Spa: Mallory Court
Ledbury: Hope End Country House Hotel
Lenham: Chilston Park
Lewdown: Fox's Earth Lewtrenchard Manor
Liskeard: The Well House
Loftus: Grinkle Park Hotel
Longhorsley: Linden Hall Hotel
Looe: Talland Bay Hotel
Lower Beeding: South Lodge
Malvern: Cottage in the Wood Hotel

Marlow: Compleat Angler Hotel
Matlock: Riber Hall
Mawnan Smith: Meudon Hotel
Moretonhampstead: Manor House Hotel
Much Birch: Pilgrim Hotel
Mullion: Polurrian Hotel
Nantwich: Rookery Hall
New Milton: Chewton Glen Hotel
Oakham: Hambleton Hall
Otley: Chevin Lodge
Portloe: Lugger Hotel
Ross-on-Wye: Pengethley Manor Hotel
Ross-on-Wye: Walford House Hotel
Rotherwick: Tylney Hall
Rothley: Rothley Court
Rusper: Ghyll Manor
St Albans: Sopwell House Hotel
St Mawes: Hotel Tresanton
Salcombe: Soar Mill Cove Hotel
Saunton: Saunton Sands Hotel
Sheffield: Hotel St George
South Walsham: South Walsham Hall Hotel
Ston Easton: Ston Easton Park
Storrington: Abingworth Hall
Storrington: Little Thakeham
Stow-on-the-Wold: Wyck Hill House
Stratford-upon-Avon: Billesley Manor
Stratford-upon-Avon: Ettington Park Hotel
Streatley-on-Thames: Swan at Streatley
Taplow: Cliveden
Thornbury: Thornbury Castle Hotel
Thornton-le-Fylde: River House
Torquay: Imperial Hotel
Torquay: Osborne Hotel
Tresco: Island Hotel
Troutbeck: Mortal Man Hotel
Uckfield: Horsted Place
Ullswater: Leeming House Hotel
Ullswater: Old Church Hotel
Ullswater: Rampsbeck Hotel
Ullswater: Sharrow Bay Hotel
Underbarrow: Greenriggs Country House
Upper Slaughter: Lords of the Manor Hotel
Veryan: Nare Hotel
Wadhurst: Spindlewood Hotel
Ware: Briggens House Hotel
Warminster: Bishopstrow House
Whitewell: Inn at Whitewell
Whitwell-on-the-Hill: Whitwell Hall Country
  House Hotel
Winchester: Lainston House
Windermere: Langdale Chase Hotel
Windermere: Miller Howe Hotel
Windsor: Oakley Court Hotel
Winsford: Royal Oak Inn
Woodbridge: Seckford Hall Hotel
Woody Bay: Woody Bay Hotel
York: Middlethorpe Hall

SCOTLAND

Aberdeen: Ardoe House Hotel
Achiltibuie: Summer Isles Hotel
Advie: Tulchan Lodge
Airth: Airth Castle Hotel

Altnaharra: Altnaharra Hotel
Ardentinny: Ardentinny Hotel
Arduaine: Loch Melfort Hotel
Arisaig: Arisaig House
Auchterarder: Auchterarder House
Auchterarder: Gleneagles Hotel
Auchterhouse: Old Mansion House Hotel
Ballater: Tullich Lodge
Balquhidder: Ledcreich Hotel
Banchory: Raemoir House Hotel
Beattock: Auchen Castle Hotel
Bonnyrigg: Dalhousie Castle Hotel
Contin: Craigdarroch Lodge Hotel
Crinan: Crinan Hotel
Drumnadrochit: Polmaily House Hotel
Dryburgh: Dryburgh Abbey Hotel
Dunblane: Cromlix House
Duror: Stewart Hotel
Eckford: Marlefield Country House Hotel
Eriska: Isle of Eriska
Ettrickbridge: Ettrickshaws Hotel
Fort William: Inverlochy Castle
Fort William: Ladbroke Mercury Motor Inn
Garve: Inchbae Lodge Hotel
Gatehouse of Fleet: Cally Palace Hotel
Gullane: Greywalls
Humbie: Johnstounburn House Hotel
Inverness: Bunchrew House Hotel
Inverness: Culloden House
Inverness: Dunain Park Hotel
Isle of Gigha: Gigha Hotel
Isle of Raasay: Isle of Raasay Hotel
Kelso: Ednam House Hotel
Kelso: Sunlaws House Hotel
Kenmore: Kenmore Hotel
Kentallen of Appin: Ardsheal House
Kilchrenan: Ardanaiseig
Kilchrenan: Taychreggan Hotel
Kildrummy: Kildrummy Castle Hotel
Killiecrankie: Killiecrankie Hotel
Kilwinning: Montgreenan Mansion House
Kinclaven by Stanley: Ballathie House
Kinloch Rannoch: Loch Rannoch Hotel
Kirkmichael: Log Cabin Hotel
Knipoch: Knipoch Hotel
Langbank: Gleddoch House Hotel
Newton Stewart: Kirroughtree Hotel
North Middleton: Borthwick Castle
Old Meldrum: Meldrum House Hotel
Onich: Onich Hotel
Peebles: Cringletie House Hotel
Peebles: Peebles Hotel Hydro
Pitcaple: Pittodrie House Hotel
Pitlochry: Green Park Hotel
Port Appin: Airds Hotel
Port William: Corsemalzie House Hotel
Portpatrick: Knockinaam Lodge Hotel
Portsonachan: Portsonachan Hotel
Rockcliffe: Baron's Craig Hotel
St Fillans: Four Seasons Hotel
Scarista: Scarista House
Scourie: Eddrachilles Hotel
Skelmorlie: Manor Park Hotel
Sleat: Kinloch Lodge
Spean Bridge: Letterfinlay Lodge Hotel
Strachur: Creggans Inn

BEAUTIFULLY SITUATED HOTELS & INNS

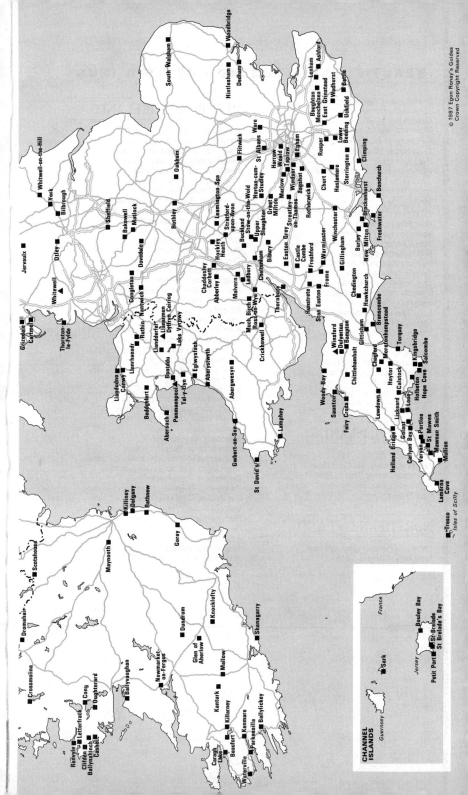

BEAUTIFULLY SITUATED HOTELS & INNS

Strathtummel: Port-an-Eilean Hotel
Talladale: Loch Maree Hotel
Tarbert: Stonefield Castle Hotel
Tiroran: Tiroran House
Turnberry: Turnberry Hotel
Tweedsmuir: Crook Inn
Uig: Uig Hotel
Whitebridge: Knockie Lodge Hotel

WALES

Abergwesyn: Llwynderw Hotel
Abersoch: Porth Tocyn Hotel
Aberystwyth: Conrah Country Hotel
Beddgelert: Royal Goat Hotel
Bontddu: Bontddu Hall Hotel
Conwy: Sychnant Pass Hotel
Crickhowell: Gliffaes Hotel
Eglwysfach: Ynyshir Hall Hotel
Gwbert-on-Sea: Cliff Hotel
Lake Vyrnwy: Lake Vyrnwy Hotel
Lamphey: Court Hotel
Llanarmon Dyffryn Ceiriog: Hand Hotel
Llandderfel: Palé Hall
Llandudno: Bodysgallen Hall
Llanrhaeadr: Llanrhaeadr Hall
Penmaenpool: George III Hotel
Ruthin: Ruthin Castle
St David's: Warpool Court Hotel
Tal-y-Llyn: Ty'n-y-Cornel Hotel

CHANNEL ISLANDS

Bouley Bay, Jersey: Water's Edge Hotel
Petit Port, Jersey: Sea Crest Hotel
St Brelade, Jersey: Atlantic Hotel
St Brelade's Bay, Jersey: Hotel l'Horizon
Sark: Stocks Hotel

NORTHERN IRELAND

Larne: Magheramorne House Hotel
Portaferry: Portaferry Hotel

REPUBLIC OF IRELAND

Ballylickey: Ballylickey House
Ballylickey: Sea View House Hotel
Ballynahinch: Ballynahinch Castle
Ballyvaughan: Gregans Castle Hotel
Beaufort: Hotel Dunloe Castle
Caragh Lake: Ard-Na-Sidhe
Caragh Lake: Caragh Lodge
Cashel (Co. Galway): Cashel House Hotel
Cashel (Co. Galway): Zetland House Hotel
Clifden: Abbeyglen Castle Hotel
Clifden: Hotel Ardagh
Clifden: Rock Glen Hotel
Cong: Ashford Castle
Crossmolina: Enniscoe House
Culleenamore: Knockmuldowney Hotel
Delgany: Glenview Hotel
Dromahair: Drumlease Glebe House
Dundrum: Dundrum House Hotel
Glen of Aherlow: Aherlow House Hotel
Gorey: Marlfield House
Kanturk: Assolas Country House
Kenmare: Park Hotel Kenmare
Killarney: Aghadoe Heights Hotel
Killarney: Cahernane Hotel
Killarney: Castlerosse Hotel
Killarney: Hotel Europe
Killiney: Court Hotel
Killiney: Fitzpatrick's Castle Hotel
Knocklofty: Knocklofty House Hotel
Letterfrack: Rosleague Manor Hotel
Mallow: Longueville House
Maynooth: Moyglare Manor
Newmarket-on-Fergus: Clare Inn
Newmarket-on-Fergus: Dromoland Castle
Oughterard: Connemara Gateway Hotel
Oughterard: Currarevagh House
Parknasilla: Parknasilla Great Southern Hotel
Rathmullan: Rathmullan House
Rathnew: Tinakilly House Hotel
Renvyle: Renvyle House Hotel
Rossnowlagh: Sand House Hotel
Scotshouse: Hilton Park
Shanagarry: Ballymaloe House
Waterville: Waterville Lake Hotel

Not another plate of boring rice

1. Basmati Rice
2. USA Brown Easy Cook
3. USA Easy Cook
4. USA Long Grain
5. USA Pudding Rice

This is Tilda rice. We think it's good enough to bring a smile to anyone's face. And at the risk of being rather cheeky, we think most rice is boring by comparison.

There's a lot more to our rice than meets the eye. For a start, we take the time to choose it from the finest grains in the world. And we take special care with cleaning, milling and sorting it.

In fact, we've made our rice surprisingly interesting. And with so many tasty varieties to choose from, you can make something really interesting with it too. Cook up a meal with Tilda rice and you'll never have to put a brave face on boring rice again.

Tilda rice

Rice is our only interest. So we make it more interesting.

EXECUTIVE HOTELS

LONDON

Belgravia-Sheraton, SW1
The Berkeley, SW1
Hotel Britannia Inter-Continental, W1
Brown's Hotel, W1
Capital Hotel, SW3
Chelsea Hotel, SW1
Chesterfield Hotel, W1
Churchill Hotel, W1
The Dorchester, W1
Dorset Square Hotel, NW1
Dukes Hotel, SW1
The Gloucester, SW7
Grosvenor House, W1
Holiday Inn (Marble Arch), W1
Holiday Inn (Swiss Cottage), NW3
Howard Hotel, WC2
Hyatt Carlton Tower, SW1
Hyde Park Hotel, SW1
Inn on the Park, W1
Inter-Continental Hotel, W1
Ladbroke Westmoreland Hotel, NW8
London Hilton on Park Lane, W1
London Marriott Hotel, W1
Londonderry Hotel, W1
Lowndes Thistle Hotel, SW1
May Fair Inter-Continental Hotel, W1
Le Meridien Piccadilly, W1
The Montcalm, W1
Park Lane Hotel, W1
Portman Inter-Continental Hotel, W1
Ramada Hotel London, W1
The Ritz, W1
Royal Garden Hotel, W8
Royal Lancaster Hotel, W2
The Savoy, WC2
The Selfridge, W1
Sheraton Park Tower, SW1
Stakis St Ermin's Hotel, SW1
Tower Thistle Hotel, E1
Westbury Hotel, W1
White House, NW1

LONDON AIRPORTS

Gatwick
Copthorne Hotel
Gatwick Hilton International
Gatwick Penta Hotel

Heathrow
Holiday Inn
Sheraton-Heathrow Hotel
Sheraton Skyline

ENGLAND

Ascot: Royal Berkshire
Birmingham: Albany Hotel
Birmingham: Copthorne Hotel
Birmingham: Holiday Inn
Birmingham: Metropole & Warwick Hotel
Birmingham: Plough & Harrow Hotel
Bournemouth: Carlton Hotel
Bournemouth: Royal Bath Hotel
Brighton: The Grand
Bristol: Holiday Inn
Bristol: Ladbroke Dragonara Hotel
Broadway: Lygon Arms
Canterbury: County Hotel
Cheltenham: The Greenway
Chester: Chester Grosvenor
Croydon: Holiday Inn
Dover: Dover Moat House
Egham: Runnymede Hotel
Harrogate: Majestic
Huntingdon: Old Bridge Hotel
Leeds: Ladbroke Dragonara Hotel
Leicester: Holiday Inn
Liverpool: Atlantic Tower Hotel
Longhorsley: Linden Hall Hotel
Manchester: Britannia Hotel
Manchester: Hotel Piccadilly
Manchester: Portland Thistle Hotel
Manchester Airport: Ladbroke International Hotel
Marlow: Compleat Angler Hotel
Newcastle upon Tyne: Gosforth Park Thistle Hotel
Newcastle upon Tyne: Holiday Inn
North Stoke: Springs Hotel
Northampton: Swallow Hotel
Nottingham: Albany Hotel
Nottingham: Royal Moat House International
Plymouth: Copthorne Hotel
Plymouth: Holiday Inn
Poole: Hospitality Inn, The Quay
Portsmouth: Holiday Inn
Reading: Ramada Hotel
Slough: Holiday Inn
South Normanton: Swallow Hotel
Stamford: George of Stamford
Stockton-on-Tees: Swallow Hotel
Stratford-upon-Avon: Ettington Park Hotel
Stratford-upon-Avon: Moat House International
Taplow: Cliveden
Torquay: Imperial Hotel
Tunbridge Wells: Spa Hotel
Warwick: Ladbroke Hotel
Winchester: Lainston House
Windsor: Oakley Court Hotel
Wishaw: Belfry Hotel
Wrotham Heath: Post House Hotel
York: Viking Hotel

continued
on page 90

Interludes

MUNSTER

Interludes
A taste of Luxury

Interludes are the First Class short break packages where the accent is on style and comfort. We have selected top quality hotels in the pick of Britain's most interesting cities and beautiful countryside so you can experience the

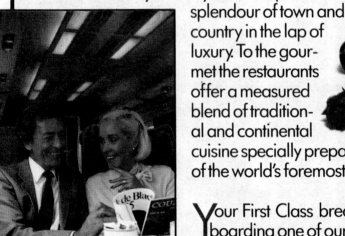

splendour of town and country in the lap of luxury. To the gourmet the restaurants offer a measured blend of traditional and continental cuisine specially prepared by some of the world's foremost chefs.

Your First Class break starts on boarding one of our fast and frequent InterCity Expresses or prestigious Pullman services which operate on numerous routes between major cities. Sit back and relax over a drink in your reserved First Class seat and start your Interlude in style. Enjoy a meal in the restaurant provided on most InterCity trains and watch the countryside slip past.

On arrival at your hotel you will be greeted with champagne or wine in your superbly appointed room. As for activities, you can please yourself – from golf to theatre or just a leisurely stroll to take in the city centre sights.

Weekend scenic Interludes are a variation on the Interludes theme. Where you can select your break in any one of seven areas of breathtaking natural beauty, most bordering a national park. The inclusion of a premier quality hire car gives you the freedom to explore the sights whenever it suits.

Take time out for a taste of Luxury

Simply ring 0904 610945 or 01-200 0200 for your copy of the Interludes brochure.

INTERCITY

EXECUTIVE HOTELS

SCOTLAND

Aberdeen: Copthorne Hotel
Aberdeen Airport: Holiday Inn
Edinburgh: Caledonian Hotel
Edinburgh: Carlton Highland Hotel
Edinburgh: Edinburgh Sheraton
Edinburgh: George Hotel
Edinburgh: King James Thistle Hotel
Edinburgh: Ladbroke Dragonara Hotel
Glasgow: The Albany
Glasgow: Hospitality Inn
Peebles: Peebles Hotel Hydro
St Andrews: Old Course Golf & Country Club

WALES

Cardiff: Holiday Inn
Cardiff: Park Hotel

CHANNEL ISLANDS

St Peter Port, Guernsey: St Pierre Park Hotel
St Brelade, Jersey: Atlantic Hotel
St Brelade's Bay, Jersey: Hotel l'Horizon

NORTHERN IRELAND

Belfast: Europa Hotel

REPUBLIC OF IRELAND

Cong: Ashford Castle
Dublin: Berkeley Court
Dublin: Burlington Hotel
Dublin: Jurys Hotel
Dublin: Shelbourne Hotel
Dublin: Westbury Hotel

Eat out in any style with Luncheon Vouchers

 Of course, business people in a hurry use their Luncheon Vouchers at Sandwich shops and Snack Bars.

But you may be surprised at some of the other places where you and your Luncheon Vouchers are more than welcome. Like country pubs, wine bars, bistros and brasseries, and some of the best known restaurants in the country – like the famous Cafe Royal for instance.

Next time you're thinking of eating out in style, remember Luncheon Vouchers have a lot of style, too. Just look for the sign that says 'LV' and you know that, whatever your style, you're welcome.

50 Vauxhall Bridge Road, London SW1V 2RS.
Telephone 01-834 6666

HOTELS WITH SPORTS FACILITIES

INDOOR SWIMMING

LONDON

The Berkeley, SW1
Grosvenor House, W1
Holiday Inn (Marble Arch), W1
Holiday Inn (Swiss Cottage), NW3
Kensington Close Hotel, W8
Le Meridien Piccadilly, W1
Rembrandt Hotel, SW7

LONDON AIRPORTS

Gatwick
Gatwick Hilton International
Gatwick Penta Hotel

Heathrow
Excelsior Hotel
Heathrow Penta Hotel
Holiday Inn
Sheraton-Heathrow Hotel
Sheraton Skyline

ENGLAND

Ascot: Royal Berkshire
Barnham Broom: Barnham Broom Hotel
Basingstoke: Ladbroke Hotel
Basingstoke: Ladbroke Lodge
Bassenthwaite: Armathwaite Hall
Birmingham: Albany Hotel
Birmingham: Copthorne Hotel
Birmingham: Holiday Inn
Blackpool: Imperial Hotel
Blackpool: Pembroke Hotel
Bolton: Last Drop Village Hotel
Borrowdale: Lodore Swiss Hotel
Bournemouth: Durley Hall Hotel
Bowness on Windermere: Belsfield Hotel
Bradford: Baron Hotel
Bramhope: Post House Hotel
Brighton: Brighton Metropole Hotel
Brighton (Hove): Courtlands Hotel
Brighton: The Grand
Brighton: Ramada Renaissance Hotel
Bristol: Crest Hotel

Bristol: Holiday Inn
Bristol: Redwood Lodge Hotel
Brockenhurst: Careys Manor Hotel
Brockenhurst: Ladbroke Balmer Lawn Hotel
Brockenhurst: Rhinefield House Hotel
Burnham: Burnham Beeches Hotel
Calbourne: Swainston Manor Hotel
Cambridge: Cambridgeshire Moat House
Cambridge: Post House Hotel
Carlisle: Ladbroke Crown & Mitre Hotel
Carlisle: Swallow Hilltop Hotel
Carlyon Bay: Carlyon Bay Hotel
Castle Donington: Donington Thistle Hotel
Chelmsford: Pontlands Park
Chester: Mollington Banastre Hotel
Chittlehamholt: Highbullen Hotel
Chollerford: George Hotel
Churt: Frensham Pond Hotel
Cobham: Ladbroke Seven Hills Hotel
Constantine Bay: Treglos Hotel
Cooden: Cooden Resort Hotel
Croydon: Holiday Inn
Croydon: Selsdon Park Hotel
Darlington: Blackwell Grange Moat House
Dover: Dover Moat House
East Grinstead: Ladbroke Felbridge Hotel
Eastbourne: Grand Hotel
Fairy Cross: Portledge Hotel
Farnborough: Queen's Hotel
Fawkham: Brandshatch Place
Ferndown: Dormy Hotel
Gateshead: Swallow Hotel Gateshead
Gillingham: Stock Hill House Hotel
Golant: Cormorant Hotel
Grasmere: Wordsworth Hotel
Guildford: University Post House Hotel
Hackness: Hackness Grange Country Hotel
Harrogate: Majestic
Harrogate: Hotel St George
Havant: Post House Hotel
Hethersett: Park Farm Hotel
Hollingbourne: Great Danes Hotel
Hope Cove: Lantern Lodge Hotel
Hythe: Hythe Imperial Hotel
Knutsford: The Cottons Hotel
Lancaster: Post House Hotel
Langdale: Langdale Hotel
Leicester: Holiday Inn
Liverpool: Britannia Adelphi Hotel
Liverpool: Liverpool Moat House
Lower Slaughter: Lower Slaughter Manor
Lymington: Passford House Hotel
Maidenhead: Crest Hotel
Manchester: Britannia Hotel
Manchester: Copthorne Hotel

Manchester: Portland Thistle Hotel
Manchester Airport: Excelsior Hotel
Manchester Airport: Ladbroke International Hotel
Matlock Bath: New Bath Hotel
Mawnan Smith: Budock Vean Hotel
Milton Damerel: Woodford Bridge Hotel
Moreton-in-Marsh: Manor House Hotel
Mottram St Andrew: Mottram Hall Hotel
Mullion: Polurrian Hotel
Newcastle upon Tyne: Gosforth Park Thistle Hotel
Newcastle upon Tyne: Holiday Inn
Newquay: Atlantic Hotel
Newquay: Hotel Bristol
Northampton: Swallow Hotel
Norwich: Post House Hotel
Oxford: Oxford Moat House
Penrith: North Lakes Gateway Hotel
Plymouth: Holiday Inn
Portsmouth: Holiday Inn
Reading: Post House Hotel
Reading: Ramada Hotel
St Ives: Garrack Hotel
Salcombe: Marine Hotel
Salcombe: Soar Mill Cove Hotel
Salcombe: South Sands Hotel
Salcombe: Tides Reach Hotel
Samlesbury: Trafalgar Hotel
Saunton: Saunton Sands Hotel
Scarborough: Palm Court Hotel
Scarborough: Royal Hotel
Shaftesbury: Royal Chase Hotel
Shedfield: Meon Valley Hotel
Sheffield: Hallam Tower Post House Hotel
Sheffield: Hotel St George
Shifnal: Park House Hotel
Sidmouth: Fortfield Hotel
Sidmouth: Victoria Hotel
Slough: Holiday Inn
South Marston: South Marston Hotel
South Milford: Selby Fork Hotel
South Mimms: Crest Hotel
South Normanton: Swallow Hotel
Stratford-upon-Avon: Billesley Manor
Stratford-upon-Avon: Ettington Park Hotel
Streatley-on-Thames: Swan at Streatley
Swindon: Blunsdon House Hotel
Swindon: Post House Hotel
Telford: Telford Hotel, Golf & Country Club
Telford: Telford Moat House
Tewkesbury: Tewkesbury Park Hotel
Thurlestone: Thurlestone Hotel
Torquay: Grand Hotel
Torquay: Imperial Hotel
Torquay: Kistor Hotel
Torquay: Palace Hotel
Tunbridge Wells: Spa Hotel
Uckfield: Horsted Place
Walberton: Avisford Park Hotel
Walsall: Barons Court Hotel
Warminster: Bishopstrow House
Warrington: Lord Daresbury Hotel
Warwick: Ladbroke Hotel
Washington: George Washington Hotel
West Runton: Links Country Park Hotel

Whitwell-on-the-Hill: Whitwell Hall Country House Hotel
Wilmslow: Valley Lodge Hotel
Wishaw: Belfry Hotel
Wrotham Heath: Post House Hotel

SCOTLAND

Aberdeen: Bucksburn Moat House
Aberdeen: Stakis Tree Tops Hotel
Aberdeen Airport: Holiday Inn
Airth: Airth Castle Hotel
Auchterarder: Gleneagles Hotel
Aviemore: Stakis Coylumbridge Resort Hotel
Edinburgh: Carlton Highland Hotel
Edinburgh: Edinburgh Sheraton
Edinburgh: Royal Scot Hotel
Forfar: Royal Hotel
Glasgow: Holiday Inn
Glasgow: Stakis Pond Hotel
Glasgow: Swallow Hotel
Irvine: Hospitality Inn
Kinloch Rannoch: Loch Rannoch Hotel
Peebles: Peebles Hotel Hydro
St Andrews: Old Course Golf & Country Club
South Queensferry: Forth Bridges Moat House
Stranraer: North West Castle Hotel
Turnberry: Turnberry Hotel

WALES

Aberdovey: Trefeddian Hotel
Abersoch: Riverside Hotel
Aberystwyth: Conrah Country Hotel
Cardiff: Holiday Inn
Cardiff: Post House Hotel
Cardiff: Stakis Inn on the Avenue
Chepstow: St Pierre Hotel
Lamphey: Court Hotel
Llandudno: Empire Hotel
Llandudno: St Tudno Hotel
Miskin: Miskin Manor
St David's: Warpool Court Hotel
Swansea: Ladbroke Hotel

CHANNEL ISLANDS

St Peter Port, Guernsey: St Pierre Park Hotel
St Brelade's Bay, Jersey: Hotel l'Horizon
St Helier, Jersey: Apollo Hotel
St Helier, Jersey: Beaufort Hotel
St Helier, Jersey: Grand Hotel

ISLE OF MAN

Douglas: Sefton Hotel
Ramsey: Grand Island Hotel

NORTHERN IRELAND

Comber: La Mon House Hotel

REPUBLIC OF IRELAND

Ballina: Downhill Hotel
Beaufort: Hotel Dunloe Castle
Bunratty: Fitzpatrick's Shannon Shamrock Hotel
Carrickmacross: Nuremore Hotel
Cork: Jurys Hotel
Dublin: Berkeley Court
Dublin: Jurys Hotel
Dundalk: Ballymascanlon Hotel
Galway: Corrib Great Southern Hotel
Galway: Great Southern Hotel
Kilkenny: Newpark Hotel
Killarney: Hotel Europe
Killarney: Killarney Great Southern Hotel
Killarney: Torc Great Southern Hotel
Killiney: Fitzpatrick's Castle Hotel
Kinsale: Actons Hotel
Knocklofty: Knocklofty House Hotel
Limerick: Limerick Inn Hotel
Parknasilla: Parknasilla Great Southern Hotel
Renvyle: Renvyle House Hotel
Rosslare: Kelly's Strand Hotel
Waterville: Waterville Lake Hotel

OUTDOOR SWIMMING

LONDON AIRPORTS

Gatwick
Chequers Thistle Hotel
Post House Hotel

Heathrow
Skyway Hotel

ENGLAND

Alton: Grange Hotel
Alveston: Post House Hotel
Ascot: Berystede Hotel
Bagshot: Pennyhill Park Hotel
Barnham Broom: Barnham Broom Hotel
Bath: Priory Hotel
Beanacre: Beechfield House
Bembridge: Highbury Hotel
Birmingham: Post House Hotel
Bodymoor Heath: Marston Farm Hotel
Bognor Regis: Royal Norfolk Hotel
Bonchurch: Winterbourne Hotel
Borrowdale: Lodore Swiss Hotel
Bournemouth: Carlton Hotel
Bournemouth: Durley Hall Hotel
Bournemouth: East Cliff Court Hotel
Bournemouth: Highcliff Hotel

Bournemouth: Royal Bath Hotel
Bowness on Windermere: Old England Hotel
Bradford: Novotel
Brentwood: Post House Hotel
Bristol: Redwood Lodge Hotel
Broadway: Collin House Hotel
Brockenhurst: Ladbroke Balmer Lawn Hotel
Brockenhurst: Rhinefield House Hotel
Broxted: Whitehall Hotel
Buckland: Buckland Manor
Burley: Burley Manor Hotel
Carlyon Bay: Carlyon Bay Hotel
Castle Combe: Manor House Hotel
Charlecote: The Charlecote Pheasant
Cheltenham: Hotel de la Bere
Chittlehamholt: Highbullen Hotel
Climping: Bailiffscourt
Coatham Mundeville: Hall Garth
Cooden: Cooden Resort Hotel
Coventry: Novotel Coventry
Croydon: Selsdon Park Hotel
Dorking: Burford Bridge Hotel
Dorking: White Horse Hotel
Dulverton: Carnarvon Arms Hotel
East Grinstead: Ladbroke Felbridge Hotel
East Horsley: Thatchers Hotel
Eastbourne: Grand Hotel
Easton Grey: Whatley Manor
Egham: Great Fosters
Evershot: Summer Lodge
Exmouth: Imperial Hotel
Falmouth: Falmouth Hotel
Farnham: Trevena House Hotel
Faugh: String of Horses
Freshwater: Farringford Hotel
Frome: Selwood Manor
Gloucester: Hatton Court
Golant: Cormorant Hotel
Great Milton: Le Manoir aux Quat' Saisons
Grimston: Congham Hall
Hatherleigh: George Hotel
Helland Bridge: Tredethy Country Hotel
Helmsley: Feversham Arms Hotel
Holbeton: Alston Hall Hotel
Hunstrete: Hunstrete House
Ipswich: Post House Hotel
Lamorna Cove: Lamorna Cove Hotel
Leamington Spa: Mallory Court
Liskeard: The Well House
Looe: Talland Bay Hotel
Lymington: Passford House Hotel
Lyndhurst: Lyndhurst Park Hotel
Lyndhurst: Parkhill Hotel
Lynmouth: Tors Hotel
Maidstone: Boxley House Hotel
Manchester: Novotel Manchester West
Matlock Bath: New Bath Hotel
Meriden: Manor Hotel
Mudeford: Avonmouth Hotel
Mullion: Polurrian Hotel
New Milton: Chewton Glen Hotel
Newquay: Atlantic Hotel
Newquay: Hotel Riviera
North Stoke: Springs Hotel
Nottingham: Novotel

The choice is yours.

At home you choose Flora for all the right reasons. You enjoy its light, delicate taste and you know it's made with pure sunflower oil, which is high in essential polyunsaturates, low in saturates, low in cholesterol.

Today you can also choose Flora when eating out because it's now available in portion packs at all the best restaurants in town.

Ormesby St Margaret: Ormesby Lodge Hotel
Oxford: TraveLodge
Paignton: Palace Hotel
Paignton: Redcliffe Hotel
Penzance: Higher Faugan Hotel
Plymouth: Mayflower Post House Hotel
Plymouth: Novotel
Preston: Novotel
Redbourn: Aubrey Park Hotel
Ross-on-Wye: Pengethley Manor Hotel
Rotherwick: Tylney Hall
Rusper: Ghyll Manor
St Ives: Boskerris Hotel
St Ives: Tregenna Castle Hotel
Salcombe: St Elmo Hotel
Salcombe: Soar Mill Cove Hotel
Sandown: Melville Hall Hotel
Sedlescombe: Brickwall Hotel
Shanklin: Cliff Tops Hotel
Sidmouth: Victoria Hotel
Silchester: Romans Hotel
Somerton: The Lynch Country House Hotel
South Marston: South Marston Hotel
South Walsham: South Walsham Hall Hotel
Southampton: Post House Hotel
Steyning: Springwells Hotel
Stoke Mandeville: Belmore Hotel
Storrington: Abingworth Hall
Storrington: Little Thakeham
Studland Bay: Knoll House Hotel
Taplow: Cliveden
Tetbury: Calcot Manor
Tewkesbury: Bredon Manor
Thurlestone: Thurlestone Hotel
Torquay: Grand Hotel
Torquay: Imperial Hotel
Torquay: Livermead Cliff Hotel
Torquay: Livermead House Hotel
Torquay: Osborne Hotel
Torquay: Palace Hotel
Torquay: Toorak Hotel
Tresco: Island Hotel
Ventnor: Royal Hotel
Veryan: Nare Hotel
Walberton: Avisford Park Hotel
Wallingford: Shillingford Bridge Hotel
Ware: Briggens House Hotel
Wareham: Springfield Country Hotel
Warminster: Bishopstrow House
Wem: Hawkstone Park Hotel
Weston-on-the-Green: Weston Manor Hotel
Weston-super-Mare: Grand Atlantic Hotel
Wincanton: Holbrook House Hotel
Yelverton: Moorland Links Hotel
York: Mount Royale Hotel

SCOTLAND

Aberdeen Airport: Skean Dhu Hotel Aberdeen
Airport
Auchterhouse: Old Mansion House Hotel
Drumnadrochit: Polmaily House Hotel
Dunblane: Stakis Dunblane Hydro
Gatehouse of Fleet: Cally Palace Hotel

Nairn: Golf View Hotel
North Berwick: Marine Hotel
Pitlochry: Atholl Palace Hotel
Selkirk: Philipburn House Hotel
Tarbert: Stonefield Castle Hotel

WALES

Abersoch: Porth Tocyn Hotel
Caernarfon: Stables Hotel
Coychurch: Coed-y-Mwstwr Hotel
Fishguard: Fishguard Bay Hotel
Gwbert-on-Sea: Cliff Hotel
Llandudno: Empire Hotel
Tal-y-Llyn: Ty'n-y-Cornel Hotel

CHANNEL ISLANDS

Herm Island: White House Hotel
St Martin's, Guernsey: St Margaret's Lodge
Hotel
St Martin's, Guernsey: La Trelade Hotel
St Peter Port, Guernsey: Duke of Richmond
Hotel
St Peter Port, Guernsey: Flying Dutchman Hotel
St Peter Port, Guernsey: Old Government House
Hotel
Bouley Bay, Jersey: Water's Edge Hotel
Gorey, Jersey: Old Court House Hotel
Petit Port, Jersey: Sea Crest Hotel
Portelet Bay, Jersey: Portelet Hotel
St Brelade, Jersey: Atlantic Hotel
St Brelade, Jersey: La Place Hotel
St Brelade's Bay, Jersey: Hotel Château
Valeuse
St Brelade's Bay, Jersey: St Brelade's Bay Hotel
St Clement's Bay, Jersey: Hotel Ambassadeur
St Lawrence, Jersey: Little Grove Hotel
St Peter, Jersey: Mermaid Hotel
St Saviour, Jersey: Longueville Manor Hotel
Sark: Hotel Petit Champ
Sark: Stocks Hotel

ISLE OF MAN

Douglas: Palace Hotel

REPUBLIC OF IRELAND

Ballylickey: Ballylickey House
Castledermot: Kilkea Castle
Clifden: Abbeyglen Castle Hotel
Cork: Jurys Hotel
Dromahair: Drumlease Glebe House
Dublin: Jurys Hotel
Glounthaune: Ashbourne House Hotel
Oughterard: Connemara Gateway Hotel
Renvyle: Renvyle House Hotel
Rosslare: Kelly's Strand Hotel
Shanagarry: Ballymaloe House

HOTELS WITH SPORTS FACILITIES

FISHING

ENGLAND

Alcester: Arrow Mill
Aldeburgh: Brudenell Hotel
Allendale: Bishopfield
Ambleside: Nanny Brow
Ambleside: Wateredge Hotel
Bagshot: Pennyhill Park Hotel
Bampton: Huntsham Court
Baslow: Cavendish Hotel
Bassenthwaite: Armathwaite Hall
Beanacre: Beechfield House
Beccles: Waveney House Hotel
Bibury: Bibury Court Hotel
Bibury: Swan Hotel
Bideford: Yeoldon House
Bigbury on Sea: Burgh Island
Bodymoor Heath: Marston Farm Hotel
Bolton Abbey: Devonshire Arms
Bredwardine: Red Lion Hotel
Bristol: Crest Hotel
Bromsgrove: Grafton Manor
Burbage: Savernake Forest Hotel
Burley: Burley Manor Hotel
Castle Combe: Manor House Hotel
Chagford: Mill End Hotel
Charlbury: Bell at Charlbury
Chittlehamholt: Highbullen Hotel
Chollerford: George Hotel
Churt: Frensham Pond Hotel
Clearwell: Clearwell Castle
Constantine Bay: Treglos Hotel
Cornhill-on-Tweed: Tillmouth Park Hotel
Crooklands: Crooklands Hotel
Dovedale: Izaak Walton Hotel
Dulverton: Carnarvon Arms Hotel
East Grinstead: Gravetye Manor
Easton Grey: Whatley Manor
Egham: Runnymede Hotel
Fairford: Bull Hotel
Falmouth: Greenbank Hotel
Felixstowe: Orwell Moat House
Flitwick: Flitwick Manor
Frome: Selwood Manor
Gittisham: Combe House Hotel
Grasmere: White Moss House
Greta Bridge: Morritt Arms Hotel
Hackness: Hackness Grange Country Hotel

Hollingbourne: Great Danes Hotel
Hope: Poachers Arms Hotel
Huntingdon: Old Bridge Hotel
Hythe: Stade Court Hotel
Kingham: Mill House Hotel
Lancaster: Post House Hotel
Langdale: Langdale Hotel
Lewdown: Fox's Earth Lewtrenchard Manor
Lifton: Arundell Arms
Lower Beeding: South Lodge
Lympsham: Batch Farm Country Hotel
Lyndhurst: Parkhill Hotel
Maiden Newton: Maiden Newton House
Marlow: Compleat Angler Hotel
Mawnan Smith: Budock Vean Hotel
Mawnan Smith: Meudon Hotel
Milton Damerel: Woodford Bridge Hotel
Moretonhampstead: Manor House Hotel
Mousehole: Lobster Pot
Mullion: Polurrian Hotel
Needingworth: Pike & Eel
Otley: Chevin Lodge
Otterburn: Percy Arms Hotel
Paignton: Redcliffe Hotel
Quorn: Quorn Country Hotel
Ross-on-Wye: Walford House Hotel
Rowsley: Peacock Hotel
Salcombe: South Sands Hotel
Samlesbury: Tickled Trout Hotel
Sheffield: Hotel St George
Shorne: Inn on the Lake
Slaidburn: Hark To Bounty Inn
South Walsham: South Walsham Hall Hotel
Staddle Bridge: McCoy's at the Tontine
Stonehouse: Stonehouse Court Hotel
Stratford-upon-Avon: Ettington Park Hotel
Stratford-upon-Avon: Moat House International
Stratford-upon-Avon: Welcombe Hotel
Sudbury: Mill
Sutton Coldfield: Penns Hall Hotel
Taplow: Cliveden
Tewkesbury: Bredon Manor
Torquay: Livermead Cliff Hotel
Torquay: Livermead House Hotel
Tresco: Island Hotel
Ullswater: Leeming House Hotel
Ullswater: Old Church Hotel
Ullswater: Rampsbeck Hotel
Ullswater: Sharrow Bay Hotel
Umberleigh: Rising Sun Hotel
Upper Slaughter: Lords of the Manor Hotel
Wallingford: Shillingford Bridge Hotel
Wansford-in-England: Haycock Hotel
Ware: Briggens House Hotel

Wareham: Priory Hotel
Warminster: Bishopstrow House
Weston-on-the-Green: Weston Manor Hotel
Whitewell: Inn at Whitewell
Windsor: Oakley Court Hotel
Winsford: Royal Oak Inn
Woodbridge: Seckford Hall Hotel

SCOTLAND

Aberdeen: Ardoe House Hotel
Achiltibuie: Summer Isles Hotel
Advie: Tulchan Lodge
Altnaharra: Altnaharra Hotel
Ardentinny: Ardentinny Hotel
Auchterarder: Gleneagles Hotel
Ballachulish: Ballachulish Hotel
Balquhidder: Ledcreich Hotel
Banchory: Raemoir House Hotel
Banchory: Tor-na-Coille Hotel
Beattock: Auchen Castle Hotel
Bridge of Cally: Bridge of Cally Hotel
Connel: Ossian's Hotel
Contin: Craigdarroch Lodge Hotel
Crinan: Crinan Hotel
Drumnadrochit: Polmaily House Hotel
Dunblane: Cromlix House
Eriska: Isle of Eriska
Ettrickbridge: Ettrickshaws Hotel
Fort William: Inverlochy Castle
Garve: Inchbae Lodge Hotel
Gatehouse of Fleet: Murray Arms
Glenlivet: Blairfindy Lodge Hotel
Isle of Gigha: Gigha Hotel
Isle of Raasay: Isle of Raasay Hotel
Kelso: Ednam House Hotel
Kelso: Sunlaws House Hotel
Kenmore: Kenmore Hotel
Kilchrenan: Ardanaiseig
Kilchrenan: Taychreggan Hotel
Kildrummy: Kildrummy Castle Hotel
Kinclaven By Stanley: Ballathie House
Kinloch Rannoch: Loch Rannoch Hotel
Kirkmichael: Log Cabin Hotel
Lanark: Cartland Bridge Hotel
Letham: Fernie Castle Hotel
Lochgair: Lochgair Hotel
Pitlochry: Green Park Hotel
Port William: Corsemalzie House Hotel
Portpatrick: Knockinaam Lodge Hotel
Portsonachan: Portsonachan Hotel
St Fillans: Four Seasons Hotel
Scourie: Eddrachilles Hotel
Scourie: Scourie Hotel
Skeabost Bridge: Skeabost House Hotel
Sleat: Kinloch Lodge
Spean Bridge: Letterfinlay Lodge Hotel
Strachur: Creggans Inn
Strathtummel: Port-an-Eilean Hotel
Talladale: Loch Maree Hotel
Tweedsmuir: Crook Inn
Whitebridge: Knockie Lodge Hotel

WALES

Beddgelert: Royal Goat Hotel
Criccieth: Bron Eifion Hotel
Crickhowell: Gliffaes Hotel
Gwbert-on-Sea: Cliff Hotel
Lake Vyrnwy: Lake Vyrnwy Hotel
Llanarmon Dyffryn Ceiriog: Hand Hotel
Llandderfel: Palé Hall
Llangollen: Hand Hotel
Llangollen: Royal Hotel
Penmaenpool: George III Hotel
Ruthin: Ruthin Castle
Tal-y-Llyn: Ty'n-y-Cornel Hotel
Tintern Abbey: Beaufort Hotel

CHANNEL ISLANDS

Herm Island: White House Hotel

NORTHERN IRELAND

Dunadry: Dunadry Inn

REPUBLIC OF IRELAND

Ballina: Downhill Hotel
Ballinasloe: Hayden's Hotel
Ballylickey: Ballylickey House
Ballynahinch: Ballynahinch Castle
Beaufort: Hotel Dunloe Castle
Caragh Lake: Ard-Na-Sidhe
Caragh Lake: Caragh Lodge
Carrickmacross: Nuremore Hotel
Cashel, Co. Galway: Zetland House Hotel
Cashel, Co. Tipperary: Cashel Palace Hotel
Cong: Ashford Castle
Crossmolina: Enniscoe House
Dromahair: Drumlease Glebe House
Dundrum: Dundrum House Hotel
Kanturk: Assolas Country House
Kilcoran: Kilcoran Lodge Hotel
Killarney: Aghadoe Heights Hotel
Killarney: Cahernane Hotel
Killarney: Castlerosse Hotel
Killarney: Hotel Europe
Kinsale: Blue Haven Hotel
Knocklofty: Knocklofty House Hotel
Letterfrack: Rosleague Manor Hotel
Mallow: Longueville House
Newmarket-on-Fergus: Dromoland Castle
Newport: Newport House
Oughterard: Currarevagh House
Parknasilla: Parknasilla Great Southern Hotel
Rathmullan: Rathmullan House
Renvyle: Renvyle House Hotel
Riverstown: Coopershill
Rossnowlagh: Sand House Hotel
Scotshouse: Hilton Park
Shanagarry: Ballymaloe House
Waterville: Waterville Lake Hotel

HOTELS WITH SPORTS FACILITIES

RIDING

ENGLAND

Bagshot: Pennyhill Park Hotel
Bromsgrove: Grafton Manor
Buckland: Buckland Manor
Burley: Burley Manor Hotel
Croydon: Selsdon Park Hotel
Exford: Crown Hotel
Hintlesham: Hintlesham Hall
Lower Beeding: South Lodge
Newbury: Chequers Hotel
Oakham: Hambleton Hall
Rusper: Ghyll Manor
South Walsham: South Walsham Hall Hotel
Stratford-upon-Avon: Ettington Park Hotel
Taplow: Cliveden
Wareham: Springfield Country Hotel

SCOTLAND

Dunblane: Cromlix House
Eriska: Isle of Eriska

Langbank: Gleddoch House Hotel
Peebles: Peebles Hotel Hydro
Tarbert: Stonefield Castle Hotel
Turnberry: Turnberry Hotel

WALES

Brechfa: Tŷ Mawr Country House Hotel
Glyn Ceiriog: Golden Pheasant Hotel

NORTHERN IRELAND

Comber: La Mon House Hotel

REPUBLIC OF IRELAND

Beaufort: Hotel Dunloe Castle
Cashel: Cashel Palace Hotel
Dundrum: Dundrum House Hotel
Killarney: Hotel Europe
Killarney: Killarney Great Southern Hotel
Renvyle: Renvyle House Hotel
Spiddal: Bridge House Hotel
Waterville: Waterville Lake Hotel

HOTELS WITH SPORTS FACILITIES

GOLF

LONDON AIRPORTS

Heathrow
Holiday Inn

ENGLAND

Bagshot: Pennyhill Park Hotel
Barnham Broom: Barnham Broom Hotel
Borrowdale: Borrowdale Hotel
Cambridge: Cambridgeshire Moat House
Carlyon Bay: Carlyon Bay Hotel
Chittlehamholt: Highbullen Hotel
Croydon: Selsdon Park Hotel
Freshwater: Farringford Hotel
Hythe: Hythe Imperial Hotel
Mawnan Smith: Budock Vean Hotel
Moretonhampstead: Manor House Hotel
New Milton: Chewton Glen Hotel
St Ives: Tregenna Castle Hotel
Shedfield: Meon Valley Hotel
Stratford-upon-Avon: Welcombe Hotel
Studland Bay: Knoll House Hotel
Telford: Telford Hotel, Golf & Country Club
Tewkesbury: Tewkesbury Park Hotel
Thurlestone: Thurlestone Hotel
Torquay: Palace Hotel
Walberton: Avisford Park Hotel
Ware: Briggens House Hotel
Washington: George Washington Hotel

Wem: Hawkstone Park Hotel
West Runton: Links Country Park Hotel
Wishaw: Belfry Hotel

SCOTLAND

Auchterarder: Gleneagles Hotel
Gatehouse of Fleet: Murray Arms
Kenmore: Kenmore Hotel
Langbank: Gleddoch House Hotel
Old Meldrum: Meldrum House Hotel
Skeabost Bridge: Skeabost House Hotel
Turnberry: Turnberry Hotel

WALES

Chepstow: St Pierre Hotel
Gwbert-on-Sea: Cliff Hotel

CHANNEL ISLANDS

St Peter Port, Guernsey: St Pierre Park Hotel

REPUBLIC OF IRELAND

Carrickmacross: Nuremore Hotel
Clifden: Abbeyglen Castle Hotel
Cong: Ashford Castle
Kenmare: Park Hotel Kenmare
Newmarket-on-Fergus: Clare Inn
Newmarket-on-Fergus: Dromoland Castle
Renvyle: Renvyle House Hotel
Rossnowlagh: Sand House Hotel
Scotshouse: Hilton Park
Waterville: Waterville Lake Hotel

How to close the deal smoothly while your biggest competitor is still in the rough

A cellphone using the Cellnet system should be part of every sportsman's kit. Small enough to carry with you wherever you go, but capable of linking you with any phone in the world, a Cellnet phone gives you a real advantage, whatever your game.

So, if you want to make sure your leisure activities are never a handicap to your business, you need to find out more about Cellnet.

For further information or a free demonstration, call 0800 400 433 today.

Cellnet
THE CELLPHONE NETWORK

HOTELS WITH SPORTS FACILITIES

SQUASH

LONDON

Kensington Close Hotel, W8
Le Meridien Piccadilly, W1

LONDON AIRPORTS

Gatwick
Copthorne Hotel
Gatwick Penta Hotel

ENGLAND

Ascot: Royal Berkshire
Barnham Broom: Barnham Broom Hotel
Bassenthwaite: Armathwaite Hall
Birmingham: Albany Hotel
Birmingham: Metropole & Warwick Hotel
Borrowdale: Lodore Swiss Hotel
Brandon: Brandon Hall Hotel
Bristol: Redwood Lodge Hotel
Brockenhurst: Ladbroke Balmer Lawn Hotel
Cambridge: Cambridgeshire Moat House
Chester: Mollington Banastre Hotel
Chittlehamholt: Highbullen Hotel
Churt: Frensham Pond Hotel
Clayton-le-Woods: Pines Hotel
Cobham: Ladbroke Seven Hills Hotel
Coventry: Novotel Coventry
Croydon: Holiday Inn
Croydon: Selsdon Park Hotel
Driffield: Bell Hotel
Fawkham: Brandshatch Place
Ferndown: Dormy Hotel
Harrogate: Majestic
Hythe: Hythe Imperial Hotel
Langdale: Langdale Hotel
Leamington Spa: Mallory Court
Ledbury: Feathers Hotel
Liverpool: Britannia Adelphi Hotel
Maidenhead: Crest Hotel
Milton Damerel: Woodford Bridge Hotel
Moretonhampstead: Manor House Hotel
Mottram St Andrew: Mottram Hall Hotel
Mullion: Polurrian Hotel
Newcastle upon Tyne: Gosforth Park Thistle
  Hotel

Newquay: Atlantic Hotel
Newquay: Hotel Riviera
North Stoke: Springs Hotel
Nottingham: Royal Moat House International
Oxford: Oxford Moat House
Paignton: Palace Hotel
Penrith: North Lakes Gateway Hotel
Portsmouth: Holiday Inn
St Ives: Tregenna Castle Hotel
Salcombe: Tides Reach Hotel
Samlesbury: Trafalgar Hotel
Saunton: Saunton Sands Hotel
Shedfield: Meon Valley Hotel
South Marston: South Marston Hotel
South Walsham: South Walsham Hall Hotel
Swindon: Blunsdon House Hotel
Taplow: Cliveden
Telford: Telford Hotel, Golf & Country Club
Tewkesbury: Tewkesbury Park Hotel
Thurlestone: Thurlestone Hotel
Torquay: Imperial Hotel
Torquay: Livermead House Hotel
Torquay: Palace Hotel
Walberton: Avisford Park Hotel
Wallingford: Shillingford Bridge Hotel
Warrington: Lord Daresbury Hotel
Washington: George Washington Hotel
Weston-on-the-Green: Weston Manor Hotel
Westonbirt: Hare & Hounds Hotel
Wetheral: Crown Hotel
Wilmslow: Valley Lodge Hotel
Wincanton: Holbrook House Hotel
Wishaw: Belfry Hotel

SCOTLAND

Aberdeen Airport: Skean Dhu Hotel Dyce
Auchterarder: Gleneagles Hotel
Auchterhouse: Old Mansion House Hotel
Banchory: Tor-na-Coille Hotel
Edinburgh: Carlton Highland Hotel
Glasgow: Holiday Inn
Inverness: Kingsmills Hotel
Kinloch Rannoch: Loch Rannoch Hotel
Langbank: Gleddoch House Hotel
North Berwick: Marine Hotel
Peebles: Cringletie House Hotel
Peebles: Peebles Hotel Hydro
Pitcaple: Pittodrie House Hotel
South Queensferry: Forth Bridges Moat House
Tarbert: Stonefield Castle Hotel
Troon: Sun Court Hotel

HOTELS WITH SQUASH

WALES

Cardiff: Holiday Inn
Chepstow: St Pierre Hotel
Gwbert-on-Sea: Cliff Hotel
Miskin: Miskin Manor
Wolf's Castle: Wolfscastle Country Hotel

NORTHERN IRELAND

Dunmurry: Conway Hotel
Holywood: Culloden Hotel

REPUBLIC OF IRELAND

Ballina: Downhill Hotel
Carrickmacross: Nuremore Hotel
Cork: Jurys Hotel
Dundalk: Ballymascanlon Hotel
Killiney: Fitzpatrick's Castle Hotel
Knocklofty: Knocklofty House Hotel
Rosslare: Kelly's Strand Hotel

HOTELS WITH SPORTS FACILITIES

TENNIS

LONDON

Cadogan Thistle Hotel, SW1
Hyatt Carlton Tower, SW1

LONDON AIRPORTS

Heathrow
Holiday Inn

ENGLAND

Abberley: Elms Hotel
Ascot: Royal Berkshire
Ashford: Eastwell Manor
Bagshot: Pennyhill Park Hotel
Bakewell: Hassop Hall Hotel
Barnham Broom: Barnham Broom Hotel
Bassenthwaite: Armathwaite Hall
Beanacre: Beechfield House
Bigbury on Sea: Burgh Island
Bodymoor Heath: Marston Farm Hotel
Bognor Regis: Royal Norfolk Hotel
Borrowdale: Lodore Swiss Hotel
Bournemouth: Highcliff Hotel
Bowness on Windermere: Belsfield Hotel
Bramley: Bramley Grange Hotel
Bristol: Redwood Lodge Hotel
Broadway: Lygon Arms
Brockenhurst: Ladbroke Balmer Lawn Hotel
Brockenhurst: Rhinefield House Hotel
Broxted: Whitehall Hotel
Buckland: Buckland Manor
Burnham: Burnham Beeches Hotel
Cambridge: Cambridgeshire Moat House
Carlyon Bay: Carlyon Bay Hotel
Castle Combe: Manor House Hotel
Chagford: Gidleigh Park Hotel
Chagford: Teignworthy
Charlecote: The Charlecote Pheasant
Cheltenham: Hotel de la Bere
Chester: Mollington Banastre Hotel
Chittlehamholt: Highbullen Hotel
Climping: Bailiffscourt
Coatham Mundeville: Hall Garth
Cobham: Ladbroke Seven Hills Hotel
Cobham: Woodlands Park Hotel

Colchester: Marks Tey Hotel
Croydon: Selsdon Park Hotel
Dane End: Green End Park Hotel
Darlington: Blackwell Grange Moat House
Dovedale: Peveril of the Peak Hotel
Droitwich Spa: Château Impney Hotel
Dulverton: Carnarvon Arms Hotel
East Dereham: King's Head Hotel
Easton Grey: Whatley Manor
Egham: Great Fosters
Evershot: Summer Lodge
Exmouth: Imperial Hotel
Fairy Cross: Portledge Hotel
Farnham: Trevena House Hotel
Fawkham: Brandshatch Place
Ferndown: Dormy Hotel
Flitwick: Flitwick Manor
Freshford: Homewood Park
Freshwater: Farringford Hotel
Great Ayton: Ayton Hall
Great Milton: Le Manoir aux Quat' Saisons
Grimston: Congham Hall
Hackness: Hackness Grange Country Hotel
Harrogate: Majestic
Harrogate: Old Swan Hotel
Haslemere: Lythe Hill Hotel
Hawkhurst: Tudor Arms Hotel
Haytor: Bel Alp House Country Hotel
Helmsley: Feversham Arms Hotel
Hintlesham: Hintlesham Hall
Holbeton: Alston Hall Hotel
Hollingbourne: Great Danes Hotel
Horton-cum-Studley: Studley Priory Hotel
Hunstrete: Hunstrete House
Hurstbourne Tarrant: Esseborne Manor
Hythe: Hythe Imperial Hotel
Ilkley: Craiglands Hotel
Leamington Spa: Mallory Court
Lenham: Chilston Park
Liskeard: The Well House
Loftus: Grinkle Park Hotel
Longhorsley: Linden Hall Hotel
Lower Beeding: South Lodge
Lower Slaughter: Lower Slaughter Manor
Lymington: Passford House Hotel
Lyndhurst: Lyndhurst Park Hotel
Marlow: Compleat Angler Hotel
Matlock: Riber Hall
Matlock Bath: New Bath Hotel
Mawnan Smith: Budock Vean Hotel
Milton Damerel: Woodford Bridge Hotel
Moreton-in-Marsh: Manor House Hotel
Moretonhampstead: Manor House Hotel
Mottram St Andrew: Mottram Hall Hotel
Mullion: Polurrian Hotel

Nantwich: Rookery Hall
Newbury: Elcot Park Hotel
Newquay: Atlantic Hotel
North Stifford: Stifford Moat House
North Stoke: Springs Hotel
Oakham: Hambleton Hall
Paignton: Palace Hotel
Penzance: Higher Faugan Hotel
Rotherwick: Tylney Hall
Rusper: Ghyll Manor
St Ives: Tregenna Castle Hotel
Salcombe: Soar Mill Cove Hotel
Saunton: Saunton Sands Hotel
Shedfield: Meon Valley Hotel
Sidmouth: Victoria Hotel
Silchester: Romans Hotel
Six Mile Bottom: Swynford Paddocks
Slough: Holiday Inn
South Milford: Selby Fork Hotel
South Walsham: South Walsham Hall Hotel
Stafford: Tillington Hall Hotel
Storrington: Abingworth Hall
Storrington: Little Thakeham
Stow-on-the-Wold: Wyck Hill House
Stratford-upon-Avon: Billesley Manor
Stratford-upon-Avon: Ettington Park Hotel
Studland Bay: Knoll House Hotel
Taplow: Cliveden
Tewkesbury: Bredon Manor
Thurlestone: Thurlestone Hotel
Torquay: Grand Hotel
Torquay: Imperial Hotel
Torquay: Livermead House Hotel
Torquay: Osborne Hotel
Torquay: Palace Hotel
Torquay: Toorak Hotel
Tunbridge Wells: Spa Hotel
Uckfield: Horsted Place
Veryan: Nare Hotel
Wadhurst: Spindlewood Hotel
Walberton: Avisford Park Hotel
Ware: Briggens House Hotel
Wareham: Springfield Country Hotel
Warminster: Bishopstrow House
Weedon: Crossroads Hotel
Wem: Hawkstone Park Hotel
Weston-on-the-Green: Weston Manor Hotel
Weston-super-Mare: Grand Atlantic Hotel
Westonbirt: Hare & Hounds Hotel
Whimple: Woodhayes
Whitwell-on-the-Hill: Whitwell Hall Country
   House Hotel
Wincanton: Holbrook House Hotel
Winchester: Lainston House
Windermere: Langdale Chase Hotel
Wishaw: Belfry Hotel
Wroxton: Wroxton House Hotel
Yelverton: Moorland Links Hotel

SCOTLAND

Aberdeen: Stakis Tree Tops Hotel
Advie: Tulchan Lodge
Auchterarder: Gleneagles Hotel
Auchterhouse: Old Mansion House Hotel

Aviemore: Stakis Coylumbridge Resort Hotel
Contin: Craigdarroch Lodge Hotel
Drumnadrochit: Polmaily House Hotel
Dunblane: Cromlix House
Dunblane: Stakis Dunblane Hydro
Eriska: Isle of Eriska
Fort William: Inverlochy Castle
Gatehouse of Fleet: Cally Palace Hotel
Gatehouse of Fleet: Murray Arms
Gullane: Greywalls
Inverness: Culloden House
Kelso: Sunlaws House Hotel
Kentallen of Appin: Ardsheal House
Kilchrenan: Ardanaiseig
Kilwinning: Montgreenan Mansion House
Kinclaven By Stanley: Ballathie House
Kinloch Rannoch: Loch Rannoch Hotel
Nairn: Golf View Hotel
Nairn: Newton Hotel
North Berwick: Marine Hotel
Peebles: Cringletie House Hotel
Peebles: Peebles Hotel Hydro
Pitcaple: Pittodrie House Hotel
Pitlochry: Atholl Palace Hotel
Pitlochry: Pitlochry Hydro Hotel
Tarbert: Stonefield Castle Hotel
Troon: Sun Court Hotel
Turnberry: Turnberry Hotel

WALES

Aberdovey: Hotal Plas Penhelig
Aberdovey: Trefeddian Hotel
Abersoch: Porth Tocyn Hotel
Chepstow: St Pierre Hotel
Coychurch: Coed-y-Mwstwr Hotel
Crickhowell: Gliffaes Hotel
Lake Vyrnwy: Lake Vyrnwy Hotel
Llanarmon Dyffryn Ceiriog: Hand Hotel
Llandudno: Bodysgallen Hall
Miskin: Miskin Manor
St David's: Warpool Court Hotel
Wolf's Castle: Wolfscastle Country Hotel

CHANNEL ISLANDS

Herm Island: White House Hotel
St Peter Port, Guernsey: St Pierre Park Hotel
Portelet Bay, Jersey: Portelet Hotel
St Brelade, Jersey: Atlantic Hotel
St Brelade's Bay, Jersey: St Brelade's Bay Hotel

NORTHERN IRELAND

Holywood: Culloden Hotel

REPUBLIC OF IRELAND

Ballina: Downhill Hotel
Ballynahinch: Ballynahinch Castle
Beaufort: Hotel Dunloe Castle
Blessington: Downshire House Hotel

HOTELS WITH TENNIS

Caragh Lake: Caragh Lodge
Cashel: Cashel House Hotel
Castledermot: Kilkea Castle
Clifden: Abbeyglen Castle Hotel
Clifden: Rock Glen Hotel
Cong: Ashford Castle
Cork: Silver Springs Hotel
Dundalk: Ballymascanlon Hotel
Dundrum: Dundrum House Hotel
Glounthaune: Ashbourne House Hotel
Gorey: Marlfield House
Kanturk: Assolas Country House
Kenmare: Park Hotel Kenmare
Kilkenny: Newpark Hotel
Killarney: Aghadoe Heights Hotel
Killarney: Cahernane Hotel
Killarney: Castlerosse Hotel
Killarney: Killarney Great Southern Hotel

Killarney: Torc Great Southern Hotel
Killiney: Fitzpatrick's Castle Hotel
Knocklofty: Knocklofty House Hotel
Letterfrack: Rosleague Manor Hotel
Limerick: Limerick Inn Hotel
Maynooth: Moyglare Manor
Newmarket-on-Fergus: Dromoland Castle
Oughterard: Connemara Gateway Hotel
Oughterard: Currarevagh House
Parknasilla: Parknasilla Great Southern Hotel
Rathmullan: Rathmullan House
Renvyle: Renvyle House Hotel
Rosslare: Kelly's Strand Hotel
Rossnowlagh: Sand House Hotel
Shanagarry: Ballymaloe House
Waterford: Ardree Hotel
Waterville: Waterville Lake Hotel

SAM TWINING'S GUIDE TO
TEA AFTER MEALS

The history of tea is a long and colourful one whose origins are shrouded in the mists of Chinese legend dating back nearly 5000 years. Health-conscious Emperor Shen Nung always boiled his drinking water, and one day leaves from a branch burning under the pot were blown into the water. The aroma so pleased the Emperor that he gathered more of the same leaf and reproduced the pleasing brew; the leaf came from a tree called *Camellia sinensis* – the tea bush.

Tea first came to our shores from China around the middle of the 17th century and soon afterwards started to be offered as an expensive novelty in the already fashionable coffee shops. Helped by a reduction in the initially punitive tax, it grew in popularity, spreading to all classes and eventually giving rise to the cherished tradition of afternoon tea with light snacks. But tea is an anytime drink par excellence, its powers to sooth, restore and refresh being equally appropriate to morning, noon and evening.

It is quite customary to drink tea throughout a meal in Chinese and Indian restaurants, but have you ever thought of asking for a cup of tea to finish lunch or dinner in restaurants serving Western cuisine?

The choice is becoming increasingly wide and tempting, and besides the familiar favourites you might like to try one of the many speciality teas. Earl Grey, a blend of China and Darjeeling scented with oil of bergamot, is the most popular, and other varieties include jasmine, Ceylon, Lapsang Souchong with its distinctive smoky smell and taste, and luxurious Oolong with its subtle suggestion of ripened peaches.

More and more restaurants are responding to these increasing calls, and some of them now provide a wide range of speciality teas. The following is a selection of establishments in Great Britain and Northern Ireland where you are offered the delights of a cup of tea after your meal.

LONDON

Le Bistroquet

273 Camden High Street, NW1
01-485 9607

Book early for a table in the conservatory of this lively brasserie, where fresh pasta is a popular choice. There are enjoyable meat dishes, too, and interesting salads. Tea drinkers can choose from jasmine, Earl Grey and a variety of infusions.

Hotel Britannia, Adams Restaurant

Grosvenor Square, W1
01-629 9400

Quiet luxury and skilled cooking with a distinctive modern touch. Typical delights are scallops with sweet turnip and potato muffins, and fillet of veal with creamed artichokes. The wine list features good Californian and English sections, and there are lots of teas available, including English breakfast and Orange Pekoe.

Le Caprice

Arlington House, Arlington Street, SW1
01-629 2239

Black and white decor, mirror panels and David Bailey portraits make a sophisticated setting for an excellent meal. Favourite dishes include eggs Benedict, salmon fishcakes and rack of lamb en croûte. Indian, mint, camomile and jasmine teas.

Churchill Hotel, The Arboury

30 Portman Square, W1
01-486 5800

Trees are the new decorative theme at what used to be No. 10. Dover sole, grills and the daily roast are traditional favourites, sharing the menu with more adventurous choices such as duck sautéed with pineapple and ginger. Good variety of teas and infusions.

English House

3 Milner Street, SW3
01-584 3002

A little, ever-so-English restaurant on three floors. The dishes are all adaptations from old English cookery books, ranging from dressed Cornish crab and traditional fish pie to lamb in a salt crust and some delectable sweets. Teas include breakfast, Earl Grey and herbal varieties.

Frith's

14 Frith Street, W1
01-439 3370

Best to book at this popular place, where British produce gets careful, unelaborate treatment. Poached meats dressed with olive oil, parsley and capers is a healthy choice. Indian and China teas, plus fruit varieties like apricot, peach and passion fruit.

Grosvenor House, Pasta, Vino e Fantasia

Park Lane, W1
01-499 6363

Pasta's the choice for economy meals in this bright, colourful restaurant, but there's plenty of other Italian fare on the menu. Note, too, an impressive selection of over 30 types of tea.

Inigo Jones

14 Garrick Street, WC2
01-836 6456

Outstanding cooking by Paul Gayler, plus youthful, polished service and the most stylish surroundings. Specialities include salmon and scallop terrine with dill cucumbers, and mille-feuille of chocolate pastry with walnut cream, raspberries and a Calvados sauce. Various teas and herbal infusions.

Inn on the Park, Lanes

Hamilton Place, Park Lane, W1
01-499 0888

The central feature here is a lavish display of cold hors d'oeuvre, which you can make your starter or main course. There's an outstanding wine list and a good variety of teas. Book.

Joe's Café

126 Draycott Avenue, SW3
01-225 2217

A fashionable spot both for dinner and for lighter lunchtime snacks such as salads and club sandwiches. Delicious sweets and well-chosen wines. Lots of teas, including jasmine, gunpowder, Earl Grey, Ceylon and Indian.

Leith's

92 Kensington Park Road, W11
01-229 4481

A favourite sophisticated dinner spot for nearly 20 years, with a splendid hors d'oeuvre trolley to get the meal under way. Duck breast with green peppercorn sauce or rib of beef could follow. Teas include Indian, China, camomile and mint.

Le Meridien, Terrace Garden Restaurant

Piccadilly, W1
01-734 8000

This smart, leafy restaurant provides a summery setting for a pleasant snack or meal throughout the day. Burgers and club sandwiches for quickies; crab soup with rouille followed by steak and Stilton pie for something more formal. Good variety of teas.

Park Lane Hotel, Bracewells

Piccadilly, W1
01-499 6321

High-quality French dishes are served in formal,

professional style in this elegant hotel restaurant. The choice embraces both traditional and modern cuisines and splendid trolleys carry cargoes of the day's roast, starters, cheeses and sweets. Extensive selection of teas.

Quincy's 84

675 Finchley Road, NW2
01-794 8499
It's always busy, so booking's a must at this lively, colourful place with bare boards and scrubbed pine. The menu deals in delights like rillettes of veal and duck, turbot with Pernod sauce and a lovely rhubarb sorbet. Super cheeseboard. Lapsang, Indian and herbal teas.

Swiss Centre, Chesa

2 New Cavendish Street, W1
01-734 1291
A delightful basement restaurant in the Swiss tourist complex. Chef André Pernet features many national specialities, including air-cured meats, raclette cheese, rösti and some splendid gâteaux. Quality teas.

London Airport, Heathrow

Sheraton Skyline, Colony Room
Bath Road, Hayes, Middlesex
01-759 2535
Formal elegance, polished service and skilled French cooking in a fine modern airport hotel. Spinach and watercress soup, veal with sorrel sauce and kiwi-fruit pancakes are typical delights, and there's a vast choice of French cheeses. Various teas available.

ENGLAND

Royal Berkshire Hotel Restaurant

Ascot, Berkshire
London Rd, Sunninghill
Ascot (0990) 23322
Set in a Queen Anne mansion, once the home of the Churchill family, this restaurant serves fine quality dishes. Specialities include grilled foie gras with fresh raspberries and ginger sauce, and rhubarb pudding spiked with pastis. A good choice of quality teas is offered.

Clos du Roy

Bath, Avon
7 Edgar Buildings, George St
Bath (0225) 64356
A central position for this pleasant little restaurant, where Philippe Roy produces French dishes that are often very imaginative and elaborate. There's a fine wine list, and teas span leaf, herbs, spice and fruit.

Flowers

Bath, Avon
27 Monmouth Street
Bath (0225) 313774
Teresa Lipin's three-course menus offer excellent value for money in this pleasant restaurant. Smoked salmon mousse, breast of pigeon and grilled steak are typical dishes, and there are some delicious sweets. To refresh the palate, a fine variety of leaf teas.

Lygon Arms Restaurant

Broadway, Hereford & Worcester
High Street
Broadway (0386) 852255
Tempting seasonal menus presented in the barrel-vaulted Great Hall of a renowned 600-year-old hotel. Duck quenelles with chestnut sauce and braised beef in Guinness are typical dishes. Low-fat and vegetarian foods available. Wide choice of teas.

Buckland Manor Restaurant

Buckland, Gloucestershire
near Broadway
Broadway (0386) 852626
Baronial furnishings and marvellous views go along with Martyn Pearn's carefully cooked, eye-pleasing dishes. Superb wines complement dishes like quail pâté, or lamb with a gentle garlic sauce. Ten varieties of quality tea.

Truffles

Manchester, Greater Manchester
63 Bridge Street
061-832 9393
A friendly city-centre restaurant with pleasing Victorian-style decor and a French accent to the cooking: piquant baked crab, snails in puff pastry, pot-roasted guinea fowl with a red wine and apricot sauce. Good-value set lunches. Oolong and Assam among the teas.

Rankin's

Sissinghurst, Kent
The Street
Cranbrook (0580) 713964
A cosy, homely restaurant near the famous castle and gardens. Fresh produce from local suppliers is used in enjoyable dishes such as Hastings smokie, and ragout of lamb with green peppercorns, orange and honey. English breakfast and Lapsang among the quality teas.

Heskyn Mill

Tideford, Cornwall
near Saltash
Landrake (075 538) 481
The old machinery has been used imaginatively in the decor of this converted corn mill. Regular favourites like steak, sole and pork with prunes are supplemented by daily specials. A variety of teas is served.

TEA AFTER MEALS

Old Beams

Waterhouses, Staffordshire
Waterhouses (053 86) 254

Pastry case of scampi on winter leaves and veal noisette with wood mushrooms are typical temptations in this roomy, attractive restaurant. Lovely light lemon tart makes a fine sweet, followed perhaps by Earl Grey or Darjeeling tea.

SCOTLAND

Nivingston House Restaurant

Cleish, Tayside
near Kinross
Cleish Hills (057 75) 216

Daily-changing menus offer plenty of good things in this elegantly appointed hotel restaurant. There's tomato and orange soup, loin of pork with apple and cranberry sauce, and brandy snaps with peach ice cream. A choice of about five teas.

Culloden House Restaurant

Inverness, Highland
near Culloden
Inverness (0463) 790461

Scottish and modern French elements combine in the daily-changing menus at this magnificent Georgian mansion. Local seafood, Brie-glazed loin of veal and medallions of venison in a pastry case are favourites. Teas of quality.

WALES

Meadowsweet Hotel Restaurant

Llanrwst, Gwynedd
Station Road
Llanrwst (0492) 640732

In a pleasant hotel overlooking Conwy Valley, John Evans prepares tasty dishes like scallop mousse, lamb with orange and ginger and a good cherry pudding. Super cheeses, outstanding wines and a large choice of leaf teas.

NORTHERN IRELAND

The Barn

Saintfield, Co. Down
120 Monlough Road
Saintfield (0238) 510396

Check directions when booking at this delightful restaurant in a converted barn. Raw materials are all important, with local fish, game from Tyrone, herbs from the garden and berries from the hedgerows contributing to delightful meals. Teas include Darjeeling and Earl Grey.

RESTAURANTS WITH ROOMS

'Restaurants with rooms' is a category based on 'restaurants avec chambres' in France. We give relevant information about accommodation in the restaurant entry.

ENGLAND

Ashbourne: Callow Hall
Bath: Hole in the Wall
Blandford Forum: La Belle Alliance
Bradford: Restaurant Nineteen
Brampton: Old Rectory
Brampton: Tarn End
Campsea Ashe: Old Rectory
Cartmel: Uplands
Cawston: Grey Gables
East Buckland: Lower Pitt
Farrington-Gurney: Old Parsonage
Grantham: Barkston House
Gulworthy: Horn of Plenty
Hastingleigh: Woodmans Arms Auberge
Helford: Riverside
Knutsford: La Belle Epoque
Lymington: Provence
Oakhill: Oakhill House
Padstow: Seafood Restaurant
Pool-in-Wharfedale: Pool Court
Ryde: Biskra House Restaurant

Shepton Mallet: Bowlish House Restaurant
Shipdham: Shipdham Place
Stockbridge: Sheriff House
Storrington: Manleys
Sturminster Newton: Plumber Manor Restaurant
Thame: Thatchers
Trebarwith Strand: Old Millfloor
Uppingham: Lake Isle
Waterhouses: Old Beams
Yeovil: Little Barwick House

SCOTLAND

Canonbie: Riverside Inn
Fort William: Factor's House Restaurant
Kingussie: The Cross
Swanbridge: Sully House
Ullapool: Altnaharrie Inn

WALES

Cardigan: Rhyd-Garn-Wen
Felingwm Uchaf: Plough Inn, Hickman's Restaurant
Welsh Hook: Stone Hall

REPUBLIC OF IRELAND

Dublin: Le Coq Hardi
Waterville: Huntsman

SEAFOOD RESTAURANTS

The following is a selection of restaurants where seafood is a major feature on the menu. For more details see the individual entries in the main section.

LONDON

Bentley's, W1
Bill Bentley's, EC2
La Croisette, SW10
Faulkners, E8 (e)
Frère Jacques, WC2
Grimes, WC2
L'Hippocampe, SW6
Lou Pescadou, SW5
Manzi's, WC2
Le Quai St Pierre, W8
Scotts, W1
Seashell, NW1 (e)
Le Suquet, SW3

ENGLAND

Birmingham, W Midlands: Biarritz
Burnham Market, Norfolk: Fishes
Burnham-on-Crouch, Essex: Contented Sole
Constantine Bay, Cornwall: Treglos Hotel
East Langton, Leicestershire: Bell Inn
Flitwick, Bedfordshire: Flitwick Manor Restaurant
Great Yarmouth, Norfolk: Seafood Restaurant
Harrogate, North Yorkshire: Drum & Monkey
Harwich, Essex: Pier at Harwich
Helford, Cornwall: Riverside
Hull, Humberside: Ceruttis
Ipswich, Suffolk: Mortimer's
Looe, Cornwall: Talland Bay Hotel
Lymington, Hampshire: Provence
Lympstone, Devon: River House
Norwich, Norfolk: Green's Seafood
Padstow, Cornwall: Seafood Restaurant
Penzance, Cornwall: Harris's
Stokesley, North Yorkshire: Chapters
Torquay, Devon: Imperial Hotel
Tresco, Isles of Scilly: Island Hotel
Waltham Abbey, Essex: Blunk's

SCOTLAND

Aberdeen, Grampian: Atlantis
Anstruther, Fife: Cellar Restaurant
Colbost, Highland: Three Chimneys
Crinan, Strathclyde: Crinan Hotel, Lock 16 Restaurant
Edinburgh, Lothian: L'Auberge
Edinburgh, Lothian: Le Marché Noir
Glasgow, Strathclyde: Rogano
Kinlochbervie, Highland: Kinlochbervie Hotel
Linlithgow, Lothian: Champany Inn Restaurant
Port Appin, Strathclyde: Airds Hotel
Tayvallich, Strathclyde: Tayvallich Inn

WALES

Llandudno, Gwynedd: Lanterns
Penarth, S Glamorgan: Caprice

CHANNEL ISLANDS

St Anne, Alderney: Nellie Gray's
St Peter Port, Guernsey: Le Nautique
St Aubin's Harbour, Jersey: Old Court House Inn Restaurant
St Brelade's Bay, Jersey: Hotel l'Horizon, Star Grill
Sark, Sark: Aval du Creux Hotel

ISLE OF MAN

Ramsey, Isle of Man: Harbour Bistro

NORTHERN IRELAND

Holywood, Co. Down: Schooner
Portrush, Co. Antrim: Ramore

REPUBLIC OF IRELAND

Baltimore, Co. Cork: Chez Youen
Cashel, Co. Galway: Cashel House Hotel
Cashel, Co. Tipperary: Chez Hans
Clifden, Co. Galway: Abbeyglen Castle Hotel
Clifden, Co. Galway: Hotel Ardagh
Cork, Co. Cork: Lovetts Restaurant
Dingle, Co. Kerry: Doyles's Seafood Bar
Dun Laoghaire, Co. Dublin: Restaurant Na Mara
Howth, Co. Dublin: King Sitric
Letterfrack, Co. Galway: Rosleague Manor House
Moyard, Co. Galway: Doon
Waterville, Co. Kerry: Huntsman
Youghal, Co. Cork: Aherne's Seafood Restaurant

LONDON RESTAURANTS WITH DISTINCTLY NATIONAL COOKING

AFGHAN

Buzkash, SW15 (e)
Caravan Serai, W1

CARIBBEAN

Caribbean Sunkissed Restaurant, W9 (e)

CHINESE

Chuen Cheng Ku, W1
Dynasty of Hampstead, NW3
Fung-Shing, WC2
Golden Chopsticks, SW7
Good Earth, NW7 & SW3
Good Friends, E14
Green Cottage, NW3 (e)
Hoizin, SW1
Hung Toa, W2 (e)
Jade Garden, W1
Ken Lo's Memories of China, SW1
Kym's, SW1
Lee Ho Fook, W1
Lok-Zen, N10
Mandarin, W8
Mandarin Kitchen, W2
Mayflower, W1
Mr Kai, W1
Nanyang, SW7
New Leaf, W5
New Loon Fung, W1
New Shu Shan, WC2
Pangs, W9
Peking Duck, NW11
Poons, WC2
Poons of Covent Garden, WC2
Pun, SW7
St James Court Hotel, Inn of Happiness, SW1
Shanghai, W8
T'ang, SW10
Tiger Lee, SW5
Weng Wah House, NW3
Youngs, N1
Yung's, W1
Zen, SW3

ENGLISH

Auntie's, W1
Blue Posts, Olde English Carving Room, SW1 (e)
Boswell's, SW5
Dorchester Grill Room, W1
Drakes, SW3
English Garden, SW3
English House, SW3
Green's Restaurant, SW1
Guinea, W1
Lindsay House, W1
Wiltons, SW1

FRENCH

L'Aquitaine, SW5
Ark, W8
L'Arlequin, SW8
Au Jardin des Gourmets, W1
L'Aventure, NW8
Bagatelle, SW10
Barnaby's, SW13
La Bastide, W1
Belvedere, W8
Bubb's, EC1
Café du Commerce, E14
Café Flo, NW3
Café Royal Grill Room, W1
Capital Hotel Restaurant, SW3
Chez Moi, W11
Christian's, W4
Ciboure, SW1
Claridge's Restaurant, W1
Connaught Hotel Restaurant, W1
Criterion Brasserie, W1 (e)
La Croisette, SW10
Daphne's, SW3
Dorchester Terrace, W1
La Fantaisie Brasserie, SW1

113

Frederick's, N1
Frère Jacques, WC2
Le Gamin, EC4
Le Gastronome, SW6
Le Gavroche, W1
Gavvers, SW1
The Grafton, SW4
Grill St Quentin, SW3 (e)
L'Hippocampe, SW6
Hyatt Carlton Tower, Chelsea Room, SW1
Inter-Continental Hotel, Le Soufflé, W1
Interlude, WC2
Keats, NW3
Langan's Bar & Grill, EC3
Langan's Bistro, W1
Ma Cuisine, SW3
Magno's Brasserie, WC2
Le Marmiton, EC2
Martin's, NW1
May Fair Inter-Continental Hotel, Le Château, W1
Le Mazarin, SW1
Le Meridien Piccadilly, Oak Room, W1
Mijanou, SW1
M'sieur Frog, N1
Monsieur Thompsons, W11
Montcalm Hotel, Les Célébrités, W1
Le Muscadet, W1
Ninety Park Lane, W1
L'Olivier, SW10
Oscar's Brasserie, EC4
Park Lane Hotel, Bracewells Restaurant, W1
Pavilion, EC2
Le Plat du Jour, NW1 (e)
Portman Inter-Continental Hotel, Truffles
   Restaurant, W1
Le Poulbot, EC2
Le Quai St Pierre, W8
Le Routier, NW1
St James Court Hotel, Auberge de Provence, SW1
St Quentin, SW3
Simply Nico, SW1
Le Suquet, SW3
La Tante Claire, SW3
Le Trou Normand, SW1
Turner's, SW3

GREEK & CYPRIOT

Andreas, W1 (e)
Anemos, W1 (e)
Bitter Lemons Taverna, SW6
Halepi, W2
Kalamaras (Mega), W2
Kolossi Grill, EC1 (e)
Lemonia, NW1 (e)
Little Akropolis, W1
Nontas, NW1 (e)
White Tower, W1
Wine & Mousaka, Richmond (e)

HUNGARIAN

Gay Hussar, W1

INDIAN & PAKISTANI

Ajanta, W12 (e)
Bombay Bicycle Club, SW12
Bombay Brasserie, SW7
Chambeli, W1
Delhi Brasserie, SW7
Great Nepalese Tandoori, W8
Gurkhas Tandoori, W1 (e)
Kensington Tandoori, W8
Khyber Pass, SW7
Kundan, SW1
Lal Qila, W1
Last Days of the Raj, W1
Maha Gopal, W1 (e)
Majlis, SW7
Malabar, W8 (e)
Memories of India, SW7
Mogul, SE10
Noorjahan, SW5 (e)
Ravi Shankar, NW1 (e)
Red Fort, W1
Sabras, NW10 (e)
Salloo's, SW1
Shezan, SW7
Shireen, W12 (e)
The Veeraswamy, W1
Woodlands, SW1 (e)
Woodlands, W1 (e)
Woodlands, Wembley (e)

INDONESIAN

Harry's Java Brasserie, E1
Sinar Matahari, W13

ITALIAN

Al Gallo d'Oro, W8
Caffé Mamma, Richmond (e)
Campanella, W11 (e)
Casa Cominetti, SE6
Como Lario, SW1
Da Gianbruno, W6 (e)
La Famiglia, SW10
Gavins, SW15 (e)
Giovanni's, WC2
Gran Paradiso, SW1
Grosvenor House, Pasta, Vino e Fantasia, W1 (e)
Luigi, SE19
Mario, SW3
Orso, WC2 (e)
Piccadilly Restaurant, W1
La Preferita, SW11 (e)
San Frediano, SW3
San Lorenzo, SW3
San Lorenzo Fuoriporta, SW19
San Martino, SW3
Santini, SW1
Ziani, SW3

JAPANESE

Ajimura, WC2
Azami, WC2
Benihana, NW3
City Miyama, EC4
Defune, W1
Fuji, W1
Ginnan, EC4
Gonbei, WC1
Hana-Guruma, EC4
Hiroko of Kensington, W11
Hokkai, W1
Ikeda, W1
Ikkyu, W1
Kitchen Yakitori, W1 (e)
Koto, NW1
Masako, W1
Miyama, W1
Ninjin Club, W1
One Two Three, W1
Saga, W1
Shogun, W1
Suntory, SW1
Wakaba, NW3
Yumi, W1

JEWISH

Bloom's, NW11 & E1
Harry Morgans, NW8 (e)

KOREAN

Arirang, W1
Arirang House, SW1
Cho Won, W1
Kaya, W1

LEBANESE

Phoenicia, W8

MEXICAN

Café Pacifico, W12 (e)

POLISH & RUSSIAN

Daquise, SW7 (e)

SOUTH-EAST ASIAN

Equatorial, W1 (e)
Penang, W2
Singapore Garden, NW6

SPANISH

Don Pepe, NW8

SWEDISH

Anna's Place, N1

SWISS

Swiss Centre, Chesa, W1

THAI

Bahn Thai, W1 & W8
Bangkok, SW7
Chaopraya Restaurant, W1
Chiang Mai, W1 (e)
Lakorn Thai, EC1
Lena's Thai Restaurant, SW11
Tui, SW7

TUNISIAN

Sidi Bou Said, W1 (e)

TURKISH

Aspava, W1 (e)
Efes Kebab House, W1, (e)

VIETNAMESE

Lindas, W9 (e)

OUTSTANDING CHEESEBOARDS

The following is a list of restaurants considered by our inspectors to have noteworthy cheeseboards. The range of cheeses offered need not always be large, but in all cases the selection is interesting and well kept.

LONDON

Bates, WC2
Boulestin, WC2
Chinon, W14
Ciboure, SW1
Corney & Barrow, EC2
Dorchester, Grill Room, W1
Dorchester, The Terrace, W1
Le Gamin, EC4
Harveys, SW17
Inigo Jones, WC2
Inn on the Park, Four Seasons, W1
Le Marmiton, EC2
May Fair Inter-Continental, Le Château, W1
Le Meridien Piccadilly, Oak Room, W1
Montcalm Hotel, Les Célébrités, W1
Quincy's '84, NW2
Rue St Jacques, W1
Simply Nico, SW1
La Tante Claire, SW3

ENGLAND

Ambleside, Cumbria: Kirkstone Foot Hotel
Ambleside, Cumbria: Rothay Manor
Ascot, Berkshire: Royal Berkshire
Ashford, Kent: Eastwell Manor
Bampton, Devon: Huntsham Court
Bath, Avon: Priory Hotel
Bath, Avon: Royal Crescent Hotel
Beanacre, Wiltshire: Beechfield House
Bedford, Bedfordshire: Woodlands Manor Hotel
Boughton Monchelsea, Kent: Tanyard Hotel
Brampton, Cumbria: Farlam Hall Hotel
Bray-on-Thames, Berkshire: Waterside Inn
Bury, Greater Manchester: Normandie Inn
Calstock, Cornwall: Danescombe Valley Hotel
Cambridge, Cambridgeshire: Midsummer House
Campsea Ashe, Suffolk: Old Rectory
Chagford, Devon: Mill End Hotel
Chagford, Devon: Teignworthy
Cheltenham, Gloucestershire: Redmonds
Chipping Norton, Oxfordshire: La Madonette
Corse Lawn, Gloucestershire: Corse Lawn House

Cricklade, Wiltshire: Whites
Dartmouth, Devon: Carved Angel
Edenbridge, Kent: Honours Mill
Ettington, Warwickshire: Chase Hotel
Evershot, Dorset: Summer Lodge Hotel
Grasmere, Cumbria: Michael's Nook
Grasmere, Cumbria: White Moss House
Great Milton, Oxfordshire: Le Manoir
Haslemere, Surrey: Morels
Huddersfield, West Yorkshire: Weavers Shed
Hurstbourne Tarrant, Hampshire: Esseborne
  Manor
Knutsford, Cheshire: La Belle Epoque
Ledbury, Hereford & Worcester: Hope End
Lower Beeding, West Sussex: South Lodge
Maiden Newton, Dorset: Maiden Newton House
Malvern, Hereford & Worcester: Cottage in the
  Wood Hotel
Malvern, Hereford & Worcester: Croque-en-
  Bouche
Nantwich, Cheshire: Rookery Hall Restaurant
New Milton, Hampshire: Chewton Glen Hotel,
  Marryat Room
Oakham, Leicestershire: Hambleton Hall
Odiham, Hampshire: La Forêt
Pangbourne, Berkshire: Copper Inn
Plumtree, Nottinghamshire: Perkins Bar Bistro
Powburn, Northumberland: Breamish House
  Hotel
Richmond, Surrey, Lichfields
Rockley, Wiltshire: Loaves & Fishes
Romsey, Hampshire: Old Manor House
Ryde, Isle of Wight: Biskra House
Scole, Norfolk: Scole Inn Restaurant
Shifnal, Shropshire: Park House Hotel, Idsall
  Rooms
Shipton-u-Wychwood, Oxfordshire: Lamb Inn
Speldhurst, Kent: George & Dragon, Oak Room
Ston Easton, Somerset: Ston Easton Park
Stonham, Suffolk: Mr Underhill's
Storrington, West Sussex: Abingworth Hall
Streatley-on-Thames, Berkshire: Swan Hotel
Stroud, Gloucestershire: Oakes
Taplow, Berkshire: Cliveden Dining Room
Taunton, Somerset: Castle Hotel
Tetbury, Gloucestershire: Calcot Manor
Thornbury, Avon: Thornbury Castle
Tresco, Isles of Scilly: Island Hotel
Tunbridge Wells, Kent: Thackeray's House
Ullswater, Cumbria: Sharrow Bay Hotel
Upper Slaughter, Gloucestershire: Lords of the
  Manor Hotel
Wareham, Dorset: Priory Hotel
Warminster, Wiltshire: Bishopstrow Hotel
Welwyn, Hertfordshire: Heath Lodge Hotel

Windermere, Cumbria: Roger's
Worcester, Hereford & Worcester: Brown's
Yattendon, Berkshire: Royal Oak Hotel

SCOTLAND

Canonbie, Dumfries & Galloway: Riverside Inn
Colbost, Highland: Three Chimneys
Drumnadrochit, Highland: Polmaily House Hotel
Inverness, Highland: Dunain Park Hotel
Kilchrenan, Strathclyde: Taychreggan Hotel
Tiroran, Strathclyde: Tiroran House
Uphall, Lothian: Houstoun House

WALES

Abersoch, Gwynedd: Porth Tocyn Hotel
Cardiff, South Glamorgan: Spanghero's

Felingwm Uchaf, Dyfed: Plough Inn, Hickmans
Llandudno, Gwynedd: Bodysgallen Hall Dining
  Room
Llandudno, Gwynedd: St Tudno Hotel
Llanrwst, Gwynedd: Meadowsweet Hotel

REPUBLIC OF IRELAND

Adare, Co. Limerick: Mustard Seed
Cashel, Co. Galway: Cashel House Hotel
Cashel, Co. Tipperary: Chez Hans
Cork, Co. Cork: Lovetts
Dublin, Co. Dublin: Locks
Dublin, Co. Dublin: Patrick Guilbaud
Dun Laoghaire, Co. Dublin: Restaurant Mirabeau
Dunworley, Co. Cork: Dunworley Cottage
Gorey, Co. Wexford: Marlfield House
Oughterard, Co. Galway: Currarevagh House
Rosses Point, Co. Sligo: Reveries

The Dairy Crest Symbol of Excellence

DAIRY CREST

Symbol of Excellence

Wherever you see this sign, you will be entering a restaurant, pub or cafe where the quality and presentation of cheese on the menu is excellent.

The inspectors for Egon Ronay's Guides will have paid a visit and decided to award the Dairy Crest Symbol of Excellence for the high standard of cheese available – whether presented on a cheeseboard or included in a meal or snack.

As Britain's leading manufacturer of cheese, Dairy Crest Foods has joined with Egon Ronay's Guides to acknowledge those catering establishments who are applying the highest standards of quality and presentation to the cheeses they offer. These are identified in three major 1988 Guides: the Hotel and Restaurant Guide, the Just A Bite Guide and the Pub Guide.

So, wherever you see the Symbol of Excellence, you will enjoy guaranteed quality of:

TASTE – through expert selection, handling and storage

VARIETY – through imaginative use of traditional, new and local cheeses

PRESENTATION – through the use of colour, texture and shape to give a mouth-watering display

INFORMATION – through the caterer's knowledge and understanding

Where you find English cheeses at their best, you will be sure to find Dairy Crest's own excellent cheeses, such as the famous Lymeswold range, the reduced-fat Tendale range and the full selection of English and Welsh traditional cheeses and prize-winning Cheddars and Stilton.

DAIRY CREST

EARLY EVENING EATING IN LONDON

Restaurants listed below open for dinner at 6pm or earlier.

LONDON

Ajimura, WC2
Arirang, W1
Arirang House, SW1
Athenaeum Hotel Restaurant, W1
Auntie's, W1
Azami, WC2
Bahn Thai, W1
Bahn Thai, W8
La Bastide, W1
Bates, WC2
Benihana, NW3
Bentley's, W1
Bitter Lemons Taverna, SW6
Bloom's, E1 & NW11
Boswell's, SW5
Café Flo, NW3
Café Royal Grill Room, W1
Le Caprice, SW1
Caravan Serai, W1
Chambeli, W1 & WC1
Cho Won, W1
Chuen Cheng Ku, W1
City Miyama, EC4
Claridge's Causerie, W1
Defune, W1
Delhi Brasserie, SW7
The Dorchester, The Terrace, W1
Dorset Square Hotel, Country Manners
    Restaurant, NW1
Dukes Hotel Restaurant, SW1
Dynasty of Hampstead, NW3
Frère Jacques, WC2
Frith's, W1
Fuji, W1
Fung-Shing, WC2
Gay Hussar, W1
Ginnan, EC4
Golden Chopsticks, SW7
Gonbei, WC1
Good Earth, NW7 & SW3
Good Friends, E14
Goring Hotel Restaurant, SW7
Gran Paradiso, SW1
Grimes, WC2
Halepi, W2
Hana-Guruma, EC4
Hankuk Koe Kwan, W1

Harry's Java Brasserie, E1
Hilton Kensington, Market Restaurant, W11
Hiroko of Kensington, W11
Hoizin, SW1
Hokkai, W1
Ikkyu, W1
Inigo Jones, WC2
Inn on the Park, Lanes, W1
Jacques, N4
Jade Garden, W1
Kaya, W1
Kensington Tandoori, W8
Koto, NW1
Lakorn Thai, EC1
Lal Qila, W1
Last Days of the Raj, W1
Lee Ho Fook, W1
Lindsay House, W1
Little Akropolis, W1
Lok-Zen, N10
Magno's Brasserie, WC2
Majlis, SW7
Mandarin, W8
Mandarin Kitchen, W2
Manzi's, WC2
Martin's, NW1
Mayflower, W1
Memories of India, SW7
Le Meridien Piccadilly, Terrace Garden
    Restaurant, W1
Mogul, SE10
Nanyang, SW7
New Leaf, W5
New Loon Fung, W1
New Shu Shan, WC2
Ninjin Club, W1
Peking Duck, NW11
Phoenicia, W8
Piccadilly Restaurant, W1
Poons, WC2
Poons of Covent Garden, WC2
Pun, SW7
Red Fort, W1
RSJ, SE1
The Savoy, Grill Room, WC2
Scotts, W1
Shogun, W1
Sinar Matahari, W13
Singapore Garden, NW6
Swiss Centre, Chesa, W1
Tiger Lee, SW5
The Veeraswamy, W1
Weng Wah House, NW3
Youngs, N1
Yumi, W1

Yung's, W1
Zen, SW3

RESTAURANTS UNDER £30 FOR TWO (see A Lot for Less)

Ajanta, W12
Andreas, W1
Anemos, W1
Aspava, W1
Blue Posts, Olde English Carving Room, SW1
Buzkash, SW15
Café Pacifico, WC2
Caffé Mamma, Richmond
Campanella, W11
Caribbean Sunkissed Restaurant, W9
Charing Cross Hotel, Betjeman Restaurant, WC2
Chiang Mai, W1
Cranks, W1
Criterion Brasserie, W1
Da Gianbruno, W6
Daquise, SW7
Diwana Bhel-Poori House, NW1 & W2
Ebury Wine Bar, SW1
Efes Kebab House, W1
Entrecôte, WC1
Equatorial, W1
Faulkners, E8
Great Nepalese Tandoori, NW1
Green Cottage, NW3

Gurkhas Tandoori, W1
Hard Rock Café, W1
Harry Morgan's, NW8
Hung Toa, W2
Joe Allen, WC2
Khyber Pass, SW7
Kitchen Yakitori, W1
Kolossi Grill, EC1
L. S. Grunts Chicago Pizza Co., WC2
Laurent, NW2
Lemonia, NW1
Lindas, W9
Maha Gopal, W1
Mélange, WC2
Nontas, NW1
Noorjahan, SW5
Nouveau Quiche, SE14
Oliver's, W14
Orso, WC2
Penang, W2
Le Plat du Jour, NW1
Punters Pie, SW11
Ravi Shankar, NW1
Sabras, NW10
Seashell, NW1
Shireen, W12
Sidi Bou Said, W1
Soho Brasserie, W1
Solopasta, N1
Topkapi, W1
Wine & Mousaka, Richmond
Wolfe's, SW3
Woodlands, W1, SW1 & Wembley

LATE NIGHT EATING IN LONDON

Restaurants listed below serve dinner at 11pm or later.

LONDON

Ajimura, WC2
Al Gallo d'Oro, W8
Alastair Little, W1
L'Aquitaine, SW5
Arirang House, SW1
Ark, W8
L'Arlequin, SW8
L'Artiste Affamé, SW5
Au Jardin des Gourmets, W1
L'Aventure, NW8
Bagatelle, SW10
Bahn Thai, W1
Bahn Thai, W8
Bangkok, SW7
La Bastide, W1
Bates, WC2
Benihana, NW3
Bentley's, W1
Le Bistroquet, NW1
Bitter Lemons Taverna, SW6
Blakes Hotel Restaurant, SW7
Bombay Bicycle Club, SW12
Bombay Brasserie, SW7
Boswell's, SW5
Boulestin, WC2
Café Flo, NW3
Le Caprice, SW1
Caravan Serai, W1
Chambeli, W1 & WC1
Chaopraya Restaurant, W1
Chez Moi, SW11
Cho Won, W1
Chuen Cheng Ku, W1
Churchill Hotel, The Arboury, W1
Ciboure, SW1
Claridge's, Restaurant & Causerie, W1
Como Lario, SW1
La Croisette, SW10
Crowthers, SW14
Dan's, SW3
Daphne's, SW3
Delhi Brasserie, SW7
Don Pepe, NW8
The Dorchester, The Terrace, W1
Drakes, SW3
Dynasty of Hampstead, NW3

Eatons, SW1
English Garden, SW3
English House, SW3
L'Escargot, W1
La Famiglia, SW10
Frederick's, N1
Frère Jacques, WC2
Frith's, W1
Fung-Shing, WC2
Le Gastronome, SW6
Gavvers, SW1
Giovanni's, WC2
Golden Chopsticks, SW7
Good Earth, NW7 & SW3
Good Friends, E14
The Grafton, SW4
Gran Paradiso, SW1
Greenhouse, W1
Grimes, WC2
Guinea, W1
Guinea Grill, W1
Halcyon, Kingfisher Restaurant, W11
Halepi, W2
Harry's Java Brasserie, E1
Harveys, SW17
Hiders, SW6
Hilaire, SW7
Hilton Kensington, Market Restaurant, W11
L'Hippocampe, SW6
Hoizin, SW1
Hyatt Carlton Tower, Rib Room, SW1
Hyde Park Hotel, Grill Room, SW1
Inigo Jones, WC2
Inn on the Park, Four Seasons Restaurant & Lanes, W1
Inter-Continental Hotel, Le Soufflé, W1
Interlude, WC2
Jade Garden, W1
Jams, W1
Joe's Café, SW3
Kalamaras (Mega), W2
Keats, NW3
Kensington Tandoori, W8
Kundan, SW1
Kym's, SW1
Lakorn Thai, EC1
Lal Qila, W1
Langan's Bistro, W1
Langan's Brasserie, W1
Last Days of the Raj, W1
Launceston Place Restaurant, W8
Lee Ho Fook, W1
Leith's, W11
Lena's Thai Restaurant, SW11
Lindsay House, W1

Lok-Zen, N10
Lou Pescadou, SW5
Luigi, SE19
Ma Cuisine, SW3
Magno's Brasserie, WC2
Majlis, SW7
Mandarin, W8
Mandarin Kitchen, W2
Manzi's, WC2
Mario, SW3
Martin's, NW1
Maxim's de Paris, SW1
Mayflower, W1
Le Mazarin, SW1
Memories of India, SW7
Ménage à Trois, SW3
Le Meridien Piccadilly, Terrace Garden
   Restaurant, W1
Mr Kai, W1
Mogul, SE10
M'sieur Frog, N1
The Montcalm, Les Célébrités, W1
Motcombs, SW1
Le Muscadet, W1
Nanyang, SW7
Neal Street Restaurant, WC2
New Leaf, W5
New Loon Fung, W1
New Shu Shan, WC2
Odette's, NW1
Odins, W1
L'Olivier, SW10
Pangs, W9
Peking Duck, NW11
Peter's, NW6
Phoenicia, W8
Piccadilly Restaurant, W1
Pollyanna's, SW11
Pomegranates, SW1
Poons, WC2
Poons of Covent Garden, WC2
Portman Inter-Continental Hotel, Truffles
   Restaurant, W1
Pun, SW7
Le Quai St Pierre, W8
Read's, SW5
Red Fort, W1
Le Routier, NW1
Royal Garden Hotel, Royal Roof Restaurant, W8
RSJ, SE1
Rue St Jacques, W1
St James Court Hotel, Auberge de Provence & Inn
   of Happiness, SW1
St Quentin, SW3
Salloos, SW1
San Frediano, SW3
San Lorenzo, SW3
San Lorenzo Fuoriporta, SW19
San Martino, SW3
Santini, SW1
The Savoy, Grill Room & Restaurant, WC2
Shanghai, W8
Shezan, SW7
Shogun, W1
Simply Nico, SW1

Sinar Matahari, W13
Le Suquet, SW3
Swiss Centre, Chesa, W1
T'ang, SW10
La Tante Claire, SW3
Tiger Lee, SW5
Le Trou Normand, SW1
Tui, SW7
Turner's, SW3
The Veeraswamy, W1
Waltons, SW3
Weng Wah House, NW3
Wok-On-By, SW11
Youngs, N1
Yung's, W1
Zen, SW3
Ziani, SW3

LONDON AIRPORTS

Heathrow
Sheraton Skyline, Colony Room

RESTAURANTS UNDER £30 FOR TWO (see A Lot for Less)

Ajanta, W12
Andreas, W1
Anemos, W1
Ark, W8
Aspava, W1
Le Bistroquet, NW1
La Bouffe, SW11
Buzkash, SW15
Café Pacifico, WC2
Caffé Mamma, Richmond
Campanella, W11
Caribbean Sunkissed Restaurant, W9
Chiang Mai, W1
La Cloche, NW6
Criterion Brasserie, W1
Da Gianbruno, W6
Diwana Bhel-Poori House, NW1
Efes Kebab House, W1
Entrecôte, WC1
Equatorial, W1
Foxtrot Oscar, SW3
Gavins, SW15
Great Nepalese Tandoori, NW1
Green Cottage, NW3
Grill St Quentin, SW3
Grosvenor House, Pasta, Vino e Fantasia, W1
Gurkhas Tandoori, W1
Hard Rock Café, W1
Hung Toa, W2
Joe Allen, WC2
Khyber Pass, SW7
Kolossi Grill, EC1
L. S. Grunts Chicago Pizza Co., WC2
Lantern, NW6
Laurent, NW2

Lemonia, NW1
Maha Gopal, W1
Malabar, W8
Manna, NW3
Mélange, WC2
Mother Huff's, NW3
Nontas, NW1
Noorjahan, SW5
Nouveau Quiche, SE14
Ormes, SW4
Orso, WC2
Penang, W2

Le Petit Prince, NW5
Pigeon, SW6
La Preferita, SW11
Le Premier Cru, SE10
Punters Pie, SW11
Shireen, W12
Sidi Bou Said, W1
Soho Brasserie, W1
Topkapi, W1
Villa Estense, SW6
Wine & Mousaka, Richmond
Wolfe's, SW3

OPEN AIR EATING IN AND AROUND LONDON

LONDON

Anna's Place, N1
L'Aquitaine, SW5
L'Artiste Affamé, SW5
Auntie's, W1
L'Aventure, NW8
Bagatelle, SW10
Le Bistroquet, NW1
Café Flo, NW3
Dan's, SW3
La Famiglia, SW10
La Fantaisie Brasserie, SW1
Frederick's, N1
Frith's, W1
Gran Paradiso, SW1
Hoizin, SW1
Lindsay House, W1
Lou Pescadou, SW5
Luigi, SE19
Mario, SW3
Memories of India, SW7
Mijanou, SW1
Odette's, NW1
Pollyanna's, SW11
Le Quai St Pierre, W8
Read's, SW5
Le Routier, NW1
St James Court Hotel, Inn of Happiness, SW1
St Quentin, SW3
San Lorenzo Fuoriporta, SW19
Singapore Garden, NW6
Le Suquet, SW3
Le Trou Normand, SW1

RESTAURANTS UNDER £30 FOR TWO (see A Lot for Less)

Anemos, W1
Ark, W8
Aspava, W1
Buzkash, SW15
Lantern, NW6
Mrs Beeton, Richmond
Mother Huff's, NW3
Nontas, NW1
La Preferita, SW11
Punters Pie, SW11
Soho Brasserie, W1
Villa Estense, SW6
Wolfe's, SW3

AROUND LONDON

Berkshire
Ascot: Royal Berkshire Hotel

Buckinghamshire
Marlow: Compleat Angler Hotel, Valaisan
   Restaurant

Surrey
Esher: Good Earth
Hersham: The Dining Room
West Clandon: Onslow Arms

SUNDAY EATING IN AND AROUND BRITAIN'S MAJOR CENTRES

LONDON

Ajimura, WC2 (D)
Al Gallo d'Oro, W8
Ark, W8 (D)
Athenaeum Hotel Restaurant, W1
L'Aventure, NW8
Azami, WC2 (D)
Bahn Thai, W1
Basil Street Hotel, Dining Room, SW3
Benihana, NW3
Berkeley Restaurant, SW1
Le Bistroquet, NW1
Blakes Hotel Restaurant, SW7
Bloom's, E1 & NW11
Bombay Bicycle Club, SW12 (L)
Bombay Brasserie, SW7
Boswell's, SW5
Hotel Britannia Inter-Continental, Adams
    Restaurant, W1 (D)
Café Flo, NW3
Café Royal Grill Room, W1 (D)
Capital Hotel Restaurant, SW3
Le Caprice, SW1
Caravan Serai, W1
Cho Won, W1
Chuen Cheng Ku, W1

Churchill Hotel, The Arboury, W1
Claridge's Restaurant & Causerie, W1
The Connaught Restaurant, W1
La Croisette, SW10
Cumberland Hotel, Wyvern Restaurant, W1
Delhi Brasserie, SW7
Don Pepe, NW8
The Dorchester, Grill Room, W1
Dorset Square Hotel, Country Manners
    Restaurant, NW1
Drakes, SW3
Dukes Hotel Restaurant, SW1
Dynasty of Hampstead, NW3
Ebury Court Hotel Restaurant, SW1
English Garden, SW3
English House, SW3
La Famiglia, SW10
Frère Jacques, WC2
Fung-Shing, WC2
Golden Chopsticks, SW7
Good Earth, NW7 & SW3
Good Friends, E14
Goring Hotel Restaurant, SW7
The Grafton, SW4
The Halcyon, Kingfisher Restaurant, W11
Halepi, W2
Harry's Java Brasserie, E1
Hilton Kensington, Market Restaurant, W11

Hyde Park Hotel, Grill Room, SW1
Inn on the Park, Four Seasons & Lanes
  Restaurants, W1
Inter-Continental Hotel, Le Soufflé, W1
Jacques, N4
Jade Garden, W1
Joe's Café, SW3 (L)
Kaya, W1 (D)
Kensington Tandoori, W8
Kym's, SW1
Lakorn Thai, EC1
Lal Qila, W1
Last Days of the Raj, W1
Launceston Place Restaurant, W8 (L)
Lee Ho Fook, W1
Leith's, W11
Lena's Thai Restaurant, SW11 (D)
Lindsay House, W1
Lok-Zen, N10 (D)
Lou Pescadou, SW5
Majlis, SW7
Mandarin, W8
Mandarin Kitchen, W2
Manzi's, WC2 (D)
Mario, SW3
May Fair Inter-Continental Hotel, Le Château, W1
Mayflower, W1
Memories of India, SW7
Le Meridien Piccadilly, Oak Room, W1 (D)
Le Meridien Piccadilly, Terrace Garden
  Restaurant, W1
Mr Kai, W1
Mogul, SE10
M'sieur Frog, N1 (D)
Monsieur Thompsons, W11
The Montcalm, Les Célébrités, W1
Nanyang, SW7
New Leaf, W5 (D)
New Loon Fung, W1
New Shu Shan, WC2
Pangs, W9
Peking Duck, NW11
Peter's, NW6 (L)
Phoenicia, W8
Pollyanna's, SW11 (L)
Portman Inter-Continental Hotel, Truffles
  Restaurant, W1

Pun, SW7
Quincy's 84, NW2
Read's, SW5
Red Fort, W1
Le Routier, NW1
St James Court Hotel, Auberge de Provence & Inn
  of Happiness, SW1
St Quentin, SW3
San Lorenzo Fuoriporta, SW19
Santini, SW1 (D)
The Savoy Restaurant, WC2
Scotts, W1
Shanghai, W8
Shogun, W1
Sinar Matahari, W13
Singapore Garden, NW6
Stafford Hotel Restaurant, SW1
Le Suquet, SW3
Swiss Centre, Chesa, W1
Tiger Lee, SW5
Tui, SW7
Turner's, SW3
The Veeraswamy, W1
Wakaba, NW3 (D)
Waltons, SW3
Weng Wah House, NW3
Youngs, N1
Yung's, W1
Zen, SW3
Ziani, SW3

LONDON AIRPORTS

Heathrow
Sheraton Skyline, Colony Room (D)

RESTAURANTS UNDER £30 FOR TWO (see A Lot for Less)

Ajanta, W12
Ark, W8 (D)
Aspava, W1
Le Bistroquet, NW1

La Bouffe, SW11 (L)
Café Pacifico, WC2
Caffé Mamma, Richmond
Charing Cross Hotel, Betjeman Restaurant, WC2
La Cloche, NW6
Da Gianbruno, W6
Daquise, SW7
Diwana Bhel-Poori House, NW1 & W2
Ebury Wine Bar, SW1
Entrecôte, WC1 (D)
Equatorial, W1
Foxtrot Oscar, SW3
Gavins, SW15
Great Nepalese Tandoori, NW1
Green Cottage, NW3
Grill St Quentin, SW3
Gurkhas Tandoori, W1
Hard Rock Café, W1
Harry Morgan's, NW8
Hung Toa, W2
Joe Allen, WC2
Khyber Pass, SW7
L. S. Grunts Chicago Pizza Co., WC2
Lantern, NW6
Laurent, NW2 (L)
Maha Gopal, W1 (D)
Malabar, W8
Manna, NW3
Mrs Beeton, Richmond (L)
Noorjahan, SW5
Nouveau Quiche, SE14
Oliver's, W14
Ormes, SW4
Orso, WC2
Penang, W2
Le Petit Prince, NW5 (D)
Pigeon, SW6
La Preferita, SW11
Le Premier Cru, SE10 (L)
Punters Pie, SW11
Ravi Shankar, NW1
Sabras, NW10
Shireen, W12
Topkapi, W1
Villa Estense, SW6 (L)
Wolfe's, SW3
Woodlands, W1, SW1 & Wembley

AROUND LONDON

Berkshire
Bray-on-Thames: Waterside
Maidenhead: Fredrick's Hotel Restaurant
Taplow: Cliveden Dining Room
Windsor: Oakley Court Hotel, Oak Leaf Room

Buckinghamshire
Chenies: Bedford Arms Thistle Hotel

Essex
South Woodford: Ho-Ho
Waltham Abbey: Blunk's

Hertfordshire
Old Hatfield: Salisbury (L)

Kent
Tatsfield: The Old Bakery

Middlesex
London Airports, Heathrow: Sheraton Skyline, Colony Room (D)

Surrey
Cobham: Il Giardino
Croydon: Tung Kum
East Molesey: Langan's Bar & Grill
East Molesey: Vecchia Roma
Esher: Good Earth
Guildford: Rumwong
Hersham: The Dining Room
Kingston-upon-Thames: Ayudhya
Limpsfield: Old Lodge
Ripley: Michel's
Tadworth: Fredericks

ENGLAND

BATH

Hole in the Wall (D)
Priory Hotel
Royal Crescent Hotel

AROUND BATH

Avon
Farrington Gurney: Old Parsonage (L)
Freshford: Homewood Park Restaurant
Hunstrete: Hunstrete House

Somerset
Ston Easton: Ston Easton Park

Wiltshire
Beanacre: Beechfield House
Lacock: Sign of the Angel (L)
Warminster: Bishopstrow House (D)

BIRMINGHAM

Dynasty
New Happy Gathering
Plough & Harrow Hotel
Rajdoot (D)

AROUND BIRMINGHAM

Belbroughton: Bell Inn (L)
Bromsgrove: Grafton Manor
Chaddesley Corbett: Brockencote Hall
Hockley Heath: Nuthurst Grange

BRIGHTON

Gar's
Old Ship Hotel
Peking
Whitehaven Hotel, Rolling Clock Restaurant

AROUND BRIGHTON

East Sussex
Jevington: Hungry Monk
Lewes: Light of Bengal
Lewes: Trumps

West Sussex
Cuckfield: Ockenden Manor
Storrington: Cottage Tandoori
Storrington: Little Thakeham (L)
Storrington: Manley's (L)

BRISTOL

Rajdoot (D)

AROUND BRISTOL

Avon
Farrington Gurney: Old Parsonage (L)
Hunstrete: Hunstrete House
Thornbury: Thornbury Castle

Somerset
Ston Easton: Ston Easton Park

AROUND BOURNEMOUTH

Poole: Mansion House Restaurant
Tarrant Monkton: Langton's
Wareham: Priory Hotel Restaurant

CAMBRIDGE

Charlie Chan
Shao Tao

AROUND CAMBRIDGE

Huntingdon: Old Bridge Hotel
Duxford: Duxford Lodge Hotel Restaurant

CANTERBURY

County Hotel, Sully's Restaurant
Howfield Manor Restaurant
Tuo e Mio

Sparkling
ASHBOURNE
Natural Water
Pure

AN EGON RONAY'S GUIDE FOR FREE!

Dear Reader,

We need your help please.

EGON RONAY'S GUIDES would like to know more about you.

To enable us to continue to publish the kind of Guides that you enjoy, please fill in this questionnaire. Simply tick the appropriate boxes or write in the spaces provided, and as a token of our appreciation, we will send you a complimentary copy of **Egon Ronay's Guide to Healthy Eating Out**.

Thank you.

Barbara Littlewood
Editor

NB. Your replies will, of course, be treated in the strictest confidence.

---

1 Where did you obtain your copy of this guide from?

2 Which other guide books, if any, do you own?

3 How do you *prefer* to pay for:

A restaurant meal?
An hotel bill?

4 Which credit or charge cards, if any, do you own?

Access   Visa
American Express   Other
Diners   None

5 Which newspaper do you read most often:

On a weekday?
On a Sunday?

6 Do you own a car phone?

Yes   No

If not, are you considering buying a car phone in the future?

Yes   No

7 Are you:

Under 35   Male
35 – 54   Female
55+

8 What is the total annual income for your household?

Under £5,000 pa.
£ 5,000 – £ 9,999 pa.
£10,000 – £14,999 pa.
£15,000 – £19,999 pa.
£20,000 or over

Name and address

2

The Automobile Association

Marketing Research Department

PO Box 50

BASINGSTOKE

Hampshire

RG21 2BR

AROUND CANTERBURY

Ashford: Eastwell Manor
Folkestone: Emilio Restaurant Portofino
St Margaret's at Cliffe: Wallets Court

CHESTER

Abbey Green (L)
Chester Grosvenor Restaurant
Crabwall Manor Restaurant

LIVERPOOL

Mandarin (D)

MANCHESTER

Rajdoot (D)
Yang Sing

AROUND MANCHESTER

Cheshire
Handforth: Belfrey Hotel
Heaton Moor: Jade Garden

OXFORD

Cherwell Boathouse (L)
Restaurant Elizabeth
15 North Parade
Le Petit Blanc
Randolph Hotel, Spires Restaurant
La Sorbonne

AROUND OXFORD

Chesterton: Woods
Cumnor: Bear & Ragged Staff (L)
Great Milton: Le Manoir aux Quat' Saisons (L)
North Stoke: Springs Hotel, Fourways
Stanton Harcourt: Harcourt Arms Restaurant
Wallingford: Brown & Boswell
Woodstock: Feathers Hotel

STRATFORD-UPON-AVON

Billesley Manor
Bunbury's Eating House
Ettington Park Hotel
Hussain's
Welcombe Hotel

AROUND STRATFORD-UPON-AVON

Gloucestershire
Buckland: Buckland Manor

Hereford & Worcester
Broadway: Collin House Hotel Restaurant (L)
Broadway: Dormy House
Broadway: Hunter's Lodge (L)
Broadway: Lygon Arms

Warwickshire
Ettington: Chase Hotel (L)
Leamington Spa: Mallory Court

SCOTLAND

EDINBURGH

L'Auberge
Caledonian Hotel, Pompadour Restaurant (D)
Number 10 (D in Summer)
One Devonshire Gardens Restaurant

AROUND EDINBURGH

Gullane: Greywalls Restaurant
Gullane: La Potinière (L)

GLASGOW

Amber (D)

AROUND GLASGOW

Langbank: Gleddoch House Hotel

WALES

CARDIFF

La Chaumière

AROUND CARDIFF

Coychurch: Coed-y-Mwstwr Hotel, Eliot Room (L)

NORTHERN IRELAND

BELFAST

Manor House

AROUND BELFAST

Holywood: Schooner
Waringstown: Grange (L)

REPUBLIC OF IRELAND

AROUND CORK

Shanagarry: Ballymaloe House

AROUND DUBLIN

Dun Laoghaire: Digby's
Maynooth: Moyglare Manor

MEALS IN PRIVATE HOSPITALS
A DOSE OF COSTLY MEDICINE

If you were shelling out around £200 a day to stay in a top London hotel like Claridge's, you would be entitled to expect something pretty special in the way of luxury accommodation, service and, not least, meals. And the chances are that you would not be disappointed.

But pay much the same upmarket price for a day's stay in a private hospital and the odds are that you will end up in an establishment which rates little better than a middle-grade hotel.

That is the inescapable conclusion of our inspectors' study of some of Britain's best known independent clinics. Their verdict: there is simply no comparison.

True, nurses and doctors are on call round the clock and the cost of this cover is built into the accommodation charge, but the extra staffing levels and facilities in a de luxe hotel more than offset this.

And no private hospital offers you comfort to the degree of, say Claridge's, where you have antique furniture in your room in addition to virtually every luxury you can imagine.

Worse, the food at some of the private hospitals we visited was little better than (and in one case below) the average served up by NHS hospitals in the same cities. This, despite the fact that the private sector on average spends four times more on food per patient than the State.

Says chief hotel and restaurant inspector, Andrew Eliel: 'There can be

little doubt for the most part that the hotel operations in private hospitals are grossly overpriced.'

By how much? By an average £75 a day if you compare the mean price charged by the hospitals we surveyed against the £90 bill from a typical mid-range hotel for three main meals and afternoon tea, and a single room with bathroom en suite.

'The clinics get away with it', says Andrew, 'because the majority of private patients these days don't know any better – the chances are that they have never even seen the inside of a top hotel. Most are employed people on average professional incomes who are able to cock a snook at the long NHS waiting lists because they have private medical insurance as part of their remuneration package.

'And you have to look no further than the car repair trade to see the effect on prices when, in most cases, the insurance company is footing the bill.'

In fact, the number of people with independent health cover has more than doubled in the last eight years to more than 5·2 million. Of these, 55 per cent have the premiums paid for them by their companies, while a further 20 per cent pay reduced subscriptions by belonging to discounted corporate schemes.

Inevitably, hotel prices in private clinics are dearest in London. At three of the hospitals we surveyed here – the Harley Street Clinic, the Lister and the Humana Wellington – you could pay as much as £220, £225 and £250 a day respectively . . . with the consultants' fees, cost of your operation and subsequent treatment on top of that.

Yet, remarkably, the Harley Street Clinic came last but one in our private hospital league, while the Lister was only one place better off. Even the Humana Wellington, the joint winner, was equalled by a small, comparatively unknown clinic whose daily tariff for a room *en suite* and meals and refreshments is almost £100 cheaper, with drugs and dressings.

Moreover, despite the fact that this clinic's daily food budget per patient is only half that of the big-name hospitals, the meal sampled there was awarded the joint highest mark in our survey. But perhaps the biggest surprise of all was the clinic's location – in the strife-ridden city of Belfast.

The establishment in question is the Ulster Independent Clinic, purpose-built in 1978 and the only private hospital in Northern Ireland. But that's not all. Belfast scores again with the Royal Victoria Hospital declared joint runner-up out of the NHS establishments we looked at.

The importance of hospital hotel services cannot be over-emphasised – especially where meals are concerned. As the Hospital Caterers' Association says: 'Food must be seen as an essential part of the cure of the patients.' And the way in which it is served, it says, is also vital: 'Meals are often the only break in the tedium of a patient's day'.

In our survey, hospitals were assessed on menu variety, balance and presentation, on whether patients could order meals the same day, and if they could change their selection at the last minute; and on whether visitors could order food.

Also checked were system of distribution; the quality of the meal and service; the procedure in the event of a patient complaining about the food; kitchen standards and hygiene; the level of accommodation; and value for money.

REFUSED ADMISSION

Altogether, we approached 38 hospitals before finalising the 22 that were subsequently surveyed.

Sixteen establishments were to turn us down – seven from the private sector, the rest NHS.

Four of the big names among the independents – the King Edward VII for Officers, the Cromwell, the Royal Masonic and the Devonshire, all in London – refused for technical reasons. These ranged from new systems and key personnel yet to be installed to an existing catering contractor being under notice.

Particularly galling was the response from BUPA, one of the best-known independent groups. After saying 'no' to visits to its hospitals in Cardiff and Manchester, it finally agreed to open the doors of its Norwich establishment to us.

But two days later, an embarrassed press officer, Philip Codd, was to tell us that one of his directors had quashed the invitation. The reason: this anonymous member of the board felt that our sole intention was to find faults.

The only answer to that is: 'If the cap fits . . .'

The NHS hospitals that refused – all on grounds of imminent major changes or lack of staff – were from the London area. These were St Mary's, the Royal Free, St Bartholomew's, the Middlesex, Moorfields, the Westminster, Great Ormond Street Hospital for Sick Children and finally Friern Psychiatric and Ealing.

Certainly the *ULSTER INDEPENDENT CLINIC* wasn't found lacking, despite a relatively low food budget (ranging from £2·75–£2·95) per patient per day and fewer beds (a mere 36) than any of the other private hospitals in the survey.

Yet, as our inspector comments: 'Overall, I felt that the lunch I tasted was well up to public restaurant standard.'

The first course of home-made mushroom soup, although judged 'a touch too salty', earned good marks for flavour and presentation, being served piping hot at ward level out of a bain-marie in a preheated china bowl on a doily-covered tray.

The main course chosen was deep-fried fillet of cod ('good, fresh, quality fish') with a 'nicely textured, fresh, thin coating of breadcrumbs' accompanied by roast and mashed potatoes, and broccoli that was 'pleasantly al dente'.

The sweet selected was a lemon soufflé ('very good indeed') – served with a freshly made pot of tea.

But the quality of the meal wasn't the only reason why the Ulster Independent scored so highly. For instance, the compact kitchen, with its array of modern equipment, was spotless. Equally apparent was the happy working atmosphere, and the care taken over presentation and garnishing.

Another 'plus' was that no course was served until the remnants of the previous dish had been cleared away.

It was perhaps small wonder that the patients interviewed were full of praise for the meals – the responsibility of contract caterers Gardner Merchant. Menus are operated on a four-week cycle and one of the few criticisms is that meals have to be ordered the previous day, though it is possible to change your selection right up to the time that the dishes are served.

Accommodation, soon to be extended to 48 single rooms, is well-equipped with carpeting, teletext colour TV and direct-dial telephones. *VERDICT: A very competent, professional food operation that appears to maintain a degree of homely appeal, with all staff only too eager to please.*

Joint-winner, London's *HUMANA WELLINGTON HOSPITAL* (just a stone's throw from Lord's cricket ground) was the largest (253 beds) and most luxurious and expensive of the private hospitals checked. But despite its classy clientele (which includes royalty, the titled and very rich) and a minimum £250 a day for accommodation and food, even this clinic doesn't match the best of the London hotels.

Wholly American owned, the Humana comprises two buildings, each with its own bar-lounge and well-equipped, well-planned kitchen. Menus change every fortnight and are printed in English, Arabic, German and Greek; in addition there is an à la carte choice featuring Beluga caviar among other delights.

Most rooms have balconies, many with good views over leafy St John's Wood. All are spacious and carpeted, with individual temperature control, radio, remote-control colour TV (and, like many private hospitals, an in-house video channel), built-in fridge, telephone (though only London calls are on direct dial) and more than adequate wardrobes. Standard bathrooms include bidets.

The dishes tasted were all specials of the day – tomato and carrot soup ('outstanding . . . excellent flavour . . . but the accompanying wholemeal roll was a little rubbery'), followed by breast of chicken stuffed with crabmeat and salmon ('colourful dish . . . artistic presentation . . . fresh tasting, moist chicken . . . with small, firm new potatoes and a cauliflower polonaise that was crunchy with a good topping').

The third course, gâteau St Honoré, had an 'exquisite wholemeal base with good crème patissière, choux and caramel topping' and, to finish, there was 'splendid coffee and . . . champagne'!

All courses, normally ordered 24 hours in advance, are served separately, and the china and cutlery are of good quality.

VERDICT: *Attention to detail evident . . . every whim catered for . . . pleasant staff . . . kitchen and store areas impeccable. (The daily food budget per patient was not disclosed.)*

A close runner-up was the largest private hospital outside London, the *ALEXANDRA HOSPITAL* at Cheadle in the southern environs of Manchester. Here again the minimum daily tariff is around £100 less than the Humana's.

At the Alexandra we sampled chilled apple and fennel soup ('well made, smooth and delicate'), steamed turbot with oyster mushrooms ('as good a turbot dish as you will find anywhere') and, for sweet, glazed fresh fruit tart ('light and delicious').

The in-house catering team changes the menu every three months or so, but there are also different specialities each week. Patients select the dishes of their choice on the day of eating, a few hours in advance.

This hospital is to add a new wing soon and increase the number of beds by 31 to 177. And given the number of meals that are assembled, a conveyor belt system is employed.

Rooms are bright and cheerfully decorated, and have a toilet and shower en suite.

VERDICT: *Well prepared, imaginative food.*

The Alexandra was one of four hospitals surveyed run by AMI Health Care. The other three were the Harley Street Clinic, London (97 beds, £99–£220), Ross Hall Hospital, Glasgow (101 beds, £150), and the Priory Hospital, Birmingham (96 beds, £131–£210). Surprisingly, in overall terms, there was a marked lack of consistency – the Priory coming equal seventh, and the Harley Street Clinic and Ross Hall occupying the bottom two places.

The daily food allocation per patient was also different at each one – £8·20, £8, £7·30 and £3·25 respectively. And strangely, the lowest of these budgets produced the best of the AMI meal offerings.

Our starter at the *PRIORY HOSPITAL* was home-made minestrone soup ('super consistency . . . full of vegetables, pasta and flavour . . . nicely seasoned . . . but

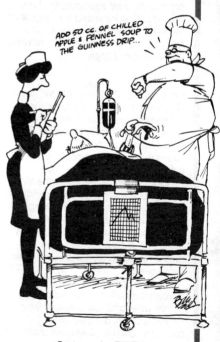

Cartoons by Bill Tidy

135

lost marks for not being hot enough').

The main course was beef fillet with pastry ('tender, good-quality meat . . . nice pastry . . . delicious creamy mushroom sauce . . . accompanying carrots were crisp . . . but potatoes a shade overcooked and, again, the meal could have been hotter'). The sweet selected was Bakewell tart ('good pastry . . . tasty, light filling').

The menu runs on a 10-day cycle which in turn changes every three months. It offers an extensive choice – four starters and at least five main courses (one or two meat, one fish, one egg, one vegetarian and a salad). In addition, there's a selection of sweets. Meals are ordered by patients the previous evening, and distributed on a conveyor belt system.

Bedrooms are comfortable, light and airy, and have intercoms, colour TV and direct-dial telephones.
VERDICT: A spotlessly clean, well organised, well equipped kitchen. Tray layout is neat and unfussy, and the staff smiling and friendly. The food is carefully cooked, attractively presented and appetising.

The *HARLEY STREET CLINIC*, in contrast, clearly suffers through not being purpose-built. As a result, patients' rooms are rather small and the kitchen is cramped and sometimes hot and uncomfortable to work in.

Not surprisingly, perhaps, the meal sampled here achieved a score no higher than the average NHS hospital.

There is a choice of four main dishes, but meals have to be chosen the previous day. The menu, which runs on a fortnightly cycle, is changed twice a year.

We tried Scotch broth ('a well flavoured mix of root vegetables, barley, peas and cubes of lean lamb served with good crusty bread'), curried chicken Madras ('well made and accompanied by a good range of pickles and condiments') and lemon meringue pie ('good pastry case and filling, with crisp, fluffy meringue').
VERDICT: The space problem affects the whole hospital.

The meal tasted at Glasgow's *ROSS HALL HOSPITAL,* on the other hand, was actually awarded a lower mark than the majority of NHS hospitals.

Although the menu (a fortnightly cycle changed twice a year) offered reasonable variety, only the lentil soup ('good, freshly made and adequately seasoned') got the thumbs up.

The main course of roast ham was 'mediocre' ('only the covering of crushed peppercorns gave the slice some interest') and the asparagus, like the fruit in the peach melba that followed, was tinned.

It is also normal practice here to serve all three courses together, unless a hot sweet has been ordered. Tray presentation wasn't particularly attractive, either.

But at least patients are able to make their selection on the same day (at the time of the previous meal, in fact) and they can change their minds at the last minute.
VERDICT: Friendly, smartly turned-out serving staff . . . clean, pleasant kitchen . . . comfortable accommodation, but unimaginative decor. The meal, though, was a big let-down.

What a difference at the 62-bed *ITALIAN HOSPITAL,* run by a registered charity in London WC1! The amount of food left on patients' plates amounts to a wastage factor of less than one per cent.

And no wonder. The cooking here surpassed most Italian restaurants. You had only to look round the kitchen stores to appreciate the quality of the produce and raw materials.

Also very apparent was the sense of pride among the staff both in front of and behind the scenes. Led by 36-year-old house services manager, Ermano Nuonno di Agnone ('Mr Nino'), the eight-strong kitchen team are all Italian and each holds a catering diploma (washer-upper included!).

The daily food budget per patient is £7·50 – and if the meal, service and menus had been the only criteria, the Italian Hospital would have been only one point behind the Ulster Independent and the Humana Wellington.

Patients make their selection at the end of the previous meal, and the menus are on a two-week cycle.

We started with minestrone ('piping hot, tasty, well made and generously laden with fresh vegetables'). Next, we selected a pâté maison ('smooth . . . certainly home-made . . . but perhaps lacking flavour') served with a side salad and fresh wholemeal roll, and garnished with lemon.

Then followed an excellent chicken pizzaiola ('tender breast . . . nice tomato sauce with herbs') or a very good escalope of veal ('hot, well cooked and much better than in most restaurants') – accompanied by mixed vegetables (some fresh, some frozen) and sautéed potatoes.

To finish, there was Italian ice cream, chocolate sponge gâteau and super-strong filter coffee.

There are five choices of accommodation, ranging from £95 a day (in a general ward) to £200 (private room with bathroom en suite). Italian nationals resident in Britain go free by right – and hotel and restaurant magnate, Lord Forte, is one of the trustees.

VERDICT: Though the building is old, it is spotlessly clean, and the staff are cheerful and obliging. The food: first class.

Two other establishments scored the same number of points overall as the Italian Hospital – the Bath Clinic (50 beds, £125–£188 a day) and the

Chalybeate Hospital, Southampton (94 beds, £127–£146).

The *BATH CLINIC* at Bath, Avon – one of six hospitals owned by the Compass organisation – is a strikingly modern two-storey building set in award-winning gardens and woodland.

The standard of accommodation is impressive: patients' rooms are air-conditoned, with large, double-glazed, solar-reflecting, one-way tinted windows; they have modern furnishings, high-tech bed, remote-control colour TV, radio and direct-dial phone; all have bath or shower room en suite.

The all-important catering operation is headed by hotel services manager Christine Miles and catering manager Eric Moore. The well designed, compact kitchen and preparation area is spotless, and food is dispatched by heated trolley. The daily meal budget was not disclosed.

Selection from the 14-day cycle menu is made at each preceding meal. If there was a criticism from the patients we spoke to, it was that having two substantial cooked meals a day was just 'too heavy' and 'too much'.

The first dish sampled was smoked trout ('cool and moist, attractively presented with a neat fresh salad garnish and separate boat of creamy, subtle horseradish sauce . . . but the small fish bones were annoying'). The next selection was escalope of veal, breadcrumbed and pan-fried to a crispy brown ('beautifully moist and tender . . . with attractive egg and olive garnish . . . simple but excellent quality'). This was accompanied by al dente, fresh broccoli and boiled potatoes.

The sweet choice, walnut gâteau, had been bought in but was reasonably good and, to follow, there was excellent, freshly brewed coffee.

Before the end of the year, patients will have the option of both light snacks and substantial meals.
VERDICT: Good standard of comfort, and a caring, efficient, obliging staff.

The CHALYBEATE HOSPITAL, Southampton, owned by the Hospital Corporation of America, is another modern, sophisticated establishment with above-average patients' rooms featuring beds that can be angled and raised at the touch of a button.

All the catering has been contracted out to the Commercial Catering Group, and meal-ordering times were the shortest of all hospitals surveyed, patients selecting lunch, dinner and the next day's breakfast at mid-morning, mid-afternoon and in the evening respectively. All meals are served one course at a time by ward maids in smart uniforms.

The menu is run on a three-week cycle and a special effort is made to avoid ingredients with saturated fats; neither is salt added, and sugar only very sparingly.

The meal sampled here began with leek and potato soup ('good flavour and consistency . . . well seasoned'). Next came seafood vol-au-vent ('good puff pastry, well baked and served crisp . . . overflowing with a well-seasoned mix of white fish, mussels and scallops in a light parsley sauce'). The vegetables and potatoes were fine, and the side salad, though devoid of dressing, was fresh and crisp. The range of simple sweets included an acceptable wine jelly.
VERDICT: A more than reasonable meal, given that the daily food budget per patient (£2·79) was one of the lowest of the private hospitals visited.

Also checked out was the NUFFIELD HOSPITAL at Newcastle upon Tyne (60 beds, £141 per day) – run by the Nuffield Organisation, the longest-established and largest private hospital group in Britain.

The daily food budget per patient (£2·84) was among the three lowest recorded in the independent sector, but the quality of the meal sampled was well below the standard found at the Ulster Independent and not as good, either, as the Chalybeate's.

The first course – a fresh cream of mushroom soup – was enjoyable enough (as was the sweet) but this was followed by a disappointing pork chop flamande ('on the dry side and slightly tough') while the creamed potato gave the impression that it had come out of a packet. One would have wished, too, for a more imaginative vegetable selection than spring cabbage, runner beans and peas. Patients were also expected to choose their meals the day before.

The food operation is supervised by Gardner Merchant and staffed by the hospital.

Accommodation, though, is well equipped and spacious with large windows and an attractive pale colour scheme. The en suite facility, however, provides only a shower, not a bath.

VERDICT: The main course left a lot to be desired. Given that the daily hotel services' rate is approaching £150, patients are entitled to something better than this.

The *LISTER HOSPITAL,* overlooking the Thames along London's Chelsea Bridge Road, could have done better, too – considering that the daily charge just to stay there ranges from £120–£225.

Part of the St Martin's Group, the hospital has contracted out its catering operation to the Gardner Merchant organisation. But though the daily food budget per patient (£5·25) is almost twice that of the Ulster Independent where Gardner Merchant are also in charge, the meal was inferior.

Patients have to order off the nine-day cycle menu the day before, but can change their selection at the last minute. All three courses are served at the same time and, on the day of our visit, something had clearly gone wrong because one patient was still waiting for his tray 45 minutes after the trolley had left the kitchen.

The hors d'oeuvre was a well presented concoction of avocado mousse, soft pâté, a slice of salami, sliced boiled egg, salad garnish and a tomato 'rose'. The home-made leek soup that followed was tasty but slightly separated, while the chicken casserole ('a good dish with plenty of chicken in a cream sauce') seemed hardly appropriate for a light diet. Also, the meat in the beef bourguignon was on the dry side, the duchesse potatoes tasted as if they were 50 per cent synthetic, sauces were not served separately, and the chocolate mousse lacked flavour.

Full marks though for a lovely baked rice pudding and the china which matched the hospital's decor. Staff, too, were impressively turned out. But in the splendid, well-equipped, airy kitchen, the floors could have been cleaner. And the pantries at ward level were cramped and poorly ventilated.

However, the fully carpeted bedrooms are spacious, double-glazed and have good en suite bathrooms.

VERDICT: The meals were reasonable but, in general, lacked the quality you should expect for your money.

SUMMING UP
THE INDEPENDENTS

■ Despite the comparatively small number of patients at most independent clinics, only in a third of those visited was it possible to order lunch and dinner at the time of the preceding meal. At most of the others, selections were asked for on the previous day.

■ In about a third of the establishments assessed, courses were not served separately.

■ Unlike their NHS counterparts, most private hospitals provided a wine list. The Ulster Independent Clinic, Belfast, in common with all Northern Ireland hospitals, dispensed free Guinness instead.

■ Also in contrast to the State sector, patients' meals were served by waiters and waitresses. In the NHS, this task was performed by nursing staff.

■ Only two hospitals, however, provided beds that could be adjusted to various positions at the touch of a button.

How Do You Fare on the NHS?

We also surveyed an equal number of NHS hospitals, so that we could have a base line to measure the private clinics by.

We had, of course, assumed a lower all-round standard. But taking into account the huge number of patients involved and the much-debated restrictions on public health spending, the food operation in the state sector proved an eye-opener.

Indeed, according to one of our inspectors who assessed four NHS hospitals and their independent counterparts, the quality and content of the fare was practically identical. 'With just one exception, I'm sure that if I had been blindfolded, I wouldn't have been able to tell the difference,' he said. 'But with accommodation charges of around £145 a day on average, the food in the private hospitals *should* have been a lot better.'

CEILING SOUP, DUCKS!

Without doubt, the pick of the NHS sector was London's 550-bed *UNIVERSITY COLLEGE HOSPITAL* (UCH) where, despite the inevitable teething troubles of a brand-new kitchen that had come on stream only days before our visit, in-house catering officer Peter Rugg and his team came up with a mass-produced meal that was better than those sampled in seven of the independent hospitals and the equal of two others.

And, incredibly, his food budget per patient is just £1·28 a day.

Of course the frills and niceties are conspicuously absent in the NHS – the china is chunky, canteen-style; the cutlery plain, heavy and cumbersome; and the trays devoid of linen and fresh flowers and so on. But there's not much wrong with the meals.

As with the private hospitals, there is a wide choice and, in addition to the main menu, there are salads, vegetarian offerings, ethnic dishes, kosher meals and special fare prescribed by dieticians.

Balance is the key, and it is noticeable that no NHS or private hospital in our survey insisted that patients consume only healthy food. Where, in a handful of cases, this has been tried (particularly at breakfast time), most patients have refused to touch it! Nevertheless, efforts are made to reduce fat and salt content and increase fibre intake.

At UCH we sampled chick pea casserole ('extremely tasty, with fresh ingredients'), cottage-cheese salad prepared the same morning ('generous . . . though the carrots were a little dry'), veal escalope ('very tasty . . . well seasoned') and 'excellent' rhubarb flan.

Two other hospitals – the Royal Victoria, Belfast (700 beds) and Northwick Park, Harrow (800 beds) – ran it close overall.

Not surprisingly, perhaps, the food at the *ROYAL VICTORIA HOSPITAL* – a huge site which, at its widest point, measures almost a mile – arrived only lukewarm in some wards. However, the emphasis on fresh ingredients, particularly vegetables, was very much a plus point – and the fact that most of the meals were produced in what was regarded as a temporary kitchen 13 years ago, made the effort even more impressive.

This 'temporary' kitchen, incidentally, may soon be replaced, given that major capital investment is planned in the next 12 months.

NORTHWICK PARK HOSPITAL has a claim to fame of a kind: it is one of only seven NHS hospitals so far that have handed the catering operation to a commercial catering organisation, in this case Spinneys.

The food here was well prepared and enjoyable – and the baked cherry sponge 'excellent'.

Standards at Birmingham's Queen Elizabeth Hospital and Southampton General were also above average in the NHS sector.

Interestingly, the catering department at the *QUEEN ELIZABETH HOSPITAL* (600 beds) was also run by Spinneys for a few months last year. But, underlining the constraints and general shortage of money within the NHS, the company was forced to pull out. So once again the in-house team is back in charge.

At *SOUTHAMPTON GENERAL HOSPITAL* (750 beds), the daily food budget is only £1·45 a head. Here, it came as a surprise to learn that catering officer John Wane and his team generated funds of more than £75,000 in the last financial year by laying on special meals at medical conferences and other functions held at the hospital. Wane, who firmly believes that there is scope and extra profit to be made in offering a contract service to outside organisations, using the hospital's facilities, also goes out of his way to make cakes for patients celebrating birthdays – a

treat, incidentally, served up by many State and Private Hospitals.

Just three hospitals – the Royal Infirmary, Manchester (700 beds), the Royal United at Bath (850 beds) and the Western Infirmary, Glasgow (556 beds) – epitomised the cartoonists' jaundiced view of NHS establishments.

Patients' reaction to the food at *MANCHESTER ROYAL INFIRMARY* was generally hostile, and the building as a whole tired and rather shabby. Arguably not before time, it is to be rebuilt in phases, with completion due in the 1990s.

The blot on the landscape at *BATH'S ROYAL UNITED,* on the other hand, was Ward 8 – an old, illegally cramped, 23-bed wing with basic toilet facilities, peeling walls and a leaking ceiling resulting in the beds having to be moved every time it rains. Many of the patients were elderly men – among them critically ill cardiac cases. Four remarkably stoical nurses – one staff, one enrolled and two novices – coped somehow, but sometimes only just.

The 30-year-old trolleys that ferry the meals to the wards weren't exactly clean either – due to a dispute. And one-third of the meals brought to one of the wards on our visit remained untouched because of administrative errors (the patients were either too poorly to eat, or couldn't swallow . . . or had already been discharged!)

The *WESTERN INFIRMARY, GLASGOW,* was also let down by the standard of accommodation. There was only one toilet and bathroom in one ward containing 24 beds and, in at least one dayroom, the wallpaper was torn and the plasterwork chipped – 'not very inviting'.

All in all, though, the NHS scene wouldn't appear to be half as bad as it is popularly painted – at least judged on the hospitals we visited.

SUMMING UP THE NHS

■ In the bulk of cases, meals were ordered the day before – and at four hospitals patients were unable to change their minds at the last minute. At two hospitals, to ease the workload, nurses selected the meals without consulting the patients.

■ All courses were served simultaneously.

■ Despite the Government's privatisation policy, only seven hospitals so far are using outside caterers. According to one contractor, Spinneys, it is unlikely that any more companies will put in tenders; this results from a change in the rules a year ago, which insists that contractors foot the complete bill of any redundancies.

■ NHS meals could be improved, according to catering officers, by an average extra 30p per patient per day. But it's more likely, they say, that budgets will be trimmed.

The Independents

POSITION	HOSPITALS	MEAL ONLY *	FOOD QUALITY & SERVICE **	ACCOMMODATION ***	TOTAL %
1 =	Ulster Independent Clinic, Belfast	9	23	8	83
1 =	Humana Wellington Hospital, London NW8	9	23	8	83
3	Alexandra Hospital, Cheadle, Manchester	7	21	8	79
4 =	Bath Clinic, Bath	7	20	8	75
4 =	Chalybeate Hospital, Southampton	6	20	8	75
4 =	Italian Hospital, London WC1	8	22	7	75
7 =	Priory Hospital, Birmingham	8	19	8	73
7 =	Nuffield Hospital, Newcastle upon Tyne	6	19	8	73
9	Lister Hospital, London SW1	7	19	7	71
10	Harley Street Clinic, London W1	5	18	7	67
11	Ross Hall Hospital, Glasgow	4	17	5	65

* Points out of 11   ** Points out of 28   *** Points out of 10

The National Health

POSITION	HOSPITALS	MEAL ONLY *	FOOD QUALITY **	ACCOMMODATION & SERVICE ***	TOTAL %
1	University College Hospital, London WC1	8	16	5	58
2=	Northwick Park Hospital, Harrow	5	12	6	54
2=	Royal Victoria Hospital, Belfast	5	13	5	54
4=	Queen Elizabeth Hospital, Birmingham	5	12	5	50
4=	St Thomas's Hospital, London SE1	5	11	6	50
6	Charing Cross Hospital, London W6	6	12½	5	49
7	Southampton General Hospital	4	11	5	48
8=	Royal United Hospital, Bath	5	13	5	46
8=	Western Infirmary, Glasgow	5	12	1	46
10	Newcastle upon Tyne General Hospital	4	11	5	44
11	Royal Infirmary, Manchester	4	6	4	31

* Points out of 11   ** Points out of 28   *** Points out of 10

**Please note that these tables are an abridged version of our findings.
Other factors, not shown here, were also taken into account.**

LACK OF QUALITY

Our investigation was triggered by a letter from former Deputy Director-General of the Confederation of British Industry, Edward James CMG, OBE, who is very critical of the meals in private hospitals where he has stayed.

The food, he says, and this is true of many independent clinics, was the responsibility of contract caterers who provide a similar daily service for business and industry in management and staff dining rooms.

'I realise that mass catering has its problems,' he declared, 'but that is no excuse for the standard frequently found.' Judged on his own experiences hospital fare was little better. 'Disgusting' was his word for it.

He goes on: 'One of the reasons' . . . 'is that patients either don't complain or don't complain enough. The truth all too often is that you get quality only if you insist on it.'

THE FIAT GUIDE
TO SUCCESSFUL
MOTORING

Fiat main and service dealers are strategically situated across the United Kingdom to offer comprehensive sales, servicing and repair facilities together with an abundant availability of spares and accessories.

At the time this guide is going to press we have 369 dealerships, as shown in the list below, bringing the stylish Fiat range close to home and ensuring you can easily contact us wherever you are.

To learn of any possible new appointment nearer to you please contact the Fiat Information Service, Dept ER87, PO Box 39, Windsor, Berks SL4 3SP. Telephone: 07535 56397 or call free on Linkline (0800) 521581
★ denotes Service Only Dealer

ENGLAND

AVON
Bath **MOTOR SERVICES (BATH) LTD** Circus Pl. 0225 27328
Bristol **AUTOTREND LTD** 724-726 Fishponds Road. 0272 659491
Bristol **BAWNS (BRISTOL) LTD** 168-176 Coronation Rd. 0272 631101
Clevedon **JEFF BROWNS (CLEVEDON)** Old Church Rd. 0272 871211
Weston-Super-Mare **JEFF BROWNS (LYMPSHAM)** Bridgwater Rd. 0934 72300/72696
★ *Thornbury Bristol* **SHIPPS OF THORNBURY** Midland Way. 0454 413130

BEDFORDSHIRE
Bedford **OUSE VALLEY MOTORS** 9 Kingsway. 0234 64491
Biggleswade **OWEN GODFREY LTD** 91-119 Shortmead St. 0767 313357
Billington **D & J AUTOS LTD** The Garage, Leighton Buzzard Rd. 0525 383068
Luton **BLACKABY & PEARCE (LUTON) LTD** Poynters Rd. 0582 67742

BERKSHIRE
Goring-on-Thames **COURTS GARAGE (GORING)** 42 Wallingford Rd. 0491 872006
Maidenhead **SOUTH BERKSHIRE MOTOR CO LTD** 264-270 Windsor Rd. 0628 71628
Newbury **BLACK AND WHITE GARAGE** Hermitage Rd, Cold Ash. 0635 200444
Reading **JACK HILL (READING) LTD** Chatham St. Multi-Storey Car Park. 0734 582521
Windsor **ANDREWS OF WINDSOR** 110 St. Leonards Rd. 0753 866108

BUCKINGHAMSHIRE
Amersham **AMERSHAM MOTORS LTD** Chesham Rd, HP6 5EX. 02403 22191
Aylesbury **AMERSHAM MOTORS** Stoke Rd. 0296 81181
Beaconsfield **MAURICE LEO LTD** 15 Gregories Rd. 049 46 6171
Bourne End **CARCHOICE LTD** Station Rd. 06285 22606

Gerrards Cross **BURWOODS GARAGE LTD** Oxford Rd. Tatling End. 0753 885216
High Wycombe **DESBOROUGH MOTOR CO LTD** 41 Desborough Ave. 0494 36331
Milton Keynes **ELMDENE MOTORS LTD** Townsend Thoresen Auto Centre, Unit 15, Erica Rd. 0908 320355

CAMBRIDGESHIRE
Cambridge **HOLLAND FIAT CENTRE** 315-349 Mill Rd. 0223 242222
March **CARL PORTER LTD** Causeway Garage, The Causeway. 0354 53340/55956
Peterborough **PETERBOROUGH AUTOS** Midland Rd. 0733 314431
St Ives **OUSE VALLEY MOTORS** Station Rd. 0480 62641

CHESHIRE
Chester **HERON** Mountview, Sealand Rd. 0244 374440
★ *Congleton* **ROBIN HOOD GARAGE** West Heath. 0260 273219
Crewe **COPPENHALL GARAGE LTD** Cross Green. 0270 583437
Macclesfield **MOSS ROSE MOTORS LTD** London Rd. 0625 28866
Northwich **STATION ROAD GARAGE (NORTHWICH) LTD** Station Rd. 0606 49957
Warrington **WILLIAM MARTYN GARAGES LTD** Wilderspool Causeway. 0925 50417

CLEVELAND
Middlesbrough **MARTINS LONGLANDS** Longlands Rd. 0642 244651
Stockton-on-Tees **WENTANE MOTORS LTD** 100 Yarm Lane. 0642 611544

CORNWALL
Newquay **TOWER OF NEWQUAY** Tower Rd. 0637 872378/877332
Pensilva **MARSH'S (GARAGES)** Princess Row. 0579 62595
Truro **W.H. COLLINS & SON (MOTORS) LTD** Kenwyn Mews. 0872 74334

CUMBRIA
Carlisle **GRIERSON & GRAHAM (CARLISLE) LTD** 33 Church St, Caldergate. 0228 25092
Flimby **DOBIE'S GARAGE** Risehow. 0900 812332
★ *Kendal* **CRAIGHILL & CO LTD** 113 Stricklandgate. 0539 20967/8
Keswick **KESWICK MOTOR CO LTD** Lake Rd Garage. Sales: 0596 72534
Barrow-in-Furness **COUNTY PARK MOTORS,** County Park Industrial Est., Park Rd 0229 36888

DERBYSHIRE
Derby **KEN IVES MOTORS (DERBY) LTD** 574-576 Burton Rd, Littleover. 0332 369723
Chesterfield **WOODLEIGH MOTOR SALES LTD** 300 North Wingfield Rd, Grassmoor. 0246 850686
Heanor **NAVIGATION GARAGE (HEANOR)** Loscoe Rd. 0773 717008
Kegworth **J.C.S. GARAGES LTD** Station Rd, Kegworth. 050 97 2523
★ *Wirksworth* **WIRKSWORTH SERVICE GARAGE** Derby Rd. 062 982 2143

DEVON
Barnstaple **NORTH DEVON MOTOR CO** Pottington Ind Est. 0271 76551
Exeter **SIDWELL STREET MOTORS LTD** 85-88 Sidwell Street. 0392 54923
Newton Abbot **QUAY GARAGE FREDDIE HAWKEN LTD** The Avenue. 0626 52525/6
★ *Okehampton* **F J GLASS & CO (1981) LTD** 57 Exeter Rd. 0837 2255
Plymouth **MUMFORDS OF PLYMOUTH** Plymouth Rd. 0752 261511
Sidmouth **CENTRAL GARAGE (SIDFORD) LTD** Crossways, Sidford. 039 55 3595

DORSET
Bournemouth **CAFFYNS P.L.C.** 674-680 Wimborne Rd, Winton. 0202 512121
Weymouth **OLDS** 172 Dorchester Rd. 0305 786311

CO DURHAM

Consett **TRAVELWISE**
Delves La. 0207 502353
★ *Crook* **BROOKSIDE GARAGE LTD**
New Rd. 0388 762551
Darlington **E. WILLIAMSON (MOTORS)**
LTD 1-7 Woodland Rd. 0325 483251
Parts: 0325 55850
Sacriston **FULTONS OF SACRISTON,**
Woodside Garage, Witton Rd.
0385 710422.

ESSEX

Basildon **H.W.S.**
Roundacre, Nethermayne. 0268 22261
Buckhurst Hill **MONTROE MOTORS**
Epping New Rd. 01-504 1171
Colchester **D SALMON CARS LTD**
Sheepen Rd. 0206 563311
Frinton-on-Sea **POLLENDINE MOTORS**
LTD 132 Connaught Ave. 02556 79123
Harlow **MOTORSALES (HARLOW) LTD**
Elizabeth Way, Burnt Mill. 0279 412161
Hutton **HUTTON GARAGES LTD**
661 Rayleigh Rd. 0277 210087
Little Waltham **MATTHAMS FIAT**
CENTRE, Braintree Rd. 0245 361731
Romford **McQUIRE MOTORS LTD**
229-307 Collier Row La. 0708 66806
Southend-on-Sea **BELLE VUE MOTORS**
LTD 460-464 Southchurch Rd. 0702 64945
Westcliff-on-Sea **H W STONE MOTOR CO**
684 London Rd. 0702 715181

GLOUCESTERSHIRE

Cheltenham **DANEWAY MOTOR CO LTD**
84 Bath Rd. 0242 523879
Cirencester **PAGE & DAVIES LTD**
10 Love La. 0285 69112/3
Stroud **PAGANHILL SERVICE STATION**
LTD 105 Stratford Rd. 04536 4781
Gloucester **WARNERS MOTORS LTD**
Quedgeley Garage, Quedgeley. 0452
720107
★ *Wotton-under-Edge* **WOTTON MOTOR**
CENTRE LTD
Gloucester St. 0453 842240

GREATER MANCHESTER

Ashton-under-Lyne **PREMIER MOTOR CO**
Manchester Rd, Mossley. 04575 67121
Bolton **KNIBBS (BOLTON) LTD**
Kay St/Higher Bridge St. 0204 386306
Bury **BLACKFORD BRIDGE CAR SHOW**
LTD 701 Manchester Rd, Blackford Bridge.
061-766 1346
Leigh **SMALLBROOK SERVICE STATION**
Smallbrook La. 0942 882201/891939
Manchester **KNIBBS (MANCHESTER)**
LTD Midland Street Garage, Ashton Old Rd.
061-273 4411
Oldham **KNIBBS (OLDHAM) LTD**
23-37 Lees Rd. 061-624 8046
Rochdale **KNIBBS (ROCHDALE) LTD**
Queensway, 0706 33222
Stockport **KNIBBS (STOCKPORT) LTD**
West End Garage, Heaton La. 061-480 6661

HAMPSHIRE

Aldershot **CLEVELAND CARS LTD**
Ash St, Ash. 0252 313033
Andover **CLOVER LEAF CARS**
(ANDOVER) Salisbury Rd. 0264 61166
Basingstoke **CLOVER LEAF CARS**
(BASING) London Rd (A30). 0256 55221
Fareham **DIBBEN MOTOR CO LTD**
244 West St. 0329 286241
Lymington **STATION GARAGE**
LYMINGTON Station St. 0590 77771
Portsmouth **CANNON GARAGES**
(PORTSMOUTH) LTD
117 Copnor Rd. 0705 691621
Ringwood **WELLS RINGWOOD**
Salisbury Rd. 04254 6111
Southampton **SEWARDS**
Rushington Roundabout, Totton Bypass.
0703 861001

HEREFORD & WORCESTER

Evesham **BRIGHTS GARAGE**
3 Cheltenham Rd. 0386 2301
Hereford **GODSELL'S (HEREFORD) LTD**
Bath St. 0432 274134
Kidderminster **STANLEY GOODWIN**
MOTORS LTD Worcester Rd. 0562 2202
Worcester **BOWLING GREEN GARAGE**
(POWICK) LTD Powick. 0905 830361
Bromsgrove **NEALE'S GARAGE (1985)**
LTD 2-12 Station St. 0527 72071

HERTFORDSHIRE

Croxley Green **CROXLEY GREEN MOTORS**
LTD 185 Watford Rd. 0923 55511
Hemel Hempstead **SHAW & KILBURN LTD**
Two Waters Rd. 0442 51212
Hitchin **SERVAL (HITCHIN) LTD**
Ickleford. 0462 54526
Knebworth **LISLES MOTOR REPAIRS LTD**
London Rd, Woolmer Green. 0438 81 1011
St Albans **I.A.P. GROUP**
2 Beech Rd. Marshalswick. 0727 50871

HUMBERSIDE

Driffield **GEORGE WILLIAMSON**
(GARAGES) LTD
82-84 Middle St. South. 0377 43130
Grimsby **ERIC C. BURTON & SONS LTD**
Station Garage, Wellowgate. 0472 55951
★ *Goole* **J WARDLE & SON LTD**
Boothferry Rd, Howden. 0430 30388
Hull **A B MOTOR CO OF HULL LTD**
96 Boothferry Rd. 0482 506976 & 54256
Hull **JUBILEE GARAGE**
Holderness Rd. 0482 701785
Scunthorpe **BRUMBY SERVICE GARAGE**
LTD The Fiat Centre, Normanby Rd.
0724 861191

ISLE OF WIGHT

Sandown **HODGE & CHILDS LTD**
Station Av. 0983 402552

KENT

Ashford **ASHFORD MOTOR CO**
Chart Rd. 0233 22281
Beckenham **BRUTONS OF BECKENHAM**
LTD 181 Beckenham Rd. 01-650 0108/9/
01-650 3333
Bexleyheath **BELLWAY MOTORS KENT**
303/307 Broadway. 01-301 0420
Brasted **MANNERING BROTHERS**
Brasted Garage, High St. 0959 62540/
64497
Bromley **THAMES**
96 Bromley Hill. 01-460/4646
Canterbury **MARTIN WALTER LTD**
41 St. George's Pl. 0227 763800
Deal **CAMPBELLS OF DEAL LTD**
6 The Marina. 0304 363166
Farnborough **FARNWAY SERVICE LTD**
2 Church Rd. 0689 50121
Gillingham **AUTOYACHTS LTD**
171 Pier Rd. 0634 28133
★ *Gravesend* **MARTINS GARAGE**
50 Singlewell Rd. 0474 66148
★ *Ham Street* **ANNINGS MARSH ROAD**
Nr. Ashford. 023 373 2275
Hythe **RAMPART GARAGE**
15-17 Rampart Rd. 0303 67088
Maidstone **UNION MOTORS**
29 Union St. 0622 55403
★ *Margate* **S & S MOTORS**
10-12 Park La. 0843 227778
Orpington **GODDINGTON SERVICE**
STATION, 318 Court Rd. 0689 20337
Ramsgate **S & S MOTORS LEVERPOINT**
LTD Willsons Rd. 0843 593465
★ *Sittingbourne* **J G BURGESS & CO**
Ufton Lane Garage. 0795 23815
Swanley **FOREMAN BROS LTD**
London Rd. 0322 68411
Tunbridge Wells **G.E. TUNBRIDGE LTD**
319 St John's Rd. 0892 511522

LANCASHIRE

Accrington **MICHAEL O'SULLIVAN**
Rising Bridge Garage, Blackburn Rd.
0706 225321

Blackburn **BARKERS**
King St. 0254 52981
Burnley **KNIBBS (BURNLEY) LTD**
Parker St. Kingsway. 0282 58271
Colne **EAGLE SERVICE STATION**
Stonebridge Works, Windybank.
0282 863254
Lancaster **G & L CAR SERVICE LTD**
Wheatfield St. 0524 39857
Preston **LOOKERS GROSVENOR**
MOTORS LTD
306-310 Ribbleton La. 0772 792823
Wigan **WILLIAM MARTYN (WIGAN) LTD**
Great George St. 0942 826390

LEICESTERSHIRE

Earl Shilton **SWITHLAND MOTORS LTD**
42 Wood St. 0455 4411
Leicester **TRINITY MOTORS (D.R.**
WATTAM)
47 Blackbird Rd. 0533 530137
★ *Market Harborough* **BADGER**
BROTHERS 109 Main St. Lubenham.
0858 66984
Melton Mowbray **ROCKINGHAM CARS**
LTD Manor Garage, Mill St. 0664 60141
Wigston **KILBY BRIDGE MOTORS LTD**
Kilby Bridge. 0533 881109/886264

LINCOLNSHIRE

Boston **LONDON ROAD GARAGE**
200 London Rd. 0205 55500
Grantham **WILLSONS OF GRANTHAM**
LTD Spittlegate Level. 0476 74117
Lincoln **MINSTER CARS**
316-322 Wragby Rd. 0522 34805
Louth **BURTONS OF LOUTH,**
Legbourne Rd. 0507 607555
★ *Rippingale* **WILLSONS OF RIPPINGALE**
Windmill Garage, Bourne. 077 835 777
Skegness **D R M MOTORS**
Beresford Ave. 0754 67131
Sleaford **RALPH DEAR**
Greylees Garage, Grantham Rd. 05298 674

LONDON

London E4 **ALLEN BRIGGS (MOTORS)**
LTD 47-59 Chingford Mount Rd.
01-527 5004/5
London N7 **CONTINENTAL MOTOR**
CENTRE LTD Campdale Rd. 01-272 4762
London N12 **LINDSAY BROTHERS LTD**
920 High Rd. 01-445 1022
London N17 **BRUCE MOTOR GROUP**
127 Lordship La. 01-808 9291
★ *London NW1* **HUNTSWORTH**
GARAGES LTD
24-28 Boston Pl. 01-724 0269/
01-723 8782
★ *London NW10* **MARN SERVICE**
CENTRE 854 Coronation Rd. 01-961 2377/
01-965 7001
London NW11 **PAMSONS MOTORS LTD**
761/3 Finchley Rd. 01-458 5968/8384
London SE9 **CLIFFORDS OF ELTHAM**
Well Hall Rd. 01-850 3834
London SE18 **WOOLWICH MOTOR CO,**
160-170 Powis St. 01-854 2550
London SE19 **S.G. SMITH MOTORS LTD**
Crown Point Service Station, Beulah Hill.
01-670 6266
London SE23 **PREMIER MOTORS**
(FOREST HILL) LTD
163/167 Stanstead Rd. 01-291 1721
London SW12 **BALHAM AUTOS**
147 Balham Hill, SW12 9DL.
01-675 6744/5/6/7
London SW15 **A.F. TANN LTD**
96-98 Upper Richmond Rd. 01-788 7681
London SW19 **SPUR GARAGE LTD**
39 Hartfield Rd. Sales: 01-540 3325
London W1 **FIAT MOTOR SALES LTD**
62-64 Baker St. 01-486 7555
London W12 **MARN WEST LONDON**
370-376 Uxbridge Rd. 01-749 6058/9
London W11 **RADBOURNE RACING LTD**
1a Clarendon Rd. 01-727 5066

THE FIAT GUIDE TO SUCCESSFUL MOTORING

MERSEYSIDE
Birkenhead FIRS GARAGE (WIRRAL) LTD
Claughton Firs, Oxton. 051-653 8555
Formby ALTCAR AUTOS LTD
Altcar Rd. 070 48 73342
Heswall, Wirral J STUART & CO
(GARAGES) LTD
Chester Rd. 051-342 6202
Southport MILNER & MARSHALL LTD
89-91 Barth Street North. 0704 35535
St. Helens FORWARD AUTOS
Gaskell St. 0744 21961
Liverpool STANLEY MOTORS
(LIVERPOOL) LTD
243 East Prescot Rd. 051-228 9151
Liverpool CROSBY PARK GARAGE LTD
2 Coronation Road, Crosby. 051-924 9101
Liverpool LAMBERT AUTOS LTD
Custom House, Brunswick Business Park.
051-708 8224

MIDDLESEX
Ashford ASHFORD MANOR MOTORS
102 Fordbridge Rd. 07842 50077
Hampton Hill SUPREME AUTOS
(HAMPTON HILL) LTD
7-11 Windmill Rd. 01-979 9061/2
Norwood Green FIRST COUNTY
GARAGES LTD
Norwood Rd. 01-571 2151
Wembley FIAT MOTOR SALES LTD
372 Ealing Rd. 01-998 8811
West Drayton PRIORS,
127 Station Rd. 0895 444672
Whitton SPEEDWELL GARAGE
(WHITTON) LTD
53/55 High St. 01-894 6893/4
Wraysbury CONCORDE GARAGE
(WRAYSBURY)
31 Windsor Rd. 078481 2927/2815

NORFOLK
★*Aylsham* WATT BROTHERS
Norwich Rd. 026 373 2134
King's Lynn DENNIS MARSHALL LTD
Scania Way. 0553 771331
Norwich POINTER MOTOR CO LTD
Aylsham Rd. 0603 45345/6
★*Norwich* ANGLIA AUTO CENTRE,
Barford. 060 545 501
Norwich WOODLAND CAR SALES LTD
Salhouse Rd. 0603 37555/6
Scole DESIRA MOTOR CO LTD
Diss Rd. 037 9740741
Sherringham EARLGATE MOTORS LTD
41 Cromer Rd. 0263 822782
Great Yarmouth DESIRA MOTOR CO LTD
North Quay. 0493 844266

NORTHAMPTONSHIRE
Corby ROCKINGHAM CARS LTD
Rockingham Rd. 0536 68991
Kettering GRADY BROTHERS
(KETTERING) LTD
Britannia Rd. 0536 51 3257
Kilsby, Nr. Rugby HALFWAY GARAGE
(1986) LTD
Crick Cross Rds. 0788 822226
Northampton MOTORVOGUE LTD
74 Kingsthorpe Rd. 0604 714555
Rushden ROCKINGHAM CARS LTD
John St. 0933 57500

NORTHUMBERLAND
Hexham MATT CLARK LTD
Tyne Mills. 0434 603013/603236
Stakeford T LIDDELL & SON
Milburn Terrace. 0670 815038

NOTTINGHAMSHIRE
Newark-on-Trent ELLIOTS GARAGE
(NEWARK) Sleaford Rd. 0636 703405
Nottingham BRISTOL STREET MOTORS
(SHERWOOD) LTD
323-333 Mansfield Rd. 0602 621000
Ruddington J C S GARAGES LTD
Manor Park Garage, Wilford Rd.
0602 844114 & 844164

Sutton-in-Ashfield J.J. LEADLEY LTD
Downing St. 0623 515222
Worksop BARRATT MOTORS LTD
7 Newcastle Ave. 0909 475124

OXFORDSHIRE
Banbury WHITE HORSE GARAGE
(BANBURY) LTD
21-27 Broad St. 0295 50733
Henley-on-Thames BELL STREET
MOTORS (HENLEY) LTD
66 Bell St. 0491 573077
Oxford J D BARCLAY LTD
Botley Rd. 0865 722444
Witney M A WILKINS
1a Bridge St. 0993 3361/2
Wantage MELLORS OF CHALLOW LTD
Faringdon Rd. 023 57 2751

SHROPSHIRE
Shrewsbury WAVERLEY GARAGE LTD
Featherbed La, Harlescott. 0743 64951
Telford T J VICKERS & SONS
Trench Rd, Trench. 0952 605301

SOMERSET
Bridgwater STACEY'S MOTORS
48 St John St. 0278 424801 & 423312
Minehead MINEHEAD AUTOS LTD
37-39 Alcombe Rd. 0643 3379/3238
Street RIZZUTI BROTHERS
West End Garage. 0458 42996
Taunton COUNTY GARAGE (TAUNTON)
LTD Priory Ave. 0823 337611
Yeovil ABBEY HILL MOTOR SALES
Boundary Rd, Lufton Trading Est.
0935 29111

STAFFORDSHIRE
Chasetown SPOT OF CHASETOWN
Highfields Rd. 054 36 5544
Newcastle-under-Lyme B S MARSON &
SONS Deansgate Garage, Keele Rd.
0782 622141
Stafford BOSTONS OF MILFORD
16 The Green, Milford. 0785 661226
Stoke-on-Trent PLATT'S GARAGE
(LONGTON) LTD
Lightwood Rd, Longton. 0782 319212/3/4
★*Uttoxeter* SMITHFIELD ROAD GARAGE
LTD Smithfield Rd. 08893 3838

SUFFOLK
Beccles BRAND (MOTOR) ENGINEERS
LTD Ringsfield Rd. 0502 716940
Bury St Edmunds DESIRA MOTOR CO
LTD Mildenhall Rd. 0284 3280 & 3479
Ipswich STATION GARAGE
Burrell Rd. 0473 690321
★*Leiston* AVENUE SERVICE STATION
King George's Ave. 0728 830654
Needham Market TURNER'S (NEEDHAM
MARKET) LTD 30 High St. 0449 721212

SURREY
Camberley MARN CAMBERLEY,
71 Frimley Rd. 0276 64672
Cheam GODFREY'S (SUTTON & CHEAM)
LTD 50 Malden Rd. 01-644 8877
Croydon THAMES
115 Addiscombe Rd. 01-655 1100
Englefield Green SAVAGE & SON (MOTOR
ENGINEERS) LTD Victoria St. 0784 39771
Epsom H F EDWARDS & CO LTD
4 Church St. 03727 25611
★*Farnham* FRENSHAM ENGINEERING
CO Shortfield, Frensham. 025125 3232
Guildford A.B.C. GUILDFORD,
Pilot Works, Walnut Tree Close.
04835 75251
Kenley MARN KENLEY
60 Godstone Rd. 01-660 4546
New Malden LAIDLER MOTOR CO LTD
69 Kingston Rd. 01-942 6075
Reigate COLIN CRONK,
Showroom: 87/89 Bell St. RH2 7AN.
0737 223304

Wallington BALHAM AUTOS
(WALLINGTON)
268 London Rd. 01-647 5527/8
Weybridge TONY BROOKS LTD
Brooklands Rd. 09323 49521
Woking TONY BROOKS LTD
College Rd, Off Maybury Hill. 04862 20622
& 21222

EAST & WEST SUSSEX
Brighton TILLEYS (SUSSEX) LTD
Showroom: 100 Lewes Rd. 0273 603244
Burgess Hill TILLEYS (SUSSEX) LTD
Chandlers Garage, London Rd.
044 46 43431
Chichester CITY SALES CENTRE
Chichester By-Pass (A27), Kingsham
0243 782478
Eastbourne CENTRAL MOTOR CO,
38 Ashford Rd. 0323 640101
East Grinstead FELBRIDGE GARAGE
Eastbourne Rd. Sales & Service: 0342
24677
Horsham WILSON PURVES LTD
Brighton Rd. Sales: 0403 61821/65637
Hailsham G.F. SHAW LTD
Cowbeech. 0323 833321
★*Isfield* ROSEHILL GARAGE
Isfield, Nr. Uckfield. 082575 313/445
Pulborough FLEET GARAGE
(FITTLEWORTH) LTD
Fittleworth. 079 882 307 & 244
Shoreham-by-Sea KEEN & BETTS
(SHOREHAM) LTD
Church Wood Dr. 0273 461333
St. Leonards-on-Sea ST LEONARDS
MOTORS LTD Church Wood Drive
0424 53493
Wadhurst EATON BROS
Forge Garage, Beech Hill. 089288 2126
Worthing P D H (GARAGES) LTD
Downlands Service Station, Upper Brighton
Rd. 0903 37487

TYNE & WEAR
Gateshead BENFIELD MOTORS,
Lobley Hill Rd. 091 490 0292
Newcastle-upon-Tyne BENFIELD
MOTORS LTD
Railway St. 091 2732131
Sunderland REG VARDY LTD
16-18 Villiers St. 091 510 0550
Whitley Bay WHITLEY LODGE MOTOR
CO Claremont Rd. 091 2523347

WARWICKSHIRE
Balsall Common CARSTINS LTD
324 Station Rd. 0676 33145
Nuneaton RESEARCH GARAGE
(NUNEATON) LTD
Haunchwood La. 0203 382807
Warwick GRAYS GARAGE LTD
Wharf St. 0926 496231

WEST MIDLANDS
Birmingham COLMORE DEPOT LTD
35 Sutton New Rd, Erdington.
021-350 1301
Birmingham COLMORE DEPOT LTD
979 Stratford Rd, Hall Green. 021-778 2323
★*Clent* HOLY CROSS GARAGE LTD
Bromsgrove Rd. 0562 730557
Coventry SMITH & SONS MOTORS LTD
Roland Ave, Holbrooks. 0203 667778
Marston Green MARSTON GREEN
GARAGE 32 Station Rd. 021-779 5140
Solihull TANWORTH GARAGE LTD
The Green, Tanworth in Arden. 056 44 2218
Tipton CALDENE AUTOLAND
Burnt Tree 021-520 2411
Walsall SPOT OF WALSALL,
44A Ward St. 0922 32911
West Bromwich COLMORE DEPOT LTD
Birmingham Rd. 021-553 7500/7509
Wolverhampton A N BLOXHAM LTD
The Fiat Centre, Raby St. 0902 57116

WILTSHIRE
Chippenham **WADHAM STRINGER (CHIPPENHAM) LTD**
21 New Rd. 0249 655757
★ *Marlborough* **SKURRAYS**
George La. 0672 53535
Salisbury **CAFFYNS**
194 Castle St. 0722 336668
Swindon **SKURRAYS**
Drove Rd. 0793 20971

YORKSHIRE
Barnsley **S.A. SNELL (BARNSLEY) LTD**
436-440 Doncaster Rd, Stairfoot.
0226 206675
Bradford **WEST YORKSHIRE MOTOR GROUP**
Keighley Rd, Frizinghall. 0274 490031
Bradford **JCT 600**
The Italian Car Centre, Sticker Lane.
0274 667234
Castleford **AIRE AUTOS LTD**
Lock La. 0977-515806
Doncaster **R ROODHOUSE LTD**
York Rd. 0302 784444
Halifax **MAYFIELD GARAGE (HALIFAX) LTD** Queens Rd. 0422 67711/3
Harrogate **CROFT & BLACKBURN LTD**
Leeds Road, Pannal. 0423 879236
Huddersfield **GALWAY SMITH OF HUDDERSFIELD**
4 Queensgate. 0484 548111
Keighley **WEST YORKSHIRE MOTOR GROUP**
Alkincote Street, Tanfield. 0535 667621
Leeds **JCT 600 (LEEDS) LTD**
Spence La. 0532 431843
Leeds **WHITEHAD & HINCH LTD**
South Broadgate Lane, Horsforth.
0532 585056
★ *Malton* **BENTLEYS GARAGE**
Amotherby. 0653 3616
Mirfield **THORNTON MOTORS OF DEWSBURY LTD**
Calder Garage, 117 Huddersfield Rd.
0924 498316
★ *Northallerton* **TIM SWALES (CAR SALES) LTD**
Clack Lane Garage, Osmotherley.
060 983 263/666
Ripon **CROFT & BLACKBURN LTD**
Harvester House, Kirkby Rd. 0765 4491/4
Rotherham **DEREK G PIKE & CO**
126 Fitzwilliam Rd. 0709 361666
Scarborough **MISKIN & KNAGGS LTD**
Manor Rd. 0723 364111/3
Selby **PARKINSON'S GARAGE LTD**
Hambleton. 075 782 396
Sheffield **G T CARS**
Suffolk Rd. 0742 21370/21378/22748
Wakefield **PICCADILLY WAKEFIELD LTD**
Bradford Rd. 0924 290220
York **PICCADILLY AUTO CENTRE LTD**
84 Piccadilly. 0904 34321

SCOTLAND
Aberdeen **CALLANDERS GARAGE (AUTOPORT) LTD**
870 Great Northern Rd. 0224 695573
Ayr **ROBERT McCALL LTD** Galloway
Avenue 0292 260416
Bathgate **J & A BROWNING LTD** 11 East
Main Street 0501 40536
Brechin **KAY'S AUTO CENTRE,**
18 Clerk St. 03562 2561
Coatbridge **R J CROSS LTD**
Sales: 206 Bank St, ML5 1EG. 0236 35774
Dollar **STEWART BROTHERS**
28-34 Bridge St. 025 94 2233/4
★ *Dumbarton* **DUNCAN McFARLANE & SON** 96 Church St. 0389 63689
Dumfries **CENTRAL CAR SALES**
77 Whitesands. 0387 61378
Dundee **MACALPINE MOTORS**
MacAlpine Rd. 0382 818004
Dunfermline **FLEAR & THOMSON LTD**
128-138 Pittencrieff St. 0383-722565/6
Edinburgh **CROALL & CROALL**
Glenogle Rd. 031 556 6404/9
Edinburgh **WADHAM HAMILTONS (EDINBURGH) LTD** 162 St. Johns Rd.
031 334 6248

Falkirk **ARNOLD CLARK AUTOMOBILES LTD**
Falkirk Road, Grangemouth. 0324 474766
Forres **DICKSON MOTORS (FORRES) LTD** Tytler St. 0309 72122/3
Glasgow **RITCHIES**
393 Shields Rd. 041 429 5611
Glasgow **PEAT ROAD MOTORS (JORDANHILL) LTD**
120 Whittingehame Drive, Jordhanhill.
041 357 1939
Gourock **MANOR VEHICLE (TURIN) LTD**
92 Manor Crescent 0475 32356
Hamilton **JAMES J NICHOLSON LTD**
136 Strathaven Rd. 0698 284606
Hawick **BORDER MOTOR CO**
12 Havelock St. 0450 73881
Invergordon **SEAFIELD MOTORS (INVERNESS) LTD**
Scotburn Road, Kildary. 086 284 2552
Inverness **DONALD MACKENZIE LTD**
62 Seafield Rd. 0463 235777/8
Parts: 0463 232285
Irvine **HARRY FAIRBAIRN LTD**
Ayr Rd. 0294 72121
Kilmarnock **GEORGE BICKET & CO LTD**
67-79 Campbell St, Riccarton.
0563 22525/6
★ *Lanark* **J & J FERGUSON**
Wellgatehead. 0555 3106
Leven **LINKS GARAGE (LEVEN)**
Sconnie Rd. 0333 27003
Oban **HAZELBANK MOTORS LTD**
Stevenson St. 0631 66476
Paisley **HAMILTON BROS LTD**
Ralston Garage, 255 Glasgow Rd.
041-882 9901
★ *Paisley* **LOCHFIELD GARAGE**
4-8 Lochfield Rd. 041-884 2281
Perth **MACALPINE OF PERTH,**
St. Leonards Bank. 0738 38511
Peterhead **CLYNE AUTOS**
Seaview, St. Fergus. 077 983 258
★ *Pitscottie by Cuper* **D.H. PATTERSON MOTOR ENGINEERS**
Burnbank Garage. 033482 200
★ *Rutherglen* **McKECHNIE OF RUTHERGLEN**
77 Farmeloan Rd. 041-647 9722/5915
St. Boswells **ST. BOSWELLS GARAGE**
St. Boswells 08352 2259/3475
Stirling **HAMILTON BROTHERS LTD**
44 Causeway Head Rd. 0786 62426
Tranent **WILLIAM B COWAN LTD**
The Garage Elphinstone 0875 610492

WESTERN ISLES
★ *Stornoway* **KIWI'S GARAGE (STORNOWAY) LTD**
Bells Rd. 0851 5033

ORKNEY ISLES
Kirkwall **J & M SUTHERLAND**
Junction Rd. 0856 2158

SHETLAND ISLES
Aith **AITH AUTOS LTD**
Aith by Bixter. 059 581 230
Lerwick **AITH AUTOS LTD**
9 Blackhill Industrial Estate. 0595 3385/4450

WALES
Pwllheli **PULROSE MOTOR SERVICES LTD** Ala Rd. 0758 612827
Abergele **SLATERS EUROCARS LTD**
Marine Road, Pensarn. 0745 822021/823387
Wrexham **N & G DICKENS LTD**
Border Service Station, Gresford.
097-883-6262
Cardigan **B.V. REES**
Abbey Garage St. Dogmaels. 0239 612025
Carmarthen **WILLIAM DAVIES & SONS**
Central Garage, St. Catherine St.
0267 236284
Aberystwyth **EVANS BROS**
Royal Oak Garage, Llanfarian.
0970 61 2311/2
Kilgetty **STEPASIDE GARAGE LTD**
Carmarthen Rd. 0834 813786

Builth Wells **PRYNNE'S SERVICE STATION LTD** Garth. 059 12 287
Abergavenny **CLYTHA MOTOR CO**
Merthyr Road, Llanfoist. 0873 6888
★ *Blackwood* **A.J. STEVENS & SONS**
High Bank Garage, Fairview. 0443 831703
★ *Cwmbran* **C.K. MOTOR CO (SOUTH WALES LTD)**
10/11 Court Road Industrial Estate.
06333 72711
Newport **L.C. MOTORS**
121 Corporation Rd. 0633 212548/598892
Bridgend **T.S. GRIMSHAW (BRIDGEND) LTD** Tremains Rd. 0656 2984
Cardiff **T.S. GRIMSHAW LTD**
Fiat House, 329 Cowbridge Road East.
0222 395322
Llanishen Cardiff **YAPP'S GARAGES LTD**
Fidlas Rd. 0222 751323
★ *Merthyr Tydfil* **CYFARTHFA MOTORS LTD** Cyfarthfa Rd. 0685 5400
★ *Tonyrefail* **VALLEY MILL MOTORS**
Gilfach Rd. 0443 670742
Swansea **MOORCROFT MOTORS LTD**
54 Sway Road, Morriston. 0792 75271
Aberdare **WILSON CAR SALES (ABERDARE) LTD**
Canal Road, Cwmbach. 0855 875577/883717

NORTHERN IRELAND
Omagh **GLENPARK MOTORS**
62 Gortini Road, Co. Tyrone. 0662 46521
Armagh **ARMAGH GARAGES LTD**
Portadown Rd. 0861 524 252
Ballymena **YOUNG'S (BROUGHSHANE) LTD** 11 Raceview Road, Broughstane.
0266 861380/861497
Ballymoney **MODEL CAR MART**
Model Rd. 026 56 63275
Banbridge **ANNAGH MOTORS (BANBRIDGE) LTD**
51 Church St. 082 06 24495
Bangor **JAMES THOMPSON**
135-141 Bryansburn Rd. 0247 463911
Dungannon **FRANCIS NEILL MOTORS (DUNGANNON) LTD**
1 Ranfurley Rd. 086 87 22552
Enniskillen **T & T TOWN & COUNTRY CARS LTD** Sligo Rd. 0365 22440
Holywood **TERENCE McKEAG**
36-38 Shore Rd. 0232 28900/1
Lisburn **DORNAN'S SERVICE STATION (LISBURN) LTD**
22 Market Pl. 08462 77412
Portadown **ANNAGH MOTORS WORKS**
Mahon Industrial Estate, Mahon Rd.
0762 332552
Newry **N.W. KEHOE & SONS**
18 Patrick St. 0693 3193/66500
Belfast **BAIRDS CARS**
7-9 Boucher Rd. 0232 247770
Belfast **B.A.S. (MOTORS) LTD**
45-47 Rosetta Rd. 0232 491049/491676
Belfast **DICK & CO (BELFAST) LTD**
43 Mallusk Road, Newtownabbey.
0232 342511
Belfast **W.J. BELL & SON**
40-50 Townsend St. 0232 241394
Comber **T.J. CHAMBERS & SON (BELFAST) LTD**
31-37 Mill Street, Comber. 0247 873565
Downpatrick **D.S.C. CARS**
10/12 Church Street, Downpatrick.
0396 2858/4322

CHANNEL ISLANDS
Guernsey **GT CARS**
Les Banques Garage, St. Sampsons.
0481 47838
Jersey **BEL ROYAL MOTOR WORKS LTD**
Bel Royal, St. Lawrence. 0534 22556

EUROPE'S DRIVING FORCE

WE STILL HOLD POLL POSITION.

After several years out front we're happy to report that the Fiat Uno is still the best selling small car in Europe. Since its launch at the British Grand Prix in 1985 the Uno Turbo i.e. has won more admirers than Murray Walker's fan club. Not surprising when you consider the Turbo i.e. is capable of 60mph in 8.0 seconds from a standing start. The mere fact it has a top speed of 125mph* should be enough to set your pulse racing, yet the Uno Turbo still manages to deliver a very conscientious 48.7mpg at 56mph. The power source for all these superlatives is a 1299cc engine which combines electronic fuel injection and mapped electronic ignition with a water cooled turbo-charger, inter-cooler and oil-cooler — a system developed by the Ferrari Formula 1 race engineers. And of course, the Uno's legendary level of refinement ensures your every creature comfort is catered for. So if you want to get off to a great start, get an Uno Turbo i.e.

FIAT UNO THE MOST WANTED SMALL CAR IN EUROPE.

*Where legal speeds permit. For more information on the Uno range contact :
The Fiat Information Service, Dept UT0587, PO Box 39, Windsor, Berks. SL4 3SP. Tel: 0753-856307.

A LOT FOR LESS

BED & BREAKFAST
UNDER £36 FOR TWO (INC VAT & SERVICE)

ENGLAND

Amberley, Gloucestershire: Amberley Inn
Askham, Cumbria: Queen's Head Inn
Barnard Castle, Co. Durham: Jersey Farm
Blandford Forum, Dorset: La Belle Alliance
Bradford, West Yorkshire: Restaurant Nineteen
Bredwardine, Hereford & Worcester: Red Lion
Buckler's Hard, Hampshire: Master Builder's House Hotel
Bury St Edmunds, Suffolk: Butterfly Hotel
Cambridge, Cambridgeshire: Arundel House Hotel
Campsea Ashe, Suffolk: Old Rectory
Canterbury, Kent: Ebury
Castle Cary, Somerset: Bond's
Cawston, Norfolk: Grey Gables
Chideock, Dorset: Chideock House
East Dereham, Norfolk: Kings Head Hotel
Fairford, Gloucestershire: Bull Hotel
Hatherleigh, Devon: George
Hexham, Northumberland: Beaumont
Long Melford, Suffolk: Black Lion Hotel
Lower Swell, Gloucestershire: Old Farmhouse
Lympsham, Somerset: Batch Farm
Newark-on-Trent, Nottinghamshire: Grange
Oakhill, Somerset: Oakhill House
Padstow, Cornwall: Seafood Restaurant
Pendoggett, Cornwall: Cornish Arms
St Austell, Cornwall: White Hart Hotel
St Ives, Cornwall: Boskerris Hotel
St Margaret at Cliffe, Kent: Walletts Court
Seahouses, Northumberland: Olde Hotel
Stonham, Suffolk: Mr Underhill's
Tarrant Monkton, Dorset: Langton Arms
Thornaby-on-Tees, Cleveland: Golden Eagle Hotel
Uppingham, Leicestershire: Lake Isle
Winkton, Dorset: Fisherman's Haunt Hotel
Wooler, Northumberland: Ryecroft
Wooler, Northumberland: Tankerville Arms Hotel

SCOTLAND

Ardnadam, Strathclyde: Firpark Hotel
Ayr, Strathclyde: Balgarth Hotel
Bridge of Cally, Tayside: Bridge of Cally
Connel, Strathclyde: Ossians
East Kilbride, Strathclyde: Bruce Hotel
Garve, Highland: Inchbae Lodge
Kinross, Tayside: Windlestrae
Lochgair, Strathclyde: Lochgair
Muir of Ord, Highland: Old Arms Hotel
Tobermory, Strathclyde: Tobermory Hotel
Ullapool, Highland: Ceilidh Place

WALES

Aberdovey, Gwynedd: Hotel Plas Penhelig
Aberdovey, Gwynedd: Trefeddian Lodge
Conwy, Gwynedd: Sychnant Pass Hotel
Llanrwst, Gwynedd: Meadowsweet Hotel
Three Cocks, Powys: Three Cocks

CHANNEL ISLANDS

Pleinmont, Guernsey: Imperial
Sark, Sark: Aval Du Creux
Sark, Sark: Hotel Petit Champ

NORTHERN IRELAND

Portballintrae, Co. Antrim: Bayview
Portaferry, Co. Down: Portaferry

REPUBLIC OF IRELAND

Riverstown, Co. Sligo: Coopershill
Waterville, Co. Derry: Huntsman

BARGAIN BREAKS

All hotels listed are included in the main section of the Guide, where individual entries should be consulted for closures and other relevant details. We have given preference to hotels offering good value compared with their everyday prices.

When are these bargains available?

Dates published are those for which prices could be obtained for bargain breaks operating from November 1987–November 1988. Most hotels do not include Bank Holidays, particularly Easter and Christmas, and many exclude periods of local festivals. Note that many hotels require a week's advance booking.

How many nights are included?

The breaks cover two consecutive nights. **'Any 2 nights'** means that breaks are available seven days a week; **'2 nights'** denotes some restrictions.

How much does it cost?

Prices are for **one night** for two people sharing a double room. We have quoted where possible for a room with private bathroom. Many hotels offer special rates for children. It is important to specify bargain breaks when booking and also to check prices. When we quote 'from £ . . .', the figure is the lowest price available and may not apply at all times.

What do you get?

Bargain-break holidaymakers are entitled to all the hotel's facilities. Meals quoted apply to every day of the stay unless stated otherwise. A full English breakfast is served unless a continental breakfast is indicated.

Hotels are listed by location in alphabetical order within the following sections:

LONDON

■ **Athenaeum Hotel** page 222
All year 2 nights from £120
Breakfast

■ **Beaufort** page 225
Nov–Apr. Any 2 nights from £85
Continental breakfast

■ **Bonnington Hotel** page 229
Nov–31 Mar 2 nights from £54
Breakfast

■ **The Cavendish** page 233
5 Nov–13 Dec & 3–27 Mar 2 nights from £82
17 Dec–28 Feb 2 nights from £72
Continental breakfast

■ **Charles Bernard Hotel** page 233
All year 2 nights from £45 Breakfast

■ **Coburg Hotel** page 237
Nov–26 Mar 2 nights from £70
27 Mar–Nov 2 nights from £75
Breakfast & lunch or dinner

■ **The Cumberland** page 239
5 Nov–13 Dec & 3 Mar–27 Mar
2 nights from £74
17 Dec–28 Feb 2 nights from £64
Breakfast

■ **Drury Lane Moat House** page 241
All year. Any 2 nights from £100
Breakfast, dinner

■ **Embassy House Hotel** page 243
1 Dec–29 Feb 2 nights from £44
1 Mar–30 Apr 2 nights from £55
Breakfast

BARGAIN BREAKS

■ **Gloucester Hotel** page 248
All year 2 nights from £80
Breakfast

■ **Gore Hotel** page 249
Nov–24 Mar 2 nights from £65
Breakfast

■ **Hendon Hall Hotel** page 255
All year 2 nights from £68
Breakfast

■ **Hilton International Kensington** page 255
All year 2 nights from £85
Breakfast

■ **Hogarth Hotel** page 256
Nov–31 Mar. Any 2 nights from £39
Continental breakfast

■ **Holiday Inn (Mayfair)** page 257
All year 2 nights from £80
Breakfast

■ **Holiday Inn (Swiss Cottage)** page 257
All year 2 nights from £80
Breakfast

■ **Hospitality Inn, Bayswater** page 258
Nov–25 Apr 2 nights from £56
26 Apr–Nov 2 nights from £70
Breakfast

■ **Hyatt Carlton Tower** page 258
All year 2 nights from £112·70
Continental breakfast

■ **Kennedy Hotel** page 264
Nov–Mar 2 nights from £48
Apr–Nov 2 nights from £58
Breakfast

■ **The Kensington Close** page 264
5 Nov–13 Dec & 3–27 Mar 2 nights from £60
17 Dec–28 Feb 2 nights from £50
Breakfast

■ **Kingsley Hotel** page 264
All year 2 nights from £60
Breakfast

■ **The Ladbroke at Hampstead** page 265
All year 2 nights from £55
Breakfast

■ **Ladbroke at Park Lane** page 266
All year 2 nights from £56
Breakfast

■ **Ladbroke Westmoreland Hotel** page 266
All year 2 nights from £52
Breakfast

■ **London Embassy Hotel** page 269
All year 2 nights from £58   Breakfast

■ **London International Hotel** page 269
Nov–31 Mar. Any 2 nights from £65
Breakfast, £11·95 towards meals

■ **London Metropole** page 269
All year 2 nights from £58
Continental breakfast

■ **London Tara Hotel** page 270
All year 2 nights from £60
Breakfast

■ **Londonderry Hotel** page 270
All year 2 nights from £136
Breakfast

■ **Mandeville Hotel** page 273
Nov–31 Mar 2 nights from £60
Breakfast

■ **Marlborough Crest** page 273
All year 2 nights from £70
Breakfast

■ **Le Meridien Piccadilly** page 276
All year 2 nights from £92
No meals

■ **Norfolk Hotel** page 282
Nov–30 Apr 2 nights from £82
Breakfast

■ **Novotel Hotel** page 282
Nov–Mar 2 nights from £42
Apr–Nov 2 nights from £59
Breakfast

■ **Pembridge Court Hotel** page 285
Nov–Mar 2 days from £46
Breakfast

■ **Portman Inter-Continental Hotel** page 286
All year 2 nights from £95
Continental breakfast

■ **The Ritz** page 289
All year 2 nights from £140
Breakfast

■ **Royal Trafalgar Thistle Hotel** page 291
All year 2 nights from £74
Breakfast

■ **Royal Westminster Thistle Hotel** page 292
All year 2 nights from £82
Breakfast, 25% discount on meals

■ **Hotel Russell** page 293
5 Nov–13 Dec & 13–27 Mar 2 nights from £66
17 Dec–28 Feb 2 nights from £56
Breakfast

■ **St George's Hotel** page 293
5 Nov–13 Dec & 13–27 Mar 2 nights from £74
17 Dec–28 Feb 2 nights from £64   Breakfast

■ **Selfridge Hotel**   page 296
All year. Any 2 nights from £78
Breakfast

■ **Sheraton Park Tower**   page 296
11 Dec–10 Jan & 1–4 Apr
2 nights from £78
No meals

■ **Stakis St Ermin's Hotel**   page 298
Nov–Mar 2 nights from £58
Apr–Nov 2 nights from £62
Breakfast, £2 towards lunch

■ **The Strand Palace**   page 299
5 Nov–13 Dec & 13–27 Mar 2 nights from £60

17 Dec–28 Feb 2 nights from £50
Breakfast

■ **The Waldorf**   page 302
5 Nov–13 Dec & 13–27 Mar 2 nights from £80
17 Dec–28 Feb 2 nights from £70
Breakfast

■ **The Westbury**   page 303
5 Nov–27 Mar 2 nights from £120
Breakfast

■ **White House**   page 303
Nov–Mar 2 nights from £60
Apr–Oct 2 nights from £70
Breakfast

LONDON AIRPORTS

■ **Gatwick**
Chequers Thistle Hotel   page 308
All year 2 nights from £50
Continental breakfast, £9 towards meals

■ **Gatwick**
Copthorne Hotel   page 308
Nov–5 May 2 nights from £53
Breakfast

■ **Gatwick**
Crest Hotel   page 308
All year 2 nights from £66
Breakfast, dinner

■ **Gatwick**
Post House Hotel   page 310
5 Nov–27 Mar 2 nights from £66
Breakfast, dinner

■ **Heathrow**
The Ariel   page 310
5 Nov–13 Dec & 3–27 Mar 2 nights from £52
17 Dec–28 Feb 2 nights from £48
Breakfast

■ **Heathrow**
The Excelsior   page 310
5 Nov–13 Dec & 3–27 Mar 2 nights from £56
17 Dec–28 Feb 2 nights from £50
Breakfast

■ **Heathrow**
Heathrow Park Hotel   page 311
All year 2 nights from £38·50 (£42·90 summer)
No meals

■ **Heathrow**
Holiday Inn   page 311
Nov–30 Apr 2 nights from £50
Breakfast, £10·95 towards meals

■ **Heathrow**
Master Robert Motel   page 311
All year 2 nights from £39
Breakfast

■ **Heathrow**
Post House Hotel   page 311
5 Nov–13 Dec & 3–27 Mar 2 nights from £54
17 Dec–28 Feb 2 nights from £48
Breakfast

■ **Heathrow**
Sheraton Skyline   page 312
Nov–31 Dec 2 nights from £63·25
Apr–Nov 2 nights from £69
No meals

■ **Heathrow**
The Skyway   page 312
5 Nov–13 Dec & 3–27 Mar 2 nights from £46
17 Dec–28 Feb 2 nights from £42   Breakfast

ENGLAND

■ **Abberley**
Elms Hotel   page 314
All year 2 nights from £99·50
Breakfast, dinner

■ **Abingdon**
Upper Reaches Hotel   page 314
Nov & Mar 2 nights from £76
Dec–29 Feb 2 nights from £72
Breakfast, dinner

■ **Alcester**
Arrow Mill   page 314
All year. Any 2 nights from £59
Breakfast, dinner

■ **Aldeburgh**
The Brudenell   page 315
Nov & Mar. Any 2 nights from £62
Dec–29 Feb. Any 2 nights from £56
Breakfast, dinner

■ **Aldeburgh**
Uplands Hotel   page 315
Nov–31 May. Any 2 nights from £54
Breakfast, dinner

■ **Aldeburgh**
Wentworth Hotel   page 315
Nov–30 Apr. Any 2 nights £55
May–15 Jul. Any 2 nights £60
Breakfast, dinner

■ **Aldridge**
Fairlawns Hotel   page 315
All year 2 nights from £55
Breakfast, dinner

■ **Alnwick**
Hotspur Hotel   page 316
All year. Any 2 nights from £55
Breakfast, £8·50 towards dinner

■ **Alnwick**
White Swan Hotel   page 316
Nov–Apr. Any 2 nights from £62
May–Nov. Any 2 nights from £70
Breakfast, dinner

■ **Altrincham**
Bowdon Hotel   page 317
All year 2 nights £52
Breakfast, dinner

■ **Altrincham**
Cresta Court Hotel   page 317
All year 2 nights £55
Breakfast, £9 towards dinner

■ **Altrincham**
George & Dragon Hotel   page 317

Nov–Mar 2 nights from £36
Apr–Nov 2 nights from £40
Breakfast

■ **Alveston**
Alveston House Hotel   page 317
All year 2 nights from £69
Breakfast, dinner

■ **Alveston**
Post House Hotel   page 318
Nov & Mar 2 nights from £66
Dec–29 Feb 2 nights from £60
Breakfast, dinner

■ **Amberley**
Amberley Inn   page 318
3 Nov–24 Mar. Any 2 nights from £55
25 Mar–31 Aug. Any 2 nights from £63
Breakfast & dinner or lunch

■ **Ambleside**
Kirkstone Foot Hotel   page 318
Nov–Mar. Any 2 nights from £52
Breakfast, dinner

■ **Ambleside**
Nanny Brow Hotel   page 318
Nov–Mar. Any 2 nights from £44
Breakfast, dinner

■ **Ampfield**
Potters Heron Hotel   page 319
All year 2 nights from £70
Breakfast, dinner

■ **Arundel**
Norfolk Arms Hotel   page 320
All year. Any 2 nights from £69
Breakfast, dinner

■ **Ascot**
The Berystede   page 320
Nov & Mar 2 nights from £76
Dec–29 Feb 2 nights from £68
Breakfast, dinner

■ **Ashford**
Eastwell Manor   page 321
All year 2 nights from £60
Breakfast

■ **Ashford-in-the-Water**
Riverside Country House Hotel   page 322
All year. Any 2 nights £95
Breakfast, dinner

■ **Aston Clinton**
Bell Inn   page 323
Jan–Mar 2 nights from £121
Continental breakfast, dinner

BARGAIN BREAKS

■ Axbridge
Oak House page 323
All year 2 nights from £65
Breakfast, dinner

■ Aylesbury
The Bell page 323
5 Nov–27 Mar 2 nights from £58
Breakfast, dinner

■ Bagshot
Pennyhill Park Hotel page 324
Nov–31 Mar 2 nights £135
Apr–Nov 2 nights £145
Breakfast, dinner

■ Bakewell
Hassop Hall Hotel page 325
Nov–31 Mar. Any 2 nights from £45
No meals

■ Bamburgh
Lord Crewe Arms Hotel page 325
Apr–Nov. Any 2 nights from £62
Breakfast, dinner

■ Banbury
Whately Hall page 326
5 Nov–27 Mar 2 nights from £64
Breakfast, dinner

■ Barford
Glebe Hotel page 326
Nov–31 Mar 2 nights from £65
Apr–Nov 2 nights from £70
Breakfast, dinner

■ Barnard Castle
Jersey Farm Hotel page 326
Nov–Mar 2 nights £42
Easter–Nov 2 nights £45
Breakfast, dinner

■ Barnby Moor
Ye Olde Bell page 326
Nov–Mar 2 nights £58 (£54 during Jan)
Breakfast, dinner

■ Barnsdale Bar
TraveLodge page 327
2 nights from £44
Breakfast, dinner

■ Barnsley
Ardsley Moat House page 327
All year. Any 2 nights from £55
Breakfast, dinner

■ Barnstaple
The Imperial page 327
Nov & Mar. Any 2 nights from £60
Dec–29 Feb. Any 2 nights from £56
Breakfast, dinner

■ Basildon
Crest Hotel page 328
All year 2 nights from £30·32
Breakfast

■ Basingstoke
Crest Hotel page 328
All year 2 nights from £40   Breakfast

■ Basingstoke
Ladbroke Hotel page 328
All year 2 nights from £46
Breakfast, 1 dinner

■ Basingstoke
Ladbroke Lodge page 328
Nov–Apr 2 nights from £50
Breakfast

■ Baslow
Cavendish Hotel page 329
Nov–31 Mar 2 nights from £50
No meals

■ Bassenthwaite
Armathwaite Hall page 329
Nov–Apr 2 nights from £85
Breakfast, £16 towards dinner

■ Bath
Apsley House Hotel page 332
Nov–Apr. Any 2 nights from £75
Breakfast, dinner

■ Bath
Bath Hotel page 332
Nov–31 Mar 2 nights from £88
Apr–Nov 2 nights from £90
Breakfast, dinner

■ Bath
The Francis page 333
Nov–Feb 2 nights from £78
Mar 2 nights from £82
Breakfast, dinner

■ Bath
Lansdown Grove Hotel page 333
All year 2 nights from £70
Breakfast, dinner (or lunch)

■ Bath
Redcar Hotel page 334
All year 2 nights from £78
Breakfast, dinner

■ Battle
Netherfield Place page 335
Nov–Mar & Oct. Any 2 nights from £90
Breakfast, dinner

■ Bawtry
Crown Hotel page 335
All year. Any 2 nights from £58
Breakfast, dinner

■ **Beaconsfield**
Bellhouse Hotel   page 336
All year 2 nights from £61·50
Breakfast, £10·75 towards dinner

■ **Beanacre**
Beechfield House   page 336
Nov–Dec 2 nights from £87·50
Breakfast, dinner

■ **Beaulieu**
Montagu Arms Hotel   page 336
Nov–Mar. Any 2 nights £75·50
Breakfast, dinner

■ **Beccles**
Waveney House Hotel   page 337
All year. Any 2 nights from £60
Breakfast, £7 towards lunch & dinner

■ **Bedford**
Woodlands Manor Hotel   page 337
All year 2 nights from £65
Breakfast, dinner

■ **Belford**
Blue Bell Hotel   page 338
All year. Any 2 nights from £58
Breakfast, dinner

■ **Bembridge**
Highbury Hotel   page 338
Nov–1 Jan. Any 2 nights from £45
Breakfast, dinner

■ **Berkhamsted**
Swan Hotel   page 338
All year 2 nights from £50
Breakfast, £10 towards dinner

■ **Berwick-upon-Tweed**
Kings Arms Hotel   page 338
Nov–23 Nov & 1 Jan–Nov 2 nights £65
Breakfast, £13·50 towards dinner

■ **Beverley**
Beverley Arms Hotel   page 339
Nov & Mar 2 nights from £60
Dec–29 Feb. Any 2 nights from £50
Breakfast, dinner

■ **Bibury**
Bibury Court Hotel   page 339
Nov–Mar (except Cheltenham Gold Cup week)
Any 2 nights from £64
Breakfast, dinner & 1 bar lunch

■ **Bibury**
Swan Hotel   page 339
Nov–Mar 2 nights from £57·50
Breakfast, dinner

■ **Bideford**
Yeoldon House   page 339

All year. Any 2 nights from £53
Breakfast, dinner

■ **Birkenhead**
Bowler Hat Hotel   page 341
All year 2 nights from £41
Breakfast

■ **Birmingham**
Albany Hotel   page 341
5 Nov–27 Mar 2 nights from £60
Breakfast, dinner

■ **Birmingham**
Cobden Hotel   page 344
All year 2 nights from £47
Breakfast, dinner

■ **Birmingham**
Grand Hotel   page 345
All year. Any 2 nights from £52
Breakfast, dinner

■ **Birmingham**
Midland Hotel   page 346
All year. Any 2 nights £35
Breakfast

■ **Birmingham**
Norfolk Hotel   page 346
All year 2 nights from £47
Breakfast, dinner

■ **Birmingham**
Plough & Harrow Hotel   page 347
All year. Any 2 nights from £98
Breakfast, dinner

■ **Birmingham**
Post House Hotel   page 347
5 Nov–27 Mar 2 nights from £52 (Dec & Jan £48)
Breakfast, dinner

■ **Birmingham**
Royal Angus Thistle Hotel   page 347
All year 2 nights from £48
Breakfast

■ **Birmingham**
Strathallan Thistle Hotel   page 348
All year. Any 2 nights from £50
Breakfast

■ **Birmingham Airport**
Excelsior Hotel   page 348
5 Nov–27 Mar 2 nights from £48
Breakfast, dinner

■ **Blackburn**
Blackburn Moat House   page 348
All year 2 nights from £59
Breakfast, dinner & 1 lunch

BARGAIN BREAKS

■ Blackpool
Imperial Hotel   page 348
All year. Any 2 nights from £64
Breakfast, dinner

■ Blackpool
New Clifton Hotel   page 349
All year. Any 2 nights from £62
Breakfast, dinner

■ Blackpool
Pembroke Hotel   page 349
All year. Any 2 nights from £75
Breakfast, dinner

■ Blockley
Lower Brook House   page 350
Nov–12 Mar. Any 2 nights from £72
Breakfast, dinner

■ Bolton
Crest Hotel   page 350
All year 2 nights from £60
Breakfast, dinner

■ Bolton
Last Drop Village Hotel   page 351
All year 2 nights from £90
Breakfast, dinner

■ Bolton Abbey
Devonshire Arms Hotel   page 351
All year. Any 2 nights from £88
Breakfast, dinner

■ Boroughbridge
Crown Hotel   page 352
All year 2 nights from £64
Breakfast, dinner

■ Borrowdale
Borrowdale Hotel   page 352
8 Nov–24 Mar. Any 2 nights from £54
Breakfast, dinner

■ Boston
New England Hotel   page 353
All year 2 nights from £70
Breakfast, dinner

■ Bournemouth
Crest Hotel   page 354
All year. Any 2 nights from £82
Breakfast, dinner

■ Bournemouth
Durley Hall Hotel   page 354
All year. Any 2 nights from £55
Breakfast, dinner

■ Bournemouth
East Cliff Court Hotel   page 355
Nov–May. Any 2 nights from £45
Breakfast, dinner

■ Bournemouth
Highcliff Hotel   page 355
All year. Any 2 nights from £80
Breakfast, dinner

■ Bournemouth
Palace Court Hotel   page 355
All year. Any 2 nights from £63
Breakfast, dinner

■ Bournemouth
Royal Bath Hotel   page 355
All year 2 nights from £116
Breakfast, dinner

■ Bowness-on-Windermere
The Belsfield   page 358
2 Nov–29 Mar 2 nights from £62 (Nov & Mar £66)
Breakfast, dinner

■ Bowness-on-Windermere
Old England Hotel   page 358
2 Nov–29 Mar 2 nights from £68 (Nov & Mar £72)
Breakfast

■ Bracknell
Ladbroke Hotel   page 359
All year 2 nights from £46   Breakfast

■ Bradford
Novotel   page 360
All year 2 nights from £32
Breakfast

■ Bradford
Victoria Hotel   page 360
5 Nov–27 Mar 2 nights from £44 (Mar £50)
Breakfast, dinner

■ Braithwaite
Ivy House Hotel   page 361
Nov–May. Any 2 nights from £49·50
Breakfast, dinner

■ Bramhope
Parkway Hotel   page 361
All year 2 nights from £62
Breakfast, dinner

■ Bramhope
Post House Hotel   page 361
Nov & Mar 2 nights from £72
Dec–Feb 2 nights from £64
Breakfast, dinner

■ Brampton
Farlam Hall Hotel   page 362
Nov–Mid Apr (except Feb). Any 2 nights from
£80
Breakfast, dinner

■ Brandon
Brandon Hall Hotel   page 363
5 Nov–27 Mar 2 nights from £58
Breakfast, dinner

■ **Branscombe**
Masons Arms page 363
All year. Any 2 nights from £70
Breakfast, dinner

■ **Bredwardine**
Red Lion Hotel page 363
All year. Any 2 nights from £64
Breakfast, dinner

■ **Brentwood**
Post House Hotel page 364
Nov & Mar 2 nights from £66
Dec–Feb 2 nights from £60
Breakfast, dinner

■ **Brighton (Hove)**
Alexandra Hotel page 364
All year 2 nights from £57·50
Breakfast, dinner

■ **Brighton (Hove)**
Courtlands Hotel page 365
Nov–Mar 2 nights £60
Mar–Oct 2 nights £65
Breakfast, dinner

■ **Brighton (Hove)**
Dudley Hotel page 365
Nov–29 Mar. Any 2 nights £74 (Jan & Feb £68)
Breakfast, dinner

■ **Brighton**
Granville Hotel page 368
All year. Any 2 nights from £73·50
Breakfast, £5 towards meals

■ **Brighton**
Old Ship Hotel page 369
All year 2 nights from £74
Breakfast, dinner

■ **Brighton**
Sheridan Hotel page 370
All year. Any 2 nights from £65
Breakfast, dinner

■ **Bristol**
Holiday Inn page 371
Nov–Apr 2 nights from £50
Breakfast

■ **Bristol**
Ladbroke Dragonara Hotel page 374
All year 2 nights from £48
Breakfast

■ **Bristol**
Redwood Lodge Hotel page 374
All year. Any 2 nights from £70
Breakfast, dinner

■ **Bristol**
Unicorn Hotel page 375

All year 2 nights from £53·50
Breakfast

■ **Brixham**
Quayside Hotel page 375
All year. Any 2 nights from £64
Breakfast, dinner

■ **Broadway**
Broadway Hotel page 375
Nov–Easter 2 nights from £50
Breakfast, dinner

■ **Broadway**
Collin House Hotel page 376
Nov–Mar. Any 2 nights from £70
Breakfast, £11·50 towards dinner

■ **Broadway**
Dormy House page 376
All year 2 nights from £108
Breakfast, dinner

■ **Broadway**
Lygon Arms page 377
Nov–Apr 2 nights from £135
Breakfast, £20 towards dinner

■ **Brockenhurst**
Careys Manor Hotel page 377
All year. Any 2 nights from £79·50
Breakfast, dinner

■ **Brockenhurst**
Ladbroke Balmer Lawn Hotel page 377
All year 2 nights from £78
Breakfast, dinner

■ **Brome**
Oaksmere page 378
All year 2 nights from £65
Breakfast, dinner

■ **Buckingham**
White Hart Hotel page 380
Nov–27 Mar 2 nights from £64 (Jan & Feb £60)
Breakfast, dinner

■ **Buckland**
Buckland Manor page 380
29 Nov–10 Mar 2 nights from £115
Breakfast, £20 towards dinner

■ **Bude**
The Strand page 381
Nov–29 Mar 2 nights from £46
Breakfast, dinner

■ **Burbage**
Savernake Forest Hotel page 381
All year. Any 2 nights from £56
Breakfast, dinner

■ **Burford**
Bay Tree Hotel   page 381
Nov–30 Apr. Any 2 nights from £69·50
Breakfast, dinner

■ **Burford**
Inn for All Seasons   page 381
Nov–Mar. Any 2 nights from £59
Apr–Nov. Any 2 nights from £66
Breakfast, dinner

■ **Burnham**
Burnham Beeches Hotel   page 382
Nov–Apr 2 nights from £69
Apr–Nov 2 nights from £75
Breakfast, dinner

■ **Burnham**
Grovefield Hotel   page 382
All year 2 nights from £61
Breakfast, £14 towards dinner

■ **Burnley**
Keirby Hotel   page 383
All year 2 nights from £45
Breakfast, dinner

■ **Burton upon Trent**
Brookhouse Inn   page 383
All year 2 nights from £70
Breakfast, £14 towards dinner

■ **Burton upon Trent**
Riverside Inn   page 383
All year 2 nights from £66
Breakfast, dinner

■ **Bury**
Normandie Hotel   page 383
All year 2 nights from £65
Breakfast, dinner

■ **Bury St Edmunds**
Angel Hotel   page 384
All year 2 nights from £50
Breakfast

■ **Bury St Edmunds**
Suffolk Hotel   page 384
Nov & Mar 2 nights from £60
Dec–Feb. Any 2 nights from £56
Breakfast, dinner

■ **Camberley**
Frimley Hall   page 385
Nov & Mar 2 nights from £70
Dec–Feb 2 nights from £60
Breakfast, dinner

■ **Cambridge**
Arundel House Hotel   page 388
Nov–31 Mar 2 nights from £56·50
Breakfast, dinner

■ **Cambridge**
Cambridge Lodge Hotel   page 388
Nov–31 Mar 2 nights from £42
Breakfast

■ **Cambridge**
Cambridgeshire Moat House   page 388
All year 2 nights from £79
Breakfast, dinner

■ **Cambridge**
Garden House Hotel   page 388
Nov–Mar 2 nights from £78·50
Apr–Nov 2 nights from £94
Breakfast, £14 towards dinner (£15 from Apr)

■ **Cambridge**
Gonville Hotel   page 389
Oct–Mar 2 nights from £57
Apr–Sep 2 nights from £65
Breakfast, £8·95 towards lunch or dinner

■ **Cambridge**
Post House Hotel   page 389
Nov & Mar 2 nights from £84
Dec–Feb 2 nights from £80
Breakfast, dinner

■ **Cambridge**
University Arms Hotel   page 389
Nov–31 Mar 2 nights £57
Apr–31 May 2 nights £61
Breakfast, dinner

■ **Canterbury**
Canterbury Hotel   page 390
Nov–June. Any 2 nights from £46
Breakfast, £8·50 towards dinner

■ **Canterbury**
Chaucer Hotel   page 390
Nov–27 Mar 2 nights from £70 (Dec & Jan £66)
Breakfast, dinner

■ **Canterbury**
County Hotel   page 390
Nov–27 Mar 2 nights from £56
Breakfast

■ **Canterbury**
Ebury Hotel   page 391
All year 2 nights from £46
Breakfast, £8·50 towards dinner

■ **Canterbury**
Falstaff Hotel   page 391
Nov–Feb 2 nights from £56
Mar–Nov 2 nights from £68
Breakfast, dinner

■ **Canterbury**
Howfield Manor   page 391
Nov–15 Mar. Any 2 nights from £60
Breakfast, dinner

■ **Canterbury**
Slatters Hotel   page 394
All year. Any 2 nights from £68
Breakfast, dinner

■ **Carlisle**
Crest Hotel   page 395
All year. Any 2 nights from £68
Breakfast, dinner

■ **Carlisle**
Swallow Hilltop Hotel   page 395
All year. Any 2 nights from £60
Breakfast, dinner & 1 lunch

■ **Carlyon Bay**
Carlyon Bay Hotel   page 395
Nov–mid Jul. Any 2 nights from £74
Breakfast, dinner, £5 towards lunch

■ **Carlyon Bay**
Porth Avallen Hotel   page 395
Nov–Apr. Any 2 nights from £53·50
Breakfast, dinner

■ **Cartmel**
Aynsome Manor Hotel   page 396
Nov–12 May. Any 2 nights from £50
Breakfast, dinner

■ **Castle Cary**
Bond's Hotel   page 396
All year. Any 2 nights from £44
Breakfast, dinner

■ **Chagford**
Great Tree Hotel   page 398
All year. Any 2 nights from £74
Breakfast, dinner

■ **Chagford**
Mill End Hotel   page 399
Nov–Mar. Any 2 nights from £70
Breakfast, dinner

■ **Chagford**
Teignworthy   page 399
Nov–Easter. Any 2 nights from £115
Breakfast, dinner

■ **Charlbury**
Bell at Charlbury   page 399
Nov–Mar. Any 2 nights from £65
Apr–Nov. Any 2 nights from £70
Breakfast, dinner

■ **Charlecote**
Charlecote Pheasant   page 400
All year. Any 2 nights from £58
Breakfast, dinner

■ **Charnock Richard**
TraveLodge   page 400
Nov–27 Mar 2 nights from £44
Breakfast, dinner

■ **Chedington**
Chedington Court   page 400
All year (except mid Jan–mid Feb)
Any 2 nights from £76
Breakfast, dinner

■ **Cheltenham**
Hotel de la Bere   page 401
All year. Any 2 nights from £68
Continental breakfast, £12 towards dinner

■ **Cheltenham**
Golden Valley Thistle Hotel   page 401
All year 2 nights from £46
Breakfast, £10 towards dinner

■ **Cheltenham**
Queen's Hotel   page 402
Nov–27 Mar 2 nights from £80
Breakfast, dinner

■ **Cheltenham**
Wyastone Hotel   page 403
All year 2 nights from £60
Breakfast, dinner

■ **Chenies**
Bedford Arms Thistle Hotel   page 403
All year 2 nights from £58
Breakfast

■ **Chester**
Abbots Well Hotel   page 404
All year. Any 2 nights from £64
Breakfast, dinner

■ **Chester**
Blossoms Hotel   page 406
Nov–14 Apr. Any 2 nights from £60
15 Apr–Nov. Any 2 nights from £74
Breakfast, dinner

■ **Chester**
Chester Grosvenor   page 406
Nov–23 Dec & 6 Apr–Nov from £72·50
Breakfast, dinner

■ **Chester**
Ladbroke Hotel   page 407
All year 2 nights from £48
Breakfast

■ **Chester**
Mollington Banastre Hotel   page 407
All year 2 nights from £75
Breakfast, £13 towards dinner

■ **Chester**
Post House Hotel   page 407
Nov & Mar 2 nights from £66
Dec–Feb 2 nights from £62
Breakfast, dinner

■ **Chester**
Rowton Hall Hotel   page 407
All year 2 nights from £79
Breakfast, dinner

■ **Chesterfield**
Chesterfield Hotel   page 407
All year 2 nights from £58
Breakfast, £9·30 towards dinner

■ **Chester-le-Street**
Lumley Castle Hotel   page 408
All year 2 nights from £69
Breakfast, dinner

■ **Chichester**
Dolphin and Anchor Hotel   page 408
Nov–27 Mar 2 nights from £72
Breakfast, dinner

■ **Chideock**
Chideock House Hotel   page 409
All year. Any 2 nights from £49
Breakfast, dinner

■ **Chipping Campden**
Kings Arms Hotel   page 409
All year. Any 2 nights from £70
Breakfast, dinner

■ **Chipping Campden**
Noel Arms Hotel   page 409
Nov–30 Apr. Any 2 nights from £60
Breakfast, dinner

■ **Chittlehamholt**
Highbullen Hotel   page 410
Nov–Mar 2 nights from £80
Continental breakfast, dinner

■ **Chollerford**
George Hotel   page 410
All year. Any 2 nights from £74
Breakfast, dinner & 1 lunch

■ **Churt**
Frensham Pond Hotel   page 410
All year 2 nights from £78
Breakfast, dinner

■ **Cirencester**
King's Head Hotel   page 411
1 Jan–24 Mar. Any 2 nights from £62
25 Mar–26 May. Any 2 nights £66
27 May–20 Oct. Any 2 nights £74
Breakfast, dinner

■ **Clanfield**
Plough at Clanfield   page 411
All year. Any 2 nights from £75
Breakfast, dinner

■ **Clayton-le-Woods**
Pines Hotel   page 412

All year 2 nights from £105
Breakfast, dinner

■ **Cleethorpes**
Kingsway Hotel   page 412
All year 2 nights from £55
Breakfast, dinner

■ **Coatham Mundeville**
Hall Garth   page 413
All year 2 nights from £69
Continental breakfast, dinner

■ **Cobham**
Ladbroke Seven Hills Hotel   page 413
All year. Any 2 nights from £52
Breakfast, £12·95 towards meals

■ **Cobham**
Woodlands Park Hotel   page 413
All year 2 nights from £61
Breakfast, dinner

■ **Colchester**
Marks Tey Hotel   page 414
All year 2 nights from £46
Breakfast, dinner

■ **Colchester**
Rose & Crown Hotel   page 414
All year 2 nights from £32·50
Breakfast

■ **Coleford**
Speech House   page 414
Nov–29 Mar. Any 2 nights from £68
Breakfast, dinner

■ **Coniston**
Coniston Sun Hotel   page 415
Nov, Dec, Mar & Apr. Any 2 nights from £30
Breakfast, dinner

■ **Copdock**
Ipswich Moat House   page 416
All year 2 nights from £56
Breakfast, dinner

■ **Cornhill-on-Tweed**
Tillmouth Park Hotel   page 416
All year. Any 2 nights from £45
Breakfast, dinner

■ **Corsham**
Methuen Arms Hotel   page 417
All year (except during Badminton weekend)
2 nights from £40
Breakfast

■ **Corsham**
Rudloe Park Hotel   page 417
All year 2 nights from £55
Breakfast

BARGAIN BREAKS

■ **Coventry**
Chace Crest Hotel   page 417
All year 2 nights from about £32
Breakfast, dinner

■ **Coventry**
Crest Hotel   page 417
All year 2 nights from £36
Breakfast, dinner

■ **Coventry**
De Vere Hotel   page 418
All year 2 nights from £39·50
Breakfast

■ **Coventry**
Novotel Coventry   page 418
All year 2 nights from £36
Breakfast

■ **Coventry**
Post House Hotel   page 418
Nov & Mar 2 nights from £56
Dec–Feb 2 nights from £46
Breakfast, dinner

■ **Cranbrook**
Willesley Hotel   page 419
Nov–30 Apr 2 nights from £60
Breakfast, dinner

■ **Crathorne**
Crathorne Hall Hotel   page 419
All year 2 nights from £60
Breakfast, dinner

■ **Crawley**
George Hotel   page 420
Nov–27 Mar 2 nights from £58
Breakfast, dinner

■ **Crick**
Post House Hotel   page 420
All year 2 nights from £54
Breakfast, dinner

■ **Crook**
Wild Boar Hotel   page 420
All year. Any 2 nights from £64
Breakfast, dinner

■ **Crosby-on-Eden**
Crosby Lodge Hotel   page 421
Oct–Apr 2 nights from £70
Breakfast, dinner

■ **Croxdale**
Bridge Hotel   page 421
All year 2 nights from £46
Breakfast, dinner

■ **Croydon**
Holiday Inn   page 421
All year 2 nights from £50
Breakfast

■ **Croydon**
Selsdon Park Hotel   page 422
Nov–Mar 2 nights from £48
Apr–Nov 2 nights from £52
Breakfast, dinner

■ **Cuckfield**
Ockenden Manor Hotel   page 422
All year. Any 2 nights from £93
Breakfast, dinner

■ **Darlington**
Blackwell Grange Moat House   page 423
All year. Any 2 nights from £64
Breakfast, dinner

■ **Darlington**
King's Head Swallow Hotel   page 423
All year. Any 2 nights from £62
Breakfast, dinner & 1 lunch

■ **Darlington**
Stakis White Horse Hotel   page 424
All year. Any 2 nights from £50
Breakfast, dinner

■ **Dartmouth**
Royal Castle Hotel   page 426
All year. Any 2 nights from £52·90
Breakfast, dinner

■ **Denton**
Old Rectory Hotel   page 427
All year 2 nights £50
Breakfast, dinner

■ **Derby**
International Hotel   page 427
All year (except December)
2 nights £110
Breakfast, dinner & 1 lunch

■ **Doncaster**
Danum Swallow Hotel   page 427
All year 2 nights £58
Breakfast, dinner & 1 lunch

■ **Doncaster**
Earl of Doncaster Hotel   page 428
All year 2 nights £56
Breakfast, dinner

■ **Dorchester-on-Thames**
George Hotel   page 428
All year 2 nights from £64
Breakfast, dinner

■ **Dorking**
Burford Bridge Hotel   page 428
Nov–27 Mar 2 nights from £80
Breakfast, dinner

■ **Dorking**
Punch Bowl Hotel   page 429
All year 2 nights from £56   Breakfast, dinner

BARGAIN BREAKS

■ **Dorking**
White Horse Hotel   page 429
Nov–27 Mar 2 nights from £56
Breakfast, dinner

■ **Dovedale**
Peveril of the Peak Hotel   page 429
Nov–29 Mar 2 nights from £62 (Dec & Jan £58)
Breakfast, dinner

■ **Dover**
Dover Moat House   page 429
All year 2 nights from £65
Breakfast, dinner

■ **Dover**
White Cliffs Hotel   page 430
Nov–June 2 nights from £52
Breakfast, dinner

■ **Driffield**
Bell Hotel Inn   page 430
All year 2 nights from £66
Breakfast, £9 towards dinner

■ **Dulverton**
Ashwick Country House Hotel   page 431
Nov–Feb. Any 2 nights from £60
Mar–Jun. Any 2 nights from £64
Breakfast, dinner

■ **Dulverton**
Carnarvon Arms Hotel   page 431
All year. Any 2 nights from £55
Breakfast, dinner & afternoon tea

■ **Dunchurch**
Dun Cow Hotel   page 431
All year. Any 2 nights from £74
Breakfast, lunch & dinner

■ **Dunkirk**
Petty France Hotel   page 431
All year (except Badminton weekend)
2 nights from £80
Continental breakfast, £14 towards dinner

■ **Dunstable**
Old Palace Lodge Hotel   page 432
All year 2 nights from £50
Breakfast

■ **Dunster**
The Luttrell Arms   page 432
Nov & Mar. Any 2 nights from £70
Dec–Feb. Any 2 nights from £64
Breakfast, dinner

■ **Durham**
Royal County Hotel   page 432
All year 2 nights from £78
Breakfast, dinner & 1 lunch

■ **Duxford**
Duxford Lodge Hotel   page 432

All year 2 nights from £70
Breakfast, £14 towards dinner

■ **East Dereham**
Kings Head Hotel   page 433
Nov–May & Oct 2 nights from £49
Breakfast, dinner

■ **East Dereham**
Phoenix Hotel   page 433
All year. Any 2 nights from £58
Breakfast, dinner

■ **East Grinstead**
Ladbroke Felbridge Hotel   page 433
All year 2 nights £52
Breakfast

■ **East Horsley**
Thatchers Hotel   page 434
All year 2 nights from £130
Breakfast, £15 towards dinner

■ **Eastbourne**
Cavendish Hotel   page 436
All year. Any 2 nights from £87
Breakfast, dinner

■ **Eastbourne**
Grand Hotel   page 436
All year 2 nights from £105
Breakfast, dinner

■ **Eastbourne**
Queens Hotel   page 437
All year. Any 2 nights from £85
Breakfast, dinner

■ **Eastbourne**
Wish Tower Hotel   page 437
Nov & Mar. Any 2 nights from £60
Dec–Feb. Any 2 nights from £56
Breakfast, dinner

■ **Easton Grey**
Whatley Manor Hotel   page 437
All year 2 nights from £95
Breakfast, dinner

■ **Ely**
Lamb Hotel   page 439
Nov–Mar. Any 2 nights from £52
Apr–Nov. Any 2 nights from £55
Breakfast, dinner

■ **Epping**
Post House Hotel   page 439
Nov–27 Mar 2 nights from £56 (Mar £60)
Breakfast, dinner

■ **Ettington**
Chase Hotel   page 440
All year. Any 2 nights from £82
Breakfast, dinner & 1 lunch

166

■ **Evershot**
Summer Lodge Hotel   page 440
All year. Any 2 nights from £77
Breakfast, dinner

■ **Evesham**
Evesham Hotel   page 441
5–24 Nov & 11 Feb–26 May
2 nights from £64
26 Nov–9 Feb 2 nights from £52
Breakfast, dinner & 1 lunch

■ **Exeter**
Buckerell Lodge Crest Hotel   page 441
All year. Any 2 nights from £74
Breakfast, dinner

■ **Exeter**
Rougemont Hotel   page 441
All year 2 nights from £48 (summer £56)
Breakfast, dinner

■ **Exeter**
White Hart Hotel   page 442
All year 2 nights from £25·50
Breakfast

■ **Exford**
Crown Hotel   page 442
All year 2 nights from £70
Breakfast, dinner

■ **Exmouth**
Imperial Hotel   page 442
Nov & Mar. Any 2 nights from £64
Dec–Feb. Any 2 nights from £58
Breakfast, dinner

■ **Fairford**
Bull Hotel   page 442
All year. Any 2 nights from £52
Breakfast, dinner

■ **Fairy Cross**
Portledge Hotel   page 443
Nov–30 Apr & 10 Oct–Nov
Any 2 nights from £58
Breakfast, dinner

■ **Falmouth**
Bay Hotel   page 443
Mar–Oct. Any 2 nights from £60
Breakfast, dinner

■ **Falmouth**
Falmouth Hotel   page 443
All year. Any 2 nights from £62·50
Breakfast, dinner

■ **Falmouth**
Greenbank Hotel   page 443
All year 2 nights from £69
Breakfast, dinner

■ **Farnham**
Bishop's Table Hotel   page 444
All year 2 nights from £50
Breakfast, dinner

■ **Farnham**
Trevena House Hotel   page 445
All year. Any 2 nights from £54
Breakfast, £10 towards dinner

■ **Fawkham**
Brandshatch Place   page 446
All year (except during Grand Prix)
Any 2 nights from £70
Breakfast, dinner

■ **Felixstowe**
Orwell Moat House   page 446
All year 2 nights from £67·50
Breakfast, lunch & dinner

■ **Ferndown**
Dormy Hotel   page 446
All year 2 nights from £95
Breakfast, dinner

■ **Folkestone**
Burlington Hotel   page 447
Nov–Mar. Any 2 nights £27·50
Apr–Oct. Any 2 nights £33
Breakfast, lunch or dinner

■ **Folkestone**
Clifton Hotel   page 448
Nov–30 Apr. Any 2 nights from £51
Breakfast, dinner

■ **Fradley**
The Fradley Arms Hotel   page 449
All year. Any 2 nights from £39
Breakfast, £4 towards dinner

■ **Framlingham**
Crown Hotel   page 449
Nov & Mar. Any 2 nights from £68
Dec–Feb. Any 2 nights from £64
Breakfast, dinner

■ **Frome**
Mendip Lodge Hotel   page 450
All year. Any 2 nights from £67
Breakfast, dinner

■ **Frome**
Selwood Manor   page 450
Nov–Mar. Any 2 nights £80
Breakfast, dinner

■ **Garforth**
Ladbroke Hotel   page 451
All year. Any 2 nights from £46
Breakfast

■ **Gateshead**
Springfield Hotel   page 451
All year 2 nights from £51
Breakfast, dinner

■ **Gittisham**
Combe House Hotel   page 452
Nov–23 Dec, 3–9 Jan & 26 Feb–31 Mar
Any 2 nights from £90
˙ Breakfast, afternoon tea, £18·50 towards dinner

■ **Glastonbury**
George & Pilgrims Hotel   page 453
All year. Any 2 nights from £66
Breakfast, dinner

■ **Gloucester**
Crest Hotel   page 453
All year 2 nights from £80
Breakfast, dinner

■ **Gloucester**
Hatton Court   page 453
Nov–Mar. Any 2 nights from £70
Apr–Nov. Any 2 nights from £75
Breakfast, dinner

■ **Goathland**
Mallyan Spout Hotel   page 454
All year. Any 2 nights from £55
Breakfast, dinner

■ **Godalming**
Inn on the Lake   page 454
All year 2 nights from £40
Breakfast

■ **Golant**
Cormorant Hotel   page 454
Nov–May. Any 2 nights from £50
Breakfast, dinner

■ **Goodwood**
Goodwood Park Hotel   page 454
Nov–Mar 2 nights from £63
Apr–Oct 2 nights from £79
Breakfast & lunch or dinner

■ **Grasmere**
Swan Hotel   page 455
Nov–29 Mar. Any 2 nights from £60
Breakfast, dinner

■ **Grasmere**
Wordsworth Hotel   page 456
Nov–Mar. Any 2 nights from £75
Breakfast, dinner

■ **Great Ayton**
Ayton Hotel   page 457
All year 2 nights from £87·50
Breakfast, dinner, 1 lunch

■ **Great Dunmow**
Saracen's Head Hotel   page 457

Nov–27 Mar 2 nights from £62 (Dec & Jan from £58)
Breakfast, dinner

■ **Great Milton**
Le Manoir aux Quat'Saisons   page 458
Nov–17 Dec & 20 Jan–28 Apr
2 nights from £150
Continental breakfast, dinner

■ **Great Snoring**
Old Rectory   page 458
Dec–Mar. Any 2 nights from £70
Breakfast, dinner

■ **Greta Bridge**
Morritt Arms Hotel   page 459
Nov–Mar. Any 2 nights from £52
Breakfast, dinner

■ **Grimsby**
Humber Royal Crest Hotel   page 459
All year 2 nights from £60
Breakfast, dinner

■ **Grimston**
Congham Hall   page 460
All year 2 nights £100
Breakfast, dinner

■ **Grindleford**
Maynard Arms Hotel   page 460
All year. Any 2 nights from £59
Breakfast, dinner

■ **Grizedale**
Grizedale Lodge Hotel   page 461
Nov–May. Any 2 nights from £48
Breakfast, dinner

■ **Guildford**
Angel Hotel   page 461
Nov–27 Mar 2 nights from £64
Breakfast, dinner

■ **Hackness**
Hackness Grange Country Hotel   page 462
All year. Any 2 nights from £65
Breakfast, afternoon tea, dinner

■ **Hadley Wood**
West Lodge Park   page 462
Nov–Mar 2 nights from £55
Breakfast

■ **Halifax**
Holdsworth House Hotel   page 463
All year 2 nights from £80
Breakfast, 1 dinner

■ **Harlow**
Harlow Moat House   page 464
All year 2 nights from £62
Breakfast, dinner

■ **Harome**
Pheasant Hotel page 464
Nov–Dec & Mar–May. Any 2 nights from £56
Breakfast, dinner

■ **Harpenden**
Harpenden Moat House Hotel page 464
All year 2 nights from £45
Breakfast

■ **Harrogate**
Crown Hotel page 465
Nov & Mar 2 nights from £60
Dec–Feb 2 nights from £54
Breakfast, dinner

■ **Harrogate**
Hospitality Inn page 465
All year 2 nights from £64
Breakfast, dinner

■ **Harrogate**
Majestic page 468
Nov & Mar 2 nights from £70
Dec–Feb 2 nights from £60
Breakfast, dinner

■ **Harrogate**
Old Swan Hotel page 468
All year. Any 2 nights from £55
Breakfast

■ **Harrogate**
Russell Hotel page 468
All year 2 nights from £66
Breakfast, dinner

■ **Harrogate**
Hotel St George page 468
Nov–Mar. Any 2 nights from £70
Apr–Nov. Any 2 nights from £83
Breakfast, dinner

■ **Harrogate**
Studley Hotel page 469
All year (except during major conferences)
2 nights from £65
Breakfast, £12·50 towards dinner

■ **Harrow Weald**
Mansion House at Grim's Dyke page 469
All year 2 nights from £68
Breakfast, dinner

■ **Hartlepool**
Grand Hotel page 469
All year. Any 2 nights from £54
Breakfast, dinner

■ **Haslemere**
Lythe Hill Hotel page 470
All year. Any 2 nights from £72
Breakfast, £11·50 towards dinner

■ **Hatch Beauchamp**
Farthings Country House Hotel page 471
Nov–Mar. Any 2 nights from £79
Breakfast, dinner

■ **Hatfield**
Comet Hotel page 471
Nov–Mar 2 nights from £52
Breakfast, dinner

■ **Havant**
Post House Hotel page 472
Nov & Mar 2 nights from £78
Dec–Feb 2 nights from £72
Breakfast, dinner

■ **Hawkchurch**
Fairwater Head Hotel page 472 ·
Mar–Nov. Any 2 nights from £70
Breakfast, afternoon tea, dinner

■ **Hawkhurst**
Tudor Arms Hotel page 472
All year. Any 2 nights from £75
Breakfast, dinner

■ **Haydock**
Post House Hotel page 472
Nov–27 Mar 2 nights from £54
Breakfast, dinner

■ **Helmsley**
Black Swan Hotel page 474
Nov–29 Mar 2 nights from £74
Breakfast, dinner

■ **Helmsley**
Feathers Hotel page 474
Oct–June. Any 2 nights from £48
Breakfast, dinner

■ **Helmsley**
Feversham Arms Hotel page 474
Oct–24 Mar. Any 2 nights from £52
25 Mar–26 May. Any 2 nights from £58
27 May–20 Oct. Any 2 nights from £64
Breakfast, dinner

■ **Hemel Hempstead**
Post House Hotel page 475
Nov–27 Mar 2 nights from £52
Breakfast, dinner

■ **Henley-on-Thames**
Red Lion Hotel page 475
Nov–Apr 2 nights from £60
Breakfast, £12 towards dinner

■ **Hereford**
Green Dragon Hotel page 475
Nov–29 Mar. Any 2 nights from £64
Breakfast, dinner

BARGAIN BREAKS

■ **Hereford**
Hereford Moat House page 475
All year 2 nights from £55
Breakfast, dinner

■ **Hertingfordbury**
White Horse Inn page 476
Nov–27 Mar 2 nights from £74
Breakfast, dinner

■ **Hethersett**
Park Farm Hotel page 476
All year 2 nights from £42
Breakfast

■ **Hintlesham**
Hintlesham Hall page 478
Nov–Mar. Any 2 nights from £105
Breakfast, dinner

■ **Hollingbourne**
Great Danes Hotel page 479
All year 2 nights from £76
Breakfast, dinner

■ **Hope**
Poachers Arms Hotel page 479
All year. Any 2 nights from £60
Breakfast, £9·75 towards dinner

■ **Hope Cove**
Cottage Hotel page 479
Nov–Mar. Any 2 nights from £47·70
Breakfast, dinner

■ **Hope Cove**
Lantern Lodge Hotel page 480
Nov, Mar–May. Any 2 nights from £53
Breakfast, dinner

■ **Horton-cum-Studley**
Studley Priory Hotel page 480
Nov–1 May. Any 2 nights from £75
Breakfast, dinner

■ **Huddersfield**
George Hotel page 481
Nov, Feb & Mar 2 nights from £48
Dec & Jan 2 nights from £44
Breakfast, dinner

■ **Huddersfield**
Ladbroke Hotel page 481
All year 2 nights from £50·50
Breakfast

■ **Hull**
Crest Hotel (Humber Bridge) page 482
All year 2 nights from £68
Breakfast, 1 dinner

■ **Hungerford**
Bear at Hungerford page 482
All year 2 nights from £62·50
Breakfast, dinner

■ **Huntingdon**
Brampton Hotel page 483
All year 2 nights from £65
Breakfast, dinner

■ **Huntingdon**
George Hotel page 483
Nov & Mar 2 nights from £62
Dec–Feb 2 nights from £58
Breakfast, dinner

■ **Huntingdon**
Old Bridge Hotel page 483
All year 2 nights from £85
Breakfast, dinner

■ **Hythe**
Hythe Imperial Hotel page 485
All year 2 nights from £70
Breakfast, dinner

■ **Hythe**
Stade Court Hotel page 485
All year. Any 2 nights from £50
Breakfast & lunch or dinner

■ **Ilkley**
Craiglands Hotel page 486
Nov–29 Mar. Any 2 nights from £56
Breakfast, dinner

■ **Ipswich**
Belstead Brook Hotel page 486
All year 2 nights from £53
Breakfast, dinner

■ **Ipswich**
Marlborough Hotel page 486
All year 2 nights from £68
Breakfast, dinner

■ **Ipswich**
Post House Hotel page 487
Nov–27 Mar 2 nights from £50
Breakfast, dinner

■ **Jervaulx**
Jervaulx Hall Hotel page 487
Nov, Mar & Apr. Any 2 nights from £64
Breakfast, dinner

■ **Kendal**
Woolpack Hotel page 488
All year 2 nights from £68
Breakfast, dinner, 1 lunch

■ **Kenilworth**
Clarendon House Hotel page 488
All year 2 nights from £55
Breakfast, dinner

■ **Kenilworth**
De Montfort Hotel page 488
Nov–Mar 2 nights from £45
Breakfast, dinner

■ **Keswick**
Keswick Hotel   page 489
Nov & Mar 2 nights from £54
Dec–Feb 2 nights from £50
Breakfast, dinner

■ **Kildwick**
Kildwick Hall   page 489
All year. Any 2 nights from £87·90
Breakfast, £13·95 towards dinner

■ **Kingham**
Mill House Hotel   page 490
All year. Any 2 nights from £40
Breakfast, dinner

■ **King's Lynn**
Duke's Head   page 490
Nov & Mar 2 nights from £62
Dec–Feb 2 nights from £58
Breakfast, dinner

■ **Kingsbridge**
Buckland-Tout-Saints Hotel   page 491
Nov–Mar. Any 2 nights from £87
Breakfast, £18·70 towards dinner

■ **Kirkbymoorside**
George & Dragon   page 492
Nov–Easter. Any 2 nights from £20
Breakfast

■ **Knaresborough**
Dower House Hotel   page 492
Nov–1 May 2 nights from £60
Breakfast, dinner

■ **Knutsford**
Cottons Hotel   page 493
All year 2 nights from £66
Breakfast, £12 towards dinner

■ **Lacock**
Sign of the Angel   page 494
All year 2 nights from £85
Breakfast, dinner

■ **Lancaster**
Post House Hotel   page 494
Nov, Feb & Mar 2 nights from £64
Dec & Jan 2 nights from £60
Breakfast, dinner

■ **Langdale**
Langdale Hotel   page 494
All year. Any 2 nights from £92
Breakfast, £15 towards dinner

■ **Langho**
Northcote Manor   page 496
All year 2 nights from £29
Breakfast

■ **Lavenham**
Swan Hotel   page 496

Nov–29 Mar. Any 2 nights from £80
Breakfast, dinner

■ **Leamington Spa**
Regent Hotel   page 497
Nov–25 Mar 2 nights from £65
26 Mar–Nov 2 nights from £70
Breakfast, dinner

■ **Ledbury**
Feathers Hotel   page 497
All year. Any 2 nights from £63
Breakfast, dinner

■ **Ledbury**
Hope End   page 497
Mar–Nov 2 nights from £90
Breakfast, dinner

■ **Leeds**
Ladbroke Dragonara Hotel   page 500
All year. Any 2 nights from £46
Breakfast

■ **Leeds**
Merrion Hotel   page 500
All year 2 nights from £62
Breakfast, dinner

■ **Leeds**
Metropole   page 500
All year 2 nights from £48
Breakfast, dinner

■ **Leeds**
Queen's Hotel   page 500
Nov & Mar 2 nights from £58
Dec–Feb 2 nights from £52
Breakfast, dinner

■ **Leicester**
Belmont Hotel   page 501
All year 2 nights from £56
Breakfast, dinner

■ **Leicester**
Grand Hotel   page 501
All year 2 nights from £56
Breakfast, dinner

■ **Leicester**
Post House Hotel   page 502
Nov & Mar 2 nights from £52
Dec–Feb 2 nights from £48
Breakfast, dinner

■ **Leicester**
Queens Hotel   page 502
All year 2 nights from £60
Breakfast, dinner

■ **Leighton Buzzard**
Swan Hotel   page 502
All year 2 nights from £72
Breakfast, dinner

■ Lenham
Chilsdon Park   page 503
All year. Any 2 nights from £110
Breakfast, 1 lunch, afternoon tea, dinner

■ Lewdown
Fox's Earth Lewtrenchard Manor   page 503
All year 2 nights from £90
Breakfast, dinner

■ Lewes
Shelleys Hotel   page 504
Nov–Apr 2 nights from £75
Breakfast, dinner

■ Leyland
Ladbroke Hotel   page 504
All year 2 nights from £46
Breakfast, £7 towards lunch, £9·50 towards dinner

■ Lichfield
George Hotel   page 505
Nov–Mar 2 nights from £52
Breakfast & lunch or dinner

■ Lifton
Arundell Arms   page 505
Nov–31 Mar. Any 2 nights from £68
Breakfast, dinner

■ Lincoln
Eastgate Post House Hotel   page 505
Nov & Mar 2 nights from £66
Dec–Feb 2 nights from £60
Breakfast, dinner

■ Lincoln
Moor Lodge Hotel   page 506
All year. Any 2 nights from £58
Breakfast, dinner

■ Lincoln
White Hart Hotel   page 506
5 Nov–27 Mar 2 nights from £76
Breakfast, dinner

■ Liskeard
The Well House   page 506
Nov–31 Mar. Any 2 nights from £80
Continental breakfast, dinner

■ Little Wymondley
Redcoats Farmhouse Hotel   page 506
All year 2 nights from £60
Breakfast, £15 towards dinner

■ Liverpool
Atlantic Tower Hotel   page 507
Nov–25 Apr 2 nights from £40   Breakfast

■ Liverpool
Britannia Adelphi Hotel   page 507
All year 2 nights from £59
Breakfast, dinner

■ Liverpool
Crest Hotel, Liverpool-City   page 507
All year. Any 2 nights from £48
Breakfast

■ Liverpool
St George's Hotel   page 511
Nov–27 Mar 2 nights from £48
Breakfast, dinner

■ Loftus
Grinkle Park Hotel   page 511
All year 2 nights from £70
Breakfast, £12·25 towards 1 dinner

■ Longhorsley
Linden Hall Hotel   page 512
All year 2 nights from £71
Breakfast, dinner

■ Longleat
Bath Arms   page 513
Nov–Mar. Any 2 nights from £48
Breakfast, 1 lunch & 1 dinner

■ Looe
Talland Bay Hotel   page 513
Nov–12 Dec & 13 Feb–8 Apr
Any 2 nights £62
9 Apr–6 May & 21 Oct–30 Nov
Any 2 nights £65
Breakfast, dinner

■ Lostwithiel
Carotel Motel   page 513
All year. Any 2 nights from £50
Breakfast, dinner

■ Loughborough
King's Head Hotel   page 513
Nov–Feb 2 nights from £50
Mar–Oct 2 nights from about £54
Breakfast, dinner

■ Lower Beeding
South Lodge   page 514
All year. Any 2 nights from £150
Breakfast, dinner

■ Lower Swell
Old Farmhouse Hotel   page 515
All year (except during Cheltenham Gold Cup)
Nov–20 Apr. Any 2 nights from £50·50
21 Apr–31 Oct. Any 2 nights from £58·50
Breakfast, dinner

■ Ludlow
Feathers Hotel   page 515
All year. Any 2 nights from £82
Breakfast, dinner

■ Luton
Crest Hotel   page 515
All year 2 nights from £64
Breakfast, dinner

■ Luton
Leaside Hotel   page 516
All year 2 nights from £65
Breakfast, dinner

■ Lyme Regis
Alexandra Hotel   page 516
Nov–19 May. Any 2 nights from £60
Breakfast, dinner

■ Lyme Regis
Mariners Hotel   page 517
Mar–May & Oct. Any 2 nights from £55
Breakfast, dinner

■ Lymington
Passford House Hotel   page 517
Nov–20 May. Any 2 nights from £80
Breakfast, dinner

■ Lymington
Stanwell House Hotel   page 517
All year 2 nights from £86
Breakfast, 1 lunch, dinner

■ Lyndhurst
Crown Hotel   page 518
All year. Any 2 nights from £68
Breakfast, dinner

■ Lyndhurst
Lyndhurst Park Hotel   page 518
All year. Any 2 nights from £69
Breakfast, dinner

■ Lyndhurst
Parkhill Hotel   page 518
All year. Any 2 nights from £68
Breakfast, dinner

■ Lytham St Anne's
Clifton Arms Hotel   page 520
All year. Any 2 nights from £64
Breakfast, dinner

■ Maiden Newton
Maiden Newton House   page 520
Nov–Mar. Any 2 nights from £78
Breakfast, dinner

■ Maidenhead
Crest Hotel   page 521
All year 2 nights from £88
Breakfast, dinner

■ Maidstone
Boxley House Hotel   page 522
All year 2 nights from £68
Breakfast, dinner

■ Maidstone
Larkfield Hotel   page 522
All year 2 nights from £60
Breakfast, £11 towards dinner

■ Maldon
Blue Boar Hotel   page 522
Nov & Mar 2 nights from £62
Dec–Feb 2 nights from £58
Breakfast, dinner

■ Malmesbury
Old Bell Hotel   page 522
All year. Any 2 nights from £73
Breakfast, dinner

■ Malvern
Cottage in the Wood Hotel   page 523
Nov & Mar. Any 2 nights from £65
Dec–Feb. Any 2 nights from £55
Apr–Oct. Any 2 nights from £75
Continental breakfast, £14 towards dinner

■ Malvern
Foley Arms Hotel   page 524
All year. Any 2 nights from £66
Breakfast, dinner

■ Malvern
Mount Pleasant Hotel   page 524
Nov–Mar. Any 2 nights from £51
Apr–Nov. Any 2 nights from £55
Breakfast, £7·50 towards dinner

■ Manchester
Britannia Hotel   page 524
All year. Any 2 nights from £59
Breakfast, dinner

■ Manchester
Grand Hotel   page 524
Nov–27 Mar 2 nights from £50
Breakfast, dinner

■ Manchester
Hotel Piccadilly   page 525
All year 2 nights from £80
Breakfast, dinner

■ Manchester
Portland Thistle Hotel   page 529
All year 2 nights from £50
Breakfast

■ Manchester
Post House Hotel   page 529
Nov–27 Mar 2 nights from £64
Breakfast, dinner

■ Manchester
Willow Bank Hotel   page 529
All year 2 nights £26
No meals

■ Manchester Airport
Excelsior Hotel   page 530
Nov–27 Mar 2 nights from £72
Breakfast, dinner

BARGAIN BREAKS

Manchester Airport
Ladbroke International Hotel   page 530
All year 2 nights from £46
Breakfast

Markington
Hob Green Hotel   page 531
Nov–Apr 2 nights from £80
Breakfast, dinner

Matlock Bath
New Bath Hotel   page 532
Nov & Mar 2 nights from £60
Dec–Feb 2 nights from £54
Breakfast, dinner

Mawnan Smith
Meudon Hotel   page 533
Oct–Apr. Any 2 nights from £74
May–Jul. Any 2 nights from £96
Breakfast, dinner

Melksham
King's Arms Hotel   page 533
All year. Any 2 nights from £53
Breakfast, dinner

Melton Mowbray
George Hotel   page 534
All year 2 nights from £60
Breakfast, dinner

Melton Mowbray
Harboro' Hotel   page 534
All year 2 nights from £52
Breakfast, dinner

Meriden
Manor Hotel   page 534
Nov–Mar 2 nights from £49
Breakfast, dinner

Mickleton
Three Ways Hotel   page 534
Nov–31 Mar 2 nights from £62
Apr–Oct 2 nights from £64
Breakfast, £11 towards dinner

Middle Wallop
Fifehead Manor   page 535
All year. Any 2 nights from £75
Breakfast, £15 towards dinner

Middlesbrough
Hotel Baltimore   page 535
All year 2 nights from £35
Breakfast, dinner

Middlesbrough
Ladbroke Dragonara Hotel   page 535
All year 2 nights from £46
Breakfast

Middleton Stoney
Jersey Arms   page 535

All year. Any 2 nights from £65
Breakfast, £13·50 towards dinner

Midhurst
Spread Eagle Hotel   page 536
25 Mar–26 May. Any 2 nights from £77·50
27 May–3 Nov. Any 2 nights from £85
Breakfast, dinner

Minster Lovell
Old Swan Hotel   page 536
Nov–31 Mar 2 nights from £65
Breakfast, dinner

Monk Fryston
Monk Fryston Hall Hotel   page 536
Nov–Mar 2 nights from £63
Apr–Oct 2 nights from £68
Breakfast, dinner

Moreton-in-Marsh
Manor House Hotel   page 537
Nov–Apr. Any 2 nights from £73·50
Breakfast, dinner

Moretonhampstead
Manor House Hotel   page 537
Nov–Mar 2 nights from £48·50
Apr–Oct 2 nights from £51
Breakfast, dinner

Moretonhampstead
White Hart Hotel   page 537
All year. Any 2 nights from £56
Breakfast, dinner

Mottram St Andrew
Mottram Hall Hotel   page 538
All year 2 nights from £64
Breakfast

Much Birch
Pilgrim Hotel   page 538
All year 2 nights from £68
Breakfast, dinner

Mudeford
Avonmouth Hotel   page 538
Nov & Mar. Any 2 nights from £66
Dec–Feb. Any 2 nights from £60
Breakfast, dinner

Mullion
Polurrian Hotel   page 539
Easter–June & Sept–Nov
Any 2 nights from £67
Breakfast, dinner

Nantwich
Rookery Hall   page 539
Nov–Mar 2 nights from £125
Breakfast, dinner

■ **Neasham**
Newbus Arms Hotel   page 539
All year 2 nights from £70
Breakfast, dinner

■ **New Milton**
Chewton Glen Hotel   page 540
Nov–31 Apr 2 nights from £154
Continental breakfast, dinner

■ **Newbury**
Chequers Hotel   page 541
Nov & Mar 2 nights from £58
Dec–Feb 2 nights from £54
Breakfast, dinner

■ **Newbury**
Elcot Park Hotel   page 541
All year. Any 2 nights from £69·50
Breakfast, dinner

■ **Newby Bridge**
Swan Hotel   page 541
Nov–25 Mar 2 nights from £64
Breakfast, dinner

■ **Newby Wiske**
Solberge Hall   page 541
All year. Any 2 nights from £80
Breakfast, dinner

■ **Newcastle-under-Lyme**
Clayton Lodge Hotel   page 544
Nov–Apr 2 nights from £55
Breakfast, dinner

■ **Newcastle-under-Lyme**
Post House Hotel   page 544
Nov–27 Mar 2 nights from £52
Breakfast, dinner

■ **Newcastle upon Tyne**
County Thistle Hotel   page 544
All year 2 nights from £39
Breakfast

■ **Newcastle upon Tyne**
Crest Hotel   page 544
All year 2 nights from £58
Breakfast, dinner

■ **Newcastle upon Tyne**
Gosforth Park Thistle Hotel   page 545
All year 2 nights from £56
Breakfast

■ **Newcastle upon Tyne**
Holiday Inn   page 545
Nov–Apr 2 nights from £50
May–Oct 2 nights from about £55
Breakfast

■ **Newcastle upon Tyne**
Stakis Airport Hotel   page 546
Nov–Mar 2 nights from £48

23 May–Oct 2 nights from £50
Breakfast, dinner

■ **Newmarket**
White Hart Hotel   page 546
All year 2 nights from £56
Breakfast, £8 towards dinner

■ **Newport Pagnell**
TraveLodge   page 547
Nov–27 Mar 2 nights from £48
Breakfast, dinner

■ **Newquay**
Atlantic Hotel   page 547
All year. Any 2 nights from £48·30
Breakfast, dinner

■ **Newquay**
Hotel Riviera   page 547
All year 2 nights from £58
Breakfast, dinner

■ **Newton Solney**
Newton Park Hotel   page 547
Nov–Feb 2 nights from £51
Mar–Apr 2 nights from £57
Breakfast, dinner

■ **North Petherton**
Walnut Tree Inn   page 548
All year 2 nights from £34   Breakfast

■ **North Stifford**
Stifford Moat House   page 548
All year 2 nights from £59
Breakfast, dinner

■ **Northampton**
Northampton Moat House   page 549
All year 2 nights from £67
Breakfast, dinner

■ **Northampton**
Swallow Hotel   page 549
Nov–Mar 2 nights from £72
Breakfast, 1 lunch, dinner

■ **Norwich**
Maid's Head Hotel   page 551
Nov–Mar 2 nights from £63·50
Apr–Aug 2 nights from £68
Sep & Oct 2 nights from £72·50
Breakfast, dinner

■ **Norwich**
Hotel Nelson   page 552
All year. Any 2 nights from £69
Breakfast, 1 dinner & 1 lunch or dinner

■ **Norwich**
Post House Hotel   page 552
Nov, Dec, Feb & Mar 2 nights from £70
Jan 2 nights from £60
Breakfast, dinner

BARGAIN BREAKS

■ Nottingham
Albany Hotel   page 552
Nov–27 Mar 2 nights from £52
Breakfast, dinner

■ Nottingham
Royal Moat House International   page 553
Nov–27 Mar. Any 2 nights from £75
Breakfast, dinner

■ Nottingham
Stakis Victoria Hotel   page 554
All year. Any 2 nights from £50
Breakfast, dinner

■ Nottingham
Strathdon Thistle Hotel   page 554
All year 2 nights from £54
Breakfast

■ Oakham
Hambleton Hall   page 554
Nov–Apr 2 nights from £41
Continental breakfast

■ Ormesby St Margaret
Ormesby Lodge Hotel   page 556
All year 2 nights from £63·80
Breakfast, £11·75 towards dinner & 1 lunch

■ Oswestry
Wynnstay Hotel   page 557
2 Nov–29 Mar. Any 2 nights from £54
Breakfast, dinner

■ Otley
Chevin Lodge   page 557
All year 2 nights from £65
Breakfast, dinner

■ Otterburn
Percy Arms Hotel   page 557
All year. Any 2 nights from £60
Breakfast, dinner

■ Oxford
Ladbroke Linton Lodge Hotel   page 559
All year 2 nights from £48
Breakfast

■ Oxford
Randolph Hotel   page 562
5 Nov–27 Mar 2 nights from £76 (Dec & Jan £72)
Breakfast, dinner

■ Oxford
TraveLodge   page 562
5 Nov–27 Mar 2 nights from £56
Breakfast, dinner

■ Paignton
Palace Hotel   page 563
Nov–Feb 2 nights from £56
Mar 2 nights from £62
Breakfast, dinner

■ Paignton
Redcliffe Hotel   page 563
Nov–31 Mar 2 nights from £52
Breakfast, dinner

■ Pangbourne
Copper Inn   page 563
All year 2 nights from £62·50
Breakfast, £15 towards dinner

■ Parkgate
Ship Hotel Inn   page 563
All year. Any 2 nights from £56
Breakfast, dinner

■ Penzance
Abbey Hotel   page 565
Nov–Apr. Any 2 nights from £40
Breakfast, £1·50 towards meals

■ Peterborough
Peterborough Moat House   page 566
All year 2 nights from £55
Breakfast, dinner

■ Petersfield
Langrish House   page 567
Nov–Mar 2 nights from £54
Breakfast, dinner

■ Plymouth
Astor Hotel   page 567
All year 2 nights from £56
Breakfast, dinner

■ Plymouth
Duke of Cornwall Hotel   page 568
All year 2 nights from £40
Breakfast

■ Plymouth
Holiday Inn   page 568
Nov–Apr 2 nights from £50
Breakfast

■ Plymouth
Mayflower Post House Hotel   page 569
Nov & Mar 2 nights from £68
Dec–Feb 2 nights from £64
Breakfast, dinner

■ Plymouth
Novotel   page 569
All year 2 nights from £39
Breakfast

■ Poole
Hospitality Inn, The Quay   page 570
All year 2 nights from £60
Breakfast, dinner

■ Portsmouth
Holiday Inn   page 571
All year 2 nights from £50
Breakfast, £12·50 towards meals

■ **Powburn**
Breamish House Hotel   page 572
Nov–Dec, Feb–Apr, Oct–Nov
Any 2 nights from £68
Breakfast, dinner

■ **Preston**
Crest House Hotel   page 572
All year. Any 2 nights from £64
Breakfast, 1 dinner

■ **Pulborough**
Chequers Hotel   page 573
Nov–Mar. Any 2 nights £49
Apr–Nov. Any 2 nights from £54
Breakfast, dinner

■ **Quorn**
Quorn Country Hotel   page 573
All year 2 nights from £65
Breakfast, dinner

■ **Reading**
Post House Hotel   page 574
5 Nov–27 Mar 2 nights from £62
Breakfast, dinner

■ **Reading**
Ramada Hotel   page 574
All year 2 nights from £73
Breakfast, 1 dinner

■ **Redbourn**
Aubrey Park Hotel   page 574
All year 2 nights from £70
Breakfast, dinner

■ **Renishaw**
Sitwell Hotel   page 575
All year 2 nights from £25
Breakfast

■ **Ripon**
Ripon Spa Hotel   page 576
All year. Any 2 nights from £65
Breakfast, dinner

■ **Rochester**
Crest Hotel   page 576
All year. Any 2 nights from £68
Breakfast, £12·95 towards dinner

■ **Romaldkirk**
Rose and Crown Hotel   page 576
Nov–June. Any 2 nights from £58
Breakfast, dinner

■ **Romsey**
White Horse Hotel   page 577
Nov & Mar 2 nights from £72
Dec–Feb 2 nights from £64
Breakfast, dinner

■ **Ross-on-Wye**
Pengethley Manor Hotel   page 578

All year. Any 2 nights from £100
Breakfast, dinner

■ **Ross-on-Wye**
Walford House Hotel   page 578
All year. Any 2 nights from £74
Breakfast, dinner

■ **Rotherham**
Rotherham Moat House   page 578
All year 2 nights from £50
Breakfast, dinner

■ **Rotherwick**
Tylney Hall   page 579
All year 2 nights from £105
Breakfast, dinner

■ **Rowsley**
Peacock Hotel   page 579
Nov–29 Feb 2 nights from £62
Mar–30 Apr 2 nights from £68
May–28 Oct 2 nights from £87
Breakfast, dinner

■ **Ryde (Isle of Wight)**
Hotel Ryde Castle   page 581
Nov–Mar 2 nights from £50   Breakfast

■ **Rye**
George Hotel   page 581
Nov–29 Mar. Any 2 nights £74 (Jan & Feb £70)
Breakfast, dinner

■ **Rye**
Mermaid Inn   page 581
All year. Any 2 nights from £76.
Breakfast, dinner

■ **Saffron Walden**
Saffron Hotel   page 581
All year 2 nights from £35
Continental breakfast

■ **St Albans**
Noke Thistle Hotel   page 582
All year 2 nights from £50
Breakfast, £10 towards meals

■ **St Albans**
Sopwell House Hotel   page 582
Nov–26 Mar 2 nights from £65
27 Mar–Nov 2 nights from £75
Breakfast, dinner

■ **St Ives**
Slepe Hall Hotel   page 582
All year 2 nights from £55
Breakfast, dinner

■ **St Ives**
Boskerris Hotel   page 583
Easter–mid May & Sept–mid Oct
Any 2 nights from £46
Breakfast, dinner

BARGAIN BREAKS

■ **St Mawes**
Idle Rocks Hotel page 584
25 Mar–31 May & 1–22 Oct
Any 2 nights from £64
Breakfast, dinner

■ **Salcombe**
Marine Hotel page 584
Nov–Mar. Any 2 nights from £82
Breakfast, dinner

■ **Salcombe**
South Sands Hotel page 585
Nov–Jun & Sep–Nov. Any 2 nights from £70
Breakfast, dinner

■ **Salisbury**
Rose & Crown Hotel page 586
All year 2 nights from £38·50
Breakfast, £9·50 towards dinner

■ **Salisbury**
White Hart Hotel page 586
Nov & Mar. Any 2 nights from £68
Dec–Feb. Any 2 nights from £60
Breakfast, dinner

■ **Samlesbury**
Tickled Trout Hotel page 586
Jan–Sept 2 nights from £60
Breakfast, dinner

■ **Samlesbury**
Swallow Trafalgar Hotel page 586
All year 2 nights from £62
Breakfast, dinner & 1 lunch

■ **Sandbach**
Chimney House Hotel page 586
All year 2 nights from £60
Breakfast, dinner

■ **Sandown**
Melville Hall Hotel page 587
Nov–27 May & 18 Sept–Nov
Any 2 nights from £50
Breakfast, dinner

■ **Saunton**
Saunton Sands Hotel page 587
All year (except 19 Jul–19 Sept)
2 nights from £75·90
Breakfast, dinner

■ **Scarborough**
Crown Hotel page 587
All year. Any 2 nights from £52
Breakfast, dinner

■ **Scarborough**
Holbeck Hall Hotel page 587
All year. Any 2 nights from £80
Breakfast, dinner

■ **Scarborough**
Palm Court Hotel page 588
All year. Any 2 nights for £59
Breakfast, dinner & 1 lunch

■ **Scarborough**
Royal Hotel page 588
Nov–Apr. Any 2 nights £72
May–Nov. Any 2 nights £88
Breakfast, dinner & 1 lunch

■ **Scole**
Scole Inn page 588
All year. Any 2 nights from £54
Breakfast, dinner

■ **Seale**
Hog's Back Hotel page 589
All year. Any 2 nights from £62
Breakfast, dinner

■ **Seaview (Isle of Wight)**
Seaview Hotel page 589
All year. Any 2 nights from £70
Breakfast, dinner

■ **Seavington St Mary**
Pheasant Hotel page 589
All year. Any 2 nights £69
Breakfast, dinner

■ **Sedlescombe**
Brickwall Hotel page 589
All year. Any 2 nights from £57
Breakfast, dinner

■ **Sennen**
Tregiffian Hotel page 590
Mar–May & Sep–Oct. Any 2 nights from £47
Breakfast, dinner

■ **Shaftesbury**
Grosvenor Hotel page 590
All year. Any 2 nights from £72
Breakfast, dinner

■ **Shaftesbury**
Royal Chase Hotel page 590
Nov–11 Feb 2 nights from £54
12 Feb–24 Mar 2 nights from £64
Breakfast, £12·50 towards dinner

■ **Shedfield**
Meon Valley Hotel page 591
All year. Any 2 nights from £70
Breakfast, dinner

■ **Sheffield**
Charnwood Hotel page 591
All year 2 nights from £39
Breakfast

- **Sheffield**
  Grosvenor House Hotel   page 591
  Nov & Mar 2 nights from £52
  Dec–Feb 2 nights from £48
  Breakfast, dinner

- **Sheffield**
  Hallam Tower Post House Hotel   page 591
  Nov & Mar 2 nights from £62
  Dec–Feb 2 nights from £56
  Breakfast, dinner

- **Sheffield**
  Hotel St George   page 592
  Nov–Mar 2 nights from £69
  Breakfast, dinner

- **Shepperton**
  Shepperton Moat House   page 592
  All year 2 nights from £56
  Breakfast, dinner

- **Shepperton**
  Warren Lodge Hotel   page 592
  All year 2 nights from £45   Breakfast

- **Sherborne**
  Post House Hotel   page 593
  Nov & Mar. Any 2 nights from £64
  Dec–Feb. Any 2 nights from £52
  Breakfast, dinner

- **Shipton-u-Wychwood**
  Lamb Inn   page 594
  Nov–Apr. Any 2 nights from £30
  Breakfast

- **Shrewsbury**
  Lion Hotel   page 595
  Nov & Mar. Any 2 nights from £66
  Dec–Feb. Any 2 nights from £62
  Breakfast, dinner

- **Sidmouth**
  Belmont Hotel   page 595
  Nov–31 Mar. Any 2 nights from £56
  Apr, May & Aug. Any 2 nights from £60
  Breakfast

- **Sidmouth**
  Fortfield Hotel   page 596
  Nov–31 Mar. Any 2 nights £54
  5 Apr–Nov. Any 2 nights £58
  Breakfast, dinner

- **Sidmouth**
  Hotel Riviera   page 596
  Nov–2 May 2 nights from £63·25
  Breakfast, dinner

- **Sidmouth**
  Victoria Hotel   page 596
  Nov, Dec, Jan–May & Oct. Any 2 nights from
  £63·25
  Breakfast, dinner

- **Silchester**
  Romans Hotel   page 596
  All year 2 nights from £66
  Breakfast, dinner

- **Six Mile Bottom**
  Swynford Paddocks   page 597
  All year 2 nights from £83
  Breakfast, £14 towards dinner

- **Slough**
  Holiday Inn   page 597
  All year. Any 2 nights from £50
  Breakfast

- **Solihull**
  George Hotel   page 598
  All year 2 nights from £59
  Breakfast, dinner

- **Somerton**
  Red Lion Hotel   page 599
  All year. Any 2 nights from £44
  Breakfast, dinner

- **South Marston**
  South Marston Hotel   page 599
  All year 2 nights from £66
  Breakfast, dinner

- **South Mimms**
  Crest Hotel   page 600
  All year 2 nights from £84
  Breakfast, dinner

- **South Normanton**
  Swallow Hotel   page 600
  All year 2 nights from £72
  Breakfast, dinner & 1 lunch

- **South Walsham**
  South Walsham Hall Hotel   page 600
  All year. Any 2 nights from £70
  Breakfast, lunch & dinner

- **Southampton**
  Dolphin Hotel   page 601
  5 Nov–27 Mar 2 nights from £54 (Feb & Mar £58)
  Breakfast, dinner

- **Southampton**
  Polygon Hotel   page 601
  5 Nov–27 Mar 2 nights from £56
  Breakfast, dinner

- **Southampton**
  Post House Hotel   page 601
  Nov & Mar 2 nights from £54
  Dec–Feb 2 nights from £52
  Breakfast, dinner

- **Southwell**
  Saracen's Head Hotel   page 602
  All year 2 nights from £62
  Breakfast, dinner

■ **Stafford**
Tillington Hall Hotel   page 604
All year 2 nights from £49·50
Breakfast, dinner

■ **Stamford**
George of Stamford   page 605
All year 2 nights from £75
Breakfast, 1 dinner

■ **Stanton Harcourt**
Harcourt Arms   page 605
All year. Any 2 nights from £54
Breakfast, £9 towards dinner

■ **Stevenage**
Roebuck Inn   page 606
5 Nov–27 Mar 2 nights from £50
Breakfast, dinner

■ **Stockbridge**
Grosvenor Hotel   page 606
1 Apr–31 Oct 2 nights from £64
1 Nov–28 Feb 2 nights from £56
Breakfast, dinner

■ **Stockport**
Alma Lodge Hotel   page 607
All year 2 nights from £46
Breakfast, £8·50 towards dinner

■ **Stockton-on-Tees**
Swallow Hotel   page 607
All year. Any 2 nights from £65
Breakfast, dinner & 1 lunch

■ **Stoke Mandeville**
Belmore Hotel   page 607
All year 2 nights from £38
Continental breakfast

■ **Stoke-on-Trent**
North Stafford Hotel   page 608
5 Nov–27 Mar 2 nights from £54
Breakfast, dinner

■ **Ston Easton**
Ston Easton Park   page 608
Nov–31 Mar 2 nights from £124
Continental breakfast, dinner

■ **Storrington**
Abingworth Hall   page 610
Nov–Apr. Any 2 nights from £86
May–Nov. Any 2 nights from £98
Breakfast, dinner

■ **Stourbridge**
Talbot Hotel Inn   page 612
All year. Any 2 nights from £42
Breakfast

■ **Stow-on-the-Wold**
Fosse Manor Hotel   page 612
Nov–Apr. Any 2 nights from £40

Jun–Aug. Any 2 nights from £52
Breakfast, dinner

■ **Stow-on-the-Wold**
Unicorn Crest Hotel   page 612
All year. Any 2 nights from £78
Breakfast, dinner

■ **Stow-on-the-Wold**
Wyck Hill Hotel   page 613
Nov–Mar. Any 2 nights from £90
Continental breakfast, dinner

■ **Stratford-upon-Avon**
Alveston Manor   page 613
Nov & Mar 2 nights from £72
Dec–Feb 2 nights from £66
Breakfast, dinner

■ **Stratford-upon-Avon**
Falcon Hotel   page 617
All year 2 nights from £66
Breakfast, dinner

■ **Stratford-upon-Avon**
Shakespeare Hotel   page 618
5 Nov–27 Mar 2 nights from £84
Breakfast, dinner

■ **Stratford-upon-Avon**
Stratford House Hotel   page 618
Nov–May 2 nights from £64
Breakfast, £10 towards lunch or dinner

■ **Stratford-upon-Avon**
Swan's Nest   page 619
Nov & Mar 2 nights from £64
Dec–Feb 2 nights from £60
Breakfast, dinner

■ **Stratford-upon-Avon**
Welcombe Hotel   page 619
All year. Any 2 nights from £94
Breakfast, dinner

■ **Stratford-upon-Avon**
White Swan   page 619
All year 2 nights from £74
Breakfast, dinner

■ **Streatley-on-Thames**
Swan at Streatley   page 620
All year 2 nights from £85·50
Breakfast, £14·50 towards dinner

■ **Street**
Bear Hotel   page 620
All year 2 nights from £56
Breakfast, dinner

■ **Street**
Wessex Hotel   page 620
All year. Any 2 nights from £52
Breakfast, dinner

■ **Stroud**
Bear of Rodborough   page 621
All year. Any 2 nights from £70
Breakfast, dinner

■ **Sunderland**
Seaburn Hotel   page 623
All year 2 nights from £60
Breakfast, dinner & 1 lunch

■ **Sutton Benger**
Bell House Hotel   page 623
All year 2 nights from £42
Continental breakfast

■ **Sutton Coldfield**
Penns Hall Hotel   page 624
All year 2 nights from £61
Breakfast, dinner

■ **Swindon**
Blunsdon House Hotel   page 624
All year. Any 2 nights from £79
Breakfast, dinner

■ **Swindon**
Post House Hotel   page 625
Nov & Mar 2 nights from £64
Dec–Feb 2 nights from £60
Breakfast, dinner

■ **Taunton**
Castle Hotel   page 626
Nov–Mar 2 nights from £99
Breakfast, dinner

■ **Taunton**
County Hotel   page 627
Nov & Mar 2 nights from £56
Dec–Feb 2 nights from £52
Breakfast, dinner

■ **Tebay**
Tebay Mountain Lodge Hotel   page 627
All year. Any 2 nights from £40
Breakfast, dinner

■ **Teignmouth**
Venn Farm Country House Hotel   page 627
Nov–May 2 nights from £55
Breakfast, dinner

■ **Telford**
Telford Hotel, Golf & Country Club   page 627
All year 2 nights from £88
Breakfast, dinner

■ **Telford**
Telford Moat House   page 627
Nov–Mar 2 nights from £57
Apr–Oct 2 nights from £62
Breakfast, dinner

■ **Tetbury**
Calcot Manor   page 628

Nov–Mar. Any 2 nights from £110
Breakfast, dinner

■ **Tetbury**
Close at Tetbury   page 628
All year (except during Badminton Horse Trials
& Cheltenham Gold Cup week)
Any 2 nights from £96
Breakfast, dinner

■ **Tewkesbury**
Bredon Manor   page 629
All year (except during Cheltenham Gold Cup
week)
Any 2 nights from £80
Breakfast, dinner

■ **Tewkesbury**
Tewkesbury Park Hotel   page 629
All year 2 nights from £70
Breakfast, dinner

■ **Thetford**
The Bell   page 630
Nov–Feb 2 nights from £60
Mar 2 nights from £64
Breakfast, dinner

■ **Thornbury**
Thornbury Castle   page 630
Oct–Mar (except during Cheltenham Gold Cup
week)
Any 2 nights from £118
Continental breakfast, dinner

■ **Thornton-le-Fylde**
River House   page 631
All year 2 nights from £70
Breakfast, dinner & 1 lunch

■ **Threshfield**
Wilson Arms Hotel   page 631
Nov–Mar. Any 2 nights from £50
Breakfast, £10 towards dinner

■ **Thurlestone**
Thurlestone Hotel   page 632
All year. Any 2 nights from £94
Breakfast, dinner

■ **Tickton**
Tickton Grange Hotel   page 632
All year 2 nights from £35
Breakfast

■ **Tonbridge**
Rose and Crown Hotel   page 632
Nov–27 Mar 2 nights from £62
Breakfast, dinner

■ **Torquay**
Homers Hotel   page 633
All year. Any 2 nights from £54
Breakfast, dinner

■ **Torquay**
Imperial Hotel   page 633
Nov–29 Mar. Any 2 nights from £120
Breakfast, dinner

■ **Torquay**
Kistor Hotel   page 633
Nov–27 May. Any 2 nights from £50
Breakfast, 1 lunch, dinner

■ **Torquay**
Livermead Cliff Hotel   page 633
All year. Any 2 nights from £56
Breakfast, 1 dinner & 1 lunch or dinner

■ **Torquay**
Livermead House Hotel   page 634
All year. Any 2 nights from £56
Breakfast, 1 dinner & 1 lunch or dinner

■ **Torquay**
Osborne Hotel   page 634
All year. Any 2 nights from £94
Breakfast, dinner

■ **Torquay**
Palace Hotel   page 634
All year. Any 2 nights from £76
Breakfast, dinner

■ **Torquay**
Toorak Hotel   page 634
Nov–Apr 2 nights from £48
May 2 nights from £54
Breakfast, dinner

■ **Tunbridge Wells**
Royal Wells Inn   page 636
All year 2 nights from £68
Breakfast, dinner

■ **Tunbridge Wells**
Spa Hotel   page 636
All year 2 nights from £79
Breakfast, dinner

■ **Ullswater**
Leeming House Hotel   page 638
All year. Any 2 nights from £100
Breakfast, dinner

■ **Ullswater**
Rampsbeck Hotel   page 639
Nov–31 Mar. Any 2 nights from £58
Apr–Jun, Sept & Oct 2 nights from £68
Breakfast, dinner

■ **Underbarrow**
Greenriggs Country House Hotel   page 640
Nov–mid Dec & Mar 2 nights from £55
Apr & May. Any 2 nights from £59
Breakfast, dinner

■ **Uppingham**
Falcon Hotel   page 640

All year 2 nights from £50
Breakfast, dinner

■ **Uttoxeter**
White Hart Hotel   page 641
All year 2 nights from £25
Breakfast

■ **Ventnor**
Royal Hotel   page 641
Nov & Mar. Any 2 nights from £54
Dec–Feb. Any 2 nights from £50
Breakfast, dinner

■ **Veryan**
Nare Hotel   page 641
Nov–Apr. Any 2 nights from £65
Breakfast, dinner

■ **Wadhurst**
Spindlewood Hotel   page 642
Nov–May & mid Oct–Nov. Any 2 nights from £60
Breakfast, dinner

■ **Wakefield**
Post House Hotel   page 642
Nov–27 Mar 2 nights from £52
Breakfast, dinner

■ **Wakefield**
Swallow Hotel   page 642
All year. Any 2 nights from £60
Breakfast, 1 lunch, dinner

■ **Walberton**
Avisford Park Country Hotel   page 642
Nov–28 Feb 2 nights from £79
4 Mar–2 Sept 2 nights from £89
Breakfast, dinner

■ **Wall**
Hadrian Hotel   page 643
All year. Any 2 nights from £56
Breakfast, £9 towards dinner

■ **Wallingford**
George Hotel   page 643
All year 2 nights from £75
Breakfast, dinner

■ **Walsall**
Baron's Court Hotel   page 643
All year 2 nights from £60
Breakfast, dinner

■ **Wansford-in-England**
Haycock Hotel   page 644
All year 2 nights from £67·50
Breakfast, 1 dinner

■ **Ware**
Briggens House Hotel   page 645
Nov–Apr 2 nights from £75
May–Nov 2 nights from £95
Breakfast, dinner

■ **Warrington**
Lord Daresbury Hotel   page 646
Nov–Mar 2 nights from £75
Apr–Nov 2 nights from £80
Breakfast, dinner

■ **Warwick**
Ladbroke Hotel   page 647
All year 2 nights from £50
Breakfast

■ **Washington**
George Washington Hotel   page 647
All year 2 nights from £64
Breakfast, dinner

■ **Wateringbury**
Wateringbury Hotel   page 648
All year 2 nights from £44
Breakfast

■ **Watford**
Ladbroke Hotel   page 648
All year 2 nights from £46
Breakfast

■ **Wem**
Hawkstone Park Hotel   page 649
Nov–Apr & Jul–Aug. Any 2 nights from £70
Breakfast, lunch, dinner

■ **Wembley**
Ladbroke International Hotel   page 649
All year 2 nights from £50·50
Breakfast

■ **West Bexington**
Manor Hotel   page 650
All year. Any 2 nights from £57·50
Breakfast, dinner

■ **West Chiltington**
Roundabout Hotel   page 650
Nov–24 Mar. Any 2 nights from £63
25 Mar–26 May. Any 2 nights from £69
27 May–3 Nov. Any 2 nights from £74
Breakfast, dinner

■ **West Runton**
Links Country Park Hotel   page 651
All year. Any 2 nights from £70
Breakfast, dinner

■ **Weston-super-Mare**
Grand Atlantic Hotel   page 651
Nov, Dec & Mar. Any 2 nights from £62
Jan & Feb. Any 2 nights from £58
Breakfast, dinner

■ **Westonbirt**
Hare & Hounds Hotel   page 652
Nov–24 Mar. Any 2 nights from £60
25 Mar–31 Aug. Any 2 nights from £68
Breakfast, dinner or lunch

■ **Wetheral**
Crown Hotel   page 652
All year. Any 2 nights from £66
Breakfast, £12 towards dinner

■ **Wetherby**
Ladbroke Hotel   page 652
All year 2 nights from £46
Breakfast

■ **Weybourne**
Maltings Hotel   page 652
Nov–Mar. Any 2 nights from £60
Apr–Oct. Any 2 nights from £65
Breakfast, dinner

■ **Weybridge**
Ship Thistle Hotel   page 653
All year 2 nights from £50
Breakfast

■ **Whimple**
Woodhayes   page 653
Nov–Mar. Any 2 nights from £98
Breakfast, dinner

■ **Whitwell-on-the-Hill**
Whitwell Hall Country House Hotel   page 654
Nov–Mar 2 nights from £65
Apr 2 nights from £75
Breakfast, dinner

■ **Wigan**
Brocket Arms Hotel   page 654
All year 2 nights from £35
Breakfast

■ **Wilmington**
Home Farm Hotel   page 655
All year. Any 2 nights from £57
Breakfast, dinner

■ **Wilmslow**
Stanneylands Hotel   page 655
All year 2 nights from £95
Breakfast, lunch, £18 towards dinner

■ **Wimborne Minster**
The Kings Head   page 656
Nov & Mar. Any 2 nights from £72
Dec–Feb. Any 2 nights from £68
Breakfast, dinner

■ **Wincanton**
Holbrook House Hotel   page 656
Jan–Mar. Any 2 nights from £40
Apr–Sept. Any 2 nights from £49·50
Oct–Nov. Any 2 nights from £45
Breakfast, dinner

■ **Winchester**
Lainston House   page 656
All year 2 nights from £135
Breakfast, dinner

■ **Winchester**
Wessex Hotel page 657
Nov–27 Mar 2 nights from £72
Breakfast, dinner

■ **Windermere**
Langdale Chase Hotel page 657
Nov–Apr 2 nights from £64
Breakfast, dinner

■ **Windsor**
Castle Hotel page 658
Nov, Feb & Mar 2 nights from £82
Dec & Jan 2 nights from £74
Breakfast, dinner

■ **Windsor**
Oakley Court Hotel page 658
All year 2 nights from £99·50
Breakfast, dinner

■ **Winterbourne**
Grange Hotel at Northwoods page 659
All year 2 nights from £59
Breakfast, dinner

■ **Wishaw**
Belfry Hotel page 659
Nov–Mar 2 nights from £95
Breakfast, dinner

■ **Witherslack**
Old Vicarage Hotel page 660
All year. Any 2 nights from £83
Breakfast, dinner

■ **Wiveliscombe**
Langley House Hotel page 660
All year. Any 2 nights from £80
Breakfast, dinner

■ **Woburn**
Bedford Arms Hotel page 660
All year 2 nights from £74
Breakfast, dinner

■ **Woodbridge**
Seckford Hall page 661
All year. Any 2 nights from £80
Breakfast, £15 towards dinner

■ **Woodford Green**
Woodford Moat House page 661
All year 2 nights from £57
Breakfast, dinner

■ **Woodhall Spa**
Golf Hotel page 661
All year. Any 2 nights from £60
Breakfast, dinner

■ **Woodstock**
Bear Hotel page 662
All year. Any 2 nights from £107
Breakfast, £13·50 towards dinner

■ **Woodstock**
Feathers Hotel page 662
Nov–Mar. Any 2 nights from £85
Breakfast, dinner

■ **Woody Bay**
Woody Bay Hotel page 663
All year. Any 2 nights from £52
Breakfast, dinner

■ **Wooler**
Ryecroft Hotel page 663
All year. Any 2 nights from £55
Breakfast, dinner

■ **Wooler**
Tankerville Arms Hotel page 663
Nov–June & Sept–Nov
Any 2 nights from £45
Breakfast, dinner

■ **Worcester**
Giffard Hotel page 663
Nov & Mar 2 nights from £66
Dec–Feb 2 nights from £60
Breakfast, dinner

■ **Worthing**
Beach Hotel page 664
Nov–Apr 2 nights from £55
Breakfast, dinner

■ **Worthing**
Chatsworth Hotel page 664
All year 2 nights from £55
Breakfast, dinner

■ **Worthing**
Eardley Hotel page 664
All year 2 nights from £50
Breakfast, dinner

■ **York**
Abbots Mews Hotel page 667
All year. Any 2 nights from £64
Breakfast, dinner

■ **York**
Hill Hotel page 667
Nov–Mar. Any 2 nights from £53
Apr–Nov. Any 2 nights from £59
Breakfast, dinner

■ **York**
Ladbroke Abbey Park Hotel page 670
Nov–Mar 2 nights from £50
Apr–Nov 2 nights from about £55
Breakfast, £10 towards dinner

■ **York**
Middlethorpe Hall page 670
Nov–Mar 2 nights from £120
Breakfast, dinner

■ **York**
Post House Hotel   page 671
Nov & Mar. Any 2 nights from £66
Dec–Feb. Any 2 nights from £62
Breakfast, dinner

■ **York**
Swallow Chase Hotel   page 671
All year 2 nights from £72
Breakfast, dinner & 1 lunch

■ **York**
Viking Hotel   page 671
All year. Any 2 nights from £72
Breakfast, £9 towards dinner

■ **Yoxford**
Satis House   page 671
All year. Any 2 nights from £55·50
Breakfast, £9·50 towards dinner

SCOTLAND

■ **Aberdeen Airport**
Holiday Inn   page 675
All year. Any 2 nights from £50
Breakfast

■ **Aberdeen Airport**
Skean Dhu Hotel   page 676
All year. Any 2 nights from £63
No meals

■ **Aberdeen Airport**
Skean Dhu Hotel Dyce   page 676
All year 2 nights from £29
No meals

■ **Achiltibuie**
Summer Isles Hotel   page 676
1 Apr–13 May. Any 2 nights from £48
Breakfast

■ **Anstruther**
Craw's Nest Hotel   page 678
All year. Any 2 nights from £60
Breakfast, dinner

■ **Auchterarder**
Auchterarder House   page 679
Nov–30 Apr 2 nights from £65
Breakfast

■ **Auchterarder**
Gleneagles Hotel   page 680
Nov–30 Apr. Any 2 nights from £125
Breakfast, dinner

■ **Auchterhouse**
Old Mansion House Hotel   page 680
All year. Any 2 nights from £55
Breakfast

■ **Aviemore**
Post House Hotel   page 680
Nov–Dec 2 nights from £58
Jan–Mar 2 nights from £60
Breakfast, dinner

■ **Aviemore**
Stakis Coylumbridge Resort Hotel   page 681
All year. Any 2 nights from £62
Breakfast, dinner

■ **Aviemore**
Stakis Four Seasons Hotel   page 681
All year. Any 2 nights from £60
Breakfast, dinner

■ **Ayr**
Caledonian Hotel   page 681
Nov–Apr. Any 2 nights from £52
May–Nov. Any 2 nights from £68
Breakfast, dinner

■ **Ballachulish**
Ballachulish Hotel   page 682
All year. Any 2 nights from £49·50
Breakfast, dinner

■ **Banchory**
Raemoir House Hotel   page 683
All year. Any 2 nights from £70
Breakfast, lunch & dinner

■ **Beattock**
Auchen Castle Hotel   page 683
All year. Any 2 nights from £50
Continental breakfast, dinner

■ **Bonnyrigg**
Dalhousie Castle   page 683
Nov–Mar. Any 2 nights from £82
Breakfast, dinner

■ **Bridge of Allan**
Royal Hotel   page 684
All year 2 nights £53·95
Breakfast, dinner

■ **Cleish**
Nivingston House   page 685
Nov–30 Apr. Any 2 nights from £65
May–31 Oct. Any 2 nights from £80
Breakfast, dinner

■ **Dirleton**
Open Arms Hotel   page 687
All year. Any 2 nights from £45
Breakfast, dinner

■ **Dryburgh**
Dryburgh Abbey Hotel   page 687
Nov–May. Any 2 nights from £65
Breakfast, dinner & 1 lunch

■ **Drymen**
Buchanan Arms Hotel   page 688
Nov–Mar 2 nights from £54
Breakfast, dinner

■ **Dundee**
Angus Thistle Hotel   page 689
All year. Any 2 nights from £40
Breakfast, £10 towards meals

■ **Dunfermline**
King Malcolm Thistle Hotel   page 689
All year 2 nights from £42
Breakfast

■ **East Kilbride**
Stuart Hotel   page 690
All year. Any 2 nights from £36
Breakfast

■ **Edinburgh**
Albany Hotel   page 690
Nov–May. Any 2 nights from £50
Breakfast, £8·50 towards dinner

■ **Edinburgh**
Barnton Thistle Hotel   page 691
Jun–Aug. Any 2 nights from £50
Breakfast

■ **Edinburgh**
Braid Hills Hotel   page 691
All year. Any 2 nights from £60
Breakfast, dinner

■ **Edinburgh**
Bruntsfield Hotel   page 691
All year. Any 2 nights from £56
Breakfast, dinner

■ **Edinburgh**
Caledonian Hotel   page 695
Nov–31 Mar 2 nights from £65
Apr–Nov 2 nights from £82
Breakfast

■ **Edinburgh**
Ellersley House Hotel   page 696
All year. Any 2 nights from £72
Breakfast, £6·95 towards dinner

■ **Edinburgh**
George Hotel   page 697
All year 2 nights from £65
Continental breakfast

■ **Edinburgh**
Howard Hotel   page 697
Nov–Mar 2 nights from £77
Breakfast, dinner

■ **Edinburgh**
King James Thistle Hotel   page 697
Nov–30 Apr 2 nights from £66
May–30 Sept 2 nights from £85
Breakfast, dinner

■ **Edinburgh**
Ladbroke Dragonara Hotel   page 698
Nov–Apr 2 nights from £52
Breakfast

■ **Edinburgh**
Post House Hotel   page 698
Nov & Mar. Any 2 nights from £62
Dec–Feb. Any 2 nights from £58
Breakfast, dinner

■ **Edinburgh**
Royal Scot Hotel   page 699
Nov–Mar 2 nights from £70
Breakfast, dinner

■ **Ellon**
Ladbroke Mercury Hotel   page 699
All year. Any 2 nights from £46
Breakfast, £10 towards meals

■ **Erskine**
Crest Hotel   page 700
Nov–Mar. Any 2 nights from £37
Breakfast, dinner

■ **Forfar**
Royal Hotel   page 702
All year 2 nights from £55
Breakfast, dinner

■ **Inchbae**
Inchbae Lodge Hotel   page 703
All year. Any 2 nights from £55
Breakfast, dinner

■ **Gatehouse of Fleet**
Murray Arms   page 703
All year. Any 2 nights from £64
Breakfast, dinner

■ **Giffnock**
Macdonald Thistle Hotel   page 703
All year 2 nights from £44
Breakfast

■ **Glasgow**
Albany Hotel   page 707
Nov–27 Mar 2 nights from £54
Breakfast, dinner

■ **Glasgow**
Central Hotel   page 707
All year 2 nights from £47
Breakfast, dinner

BARGAIN BREAKS

■ **Glasgow**
Copthorne   page 708
All year 2 nights £42
Breakfast

■ **Glasgow**
Holiday Inn   page 708
Nov–Apr 2 nights from £76
Breakfast

■ **Glasgow**
Hospitality Inn   page 709
All year 2 nights from £32
No meals

■ **Glasgow**
Stakis Grosvenor Hotel   page 710
Nov–Mar. Any 2 nights from £64
Apr–Nov. Any 2 nights from £74
Breakfast, dinner

■ **Glasgow**
Stakis Pond Hotel   page 710
All year. Any 2 nights from £64
Breakfast, dinner

■ **Glasgow**
Swallow Hotel   page 710
All year 2 nights from £60
Breakfast, dinner & 1 lunch

■ **Glasgow Airport**
Excelsior Hotel   page 711
Nov–27 Mar 2 nights from £54
Breakfast, dinner

■ **Glasgow Airport**
Stakis Normandy Hotel   page 711
All year. Any 2 nights from £48
Breakfast, £8 towards dinner

■ **Glenrothes**
Balgeddie House Hotel   page 711
All year 2 nights from £49·50
Breakfast, dinner

■ **Hawick**
Kirklands Hotel   page 712
All year 2 nights from £48
Breakfast, dinner

■ **Humbie**
Johnstounburn House Hotel   page 714
Nov–Apr 2 nights from £100
Breakfast, dinner

■ **Inverness**
Kingsmills Hotel   page 715
All year 2 nights from £75
Breakfast, dinner & 1 lunch

■ **Inverness**
Station Hotel   page 715
Nov–13 Apr. Any 2 nights from £66
Breakfast, dinner

■ **Kenmore**
Kenmore Hotel   page 717
All year. Any 2 nights from £78
Breakfast, dinner

■ **Kildrummy**
Kildrummy Castle Hotel   page 719
Nov–21 Dec & 14 Mar–21 May. Any 2 nights
from £72
Breakfast, dinner

■ **Kilwinning**
Montgreenan Mansion House   page 719
All year 2 nights from £65
Breakfast, dinner

■ **Kinclaven by Stanley**
Ballathie House   page 720
Nov–Jun & Oct–Nov. Any 2 nights from £69
Breakfast, dinner

■ **Kinlochbervie**
Kinlochbervie Hotel   page 720
All year. Any 2 nights from £84
Breakfast, dinner

■ **Lanark**
Cartland Bridge Hotel   page 722
All year 2 nights from £65
Breakfast, dinner, 1 lunch

■ **Langbank**
Gleddoch House Hotel   page 722
All year 2 nights from £88
Breakfast, dinner

■ **Lochgair**
Lochgair Hotel   page 723
Nov–31 Mar. Any 2 nights from £24   Breakfast

■ **Lundin Links**
Old Manor Hotel   page 723
Nov–Apr 2 nights from £116·20
Breakfast, dinner

■ **Milngavie**
Black Bull Thistle Hotel   page 723
All year 2 nights from £42
Continental breakfast, £6·50 towards lunch,
£11·50 towards dinner

■ **Moffat**
Ladbroke Mercury Hotel   page 724
All year. Any 2 nights from £66
Breakfast, dinner

■ **Newburgh**
Udny Arms Hotel   page 725
All year 2 nights from £75
Breakfast, lunch & dinner

■ **Newton Stewart**
Bruce Hotel   page 725
Nov–May. Any 2 nights from £56
Breakfast, dinner

■ **Newton Stewart**
Creebridge House Hotel page 725
All year. Any 2 nights from £64
Breakfast, dinner

■ **Old Meldrum**
Meldrum House Hotel page 727
Mid Mar–Nov 2 nights from £82·35
Breakfast, dinner & 1 lunch

■ **Peebles**
Park Hotel page 728
Nov–Mar. Any 2 nights from £62
Apr–Nov. Any 2 nights from £69·50
Breakfast, dinner & 1 lunch

■ **Peebles**
Tontine Hotel page 729
Nov–29 Mar 2 nights from £50
Breakfast, dinner

■ **Perth**
Royal George Hotel page 729
Nov–27 Mar 2 nights from £58 (Mar £66)
Breakfast, dinner

■ **Perth**
Stakis City Mills Hotel page 729
All year. Any 2 nights from £50
Breakfast, dinner

■ **Perth**
Station Hotel page 729
All year 2 nights from £47
Breakfast, dinner

■ **Pitcaple**
Pittodrie House Hotel page 729
Nov–1 May. Any 2 nights from £70
Breakfast, dinner

■ **Pitlochry**
Atholl Palace Hotel page 730
Nov–29 Mar 2 nights from £54
Breakfast, dinner

■ **Pitlochry**
Green Park Hotel page 730
29 Mar–10 May. Any 2 nights from £50
Breakfast

■ **Portpatrick**
Knockinaam Lodge Hotel page 731
Nov–23 Dec. Any 2 nights from £90
Breakfast, dinner

■ **Portsonachan**
Portsonachan Hotel page 731
Nov, Mar, Apr & Oct. Any 2 nights from £45
Breakfast, dinner

■ **Prestwick**
Carlton Hotel page 732
All year 2 nights from £45
Breakfast, dinner

■ **St. Andrews**
Old Course Hotel page 732
Nov–Apr. Any 2 nights from £89·50
Breakfast, dinner

■ **St. Andrews**
Rufflets Hotel page 732
Nov–Apr 2 nights from £69
Breakfast, dinner

■ **St. Andrews**
Rusacks Marine Hotel page 733
Dec–Feb 2 nights from £48
Nov & Mar 2 nights from £52
Breakfast, dinner

■ **Sleat**
Kinloch Lodge page 735
Nov–30 Apr. Any 2 nights from £80
Breakfast, dinner

■ **South Queensferry**
Forth Bridges Moat House page 735
All year 2 nights from £62
Breakfast & 1 dinner

■ **Stornoway**
Caberfeidh Hotel page 736
All year. Any 2 nights from £80
Breakfast, £13·50 towards dinner

■ **Strachur**
Creggans Inn page 736
Nov–Mar. Any 2 nights from £76
Breakfast, £15 towards dinner

■ **Stranraer**
North West Castle Hotel page 736
Nov–Jun 2 nights from £64
Jul–Nov 2 nights from £68
Breakfast, dinner & 1 lunch

■ **Troon**
Marine Hotel page 738
All year. Any 2 nights from £60
Breakfast, dinner

■ **Troon**
Piersland House Hotel page 738
Nov–Apr 2 nights from £44·50
Breakfast, dinner

■ **Troon**
Sun Court Hotel page 738
All year 2 nights from £74
Breakfast, lunch & dinner

■ **Tweedsmuir**
Crook Inn page 739
Dec–Jan. Any 2 nights from £40
Breakfast

■ **Ullapool**
Ceilidh Place page 740
Nov–mid Mar. Any 2 nights from £50
Breakfast, dinner

WALES

■ **Aberdovey**
Hotel Plas Penhelig   page 744
Feb–Nov. Any 2 nights from £52·25
Breakfast, dinner

■ **Aberdovey**
Trefeddian Hotel   page 744
Nov–18 Dec. Any 2 nights from £56
19 Mar–31 Oct. Any 2 nights from £68
Breakfast, dinner

■ **Abersoch**
Riverside Hotel   page 745
All year. Any 2 nights from £70
Breakfast, dinner

■ **Barry**
Mount Sorrel Hotel   page 745
All year 2 nights from £48
Breakfast, dinner

■ **Beddgelert**
Royal Goat Hotel   page 746
Nov–Apr. Any 2 nights from £60
Breakfast, dinner

■ **Brechfa**
Tŷ Mawr Country House Hotel   page 746
All year. Any 2 nights from £55
Breakfast, dinner

■ **Cardiff**
Crest Hotel   page 747
All year 2 nights from £66
Breakfast, dinner

■ **Cardiff**
Holiday Inn   page 747
All year 2 nights from £50
Breakfast

■ **Cardiff**
Park Hotel   page 747
All year 2 nights from £56
Breakfast, dinner

■ **Cardiff**
Post House Hotel   page 750
Nov–27 Mar 2 nights from £60
Breakfast, dinner

■ **Cardiff**
Stakis Inn on the Avenue   page 750
All year. Any 2 nights from £56
Breakfast, dinner

■ **Carmarthen**
Ivy Bush Royal   page 750
Nov–27 Mar 2 nights from £54
Breakfast, dinner

■ **Chepstow**
Castle View Hotel   page 751
Nov–22 May. Any 2 nights from £52
23 May–10 Oct. Any 2 nights from £60
Breakfast, dinner

■ **Chepstow**
St. Pierre Hotel   page 751
All year 2 nights from £74
Breakfast, dinner

■ **Colwyn Bay**
Hotel Seventy Degrees   page 751
All year. Any 2 nights from £75
Breakfast, dinner

■ **Conwy**
Sychnant Pass Hotel   page 751
All year. Any 2 nights from £59
Breakfast, dinner

■ **Coychurch**
Coed-y-Mwstwr Hotel   page 752
All year 2 nights from £70
Continental breakfast, dinner

■ **Criccieth**
Bron Eifion Hotel   page 752
Nov–29 Mar 2 nights from £56
Breakfast, dinner

■ **Eglnysfach**
Ynyshir Hall Hotel   page 752
Mar & Apr. Any 2 nights £56
Breakfast, dinner

■ **Fishguard**
Fishguard Bay Hotel   page 753
Nov–30 Apr. Any 2 nights from £48
Breakfast, dinner

■ **Lake Vyrnwy**
Lake Vyrnwy Hotel   page 753
All year. Any 2 nights from £59·50
Breakfast, packed lunch, dinner

■ **Lamphey**
Court Hotel   page 754
All year. Any 2 nights from £49
Breakfast, dinner

■ **Llanarmon Dyffryn Ceiriog**
Hand Hotel   page 754
Nov–Mar. Any 2 nights from £70
Apr–Nov. Any 2 nights from £75
Breakfast, dinner

■ **Llandeilo**
Cawdor Arms Hotel   page 754
All year 2 nights from £65
Breakfast, lunch & dinner

■ Llandudno
Bodysgallen Hall page 755
Nov–31 Mar. Any 2 nights from £99
Breakfast, dinner

■ Llandudno
Empire Hotel page 755
All year. Any 2 nights from £58
Breakfast, dinner

■ Llandudno
St. George's Hotel page 755
All year. Any 2 nights from £62
Breakfast, dinner

■ Llanelli
Stradey Park Hotel page 756
Nov–29 Mar 2 nights from £46
Breakfast, dinner

■ Llangollen
Royal Hotel page 756
Nov & Mar. Any 2 nights from £64
Dec–Feb. Any 2 nights from £56
Breakfast, dinner

■ Llanrwst
Meadowsweet Hotel page 757
All year 2 nights from £62
Breakfast, dinner

■ Machynlleth
Wynnstay Hotel page 758
Nov & Feb. Any 2 nights from £56
Dec–Feb. Any 2 nights from £52
Breakfast, dinner

■ Monmouth
King's Head Hotel page 758
All year 2 nights from £70
Breakfast, dinner

■ Penmaenpool
George III Hotel page 760
Nov–30 Apr. Any 2 nights from £50
Breakfast, dinner

■ Presteigne
Radnorshire Arms Hotel page 760
Nov & Mar. Any 2 nights from £62
Dec–Feb. Any 2 nights from £56
Breakfast, dinner

■ Ruthin
Castle Hotel & Myddleton Arms page 760
All year 2 nights from £49·50
Breakfast, dinner & 1 lunch

■ Ruthin
Ruthin Castle page 760
All year. Any 2 nights from £59
Breakfast, dinner

■ St. David's
St. Non's Hotel page 761
All year. Any 2 nights from £47·50
Breakfast, dinner

■ St. David's
Warpool Court Hotel page 761
Nov–23 Dec, 12 Feb–12 May & 25 Sep–Nov
Any 2 nights from £60
Breakfast, dinner

■ Swansea
Dragon Hotel page 761
Nov–29 Mar. Any 2 nights from £54
Breakfast, dinner

■ Swansea
Ladbroke Hotel page 761
All year 2 nights from £51
Breakfast

■ Talsarnau
Maes-y-Neuadd Hotel page 762
Nov–23 Apr & 9 Oct–Nov. Any 2 nights from £70
Breakfast, dinner

■ Tintern Abbey
Beaufort Hotel page 762
All year 2 nights from £62
Breakfast, dinner

■ Wolf's Castle
Wolfscastle Country Hotel page 763
Nov–30 Jun 2 nights from £47·50
Breakfast, £9 towards dinner

CHANNEL ISLANDS

■ Guernsey, St Peter Port
Old Government House Hotel page 767
Nov–31 Mar. Any 2 nights from £119 (incl. flight)
Breakfast, dinner

■ Jersey, St Aubin
La Haule Manor page 770
Nov–Mar. Any 2 nights from £44·50
Breakfast, dinner

■ **Jersey, St Brelade**
La Place Hotel page 770
Nov–Mar. Any 2 nights £48
Breakfast, dinner

■ **Jersey, St Lawrence**
Little Grove Hotel page 773
Nov–31 Mar. Any 2 nights from £85
Breakfast, dinner

■ **Jersey, St Helier**
Beaufort Hotel page 772
Nov–Mar. Any 2 nights from £54
Breakfast, dinner

■ **Jersey, St Saviour**
Longueville Manor Hotel page 774
Nov–1 Apr 2 nights from £78
Breakfast, dinner

■ **Jersey, St Helier**
Pomme d'Or Hotel page 773
Nov–Mar. Any 2 nights from £30
Breakfast

ISLE OF MAN

■ **Douglas**
Sefton Hotel page 775
Nov–24 Apr 2 nights £46
Breakfast, dinner

NORTHERN IRELAND

■ **Crawfordsburn**
Old Inn page 779
All year. Any 2 nights from £49
Breakfast

■ **Newtownards**
Strangford Arms Hotel page 783
All year 2 nights from £27
No meals

■ **Dunmurry**
Conway Hotel page 779
Xmas, Feb–June & Sept–Nov
Any 2 nights from £54
Breakfast, dinner

■ **Portballintrae**
Bayview Hotel page 783
All year. Any 2 nights from £52·50
Breakfast, lunch & high tea

■ **Holywood**
Culloden Hotel page 782
All year 2 nights £65
Breakfast

REPUBLIC OF IRELAND

■ **Ballynahinch**
Ballynahinch Castle page 787
Nov–Mar 2 nights from £36
Breakfast, £15 towards meals

■ **Cashel**
Cashel Palace Hotel page 791
Nov–Apr. Any 2 nights from £72
Breakfast, 1 dinner

■ **Cashel**
Cashel House Hotel page 791
Mar–Oct. Any 2 nights from £101
Breakfast, dinner

■ **Clonmel**
Clonmel Arms Hotel page 794
All year 2 nights from £30
Breakfast

BARGAIN BREAKS

■ **Cork**
Arbutus Lodge Hotel   page 795
All year 2 nights from £75
Breakfast, dinner

■ **Cork**
Jurys Hotel   page 798
All year 2 nights from £52·90
Breakfast

■ **Cork**
Silver Springs Hotel   page 798
All year 2 nights from £61
Breakfast, 1 dinner

■ **Dromahair**
Drumlease Glebe House   page 799
4 Apr–1 Jun. Any 2 nights from £85
Breakfast, dinner

■ **Dublin**
Blooms Hotel   page 802
All year 2 nights from £50
Breakfast

■ **Ennis**
Old Ground Hotel   page 808
All year. Any 2 nights from £59
Breakfast, dinner

■ **Glen of Aherlow**
Aherlow House Hotel   page 809
All year. Any 2 nights from £40
Breakfast

■ **Kilcoran**
Kilcoran Lodge Hotel   page 811
Nov–Dec & Feb–Nov. Any 2 nights from £66
Breakfast, dinner

■ **Killarney**
Aghadoe Heights Hotel   page 811
All year 2 nights from £56
Breakfast, dinner

■ **Kinsale**
Actons Hotel   page 813
Nov–1 Jun & 4 Oct–Nov. Any 2 nights from £75
Breakfast, dinner

■ **Letterfrack**
Rosleague Manor House   page 814
Apr–Jun & Sept–Oct. Any 2 nights from £80
Breakfast, dinner

■ **Oughterard**
Connemara Gateway Hotel   page 818
Feb–Oct 2 nights from £45
Breakfast, dinner

■ **Rathnew**
Tinakilly House Hotel   page 820
Nov–23 Dec, Feb–Jun & Oct. Any 2 nights from
£90
Breakfast, dinner

■ **Waterford**
Granville Hotel   page 824
All year 2 nights from £40·50
Breakfast

■ **Wicklow**
Old Rectory   page 825
Apr–30 Jun & 1 Sept–3 Oct. Any 2 nights £79
Jul–31 Aug. Any 2 nights £84
Breakfast, dinner

A LOT FOR LESS

LONDON RESTAURANTS
UNDER £30 FOR TWO

Two courses, half a carafe of wine, coffee, service, VAT – at time of going to press. Reasonable quality of food, although not always up to our usual restaurant standards. Restaurants with comparable prices in the main London section are listed separately at the end (note that prices there include three courses and a full bottle of wine).

Ajanta

Map 21 A4
12 Goldhawk Road W12
01-743 5191
Credit Access, Amex, Visa
This popular tandoori restaurant is, like many of its enthusiastic customers, expanding thanks to the success of richly-flavoured dishes like murghi massallam, prawn biryani and curries that range from the mild Malaya to the fiery Bangalore phal.
■ *L 12–2.30*   *D 6–11.30*
About £22 for two   *Parking Difficult*
Closed 24–26 Dec

Andreas

Map 27 A2
15 Frith Street W1
01-437 3911
Credit Access, Amex, Diners, Visa
An unpretentious Soho restaurant that specialises in simple, well-cooked Greek dishes. Piping-hot pitta bread is served with various dips and main courses range from spicy meatballs to kebabs and moussaka. There's also an extensive international menu. ✆
■ *L 12–3*   *D 5.30–11,*
About £23 for two   *Sat 5.30–11.30*
Closed L Sat, all Sun   *Parking Difficult*
& Bank Hols

Anemos

Map 24 B2
32 Charlotte Street W1
01-636 2289
Credit Access, Amex, Diners, Visa
Sit outside on summer days at this lively Greek restaurant, where new owners have made few changes. Authentic Aegean dishes like souvlakia, moussaka and afelia are confidently seasoned, carefully cooked and served in a friendly, convivial atmosphere. Book for dinner.
■ *Meals noon–1am*
About £28 for two   *Parking Difficult*
Closed Sun, Bank Hols, 1 Jan & 3 days Xmas

Ark

♨ **Map 22 A2**
122 Palace Gardens Terrace W8
01-229 4024
Credit Access, Amex, Visa
Be sure to book at this popular little pine-walled restaurant. The food is unpretentious and enjoyable, with dishes like ratatouille, coq au vin and steak and kidney pie. Good profiteroles.
■ *L 12–3*   *D 6.30–11.15*
About £25 for two   *Parking Limited*
Closed L Sun, all Bank Hols, 4 days Easter & 4 days Xmas

Aspava

Map 25 A4
18 Shepherd Street W1
01-491 8739
Just 20 seats at this busy Turkish restaurant in Shepherd Market. The house speciality is mixed meze (hot and cold hors d'oeuvre), and main courses span a good range of casseroles and grills served with rice and vegetables.
■ *Meals noon–midnight*   *Parking Ample*
About £23 for two   *Closed 25 Dec*

Le Bistroquet

Map 20 C3
273 Camden High Street NW1
01-485 9607
Credit Access, Amex, Visa
Best bet for budget eaters is the bar menu at this popular French restaurant. Smoked Toulouse sausage with flageolet beans is a popular choice, as is poached cod provençale. For an inexpensive snack, try a salami baguette. ✆
■ *L 12–3*   *D 7–11.30*
About £24 for two   *Parking Limited*
Closed 3 days Xmas

Blue Posts, Olde English Carving Room

Map 25 B4
6 Bennet Street SW1
01-493 3350
Credit Access, Amex, Visa
Good English cooking at affordable prices makes this carvery above a pub a popular choice with tourists and local businessmen alike. Chicken liver pâté makes a fine starter, roasts are cooked to succulent perfection and puds include a tasty apple pie. ✆
■ *L 12–2.30*   *D 6–9*
About £26 for two   *Parking Difficult*
Closed Sat, Sun & Bank Hols

Bon Ton Roulet

♀ **Map 21 D6**
127 Dulwich Road SE24
01-733 8701
　　Simple, wholesome food is skilfully prepared in this cheerful, friendly restaurant. A short but well-balanced menu embraces such dishes as beef olives, casserole of hare, kidneys turbigo and nut roast. Fresh fish dishes are listed on the blackboard. ⊖
■ *D only 7–10.30* 　　　*Parking* Ample
About £18 for two 　　*Closed* Sun, Bank Hols
exc. 1 May, 2 wks Aug & 2 wks Xmas

La Bouffe

Map 21 C6
13 Battersea Rise SW11
01-228 3384
Credit Access, Visa
　　Seats for 44 at this agreeably relaxed restaurant where the short set menus start at £6·95. Typical dishes run from boudin noir with apples and lentil soup with lardons to salmon with chives and blanquette of pork. Simple sweets like crème caramel. ⊖
■ *L 12–2.30,* 　　　　*D 7.30–11*
Sun 12.30–3.30 　　*Parking* Ample
About £25 for two 　　*Closed* L Sat, D Sun &
1 wk Xmas

Buzkash

Map 21 A6
4 Chelverton Road SW15
01-788 0599
Credit Access, Amex, Diners, Visa
　　Buzkash is a stylish, immaculately-run restaurant serving Afghan food in authentic surroundings. The informative menu introduces starters like meat soup with pomegranate juice and main courses such as barbecued lamb, baked aubergines and king prawns cooked in a clay oven. Excellent basmati rice.
■ *L 12–3* 　　　　　*D 6–11, Fri & Sat*
About £28 for two 　　*6–11.30*
Closed Sun & 25/26 Dec 　*Parking* Ample

Café Pacifico

Map 27 B2
5 Langley Street WC2
01-379 7728
Credit Access, Visa
　　Despite its size (there is seating for 132), tables are often at a premium at this popular Mexican restaurant. There's no booking so queues are commonplace. Customers clamour for guacamole, ceviche, chilli, tacos, enchiladas and creamy lemon pie.
■ *Meals 11.30am–11.45pm, Sun noon–10.45pm*
About £21 for two 　　*Parking* Difficult
Closed Bank Hols exc. Good Fri

Caffé Mamma

Map 7 A5
24 Hill Street, Richmond
01-940 1625
Credit Access, Amex, Visa
　　Pasta is the main attraction at this atmospheric Italian restaurant. Keep it simple with spaghetti aglio e olio, or try the more elaborate conchiglie with aubergines, mozzarella and tomato sauce. Also super salads, starters and sweets.
■ *Meals noon–midnight* 　*Parking* Limited
About £20 for two 　　*Closed* 25 & 26 Dec

Campanella

& **Map 22 A2**
145 Notting Hill Gate W11
01-229 9882
Credit Access, Amex, Diners, Visa
　　Focal point of this rustic Italian restaurant is the antipasto table, where stuffed aubergines and marinated peppers are part of a colourful display. The extensive menu also offers pasta, fish (including swordfish when available) and Italian favourites like scaloppine and bistecca al Barolo. ⊖
■ *L 12–3* 　　　　　*D 6–11.30*
About £30 for two 　　*Parking* Limited
Closed L Sat, all Sun & Bank Hols

Caribbean Sunkissed Restaurant

Map 20 B3
49 Chippenham Road W9
01-286 3741
Credit Access, Amex, Visa
　　West Indian delights like pumpkin soup, escovitch, ackee and saltfish star alongside more familiar dishes (beef and vegetable stew, crab cocktail) at this relaxed restaurant. Order vegetables and have the fun of encountering yam, dasheen, green bananas and breadfruit purée.
■ *L 12–3* 　　　　　*D 6–12*
About £25 for two 　　*Parking* Limited
Closed Sun & Bank Hols

Charing Cross Hotel, Betjeman Restaurant

Map 25 C4
Strand WC2
01-839 7282
Credit Access, Amex, Diners, Visa
　　Housed in a high-ceilinged room, this imposing restaurant serves hearty English roasts, both hot and cold, plus a dish of the day such as steak and kidney pie. Nice starters and sweets complete the bill of fare. ⊖
■ *L 12–3* 　　　　　*D 5.30–10.30, Sun 6–10*
About £25 for two 　　*Parking* Difficult
Closed 25 & 26 Dec

Chiang Mai

Map 27 A2
48 Frith Street W1
01-437 7444
Credit Access, Amex, Visa
Dependable cooking over a wide range of Thai dishes. Satay sticks, spring rolls, quick-fried beef with coriander, steamed crab claws and tempura show the variety, and many dishes make good use of fresh herbs and spices.
- *L 12–3*   *D 6–11.30*
About £30 for two   *Parking Difficult*
Closed Sun, 2 days Xmas & 2 days Easter

La Cloche

Map 20 B3
304 Kilburn High Road NW6
01-328 0302
Credit Access, Visa
A friendly bistro-style restaurant where it's best to book for dinner. Starters (all at £1·65) include deep-fried Gouda and crab profiteroles; main courses (all at £3·85) span duck en croûte, marinated lamb steak, vegetable pancakes and the day's fish choice. ✆
- *L 12–3*   *D 7–12*
About £22 for two   *Parking Ample*
Closed 25 & 26 Dec

Cranks

Map 24 B3
8 Marshall Street W1
01-437 9431
Credit Access, Amex, Diners, Visa
The daytime buffet at this famous health-food restaurant is now supplemented six nights a week by candlelit suppers. After-dark delights might include crudités with houmous and garlic mayonnaise, and mushroom stroganoff with brown rice and steamed vegetables.
- *Meals 8am–7pm*   *Dine & Wine 6.30–11pm*
About £12 for two (buffet) or £22 (Dine & Wine)
Parking Limited
Closed Sun, Easter, Xmas & Bank Hols

Criterion Brasserie

Map 24 B3
222 Piccadilly W1
01-839 7133
Credit Access, Amex, Diners, Visa
The prices at this marble-walled brasserie put it just above our limit, but there's no minimum charge. Portions are generous, and typical dishes include garlic snails, rillettes, choucroute, omelettes and pan-fried veal with lime.
- *L 12–3,*   *D 6–11*
Sat 12.30–2.30   *Parking Difficult*
About £32 for two   *Closed Sun & Bank Hols*

Da Gianbruno

Map 21 A5
6 Hammersmith Broadway W6
01-748 9393
Credit Access, Amex, Diners, Visa
Pick pasta and enjoy an economical feast at this cheerful Italian restaurant. Spaghetti with seafood sauce is perennially popular; other options include excellent veal scaloppine with aubergine, tomato sauce and mozzarella.
- *L 12–3*   *D 6–11.30*
About £26 for two   *Parking Difficult*
Closed 25 & 26 Dec

Daquise

Map 23 C4
20 Thurloe Street SW7
01-589 6117
Credit Visa
Robust Polish and Russian dishes are served seven days a week at this durable restaurant hard by South Kensington Station. Tasty soups, stuffed cabbage, minced veal, meatballs and beef casserole typify the hearty choice, and there's some good pâtisserie.
- *Meals 10am–11.30pm Parking Difficult*
About £20 for two   *Closed 25 & 26 Dec*

Dining Room

Map 26 C3
Winchester Walk SE1
01-407 0337
The vegetable market area behind Southwark Cathedral is an appropriate location for this vegetarian restaurant. Excellent organically-grown produce is used to imaginative effect in dishes like parsnip fritters with sesame and chilli sauce or baked mushrooms with carrots, chervil and cheese. Healthy puddings.
- *L 12.30–2.30*   *D 7–10*
About £22 for two   *Parking Limited*
Closed Sat, Sun, Mon, Bank Hols & 2 wks Aug

Diwana Bhel-Poori House

Map 20 C3
121 Drummond Street NW1
01-387 5556
Credit Access, Diners, Visa
No bookings, so you might have a short wait at this popular Indian vegetarian restaurant. The food is excellent and the prices very kind throughout the range of pooris, samosas, dosas and idli sambar – rice cakes in a splendid savoury sauce. Bring your own wine.
- *Meals noon–midnight Parking Ample*
About £15 for two   *Closed 25 Dec*

Diwana Bhel-Poori House

Map 22 A1
50 Westbourne Grove W2
01-221 0721
Credit Access, Diners, Visa
Whether you are on a budget or a binge, there is plenty on offer at this popular vegetarian restaurant. Try black pea fritters, samosas or bhel-poori for starters, with perhaps a filled dosa to follow. Good-quality raw materials, carefully prepared. Unlicensed; bring your own.
- *L 12–3*   *D 6–10.45*
About £14 for two   *Parking Limited*
Closed Mon & Bank Hols

Ebury Wine Bar

Map 23 D4
139 Ebury Street SW1
01-730 5447
Credit Access, Amex, Diners, Visa
Perennially popular for both enjoyable food and good wines (many by the glass). Dishes range from flavoursome chicken and veal terrine to seafood tart, steaks and spiced lamb. Traditional Sunday lunch.
- *L 12–2.45,*   *D 6–10.30, Sun 6–10*
Sun 12–2.30   *Parking Difficult*
About £25 for two   *Closed 25 & 26 Dec*

Efes Kebab House

♵ **Map 24 B2**
80 Great Titchfield Street W1
01-636 1953
Credit Access, Amex, Visa
The charcoal grill of this busy Turkish restaurant is open to view, so you can watch your kebabs being prepared. They're based on lamb or chicken and come in 20 varieties. Start with assorted hors d'oeuvre and end with a nice syrupy sweet. Book.
- *Meals noon–11.30pm*   *Parking Difficult*
About £24 for two   *Closed Sun, 25 Dec & 1 Jan*

Entrecôte

Map 24 C1
124 Southampton Row WC1
01-405 1466
Credit Access, Amex, Diners, Visa
Dine and dance at this attractive basement restaurant with cosy alcoves and soft lighting: a band plays from 9pm to 1am every day except Sunday. The food is French – lobster bisque, snails, steaks, fish dishes – and smart waiters offer polished service. ℮
- *L 12–2.45*   *D 6–11.45, Sun 6–10.45*
About £26 for two   *Parking Difficult*
Closed L Sat, Sun & Bank Hols, & 4 days Xmas

Equatorial

Map 27 A2
37 Old Compton Street W1
01-437 6112
Credit Access, Amex, Diners, Visa
Chef-patron Henry Tan specialises in the spicy, succulent cooking of Singapore in his agreeable two-room restaurant. Try lamb satay with cubes of rice cake, fish ball soup, chilli crab, or braised pork in soya sauce. The set lunch is very good value.
- *L 12–3*   *D 6–11.30*
About £25 for two   *Parking Ample*
Closed 5 days Xmas

Faulkners

Map 20 D3
424 Kingsland Road E8
01-254 6152
Now licensed, and with the restaurant expanded, a fish and chip meal here is an absolute delight. The huge portions will satisfy the hungriest eaters, and you can be sure of the freshest fish (plenty of variety) and chips that are the real McCoy.
- *L 12–2*   *D 5–10*
Meals Sat 11.30am–10pm
About £20 for two   *Parking Ample*
Closed Sun, Mon & 1 wk Xmas

Foxtrot Oscar

Map 23 C6
79 Royal Hospital Road SW3
01-352 7179
Credit Access, Visa
Little has changed at this fashionable Chelsea establishment: service remains swift and friendly and food continues varied and good. It's best to book as regulars come early and stay late for excellent salads, juicy hamburgers and hearty main dishes like steak and kidney pie. ℮
- *L 12.30–2.30*   *D 7.30–11.30, Sun*
About £22 for two   *7.30–10.30*
Closed Bank Hols   *Parking Limited*

Gavins

Map 21 A6
5 Lacy Road, Putney SW15
01-785 9151
Credit Access, Amex, Visa
The promise of pasta made on the premises entices customers to this bright and cheerful establishment. Fettuccine alla carbonara is a perennial favourite among a traditional selection that also includes spaghetti alle vongole. Simple sweets. ℮
- *L 12.30–3.30*   *D 6.30–11*
About £16 for two   *Parking Difficult*
Closed Bank Hols

Great Nepalese Tandoori

Map 20 C3
48 Eversholt Street NW1
01-388 6737
Credit Access, Amex, Diners, Visa
   Good fresh ingredients go into the tasty dishes served in a friendly restaurant specialising in Nepalese cooking. The menu offers a very good spread, from black lentil bread and assorted tandoori dishes to curries based on chicken, lamb, fish, pork, duck or vegetables.
■ *L 12–2.45*   *D 6–11.45*
About £20 for two   *Parking Ample*
Closed 25 & 26 Dec

Green Cottage

Map 20 B3
9 New College Parade, Finchley Road NW3
01-722 5305
   Passers-by unable to resist the sight of meat being barbecued come inside this modest Chinese restaurant to try the Cantonese-style roast duck, barbecued spare ribs or crispy belly pork. Also well-flavoured soups and seafoods. Staff are efficient and helpful.
■ *Meals noon–11.30pm*
About £20 for two   *Parking Difficult*
Closed 25 & 26 Dec

Grill St Quentin

Map 23 C4
136 Brompton Road SW3
01-581 8377
   Main courses in this smart modern restaurant are hearty French specialities like confit de canard plus charcoal grills. Pâtés, salads, nice pâtisserie, excellent French bread. Pleasant service.
■ *L 12–3,*   *D 7–12,*
Sat & Sun 12–4   *Sun 7–11.30*
About £25 for two   *Parking Difficult*

Grosvenor House, Pasta, Vino e Fantasia

   Map 22 D2
Park Lane W1
01-499 6363
Credit Access, Amex, Diners, Visa
   Tagliatelle al pesto is a good choice for budget-conscious diners at this colourful establishment. Home-made spaghetti with garlic butter is equally popular and dishes like saltimbocca and fegato di vitello alla veneziana cater for those willing to spend a little more. ℮
■ *L 12.30–2.30*   *D 7.30–11.30*
About £28 for two   *Parking Difficult*
Closed L Sat, all Sun, 26 Dec & 1 Jan

Gurkhas Tandoori

Map 24 B1
23 Warren Street W1
01-388 1640
Credit Access, Amex, Diners, Visa
   There are few frills at this unpretentious Nepalese restaurant but the food is very good – full of flavour, subtly spiced and including lots of interesting vegetable dishes. Tandoori king prawns and chicken tikka are among the more familiar dishes.
■ *L 12–2.45*   *D 6–11.45*
About £20 for two   *Parking Difficult*
Closed 25 & 26 Dec

Hard Rock Café

Map 22 D3
150 Old Park Lane W1
01-629 0382
   This is one of London's most popular restaurants, and the queues prove it. High-quality hamburgers, king-size sandwiches and super steaks are what the punters come for, along with salads, sundaes, splits and pies, plus the loud and lively atmosphere.
■ *Meals noon–12.15am, Fri & Sat noon–12.45am*
About £20 for two   *Parking Limited*
Closed 3 days Xmas

Harry Morgan's

Map 20 B3
31 St John's Wood High Street NW8
01-722 1869
   Homely Jewish (but not kosher) cooking is the speciality of this long-established restaurant. Try the chicken kreplach, lean salt beef or goulash, and a portion of lockshen pudding or fruit compote to follow.
■ *L Tues–Sat 12–3*   *D 6–10*
Meals Sun noon–10pm   *Parking Limited*
About £20 for two   *Closed D Fri, all Mon,*
10 days Easter & 3 wks Sept

Hung Toa

Map 22 B2
54 Queensway W2
01-727 6017
   A popular restaurant in teeming, cosmopolitan Queensway, serving simple, satisfying Cantonese food from noon onwards. Roast duck and pork are among the best in town, and the one-plate rice and noodle dishes are good, too.
■ *Meals noon–11pm*   *Parking Difficult*
About £20 for two   *Closed 25 & 26 Dec*

Joe Allen

Map 24 D3
13 Exeter Street WC2
01-836 0651
There's a transatlantic flavour to the fare at this popular basement restaurant in a Covent Garden side street. A blackboard lists soups, salads and starters like chopped liver alongside main dishes such as barbecue ribs and chilli con carne. Booking is advised.
■ *Meals noon–1am, Sun noon–midnight*
About £25 for two   *Parking Difficult*
Closed 25 & 26 Dec

Khyber Pass

Map 23 B5
21 Bute Street SW7
01-589 7311
Credit Access, Amex, Diners, Visa
This popular, long-established Indian restaurant is a friendly, relaxing spot for a meal. Tandoori dishes are usually very good, with lamb pasanda and keema also popular. Drink mugs of lager.
■ *L 12–2.30*   *D 6–11.30*
About £25 for two   *Parking Limited*
Closed 25 & 26 Dec

Kitchen Yakitori

Map 24 A3
12 Lancashire Court, New Bond Street W1
01-629 9984
A tiny restaurant with a big reputation, Kitchen Yakitori specialises in eel. Also sashimi, chicken teriyaki, octopus with green mustard, tofu steak and tempura. Lunch is particularly good value – about a dozen set-price dishes with starter, soup, rice, pickle and dessert.
■ *L 12–2.30*   *D 6–9.30*
About £26 for two   *Parking Difficult*
Closed D Sat, all Sun, Bank Hols, 10 days Aug & 24 Dec–3 Jan

Kolossi Grill

Map 20 D3
56 Rosebery Avenue EC1
01-278 5758
Credit Visa
Handy for Sadlers Wells, this is an unpretentious, friendly taverna. Sit at snug tables to sample starters like houmus, taramasalata and grilled Greek cheese. Blackboard specials change daily and might include kleftico, pork kebabs or stuffed vine leaves. Book for lunch. ✆
■ *L 12–3*   *D 6–11*
About £16 for two   *Parking Limited*
Closed L Sat, all Sun & Bank Hols

L. S. Grunts Chicago Pizza Co.

Map 27 B2
12 Maiden Lane WC2
01-379 7722
Credit Access, Visa
It's worth waiting 20 minutes or so for the freshly made deep-dish pizzas that are the speciality of this bustling restaurant. Minced spicy sausage is a favourite topping but the choice also includes peperoni and fresh mushrooms. Help yourself to salad served in a bathtub (one visit only) and finish with chocolate cheesecake.
■ *Meals noon–11.30pm, Sun noon–9pm*
About £19 for two   *Parking Difficult*
Closed 1 Jan, Easter Sun & 25 & 26 Dec

Lantern

✆ **Map 20 B3**
23 Malvern Road NW6
01-624 1796
Credit Visa
Robust cooking and generous portions are a winning combination at this cheerful restaurant. Chef-patron Peter Ilic offers interesting dishes like crab-filled choux buns with hollandaise sauce, and calf's liver with avocado. Service is friendly. Best to book for dinner. ✆
■ *L 12–3*   *D 7–midnight,*
About £22 for two   *Sun 7–11*
Closed 25 & 26 Dec   *Parking Ample*

Laurent

Map 20 B2
428 Finchley Road NW2
01-794 3603
Credit Access, Visa
So many customers ordered couscous that this is now the only main course served at this friendly little restaurant. Three versions are available: one vegetarian, another with lamb and spicy sausage, and a third with the addition of a mixed grill.
■ *L 12–2*   *D 6–11*
About £25 for two   *Parking Ample*
Closed D Sun, all Bank Hols & Aug

Lemonia

Map 20 C3
154 Regent's Park Road NW1
01-586 7454
It's best to book for this popular Greek restaurant in Chalk Farm village, where Tony Evangelou and chef George Ioannou continue to offer tasty dishes like spanakopitta, stifado, squid and an excellent afelia. Also tasty charcoal grills and fish.
■ *D only 6–11.30*
About £20 for two   *Parking Ample*
Closed Sun, Bank Hols, 2 wks Aug & 3 days Xmas

Lindas

♨ **Map 20 B3**
4 Fernhead Road W9
01-969 9387
Credit Access, Diners, Visa
   Authentic Vietnamese dishes are Linda
Blaney's speciality and husband Robin is happy
to guide guests through the menu. Try rice stick
soup, spring rolls, spiced spare ribs or mixed
omelette – or select a set meal. Very good value.
■ *L 12–2.15*   *D 6–10.15*
About £22 for two   **Parking** *Ample*
*Closed L Sat, all Sun, Bank Hols & 2 wks Xmas &
2 wks summer*

Maha Gopal

Map 24 B1
160 New Cavendish Street W1
01-580 5607
Credit Access, Amex, Diners, Visa
   Duck is one of the more unusual offerings from
the tandoor of this traditional Indian restaurant.
The extensive menu also offers curries (including
a vegetarian variety from Kashmir), plus chicken
tikka, biryanis and dansaks. Service is friendly
and helpful.
■ *L 12–3*   *D 6–11.45, Sun 7–11.45*
About £20 for two   **Parking** *Difficult*
Closed L Sun & all Bank Hols

Malabar

Map 22 A2
27 Uxbridge Street W8
01-727 8800
Credit Access, Visa
   Mixed among the familiar tikkas and curries at
this pleasant Indian restaurant you will find a few
more unusual dishes such as venison marinated
in tamarind, pumpkin with herbs and Friday's
special fish curry with mullet, eel, trout or pomfret.
Sunday buffet lunch.
■ *L 12–3*   *D 6.30–11.30,*
About £25 for two   *Sun 6.30–11*
Closed 25 & 26 Dec   **Parking** *Ample*

Manna

Map 20 C3
4 Erskine Road NW3
01-722 8028
   Good value for money is the key to this long-
established vegetarian restaurant. Starters
include avocado and cottage cheese and houmus
with home-made bread. Salads are super and the
blackboard lists casseroles, bakes and flans.
Good puds. Non-smoking area.
■ *D only 6.30–midnight*   **Parking** *Limited*
About £15 for two   *Closed 24–26 Dec*

Mélange

Map 27 B1
59 Endell Street WC2
01-240 8077
Credit Access, Amex, Diners, Visa
   A relaxed atmosphere greets the diner at this
French-style Covent Garden restaurant. The short
menu is full of interest, featuring items such as
spinach parcels with yoghurt and mint or mixed
beans with marinated fish.
■ *L 12–2.30*   *D 6–11.30*
About £30 for two   **Parking** *Limited*
*Closed L Sat, all Sun & Mon, Bank Hols & 2 wks
Xmas*

Mrs Beeton

Map 7 A5
58 Hill Rise, Richmond
01-940 9561
   Mrs Beeton would have approved the system at
this simply decorated restaurant, where local
women take it in turns to cook. Standards are
generally high, and dishes range from soups and
simple starters to main courses like navarin of
lamb. Very good vegetables and irresistible afters.
Bring your own wine.
■ *L 10–5*   *D 6.30–10.30*
About £15 for two   **Parking** *Difficult*
Closed D Sun, Mon & Tues & all 24 Dec–1 Jan

Mother Huff's

♨ **Map 20 B2**
12 Heath Street NW3
01-435 3714
Credit Amex, Visa
   No one goes hungry at Mother Huff's, where
the hearty bill of fare includes soups and pâtés,
meat and fish pies, rack of lamb and duckling with
a choice of fruit sauces. Delicious puds, too.
There's a little terrace for alfresco summer
eating. ☺
■ *L 12–3*   *D 7–11*
About £25 for two   **Parking** *Limited*
Closed D Mon, all Sun & 25 & 26 Dec

Nontas

♨ **Map 20 C3**
16 Camden High Street NW1
01-387 4579
Credit Access, Amex, Diners
   Great Greek grub – stuffed vegetables,
delicious dips, kebabs of all kinds, mezes and
more – is now also available in the garden of this
popular restaurant, weather permitting. Snacks
and drinks are served in the bar.
■ *L 12–2.45*   *D 6–11.30*
About £17 for two   **Parking** *Limited*
Closed Sun, Bank Hols & 3 days Xmas

Noorjahan

Map 23 B5
2a Bina Gardens SW5
01-373 6522
Credit Access, Amex, Diners, Visa
  Reliable cooking and friendly, willing service in a long-established Indian restaurant just off Old Brompton Road. A fairly standard range of lamb, chicken and prawn curries runs from mild to distinctly torrid. Tandoori dishes, too, plus good vegetables, rice and bread.

■ *L 12–2.45,*   *D 6–11.45, Sun 6–11.30*
Sun 12–2.30   *Parking Limited*
About £21 for two   *Closed 24–26 Dec*

Nouveau Quiche

♧ **Map 7 B5**
301 New Cross Road SE14
01-691 3686
Credit Access, Visa
  A stylishly simple restaurant opposite Deptford Town Hall. The location is rather noisy (heavy traffic thundering past) but the food is delightfully imaginative, with choice for both meat-eaters and vegetarians. Typical dishes are miso and vegetable soup, walnut-stuffed aubergines, mussels with herb butter, Szechuan beef with brown rice.

■ *L Sun only 12–2.30*   *D 6–11, Sun 7–11*
About £22 for two   *Parking Limited*
Closed 2 wks Aug & 1 wk Xmas

Oliver's

Map 21 B4
10 Russell Gardens W14
01-603 7645
  The style is French brasserie, the cooking international, the service speedy and amiable. Typical main dishes include grills, duck à l'orange and pork in honey sauce. There is also soup and lasagne, plus good satisfying sweets. Set lunches and an evening party menu.

■ *Meals noon–10.30*   *Parking Limited*
About £22 for two   *Closed 25 & 26 Dec*

Ormes

♧ **Map 21 C6**
67 Abbeville Road SW4
01-673 2568
Credit Access, Amex, Diners, Visa
  Fresh raw materials are thoughtfully cooked at this informal wine bar. Staff will gladly make informed suggestions on both food and wine. Imaginative dishes include sole rolled around mousses of smoked trout and smoked salmon in a cream sauce. The summer pudding is first class. ℮

■ *L 12–2.30*   *D 6.30–11, Sun 7–10.30*
About £26 for two   *Parking Ample*
Closed 4 days Xmas

Orso

Map 24 D3
27 Wellington Street WC2
01-240 5269
  The nicely-balanced menu at this modern Italian restaurant ranges from pasta and pizzas to main courses like grilled stuffed swordfish and calf's liver with onions. It is tempting to splurge, but those who choose wisely can still enjoy a delicious budget meal.

■ *Meals noon–11.30pm*   *Parking Difficult*
About £30 for two   *Closed 25 Dec*

Penang

♧ **Map 22 A2**
41 Hereford Road W2
01-229 2982
Credit Access, Amex, Diners, Visa
  Mrs Tung specialises in Malaysian cooking at this cheerful little basement restaurant. Satay, prawn toast and squid balls could precede lemon chicken, garlic pork or deep-fried fish with a sweet and sour sauce and a garnish of lychees. Lots of vegetable dishes.

■ *D only 6–11, Sun 6–10.30*
About £23 for two   *Parking Ample*
Closed Good Fri, 1 wk June & 1 wk Xmas

Le Petit Prince

Map 20 C2
5 Holmes Road NW5
01-267 0752
  A lively, unpretentious and frequently crowded little restaurant just a few steps from Kentish Town Road. Couscous is the speciality, and the basic vegetable version can be boosted by meatballs, merguez, lamb or chicken (or all of them).

■ *L 12–2.30*   *D 7–11.30, Sat 7–11.45,*
About £22 for two   *Sun 7–11.15*
Closed L Sat, Sun &   *Parking Limited*
Mon, L Jul–Oct, 4 days Easter, 1 wk Xmas &
2 wks Aug

Pigeon

Map 21 B5
606 Fulham Road SW6
01-736 4618
Credit Access, Visa
  Cheerful bistro serving satisfying fare with a French flavour: smoked chicken and mushroom feuilleté, seafood salad on a bed of spinach, calf's liver with sage, chunky cassoulet. Roast beef for Sunday lunch.

■ *L 12–3*   *D 7–1am, Sun 7–12*
About £25 for two   *Parking Limited*
Closed 25 & 26 Dec

Le Plat du Jour

Map 20 C3
19 Hampstead Road NW1
01-387 9644
Credit Access, Amex, Visa
   Enjoyable eating from lunchtime on in a bright, brasserie-style restaurant. The French menus tempt with dishes like mushroom feuilleté and moules marinière. Delicious sweets (iced nougat with raspberry coulis, mousse aux deux chocolats).
■ *Meals* noon–10pm   *Parking* Limited
About £25 for two   *Closed* Sat, Sun, Bank
Hols & 2 wks Xmas

La Preferita

Map 21 C6
163 Lavender Hill SW11
01-223 1046
Credit Access, Amex, Diners, Visa
   A bright and airy Italian restaurant open seven days a week. Pasta (starter or main course) includes the house speciality spaghetti al cartoccio, with seafood and tomato sauce. Main courses span sole, scampi, veal, chicken and steaks. ⊖
■ *L 12–2.30*   *D 7–11.30*
About £30 for two   *Parking Ample*
Closed 25 & 26 Dec

Le Premier Cru

⊊ **Map 7 B4**
328 Creek Road, Greenwich SE10
01-858 9222
Credit Access, Amex, Diners, Visa
   A pleasant restaurant serving an enjoyable variety of dishes. Eggs come sauced in soubise and seafood versions, and main courses include salmon cutlets, sole bonne femme, chicken véronique and steak chasseur. Sweets and cheese from the trolley. Traditional Sunday lunch. ⊖
■ *L 12–3*   *D 7–11*
About £25 for two   *Parking Ample*
Closed L Sat, D Sun, all Mon (exc. Bank Hols),
Tues after Bank Hols & 2 wks Xmas

Punters Pie

Map 21 C6
183 Lavender Hill SW11
01-228 2660
Credit Access, Amex, Diners, Visa
   Tasty home-baked pies come in a great variety at this colourful modern restaurant: cod and shellfish, steak and mushroom, pizza, pasta, soufflés. Also interesting purées like mushroom, garlic and coriander. Traditional Sunday lunch.
■ *L 12–3*   *D 6–11.30, Sun 7–11.30*
About £25 for two   *Parking Ample*
Closed 8 days Xmas

Ravi Shankar

Map 20 C3
135 Drummond Street NW1
01-388 6458
Credit Access, Amex, Diners, Visa
   A popular Indian restaurant offering delicious vegetarian dishes in a simple setting. Start with samosas or potato pooris and continue with a vegetable curry or spiced lentil pizza. Extras are individually priced so you can build a meal within your budget.
■ *Meals* noon–10.45pm   *Parking* Difficult
About £16 for two

Sabras

⊊ **Map 20 A3**
263 High Road, Willesden Green NW10
01-459 0340
Credit Access, Visa
   Indian vegetarian dishes make memorable meals at this cheerful establishment. The menu is as detailed as it is diverse, identifying dishes like bateta vada as potatoes and nuts in batter, and palak as curried spinach in a yoghurt sauce. Non-smoking area. Bring your own wine.
■ *L Tues–Fri 12.30–3   D Tues–Fri 6–9.30*
Meals Sat & Sun 12.30–9.30
About £15 for two   *Parking* Limited
Closed Mon, 2 wks Aug & 2 wks Xmas

Seashell

Map 21 B4
49 Lisson Grove NW1
01-723 8703
Credit Access, Visa
   Close to Marylebone Road, this is one of London's best fish and chip restaurants, where only the freshest of fish is allowed to appear on diners' plates and is served in monstrous portions.
■ *L 12–2*   *D 5.15–10.30*
About £25 for two   *Parking* Limited
Closed Sun, Mon & 10 days Xmas

Shireen

Map 21 A4
270 Uxbridge Road W12
01-749 5927
Credit Access, Amex, Diners, Visa
   Pleasant Indian restaurant maintaining a good standard of cooking, with good ingredients and plenty of fresh herbs. As well as familiar favourites there are some more unusual dishes such as karahi-cooked lamb's liver, Bengali king prawns and beef tikka kebabs.
■ *L 12–3*   *D 6–11.30*
About £22 for two   *Parking* Limited
Closed 25 & 26 Dec

Sidi Bou Said

♵ **Map 22 C1**
9 Seymour Place W1
01-402 9930
Credit Access, Amex, Diners, Visa
All the rich flavours and bright colours that typify North African cooking are to be found at this bustling Tunisian restaurant. It's a popular spot, so be sure to book for a meal of briks (pastry parcels) followed by excellent couscous. Bring your own wine.
■ *L 12–3*   *D 6–12*
About £18 for two   **Parking** *Difficult*
Closed Sun & 25 & 26 Dec

Soho Brasserie

Map 27 A2
23 Old Compton Street W1
01-439 3758
Credit Access, Amex, Diners, Visa
Fish soup remains a favourite starter at this bustling Soho rendezvous. Served with croûtons, rouille and Gruyère, it's the perfect prelude to main courses like home-made herb sausages with potato purée and calf's liver with onions. ⊖
■ *Meals 10am–11.30pm*
About £27 for two   **Parking** *Difficult*
Closed Sun, Bank Hol Mons & 25 & 26 Dec

Solopasta

Map 20 D3
26 Liverpool Road N1
01-359 7648
Small, simple premises for enjoying pasta dishes served quickly and efficiently. The pasta is home-made and comes plain or wholemeal with tasty sauces, including bolognese, pesto and vongole. Good fresh salads, chunky garlic bread, delicious sweets and excellent coffee.
■ *L 12–3*   *D 6–10.30*
About £16 for two   **Parking** *Ample*
Closed Sun, Mon, Bank Hols & 3 wks Aug

Topkapi

Map 22 D1
25 Marylebone High Street W1
01-486 1872
Credit Access, Amex, Diners, Visa
Long opening hours are a plus at this cheerful Turkish restaurant. Mixed hors d'oeuvre is a popular prelude to one of the very good main-course grills – perhaps lamb fillets, lamb's kidneys, spicy meatballs or breast of chicken with green peppers.
■ *Meals noon–midnight* **Parking** *Limited*
About £25 for two   **Closed** *25 & 26 Dec*

Villa Estense

♿ **Map 21 B5**
642 King's Road SW6
01-731 4247
Credit Access, Amex, Visa
King's Road cognoscenti choose the pasta at this popular Italian restaurant. There are 15 varieties in all, with flavoursome sauces. Also on the menu are filling pizzas of generous proportions, plus starters, meat and chicken dishes and a selection of ice creams.
■ *L 12.30–2.30, Sat &*
Sun 12.30–3   *D 7–11.30*
About £20 for two   **Parking** *Difficult*
Closed D Sun & all Bank Hols

Wine & Mousaka

Map 7 A5
12 Kew Green, Richmond
01-940 5696
Credit Access, Amex, Diners, Visa
It's best to book at this welcoming restaurant overlooking Kew Green. Most well-known Greek dishes are on the menu, from dolmades and calamari to moussaka, kleftiko, wine sausages and kebabs. Children's portions and set meals (for two or more) are available.
■ *L 12–2.30*   *D 6–11.30*
About £22 for two   **Parking** *Ample*
Closed Sun, Bank Hols, 4 days Easter & 3 days Xmas

Wolfe's

Map 23 C4
25 Basil Street SW3
01-584 7217
Credit Access, Amex, Diners, Visa
The best beef goes into the most popular product, meaty Wolfburgers served in all sorts of ways – plain, with melted cheese or provençale style with tomatoes, onions, garlic, herbs and croquette potatoes. Also grills, fried sole, potato pancakes, chicken kebabs, salads.
■ *L 11.30am–midnight*   **Parking** *Ample*
About £22 for two   **Closed** *25 & 26 Dec*

Woodlands

Map 22 D1
77 Marylebone Lane W1
01-486 3862
Credit Access, Amex, Diners, Visa
Just off Marylebone High Street, this is a friendly restaurant with booth seating, serving a good range of South Indian vegetarian dishes: vegetable samosas, rice and lentil pancakes, lentil pizzas, eggless (creamed milk) omelettes, curries and a choice of set meals.
■ *L 12–3*   *D 6–11*
About £22 for two   **Parking** *Limited*
Closed 25 Dec

Woodlands

Map 27 A3
37 Panton Street SW1
01-839 7258
Credit Access, Amex, Diners, Visa
   The newest of the three Woodlands, with the same menu of South Indian vegetarian dishes. Potato-stuffed patties, lentil pizzas and vegetable samosas are typical fare, and there are various curries and set meals. Delicious coconut chutney enhanced by fresh coriander goes well with almost everything.
■ *L 12–3*   *D 6–11*
About £22 for two   **Parking** Limited
Closed 25 & 26 Dec

Economy evening meals can be had at the following restaurants, which are listed in the main London section of the Guide. (Note that prices in the main section include three courses and a full bottle of wine.)

Arirang
Map 24 B2

Bangkok
Map 23 B5

Bitter Lemons Taverna
Map 21 B5

Bloom's, Golders Green
Map 20 B1

Bloom's, Whitechapel
Map 21 D4

Café du Commerce
Map 5 F2

Café Flo
Map 20 B2

Chambeli, Oxford Circus
Map 24 B2

Chambeli, Southampton Row
Map 24 C1

Cho Won
Map 27 A2

Chueng Cheng Ku
Map 27 A2

Como Lario
Map 23 D5

Delhi Brasserie
Map 23 B4

Dynasty of Hampstead
Map 20 B2

Woodlands

Map 7 A4
402a High Road, Wembley
01-902 9869
Credit Access, Amex, Diners, Visa
   South Indian vegetarian dishes are expertly prepared in this neat, friendly place. Try spicy steamed rice cakes, lentil pizzas and dosas – wheat pancakes with delicious fillings.
■ *L 12–3*   *D 6–11*
About £22 for two   **Parking** Ample
Closed 25 Dec

Ebury Court Hotel Restaurant
Map 25 A6

Fung-Shing
Map 27 A2

Golden Chopsticks
Map 23 B4

Good Friends
Map 7 B4

Jade Garden
Map 25 C6

Kalamaras (Mega)
Map 22 B2

Kensington Tandoori
Map 23 A4

Lakorn Thai
Map 20 D3

Last Days of the Raj
Map 27 A2

Lee Ho Fook
Map 27 A2

Lena's Thai Restaurant
Map 21 C6

Lok-Zen
Map 20 C1

Lou Pescadou
Map 23 A5

Majlis
Map 23 B4

Mandarin Kitchen
Map 22 B2

Mayflower
Map 24 B3

Memories of India
Map 23 B4

RESTAURANTS UNDER £30 FOR TWO

Mogul
Map 7 B5

Nanyang
Map 23 B4

New Leaf
Map 7 A4

New Loon Fung
Map 27 A2

New Shu Shan
Map 27 A2

Pangs
Map 20 B3

Peking Duck
Map 20 B1

Piccadilly Restaurant
Map 24 B3

Poons
Map 27 A2

Le Routier
Map 20 C3

Sinar Matahari
Map 7 A4

Singapore Gardens
Map 20 B3

Weng Wah House
Map 20 B2

Wok-on-By
Map 21 B5

Young's, Upper Street
Map 20 D3

Yung's
Map 24 B3

A LOT FOR LESS

LONDON HOTELS
UNDER £60 FOR TWO

This is a category comprising modest hotels with limited facilities and accommodation of a reasonable standard but below our 50% grading. Hotels in the main London section, where prices are comparable to those in this section, are listed separately at the end.

Academy Hotel

£D/E Map 24 C1
17 Gower Street WC1E 6HG
01-631 4115. Tlx 24364
Credit Access, Amex, Diners, Visa
    Two sensitively restored Georgian houses make up a comfortable, well-run hotel. Handsome darkwood furniture is used in day rooms and bedrooms, where original fireplaces are among period features. No dogs. *Amenities* porterage, laundry service, 24-hour lounge service.

■ *Rooms* 35	*Direct dial* Yes
en suite bath/shower 25	*Room TV* Yes
Parking Limited	

Adelphi Hotel

£E Map 23 B4
127 Cromwell Road SW7 4DT
01-373 7177. Tlx 8813164
Credit Access, Amex, Diners, Visa
    Public rooms in this Victorian town house include a modern lounge area, panelled bar and cheerful breakfast room. Neat bedrooms offer TVs and radios, some also have trouser presses and hairdryers. Two rooms have showers only. *Amenities* in-house movies, laundry service.

■ *Rooms* 55	*Direct dial* Yes
en suite bath/shower 55	*Room TV* Yes
Parking Difficult	

Alison House Hotel

£E/F Map 23 D4
82 Ebury Street SW1W 9QD
01-730 9529
    Behind its Georgian facade this is a hotel of simple, friendly charm. Bedrooms are small and neat, with TVs, hairdryers and various styles of furniture. One has its own shower room, the rest share two. Unlicensed. No children under 12. No dogs.

■ *Rooms* 11	*Room phone* No
en suite bath/shower 1	*Room TV* Yes
Parking Difficult	*Closed* Jan

Apollo Hotel

£E Map 23 A4
18 Lexham Gardens W8 5JE
01-373 3236. Tlx 264189
Credit Access, Amex, Diners, Visa
    Practical accommodation for the tourist and businessman in a Victorian terrace off Cromwell Road. Ten of the bedrooms are family size, and nearly all have their own bathrooms. There's a neat bar and restaurant. No dogs. *Amenities* porterage, lift, laundry service.

■ *Rooms* 59	*Direct dial* Yes
en suite bath/shower 50	*Room TV* Yes
Parking Difficult	

Aster House

£E Map 23 B5
3 Sumner Place SW7 3EE
01-581 5888
Credit Access, Amex, Diners, Visa
    A recently added conservatory enhances the fresh, bright feel of this charming little end-of-terrace hotel. One of the bedrooms has two single four-posters. Buffet breakfast. Unlicensed. No dogs. *Amenities* garden, laundry service.

■ *Rooms* 14	*Direct dial* Yes
en suite bath/shower 12	*Room TV* Most
Parking Limited	

Atlas Hotel

£E Map 23 A4
24 Lexham Gardens W8 5JE
01-373 7873. Tlx 264189
Credit Access, Amex, Diners, Visa
    In the same family management as the neighbouring Apollo, and providing similar standards of accommodation. Bedrooms vary in size, and most have showers and WCs (bath and WC the norm at the Apollo). No dogs. *Amenities* porterage, lift, laundry service.

■ *Rooms* 70	*Direct dial* Yes
en suite bath/shower 50	*Room TV* Yes
Parking Difficult	

Avonmore Hotel

£F Map 21 B5
66 Avonmore Road W14 8RS
01-603 4296. Tlx 298842
    A very pleasant little hotel, spick and span both outside and in. Good-sized bedrooms, all with radio-alarms and fridges, share five smart tiled bathrooms. There is a combined reception, lounge, bar and breakfast room. No dogs. *Amenities* garden, porterage.

■ *Rooms* 9	*Room phone* Yes
en suite bath/shower 0	*Room TV* Yes
Parking Ample	

Bryanston Court

£E Map 22 C1
56 Great Cumberland Place W1H 7FD
01-262 3141. Tlx 262076
Credit Access, Amex, Diners, Visa
   Recent improvements at this family-run hotel
near Hyde Park include refurbishment of the
comfortable lounge, mirrored bar, corridors and
reception. Compact bedrooms, all furnished in
smart contemporary style, have neat little tiled
shower rooms. *Amenities* porterage, lift, laundry
service.

■ *Rooms* 56	*Direct dial* Yes
en suite bath/shower 56	*Room TV* Yes
Parking Limited	

Chesham House Hotel

£E/F Map 23 D4
64 Ebury Street SW1W 9QD
01-730 8513. Tlx 912881
Credit Amex, Diners, Visa
   Housekeeping is excellent at this modest hotel
in a terrace of town houses. Bedrooms are neat
and bright, with televisions and trouser presses
(hairdryers available). There's no room service,
but a decent breakfast is served in the only public
room. Unlicensed. No dogs.

■ *Rooms* 23	*Room phone* No
en suite bath/shower 0	*Room TV* Yes
Parking Difficult	*Closed* 5 days Xmas

Collin House

£E/F Map 23 D4
104 Ebury Street SW1W 9QD
01-730 8031
   Dafydd Thomas and his wife run this spotless
terrace hotel with efficiency and charm. It's very
convenient for Victoria's coach and rail stations
and the accommodation is neat and comfortable
(some rooms are quite small). Unlicensed. No
dogs. *Amenities* porterage.

■ *Rooms* 13	*Room phone* No
en suite bath/shower 8	*Room TV* No
Parking Difficult	

Columbia Hotel

£D/E Map 22 B2
95 Lancaster Gate W2 3NS
01-402 0021. Tlx 21879
Credit Access, Amex, Visa
   Lofty, elegant public areas, conference suites
and comfortable bedrooms in an attractive owner-
managed hotel. Variously sized bedrooms are
well kept, and some enjoy nice views over Hyde
Park. *Amenities* garden, laundry service, 24-hour
lounge service, porterage, lift.

■ *Rooms* 93	*Room phone* Yes
en suite bath/shower 93	*Room TV* Yes
Parking Limited	

Concord Hotel

£E/F Map 23 A4
155 Cromwell Road SW5 0TQ
01-370 4151
Credit Amex, Visa
   Straightforward accommodation in a terraced
town house on busy Cromwell Road. Furnishings
are functional, and most rooms are of quite a
decent size. There's a roomy TV lounge and
bright breakfast room. *Amenities* porterage,
laundry service, 24-hour lounge service.

■ *Rooms* 40	*Room phone* Yes
en suite bath/shower 15	*Room TV* No
Parking Limited	

Craven Gardens Hotel

£D/E Map 22 B2
16 Leinster Terrace W2 3ES
01-262 3167. Tlx 8955622
Credit Access, Amex, Diners, Visa
   A spacious open-plan foyer with rattan-
furnished bar greets guests at this modest
Victorian hotel. There's also a small lounge at the
rear of the building. Compact bedrooms have
built-in units with bedside radios. Compact
bathrooms. No dogs. *Amenities* lift.

■ *Rooms* 45	*Room phone* Yes
en suite bath/shower 41	*Room TV* Yes
Parking Difficult	

Diplomat Hotel

£D Map 23 D4
2 Chesham Street, Belgrave Square SW1X 8DT
01-235 1544. Tlx 9413498
Credit Access, Amex, Diners, Visa
   At the top of the budget range is this friendly
and well-managed hotel in Belgravia. Recently
refurbished bedrooms have attractive wall
coverings and smart free-standing furniture. TVs,
hairdryers and beverage facilities are all standard.
Attractively tiled bathrooms. *Amenities* laundry
service, lift.

■ *Rooms* 28	*Direct dial* Yes
en suite bath/shower 28	*Room TV* Yes
Parking Limited	

Eden Plaza Hotel

£D/E Map 23 B4
68 Queen's Gate SW7 5JT
01-370 6111. Tlx 916228
Credit Access, Amex, Diners, Visa
   A friendly, well-equipped hotel, recently
refurbished throughout. Day rooms are bright and
modern, and double-glazed bedrooms have
compact shower rooms (just six with tubs).
Amenities sauna, solarium, lift, porterage, laundry

service, coffee shop (7am–midnight), 24-hour
lounge service.
- Rooms 65　　　　　Direct dial Yes
en suite bath/shower 65　Room TV Yes
Parking Difficult

Elizabeth Hotel

£D/E　Map 21 C5
37 Eccleston Square SW1V 1PB
01-828 6812
　Traditionally-styled bedrooms range from small
singles to twins and family rooms at this friendly,
well-kept hotel overlooking a garden square near
Victoria's coach and railway stations. There's a
roomy TV lounge and a neat, functional breakfast
room. Unlicensed. No dogs.
- Rooms 24　　　　　Room phone No
en suite bath/shower 3　Room TV Some
Parking Difficult

Executive Hotel

£C/D　Map 23 C4
57 Pont Street SW1X 0BD
01-581 2424
Credit Access, Amex, Diners, Visa
　Just over the price limit for this section, but this
well-maintained Knightsbridge hotel offers many
more extras than the usual budget establishment,
including hairdryers, colour TVs, tea-makers and
tiled bath/shower rooms for all bedrooms. There's
a bright breakfast room and cosy bar. Amenities
laundry service, 24-hour lounge service,
porterage, lift.
- Rooms 30　　　　　Direct dial Yes
en suite bath/shower 30　Room TV Yes
Parking Limited

George Hotel

£E/F　Map 20 C3
58 Cartwright Gardens WC1H 9EL
01-387 6789
Credit Access, Amex, Diners, Visa
　Part of a Georgian crescent overlooking
gardens and tennis courts (available for hotel
guests). Bedrooms range from compact singles to
large family rooms. The television lounge is roomy
and comfortable, and there's a cheerful breakfast
room. Unlicensed. No dogs.
- Rooms 40　　　　　Room phone No
en suite bath/shower 3　Room TV No
Parking Difficult

Kensington Court Hotel

£D/E　Map 23 A5
33 Nevern Place SW5 9NP
01-370 5151. Tlx 8814451
Credit Access, Amex, Diners, Visa
　This friendly commercial hotel is a modern
building standing among older neighbours.
Bedrooms are roomy and well equipped,

bathrooms tiled and practical. There is a
comfortable bar-lounge. Own parking. Amenities
laundry service, 24-hour lounge service, lift.
- Rooms 35　　　　　Direct dial Yes
en suite bath/shower 35　Room TV Yes
Parking Limited　　　Closed 3 days Xmas

Knightsbridge Green Hotel

£D　Map 22 C3
159 Knightsbridge SW1X 7PD
01-584 6274
Credit Access, Amex, Visa
　Much of the accommodation at this recently
refurbished hotel is now in suites. Rooms are
spacious, with smart bathrooms. Direct-dial
telephones, TVs, beverage facilities and trouser
presses are standard. Breakfast served in the
rooms. Unlicensed. No dogs. Amenities
porterage, lift, laundry service.
- Rooms 22　　　　　Direct dial Yes
en suite bath/shower 22　Room TV Yes
Parking Difficult　　　Closed 5 days Xmas

Lancaster Court Hotel

£E　Map 22 B2
202 Sussex Gardens W2 3AU
01-402 8438. Tlx 21879
Credit Access, Amex, Diners, Visa
　A four-storey Victorian terraced property near
Paddington Station. Most of the bedrooms have
both double and single beds, and all but a few
have shower cubicles. There's a neat breakfast
room (continental breakfast only). Unlicensed. No
dogs.
- Rooms 42　　　　　Room phone No
en suite bath/shower 14　Room TV Yes
Parking Limited　　　Closed 25 Dec

Hotel Lexham

£E/F　Map 23 A4
32 Lexham Gardens W8 5JU
01-373 6471
Credit Access, Visa
　A well-run hotel, quietly situated though near
Cromwell Road. There are two lounges, one with
TV, and an attractive dining room. Neatly kept
bedrooms, half with private facilities. Unlicensed.
No dogs. Amenities garden, lift, porterage,
laundry service, 24-hour lounge service.
- Rooms 63　　　　　Room phone Yes
en suite bath/shower 30　Room TV No
Parking Difficult　　　Closed 23 Dec–2 Jan

Hotel Lily

£D/E　Map 23 A6
23 Lillie Road SW6 1UG
01-381 1881. Tlx 918922
　Near Earl's Court Exhibition Centre, a modern
hotel with likeable, efficient staff. Day rooms sport
new carpets, and the compact, well-equipped

bedrooms have been redecorated. Decent breakfasts. Own parking. *Amenities* porterage, tea-making facilities, lift, sauna.

- *Rooms 106*   *Direct dial* Yes
en suite bath/shower 106   *Room TV* Yes
Parking Limited

London Park Hotel

£D/E   **Map 21 D5**
Brook Drive SE11 4QU
01-735 9191. Tlx 919161
Credit Access, Amex, Diners, Visa

Large, cheerful grey-brick hotel close to the Elephant & Castle. Public rooms are quite extensive, bedrooms compact and simply furnished. Most have shower cabinets. *Amenities* garden, porterage, lift, laundry service, in-house movies (free).

- *Rooms 376*   *Room phone* Yes
en suite bath/shower 323   *Room TV* Yes
Parking Ample

Lonsdale Hotel

£E   **Map 24 C1**
9 Bedford Place WC1B 5JA
01-636 1812. Tlx 296012

Modest, neat and cheerful overnight accommodation in a Georgian terrace close to the British Museum. Rooms have central heating and wash-basins. There is a smart TV lounge and breakfast room. Unlicensed. No children under two. No dogs.

- *Rooms 34*   *Room phone* No
en suite bath/shower 0   *Room TV* No
Parking Difficult

Merryfield House

£F   **Map 22 C1**
42 York Street W1H 1FN
01-935 8326

A civil welcome awaits visitors to this unpretentious little hotel, run by the same family for over 30 years. Fair-sized bedrooms are comfortable and homely, bathrooms well cared for. There is a drinks machine on the landing. Unlicensed. No dogs.

- *Rooms 7*   *Room phone* No
en suite bath/shower 7   *Room TV* No
Parking Limited

Number Eight Hotel

£D/E   **Map 23 B4**
8 Emperor's Gate SW7 4HH
01-370 7516
Credit Access, Amex, Diners, Visa

Just off Cromwell Road (north side), this stylishly refurnished hotel is part of a Victorian terrace. Decent-sized bedrooms are comfortable,

attractive and quite well equipped (hairdryers, tea-makers). Basement breakfast room. Unlicensed. No dogs. *Amenities* laundry service.

- *Rooms 14*   *Direct dial* Yes
en suite bath/shower 13   *Room TV* Yes
Parking Difficult

Parkwood Hotel

£E   **Map 22 C2**
4 Stanhope Place W2 2HB
01-402 2241. Tlx 8812714
Credit Access, Visa

New owners have refurbishment plans for this comfortable hotel near Hyde Park and the Oxford Street stores. Bedrooms are bright, cheerful and well equipped. There is a pleasant high-ceilinged lounge and a basement breakfast room. Unlicensed. No dogs.

- *Rooms 18*   *Direct dial* Yes
en suite bath/shower 12   *Room TV* Yes
Parking Limited

President Hotel

£E   **Map 24 C1**
Russell Square WC1N 1DB
01-837 8844. Tlx 21822
Credit Access, Amex, Diners, Visa

Sixties hotel with very spacious and quite striking public areas that include a row of shops. Comfortable bedrooms (front ones double-glazed). No dogs. *Amenities* porterage, laundry service, in-house movies (free), 24-hour lounge service, coffee shop (10.30am–2am), lift.

- *Rooms 447*   *Direct dial* Yes
en suite bath/shower 447   *Room TV* Yes
Parking Ample

Prince Hotel

£E   **Map 23 B5**
6 Sumner Place SW7 3AB
01-589 6488
Credit Access, Amex, Visa

Public areas have been redecorated, keeping things smart and shipshape at this comfortable hotel in a Victorian terrace. Bedrooms are generally spacious, with good wardrobes and linen. TV lounge, garden room, breakfast room. No dogs. *Amenities* garden, porterage.

- *Rooms 20*   *Direct dial* Yes
en suite bath/shower 12   *Room TV* Yes
Parking Limited

Sorbonne Hotel

£E/F   **Map 23 B4**
39 Cromwell Road SW7 2DH
01-589 6636
Credit Access, Amex, Visa

Next to the Lycée, and opposite the Natural History Museum. Most bedrooms are of a fair size, ranging up to a four-person family room. TV lounge. Continental breakfast. Unlicensed. No children under ten. No dogs. *Amenities* lift.

■ *Rooms* 20   *Room phone* Yes
en suite bath/shower 9   *Room TV* Most
Parking Difficult

Surtees Hotel

£F   Map 21 C5
94 Warwick Way SW1V 1SB
01-834 7163

Bedrooms are neat, compact and modern at this hotel in a Victorian terrace. Among other improvements, the new owner is increasing the number of en suite shower rooms. A basement breakfast room doubles as a lounge. Unlicensed. *Amenities* coffee shop (11am–10pm).

■ *Rooms* 10   *Room phone* No
en suite bath/shower 3   *Room TV* Yes
Parking Limited

Terstan Hotel

£F   Map 23 A5
29 Nevern Square SW5 9PE
01-373 5368
Credit Access, Visa

No major changes, but continual upgrading goes on at this family-run red-brick hotel in a garden square. Bedrooms are neat and compact; public areas include lounge, bar, breakfast room and pool table room. No dogs. *Amenities* garden, lift.

■ *Rooms* 50   *Room phone* Yes
en suite bath/shower 34   *Room TV* Yes
Parking Difficult

Willett Hotel

£E   ♿   Map 23 D5
32 Sloane Gardens SW1W 8DJ
01-824 8415

Well-equipped bedrooms, some of family size, provide comfortable accommodation in quiet surroundings near Sloane Square. TVs, direct-dial phones, tea-makers and hairdryers are provided in all rooms, and all but two have private facilities. Unlicensed. No dogs. *Amenities* garden, laundry service.

■ *Rooms* 19   *Direct dial* Yes
en suite bath/shower 17   *Room TV* Yes
Parking Limited

Yardley Court

£E/F   Map 7 B5
18 Court Yard, Eltham SE9 5PZ
01-850 1850

A homely atmosphere pervades this Victorian house, bolstered by bookshelves and bric-a-brac in the comfortable lounge and breakfast room. Individually-decorated bedrooms have modern furniture and remote-controlled colour TV. *Amenities* garden, porterage, laundry service.

■ *Rooms* 9   *Room phone* No
en suite bath/shower 6   *Room TV* Yes
Parking Ample   *Closed* 1 wk Xmas

Hotels in the main London section of the Guide where prices are comparable to those in this section:

Bardon Lodge Hotel
Map 7 B5

Colonnade Hotel
Map 20 B3

Hogarth Hotel
Map 23 A5

Mornington Hotel
Map 22 B2

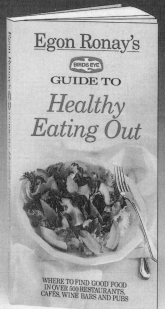

THE **Cellnet** THEATRE GUIDE

A theatre visit can be easy to arrange with your cellphone. A call to the box office will usually reserve your tickets - or you can pay for them right away over the phone with your credit card.

Here is a list of most major theatres throughout Britain - compliments of Cellnet!

LONDON THEATRES	Box Office
ADELPHI Strand WC2E 7NH	01-836 7611
ALBERY St Martin's Lane WC2	01-836 3878
ALDWYCH Aldwych WC2	01-836 6404
AMBASSADORS West St WC2	01-836 6111
APOLLO Shaftesbury Ave W1	01-437 2663
APOLLO VICTORIA Wilton Rd SW1	01-630 6262
ARTS 6-7 Gt Newport St WC2	01-836 3334
ASTORIA Charing Cross Road WC2	01-434 0403
BARBICAN Barbican EC2Y 8BQ	01-628 8795
BLOOMSBURY Gordon St WC1H 0AH	01-387 9629
COLISEUM (English National Opera) St Martin's Lane WC2	01-836 3161
COMEDY Panton ST SW1	01-930 2578
COVENT GARDEN (Royal Opera House) WC2	01-240 1066
CRITERION Piccadilly Circus W1	01-930 3216
DRURY LANE (Theatre Royal) WC2	01-836 8108
DUCHESS Catherine St WC2	01-836 8243
DUKE OF YORK'S St Martin's Lane WC2	01-836 5122
FORTUNE Russell St WC2B 5HH	01-836 2238
GARRICK Charing Cross Rd WC2	01-836 4601
GLOBE Shaftesbury Ave W1	01-437 3667
HAYMARKET (Theatre Royal) SW1	01-930 9832
HER MAJESTY'S Haymarket SW1Y 4QL	01-930 4025
LYRIC King St Hammersmith W6 0QL	01-741 2311
LYRIC Shaftesbury Ave W1	01-437 3686
MAYFAIR Stratton St W1	01-629 3036
MERMAID Puddle Dock Blackfriars EC4	01-236 5568
NATIONAL Upper Ground South Bank SE1 9PX	01-928 2252
NEW LONDON Drury Lane WC2	01-405 0072
OLD VIC Waterloo Rd SE1 8NB	01-928 7616
PALACE Shaftesbury Ave W1	01-434 0909
PALLADIUM 8 Argyll St W1	01-437 7373
PHOENIX Charing Cross Rd WC2	01-836 2294
PICCADILLY Denman St W1	01-437 4506
PRINCE EDWARD Old Compton St W1	01-734 8951
PRINCE OF WALES Coventry St W1	01-839 5987
QUEEN'S Shaftesbury Ave WC2	01-734 1166
REGENT'S PARK (Open Air)	01-486 2431
ROYAL COURT Sloane Sq SW1	01-730 1745
SADLER'S WELLS Rosebery Ave EC1	01-278 8916
ST MARTIN'S West St WC2	01-836 1443
SAVOY Strand WC2	01-836 8888
SHAFTESBURY Shaftesbury Ave WC2	01-379 5399
SHAW 100 Euston Rd NW1 2AJ	01-388 1394
STRAND Aldwych WC2	01-836 2660

VAUDEVILLE Strand WC2	01-836 9987
VICTORIA PALACE Victoria St SW1	01-834 1317
WESTMINSTER Palace St SW1	01-834 0283
WHITEHALL Whitehall SW1	01-930 7765
WYNDHAM'S Charing Cross Rd WC2	01-836 3028
YOUNG VIC 66 The Cut SE1	01-928 6363

REGIONAL THEATRES

BELFAST "Lyric" 55 Ridgeway St Stranmillis Rd Belfast 9	0232 660081
BIRMINGHAM "Repertory" & "Studio" Broad St Birmingham B1 2EP	021-236 4455
BRISTOL "Theatre Royal & New Vic Studio" King St Bristol BS1 4ED	0272 264388
CHELTENHAM "Everyman" Regent St Cheltenham Glos GL5 1HQ	0242 512515
CHESTER "Gateway" Hamilton Pl Chester Cheshire CH1 2BH	0244 40393
COVENTRY "Belgrade" Belgrade Sq Coventry Warwickshire CV1 1GS	0203 553055
CREWE "Lyceum" 10 Heath St Crewe Cheshire CW1 2DA	0270 211149
DERBY "Playhouse" Theatre Walk Eagle Centre Derby Derbyshire DE1 2NF	0332 363275
DUNDEE "Repertory" Tay Square Dundee DD1 1PB	0382 23530
EASTBOURNE "Devonshire Park" Compton St Eastbourne Sussex	0323 36363
EDINBURGH "Royal Lyceum" Grindlay St Edinburgh EH3 9AX	031-229 9697
EXETER "Northcott' Stocker Rd Exeter Devon EX4 4QB	0392 54853
GLASGOW "Citizens" 119 Gorbals St Glasgow G5 9DS	041-429 0022
IPSWICH "Wolsey Theatre" Civic Dr Ipswich Suffolk IP1 2AS	0473 53725
LANCASTER "Duke's Playhouse" Moor La Lancaster Lancs LA1 1QE	0524 66645
LEEDS "Playhouse" Calverley St Leeds W Yorks LS2 3AJ	0532 442111
LEICESTER "Phoenix Arts" 11 Newarke St Leicester Leics LE1 5TA	0533 554854
LIVERPOOL "Playhouse" Williamson Sq Liverpool L2 1EL	051-709 8363
MANCHESTER "Royal Exchange" Cross St Manchester M2 7DH	061-833 9833
MILFORD HAVEN "Torch Theatre" St Peter's Rd Milford Haven SA73 2BU	064-62 5267
NEWCASTLE UPON TYNE "Playhouse" Barras Bridge Newcastle upon Tyne NE1 7RH	091-232 3421
NORTHAMPTON "Royal Theatre" & "Opera House" 19-21 Guildhall Rd Northampton Northants NN1 1DP	0604 32533
NOTTINGHAM "Playhouse" (Theatre Trust Ltd) Wellington Circus Nottingham NG1 5AF	0602 419419
OXFORD "Playhouse" Beaumont St Oxford OX1 2LW	0865 247134
PLYMOUTH "Theatre Royal" Royal Parade Plymouth Devon PL1 2TR	0752 669595
SALISBURY "Playhouse & Studio" Malthouse La Salisbury Wilts SP2 7RA	0722 20333
SHEFFIELD "Crucible" & "Studio" 55 Norfolk St Sheffield S1 1DA	0742 769922
SWANSEA "Grand" Singleton St Swansea SA1 3QJ	0792 475715
WINDSOR "Theatre Royal" Thames St Windsor Berks S14 1PS	0753 853888
YORK "Theatre Royal" St Leonard's Pl York YO1 2HD	0904 23568

Cellnet

THE CELLPHONE NETWORK

HOTELS
RESTAURANTS
AND INNS

HOTELS
RESTAURANTS
AND INNS

LONDON

Ajimura

R **Map 27 B1**
51 Shelton Street WC2
01-240 0178
Japanese cooking
Owner manager Susumu Okada
Credit Access, Amex, Diners, Visa
   Sit at the sushi bar and watch the deft chefs, or
go for one of the small pine tables in this cheerful,
unfussy Japanese restaurant. Set meals offer a

good introduction to sashimi (raw fish), teriyaki
and tempura dishes, or make a creative choice
with the help of friendly waiters. Try the o-cha tea.
Booking essential.
■ *Set L* £5·50	*L 12–3*
Set D from £9·90	*D 6–11, Sun 6–10.30*
About £36 for two	*Parking Difficult*
Seats 56	*Parties 25*
Closed L Sat & Sun & all Bank Hols	

Al Gallo d'Oro

R **Map 21 B5**
353 Kensington High Street W8
01-603 6951
Italian cooking
Manager Mr Fernando
Credit Access, Amex, Diners, Visa
   Regular favourites and seasonal specialities
provide plenty of choice in this neat Italian
restaurant with stylish modern decor. There's an

attractive hors d'oeuvre trolley, and pasta can be
ordered as a starter or main course. Plenty of
steak, chicken and veal dishes, plus sole, trout
and scampi. Conventional sweets. Good, reliable
cooking and attentive service. ℮
■ *About £45 for two*	*L 12.15–2.45*
Seats 56	*D 6.45–11.45*
Parties 26	*Parking Difficult*
Closed L Sat & all Bank Hols	

■ Any person using our name
to obtain free hospitality is
a fraud. Proprietors, please
inform the police and us.

Alastair Little ★

R ★ ⌀ **Map 27 A2**
49 Frith Street W1
01-734 5183
Credit Visa
   Owner-chef Alastair Little favours a robust,
forthright style of cooking at his strikingly modern
restaurant with its jet black tables and chairs,
varnished floorboards and abstract prints on the
walls. Portions are generous, flavours clear and
strong and the imaginative combinations
displayed are never merely gimmicky but always
successfully realised. Plenty of fresh fish dishes
are on offer. Typical treats from the well-balanced
menu (which changes daily) might include a
triumphant, oriental-influenced seafood
consommé with king prawn ravioli and flavour-
packed venison terrine, perfectly complemented
by onion marmalade and a simple salad, among
starters, followed by such masterly main courses
as red mullet with pesto, pot-roast saddle of veal
with a pungent fumet of cèpes or braised

pheasant with cabbage and zampone sausage.
Delicious sweets like rich chocolate truffle and
chestnut gâteau to finish, and a concise selection
of classic and New World wines to accompany
your meal. Service is informal and friendly. ℮
■ *About £45 for two*	*L 12.30–2.30*
Seats 34	*D 7.30–11.15*
Parking Difficult	*Closed Sat, Sun,*
Bank Hols & 3 wks Aug	

Alexander Hotel

H **67% £C Map 23 B5**
9 Sumner Place SW7 3EE
01-581 1591. Tlx 917133
Credit Access, Amex, Diners, Visa
   Behind the facade of this lovely 19th-century
house is an air of quiet sophistication and
elegance. Period furniture and comfortable sofas
grace the restful reception-lounge, while the bar-
lounge in the basement is more modern.

Bedrooms have attractive free-standing furniture,
pretty coordinating fabrics and good lighting.
Bathrooms are fitted with showers and plenty of
mirrors. No dogs. *Amenities* garden, in-house
movies (free), laundry service.
■ *Rooms 40*	*Confirm by arrang.*
en suite bath/shower 40	*Last dinner 8*
Direct dial Yes	*Parking Difficult*
Room TV Yes	*Room service All day*

Anna's Place

R Map 20 D2
90 Mildmay Park N1
01-249 9379
Swedish cooking
Owner manager Anna Hegarty
  Anna Hegarty personally ensures that everyone is happy at this exceptionally friendly place. The menu is mainly Swedish, with gravad lax, herrings, meatballs and roast breast of duck with red cabbage among the popular items. Burgundy pears with cinnamon ice cream is a pleasant pud. There's a little courtyard for summer eating.

■ *About £33 for two*   *L 12.15–2.15*
Seats 44   *D 7.15–10.15*
Parties 10   *Parking Limited*
Closed Sun, Mon, Bank Hols, 2 wks Easter, 2 wks Xmas & all Aug

♀ indicates a **well-chosen** house wine.

L'Aquitaine

R Map 23 B5
158 Old Brompton Road, SW5
01-373 9918
French cooking
Manager Fernand Casteras
Credit Access, Amex, Visa
  Foie gras, pipérade, cassoulet and confits typify the robust cuisine of south-western France served in this basement restaurant. There's also fish soup, snails and rack of lamb. Live music from 10pm. Lunch (similar, shorter menu) is served in the ground-floor bistro. Interesting regional wines.
♀ Well-chosen ☺

■ *About £40 for two*   *L 12–3*
Seats 70   *D 7.30–2am*
Parties 20   *Parking Limited*
Closed L Sat, all Sun & 25 Dec

Arirang

R Map 24 B2
31 Poland Street W1
01-437 6633
Korean cooking
Owner manager Tony Wee
Credit Access, Amex, Diners, Visa
  Owner Tony Wee and his friendly staff are always ready to guide your choice at this excellent Korean restaurant. Fresh, assertive flavours come through in classic dishes like bulgogi (thin strips of spicy marinated beef) and there are tempting appetisers such as garlicky bracken stalks.

■ *Set L £3·95*   *L 12–3*
Set D from £7·50   *D 6–11*
About £30 for two   *Parking Difficult*
Seats 80   *Parties 40*
Closed Sun, Easter Mon & 25 & 26 Dec

▷ is our symbol for an **outstanding** wine list.

Arirang House

R Map 22 C3
3 Park Close SW1
01-581 1820
Korean cooking
Owner managers Mr & Mrs Bae
Credit Access, Amex, Diners, Visa
  Booking is essential at this friendly little Korean restaurant. Charming staff are on hand to guide you through the menu, which ranges from fiery pickled cabbage to yuk hue – spiced raw minced beef with pears – and a nourishing soup with meat dumplings and soya bean cake. Try soju, a spirit made with ginseng.

■ *Set L from £6·50*   *L 12–3*
Set D £28 for two   *D 6–11*
About £40 for two   *Parking Difficult*
Seats 40 Parties 10
Closed Sun, some Bank Hols

Ark

R Map 22 A3
35 Kensington High Street W8
01-937 4294
French cooking
Manager Mr J. Molina
Credit Access, Amex, Diners, Visa
  A long-established and popular restaurant with an entrance just off Kensington High Street. The food is French bourgeois, satisfying and soundly prepared, with generous portions. Favourite fixtures include oeufs en cocotte, French onion soup and rack of lamb; daily specials may be skate with black butter, or venison with green peppercorn sauce. ☺

■ *About £37 for two*   *L 12–3*
Seats 90   *D 7–11.30, Sun 7–11*
Parties 20   *Parking Limited*
Closed L Sun, 4 days Easter & 4 days Xmas

L'Arlequin ★★

R ★★ ♕ ⑨ ♿ **Map 21 C6**
123 Queenstown Road SW8
01-622 0555
French cooking
Credit Access, Diners, Visa

One of London's most sophisticated restaurants, with a clientele to match, L'Arlequin is run with impeccable taste and flair by the Delteils. Recent expansion has enlarged both the kitchen and dining area. While Geneviève masterminds the smooth running of the two dining rooms, self-effacing chef-patron Christian performs his brilliant magic in the kitchen. Recent memorable delights have included a faultless terrine of asparagus, seabass baked in a sea-salt crust, sweetbreads served on a bed of raspberry vinegar coulis, and the superb assiette gourmande – a taste of some seven different exquisite sweets. Service is very French, smooth and unobtrusive. A conservative but fine wine list (Château d'Angludet 1978, Pommard Comte Armand 1979). *Specialities* émincé de coquilles St Jacques gingembre, rable de lièvre aux pâtes fraîches, roulé de sole, sauce mirepoix, chaud-froid de framboises. ♀ **Well-chosen** ℮

■ *Set L* £13·50   L 12.30–2
About £75 *for two*   D 7.30–11
Seats 45 *Parties* 12   *Parking* Ample
Closed Sat, Sun, Bank Hols, 1 wk Xmas & 3 wks Aug

L'Artiste Affamé

R **Map 23 A5**
243 Old Brompton Road SW5
01-373 1659
Owner manager Peter Durrant
Credit Access, Amex, Diners, Visa

Enjoyable cooking of popular favourites in a cheerful, colourful restaurant comprising ground floor, basement and small patio garden. Avocado and mushroom salad, herby stuffed aubergine and creamy-sauced smoked haddock are typical starters, with coquilles St Jacques provençale, entrecôte Café de Paris and chicken breast with a well-made béarnaise among the mains. To finish, try chocolate mousse. ℮

■ *Set L & D* £11·50   L 12.30–2.30
About £42 *for two*   D 6.30–11.15
Seats 75 *Parties* 50   *Parking* Limited
Closed Sun & Bank Hols (exc. D Good Fri)

■ For a discount on next year's guide, see Offer for Answers.

Athenaeum Hotel

HR **80% £A Map 25 A4**
116 Piccadilly W1
01-499 3463. Tlx 261589
Credit Access, Amex, Diners, Visa

The urbane general manager Mr Rettie is very much in evidence, chatting to guests and generally assisting the civilised, up-market atmosphere of the hotel. It's a modern building overlooking Green Park, and the day rooms, though not large, are stylish and comfortable. On the accommodation side, the suites and Executive rooms have benefited from refurbishment, the rather dated bold wall coverings giving way to softer colours, and the bathrooms luxuriating in marble tiling and panelled baths. Standard rooms, with smaller bathrooms, are to be improved over the next year or two. Furniture in all rooms is of the durable brass-inlaid, leather-topped variety in yew, mahogany and other woods.
Amenities hairdressing, in-house movies (free), valeting, laundry service, 24-hour lounge service.

■ *Rooms* 112   *Confirm by* 6
en suite bath/shower 112 *Last dinner* 10.30
Direct dial Yes   *Parking* Limited
Room TV Yes   *Room service* 24 hours

Athenaeum Hotel Restaurant ♕

Cooking in the plush-pretty restaurant is consistently capable, if not particularly exciting. A tempting choice of dishes runs from light, well-constructed quenelles of sole to saddle of hare with sour cream and beautifully tender lamb accompanied by a pleasant garlic-flavoured jus. Average sweet trolley; cheeses not always in their prime. Good wines. ♀ **Well-chosen** ℮

■ *Set L from* £15·50   L 12.30–3,
About £65 *for two*   Sun 12.30–3.30
Seats 50 *Parties* 48   D 6–10.30, Sun 7–10

Au Jardin des Gourmets

R ☟ ♿ **Map 27 A1**
5 Greek Street W1
01-437 1816
French cooking
Manager Franco Zoia
Credit Access, Amex, Diners, Visa
A comfortable, well-run French restaurant, with very decent cooking and quite magnificent wines. The menu mixes classics like onion soup and sole meunière with less everyday choices like salmon quenelles or lamb fillets with raspberry vinegar and redcurrant sauce. Special theatre menu.
◷ Outstanding ♟ Well-chosen ℮

■ *Set L & D from £12.95* *L 12.15–2.30*
About £50 for two *D 6.30–11.30*
Seats 95 Parties 20 *Parking Difficult*
Closed L Bank Hols, all Sun & 4 days Easter

■ Our inspectors are our full-time employees; they are professionally trained by us.

Auntie's

R **Map 24 B1**
126 Cleveland Street W1
01-387 1548
English cooking
Credit Access, Amex, Diners, Visa
Shaun Thomson is continuing the tradition of English cooking at this former tea room. Seasonally changing menus tempt with potted meat, creamy fish soup, chicken cobbler with herby dumplings and excellent bangers and mash with onion sauce. Gargantuan grills, splendidly crisp vegetables and lovely diet-obliterating sweets. Good-value English wines.
♟ Well-chosen
■ *About £40 for two* *L 12–3*
Seats 28 Parties 28 *D 6–11*
Closed L Sat, all Bank *Parking Limited*
Hols, 2 wks Aug & 10 days Xmas

L'Aventure

R ♿ **Map 20 B3**
3 Blenheim Terrace NW8
01-624 6232
French cooking
Owner manager Catherine Parisot
Credit Amex, Visa
Very appealing and very French, with beige-clothed tables, original works of art and an attractive flagstoned terrace. Cooking is reliable through a well-balanced selection of dishes, from smoked salmon pancakes or sweetbread and broccoli salad to fillet of beef with Roquefort and the day's fish specials. ℮
■ *Set L & D Sun only* *L 12.30–2.30, Sun 12–2*
£10.50 *D 7–11 Sun 7–10*
About £45 for two *Parking Limited*
Seats 38 *Parties 40*
Closed L Sat, 4 days Easter & 1 wk Xmas

Azami *NEW ENTRY*

R **Map 27 A2**
13 West Street WC2
01-240 0634
Japanese cooking
Credit Access, Amex, Diners, Visa
Long-established Japanese restaurant with two menus, one in English and geared to Western palates, the other in Japanese. Whichever you choose you'll get an excellent meal: fish is particularly good – try strongly-flavoured sardine fish balls with tofu or superb salmon teriyaki. Staff are extremely friendly and helpful – and much smarter than the slightly fading decor.
■ *Set L £5* *L 12–2.30*
Set D from £23 *D 6–9.30*
About £60 for two *Parking Difficult*
Seats 50 *Parties 40*
Closed L Sat & Sun, all Mon

Bagatelle

R **Map 23 B6**
5 Langton Street SW10
01-351 4185
French cooking
Credit Access, Amex, Diners, Visa
A charming French restaurant with garden tables which are much in demand in sunny weather. Casually-dressed French waiters provide pleasant and efficient service. Typical dishes are vegetable pâté, salmon crêpes, medallions of lamb cooked with white wine and tarragon, duck legs cooked with Madeira sauce and prunes and breast of duck in green peppercorn sauce. Finish with sorbets and sweets of the day. ℮
■ *Set L £14* *L 12–2*
About £55 for two *D 7–11*
Seats 50 Parties 8 *Parking Limited*
Closed Sun & Bank Hols

Bahn Thai ▶

Bahn Thai

R   **Map 27 A2**
21a Frith Street W1
01-437 8504
Thai cooking
Credit Access, Amex, Visa
   Authentic and excellent Thai cooking in a ground and first-floor Soho restaurant. Fragrant herbs and roots, coconut and chilli are used to sensational effect in a wide range of dishes,

including delicious soups, spicy fish cakes, roast duck curry and fried pomfret coated in chilli and tamarind sauce. Carefully selected wines. Amiable, helpful owners. ♀ **Well-chosen**
■ *Set L £8·75*   *L 12–2.45,*
About £40 for two   *Sun 12.30–2.30*
Seats 100 Parties 60   *D 6–11.15,*
Parking Difficult   *Sun 6.30–10.30*
Closed 4 days Easter & Xmas

Bahn Thai   *NEW ENTRY*

R **Map 27 A2**
35a Marloes Road W8
01-937 9960
Thai cooking
Owner managers Noi & Philip Harris
Credit Access, Amex, Visa
   A friendly basement restaurant serving enjoyable Thai food, with a menu that is both extensive and informative. King prawns with

sweet or fiery dips, delicious seafood soup with spices and lemon grass, charcoal-grilled pork and beef in a red curry sauce are typical items, and there are lots of salads and vegetables, plus composite rice and noodle dishes. Carefully selected wines. ♀ **Well-chosen**
■ *About £40 for two*   *D 6–11.15*
Seats 32 Parties 35   *Parking Ample*
Closed Sun, Bank Hols, 2 wks Aug & 2 wks Xmas

Bangkok

R ♀ **Map 23 B5**
9 Bute Street SW7
01-584 8529
Thai cooking
   A popular, long-established restaurant providing some excellent Thai cooking. The short menu offers chicken and crab soup, savoury beef omelette and satay with peanut sauce and cucumber salad among starters; beef with ginger

and mushrooms, chicken with mushrooms and bamboo shoots, or beef with oyster sauce and green pepper for a main course. Delicious Thai rice noodles and crisp, tasty vegetables are recommended.
■ *About £32 for two*   *L 12.15–2.15*
Seats 60   *D 6.30–11*
Parties 20   *Parking Limited*
Closed Sun, Bank Hols & 2 wks late Aug

Bardon Lodge Hotel

H **58% £D/E** **Map 7 B5**
15 Stratheden Road SE3 7TH
01-853 4051
Owner managers Donald & Barbara Nott
Credit Access, Visa
   The linking of two Victorian houses completes a major improvement programme at this friendly, family-run hotel. Bedrooms vary in size, but all are neat and well equipped (remote-control TVs,

hairdryers, trouser presses); the majority have their own shower rooms. There's a cosy little lounge area and a comfortable cocktail bar with leather chesterfields and plush banquette seating. *Amenities* garden.
■ *Rooms 41*   *Confirm by arrang.*
en suite bath/shower 28   *Last dinner 9.30*
Direct dial Yes   *Parking Limited*
Room TV Yes   *Room service All day*

■ We welcome complaints and bona fide recommendations on the tear-out pages for readers' comments. They are followed up by our professional team. Please also complain to the management instantly.

RECEPTION

Barnaby's

R ♀ **Map 21 A6**
39b High Street, Barnes, SW13
01-878 4750
French cooking
Owner managers Claude & Jenny Harry
Credit Access, Amex, Diners, Visa
   Jenny Harry provides the charming service while husband Claude prepares delicious dishes from his native France at this homely restaurant

near the river. Start perhaps with creamy mussel soup before moving on to venison in red wine sauce, brochette of monkfish or a traditional Perigord cassoulet. Finish with tarte tatin or flavoursome chocolate bavarois.
■ *About £36 for two*   *L 12.30–1.30*
Seats 24   *D 7–10.15*
Closed L Mon & Sat,   *Parking Ample*
all Sun, Bank Hols & 3 wks Sept

Basil Street Hotel

HR **69%** **£B** **Map 22 C3**
Basil Street SW3 1AH
01-581 3311. Tlx 28379
Owner manager Stephen Korany
Credit Access, Amex, Diners, Visa. LVs
   Much of its original Edwardian charm survives
at this splendid Knightsbridge hotel. English and
Oriental antiques and objets d'art abound in the
public rooms, with fresh flowers adding an extra
sparkle. Bedrooms – some with old-fashioned
high beds, others sympathetically modernised –
are spacious and well kept. Superb breakfasts.
Amenities valeting, laundry service, 24-hour
lounge service.

■ *Rooms* 100	*Confirm by* 6
en suite bath/shower 90	*Last dinner* 9.45
Direct dial Yes	*Parking* Difficult
Room TV Yes	*Room service* 24 hours

The Dining Room ⌘

Setting and menu are in perfect accord at this
peaceful, eminently traditional dining room.
Starters range from a classic beef consommé with
vegetable julienne to quenelles of trout with
mousseline sauce. To follow, prime Scottish beef
from the trolley is the chief speciality, with equally
reliable favourites like steak and kidney pie, Dover
sole or poached salmon as alternatives. Other
choices might be veal escalopes florentine or
duckling braised in vermouth and brandy.
Enjoyable desserts like fruit tarts and cream
gâteaux. ⌘ Well-chosen ⊖

■ *Set L* £10·75	*L* 12.30–2.15
About £44 *for two*	*D* 6.30–9.45,
Seats 90 *Parties* 50	*Sun* 7–9.30
Closed L Sat	

⌘ indicates a **well-chosen** house wine.

La Bastide

R ⌘ ⊊ **Map 27 A2**
50 Greek Street W1
01-734 3300
French cooking
Credit Access, Amex, Diners, Visa
   Nicolas Blacklock's sound, careful French
cooking finds an elegant setting in this gracious
Georgian house. Good-quality ingredients are
attractively presented; sauces are excellent. The
regularly changing menu offers unusual items
such as hake poached with morels and lamb in
champagne sauce, as well as simpler dishes like
moules marinière. The selection of Armagnacs is
impressive. ⌘ Well-chosen ⊖

■ *Set L & D from* £13·90	*L* 12.30–2.30
About £48 *for two*	*D* 6–11.30
Seats 45 *Parties* 100	*Parking* Difficult
Closed L Sat, all Sun & Bank Hols	

⊳ is our symbol for an **outstanding** wine list.

Bates

R **Map 27 B2**
11 Henrietta Street WC2
01-240 7600
Credit Access, Amex, Diners, Visa
   Framed cartoons decorate the walls of this
attractive restaurant, where Richard Williams is
the talent behind a short, well-conceived
lunchtime set menu and an equally judicious
evening carte. Fine ingredients and attractive
presentation enhance deceptively simple
offerings such as broccoli and almond soup
followed by, say, calf's liver with Calvados and
apples, rosemary-scented lamb or salmon with dill
and saffron sauce. Colourful, fruity sweets. ⊖

■ *Set L* £15	*L* 12–2.30
About £44 *for two*	*D* 5.30–11.30
Seats 65 *Parties* 50	*Parking* Limited
Closed L Sat, all Sun & Bank Hols	

Beaufort

H **67%** **£B** **Map 23 C4**
33 Beaufort Gardens SW3 1PP
01-584 5252. Tlx 929200
Credit Access, Amex, Diners, Visa
   This truly delightful hotel in a Victorian garden
square offers style and comfort in a setting that is
both elegant and civilised. The only public room is
a gracious sitting room with inviting sofas, lots of
magazines and an honour bar. The rest of the
hotel is given over to comfortable, well-furnished
bedrooms, some quite small, others large enough
to have sitting areas, all fitted with thoughtful
extras, from chocolates and teddy bears to fold-
out maps and cassette players. Bathrooms (three
shower only) have quality toiletries and luxurious
bathrobes. A superb continental breakfast is
served in the rooms. No other meals available.
Original watercolours are a feature throughout.
Amenities laundry service.

■ *Rooms* 29	*Confirm by* arrang.
en suite bath/shower 29	*Last dinner* None
Direct dial Yes	*Parking* Difficult
Room TV Yes	*Room service* All day
Closed 10 days Xmas	

Belgravia-Sheraton

H 78% **£A** *E* **Map 23 D4**
20 Chesham Place SW1X 8HQ
01-259 6243. Tlx 919020
Credit Access, Amex, Diners, Visa
   Occupying a prime corner site in Belgravia, this
fine modern hotel provides comfort, style and
service in good measure. Steps lead down into
the pleasant lobby-lounge, in one corner of which
nestles the little library bar. Bedrooms, generally
of a decent size, include a dozen designated non-
smoking; all rooms have king-size beds, mini-bars
and hairdryers, and their colour schemes and
darkwood military-style furnishings impart a
traditional feel. Bathrooms are well supplied with
towels and toiletries. Good valeting and
comprehensive room service. No dogs.
Amenities laundry service, valeting, in-house
movies (free), 24-hour lounge service.

■ *Rooms 89*	*Confirm by 4*
en suite bath/shower 89	*Last dinner 10.30*
Direct dial Yes	*Parking Difficult*
Room TV Yes	*Room service 24 hours*

■ Changes in data may occur in
establishments after the Guide
goes to press. Prices should be taken
as indications rather than firm quotes.

menu & WINE LIST 1987-8

Belvedere

R ♨ ♿ **Map 21 B4**
Holland House, Holland Park W8
01-602 1238
French cooking
Credit Access, Amex, Diners, Visa
   A spacious and elegant restaurant set in
Holland Park. The ambitious menu is classical
French with a modern influence and uses good
raw materials to produce satisfying dishes.

Typical offerings are breast of mallard duck with
mushrooms and chestnuts, and sole and salmon
fillets served with sea urchin sauce. Good choice
of sweets. Sound wine list. ℮

■ *Set L £35*	*L 12–2.30*
Set D £35	*D 6.30–10.30,*
About £70 for two	*Sat 6.30–11*
Seats 70 Parties 250	*Parking Ample*
Closed L Sat, all Sun & Bank Hols	

Benihana *NEW ENTRY*

R **Map 20 B3**
100 Avenue Road NW3
01-586 9508
Japanese cooking
Credit Access, Amex, Diners, Visa
   Diners are seated eight to a table at this
spacious ultra-modern Japanese restaurant,
where you can watch your meal being cooked by
the accomplished chef. Appetiser, soup, salad,

vegetables, rice and green tea are included in the
price of main dishes. Try the seafood combination
– cold water lobster tail, king prawns and scallops.
Finish with sorbet or fresh fruit. Children's menu
Sunday lunchtime. Booking essential.

■ *Set D from £11·25*	*L Sun only 12–3*
About £60 for two	*D 5.30–11, Sun 7–11*
Seats 112 Parties 112	*Parking Limited*
Closed 25 Dec.	

Bentley's

R **Map 24 B3**
11 Swallow Street W1
01-734 4756
Seafood cooking
Credit Access, Amex, Diners, Visa. **LVs**
   First-class seafood draws the crowds to this
simply appointed West End restaurant. Oysters,
whitebait and smoked salmon pâté are all
favourite starters, while the wide choice of main

courses embraces grilled plaice and fish-cakes as
well as elaborately sauced dishes like Dover sole
mille-feuille served with a typically flavoursome
saffron sauce. Excellent white burgundies. Simple
sweets like fresh strawberry cheesecake or
wholesome apple pie. ♀ **Well-chosen** ℮

■ *About £52 for two*	*L 12–3*
Seats 120 Parties 50	*D 6–11*
Closed Sun & Bank Hols	*Parking Difficult*

The Berkeley

HR **90% £A *E* Map 22 D3**
Wilton Place SW1
01-235 6000. Tlx 919252
Manager Stefano Sebastiani
Credit Access, Amex, Diners, Visa

Discreet and dignified, this quintessential English hotel offers superlative service and outstanding comfort. Many fine features come from the old Berkeley, including the Lutyens panelling and an impressive cut-glass chandelier in one of the beautiful lounges. The restaurant, which incorporates a private dining room, is decorated with Holbein prints from the Queen's collection. There are two bars, one of them overlooking the roof-top pool. Bedrooms are large and superbly furnished, with sumptuously

appointed marble-floored bathrooms equipped with unusually large baths. No dogs.
Amenities indoor swimming pool, sauna, solarium, keep-fit equipment, beauty salon, hairdressing, cinema, valeting, laundry service, kiosk.

■ *Rooms* 160	*Confirm by* arrang.
en suite bath/shower 160	*Last dinner* 11.15
Direct dial Yes	*Parking* Ample
Room TV Yes	*Room service* 24 hours

Berkeley Restaurant ♔ ♔

Panelled walls and stylish drapes provide a luxurious setting for a lengthy menu that largely follows standard French lines. Soufflés and quenelles, sauced entrées and grills are all soundly prepared using quality ingredients; a strong English element is apparent with seasonal game dishes, a daily roast and grills. A good sweet trolley includes traditional puddings. Service under Carlo Tanzi is polished and professional. A fine range of champagnes on a classic wine list. ☺

■ *Set L* £15	*L* 12.30–2.15,
About £70 *for two*	*Sun* 1–2.15
Seats 60 *Parties* 200	*D* 6.30–10.45,
Closed Sat	*Sun* 7–10.15

Berners Hotel

See under Ramada Hotel

Bill Bentley's

R **Map 26 D1**
Swedeland Court, 202 Bishopsgate EC2
01-283 1763
Seafood
Credit Access, Visa

Seafood is the obvious choice at this well-patronised cellar restaurant opposite Liverpool Street Station. What's best depends on the season – seek the head waiter's advice. Start perhaps with oysters – a speciality here – then proceed to skate in black butter or suprême of salmon with sorrel sauce. For meat-lovers the choice might include roast pheasant, and vegetarians are also well catered for. Booking advised. ♟ Well-chosen ☺

■ *About* £55 *for two*	*L only* 11.30–3
Seats 90 *Parties* 90	*Parking* Difficult
Closed Sat, Sun & Bank Hols	

Le Bistroquet

R **Map 20 C3**
273 Camden High Street NW1
01-485 9607
Credit Access, Amex, Visa

In essence, this lively brasserie is best visited in a party, although there are some quiet alcoves for dining à deux. Book early for a table in the conservatory, with its novel glass sliding roof and flower-decked tables. Cooking is of a good standard with excellent salads and interesting vegetables. Fresh pasta is popular. Desserts include glazed fruits and sorbets.
♟ Well-chosen ☺

■ *Set L* £7·50	*L* 12–3
Set D £7·50	*D* 7–11.30, Sun 7–11
About £45 *for two*	*Parking* Ample
Seats 130 *Parties* 15	*Closed* 3 days Xmas

Bitter Lemons Taverna

R ♘ **Map 21 B5**
98 Lillie Road SW6
01-381 1069
Greek cooking
Credit Access, Visa

Generous portions of traditional Greek Cypriot dishes are reliably prepared by the Zarvos family at this unpretentious restaurant. Start with a deliciously salty grilled Greek cheese and choose from favourites like moussaka and afelia. Excellent mezes (dips, spicy sausages, stuffed vine leaves, kebabs) are good value and ideal for two or more. Friendly service.

■ *Set L & D* £8·15	*L* 12–3
About £33 *for two*	*D* 6–12
Seats 80 *Parties* 80	*Parking* Limited
Closed Sun & 2 wks Aug	

Blakes Hotel

HR 76% £A **Map 23 B5**
33 Roland Gardens SW7 3PF
01-370 6701. Tlx 8813500
Credit Access, Amex, Diners, Visa

A unique hotel created from several Victorian terraced houses, where the interior is a veritable Aladdin's cave of rich carpets, fabrics and treasures. The foyer has exotic black walls, leather and bamboo furniture. An intimate bar is boldly decorated in black and white while the lounge has striking Chinese enamelled screens and colourful cushions. Upstairs, one floor has been redecorated entirely in black. Bedrooms are stunning, with voluminous drapes, huge carved beds and exquisite antiques. Sumptuous

bathrooms have black marble fittings. The tone gradually lightens to grey on the ascent to the next floor, which shows the same astonishing artistry. A new suite in deepest peach is just as awe-inspiring. Superb service. No dogs.
Amenities laundry service.

■ *Rooms* 55	*Confirm by arrang.*
en suite bath/shower 55	*Last dinner* 11.30
Direct dial Yes	*Parking* Difficult
Room TV Yes	*Room service* 24 hours

Blakes Hotel Restaurant ♕

This smart, stylish basement restaurant has a Far-Eastern feel in design and decor. The menu incorporates dishes from many nations with plenty of imaginative choices cooked with skill. Start with game and chicory soup or salad of foie gras and black truffles; move on to mousseline of veal sweetbreads, or prawn satay before tackling noisettes of venison with celeriac purée or salmis of guinea fowl with fruit seasoning. Fine sweets such as passion fruit soufflé to finish. Friendly service. ℗

■ *About £90 for two*	*L* 12.30–2.30
Seats 36	*D* 7.30–11.30
Closed 25 & 26 Dec	

Bloom's

R ♿ 130 Golders Green Road NW11
01-455 3033 **Map 20 B1**

90 Whitechapel High Street E1
01-247 6001 **Map 21 D4**
Jewish cooking
Credit Access, Visa

Excellent kosher cooking and a stream of banter from quick-serving staff are what Bloom's is famous for. The twin restaurants serve a variety of dishes from the classic salt beef with potato latkes and pickled cucumber to other traditional delights, including viennas, chopped liver and

frankfurters; you can also choose daily specials like giblet soup and curried turkey. Formidable eaters not overwhelmed by the substantial main courses can tackle desserts such as lockshen pudding.

■ *Golders Green*	*Meals* noon–9.30,
Seats 80 *Parties* 80	Sun 11.30–9.30
Whitechapel High St	*Meals* 11.30–10, Fri
Seats 150	11.30–3pm (2pm in
Parties 150	winter)
About £28 for two	*Parking* Ample
Closed Sat, Good Fri, 25 Dec & Jewish hols	

Bloomsbury Crest Hotel

H 62% £C **Map 24 C1**
Coram Street, Russell Square WC1N 1HT
01-837 1200. Tlx 22113
Credit Access, Amex, Diners, Visa. **LVs**

A comfortable modern hotel well placed for the West End. Bloomsbury's literary associations are recalled in the pubby Dickens Bar and the plusher Lady Ottoline Bar. There's a non-smoking option on both standard and Executive bedrooms. The

latter offer extras like mini-bars, remote-control TVs, hairdryers, fresh fruit, trouser presses and bath robes. *Amenities* in-house movies (charge), laundry service.

■ *Rooms* 239	*Confirm by* 6
en suite bath/shower 239	*Last dinner* 10.45
Direct dial Yes	*Parking* Ample
Room TV Yes	*Room service* All day

Bombay Bicycle Club *NEW ENTRY*

R **Map 21 C6**
95 Nightingale Lane SW12
01-673 6217
Indian cooking
Credit Visa

Perry and Amanda de Samarkandi drive the wheels of this lively and popular Indian restaurant where booking's a must. The menu is particularly well laid out, and the food is very enjoyable.

Among their specialities are tandoori prawns, chicken channa, whole leg of lamb (advance order) and machli masala, a highly spiced fish curry 'as eaten among the northern tribesmen'. Buffet lunch Sat & Sun.

■ *About £40 for two*	*L* 12–3
Seats 65	*D* 7–11.30
Parties 75	*Parking* Ample
Closed L Mon–Fri, D Sun & Xmas	

Bombay Brasserie

R ⛉ **Map 23 B4**
Courtfield Close, Courtfield Road SW7
01-370 4040
Indian cooking
Credit Access, Amex, Diners, Visa
    The lunchtime buffet brings the chance to sample dishes from the North-West Frontier, Kashmir and the Punjab, as well as Bombay, at this spacious and elegant Indian restaurant.

Spicing is authentic and the choice includes fish, chicken, lamb, and lentil dishes, plus hot and cold desserts. Booking is essential in the evening, when the menu is more elaborate. Friendly, helpful service.

■ *Set L* £8.95	*L 12.30–3*
About £42 for two	*D 7.30–12*
Seats 175	*Parking Limited*

■ For a discount on next year's guide, see Offer for Answers.

Bonnington Hotel

H **59% £D Map 24 C1**
92 Southampton Row WC1B 4BH
01-248 2828. Tlx 261591
Manager Mr A. D. Bostock
Credit Access, Amex, Diners, Visa. LVs
    A competently run Edwardian hotel, where a continuing programme of bedroom refurbishment keeps standards up. Improved rooms have light, attractive decor, practical units and neatly

designed bathrooms. The foyer is airy and well planned, and there's a fine balconied lounge and cane-furnished bar. Pleasant staff.
Amenities laundry service, in-house movies (free).

■ *Rooms 228*	*Confirm by 6*
en suite bath/shower 180	*Last dinner 9.30*
Direct dial Yes	*Parking Difficult*
Room TV Yes	*Room service 24 hours*

Boswell's

R **Map 23 A5**
229 Old Brompton Road SW5
01-373 3502
English cooking
Owner manager Mr D. Harding
Credit Access, Amex, Diners, Visa
    The cooking is characteristically English at this pleasant, simple restaurant on the fringes of cosmopolitan Earls Court. The seasonally-

changing menu, amplified by daily blackboard specials, offers a good selection of dishes, from baked egg with madeira and prawns to steak, kidney, mushroom and oyster pie, rack of lamb and roast pheasant served with Cumberland sauce. To finish, perhaps Lord Mayor's trifle. ☺

■ *About £40 for two*	*L Sun only 12.30–2.30*
Seats 40	*D 6–11*
Parties 30	*Parking Ample*

Boulestin

R ⛉ ⛉ **Map 27 B2**
1a Henrietta Street WC2
01-836 7061
Credit Access, Amex, Diners, Visa
    As busy and popular as ever, so booking remains a must at this elegant basement restaurant in Covent Garden. Kevin Kennedy's menu is varied and imaginative, and dishes tried on our latest visit included asperges en filo au beurre de poivre vert (lovely sauce, pastry a touch hard); brioche de langoustines (the brioche surprisingly filled with mushrooms, with langoustines as a garnish); and carré d'agneau

(beautifully cooked, but a very dainty portion). Good selection of plainly prepared vegetables, average sweets. There's an outstanding cheeseboard from Androuet, and the coffee is superb. An impeccable classic cellar has a particularly powerful burgundy showing. Staff are very efficient and courteous.
⊃ Outstanding ♀ Well-chosen ☺

■ *Set L* £15	*L 12–2.30*
About £85 for two	*D 7–11.15*
Seats 70	*Parking Difficult*
Closed L Sat, all Sun, Bank Hols, 3 wks Aug & 1 wk Xmas	

Boyd's Glass Garden Restaurant *NEW ENTRY*

R � **Map 22 A3**
135 Kensington Church Street W8
01-727 5452
Credit Access, Amex, Visa
    Chef-patron Boyd Gilmour gives his name to a chic, summery little restaurant. His cooking is modern and thoughtful. Typical dishes could include mousseline of scallops, calf's kidney with a trio of mustards and veal roulade with game and

sweetbread stuffing. Blackberry délice with pear coulis a pleasant sweet. Carefully chosen French wines, with plenty of half-bottles.
♀ Well-chosen ☺

■ *Set L from* £11	*L 12.30–2.30*
Set D from £19.50	*D 7.30–10.30*
About £55 for two	*Parking Limited*
Seats 36	*Closed L Sat, all Sun,*
Bank Hols & 2 wks Aug	

Hotel Britannia Inter-Continental

HR **80% £A E Map 22 D2**
Grosvenor Square W1A 3AN
01-629 9400. Tlx 23941
Credit Access, Amex, Diners, Visa

Very high standards of comfort, style and
service are offered at this Corinthian-columned
hotel overlooking Grosvenor Square. The roomy
lobby has separate reception, concierge and
customer relations desks, plus a capacious
carpeted island of easy chairs and settees under
modern crystal chandeliers. There's plenty more
space to relax in the cocktail lounge and bars, and
the arcade of bow-fronted shops is quite a
feature. Standard bedrooms, though not
particularly large, are very well equipped, with air-
conditioning, remote-control TVs, mini-bars and

hairdryers. All rooms have good walnut veneered
furniture; compact, tiled bathrooms are also well
appointed. Studio rooms are more spacious, and
there are some well laid-out suites. *Amenities*
laundry service, hairdressing, shopping arcade,
in-house movies (free), teletext, kiosk.

■ *Rooms 354*	*Confirm by 6*
en suite bath/shower 354	*Last dinner 10.30*
Direct dial Yes	*Parking Limited*
Room TV Yes	*Room service 24 hours*

Adams Restaurant ♛

Raw materials are garnered from far and wide to
prepare the excellent meals served in this quietly
luxurious hotel restaurant. Chef David Nicholls
cooks with a distinctive modern touch, his skills
typified in dishes like scallops with sweet turnip
and potato muffins, fillet of veal crowned with
creamed artichokes or apple and orange turnover
with Oregon syrup ice cream. The wine list
includes good Californian and English sections.
♀ Well-chosen ℮

■ *Set L £15·50*	*L 12.30–2.30*
Set D £21·50	*D 6.30–10.30*
About £62 for two	*Seats 45*
Closed L Sat, L Sun & Bank Hols	

Brown's Hotel

H **77% £A E Map 25 B4**
Albemarle Street W1A 4SW
01-493 6020. Tlx 28686
Manager Bruce Banister
Credit Access, Amex, Diners, Visa

Excellent old-fashioned standards of service
and a strong sense of tradition have helped to
make this beautifully-kept hotel the favourite it is
today. The atmosphere of the public areas, with
their mellow wood panelling, is not unlike that of
an English country house. Afternoon tea may be
taken in the splendidly chintzy, flower-filled
lounge; letters composed in the peaceful writing
room; or a pre-dinner aperitif sipped in the warmly
elegant St George's Bar. Scrupulous
refurbishment keeps bedrooms looking fresh and
bright, whether furnished in sleek contemporary
style or adorned with fine antique pieces; all

rooms have mini-bars. Bathrooms, equally varied
in style, are well equipped. *Amenities* men's
hairdressing, valeting, laundry service, 24-hour
lounge service.

■ *Rooms 125*	*Confirm by 6*
en suite bath/shower 125	*Last dinner 10*
Direct dial Yes	*Parking Difficult*
Room TV Yes	*Room service 24 hours*

℮ is our symbol for an **outstanding** wine list.

Bubbles Bistro

R ⌕ **Map 22 D2**
41 North Audley Street W1
01-491 3237
Owner managers David & Susan Nichol
Credit Access, Amex, Diners, Visa

The monthly-changing menu keeps the chef on
his toes at this smart bistro in the downstairs
section of Bubbles Wine Bar. Delicious choices
range from chicken and pink peppercorn terrine

and tender veal in a superb lime and chive sauce
to a scallop, ginger and spring onions salad
garnished with mange-touts. Mouthwatering
sweets, too.
♀ Well-chosen ℮

■ *Set L £12·50*	*L 12–3*
About £38 for two	*D 6–10.30*
Seats 50 Parties 50	*Parking Limited*
Closed Sat, Sun & Bank Hols	

Bubb's

R **Map 26 A1**
329 Central Markets, Smithfield EC1
01-236 2435
French cooking
   Lunchtime booking's essential at this agreeable French restaurant at the edge of Smithfield Market. The short menu, supplemented by plats du jour, tempts with well-prepared dishes like consommé with sorrel, duck breast au poivre and veal chop with mustard. Despite the meaty milieu, there are also several fish dishes. Crisply cooked vegetables, nice sweets. Fast, efficient French service. ℮
■ *About £50 for two*   *L 12.15–2*
Seats 80   *D 7–9.30*
Parties 40   *Parking* Difficult
Closed Sat, Sun, Bank Hols, 2 wks Aug & 10 days Xmas

Cadogan Thistle Hotel

H **71% £A/B Map 23 D4**
75 Sloane Street SW1X 9SG
01-235 7141. Tlx 267893
Credit Access, Amex, Diners, Visa
   Once the London home of Lillie Langtry, and frequently linked with such distinguished names as Oscar Wilde and J. A. M. Whistler, this turreted hotel still preserves an elegant period feel and retains a great deal of character. Fine panelling and chintzy drapes distinguish the charming foyer and lounge, and there's an intimate cocktail bar decorated with an interesting collection of Victorian and Edwardian photographs. Spacious bedrooms featuring attractive coordinating fabrics in pastel shades and darkwood furnishings are also in traditional style, though accessories such as hairdryers, trouser presses, mini-bars and wall safes are thoroughly up to

date. A number of rooms are more modestly fitted. Original hand-painted tiles remain in some bathrooms. *Amenities* garden, tennis, in-house movies, valeting, 24-hour lounge service.
■ *Rooms* 69   *Confirm by* 6
en suite bath/shower 69   *Last dinner* 10
Direct dial Yes   *Parking* Limited
Room TV Yes   *Room service* 24 hours

Café du Commerce *NEW ENTRY*

R & **Map 5 F2**
The Business Efficiency Centre,
Limeharbour E14
01-538 2030
Credit Access, Diners, Visa
   In the heart of the new Docklands complex, this brasserie-style restaurant is popular for morning coffee, lunch and early evening snacks. The lunchtime menus feature seafood (mussel omelette, sea bass en papillote, Danish pickled herrings) alongside meat dishes such as grilled rabbit, veal cordon bleu or beef bordelaise. For private parties there's an old Dutch clipper moored in West India Docks. ♀ Well-chosen
■ *Set L £11·75*   *L 11.45–3*
About £30 for two   *Parking* Ample
Seats 45   *Parties* 80
Closed Sat, Sun & Bank Hols

Café Flo *NEW ENTRY*

R **Map 20 B2**
205 Haverstock Hill NW3
01-435 6744
Credit Access, Visa
   Skilled cooking and delightful friendly service in a cheerful and informal atmosphere in this modern brasserie opposite Belsize Park Underground Station. The menu, though not lengthy, holds plenty of interest with items like beautifully cooked pasta spirals au pistou, confit de canard with sautéed potatoes, and poached cod with a provençale sauce. Desserts always include a tart – ours was a really delicious tarte tatin. A roast or pot au feu is the centrepiece of the set Sunday lunch; brunch menu also available. ℮
■ *Set L £4·95*   *L 12–3, Sat & Sun 11–3*
About £30 for two   *D 6–12, Sun 7–11*
Seats 40 *Parties* 12   *Parking* Difficult

Café Royal Grill Room

R ⍩⍩⍩ & **Map 24 B3**
68 Regent Street W1
01-437 9090
French cooking
Manager Carlo Ambrosini
Credit Access, Amex, Diners, Visa. LVs
   Splendour unlimited, with carved caryatids, ornate gilt mirrors and rich red plush. The menu is classical French, with a choice of luxury starters, grills, flambés, fish dishes and sauced entrées. Cooking is very acceptable, if rarely particularly exciting or imaginative. A classic cellar includes several 1961 clarets.
♀ Well-chosen ℮
■ *Set L £18·50*   *L 12.30–3*
About £56 for two   *D 6–11, Sun 7–10.30*
Seats 55   *Parking* Difficult
Closed L Sat & Sun

Capital Hotel

HR **81% £A E Map 23 C4**
22 Basil Street SW3 1AT
01-589 5171. Tlx 919042
Manager Keith Williams
Credit Access, Amex, Diners, Visa

An immaculate hotel just a stone's throw from Harrods. A continuing programme of improvements has resulted in cosy and traditional public areas enhanced with rich fabrics and antique furniture. The foyer has a fin de siècle feel and the lounge, with its dark green walls and contrasting wine-coloured fabric, is full of interest. An engraved mirror adorns the bar, which has pickled pine walls and comfortable seating. Bedrooms are gradually being refurbished to a high standard with beautiful fabrics and delicate pastel colours combining to give stunning effects.

The superb bathrooms are well equipped with lots of thoughtful extras including hairdryers, bathrobes and sewing kits. *Amenities* laundry service, 24-hour lounge service.

■ *Rooms* 56	*Confirm by* arrang.
en suite bath/shower 56	*Last dinner* 10.30
Direct dial Yes	*Parking* Limited
Room TV Yes	*Room service* 24 hours

Capital Hotel Restaurant ♔ ᕼ

French cooking
An elegantly appointed restaurant with a concise French menu. Starters include brandade de sole aux endives and timbale de légumes; main course might be ris de veau au coulis de poivrons or foie de veau poêlé aux échalotes. Finish with mousse de crème brûlée aux fruits de passion or marquise au chocolat blanc sauce au café. Wine list is strong in fine clarets. Service is disappointing.
♀ Well-chosen ☺

■ *Set L* £17·50	*L* 12.30–2.15,
Set D £25	*Sun* 12.30–2
About £80 for two	*D* 6.30–10.30, *Sun* 7–10
Seats 40	*Parties* 24

■ For a discount on next year's guide, see Offer for Answers.

Le Caprice

R **Map 25 B4**
Arlington House, 17 Arlington Street SW1
01-629 2239
Owner managers Christopher Corbin & Jeremy King
Credit Access, Amex, Diners, Visa

Coolly sophisticated in black and white, with mirror panels and David Bailey portraits. The menu, boosted by daily specials, is full of interest and imagination, ranging from eggs Benedict and a salad of raw tuna to salmon fishcakes, veal steak with kidneys and really excellent rack of lamb en croûte. Sweets are not to be missed. Sunday brunch. ♀ Well-chosen ☺

■ *About £46 for two*	*L* 12–2.30
Seats 75	*D* 6–12, Sat 7–12
Closed L Sat & Bank	*Parking* Limited
Hols & 10 days Xmas	

Caravan Serai

R **Map 22 D1**
50 Paddington Street W1
01-935 1208
Afghan cooking
Owner manager Mr Nayeb
Credit Access, Amex, Diners, Visa

At its busiest at lunchtime, this colourful Afghan restaurant teams tasty cooking with friendly service. Many of the dishes feature chicken or lamb, and the clay-oven specialities such as chopan kebab are particularly good. The pan-fried fish, veal and beef dishes are also excellent. Ashak – a leek-filled pasta with minced lamb – makes a delicious starter.

■ *About £40 for two*	*L* 12–3
Seats 50	*D* 6–11, Sat 6–11.30,
Parties 50	*Sun* 6–10.30
Closed 25 & 26 Dec	*Parking* Difficult

Casa Cominetti

R ♪ **Map 7 B5**
129 Rushey Green, Catford SE6
01-697 2314
Italian cooking
Credit Amex, Diners, Visa

A long-established restaurant offering a good selection of mainly Italian dishes capably prepared by Luigi Lipparelli. Starters include sardines in mustard sauce, artichoke hearts and seafood salad; main courses range from classics such as spaghetti bolognese to skate with capers and bitter lemon sauce, and steak with pineapple and sweetcorn. Good sweets and ice cream. Both dining rooms are air-conditioned. ☺

■ *About £36 for two*	*L* 12–2.30
Seats 40	*D* 7–10.30
Parties 32	*Parking* Ample
Closed Sun, Mon, Bank Hols & 3 days Xmas	

Cavendish Hotel

H **70% £A/B** **Map 25 B4**
Jermyn Street SW1Y 6JF
01-930 2111 Tlx 263187
Credit Access, Amex, Diners, Visa. LVs
A splendid marble-floored foyer, with oil paintings brightening the mahogany-panelled walls, sets the tone of comfort and luxury at this fine modern hotel. The adjoining lounge bar is quietly intimate – soft lighting and contemporary prints adding to the air of sophistication. Up on the first floor, decor continues cool and elegant with cream walls and plum upholstery. Here there's a second bar, a relaxing lounge area and a coffee shop (called The Gallery). Bedrooms, styled in pale blue and cream, have simple traditional-style furniture – including a writing desk and two armchairs apiece. Mini-bars, hairdryers and trouser presses are standard,

while smallish bathrooms are well equipped with bathtime extras. *Amenities* in-house movies (charge), valeting, laundry service, coffee shop (8am–11pm), 24-hour lounge service, kiosk.

■ *Rooms* 253	*Confirm by* 6
en suite bath/shower 253	*Last dinner* 11
Direct dial Yes	*Parking* Limited
Room TV Yes	*Room service* 24 hours

Chambeli

R 12 Great Castle Street W1
01-636 0662 **Map 24 B2**
146 Southampton Row WC1
01-837 3925 **Map 24 C1**
Indian cooking
Credit Access, Amex, Diners, Visa
Two smart Indian restaurants offering enjoyable food and good service. The menu is fairly standard, with popular choices like tandoori mixed grill, chicken, lamb and prawn curries, tandooris and tikkas. Good selection of vegetable dishes and well-made nan; simple sweets.

■ *Great Castle Street*	*L* 12–3 *D* 6–11.30
Seats 86	*Parties* 86
Southampton Row	*Meals* noon–midnight
Seats 65	*Parties* 65
About £30 for two	*Parking* Difficult
Closed 25 Dec, also Sun at Great Castle Street	

Chaopraya Restaurant

R 〰 **Map 22 D1**
22 St Christopher's Place W1
01-486 0777
Thai cooking
Owner manager Mr S. I. Nilawonese
Credit Access, Amex, Diners, Visa
Authentic Thai cooking, graceful service and ready smiles in this smart basement restaurant, a civilised spot to get over a shopping trip to Oxford Street. Fresh herbs and spices play subtle leading roles in the soups, the satays, the steamed fish, the grilled beef with hot basil, the excellent Thai rice noodles. Fresh fruits and ices for a cooling conclusion.

■ *Set L & D from* £11	*L* 12–3
About £35 for two	*D* 6.30–11
Seats 85 *Parties* 85	*Parking* Limited
Closed L Sat, all Sun & Bank Hols	

Charing Cross Hotel

H **60% £C** ♿ **Map 27 B3**
Strand, WC2N 5HX
01-839 7282. Tlx 261101
Manager Hans Pearson
Credit Access, Amex, Diners, Visa. LVs
The handsome Victorian facade of this railway hotel is a well-known sight to travellers. Inside, there's still considerable traditional appeal, particularly in the restaurant and main lounge. Bedrooms are light and quite roomy. The 80 singles are being converted into twins. Staff are cheerful and helpful. *Amenities* sauna, solarium, keep-fit equipment, beauty salon, hairdressing, 24-hour lounge service.

■ *Rooms* 218	*Confirm by* 6
en suite bath/shower 218	*Last dinner* 10.30
Direct dial Yes	*Parking* Difficult
Room TV Yes	*Room service* None

Charles Bernard Hotel

H **55% £D** **Map 20 B2**
5 Frognal NW3 6AL
01-794 0101. Tlx 23560
Manager Mr M. J. Muir
Credit Access, Amex, Diners, Visa
A purpose-built 70s-style hotel situated in a quiet residential street just off the busy Finchley Road. Open-plan public areas include a spacious bar-lounge and an adjoining TV lounge. Neat well-kept bedrooms feature the vibrant colour schemes and hessian walls typical of the period. All have remote-control TVs and tea/coffee-makers.
Amenities laundry service.

■ *Rooms* 57	*Confirm by* 6
en suite bath/shower 57	*Last dinner* 9.15
Direct dial Yes	*Parking* Limited
Room TV Yes	*Room service* All day

Chelsea Hotel

H 74% £A/B *E* Map 23 D4
Sloane Street SW1X 9NU
01-235 4377. Tlx 919111
Credit Access, Amex, Diners, Visa
   A modern hotel in a prime Knightsbridge location, within strolling distance of Harrods. Marble floors, leather chesterfields and glittering chandeliers create an unashamedly luxurious effect in the lobby, while the lounge with its rich red tones, period-style furnishings and portraits is comfortably elegant. Good-sized bedrooms – many with magnificent views over London – offer large beds, modern darkwood units, brass light fittings and plenty of writing space. Mini-bars, hairdryers and remote-control TVs are standard. Marble-effect wallcoverings create a stylish effect in the neat, well-equipped bathrooms. No dogs. *Amenities* hairdressing, in-house movies, laundry

service, coffee shop (7am–10.30pm), 24-hour lounge service, kiosk.

■ *Rooms* 215	*Confirm by 6*
en suite bath/shower 215	*Last dinner* 10.30
Direct dial Yes	*Parking* Ample
Room TV Yes	*Room service* 24 hours

Chesterfield Hotel

H 75% £A *E* Map 25 A4
35 Charles Street W1X 8LX
01-491 2622. Tlx 269394
Manager Graham Tomlinson
Credit Access, Amex, Diners, Visa
   Once the home of the fourth Earl of Chesterfield, this attractive Georgian building is an elegant and very comfortable hotel, where smart staff provide willing, pleasant service. The foyer, with its marble floor, Venetian chandelier, fine oil paintings and fresh flowers in abundance, sets a tone of quiet luxury that extends to the panelled lounge, situated in the library, and the clubby bar which features family portraits of the Chesterfield house. Good-sized bedrooms with handsome furnishings and fittings and colourful coordinated fabrics offer extras large and small, from remote-control TVs to fresh flowers and

mineral water. Bathrobes and quality toiletries are provided. No dogs. *Amenities* 24-hour lounge service, coffee shop (10am–midnight), in-house movies (free), laundry service.

■ *Rooms* 113	*Confirm by 6*
en suite bath/shower 113	*Last dinner* 10.30
Direct dial Yes	*Parking* Difficult
Room TV Yes	*Room service* 24 hours

♀ indicates a **well-chosen** house wine.

Chez Moi

R ♨ ♀ Map 21 A4
1 Addison Avenue, Holland Park W11
01-603 8267
French cooking
Credit Access, Amex, Diners, Visa
   Lamb is Richard Walton's speciality, and on our visit to this inviting French restaurant he was offering garlicky or mustard-coated racks, cutlets with sauce paloise and grilled medallions with an

apricot sauce. Other choices included onion soup, quenelles of turbot, and boned poussin with a creamy shrimp sauce. Partner Colin Smith ensures efficient service front of house.
♀ Well-chosen ⊜

■ *Set D* £16.50	*D only* 7–11.30
About £55 *for two*	*Parking* Ample
Seats 45	*Closed* Sun, Bank

Hols, 2 wks Aug & 2 wks Xmas

Chinon *NEW ENTRY*

R ♀ Map 21 A4
25 Richmond Way W14
01-602 5968
Credit Access, Amex, Visa
   Barbara Dean and Jonathan Hayes have transferred their talents from the Perfumed Conservatory to this small, chic new restaurant. Their menu changes with whatever's good, and inventiveness stamps dishes like pea, pear and

nettle soup or breast of duck with orange and rowan jelly sauce. Good cheeseboard. A carefully considered wine list contains some excellent lesser-known items. ♀ Well-chosen ⊜

■ *Set D* £17.50	*L* 12–2.30
About £55 *for two*	*D* 7–10.30
Seats 28 *Parties* 28	*Parking* Limited

Closed L Sat, all Sun, Bank Hols, Aug &
1 wk Xmas

Cho Won

R **Map 27 A2**
27 Romilly Street W1
01-437 2262
Korean cooking
Credit Access, Amex, Diners, Visa
  A small, unpretentious Korean restaurant with an extensive menu which is helpfully explained. You might sample thinly sliced sirloin of beef with a julienne of vegetables, served with a

flavoursome soup, or fried rice with tiny prawns. Pickled vegetables are popular, as is grilled fish. The dishes are authentic, varied and carefully cooked, with a good choice available for those who prefer vegetarian meals.

■ *Set L £3·90*	*L 12–3*
Set D from £9	*D 6–11*
About £26 for two	*Parking Difficult*
Seats 70 Parties 30	*Closed 25 Dec*

▷ is our symbol for an **outstanding** wine list.

Christian's

R ♵ **Map 21 A5**
Station Parade, Burlington Lane,
Chiswick W4
01-995 0382
French cooking
  Chef-patron Christian Gustin cooks with flair and imagination at this informal, leafy restaurant. His short, well-balanced menus offer such thoroughly modern temptations as salmon

dumplings in a light watercress sauce followed by quails en papillote sauced with red wine or fillet steak with oyster mushrooms, cream and vermouth. Attractively presented sweets to finish. ⊖

■ *About £40 for two*	*L 12.30–2*
Seats 35	*D 7.30–10.15*
Parties 8	*Parking Ample*
Closed L Sat, all Sun & Mon, 1 wk Xmas	
& 2 wks in winter	

Chuen Cheng Ku

R **Map 27 A2**
17 Wardour Street W1
01-734 3281
Chinese cooking
Manager Mr K. W. Charm
Credit Access, Amex, Diners, Visa
  One of the Soho stalwarts, a cavernous 400-seat Chinese restaurant that's always busy. Three kitchens support this frenzy, one for dim sum

(served until 6pm), one for soups, roast meats, etc, and one for the huge Cantonese main menu listing familiar favourites and more unusual specialities. Manager Mr Charm keeps it all together and lives up to his name.

■ *Set meals from £13*	*Meals 11am–midnight,*
About £30 for two	*Sun 11am–11.30pm*
Seats 400 Parties 250	*Parking Difficult*
Closed 24 & 25 Dec	

Churchill Hotel

HR **80% £A *E* Map 22 D1**
30 Portman Square W1A 4ZX
01-486 5800. Tlx 264831
Credit Access, Amex, Diners, Visa
  Built in 1970, with a subtle Regency feel to its interior design, the Churchill offers very high standards of service, maintenance and housekeeping. A continuous programme of redecoration keeps everything pristine, and the bedrooms, including numerous suites, are stylish and very comfortable, with individual air-conditioning, remote-control TVs and mini-bars. Room service is extensive. There's also abundant comfort in the marble foyer, the sunken lounge (sometimes used for functions) and the walnut-panelled Churchill Bar. Note, too, the coffee shop,

cheerful in yellow and blue. No dogs.
Amenities garden, hairdressing, satellite TV, teletext, valeting, laundry service, coffee shop (7am–1am), 24-hour lounge service, shopping arcade.

■ *Rooms 489*	*Confirm by 6*
en suite bath/shower 489	*Last dinner 11*
Direct dial Yes	*Parking Limited*
Room TV Yes	*Room service 24 hours*

The Arboury 🛏 ♿

Manager Sergio Filotrani
A name change (it used to be called 'No 10') accompanies a new decorative theme of trees at this comfortable restaurant. The daily roast and grills remain popular lunchtime choices, while both sessions also offer slightly more elaborate choices like beef fillet with foie gras sauce or breast of duck sautéed with pineapple and ginger, deglazed with wine vinegar. Polished service. Sound wines: Riesling from Beyer, Montagny from Steinmaier, Sancerre from Dezat.
♟ Well-chosen ⊖

■ *Set L from £16·50*	*L 12–2.30*
Set D £25	*D 7–11*
About £70 for two	*Seats 72*

Ciboure

R **Map 23 D4**
21 Eccleston Street SW1
01-730 2505
Owner manager Jean-Louis Journade
Credit Access, Amex, Diners, Visa
An attractively contemporary restaurant where Richard Price gives French dishes the modern treatment. Vegetable terrine and leek butter, sautéed beef sauced with beetroot and chicken poached with mussels in saffron sauce typify his masterly blend of the subtle and the distinct. Exquisite sweets and unpasteurised English cheeses. Post-theatre set menu after 10pm.
♥ Well-chosen ©

■ Set L £12.50	L 12–2.30
About £54 for two	D 7–11
Seats 36 Parties 8	*Parking Limited*
***Closed** L Sat, all Sun, Bank Hols & 22 Aug–1 Sept*	

City Brasserie

R **Map 26 D2**
Plantation House, Mincing Lane EC3
01-220 7094
French cooking
Credit Access, Amex, Diners, Visa
In the basement of Plantation House, Peter Langan's City venture offers comfortable lunch-time eating in pleasantly relaxed surroundings, with good wines and expert service. Frequently changing menus span a tempting range, from soups like wild mushroom and almond to roasts like guinea fowl stuffed with celeriac mousse. Some nice fruity desserts. Carefully selected wines include an excellent 1985 Brouilly from Pierre Ferraud. ♥ Well-chosen ©

■ *About £44 for two*	L only 11.30–3
Seats 225 Parties 250	*Parking Difficult*
***Closed** Sat, Sun & Bank Hols*	

City Miyama *NEW ENTRY*

R ♟ **Map 26 B2**
17 Godliman Street EC4
01-489 1937
Japanese cooking
Credit Access, Amex, Diners, Visa
In a side street near St Paul's Cathedral, this Japanese restaurant has all the sophistication of its Mayfair counterpart. The griddle and sushi bars are on the ground floor, the main restaurant – all in white, with mirrors and subtle lighting – downstairs. Seafood is of superb quality, though some of it, such as ark shell or sea urchin, is definitely an acquired taste. Various inexpensive set lunches.

■ Set L from £5·60	L 12–2.30
About £60 for two	D 6–10
Seats 80 Parties 20	*Parking Difficult*
***Closed** Sat, Sun & Bank Hols*	

Claridge's

HR **90% £A** ♿ **Map 24 A3**
Brook Street W1A 2JQ
01-629 8860. Tlx 21872
Credit Access, Amex, Diners, Visa
From the instant you enter this London landmark, liveried staff are at your service. In the newly decorated lounge (there is no bar), drinks are served to the dulcet tones of an orchestra, while the peace of the reading room is broken only by the chink of tea cups. Climb the grand staircase or take the elegant lift to Art Deco or traditional bedrooms that are spacious and well appointed. Bathrooms come in two sizes – large and enormous – with reassuringly old-fashioned suites, superb showers and lots of thoughtful extras. No dogs. *Amenities* hairdressing, valeting, laundry service, 24-hour lounge service.

■ *Rooms 205*	*Confirm by arrang.*
en suite bath/shower 205	*Last dinner 11.15*
Direct dial Yes	*Parking Difficult*
Room TV Yes	*Room service 24 hours*

Claridge's Restaurant ♛ ♛ ♿

French cooking
Run on classic French lines (with staff sometimes volatile and voluble), this pink and peach restaurant serves a nicely-balanced selection of dishes ranging from a simple T-bone steak to a highly-sauced feuilleté aux champignons de prairie à la crème. There's a good choice of carefully cooked vegetables, plus some delectable desserts. Excellent burgundies.
♥ Well-chosen ©

■ *About £70 for two*	L 12.30–3
Seats 100	D 7.30–11.15, Sat
Parties 12	7–11.15

The Causerie ♛ ♿

Manager Peter Mand
Service is charming and efficient at this intimate little establishment. Sample the lavish lunchtime smörgåsbord or settle for a simple starter like scallops and langoustines in herb butter, followed perhaps by rosettes of lamb with basil and tomato sauce. Raw materials are outstanding, cooking very assured. Pre- and post-theatre menu.
♥ Well-chosen ©

■ *About £60 for two*	L 12–3
Seats 40 Parties 10	D 6–11,
***Closed** Sat*	Sun 7–10.30

Clarke's

R ⚑ **Map 22 A3**
124 Kensington Church Street W8
01-221 9225
Credit Access, Visa
    Sally Clarke manages the kitchens by day and the dining room at night at this smart modern restaurant. Her daily changing menus provide a small choice at lunchtime and none in the evening. Imaginative dishes like pork loin with rosemary and prune sauce, pheasant with pecan nuts and spinach and char grilled corn-fed chicken are cooked with skill and dedication. Delicious home-made breads. ⚑ Well-chosen ☺

■ Set L from £11	L 12.30–2
Set D £19	D 7.30–10
About £50 for two	Parking Limited
Seats 60 Parties 8	Closed Sat, Sun, Bank
Hols, 1 wk Easter, 3 wks Aug & 2 wks Xmas	

The Clifton-Ford

H **70% £B Map 22 D1**
47 Welbeck Street W1M 8DN
01-486 6600. Tlx 22569
Manager Andrew Schlemmer
Credit Access, Amex, Diners, Visa
    Enjoying a quiet location just north of Oxford Street, this friendly modern hotel is notably well kept throughout public and private areas. The elegant and airy foyer-lounge, where a pianist plays at night, offers delightfully comfortable seating and a peaceful atmosphere, while the panelled Howard de Walden Bar, decorated in rich burgundy, has a warm, convivial air. Bedrooms, all of a good size, have pretty coordinating decor and built-in modern units, plus up-to-date accessories like hairdryers and direct-dial telephones. Compact tiled bathrooms are all en suite. No dogs. Amenities in-house movies

(free), valeting, laundry service, 24-hour lounge service.

■ Rooms 220	Confirm by arrang.
en suite bath/shower 220	Last dinner 10.15
Direct dial Yes	Parking Limited
Room TV Yes	Room service 24 hours

Coburg Hotel

H **62% £C/D Map 22 A2**
129 Bayswater Road W2 4RJ
01-229 3654. Tlx 268235
Manager Edward E. Gray
Credit Access, Amex, Diners, Visa
    Three terracotta domes distinguish this elegant Edwardian hotel above Queensway tube station. The welcoming panelled foyer creates a stylish first impression and there's a spacious lounge bar. Pleasantly decorated bedrooms (front ones are double glazed) offer tea-makers, trouser presses and hairdryers.
Amenities in-house movies (free), laundry service.

■ Rooms 125	Confirm by 6
en suite bath/shower 70	Last dinner 9.30
Direct dial Yes	Parking Ample
Room TV Most	Room service All day

Colonnade Hotel

H **58% £D/E ♿ Map 20 B3**
2 Warrington Crescent W9 1ER
01-289 2167. Tlx 298930
Owner manager Mr A. R. Richards
Credit Access, Amex, Diners, Visa
    Continuing improvements including a new bar emphasise the clever conversion of this handsome Georgian building near Little Venice. Well-equipped bedrooms of varying sizes (several with four-posters) include the ingenious Captain's Quarters, a box room with a bunk bed and porthole window; spacious suites have their own whirlpool baths. No dogs. Amenities garden, laundry service.

■ Rooms 53	Confirm by 6
en suite bath/shower 40	Last dinner 10
Room phone Yes	Parking Limited
Room TV Yes	Room service 24 hours

Como Lario

R ⚑ **Map 23 D5**
Pimlico Road SW1
01-730 2954
Italian cooking
    Signor Bellini, the simpatico owner of this popular trattoria, insists on quality ingredients, reliable cooking, and cheerful service. Tagliatelle in a tomato sauce with just the right amount of basil is his speciality, but the beautifully tender calf liver alburro is a great favourite, along with familiar steak and veal dishes. Vegetables are good. Simple sweets include excellent zabaglione and fresh fruit salad.

■ About £34 for two	L 12.30–2.30
Seats 70	D 6.30–11.30 `
Parties 20	Parking Limited
Closed Sun, Bank Hols & Xmas	

The Connaught

HR **91%** **£A** & **Map 22 D2**
Carlos Place W1
01-499 7070
Manager Paolo Zago
Credit Access

One of the smallest of London's grand hotels and probably the most discreet, the Connaught has no brochure and even the telex is ex-directory. The warm glow of richly polished oak gives the bar the atmosphere of an exclusive gentleman's club while the sumptuously comfortable antique-furnished lounges have the graceful charm of private drawing rooms. Bedrooms and suites with antique furniture, fresh flowers and high-quality carpets and curtains have an air of restrained luxury and bathrooms, equipped with the finest toiletries, are equally elegant. Housekeeping is impeccable throughout, as is the service from well-groomed, unobtrusive staff. *Amenities* valeting, 24-hour lounge service.

■ Rooms 90	*Confirm by arrang.*
en suite bath/shower 90	*Last dinner 10.30*
Direct dial Yes	*Parking Difficult*
Room TV Yes	*Room service 24 hours*

The Connaught Restaurant ★ ♕♕♕

Manager Mr J. P. Chevallier
Gleaming mahogany panelling, crystal chandeliers and generously spaced tables only partly compensate for some of the dishes which fail to reach the high standard of taste and presentation previously expected of this classically elegant restaurant. The menu is French augmented by traditional English fare including regular daily lunch dishes such as oxtail, steak, kidney and mushroom pie and roast sirloin. Sweets – a splendid bread and butter pudding, apricot tart, delicious feuilleté of fresh raspberries and delicate summer pudding – excel. The liveried service is polished but rather mechanical. Conventional list of classic wines.
Specialities pâté de turbot froid au homard, sauce pudeur; salmi de canard strasbourgeoise en surprise; feuilles d'automne en surprise.
♟ Well-chosen ☺

■ Set L £22·50	*L 12.30–2.30*
Set D £26	*D 6.30–10.15*
About £90 for two	*Seats 80 Parties 10*

Corney & Barrow   *NEW ENTRY*

R ♕ **Map 26 C1**
109 Old Broad Street EC2
01-638 9308
Credit Access, Amex, Diners, Visa

Booking is essential at this exclusive and expensive City restaurant, where fine food is matched by very polished and attentive service. Quality is the keynote throughout, typified by dishes such as whole poached Scottish lobster with a shellfish and tarragon sauce, marinated medallions of venison on pommes Anna, or fillet of beef with a foie gras sauce and a garnish of morels. A splendid wine list, admirably concise, includes some superb clarets and lovely burgundies. ♟ Well-chosen ☺

■ Set L £32	*L only 12–2.30*
About £110 for two	*Parking Difficult*
Seats 30 Closed Sat, Sun & Bank Hols	

La Croisette

R & **Map 23 A6**
168 Ifield Road SW10
01-373 3694
Manager Jean-Marc Fourastie
Credit Access, Amex, Diners, Visa

Seafood is the stock in trade of this stylish basement restaurant, the choice ranging from oysters, langoustines and the imposing mixed platter to daily-changing main courses like salmon with cucumber sauce or sea bass beurre blanc. The fixed price includes kir, nibbles, two fish courses, cheese and salad, sweet and coffee. For a supplement, you can choose a lobster from the tank. ♟ Well-chosen ☺

■ Set L & D £20	*L 12.30–2.30*
About £55 for two	*D 7–11.30*
Seats 55 Parties 10	*Parking Difficult*
Closed Tues, all Mon & 2 wks Xmas	

Crowthers

R ♗ **Map 21 A6**
481 Upper Richmond Road West, East Sheen SW14
01-876 6372
Credit Access, Amex

Philip Crowther cooks with panache in the modern French style at this pretty little restaurant. Menus, changing monthly, offer imaginative combinations of flavour and texture in dishes such as Gruyère cheese ramekins served with a fresh tomato sauce, and spinach-wrapped salmon sauced with leeks. Tempting sweets. ☺

■ Set L £12	*L 12–2*
Set D £18	*D 7–11*
About £46 for two	*Parking Ample*
Seats 30	*Parties 30*
Closed L Sat, all Sun & Mon, 1 wk late Feb–Mar & 1 wk Xmas	

Cumberland Hotel

HR **69% £B &** Map 22 D2
Marble Arch W1A 4RF
01-262 1234. Tlx 22215
Credit Access, Amex, Diners, Visa. **LVs**

A hive of activity confronts the visitor to this
large hotel conveniently placed at Marble Arch.
There's a contemporary bar, a relaxing panelled
one with a quieter atmosphere and a comfortable
lounge. The bedrooms have co-ordinating fabrics,
smart bathrooms, mini-bars and remote-control
TVs; executive rooms also have trouser presses
and hairdryers. *Amenities* sauna, hairdressing,
beauty salon, laundry service, coffee shop
(6.30am–midnight), 24-hour lounge service.

■ *Rooms 907*	*Confirm by 6*
en suite bath/shower 907	*Last dinner 10.30*
Direct dial Yes	*Parking Limited*
Room TV Yes	*Room service 24 hours*

Wyvern Restaurant �

A restaurant with a pleasingly elegant air and a
classic menu. The cooking is enjoyable, with
well-defined flavours and innovative touches.
Starters might be Jerusalem artichoke and
sorrel soup or fresh asparagus and quail's eggs
with lemon butter sauce; leading to a main
course of monkfish brochette marinated in lime
and ginger or breast of chicken with pimento
mousse, braised with a green pepper sauce.
Simple choice of good, enjoyable vegetables and
a conventional selection of sweets from the
trolley. ℮

■ *Set L £14·75*	*L 12–2.30*
Set D £16·75	*D 6.30–10.30*
About £58 for two	*Seats 80 Parties 120*

Dan's

R **Map 23 C5**
119 Sydney Street SW3
01-352 2718
Credit Amex, Diners, Visa

Skilled cooking and attractive presentation
make for an agreeable meal at this pretty, informal
restaurant with a neat walled garden. Spinach
mousse with mushroom sauce, snails in pastry
and mussels in white wine are typical of the
starters, with sorrel-sauced medallions of pike in
pastry, roast poussin and grilled steaks among
the main course choices. ℮

■ *Set L £12*	*L 12.30–2.30*
Set D £13·50	*D 7.30–11.15*
About £45 for two	*Parking Limited*
Seats 50	*Parties 30*

*Closed L Sat, also D Sat in winter, all Sun, Bank
Hols & 25 Dec–1 Jan*

Daphne's

R & **Map 23 C5**
112 Draycott Avenue SW3
01-589 4257
French cooking
Director Giordano Ponticelli
Credit Access, Amex, Diners, Visa

Consistency is the strong point at this stylish,
well-run restaurant, for if the cooking rarely
excites it also hardly ever disappoints. The regular
menu plays it safe with dishes like potted
shrimps, sole véronique and entrecôte béarnaise,
but there are always lots of plats du jour, including
seasonal game. Crêpes, sorbets, superior soufflés
to finish. ♀ Well-chosen

■ *About £45 for two*	*L 12.30–2.30*
Seats 85	*D 7.15–11.45*
Parties 30	*Parking Limited*

Closed Sun, Bank Hols & 4 days Xmas

Defune *NEW ENTRY*

R **Map 22 D1**
61 Blandford Street W1
01-935 8311
Japanese cooking
Credit Amex, Diners

Tiny and usually busy, so booking's a must at
this simple Japanese restaurant just off Baker
Street. There are no set meals, but the menu is
clear enough to take the ordeal out of ordering.
Sushi is the house speciality, and other good
choices are yakitori (Japanese kebabs), sizzling
beef teriyaki and sakanachiri – a huge pot of fish,
vegetables and bean curd simmering in a special
stock.

■ *About £65 for two*	*L 12–2.30*
Seats 30	*D 6–10.30*
Closed Sun, Bank	*Parking Difficult*

Hols, 1st wk Jan & 1 wk Aug

Delhi Brasserie

R ♀ **Map 23 B4**
134 Cromwell Road SW7
01-370 7617
Indian cooking
Owner manager Mr A. Jabbar
Credit Access, Amex, Diners, Visa

A three-storey restaurant with attractive
modern decor. Good-quality ingredients are
cooked with great care and experience, and there
are interesting and original touches. Popular
dishes are tandoori quails and trout, along with
old favourites such as lamb pasanda and chicken
makhani. Meat and vegetarian thali are available.
Sweets include good home-made ice cream and
fresh mango.

■ *About £28 for two*	*L 12–2.30*
Seats 65 Parties 45	*D 6–11.30*
Closed 25 Dec	*Parking Difficult*

Don Pepe *NEW ENTRY*

R ♔ **Map 20 B3**
99 Frampton Street NW8
01-262 3834
Spanish cooking
Owner manager Mr J. Garcia
Credit Access, Amex, Diners, Visa

Hearty Spanish cooking in a boisterous restaurant that's a favourite with families. Quality ingredients get the simple Spanish treatment to produce wholesome dishes like octopus with olive oil and pimento, chicken in rioja or hake with potatoes and a sauce of onions and peppers – a true Galician classic. There's also a tapas (snack) bar. Evening guitarist.

♟ **Well-chosen**

■ *About £40 for two*	*L 12–3, Sun 12–2*
Seats 70 Parties 30	*D 7–12, Sun 7–10*
Closed 24, 25 & 26 Dec	*Parking Limited*

The Dorchester

HR **90% £A *E* Map 22 D3**
Park Lane W1A 2HJ
01-629 8888. Tlx 887704
Credit Access, Amex, Diners, Visa

A world-renowned hotel of immense style and luxury in a prime site overlooking Hyde Park. The long and elegant Promenade, with its marble pillars, gold-leaf ceiling and sumptuous furnishings is perhaps the most magnificent of the public rooms, but the Art Deco bar, the library, the restaurants and the function suites are hardly less impressive. Outstandingly quiet and comfortable bedrooms boast traditional furnishings, exquisite fabrics and splendid bathrooms, many with old-fashioned fittings. The famous Oliver Messel suites are in a class of their own. No dogs.
Amenities laundry service, valeting, in-house movies (free), cable TV, 24-hour lounge service, kiosk.

■ *Rooms 275*	*Confirm by arrang.*
en suite bath/shower 275	*Last dinner 11.30*
Direct dial Yes	*Parking Difficult*
Room·TV Yes	*Room service 24 hours*

The Terrace ★★ ♚♚

Manager Peter Buderath
The twin talents of Anton Mosimann in the kitchen and Peter Buderath, the restaurant manager, combine to make an evening here a memorable gastronomic experience. The live music won't please everyone, but the cooking is brilliant, whether you choose from the à la carte selection or take the menu surprise – a series of inspired creations, featuring some of Anton's famous cuisine naturelle, which uses the very finest raw materials to produce the very finest and most natural flavours. When choosing the menu surprise, it's as well to check what the courses are beforehand, just in case there are dishes you might not enjoy. Superb wines, but at a price.
Specialities feuilleté de ris de veau et homard, loup de mer cuit à la vapeur 'Orientale', mignon de veau à la crème d'échalote, symphonie de sorbets.

▭ **Outstanding**   ♟ **Well-chosen** ☺

■ *Set D £75 for two*	*D only 6–11.30*
About £90 for two	*Seats 80*
Closed Sun	

Grill Room ★ ♛ ♿

Manager John Curry
Anton Mosimann and Grill Room manager John Curry have compiled a menu of British national and regional dishes, one or two prepared à la cuisine naturelle. Recent visits have produced slightly mixed results: ragout of samphire and woodland mushrooms, and fillets of Dover sole with a subtle mustard and pear sauce were dishes that delighted; Glamorgan sausage with leek sauce (both elements rather bland) and apple pie with undercooked pastry were disappointments. Lunchtime brings one or two specials for each day of the week, and the trolley-borne roast sirloin is popular both lunchtime and evening. *Specialities* terrine of forest mushrooms with grain mustard sauce (cuisine naturelle); cucumber and smoked trout salad; North Sea halibut with a lobster coat; fillet of veal with a cider and yarg sauce.

▭ **Outstanding**   ♟ **Well-chosen** ☺

■ *Set L & D from £17*	*L 12.30–3,*
About £60 for two	*Sun 12.30–2.30*
Seats 85	*D 6.30–10.30,*
Closed D 25 Dec	*Sun 7–10.30*

The Dorchester, The Terrace

■ Also see INSPECTOR FOR A DAY

■ We publish annually, so make sure you use the current edition. It's worth it!

Dorset Square Hotel

HR **76%** **£B/C** **E** **Map 21 C4**
39 Dorset Square NW1 6QN
01-723 7874. Tlx 263964
Credit Access, Amex, Visa

An immensely civilised little town-house hotel, where delightful management and staff create an atmosphere that is particularly warm and welcoming. The elegant foyer does double duty as a lounge, with lovely comfortable sofas and other period pieces, and there's a cosy sitting room with a drinks cabinet. Bedrooms, too, are decorated in the best of English taste, and are

provided with books, magazines, mini-bars and remote-control TVs. Sparkling bathrooms have liberal supplies of luxury toiletries. Another stylish note: the hotel car, available with a chauffeur, is a Bentley Continental. No children under ten. *Amenities* laundry service, 24-hour lounge service, restaurant (7am–10.30pm).

■ *Rooms* 29	*Confirm by 6*
en suite bath/shower 29	*Last dinner* 10
Direct dial Yes	*Parking* Difficult
Room TV Yes	*Room service* 24 hours

Country Manners Restaurant ♀

Frances Warde and Lucy Hill share the cooking at this delightful little restaurant on the lower ground floor of the hotel. Their style is English, and enjoyably gimmick free. Short, daily-changing menus include carefully prepared, tasty dishes like bacon and lentil soup, mange-tout and monkfish salad, tender, succulent lamb chops with redcurrant sauce, and cranberry and apple crumble. Charming service. ♀ **Well-chosen** ☺

■ *Set L & D* £10-50,	*L* 12–2.30
Sun £15	*D* 6–10
About £50 for two	*Seats* 20

■ For a discount on next year's guide, see Offer for Answers.

Drakes

R **Map 23 C5**
2a Pond Place SW3
01-584 4555
English cooking
Credit Access, Amex, Diners, Visa

An informal but quite smart restaurant with enjoyable English cooking under the charge of David Bickford. Spit-roast dishes remain popular; other choices run from fresh asparagus (ours not

helped by an insipid lemon hollandaise), to Dover sole and venison with blackcurrant sauce. Passion fruit posset makes a nice ending. Traditional Sunday menu.
♀ **Well-chosen** ☺

■ *Set L & D* Sun £15	*L* 12.30–2.30, Sun
About £60 for two	12.30–3
Seats 85	*D* 6.30–11, Sun 7–10.30
Closed 1 wk Xmas	*Parking* Difficult

Drury Lane Moat House Hotel

H **68%** **£B** **Map 27 B1**
10 Drury Lane WC2B 5RE
01-836 6666. Tlx 8811395
Manager Oliver Sweeney
Credit Access, Amex, Diners, Visa

A smart, comfortable hotel in London's theatreland. The lobby incorporates a cool, relaxing lounge area, and Maudie's Bar, with its original cartoons by Sir Osbert Lancaster, is a

good spot for a drink. Bedrooms are neat and up-to-date with trouser presses and individually controlled central heating. *Amenities* laundry service, 24-hour lounge service.

■ *Rooms* 129	*Confirm by 6*
en suite bath/shower 129	*Last dinner* 11
Direct dial Yes	*Parking* Limited
Room TV Yes	*Room service* 24 hours
Closed 4 days Xmas	

Dukes Hotel

HR 81% £A *E* Map 25 B4
35 St James's Place SW1A 1NY
01-491 4840. Tlx 28283
Credit Access, Amex, Diners, Visa
  The quiet courtyard setting is a marvellous feature of this beautifully preserved Edwardian hotel which is just a few minutes' walk from the hustle and bustle of London's West End shops, theatres and tourist sights. The foyer is warm, cosy and clubby, with fresh flowers and period furnishings adding to the charm. The bar, with its oil paintings of dukes, and the comfortably appointed lounge are splendid places in which to relax. Good-sized bedrooms provide a high

degree of comfort and style: fabrics and furnishings are of excellent quality, and accessories include remote-control TVs and hairdryers. Spotless tiled bathrooms offer bathrobes and good toiletries. Smart, extremely efficient management and staff. No dogs. *Amenities* laundry service, valeting, 24-hour lounge service.

■ *Rooms* 52	*Confirm by* 6
en suite bath/shower 52	*Last dinner* 10
Direct dial Yes	*Parking* Difficult
Room TV Yes	*Room service* 24 hours

Dukes Hotel Restaurant ♛

Tony Marshall and his team are equally adept at traditional English cooking and more modern French-inspired methods. The trolley-borne lunchtime special is always a favourite, and other choices run from feuilleté of salmon with a super chive sauce to honey-basted quail and sirloin steak; bread and butter pudding is hard to beat for a sweet—light and fluffy with a crisp topping. Good classic cellar. ♀ **Well-chosen** ☺

■ *Set L from* £15	*L* 12.30–2.30
About £70 *for two*	*D* 6–10
Seats 35	

Durrants Hotel

H 63% £C Map 22 D1
George Street W1H 6BJ
01-935 8131. Tlx 894919
Owner manager Mr R. C. Miller
Credit Access, Amex, Visa
  A handsome Georgian hotel, where panelled walls and period furniture are much in evidence. The lounges are comfortably furnished with leather armchairs or red velour seating. Bedrooms

are attractively traditional in style; most have en suite bathrooms which are small, bright and clean, with fine tiling. No dogs. *Amenities* laundry service, coffee shop (7.30–12am), 24-hour lounge service.

■ *Rooms* 96	*Confirm by* 6
en suite bath/shower 87	*Last dinner* 10.30
Direct dial Yes	*Parking* Difficult
Room TV Most	*Room service* Limited

Dynasty of Hampstead

R Map 20 B2
291 Finchley Road NW3
01-794 5920
Chinese cooking
Owner manager Frank Wu
Credit Access, Amex, Diners, Visa
  Szechuan dishes are the speciality at this friendly Chinese restaurant on Finchley Road, but the careful preparation of good fresh ingredients

also encompasses Peking cuisine, including excellent crispy duck. Note, too, delicious griddle-fried dumplings and fine seafood. Above average food, helpful service.

■ *Set L from* £10·95	*L* 12–2.30 *Fri & Sat*
Set D from £10·95	*D* 6–11.15 *Mon–Sat*
About £30 *for two*	*Meals Sun* 1–11pm
Seats 70 *Parties* 40	*Parking* Ample
Closed L Mon–Thurs & 4 days Xmas	

Eatons

R ♛ Map 23 D5
49 Elizabeth Street SW1
01-730 0074
Credit Access, Amex, Diners, Visa
  Santosh Bakshi's cooking remains consistently enjoyable at this comfortable little restaurant, where most of the customers are staunch regulars. Forthright flavours are a feature of carefully prepared dishes like smoked salmon

croquettes with orange sauce, fillet of lamb and lambs' kidneys provençale, and there's a particularly good lemon cheesecake. On our last visit the service was much warmer than the coffee.

■ *About* £40 *for two*	*L* 12–2
Seats 40	*D* 7–11.15
Closed Sat, Sun	*Parking* Limited
& Bank Hols	

Ebury Court Hotel

HR 57% £C/D **Map 25 A6**
26 Ebury Street SW1W 0LU
01-730 8147
Owner managers Mr & Mrs Topham
Credit Access, Visa. LVs

The delightful Tophams take positive pleasure in considering guests' needs at this charming hotel in a Victorian terrace. Appealing day rooms include a writing room-cum-lounge and a club bar (guests can become temporary members) with a small patio. Bedrooms of various shapes and sizes have certain charm; bathrooms, both public and private, are pleasantly old-fashioned. *Amenities* laundry service.

■ Rooms 39	Confirm by arrang.
en suite bath/shower 12	Last dinner 9
Room phone Yes	Parking Difficult
Room TV No	Room service 24 hours

Ebury Court Hotel Restaurant

Excellent cooking of straightforward, unpretentious dishes and homely, welcoming surroundings are the great attractions of this basement hotel restaurant. Typical dishes on long-serving (over 25 years) chef Patrick O'Connor's menu include halibut with orange and celery salad, and roast lamb. Cheese soufflé makes a delicious starter and there are ice creams and sorbets for afters – or perhaps highland flummery or mince pies and cream. Service is polite and friendly. ☺

■ Set L £6	L 12–2
Set D £5·15	D 7–9
About £34 for two	Seats 35 Parties 12

Embassy House Hotel

H 58% £C/D **Map 23 B4**
31 Queen's Gate SW7 5LA
01-584 7222. Tlx 8813386
Manager Jonathan Peters
Credit Access, Amex, Diners, Visa

The 19th-century stuccoed facade of this hotel hides a bright, up-to-date interior with colourful carpets and upholstery in the lofty foyer-lounge. The basement bar is pleasantly light and summery. Good-sized bedrooms (many ideal for families) have fitted lightwood units, tea-makers and practical tiled bathrooms. *Amenities* laundry service, 24-hour lounge service.

■ Rooms 69	Confirm by 6
en suite bath/shower 69	Last dinner 9.45
Direct dial Yes	Parking Limited
Room TV Yes	Room service Limited

English Garden

R ♨ **Map 23 C5**
10 Lincoln Street SW3
01-584 7272
Owner managers Malcolm & Colin Livingston
Credit Access, Amex, Diners, Visa

A summery conservatory-style decor creates a pleasant atmosphere at this stylish restaurant. The menu offers traditional English dishes like roast rack of lamb as well as modern inventive items. Try quail egg patty with sorrel and green peppercorn sauce to start; then perhaps fillet of sole with lobster and brandysnap baskets filled with strawberry cream to finish. ☺

■ About £50 for two	L 12.30–2.30,
Seats 65	Sun 12.30–2
Parties 30	D 7.30–11.30,
Closed 25 & 26 Dec	Sun 7.30–10
	Parking Difficult

English House

R **Map 23 C4**
3 Milner Street SW3
01-584 3002
English cooking
Owner manager Malcolm Livingston
Credit Access, Amex, Diners, Visa

Dishes at this charming Victorian-style restaurant are based on English court and country cooking, with old recipes adapted to modern palates. Casserole of wild mushrooms, Gloucester and Cheddar cheese tart, fish pie and collops of veal with fresh herbs show the range. Leave room for delicious puddings like ginger trifle with butterscotch custard. ☺

■ Set L £11·50	L 12–2.30, Sun 12–2
About £55 for two	D 7–11.30, Sun 7–10
Seats 45 Parties 12	Parking Limited
Closed Good Fri & 25 & 26 Dec	

L'Escargot

R ♨ **Map 27 A2**
48 Greek Street W1
01-437 2679
Owner manager Nick Lander
Credit Access, Amex, Diners, Visa

Martin Lam cooks with skill and confidence at this elegant upstairs restaurant (downstairs for the more informal brasserie). His imaginative, regularly changing menus might include a hot terrine of salmon and scallops or marinated crispy duck salad, to be followed by ragoût of wild rabbit or calf's sweetbreads in puff pastry with chicken mousse. Good fresh vegetables and enjoyable sweets. ♀ Well-chosen

■ About £50 for two	L 12.30–2.30
Seats 100	D 6.30–11.15
Parties 10	Parking Difficult
Closed L Sat, all Sun, Bank Hols & 1 wk Xmas	

La Famiglia

R **Map 23 B6**
7 Langton Street SW10
01-351 0761
Italian cooking
Owner manager Alvaro Maccioni
Credit Access, Amex, Diners, Visa
Long-established, bustling restaurant with an attractive patio and evening bar. There's plenty of variety on the largely classical menu, with weekly specials too like cold avocado soup or monkfish with a delicious lemon and garlic sauce. Home-produced wild boar is a special feature. Comprehensive Italian wine list with the occasional star (Bricco dell Uccellone Barbera). ℮

■ *About £36 for two*	*L 12–3*
Seats 48 Parties 14	*D 7–12*
Closed Bank Hols	*Parking* Limited

La Fantaisie Brasserie

R **Map 22 C3**
14 Knightsbridge Green SW1
01-589 0509
French cooking
Credit Access, Amex, Diners, Visa
The French menu is full of interest at this smart, busy brasserie a few steps away from the Knightsbridge shops. Mussel soup spiked with saffron or smoked trout and Roquefort on a bed of chicory might precede sliced duck breast with a pink peppercorn and pistachio sauce, a simple grilled steak or perhaps brill baked in puff pastry. To follow, there are delicious fresh fruit desserts like raspberry mousse. ℮

■ *About £42 for two*	*L 12–3*
Seats 65	*D 7–10.30*
Parties 50	*Parking* Limited
Closed Sun, Bank Hols & 10 days Xmas	

The Fenja *NEW ENTRY*

H **76% £B Map 23 D5**
69 Cadogan Gardens SW3
01-589 7333. Tlx 934272
Credit Access, Amex, Diners, Visa
Overlooking Cadogan Gardens, this exquisitely-restored house is a welcome addition to London's list of superior hotels. The relaxed atmosphere is almost Edwardian and guests are well and truly pampered. Although there is no restaurant, room service includes meals, and elegant drinks trays are provided. Public areas include a beautifully-proportioned drawing room. Designer Rupert Lord assisted in the hotel's transformation, and his inimitable touch is obvious in bedrooms furnished with fine antiques, paintings and sculptures. Fresh flowers, fruit baskets, linen sheets and fluffy towels add the luxury touch, and standard equipment includes

TVs, portable radios, trouser presses and hairdryers. Compact bathrooms are expensively equipped. No dogs. *Amenities* garden, laundry service.

■ *Rooms 14*	*Confirm by* arrang.
en suite bath/shower 14	*Last dinner 9*
Direct dial Yes	*Parking* Difficult
Room TV Yes	*Room service 24 hours*

Forum Hotel

H **62% £C & Map 23 B4**
97 Cromwell Road SW7 4DN
01-370 5757. Tlx 919663
Credit Access, Amex, Diners, Visa. **LVs**
Continuing refurbishment keeps standards high at this skyscraper hotel on the main road to Heathrow and the West. Public areas on the ground and first floors include a Victorian-style bar, smart lounges and cafés (two with pianists), and a splendid gift shop. Practical twin or double bedrooms – all with compact bathrooms – are well equipped. *Amenities* garden, in-house movies (free), laundry service, coffee shop (6.30am–11pm).

■ *Rooms 907*	*Confirm by 6*
en suite bath/shower 907	*Last dinner 11*
Direct dial Yes	*Parking* Ample
Room TV Yes	*Room service* None

Frederick's

R ♕ **Map 20 D3**
Camden Passage N1
01-359 2888
French cooking
Owner manager Louis Segal
Credit Access, Amex, Diners, Visa
The menu changes fortnightly at this popular French restaurant with a pink-plush dining room and a light, leafy conservatory. A typical choice of dishes runs from smoked salmon and trout mousse to herby rack of lamb and diced venison Grand Veneur. Vegetarian dishes, tempting sweets. Note good-value burgundies and Rhônes.

■ *Set L £8-25*	*L 12–2.30*
About £50 for two	*D 7–11.30*
Seats 155 Parties 120	*Parking* Limited
Closed Sun & Bank Hols	

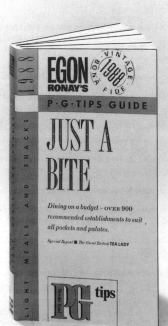

Frère Jacques

R **Map 27 B2**
38 Long Acre WC2
01-836 7823
French cooking
Owner manager Barry Jones
Credit Access, Amex, Diners, Visa
 Good fresh seafood draws the crowds to this lively, informal restaurant. Consult the blackboard for seasonal delights such as oysters served in a

warm brioche with a cream and chive sauce, or crayfish with garlic butter. Other choices include the popular plateau de fruits de mer, plus a few meat dishes and simple sweets like rich, dark chocolate mousse. ⊖
■ About £40 for two
Seats 130
Parties 120
Closed 25 & 26 Dec
L 12–3, Sun 12–2.30
D 5.30–11.30,
Sun 7–10.30
Parking Limited

Frith's

R **Map 27 A2**
14 Frith Street W1
01-439 3370
Credit Access, Amex, Diners, Visa
 British produce cooked without undue elaboration by Charles Mumford. It's a popular place, so booking's advisable. Poached meats dressed with olive oil, parsley and capers is a healthy choice, and other options could include

apple and sage soup, calf's liver with bacon and an enjoyable salmon, bream and red mullet stew. Nice sweets, home-made ices and British farmhouse cheeses. ⊖
■ Set L £14·00
Set D £14·00
About £50 for two
Seats 60 Parties 40
Bank Hols & 1 wk Xmas (exc. L 25 Dec)
L 12–2.30
D 6–11.30
Parking Difficult
Closed L Sat, all Sun,

Fuji

R **Map 24 B3**
36 Brewer Street W1
01-734 0957
Japanese cooking
Owner manager Mr H. Taoka
Credit Access, Amex, Diners, Visa
 The menu in this unpretentious Japanese restaurant features a good selection of set dinners. The à la carte is extensive, too, and

waitresses will gladly advise on ordering. There's a heavy reliance on seafood, with a few meat choices. Preparation and cooking are of a very high standard.
■ Set L & D from £18
About £45 for two
Seats 54 Parties 15
Closed L Sat & Sun, L Bank Hols & 2 wks Xmas
L 12.30–2.30
D 6–10.45, Sun 6–10.15
Parking Difficult

Fung-Shing

R **Map 27 A2**
15 Lisle Street WC2
01-437 1539
Chinese cooking
Owner manager Yau Fook Jim
Credit Access, Amex, Diners, Visa
 A good Soho Chinese restaurant with smart, relaxing decor and affable staff. The long menu of well-prepared, nicely presented dishes offers old

favourites – including a tasty fishball soup – and less familiar items such as crispy tender-pink roast quail with barbecue sauce, eel with coriander and duck hot pot with preserved plum sauce. Sliced oranges make a refreshing finale.
♀ Well-chosen
■ Set meals £8
About £32 for two
Seats 90 Parties 30
Meals noon–11.30
Parking Limited
Closed 25 & 26 Dec

Le Gamin

R ♀ **Map 26 B1**
31 Old Bailey EC4
01-236 7931
French cooking
Credit Access, Amex, Diners, Visa
 Fixed-price lunches including kir, three courses, wine and coffee are the sole offering at this French brasserie-style basement restaurant. Choose from a variety of well-cooked dishes:

monkfish in a ginger sauce; blanquette de veau; or roast pheasant in a creamy fig sauce. Good vegetables, excellent French cheeses, and simple tempting sweets. ⊖
♀ Well-chosen
■ Set L £19·25
About £39 for two
Seats 120
Closed Sat, Sun & Bank Hols
L only 12–2.30
Parking Difficult
Parties 160

Le Gastronome

R **Map 21 B6**
309 New King's Road SW6
01-736 8833
French cooking
Manager Mr M. Wallis

Credit Access, Amex, Visa. **LVs**
 Gastronome One changed its name and telephone number when moving next door, but kept the services of a very able French chef, Thierry Aubugeau. Specialities on his modern

menu (now à la carte only) include grilled carp sauce diable, fillet of lamb with oyster mushrooms and delicate apple tart with Calvados. Fine classic wines. ♀ Well-chosen

■ *About £50 for two*	*L 12–2*
Seats 50	*D 7–11*
Parties 20	*Parking Limited*
Closed Sun, Bank Hols, 3 wks Aug & 1 wk Xmas	

Le Gavroche ★★

R ★★ ய ய ⌀ **Map 22 D2**
43 Upper Brook Street W1
01-408 0881
French cooking
Credit Access, Amex, Diners, Visa

A chic, comfortable setting and service beyond reproach highlight the considerable talents of chef Steven Doherty at the Roux brothers' admirable establishment. Recent quite remarkable dishes have included the lightest, most delicately flavoured of vegetable mousses, a mouthwatering warm terrine of turbot and oyster mushrooms accompanied by a brilliantly successful combination of beurre blanc with fresh truffles, and a richly sauced, pungently garlicky ragout of pink-cooked kidneys, golden sweetbreads and tender veal tongue. Sweets are a delight – notably the exquisitely light and delicate vanilla-flavoured soufflé Lamberty with its chocolate base, and the equally splendid assiette gourmande de chocolat. A classic cellar at high

prices, strongest in Bordeaux. *Specialities* soufflé suissesse, mousseline de homard au champagne, homard à l'escargot, assiette du boucher, soufflé aux fraises.

⌔ Outstanding ♀ Well-chosen ☺

■ *Set L £19.50*	*L 12–2*
Set D £80 for 2	*D 7–10.30*
About £100 for two	*Parking Difficult*
Seats 70	*Parties 22*
Closed Sat, Sun, Bank Hols & 12 days Xmas	

Gavvers

R **Map 23 D5**
61 Lower Sloane Street SW1
01-730 5983
French cooking
Credit Access, Amex, Diners, Visa. LVs

Part of the Roux brothers' empire, so the closely-packed tables are crowded, and booking is a must. The set menu includes kir, three courses, wine and coffee; starters may be a salad tiède, timbale of mussels or onion soup, while typical main dishes could include a daube de boeuf, cassoulet or veal escalopes. There are delicious sweets too and a choice of tisanes to follow. ♀ Well-chosen

■ *Set D £19.25*	*D 7–11*
About £39 for two	*Parking Difficult*
Seats 66	*Parties 60*
Closed Sun, Bank Hols & 10 days Xmas	

Gay Hussar ★

R ★ **Map 27 A1**
2 Greek Street W1
01-437 0973
Hungarian cooking

Victor Sassie's long-established Soho restaurant still manages to thrill and excite with a wonderful selection of richly-flavoured traditional Hungarian dishes. It is, quite simply, the undisputed best of its kind. Be guided by Victor himself, or his manager, when selecting from the regular menu or list of daily specials. Follow their suggestions and you're most unlikely to be disappointed. Start perhaps with succulent cold pike with beetroot sauce and cucumber, or with the more robust pressed boar's head. A main-course choice could be roast saddle of carp, minced goose and pungent smoked beans, or a hearty veal goulash with thimble egg dumplings. To round it all off, there is a small but balanced selection of delicious desserts such as sweet cheese pancakes or soft fruit pudding. A keen

appetite is required for proper appreciation of this full-bodied fare. But relax, take your time and enjoy the friendly, professional service. Booking is absolutely essential. *Specialities* chicken in paprika and cucumber sauce, Transylvanian stuffed cabbage, jugged hare, raspberry and chocolate torta. ♀ Well-chosen

■ *Set L £11*	*L 12.30–2.30*
About £45 for two	*D 5.30–10.30*
Seats 35	*Parking Difficult*
Parties 10	*Closed Sun, Bank Hols*

Ginnan

R **Map 26 B1**
5 Cathedral Place EC4
01-236 4120
Japanese cooking
Manager Mr F. Inomata
Credit Access, Amex, Diners, Visa
That this small restaurant is so popular with
Japanese businessmen attests to its authenticity.
Situated in a shopping precinct next to St. Paul's,

Ginnan offers set lunches that are excellent value,
plus à la carte favourites like sukiyaki and shabu.
Sashimi is available, but not sushi, and there's a
good range of starters. Efficient and courteous
staff.

■ *Set L from £5·20*　*L 12–2.30*
Set D from £18·50　*D 6–10*
About £40 for two　*Parking Difficult*
Seats 45 Closed D Sat, all Sun & Bank Hols

Giovanni's

R **Map 27 B2**
10 Goodwin's Court, 55 St Martin's
Lane WC2
01-240 2877
Owner manager Giovanni Colla
Credit Access, Amex, Diners, Visa
A small Italian restaurant, popular with
businessmen at lunchtime and actors and
theatregoers in the evening. Ramon Pareden,

chef for 17 years, provides tasty dishes like
mozzarella alla caprese (avocado), various ways
with veal (scaloppine del chef is cooked with port
and mushrooms) and, to finish, zuppa inglese,
Italy's answer to the English trifle.

■ *About £44 for two*　*L 12.30–2.30*
Seats 40　*D 6.30–11*
Parties 12　*Parking Ample*
Closed L Sat, all Sun, Bank Hols

The Gloucester

H **78%　£A　E　Map 23 B5**
4 Harrington Gardens SW7 4LH
01-373 6030. Tlx 917505
Credit Access, Amex, Diners, Visa
Behind a fairly ordinary facade the Gloucester
is an impressively run hotel with a considerable
sense of style and luxury. The large lobby with its
marble floor, modern chandeliers and mezzanine
gallery makes a favourable first view, and there
are bars to suit many moods. Air-conditioned
bedrooms are large, very comfortable and well
designed, with writing desks and small dressing
areas; mini-bars and hairdryers are standard.
Bathrooms are also well equipped. There are two
private lounges, and butler service, for guests
staying in the sixth-floor Reserve Club rooms.
Amenities sauna, solarium, whirlpool bath,
beauty salon, hairdressing, in-house movies

(charge), laundry service, 24-hour lounge service,
coffee shop (6.30am–1am).

■ *Rooms 531*　*Confirm by 6*
en suite bath/shower 531　*Last dinner 10.15*
Direct dial Yes　*Parking Ample*
Room TV Yes　*Room service 24 hours*

Golden Chopsticks　*NEW ENTRY*

R ⌕ **Map 23 B4**
1 Harrington Road, SW7
01-584 0855
Chinese cooking
Credit Access, Amex, Diners, Visa
A good modern Chinese restaurant just a few
steps from South Kensington Station. The Choi
family offer an unusually long seafood selection,
and other dishes to note include Capital spare

ribs, Hunan lamb and various ways with duck
(fragrant and aromatic, barbecued Peking-style,
camphorwood and tea-smoked, braised with
mixed vegetables). Ask about specials like quail
and soft-shell crab not listed on the menu.

■ *Set D £12*　*L 12–2.45*
About £30 for two　*D 6–11.45,*
Seats 75 Parties 40　*Sun 6–10.45*
Closed 3 days Xmas　*Parking Limited*

Gonbei

R **Map 20 D3**
151 King's Cross Road WC1
01-278 0619
Japanese cooking
Owner manager Mr S. Uno
Booking is a must at this simple little restaurant
with a menu of enjoyable Japanese dishes. Plenty
of attention is paid to both preparation and
presentation, and friendly staff will help you make

your choice. Popular items include excellent
sashimi and sushi, sukiyaki for two and lean,
tender beef with a splendid teriyaki sauce. Good
Japanese tea is served but there are no
sweets.

■ *About £40 for two*　*D only 6–10.30*
Seats 24 Parties 20　*Parking Ample*
Closed Sun, Bank Hols & wks Xmas

Good Earth

R 143 The Broadway NW7
01-959 7011 **Map 7 B4**

223 Brompton Road SW3
01-584 3658 **Map 23 C4**

91 Kings Road SW3
01-352 9231 **Map 23 C5**
Chinese cooking
Credit Access, Amex, Diners, Visa
   Sound Chinese cooking in three restaurants with stylish modern decor and friendly, helpful staff. The menu provides an abundant choice,

from satay, seaweed and rice paper-wrapped chicken to squid with soya beans, barbecued pork and dry shredded chilli beef. Lots of rice and noodle dishes, plus a good selection of vegetarian items. Enjoy it all with fragrant jasmine tea.

■ *Meals* The Broadway	*12–2.30, Sun 12.30–3*
Brompton Road	*12–11, Sun 12.30–11*
Kings Road	*12.30–11.45*
Set L & D £12	*Parking Ample*
About £38 for two	*Seats 60*
Closed 4 days Xmas	*Parties 45*

Good Friends

R ♕ **Map 7 B4**
139 Salmon Lane, Limehouse E14
01-987 5541
Chinese cooking
Credit Access, Amex, Diners, Visa
   Set in a parade of shops in London's original Chinatown, this long-established restaurant has made many good friends over the years. The two Mr Cheungs are owners and chefs, and their

mainly Cantonese menu spans a very wide range, from beef and salt cabbage soup to crispy duck, stuffed mushrooms and pork with walnuts. A cheerful, reliable place offering good eating for 11 hours a day.

■ *Set L from £10*	*Meals noon–11*
Set D from £10	*Parking Difficult*
About £24 for two	*Seats 144*
Closed 24, 25 & 26 Dec	*Parties 60*

Gore Hotel

H **64% £B/C Map 22 B3**
189 Queen's Gate SW7 5EX
01-584 6601. Tlx 296244
Owner managers Brian & Aminge Dale-Thomas
Credit Access, Amex, Diners, Visa
   Check in at the reception desk and look forward to a pleasant, comfortable stay in this family-run hotel. Tastefully decorated bedrooms, all with safes, hairdryers and private facilities include

several luxurious rooms with striking individual themes. The cocktail bar houses a picture collection, and there's a fresh, bright brasserie. No dogs. *Amenities* laundry service, coffee shop (8am–3pm, 6–9pm), 24-hour lounge service.

■ *Rooms 54*	*Confirm by arrang.*
en suite bath/shower 54	*Last dinner 9*
Direct dial Yes	*Parking Difficult*
Room TV Yes	*Room service 24 hours*

Goring Hotel

HR **77% £A Map 25 A6**
Beeston Place, Grosvenor Gardens,
SW1W 0JW
01-834 8211. Tlx 919166
Manager William Cowpe
Credit Access, Amex, Diners, Visa
   The emphasis at this traditional hotel near Victoria Station is on good service, and it shows right through from valeting to laundering, room service and breakfast. The foyer has an old-fashioned, welcoming feel, and beyond it the handsomely proportioned lounge is equally charming; there's also a long bar that overlooks the hotel's garden. Bedrooms, with comfortable sitting areas and well-lit desk space, have mainly

pastel colour schemes. The quality of furnishings is high, and all rooms offer remote-control TVs, radios and hairdryers. Bathrooms, too, are impressive, especially those done out with soon-to-be-standard marble tiling. No dogs. *Amenities* valeting, laundry service, 24-hour lounge service.

■ *Rooms 90*	*Confirm by arrang.*
en suite bath/shower 90	*Last dinner 10*
Direct dial Yes	*Parking Limited*
Room TV Yes	*Room service 24 hours*

Goring Hotel Restaurant

A comfortable and civilised restaurant, and one of the better meeting places in Victoria. Set menus are offered alongside an extensive à la carte; grills and roasts are always available, and other good dishes include rabbit and pigeon terrine, scallops in a lime and dill marinade, sea bass in puff pastry and saddle of hare with stuffed morels. Nice hors d'oeuvre and sweet trolleys. Excellent clarets: Châteaux Léoville Lascases 1970, Pape-Clément 1970. ♀ Well-chosen ⊖

■ *Set L £15·50*	*L 12.30–2.30*
Set D £17·50	*D 6–10*
About £55 for two	*Seats 75 Parties 50*

The Grafton *NEW ENTRY*

R **Map 21 C6**
45 Old Town, Clapham SW4
01-627 1048
French cooking
Owner manager Wafik Gabr
Credit Access, Visa
The oldest building in Clapham is the setting for this elegant French restaurant. Starters include excellent home-prepared salmon, while main dishes include herby fillet of lamb and breast of duck with apricot sauce. Finish with a delicious crêpe soufflé – our flavour of the day was lime. Three-course Sunday brunch. ☺

- *Set L* £11·50 — L 12.30–3, Sun 12–3.30
- *Set D* £18·50 — D 7–11.30, Sun 7.30–11
- *About £50 for two* — *Parking Ample*
- *Seats 70* — *Parties 60*
- *Closed Mon & last 3 wks Aug*

- Our inspectors never book in the name of Egon Ronay's Guides; they disclose their identity only after paying their bills.

Grafton Hotel

H **61% £B Map 24 B1**
130 Tottenham Court Road W1P 9HP
01-388 4131. Tlx 297234
Credit Access, Amex, Diners, Visa. LVs
After extensive refurbishment the Grafton now has more of an Edwardian feel, in keeping with its original character. There's an elegant pillared drawing room, resplendent with oil paintings and red plush, where drinks are served. Or, if you prefer something more informal, you can choose the lively cellar bar. Bedrooms, including 70 smart new ones with remote-control TV, have private bath or shower plus hairdryers.
Amenities in-house movies (free), laundry service.

- *Rooms 236* — *Confirm by 6*
- *en suite bath/shower 236* — *Last dinner 10*
- *Direct dial Yes* — *Parking Difficult*
- *Room TV Yes* — *Room service 24 hours*

Gran Paradiso

R ♿ **Map 25 B6**
52 Wilton Road SW1
01-828 5818
Italian cooking
Owner manager Sandro Maldini
Credit Access, Amex, Diners, Visa
Robust flavours are the key to this long-established Italian restaurant, where attentive and courteous staff serve a taste of country cooking in dishes like minestrone, pasta, pollo alla contadina (chicken with wild mushrooms and wine) and a superb saddle of lamb with rosemary and garlic. Simple sweets and good coffee. ☺

- *About £38 for two* — L 12–2.30
- *Seats 50* — D 6–11.15
- *Parties 25* — *Parking Ample*
- *Closed L Sat, all Sun, Bank Hols & 2 wks Aug*

Great Eastern Hotel

H **56% £C Map 26 D1**
Liverpool Street EC2M 7QN
01-283 4363. Tlx 886812
Credit Access, Amex, Diners, Visa. LVs
Complimentary copies of the *Financial Times* for guests each morning underline the City location of this splendid railway hotel. Victorian grandeur survives in the marble foyer and fine staircase. The spacious bar and first-floor bedrooms have been refurbished, and rooms on the top two floors have polished pine furniture. All have mini-bars and tea-makers. No dogs.
Amenities solarium, hairdressing, laundry service.

- *Rooms 163* — *Confirm by 6*
- *en suite bath/shower 126* — *Last dinner 10*
- *Direct dial Yes* — *Parking Difficult*
- *Room TV Yes* — *Room service None*
- *Closed 8 days Xmas*

Great Northern Hotel

H **63% £C/D** ♿ **Map 20 C3**
Kings Cross N1 9AN
01-837 5454. Tlx 299041
Credit Access, Amex, Diners, Visa
Opened in 1854, the Great Northern was London's first purpose-built hotel. Northbound rail travellers find it handy as it's just a few paces from King's Cross and St Pancras stations. Bedrooms have been pleasantly modernised and furnished, and all have trouser presses and mini-bars. Agreeable staff. Poor buffet-style breakfast.
Amenities in-house movies (free), laundry service.

- *Rooms 88* — *Confirm by 6*
- *en suite bath/shower 68* — *Last dinner 10*
- *Direct dial Yes* — *Parking Ample*
- *Room TV Yes* — *Room service 24 hours*
- *Closed 3 days Xmas*

Greenhouse

R ♨ **Map 25 A4**
27a Hay's Mews W1
01-499 3331
Owner manager Andrew Baker
Credit Access, Amex, Diners, Visa
   A delightful and immensely popular restaurant with enjoyable cooking and cheerful service. Typical dishes on a menu that changes every two months could include shrimp bisque or noodles

with cream and Parmesan to start, followed by sautéed salmon with sorrel, duck with fig and blackcurrant sauce, or a charcoal grill. Traditional puds like rice pudding with strawberry jam. Concise but classy wine list. ♀ **Well-chosen** ⊖

■ About £44 for two	L 12–2.30
Seats 85	D 7–11, Sat from 7.30
Parties 10	Parking Difficult
Closed Sun, Bank Hols & 10 days Xmas	

Green's Restaurant

R ♨ & **Map 25 B4**
36 Duke Street, St James's SW1
01-930 4566
English cooking
Credit Access, Amex, Diners, Visa
   The emphasis at this mahogany-panelled restaurant is on very fresh seafood, with oysters, dressed crab and Dover sole among the favourites. Traditional lunchtime specials include

liver and bacon, tasty salmon fishcakes and steamed syrup sponge with a jolt of ginger. Steaks and grills in the evening. Polished service. Excellent wines – note the superb Soave Classico 1985 from Roberto Anselmi. ♀ **Well-chosen** ⊖

■ About £46 for two	L 12.30–2.30
Seats 60	D 6.30–10.45
Parties 30	Parking Difficult
Closed Sat, Sun & Bank Hols	

Grimes

R ♀ **Map 27 B2**
6 Garrick Street WC2
01-836 7008
Seafood
Credit Access, Amex, Diners, Visa
   Excellent fresh seafood in tempting variety is offered at this simple little restaurant. Cold choices include seasonal oysters, Norfolk smoked eel and salmon mayonnaise, while among hot

options are warming fish soup with rouille, pan-fried Dover sole, and langoustines with garlic herb butter. Also available are one or two meat dishes. Booking is essential. ⊖

■ About £42 for two	L 12–3
Seats 50	D 5.30–11.30
Parties 40	Parking Limited
Closed L Sat, all Sun & Bank Hols	

Grosvenor Hotel

H **61% £C Map 25 A6**
101 Buckingham Palace Road SW1W 0SJ
01-834 9494. Tlx 916006
Credit Access, Amex, Visa. LVs
   Much refurbishment is completed, in progress or planned at this handsome neighbour of Victoria Station. Many of the bedrooms have stylish new fabrics and decent lightwood furniture; bathrooms and corridors have also received attention. Most

impressive of the public areas is the entrance hall with its fine marble staircase and gallery. *Amenities* hairdressing, laundry service, laundry room, restaurant (7am–11pm), 24-hour lounge service, kiosk.

■ Rooms 360	Confirm by 6
en suite bath/shower 360	Last dinner 10
Direct dial Yes	Parking Difficult
Room TV Yes	Room service None

Grosvenor House

H **85% £A E Map 22 D2**
Park Lane W1A 3AA
01-499 6363. Tlx 24871
Manager Mr M. Buccianti
Credit Access, Amex, Diners, Visa
   Overlooking Hyde Park, this Lutyens-designed building dates from the late 1920s. Superb service is provided by splendidly turned-out staff, from doormen in green top hats to tailcoated under-managers, smiling receptionists, affable barmen and nippy pages. Accommodation is of three basic types: luxurious antique-furnished suites; stylish Superior rooms, including a floor of Crown Club rooms with its own check-in, lounge, boardroom, manager and staff; and Standard rooms, of which some on the top floor are badly in need of the upgrading planned for 1988. Public rooms are particularly spacious and comfortable.

No dogs. *Amenities* indoor swimming pool, sauna, solarium, whirlpool bath, gymnasium, beauty salon, hairdressing, valeting, laundry service, coffee shop (7am–10pm), 24-hour lounge service.

■ Rooms 466	Confirm by arrang.
en suite bath/shower 466	Last dinner 10.30
Direct dial Yes	Parking Limited
Room TV Yes	Room service 24 hours

Guinea

R **Map 24 A3**
30 Bruton Place W1
01-499 1210
English cooking
Credit Access, Amex, Diners, Visa

A simply and traditionally furnished restaurant reached through the Guinea pub. Its main appeal is the tender and succulent quality of the charcoal-grilled Aberdeen Angus steaks. Starters include Colchester oysters, smoked salmon and Beluga caviar. Alternatives to steak are lobster, lamb cutlets and poached salmon. Luxurious ingredients, admirably and capably cooked. Simple sweets. Pleasant service. ☺

■ *Set L £12·95*   *L 12.30–2.30*
About £80 for two   *D 6.30–11*
Seats 60 Parties 30   *Parking* Limited
Closed L Sat, all Sun & Bank Hols

Guinea Grill

R ♔ ♀ **Map 24 A3**
26 Bruton Place W1
01-629 5613
Credit Access, Amex, Diners, Visa

A friendly restaurant with smart plush decor. The splendid table just inside, laden to overflowing with fine fresh produce, almost obviates the need for a menu, although there is one on display. A simple choice of food is based on a wonderful selection of superbly-flavoured meats, which include spring chicken, baby lamb cutlets, various steaks and a dish of kidneys and bacon. The choice of starters and sweets is uncomplicated too. ♀ Well-chosen ☺

■ *About £65 for two*   *L 12.30–2.30*
Seats 60   *D 7–11*
Closed L Sat, all Sun   *Parking* Limited
                        & 25 & 26 Dec

The Halcyon *NEW ENTRY*

HR **80% £A Map 21 B4**
81 Holland Park W11 3RZ
01-727 7288. Tlx 266721
Credit Access, Amex, Diners, Visa

No expense has been spared to turn two early Victorian town houses on a tree-lined avenue into a hotel which reproduces the splendid style of the Belle Epoque. The suppliers read like an interior designers' roll of honour, and the handsome public areas, including the antique-furnished reception lounge and opulent cocktail bar, are fittingly impressive. Bedrooms and suites – some with four-posters – breathe luxury, from plush carpets and plump-cushioned chairs to a host of cosseting extras such as night safes and mini-bars. Marble bathrooms (some with jacuzzis) are equally lavish, with pampering bathrobes, telephones, hairdryers and bidets. No dogs.
Amenities satellite TV, in-house movies, teletext, valeting, laundry service, 24-hour lounge service, courtesy car.

■ *Rooms 44*   *Confirm by 6*
en suite bath/shower 44   *Last dinner 11.30*
Direct dial Yes   *Parking* Limited
Room TV Yes   *Room service 24 hours*

Kingfisher Restaurant ♔

01-221 5411

Soft pinks and greens create a restful ambience in this basement restaurant with a small patio. Much skill and flair go into James Robbins' tempting menus, which show an Italian bias in such dishes as black tagliatelle with scallops; crab, squid and saffron risotto; and medallions of beef with peperonata and wild rice. To finish try the exquisite amaretto and honey soufflé. Small but select wine list with some very fine Italians: a splendid '83 Valpolicella Classico Superiore, Serego Alighieri, from Masi. ♀ Well-chosen ☺

■ *Set L from £13·50*   *L 12.30–2.30*
About £50 for two   *D 7.30–11.30*
Seats 66 Parties 60   *Parking* Limited

Halepi

R **Map 22 B2**
18 Leinster Terrace W2
01-723 4097
Greek cooking
Owner manager Mr K. Kazolides
Credit Access, Amex, Diners, Visa

A cheerful, busy restaurant off Bayswater Road serving a selection of international dishes as well as plenty of Greek specialities. Meze is a favourite order as a starter, featuring a good medley of dips and salads with pitta bread. Good-quality meat is the basis for the main courses, which include kebabs, kleftiko and moussaka. For a sweet, go for fresh fruit or nice sticky pastries.

■ *About £35 for two*   *Meals noon–midnight*
Seats 100 Parties 70   *Parking* Limited
Closed 25 & 26 Dec

Hana-Guruma *NEW ENTRY*

R ⌇ **Map 26 B2**
49 Bow Lane EC4
01-236 6451
Japanese cooking
Credit Access, Amex, Diners, Visa
Spot the window display of dishes as you walk down the little lane. This Japanese restaurant on two floors is very popular at lunchtime, so book. Fuller version of Mr Takeuchi's set menus (up to

11 items) provides an excellent introduction for the uninitiated – or try his special appetiser with soup and one main dish. In the evening it's à la carte only, from a fairly short menu.

■ *Set L from £22*   *L 11.30–2.30*
About £50 for two   *D 6–10*
Seats 200 Parties 10   *Parking Difficult*
Closed Sat, Sun, Bank Hols & 10 days Xmas

⚑ indicates a **well-chosen** house wine.

Harewood Hotel

H **56% £C Map 21 C4**
Harewood Row NW1 6SE
01-262 2707. Tlx 297225
Credit Access, Amex, Diners, Visa
1974 saw the opening of this purpose-built hotel on a corner site near Marylebone Station. The split-level lobby-lounge features marble, brass and healthy house plants, and below there's a large bar with a clubby colonial feel.

Bedrooms, whether singles, doubles or twins, have decent fitted furniture and a good range of accessories, including radio-alarms, hairdryers and trouser presses. No dogs. *Amenities* in-house movies (charge).
■ *Rooms 93*   *Confirm by 6*
en suite bath/shower 93   *Last dinner 10*
Direct dial Yes   *Parking Difficult*
Room TV Yes   *Room service Limited*

Harry's Java Brasserie *NEW ENTRY*

R ⍶ **Map 7 B4**
78 Wapping Lane E1
01-481 4282
Indonesian cooking
Owner manager Harry McHugh
Credit Access, Amex, Diners, Visa
Large, lively and fashionable, Harry's Java Brasserie is set in an elegantly converted warehouse alongside the new Docklands. The

Indonesian menu includes chargrilled satay, curries from Sumatra, spicy beef rendang and fish roasted in banana leaves. Fresh fruit and coconut ice cream to finish. Coffee and light meals are served throughout the day. A ristaffel feast is available with advance booking for parties.

■ *About £35 for two*   *Meals noon–11.30*
Seats 250 Parties 20   *Parking Ample*

Harveys ★ *NEW ENTRY*

R ★ ⍶ ⌇ **Map 21 B6**
2 Bellevue Road, Wandsworth Common
SW17
01-672 0114
Credit Access, Amex, Visa
The City had its Big Bang, and the equivalent for Wandsworth has been the explosive arrival of Marco-Pierre White on the restaurant scene. With the help of a young and dedicated all-British team he achieves splendid results in dishes that combine visual appeal with truly distinctive flavours. Menus change daily to take advantage of the best and freshest ingredients. Exciting starters range from mosaic of lamb with ratatouille to ballotine of rabbit with wild mushrooms, while main dishes include delights like fillet of veal topped with veal purée and tagliatelle of carrots, and roast saddle of rabbit with wild mushrooms and kidneys. Finish with mouthwatering honey ice cream with fresh apricot sauce. A concise, skilfully chosen wine list: Mercurey (Michel Juillot)

'83, Rosemount Chardonnay Show Reserve '85. *Specialities* nage of fresh fishes with coriander and carrot, escalopes of salmon with fresh chervil and wild mushrooms, noisettes of English lamb en crêpinette, pavè of dark chocolate with caramel sauce. ⚑ **Well-chosen** ℮
■ *Set L from £11·50*   *L 12.30–2.30*
Set D from £22·50   *D 7.30–11.30*
About £65 for two   *Parking Ample*
Closed Sun, Bank Hols   *Seats 44*
& 2 wks Xmas

■ See INSPECTOR FOR A DAY

Hendon Hall Hotel

H 66% £C Map 20 A1
Ashley Lane NW4 1HE
01-203 3341. Tlx 8956088
Credit Access, Amex, Diners, Visa

Actor and theatre manager David Garrick once lived in this handsome red-brick house, behind whose Georgian facade is now an essentially modern hotel. Comfortable public areas are very smart after total refurbishment, and attention has turned to the slightly dated, but roomy and tidy, bedrooms. Service could be warmer. No dogs. *Amenities* garden, in-house movies (free), laundry service.

■ *Rooms* 52   *Confirm by* 6
en suite bath/shower 52   *Last dinner* 10.30
Direct dial Yes   *Parking* Ample
Room TV Yes   *Room service* 24 hours

Hiders

R Map 21 B6
755 Fulham Road SW6
01-736 2331
Credit Access, Amex, Visa

Dishes in this quietly opulent restaurant please the eye with their artistic presentation and the palate with their fresh, clean flavours. Typical evening dishes include lovely fish terrine with roulades of smoked salmon, scallops, crab and mussels; pan-fried liver with herbs; and sliced breast of duck with port wine sauce and a light lemony stuffing. Simpler lunchtime choice. Friendly professional service. ♀ Well-chosen ⓔ

■ *Set D* £14·50   L 12.30–2.30
About £40 *for two*   D 7.30–11.30
Seats 65 *Parties* 35   *Parking* Ample
Closed L Sat, all Sun, Bank Hols, 2 wks Aug & 1 wk Xmas

Hilaire

R Map 23 B5
68 Old Brompton Road SW7
01-584 8993
Credit Access, Amex, Diners, Visa

New chef Brian Webb creates appealing, well-presented meals while Dominic Ford runs the front of house with great charm. The fixed-price dinner menu changes fortnightly, luncheon daily. Starter might be crab ravioli or hot mousseline of chicken, with steamed turbot or fillet of lamb to follow. Delicious sweets. An impeccably refined wine list with some notable dessert wines. ⬔ Outstanding ♀ Well-chosen ⓔ

■ *Set L* £13·50   L 12.30–2.30
Set D £21   D 7.30–11
About £60 *for two*   *Parking* Limited
Closed L Sat, all Sun &   *Seats* 45
Bank Hols

Hilton International Kensington

HR 70% £B ⓖ Map 21 A4
179 Holland Park Avenue, W11 4UL
01-603 3355. Tlx 919763
Credit Access, Amex, Diners, Visa

A '70s high-rise hotel where renovation work goes on apace. Public areas include a smart wine bar-cum-restaurant, a contemporary lounge and extensive conference facilities. The refurbished bedrooms are of a high standard, with good-quality furniture, attractive colour schemes and coordinating fabrics. All have controlled heating, dispense bars for breakfast trays, beverages and alcoholic drinks and tea/coffee-making facilities.

The well-equipped bathrooms have good toiletries. The rooms yet to be attended to are simpler but still comfortable. *Amenities* in-house movies (free), laundry service, 24-hour coffee shop and lounge service.

■ *Rooms* 606   *Confirm by* 6
en suite bath/shower 606 *Last dinner* 10.30
Room phone Yes   *Parking* Ample
Room TV Yes   *Room service* None

Market Restaurant ⓖ

A central buffet displaying an attractive array of food dominates this pleasant, conservatory-style restaurant, with glass skylights and attractive lightwood decor. A good range of well-prepared fish and meat dishes is on offer; a luncheon club offers discounts and Sunday brunch is accompanied by jazz. Good bread rolls and excellent coffee. Over a dozen quality wines available by the glass. Service is commendably courteous and friendly.
♀ Well-chosen ⓔ

■ *Set L & D from* £9·60   L 12.15–3
About £46 *for two*   D 5.30–11
Seats 98

L'Hippocampe

R **Map 21 B5**
131a Munster Road SW6
01-736 5588
French cooking
Owner manager Pierre & Kathy Condou
Credit Access, Amex, Visa
Grilled salmon with herb butter, John Dory in a pink pepper sauce, pan-fried red mullet à la provençale . . . these are typical main dishes at

this French seafood restaurant in Fulham. Starters also smack of the sea, while for dessert there are fruity delights like mixed sorbets or orange cream with caramel. Also a selection of French cheeses.
♀ **Well-chosen** ℮

■ *Set L £9·50*	*L 12–2.30*
About £45 for two	*D 7.30–11*
Seats 35 Parties 8	*Parking Ample*
Closed L Sat, all Sun, Bank Hols & 1 wk Xmas	

Hiroko of Kensington Hilton

R ♿ **Map 21 A4**
Kensington Hilton Hotel, 179 Holland Park Avenue W11
01-603 5003
Credit Access, Amex, Diners, Visa
Approached either through the hotel foyer or its own separate entrance, this is a bright, comfortable Japanese restaurant. The set menus provide a well-balanced meal. Dishes include

sukiyaki, shabu shabu and sankaiyaki – a Japanese-style barbecue with beef, chicken, pork, oysters, scallops, prawns and vegetables.

■ *Set L from £8*	*L 12–2.30*
Set D from £19	*D 6–10.30*
About £45 for two	*Parking Limited*
Seats 80	*Parties 15–30*
Closed L Mon, some Bank Hols, 25 & 26 Dec & 1–4 Jan	

Hogarth Hotel

H **58% £D/E Map 23 A5**
Hogarth Road SW5 0QQ
01-370 6831. Tlx 8951994
Credit Access, Amex, Diners, Visa
New carpet, curtains, lighting and redecoration have smartened this five-storey modern hotel close to the Earls Court Exhibition Centre. There's a neat little lounge area in the foyer, a bright, comfortable bar and two popular function rooms.

Well-kept bedrooms with practical contemporary furnishings have hairdryers, tea-makers, and tiled bathrooms (shower only in singles). **Amenities** 24-hour lounge service, laundry service.

■ *Rooms 86*	*Confirm by 4*
en suite bath/shower 86	*Last dinner 9.30*
Direct dial Yes	*Parking Limited*
Room TV Yes	*Room service Limited*
Closed 2 days Xmas	

Hoizin

R **Map 21 C5**
72 Wilton Road SW1
01-630 5108
Chinese cooking
Credit Access, Amex, Visa
Hoizin means 'good, fresh taste of the sea' and the seafood certainly seems fresh at this neat, contemporary Chinese restaurant. Crab and lobster, scallops and prawns, eels and oysters,

sea bass and sole are prepared in various tempting ways, both plain and sauced. There are meat and poultry dishes, too, including salt-baked chicken, and many of the vegetables are supplied straight from the owners' farm.

■ *Set L from £6·50*	*L 12–2.30*
Set D from £6·50	*D 6–11.30*
About £40 for two	*Parking Ample*
Seats 85 Parties 80	*Closed Sun*

■ See INSPECTOR FOR A DAY

Hokkai *NEW ENTRY*

R **Map 24 B3**
59 Brewer Street W1
01-734 5826
Japanese cooking
Credit Access, Amex, Diners, Visa
Simple and unelaborate in typical Japanese style, with bamboo screens and paper panels. The menu's fairly concise, featuring a well-chosen selection of dishes to appeal to both Western and

Japanese palates. Set meals offer good value and centre round the main dish, maybe tempura, beef teriyaki or hokkai nabe (a fish and vegetable stew). Well-cooked rice, refreshing green tea.

■ *Set L £6·50*	*L 12.30–2.30*
Set D £13·80	*D 6–10.30*
About £40 for two	*Parking Difficult*
Seats 40	*Parties 16*
Closed Sun & Bank Hol Mons	

Holiday Inn Chelsea

See under The Chelsea Hotel

Holiday Inn (Marble Arch)

H **74%** **£A** *E* **Map 22 C1**
134 George Street W1H 6DN
01-723 1277. Tlx 27983
Credit Access, Amex, Diners, Visa

The private basement car park is a real bonus at this well-maintained modern hotel, which stands just north of Marble Arch, near Hyde Park and Oxford Street. Stylishly contemporary lounges flank the reception area, and the cane-furnished bar is popular with both residents and casual callers. Guests wishing to take a little exercise will welcome the pool and keep-fit facilities. Bedrooms are excellent, with easy-on-the-eye colour schemes, comfortable chairs, plenty of space and all the usual modern accessories like trouser presses and hairdryers. Individually controlled air conditioning throughout. Neat compact bathrooms. *Amenities* indoor

swimming pool, sauna, solarium, whirlpool bath, keep-fit equipment, beauty salon , in-house movies, laundry service, coffee shop (7.30am–10.30pm), 24-hour lounge service.

■ *Rooms* 241	*Confirm by 6*
en suite bath/shower 241	*Last dinner 12*
Direct dial Yes	*Parking* Ample
Room TV Yes	*Room service* 24 hours

■ If we recommend meals in a hotel or inn, a separate entry is made for its restaurant.

Holiday Inn (Mayfair)

H **76%** **£A** **Map 25 B4**
3 Berkeley Street W1X 6NE
01-493 8282. Tlx 24561.
Credit Access, Amex, Diners, Visa

Converted from an office block in the 1970s, this particular Holiday Inn stands on the corner of Berkeley Street and Piccadilly. This location puts it near shops, theatres and tourist sights, and must be counted as one of its chief assets. The reception area is attractively tiled in marble, and refurbishment has left the lounge bar and restaurant looking very smart. Spacious bedrooms, with large beds and standardised modern furniture (not all of it pristine), are very comfortable and well equipped, with individual heating and air conditioning controls, mini-bars, trouser presses and hairdryers. Compact bathrooms have a lot of mirror space. Some staff

seem to lack sparkle. No dogs.
Amenities in-house movies (charge), laundry service.

■ *Rooms* 185	*Confirm by 6*
en suite bath/shower 185	*Last dinner 10.30*
Direct dial Yes	*Parking* Limited
Room TV Yes	*Room service* 24 hours

Holiday Inn (Swiss Cottage)

H **79%** **£A/B** *E* & **Map 20 B3**
128 King Henry's Road NW3 3ST
01-722 7711. Tlx 267396
Credit Access, Amex, Diners, Visa

A major programme of improvements is nearing completion at this multi-storey hotel not far from Regent's Park. The redesigned ground floor now has a spacious cocktail bar and lounge area leading off the reception. Roomy, comfortable bedrooms all have small balconies, good-quality furniture and drapes, and plenty of writing and storage space; air-conditioning, mini-bars and trouser presses are standard. The smart bathrooms have shower attachments and hairdryers. Top-floor penthouse rooms and suites are luxurious in the extreme and some boast whirlpool baths. *Amenities* garden, indoor swimming pool, sauna, solarium, keep-fit

equipment, beauty salon, hairdressing, pool table, in-house movies (charge), laundry service, 24-hour lounge service, kiosk.

■ *Rooms* 305	*Confirm by 6*
en suite bath/shower 305	*Last dinner 10.30*
Direct dial Yes	*Parking* Ample
Room TV Yes	*Room service* 24 hours

Hospitality Inn, Bayswater

H **62% £C Map 22 B2**
104 Bayswater Road W2 3HL
01-262 4461. Tlx 22667
Credit Access, Amex, Diners, Visa
   Bedrooms at this modern hotel offer a good measure of space, comfort and practicality. Front rooms with park views are the most desirable, but all offer air conditioning, mini-bars, hairdryers and other up-to-date extras. Chandeliers and large plants feature in the relaxing first-floor public area. Service can be a shade remote, and the buffet breakfast is nothing special. *Amenities* in-house movies (free), laundry service.

■ *Rooms* 175	*Confirm by* 6
en suite bath/shower 175	*Last dinner* 10.15
Direct dial Yes	*Parking* Ample
Room TV Yes	*Room service* 24 hours

L'Hotel

H **65% £B/C Map 23 C4**
28 Basil Street SW3 1AT
01-589 6286. Tlx 919042
Credit Visa
   Paris rather than nearby Knightsbridge is the inspiration of this stylish, friendly little hotel. There are no public areas apart from the spacious foyer and the brasserie-style wine bar, where a delicious continental breakfast is served.

Individually furnished bedrooms have a charming country air, as well as TVs, direct-dial telephones, and spacious, gleaming bathrooms.

Amenities laundry service.

■ *Rooms* 12	*Confirm by* 6
en suite bath/shower 12	*Last dinner* 10
Direct dial Yes	*Parking* Difficult
Room TV Yes	*Room service* None

Howard Hotel

HR **87% £A E Map 24 D3**
Temple Place, Strand WC2 2PR
01-836 3555. Tlx 268047
Manager Mr N. Martini
Credit Access, Amex, Diners, Visa
   Close to The Strand, Fleet Street and theatreland, this modern luxury hotel by the Thames is also a convenient prestige base for those with business in the City. Staff are unfailingly courteous, and there's a great sense of style about the place, notably the superb foyer-lounge with its Adam-style friezes, Oriental carpets, chandeliers and Ionic columns in Italian marble. Bedrooms, all of a good size, include some splendid balconied penthouse suites with wonderful sweeping views of the river. Furnishings are French reproduction and there are no less than three phones – by the bed, on the desk and in the marble-clad bathroom. No dogs. *Amenities* satellite TV, in-house movies (free), valeting, laundry service, 24-hour lounge service.

■ *Rooms* 136	*Confirm by* 6
en suite bath/shower 136	*Last dinner* 11
Direct dial Yes	*Parking* Ample
Room TV Yes	*Room service* 24 hours

Quai D'or Restaurant ⚌ ⚌ &

The renaissance decor and the stylish service complement the excellent cooking of Gerhard Reisepatt, who has been in charge of the kitchens for more than a decade. His long classic menu includes splendid soup (minestrone with fresh basil; vichyssoise; seafood soup topped by a puff-pastry hat), grills and sauced entrées, and a daily special such as coq au vin served from the silver trolley. Fine wines including burgundies from top growers (Dujac, Trapet). ⊖

■ *About £85 for two*	*L* 12.30–3,
Seats 60	*Sun* 12.30–2.30
Parties 200	*D* 6.30–11

Hyatt Carlton Tower

HR **89% £A E Map 23 D4**
2 Cadogan Place SW1X 9PY
01-235 5411. Tlx 21944
Credit Access, Amex, Diners, Visa
   Opulent public areas create a favourable first impression at this luxury hotel overlooking Cadogan Gardens. Bedrooms combine elegance and luxury with up-to-the-minute facilities like satellite TV, video and room safes. Bathrooms are exemplary. The new leisure complex, though not so extensive as originally planned, adds a new dimension. Additional improvements include a new business centre and a luxury suite. No dogs.

Amenities garden, sauna, solarium, steam bath, keep-fit equipment, hairdressing, tennis, in-house movies (free), 24-hour lounge service, kiosk, courtesy car.

■ *Rooms* 223 *Confirm by 6*
en suite bath/shower 223 *Last dinner* 11.15

Direct dial Yes *Parking* Ample
Room TV Yes *Room service* 24 hours

CHELSEA ROOM &

The Chelsea Room closed for a major refit in May 1987 so our earlier visit could no longer be the basis for an accurate assessment. However, there is every reason to suppose that standards still match the gradings in our 1987 Guide, namely two stars for Bernard Gaume's marvellous French cooking, two crowns for the luxurious ambience, an outstanding wine list and praise for superb service led by Jean Quéro. ©

■ *Set L* £18·50 incl. wine L 12.30–2.45
About £90 for two D 7–10.45,
Seats 60 Sun 7–10.15

Rib Room ♔♔

A major refit has added more flesh to the Rib Room without altering its essential character or mode of operation. Superb Aberdeen Angus beef with all the traditional trimmings remains the prime choice, with grills and seafood as alternatives. The concise but delightful wine list includes fine burgundies and an excellent Petaluma Chardonnay. ♛ **Well-chosen** ©

■ *L* 12.30–2.45, D 6.30–11.15
Sun 12.30–2.30 Sun 7–10.30
About £58 for two *Parking* Ample
Seats 86 *Parties* 40

Hyde Park Hotel

HR **85% £A E & Map 22 C3**
66 Knightsbridge SW1Y 7LA
01-235 2000. Tlx 262057
Manager Aldo Grosso
Credit Access, Amex, Diners, Visa

Behind the richly ornate Edwardian frontage is an air of luxury and grandeur. The imposing entrance is graced by multi-coloured marble, chandeliers and ornate filigree, and the day rooms are similarly opulent. Palatial rooms with large balconies overlook Hyde Park at the rear. All rooms have double glazing to ensure a peaceful stay, solid period furniture, quality fittings, air-conditioning and a multitude of extras; some have

fine antiques and four-posters. Bathrooms are equally magnificent. The Park Room overlooking Rotten Row is a delightful setting for breakfast. *Amenities* hairdressing, laundry service, 24-hour lounge service.

■ *Rooms* 180 *Confirm by 6*
en suite bath/shower 180 *Last dinner* 11
Direct dial Yes *Parking* Difficult
Room TV Yes *Room service* 24 hours

Grill Room ♔♔ &

A panelled dining room and fine tableware make for a smart setting in which to enjoy Jean-Michel Bonin's classically-based menus. The cooking is consistently pleasing and the three-course menu (which includes a splendid roast of the day) offers good value. Start with salade de canard, followed by fillet of beef with foie gras, truffle and redcurrant sauce or delicately-flavoured turbot and langoustines in a chive sauce. Good Bordeaux wines.
♛ **Well-chosen** ©

■ *Set L* £15 L 12.30–2.30
About £65 for two D 7–11, Sun 7–10
Seats 74 *Parties* 20
Closed Sat & Bank Hols

Ikeda

R **♙ Map 24 A3**
30 Brook Street W1
01-629 2730
Japanese cooking
Credit Access, Amex, Diners, Visa

Whether you want a table or a counter seat you should book at least a week in advance, for Shigeru Ikeda's tiny, well-run restaurant is very popular. All the food is wonderfully fresh and

beautifully prepared, and if you're not sure what to order the staff will muster enough English to help you decide. There's a separate sushi and sashimi bar.

■ *Set L* from £9·50 L 12–2.30
Set D from £23 D 6.30–10.30
About £65 for two *Parking* Difficult
Seats 32 *Parties* 8
Closed Sat, Sun & 1 wk Xmas

Ikkyu *NEW ENTRY*

R **Map 24 B2**
67 Tottenham Court Road W1
01-636 9280
Japanese cooking
Credit Access, Amex, Diners, Visa

Booking is essential at this hectically busy Japanese basement restaurant. The atmosphere is relaxed and informal, and staff will help with menu choice. A good selection of dishes (but no

red meat) includes yakitori, using most parts of the chicken, sashimi and sushi, the last being served in fairly large pieces. Excellent fresh fruit and good brown tea with more body and flavour than the usual green.

■ *About £35 for two* L 12.30–2.30
Seats 70 D 6–10.30, Sun 7–10.30
Parties 40 *Parking* Difficult
Closed L Sun, all Sat & 8 days Xmas

Inigo Jones ▶

Inigo Jones ★★

R ★★ ♔ ♩ **Map 27 B2**
14 Garrick Street WC2
01-836 6456
Manager Denis Flouvat
Credit Access, Amex, Diners, Visa

Quality of produce, a marvellous sense of design, plus abundant flair and expertise ensure that Paul Gayler always meets – and invariably exceeds – expectations at this most stylish of restaurants. His menus offer much to delight, from starters like our visually superb pastry cornucopia of scallops and baby vegetables to mouthwatering main courses such as baked wood pigeon with savoy cabbage and thyme, or a fragrantly simple cod dish of melting freshness. Wonderfully indulgent yet delicate sweets include a rich glazed coffee cream with prunes marinaded in Tia Maria. Superlative cheeses and a wine list of great finesse complete the triumphant picture. Youthful, polished service admirably complements the culinary skills.

■ **See INSPECTOR FOR A DAY**

Specialities salmon and scallop terrine with dill cucumber, suprême of duck with black olive and mushroom purée and lavender honey sauce, mille-feuille of chocolate pastry filled with walnut cream, raspberries and a Calvados sauce.
▭ Outstanding ♀ Well-chosen ℮

■ Set L £16·25	L 12.30–2.30
Set D £29·50	D 5.30–11.30
About £100 for two	Parking Difficult
Seats 85	Parties 30
Closed L Sat, Sun & Bank Hols	

Inn on the Park

HR **90% £A** **E** **Map 22 D3**
Hamilton Place, Park Lane W1A 1AZ
01-499 0888. Tlx 22771
Manager Ramon Pajares
Credit Access, Amex, Diners, Visa

First-class management and impressively high standards of service and maintenance mark out this hotel as a model of its kind. Crystal chandeliers and a polished marble floor create an air of unashamed luxury in the foyer, while the lounge area, bars and banqueting rooms strike a similarly elegant note. Bedrooms are just as delightful; king-sized beds and attractive soft furnishings are standard, and there are numerous extras like mini-bars. Sumptuous bathrooms have bidets, bath robes and telephone extensions. *Amenities* garden, in-house movies (free), valeting, shopping arcade.

■ Rooms 228	Confirm by 6
en suite bath/shower 228	Last dinner 11
Direct dial Yes	Parking Ample
Room TV Yes	Room service 24 hours

Four Seasons Restaurant ★ ♔ ♔ &

Manager Vinicio Paolini
A highly civilised restaurant where John McManus' seasonal à la carte menus are full of interest. Natural flavours and quality produce take starring roles, while skilful saucing and artistic presentation add to the overall success. Your starter might be avocado with smoked salmon mousse, followed perhaps by best end of lamb in

puff pastry. Superb cheeses and wickedly rich sweets. There's also a special menu for health-watchers. A great cellar strongest in the classics: 15 vintages of Ch. Latour including the legendary 1945. *Specialities* seafood sausage with julienne of celeriac and creamy leek sauce, feuilleté of wild mushrooms with champagne butter sauce, sautéed baby chicken with cream chive sauce, apple charlotte.
⊃ Outstanding ♀ Well-chosen ℮

■ *Set L £16·75*   *L 12–3*
About £80 for two   *D 7–11*
Seats 62

Lanes ₩ ₩ &

Manager Peter Romerio
A justly popular, elegant restaurant where the main attraction is a lavish display of cold hors d'oeuvre. The fixed-price luncheon menu offers a small choice of delicious dishes, and there's a slightly extended version for dinner. Apart from grills, main dishes might include poached salmon or emincé of veal. To follow, there are simple but delicious desserts like crème brûlée. Book.
⊃ Outstanding ♀ Well-chosen ℮

■ *Set L from £17*   *L 12–3*
Set D from £22   *D 6–12, Sun 6.30–11*
About £52 for two   *Seats 72 Parties 10*

Inter-Continental Hotel

HR 86% £A *E* & **Map 22 D3**
1 Hamilton Place W1V 0QY
01-409 3131. Tlx 25853
Manager Graham Jeffrey
Credit Access, Amex, Diners, Visa
   A prime position on Hyde Park Corner and excellent conference facilities that include a satellite link with the United States make this modern hotel popular with tourists and business people alike. The luxurious foyer-lounge is a favourite place for tea and there are two bars, one with stylish, seductive decor and panoramic views. Spacious supremely comfortable bedrooms with thick carpets and writing desks have air-conditioning, double-glazing and mini-bars. Marble-clad bathrooms offer cosseting extras. *Amenities* sauna, solarium, whirlpool bath, steam bath, gymnasium, beauty salon, hairdressing, in-house movies (free), valeting, laundry service, coffee shop (7am–midnight), shopping arcade, courtesy car.
■ *Rooms 496*   *Confirm by 6*
en suite bath/shower 496   *Last dinner 11.30*
Direct dial Yes   *Parking Ample*
Room TV Yes   *Room service 24 hours*

Le Soufflé ★★ ₩ &

French cooking
Rich colours and striking decor provide a smart, comfortable background for Peter Kromberg's exciting, imaginative menu of splendid French dishes. From a simple starter such as the grande assiette of salmon through unusual dishes like the parcels of sweetbread on a potato pancake with a green lentil salad to the complexities of chicken leg filled with crabmeat and prawn in a garlic and basil sauce, his skill and flair create a truly memorable experience. Also on the menu are simple grills and the most superb soufflés. Beautifully balanced list of exceptional wines (wonderful clarets) at fair prices.
Specialities grande assiette de saumon, soufflé de haddock à la moutarde de Dijon, dodine de canard de Barbarie aux cèpes, soufflé aux fruits de la passion.
⊃ Outstanding ♀ Well-chosen ℮
■ *Set L £19*   *L 12.30–3, Sun 12–4*
Set D £29·50   *D 7–11.30, Sun 7–11*
About £70 for two   *Seats 76*
Closed L Sat, 26 Dec & 1 Jan

Interlude

R **Map 27 B2**
7 Bow Street WC2
01-379 6473
French cooking
Credit Access, Amex, Diners, Visa
   Prix fixe menus offer a good choice of imaginative dishes in this attractive restaurant by the Royal Opera House. David Lawrence is the head chef, and saucing is a strong point – port and Stilton for sirloin steak, red, green and yellow peppers for a pike and salmon terrine, a classic normande with calf's liver. Good wine list, strong in Burgundies. ♀ Well-chosen ℮
■ *Set L £19·50*   *L 12.15–2.15*
Set D £22·50   *D 7.15–11.30*
About £60 for two   *Parking Difficult*
Seats 50   *Parties 24*
Closed L Sat, Sun & Bank Hols

Jacques ▶

Jacques NEW ENTRY

R ♀ **Map 20 D2**
130 Blackstock Road N4
01-359 3410
Credit Access
A lively, relaxed restaurant run with panache by Jacques Herbert, who also shares the cooking. Good fresh ingredients are used in a short menu that includes soups, terrines, a fish dish and the excellent speciality, duck breast with a cream and peppercorn sauce. Sunday brunch. Some very good wines at keen prices: Tokay (Albrecht) 1983, Beaune Les Boucherottes (Parent) 1982. Must book. ♀ **Well-chosen** ☙

■ *Set D Sun only £20* *L Sun only 12.15–1.30*
About £42 for two *D 6–10.45, Sun 7–10*
Seats 44 *Parking Ample*
Closed Mon, Bank Hols, 2 wks Aug, 10 days Xmas

Jade Garden

R **Map 27 A3**
15 Wardour Street W1
01-439 7851
Chinese cooking
Manager David Chung
Credit Access, Amex, Diners, Visa
Proximity to theatreland and an extensive choice of reliably prepared Cantonese dishes guarantee full tables at this spacious restaurant. Deep-fried squid or oyster with chilli and black bean sauce make tasty starters, to be followed perhaps by steamed pork with plum sauce or sizzling hot beef with crisp vegetables.

■ *Set D from £7-20* *Meals noon–11,*
About £33 for two *Sat & Sun 11.30–11*
Seats 150 Parties 150 *Parking Difficult*
Closed 25 & 26 Dec

Jams NEW ENTRY

R **Map 25 B4**
42 Albermarle Street W1
01-493 3600
Owner managers Jonathan Waxman & Melvyn Master
Credit Access, Amex, Visa
The owners have had great success with their New York restaurants, and this stylish London offshoot has also hit the jackpot. In Californian cooking the quality of the produce speaks for itself in fairly simple treatments – the charcoal grill is the principal tool here. Corn-fed chicken comes with super French fries, rainbow trout with leek and walnut vinaigrette, pork tenderloin with Zinfandel sauce and a gratin of potato and red pepper. Angel hair pasta with scallops and asparagus is a nice starter; salads and vegetables abound, and sweets include mocha fudge cake (heaped with freshly whipped cream) and key lime pie. The wine list includes some good, but fairly pricy, Californians.

■ *About £60 for two* *L 12–3*
Seats 95 *D 7–11.30*
Parties 55 *Parking Difficult*
Closed L Sat, all Sun & Bank Hols

☙ is our symbol for an **outstanding** wine list.

Joe's Café

R **Map 23 C4**
126 Draycott Avenue SW3
01-225 2217
Credit Access, Amex, Diners, Visa
A chic, split-level restaurant in black, white and chrome where the fashionable gather to enjoy carefully prepared and attractively presented dishes. Boned quail and endive salad, champagne sausages with mash and onions, cassoulet, and grilled tuna with a soy ginger sauce are typical of the eclectic range. Lighter offerings at lunchtime (salads, club sandwiches), and delicious sweets like lemon mousse tart to finish. ♀ **Well-chosen**

■ *About £45 for two* *L 12–3.30*
Seats 80 *D 7.30–11.30*
Parties 20 *Parking Limited*
Closed D Sun, 25 & 26 Dec & 1 Jan

Kalamaras (Mega)

R ♀ & **Map 22 BZ**
76 Inverness Mews W2
01-727 9122
Greek cooking
Owner manager Stellos Platonos
Credit Access, Amex, Diners, Visa
A busy restaurant serving well-cooked fresh meals for the hearty eater. There is a good regular menu with interesting daily specials, such as good garlicky aubergine dip, chicken-stuffed courgettes and salmon and hake in filo pastry with a rosemary sauce. Try the tyropites (flaky pastry puffs filled with melting cheese) as a starter. Delicious salads with plenty of crumbled feta.

■ *Set D £13-50* *D only 6.30–midnight*
About £32 for two *Parking Limited*
Seats 86 Parties 26 *Closed Sun & Bank Hols*

Kaya

R ♕ **Map 27 A2**
22 Dean Street W1
01-437 6630
Korean cooking
Owner manager Mr B. W. Suh
Credit Access, Amex, Diners, Visa
　Korean specialities are skilfully executed and full of flavour at this smart, friendly restaurant. Rice-based meals traditionally include appetisers

(try savoury green bean pancake and fried fish fillets), plus main dishes such as sirloin steak barbecued at your table and accompanied by a variety of piquant side dishes.
■ *Set L from £5*　　　*L 12–3*
Set D £19　　　　　*D 6–11*
About £45 for two　　*Parking Difficult*
Seats 80　　　　　　*Parties 60*
Closed L Sat & Sun & all 24 & 25 Dec

■ Our inspectors are our full-time employees; they are professionally trained by us.

Keats

R **Map 20 B2**
3 Downshire Hill NW3
01-435 3544
French cooking
Owner manager Aron Misan
Credit Access, Amex, Diners, Visa
　A long-established restaurant providing skilled French cooking. The seasonally-changing menu offers delights such as stuffed mussels in cream

sauce or Roquefort cheese soufflé for starters; breast of chicken rolled with lobster or venison in chestnut sauce as a main course. First-class vegetables, excellent sweets and good French cheeses. Carefully chosen wines, notably Chablis. ℮
■ *Set D £19*　　　*D only 7–11*
About £60 for two　*Parking Ample*
Seats 55　　　　　*Parties 55*
Closed Sun & Bank Hols

Ken Lo's Memories of China ★

R ★ ♿ **Map 25 A6**
67 Ebury Street, SW1
01-730 7734
Chinese cooking
Owner manager Kenneth Lo
Credit Access, Amex, Diners, Visa
　Ken Lo, known through his books and TV appearances as the doyen of Chinese food experts, is ably supported by his English wife Anne and chef Kam-Po But at this superb Chinese restaurant which is regarded as one of Europe's finest. Attracting a sophisticated, cosmopolitan clientele, the atmosphere in this restaurant fairly buzzes with electricity and activity, especially in the evening. Many of Ken Lo's gastronomic discoveries find a place on a menu that provides an impressive tour of his native country, with dishes from as far afield as Mongolia, Shantung and Shanghai. Highlights include incomparable Peking Duck, fresh crab with a flavoursome onion, ginger and yellow bean sauce, and deliciously

spicy fingers of pork, as well as a section of 'Family Favourites'. Superb sweets such as the beautifully prepared Peking glazed apples and bananas. *Specialities* Peking duck, steamed cabbage meat rolls, lotus leaf-wrapped steamed chicken, Sichuan crispy beef.　🍷 Well-chosen
■ *Set L from £16*　　*L 12–2.30*
Set D from £22　　　*D 7–10.45*
About £59 for two　　*Parking Limited*
Seats 100 Parties 100　*Closed Bank Hols*

Kenilworth Hotel

H **62% £B Map 24 C2**
97 Great Russell Street WC1B 3LB
01-637 3477. Tlx 25842
Credit Access, Amex, Diners, Visa
　A well-placed hotel, handy for theatreland, West End shopping and the City – and just a stone's throw from the British Museum. The marbled foyer doubles as a spacious, airy lounge, and there's a sophisticated cocktail bar.

Bedrooms are comfortable and quite stylish, with plants, brass light fittings, floral fabrics and neat lightwood units. Smart tiled bathrooms.
Amenities laundry service, 24-hour lounge service, in-house movies (free).
■ *Rooms 182*　　　　*Confirm by 6*
en suite bath/shower 182 Last dinner 10.30
Direct dial Yes　　　*Parking Difficult*
Room TV Yes　　　　*Room service 24 hours*

Kennedy Hotel

H **64%** **£D** **Map 20 C3**
Cardington Street NW1 2LP
01-387 4400. Tlx 28250
Manager Adrian Allen
Credit Access, Amex, Diners, Visa
Accommodation has benefited much from the continuing improvements at this late-'60s hotel near Euston Station. Bedrooms have now been attractively redecorated and refurbished. Smart bathrooms, plus extras like mini-bars, hairdryers and trouser presses. Day rooms – approached from the elegant foyer – include a stylish cocktail bar and lounge. *Amenities* garden, in-house movies (free), laundry service.

■ *Rooms* 324		*Confirm by* 6
en suite bath/shower 324		*Last dinner* 10.30
Direct dial Yes		*Parking* Limited
Room TV Yes		*Room service* Limited

Kensington Close Hotel

H **64%** **£B/C** **Map 23 A4**
Wright's Lane W8 5SP
01-937 8170. Tlx 23914
Credit Access, Amex, Diners, Visa
Stylish features of this large redbrick hotel include a leafy patio garden and a striking open-plan area that combines restaurant, coffee shop and bar. Well-kept bedrooms are seeing gradual improvements – smart darkwood furniture, brass light fittings, pastel quilted bedspreads. *Amenities* garden, indoor swimming pool, sauna, solarium, gymnasium, squash, laundry service, coffee shop (11am–11pm), kiosk.

■ *Rooms* 522		*Confirm by* 6
en suite bath/shower 522		*Last dinner* 10.30
Direct dial Yes		*Parking* Limited
Room TV Yes		*Room service* None

Kensington Palace Thistle

H **71%** **£D** **Map 22 B3**
De Vere Gardens W8 5AF
01-937 8121. Tlx 262422
Credit Access, Amex, Diners, Visa. **LVs**
A large white-painted hotel in a convenient position opposite Kensington Gardens, and close to the Albert Hall and the shops of Kensington High Street. Many of the bedrooms have been upgraded with smart darkwood units, brass fittings and coordinating fabrics; some of those still awaiting improvement are looking a little tired. The foyer, with its chandeliers and potted palms, makes a grand first impression, and there's a plush, peaceful lounge and cocktail bar. Alternative refreshment spots are a convivial pub-style bar and a popular coffee shop that overlooks the park. Staff standards have slipped slightly. No dogs. *Amenities* in-house movies (charge), coffee

shop (7am–11.45pm).

■ *Rooms* 299		*Confirm by* 6
en suite bath/shower 299		*Last dinner* 10.30
Direct dial Yes		*Parking* Limited
Room TV Yes		*Room service* 24 hours

Kensington Tandoori

R **Map 23 A4**
1 Abingdon Road W8
01-937 6182
Indian cooking
Manager Pan Sing Rana
Credit Access, Amex, Diners, Visa
Pretty decor and a sense of privacy offered by glass screens and a trough of greenery isolating each pair of tables are bonuses here. There's a variety of tikkas, curries, kormas and biryanis on offer, with the moist and tender chicken and lamb tikkas, accompanied by sizzling onions, lemon and crisp salads, being particularly well-cooked. Good quality thalis too.

■ *Set L from* £5·95		*Meals* noon–midnight
About £30 *for two*		*Parking* Limited
Seats 76 *Parties* 30		*Closed* 25 Dec

Kingsley Hotel

H **64%** **£B/C** **Map 24 C2**
Bloomsbury Way WC1A 2SD
01-242 5881. Tlx 21157
Manager Mr John Stewart
Credit Access, Amex, Diners, Visa. **LVs**
The Kingsley is ideally located for theatres, shopping and sightseeing. Behind the impressive turreted red-brick facade, refurbishment continues, and most bedrooms now have luxurious thick carpets, attractive decor in sage green or salmon pink and good modern bathrooms. Day rooms are pleasantly traditional. No dogs. *Amenities* in-house movies (free), laundry service, 24-hour lounge service.

■ *Rooms* 145		*Confirm by* 6
en suite bath/shower 145		*Last dinner* 10
Direct dial Yes		*Parking* Difficult
Room TV Yes		*Room service* 24 hours

Koto

R **Map 20 C3**
75 Parkway NW1
01-482 2036
Japanese cooking
Credit Visa
A very good place for a first taste of Japanese cuisine, Koto provides excellent eating and notable value for money in friendly, relaxed surroundings. The choice is very varied, from

splendid sushi to teriyaki and tempura. Japanese roast duck and a robust salmon and noodle stew. Fresh fruit is eye-catchingly arranged for a refreshing sweet. A sushi bar is planned.

■ *Set L £5·50*   *L 12.30–2.30*
Set D £13·50   *D 6–10.30*
About £35 for two   *Parking Ample*
Seats 45 Parties 20   *Closed Sun, Bank Hols, 4 days Xmas & 3 days New Year*

Kundan

R **Map 21 C5**
3 Horseferry Road SW1
01-834 3434
Indian & Pakistani cooking
Owner manager Nayab Abbasi
Credit Access, Amex, Diners, Visa
Expertly prepared North Indian and Pakistani dishes are the speciality of this comfortable basement restaurant, one of the best of its kind in

London. Delicate spicing distinguishes appetising offerings which range from sizzling chicken or tandoori lamb chops to enjoyable vegetarian dishes. Lovely breads and Basmati rice.

■ *Set L £10*   *L 12–3*
Set D £15   *D 7–12*
About £38 for two   *Parking Ample*
Seats 140   *Parties 200*
Closed Sun & Bank Hols

Kym's

R ᕙ **Map 21 C5**
70 Wilton Road SW1
01-828 8931
Chinese cooking
Credit Access, Amex, Visa
Careful cooking does justice to quality ingredients at this bright, simple Chinese restaurant. Szechuan specialities are particularly popular, and the interesting menu offers a wide

choice of dishes, from hot and cold appetisers (try the delicious fried Peking dumplings) to seafood like sole in black bean sauce, plus chicken, pork, beef and griddle-sizzled dishes.

■ *Set L £7·50*   *L 12–3*
Set D £15   *D 6.30–11.30*
About £36 for two   *Parking Ample*
Seats 120   *Parties 100*
Closed 25 & 26 Dec

Ladbroke at Hampstead

H **64% £B/C Map 20 C3**
Primrose Hill Road, Hampstead NW3 3NA
01-586 2233. Tlx 22759
Credit Access, Amex, Diners, Visa
Comfortable accommodation and useful conference facilities are provided at this modern block hotel in a residential area north of Regent's Park. Good-sized bedrooms with attractive furnishings all have tea-makers, trouser presses

and neat bathrooms (some with shower only). The open-plan foyer, lounge and bar are smart and relaxing.
Amenities in-house movies (free), laundry service, 24-hour lounge service.

■ *Rooms 96*   *Confirm by 6*
en suite bath/shower 96   *Last dinner 10*
Direct dial Yes   *Parking Limited*
Room TV Yes   *Room service 24 hours*

Ladbroke at Park Lane

H **71% £A/B Map 22 D3**
2 Stanhope Row, Park Lane W1Y 7HE
01-493 7222. Tlx 24665
Credit Access, Amex, Diners, Visa
Tucked away just off Park Lane, this discreet modern hotel has undergone a £2 million face-lift and a change of name (it was the Ladbroke Curzon). Style and comfort are provided in generous measure in the public rooms, where indoor plants, bleached wood and chintzy fabrics give a traditional feel. Bedrooms, though not large, are well designed, and their pastel colour schemes and light pine furnishings are very easy on the eye. Air-conditioning has recently been installed, and accessories include tea-makers, hairdryers and remote-control TVs. Compact bath or shower rooms. Service is friendly if occasionally a touch haphazard. No dogs.

Amenities 24-hour lounge service.
■ *Rooms 71*   *Confirm by 6*
en suite bath/shower 71   *Last dinner 11*
Direct dial Yes   *Parking Limited*
Room TV Yes   *Room service 24 hours*

Ladbroke Westmoreland Hotel

H **72%** **£B** *E* **Map 20 B3**
Lodge Road, St John's Wood NW8 7JT
01-722 7722. Tlx 23101
Credit Access, Amex, Diners, Visa

Overlooking Lord's cricket ground and affording the fortunate few a fine view of the day's play, this is a popular meeting place for watchers and players alike. They congregate in the Nursery End pub or in the spacious and comfortable lounge-cum-bar above the gleaming contemporary foyer, with its polished marble floors and mirror-clad columns. Bedrooms range from the standard (with neat bathrooms and tea-making facilities) to the Gold Star, in which all the beds are double and where you can have a chocolate biscuit with your Ovaltine (or complimentary miniature of whisky). Trouser presses and hairdryers are also supplied. Many bedrooms have just been refurbished, and a recent extension has added 30 mini-suites.
Amenities in-house movies (charge), laundry service, coffee shop (10am–1am), kiosk.

■ *Rooms* 377	*Confirm by* 6
en suite bath/shower 377	*Last dinner* 10
Direct dial Yes	*Parking* Ample
Room TV Yes	*Room service* 24 hours

Lakorn Thai

R **Map 20 D3**
197 Rosebery Avenue EC1
01-837 5048
Thai cooking
Credit Access, Amex, Diners, Visa

Tasty, spicy food that is excellent value for money brings the customers to this simple little restaurant close to Sadler's Wells. The menu offers a good sample of Thai cuisine, from exotic soups and satay to stuffed tomatoes, fried butter fish, delicious spring rolls, and crunchy quick-fried vegetables. Lovely refreshing jasmine tea. Booking advisable.

■ *Set L* £7·50	*L* 12–3
About £25 *for two*	*D* 6–12
Seats 90 *Parties* 30	*Parking* Ample
Closed L Sun & 25 & 26 Dec	

Lal Qila

R **Map 24 B1**
117 Tottenham Court Road W1
01-387 5332
Indian cooking
Manager Enam Ul Haque
Credit Access, Amex, Diners, Visa

A pleasantly uncluttered restaurant where prime ingredients, enhanced by fresh herbs and aromatic spices, are carefully prepared in a variety of appetising ways. Specialities include marinated rainbow trout cooked over charcoal, quails and lamb chops masala, as well as tandooris and tasty starters like juicy chicken with hot and sour sauce. Help-yourself Sunday buffet.

■ *Set L & D* Sun £7·95	*L* 12–3
About £34 *for two*	*D* 6–11.30
Seats 70 *Parties* 20	*Parking* Ample
Closed 25 & 26 Dec	

Langan's Bistro

R **Map 24 A1**
26 Devonshire Street W1
01-935 4531
French cooking
Credit Amex

A stylish bistro with an intimate atmosphere. The unfussy menu offers imaginative dishes, expertly prepared. Start perhaps with halibut mousse, or sautéed cabbage with quail's eggs, bacon and walnut; then follow with loin of pork glazed with Stilton and green peppercorns, or calf's liver with kumquats and cranberries. Don't miss Mrs Langan's chocolate pudding. Book well in advance. ♀ **Well-chosen** ☺

■ *About* £42 *for two*	*L* 12.30–2.30
Seats 38	*D* 7–11.30
Closed L Sat, all Sun	*Parking* Difficult
& Bank Hols	

RECEPTION

Langan's Brasserie

R ♌ **Map 25 A4**
Stratton Street W1
01-491 8822
Owner Messrs Langan, Shepherd & Caine
Credit Access, Amex, Diners, Visa
  Customers compete for tables at this popular
venue, and are rewarded by a vast and varied
menu, admirably executed by Richard Shepherd
and his staff. Starters range from pea soup to

oyster mushroom salad, and a main course may
be humble liver and onions or sophisticated filet
mignon de porc en croûte. Plenty of puds, good
cheeses and lively crowds (upstairs is more
sedate). ℮

■ *About £52 for two*	*L 12.30–2.45*
Seats 200	*D 7–11.45, Sat 8–12.45*
Closed L Sat, all Sun	*Parking Limited*
& all Bank Hols	

Last Days of the Raj

R ⛺ ♌ ♿ **Map 27 A2**
42 Dean Street W1
01-439 0972
Indian cooking
Manager Mohammed Hanif
Credit Access, Amex, Diners, Visa
  Stylish surroundings and splendid cooking are
to be found at this up-market branch of the
Covent Garden restaurant. Exciting dishes such

as Chuzza Zaffrani (baby chicken marinated and
cooked in a spiced sauce, served with herbs and
egg) and lamb tikka tempt the palate with their
subtle spices. There is a good choice of
vegetarian dishes and delicious breads. Non-
smoking area.

■ *About £32 for two*	*L 12–3*
Seats 100 Parties 100	*D 6–11.30*
Closed 25 & 26 Dec	*Parking Limited*

■ Changes in data may occur in
  establishments after the Guide
  goes to press. Prices should be taken
  as indications rather than firm quotes.

Launceston Place Restaurant

R **Map 23 B4**
1a Launceston Place W8
01-937 6912
Credit Access, Visa
  Smart residential Kensington is the home of this
stylish restaurant where fresh ingredients are
used to good effect in dishes like warm lobster
and spinach tart, John Dory with saffron and
tomato, and breast of chicken with watercress

sauce. Vegetables are first rate and sauces have
good consistency and fine flavour. Desserts
include a tasty tropical fruit salad.
🍷 **Well-chosen** ℮

■ *Set L £8·50*	*L 12.30–2.30*
Set D 7–8pm £10·50	*D 7–11.30*
About £44 for two	*Parking Limited*
Seats 58 Parties 14	*Closed L Sat, D Sun,*
Bank Hols, 4 days Easter & Xmas	

Lee Ho Fook

R ♿ **Map 27 A2**
15 Gerrard Street W1
01-734 9578
Chinese cooking
Credit Access, Amex, Diners, Visa
  Soho stalwart in the main street of Chinatown.
Cantonese and Peking dishes are the mainstay of
a lengthy menu, and generally sound,
straightforward cooking is backed up by

proficient service with a smile. Dim sum are
served in the daytime (paper prawns were
particularly good on our last visit – fresh tasting
and not greasy) and the pork is good, with very
little fat. There are various set menus. Tea arrives
at the table just after you.

■ *Set meals from £7*	*Meals noon–midnight*
About £32 for two	*Parking Difficult*
Seats 147 Parties 40	*Closed 2 days Xmas*

Leinster Towers Hotel

H **55% £D Map 22 B2**
Leinster Gardens W2 3AU
01-262 4591. Tlx 291634
Credit Access, Amex, Diners, Visa
  Simple comfort is the key to this Bayswater
hotel. Large windows; light colours and green
carpets lend a cool spaciousness to the entrance
foyer-lounge. In contrast, the 'Duke of Leinster' is
a bright, cosy little bar, hung with banners. Simply

decorated bedrooms offer modest overnight
accommodation with modern fitted units, floral
curtains and tea-makers. Bathrooms are
compact and functional. *Amenities* in-house
movies (charge), laundry service.

■ *Rooms 163*	*Confirm by arrang.*
en suite bath/shower 163	*Last dinner 10*
Room phone Yes	*Parking Difficult*
Room TV Yes	*Room service Limited*

Leith's

R ♔ **Map 21 B4**
92 Kensington Park Road, W11
01-229 4481
Credit Access, Amex, Diners, Visa

A long-established restaurant with a sophisticated decor and clientele, the fixed price seasonal menu here draws on Prudence Leith's own farm for fresh produce. The hors d'oeuvres trolley has been a favoured choice for many years.

Typical main dishes are duck breast with fried apple and green peppercorn sauce and brill stuffed with crab mousseline, all well-presented. Competent cooking using quality ingredients, and good service too. ☻ Well-chosen ⊜
■ *Set D £33–£35*   *D only 7.30–11.30*
About £70 for two   *Parking Ample*
Seats 90 Parties 35   *Closed 2 days during Notting Hill Festival (Aug) & 4 days Xmas*

■ We publish annually, so make sure you use the current edition. It's worth it!

Lena's Thai Restaurant *NEW ENTRY*

R ♀ **Map 21 C6**
196 Lavender Hill SW11
01-228 3735
Thai cooking
Credit Access, Amex, Diners, Visa

Evenings are especially popular at Lena Limnamkam's pleasant Thai restaurant, where it's fun to go in a group and share the tasty dishes. Our choice included a delicious potato basket

filled with prawns and sweetcorn, king prawns stuffed with crabmeat, a hot-sour soup of prawns and mushrooms, and a green beef curry flavoured with coconut. Don't miss the house special: a hotpot of mixed seafood in a subtly spiced sauce.
■ *About £30 for two*   *L 12–2.45*
Seats 50   *D 6.30–11.30*
Closed L Sun & Mon   *Parking Limited*

Lindsay House *NEW ENTRY*

R ♔ **Map 27 A2**
21 Romilly Street W1
01-439 0450
English cooking
Credit Access, Amex, Diners, Visa

Ring the bell to gain admission to this pleasant little restaurant, where owner Malcolm Livingston has recreated the private house style of his English House and English Garden. The menu is

similar, too, with traditional English dishes like home-smoked meats with spicy fruit chutney, Cornish fish pies, fillet steak Guinness and yummy ginger and rum junket. Paul Hodgson, once at Carrier's, is the chef. ☻ Well-chosen ⊜
■ *About £60 for two*   *L 12.30–2.30*
Seats 35   *D 6–12*
Parties 20   *Parking Difficult*
Closed 25 Dec & Good Fri

Little Akropolis

R ♀ ♿ **Map 24 B2**
10 Charlotte Street W1
01-636 8198
Greek cooking
Credit Access, Amex, Diners, Visa

Robust, positively flavoured Greek dishes from chef/patron Michael Ktori are the speciality of this long-established restaurant, run by two brothers. A plate of traditional hors d'oeuvre, including

taramasalata, houmus and stuffed vine leaves, makes a fine introduction, followed by a classic such as kleftiko or stifado. Moussaka appears in meat or vegetarian form, and the feta salad is notably good.
■ *About £37 for two*   *L 12–2.30*
Seats 32   *D 6–10.30*
Parties 25   *Parking Limited*
Closed L Sat, all Sun & Bank Hols

Lok-Zen

R ♀ **Map 20 C1**
138 Fortis Green Road, N10
01-883 4202
Chinese cooking
Credit Access, Amex, Diners, Visa

A light and airy restaurant with hanging plants, Chinese prints and fans and attractively presented tables. Chef Lo offers a menu of Peking and Cantonese dishes, as well as specials such

as bang bang chicken (poached chicken in peanut and chilli sauce – a delicious cold dish ideal for a summer starter), drunken fish (in wine sauce!) and sesame toffee bananas. Service is friendly and efficient. ☻ Well-chosen
■ *About £26 for two*   *L 12–2.30*
Seats 40   *D 6–midnight*
Closed L Sun, all Mon   *Parking Ample & Bank Hols*

London Embassy Hotel

H 68% £C Map 22 A2
150 Bayswater Road W2 4RT
01-229 1212. Tlx 27727
Credit Access, Amex, Diners, Visa
A summer patio leading from the smart bar is a popular feature of this comfortable modern hotel overlooking Kensington Gardens. Other day rooms include a cool and spacious marble-floored foyer and a small, comfortable lounge. Attractively

decorated bedrooms on seven floors, each with its own colour scheme, have tea-makers, radio-alarms and compact, tiled bathrooms. Executive rooms offer extra accessories. *Amenities* in-house movies (charge), laundry service.
■ *Rooms 192*　　　　　*Confirm by 6*
en suite bath/shower 192 *Last dinner 10.15*
Direct dial Yes　　　　*Parking Ample*
Room TV Yes　　　　*Room service 24 hours*

London Hilton on Park Lane

H 85% £A E ₺ Map 22 D3
Park Lane W1
01-493 8000. Tlx 24873
Credit Access, Amex, Diners, Visa
The day rooms at this superb high-rise hotel have been the subject of a massive improvement programme, and the opulent lobby-lounge, the Victorian-style bar and the top-floor cocktail lounge are looking splendid. The exception is the marble foyer, which is beginning to have a slightly tired appearance. Bedrooms, including one floor designated non-smoking, are very comfortable and attractive, with Georgian-style furnishings, deep carpets and chintz. Accessories include satellite TV, refrigerator, hairdryer and luxury toiletries. Four floors of superior executive rooms have their own lounge, bar, meeting rooms and check-in arrangements. *Amenities* hairdressing,

in-house movies (free), laundry service, shopping arcade.
■ *Rooms 501*　　　　　*Confirm by 6*
en suite bath/shower 501 *Last dinner 1am*
Direct dial Yes　　　　*Parking Ample*
Room TV Yes　　　　*Room service 24 hours*

London International Hotel

See under Swallow International Hotel

London Marriott Hotel

H 85% £A E Map 22 D2
Grosvenor Square W1A 4AW
01-493 1232. Tlx 268101
Credit Access, Amex, Diners, Visa
An ultra-modern hotel, fitted to the highest standards, where computerisation aids the efficient organisation. Guests have coded key cards with which to gain entrance to the spacious bedrooms, equipped with ample wardrobe and desk space and large beds. Roomy sitting areas are provided in the executive rooms and the beautifully fitted bathrooms have marble surfaces. The bar, amply supplied with easy chairs, is relaxing, while the lounge is luxurious to a degree, with deep carpets, fine furniture and flower arrangements. Helpful porterage and comprehensive room service. No dogs. *Amenities* in-house movies (free), valeting, coffee

shop (24 hours), 24-hour lounge service.
■ *Rooms 228*　　　　　*Confirm by 6*
en suite bath/shower 228 *Last dinner 11*
Direct dial Yes　　　　*Parking Ample*
Room TV Yes　　　　*Room service 24 hours*

London Metropole

H 68% £B Map 22 C1
Edgware Road W2 1JU
01-402 4141. Tlx 23711
Credit Access, Amex, Diners, Visa
Accommodation here is on 23 floors, and the higher you go the more spectacular the views. Built in the 1970s, the hotel is kept smartly up to date by continuous refurbishment. Executive rooms offer extras like electronic message

systems and adjustable air-conditioning. Public areas are stylish. No dogs.
Amenities hairdressing, in-house movies (charge), laundry service, coffee shop (7am–11.30pm), 24-hour lounge service, kiosk.
■ *Rooms 586*　　　　　*Confirm by 6*
en suite bath/shower 586 *Last dinner 11*
Direct dial Yes　　　　*Parking Ample*
Room TV Yes　　　　*Room service 24 hours*

London Tara Hotel ▶

London Tara Hotel

H **69% £C** ♿ **Map 23 A4**
Scarsdale Place, Kensington W8 5SR
01-937 7211. Tlx 918834/5
Manager Eoin Dillon
Credit Access, Amex, Diners, Visa
  Vast and modern it may be, but the London Tara is also a place of warmth and welcome, and general manager Eoin Dillon heads a friendly and highly efficient team. Bright, airy bedrooms. Note

the new Twizzles Parade, with library-style piano-lounge, champagne bar, and a colourful brasserie with a carousel theme. No dogs. *Amenities* in-house movies, laundry service, brasserie (7am–11pm).

■ *Rooms 831*	*Confirm by 6*
en suite bath/shower 831	*Last dinner 1am*
Direct dial Yes	*Parking Ample*
Room TV Yes	*Room service 24 hours*

London West Hotel

See under Ramada Inn West London

Londonderry Hotel

H **85% £A** *E* **Map 22 D3**
19 Old Park Lane W1Y 8AP
01-493 7292. Tlx 263292
Credit Access, Amex, Diners, Visa
  Opulence and impeccable service are the keynotes here: lavish investment has produced a truly de luxe hotel. Sumptuous interiors hint at the classical lines of a palazzo. Plush Italianate chairs are set amid marble columns in the elegant foyer-lounge and there's an inviting club-style bar with mirrored ceiling. Hand-painted and gilded decoration abounds, culminating in a delightful domed ceiling. Double-glazed, air-conditioned bedrooms, including studio and penthouse suites, are equally impressive with their stylishly coordinated quilts and curtains, and hand-painted furniture. Remote-control TVs, radio consoles and mini-bars are standard. Gleaming marble

bathrooms offer hairdryers and excellent towels and soaps. No dogs. *Amenities* satellite TV, in-house movies (free), valeting, 24-hour lounge service.

■ *Rooms 150*	*Confirm by 6*
en suite bath/shower 150	*Last dinner 11*
Direct dial Yes	*Parking Ample*
Room TV Yes	*Room service 24 hours*

Lou Pescadou

R ♿ **Map 23 A5**
241 Old Brompton Road SW5
01-370 1057
Credit Access, Amex, Diners, Visa
  Rough plaster walls displaying numerous Mediterranean paintings give the genuine feel of Provence to this bistro-style establishment. Extensive seafood menu includes flavoursome fish soup, simply cooked red mullet and

skate, as well as shellfish. There's also a good selection of pizzas, pâtés, omelettes and steaks, and daily specials such as kidneys dijonnaise and beef with lentils. Service both relaxed and friendly.

■ *About £35 for two*	*L 12.30–3*
Seats 55	*D 7.30–12*
Parking Limited	

Lowndes Thistle Hotel

H **79% £A** *E* **Map 23 D4**
21 Lowndes Street SW1X 9ES
01-235 6020. Tlx 919065
Manager Peter N. Proquitte
Credit Access, Amex, Diners, Visa
  Service and comfort are of equal importance at this fine modern hotel in a peaceful Belgravia setting. Luxurious day rooms on an intimate scale include the handsome marble-floored lobby and lounge with moulded ceilings and crystal chandeliers, plus a most striking bar in Chinese Chippendale style. Bedrooms are delightful, featuring Regency-style furniture and lovely coordinating colour schemes. Modern accessories provided range from hairdryers and trouser presses to wall safes. The marble-walled bathrooms, all fully carpeted, provide plenty of toiletries and bathrobes, and have separate

telephone extensions. An excellent hotel and a credit to this hotel chain. No dogs.
Amenities in-house movies (one free), valeting, laundry service.

■ *Rooms 79*	*Confirm by 6*
en suite bath/shower 79	*Last dinner 10.15*
Direct dial Yes	*Parking Ample*
Room TV Yes	*Room service 24 hours*

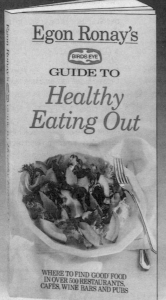

Luigi

R **Map 7 B5**
129 Gypsy Hill, Dulwich SE19
01-670 1843
Italian cooking
Credit Access, Amex, Diners, Visa
   Choose the simplest, most straightforward dishes at this stylish Italian restaurant with a terrace for summer eating. A typically rewarding meal might start with grilled sardines or home-made linguine and clam sauce, then move on to tender calf's liver with sage, grilled lamb cutlets or baby chicken en cocotte – with fresh fruit salad or zabaglione for a classic finale.

♀ Well-chosen ☺

■ About £43 for two	L 12–3
Seats 55	D 6.30–11.30
Parties 25	Parking Ample
Closed L Sat, all Sun, Bank Hols & Aug	

■ For a discount on next year's guide, see Offer for Answers.

Ma Cuisine

R ♀ **Map 23 C4**
113 Walton Street SW3
01-584 7585
French cooking
Credit Amex, Diners
   As we closed research, Guy Mouilleron remained at the helm in Ma Cuisine's tiny kitchen, displaying his skills in classical French dishes such as daube de canard. His largely unchanging menu is supplemented by specials like vegetable terrine with tomato coulis, or breast of chicken with langoustine and lobster sauce. Sweets include seasonal fruit tartlets and bavarois. Not every dish is an unqualified success. ☺

■ About £65 for two	L 12.30–2
Seats 30	D 7.30–11
Closed Sat, Sun, Bank	Parking Difficult
Hols, 1 wk Easter, 1 wk Xmas & mid July–mid Aug	

Magno's Brasserie

R **Map 27 B2**
65a Long Acre, Covent Garden WC2
01-836 6077
French cooking
Credit Access, Amex, Diners, Visa
   Good-quality ingredients, with the emphasis on seasonal produce, are soundly if rather unimaginatively prepared by Luc Ferrand at this busy bistro. Mussels in puff pastry and sautéed sweetbreads are typical starters, while main courses range from simple pan-fried liver and bacon and steak béarnaise to baked fillets of John Dory, sea bream and hake in a dill and cucumber sauce. Booking is advisable. ☺

■ D pre-theatre £8·45	L 12–2.30
About £50 for two	D 6–11.30
Seats 54 Parties 60	Parking Difficult
Closed L Sat, all Sun, Bank Hols & 1 wk Xmas	

Majlis *NEW ENTRY*

R **Map 23 B4**
32 Gloucester Road SW7
01-584 3476
Indian cooking
Credit Access, Amex, Diners, Visa. LVs
   Just a few steps along the road from Memories of India, and now in the same ownership. The menu – centred around lamb, chicken and prawns – is more or less the same, and cooking is of a similar enjoyable standard. Dishes relished on a recent visit include tandoori mixed grill, jheenga chat (spicy prawns on fried bread) and lamb chat mossala in a rich, buttery sauce.

■ Set L & D £11·95	L 12–2.30
About £32 for two	D 5.30–11.30
Seats 32	Parties 32
Closed 25 & 26 Dec	Parking Limited

♀ indicates a **well-chosen** house wine.

Mandarin

R **Map 23 A4**
197c Kensington High Street W8
01-937 1551
Chinese cooking
Owner manager Alan Man
Credit Access, Amex, Diners, Visa
   A welcoming Chinese restaurant in smart basement premises (entrance in Allen Street). The cooking is sound and reliable, and favourites on the inter-regional menu include succulent spare ribs, griddle-fried dumplings, spicy Singapore noodles, crab with black bean sauce and duck dishes. The steamboat, a sort of Chinese fondue, is a popular party choice. Sweets are sorbets or toffee-glazed fruits.

■ Set meals from £8	Meals noon–11.30
About £35 for two	Parking Limited
Seats 60 Parties 50	Closed 24–26 Dec

Mandarin Kitchen

R **Map 22 B2**
14 Queensway W2
01-727 9012
Chinese cooking
Credit Access, Amex, Diners, Visa
   At the park end of Queensway, this is a smart friendly Chinese restaurant with a long menu that leans towards seafood. Poached scallops in garlic, king prawns served sizzling with a fruity

sauce, steamed sea bass and carp with ginger are typical temptations. Also a wide variety of meat and vegetable dishes. Good soups, carefully cooked rice and noodles. Note long opening hours.

■ *Set meals £7·30*   *Meals noon–11.30*
About £35 for two   *Parking Ample*
Seats 95 Parties 95   *Closed 25 & 26 Dec*

Mandeville Hotel

H **66% £B   Map 22 D1**
Mandeville Place W1M 6BE
01-935 5599. Tlx 269487
Manager Mr Serrano
Credit Access, Amex, Diners, Visa. **LVs**
   A strikingly contemporary, marble-floored foyer sets the tone at this elegant hotel near the key West End shopping areas. Modern artwork adorns the walls of the pretty little lounge, and the

two bars include one in traditional pub style. Cane and rattan furnish the attractive bedrooms, which are of uniform size and have neat tiled bathrooms. *Amenities* in-house movies, laundry service, coffee shop (7am–11am & noon–11.30pm).
■ *Rooms 165*   *Confirm by 6*
en suite bath/shower 165 *Last dinner 11.30*
Direct dial Yes   *Parking Difficult*
Room TV Yes   *Room service 24 hours*

Manzi's

R **Map 27 A2**
1 Leicester Street WC2
01-734 0224
Seafood
Owner manager Louis G. Manzi
Credit Access, Amex, Diners, Visa
   London's oldest seafood restaurant, Manzi's is a perennial favourite just by Leicester Square. Sit in the bustling ground-floor room and order from

one of the affable waiters; simplest things are best, like potted shrimps, crab salad, fine large Dover sole meunière and skate with black butter. Determined meat-eaters can settle for a steak. Fresh fruit salad to finish. ☺
■ *About £40 for two*   *L 12–2*
Seats 80   *D 5.30–11.30,*
Closed L Sun   *Sun 6–10.30*
Parking Difficult

Mario

R ♔ **Map 23 C4**
260 Brompton Road SW3
01-584 1724
Italian cooking
Credit Access, Amex, Diners, Visa
   A stylish Italian restaurant which opens its sliding windows on to pavement tables in fine weather. A change of chef has made for greater consistency throughout an interesting range of

dishes: smoked mozzarella grilled with ham; linguine with clams; Scotch salmon cooked in Pernod sauce; a splendid osso buco with saffron rice; tira-mi-su and zabaglione. Note Masi wines on a good Italian list. ♀ **Well-chosen** ☺
■ *Set L £9·50*   *L 12–3*
About £54 for two   *D 7–11.30, Sun 7–11*
Seats 74   *Parking Limited*
Closed Mon & Bank Hols

Marlborough Crest

H **73% £B ঙ Map 24 C2**
Bloomsbury Street WC1B 3QD
01-636 5601. Tlx 298274
Credit Access, Amex, Diners, Visa
   Elegance and luxury are the keynotes of this handsome Edwardian hotel conveniently placed for Oxford Street. Fresh flowers and plants fill the spacious, traditionally appointed foyer, and the intimate residents' lounge offers comfortable seating and a period writing desk for private correspondence. Contrasting drinking venues are provided by the smart, '20s-style Brasserie Saint Martin and the more traditional Duke's Head Bar. Light, airy bedrooms (including a number of sumptuous suites) have attractive lightwood units and are all of a good size. Useful accessories range from tea-makers and mini-bars to hairdryers, trouser presses and fruit, and the

bright, tiled bathrooms provide bathrobes and baskets of quality toiletries. No dogs.
Amenities in-house movies (charge), laundry service, brasserie (7am–11.30pm).
■ *Rooms 169*   *Confirm by 6*
en suite bath/shower 169 *Last dinner 11.30*
Direct dial Yes   *Parking Difficult*
Room TV Yes   *Room service 24 hours*

Le Marmiton

R Map 26 C1
11 Blomfield Street EC2
01-588 4643
French cooking
Owner manager Mr M. Trouard-Riolle
  More comfortable premises for this busy city bistro, where tasty French dishes are served in fast, friendly fashion. Robust fare includes fish soup, country terrine, rillettes as good as you'd find in Tours, civet de lièvre, gigot d'agneau and a pepper steak that's not to be sneezed at. Excellent French cheeses (three chèvres among them) and a decent French wine list with good Beaujolais crus ☺

- About £40 for two
- Seats 95
- Closed Sat, Sun, Bank Hols & 1 wk Xmas

L only 12–2.45
Parking Difficult

☞ is our symbol for an **outstanding** wine list.

Martin's

R ⅙ Map 20 C3
239 Baker Street NW1
01-935 3130
Owner manager Martin Coldicott
Credit Access, Amex, Diners, Visa
  Beautifully decorated menus and a soft peach decor contribute to the chic look of this newly-relocated restaurant. Expectations are raised by enticing dishes like gâteau of wild mushrooms, roast monkfish with garlic sauce, and veal sauced with broccoli, but results on the plate can disappoint. Carefully chosen wines include some lovely burgundies. 🍷 **Well-chosen** ☺

- Set L from £12·50
- About £50 for two
- Seats 60 Parties 20
- Closed L Sat, all Sun & Bank Hols

L 12–2.30
D 6–11, Sat 7–11
Parking Limited

Masako

R ♕ Map 22 D1
6 St Christopher's Place W1
01-935 1579
Japanese cooking
Credit Access, Amex, Diners, Visa
  Waitresses in kimonos, paper lanterns and screens and shiny black tables bring a simple elegance to this appealing Japanese restaurant. Attractively presented fresh fish is a feature of the downstairs sushi bar, and also of a menu that includes delicately flavoured soups and a tasty, tender beef teriyaki. Try the o-cha tea, and finish with fresh fruit. Booking advisable at lunchtime.

- Set L £10·50
- Set D £20·50
- About £55 for two
- Seats 100
- Closed Sun & Bank Hols

L 12–2
D 6–10
Parking Difficult
Parties 14

Maxim's de Paris

R ♕ Map 27 A3
32 Panton Street SW1
01-839 4809
Credit Access, Amex, Diners, Visa
  In spite of an upstairs move into a more intimate room the decor is still Belle Epoque, with mirrors, murals and a canopied ceiling. The food is classical, with attractive modern presentation; a typical starter might be terrine de pintadeau à la vinaigrette tomatée, with tournedos farci aux noix to follow. Exceptional clarets (Ch. Lynch Bages '61, Ch. La Fleur Pétrus '71) and splendid white burgundies.
☞ **Outstanding** ☺

- Set D £25
- About £90 for two
- Seats 80
- Closed Sun, Mon & Bank Hols

D only 7–11.30
Parking Ample
Parties 120

May Fair Inter-Continental Hotel

HR 85% £A E ⅙ Map 25 A4
Stratton Street W1A 2AN
01-629 7777. Tlx 262526
Credit Access, Amex, Diners, Visa. LVs
  The hotel's atmosphere of luxury and style envelops guests immediately on entering the marble-floored foyer. The lounge and two bars are graced with antiques, period chairs, fine rugs and plenty of flowers and greenery, continuing the ambience of relaxing elegance. Bedrooms have silk wallpaper, light colour schemes and splendid fabrics: the tiled bathrooms are light and pretty. An even higher standard of comfort is to be found in the de luxe rooms, which have writing desks, leather chesterfields and marble bathrooms. Superb staff. No dogs.
Amenities satellite TV, in-house movies (free), laundry service, coffee shop (7.30am–11pm).

- Rooms 310
- en suite bath/shower 310
- Direct dial Yes
- Room TV Yes

Confirm by 6
Last dinner 11
Parking Difficult
Room service 24 hours

Le Château ♔

Quality ingredients are skilfully cooked by Michael Coaker, who has introduced some individual touches to the menu – try Chinese-style foie gras (with stir-fried vegetables). Tempting sweet trolley and excellent cheeses. Very good wine list.

♟ Well-chosen ♙

■ Set L £15·50	L 12.30–2.30
Set D £23	D 6.30–10.30
About £62 for two	Seats 65
Closed L Sat	Parties 25

Mayflower

Ｒ **Map 27 A2**
68 Shaftesbury Avenue W1
01-734 9207
Chinese cooking
Owner manager Mr Tsang
Credit Access, Amex, Diners, Visa

Perfectly placed for theatre-goers, this smart Chinese restaurant has a vast repertoire of dishes, with Cantonese specialities predominating. Deep-fried wun-tun or crispy pancake rolls stuffed with vegetables and prawns make tasty starters, while main courses range from sweet and sour chicken or beef with sweet green peppers to sea bass in black bean sauce or abalone with sea cucumbers.

■ Set D £17 for two	Meals noon–3.30am
About £34 for two	Parking Difficult
Seats 122 Parties 40	Closed 3 days Xmas

Le Mazarin ★

Ｒ ★ ♔ ♙ **Map 21 C5**
30 Winchester Street SW1
01-828 3366
French cooking
Credit Access, Amex, Diners

Soft lighting and contemporary decor create a pleasing, intimate atmosphere at this pretty, alcoved basement restaurant. René Bajard's imaginative menu reflects his association with the Roux brothers, as do the high standard of cooking and beautiful presentation. There is a fixed-price multiple-choice menu and a five-course menu gastronomique. Typical starters might be mousseline of duck with green peppercorns, red mullet with tomato and basil coulis; main courses could include suprême of turbot in champagne, breast of duck with morels or noisettes of lamb provençale. Delicate flavours and superb sauces, perfectly balanced to complement the main ingredient. Excellent sweets may tempt with delicate strawberry-filled pastries or a well-made

bavarois au chocolat. Good list of young French wines, strongest in burgundies.
Specialities fricassée de poulet fermier au basilic, filets de sole Mazarin, tranchettes d'onglet poêlées aux échalotes, délice aux deux chocolats et sa crème anglaise à la menthe fraîche.

♟ Well-chosen ♙

■ Set D from £17·50	D only 7–11.30
About £50 for two	Parking Limited
Seats 50	Parties 10
Closed Sun, Bank Hols & 1 wk Xmas	

■ Our inspectors never book in the name of Egon Ronay's Guides; they disclose their identity only after paying their bills.

Memories of India

Ｒ **Map 23 B4**
18 Gloucester Road SW7
01-589 6450
Indian cooking
Credit Access, Amex, Diners, Visa.

Friendly Indian restaurant with a comfortable, dimly lit dining area and a little back patio. Cooking is very sound and reliable throughout a range of tandoori dishes and curries based on lamb, chicken and prawns. There's also a very good choice of vegetables, available as side dishes or main courses. Sweets include syrupy guleb jamon and home-made ice cream.

■ Set L & D £10·70	L 12–2.30
About £32 for two	D 5.30–11.30
Seats 50	Parties 50
Closed 25 & 26 Dec	Parking Limited

Ménage à Trois

R Map 23 C4
14 Beauchamp Place SW3
01-589 4252
Credit Access, Visa

An attractively contemporary basement restaurant where the menu announces that there are only 'befores' and 'afters' and from the five pages of enticing dishes, as well as daily specials, a meal can be put together to satisfy any appetite. The cooking is modern and well-executed, with excellent flavours and balanced sauces. Dishes come in some wonderful combinations like the lime-scented sea bass with scallops, oriental

dressing and coriander. Try the quail with game mousse, red cabbage and diced duck in flaky pastry; chicken julienne on pickled cucumber with a peanut dressing or a salad tiède for lighter appetites. Finish with a wonderful chocolate pudding. Exciting wines, as strong in Alsace (Domaine Weinbach) and California (Ridge) as in Bordeaux and burgundy.
◁▷ Outstanding ♀ Well-chosen ℰ

■ About £52 for two | L 11.45–3
Seats 75 | D 7–12.15
Closed Sun, 25 & 26 Dec | Parking Ample

■ For a discount on next year's guide, see Offer for Answers.

Le Meridien Piccadilly

HR 86% £A E Map 25 B4
Piccadilly W1V 0BH
01-734 8000. Tlx 25795
Credit Access, Amex, Diners, Visa

No expense has been spared to transform this handsome turn-of-the-century building into one of the capital's leading hotels. The marble entrance hall leads to a domed and galleried reception, which in turn leads to the impressive Oak Lounge with its ornate panelling and extravagant Venetian glass chandeliers. Edwardian splendour is seen also in the conservatory-style restaurant bar and the clubby dark green cocktail bar, while the basement houses a superb leisure complex and a quiet, relaxing drawing room/library. Bedrooms are equally luxurious, with quality furniture and designer fabrics, many extras and lavish marble-clad bathrooms. Impeccable staff provide first-class service. *Amenities* indoor swimming pool, sauna, solarium, whirlpool bath, gymnasium, beauty salon, squash, billiards, snooker, satellite TV, valeting, kiosk.

■ Rooms 284 | Confirm by 6
en suite bath/shower 284 | Last dinner 11.30
Direct dial Yes | Parking Difficult
Room TV Yes | Room service 24 hours

Oak Room ★ 👑👑👑 ♿

French cooking
An opulent room with Venetian chandeliers and limed oak panelling is the setting for some interesting and excellent eating, with many dishes re-created from a famous restaurant in Burgundy. David Chambers is the man in charge here, and

his sometimes inspired cooking is complemented by high-class service. Start perhaps with fillets of red mullet served on a bed of French salads and follow with sautéed veal sweetbreads, finishing with either splendid cheeses or an indulgent chocolate soufflé. Fine clarets (Ch. Figeac 1971) on a good list. A violinist and pianist play each evening. The fixed-price business lunch gives good value. *Specialities* le gaspacho de langoustines à la crème de courgette, papillote de bar aux tomates fraîches et à l'estragon, filet d'agneau en robe de veau et son gratin dauphinois, tarte tiède aux figues.
♀ Well-chosen ℰ

■ Set L £17·50 | L 12–2.30
Set D from £26 | D 7–10.30
About £80 for two | Seats 50 Parties 10
Closed L Sat & Sun & some Bank Hols

Terrace Garden Restaurant 👒

This smart, leafy restaurant provides a summery setting for an agreeable meal. Crab soup with rouille or ceviche of scallops and salmon marinated in lime and orange to start, then maybe steamed breast of chicken flavoured with tomatoes and spring onions, or steak and Stilton pie. Lighter choices include burgers and club sandwiches. Splendid sweets – a faultless tarte tatin. Last orders 11.30pm.
♀ Well-chosen ℰ

■ Set L £13·50 | Meals 7am–1am,
Set D £15·50 | Sun 8am–1am
About £42 for two | Seats 140 Parties 25

Mijanou

R ♧ **Map 23 D5**
143 Ebury Street SW1
01-730 4099
French cooking
Credit Access, Amex, Diners, Visa
   Ring the doorbell to gain entry to this popular haunt of MPs and top civil servants. Neville Blech directs front of house while wife Sonia creates elaborate dishes like seafood-stuffed squid and

paupiettes of chicken breast and crab with lemon grass and Cognac sauce. Acceptable sweets.
▷ Outstanding   ♀ Well-chosen ✆
■ *Set L £10·95*   *L 12.30–2*
Set D £26·50   *D 7.30–11*
About £62 for two   *Parking Difficult*
Seats 30   *Parties 24*
Closed Sat, Sun, Bank Hols, 1 wk Easter, 3 wks Aug & 2 wks Xmas

Mr Kai

R **Map 22 D2**
65 South Audley Street, Mayfair W1
01-493 8988
Chinese cooking
Owner manager Duncan Tong
Credit Access, Amex, Diners, Visa
A stylishly appointed restaurant offering sound, careful cooking of a wide range of mainly Pekinese dishes. Evocatively named items such

as the Surprise of the Encircled Piglet – minced pork and bamboo shoots wrapped in pastry – are available along with classics like wun tun soup or baked crab. Finish with toffee banana, fruit mountain or pancake with red bean paste.
♀ Well-chosen
■ *About £43 for two*   *L 12–2.30*
Seats 120 Parties 40 *D 7–11.15*
Closed Bank Hols   *Parking Limited*

Miyama

R ♛ ♧ **Map 25 A4**
38 Clarges Street W1
01-499 2443
Japanese cooking
Credit Access, Amex, Diners, Visa
   Delightful waitresses in traditional costume serve Mr Miyama's freshly prepared, beautifully presented Japanese food at this elegant modern restaurant. Fish dishes, both raw and cooked, are

particularly good, while meaty options such as beef teriyaki and deep-fried loin of pork merit similar approval. Seasonal fruit makes a light, refreshing finale.
■ *Set L £6·40*   *L 12.30–3*
Set D £19   *D 6.30–11*
About £60 for two   *Parking Limited*
Seats 64   *Parties 20*
Closed L Sat, all Sun & Bank Hols

Mogul

R **Map 7 B5**
10 Greenwich Church St, Greenwich SE10
01-858 6790
Indian cooking
Credit Access, Amex, Diners, Visa
   A basement and ground-floor Indian restaurant in the centre of Greenwich. The menu features tandoori specialities and a wide range of curries based on lamb, chicken and prawns. Cooking is

enjoyable throughout, and those who want to sample a selection of dishes should try the meat or vegetarian thali (set meals). Note an unusual vegetable dish with potatoes, bamboo shoots and black-eyed beans.
■ *Set L from £5·50*   *L 12–2.30*
Set D from £5·50   *D 6–11.30*
About £28 for two   *Parking Difficult*
Seats 60 Parties 10   *Closed 25 & 26 Dec*

■ If we recommend meals in a
  hotel or inn, a separate entry is
  made for its restaurant.

M'sieur Frog

R **Map 20 D3**
31a Essex Road N1
01-226 3495
French cooking
Owner managers Howard & Tina Rawlinson
Credit Access, Visa
   An immensely popular, bistro-style restaurant where modern French dishes are most enjoyably prepared. Typical treats include fish terrine with

sauces of saffron and watercress, roast quails with kumquats served on a bed of wild rice, and simple grilled calf's liver with fresh sage. Sticky toffee pudding to finish.   ♀ Well-chosen ✆
■ *Set L £9·95*   *L 12–2.30*
About £38 for two   *D 7–11.30*
Seats 63 Parties 12   *Parking Ample*
Closed L Sun, all Bank Hol Mons, 1 wk Aug & 1 wk Xmas

Monsieur Thompsons

R **Map 21 B4**
29 Kensington Park Road W11
01-727 9957
French cooking
Owner manager Dominique Rocher
Credit Access, Amex, Diners, Visa

Chef Rémy Dieu produces a good variety of dishes at this cheerful restaurant, enhancing many of them with tasty, well-balanced sauces: lime with coquilles St Jacques, Meaux mustard with leg of lamb, deliciously rich black olive with beautifully cooked breast of duck. Excellent vegetables and very enjoyable desserts. Service could be more efficient. ☺

■ *Set L* £10·50	*L 12.30–2.30*
Set D £13.50	*D 7.30–10.30*
About £45 *for two*	*Parking* Difficult
Seats 55 *Parties* 40	*Closed* Bank Hols

♀ indicates a **well-chosen** house wine.

The Montcalm

HR **78% £A *E* Map 22 D1**
Great Cumberland Place W1A 2LF
01-402 4288. Tlx 28710
Manager Jonathan Orr Ewing
Credit Access, Amex, Diners, Visa

Exemplary service is the strong suit of this discreet luxury hotel, which stands in an attractive and surprisingly quiet Georgian crescent just two minutes' walk from Marble Arch. Jonathan Orr Ewing is an outstanding general manager, and, in terms of friendliness, efficiency and generally being looked after, guests could hardly ask for more. Louis-style French furnishings add extra elegance to the comfortable lounge and bar areas, which also retain their stylish,

contemporary leather armchairs and sofas. Well-equipped bedrooms range from standard through more luxurious studio rooms to the sumptuous duplex suites. First-rate modern bathrooms. Good breakfasts are a further plus. *Amenities* valeting, laundry service.

■ *Rooms* 116	*Confirm by* 6
en suite bath/shower 116	*Last dinner* 11
Direct dial Yes	*Parking* Ample
Room TV Yes	*Room service* 24 hours

Les Célébrités ♔

French cooking
Refined French cooking by Gary Houiellebecq combines with superb service orchestrated by Armando Calero in a comfortable, stylish setting. Leek and potato soup, salmon quenelles, calf's liver with mustard sauce and fillet steak marchand de vin are typical delights. The chocolate marquise is as good as ever, so too are the coffee and friandises, and there's a splendid cheeseboard. Aristocratic list of classic wines, particularly fine Bordeaux from the best years. ☺

■ *Set L* £15	*L 12.30–2.30*
About £60 *for two*	*D 7–11*
Seats 55	

Mornington Hotel

H **62% £D/E Map 22 B2**
12 Lancaster Gate W2 3LG
01-262 7361. Tlx 24281
Manager Robert Bellhouse
Credit Access, Amex, Diners, Visa

Friendly staff and excellent housekeeping make for a pleasant stay at this Swedish-owned hotel near Kensington Gardens. It's easy to relax in the stylish foyer-lounge with its mahogany panelling or equally comfortable book-lined bar. Most bedrooms have been refurbished to a high standard, with smart decor and thoughtfully fitted bathrooms. *Amenities* sauna.

■ *Rooms* 70	*Confirm by* 6
en suite bath/shower 70	*Last dinner* None
Direct dial Yes	*Parking* Difficult
Room TV Yes	*Room service* 24 hours
Closed 10 days Xmas	

Mostyn Hotel

H **65% £B Map 22 D2**
Bryanston Street W1H 0DE
01-935 2361. Tlx 27656
Credit Access, Amex, Diners, Visa

An elegant, centrally located hotel converted from four adjoining period houses. Attractive pink-upholstered blue-cane chairs and lots of potted greenery give a light and airy feel to the spacious marble-floored foyer. Remaining public areas are equally stylish too. Bedrooms have smart darkwood units and fully tiled bathrooms. No dogs.
Amenities in-house movies (charge), laundry service, 24-hour lounge service.

■ *Rooms* 125	*Confirm by* 6
en suite bath/shower 125	*Last dinner* 9.30
Direct dial Yes	*Parking* Ample
Room TV Yes	*Room service* 24 hours

Motcombs

R **Map 23 D4**
26 Motcomb Street SW1
01-235 6382
Credit Access, Amex, Diners, Visa.
Prime meat and fresh fish are the basis of the enjoyable meals served in this club-like restaurant below a fashionable wine bar. Oysters (the rock variety available all year), warm salad starters, sea bass, liver with bacon and rack of lamb are among the favourites, and sweets include a first-rate fruit salad. Very good wines, notably burgundies from Heyman Frères. Friendly, mainly Italian, staff.
🍾 Well-chosen ⊘

■ *About £50 for two*   *L 12–3*
Seats 70   *D 7–11, Sat 7.30–11*
Parties 16   *Parking Limited*
Closed L Sat, all Sun, Bank Hols & 25 & 26 Dec

Mount Royal Hotel

H **59% £C**   **Map 22 D2**
Marble Arch W1A 4UK
01-629 8040. Tlx 23355
Manager Mr J. A. Rios
Credit Access, Amex, Diners, Visa
Two minutes' walk from Marble Arch, a large red-brick hotel with spacious, practical accommodation. Many bedrooms have sitting and dressing areas, and all have well-equipped bathrooms. There's a mellow panelled bar, a comfortable enough lounge and a brightly decorated coffee shop. Refurbishment planned. No dogs. *Amenities* laundry service, coffee shop (7am–10.30pm), kiosk.

■ *Rooms 701*	*Confirm by 6*
en suite bath/shower 701	*Last dinner 10.30*
Direct dial Yes	*Parking Ample*
Room TV Yes	*Room service Limited*

Mountbatten Hotel

H **74% £A Map 27 B2**
Seven Dials, Covent Garden WC2H 9HD
01-836 4300. Tlx 298087
Credit Access, Amex, Diners, Visa
Named after the late Lord Mountbatten, this stylish hotel in the heart of Covent Garden displays drawings, paintings and personal possessions as reminders of the man and his life. Revolving doors lead into an impressive marble-floored foyer laid with oriental carpets. Day rooms include the elegantly furnished Broadlands drawing room and the inviting, softly-lit Burma bar. Beautifully decorated bedrooms, with fine fabrics and furniture, include seven sumptuous suites with whirlpool baths and fifteen Executive singles with double beds. All have smart units, hairdryers, trouser presses and satellite TV. Italian marble bathrooms have luxury extras including

phones. Dogs at the discretion of the management.
Amenities in-house movies (free), laundry service, 24-hour lounge service.

■ *Rooms 127*	*Confirm by 6*
en suite bath/shower 127	*Last dinner 10.30*
Direct dial Yes	*Parking Difficult*
Room TV Yes	*Room service 24 hours*

Le Muscadet

R ♫ **Map 22 D1**
25 Paddington Street W1
01-935 2883
French cooking
Credit Access, Visa
A little enclave of French Provincial cuisine just off Baker Street. Staples on Alex Grant's menu include fish soup, boudin noir with apples, and garlicky king prawns. Daily specials bring salmon terrine with champagne sauce or succulent guinea fowl marchand de vin. A short list of good French wines includes the excellent Brouilly Ch. Thivin 1985. ⊘

■ *About £40 for two*	*L 12.15–2.30*
Seats 30	*D 7.15–10.15*
Closed L Sat, all Sun,	*Parking Difficult*
Bank Hols, 3 wks Aug & 2 wks Xmas	

Nanyang *NEW ENTRY*

R **Map 23 B4**
112 Cromwell Road SW7
01-370 0803
Chinese cooking
Credit Access, Amex, Diners, Visa
A comfortable modern Chinese restaurant just west of Gloucester Road. The extensive menu features Szechuan and Singapore cuisines and includes favourites like grilled pork dumplings with vinegar dip, above-average crispy aromatic duck, and succulent, sizzling pork with ginger and spring onions. Very spicy dishes are marked with a warning red flame. Pleasant service.

■ *Set L £11·50*	*L 12–2.30*
Set D £11·50	*D 6–11.30*
About £32 for two	*Parking Difficult*
Seats 80 Parties 50	*Closed 3 days Xmas*

Neal Street Restaurant

R   **Map 27 B2**
26 Neal Street WC2
01-836 8368
Owner manager Antonio Carluccio
Credit Access, Amex, Diners, Visa
  Booking is recommended at this stylish modern restaurant. Cooking is sound, and the menu holds much interest, with dishes like pasta spirals with a simple, delicious broccoli sauce; offal soup, based

on lamb's liver and heart; loin of venison with fresh cèpes; and hunger-banishing bollito misto. Excellent house wines include a delicious Italian Pinot Noir from the Alto Adige.
♥ Well-chosen   ⊕

■ About £60 for two	L 12.30–2.30
Seats 70	D 7.30–11.00
Closed Sat, Sun, Bank	Parking Difficult
Hols & 1 wk Xmas	

New Leaf

R   **Map 7 A4**
35 Bond Street, Ealing W5
01-567 2343
Chinese cooking
Credit Access, Amex, Visa
  The hardworking Lees and their long-serving manager Henry Soon (now a partner) have built up a loyal local following over the years here in downtown Ealing. Cooking at their pleasant

Chinese restaurant is careful and consistently enjoyable throughout a wide range of favourites, from crispy duck and spicy boiled dumplings to prawns with ginger and spring onions or beef in oyster sauce.

■ Set meals from £7·50	L 12–2.15
About £33 for two	D 6–11.30
Seats 70 Parties 50	Parking Ample
Closed L Sun & all 25 & 26 Dec	

New Loon Fung

R   **Map 27 A2**
42 Gerrard Street W1
01-437 6232
Chinese cooking
Manager Andrew Cheng
Credit Access, Amex, Visa
  Chinese families enjoying lunch together indicate the authenticity of this spacious first-floor restaurant. Mainly Peking and Cantonese dishes

feature on the lengthy menu, with fish something of a speciality (look out for whole steamed sea bass), as well as unusual offerings such as roast belly of pork fondu with oysters. Daytime dim sum include over 30 items.

■ Set meals from £6·50	Meals 12–11.30, Sun
About £30 for two	11–10.30
Seats 450	Parking Difficult
Parties 400	Closed 25 Dec

New Shu Shan

R   **Map 27 A2**
36 Cranbourn Street, WC2
01-836 7501
Chinese cooking
Credit Amex, Diners, Visa
  A friendly little Chinese restaurant near Leicester Square, offering an interesting variety of Cantonese and Szechuan dishes. Red type on the menu indicates items with an extra fiery kick –

like sliced pork with a garlic and chilli sauce or hot and sour soup among starters. Follow with something a little milder, say beef with white mushrooms or crab in a black bean sauce, adding red bean paste pancakes for a delicious finale.

■ Set meals from £13	Meals noon-midnight
About £32 for two	Parking Difficult
Seats 60 Parties 30	Closed 25 Dec

Ninety Park Lane

R   ♛♛   **Map 22 D2**
90 Park Lane W1
01-409 1290
French cooking
Credit Access, Amex, Diners, Visa
  Setting and service are both superb at this sumptuous restaurant, where dishes such as diced lobster on a fresh mint dressing with pink grapefruit, or duck breast with juniper berry

liqueur and crystallised orange zest are presented with style and panache. Impeccably chosen cellar: note the excellent Alsace wines from Lucien Albrecht. ▷ Outstanding ⊕

■ Set L £22·50	L 12–2.30
Set D £32·50	D 7.30–10.45
About £96 for two	Parking Ample
Seats 80	Parties 80
Closed L Sat, all Sun & Bank Hols	

■ See INSPECTOR FOR A DAY

Ninjin Club *NEW ENTRY*

R **Map 24 A1**
244 Great Portland Street W1
01-388 4657
Japanese cooking
Credit Access, Amex, Diners, Visa
A fresh, bright basement restaurant with friendly, obliging staff and excellent Japanese food. Order à la carte or choose a set meal (several variations at lunchtime, just one in the evening). Among many items alluring both in look and taste are miso soup, rice with nori seaweed, and sashimi. Ask about the appetisers, as that part of the menu is in Japanese.

■ *Set L from* £8	*L* 12–2.30
Set D £15	*D* 6–10.30
About £35 *for two*	*Parking* Difficult
Closed D Sat, all Sun & some Bank Hols	*Seats* 50

Norfolk Hotel

H **69% £B Map 23 B4**
Harrington Road SW7 3ER
01-589 8191. Tlx 268852
Manager Michael Lucas
Credit Access, Amex, Diners, Visa. **LVs**
A smart red-brick hotel located close to South Kensington station and the Cromwell Road museums. Quietly elegant public areas include a handsome foyer with fine chandelier and giant parlour plants, and a small sunken lounge and cosy cocktail bar. There's also a pubby tavern and cellar wine bar-cum-coffee shop. Good-sized bedrooms have light pastel colour schemes, coordinating fabrics and reproduction furniture. Extras range from hairdryers to trouser presses. A heater booster button is also provided – but we found room temperatures already on the high side and think you'd be unlikely to need this. Most rooms have whirlpool baths. No dogs.
Amenities sauna, solarium, keep-fit equipment, in-house movies (free), laundry service, coffee shop (10am–11pm), 24-hour lounge service.

■ *Rooms* 97	*Confirm by* 6
en suite bath/shower 97	*Last dinner* 10.30
Direct dial Yes	*Parking* Limited
Room TV Yes	*Room service* 24 hours

⮂ is our symbol for an **outstanding** wine list.

Novotel London

H **65% £C ♿ Map 21 A5**
1 Shortlands, Hammersmith W6 8DR
01-741 1555. Tlx 934539
Credit Access, Amex, Diners, Visa. **LVs**
Large, modern and efficient, this smartly maintained hotel stands by Hammersmith flyover. It's a comfortable place, if a trifle lacking in soul, and there's ample space to unwind in the foyer-lounge, bar and coffee shop. Bedrooms – some designated non-smoking – are pleasantly functional, with air conditioning, double glazing, remote-control TVs and mini-bars.
Amenities hairdressing, in-house movies (free), laundry service, coffee shop (7am–6pm), kiosk.

■ *Rooms* 640	*Confirm by* arrang.
en suite bath/shower 640	*Last dinner* 12
Direct dial Yes	*Parking* Limited
Room TV Yes	*Room service* All day

Number Sixteen

H **62% £C Map 23 B5**
16 Sumner Place SW7 3EG
01-589 5232. Tlx 266638
Manager Tim Daniel
Credit Access, Amex, Diners, Visa
A charming little hotel created from a row of Victorian houses. Fresh flowers grace the antique-furnished lounges, and a new conservatory supplements the delightful garden. Bedrooms are well furnished and thoughtfully equipped, but some look a little tired. Good continental breakfast; no other meals. No children under 12. No dogs.
Amenities garden, laundry service.

■ *Rooms* 32	*Confirm by* arrang.
en suite bath/shower 28	*Last dinner* N/A
Direct dial Yes	*Parking* Difficult
Room TV No	*Room service* All day

Odette's

R **Map 20 C3**
130 Regent's Park Road NW1
01-586 5486
Owner manager Simone Green
Credit Access, Amex, Diners, Visa
A delightfully elegant restaurant with an airy conservatory section. Talented chef John Armstrong offers a varied and imaginative menu with dishes like sea bass sashimi and roast partridge aux croûtes. Preparation and presentation are first-class. Super sweets include delights like hot prune and Armagnac tart and rice pudding with home-made jam.
🍷 Well-chosen ©

■ *About* £50 *for two*	*L* 12.30–2.30
Seats 50	*D* 7.30–11
Parties 30	*Parking* Ample
Closed L Sat, all Sun, Bank Hols & 1 wk Xmas .	

Odins ★

R ★ ⊌ **Map 24 A1**
27 Devonshire Street W1
01-935 7296
Owner Peter Langan
Credit Amex

A stunning collection of paintings and prints lines the walls of this elegant restaurant, where Chris German's innovative menus continue to win enthusiastic approval. Dishes combine textures and flavours in perfect harmonies, and the descriptions alone sound so marvellous that making a choice can prove a delightful predicament. Typical starters range from wild mushroom consommé with a pastry crust to hot sweetbread terrine with Pommery mustard sauce; followed perhaps by Dover sole and salmon paupiettes with chive and butter sauce, or breast of chicken stuffed with lobster mousseline. Beautifully cooked vegetables and magnificent sweets. Friendly, efficient service. Excellent classic wines. ⊖

Specialities salmon and smoked eel rillette, sautéed goose with pink peppercorns and baby spinach, suprême of halibut baked with a lemon and thyme topping, medallions of venison with plum and apple purée and Calvados sauce, Poire William parfait with caramelised pears.
♀ Well-chosen
■ *Set L* £12·50   *L* 12.30–2.30
About £65 *for two*   *D* 7–11.30
Seats 60 *Parties* 8   *Parking* Difficult
Closed L Sat, all Sun & Bank Hols

L'Olivier

R **Map 23 B6**
116 Finborough Road SW10
01-370 4183
French cooking
Owner manager Pierre Martin
Credit Access, Amex, Diners, Visa

Ring the bell for admission to this attractive basement restaurant with fresh, flowery decor. It's best known for its superb roasts (chicken, duck,

rack of lamb, rib of beef) and sauced plats du jour. There's also a splendid hors d'oeuvre basket, along with soups and salads, pâtés and very good feuilletés. Simple sweets and good French cheeseboard. ♀ Well-chosen ⊖
■ *Set D from* £15   *L by arrang.*
About £55 *for two*   *D* 7.30–1.30
Seats 60 *Parties* 60   *Parking* Limited
Closed Sun

■ Any person using our name to obtain free hospitality is a fraud. Proprietors, please inform the police and us.

One Two Three

R **Map 24 A3**
27 Davies Street W1
01-409 0750
Japanese cooking
Credit Access, Amex, Diners, Visa

Excellent Japanese food is charmingly served in simple, stylish surroundings. One of the favourite dishes at this Mayfair restaurant is belly of pork simmered in saké, and the tempura

vegetables and beautifully presented sashimi (raw salmon, turbot and cuttlefish with tangy dips and sauces) are also popular. Strongly perfumed Japanese tea is a good accompaniment.
■ *Set L* £7·50   *L* 12–2.30
Set D £25   *D* 6.30–10.30
About £50 *for two*   *Parking* Limited
Seats 50   *Parties* 50
Closed Sat, Sun, Bank Hols & Xmas–early Jan

Oscar's Brasserie

R ⊄ **Map 26 A2**
5 Temple Avenue, Temple Chambers EC4
01-353 6272
French cooking
Credit Access, Amex, Diners, Visa. LVs

Lunchtime booking is recommended at this basement restaurant where José-Antonio Skelton's enterprising French menu draws an appreciative crowd. Ambitious dishes like

scallops, monkfish and prawns in a puff pastry case are prepared with as much confidence as simple things like grilled sardines and carré d'agneau. Grace Skelton oversees the speedy service front of house. ⊖
■ *About* £45 *for two*   *L* 12–3
Seats 40 *Parties* 35   *D* 6.30–9.30
Closed Sat, Sun, Bank   *Parking* Limited
Hols, 10 days Xmas & 3 wks Aug

Pangs

R **Map 20 B3**
215 Sutherland Avenue W9
01-289 2562
Chinese cooking
Owner manager Tony Ng
Credit Access, Amex, Diners, Visa
    Quality ingredients and sound cooking make for
enjoyable eating at this spacious and
sophisticated Chinese restaurant. Largely

Cantonese dishes range from deep-fried prawns
and wun tun soup to crispy duck with pancakes
and fried beef with black beans and chilli. Good
variety of bean and noodle dishes; toffee bananas
or apples to finish. Service is attentive and
efficient.

■ About £36 for two	L 12–2.30
Seats 120 Parties 30	D 6.30–11
Closed Bank Hols	Parking Ample

■ For a discount on next year's guide, see Offer for Answers.

Park Lane Hotel

HR **80% £A E Map 25 A4**
Piccadilly W1Y 8BX
01-499 6321. Tlx 21533
Credit Access, Amex, Diners, Visa
    Old-world charm and a tradition of personal
service continue to win friends for this fine hotel
overlooking Green Park. Stylish public rooms such
as the magnificent Art Deco ballroom, the inviting
Palm Court lounge and the smart bar (where a
pianist plays), combine space and elegance.
Refurbishment has brought air conditioning to
many of the bedrooms, all of which have double
glazing, radio-alarms and mini-bars. The best of
the bathrooms offer whirlpool baths and white

marble. There are 53 very attractive suites, and
housekeeping throughout is excellent. No dogs.
Amenities keep-fit equipment, beauty salon,
hairdressing, teletext, valeting, laundry service,
coffee shop (12am–12pm), 24-hour lounge
service, kiosk.

■ Rooms 325	Confirm by 6
en suite bath/shower 325	Last dinner 10.30
Direct dial Yes	Parking Ample
Room TV Yes	Room service 24 hours

Bracewells Restaurant 😀 😀

French cooking
Ian Whittock continues to delight patrons with
high-quality, richly-sauced French dishes in both
classical and nouvelle cuisine styles. Choice
ranges from poached sea bass and grilled beef
béarnaise to such confections as duck in a
vermouth sauce garnished with truffles, pistachio
nuts and grapefruit. Tempting trolleys offer the
day's roast, hors d'oeuvres, and some attractive
desserts. Attentive service. 🍷

■ Set L £15	L 12.30–2.30
Set D £19.50	D 7–10.30
About £62 for two	Seats 80 Parties 10
Closed Sat, Sun & Bank Hols exc. Xmas	

Pastoria Hotel

H **63% £C Map 27 A3**
St Martins Street WC2H 7HL
01-930 8641. Tlx 25538
Manager Mr Z. Lalji
Credit Access, Amex, Diners, Visa
    The Pastoria is a modern hotel located just a
few steps away from Leicester Square. It has
recently been considerably smartened up, from
the marble-floored foyer to the bedrooms which

now have attractive pastel decor and stylish
window blinds. No dogs. Amenities laundry
service, coffee shop (11.30am–10.30pm) 24-hour
lounge service.

■ Rooms 58	Confirm by arrang.
en suite bath/shower 58	Last dinner 10.30
Direct dial Yes	Parking Difficult
Room TV Yes	Room service Limited
Closed 25 & 26 Dec	

Pavilion

R **Map 26 C1**
Finsbury Circus EC2
01-628 8224
French cooking
Owner manager David Gilmour
Credit Access, Amex, Diners, Visa. LVs
    A cosy restaurant, where simple French food
provides the perfect accompaniment to specially
selected wines. The menu changes frequently. A

typical choice might be duck terrine, followed by
grilled turbot with beurre blanc. The impeccably
chosen wines include a superb Chiroubles
(Georges Boulon) 1985.
🍷 Outstanding 🍷 Well-chosen

■ Set L £20	L 12–2.30
About £50 for two	Parking Limited
Seats 28	Parties 24
Closed Sat, Sun & Bank Hols	

Peking Duck

R 🍸 ♿ **Map 20 B1**
30 Temple Fortune Parade NW11
01-458 3558
Chinese cooking
Credit Access, Amex, Diners, Visa
Owner Mr Wong prepares a good variety of Pekinese and other Chinese dishes in his neat, simple restaurant. Items recently enjoyed include nice crunchy spring rolls; succulent aromatic crispy duck; delicious Chinese cabbage quick-fried in chicken oil; and sticky satisfying hot toffee bananas. Only a rather gloopy hot and sour soup disappointed.

■ *Set L & D from £8*
About £30 for two
Seats 40
Closed Tues & 25 & 26 Dec

L 12–2.30
D 6–11.30, Sat 6–12
Parking Limited

Pembridge Court Hotel

H **61% £D Map 22 A2**
34 Pembridge Gardens W2 4DX
01-229 9977. Tlx 298363
Owner manager Paul Capra
Credit Access, Amex, Diners, Visa
Several bedrooms have been upgraded at this welcoming converted Victorian house near the Portobello Road antiques market, and a lift has been installed. Prints and plants adorn the neat entrance and there is a relaxing lounge and attractive basement bar. All the bedrooms are well-kept, light and airy, with hair dryers, trouser presses and private bath or shower rooms. *Amenities* laundry service.

■ *Rooms 26*
en suite bath/shower 26
Direct dial Yes
Room TV Yes

Confirm by 4
Last dinner 11.15
Parking Difficult
Room service 24 hours

■ Our inspectors are our full-time employees; they are professionally trained by us.

Peter's

R **Map 20 B3**
65 Fairfax Road NW6
01-624 5804
Owner manager Peter Simonyi
Credit Access, Amex, Diners, Visa
Sound French cooking and amiable service go hand in hand at this cheerful little restaurant. The fixed-price lunch allows free choice of two or three courses from the à la carte menu, and popular dishes include honey-glazed duck and chicken Kiev. A pastry parcel of avocado, salmon and spinach makes a delicious starter, and there are tempting sweets. Traditional Sunday lunch.
♉ Well-chosen ☻

■ *Set L from £10*
About £40 for two
Seats 55 Parties 60
Closed L Bank Hols & L 10 days Xmas

L 12–2.30, Sun 12.30–3
D 6.30–11.30
Parking Limited

Phoenicia

R 🍸 **Map 23 A4**
11 Abingdon Road W8
01-937 0120
Lebanese cooking
Owner manager Hani Khalifé
Credit Access, Amex, Diners, Visa
A very good Lebanese restaurant with abundant comfort and friendly, helpful staff. Order one of the mezze meals and share a succession of delights, from houmus and falafel to lemony chicken wings, assorted kebabs from the charcoal grill and delicious Lebanese desserts. Château Musar is an excellent accompaniment. The lunchtime buffet is particularly good value.

■ *Set L from £6·50*
Set D from £8·95
About £42 for two
Closed 25 & 26 Dec

Meals noon–midnight
Parking Limited
Seats 90 Parties 90

Piccadilly Restaurant

R **Map 24 B3**
31 Great Windmill Street W1
01-734 4956
Italian cooking
Credit Access, Amex, Visa
A homely, bustling Italian restaurant (also known as Little Cottage) that's immensely popular both for its highly enjoyable food and good value for money. Excellent pasta competes with nicely sauced veal dishes plus familiar ways with chicken and steak. The choice also includes fish and straightforward grills with good fresh vegetables. Simple sweets and simpatico service.

■ *About £30 for two*
Seats 50
Parties 12
Closed Sun & Bank Hols

L 12–2.45
D 6–11
Parking Limited

Pollyanna's

R **Map 21 C6**
2 Battersea Rise SW11
01-228 0316
Owner manager Norman Price
Credit Access, Amex, Visa
   Chef Eamonn Connolly prepares varied and imaginative fare for this lively, bistro-style restaurant. Start with the popular Cantal cheese soufflé, unusual lamb's offal pâté, or scallop and crab terrine on a watercress sauce. Next choose fillets of red mullet and sea bass teamed with aubergine purée, veal served with mushroom and beetroot mousses and a champagne and chive

sauce, or roast venison with two William pear sauces. Super sweets like white chocolate and kümmel mousse. Traditional Sunday lunch. The wine list offers a very fine, exceptionally well-judged selection of French wines at keen prices: Château Fourcas Hosten '78, Corton Charlemagne (Bonneau du Martray) '82, Côte Rôtie (Guigal) '80.
   ~ Outstanding   🍷 Well-chosen   ℗
■ *Set L Sun only £9.95*   *L 1–3*
About £45 for two   *D 7–12*
Seats 80 Parties 30   *Parking Ample*
Closed D Sun, 1 Jan & 4 days Xmas

Pomegranates

R **Map 21 C5**
94 Grosvenor Road SW1
01-828 6560
Owner manager Patrick Gwynn-Jones
Credit Access, Amex, Visa
   The menu spans the globe at this friendly restaurant, giving Patrick Gwynn-Jones and chef Jeremy Davies a chance to show their talents. Imaginative dishes include lime-pickled raw

salmon, powerfully-flavoured curried goat and Welsh salt duck. Home-made ices, gâteaux and tarts sustain the pleasure to the end. Good burgundies on a rambling list.   🍷 Well-chosen ℗
■ *Set L from £12*   *L 12.30–2.15*
Set D from £13.50   *D 7.30–11.15*
About £60 for two   *Parking Difficult*
Seats 40   *Parties 12*
Closed L Sat, all Sun & Bank Hols

Poons

R **Map 27 A2**
4 Leicester Street WC2
01-437 1528
Chinese cooking
Owner manager Mr W. Poon
   Wind-dried meats and sausages hanging in the window of this unpretentious Soho restaurant indicate the speciality of the house – although the lengthy menu features many other favourites too.

Stir-fried chicken in a gingery bean paste sauce, stewed crab with chilli and black beans, plus delicious fried rice and noodles are all worth looking out for. Booking advised in the evening.

■ *Set meals from £9·50 for two*
About £23 for two   *Meals 12–11.30*
Seats 100 Parties 50   *Parking Limited*
Closed Sun & 24–27 Dec

Poons of Covent Garden

R ♀ ♿ **Map 27 B2**
41 King Street WC2
01-240 1743
Chinese cooking
Credit Amex, Diners, Visa
   High-flame cooking in the open-view kitchen gives customers plenty of excitement while they tuck into the range of Cantonese dishes, some aimed at Western palates. Try the three-course

duck Kam Ling style – crispy duck skin served with Cantonese hot cakes; delicious duck bone soup with fresh vegetables and bean curd; and meat of the duck stir-fried with seasonal greens.

■ *Set L £7·80*   *Meals noon–midnight*
Set D £15   *Parking Difficult*
About £45 for two   *Seats 120 Parties 120*
Closed Sun & 4 days Xmas

Portman Inter-Continental Hotel

HR **79% £A E Map 22 D1**
22 Portman Square W1H 9FL
01-486 5844. Tlx 261526
Credit Access, Amex, Diners, Visa
   Popular with both business people and tourists, this luxurious modern hotel has a central position near Marble Arch and Park Lane. Plush sofas and elegant chesterfields provide inviting seating in the vast wood-panelled foyer, which doubles as a lounge and at teatime echoes to the soothing music of a harp. Other public areas include a smart, split-level bar with the opulent decor of a plush Edwardian pub, and numerous function suites. Very comfortable, attractively-decorated bedrooms have up-to-date facilities and stylish

reproduction period furnishings. Single rooms are particularly pleasing, having matching wallpaper and soft furnishings. Compact, modern bathrooms are equipped with hairdryers.
Amenities in-house movies (free), valeting, laundry service, coffee shop (11am–11pm), kiosk.

■ *Rooms 278*   *Confirm by 6*
en suite bath/shower 278   *Last dinner 11*
Direct dial Yes   *Parking Ample*
Room TV Yes   *Room service 24 hours*

Truffles Restaurant ♕♕ &

Ambitious French dishes, some on a truffle theme, match the ambience of this smart, split-level restaurant. Choices range from pigeon and scallop salad to sole and crayfish on a Brouilly wine sauce, veal fillets flavoured with honey, and a superb chocolate truffle gâteau. Sunday offers brunch with Creole cooking and live jazz. ℮

- Set L £15   L 12–3
  Set D from £20   *D 7–11*
  About £75 for two   *Seats 80 Parties 40*

- We welcome complaints and bona fide recommendations on the tear-out pages for readers' comments. They are followed up by our professional team. Please also complain to the management instantly.

RECEPTION

Portobello Hotel

H **62% £C Map 21 B4**
22 Stanley Gardens W11 2NG
01-727 2777. Tlx 268349
Manager Eva Lofstad
Credit Access, Amex, Diners, Visa
   A town-house hotel in a Victorian terrace near Portobello Road. It's got plenty of personality, generated by the Norwegian-born manager. Public rooms include a bright basement bar.

Bedrooms range from compact cabin rooms to suites with private sitting rooms.
Amenities laundry service, restaurant (24 hours).

- Rooms 25   *Confirm by arrang.*
  en suite bath/shower 25   *Last dinner Any time*
  Direct dial Yes   *Parking Difficult*
  Room TV Yes   *Room service None*
  Closed 24 Dec–2 Jan

Post House Hotel (Hampstead)

H **64% £C Map 20 B2**
215 Haverstock Hill NW3 4RB
01-794 8121. Tlx 262494
Credit Access, Amex, Diners, Visa. **LVs**
   Bedrooms had the priority when this modern hotel was built, and they continue to provide attractive accommodation with marvellous views from the top floors. The best rooms have darkwood units, armchairs and sofas, and a range

of luxury extras. Small bathrooms all have showers. There is a comfortable foyer-lounge and a bright bar with picture windows. *Amenities* in-house movies (charge), restaurant (7am–10.30pm), laundry service.

- Rooms 140   *Confirm by 6*
  en suite bath/shower 140   *Last dinner 10.30*
  Room phone Yes   *Parking Ample*
  Room TV Yes   *Room service Limited*

Le Poulbot ★

R **★ ♕ Map 26 B2**
45 Cheapside EC2
01-236 4379
French cooking
Manager Jean Cottard
Credit Access, Amex, Diners, Visa
   Book for one of the City's favourite lunchtime venues, an intimate basement restaurant that is part of the Roux Brothers' organisation. The menu is French, and young French staff provide deft, efficient service, but the highly skilled chef, Roland Leigh, is an Englishman. His short, fixed-price menu (the price includes an aperitif and canapés) changes each week; there are also a few daily variations, so seasonal produce is well represented, with game a popular choice. Dishes are skilfully conceived and executed, with well-balanced flavours; top-quality produce is complemented by particularly good sauces, typified by our tender, well-flavoured loin of hare served with a gentle cream sauce garnished with

tiny beetroot slices. Imaginative sweets. There's a good, concise wine list. *Specialities* sous-presse de foie gras aux fenouils, escalope de saumon cressonière, pigeonneau à la vanille, marquise aux deux chocolats, pudding froid de fraise de bois. ♀ **Well-chosen** ℮

- Set L £24·50   *L only 12–3*
  About £65 for two   *Parking Difficult*
  Closed Sat, Sun,   *Seats 55*
  Bank Hols & 1 wk Xmas

Pun

R **Map 23 B5**
53 Old Brompton Road SW7
01-225 1609
Chinese cooking
Credit Access, Amex, Diners, Visa
  Notably helpful staff run this modern Chinese restaurant. There's lots of seafood, and a fine variety of enjoyable Szechuan, Peking and Cantonese dishes. Favourites include mixed hors

d'oeuvre (seaweed, prawn toast, tiny spring rolls, honeyed spare ribs), crisp-skinned duck and sizzling lamb. Toffee apples and bananas for a sticky end. ♀ Well-chosen

■ *Set L £7.50*	*L 12–3*
Set D £12.80	*D 6–11.30, Sat 12–*
About £42 for two	*11.30, Sun 12–11*
Seats 60	*Parking Ample*
Parties 30	*Closed 25 Dec*

Le Quai St Pierre

R **Map 23 A4**
7 Stratford Road W8
01-937 6388
French cooking
Owner manager Pierre Martin
Credit Access, Amex, Diners, Visa
  Live lobsters in a glass tank are proof positive that the shellfish in this popular French restaurant is wonderfully fresh. Customers unwilling to

consume the cabaret may sample a wide range of fish dishes (including six daily specials) or select scallops, oysters or mussels. Also excellent salads, some steaks, nicely cooked vegetables and a simple choice of sweets.

■ *About £57 for two*	*L 12.30–2.30*
Seats 50	*D 7–11.30*
Closed L Mon, all Sun	*Parking Difficult*
& 10 days Xmas	

Quincy's 84

R ♀ **Map 20 B2**
675 Finchley Road NW2
01-794 8499
Credit Access, Visa
  Be sure to book at this delightful little place with charming decor and super food. Chef-partner Sandy Anderson allies imagination to artistry in such dishes as rillettes of veal and duck, fillet of turbot in pernod sauce and iced amaretto soufflé.

There's a distinguished cheeseboard and a first-rate house muscadet. Partner David Wardle guarantees excellent service throughout the meal. ♀ Well-chosen ℮

■ *Set L £12*	*L Sun only 12–2*
Set D £14.75	*D 7.30–10.30*
About £38 for two	*Parking Ample*
Seats 30	
Closed 3 wks Xmas & 1 wk Aug	

Ramada Hotel

H **71% £A/B E ⅾ Map 24 B2**
10 Berners Street W1A 3BE
01-636 1629. Tlx 25759
Credit Access, Amex, Diners, Visa
  The Edwardian grandeur of what was formerly Berners Hotel is evident immediately on entering the large lobby-lounge with its spectacularly moulded ceilings. Comfortable chairs and sofas abound, and the bar is equally impressive. The well-kept, good-sized bedrooms vary in shape and have natural polished wood furniture, brass light fittings, attractive quilted bedcovers, and pink dralon easy chairs, curtains and padded headboards. All are equipped with direct-dial phones, radios, hairdryers and trouser presses. Bathrooms are tiled, with shower fittings and good towels and toiletries; telephone extensions are gradually being installed.

Amenities hairdressing, in-house movies (charge), laundry service, 24-hour lounge service, kiosk.

■ *Rooms 232*	*Confirm by 6*
en suite bath/shower 232	*Last dinner 10*
Direct dial Yes	*Parking Difficult*
Room TV Yes	*Room service 24 hours*

Ramada Inn West London

H **59% £C/D Map 23 A6**
47 Lillie Road, SW6 1UQ
01-385 1255. Tlx 917728
Credit Access, Amex, Diners, Visa
  Refurbishment is under way to boost the appeal of this large modern hotel, formerly the London West. Its location near Earl's Court and Olympia makes it a handy stopover for visitors to exhibitions. Overnight accommodation is

functionally contemporary, and day rooms include a cheerful public bar and a smart lounge bar. No dogs. *Amenities* laundry service, coffee shop (11am–11pm), in-house movies (charge).

■ *Rooms 510*	*Confirm by 6*
en suite bath/shower 510	*Last dinner 10.30*
Room phone Yes	*Parking Ample*
Room TV Yes	*Room service None*

Read's

R ♨ **Map 23 B5**
152 Old Brompton Road SW5
01-383 2445
Credit Access, Amex, Diners, Visa
The aptly named and talented young Norman
Cook has replaced Caroline Read at this delightful
summery restaurant. His presentation of dishes
and saucing are particularly fine, and fixed-price
menus offer many treats – beautifully crisp

feuilleté of veal sweetbreads with a light
mushroom sauce, steamed dariole of pike
splendidly sauced with lobster, and a faultless
brandy snap tulip. 🍷 Well-chosen ⊖

■ *Set L* £11·50	*L 12.30–2.30,*
Set D £19·50	*Sun till 3*
About £62 for two	*D 7.30–11*
Seats 70 Parties 20	*Parking Limited*
Closed D Sun & all Mon	

Red Fort

R ♨ **Map 27 A2**
77 Dean Street W1
01-437 2525
Indian cooking
Credit Access, Amex, Diners, Visa
Named after Shahjehan's famous fort in Delhi,
this authentic Mogul restaurant offers tasty dishes
in stylish surroundings. Starters include momo
(spiced minced beef in pastry) and tandoori

quails. Also from the tandoor – seekh kebab and
chicken tikka. Spiced grilled trout is excellent and
thalis are popular. For excellent value, and the
chance to sample a wide variety of dishes, try the
Sunday buffet.

■ *Set L Sun only* £8·95	*L 12–3*
About £40 for two	*D 6–11.30*
Seats 160 Parties 100	*Parking Difficult*
Closed 25 & 26 Dec	

Regent Crest Hotel

H **64% £C** ♿ **Map 24 A1**
Carburton Street W1P 8EE
01-388 2300. Tlx 22453
Credit Access, Amex, Diners, Visa
An elegant and spacious foyer sets the tone of
this smart modern hotel situated close to the
West End. The first-floor public rooms are similarly
elegant, with an inviting bar and attractive Cafe
Boulevard. Bedrooms (all doubles) have tea-

makers and trouser presses. Executive and
ladies' rooms have better coordinated colour
schemes and feature more extras. No dogs.
Amenities in-house movies (charge), coffee shop
(11am–12.30am), laundry service, kiosk.

■ *Rooms 320*	*Confirm by 6*
en suite bath/shower 320	*Last dinner 10.30*
Direct dial Yes	*Parking Ample*
Room TV Yes	*Room service 24 hours*

Rembrandt Hotel

H **67% £B Map 23 C4**
11 Thurloe Place SW7 2RS
01-589 8100. Tlx 295828
Credit Access, Amex, Diners, Visa
There's style and elegance at this popular hotel
opposite Brompton Oratory. Marble steps link the
foyer to the bar-lounge and there's an attractive
conservatory and luxurious health club.
Comfortable, well-equipped bedrooms have

excellent bathrooms. *Amenities* indoor
swimming pool, sauna, solarium, whirlpool bath,
steam bath, gymnasium, beauty salon, in-house
movies (free), laundry service, 24-hour lounge
service.

■ *Rooms 200*	*Confirm by 6*
en suite bath/shower 200	*Last dinner 10*
Direct dial Yes	*Parking Difficult*
Room TV Yes	*Room service 24 hours*

The Ritz

H **87% £A E Map 25 B4**
Piccadilly W1V 9DG
01-493 8181. Tlx 267200
Manager Mr Julian Payne
Credit Access, Amex, Diners, Visa
The fabled Ritz remains as flamboyant and
opulent as ever, even if the Louis XVI decor is not
as fresh as it once was. Conversions in recent
years have created twenty-two superlative
bedrooms with silk curtains, marble fireplaces
from French châteaux, pickled pine furniture and
gold-leaf mouldings; gold-plated taps adorn the
Italian marble bathrooms. Thirty-five more
bedrooms have been recently refurbished in the
original style, with some of the furniture (including
the brass bedsteads) being retained and
restored. No dogs. *Amenities* garden,
hairdressing, in-house movies (free), valeting,

laundry service, 24-hour lounge service, kiosk.

■ *Rooms 128*	*Confirm by 6*
en suite bath/shower 128	*Last dinner 11*
Direct dial Yes	*Parking Limited*
Room TV Yes	*Room service 24 hours*

Le Routier

R **Map 20 C3**
Camden Lock, Chalk Farm Road NW1
01-485 0360
French cooking
Credit Access, Amex, Diners, Visa

Seasonally changing menus of interesting, carefully prepared dishes and a price range to suit all pockets make up the successful formula at this cheerful informal restaurant overlooking the lock. (If you want a window table you'll need to book.) Warm duck liver salad or pasta with prawns and mushrooms might be your starter, followed perhaps by homely calf's liver and bacon or more exotic monkfish with ginger and spring onions. Simplest sweets are best. ℮

■ About £35 for two	L 12.30–3
Seats 62 Parties 100	D 7–11.45
Closed Jan	Parking Limited

■ Changes in data may occur in establishments after the Guide goes to press. Prices should be taken as indications rather than firm quotes.

menu & WINE LIST 1987/8

Royal Court Hotel

H **69% £B Map 23 D5**
Sloane Square SW1W 8EG
01-730 9191. Tlx 296818
Manager Robin Winter
Credit Access, Amex, Diners, Visa. LVs

This comfortable hotel immediately impresses with its handsome chandelier-hung foyer-lounge. There's a choice of bars – try the intimate cocktail bar. Attractive bedrooms are elegantly furnished in French reproduction style. Compact bathrooms are fully tiled and well equipped. No dogs. *Amenities* in-house movies, laundry service, coffee shop (10.30am–11pm).

■ Rooms 99	Confirm by 6
en suite bath/shower 99	Last dinner 10.30
Direct dial Yes	Parking Limited
Room TV Yes	Room service 24 hours

Royal Garden Hotel

HR **81% £A E Map 22 A3**
Kensington High Street W8 4PT
01-937 8000. Tlx 263151
Manager James Brown
Credit Access, Amex, Diners, Visa

This superbly run hotel stands on bustling Kensington High Street, but inside the atmosphere is relaxing, especially in the areas that overlook Kensington Gardens. These include the bar lounge and coffee shop. The striking marble-floored foyer doubles as a lounge and, above it, there's the restful Gallery Bar. Bedrooms are all very stylish, comfortable and well equipped, with individual heating controls, mini-bars, hairdryers and remote-control TVs.

Armchairs and coffee tables add to the comforts. Luxuriously equipped bathrooms have heated towel rails. No dogs. *Amenities* beauty salon, hairdressing, in-house movies, valeting, laundry service, coffee shop (7am–11pm), 24-hour lounge service, kiosk, casino.

■ Rooms 390	Confirm by 6
en suite bath/shower 390	Last dinner 11.30
Room phone Yes	Parking Ample
Room TV Yes	Room service 24 hours

Royal Roof Restaurant

Whizz up in the express lift to the 10th floor, and relax with the food and the views. Modern French cooking shows care and imagination, and dishes are plated with panache. Some typical choices: ham mousse with a mustard seed sauce, trout with grapes and almonds, crab-topped veal medallions, poached pear with black cherry sorbet. Good classic wine list and some excellent Californians. ℮

■ Set L from £17	L 12–2.30
Set D £22	D 7–11.30
About £65 for two	Parking Ample
Closed L Sat, all Sun,	Seats 68
Bank Hols & L last 3 wks Aug	

Royal Horseguards Thistle Hotel

H 72% £B Map 25 C4
Whitehall Court SW1A 2EJ
01-839 3400. Tlx 917096
Credit Access, Amex, Diners, Visa
Only Victoria Embankment separates this handsome hotel from the Thames, and many rooms are able to take advantage of the splendid setting. The building dates from 1884 and is in the style of a Gothic French château. Public areas include a hall with panelling and a marble floor, a quietly luxurious lounge/writing room and a stylish coffee shop that opens on to a pleasant terrace. Bedrooms range from snug to spacious, the latter with river views. Most rooms have been quite elegantly refurbished, and all are equipped with tea-makers, trouser presses and hairdryers. Neat tiled bathrooms throughout. Service is not always the warmest. No dogs. *Amenities* terrace, in-

house movies (free), laundry service, coffee shop (10.30am–11pm).
■ *Rooms* 285 | *Confirm by* 6
en suite bath/shower 285 | *Last dinner* 10.30
Direct dial Yes | *Parking* Limited
Room TV Yes | *Room service* 24 hours

Royal Lancaster Hotel

H 81% £B E Map 22 B2
Lancaster Terrace W2 2TY
01-262 6737. Tlx 24822
Manager Mr M. K. Amer
Credit Access, Amex, Diners, Visa
Notably high standards of service and housekeeping prevail at this tall modern hotel overlooking the Italian Gardens at Lancaster Gate. Public rooms are very impressive: the spacious lobby with marble-topped reception counters; chic, comfortable lounges and cocktail lounge bar; superb airy coffee shop, with staff uniforms designed by Zandra Rhodes. In the bedrooms, the easy elegance of ash furnishings and the restfulness of the cream and grey colour schemes make a fine combination. All the modern comforts are provided, and the luxurious Reserve Club rooms on the upper floors have their own

communal lounge and little boardroom. No dogs. *Amenities* hairdressing, beauty salon, in-house movies (charge), laundry service, coffee shop (7am–12pm), 24-hour lounge service.
■ *Rooms* 418 | *Confirm by* 6
en suite bath/shower 418 | *Last dinner* 11.15
Direct dial Yes | *Parking* Ample
Room TV Yes | *Room service* 24 hours

Royal Scot Hotel

H 57% £C/D Map 20 D3
100 King's Cross Road WC1 X 9DT
01-278 2434. Tlx 27657
Credit Access, Amex, Diners, Visa. LVs
Business people and groups find that this friendly modern hotel near King's Cross makes a useful stopover when visiting the capital. The spacious foyer and two bars have simple, up-to-date appeal. Best of the bedrooms are in

Georgian style (some with four-posters), and all have practical tiled bathrooms.
Amenities in-house movies (free), laundry service, coffee shop (9am–11pm), 24-hour lounge service.
■ *Rooms* 350 | *Confirm by* 6
en suite bath/shower 350 | *Last dinner* 10
Direct dial Yes | *Parking* Limited
Room TV Yes | *Room service* None

Royal Trafalgar Thistle Hotel

H 68% £B Map 27 A3
Whitcomb Street, Trafalgar Square
WC2H 7HG
01-930 4477. Tlx 298564
Credit Access, Amex, Diners, Visa. LVs
A neighbour of the National Gallery, this modern hotel is popular with both tourists and business visitors. There's a comfortable little lounge, bright brasserie and naval-themed bar.

Bedrooms are well designed with excellent bathrooms. Less than perfect housekeeping on a recent visit. *Amenities* patio, in-house movies (charge), 24-hour lounge service.
■ *Rooms* 108 | *Confirm by* 6
en suite bath/shower 108 | *Last dinner* 11.30
Direct dial Yes | *Parking* Difficult
Room TV Yes | *Room service* 24 hours
Closed 4 days Xmas

♀ indicates a **well-chosen** house wine.

Royal Westminster Thistle Hotel ▶

Royal Westminster Thistle Hotel

H **70% £A/B Map 25 A6**
Buckingham Palace Road SW1W 0QT
01-834 1821. Tlx 916821
Manager Mike Charman
Credit Access, Amex, Diners, Visa. LVs

Style and comfort go hand in hand at this fine
modern hotel, following last year's programme of
total refurbishment. The spacious foyer, with its
leafy plants, oriental vases and wide expanse of
cream and brown marble floor, sets the tone of
cool elegance, while the traditionally appointed
lounge boasts a splendid Chinese carpet.
Contrasting venues for refreshment are provided
by the French-style café and comfortable little
cocktail bar. Smartly furnished, air-conditioned
bedrooms of varying shapes provide hairdryers,
trouser presses and wall safes; bathrooms, too,
are superbly equipped. No dogs.

Amenities in-house movies (one free), laundry
service, coffee shop (7am–midnight), 24-hour
lounge service.

■ *Rooms* 135	*Confirm by* 6
en suite bath/shower 135	*Last dinner* 11.15
Direct dial Yes	*Parking* Difficult
Room TV Yes	*Room service* 24 hours

RSJ

R **♿ Map 26 A3**
13a Coin Street SE1
01-928 4554
Owner manager Nigel Wilkinson
Credit Access, Visa

A smartly modern restaurant near the South
Bank complex where imaginative dishes are
skilfully prepared. Typical delights might include
salmon and turbot pâté studded with green beans
and scampi, apple-stuffed goose breast
accompanied by a sharp redcurrant jelly sauce,
and a mouthwatering finale of white and dark
chocolate quenelles. Book. ⬛ Well-chosen ⊕

■ *Set L* £11·25	*L* 12–2
Set D £11·95	*D* 6–11
About £50 for two	*Parking* Ample
Seats 50 *Parties* 25	*Closed* L Sat, all Sun,
Bank Hols (exc. D Good Fri) & 1 wk Xmas	

Rubens Hotel

H **65% £B Map 25 A6**
Buckingham Palace Road SW1W 0PS
01-834 6600. Tlx 916577
Manager Mrs V. Barlow
Credit Access, Amex, Diners, Visa

The grand, marble-floored foyer leads into an
open-plan lounge and bar area decorated in soft
pastel shades. Downstairs there's another stylish
lounge – a quiet room lined with well-stocked
bookshelves. Identically decorated bedrooms
with smart built-in units offer extras like hairdryers
and bathroom telephone extensions. No dogs.
Amenities in-house movies (free), teletext,
laundry service, 24-hour lounge service.

■ *Rooms* 191	*Confirm by* 6
en suite bath/shower 191	*Last dinner* 10
Direct dial Yes	*Parking* Difficult
Room TV Yes	*Room service* 24 hours

Rue St Jacques ★

R **★ ♔ Map 24 B2**
5 Charlotte Street W1
01-637 0222
Credit Access, Amex, Diners, Visa

Neighbourhood television and advertising
executives provide an appreciative clientele for
Gunther Schlender's sophisticated, artistic
cooking. Lunch offers a choice of set menus while
dinner brings an ambitious and imaginative à la
carte into play. A pike mousse filled with snails
and a galantine of monkfish with a foie gras filling
are typical starters, while main courses such as a
selection of seafood with a beetroot sauce or
nuggets of lamb with a parsley purée epitomise
Schlender's simple way with quality produce.
Make room both for the superb French farmhouse
cheeses and for a delicious dessert such as the
outstanding peach and champagne mousse. An
exceptional wine list, still with some Château
Latour '59, offers exquisite burgundies from top
growers (de Montille, Duc de Magenta). Vincent

Calcerano directs a friendly, professional service.
Specialities arlequin de poissons aux pâtes
fraîches dans un coulis de tomates, caille farcie au
foie gras tiède aux deux choux, noix de ris de
veau aux champignons sauvages.
▱ Outstanding ⬛ Well-chosen ⊕

■ *Set L* from £15	*L* 12.30–2.30
About £72 for two	*D* 7.30–11.15
Seats 65 *Parties* 36	*Parking* Difficult
Closed L Sat, all Sun, Bank Hols, 4 days Easter &	
10 days Xmas	

Hotel Russell

H **68% £C Map 24 C1**
Russell Square WC1B 5BE
01-837 6470. Tlx 24615
Credit Access, Amex, Diners, Visa. **LVs**
Service and accommodation are on a grand scale here in the heart of fashionable Edwardian Bloomsbury. Italian marble, crystal chandeliers and fresh flowers grace the elegant foyer and there are two bars – one club-style, the other more relaxed and pub-like in atmosphere. Bedrooms are comfortably and attractively furnished and have modern shower/bathrooms. *Amenities* in-house movies (charge), valeting, laundry service, 24-hour lounge service.

■ *Rooms* 318	*Confirm by* 6
en suite bath/shower 318	*Last dinner* 10.30
Direct dial Yes	*Parking* Difficult
Room TV Yes	*Room service* 24 hours

Saga *NEW ENTRY*

R **Map 22 D2**
43 South Molton Street W1
01-408 2236
Japanese cooking
Credit Access, Amex, Diners, Visa
At street level a 12-seater griddle bar, downstairs the main restaurant and a sushi bar. Decor is quite formal, the menu concise but very interesting, the cooking particularly careful. Try beautifully prepared, dainty sushi (eating them with the fingers is allowed!), seaweed salad, fillet steak or raw beef with ginger and garlic. Fresh fruit and sorbets for sweets. Book.

■ *Set L from* £5	*L* 12–2.30
Set D from £20	*D* 6.30–10
About £65 *for two*	*Parking* Difficult
Seats 74 *Parties* 40	*Closed* Sun, Bank
Hols, 10 days Xmas & 1 week Aug	

St George's Hotel

H **68% £A Map 24 A2**
Langham Place W1N 8QS
01-580 0111. Tlx 27274
Credit Access, Amex, Diners, Visa
Proximity to the big stores and the tourist sights is a plus for this modern hotel on the upper floors of a tower block. Check in at street level, then take a fast lift up to the comfortable bar-lounge, the bedrooms and the splendid views. Bedroom accessories include remote-control TVs, hairdryers and mini-bars. Housekeeping could be improved.
Amenities laundry service, 24-hour lounge service.

■ *Rooms* 86	*Confirm by* 6
en suite bath/shower 86	*Last dinner* 10
Direct dial Yes	*Parking* Difficult
Room TV Yes	*Room service* 24 hours

St James Court Hotel

HR **76% £A Map 25 B5**
Buckingham Gate SW1E 6AF
01-834 6655. Tlx 938075
Credit Access, Amex, Diners, Visa
Work continues on the £40 million face-lift given to this turn-of-the-century apartment block which is now a sparkling hotel with a modern business centre. Attractive features include an elegant courtyard with a fountain, the world's longest brick frieze depicting scenes from Shakespeare and an impressive marble-floored foyer-lounge. Bedrooms are furnished to a high standard with smart reproduction furniture, satellite TVs and mini-bars. De-luxe rooms have extras like air-conditioning. Bathrooms are sumptuous. No dogs. *Amenities* satellite TV, teletext, laundry service, 24-hour lounge service.

■ *Rooms* 391	*Confirm by* 6
en suite bath/shower 391	*Last dinner* 11.30
Direct dial Yes	*Parking* Difficult
Room TV Yes	*Room service* 24 hours

Auberge de Provence

French cooking
Chef Marc Besançon's Provençal-style cooking brings an authentic taste of France to this smart hotel restaurant. Garlic and other herbs are much in evidence, and regional specialities range from the traditional Mediterranean fish soup to a leg of lamb en croûte, hearty beef casserole in red wine and ratatouille Niçoise. Fine cheeseboard, super sweet trolley, and splendid coffee.
🍷 Well-chosen ☺

■ *Set L* £15	*L* 12–2.30
Set D £25	*D* 7.30–11
About £50 *for two*	*Seats* 80 *Parties* 20

Inn of Happiness ♨ ⅊

01-821 1913
Chinese cooking
Hand-painted clouds adorn the ceiling of this stylish Chinese restaurant, but if the weather's fine it's nice to sit under a real sky in the courtyard. The menu sticks mainly to familiar Szechuan, Cantonese and Peking dishes, with a few more adventurous items like shredded jelly fish tossed in sesame oil. Capable cooking, attentive service.

■ *Set L* £10	*L* 12.30–2.45
About £40 *for two*	*D* 7.30–11.30
Seats 110	*Parties* 60

St Quentin

R **Map 23 C4**
243 Brompton Road SW3
01-589 8005
French cooking
Owner manager Didier Garnier
Credit Access, Amex, Diners, Visa
   The decor is French chic, the waiters French professional, the cooking French and mainly modern. Boudin of chicken and wild mushrooms,

monkfish with a zappy lime sauce, kidneys with mustard and grilled rib of beef show the range; dishes are generally very enjoyable, but some are served lukewarm. The wine list is concise and carefully compiled. ♀ **Well-chosen** ☺

■ *Set L £9.50*	*L 12–3, Sat 12–4*
Set D £12.90	*D 7–12, Sun 7–11.30*
About £46 for two	*Parking Difficult*
Seats 85	*Parties 30*

▷ is our symbol for an **outstanding** wine list.

Salloos

R ⛺ **Map 22 D3**
62 Kinnerton Street SW1
01-235 4444
Pakistani cooking
Owner manager Mr M. Salahuddin
Credit Access, Amex, Diners, Visa
   High standards are maintained at this comfortable Pakistani restaurant. The cooking is subtle, distinctive and different: try yakhni (a herb-

flavoured consommé); terrific tandoori lamb chops (marinated for a whole day); lamb with wholewheat germ, lentils and spices; chicken karahi with ginger and chilli; irresistible ice cream. Impressive service. Above average wine list.

■ *About £42 for two*	*L 12–2.30*
Seats 65	*D 7–11.30*
Closed Sun & Bank Hols	*Parking Limited*

San Frediano

R **Map 23 C5**
62 Fulham Road SW3
01-584 8375
Italian cooking
Owner manager Franco Buonaguidi
Credit Access, Diners, Visa
   A warm welcome and sound, tasty Italian food continue to ensure a full house at San Fred's. The wide choice of daily specials might include garlic

mussels; duck with orange and grapes; pigeon and polenta; skate in butter and capers. Vegetables are crisp, and sweets mouthwatering. Wise to book. ♀ **Well-chosen** ☺

■ *About £42 for two*	*L 12.30–2.30*
Seats 85	*D 7.15–11.15*
Parties 12	*Parking Ample*
Closed Sun & Bank Hols	

San Lorenzo   *NEW ENTRY*

R ♿ **Map 23 C4**
22 Beauchamp Place SW3
01-584 1074
Italian cooking
Owner manager Lorenzo & Mara Berni
   The menu at this popular chic Italian restaurant is full of interest ranging from excellent pasta and top-quality calf's liver to grilled sea bass and zampone (pig's trotter sausages). Vegetarians

are well catered for, and sweets include pancakes with amaretto-flavoured cream. Strong Italian wine list – note the exceptional Barbaresco (Vignaiola) 1980. Friendly, laid-back service but simpatico. Book. ☺

■ *About £45 for two*	*L 12.30–3*
Seats 120	*D 7.30–11.30*
Closed Sun & Bank Hols	*Parking Difficult*

■ For a discount on next year's guide, see Offer for Answers.

San Lorenzo Fuoriporta

R ♿ **Map 7 A5**
38 Worple Road Mews SW19
01-946 8463
Italian cooking
Manager Gandolfo Vilardo
Credit Access, Amex, Diners, Visa
   Familiar dishes are consistently enjoyable at this attractive, popular Italian restaurant with a delightful terrace for alfresco eating. Home-made

pasta such as the excellent fettucine is not to be missed, nor the tender calf's liver with sage, served with nicely firm vegetables. The San Lorenzo special – a cold pancake filled with amaretto cream – makes the perfect ending.

■ *About £44 for two*	*L 12.30–3*
Seats 100	*D 7–11, Sun 7–10*
Parties 35	*Parking Limited*
Closed Bank Hols	

San Martino

R ♿ **Map 23 C4**
103 Walton Street SW3
01-589 3833
Italian cooking
Owner manager Costanzo Martinucci
Credit Access, Amex, Diners, Visa
   Good market-fresh produce is well handled to provide enjoyable, tasty meals in this attractive Italian restaurant. The printed menu is largely familiar – antipasti, pasta, chicken sorpresa, steaks, veal – while daily specials might include comparative rarities like crab-stuffed papaya, swordfish stew and braised baby goat. Spaghetti cooked with fish in cartoccio is a speciality.

■ *About £45 for two*   *L 12–2.45*
Seats 48 Parties 24   *D 7–11.30*
Closed Sun & Bank Hols   *Parking Limited*

Santini

R ⏤ 🍴 ♿ **Map 25 A6**
29 Ebury Street SW1
01-730 4094
Italian cooking
Credit Access, Amex, Diners, Visa
   Gleaming marble and well-spaced tables create a coolly stylish look at this popular Italian restaurant. Pasta made on the premises is particularly tasty, while main courses include such interesting offerings as veal escalopes with orange, calf's liver with raw spinach and grilled langoustines. The sweet trolley is full of temptation.
🍷 **Well-chosen** ℮
■ *Set L £12·50*   *L 12.30–2.30*
About £60 for two   *D 7–11.30*
Seats 65 Parties 12   *Parking Limited*
Closed L Sat & Sun & all Bank Hols

The Savoy

HR **90% £A *E* Map 24 D3**
Strand WC2R 0EU
01-836 4343. Tlx 24234
Manager Willy Bauer
Credit Access, Amex, Diners, Visa
   Staying at the Savoy is a unique and memorable experience, partly from the sense of history so rigorously preserved, partly from the superb service from immaculately groomed staff, partly from the sheer style of the place. That style is epitomised in the river-facing suites that combine hi-tech cable TV with wonderful original decor of ornate plasterwork, fading gilt and period furnishings. Their bathrooms are equally splendid, especially those with the old fittings. Other bedrooms, some quite compact, are in Art Deco style, and all rooms have the best-quality bed linen. Renowned day rooms like the American Bar and Thames Lounge have been joined by the new Upstairs Bar serving excellent light meals and fine wines by the glass. The hotel has one of London's best and most charming general managers in Willy Bauer. No dogs. *Amenities* hairdressing, laundry service, valeting, in-house movies (free), 24-hour lounge service.

■ *Rooms 202*   *Confirm by arrang.*
en suite bath/shower 202   *Last dinner 11.30*
Direct dial Yes   *Parking Ample*
Room TV Yes   *Room service 24 hours*

The Savoy Restaurant ⏤ ⏤ ♿

Manager Luigi Zambon
George Gershwin played 'Rhapsody in Blue' for the first time in this luxurious restaurant, and these days chef Anton Edelmann matches history with menus that combine tradition with originality. Haddock parisien and roast beef with Yorkshire pudding are old favourites, along with sole, salmon and simple grills. In a more modern mode are the little salad of asparagus tips and sweetbreads and the breast of pigeon served on a bed of Kohlrabi and courgettes with red wine and white wine sauces. Staff perform stylishly but at no great pace. There's a conventional range of wines, surprisingly on the young side.
🍷 **Well-chosen** ℮
■ *Set L from £17·50*   *L 12.30–2.30,*
Set D £22   *Sun 12.30–2*
About £65 for two   *D 7.30–11.30,*
Seats 180   *Sun 7–10.30*

Grill Room ⏤ ♿

Manager Angelo Maresca
The yew-panelled interior of the handsome Grill Room has framed many a famous face, and it's still very much a place to see and be seen. The menu combines long-time favourites like haddock Monte Carlo, roast saddle of lamb and the renowned grills with more original offerings such as consommé of smoked quail or wild salmon baked with crab on a broccoli and crab sauce.
🍷 **Well-chosen** ℮
■ *Set D from £15*   *L 12.30–2.30*
About £70 for two   *D 6–11.15*
Closed L Sat, all Sun,   *Seats 85*
Bank Hols & Aug

Scotts

R ♔ ♔ **Map 22 D2**
20 Mount Street W1
01-629 5248
Manager Mr J. Paissoni
Credit Access, Amex, Diners, Visa
A civilised, elegant restaurant specialising in seafood. The menu spreads its net widely, from oysters and mussels to scampi, halibut, skate and suprême of turbot with a subtle Chablis sauce

and a garnish of lobster. Meaty options, too, and nice, simple sweets. Service is polite and professional. Splendid older wines (Hermitage '67, Latour '61, Châteauneuf du Pape '59).

⊃ **Outstanding**   ♀ **Well-chosen** ☺

■ *About £90 for two*	*L 12.30–2.45*
Seats 125	*D 6–10.45, Sun 7–10*
Parties 12	*Parking Difficult*
Closed L Sun & Bank Hols	

The Selfridge

H **80% £A/B E Map 22 D1**
Orchard Street W1H 0JS
01-408 2080. Tlx 22361
Credit Access, Amex, Diners, Visa
Behind the renowned department store, this impressive hotel makes a civilised retreat from the bustle of Oxford Street. Fine panelling, elegant chandeliers and Italian marble create a splendid atmosphere in the foyer, from which a handsome marble staircase leads to the rest of the public areas – inviting day rooms like the cedar-panelled lounge with its deep leather armchairs and the attractively rustic Stoves Bar featuring wooden beams, old stoves and antique furnishings. Soundproofed bedrooms have luxurious coordinating fabrics and quality darkwood furniture. Individually controlled air conditioning is provided, together with hairdryers, trouser

presses and thoughtfully equipped tiled bathrooms. No dogs. *Amenities* in-house movies (one free), valeting, laundry service, coffee shop (7am–11pm), 24-hour lounge service.

■ *Rooms 298*	*Confirm by 6*
en suite bath/shower 298	*Last dinner 11*
Direct dial Yes	*Parking Ample*
Room TV Yes	*Room service 24 hours*

Shanghai *NEW ENTRY*

R **Map 22 A3**
38c Kensington Church Street W8
01-938 2501
Chinese cooking
Owner managers Mr Lai & Mr Lok
Credit Access, Amex, Diners, Visa
A smart, modern restaurant specialising in the aromatic cuisine of Shanghai. Try meaty spare ribs, delicious deep-fried eel served in a potato

basket or superior duck with pancakes as tasty starters, perhaps followed by prawns with chilli sauce, garlicky Tibetan lamb or sliced beef with spring onions. Lovely toffee bananas to finish. Efficient service.

■ *Set D £12·50*	*L 12–2.30*
About £38 for two	*D 6.30–11.30*
Seats 80 Parties 80	*Parking Difficult*
Closed Bank Hols	

Shares

R **Map 26 C2**
12 Lime Street EC3
01-623 1843
Manager Mr Moreno
Credit Access, Amex, Diners, Visa
A popular, well-run City restaurant offering fixed-price lunch menus of three or four courses. Cooking is very dependable throughout an interesting variety of dishes, from smoked salmon

mousse and pigeon terrine to subtly sauced pork smitane, breast of duck with cranberries, and orange towers – a lovely sweet of sponge and orange mousse, coated with a zabaglione sauce. Book.

♀ **Well-chosen** ☺

■ *Set L £18·50*	*L only 11.30–3*
About £54 for two	*Parking Difficult*
Seats 78 Parties 50	*Closed Sat & Sun*

Sheraton Park Tower

H **85% £A E Map 22 D3**
101 Knightsbridge SW1X 7RN
01-235 8050. Tlx 917222
Credit Access, Amex, Diners, Visa
A luxurious, marble-floored foyer with large floral displays creates a good first impression at this striking, modern hotel. Lounge areas are equally stylish, with elegant period furniture and inviting settees giving a relaxing atmosphere. The

decor of the Rotunda area, used as a coffee lounge, is also most impressive. Two bars, one small and intimate and the other more sophisticated, are very pleasant. Bedrooms are spacious with fine views of the city; many refurbished in period style have armchairs, desks and mini-bars. Excellent tiled bathrooms are thoughtfully equipped with personalized toiletries,

hairdryers, bathrobes and direct-dial telephones. There are also 29 superb suites. No dogs. *Amenities* hairdressing, in-house movies (charge), valeting, laundry service.

■ *Rooms* 295
en suite bath/shower 295
Direct dial Yes
Room TV Yes

Confirm by 4
Last dinner Midnight
Parking Limited
Room service 24 hours

Shezan

R **Map 23 C4**
16 Cheval Place SW7
01-589 7918
Pakistani cooking
Owner manager Shah Nawaz
Credit Access, Amex, Diners, Visa
   Lamb and chicken are the principal meats featured throughout the menu of this renowned Pakistani restaurant. Specialities include gosht

kata masala (braised lamb) and sautéed poussin, and there's a choice of tandooris, curries and seafood. Good Basmati rice and breads, plus interesting regional sweets like milk pudding garnished with nuts.

■ *Set L* £9·95
About £50 for two
Seats 120 *Parties* 100
Closed Sun & Bank Hols

L 12–2.30
D 7–11.30
Parking Ample

Shogun

R **Map 22 D2**
Adams Row W1
01-493 1877
Japanese cooking
Owner manager Hiromi Mitsuka
Credit Access, Amex, Diners, Visa
   A characterful Japanese basement restaurant with discreet screens made of arrows separating the tables. The traditional menu features yakitori,

sashimi and tempura, with sushi as the speciality. Also popular is ebi age shinjo – delicious deep-fried prawn balls with a salt dip. A section of the menu written in Japanese contains dishes for the more adventurous.

■ *Set D* from £18·80
About £60 for two
Closed Mon, Bank
Hols, 4 days Easter, 10 days Aug & 10 days Xmas

D only 6–11
Parking Difficult
Seats 65

Simply Nico ★★ *NEW ENTRY*

R ★★ ⌂ ♧ **Map 25 B6**
48a Rochester Row SW1
01-630 8061
French cooking
Credit Access, Amex, Diners, Visa
   Dinah-Jane and Nico Ladenis have settled in Victoria – an area not previously known for its gastronomic excellence – where their coolly elegant restaurant is the setting for cooking of outstanding brilliance. As passionate and enthusiastic as ever, Nico continues to produce dishes that excite all the senses with their sublime flavours and superb eye-appeal. Splendid staff include Jonathan Fox, one of London's most charming sommeliers. Booking is absolutely essential. Intelligently chosen wines, particularly burgundies from good though not always fashionable years: Beaune Clos du Roi 1980 (Ampeau), Morey St Denis Clos des Ormes 1976 (Faiveley). *Specialities* foie gras chaud en salade d'haricots verts; salade de caille aux raisins; noix

de ris de veau braisé au Madère, au jus de carottes et de Sauternes; tulipe vanille aux fruits frais assortis et au coulis de framboises.
♚ Well-chosen ℮
■ *Set L* from £16·50
Set D from £32
About £80 for two
Seats 34
Closed Sat, Sun, Bank Hols, 2 wks Aug & 8–10 days Xmas

L 12.30–2
D 7.15–11
Parking Ample
Parties 6

Sinar Matahari

R **Map 7 A4**
146 The Broadway, West Ealing W13
01-567 6821
Indonesian cooking
Owner manager David Foster
Credit Access, Amex, Visa
   Imaginative Indonesian cooking is the order of the day at this jolly restaurant, where potted palms and bamboo seating help create the right

ethnic backdrop. Set menus and carte provide an exciting range of meat, fish and vegetable dishes, featuring traditional hot chilli, coconut and peanut sauces.

■ *Set meals* from £19
for two
About £32 for two
Seats 78
Closed L Sat, all Mon & 25 & 26 Dec

L 12–2.30, Sun 1–2
D 6–11, Sun 6–10.30
Parking Ample
Parties 50

Singapore Garden

R ♧ **Map 20 B3**
83 Fairfax Road NW6
01-328 5314
South-East Asian cooking
Credit Access, Amex, Diners, Visa

A variety of enjoyable dishes, from curries to noodles and bean curd dishes, is offered at this friendly restaurant where both cooking and service are provided by the Lim family. Fresh,

good-quality ingredients are well presented. Chicken in paper parcels with ginger and spring onion makes a pleasingly different starter, other choices include Chinese roast duck and scallops in oyster sauce.

■ *Set D* £9·50   *L 12–2.45*
About £30 for two   *D 6–10.45*
Seats 50   *Parking* Limited
Parties 10   *Closed* Xmas

♀ indicates a **well-chosen** house wine.

Stafford Hotel

HR **77% £A Map 25 B4**
St James's Place SW1A 1NJ
01-493 0111. Tlx 28602
Credit Access, Amex, Diners, Visa

A stylish red-brick hotel where the air of calm and relaxation evokes the atmosphere of a private club. A smart foyer with leather chesterfields leads onto an attractive lounge with comfortable seating, fine antiques and plenty of fresh flowers, and a cosy bar hung with sailing mementoes. Bedrooms are individually furnished and

decorated with quality fabrics and furniture which ranges from period style to modern cane. Seven splendid suites offer even more luxury. The pretty tiled bathrooms have telephones and bathrobes. Cheerful, efficient staff. No dogs.
Amenities garden, in-house movies (free), laundry service.

■ *Rooms 62*   *Confirm by arrang.*
en suite bath/shower 62   *Last dinner 10.30*
Direct dial Yes   *Parking* Difficult
Room TV Yes   *Room service 24 hours*

Stafford Hotel Restaurant ❦ &

A civilised, chandeliered dining room where chef Armando Rodriguez has been demonstrating his talents for a number of years. This friendly restaurant offers top-quality produce skilfully cooked: try creamy salmon mousse in puff pastry or venison terrine for a starter; follow with fillet steak Brillat-Savarin or veal with Marsala sauce. Finish with crêpes Suzette or lemon soufflé. Extensive list of clarets. ♀ **Well-chosen** ☙
■ *Set L* £17   *L 12.30–2.30*
Set D £20   *D 6.30–10.30*
About £70 for two   *Seats 65 Parties 28*

☙ is our symbol for an **outstanding** wine list.

Stakis St Ermin's Hotel

H **74% £B E Map 25 B5**
Caxton Street SW1H 0QW
01-222 7888. Tlx 917731
Manager Stephen Elliott
Credit Access, Amex, Diners, Visa. LVs

Just a stroll from Westminster Abbey and the Houses of Parliament, this comfortable Victorian hotel provides ideal accommodation for businessmen and is also a popular choice for private functions. A marble floor, ornate ceiling and fine central staircase lend a rococo air to the foyer-lounge, and there's also a cosy bar. Good-sized bedrooms are tastefully styled in pastel shades with floral bedspreads and darkwood units; trouser presses, tea-makers, hairdryers and fresh fruit are standard. Bathrooms are adequate. The seven suites and 40 club rooms are larger and more luxurious, with better bathrooms and

extras like mini-bars and sofas. *Amenities* in-house movies (charge), valeting, laundry service, 24-hour lounge service.
■ *Rooms 300*   *Confirm by 6*
en suite bath/shower 300   *Last dinner 10.15*
Direct dial Yes   *Parking* Limited
Room TV Yes   *Room service 24 hours*

Strand Palace Hotel

H **63% £C** **Map 24 D3**
Strand WC2R 0JJ
01-836 8080. Tlx 24208
Credit Access, Amex, Diners, Visa. **LVs**
The central location makes this hotel a favourite with tourists and businessmen alike. There's a spacious foyer-lounge with tiled floor, sofas and easy chairs; also two smart, comfortable bars. Standard bedrooms have tiled bathrooms and

tea/coffee-makers but would benefit from some refurbishment. Superior rooms have better fittings, also trouser presses and hairdryers. *Amenities* laundry service, coffee shop (6.30am–12.15am), kiosk.

■ *Rooms* 771	*Confirm by* 6
en suite bath/shower 771	*Last dinner* 10
Direct dial Yes	*Parking* Difficult
Room TV Yes	*Room service* None

Suntory

R **⚘ Map 25 B4**
72 St James's Street SW1
01-409 0201
Japanese cooking
Credit Access, Amex, Diners, Visa
One of London's original Japanese restaurants, and still immensely popular, Suntory offers two distinct styles of eating. Downstairs is the relaxed tappan-yaki room, where guests sit around

individual iron griddles set in each table and marvel at the mastery of the chef. The upper rooms are more formal serving superb sushi, sashimi and tempura.

■ *Set L from* £15	*L* 12–2
Set D from £20	*D* 7–10
About £70 *for two*	*Parking* Difficult
Seats 142 *Parties* 200	*Closed* Sun, Bank
Hols, 25–28 Dec & 31 Dec–4 Jan	

Le Suquet

R **Map 23 C5**
104 Draycott Avenue SW3
01-581 1785
French cooking
Manager Francis Mornay
Credit Access, Amex, Diners, Visa
Pictures of French seaports adorn one of London's best loved fish restaurants. Oysters are popular all year round – order them on their own or

in the splendid seafood platter. Feuilletés are another favourite, and main dishes range from grilled sole to sea bass beurre blanc and turbot with sorrel sauce. Simple sweets. Service can be a little casual. Book.
♥ Well-chosen

■ *About* £55 *for two*	*L* 12.30–2.30
Seats 58	*D* 7–11.30
Parties 16	*Parking* Difficult

Swallow International Hotel

H **65% £C** **Map 23 A4**
147c Cromwell Road SW5 0TH
01-370 4200. Tlx 27260
Manager Mr G. Gold
Credit Access, Amex, Diners, Visa
Tour groups and business people are the main clientele at this large, modern hotel, formerly the London International. Bedrooms are being rejuvenated with pastel shades, better furniture

and more accessories. Public rooms include the popular Heritage Bar. Standards can slip at busy times. *Amenities* in-house movies (charge), laundry service, coffee shop (7am–12pm), 24-hour lounge service, kiosk.

■ *Rooms* 417	*Confirm by* 6
en suite bath/shower 417	*Last dinner* 11
Direct dial Yes	*Parking* Ample
Room TV Yes	*Room service* 24 hours

Swiss Centre, Chesa

R **Map 27 A3**
2 New Coventry Street W1
01-734 1291
Credit Access, Amex, Diners, Visa
Tucked away in Switzerland's tourist complex like a farmhouse in the Engadine is this delightful basement restaurant. Chef André Pernet and manageress Lydie Nunez demonstrate national skill and efficiency with a menu that features

traditional specialities such as grisons (air-cured beef and ham), raclette cheese with boiled potatoes and veal steak with Gruyère. Hedonists insist on the rösti and home-made gâteaux. Selective range of Swiss wines. ☜

■ *Set L* £13·50	*Meals* noon–midnight,
Set D £19·50	Sun noon–11
About £48 *for two*	*Parking* Limited
Seats 50 *Parties* 45	*Closed* 25 & 26 Dec

■ We publish annually, so make sure you use the current edition. It's worth it!

Swiss Cottage Hotel

H **64%** **£C/D** **Map 20 B3**
4 Adamson Road, Swiss Cottage NW3
01-722 2281. Tlx 297232
Credit Access, Amex, Diners, Visa
Part of a handsome Victorian terrace, this very individual hotel is filled with fine paintings and antiques collected by the founder. There's a little reception hall with a Persian rug and gilded desk; an attractive lounge and a cosy bar. Bedrooms of various sizes also feature some nice old pieces. Cheerful, charming staff add a very pleasant personal touch. No dogs.
Amenities patio garden, laundry service.

■ *Rooms* 65	*Confirm by* 6
en suite bath/shower 65	*Last dinner* 9
Direct dial Yes	*Parking* Ample
Room TV Yes	*Room service* 24 hours

T'ang

R ♨ **Map 23 B6**
294 Fulham Road SW10
01-351 2599
South-East Asian cooking
Credit Access, Amex, Diners, Visa
Partner Tony Pat heads the kitchen brigade in this sophisticated restaurant, whose menu takes a mouthwatering trip around the Orient. Cooking is highly refined, presentation a picture, and among many splendid dishes we remember the speciality crackling duck (crisply fried with ginger, garlic and chilli and served in a crunchy pancake shell); steamed pork dumplings with a soy/garlic dip; and beautifully tender Mongolian lamb with the zip of chilli and a garnish of vegetable strips. Other specialities include egg 'money purses' with a filling of minced scallop, mushroom and asparagus, and fuye beef – shreds of beef marinated in yellow bean paste and served with shallots and chicken roti. Minimum charge £15.

■ *About £47 for two*	*L* 12–2.30
Seats 70	*D* 7–11.30
Parties 30	*Parking* Limited
Closed L Sat, Sun, Bank Hols, 4 days Easter & 4 days Xmas	

La Tante Claire ★★★

R ★★★ ♕♕ ♨ **Map 23 C6**
68 Royal Hospital Road SW3
01-352 6045
French cooking
Credit Access, Amex, Diners, Visa
Ambience, service and exquisite food are in constant harmony at this wonderful restaurant. Pierre Koffmann is a chef of quite remarkable talent, making every meal a masterpiece yet happily avoiding the cult of the megachef. Recent memories include superlative ravioli of langoustines with asparagus and basil, the pasta mouthwateringly light, the shellfish succulently perfect, the sauce of delicate but positive flavour; and little slices of the tenderest venison fillet served in an adventurous sauce of bitter chocolate and raspberry vinegar. The cheeseboard is impeccable, and there's an aristocratic French cellar with several '61 clarets and a good variety of half-bottles. The room is light and airy, done out in white and pastels, with

a nod towards art deco. Service is superb from staff who are polished and polite, discreet yet approachable. *Specialities* galette de foie gras aux échalotes rôties, pied de cochon aux morilles, rougets au cumin, croustade aux pommes caramelisées.

➥ Outstanding	♀ Well-chosen ☺
■ *Set L* £17·50	*L* 12.30–2
About £95 for two	*D* 7–11.15
Seats 45	*Parking* Limited
Closed Sat, Sun, Bank Hols, 10 days Easter, 10 days Xmas & 3 wks Aug/Sept	

Tiger Lee

R ♕ ♿ **Map 23 A5**
251 Old Brompton Road, SW5
01-370 2323
Chinese cooking
Manager Stanley Lau
Credit Amex, Diners, Visa
Seafood tops the bill at this chic, discreetly luxurious Chinese restaurant, where you can enjoy anything from steamed fish with black bean sauce to grilled lobster with ginger and spring onions. Soups are excellent – the delicious pin yee is absolutely packed with good things – and the rice and quick-fried vegetables are first class. Meat and poultry dishes, too.

■ *Set D from* £20	*D* only 6–11.15
About £52 for two	*Parking* Limited
Seats 56	*Parties* 56
Closed 24 & 26 Dec	

■ For a discount on next year's guide, see Offer for Answers.

Tower Thistle Hotel

H **76% £B *E* Map 26 D3**
St Katherine's Way E1 9LD
01-481 2575. Tlx 885934
Manager Michael Holland
Credit Access, Amex, Diners, Visa. LVs
The Thames-side setting is spectacular, with almost all rooms overlooking the river and Tower Bridge or the colourful comings and goings of St Katherine's Dock. Bedrooms, including two wings of non-smoking rooms, are done out in relaxing pastel shades and offer, among other things, air-conditioning, radio-alarms, trouser presses, hairdryers and a range of toiletries. Executive rooms are even better equipped, and at the top of the range (and the hotel) are 22 luxury penthouse suites. The lobby, lounge and coffee shop were part of a major 1987 refurbishment programme. The Thames Bar with a nautical theme is a great

place for drinking in the views. There are very few single rooms. No dogs. *Amenities* in-house movies (charge), coffee shop (7am–midnight), laundry service, 24-hour lounge service.

■ *Rooms 826*	*Confirm by 6*
en suite bath/shower 826	*Last dinner 10*
Direct dial Yes	*Parking Ample*
Room TV Yes	*Room service 24 hours*

Le Trou Normand

R **Map 23 D4**
27 Motcomb Street SW1
01-235 1668
French cooking
Owner managers Bracci family
Credit Access, Amex, Diners, Visa
The sturdy bourgeois cuisine of northern France characterises the simple, sustaining menu of this stylishly informal French restaurant. Fish

features prominently, but there are steaks, lamb chops and duck for the carnivorous. Dishes are acceptably prepared; most come with a crisp salad and new potatoes. Sweets include a good crème brûlée. Brisk, cheerful service. ⊜

■ *About £40 for two*	*L 12.30–3*
Seats 40	*D 7.15–11.45*
Parties 28	*Parking Difficult*
Closed Sun & 2 wks Xmas	

Tui

R **Map 23 C4**
19 Exhibition Road, SW7
01-584 8359
Thai cooking
Credit Access, Amex, Diners, Visa
Decor is coolly modern, service affable and stylish at this popular Thai restaurant near the South Kensington museums. The cooking's excellent and dependable on a menu that runs

from classic tom yum soup and delicious steamed dumplings to crab claw and prawn hot pot, chicken with cashew nuts and green beef curry. Also noodles and rice dishes. Fresh fruit is the best way to finish. Quick lunch menu available.

■ *About £45 for two*	*L 12–2.30, Sun 12.30–3*
Seats 52	*D 6.30–11, Sun 7–10.30*
Parties 25	*Parking Difficult*
Closed Sun preceding Bank Hols & 2 days Xmas	

Turner's *NEW ENTRY*

R ⨆ ◁ **Map 23 C4**
87 Walton Street SW3
01-584 6711
Credit Access, Amex, Diners, Visa
Chef-patron Brian Turner shares in the greeting, the cooking and the service at this coolly elegant restaurant. His style is modern, with subtle combinations of sauces and careful presentation. Steamed brill with crab and ginger, and roulé au

chocolat blanc are happy memories of a recent visit. Fine wines: Ch. Dassault '82, Quarts de Chaume (Baumard) '83.

♊ Well-chosen ⊜	
■ *Set L from £13.25*	*L 12.30–2.30*
Set D from £19.50	*Sun 1–2.30*
About £60 for two	*D 7.30–11, Sun 7–10*
Seats 50 Parties 20	*Parking Limited*
Closed L Sat & all Bank Hols	

The Veeraswamy ▶

The Veeraswamy *NEW ENTRY*

R 👑 **Map 24 B3**
99 Regent Street W1
01-734 1401
Indian cooking
Owner manager Shakti Behal
Credit Access, Amex, Diners, Visa

Remember the old Veeraswamy's with its Raj-rich red decor, its exotically garbed staff and its effete colonial curries? It's all very different now after an expensive facelift and a complete revision of the menu. The L-shaped room is bright and airy, with pretty peach and grey decor, and the menu spans India's culinary regions, with a specialist chef for each. Great care goes into the choice and preparation of top ingredients, and among the many delights are mint-marinated chicken tikka nilgin, sole fritters with coriander chutney, chicken livers with spicy onion kulcha, tandoori trout and creamy-rich chicken Kashmiri. Good breads and rice and superior sweets. Lunch is an excellent self-service hot buffet to which return trips are in order.

■ *Set L* £9·50   *L* 12–2.30
About £45 *for two*   *D* 6–11.30, *Sun* 7–10.30
Seats 129 *Parties* 60   *Parking* Ample

■ If we recommend meals in a hotel or inn, a separate entry is made for its restaurant.

Wakaba

R 👑 **Map 20 B3**
31 College Crescent NW3
01-722 3854
Japanese cooking
Credit Access, Amex, Diners, Visa

A short but varied selection of traditional Japanese dishes is presented by chef-patron Minoru Yoshihara at this informal little restaurant with its own sushi bar. Set dinner menus provide a carefully balanced assortment, or make your own choices – perhaps raw tuna, turbot and salmon sushimi, grilled pork or beef with ginger (shoga-yaki) or king prawns deep-fried in a nice light batter.

■ *Set D from* £14·80   *D only* 6–10.45
About £40 *for two*   *Parking* Ample
Seats 38 *Parties* 20   *Closed Mon, 4 days*
Easter, 1 wk Aug & 5 days Xmas

The Waldorf

H **77% £B Map 24 D3**
Aldwych WC2
01-836 2400. Tlx 24574
Credit Access, Amex, Diners, Visa

The imposing classical facade of this renowned hotel follows the gracious sweep of Aldwych, and inside there's a lot of style and splendour. Chandeliers and marble grace the foyer, rich panelling and chesterfields the bar, and in the Edwardian ambience of the Palm Court lounge the tea dance continues its revival. Bedrooms vary in size and style, many having been upgraded with plush fabrics, more attractive furniture and brass fittings. All are well equipped, and their bathrooms have plenty of towels and toiletries. Rooms facing the street, including some grand suites, suffer somewhat from traffic noise. *Amenities* hairdressing, valeting, 24-hour lounge

service, brasserie (10am–midnight), kiosk.
■ *Rooms* 311   *Confirm by* 6
en suite bath/shower 311   *Last dinner* 10.15
Direct dial Yes   *Parking* Difficult
Room TV Yes   *Room service* 24 hours

Waltons

R 👑 **Map 23 C4**
121 Walton Street SW3
01-584 0204
Manager Rolf Amberge
Credit Access, Amex, Diners, Visa

A smart setting for stylish cooking using the best seasonal produce. Attractively presented dishes range from chilled pheasant mousse with Cumberland sauce to calf's liver with avocado and orange and monkfish with cider vinegar sauce. Tempting sweets. Traditional Sunday lunch. Classic wine list with three '82 Chambertins from Armand Rousseau. 🍷 Well-chosen ⊝
■ *Set L from* £13·80   *L* 12.30–2.30,
Set D £20 15   *Sun* 12.30–2
About £90 *for two*   *D* 7.30–11.30,
Seats 65 *Parties* 65   *Sun* 7.30–10.30
Closed Bank Hols   *Parking* Limited

Weng Wah House

R **Map 20 B2**
240 Haverstock Hill NW3
01-794 5123
Chinese cooking
Credit Access, Amex, Diners, Visa
  A comfortable and stylish Chinese restaurant featuring an ornamental tank of tropical fish. Cooking is sound, service fast and efficient. The menu runs the gamut from butterfly prawns and

barbecued quail to crispy duck, stir-fried squid with black bean sauce and sizzling lamb. Also spicy Singaporean dishes – meat and vegetable curries, and pan-fried noodles.

■ *Set L & D from £9.50*	*L Mon–Fri 12–3*
About £25 for two	*D Mon–Fri 6–11.30*
Seats 80	*Sat noon–midnight,*
Parties 80	*Sun noon–11.30*
Closed 25 & 26 Dec	*Parking Ample*

Westbury Hotel

H **78% £A *E* Map 24 A3**
New Bond Street W1A 4UH
01-629 7755. Tlx 24378
Credit Access, Amex, Diners, Visa
  Continuing high standards of personal service maintain the reputation of this fine traditional Mayfair hotel, built in 1955 as a sister to the New York original. The elegant public areas include a plush foyer, a polo-themed bar housing many photos and paintings on the subject and, most notably, the Tennyson Room lounge, oak-panelled with red-leather winged armchairs and settees. Afternoon tea is served in this sumptuous room which retains a warm and very comfortable feel. Traditionally styled bedrooms with darkwood furniture are most attractive, especially the new rooms, brightly decorated and well coordinated in pale pinks and lavender. De luxe rooms have

sitting areas and dressing gowns. All rooms have well-equipped bathrooms together with hairdryers and radio-alarms. *Amenities* valeting, 24-hour lounge service.

■ *Rooms 243*	*Confirm by 6*
en suite bath/shower 243	*Last dinner 10.30*
Direct dial Yes	*Parking Difficult*
Room TV Yes	*Room service 24 hours*

White House

H **73% £C *E* ♿ Map 24 A1**
Albany Street NW1 3VP
01-387 1200. Tlx 24111
Credit Access, Amex, Diners, Visa. **LVs**
  Converted from a block of flats built in the 1930s, this distinctive hotel stands just north of the busy Marylebone/Euston Road not far from Regent's Park. Double-glazed bedrooms, all with mini-bars, have excellent fully-tiled bathrooms with radio speakers, hairdryers and a good range of toiletries. Top-floor bedrooms are more luxurious and have their own check-in and residents' lounge. Day rooms include a spacious pillared foyer, stylish bar and coffee shop. The cellar wine bar provides a cosy meeting-place, and there are also well-designed function suites. Efficient, but not particularly warm, staff. Only average breakfast. No dogs. *Amenities* in-house

movies, laundry service, coffee shop (7am–11pm), 24-hour lounge service.

■ *Rooms 580*	*Confirm by 6*
en suite bath/shower 580	*Last dinner 11*
Room phone Yes	*Parking Difficult*
Room TV Yes	*Room service 24 hours*

White Tower

R 👑 **Map 24 B2**
1 Percy Street W1
01-636 8141
Greek cooking
Credit Access, Amex, Diners, Visa
  With a long history of excellent Greek cooking, this elegant restaurant has a great reputation. The chatty menu, with its appetising descriptions, offers such favourites as dolmades and moussaka

or renowned specialities like tender, flavourful duckling with an exquisitely crisp skin and a bulghur wheat stuffing. Good vegetables. Simple sweets followed by Greek coffee. ⊖

■ *About £46 for two*	*L 12.30–2.30*
Seats 70	*D 6.30–10.30*
Parties 16	*Parking Limited*
Closed Sat, Sun, Bank Hols, 1 wk Xmas & 3 wks Aug	

🍷 indicates a **well-chosen** house wine.

Whites Hotel

H 75% £A Map 22 B2
Lancaster Gate W2 3NR
01-262 2711. Tlx 24771
Manager Michael Wills
Credit Access, Amex, Diners, Visa
  Exuberant splendour is one's first impression of this luxurious and stylish terrace hotel overlooking Kensington Gardens. Deep-pile rugs soften marble floors, chandeliers and plush sofas adorn the foyer, which leads to a lofty panelled bar with clubby seating, and a relaxing reading room-cum-lounge. Air-conditioned bedrooms – some with balconies and lounge areas and one with a four-poster – are positively opulent, with chandeliers, fine furnishings and sumptuous drapes. Accessories include mini-bars and personal safes; all have superbly equipped marble-clad bathrooms with radio and telephone extensions.

No dogs. *Amenities* in-house movies (free), teletext, laundry service, 24-hour lounge service.

■ *Rooms* 54	*Confirm by* 6
en suite bath/shower 54	*Last dinner* 10.30
Direct dial Yes	*Parking* Limited
Room TV Yes	*Room service* 24 hours

Wilbraham Hotel

H 57% £C/D Map 23 D4
Wilbraham Place, Sloane Street SW1X 9AE
01-730 8296
Manager Daniel Mullane
  Just a minute's walk from Sloane Square, this modest but appealing hotel has an exceptionally courteous manager in Daniel Mullane, whose example is passed on to unfailingly attentive staff. Day rooms are studiously old-fashioned, while

functionally furnished bedrooms range from very large panelled rooms on the ground floor to smaller ones above. There's been a lot of redecoration recently. Decent breakfasts served in bedrooms. No dogs. *Amenities* valeting.

■ *Rooms* 53	*Confirm by* arrang.
en suite bath/shower 45	*Last dinner* 9.45
Direct dial Yes	*Parking* Difficult
Room TV Some	*Room service* 24 hours

Wiltons

R ⌂ Map 25 B4
55 Jermyn Street SW1
01-629 9955
English cooking
Credit Access, Amex, Diners, Visa
  Tradition is embodied in the decor, the staff, the clientele and the classic English menu. The oysters are famous – take them plain, in a cocktail or with a mornay sauce – and other delights run

from turtle soup and smoked turkey to Dover sole, haddock with parsley sauce and an excellent mixed grill. English cheeses, savoury toasts and simple sweets such as crème caramel or pear Belle Hélène. ♀ Well-chosen ⊗

■ *About £75 for two*	*L* 12.30–2.30
Seats 90	*D* 6.30–10.30
Parties 60	*Parking* Difficult
Closed L Sat, all Sun, last wk July & 2 wks Aug	

Wok-On-By *NEW ENTRY*

R Map 21 B5
62 Battersea Bridge Road SW11
01-228 0888
Owner manager Mr S. Chanachit
Credit Visa
  A dimly lit restaurant with plain black furnishings and a short menu that includes Chinese, Japanese and Thai dishes. The novelty behind the joky name is that some dishes are do-it-yourself:

diners simmer their own steak strips or seafood assortment in electric woks plugged in at the table. Other main dishes and starters like satay or mussels tempura are prepared more conventionally, in the kitchen. Mediocre house wine.

■ *Set D* £10.25	*L* by arrang.
About £28 for two	*D* 7.30–11
Seats 65 *Parties* 75	*Parking* Ample
Closed Sun, all Bank Hols & 2 wks Xmas	

Youngs

R ◊ ⛶ Map 20 D3
19 Canonbury Lane N1
01-226 9791
Chinese cooking
Owner managers T. H. Koo & J. Ngan
Credit Access, Amex, Diners, Visa
  A smart and justly popular Chinese restaurant offering Szechuan and Peking dishes. Try chicken with chilli and sesame sauce, squid in spiced hot

and sour sauce or spiced cold beef for a starter; prawns with cashew nuts and chilli, chicken with green pepper or beef in oyster sauce for a main course. Finish with pickled sweet baby ginger. Book

■ *Set D* from £7·50	*D* only 5–12.30
About £37 for two	*Parking* Ample
Seats 70	*Parties* 80
Closed Bank Hols & 2/3 days Xmas	

Youngs

R ⚘ **Map 20 D3**
154 Upper Street N1
01-226 8463
Chinese cooking
Credit Access, Amex, Diners, Visa
  The newer and less formal of the two Islington restaurants, specialising in Cantonese and Peking dishes. Service is outstanding and the cooking by Mr Leung is excellent, using the best raw

materials. The duck and prawn dishes are superb, soups (particularly wun tun) are tasty, the rice could not be bettered, and the sauces are a delight. Booking here is essential because it is deservedly popular.

■ Set D from £5·60 | Meals noon–midnight
About £35 for two | Parking Limited
Seats 100 Parties 100 | Closed 25 Dec

Yumi *NEW ENTRY*

R **Map 22 D1**
110 George Street W1
01-935 8320
Japanese cooking
Owner manager Yumi Fujii
Credit Access, Amex, Diners, Visa
  A delightful place, run with charm and civility by owner Yumi Fujii and her staff, all clad in kimonos. Eat sushi in the upstairs bar or go to the stylish

little restaurant, where there's an ample choice of well-prepared dishes among which charcoal-grills in all guises feature strongly. Set meals are a good idea for the uninitiated.

■ Set L £7·50 | L 12–2.30
Set D £22·50 | D 6–10.45
About £50 for two | Parking Limited
Seats 84 | Parties 16
Closed Sun, Bank Hols, 1 wk Xmas & 1 wk Aug

Yung's

R ⚘ **Map 27 A2**
23 Wardour Street W1
01-437 4986
Chinese cooking
Credit Access, Amex, Diners, Visa
  You can dine until dawn at this Soho restaurant which specialises in Cantonese cooking, although Szechuan and Peking dishes are also on the menu. A high proportion of Chinese customers

testifies to the authenticity and high standard of the cooking. Classics such as moist and tender crispy duck and quick-fried scallops are reliably prepared and the special fried rice is excellent.

■ Set meals from £6·50 | Meals 4 pm–5 am
About £25 for two | Parking Difficult
Seats 100 | Closed 24 & 25 Dec
Parties 20

Zen

R ⚲ ⚘ **Map 23 C5**
Chelsea Cloisters, Sloane Avenue, SW3
01-589 1781
Chinese cooking
Credit Access, Amex, Diners, Visa
  A pleasant Chinese restaurant, where the service is obliging and the surroundings are luxurious. The menu, drawn from all parts of China, is full of interest, from fried crisp veal sticks

and lettuce-wrapped minced quail to baked crab, aromatic Szechuan duck and sizzling Hunan lamb. Also vegetarian dishes and desserts like tapioca pudding with melon.

■ About £44 for two | L 12–3, Sat 12–11.30,
Seats 110 | Sun 12–11
Parties 20 | D 6–11.30
Closed 3 days Xmas | Parking Ample

Ziani

R ⚘ **Map 23 C5**
45 Radnor Walk SW3
01-351 5297
Italian cooking
Credit Access, Amex, Diners, Visa
  Roberto Colussi and Luciano Amato are the welcoming hosts at this smart little restaurant, where Luciano prepares an interesting selection of North Italian dishes. Wind-dried raw beef, sole

sauced with mushrooms and olives, and quail with polenta are typically flavoursome offerings, and there's a good variety of pasta. The sweets are enjoyable.
🍷 Well-chosen ℮

■ About £39 for two | L 12.30–2.45
Seats 50 Parties 20 | D 7–11.30
Closed Bank Hols | Parking Ample

HOTELS RESTAURANTS AND INNS

LONDON AIRPORTS

GATWICK

Chequers Thistle Hotel

H 66% £C Map 7 B5 Surrey
Brighton Road, Horley RH6 8PH
Crawley (0293) 786992. Tlx 877550
Manager Mr R. Grear
Credit Access, Amex, Diners, Visa. **LVs**

Much changed since its coaching inn days, this well-run hotel stands on a roundabout by the A23, north of the airport. Entrance is from the car park into a library-style lounge, and there's a choice of bars. Pastel bedrooms have remote-control TV, hairdryers and trouser presses.
Amenities garden, outdoor swimming pool, in-house movies (free), laundry service, airport coach.

■ *Rooms 78*	*Confirm by 6*
en suite bath/shower 78	*Last dinner 10*
Direct dial Yes	*Parking Ample*
Room TV Yes	*Room service 24 hours*

Copthorne Hotel

HR 71% £C E &
Map 7 B5 West Sussex
Copthorne, Nr Crawley RH10 3PG
Copthorne (0342) 714971. Tlx 95500
Credit Access, Amex, Diners, Visa

Fronted by a 16th-century farmhouse, this attractive modern hotel is peacefully situated in eight acres of landscaped gardens and yet lies only four miles from the airport, just off junction 10 of the M23. The spacious reception-lounge area and conference suites are smartly contemporary while the beamed bar retains much old-world charm. A stylish, tile-floored garden room overlooks an ornamental water garden. Neatly fitted bedrooms – the majority sporting black beams – offer a good range of modern comforts and well-equipped bathrooms. *Amenities* garden, sauna, solarium, gymnasium, hairdressing, squash, putting, croquet, in-house movies (charge), laundry service, restaurant (5.30am–11pm), 24-hour lounge service, kiosk, children's playground, airport coach.

■ *Rooms 223*	*Confirm by 6*
en suite bath/shower 223	*Last dinner 11*
Direct dial Yes	*Parking Ample*
Room TV Yes	*Room service 24 hours*

Lyon d'Or Restaurant ♛ &

A smart, spacious restaurant where sound, largely French-inspired cooking attracts locals and travellers alike. The lengthy menu ranges from garlicky snails, avocado mousse with grapefruit sauce and a terrine of chicken and pink trout to straightforward grills and roasts plus more exotic offerings such as scampi with fennel in Pernod and yoghurt, pork with cream and apple brandy or rich hare casserole. Simple, pleasant sweets. ⊖

■ *Set L £13·50*	*L 12.30–2*
About £55 for two	*D 7.30–10*
Seats 70	*Parties 120*
Closed L Sat, all Sun, Bank Hols, 25 & 26 Dec	

Crest Hotel, Gatwick

H 58% £C/D Map 7 B5 West Sussex
Langley Drive, Crawley RH11 7SX
Crawley (0293) 29991. Tlx 877311
Credit Access, Amex, Diners, Visa

A modern hotel conveniently located just 4 miles south of the airport. Open-plan public areas are bright and cheerful. Bedrooms are small but well equipped, with tea/coffee-makers and trouser presses; some are reserved for non-smokers, others for ladies. Tiled bathrooms throughout. *Amenities* garden, games room, pool table, in-house movies (charge), laundry service, coffee shop (5am–11pm), courtesy transport.

■ *Rooms 230*	*Confirm by 6*
en suite bath/shower 230	*Last dinner 11*
Direct dial Yes	*Parking Ample*
Room TV Yes	*Room service Limited*

Gatwick Concorde Hotel

H **56% £C Map 7 B5** West Sussex
Church Road, Lowfield Heath RH11 0PQ
Crawley (0293) 33441. Tlx 87287
Manager Tony Colas
Credit Access, Amex, Diners, Visa
A modern hotel just off the A23 and alongside
one of the airport runways. Double-glazed, air-
conditioned bedrooms include new rooms with
smart lightwood furnishings; older ones have
simple white units. Refurbishment will be
welcome in the day rooms, which include a
reception-lounge and a pub-style bar.
Amenities garden, in-house movies (charge),
laundry service, airport coach.

■ *Rooms 121*	*Confirm by 6*
en suite bath/shower 121	*Last dinner 10.30*
Direct dial Yes	*Parking Ample*
Room TV Yes	*Room service None*

Gatwick Hilton International

H **76% £B *E* &**
Map 7 B5 West Sussex
Gatwick Airport RH6 0LL
Gatwick (0293) 518080. Tlx 877021
Manager Mr H. Angelkotter
Credit Access, Amex, Diners, Visa
Built in 1981 and extended in June 1987, this
superbly equipped hotel lies within the Gatwick
Airport complex and is linked to the main
terminals by a covered walkway. The leafy, lofty
foyer has a replica of a Gypsy Moth aeroplane
hanging from its glazed ceiling; there's a smart
split-level coffee shop and a traditionally styled
bar featuring prints of jockeys. Good-sized
bedrooms, with easy chairs and ample writing
space, are provided with mini-bars, hairdryers,
computerised door locks and TV flight
information. *Amenities* garden, indoor swimming

pool, sauna, solarium, whirlpool bath, gymnasium,
massage parlour, hairdressing, in-house movies
(free), valeting, laundry service, 24-hour coffee
shop & lounge service.

■ *Rooms 552*	*Confirm by arrang.*
en suite bath/shower 552	*Last dinner 11*
Direct dial Yes	*Parking Ample*
Room TV Yes	*Room service 24 hours*

Gatwick Moat House

H **62% £C & Map 7 B5** Surrey
Longbridge Roundabout, Horley RH6 0AB
Horley (0293) 785599. Tlx 877138
Credit Access, Amex, Diners, Visa
Behind the functional nondescript facade, here
just off the A23, is a bright and attractive hotel,
with cheerful, friendly staff to match. Light wood
and greenery create an appealing foyer-lounge
and there's a smart bar with dark cane furniture.
Prettily coordinated bedrooms have air-
conditioning.
Amenities in-house movies (free), laundry
service, coffee shop (2.30–11pm), courtesy
transport.

■ *Rooms 120*	*Confirm by 6*
en suite bath/shower 120	*Last dinner 10.15*
Direct dial Yes	*Parking Ample*
Room TV Yes	*Room service Limited*

Gatwick Penta Hotel

H **71% £B/C *E***
Map 7 B5 Surrey
Povey Cross Road, Horley RH6 0BE
Crawley (0293) 820169
Credit Access, Amex, Diners, Visa
A recently completed leisure complex adds to
the facilities at this modern streamlined hotel just
off the A23, where there's already a self-contained
conference centre that features a facsimile
service. Public areas include a leafy relaxing foyer
lounge attractively furnished with leather sofas
and table lamps, a cane furnished coffee shop
that stays open until 6am, and a plush bar styled
on the old Brighton Belle Pullman car. Spacious
bedrooms are air-conditioned and soundproofed,
some are equipped with mini-bars and trouser
presses. Bathrooms are spick and span and
fully tiled.

Amenities garden, indoor swimming pool, sauna,
solarium, whirlpool bath, keep-fit equipment,
squash, in-house movies (free), laundry service,
coffee shop (11am–6am), kiosk.

■ *Rooms 260*	*Confirm by 6*
en suite bath/shower 260	*Last dinner 11*
Direct dial Yes	*Parking Ample*
Room TV Yes	*Room service All day*

Post House Hotel ▶

Post House Hotel

H **62%** **£C** **Map 7 B5** Surrey
Povey Cross Road, Horley RH6 0BA
Horley (0293) 771621. Tlx 877351
Credit Access, Amex, Diners, Visa. LVs
   A new block of 70 bedrooms has greatly
increased accommodation at this red-brick airport
hotel. Standard rooms offer mini-bars, tea-makers
and neat bathrooms, while executive rooms have
useful extras. Public rooms include a sunken bar.

Amenities patio, outdoor swimming pool, in-
house movies (charge), laundry service, coffee
shop (10.45am–10.45pm), 24-hour lounge service,
kiosk, courtesy coach.

■ *Rooms* 220   *Confirm by* 6
en suite bath/shower 220 *Last dinner* 10.30
Direct dial Yes   *Parking* Ample
Room TV Yes   *Room service* 24 hours

HEATHROW

Ariel Hotel

H **65%** **£C** **Map 5 E2** Middlesex
Bath Road, Hayes UB3 5AJ
01-759 2552. Tlx 21777
Credit Access, Amex, Diners, Visa. LVs
   An ornamental fountain and spiral staircase are
attractive features of the open-plan foyer-lounge
of this distinctive circular hotel built around a
garden terrace. There's also a stylish cocktail bar
and several function rooms. Most bedrooms boast

smart darkwood units and pleasant pastel colour
schemes.
Amenities garden, in-house movies (charge),
laundry service, 24-hour lounge service, kiosk,
courtesy coach.
■ *Rooms* 177   *Confirm by* 6
en suite bath/shower 177 *Last dinner* 10.30
Direct dial Yes   *Parking* Ample
Room TV Yes   *Room service* 24 hours

Berkeley Arms Hotel

H **65%** **£C/D** **Map 5 E2** Middlesex
Bath Road, Cranford TW5 9QE
01-897 2121. Tlx 935728
Credit Access, Amex, Diners, Visa. LVs
   A pretty garden complete with aviary is an
attractive feature of this pleasant hotel east of the
airport. The open-plan bar and lounge have a
coolly elegant feel, with their bamboo furniture
and plants. Bedrooms, too, appeal. All have

armchairs and built-in white units, plus hairdryers,
tea-makers and well-equipped bathrooms.
Amenities garden, laundry service, 24-hour
lounge service, courtesy coach.

■ *Rooms* 40   *Confirm by* 6
en suite bath/shower 40   *Last dinner* 10
Direct dial Yes   *Parking* Ample
Room TV Yes   *Room service* 24 hours

Excelsior Hotel

H **72%** **£B/C** &
Map 5 E2 Middlesex
Bath Road, West Drayton UB7 0DU
01-759 6611. Tlx 24525
Credit Access, Amex, Diners, Visa
   Many improvements to report at this well-
equipped hotel located on the A4 very close to the
airport terminals. The marble foyer and other
public areas have been revamped to reflect a
more traditional, elegant style, and a new leisure
complex has been built where the outdoor
swimming pool used to be. Bedrooms are
furnished in pleasant contemporary style and all
have excellent fully-tiled bathrooms. Executive
rooms offer a larger range of accessories, such as
trouser presses, mini-bars, and dressing gowns,
and there are seven spacious suites. No dogs.
Amenities garden, indoor swimming pool, sauna,

solarium, whirlpool bath, keep-fit equipment,
massage parlour, hairdressing, in-house movies
(free), laundry service, coffee shop (8am–1am),
kiosk, airport coach.
■ *Rooms* 600   *Confirm by* 6
en suite bath/shower 600 *Last dinner* 11
Direct dial Yes   *Parking* Ample
Room TV Yes   *Room service* 24 hours

Heathrow Park Hotel

H **57% £C**
Map 5 E2 Middlesex
Bath Road, Longford, West Drayton UB7 6EQ
01-759 2400. Tlx 934093
Credit Access, Amex, Diners, Visa
  A modern two-storey hotel with runway views. New owners have redecorated some of the bedrooms in attractive pink and grey, but no longer provide room service. All rooms are air-conditioned and triple-glazed, the largest being those in the Concorde wing. There are two bars. No dogs. *Amenities* games room, kiosk, hairdressing, in-house movies (charge), coffee shop (10.30am–11.30pm), airport coach.

■ *Rooms* 305	*Confirm by* 6
en suite bath/shower 305	*Last dinner* 10.30
Direct dial Yes	*Parking* Ample
Room TV Yes	*Room service* None

Heathrow Penta Hotel

H **69% £B/C** ♿ **Map 5 E2** Middlesex
Bath Road, Hounslow TW6 2AQ
01-897 6363. Tlx 934660
Credit Access, Amex, Diners, Visa
  This striking low-rise hotel stands within the airport boundary. Double-glazed bedrooms offer plenty of writing and storage space, but not all are in the best of repair. There are two bars, a coffee shop and superb function rooms. *Amenities* garden, indoor swimming pool, hairdressing, in-house movies (free), 24-hour coffee shop & lounge service, shopping arcade, airport coach.

■ *Rooms* 645	*Confirm by* 6
en suite bath/shower 645	*Last dinner* 10.30
Direct dial Yes	*Parking* Ample
Room TV Yes	*Room service* 24 hours

Holiday Inn

H **73% £C** *E* **Map 5 E2** Middlesex
Stockley Road, West Drayton UB7 9NA
West Drayton (0895) 445555. Tlx 934518
Manager Mr Leslie Ritson
Credit Access, Amex, Diners, Visa
  Located immediately north of junction 4 of the M4, this modern hotel is particularly strong on the accommodation side. Bedrooms are all of a good size, with smart, practical furnishings, ample writing space and a couple of easy chairs, plus mini-bars, trouser presses and radio-alarms. Bathrooms, too, are very well equipped, with a good supply of towels. The lobby-lounge with a central fireplace is roomy and comfortable, and there's an agreeable beamed bar in mock-Tudor style. *Amenities* garden, indoor swimming pool, sauna, solarium, keep-fit equipment, tennis, 9-hole golf course, in-house movies (charge),

laundry service, coffee shop (6.30am–11.30pm), kiosk, airport coach.

■ *Rooms* 396	*Confirm by* 6
en suite bath/shower 396	*Last dinner* 10.30
Direct dial Yes	*Parking* Ample
Room TV Yes	*Room service* 24 hours

Master Robert Motel

H **57% £D** **Map 5 E2** Middlesex
366 Great West Road, Hounslow TW5 0BD
01-570 6261. Tlx 9413782
Credit Access, Amex, Diners, Visa
  Practical overnight accommodation is provided in decent-sized motel-style rooms, 29 of which have their own car ports. Furnishings are simple fitted units, and all rooms offer tea-making facilities (complete with biscuits). The nicest day room is an attractive bar-lounge with comfortable sofas. No room service apart from breakfast. No dogs. *Amenities* garden, laundry service, coffee shop (10am–6pm).

■ *Rooms* 63	*Confirm by* 6
en suite bath/shower 63	*Last dinner* 10.45
Direct dial Yes	*Parking* Ample
Room TV Yes	*Room service* Limited

Post House Hotel

H **69% £C** **Map 5 E2** Middlesex
Sipson Road, West Drayton UB7 0JU
01-759 2323. Tlx 934280
Credit Access, Amex, Diners, Visa. LVs
  A tall modern hotel standing alongside the M4. The lobby-lounge is seldom empty, and there are two pleasant bars. Standard bedrooms offer ample writing and storage space, plus mini-bars and tea-makers and good tiled bathrooms. Furnishings are practical, but not all pristine. Club room occupants enjoy leisure facilities and limited room service. *Amenities* garden, in-house movies (free), coffee shop (6am–1.30am), airport coach.

■ *Rooms* 585	*Confirm by* 6
en suite bath/shower 585	*Last dinner* 10.30
Direct dial Yes	*Parking* Ample
Room TV Yes	*Room service* None

Sheraton-Heathrow Hotel

H 70% £C *E* **Map 5 E2** Middlesex
Bath Road, West Drayton UB7 0HJ
01-759 2424. Tlx 934331
Credit Access, Amex, Diners, Visa

Soundproofing is a useful (possibly essential) attribute of the pretty pink and plum bedrooms of this low-rise executive hotel to the west of the airport. Trouser presses are a standard accessory and modern bathrooms sport hairdryers, face flannels and complimentary toiletries. Public rooms include an elegant and well-proportioned foyer with steps up to the lounge-cum-cocktail bar. There are two more bars – one dark and intimate, the other plush and pubby. Some attention should be given to the swimming pool and enclosed patio. *Amenities* garden, indoor swimming pool, sauna, solarium, keep-fit equipment, snooker, in-house movies (charge),

laundry service, coffee shop (6.30am–11.30pm), 24-hour lounge service, courtesy coach.

■ *Rooms* 440	*Confirm by arrang.*
en suite bath/shower 440	*Last dinner 11.30*
Direct dial Yes	*Parking* Limited
Room TV Yes	*Room service* 24 hours

Sheraton Skyline

HR 77% £A/B *E* **Map 5 E2**
Middlesex
Bath Road, Hayes UB3 5BP
01-759 2535. Tlx 934254
Manager Paul James
Credit Access, Amex, Diners, Visa

An indoor tropical garden complete with palm trees, swimming pool and lounge bar provides the centrepiece of this popular modern hotel on the A4 near the airport entrance. Guests can also enjoy a six-nights-a-week cabaret in Diamond Lil's Saloon, or a quieter drink in the Edwardian-style cocktail bar. Extensive conference facilities are also available, together with good shopping areas. Spacious bedrooms with stylish decor have quality furnishings, co-ordinated fabrics, double glazing, air conditioning and smart bathrooms

(8 with shower only). *Amenities* patio, indoor swimming pool, sauna, solarium, beauty salon, hairdressing, in-house movies (charge), laundry service, coffee shop (6am–1am), shopping arcade, courtesy coach.

■ *Rooms* 355	*Confirm by* 4
en suite bath/shower 355	*Last dinner* 11
Direct dial Yes	*Parking* Ample
Room TV Yes	*Room service* 24 hours

Colony Room ♛ &

French cooking
Formal elegance and polished service support skilled French cooking. Dinner could start with turtle or spinach and watercress soup, followed perhaps by salmon en croûte (with a gingery, buttery sauce), veal with sorrel sauce, or freshly carved roast beef from the trolley. Tempting desserts include strawberries with black pepper and whisky or kiwi fruit-filled pancakes. Vast choice of French cheeses. €

■ *Set L* £15.95	*L* 12.30–2.30
About £60 for two	*D* 7–11,
Seats 155	Fri & Sat 7–11.30
Parties 60	*Closed L* Sat & Sun &
all lunches in Aug	

Skyway Hotel

H 63% £C/D **Map 5 E2** Middlesex
Bath Road, Hayes UB3 5AW
01-759 6311. Tlx 23935
Credit Access, Amex, Diners, Visa. **LVs**

Sound-proofed bedrooms are comfortably fitted at this purpose-built hotel on the A4. Superior rooms have air conditioning and extras like hairdryers and trouser presses. Downstairs, reception is bright and spacious and there's a

smart lounge and bar.
Amenities outdoor swimming pool, whirlpool bath, hairdressing, games room, snooker, valeting, laundry room, coffee shop (10am–12pm), courtesy coach.

■ *Rooms* 412	*Confirm by* 6
en suite bath/shower 412	*Last dinner* 10.30
Direct dial Yes	*Parking* Ample
Room TV Yes	*Room service* Limited

HOTELS RESTAURANTS AND INNS

ENGLAND

Elms Hotel · Abberley

HR 74% £C/D
Map 10 B4 Hereford & Worcester
Nr Worcester WR6 6AT
Great Witley (029 921) 666
Manager Rita Mooney
Credit Access, Amex, Diners, Visa

Beautiful formal gardens and parkland surround this imposing Queen Anne mansion, which commands fine views from its elevated setting. Log fires warm and cheer the traditionally-furnished lounges, and the library bar, with its carved wooden mantelpiece and handsome mahogany bookcases, is particularly appealing. Comfortable main-house bedrooms combine fine fabrics and furnishings with a host of cosseting

extras—from sewing kits and sherry to hairdryers, trouser presses and wall safes. Equally well-equipped annexe rooms are more contemporary in style, and some have balconies. Excellent bathrooms throughout. No dogs.
Amenities garden, tennis, putting, croquet, laundry service, 24-hour lounge service.

■ *Rooms* 27	*Confirm by* arrang.
en suite bath/shower 26	*Last dinner* 9
Direct dial Yes	*Parking* Ample
Room TV Yes	*Room service* 24 hours

Brooke Room Restaurant 🔥

English cooking with a contemporary if slightly inconsistent touch is the style at this formal restaurant. Dishes can be simple – mushroom soup, Dover sole, grilled veal cutlets – or more elaborate and ambitious like a fish consommé with sole quenelles or artichoke and asparagus in puff pastry and Madeira-sauced chicken breast filled with mushroom and herb mousse or fricassée of sweetbreads in mustard and taragon sauce. Good selection of farmhouse cheeses. ⊖

■ *Set L £10·95*	*L 12.30–2*
Set D £17	*D 7.30–9*
About £55 for two	*Seats 80 Parties 42*

Upper Reaches Hotel · Abingdon

H 64% £C
Map 5 D2 Oxfordshire
Thames Street OX14 3TA
Abingdon (0235) 22311
Credit Access, Amex, Diners, Visa

Good management and staff are a real plus at this delightful hotel overlooking the Thames and an old mill stream. A friendly, personal welcome awaits in the flagstoned foyer, and there's a cosy

lounge-bar, too. Decently furnished bedrooms (six in an annexe) offer many extras, from fresh fruit and mineral water to hairdryers and remote-control TVs. Bright modern bathrooms.
Amenities garden, mooring.

■ *Rooms* 26	*Confirm by* 6
en suite bath/shower 26	*Last dinner* 9.30
Room phone Yes	*Parking* Ample
Room TV Yes	*Room service* All day

Arrow Mill · Alcester

I £D/E
Map 4 C1 Warwickshire
Arrow B49 5NL
Alcester (0789) 762419
Owner managers Mr & Mrs S. Woodhams
Credit Access, Amex, Diners, Visa

Standing in extensive grounds by the A435, 2 miles from Alcester, this converted flour mill (records go back to 1086!) retains old-world

charm. Flagstoned floors, beams, waterwheel and wildfowl, farmyard animals too! Well-converted bedrooms are smartly fitted, bathrooms are excellent. *Amenities* garden, clay-pigeon shooting, coarse & game fishing, laundry service.

■ *Rooms* 15	*Confirm by* arrang.
en suite bath/shower 11	*Last dinner* 9.30
Direct dial Yes	*Parking* Ample
Room TV Yes	*Room service* All day

Old Red Lion Restaurant *NEW ENTRY* · Aldborough

R 🍴 🔥 **Map 6 C1** Norfolk
Norwich
Cromer (0263) 761451
Owners Mr & Mrs Eyles & Mr & Mrs Diluzio
Credit Access, Visa

A very traditional and welcoming restaurant by the large village green. The menu is a predictable digest of international dishes, but raw materials are good and fresh, and Bruno Diluzio's cooking is

certainly capable. Snails, fish soup or tasty lasagne could precede calf's kidneys in mustard sauce or fillet of sole véronique. Copious fresh vegetables, decent sweets. Some good clarets on a sound wine list. ⊖

■ *Set L £8·45*	*L 12.30–2.30*
Set D £9·25	*D 7–10.30*
About £30 for two	*Parking* Ample
Seats 40 Parties 65	*Closed D Sun & all Mon*

Brudenell Hotel
Aldeburgh

H **60% £D**
Map 6 D3 Suffolk
The Parade IP15 5BU
Aldeburgh (072 885) 2071
Credit Access, Amex, Diners, Visa. LVs

The discreet charms of Aldeburgh are echoed
in this traditional hotel. There are spectacular
North Sea views from the lounge and half of the
bedrooms, while other rooms overlook Snape

Marshes. A quarter of the bedrooms have smart
darkwood furnishings; those awaiting attention
range from stark '60s to trusty traditional.
Amenities hotel boat, sea fishing, games rooms,
laundry service, children's play area.

■ *Rooms 47*	*Confirm by arrang.*
en suite bath/shower 47	*Last dinner 9*
Room phone Yes	*Parking Ample*
Room TV Yes	*Room service 24 hours*

Uplands Hotel
Aldeburgh

H **60% £E** &
Map 6 D3 Suffolk
Victoria Road 1P15 5DX
Aldeburgh (072 885) 2420
Owner managers Tidder family
Credit Access, Amex, Diners, Visa

Just a few minutes walk from the sea, Uplands
is a family-run hotel with a long tradition of
hospitality. The bar is small and convivial, and the

cosy lounge has a conservatory extension. Main-
house bedrooms have been attractively
redecorated, and most now have their own up-to-
date bathrooms. Other rooms, equally pleasant,
are in chalets in the well-tended gardens.

■ *Rooms 20*	*Confirm by 6*
en suite bath/shower 17	*Last dinner 8.30*
Direct dial Yes	*Parking Ample*
Room TV Yes	*Room service All day*

Wentworth Hotel
Aldeburgh

H **65% £D/E**
Map 6 D3 Suffolk
Wentworth Road IP15 5BD
Aldeburgh (072 885) 2312
Owner manager Michael Pritt
Credit Amex, Diners

The Pritt family have owned and run this
friendly seafront hotel since the '20s. There are
two lounges; one traditional, the other recently

refurbished in cane. Bedrooms, being gradually
updated, have fitted furniture. Bathrooms range
from adequate to ultra-modern. First-rate staff.
Amenities garden, laundry service.

■ *Rooms 33*	*Confirm by arrang.*
en suite bath/shower 23	*Last dinner 8.45*
Direct dial Yes	*Parking Ample*
Room TV Yes	*Room service All day*
Closed 27 Dec–16 Jan	

Fairlawns Hotel
Aldridge

H **58% £E**
Map 10 C4 West Midlands
Little Aston Road, Walsall WS9 0NU
Walsall (0922) 55122. Tlx 339873
Owner manager John Pette
Credit Access, Amex, Diners, Visa

A well-kept and keenly run modern hotel
standing in its own grounds just off the A454. A
pleasant welcome awaits in the reception area

which, like the other day rooms, was recently
refurbished. Decent-sized bedrooms have trouser
presses, hairdryers and tea-makers, plus neat,
bright bathrooms. *Amenities* garden, laundry
service, 24-hour lounge service.

■ *Rooms 30*	*Confirm by 6*
en suite bath/shower 30	*Last dinner 10*
Direct dial Yes	*Parking Ample*
Room TV Yes	*Room service Limited*

Moonrakers Restaurant
Alfriston

R ♪ **Map 7 B6** East Sussex
High Street, Nr Polegate
Alfriston (0323) 870472
Credit none

Elaine Wilkinson cooks with skill, subtlety and a
pleasant lack of pretension in this cosy beamed
restaurant. Enjoy a glass of mulled wine in the bar-
lounge while perusing the menu. Carrot and
coriander soup is a delicious starter, and main
courses – served with plenty of varied vegetables
– run the gamut from poached fresh salmon and
roast duck with kumquats to lamb cassoulet with
a good tang of herbs. Sweets could include

blackcurrant ice cream and hot frangipan flan.
Excellent teas and filter coffee are served with
home-made truffles. Exciting wine list, strong
on burgundies and some other gems
(Sassicaia, Petaluma Riesling, Heitz Cabernet
Sauvignon).
▷ Outstanding ♀ Well-chosen ⊖

■ *About £36 for two*	*L by arrang. only*
Seats 32	*D 7–9.15, Sat 6.45–9.45*
Parties 32	*Parking Ample*
Closed L Sat, all Sun & Mon, Bank Hols exc.	
Good Fri & mid Jan–mid Feb	

315

Bishopfield *NEW ENTRY*   Allendale

H **63% £F**
Map 15 B4 Northumberland
Hexham NE47 9EJ
Allendale (043 483) 248
Owner managers Keith & Kathy Fairless
Credit Access, Diners

There's a warm, family atmosphere at this handsome Georgian farmhouse on the B6295, a mile outside Allendale. Three spacious bedrooms

are in the main building, while a converted milking byre houses six further rooms, plus an attractive lounge and snooker room. No dogs.
Amenities garden, coarse fishing, snooker.

■ *Rooms* 9	*Confirm by* arrang.
en suite bath/shower 9	*Last dinner* 8
Direct dial Yes	*Parking* Ample
Room TV Yes	*Room service* All day
Closed 1 wk Xmas & all Feb	

Hotspur Hotel   Alnwick

H **54% £E**
Map 14 B3 Northumberland
Bondgate Without NE66 1PR
Alnwick (0665) 602924
Credit Access, Visa

Modest it may be, but this one-time coaching inn is a very acceptable place for an overnight stay. The atmosphere is lively and friendly, particularly in the Billy Bones Buttery. There's

another bar, a sunny lounge and a TV room. Bedrooms have neat fitted units, tea-makers and bedside consoles; a few at the back open on to a garden. Well-kept bathrooms. *Amenities* garden.

■ *Rooms* 28	*Confirm by* arrang.
en suite bath/shower 18	*Last dinner* 9
Direct dial Yes	*Parking* Ample
Room TV Yes	*Room service* None
Closed 25 Dec & 1 Jan	

White Swan Hotel   Alnwick

H **58% £D/E**
Map 14 B3 Northumberland
Bondgate Within NE66 1TD
Alnwick (0665) 602109
Credit Access, Amex, Diners, Visa. **LVs**

The cheerful, young general manager contributes greatly to the happy atmosphere in this traditional town-centre coaching inn. The stylishly revamped bar holds a fine collection of fly

fishing rods, and the splendid function room is clad with panelling salvaged from the Titanic's sister ship the Olympic. Simply appointed bedrooms and bathrooms are gradually being refurbished. *Amenities* garden, laundry service.

■ *Rooms* 41	*Confirm by* 6
en suite bath/shower 40	*Last dinner* 9
Direct dial Yes	*Parking* Ample
Room TV Yes	*Room service* 24 hours

■ Our inspectors are our full-
time employees; they are
professionally trained by us.

Manor House Hotel   Alsager

H **60% £E**
Map 10 B3 Cheshire
Audley Road ST7 2QQ
Alsager (093 63) 78013
Credit Access, Amex, Diners, Visa

An old farmhouse and associated buildings are the basis of this friendly hotel just a short drive from the M6. Eight traditionally styled bedrooms in what was the old barn have been supplemented

by 20 smart new rooms with carved freestanding furniture, plain walls and chunky carpets. There's also a comfortable new lounge to add to the beamy bar. No dogs. *Amenities* garden, laundry service.

■ *Rooms* 28	*Confirm by* arrang.
en suite bath/shower 28	*Last dinner* 9.30
Direct dial Yes	*Parking* Ample
Room TV Yes	*Room service* All day

Grange Hotel   Alton

H **59% £E**
Map 5 D3 Hampshire
London Road, Holybourne GU34 4EG
Alton (0420) 86565
Owner managers Andrea & David Levene
Credit Access, Amex, Diners, Visa

The M3 is within easy reach of this homely hotel set in attractive gardens on the outskirts of Alton. Pleasant public rooms range from a cheerful

foyer-lounge to a little sun room overlooking the terrace. Simply furnished bedrooms have pretty duvets, tea-makers and radio-alarms.
Amenities garden, outdoor swimming pool, putting, laundry service, children's play area.

■ *Rooms* 15	*Confirm by* arrang.
en suite bath/shower 15	*Last dinner* 9
Room phone Yes	*Parking* Ample
Room TV Yes	*Room service* All day

Swan Hotel

Alton

H **58%** **£D/E**
Map 5 D3 Hampshire
High Street GU34 1AT
Alton (0420) 83777
Credit Access, Amex, Diners, Visa. **LVs**
   A former coaching inn whose history can be
traced back to 1554, the Swan has an assortment
of rooms of varying sizes and shapes. This is
charming in the bedrooms, with their pretty

furnishings and free-standing furniture, but can
create difficulties in public rooms like the long,
narrow lounge. Bedrooms have TVs, tea-making
facilities and direct-dial telephones.
Amenities laundry service.

■ *Rooms* 38	Confirm by 6
en suite bath/shower 38	Last dinner 9.30
Direct dial Yes	Parking Ample
Room TV Yes	Room service Limited

■ We welcome complaints and bona
fide recommendations on the
tear-out pages for readers' comments.
They are followed up by our professional
team. Please also complain to the
management instantly.

RECEPTION

Bowdon Hotel

Altrincham

H **57%** **£D/E**
Map 10 B2 Greater Manchester
Langham Road, Bowdon WA14 2HT
061-928 7121. Tlx 668208
Manager Mr B. Kilcoyne
Credit Access, Amex, Diners, Visa
   On the outskirts of town, the Bowdon
comprises a sturdy Victorian house and a modern
bedroom extension, with plans under way for an

additional one. Public areas like the lounge and
comfortable bar are modestly equipped.
Bedrooms are generally furnished in straightforward contemporary style; bathrooms have
showers over tubs. *Amenities* laundry service.'

■ *Rooms* 41	Confirm by 6
en suite bath/shower 38	Last dinner 10
Direct dial Yes	Parking Ample
Room TV Yes	Room service 24 hours

Cresta Court Hotel

Altrincham

H **59%** **£E**
Map 10 B2 Greater Manchester
Church Street WA14 4DP
061-928 8017. Tlx 667242
Manager Mr D. Roe
Credit Access, Amex, Diners, Visa. **LVs**
   Standing on the main A56, this 1970s hotel is a
red-brick building on four floors. The lobby-lounge
is quite roomy, and there are two bars and several

function suites. Simply furnished bedrooms –
open hanging space but no wardrobes – offer a
good range of accessories, including trouser
presses, hairdryers and remote-control TVs.
Amenities in-house movies (free), laundry service.

■ *Rooms* 139	Confirm by 6
en suite bath/shower 138	Last dinner 11
Direct dial Yes	Parking Ample
Room TV Yes	Room service 24 hours

George & Dragon Hotel

Altrincham

H **59%** **£D/E**
Map 10 B2 Greater Manchester
26 Manchester Road WA14 4PH
061-928 9933. Tlx 665051
Credit Access, Amex, Diners, Visa. **LVs**
   A former coaching inn on the A56. The foyer is
rather functional and there's no separate lounge,
but the recently redecorated main bar provides
ample space for relaxing, and there's a little public

bar. Bedrooms in the newer wing are decorated in
soft pastel shades and have decent freestanding
furniture; main-house rooms, some in similar style,
others a bit dated, are generally a little roomier.
Amenities laundry service.

■ *Rooms* 47	Confirm by arrang.
en suite bath/shower 47	Last dinner 9.45
Direct dial Yes	Parking Ample
Room TV Yes	Room service All day

Alveston House Hotel

Alveston

H **63%** **£D/E**
Map 4 B2 Avon
Nr Bristol BS12 2LJ
Thornbury (0454) 415050. Tlx 449212
Owner manager Mr M. Bland
Credit Access, Visa
   Just five minutes from the junction of the M4
and M5 motorways, this extended period house is
a popular overnight stopping place. Up-to-date

bedrooms (mainly singles) offer tea-makers and
carpeted bathrooms. Downstairs, guests can relax
on smart modern chesterfields in the comfortable lounge, or enjoy a drink amid the greenery in
the conservatory-style bar. *Amenities* garden.

■ *Rooms* 30	Confirm by arrang.
en suite bath/shower 30	Last dinner 9.30
Direct dial Yes	Parking Ample
Room TV Yes	Room service All day

Post House Hotel — Alveston

H 60% £C/D
Map 4 B2 Avon
Thornbury Road, Nr Bristol B12 2LL
Thornbury (0454) 412521. Tlx 444753
Credit Access, Amex, Diners, Visa. **LVs**

A much-extended Tudor inn located on the A38. Reminders of the past are most evident in the public bar, which has old beams, cosy nooks and an open fireplace. Best of the bedroom extensions is the most recent: rooms have fitted units, attractive furnishings and extras like tea-makers and mini-bars. *Amenities* garden, outdoor swimming pool, pitch & putt, laundry service, 24-hour lounge service.

■ *Rooms* 75	*Confirm by* 6
en suite bath/shower 75	*Last dinner* 10
Direct dial Yes	*Parking* Ample
Room TV Yes	*Room service* None

Amberley Inn — Amberley

H 56% £E
Map 4 B2 Gloucestershire
Nr Stroud GL5 5AF
Amberley (045 387) 2565
Credit Access, Amex, Visa

Splendidly traditional surroundings are the attraction of this sturdy stone-built inn high up on Minchinhampton Common. A log fire warms the entrance hall, and residents can toast themselves in the delightful panelled bar with its mullioned windows or relax in the comfortable lounge. The bedrooms are pretty and homely. *Amenities* garden.

■ *Rooms* 14	*Confirm by* 6
en suite bath/shower 13	*Last dinner* 9.30
Room phone Yes	*Parking* Ample
Room TV Yes	*Room service* Limited

■ Changes in data may occur in establishments after the Guide goes to press. Prices should be taken as indications rather than firm quotes.

Kirkstone Foot Hotel — Ambleside

HR 65% £E
Map 13 D5 Cumbria
Kirkstone Pass Road LA22 9EH
Ambleside (05394) 32232
Owner managers Jane and Simon Bateman
Credit Access, Amex, Diners, Visa

The Batemans see that everything is spotless at their converted manor house, a favourite base for walking, touring or simply staying put. Public rooms include a cosy bar and a quiet lounge. Bedrooms combine traditional appeal and modern comfort. No dogs. *Amenities* garden, croquet, laundry service.

■ *Rooms* 16	*Confirm by* arrang.
en suite bath/shower 16	*Last dinner* 8
Direct dial Yes	*Parking* Ample
Room TV Yes	*Room service* None
Closed 29 Nov–11 Feb	

Kirkstone Foot Hotel Restaurant ♿

English cooking
Dinner starts at 8 o'clock and proceeds at the same pace at each table. Carefully cooked five-course meals begin on a fishy note (prawn and egg mousse, whiting with fennel sauce) and continue via soup with hot rolls to the main course, usually a roast. Good, fresh vegetables. Some rather good sweets (the only course with choice) – such as cheesecake with a good crisp base and excellent flavour. Well-kept English cheeses, then coffee and home-made chocolates in the lounge. No smoking in the restaurant. ℮

■ *Set D* £12·50	*D* 7.30 for 8
About £33 for two	*Seats* 60
Closed 29 Nov–11 Feb	*Parties* 12

Nanny Brow — Ambleside

H 60% £E ♿
Map 13 D5 Cumbria
Clappersgate LA22 9NF
Ambleside (05394) 32036
Owner managers Geoff & Cheryl Kershaw
Credit Access, Visa

Perched on a hillside just west of Ambleside, Nanny Brow numbers its superb gardens and lovely valley views among its attractions. The main part was built in 1908, and its leaded windows and creeper-clad walls are most appealing. The lounge, done out in various shades of green, is a good place to curl up with a book, and there's a pleasant bar that opens on to a patio. Main-house bedrooms are comfortably traditional, with an assortment of nice old furniture; garden wing rooms have separate sitting rooms, and some even have their own little kitchens. Modern bathrooms.
Amenities garden, solarium, whirlpool bath, coarse fishing, games room, snooker.

■ *Rooms* 18	*Confirm by* 6
en suite bath/shower 17	*Last dinner* 8
Direct dial Yes	*Parking* Ample
Room TV Yes	*Room service* Limited

Rothay Manor · Ambleside

HR **71% £C/D**
Map 13 D5 Cumbria
Rothay Bridge LA22 0EH
Ambleside (053 94) 33605
Owner managers Nigel & Stephen Nixon
Credit Access, Amex, Diners, Visa

A verandah with cast-iron railings, a splendid doorway and an unusual glasshouse are among the original features remaining at this fine old Regency hotel. Family-run, Rothay manor maintains a warm and friendly atmosphere. Period details, including some antiques, are also included in the comfortable lounge and bar, where paintings and fresh flowers add a homely note. Books, fresh fruit, magazines and electric blankets are typically thoughtful extras in the good-sized bedrooms, many with bespoke pine

furnishings. All have smart modern bathrooms. One of the two lodge suites in the grounds is suitable for wheelchairs. No dogs.
Amenities garden, croquet, laundry service.
■ *Rooms* 18   *Confirm by arrang.*
en suite bath/shower 18   *Last dinner* 9
Direct dial Yes   *Parking* Ample
Room TV Yes   *Room service* All day
Closed early Jan–mid Feb

Rothay Manor Restaurant ⌬ &

Two smartly appointed formal dining rooms with strong period feel provide an elegant setting for Jane Binns' capably-prepared set dinners. Potted Stilton might precede cream of pepper soup, to be followed by sole Colbert or guinea fowl Normande. Good vegetables. Tempting sweets such as traditional trifle or spiced apple cake and excellent English cheeses to finish. Buffet lunches except for Sunday. No smoking.   ♀ **Well-chosen** ⊖
■ *Set L* £9   *L* 12.30–2,
Set D £17·50   *Sun* 12.45–1.30
About £48 for two   *D* 8–9
Seats 60   *Parties* 30
Closed early Jan–mid Feb

Wateredge Hotel · Ambleside

H **60% £D/E**
Map 13 D5 Cumbria
Borrans Road LA22 0EP
Ambleside (0966) 32332
Owner managers Mr & Mrs D. Cowap
Credit Access, Visa

A lakeside hotel – originally two fishermen's cottages. There's a cosy bar with beams, and three pleasant lounges with splendid views of the

lake and the fells. Bedrooms and bathrooms have all been redecorated, and there are five new suites. Half board only. No under 7s. *Amenities* garden, coarse fishing, boating, laundry service.
■ *Rooms* 23   *Confirm by* 5
en suite bath/shower 23   *Last dinner* 8
Direct dial Yes   *Parking* Ample
Room TV Some   *Room service* Limited
Closed Dec–Jan

Potters Heron Hotel · Ampfield

H **60% £D/E** &
Map 5 D3 Hampshire
Nr Romsey SO51 9ZF
Chandler's Ford (042 15) 66611. Tlx 47459
Manager Mr A. J. Flemming
Credit Access, Amex, Diners, Visa

Rustic features add charm to the refurbished public rooms of this thatched hotel on the A31, where guests can relax in a cosy lounge or smart

cocktail bar. Bedrooms, many with patios or balconies, are in modern style, with en suite bathrooms. No dogs. *Amenities* garden, sauna, keep-fit equipment, snooker room, laundry service, in-house movies (free).
■ *Rooms* 60   *Confirm by arrang.*
en suite bath/shower 60   *Last dinner* 10
Direct dial Yes   *Parking* Ample
Room TV Yes   *Room service* Limited

White Hart Hotel · Andover

I **£D/E**
Map 4 C3 Hampshire
Bridge Street SP10 1BH
Andover (0264) 52266
Manager Mr A. Lass
Credit Access, Amex, Diners, Visa. LVs

A pleasant, town-centre inn with a friendly atmosphere, some character and modest but acceptable overnight accommodation. Bedrooms

vary in size, shape and decor, but all have decent bathrooms with coloured modern suites, and good towels. The open-plan bar-lounge area has some nice old country furnishings, and there's an oak-panelled function room.
■ *Rooms* 21   *Confirm by* 6
en suite bath/shower 21   *Last dinner* 9.30
Room phone Yes   *Parking* Limited
Room TV Yes   *Room service* Limited

Underscar Hotel   Applethwaite

H **63% £D**
Map 13 C5 Cumbria
Nr Keswick CA12 4PH
Keswick (07687) 72469. Tlx 64354
Credit Access, Amex, Diners
  Built in 1860, this handsome Italianate house
enjoys breathtaking views of Derwentwater.
Public rooms include a domed and galleried hall
and have fine fabrics, mouldings, and chandeliers.

Comfortable bedrooms have good carpeted
bathrooms (two shower only); stable block rooms
have showers. *Amenities* garden, putting,
croquet, laundry service.

■ *Rooms* 18	*Confirm by* arrang.
en suite bath/shower 18	*Last dinner* 8.30
Direct dial Yes	*Parking* Ample
Room TV Yes	*Room service* All day
Closed Dec–mid Feb	

Norfolk Arms Hotel   Arundel

H **61% £D/E** &
Map 5 E4 West Sussex
22 High Street BN18 9AD
Arundel (0903) 882101. Tlx 878436
Manager David Horridge
Credit Access, Amex, Diners, Visa
  A Georgian coaching inn built by the tenth
Duke of Norfolk. Bedrooms are traditional in the
main part, more modern in the courtyard block; all

are comfortable and well equipped, and have neat
carpeted bathrooms. Pleasant day rooms include
a comfortable lounge and bar.
Amenities games room, in-house movies (free),
laundry service.

■ *Rooms* 34	*Confirm by* 6
en suite bath/shower 34	*Last dinner* 10
Direct dial Yes	*Parking* Ample
Room TV Yes	*Room service* All day

Berystede Hotel   Ascot

H **68% £C**
Map 5 E2 Berkshire
Bagshot Road, Sunninghill SL5 9JH
Ascot (0990) 23311. Tlx 847707
Credit Access, Amex, Diners, Visa
  An elegant foyer-lounge featuring a fine oak
staircase and an elaborate gilt chandelier sets the
gracious tone of this well-run hotel, a turreted
Victorian mansion with modern additions. There's
also a relaxing bar with comfortable sofas,
paintings of racehorses and views over the
terraced lawns and woods beyond. Characterful
main-house bedrooms, including four luxurious

turret rooms with antique beds, are particularly
pleasing, though all rooms are stylishly furnished
and well equipped. Remote-control TVs, radios
and tea-makers are standard. Good modern
bathrooms throughout.
Amenities garden, outdoor swimming pool, golf
practice net, putting, croquet, games room, pool
table, in-house movies (free), laundry service, 24-
hour lounge service.

■ *Rooms* 88	*Confirm by* 6
en suite bath/shower 88	*Last dinner* 9.45
Room phone Yes	*Parking* Ample
Room TV Yes	*Room service* 24 hours

Royal Berkshire   Ascot

HR **77% £B** *E*
Map 5 E2 Berkshire
London Rd, Sunninghill SL5 0PP
Ascot (0990) 23322. Tlx 847280
Credit Access, Amex, Diners, Visa
  For more than a century, this mellow red-brick
Queen Anne mansion was the home of the
Churchill family. Today a wider audience
appreciates the beautifully proportioned public
rooms with their fine views of the 15-acre grounds.
The original panelling has been drag-painted a
pale blue grey to provide a stylish backdrop for
comfortable chairs and sofas. Bedrooms, all very
spacious and attractive, have good quality
lightwood furniture and accessories like trouser

presses, remote-control TVs and stationery.
Bathrooms have good towels and complimentary
toiletries. *Amenities* garden, indoor swimming
pool, sauna, whirlpool bath, keep-fit equipment,
tennis, squash, putting, croquet, laundry service,
24-hour lounge service, helipad.

■ *Rooms* 65	*Confirm by* 6
en suite bath/shower 65	*Last dinner* 9.30
Direct dial Yes	*Parking* Ample
Room TV Yes	*Room service* 24 hours

Royal Berkshire
Restaurant ★ ♛

An attractive setting, smooth attentive service
and outstanding cooking help to make this an
exceptional establishment. Jonathan Fraser is a
highly talented chef in the modern style. His well-
conceived dishes are expertly executed and
attractively presented on a range of colourful
plates made by a local potter. Ingredients are of
the finest quality. Our inspector had only praise
for his monkfish galette and perfectly-cooked loin
of beef topped with crunchy marrow glaze served
with a subtle cream sauce. He voted the Bramley
apple charlotte 'scrumptious' and lauded the all-

English cheeseboard. The well-annotated list embraces interesting wines from around the world. *Specialities* scallop and truffle galette with a Pommery butter sauce, grilled foie gras with fresh raspberries and ginger sauce, roast wild duck with orange sauce, rhubarb pudding spiked with pastis and served with iced vanilla cream.
♀ Well-chosen ℮

■ *Set L £14·50*	*L 12.30–2*
Set D £21	*D 7.30–9.30*
About £80 for two	*Parking Ample*
Seats 46	*Parties 75*

Wychwood Arms Hotel — Ascott-under-Wychwood

I £E
Map 4 C1 Oxfordshire
OX7 6AN
Shipton-u-Wychwood (0993) 830271
Owner managers John & Julie Ingram-Johnson
Credit Access, Amex, Diners, Visa

The bedrooms at this agreeable Cotswold-stone inn facing the village green now sport new pine furniture in cottage style with nicely coordinated fabrics, trouser presses and hairdryers. The residents' lounge is a plant-screened part of the bar. No under tens. No dogs.
Amenities garden, laundry service.

■ *Rooms 5*	*Confirm by 5*
en suite bath/shower 5	*Last dinner 10*
Room phone No	*Parking Ample*
Room TV Yes	*Room service Limited*
Closed 1st 2 weeks Jan	

Callow Hall *NEW ENTRY* — Ashbourne

RR ♕ ♿ **Map 10 C3** Derbyshire
Mappleton Road DE6 2AA
Ashbourne (0335) 43403
Credit Access, Amex, Diners, Visa

Callow Hall is an imposing house standing in beautiful countryside above the valleys of Bentley Brook and the river Dove. In the traditionally appointed restaurant chef-patron David Spencer offers a regularly changing menu featuring enjoyable dishes like dried duck and avocado salad, medallions of monkfish with pink peppercorn sauce and breast of chicken cooked en papillote with a fresh herb cream. Sunday lunch includes traditional roasts. There's a sound wine list, with excellent Beaujolais from Louis Tête. ♀ Well-chosen ℮

■ *Set L £8·50*	*L Sun only 12.30–1.30*
Set D £15·50	*D 7.30–9.30*
About £40 for two	*Parking Ample*
Seats 60	*Parties 60*
Closed D Sun, all Mon, Bank Hols & 2 wks Feb	

Bedrooms £E/F

Rooms 9	*With bath/shower 3*

The bedrooms are roomy and comfortable, with traditional furnishings and splendid views; three already have private facilities – more will follow.

Eastwell Manor — Ashford

HR **82% £C/D**
Map 7 C5 Kent
Eastwell Park, Boughton Aluph TN25 4HR
Ashford (0233) 35751. Tlx 966281
Credit Access, Amex, Diners, Visa

Rolling parkland that includes a two-mile stretch of the Pilgrims' Way and immaculate formal gardens provides an appropriate setting for this splendid country-house mansion with historic origins, built to a Tudor style in the 1920s. An impressive gatehouse guards the entrance to a flagstoned courtyard that leads to spacious public rooms with carved stone fireplaces. Inviting chesterfields and armchairs are in the large bar and oak-panelled lounge which, like the conference room, has a fine moulded ceiling. A handsome oak staircase leads to good-sized, very comfortable bedrooms, each with its own sitting room and characterful bathroom. No dogs.
Amenities garden, tennis, croquet, billiards, snooker, laundry service, 24-hour lounge service.

■ *Rooms 24*	*Confirm by arrang.*
en suite bath/shower 24	*Last dinner 9.30*
Direct dial Yes	*Parking Ample*
Room TV Yes	*Room service 24 hours*

Eastwell Manor Restaurant ⌣ ♿

Chef Anthony Blake comes up with some imaginative dishes that combine classical and modern cuisine for this baronial dining room, with its lofty, heavily-beamed ceiling. Main courses range from steamed sea bass with a mussel sauce to medallions of venison in a sage and Calvados sauce. Tempting sweets include a tangerine soufflé filled with lemon curd served with thick orange Curaçao cream.
♀ Well-chosen ℮

■ *Set L £12, Sun £12·50*	*L 12.30–2*
Set D £17	*D 7.30–9.30,*
About £65 for two	*Sat 7.30–10*
Seats 75	*Parties 30*

Terraza

R **Map 5 E2** Middlesex
45 Church Road
Ashford (078 42) 244887
Italian cooking
Owner managers A. Cepollina & E. Maffi
Credit Access, Amex, Diners, Visa

Flavours are robust and portions generous at this neat, popular, high street restaurant. Tempting trolleys of antipasti, seafood and sweets are a fitting introduction to the long, interesting menu of reliably prepared Italian dishes, ranging from tasty pasta to scampi alla diavola, fegato alla Veneziana, chicken sorpresa and steaks from the grill. ⊖

■ *Set L & D £13·75*   *L 12–2.30*
About £48 for two   *D 7–10.30*
Seats 65 Parties 65   *Parking Ample*
Closed L Sat, all Sun & Bank Hols

Riverside Country House Hotel

HR **62% £D/E**
Map 10 C2 Derbyshire
Fennell Street DE4 1QF
Bakewell (062 981) 4275
Owner managers Roger & Susan Taylor
Credit Access, Amex, Visa

A peaceful riverbank and garden setting is just one of the attractions of the Taylors' converted period home. The welcoming panelled hallway doubles as a bar, and the relaxing lounge enjoys lovely views. Individually decorated bedrooms, many featuring antique furnishings, all have good modern bathrooms. No children.
Amenities garden, laundry service.

■ *Rooms 7*   *Confirm by arrang.*
en suite bath/shower 7 *Last dinner 9.30*
Direct dial Yes   *Parking Ample*
Room TV Yes   *Room service All day*

Riverside Hotel Restaurant &

The nicely-balanced menus change frequently at this comfortably traditional restaurant, offering a successful blend of simple and more elaborate dishes. Home-made soup, pork and herb terrine or smoked trout mousseline could precede guinea fowl in a rich Madeira sauce, an impressive seafood platter accompanied by a creamy chive sauce, or juicy sirloin steak. Excellent vegetables and delicious sweets like pineapple shortcake and homemade sorbets to finish. ⊖

■ *Set L £8·20*   *L Sun only at 1*
Set D from £16   *D 7–9.30*
About £45 for two   *Seats 50 Parties 50*
Closed D Sun to non-residents

■ We publish annually, so make sure you use the current edition. It's worth it!

Mill House Hotel

I **£D/E**
Map 5 E3 West Sussex
Mill Lane RH20 3BZ
Ashington (0903) 892426
Owner managers Mr & Mrs E. Falconer Wright
Credit Access, Amex, Diners, Visa

A rustic lane leads to this attractive family-run inn, where hospitality and comfort top the list of priorities. Guests can enjoy a drink in the cosy cocktail bar that overlooks the garden, or relax by the fire in the lounge. Compact bedrooms with traditional furnishings and homely charm.
Amenities garden, laundry service.

■ *Rooms 10*   *Confirm by arrang.*
en suite bath/shower 8 *Last dinner 10*
Direct dial Yes   *Parking Ample*
Room TV Yes   *Room service Limited*
Closed 25 & 26 Dec

Queen's Head Inn

I **£E/F**
Map 13 D5 Cumbria
Nr Penrith CA10 2PF
Hackthorpe (093 12) 225
Managers John & Anne Askew

A 17th-century inn with a delightful lounge bar that boasts old beams, open fires, copper kettles and horse brasses. Children are allowed in a second bar. The residents' lounge is a homely room, with some nice antiques. Bright, well-kept bedrooms are simply furnished, and there are two smart bathrooms. The model railway in the garden will please children and adults alike. No dogs.
Amenities terrace.

■ *Rooms 6*   *Confirm by arrang.*
en suite bath/shower 0 *Last dinner 7.30*
Room phone No   *Parking Ample*
Room TV No   *Room service All day*

Bell Inn   Aston Clinton

HR 74% £B/C
Map 5 E2 Buckinghamshire
London Road HP22 5HP
Aylesbury (0296) 630252. Tlx 83252
Owner manager Michael Harris
Credit Access, Visa

The original house dates from the 17th century, and the whole place has a splendidly traditional appeal. Michael Harris, owner for 20 years, provides a genuinely warm welcome, and service is invariably courteous. The flagstoned bar and smoking room recall coaching days, and guests find relaxation an easy matter in the inviting oak-panelled drawing room. Fine furnishings and lovely fabrics extend to the bedrooms – six in the house, the others set around a courtyard. Decor and appointments are individual, but thoughtful

extras ranging from potpourris to mini-bars are to be found throughout, along with sumptuous bathrooms. *Amenities* garden, croquet, laundry service, helipad.

■ *Rooms* 21	*Confirm by arrang.*
en suite bath/shower 21	*Last dinner 9.45*
Direct dial Yes	*Parking* Ample
Room TV Yes	*Room service* All day

Bell Inn Restaurant ☖ ♿

Young Kevin Cape, formerly at the Connaught, is making his mark at this charming restaurant whose walls are decorated with delightful pastoral scenes. Old favourites like Bell Inn smokies and Aylesbury duckling stay on the menu, along with a roast carved on the trolley. Other excellent choices include a trio of pâtés (fish, vegetable, meat) and succulent escalope of guinea fowl with a lovely truffle-specked sauce. Desserts might include a well-laced and very enjoyable tipsy pudding. A model cellar includes exceptional Bordeaux and a careful selection of the best Italian wines. Michael Harris presides with charm, and service throughout shows a high degree of polish and professionalism.

🗢 Outstanding ♟ Well-chosen ☺

■ *Set L from £12·50,*	*L 12.30–1.45*
Mon £15, Sun £18·50	*D 7.30–9.45*
Set D Sun & Mon £15	*Seats* 120
About £64 for two	*Parties* 200

Oak House   Axbridge

I £E
Map 4 A3 Somerset
The Square BS26 2AP
Axbridge (0934) 732444
Owner managers Douglas & Therese Hack
Credit Access, Amex, Diners, Visa

A charming inn of great character on a picture-book market square. Go-ahead new owners have already begun making improvements, starting

with new stair and hallway carpets and a direct-dial telephone system for the comfortable, cottagey bedrooms. Next in line is the rustic bar-lounge. No dogs. *Amenities* laundry service.

■ *Rooms* 9	*Confirm by arrang.*
en suite bath/shower 7	*Last dinner 9.30*
Direct dial Yes	*Parking* Ample
Room TV Yes	*Room service* All day
Closed 1 wk Xmas	

Bell Hotel   Aylesbury

H 59% £C/D
Map 5 D2 Buckinghamshire
Market Square HP20 1TX
Aylesbury (0296) 89835
Credit Access, Amex, Diners, Visa. **LVs**

Located in a corner of the market square, the beamed bar of this friendly hotel is a popular meeting place for locals. There's a club-style lounge bar, too, with a relaxing, traditional

atmosphere. Bedrooms are prettily decorated in shades of sage green, and are furnished with simple wooden units and attractive brass lights. All have tea-makers and neat bathrooms. *Amenities* laundry service.

■ *Rooms* 17	*Confirm by* 6
en suite bath/shower 17	*Last dinner 9.30*
Direct dial Yes	*Parking* Difficult
Room TV Yes	*Room service* Limited

Pebbles   Aylesbury

R ☖ ♟ **Map 5 D2** Buckinghamshire
Pebble Lane
Aylesbury (0296) 86622
Credit Access, Amex, Diners, Visa

The menu changes seasonally at this pretty, beamed restaurant, where David Cavalier's cooking is serious, skilful and enthusiastic. Typical dishes are galantine of wild rabbit with a port wine and prune confit; warm salad of veal

sweetbreads and asparagus on a sorrel butter sauce; pot-roasted baby quail with Stilton mousse and muscat sauce. ☺

■ *Set L* £12·50	*L* 12–2
Set D from £15	*D* 7–10,
About £44 for two	*Fri & Sat* 7–10.30
Seats 26 *Parties* 18	*Parking* Limited
Closed L Sat, D Sun, all Mon, 3 wks Aug & 1 wk Xmas	

Pennyhill Park Hotel   Bagshot

H **78% £C**
Map 5 E3 Surrey
College Ride GU19 5ET
Bagshot (0276) 71774. Tlx 858841
Credit Access, Amex, Diners, Visa

Turn off the A30 by the 'Hope' pub to find this creeper-clad country house set in lovely terraced gardens and parkland. The main strength is undoubtedly the bedrooms, which are very spacious (many have separate sitting areas) and all individually and stylishly appointed, with lovely fabrics and good, mainly reproduction, furniture. Accessories include teletext TVs, and a glass of sherry is offered on arrival. Bathrooms are superb, too, with high-quality towelling and toiletries and, in many cases, separate proper shower cubicles. The majority also have TVs (yes, in the bathrooms – presumably for watching soap operas!). The only lounge area, apart from some seating in the entrance hall, is a pleasant little sun-trap conservatory. There's also a comfortable and

characterful Tudor-style bar. *Amenities* garden, outdoor swimming pool, sauna, keep-fit equipment, tennis, 9-hole golf course, putting, riding, stabling, clay-pigeon shooting, game fishing, laundry service, 24-hour lounge service, helipad.

■ *Rooms* 48	*Confirm by* arrang.
en suite bath/shower 48	*Last dinner* 10.30
Direct dial Yes	*Parking* Ample
Room TV Yes	*Room service* 24 hours

Rose & Crown Hotel *NEW ENTRY*   Bainbridge

I **£E**
Map 15 B6 North Yorkshire
Nr Leyburn DL8 3EE
Wensleydale (0969) 50225
Owner manager Penny Thorpe
Credit Access, Visa

Dating back to the 15th century, the Rose & Crown overlooks the village green. In the entry stands the famous Bainbridge horn, traditionally

blown to guide lost travellers. There are several cosy little bar and lounge areas, and a larger bar with pub games. Well-kept bedrooms are comfortably furnished; three have four-posters. *Amenities* pool table.

■ *Rooms* 13	*Confirm by* 6
en suite bath/shower 11	*Last dinner* 9.15
Room phone No	*Parking* Ample
Room TV Yes	*Room service* None

Fischer's ★   Bakewell

R ★ ♨ ♋ ♿ **Map 10 C2** Derbyshire
Woodhouse, Bath Street
Bakewell (062 981) 2687
Credit Access, Amex, Diners, Visa

Max Fischer's enthusiasm continues unabated; a meal in ths sophisticated but very unpretentious stone-walled restaurant is a delightful experience from the first mouthful to the last. Fish and game terrines make a memorable start, and main courses like crown of salmon and turbot with chervil sauce, veal fillet with Stilton sauce or rack of venison with game pepper sauce and French wild mushrooms are accompanied by copious fresh vegetables. There's a good cheeseboard, and mille-feuille with dark and white chocolate is a sensational sweet. Tempting home-made chocolates are served with coffee. Interesting wines including splendid Brouilly Pissevieille 1985 (Gobet) and Kiedricher Wasseros Riesling Spätlese 1983. Max's wife Susan runs front of house with great warmth and friendliness.

Specialities game terrine, galantine of salmon with fresh herb sauce, fillet of sea bass with tomato sauce and ginger, roast saddle of spring lamb with herbs and garlic, the best of game (breast of wild duck and pheasant served with a medallion of venison). ☺

■ *Set L from* £7·50	*L* 12–2
About £48 *for two*	*D* 7.30–9.30
Seats 35 *Parties* 14	*Parking* Ample
Closed L Sat, D Sun, all Mon, Bank Hols, last wk Aug, 1st wk Sept & 2 wks Xmas	

■ Our inspectors never book in the name of Egon Ronay's Guides; they disclose their identity only after paying their bills.

Hassop Hall Hotel   Bakewell

H **77% £C/D**
Map 10 C2 Derbyshire
Hassop DE4 1NS
Great Longstone (062 987) 488. Tlx 378485
Owner manager Mr T. H. Chapman
Credit Access, Amex, Diners, Visa

Love and care are lavished on this handsome building, whose history is documented back to the Domesday Book. It's set in beautiful countryside, and its grounds include a secluded Italian garden. Beyond the flagstoned entrance hall, various spacious rooms are used as lounges or function rooms, and there's a fine oak-panelled bar. Antiques, oils and crackling log fires contribute to the delightful ambience. Good-sized bedrooms are decorated and furnished in appropriate style, and the monogrammed bed linen is a lovely touch. Bathrooms are

sumptuously fitted. Breakfast is normally served in the bedrooms. No dogs. *Amenities* garden, tennis, croquet, laundry service, helipad.

■ *Rooms* 12	*Confirm by arrang.*
en suite bath/shower 12	*Last dinner 9.30*
Direct dial Yes	*Parking* Ample
Room TV Yes	*Room service* All day
Closed 2 days Xmas	

■ If we recommend meals in a hotel or inn, a separate entry is made for its restaurant.

Lord Crewe Arms Hotel   Bamburgh

H **57% £E/F**
Map 14 B2 Northumberland
Front Street NE69 7BL
Bamburgh (066 84) 243
Owner managers Mr & Mrs B. R. Holland

Friendly, very helpful owners create a welcoming country atmosphere at this neat hotel in the shadow of Bamburgh Castle. The two cosy lounges (one for non-smokers) and two beamed bars are most hospitable. Compact bedrooms with fitted units are well-kept. No children under five. *Amenities* coffee shop (10am–10pm in summer).

■ *Rooms* 25	*Confirm by* 5
en suite bath/shower 14	*Last dinner* 8.45
Room phone No	*Parking* Ample
Room TV Yes	*Room service* Limited
Closed end Oct–week before Easter	

Huntsham Court   Bampton

HR **72% £D**
Map 3 E2 Devon
Huntsham EX16 7NA
Clayhanger (039 86) 210
Owner managers Mogens & Andrea Bolwig
Credit Visa

A splendid welcome makes guests feel really at home as soon as they step inside the marble pillared hall of the Bolwigs' handsome Victorian mansion. Antiques abound in the relaxing lounge, drinks are serve-yourself in the cosy bar, and books, pianos and a huge collection of classical records create a pleasingly civilised atmosphere. Log fires crackle in the vast bedrooms (and in some of the bathrooms, too), in tune with pre-war radios and comfortingly old-fashioned furnishings (duvets apart). First-class breakfast. No dogs.

Amenities garden, sauna, solarium, keep-fit equipment, croquet, coarse & game fishing, bicycles, billiards, laundry service, 24-hour lounge service.

■ *Rooms* 15	*Confirm by arrang.*
en suite bath/shower 15	*Last dinner* 10
Room phone No	*Parking* Ample
Room TV No	*Room service* All day
Closed mid Jan–mid Feb	

Huntsham Court Restaurant 👑 ♧

English cooking

Guests are encouraged to choose their wine from the cellar before settling down round one large table to enjoy Andrea Bolwig's traditional English cooking. A typical set menu begins with soup and continues with fish (or perhaps sweetbreads), then roast lamb (or maybe duck or quail) and superb vegetables. Lovely cheeses and delicious puds to follow.

♀ Well-chosen ☙

■ *Set D* £18·50	*L by arrang. only*
About £48 for two	*D* 8–9.30
Seats 24	*Parties* 24
Closed mid Jan–mid Feb	

Banbury Moat House — Banbury

H 59% £D/E
Map 5 D1 Oxfordshire
27 Oxford Road OX16 9AH
Banbury (0295) 59361. Tlx 838967
Manager Mr J. M. Fowlds
Credit Access, Amex, Diners, Visa

Behind its white-painted Georgian facade, this hotel has been extensively modernised and provides an additional 22 bedrooms. Pleasantly decorated, all the rooms offer remote-control TVs, tea-makers and spacious, carpeted bathrooms. There's a comfortable lounge area in the foyer, and a cosy bar, too. *Amenities* clay-pigeon shooting, laundry service, 24-hour lounge service.

■ *Rooms 52* — *Confirm by 6*
en suite bath/shower 52 — *Last dinner 9.45*
Direct dial Yes — *Parking Ample*
Room TV Yes — *Room service 24 hours*

is our symbol for an **outstanding** wine list.

Whately Hall — Banbury

H 67% £C/D ♿
Map 5 D1 Oxfordshire
Banbury Cross OX16 0AN
Banbury (0295) 3451. Tlx 837149
Credit Access, Amex, Diners, Visa. LVs

A high standard of accommodation is provided at this Cotswold-stone hotel. Bedrooms have recently been smartly refurbished – attractive Italian furnishings, pastel shades, pretty co-ordinated fabrics – and all have well-stocked bathrooms. Day rooms offer an elegant ambience and deep-cushioned comfort. *Amenities* garden, croquet, games room, pool table, laundry service, coffee shop (9am–6pm), 24-hour lounge service.

■ *Rooms 74* — *Confirm by 6*
en suite bath/shower 74 — *Last dinner 10*
Direct dial Yes — *Parking Ample*
Room TV Yes — *Room service 24 hours*

Glebe Hotel *NEW ENTRY* — Barford

H 60% £D/E
Map 10 C4 Warwickshire
Church Street CV35 8BS
Warwick (0926) 624218
Owner managers Mr & Mrs J. M. Price
Credit Access, Amex, Diners, Visa

Once a rectory, the Glebe is a Georgian house standing in its own acre alongside the village church. It's a friendly hotel, and the bar and little residents' lounge are nice, peaceful places to while away an hour or two. Most of the decent-sized bedrooms are furnished in traditional style. Upgrading planned. No dogs. *Amenities* garden, laundry service.

■ *Rooms 15* — *Confirm by arrang.*
en suite bath/shower 13 — *Last dinner 9.30*
Direct dial Yes — *Parking Ample*
Room TV Yes — *Room service All day*

Jersey Farm Hotel — Barnard Castle

H 59% £F
Map 15 B5 Co. Durham
West Town Pastures, Darlington Rd DL12 8TA
Teesdale (0833) 38223
Owner manager Mr J. Watson

Take a signposted drive off the A67 to reach this modest, white-painted hotel, which is part of the cheerful Watson's working farm. Pretty, cottagy bedrooms with lovely views and thoughtful extras all have smart, spotless bath or shower rooms. There are 5 new suites in nearby cottages. Public rooms include a convivial cocktail lounge. *Amenities* garden, laundry service.

■ *Rooms 13* — *Confirm by arrang.*
en suite bath/shower 13 — *Last dinner 9*
Direct dial Yes — *Parking Ample*
Room TV Yes — *Room service All day*

■ For a discount on next year's guide, see Offer for Answers.

Ye Olde Bell — Barnby Moor

H 61% £C/D
Map 11 D2 Nottinghamshire
Nr Retford DN22 8QS
Retford (0777) 705121
Credit Access, Amex, Diners, Visa

Open fires, beams and traditional furnishings create a mellow, welcoming atmosphere in the lounge and bar of this former coaching inn on the A638. Equally appealing bedrooms, some with polished maghogany pieces (including two four-posters), others sporting smartly coordinated fabrics and colour schemes, offer tea-makers and private bath/shower rooms. *Amenities* garden, croquet, laundry service.

■ *Rooms 55* — *Confirm by 6*
en suite bath/shower 55 — *Last dinner 9.45*
Direct dial Yes — *Parking Ample*
Room TV Yes — *Room service Limited*

Barnham Broom Hotel   Barnham Broom

H **62%** **£D/E** 🔥
Map 6 C1 Norfolk
Honnington Road NR9 4DD
Barnham Broom (060 545) 393. Tlx 975711
Credit Access, Amex, Diners, Visa
    Sports facilities are superb at this lively modern
hotel set in peaceful Norfolk country. Two bars are
popular spots for elbow exercise, and
accommodation, including a new 12-bedroom

wing, is neat and practical. *Amenities* garden,
indoor & outdoor swimming pools, sauna,
solarium, beauty salon, hairdressing, tennis,
squash, golf course, putting, laundry service,
coffee shop (9am–11pm).

■ *Rooms* 52	*Confirm by arrang.*
en suite bath/shower 52	*Last dinner* 9.30
Direct dial Yes	*Parking* Ample
Room TV Yes	*Room service* Limited

TraveLodge   Barnsdale Bar

H **54%** **£E**
Map 11 D1 West Yorkshire
A1 Trunk Road, Nr Pontefract WF8 3JB
Pontefract (0977) 620711. Tlx 557457
Credit Access, Amex, Diners, Visa
    Practical overnight accommodation to suit both
business and family travellers is provided at this
neat modern hotel in a service area on the
southbound A1. All the neatly furnished bedrooms

are equipped with tea-makers, complimentary
soft drinks and remote-control TVs. Refurbished
rooms are brighter, with good deep carpets.
Limited lounge seating is available in the foyer.

■ *Rooms* 72	*Confirm by* 6
en suite bath/shower 72	*Last dinner* 10.15
Direct dial Yes	*Parking* Ample
Room TV Yes	*Room service* None

■ Any person using our name
to obtain free hospitality is
a fraud. Proprietors, please
inform the police and us.

Ardsley Moat House   Barnsley

H **66%** **£D/E**
Map 10 C2 South Yorkshire
Doncaster Road, Ardsley S71 5EH
Barnsley (0226) 289401. Tlx 547762
Manager Mr D. Petherbridge
Credit Access, Amex, Diners, Visa
    An 18th-century house is at the heart of this
much-extended hotel. There's a spacious foyer-
lounge with comfortable seating, a lively public

bar and an elegant cocktail bar. Bedrooms are
well equipped and pleasantly furnished, some
with four-posters. Carpeted bathrooms
throughout. *Amenities* garden, laundry service,
24-hour lounge service.

■ *Rooms* 62	*Confirm by* 6
en suite bath/shower 62	*Last dinner* 10.30
Direct dial Yes	*Parking* Ample
Room TV Yes	*Room service* 24 hours

Imperial Hotel   Barnstaple

H **59%** **£D**
Map 3 D2 Devon
Taw Vale Parade EX32 8NB
Barnstaple (0271) 45861
Credit Access, Amex, Diners, Visa. LVs
    An Edwardian hotel on the river Taw. The
elegant main lounge sometimes doubles as a
meeting room, but there's also an attractive cane-
furnished sun lounge. The public bar has a strong

seafaring theme, while the cocktail bar is smartly
contemporary. Bedrooms have fairly basic
furnishings and vary in size, but some have a
good range of extras. *Amenities* garden, laundry
service, 24-hour lounge service.

■ *Rooms* 56	*Confirm by* 6
en suite bath/shower 56	*Last dinner* 9.30
Room phone Yes	*Parking* Ample
Room TV Yes	*Room service* All day

Lynwood House   Barnstaple

R 🍷 **Map 3 D2** Devon
Bishop's Tawton Road
Barnstaple (0271) 43695
Credit Access, Visa
    The Roberts family run two restaurants in a
Victorian house, an informal downstairs room with
a simple menu of fish and meat dishes, and a
more stylish upstairs room where it's nearly all
fish. The emphasis is on good fresh ingredients,

and choice ranges from chunky fish soup and
grilled sprats to prawn-stuffed sole, wing of skate,
duckling pancakes and pork steak. Nice
meringues for sweet. 🍷 Well-chosen 🗓

■ *About £40 (upstairs)*	*L* 12.2
for two	*D* 7–9.30
About £32 (downstairs)	*Parking* Ample
Seats 50	*Parties* 60
Closed Sun & Bank Hols	

Crest Hotel   Basildon

H 59% £D
Map 7 B4 Essex
Cranes Farm Road SS14 3DG
Basildon (0268) 3955. Tlx 995141
Credit Access, Amex, Diners, Visa
   A modern hotel pleasantly situated by a lake, midway between Basildon town centre and the A127. There's a leafy foyer-lounge with comfortable contemporary seating. Bedrooms are

functional, with tea-makers and trouser presses, and most have hairdryers. Neat practical bathrooms. *Amenities* garden, putting, games room, pool table, laundry service, 24-hour lounge service.

■ *Rooms 116*	*Confirm by 6*
en suite bath/shower 116	*Last dinner 9.45*
Direct dial Yes	*Parking Ample*
Room TV Yes	*Room service 24 hours*

■ Our inspectors are our full-time employees; they are professionally trained by us.

Crest Hotel   Basingstoke

H 64% £C/D
Map 5 D3 Hampshire
Venture Roundabout, Grove Road RG21 3EE
Basingstoke (0256) 468181. Tlx 858501
Credit Access, Amex, Diners, Visa
   A modern hotel just south of the town centre, with two pleasantly appointed bars. Bedrooms (some non-smoking) are bright and fresh, with lightwood units and nice fabrics. All are equipped

with radio-alarms and trouser presses. Smartly tiled bathrooms offer plenty of shelf space and good towels; all have shower fitments. *Amenities* garden, whirlpool bath, snooker, pool table, laundry service, 24-hour lounge service.

■ *Rooms 86*	*Confirm by 6*
en suite bath/shower 86	*Last dinner 9.45*
Direct dial Yes	*Parking Ample*
Room TV Yes	*Room service 24 hours*

Ladbroke Hotel   Basingstoke

H 65% £C
Map 5 D3 Hampshire
Aldermaston Roundabout, Ringway North
RG24 9NV
Basingstoke (0256) 20212. Tlx 858223
Credit Access, Amex, Diners, Visa
   A fountain graces the attractive foyer-lounge-cum-cosy bar of this splendidly maintained hotel. Bedrooms range from smart standards with radio-

alarms and tea-makers to Gold Star rooms and two suites with whirlpool baths. *Amenities* indoor swimming pool, sauna, keep-fit equipment, games room, snooker, in-house movies (charge), laundry service, 24-hour lounge service, helipad.

■ *Rooms 108*	*Confirm by 6*
en suite bath/shower 108	*Last dinner 10*
Direct dial Yes	*Parking Ample*
Room TV Yes	*Room service 24 hours*

Ladbroke Lodge   Basingstoke

H 66% £C &
Map 5 D3 Hampshire
Old Common Road, Black Dam RG21 3PR
Basingstoke (0256) 460460. Tlx 859038
Credit Access, Amex, Diners, Visa
   On the outskirts of town, near junction 6 of the M3, this modern hotel has comfortable open-plan public areas and comprehensive conference and leisure facilities. Smart bedrooms include 20 Gold

Star rooms.
Amenities garden, indoor swimming pool, sauna, keep-fit equipment, in-house movies (charge), laundry service, 24-hour lounge service.

■ *Rooms 120*	*Confirm by 6*
en suite bath/shower 120	*Last dinner 10*
Direct dial Yes	*Parking Ample*
Room TV Yes	*Room service 24 hours*

Red Lion Hotel   Basingstoke

H 56% £D/E
Map 5 D3 Hampshire
24 London Street RG21 1NY
Basingstoke (0256) 28525. Tlx 859504
Manager Austin Wadkins
Credit Access, Amex, Diners, Visa
   Beams give a pleasant traditional feel to the public bar of this former coaching inn, and some of the bedrooms in the original building boast

handsome oak panelling. Other day rooms and the bedrooms in the extension are more contemporary in style. Tea-makers, remote control TVs and radio-alarms are standard. *Amenities* laundry service.

■ *Rooms 63*	*Confirm by arrang.*
en suite bath/shower 63	*Last dinner 10.30*
Direct dial Yes	*Parking Ample*
Room TV Yes	*Room service Limited*

Cavendish Hotel

Baslow

HR **74% £C**
Map 10 C2 Derbyshire
DE4 1SP
Baslow (024 688) 2311. Tlx 547150
Owner manager Mr Eric Marsh
Credit Amex, Diners, Visa

A charming, well-run hotel standing alongside the A619 and enjoying lovely rear views over the Chatsworth Estate. The 18th-century and more modern parts blend well, and the interior tone is set by the entrance hall with its paintings, prints and splendid herringbone patterned red-brick floor. A bright, sunny drawing room leads on to

the bar, which is divided into two areas by an arch. Bedrooms, generally of a good size, are furnished in traditional style, and each has a couple of armchairs and a supply of books. The best boast brass fittings and antique furniture. Bathrooms are very thoughtfully equipped. No dogs. *Amenities* garden, golf practice net, putting, game fishing, laundry service.

■ *Rooms* 24 — *Confirm by* arrang.
en suite bath/shower 24 — *Last dinner* 10
Direct dial Yes — *Parking* Ample
Room TV Yes — *Room service* 24 hours

Cavendish Hotel Restaurant

Chef Nick Buckingham turns out a good variety of imaginative dishes, with particularly successful sauces: creamed dill for a trio of pastry parcels; warm foie gras with cold galantine of duck; delicate wild mushrooms in a glaze for lemon sole; mango with a zippy lime mousse. Coffee comes with nice home-made truffle chocolates. Good wines with some excellent burgundies. There's a table for two actually within the kitchen. ☺

NEW ENTRY

■ *About £52 for two* — L 12.30–2
Seats 50 Parties 10 — D 7–10

Armathwaite Hall

Bassenthwaite

H **66% £D** &
Map 13 C5 Cumbria
Nr Keswick CA12 4RE
Bassenthwaite Lake (059 681) 551. Tlx 64319
Owner managers Graves family
Credit Access, Amex, Diners, Visa

Glorious views along lake Bassenthwaite can be enjoyed from this fine old mansion set in 133 acres of park and woodland. A warmly panelled entrance hall leads to the elegantly furnished lounge and there's a cosy bar featuring a massive carved mantel. The smartly appointed leisure centre is housed in a converted coach house and

sports its own bar. Good-sized bedrooms, in traditional or modern style, have hairdryers and trouser presses.

Amenities garden, indoor swimming pool, sauna, solarium, whirlpool bath, gymnasium, tennis, squash, coarse fishing, snooker, pool table, in-house movies (free), valeting, laundry service, 24-hour lounge service.

■ *Rooms* 39 — *Confirm by* 4
en suite bath/shower 39 — *Last dinner* 9.30
Direct dial Yes — *Parking* Ample
Room TV Yes — *Room service* 24 hours

Pheasant Inn

Bassenthwaite Lake

H **65% £D/E**
Map 13 C5 Cumbria
Cockermouth CA13 9YE
Bassenthwaite Lake (059 681) 234
Owner manager Mr W. E. Barrington-Wilson

Friendly owners and staff keep standards commendably high at this peaceful inn just off the A66. The mellow panelled bar oozes old-world charm, and the three lounges are delightfully

civilised, with their open fires, fresh flowers and lovely old tapestry work. Refurbished bedrooms are attractively furnished and all now offer private facilities. *Amenities* garden.

■ *Rooms* 20 — *Confirm by* 4
en suite bath/shower 20 — *Last dinner* 8.15
Room phone No — *Parking* Ample
Room TV No — *Room service* All day
Closed Xmas

■ We welcome complaints and bona fide recommendations on the tear-out pages for readers' comments, They are followed up by our professional team. Please also complain to the management instantly.

RECEPTION

BATH

Map 4 B3
Town plan opposite

Population 84,000

The Romans settled in Bath because of the waters and built baths used for therapy and recreation. In the 18th century spa treatment reached the peak of fashion and Bath was greatly enlarged at this time. Being wholly built within the space of a century, all its buildings are of the same classic, elegant style. Its Georgian character and charm remained unchanged until very recently. Yet Bath has become the centre of much environmental controversy: should the face of Bath be gradually eroded to develop it as a 20th-century commercial city, or should it be enshrined for ever as a masterpiece of urban architecture?

Annual Events
Bath Festival (music and drama)
22nd May–7th June
Royal Bath and West Show

Sights Outside City
Cheddar Gorge, Wooky Hole Caves, Wells Cathedral, Glastonbury Abbey, Longleat House and Safari Park, Castle Combe Village, Lacock Abbey and Village, Stourhead House and gardens, Avebury Circles, Corsham Court

Tourist Information Centre
Abbey Church Yard
Telephone Enquiries Bath 62831

Fiat Dealer
Motor Services (Bath) Ltd
Margaret's Buildings
Circus Place
Bath
Avon BA1 2PW
Tel. Bath 27328
Map reference 2A

1 Abbey *15th c* B4

2 American Museum at Claverton Manor *2¼ miles, life in the New World from 17th c to 1860* C3

3 Assembly Rooms *Finely restored Georgian suite, also houses world-famous Museum of Costume* A2

4 Bath Industrial Heritage Centre A2

5 Bath Spa Station B5

6 Botanical Gardens in Victoria Park A2

7 Burrows Toy Museum B4

8 The Circus, Royal Crescent and Lansdown Crescent *superb examples of Georgian town-planning* A1 & A2

9 Guildhall Banqueting Room *fine Adam-style room* B3

10 Herschel House A3

11 Holburne of Menstrie Museum *paintings, silver, objects d'art* C2

12 Huntingdon Centre B2

13 Lansdown Race-course A1

14 Museum of Bookbinding B4

15 National Museum of Photography B3

16 Postal Museum B3

17 Pulteney Bridge *Adam bridge lined with shops* B3

18 Pump Room and Roman Baths *the heart of Bath, includes Britain's finest Roman remains* B4

19 Sham Castle *18th-c folly and viewpoint* C2

20 Theatre Royal A3

21 Tourist Information Centre B4

22 University C3

23 Victoria Art Gallery *works by mainly West Country artists; glass; Delft; horology* B3

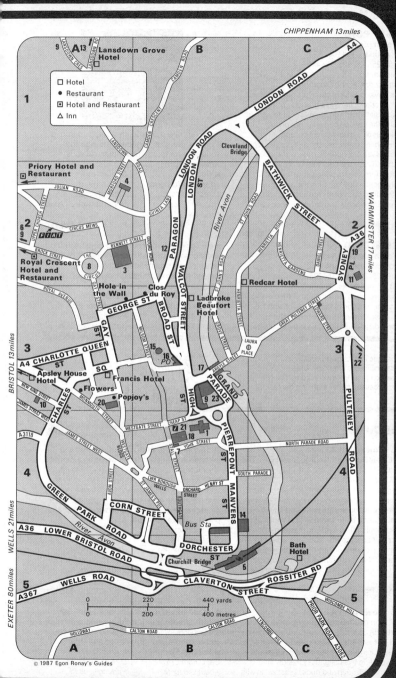

Bath FIAT

CHIPPENHAM 13 miles

A13 Lansdown Grove Hotel

Hotel ☐
Restaurant ●
Hotel and Restaurant ☒
Inn △

Priory Hotel and Restaurant

Cleveland Bridge

Royal Crescent Hotel and Restaurant

Hole in the Wall

Clos du Roy

Redcar Hotel

Ladbroke Beaufort Hotel

Laura Place

Apsley House Hotel

Francis Hotel

Flowers

Popjoy's

Bus Sta

Bath Hotel

Churchill Bridge

BRISTOL 13 miles
WELLS 21 miles
EXETER 80 miles
WARMINSTER 17 miles

| 0 | 220 | 440 yards |
| 0 | 200 | 400 metres |

© 1987 Egon Ronay's Guides

Apsley House Hotel   Bath

H 76% £C/D
Town plan A3 Avon
141 Newbridge Hill BA1 3PT
Bath (0225) 336 966. Tlx 449212
Owner managers Mr G. A. & Mrs M. I. Davidson
Credit Access, Amex, Diners, Visa

The Davidsons have created a most civilised and comfortable hotel in a gracious William IV mansion that stands on the A431 to the west of the city. The comfort of guests is a priority, cleanliness almost an obsession, and maintenance standards stay impressively high. Bedrooms are of a good size, even the attic rooms (which also have the best views); they are tastefully furnished in period style and have prettily coordinated soft furnishings and up-to-date features. Bathrooms are all fitted with shower attachments and bidets. The elegant

restaurant overlooks a south-facing garden, and there's a splendidly comfortable lounge and equally agreeable bar. No children. No dogs. *Amenities* garden, laundry service.

■ Rooms 7	Confirm by 6
en suite bath/shower 7	Last dinner 9
Direct dial Yes	Parking Ample
Room TV Yes	Room service 24 hours

Bath Hotel   Bath

H 65% £C/D &
Town plan C5 Avon
Widcombe Basin BA2 4JP
Bath (0225) 338855. Tlx 23639
Credit Access, Amex, Diners, Visa

Attractive views are a feature of this newly built hotel at the junction of the river Avon and the canal. Plush carpeting, cane seating and much greenery distinguish the main lounge-cum-bar

area. Compact bedrooms are equally stylish and boast good lightwood furnishings, pastel colour schemes and smartly fitted bathrooms. *Amenities* garden, in-house movies (free), 24-hour lounge service, kiosk.

■ Rooms 96	Confirm by 6
en suite bath/shower 96	Last dinner 9.30
Direct dial Yes	Parking Ample
Room TV Yes	Room service None

■ Changes in data may occur in establishments after the Guide goes to press. Prices should be taken as indications rather than firm quotes.

Clos Du Roy   Bath

R ♀ **Town plan B3** Avon
7 Edgar Buildings, George Street BA1 2EE
Bath (0225) 64356
Credit Access, Amex, Diners, Visa

Philippe Roy is a skilled chef with a penchant for preparing intricate and ornate dishes. Some succeed, while others are perhaps a little *too* intricate (taking up to seven lines of explanation on the menu!), with a resulting masking of the flavour and quality of the 'main' ingredients. Examples include a dodine of wild duck, quail, guinea fowl and pheasant, or paquet surprise, a starter comprising a pastry parcel of monkfish

and a mirepoix, a pancake filled with crab and avocado, and a cabbage leaf wrapping turbot and mushrooms – pretty enough, pleasant enough, but over-elaborate. Sweets such as vacherin aux pralines are lavishly garnished with flowers and exotic fruits. An expanded wine list includes some great champagnes and Chardonnays at highish prices. ♀ Well-chosen ☺

■ Set L from £8·95	L 12–2
Set D from £18·50	D 7–10.15
About £60 for two	Parking Limited
Seats 26 Parties 30	Closed Sun, Mon, 24–
26 Dec, 1st wk Jan, 1st wk Feb & 3rd wk Aug

Flowers   Bath

R ♀ **Town plan A3** Avon
27 Monmouth Street
Bath (0225) 313774
Credit Access, Amex, Diners, Visa

Teresa Lipin changes her fixed-price menus twice weekly in this delightfully friendly little restaurant. Fish soup and duck breast salad with plum sauce are popular starters, while main courses could include salmon, turbot and monkfish

poached in cider, rack of lamb in red wine, and grilled venison steak. Hazelnut meringue remains the favourite sweet. Good cooking with just the odd inconsistency. ♀ Well-chosen ☺

■ Set L £8·50	L 12–2.30
Set D from £13·50	D 7–10.30
About £40 for two	Parking Limited
Seats 26	Parties 30
Closed Sun, Mon, 2 wks Aug & 2 wks Xmas

Francis Hotel — Bath

H **69% £C**
Town plan A3 Avon
Queen Square BA1 2HH
Bath (0225) 24257. Tlx 449162
Credit Access, Amex, Diners, Visa. **LVs**

Six Georgian houses on an elegant square make up this handsome hotel with gracious public areas. Spacious bedrooms are divided into individually furnished ones in the main building and equally bright but more uniform rooms in the modern wing. All have tea-makers, direct-dial phones, remote-control TVs, and spotless, up-to-date bathrooms. *Amenities* laundry service, 24 hour lounge service.

■ *Rooms* 94	*Confirm by 6*
en suite bath/shower 94	*Last dinner 10.30*
Direct dial Yes	*Parking Limited*
Room TV Yes	*Room service 24 hours*

Hole in the Wall — Bath

RR **Town plan A3** Avon
16 George Street BA1 2EN
Bath (0225) 25242
French cooking
Credit Access, Amex, Diners, Visa

Stepping into the Hole in the Wall is pure pleasure, thanks to owner managers John and Christine Cunliffe. When they purchased this city-centre restaurant it had a marvellous reputation but a somewhat tired decor. Redecoration has corrected the latter; the former has been enhanced by the accomplished cooking of partner Bernard Habert. The menu includes venison terrine, gurnard en papillote and loin of veal with apple, spinach and cheese sauce. Dessert might be apricot and pear tart. ♀ Well-chosen ☺

■ *Set L from £18·50*	*L 12.30–2*
Set D from £18·50	*D 7–10*
About £65 for two	*Parking Difficult*
Seats 55	*Parties 16*
Closed L Sun & L Bank Hols	

Bedrooms £D/E
Rooms 8 — *With bath/shower 8*
Beautiful bedrooms have direct-dial telephones, TVs and mini-bars. There's a residents' lounge and breakfast room. No dogs.

Ladbroke Beaufort Hotel — Bath

H **64% £C**
Town plan B3 Avon
Walcot Street BA1 5BJ
Bath (0225) 63411. Tlx 449519
Credit Access, Amex, Diners, Visa

Refurbishment of many bedrooms and the ground floor has given a facelift to this centrally placed modern hotel near the river Avon. Spacious public rooms include a bar-lounge with river views. The best of the good-size bedrooms have smart colour schemes and furnishings. All have tea-makers, trouser presses and tiled bathrooms. *Amenities* in-house movies (charge), laundry service, coffee shop (10am–11pm).

■ *Rooms 124*	*Confirm by 6*
en suite bath/shower 124	*Last dinner 10*
Direct dial Yes	*Parking Ample*
Room TV Yes	*Room service 24 hours*

Landsdown Grove Hotel — Bath

H **66% £C/D**
Town plan A1 Avon
Landsdown Road BA1 5EH
Bath (0225) 315891. Tlx 444850
Credit Access, Amex, Diners, Visa

1988 is the centenary year for the Jackman family at this Georgian hotel high above the city centre. Refurbishment keeps pace with the times, and standards of housekeeping and repair are high. Bedrooms – some with spectacular views of Bath – vary in size and style, and all are well equipped. There's an attractive, roomy bar and a gracious first-floor drawing room. *Amenities* garden, 24-hour lounge service.

■ *Rooms 41*	*Confirm by 6*
en suite bath/shower 41	*Last dinner 9*
Direct dial Yes	*Parking Ample*
Room TV Yes	*Room service 24 hours*

Popjoy's — Bath

R **Town plan A3** Avon
Beau Nash's House, Sawclose
Bath (0225) 460494
Credit Access, Visa

Edgar Bührs is the talented and creative new chef at this plushly-elegant Georgian dining room. Style and menu format remain the same; a seasonally-changing selection might include fragrant calf's liver and green peppercorn mousse followed by succulent wood pigeon served on a masterly sauce of chocolate and pine nuts. Enticing sweets and local cheeses to finish. ➦ Outstanding ♀ Well-chosen ☺

■ *Set L from £12·50*	*L Thurs & Fri only,*
Set D £17·50	*June–Sept 12–2.30*
About £48 for two	*D 6–10.30*
Seats 34 Parties 34	*Parking Difficult*
Closed Sun & 2 wks Xmas	

Priory Hotel

Bath

HR 82% £B
Town plan A2 Avon
Weston Road BA1 2XT
Bath (0225) 331922. Tlx 44612
Owner manager John Donnithorne
Credit Access, Amex, Diners, Visa

This 1835 'gentleman's residence', sited a mile west of the city centre, has been sympathetically extended to create an immensely civilised hotel. John Donnithorne takes a keen interest in the running of the Priory and the influence of his style and personality extends throughout. Public areas are exceedingly comfortable, with a harmonious blend of modern and antique furnishings, fine fabrics and fresh flowers. The individually-designed bedrooms are graced by luxurious drapes and stylish wallpapers; all have remote-control TV, radios, hairdryers and direct-dial telephones. Bathrooms have quality fittings and toiletries. No children under ten. No dogs.
Amenities garden, outdoor swimming pool, croquet, laundry service.

■ *Rooms 21*   *Confirm by arrang.*
en suite bath/shower 20   *Last dinner 9.15*
Direct dial Yes   *Parking Ample*
Room TV Yes   *Room service All day*

Priory Hotel
Restaurant ★ ♔

French cooking
This is a splendid setting for Michael Collom's skilful, self-assured cooking. Well conceived and nicely balanced menus combine tried and tested favourites like crab-filled soufflé omelette with leek sauce, and roast partridge, with interesting new dishes like hot brioche with wild mushroom purée, quail's eggs and truffle sauce, and medallions of venison with poached pear, redcurrant and game sauce. Good presentation and service complete the picture. Sound selection of British cheeses and excellent sweets. Fine classic wines and the outstanding Chianti Castell'in Villa 1975. No smoking.
Specialities warm salad of guinea fowl and duck confit, poached sea bass with mange-tout and caviar and dill sauce, 'palais de glace', a caramel and praline mousse with Tia Maria coffee sauce.

◠ Outstanding   ♀ Well-chosen ⊖
■ *Set L from £12·50*   *L 12.30–2*
Set D from £26   *D 7.15–9.15*
About £70 for two   *Seats 64 Parties 40*

Redcar Hotel

Bath

H 61% £D
Town plan C3 Avon
Henrietta Street BA2 6LR
Bath (0225) 69151. Tlx 444842
Credit Access, Amex, Diners, Visa

Part of a Georgian terrace, this friendly hotel is just a short stroll from the city centre. Chandeliers and a baby grand lend a touch of elegance to the restful bar-lounge, and there is a smart

conference room. Sensible design makes maximum use of space in bedrooms, which have contemporary furnishings, tea-makers and radio consoles. *Amenities* 24-hour lounge service, in-house movies (free).

■ *Rooms 31*   *Confirm by 6*
en suite bath/shower 22   *Last dinner 10.30*
Direct dial Yes   *Parking Limited*
Room TV Yes   *Room service 24 hours*

Royal Crescent Hotel

Bath

HR 88% £A/B
Town plan A2 Avon
16 Royal Crescent BA1 2LS
Bath (0225) 319090. Tlx 444251
Credit Access, Amex, Diners, Visa

As gracious as the Royal Crescent in which it resides, this is without doubt one of Britain's finest hotels. Aesthetically it is a joy, with beautifully-proportioned public rooms enhanced by deep sofas, open fires, handsome antique furniture and oil paintings. Bedrooms in the main house remain opulent and well equipped, with magnificent drapes, four-posters or canopied

beds. Sixteen bathrooms have recently been lavishly remodelled in marble. The separate Dower House is designed as a superior conference centre, and also contains some of the bedrooms, as well as the restaurant. No dogs. *Amenities* garden, whirlpool bath, croquet, valeting, laundry service, 24-hour lounge service.

■ *Rooms 45*	*Confirm by arrang.*
en suite bath/shower 43	*Last dinner 9.30*
Direct dial Yes	*Parking Limited*
Room TV Yes	*Room service 24 hours*

Restaurant ★ ⋓⋓

Michael Croft is a dedicated and innovative young chef. Already he displays enviable culinary skills, and flashes of brilliance hint at boundless potential. His talent for combining flavours in unusual yet highly successful combinations is displayed in starters like lobster and langoustine salad with mango and mint dressing, and main courses such as brioche-crumbed lamb with aubergine and courgette gâteau or monkfish and scallops in cider and bacon butter sauce. Raw

materials are outstanding and presentation is artistic. English farmhouse cheeses precede super sweets, including featherlight soufflés. The Dower House setting is summery by day, romantic by night, and always sumptuous. A well-managed wine list features classic vintages and producers. Clarets are particularly well represented. *Specialities* timbale of trout with shellfish ragoût, smoked monkfish salad with oyster vinaigrette, grilled sea bass with smoked ham and fennel, hot dessert soufflés.

⇨ Outstanding 🍷 Well-chosen ℰ

■ *Set L from £15*	*L 12.30–2*
About £70 for two	*D 7–9.30*
Seats 62	*Parties 40*

Netherfield Place   Battle

HR 77% £D/E
Map 7 B6 East Sussex
Netherfield TN33 9PP
Battle (042 46) 4455. Tlx 95284
Owner managers Helen & Michael Collier
Credit Access, Amex, Diners, Visa

A splendidly proportioned Georgian-style 1920s country house in 30 acres of beautifully kept parkland and gardens. All rooms have been recently refurbished and upgraded. Public rooms include a pleasant lounge with open fire, an adjoining cocktail bar and a sun lounge. Bedrooms vary in size from spacious to smaller attic rooms, and are individually decorated and furnished, with period pieces (including brass

beds), good fabrics, colour TVs and extras such as portable radios, plants and fresh fruit. Bathrooms have modern fittings and are lavishly equipped with good towels, bathrobes and quality toiletries. No dogs. *Amenities* garden, laundry service, teletext.

■ *Rooms 12*	*Confirm by arrang.*
en suite bath/shower 12	*Last dinner 10*
Direct dial Yes	*Parking Ample*
Room TV Yes	*Room service All day*

Netherfield Place
Restaurant ⋓ 🍷 &

A panelled dining room provides a gracious setting in which to enjoy chef-patron Michael Collier's praiseworthy cooking. Light modern dishes are carefully prepared and colourfully presented, using vegetables and herbs from the hotel garden. Starter might be pigeon breast on wild lettuce, followed by venison with pear and cranberry sauce. Mandarin gâteau is one choice from the good sweet trolley. The wine list contains some splendid Bordeaux and burgundies. ℰ

■ *Set L £12.95*	*L 12–2*
Set D £15	*D 7–10*
About £47 for two	*Seats 40 Parties 80*

Crown Hotel   Bawtry

H 63% £D/E
Map 11 D2 South Yorkshire
High Street DN10 6JW
Doncaster (0302) 710341. Tlx 547089
Credit Access, Amex, Diners, Visa

Modern comforts are a feature of this historic posting house in the town centre. The cocktail bar/lounge has been smartly revamped, while the main bar remains traditional. Bedrooms are being refurbished with darkwood units and floral furnishings; the six club rooms have many extras apart from the standard tea-makers. *Amenities* garden, laundry service, 24-hour lounge service.

■ *Rooms 57*	*Confirm by 6*
en suite bath/shower 57	*Last dinner 9.45*
Direct dial Yes	*Parking Ample*
Room TV Yes	*Room service 24 hours*

Bellhouse Hotel

Beaconsfield

H 67% £C
Map 5 E2 Buckinghamshire
Oxford Road HP9 2XE
Gerrards Cross (0753) 887211. Tlx 848719
Manager Mr H. Waser
Credit Access, Amex, Diners, Visa
   All credit here to management and staff at this modern hotel on the A40 (convenient for London and Heathrow). Bedrooms impress with their smart decor and all have sparkling tiled bathrooms. Day rooms include a leafy foyer-lounge and nautically-themed bar. *Amenities* garden, games rooms, pool table, in-house movies (charge), 24-hour lounge service.

■ *Rooms* 118	*Confirm by arrang.*
en suite bath/shower 118	*Last dinner* 9.45
Direct dial Yes	*Parking* Ample
Room TV Yes	*Room service* 24 hours

Beechfield House

Beanacre

HR 77% £C/D
Map 4 B2 Wiltshire
Nr Melksham SN12 7PU
Melksham (0225) 703700
Credit Access, Amex, Diners, Visa
   On the A350 between Chippenham and Melksham, this Victorian mansion is a most civilised hotel. Guests are warmly greeted in the entrance hall, beyond which drinks are served from a huge mahogany dresser. Antiques, chandeliers and fine marble fireplaces are notable features, and the elegant lounge enjoys splendid views over the grounds. Spacious bedrooms, decorated and furnished with great flair and taste, are provided with many extras, from magazines and mineral water to sewing kits and hairdryers. Bathrooms, too, are superbly appointed and, like the rest of the hotel, are kept in impeccable order. New owners, but no other changes. No dogs. *Amenities* garden, outdoor swimming pool, tennis, croquet, coarse fishing.

■ *Rooms* 16	*Confirm by arrang.*
en suite bath/shower 16	*Last dinner* 9.15
Direct dial Yes	*Parking* Ample
Room TV Yes	*Room service* All day

Beechfield House Restaurant ⌂ ♃ ㅤ

Two elegant dining rooms make a fine setting in which to enjoy Jeremy Shutter's imaginative and sophisticated cooking. Warm salad of prawns and scallops or terrine of sweetbreads are typical starters; to follow, perhaps flavoursome roast partridge with game chips or sea bass with a champagne butter sauce. Sweets include excellent sorbets. Polished service. Splendid classic cellar (note old vintages of Ch. Coutet) plus excellent Clos du Val California wines.
⌦ Outstanding ♥ Well-chosen ✪

■ *Set L from* £10·95	*L* 12.15–1.45
About £55 *for two*	*D* 7–9.15,
Seats 50 *Parties* 40	*Fri & Sat* 7–9.30

Soufflé

Bearsted

R **Map 7 C5** Kent
The Green, Nr Maidstone
Maidstone (0622) 37065
Owner manager Sue Dunderdale
Credit Access, Amex, Diners, Visa
   Once the village bakehouse, now a delightful setting for imaginative cooking by Mark Fosh. Lunch is a daily-changing set menu, dinner a short, select carte. Typical dishes include terrine of winter game, crab-stuffed sole and super lamb noisettes. Tempting sweets, well-kept cheeses. Sue Dunderdale heads a charming service team. Reasonably priced wine list. ♥ Well-chosen ✪

■ *Set L* £9·95	*L* 12–2
Set D £27	*D* 7–10
About £45 *for two*	*Parking* Ample
Seats 40	*Parties* 44
Closed L Sat, D Mon, all Sun & 3 days Xmas	

Montagu Arms Hotel

Beaulieu

H 65% £D/E
Map 4 C4 Hampshire
Palace Lane SO42 7ZL
Beaulieu (0590) 612324. Tlx 47276
Credit Access, Amex, Diners, Visa
   A hostelry has stood here for seven centuries, and today's creeper-covered former coaching inn is a popular base for touring the New Forest. Traditionally-styled lounges look out over the secluded gardens, and there's a pleasant bar with a wine press theme. Well-equipped bedrooms include several with four-posters or Victorian brass beds. Friendly staff. *Amenities* garden, laundry service.

■ *Rooms* 26	*Confirm by* 6
en suite bath/shower 26	*Last dinner* 9.30
Direct dial Yes	*Parking* Ample
Room TV Yes	*Room service* 24 hours

Waveney House Hotel
Beccles

H **60%** **£E**
Map 6 D2 Suffolk
Puddingmoor NR34 9PL
Beccles (0502) 712270
Owner manager Michael Hepton
Credit Access, Amex, Diners, Visa
　A quiet lane runs from one-way Northgate to this attractive stone hotel on the river Waveney. The main day rooms are a peaceful lounge and a

bar that opens on to a riverside terrace. Bedrooms, some with beams, are very neat and tidy. Staff are efficient if not especially friendly. *Amenities* garden, coarse fishing, laundry service.

■ *Rooms 13*	*Confirm by 6*
en suite bath/shower 11	*Last dinner 9.30*
Direct dial Yes	*Parking Ample*
Room TV Yes	*Room service All day*

Bedford Moat House
Bedford

H **63%** **£D**
Map 5 E1 Bedfordshire
2 St Marys Street MK42 0AR
Bedford (0234) 55131. Tlx 825243
Manager Keith Timewell
Credit Access, Amex, Diners, Visa
　1987 saw many improvements at this 60s town-centre hotel by the Ouse. Bedrooms have emerged quite chic and stylish. There's a new

and very smart riverside coffee shop-cum-wine bar. *Amenities* sauna, whirlpool bath, keep-fit equipment, in-house movies (charge), laundry service, coffee shop (10am–11pm).

■ *Rooms 117*	*Confirm by arrang.*
en suite bath/shower 117	*Last dinner 9.45*
Direct dial Yes	*Parking Ample*
Room TV Yes	*Room service 24 hours*
Closed 25 Dec	

Woodlands Manor Hotel
Bedford

HR **72%** **£C/D**
Map 5 E1 Bedfordshire
Green Lane, Clapham MK41 6EP
Bedford (0234) 63281. Tlx 825007
Owner manager Richard Lee
Credit Access, Amex, Visa
　Set back from the A6, overlooking gardens and wooded grounds, this late-Victorian mansion makes a fine traditional hotel. The roomy foyer, with its wood panelling, rich red carpet and cheerful fire, has a welcoming feel that extends to the handsomely proportioned and comfortably furnished lounge where drinks are served. Best of the bedrooms are very spacious, with sitting areas; again, traditionally furnished, and full of nice touches, from tissues and potpourris to mini-bars and radios. Some smallish singles are not of

quite the same standard, looking a little dated – though they're certainly well kept. Bathrooms are fully equipped. No children under seven. No dogs. *Amenities* garden, laundry service.

■ *Rooms 21*	*Confirm by 6*
en suite bath/shower 21	*Last dinner 9.45*
Direct dial Yes	*Parking Ample*
Room TV Yes	*Room service 24 hours*
Closed 10 days Xmas	

Woodlands Manor Restaurant 🍴

The menu at this elegant restaurant offers a particularly varied and interesting choice, and careful cooking ensures enjoyable results on the plate. Dishes can be traditional (mutton, vegetable and barley broth; game pie; roast beef and Yorkshire pudding) or a little more out of the ordinary (melon filled with ginger sorbet; garlicky pan-fried pork stuffed wtih pistachio nuts). Super sweets, and a separate vegetarian menu. Wines include good clarets and burgundies. 🍷

■ *Set L £9·75*	*L 12.30–1.45*
Set D £13·30	*D 7.30–9.45*
About £45 for two	*Seats 30 Parties 35*
Closed L Bank Hols & 10 days Xmas	

WILD BOAR INN
Beeston

H **£E**
Map 10 B2 Cheshire
Nr Tarporley CW6 9NN
Bunbury (0829) 260309. Tlx 61455
Credit Access, Amex, Diners, Visa
　The main building's half-timbered facade is a striking feature of this distinctive hotel, which enjoys a quiet rural setting just off the A49. New owners have extensive improvement plans,

including the conversion of the motel-style accommodation into 50 new rooms, and the building of a leisure complex. Graded at 60% in 1987 Guide. *Amenities* garden.

■ *Rooms 30*	*Confirm by 6*
en suite bath/shower 30	*Last dinner 9.45*
Direct dial Yes	*Parking Ample*
Room TV Yes	*Room service Limited*
Closed 25 & 26 Dec	

Belbroughton ▶

The Bell at Belbroughton
Belbroughton

R ♛ ♧ ♿ **Map 10 B4**
Hereford & Worcester
Bell End
Kidderminster (0562) 730232
Credit Access, Amex, Diners, Visa
    Trencherman portions of masterly French dishes are the hallmark of this formal, comfortable restaurant behind a pub on the A491. Fish soup with rouille, breast of Barbary duck with a sauce of Beaujolais and figs, and poached pears with poire William sabayon were excellent from start to finish. Other delights include salmon mille-feuille and rib of beef. Sadly, the owners will be leaving in January. ♀ Well-chosen ⊜

■ *Set L £9.50*   *L 12.30–2, Sun 12.15–2*
Set D £19   *D 7.30–9.45*
About £52 for two   *Parking Ample*
Seats 60 Closed L Sat, D Sun & all Mon

Blue Bell Hotel
Belford

I **£D/E**
Map 14 B2 Northumberland
Market Square NE70 7NE
Belford (066 83) 543
Credit Access, Amex, Diners, Visa
    A fine old creeper-covered inn on the market square. Staff are friendly and engagingly forthright, and the mellow bar and lounge are nice places to relax. Bedrooms, all of a good size, are furnished mainly in solid traditional style, and all now have their own bathrooms. Half the rooms overlook the pretty garden, the church and the open fields beyond. Good breakfasts.
Amenities garden, putting.

■ *Rooms 15*   *Confirm by 6*
en suite bath/shower 15   *Last dinner 9*
Direct dial Yes   *Parking Ample*
Room TV Yes   *Room service Limited*

Highbury Hotel
Bembridge

H **60% £E/F**
Map 5 D4 Isle of Wight
Lane End Road PO35 5SU
Isle of Wight (0983) 872838
Owner manager Mr A. B. Cobb
Credit Access, Amex, Diners, Visa
    Period furniture and bric-a-brac impart a homely air to the comfortable lounges and snug bar of this friendly, family-run hotel in an extended Edwardian villa. An impressive range of useful extras complement the spick-and-span bedrooms. *Amenities* garden, outdoor swimming pool, sauna, solarium, croquet, laundry service.

■ *Rooms 9*   *Confirm by arrang.*
en suite bath/shower 7   *Last dinner 10*
Room phone Yes   *Parking Limited*
Room TV Yes   *Room service All day*
Closed Oct & 24–28 Dec

■ We publish annually, so make sure you use the current edition. It's worth it!

Swan Hotel
Berkhamsted

I **£E/F**
Map 5 E2 Hertfordshire
139 High Street HP4 3HJ
Berkhamsted (044 27) 71451. Tlx 82257
Manager Elizabeth Prochnik
Credit Access, Visa
    Easy to spot with its distinctive red frontage, this town-centre inn dates back to Tudor times and beyond. Old oak beams and sloping floors are much in evidence, and day rooms like the flagstoned bar and homely lounge have a ready appeal. The little bedrooms are no less charming, and carpeted bathrooms are kept in very good order. *Amenities* laundry service.

■ *Rooms 19*   *Confirm by arrang.*
en suite bath/shower 13   *Last dinner 10*
Direct dial Yes   *Parking Limited*
Room TV Yes   *Room service None*

Kings Arms Hotel
Berwick-upon-Tweed

H **59% £E**
Map 14 B2 Northumberland
Hide Hill TD15 1EJ
Berwick-upon-Tweed (0289) 307454
Credit Access, Amex, Diners, Visa
    Accommodation at this 18th-century town-centre hotel is spacious, with pretty fabrics and smark darkwood furniture; eleven rooms boast four-posters. Trouser presses, tea-makers and hairdryers are standard. Fresh flowers brighten the simple lounge, and there's a choice of bars – one intimate, the other young and lively.
Amenities garden, snooker, laundry service, 24-hour lounge service.

■ *Rooms 36*   *Confirm by arrang.*
en suite bath/shower 36   *Last dinner 9.30*
Room phone Yes   *Parking Difficult*
Room TV Yes   *Room service 24 hours*

The Anvil *NEW ENTRY* Beverley

R ♫ **Map 11 E1** Humberside
Market Place
Hull (0482) 862860
Owner manager David John Barker
Credit Access, Amex, Visa
   Pretty prints and antique pine give a cosy,
cottage feel to this attractive first-floor restaurant.
David Barker's menu provides a balanced choice
of enjoyable dishes, from spicy beetroot and
cabbage soup and garlic prawns with saffron rice
to rainbow trout, chicken with Pernod and pork
fillet with a tasty Madeira and walnut sauce.
Limited but decent wine list. Friendly, helpful
service. ♀ **Well-chosen**

■ *About £30 for two*	*D only 7–10,*
Seats 60	*Sat 7–10.30*
Closed Sun, Mon, Bank	**Parking** *Ample*
Hols & 2 days Xmas	

♀ indicates a **well-chosen** house wine.

Beverley Arms Hotel Beverley

H **60% £C/D**
   Map 11 E1 Humberside
North Bar Within HU17 8DD
Hull (0482) 869241. Tlx 597568
Credit Access, Amex, Diners, Visa. **LVs**
   A Georgian facade fronts this 300-year-old
hostelry, where Dick Turpin once stood before
local justices. A friendly welcome is delivered in
the reception area, and guests can relax in the
two bars, coffee shop or courtyard. A little lounge
doubles as a meeting room. Decent-sized
bedrooms have mostly now been upgraded.
Amenities coffee shop (9.30am–7.30pm, Sat &
Sun 10.30am–5pm).

■ *Rooms 61*	*Confirm by 6*
en suite bath/shower 61	*Last dinner 9.45*
Room phone Yes	**Parking** *Ample*
Room TV Yes	*Room service 24 hours*

Bibury Court Hotel Bibury

H **64% £E**
   Map 4 C2 Gloucestershire
Nr Cirencester GL7 5NT
Bibury (028 574) 337
Owner managers Messrs Collier & Johnston
Credit Access, Amex, Diners, Visa
   A splendid 17th-century mansion set on the
banks of the river Coln. Extensively remodelled in
the 1920s, the public rooms include an impressive
panelled lounge and an Art Deco bar with river
views. Spacious bedrooms are equipped with a
mixture of antique and '20s furniture.
Amenities garden, croquet, game fishing.

■ *Rooms 16*	*Confirm by 6*
en suite bath/shower 15	*Last dinner 8.45*
Direct dial Yes	**Parking** *Ample*
Room TV Some	*Room service All day*
Closed 1 week Xmas	

Swan Hotel Bibury

H **61% £D**
   Map 4 C2 Gloucestershire
Nr Cirencester GL7 5NW
Bibury (028 574) 204
Owner manager Colin Morgan
Credit Access, Visa
   Facing the river Coln, this creeper-clad former
coaching inn retains its old-world charm.
Grandfather clocks, fresh flowers and antiques
dot public areas like the cosy writing room and
restful lounge. Traditionally furnished bedrooms,
some with beams and sloping ceilings, have
coordinated fabrics and pretty little carpeted
bathrooms. *Amenities* garden, game fishing.

■ *Rooms 23*	*Confirm by 6*
en suite bath/shower 23	*Last dinner 8.30*
Room phone Yes	**Parking** *Ample*
Room TV Yes	*Room service All day*

Yeoldon House Bideford

H **59% £D/E**
   Map 2 C2 Devon
Durrant Lane Northamptonshire EX39 2RL
Bideford (023 72) 74400
Owner managers Mr & Mrs N. M. Turner
Credit Access, Amex, Diners, Visa
   Improvements continue at this solidly attractive
Victorian hotel. The dining room, which overlooks
the River Torridge, has been enlarged and an
extra bedroom created. Public rooms have
modern and period furniture coexisting happily in
lounge and intimate bar. Some bedrooms have
modern fittings; others are traditional.
Amenities garden, sea fishing, laundry service.

■ *Rooms 10*	*Confirm by arrang.*
en suite bath/shower 10	*Last dinner 9*
Direct dial Yes	**Parking** *Ample*
Room TV Yes	*Room service All day*

Burgh Island *NEW ENTRY*

H 59% £D/E
Map 3 D3 Devon
TQ7 4AU
Bigbury on Sea (0548) 810514
Owner managers Beatrice & Tony Porter
Credit Access, Visa

When the tide is in, guests can only reach Burgh Island by sea tractor – a typically novel start to a stay at the Porters' 1930s hotel. Constant improvements are being made to restore its original splendour, and the Art Deco ground floor is particularly fine. Note the curved glass peacock dome in the Palm Court, the glassed sun lounge and magnificent ballroom reached by a wide staircase flanked by jet black glass and pink mirrors. The 13 simply furnished suites (five with authentic Art Deco bathrooms, the rest modern) offer colour TVs and kitchenettes. Half-board terms only. No dogs. *Amenities* garden, keep-fit equipment, tennis, sea fishing, snooker, laundry service.

- **Rooms** 13
- en suite bath/shower 13
- **Room phone** No
- **Room TV** Yes
- **Closed** Jan 2 to mid Mar

Confirm by arrang.
Last dinner 9
Parking Ample
Room service None

Dragon House Hotel

H 64% £E
Map 3 E1 Somerset
Nr Minehead TA24 6HQ
Washford (0984) 40215
Owner managers Paul Hinsley & William Biddle
Credit Access, Amex, Diners, Visa

Once a drinking den used by smugglers, today's characterful old inn beside the A39 has an altogether more restful appeal. A galleried staircase dominates the entrance hall, and open fires warm the cosily traditional lounge and bar. Cottage bedrooms with pretty floral decor have tea-makers and modern bath/shower rooms. *Amenities* garden, croquet, laundry service.

- **Rooms** 10
- en suite bath/shower 8
- **Room phone** No
- **Room TV** Yes

Confirm by arrang.
Last dinner 9.30
Parking Ample
Room service Limited

Bilbrough Manor Hotel *NEW ENTRY*

HR 77% £C
Map 11 D1 North Yorkshire
Nr York YO2 3PH
Tadcaster (0937) 834002
Owner managers Colin & Sue Bell
Credit Access, Amex, Diners, Visa

The illustrious Fairfax family have a seven-century association with Bilbrough, and it was Guy Fairfax who built the present manor in 1901. It stands about five miles south-west of York in delightful gardens and countryside, and the efforts of Colin and Sue Bell have transformed it into a most comfortable and relaxing country house hotel. Mullion windows, antiques and coats of arms set a traditional tone in the day rooms, which include a really lovely panelled drawing room. Spacious, well-equipped bedrooms are individually decorated and furnished to a high standard, and the Fairfax Room has a four-poster. Excellent bathrooms with carpets, pretty tiles and brass fittings. Service is notably friendly and professional. No children under 12. No dogs. *Amenities* garden, croquet, laundry service, 24-hour lounge service.

- **Rooms** 12
- en suite bath/shower 12
- **Direct dial** Yes
- **Room TV** Yes

Confirm by arrang.
Last dinner 9.30
Parking Ample
Room service 24 hours

Bilbrough Manor Restaurant 🍴 ⅋

Idris Caldora has moved from the Bell at Belbroughton to the Bells at Bilbrough, and the panelled dining room is a splendid setting for sampling his skills. His French menus provide a tempting variety, from crème vichyssoise and juicy scallops in a light saffron sauce to veal with grain mustard and delightful mignons of beef with foie gras and Madeira sauce. Very good sweets, too. 🕭

- **Set L** from £10
- Set D £17·50
- About £56 for two

L 12–2
D 7–9.30
Seats 48 Parties 14

Billingham Arms Hotel

H 59% £E
Map 15 C5 Cleveland
The Causeway TS23 2HD
Stockton-on-Tees (0642) 553661. Tlx 587746
Credit Access, Amex, Diners, Visa. **LVs**

Public areas – including a wide choice of bars – have received a facelift at this modern town-centre hotel. Bedrooms, too, have been upgraded and range from bright, attractive Club rooms with darkwood units, hairdryers and trouser presses to standard rooms in simple, modern style. *Amenities* solarium, games room, in-house movies (free), laundry service, coffee shop (11am–2pm & 6pm–11pm), 24-hour lounge service.

- **Rooms** 63
- en suite bath/shower 54
- **Direct dial** Yes
- **Room TV** Yes

Confirm by arrang.
Last dinner 11
Parking Ample
Room service 24 hours

Bankfield Hotel
Bingley

H 62% £D
Map 10 C1 West Yorkshire
Bradford Road BD16 1TV
Bradford (0274) 567123
Credit Access, Amex, Diners, Visa
An impressive Gothic-style Victorian building with somewhat incongruous modern extensions, the Bankfield has a splendid oak-panelled entrance hall and comfortable, newly refurbished

cocktail bar and lounge. Many of the spacious bedrooms have been up-dated, giving them a fresh, new look. Executive rooms have good accessories and all rooms have en suite facilities. *Amenities* garden, games room, laundry service.

■ *Rooms* 69	*Confirm by* 6
en suite bath/shower 69	*Last dinner* 9.15
Direct dial Yes	*Parking* Ample
Room TV Yes	*Room service* Limited

Bowler Hat Hotel
Birkenhead

H 65% £D
Map 10 A2 Merseyside
1 Talbot Road, Oxton L43 2HH
051-652 4931. Tlx 628761
Credit Access, Amex, Diners, Visa
Major pluses at this tile-hung period hotel are the friendly atmosphere and the range of bedroom extras. These include mini-bars, trouser presses, hairdryers, fresh fruit, sherry and, in the

bathrooms, telephone extensions. The entrance hall keeps a traditional feel, and there's a roomy bar-lounge. The hotel lies about 4 minutes from junction 3 of the M53. *Amenities* garden, in-house movies (free), laundry service.

■ *Rooms* 29	*Confirm by* 6
en suite bath/shower 28	*Last dinner* 10
Direct dial Yes	*Parking* Ample
Room TV Yes	*Room service* Limited

Albany Hotel
Birmingham

HR 72% £C **E**
Town plan C3 West Midlands
Smallbrook, Queensway B5 4EW
021-643 8171. Tlx 337031
Credit Access, Amex, Diners, Visa. LVs
A comprehensive range of business and leisure facilities is provided at this fine modern hotel in the heart of the city. Public areas range from a foyer with fashionable grey sofas, and a traditional mezzanine lounge with chesterfields and writing tables, to the smart Gun Room bar with its chic French atmosphere. Best bedrooms have attractive furnishings and smart Italian units; all rooms have mini-bars, remote-control TVs, individual air conditioning and well-equipped modern bathrooms. *Amenities* indoor swimming

pool, sauna, solarium, gymnasium, squash, snooker, laundry service, 24-hour lounge service.

■ *Rooms* 257	*Confirm by* 6
en suite bath/shower 257	*Last dinner* 11
Direct dial Yes	*Parking* Difficult
Room TV Yes	*Room service* 24 hours

Four Seasons Restaurant 😋 ᵹ

Talented chef Peter Inger has led the team here for more than 20 years and his thoughtfully composed menus continue as interesting and imaginative as ever. Top-quality ingredients and confident, sure-handed preparation make a winning combination, and sauces are a particularly strong point. You might start with a puff pastry cornet of scampi, scallops, salmon and sole in a creamy vermouth sauce, and follow this with medallions of venison sauced with blackberries and served with braised red cabbage. Good Italian wines on a well-balanced list. 🅴

■ *Set L* £9.45	*L* 12.30–2.30
About £45 *for two*	*D* 7.30–11
Seats 70	*Closed L* Sat, all Sun &
Bank Hols	

Apollo Hotel
Birmingham

H 63% £C/D
Town plan A3 West Midlands
243 Hagley Road, Edgbaston B16 9RA
021-455 0271. Tlx 336759
Manager Malcolm Hancock
Credit Access, Amex, Diners, Visa
A modern suburban hotel offering pleasant, comfortable accommodation and good conference facilities. Decent-sized bedrooms,

appointed in practical modern style, have hairdryers and trouser presses. Day rooms include an inviting lounge bar. More bedrooms and a leisure centre are planned. *Amenities* laundry service, 24-hour lounge service.

■ *Rooms* 118	*Confirm by* 6
en suite bath/shower 118	*Last dinner* 10.30
Direct dial Yes	*Parking* Ample
Room TV Yes	*Room service* Limited

BIRMINGHAM

Map 10 C4
Town plan opposite

Population 1,006,000

Birmingham is the centre of one of Britain's most dynamic regions. It achieved industrial fame as a result of a fine tradition of craftsmanship. Today the city is noted for its production of motor cars, electrical equipment, machine tools and plastics. It has a splendid tradition in metal ware, including gold and silver work. Birmingham sponsored the £20m plus National Exhibition Centre at Bickenhill, just nine miles south-east of the city. This exhibition centre is Britain's first ever purpose-designed centre and ranks among the most modern in the world.

Sights Outside City
Airport, Coughton Court, Black Country Museum, Ragley Hall, Packwood House, Warwick Castle, West Midland Safari Park, Arbury Hall, Charlecote Park, Stratford-upon-Avon

Information Office
Birmingham Convention & Visitor Bureau, Ticket Shop & Tourist Information Centre, City Arcade, Birmingham B2 4TX
Telephone 021–643 2514

Fiat Dealers
Colmore Depot Ltd
35 Sutton New Road
Erdington, Birmingham B23 6DT
Tel. 021–350 1301

Colmore Depot Ltd
979 Stratford Road
Hall Green, Birmingham B28 8BG
Tel. 021–778 2323

Marston Green Garage
32 Station Road, Marston Green
B37 7AX
Tel. 021–779 5140

1 Alexandra Theatre C3
2 Aston Hall *Jacobean masterpiece open to public* D1
3 Baskerville House B2
4 Botanical Gardens A3
5 Bull Ring Shopping Centre *rotunda, multi-level shopping centre and market* C/D3
6 Cannon Hill Park C3
7 Central Libraries B2
8 Council House B2
9 Hall of Memory B2
10 Hippodrome Theatre C3
11 Lickey Hills *500 beautiful acres with views from Beacon Hill of ten counties* C3
12 Midland Red Bus Station C3
13 Museum and Art Gallery *from Veronese to Picasso via Hogarth and Constable* B2
14 Museum of Science and Industry *a link with the Industrial Revolution* B1
15 Repertory Theatre A/B2
16 New Street Station C3
17 Post Office Tower B1
18 St Chad's Cathedral *first English Roman Catholic Cathedral since Reformation* C1
19 St Philip's Cathedral *18th-c Palladian with later Burne-Jones windows* C2
20 Town Hall *meeting-place and home of Symphony orchestra* B2
21 University of Aston D1
22 University of Birmingham C3

Birmingham

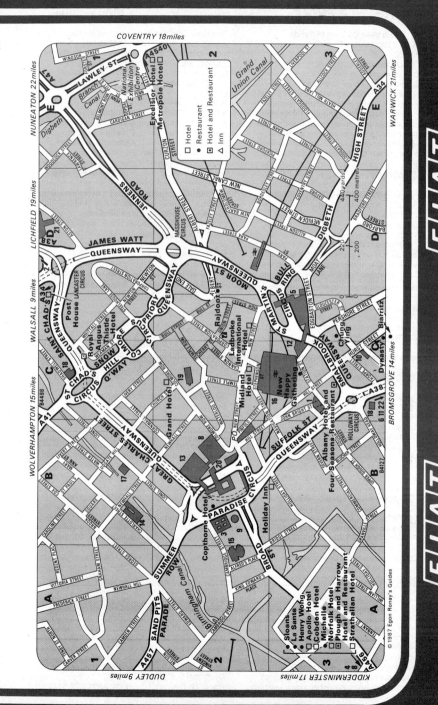

COVENTRY 18 miles

NUNEATON 22 miles

LICHFIELD 19 miles

WALSALL 9 miles

WOLVERHAMPTON 15 miles

KIDDERMINSTER 17 miles

DUDLEY 9 miles

WARWICK 21 miles

BROMSGROVE 14 miles

□ Hotel
● Restaurant
◨ Hotel and Restaurant
△ Inn

© 1987 Egon Ronay's Guides

Biarritz *NEW ENTRY*   Birmingham

R **Town plan C3** West Midlands
148 Bromsgrove Street
021-622 1989
French cooking
Owner manager Andrea Lo Coco
Credit Access, Amex, Diners, Visa

Daily trips to Birmingham's excellent markets ensure the quality of the produce in this friendly French restaurant, and chef Carl Timms does full justice to his ingredients. Fish and seafood are strongly featured, with delicious dishes like fennel-flavoured fish soup, goujons of sole with orange sauce, salmon with sorrel and lobster

Thermidor. Goat's cheese served hot in a flaky pastry case is a nice starter, and there are a few meaty main courses and some tempting sweets (hazelnut parfait with chocolate sauce, hot honey and lemon soufflé). Good French wines: note Ch. Ramage la Batisse '81, Vouvray Marc Brédif '83.
♀ Well-chosen ☺

■ Set L £7·50	L 12–2
Set D £18	D 7–10.30
About £40 for two	Parking Ample
Seats 40	Closed L Sat, all Sun,
Bank Hols & 1 wk Xmas	

Chung Ying *NEW ENTRY*   Birmingham

R ♫ ♿ **Town plan C3** West Midlands
16/18 Wrottesley Street
021-622 5669
Chinese cooking
Credit Access, Amex, Diners, Visa

The menu at the Wongs' smart Cantonese restaurant is long even by Chinese standards, with over 300 items including 40 varieties of Dim Sum. This doesn't affect the quality, and both the

food and ambience are very good. Choose familiar favourites like prawn toast, cashew chicken or beef with vegetables, or be a little more adventurous with casserole made from stewed eels, fish head or ox tripe.

■ Set meals from £6·40	Meals noon–11.30
About £20 for two	Parking Limited
Seats 240 Parties 240	Closed Xmas Day

■ Our inspectors never book in the name of Egon Ronay's Guides; they disclose their identity only after paying their bills.

Cobden Hotel *NEW ENTRY*   Birmingham

H **56% £D/E**
Town plan A3 West Midlands
166 Hagley Road, Edgbaston B16 9RA
021-454 6621. Tlx 339715
Credit Access, Amex, Diners, Visa

In a suburban setting on the busy A456, this extended Victorian house stands in its own grounds. The foyer-lounge, like the bar, is bright and welcoming, and bedrooms provide straight-

forward, practical comforts. Recent additions include 56 new Executive rooms, and a leisure centre and private facilities throughout are in the pipeline. *Amenities* garden, keep-fit equipment, laundry service, 24-hour lounge service.

■ Rooms 264	Confirm by 6
en suite bath/shower 193	Last dinner 9.45
Direct dial Yes	Parking Ample
Room TV Yes	Room service 24 hours

Copthorne Hotel *NEW ENTRY*   Birmingham

H **74% £C E ♿**
Town plan B2 West Midlands
Paradise Circus B3 2HJ
021-200 2727. Tlx 339026
Credit Access, Amex, Diners, Visa

Locals call this brand new hotel the Black Box, as its exterior is predominantly black glass. Inside, there's style and abundant space in the open-plan lounge and bar areas. There are also well-equipped conference and health centres. Bedrooms, all of a good size, are attractively done out in subtle greys and pinks, with brass light fittings and contemporary prints. Accessories include remote-control TVs, mini-bars, trouser presses and hairdryers, and there are plenty of toiletries in the smartly tiled bathrooms. Staff, initially not particularly efficient, will no doubt warm to their tasks. *Amenities* indoor swimming

pool, sauna, solarium, whirlpool bath, steam bath, keep-fit equipment, in-house movies (charge), laundry service, 24-hour lounge service.

■ Rooms 215	Confirm by 6
en suite bath/shower 215	Last dinner 10.30
Direct dial Yes	Parking Ample
Room TV Yes	Room service 24 hours

Dynasty   Birmingham

R ᕃ **Town plan C3** West Midlands
93 Hurst Street
021-622 1410
Chinese cooking
Owner manager Stewart So
Credit Access, Amex, Diners, Visa
  This fresh, bright restaurant serves very good
Peking and Cantonese food. Crispy duck is a
speciality you mustn't miss, and the seafood
selection includes unusual choices like steamed
yellow croaker or sizzling squid with black bean
sauce. Dim sum for starters or snacks – soups
and assorted hors d'oeuvre. Excellent
presentation, helpful service.

- **Set meals** from £7   D Meals noon–11.30,
  About £36 for two   Thurs noon–12
  Seats 120   **Parking** Ample
  Parties 130   Closed 25 & 26 Dec

Grand Hotel   Birmingham

H **63% £D**
  Town plan C2 West Midlands
Colmore Row B3 2DA
021-236 7951. Tlx 338174
Credit Access, Amex, Diners, Visa. LVs
  The Grand is well named if the title refers to the
magnificent Grosvenor Suite with its columns,
gallery balconies and remarkable plasterwork.
Various bars and lounges include the Penny Black
bar/coffee shop, its walls adorned with philatelic
prints. Cheerful bedrooms are furnished to a
decent standard, with smart units and good tiled
bathrooms. *Amenities* in-house movies (charge),
laundry service, 24-hour lounge service.

- **Rooms** 167   Confirm by arrang.
  en suite bath/shower 167 Last dinner 9.45
  Direct dial Yes   **Parking** Difficult
  Room TV Yes   **Room service** 24 hours

Henry Wong *NEW ENTRY*   Birmingham

R ᕃ **Town plan A3** West Midlands
283 High Street, Harborne
021-427 9799
Chinese cooking
Owner manager Henry Wong
Credit Access, Amex, Diners, Visa
  A wide range of mainly Cantonese dishes is on
offer in this smart and spacious suburban
restaurant. Starters include delicious sesame king
prawn toasts and deep-fried squid; tempting main
dishes include sizzling chicken with ginger and
spring onion, steamed fish with black bean sauce
and Cantonese-style fillet steak. Good-quality
ingredients are cooked to a high standard.

- **Set L & D** from £8   L 12–2
  About £25 for two   D 6–11
  Seats 130 **Parties** 20 **Parking** Ample
  Closed Sun, L Bank Hols, 24–26 Dec & 1 wk Aug

Holiday Inn   Birmingham

H **72% £C** *E* ᕃ
  Town plan B2 West Midlands
Central Square, Holliday Street B1 1HH
(021) 631 2000. Tlx 337272
Manager Stephen Carter
Credit Access, Amex, Diners, Visa
  Refurbishment of the public rooms has much
improved this eye-catching modern hotel not far
from the city centre. The spacious, marble floored
foyer leads to a smart lounge with inviting
chesterfields; the pool-side bar has attractively
tropical greenery, and the warm red lounge bar
has intimate lighting. Bedrooms (one floor for non-
smokers) come in three styles, all equipped with
useful accessories including mini-bars, trouser
presses and hairdryers. Well-kept bathrooms
feature non-slip floors. Smart, friendly staff.
Amenities indoor swimming pool, sauna,

solarium, keep-fit equipment, in-house movies
(free & charge), laundry service, coffee shop
(11am–11pm), 24-hour lounge service, kiosk.

- **Rooms** 295   Confirm by 6
  en suite bath/shower 295 Last dinner 11
  Direct dial Yes   **Parking** Ample
  Room TV Yes   **Room service** 24 hours

Ladbroke International Hotel   Birmingham

H **63% £C/D**
  Town plan C2 West Midlands
New Street B2 4RX
021-631 3331. Tlx 338331
Credit Access, Amex, Diners, Visa
  Restyling of bedrooms is nearing completion at
this modern city-centre hotel. Rooms now sport
brass light fittings, framed prints and cheerful
fabrics. Guests can consult the foyer's Ceefax
screens to keep in the picture, or switch off and
relax in the stylish lounge or bar.
Amenities in-house movies (charge), laundry
service, 24-hour lounge service.

- **Rooms** 193   Confirm by 6
  en suite bath/shower 193 Last dinner 9.45
  Direct dial Yes   **Parking** Difficult
  Room TV Yes   **Room service** 24 hours
  Closed 1 wk Xmas

Metropole & Warwick Hotel

Birmingham

H **81% £C/D** *E* &
Town plan E1 West Midlands
National Exhibition Centre B40 1PP
021-780 4242. Tlx 336129
Credit Access, Amex, Diners, Visa

Large, impressive hotel in the grounds of the
National Exhibition Centre. Up-to-the-minute
comfort is provided for the private guest, and
there are fine facilities for conferences and
functions. Bedrooms (twins and doubles in the
Metropole, singles in the Warwick) are spacious,
comfortable and well maintained. Newly
refurbished rooms have trouser presses,
hairdryers and attractive pastel decor. Superb
public rooms include a large marble-floored lobby
with a central seating area, an elegant, relaxing
lounge bar (evening pianist) and the popular
Cotswold Arms pub. *Amenities* garden, sauna,

solarium, hairdressing, squash, in-house movies
(charge), cinema, laundry service, 24-hour lounge
service, kiosk, courtesy coach.

■ *Rooms* 694	*Confirm by* arrang.
en suite bath/shower 694	*Last dinner* 10.30
Direct dial Yes	*Parking* Ample
Room TV Yes	*Room service* 24 hours
Closed 10 days Xmas	

Michelle

Birmingham

R **Town plan A3** West Midlands
182 High Street, Harborne
021-426 4133
Credit Access, Visa

Christian Bishop's cooking at this popular
bistro is unpretentious, and all the better for being
so. His menus offer a straightforward selection of
tasty dishes from beignets de fromage and
moules marinière to fillet of plaice with a seafood

sauce, chicken cordon bleu and steaks served
either plain or sauced. Service is keen, sometimes
overkeen. Lighter lunches available. The coffee's
not brilliant. ⬛ **Well-chosen**

■ *Set L from* £4·20	*L* 12–2
Set D from £8·90	*D* 7–10, Fri & Sat
About £30 *for two*	7–10.30
Seats 44	*Parking* Limited
Closed Sun, D 25 & all 26 Dec, also L Bank Hols	

Midland Hotel

Birmingham

H **65% £D/E**
Town plan C2 West Midlands
New Street B2 4JT
021-643 2601. Tlx 338419
Credit Access, Amex, Diners, Visa. **LVs**

One of Birmingham's longest established
hotels, and one that moves with the times.
Bedrooms have mostly been upgraded, with cane
or darkwood furniture, good-quality fabrics and

double glazing. A few standard rooms are plainer.
The foyer is quite striking with its panelling and
marble pillars, and there are bars to suit a variety
of moods. Many conference rooms. *Amenities*
laundry service, 24-hour lounge service.

■ *Rooms* 107	*Confirm by* 6
en suite bath/shower 107	*Last dinner* 10.30
Direct dial Yes	*Parking* Ample
Room TV Yes	*Room service* 24 hours

New Happy Gathering

Birmingham

R ⬛ **Town plan C3** West Midlands
43 Station Street
021-643 5247
Chinese cooking
Credit Access, Amex, Diners, Visa

A wide and tempting variety of expertly
prepared Cantonese dishes ensures a faithful
clientele at the Chan family's roomy first-floor
restaurant. Dim sum are favourite appetisers, and

main dishes run from stir-fried scallops and
stuffed king prawns to steamed duck with plum
sauce, sweet and sour pork and succulent fried
beef with cashew nuts. End your meal with a
lovely hot lotus paste bun.

■ *Set meals from* £16 *for two*	
About £20 *for two*	*Meals* noon-midnight
Seats 120 *Parties* 120	*Parking* Ample
Closed 3 days Xmas	

Norfolk Hotel

Birmingham

H **55% £E**
Town plan A3 West Midlands
257 Hagley Road, Edgbaston B16 9NH
021-454 8071. Tlx 339715
Manager S. H. Barlow
Credit Access, Amex, Diners, Visa

Refurbishment of public areas has given a
bright, stylish look to this substantial hotel sited
only about two miles from the city centre.

Bedrooms are roomy and practical, if a little
dated. *Amenities* garden, keep-fit equipment,
pitch & putt, laundry service, 24-hour lounge
service.

■ *Rooms* 175	*Confirm by* 6
en suite bath/shower 88	*Last dinner* 8.45
Direct dial Yes	*Parking* Ample
Room TV Most	*Room service* 24 hours
Closed 1 wk Xmas	

Plough & Harrow Hotel — Birmingham

HR 79% £B *E*
Town Plan A3 West Midlands
135 Hagley Road, Edgbaston B16 8LS
021-454 4111. Tlx 338074
Credit Access, Amex, Diners, Visa. LVs

Superb service is maintained by courteous management and staff at this splendid red-brick Victorian hotel, standing amidst modern office blocks on the edge of the city. Stepping into the welcoming foyer is like entering a bygone era when courtesy was king. The high-ceilinged lounge-cum-bar, with its period furniture, combines elegance and comfort while the public bar has a rustic charm. Some areas would, however, benefit from being spruced up. Bedrooms – most in a modern extension – have period-style furnishings brought up to date with accessories like hairdryers, teletext TVs and trouser presses. Carpeted bathrooms are luxurious.

Amenities garden, sauna, laundry service, 24-hour lounge service.

■ *Rooms 44* — *Confirm by arrang.*
en suite bath/shower 44 — *Last dinner 10.30*
Direct dial Yes — *Parking Ample*
Room TV Yes — *Room service 24 hours*

Plough & Harrow Hotel Restaurant

French cooking

Service is polished and efficient in the elegant restaurant, where you can choose between the set menu or à la carte, or indulge in the menu gastronomique. A typical selection from this might be scallop and prawn mousse with shellfish sauce, followed by fillet of lamb wrapped in spinach and pastry with an excellent celeriac mousse and orange-flavoured port sauce. Interesting dessert menu includes Benedictine soufflé and a tropical fruit pavlova. Service is polished and efficient. The cellar is strongest in Bordeaux, with classic vintages of Mouton Rothschild.

Well-chosen

■ *Set L £16·50* — *L 12.30–2.30*
Set D £23·50 — *D 7–10.30*
About £80 for two — *Seats 80*
Closed 25 & 26 Dec

Post House Hotel — Birmingham

H 60% £C/D
Town plan C1 West Midlands
Chapel Lane, Great Barr B43 7BG
021-357 7444. Tlx 338497
Credit Access, Amex, Diners, Visa. LVs

Businessmen using the M6 find this smart, modern hotel near exit 7 an ideal base. Public areas include the leafy Raffles lounge-bar and a foyer with clusters of inviting chesterfields. Decent-sized bedrooms (many of Executive standard) have fitted units and cosseting extras.

Amenities garden, outdoor swimming pool, laundry service, coffee shop (7am–10.30pm), 24 hour lounge service, children's playground.

■ *Rooms 204* — *Confirm by 6*
en suite bath/shower 204 — *Last dinner 10*
Direct dial Yes — *Parking Ample*
Room TV Yes — *Room service Limited*

Rajdoot — Birmingham

R ♿ **Town plan C2** West Midlands
12 Albert Street
021-643 8805
Indian cooking
Manager Mr S. K. Sharma
Credit Access, Amex, Diners, Visa

Authentic cooking in a smart, roomy restaurant. From the clay oven come various kebabs and tikkas (including lamb's kidneys and white fish), and there's a good range of curries, mostly quite mild. Enjoyable sundries and vegetables. Hot scented towels for sticky fingers, which you can then make sticky again with Indian pastries.

■ *Set L from £5·50* — *L 12–2.30*
Set D from £9·50 — *D 6.30–11.30*
About £38 for two — *Parking Difficult*
Seats 74 — *Parties 40*
Closed L Bank Hols & all 25 & 26 Dec

Royal Angus Thistle Hotel — Birmingham

H 65% £C/D
Town plan C1 West Midlands
St Chaps, Queensway B4 6HY
021-236 4211. Tlx 336889
Credit Access, Amex, Diners, Visa. LVs

After a three-year refurbishment programme this modern city-centre hotel is in pretty good shape. Throughout the public areas, abundant greenery and well-chosen furnishings create a most inviting ambience. Good-sized bedrooms offer trouser presses, hairdryers and remote-control TVs. The manager is friendly and helpful.

Amenities laundry service, 24-hour lounge service, in-house movies.

■ *Rooms 135* — *Confirm by 6*
en suite bath/shower 135 — *Last dinner 10.15*
Direct dial Yes — *Parking Ample*
Room TV Yes — *Room service 24 hours*

La Santé *NEW ENTRY*

R **Town plan A3** West Midlands
182 High Street, Harborne
021-426 4133
Credit Access, Visa
  An elegant French vegetarian restaurant located above the popular bistro Michelle on the main street of a Birmingham suburb. The evenings-only menu changes fortnightly to provide plenty of interest, with starters like

cheese beignets or spicy lentil soup preceding fondue savoyarde, hazelnut-stuffed courgettes, Turkish-style pilaff or Provençale crépinettes. End your meal with a delicately flavoured dessert like mango mousse.

■ *About £15 for two*   *D only 7–10*
Seats 40 Parties 50   *Parking Limited*
Closed Sun, Mon & Bank Hols

Sloans *NEW ENTRY*

R ♫ & **Town plan A3** West Midlands
27 Chad Square, Hawthorne Road,
Edgbaston
021-455 6697
Credit Access, Amex, Diners, Visa
  The Narbett family, previously of the Bell at Belborough, are making a name at this smart restaurant in a group of shops. French-inspired menus are full of interest and variety, with dishes

such as duck terrine with a port jelly sauce, wild duck roasted with figs and a hot lime and honey soufflé. Vegetables are outstanding. Service is skilled and friendly. ♀ **Well-chosen** ☙
■ *Set L £10·50*   *L 12–2*
Set D £21   *D 7–9.45*
About £55 for two   *Parking Ample*
Seats 60   *Parties 60*
Closed L Sat, Sun, Bank Hols & 1 wk Jan

Strathallan Thistle Hotel

H **66% £C/D**
Town plan A3 West Midlands
225 Hagley Road, Edgbaston B16 9RY
021-455 9777. Tlx 336680
Credit Access, Amex, Diners, Visa
  Close to the M5 and M6, this modern hotel makes a useful overnight stopover. Smart public areas include an elegant, marble-floored foyer-lounge, peaceful lounge bar and lively American

cocktail bar. Above, circular upper storeys house unusually shaped little bedrooms (best face outwards). Comprehensively equipped, all have good tiled bathrooms. *Amenities* in-house movies, laundry service, 24-hour lounge service.
■ *Rooms 166*   *Confirm by 6*
en suite bath/shower 166 *Last dinner 11*
Direct dial Yes   *Parking Ample*
Room TV Yes   *Room service 24 hours*

☙ is our symbol for an **outstanding** wine list.

Excelsior Hotel

H **62% £C/D**
Town plan E2 West Midlands
Coventry Road B26 3QW
021-782 8141. Tlx 338005
Credit Access, Amex, Diners, Visa. **LVs**
  Both the airport and the National Exhibition Centre are but a mile from this modernised red-brick 1930s hotel. Public rooms are stylish, some of which are grouped round an attractive patio.

Well-kept bedrooms – the best with co-ordinating fabrics, quilted bedspreads and darkwood units – have tea-makers and remote control TVs.
Amenities garden, snooker, laundry service, 24-hour lounge service, courtesy coach.
■ *Rooms 141*   *Confirm by 6*
en suite bath/shower 141 *Last dinner 10.15*
Direct dial Yes   *Parking Ample*
Room TV Yes   *Room service 24 hours*

■ For a discount on next year's guide, see Offer for Answers.

Blackburn Moat House

H **58% £D/E**
Map 10 B1 Lancashire
Preston New Road BB2 7BE
Blackburn (0254) 64441. Tlx 63271
Credit Access, Amex, Diners, Visa
  A familiar landmark on the A677 between Blackburn and the M6, this pitched-roofed hotel welcomes guests in a spacious reception area with comfortable seating. Half of the agreeably-

sized bedrooms have recently acquired new carpets, curtains and easy chairs. Hairdryers are now supplied. *Amenities* garden, solarium, snooker, in-house movies (charge), laundry service, 24-hour lounge service.
■ *Rooms 98*   *Confirm by 6*
en suite bath/shower 98   *Last dinner 10*
Direct dial Yes   *Parking Ample*
Room TV Yes   *Room service 24 hours*

Bardon Lodge Hotel   Blackheath

See under London

Imperial Hotel   Blackpool

H 66% £C/D
Map 10 A1 Lancashire
North Promenade FY1 2HB
Blackpool (0253) 23971. Tlx 677376
Manager John Herdman
Credit Access, Amex, Diners, Visa
   This grand-style Victorian seafront hotel has
played host to such notables as Charles Dickens
and Margaret Thatcher. The impressive public

rooms could be smarter; bedrooms are practical
and modern. *Amenities* indoor swimming pool,
sauna, solarium, hairdressing, in-house movies
(charge), laundry service, coffee shop (24 hours),
24-hour lounge service, kiosk.
- *Rooms 159* — *Confirm by 6*
- *en suite bath/shower 159* — *Last dinner 10.30*
- *Direct dial Yes* — *Parking Ample*
- *Room TV Yes* — *Room service 24 hours*

New Clifton Hotel   Blackpool

H 63% £D/E
Map 10 A1 Lancashire
Talbot Square FY1 1ND
Blackpool (0253) 21481. Tlx 67570
Credit Access, Amex, Diners, Visa
   A handsome foyer and a smart bar are among
the Victorian features of this Georgian seafront
hotel opposite the renovated North Pier. Sizeable
bedrooms (best ones face the sea) have practical

· modern furnishings and good bathrooms. Friendly
staff and good housekeeping.
Amenities laundry service, 24-hour lounge
service.
- *Rooms 83* — *Confirm by 6*
- *en suite bath/shower 83* — *Last dinner 10*
- *Direct dial Yes* — *Parking Difficult*
- *Room TV Yes* — *Room service 24 hours*

Pembroke Hotel   Blackpool

H 68% £C
Map 10 A1 Lancashire
North Promenade FY1 2JQ
Blackpool (0253) 23434. Tlx 677469
Credit Access, Amex, Diners, Visa
   Almost all the bedrooms enjoy sea views at this
early-80s high-rise hotel, a popular venue for
conferences and banquets. Rooms are smart and
comfortable with newly modernised bathrooms.

The leisure centre includes a poolside night spot.
Amenities garden, indoor swimming pool, sauna,
solarium, keep-fit equipment, games room, pool
table, in-house movies (charge), 24-hour lounge
service, children's play area.
- *Rooms 201* — *Confirm by 6*
- *en suite bath/shower 201* — *Last dinner 11*
- *Direct dial Yes* — *Parking Ample*
- *Room TV Yes* — *Room service 24 hours*

Manor Hotel   Blakeney

H 57% £E
Map 6 C1 Norfolk
Nr Holt NR25 7ND
Cley (0263) 740376
Manager Mr G. Murray
   Inside this converted farmhouse the
atmosphere is solidly traditional, with a dark wood
and leather-look bar and comfortable lounge on
two levels, the upper part opening into the

garden. Bedrooms (including four across the
courtyard) are bright and cheerful, with modern
furnishings and coffee and tea-making facilities.
Amenities garden, laundry service.
- *Rooms 26* — *Confirm by arrang.*
- *en suite bath/shower 26* — *Last dinner 8.45*
- *Room phone No* — *Parking Ample*
- *Room TV Yes* — *Room service All day*
- *Closed 3 wks Dec.*

Lord Crewe Arms Hotel   Blanchland

H 65% £D/E
Map 15 B4 Northumberland
Nr Consett, Co. Durham DH8 9SP
Blanchland (043 475) 251
Owner manager Mr C. J. Simpson
Credit Access, Amex, Diners, Visa
   A historic building standing in a wonderfully
unspoilt village setting. This old abbot's house
boasts characterful public rooms, and delightful

bedrooms that vary in size and shape, many with
handsome old oak furnishings, others with '30s
furniture. Bathrooms are mostly modern.
Amenities garden, laundry service.
- *Rooms 15* — *Confirm by arrang.*
- *en suite bath/shower 15* — *Last dinner 9.15*
- *Direct dial Yes* — *Parking Ample*
- *Room TV Yes* — *Room service All day*

La Belle Alliance
Blandford Forum

RR ♕ ♟ **Map 4 B4** Dorset
Whitecliffe Mill Street DT11 7BP
Blandford Forum (0258) 52842
Credit Access, Amex, Diners, Visa
Nothing is too much trouble for the enthusiastic Davisons. Lauren goes to great lengths to welcome guests while Philip shows similar consideration in planning menus with something for everyone. Ingredients are carefully combined with a view to complementary flavours and textures. A hot tart of wild mushrooms with fresh garden herbs makes a tasty starter. To follow, try poached lemon sole in vermouth and cream.

Desserts include butterscotch and chocolate syllabub. Smoking discouraged. ☺

■ *Set L £7·50*	*L Sun only 12–2*
Set D £14·50	*D 7–9.30, Sat 7–10*
About £36 for two	*Parking Ample*
Seats 25	*Parties 36*
Closed D Sun & 1st 2 wks Jan	

Bedrooms £F

Rooms 5	*With bath/shower 4*

Welcome touches in recently refurbished bedrooms include TVs, complimentary newspapers, mineral water and sewing kits. Bright bathrooms are functional.

Lower Brook House
Blockley

H 60% £C/D
Map 4 C1 Gloucestershire
Moreton-in-Marsh GL56 9DS
Broadway (0386) 700286
Owner manager Ewan Wright
Credit Access
A babbling brook in the garden is only one of the charms of this 17th-century Cotswold stone house with its huge inglenook fireplace and

wealth of old beams and uneven flagstones. Sloping ceilings bring character to simple, cosy bedrooms. Half-board terms only.
Amenities garden.

■ *Rooms 8*	*Confirm by arrang.*
en suite bath/shower 8	*Last dinner 9*
Room phone No	*Parking Ample*
Room TV Yes	*Room service Limited*
Closed Jan	

Marston Farm Hotel
Bodymoor Heath

H 63% £E
Map 10 C4 Warwickshire
Dog Lane, Nr Sutton Coldfield B76 0EA
Tamworth (0827) 872133
Owner managers Mr & Mrs J. W. Broadbent
Credit Access, Amex, Diners, Visa
Handy for Birmingham but this converted farmhouse seems a world away with its quiet rural setting. There's a pleasant, relaxing lounge and

two bars, one a lively bistro. Neat, spacious bedrooms have cosy colour schemes. Expansion under way. No dogs. *Amenities* garden, outdoor swimming pool, tennis, coarse fishing, laundry service, 24-hour lounge service.

■ *Rooms 17*	*Confirm by 6*
en suite bath/shower 17	*Last dinner 10*
Direct dial Yes	*Parking Ample*
Room TV Yes	*Room service Limited*

Royal Norfolk Hotel
Bognor Regis

H 62% £D
Map 5 E4 West Sussex
The Esplanade PO21 2LH
Bognor Regis (0243) 826222. Tlx 837921
Credit Access, Amex, Diners, Visa
Plans to restore the Royal Norfolk to its original Regency splendour are well under way, and the public rooms have been made much more attractive. Refurbishment is also improving the

bedrooms, which are generally spacious and comfortable; front ones look out to sea. Good traditional breakfast. Staff could be more helpful.
Amenities garden, outdoor swimming pool, tennis, croquet.

■ *Rooms 51*	*Confirm by arrang.*
en suite bath/shower 45	*Last dinner 9.30*
Room phone Yes	*Parking Ample*
Room TV Yes	*Room service Limited*

Crest Hotel
Bolton

H 58% £D
Map 10 B1 Greater Manchester
Beaumont Road BL3 4TA
Bolton (0204) 651511. Tlx 635527
Credit Access, Amex, Diners, Visa
A purpose-built hotel close to junction 5 of the M61. A cheery, welcoming foyer with comfortable seating leads to the smart modern cocktail bar. There are three well-equipped function rooms.

Neatly designed bedrooms with colourful curtains offer trouser presses and tea/coffee-makers. Bathrooms have shower fitments and good tiling.
Amenities games room, laundry service, 24-hour lounge service.

■ *Rooms 100*	*Confirm by 6*
en suite bath/shower 100	*Last dinner 9.45*
Direct dial Yes	*Parking Ample*
Room TV Yes	*Room service 24 hours*

Last Drop Village Hotel · **Bolton**

H 68% £D
Map 10 B1 Greater Manchester
Hospital Road, Bromley Cross BL7 9PZ
Bolton (0204) 591131. Tlx 635322
Credit Access, Amex, Diners, Visa
Ask the hotel for directions before you make
your way to this most unusual 'village' near the
A666. Consisting of a carefully restored collection
of old farm buildings, it has its own pub, tea shop,
crafts shops, hotel and restaurants. The hotel
itself is full of character, with a mass of fascinating
collectors' items enlivening the split-level cocktail
bar – don't miss the old carriage housing the

telephone! Good-sized bedrooms, mostly with
pine furniture, are comfortable and well equipped.
Executive rooms offer more luxurious bathrooms
and extras like towelling robes.
Amenities garden, indoor swimming pool, sauna,
solarium, whirlpool bath, gymnasium,
hairdressing, satellite TV, laundry service, coffee
shop (10am–4.30pm winter, 10am–5.30pm
summer), 24-hour lounge service.
- *Rooms* 80 — *Confirm by* 6
- *en suite bath/shower* 80 — *Last dinner* 10
- *Direct dial* Yes — *Parking* Ample
- *Room TV* Yes — *Room service* Limited

Pack Horse Hotel · **Bolton**

H 58% £D/E
Map 10 B1 Greater Manchester
Bradshawgate BL1 1DP
Bolton (0204) 27261. Tlx 635168
Credit Access, Amex, Diners, Visa. **LVs**
Overlooking a garden square in the centre of
town, this redbrick Georgian hotel provides
pleasant, modern accommodation in bright,
cheerful bedrooms, some with hairdryers and

trouser presses, all with tea-makers. There is
lounge seating in the foyer and two bars include
one in an attractive Regency style.
Amenities garden.
- *Rooms* 78 — *Confirm by* arrang.
- *en suite bath/shower* 73 — *Last dinner* 10
- *Direct dial* Yes — *Parking* Difficult
- *Room TV* Yes — *Room service* 24 hours

- If we recommend meals in a hotel or inn, a separate entry is made for its restaurant.

Devonshire Arms · **Bolton Abbey**

H 75% £C/D &
Map 15 B6 North Yorkshire
Nr Skipton BD23 6AJ
Bolton Abbey (075 671) 441. Tlx 51218
Credit Access, Amex, Diners, Visa
Restored and enlarged since its days as a
coaching inn, the Devonshire Arms offers very
comfortable accommodation in an attractive
setting near the river Wharfe in the heart of the
Yorkshire Dales National Park. Best bedrooms are
the nine in the original part, featuring handsome
antiques and including some with four-posters.
Bedrooms in the modern wing are more compact,
bright and cheerful, and all rooms have duvets,
remote-control TVs, radio-alarms and well-
provisioned bathrooms with lovely thick towels
and quality soaps. An open fire warms the
reception hall, beyond which are two inviting,

stylish lounges with fine furnishings, paintings
and antiques, and an equally appealing bar with
lots of character. *Amenities* garden, coarse
fishing, snooker, laundry service.
- *Rooms* 38 — *Confirm by* arrang.
- *en suite bath/shower* 38 — *Last dinner* 9.30
- *Direct dial* Yes — *Parking* Ample
- *Room TV* Yes — *Room service* 24 hours

Winterbourne Hotel · **Bonchurch**

H 68% £C/D
Map 5 D4 Isle of Wight
Nr Ventnor PO38 1RQ
Isle of Wight (0983) 852535
Owner managers Terry & Pat O'Connor
Credit Access, Amex, Diners, Visa
Lush gardens and sea views make a lovely
setting for this peaceful hotel. Day rooms include
an attractive lounge opening on to a terrace, and

a little cocktail bar. Bedrooms are comfortable
and well equipped. *Amenities* garden, outdoor
swimming pool, putting, in-house movies (free),
laundry service, hotel car.
- *Rooms* 19 — *Confirm by* arrang.
- *en suite bath/shower* 17 — *Last dinner* 10
- *Direct dial* Yes — *Parking* Ample
- *Room TV* Yes — *Room service* All day
- *Closed* mid Dec–mid Feb

White Friars Hotel   Boreham Street

H **63% £D/E**
Map 7 B6 East Sussex
Nr Herstmonceux BN27 4SE
Herstmonceux (0323) 832355
Owner manager Michael Hounsome
Credit Access, Amex, Diners, Visa
   A much-extended 18th-century building, set
back from the A271 in lovely, well-tended
gardens. There's a comfortable lounge with

chintz-covered sofas, and a choice of two bars.
Bedrooms in the main house and an adjacent
cottage are prettily furnished and have good
modern bathrooms. *Amenities* garden.

■ *Rooms* 20	*Confirm by arrang.*
en suite bath/shower 20	*Last dinner* 9
Direct dial Yes	*Parking* Ample
Room TV Yes	*Room service* All day
Closed 1–10 Jan	

■ Any person using our name
   to obtain free hospitality is
   a fraud. Proprietors, please
   inform the police and us.

Crown Hotel   Boroughbridge

H **65% £D/E** &
Map 15 C6 North Yorkshire
Horsefair YO5 9LB
Boroughbridge (090 12) 2328. Tlx 57906
Manager Mr C. Dellapuppa
Credit Access, Amex, Diners, Visa. LVs
   In the centre of Boroughbridge and only a mile
from the A1 lies the Crown, originally an old
coaching inn. Staff are friendly, and relaxation is

easy in the comfortable bar and lounge.
Bedrooms are mostly modern, with good private
bathrooms. *Amenities* sauna, solarium, laundry
service, in-house movies (free), 24-hour lounge
service, coffee shop (10am–10pm).

■ *Rooms* 43	*Confirm by arrang.*
en suite bath/shower 43	*Last dinner* 9.15
Direct dial Yes	*Parking* Ample
Room TV Yes	*Room service* 24 hours

Three Arrows Hotel   Boroughbridge

H **61% £E**
Map 15 C6 North Yorkshire
Horsefair YO5 9LL
Boroughbridge (090 12) 2245
Manager R. Korda   -
Credit Access, Amex, Diners, Visa
   Extensive grounds surround this Victorian
country mansion situated just one mile from the
A1. Guests can enjoy the views from the lounge,

and there's a pleasant bar and a useful meeting
room, too. Spacious bedrooms are furnished with
darkwood pieces and have simple, well-kept
bathrooms. *Amenities* garden, putting.

■ *Rooms* 17	*Confirm by arrang.*
en suite bath/shower 17	*Last dinner* 9
Room phone Yes	*Parking* Ample
Room TV Yes	*Room service* All day
Closed 28–30 Dec	

■ Our inspectors are our full-
   time employees; they are
   professionally trained by us.

Borrowdale Hotel   Borrowdale

H **60% £E**
Map 13 C5 Cumbria
Nr Keswick CA12 5UY
Borrowdale (059 684) 224
Credit Access, Visa
   Mountains frame this handsome hotel
overlooking Derwentwater. A slate fireplace
flanked by armchairs gives the foyer a welcoming
appearance and there are comfortable sofas and

fine antiques in the lounge. The bar is oak
panelled. Bedrooms are well kept and bathrooms
are carpeted. Guests have free weekday use of a
nearby golf course. Half-term board terms only.
Amenities garden, laundry service.

■ *Rooms* 35	*Confirm by* 4
en suite bath/shower 35	*Last dinner* 9.30
Direct dial Yes	*Parking* Ample
Room TV Yes	*Room service* Limited

Lodore Swiss Hotel — Borrowdale

HR **77% £C/D**
Map 13 C5 Cumbria
Nr Keswick CA12 5UX
Borrowdale (059 684) 285. Tlx 64305
Owner managers England family
Credit Amex

Whether you're active or idle, this long-established family hotel is a great place to be. Staff are superb, the views are magnificent, and there's a fine range of leisure activities. The lounge is spacious and attractively decorated with lots of comfortable, modern seating. There is also a bar and a small, quiet writing room. Stylish bedrooms offer modern comforts and their bathrooms are very well equipped. No dogs. *Amenities* garden, indoor & outdoor swimming pools, sauna, solarium, keep-fit equipment,

beauty salon, tennis, squash, games room, in-house movies, laundry room & service, 24-hour lounge service, kiosk, nanny, children's playground.

■ *Rooms* 72	*Confirm by arrang.*
en suite bath/shower 72	*Last dinner* 9.30
Direct dial Yes	*Parking* Ample
Room TV Yes	*Room service* 24 hours
Closed 2 Nov–late March	

Lodore Swiss Hotel Restaurant ৬

The kitchen brigade does a consistently fine job, and the restaurant staff work with almost unmatched efficiency and precision. Kurt Hartmann's fixed-price menus (five courses including sorbet) offer a succession of delights, from terrines and mousses to fresh fish, high-quality meats, interesting vegetables and some sensational pâtisserie. There's choice for every course except the fish. Some excellent wines at reasonable prices. ♀ **Well-chosen** ☺

■ *Set D from* £14	*L* 12.30–2
About £34 *for two*	*D* 7.30–9.30
Seats 150	*Parties* 40
Closed 2 Nov–26 March	

Millstream Hotel — Bosham

H **65% £D/E** ৬
Map 5 E4 West Sussex
Bosham Lane, Nr Chichester PO18 8HL
Bosham (0243) 573234
Credit Access, Amex, Diners, Visa

Take a 16th-century malthouse, add some 18th century cottages and an Edwardian manor house, set them in a pretty stream-bordered garden, and you have a delightful home-from-home hotel.

Public rooms are bright and airy, bedrooms attractively decorated, well-equipped and generally spacious. Excellent standards of housekeeping and maintenance. Helpful, friendly staff. *Amenities* garden, laundry service.

■ *Rooms* 29	*Confirm by* 6
en suite bath/shower 29	*Last dinner* 9.30
Direct dial Yes	*Parking* Ample
Room TV Yes	*Room service* Limited

New England Hotel — Boston

I **£E/F**
Map 11 F3 Lincolnshire
49 Wide Bargate PE21 6SH
Boston (0205) 65255
Credit Access, Amex, Diners, Visa

Easy parking is a plus of this friendly red-brick inn on a wide thoroughfare near the town centre, whose large panelled bar-lounge is very popular with the locals. Bedrooms have been well

modernised and equipped with well-designed units that provide useful writing space, tea-makers and digital radio-alarms. All have compact, practical bathrooms. *Amenities* laundry service.

■ *Rooms* 25	*Confirm by* 6
en suite bath/shower 25	*Last dinner* 10
Room phone Yes	*Parking* Ample
Room TV Yes	*Room service* Limited

Cobbett's — Botley

R ♀ **Map 5 D4** Hampshire
13 The Square
Botley (048 92) 2068
French cooking
Credit Access, Amex, Visa

A charming, cottagy restaurant with lots of beams, a cheerful log fire and a cosy bar. Lucie Skipwith, a native of St Emilion, runs a kitchen team that produces dishes to please throughout

the range, from prettily presented vegetable mousse and warm salad of pigeon breast to loin of pork Vallée D'Auge. ♀ **Well-chosen** ☺

■ *Set L* £8·50	*L* noon–2.30
Set D £14	*D* 7–10
About £50 *for two*	*Parking* Ample
Seats 40	*Parties* 14
Closed D Sun, *L* Mon, Bank Hols & 2 wks summer	

NEW ENTRY

Tanyard Hotel *NEW ENTRY*   Boughton Monchelsea

HR 63% £E
Map 7 C5 Kent
Wierton Hill, Nr Maidstone ME17 4JT
Maidstone (0622) 44705
Owner manager Jan Davies
Credit Access, Amex, Diners, Visa

Check directions as the hotel is tucked away on the side of the Downs. A converted medieval yeoman's house, it boasts a plethora of beams, leaded windows and inglenooks. An informal, cosy lounge encourages guests to mingle. Comfortable bedrooms have modern furniture and many extras. No dogs. *Amenities* garden.

■ *Rooms* 5	*Confirm by arrang.*
en suite bath/shower 5	*Last dinner* 8
Direct dial Yes	*Parking* Ample
Room TV Yes	*Room service* All day
Closed Jan & Feb	

Tanyard Hotel Restaurant 🍴

The wonderful beamed dining room with bread oven, open fire and leaded windows, offering breathtaking views of the Weald, provides a delightful setting in which to sample Jan Davies' good, simple cooking. Pre-dinner drinks are taken in the comfortable drawing room where guests may peruse the no-choice set menu. An excellent avocado terrine might be the starter, followed by duck breast with orange sauce accompanied by perfect vegetables, with choux pastry ring to finish. Good local produce features strongly and the cheeses are outstanding. RESIDENTS ONLY. ⊖

■ *Set D* £13·80	*D at* 8
About £35 *for two*	*Seats* 14
Closed Jan & Feb	

Carlton Hotel   Bournemouth

H 76% £B *E*
Town plan E2 Dorset
East Overcliff BH1 3DN
Bournemouth (0202) 22011. Tlx 41244
Credit Access, Amex, Diners, Visa

Courteous, old-fashioned service prevails at this fine clifftop hotel, and there are excellent facilities for the health- and fitness-conscious guest. An open-plan reception leads to the lounge and bar areas, both overlooking the patio and pool. There's also a smaller, more intimate cocktail bar. Spacious, very comfortable bedrooms, some with balconies and sweeping views of the coastline, feature well-chosen fabrics and good-quality modern furnishings; all have smartly tiled, splendidly equipped bathrooms. Good conference facilities.
Amenities garden, outdoor swimming pool,

sauna, solarium, whirlpool bath, gymnasium, beauty salon, hairdressing, games room, snooker, in-house movies (free), laundry service, 24-hour lounge service.

■ *Rooms* 65	*Confirm by* 6
en suite bath/shower 65	*Last dinner* 11
Direct dial Yes	*Parking* Ample
Room TV Yes	*Room service* 24 hours

Crest Hotel   Bournemouth

H 60% £D
Town plan E1 Dorset
The Lansdowne BH1 2PR
Bournemouth (0202) 23262. Tlx 41232
Manager Mr C. Tomkinson
Credit Access, Amex, Diners, Visa. LVs

Towards the Lansdowne, just a few minutes' walk from the seafront, this distinctive circular hotel is a good family holiday base. Friendly staff

continue to chalk up the daily weather forecast, and local information is posted in the spacious lobby lounge. The largest of the well-equipped bedrooms face outwards; all rooms are neat and practical. *Amenities* games room, snooker.

■ *Rooms* 102	*Confirm by* 6
en suite bath/shower 102	*Last dinner* 9.30
Direct dial Yes	*Parking* Ample
Room TV Yes	*Room service* Limited

Durley Hall Hotel   Bournemouth

H 55% £D/E
Town plan A3 Dorset
7 Durley Chine Road BH2 5JS
Bournemouth (0202) 766886
Manager Mr S. J. Badger
Credit Access, Amex, Diners, Visa

A sturdy red-brick hotel popular with both holiday makers and conference visitors. Some bedrooms are traditional in style, others airy and

more modern. *Amenities* garden, indoor & outdoor swimming pools, sauna, solarium, steam & whirlpool baths, hairdressing, beauty salon, keep-fit equipment, putting, games room, snooker, pool table, in-house movies (free), laundry room.

■ *Rooms* 80	*Confirm by* 6
en suite bath/shower 80	*Last dinner* 8.45
Direct dial Yes	*Parking* Ample
Room TV Yes	*Room service* 24 hours

East Cliff Court Hotel

H **60%** **£C/D**
Town plan E2 Dorset
East Overcliff Drive BH1 3AN
Bournemouth (0202) 24545
Owner managers Messrs A. & N. Michael
Credit Access, Amex, Visa

A clifftop position affording spectacular views is a feature of this well-kept hotel. Relaxing public rooms include three recently refurbished lounges and cosy bar. The best and most spacious bedrooms have balconies and sea views. En-suite bathrooms are adequately equipped.
Amenities outdoor swimming pool, sauna, solarium, 24-hour lounge service.

■ *Rooms 70*	*Confirm by 6*
en suite bath/shower 70	*Last dinner 9*
Direct dial Yes	*Parking Ample*
Room TV Yes	*Room service 24 hours*

Highcliff Hotel

H **70%** **£C**
Town plan B3 Dorset
St Michael's Road, West Cliff BH2 5DU
Bournemouth (0202) 27702. Tlx 417153
Manager Mr C. T. Smith
Credit Access, Amex, Diners, Visa

Wise investment, sound management and energetic, friendly staff ensure the continuing popularity of this fine seafront hotel. Delightful colour schemes and elegant furnishings highlight the lounges and bar; the sun lounge is a peaceful spot, while the action is livelier in the pub and night club. Bedrooms are spacious and practical, with well-equipped bathrooms. Luxury rooms in converted coastguard cottages feature many extras like trouser presses and wall safes.
Amenities garden, outdoor swimming pool, sauna, solarium, tennis, putting, games room,

snooker, pool table, in-house movies (free), laundry service, 24-hour lounge service, nanny (in summer), children's play area.

■ *Rooms 110*	*Confirm by 6*
en suite bath/shower 110	*Last dinner 9*
Direct dial Yes	*Parking Ample*
Room TV Yes	*Room service 24 hours*

♟ indicates a **well-chosen** house wine.

Palace Court Hotel

H **66%** **£D**
Town plan D2 Dorset
Westover Road BH1 2BR
Bournemouth (0202) 27681. Tlx 418451
Credit Access, Amex, Diners, Visa

Many of the bedrooms at this modernised 1930s hotel enjoy sea views, and those in the main part have private balconies. Spacious, comfortable public rooms include a lounge and bar, both flamboyantly revamped. Long-standing owner manager Mr Ronco has an even longer-standing head porter, at his desk since 1946! *Amenities* sauna, solarium, whirlpool bath, keep-fit equipment, games room, laundry service.

■ *Rooms 107*	*Confirm by arrang.*
en suite bath/shower 107	*Last dinner 9*
Direct dial Yes	*Parking Ample*
Room TV Yes	*Room service 24 hours*

Royal Bath Hotel

H **75%** **£B** *E* &
Town plan D2 Dorset
Bath Road BH1 2EW
Bournemouth (0202) 25555
Credit Access, Amex, Diners, Visa

Courteous, helpful and friendly staff are on hand from the moment you arrive at this gleaming white building overlooking the bay. Public rooms, including a pillared lounge and mellow, panelled bar, are of handsome proportions, though some of their carpets and upholstery are looking tired. Most bedrooms are of a decent size, with restful colour schemes, traditional furnishings and remote-control teletext TVs (ours wasn't working). In the bathrooms, good-quality toiletries and excellent thick towels. No dogs.
Amenities garden, outdoor swimming pool, sauna, solarium, keep-fit equipment, hairdressing,

putting, games room (summer), in-house movies (charge), valeting, laundry service, 24-hour lounge service, nanny (summer), helipad.

■ *Rooms 133*	*Confirm by arrang.*
en suite bath/shower 133	*Last dinner 9.30*
Direct dial Yes	*Parking Ample*
Room TV Yes	*Room service 24 hours*

BOURNEMOUTH

Map 4 C4
Town plan opposite

Population 144,800

The founding of Bournemouth can be dated to 1810 when a Dorset squire built a summer residence and let it to friends. It has developed from this beginning into a seaside resort receiving nearly 2 million visitors a year. The town is mainly Victorian but contains interesting additions, particularly from the 1930s. It is noted for its parks and gardens as well as its entertainment facilities.

Annual Events
Daffodil Vintage Car Rally *April*
Thirties Revival Festival, TVS air Show *May*
Health Week Flower Festival *June*
Dance Festival *July*
Beer Festival *July/August*
Folk Festival, Regatta and Carnival *July/August*
Summer Pops and Kite Festival *August*

Sights Outside City
Hengistbury Head, Christchurch Priory, Christchurch Tricycle Museum, Corfe Castle, Compton Acre Gardens, Brownsea Island, Kingston Lacy House and Park, Merley Tropical Bird Gardens, Wimbourne Minster.

Information Centre
Westover Road
BH1 2BLL
Telephone Bournemouth 291715

Fiat Dealer
Caffyns PLC
674–680 Wimbourne Road, Winton
Bournemouth
BH9 2EF
Tel. Bournemouth 512121

1   Big Four Railway Museum and Model Exhibiton **C1**
2   Boscombe Pier **E2**
3   Bournemouth Natural Science Society Museum **E1**
4   Bournemouth Pier and Leisure Centre *including a theatre, discothèque, shops and amusements* **D3**
5   Bournemouth Transport Museum **E1**
6   Casa Magni Shelley Museum **E2**
7   Ice Skating Rink **D2**
8   International Centre *including concert halls, swimming pool and fitness centre* **C3**
9   King's Park with Miniature Railway **E1**
10 Meyrick Park **A1/B1**
11 Pavilion Theatre **D2**
12 Queen's Park **E1**
13 R. L. Stevenson Memorial Gardens **A3**
14 Russell Cotes Art Gallery and Museum **D2**
15 Shell House **E2**
16 Winter Gardens Theatre **B3**

Bournemouth

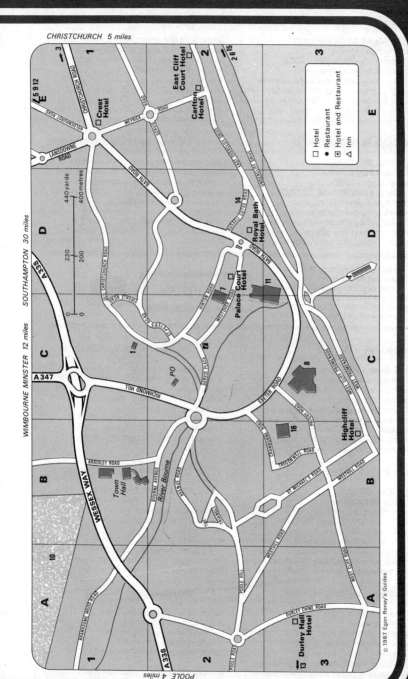

© 1987 Egon Ronay's Guides

Rose Tree
Bourton-on-the-Water

Ŕ ♧ **Map 4 C1** Gloucestershire
Riverside
Bourton-on-the-Water (0451) 20635
Credit Access, Amex, Diners, Visa
    Sound home cooking in a quaint, beamed
cottage by the river Windrush. Val Grundy's fixed-
price menus tempt with dishes such as smoked
salmon and prawn terrine, tuna and water
chestnuts in puff pastry, halibut baked with

yoghurt and fennel, sautéed pheasant breast with
orange sauce, all accompanied by copious
vegetables. Super sweets or Stilton. Sunday
roasts. ♀ Well-chosen

■ *Set L £8·95*	*L Sun only 12.30–2*
Set D from £9·50	*D 7.30–10*
About £40 for two	*Parking Limited*
Seats 26 Parties 30	*Closed D Sun & Mon,*
Bank Hols & 5 wks from mid-Jan	

Belsfield Hotel
Bowness on Windermere

Ĥ **62% £C/D** &
Map 13 D5 Cumbria
Kendal Road LA23 3EL
Windermere (096 62) 2448. Tlx 65238
Credit Access, Amex, Diners, Visa
    Lawns rolling down to the lake front this
extended Victorian house, whose comfortable
public rooms have lofty ceilings and large
windows. Bedrooms are also generally spacious,

and many have marvellous views. Some are in
need of (planned) refurbishment. Pleasant staff.
Amenities garden, indoor swimming pool, sauna,
solarium, tennis, putting, games rooms, snooker,
pool table, children's playground.

■ *Rooms 66*	*Confirm by 6*
en suite bath/shower 66	*Last dinner 9.30*
Direct dial Yes	*Parking Ample*
Room TV Yes	*Room service 24 hours*

■ We welcome complaints and bona
fide recommendations on the
tear-out pages for readers' comments.
They are followed up by our professional
team. Please also complain to the
management instantly.

RECEPTION

Jackson's Bistro
Bowness on Windermere

Ŕ ♧ **Map 13 D5** Cumbria
West End Buildings
Windermere (096 62) 6264
Credit Access, Amex, Visa
    Sound, unpretentious cooking is offered by
Frank Jackson and team in this cosy basement
restaurant with stylish Victorian decor. Barbecued
chicken wings, duck liver pâté or seafood
pancakes could precede main dishes like veal

cordon bleu, steak chasseur or delicious lemon
sole with a filling of salmon mousse. Vegetarian
dishes available, too, plus very good side salads
and vegetables of the day. Shame about the
background music.

■ *About £28 for two*	*D only 6.30–10.30*
Seats 45	*Parking Limited*
Closed Sun or Mon in winter, 25 & 26 Dec &	
2–3 wks Jan	

Old England Hotel
Bowness on Windermere

Ĥ **65% £C**
Map 13 D5 Cumbria
Church Street LA23 3DF
Windermere (096 62) 2444. Tlx 65194
Credit Access, Amex, Diners, Visa
    Victorian charm and character are much in
evidence at this handsome lakeside hotel, where
antiques, paintings and period pieces furnish the
public rooms, which include a relaxing lounge and

two bars. The most attractive bedrooms are in a
new block. *Amenities* garden, outdoor swimming
pool, solarium, beauty salon, hairdressing, golf
practice net, snooker, laundry service, 24-hour
lounge service.

■ *Rooms 82*	*Confirm by 6*
en suite bath/shower 82	*Last dinner 9.15*
Direct dial Yes	*Parking Limited*
Room TV Yes	*Room service 24 hours*

Porthole Eating House
Bowness on Windermere

Ŕ **Map 13 D5** Cumbria
3 Ash Street
Windermere (096 62) 2793
Owner manager Gianni & Judy Berton
Credit Access, Amex, Diners, Visa
    The Berton's delightful beamed restaurant is
very much a part of the Lakeland landscape, and
regular customers attest to the appeal of Italian
favourites like spaghetti aglio and chicken

parmiggiana. Steaks are also a speciality, and
Judy's liqueur-laced fruit desserts (she also bakes
the bread) are a treat. The wine list is a joy, the
collection of a real enthusiast.
⊃ Outstanding ♀ Well-chosen ⊜

■ *About £38 for two*	*D only 6.30–11*
Seats 36 Parties 24	*Parking Difficult*
Closed Tues & mid Dec–mid Feb	

Ladbroke Hotel

Bracknell

H **67%** **£C**
Map 5 E2 Berkshire
Bagshot Road RG12 3QJ
Bracknell (0344) 424801. Tlx 848058
Credit Access, Amex, Diners, Visa
Day rooms are kept bright and fresh at this well-ordered red-brick hotel. Standard bedrooms have thermostats and remote-control TVs while Gold Star rooms offer superior decor and a wide range

of extras. Good conference and leisure facilities.
Amenities plunge pool, sauna, whirlpool bath, keep-fit equipment, games room, pool table, in-house movies (charge), laundry service, 24-hour lounge service.

■ *Rooms* 147	*Confirm by 6*
en suite bath/shower 147	*Last dinner 10*
Direct dial Yes	*Parking Ample*
Room TV Yes	*Room service 24 hours*

Bradfield House

Bradfield Combust

R ⌕ ⌕ **Map 6 C3** Suffolk
Nr Bury St Edmunds
Sicklesmere (028 486) 301
English cooking
Credit Access, Diners, Visa
A typical 17th-century Suffolk timbered house, filled with an attractive hotch-potch of antiques, knick-knacks and curios. The real magnet, though, is undoubtedly Victoria Stephenson's skilled, thoughtful English cooking, in which she employs the freshest ingredients. Set-price menus deal in delights like pea and ham soup; chicken quenelles in a leek and crème fraîche

sauce; and superb oxtail casserole with white wine and grapes. Our orange crème caramel with poached kumquats (made with Jersey cream and home-produced eggs) was magnificent. Traditional Sunday lunch. Short list of good wines, including an excellent Chinon Couly Dutheil 1982. ⊖

■ *Set L £8·95*	*L Sun only 12.30–2.30*
Set D £15	*D 7.30–9.30*
About £42 for two	*Parking Ample*
Seats 24	
Closed L Mon–Sat & D Sun–Tues	

Baron Hotel

Bradford

H **57%** **£D/E**
Map 10 C1 West Yorkshire
Highfield Road, Idle BD10 8QH
Bradford (0274) 611914. Tlx 517229
Manager J. A. Maron
Credit Access, Amex, Diners
Strong '70s decor is gradually giving way to tastefully-toned Liberty prints at this spacious hotel. Large bedrooms have semi-separate sitting

areas. Generous bathrooms. *Amenities* indoor swimming pool, sauna, solarium, whirlpool bath, keep-fit equipment, in-house movies (free), laundry service, 24-hour lounge service.

■ *Rooms* 45	*Confirm by 7*
en suite bath/shower 45	*Last dinner 9*
Direct dial Yes	*Parking Ample*
Room TV Yes	*Room service All day*
Closed 1 wk Xmas	

Restaurant Nineteen ★

Bradford

RR ★ ♔ ⌕ **Map 10 C1** West Yorkshire
19 North Park Road, Heaton BD9 4NT
Bradford (0274) 492559
Owner managers Stephen Smith & Robert Barbour
Credit Amex, Diners, Visa
Chef-partner Stephen Smith takes immense care over both cooking and presentation in this elegant candlelit restaurant. He calls his style imaginative English, and his four-course dinner menus let him show his skills in superb dishes like brill wrapped in a Savoy cabbage leaf, steamed with the gentle pep of ginger and served with a subtle saffron sauce; fillet of beef with onion marmalade and port and orange sauce; and a dreamy dessert of three different chocolate creations. Well-balanced wine list with Marlborough Chardonnay 1985 from New Zealand.
Specialities sautéed rabbit with apples and Calvados, three medallions of Scottish roe deer coated with beetroot purée, mushroom purée and

onion compote, passion fruit mousse with its own sauce. ♀ Well-chosen ⊖

■ *Set D from £11·50*	*D only 7–9.30,*
About £48 for two	*Fri & Sat 7–10*
Seats 38	*Parking Ample*
Closed Sun, Mon, 1 wk Jan & 1 wk Aug	
Bedrooms £F	
Rooms 10	*With bath/shower 0*

Three of the homely bedrooms have their own shower cubicles; the rest share nice old-fashioned bathrooms. Black-and-white TVs. No children. No dogs.

Bradford ▶

Novotel   Bradford

H **60% £D/E** &
Map 10 C1 West Yorkshire
Merrydale Road BD4 6SA
Bradford (0274) 683683. Tlx 517312
Manager Mr Bernard Houssin
Credit Access, Amex, Diners, Visa
  Businessmen are well catered for at this
modern hotel three miles south of the city centre
off the M606. Spacious public areas with

comfortable seating and potted plants are
pleasantly relaxing. Smart bedrooms with picture
windows have settee beds and practical units.
Amenities garden, outdoor swimming pool, in-
house movies (free), laundry service.
■ *Rooms 136*   *Confirm by 7*
en suite bath/shower 136 *Last dinner* Midnight
Direct dial Yes   *Parking Ample*
Room TV Yes   *Room service* All day

Stakis Norfolk Gardens Hotel   Bradford

H **64% £C/D**
Map 10 C1 West Yorkshire
Hall Ings BD1 5SH
Bradford (0274) 734734. Tlx 517573
Credit Access, Amex, Diners, Visa
  A popular modern hotel in the city centre, with
first-class conference facilities. Bright blues and
green give a cheerful contemporary feel to the
spacious open-plan foyer-lounge and adjoining

bar. Most bedrooms are now smartly refitted and
have good reproduction antiques. Extras include
radio-alarms, hairdryers and fresh fruit.
Amenities in-house movies (charge), laundry
service, 24-hour lounge service.
■ *Rooms 126*   *Confirm by* arrang.
en suite bath/shower 126 *Last dinner 10*
Direct dial Yes   *Parking Ample*
Room TV Yes   *Room service 24 hours*

Victoria Hotel   Bradford

H **61% £C/D**
Map 10 C1 West Yorkshire
Bridge Street BD1 1JX
Bradford (0274) 728706. Tlx 517456
Credit Access, Amex, Diners, Visa
  Opposite the Transport Exchange, in the heart
of Bradford, stands this imposing Victorian hotel.
The vast foyer, with its classical pillars, is
softened by sofas and heavy drapes and the bar

has a fine tented ceiling. Bedrooms have smart
traditional freestanding furniture and modern
accessories. All have en suite bathrooms, some
with showers.
Amenities laundry service.
■ *Rooms 59*   *Confirm by 6*
en suite bath/shower 59   *Last dinner 10*
Direct dial Yes   *Parking Limited*
Room TV Yes   *Room service 24 hours*

■ Changes in data may occur in
  establishments after the Guide
  goes to press. Prices should be taken
  as indications rather than firm quotes.

Antonio's   Braintree

R **Map 6 C3** Essex
Little Square
Braintree (0376) 45349
Owner managers Antonino & Christina Finazzo
Credit Access, Amex, Diners, Visa
  Antonino and Christina Finazzo are delightfully
friendly hosts at this cosy beamed restaurant in a
400-year-old house. Their fresh pasta is quite
excellent, as is the quality of the meat featuring in

such flavour-packed offerings as beef in red wine,
veal Marsala and pork fillet sauced with cider,
cream and apples. Steak specialities and
delicious fish, duck and chicken dishes also
available. ☺
■ *About £40 for two*   *L 12–2*
Seats 50   *D 7–10 (Sat 7–10.30)*
Parties 60   *Parking Limited*
Closed L Sat, all Sun, Mon & Bank Hols

Braintree Curry Palace   *NEW ENTRY*   Braintree

R ⌂ & **Map 6 C3** Essex
28 Fairfield Road
Braintree (0376) 20083
Indian cooking
Owner manager M. A. Noor
Credit Access, Amex, Diners, Visa. **LVs**
  Care is the keynote at this spotless Indian
restaurant, where Mr Malick, the owner's uncle, is
in charge of the kitchen. Tandoori dishes are

available for starters or main meals, and curries
range from mild Korma or fruity Kashmir to
medium or fairly fierce Ceylon and vindaloo.
House specials include butter chicken and lamb
pasanda. Service is friendly and courteous.
■ *Set L & D £9.95*   *L 12–2*
About £25 for two   *D 6–11*
Seats 60   *Parking Limited*
Closed 25 & 26 Dec

Ivy House Hotel   Braithwaite

H 60% £E/F
Map 13 C5 Cumbria
Nr Keswick CA12 5SY
Braithwaite (059 682) 338
Owner managers Peck family
Credit Access, Visa
   In the middle of the village, a dark green
pebble-dash hotel with parts dating back to the
16th century. Focal point of the day rooms is the

main lounge, with beams, chintz and a log fire to
keep things cosy. Drinks are served here as
there's no separate bar. Bedrooms are
individually decorated – and a couple have four-
posters. No children under 12. No dogs.
■ *Rooms* 10   Confirm by *arrang.*
en suite bath/shower 9   Last dinner 7.30
Room phone No   Parking *Ample*
Room TV Yes   Room service *Limited*

■ We publish annually, so make
  sure you use the current
  edition. It's worth it!

Bramhall Moat House   Bramhall

H 55% £D/E
Map 10 B2 Cheshire
Bramhall Lane South SK7 2 EB
061-439 8116
Manager Mr W Cottan
Credit Access, Amex, Diners, Visa. LVs
   Functional, no-frills accommodation is provided
at this modern businessman's hotel, which stands
alongside the A5102. Bedrooms offer quite a lot of

space but little in the way of decor; there are
bedside controls for TV and radio, plus tea-
makers and trouser presses. Roomy lounge bar.
Amenities solarium, laundry service.
■ *Rooms* 40   Confirm by *arrang.*
en suite bath/shower 40   Last dinner 10
Direct dial Yes   Parking *Ample*
Room TV Yes   Room service *24 hours*
Closed 1 week Xmas

Parkway Hotel   Bramhope

H 63% £C/D &
Map 10 C1 West Yorkshire
Otley Road, Bramhope, Nr Leeds LS18 8AG
Leeds (0532) 672551. Tlx 556614
Manager David Collett
Credit Access, Amex, Diners, Visa
   A new wing of 80 bedrooms has vastly
increased the capacity of this mock-Tudor hotel
standing in its own grounds alongside the A660.

All the new rooms have balconies, plus the same
accessories as the older rooms (remote-control
TVs, hairdryers, trouser presses, tea-makers).
Public areas include a roomy foyer and bar-lounge.
Amenities garden, laundry service.
■ *Rooms* 103   Confirm by 6
en suite bath/shower 103 Last dinner 10
Direct dial Yes   Parking *Ample*
Room TV Yes   Room service *24 hours*

Post House Hotel   Bramhope

H 64% £C
Map 10 C1 West Yorkshire
Leeds Road LS16 9JJ
Leeds (0532) 842911. Tlx 556367
Manager Steven L. Broome
Credit Access, Amex, Diners, Visa
   A splendid leisure complex is a popular feature
of this modern hotel on the A660. Day rooms
include a bright cocktail lounge and smart main

bar. Attractive bedrooms offer tea-makers, mini-
bars and compact bathrooms. *Amenities* garden,
indoor swimming pool, sauna, solarium, whirlpool
bath, gymnasium, laundry service, coffee shop
(10.30am–10.30pm).
■ *Rooms* 130   Confirm by 6
en suite bath/shower 130 Last dinner 10.15
Direct dial Yes   Parking *Ample*
Room TV Yes   Room service *Limited*

Bramley Grange Hotel   Bramley

H 62% £C/D
Map 5 E3 Surrey
Horsham Road, Nr Guildford GU5 0BL
Guildford (0483) 893434. Tlx 859948
Credit Access, Amex, Visa
   Alterations and refurbishment are under way at
this mock-Tudor building, whose rear rooms look
out over attractive lawns towards a wooded
hillside. The bar, restaurant and function rooms

have all been improved, and new accommodation
includes five singles with shower rooms. Earlier
bedrooms are generally of a good size, not
particularly stylish but comfortable. No dogs.
Amenities garden, tennis, putting, croquet.
■ *Rooms* 26   Confirm by 6
en suite bath/shower 22   Last dinner 10
Direct dial Yes   Parking *Ample*
Room TV Yes   Room service *24 hours*

Farlam Hall Hotel

Brampton

HR 72% £D/E
Map 13 D4 Cumbria
Hallbankgate CA8 2NG
Hallbankgate (069 76) 234
Owner managers Quinion family
Credit Access, Amex, Visa

The Quinion family's charming country house hotel started life in the 17th century as a farmhouse and was enlarged to form a manor house in Victorian times. Lovely grounds (complete with stream and ornamental lake) provide the setting, and antiques, fine paintings and rich fabrics enhance the day rooms. Spacious, individually decorated bedrooms, most with a small sitting area, offer books, magazines

and mineral water. Well-equipped bathrooms are modern, except for one with handsome Victorian mahogany fittings. Inclusive terms only. No children under five. *Amenities* garden, croquet.

■ *Rooms* 13	*Confirm by arrang.*
en suite bath/shower 13	*Last dinner* 8
Room phone No	*Parking* Ample
Room TV Yes	*Room service* All day

Closed Mon & Tues in Dec & Jan, all Feb, 1st 2 wks Nov & 1 wk Xmas

Farlam Hall Hotel Restaurant ♛ ♧

An elegant, formal restaurant where Barry Quinion's short set dinner menus offer enjoyable dishes like pheasant quenelles with Madeira and mushroom sauce, roast lamb with onion tart and rosemary sauce, and venison served with green noodles and pink peppercorn sauce. Nicely made sweets include an enjoyable toffee and banana pie. Guests are asked to arrive at 7.30 and order in the cosy bar or front lounge. ⊖

■ *Set D* £16	*D only* 7.30 for 8
About £40 *for two*	*Seats* 45 *Parties* 45

Closed Mon & Tues in Dec & Jan, all Feb, 1st 2 wks Nov & 1 wk Xmas

Tarn End

Brampton

RR ♧ **Map 13 D4** Cumbria
Talkin Tarn
Brampton (069 77) 2340
French cooking
Credit Access, Amex, Diners, Visa

There are grand views of Talkin Tarn from this old stone restaurant with rooms. The menu, in the capable hands of Domenico Tellatin, is solidly French, with specialities like oysters with shallots in vinègar or langoustines providing the prelude to main courses like sweetbreads with sorrel sauce and roasted monkfish with herbs and peppercorns. There are always vegetarian dishes

and desserts include crêpes Suzette. It is essential to book for the set lunch (otherwise à la carte). ⊖

■ *Set L from* £10	*L* 12.30–1.45
Set D £15·50	*D* 7.30–9
About £49 *for two*	*Parking* Ample
Seats 25	*Parties* 45

Closed D Sun Nov–Jan & all Feb

Bedrooms £E
Rooms 6   *With bath/shower* 4
Charming bedrooms have dark fitted furniture, TVs and tea-makers. Three of the neat and smartly-tiled bathrooms are en suite. No dogs.

Old Rectory ★ NEW ENTRY

Brampton

RR ★ ♛ ♧ & **Map 6 D2** Suffolk
Nr Beccles NR34 8EA
Brampton (050 279) 616
Credit Access

As many as 30 different species of waterfowl frequent the ponds in the grounds of this Georgian house, making a fine spectacle to accompany a sublime meal. Chef and co-owner Anthony Rudge prepares top-quality produce with great skill and his presentation is flawless. Dishes such as asparagus roulade and chicken breast with mozzarella and avocado combine good honest cooking with more than a touch of sophistication. Simple, delightful sweets. A short, carefully compiled wine list includes lovely Bourgogne Aligoté (Aubert de Villaine). *Specialities* creamed seafood soup spiced with saffron; roast best end of lamb with a mousse of aubergine, courgette and tomato; trio of sorbet and ice creams with fruit liqueur sauce.
♀ Well-chosen

■ *Set D* £16·50	*L by arrang. only*
About £45 *for two*	*D* 7.30–9
Seats 16 *Parties* 16	*Parking* Ample

Closed Sun & Mon to non-residents, 10 days Xmas & Feb

Bedrooms £D/E
Rooms 2   *With bath/shower* 2
Bedrooms are spacious, with antiques, tastefully flamboyant decor, luxurious bathrooms and many extras. Outstanding breakfast. No children.

Brandon Hall Hotel — Brandon

H 64% £C/D
Map 11 D4 Warwickshire
Brandon, Nr Coventry CV8 3FW
Coventry (0203) 542571. Tlx 31472
Credit Access, Amex, Diners, Visa

A converted country residence just four miles from the centre of Coventry. Day rooms are comfortably traditional, while bedrooms now sport attractive pastel shades and smart darkwood

furniture. Remote-control TVs are standard, along with decent-sized bathrooms. Good management, pleasant staff. *Amenities* garden, squash, putting, games room, snooker, laundry service, 24-hour lounge service.

■ *Rooms* 60 — *Confirm by* 6
en suite bath/shower 60 — *Last dinner* 9.45
Direct dial Yes — *Parking* Ample
Room TV Yes — *Room service* Limited

■ Our inspectors never book in the name of Egon Ronay's Guides; they disclose their identity only after paying their bills.

Masons Arms — Branscombe

H 64% £E
Map 3 E2 Devon
Nr Seaton EX12 3DJ
Branscombe (029 780) 300
Manager Graham Williams
Credit Access, Visa

Set among terraced gardens at the heart of an unspoilt village, this creeper-clad inn combines rustic appeal with modern comfort and efficiency.

The bar features a large log fireplace, slate floors and exposed beams, the lounge boasts some fine period furniture while charmingly converted cottages provide most of the accommodation. Bedrooms are well-equipped. *Amenities* garden.

■ *Rooms* 20 — *Confirm by* arrang.
en suite bath/shower 18 — *Last dinner* 9
Direct dial Yes — *Parking* Ample
Room TV Yes — *Room service* All day

Waterside Inn ★★ — Bray-on-Thames

R ★★ ⛯⛯ ⌕ ⌕Map 5 E2
Berkshire
Ferry Road
Maidenhead (0628) 20691
French cooking
Credit Access, Amex, Diners, Visa

The riverside setting is enchanting, the decor elegant and stylish, but it's Michel Roux's talents in the kitchen that have won the Waterside Inn such high standing. Many of his dishes show the spark of real brilliance, and marvellous memories of a recent visit include wonderfully aromatic morels with tagliatelle, and impeccable veal sweetbreads and kidneys served with the subtlest of sauces on a fondue of shallots. Desserts too are spectacular, and the cheeseboard outstanding. A magnificent cellar of classics also offers some less usual French wines: note Côte de Beaune Blanc (Joliette) '83 and Bonnezeaux Ch. des Gauliers '59. Service is correct and professional but a shade short on

charm. *Specialities* pâté de poisson à la Guillaume Tirel, canette croisée challandaise aux figues et vin de Bordeaux, entremets aux fruits de la passion et aux fraises des bois.
⌔ Outstanding ☺
■ *Set L* Wed–Fri £19.50, *L* 12–2, Sun 12–2.30
also Sat & Sun £22.50 — *D* 7–10
Set D £38.50 — *Parking* Ample
About £100 for two — *Seats* 80
Closed Mon, L Tues, also D Sun Oct–Easter, all Bank Hols & 25 Dec–mid Feb (excl. L 25 Dec)

Red Lion Hotel — Bredwardine

I £F
Map 4 A1 Hereford & Worcester
Nr Hereford HR3 6BU
Moccas (098 17) 303
Owner manager Mr M. J. Taylor
Credit Access, Amex, Diners, Visa

A 17th-century red-brick country house located in a beautiful stretch of the Wye valley. First-rate fishing facilities are the main attraction here.

Accommodation is modest though cheerful, with open fires in the bar and two lounges.
Amenities garden, coarse and game fishing, laundry service.

■ *Rooms* 10 — *Confirm by* arrang.
en suite bath/shower 7 — *Last dinner* 8.30
Room phone No — *Parking* Ample
Room TV Some — *Room service* All day
Closed Nov–Mar

Brentwood ▶

Brentwood Moat House
Brentwood

H **67%** **£C/D** &
Map 7 B4 Essex
London Road CM14 4NR
Brentwood (0277) 225252. Tlx 995182
Manager Mr S. P. Pearson
Credit Access, Amex, Diners, Visa
History lies easy on this gracious Tudor hunting lodge. Public areas have been carefully preserved, with features like splendid beaming and diamond-paned windows. Bedrooms vary in style: antiques in the suites in the main house; fitted units in the modern garden wing. Standards of comfort and decoration are high. *Amenities* garden, laundry service, 24-hour lounge service.

■ *Rooms* 38	*Confirm by* 12
en suite bath/shower 38	*Last dinner* 10.15
Room phone Yes	*Parking* Ample
Room TV Yes	*Room service* 24 hours

Post House Hotel
Brentwood

H **60%** **£C**
Map 7 B4 Essex
Brook Street CM14 5NF
Brentwood (0277) 260260
Credit Access, Amex, Diners, Visa. **LVs**
Near the M25 and A12, this modern red-brick hotel is popular both for its practical overnight accommodation and as a conference venue. Standard bedrooms offer tea-makers and mini-bars; Executive rooms have superior furnishings and extra accessories. There are two bars and a spacious foyer-lounge. *Amenities* garden, outdoor swimming pool, laundry service, coffee shop (7am–10.15pm), 24-hour lounge service.

■ *Rooms* 120	*Confirm by* 6
en suite bath/shower 120	*Last dinner* 10
Direct dial Yes	*Parking* Ample
Room TV Yes	*Room service* Limited

Duck Inn
Bridge

R & **Map 7 C5** Kent
Pett Bottom, Nr Canterbury
Canterbury (0227) 830354
English cooking
Owner managers Les & Carol Boothright
Credit Access, Amex
A charming pub restaurant worth seeking out for its thoroughly enjoyable English cooking. Monthly-changing menus feature prime steaks, seasonal game and salmon, all served with crisply delicious vegetables and perhaps preceded by a creamy mushroom soup. Lovely treacle tart to finish. ☺

■ *Set L* Sun only £8·25	*L* 12–1.30
About £40 for two	*D* 7.15–9.30
Seats 30 *Parties* 30	*Parking* Ample
Closed D Sun, all Mon, 25 & 26 Dec & 2 wks early Oct	

Expanse Hotel
Bridlington

H **59%** **£E**
Map 15 D6 Humberside
North Marine Drive YO15 2LS
Bridlington (0262) 675347
Owner managers Mr & Mrs Arthur F. Seymour
Credit Access, Amex, Diners, Visa
Friendly, old-world courtesy prevails at this 1930s seaside hotel. Looking out to sea is a favourite occupation in the homely lounges; things are livelier in the popular public bar. Bright, spacious, well-kept bedrooms, furnished in various styles, have radio-alarms and tea-makers. No dogs. *Amenities* laundry room, 24-hour lounge service.

■ *Rooms* 49	*Confirm by* arrang.
en suite bath/shower 43	*Last dinner* 8.30
Direct dial Yes	*Parking* Ample
Room TV Yes	*Room service* 24 hours

■ If we recommend meals in a hotel or inn, a separate entry is made for its restaurant.

Alexandra Hotel
Brighton (Hove)

H **58%** **£D/E**
Town plan B3 East Sussex
42 Brunswick Terrace BN3 1HA
Brighton (0273) 202722. Tlx 877579
Manager Steven Johnson
Credit Access, Amex, Diners, Visa. **LVs**
Recent improvements at this listed Regency hotel include a remodelled reception area and refurbishment of some bedrooms. Well-equipped bedrooms – now double-glazed – have tidy bathrooms (2 with shower only). Suites have balconies and mini-bars. *Amenities* sauna, solarium, whirlpool bath, games room, snooker, laundry service.

■ *Rooms* 63	*Confirm by* 6
en suite bath/shower 63	*Last dinner* 9.30
Direct dial Yes	*Parking* Limited
Room TV Yes	*Room service* Limited

Bedford Hotel   Brighton

H **66% £C/D**
Town plan B3 East Sussex
King's Road BN1 2JF
Brighton (0273) 29744. Tlx 878397
Credit Access, Amex, Diners, Visa
　A bright modern hotel on the seafront with
outstanding conference facilities. Stylish public
areas include a bar with a Dickensian theme (the
great man used to stay at an earlier hotel on this

site). Best bedrooms have sea views, smart cane
furniture and well-equipped bathrooms. Guests
may use the leisure facilities of the nearby
Brighton Metropole. *Amenities* in-house movies
(charge), laundry service, 24-hour lounge service.

■ *Rooms* 127	*Confirm by* 6
en suite bath/shower 127	*Last dinner* 10.30
Direct dial Yes	*Parking* Limited
Room TV Yes	*Room service* All day

Brighton Metropole Hotel   Brighton

H **70% £B/C**
Town plan C3 East Sussex
Kings Road BN1 2FU
Brighton (0273) 775432. Tlx 877245
Manager Mr F. Hutchings
Credit Access, Amex, Diners, Visa
　Period elegance, combined with modern
amenities, is to be found within the portals of this
splendidly restored Victorian hotel. The public
areas include a restful lounge, a traditional English
'pub' and a plush cocktail bar. Bedrooms are
spacious and practically furnished with melamine
units and smart fabrics; hairdryers, trouser
presses and tea/coffee-makers are standard.
Excellent bathrooms with splendid shower
pressure. There are several luxury suites and two
apartments with antique furniture and balconies.
Amenities indoor swimming pool, sauna,

solarium, whirlpool bath, gymnasium,
hairdressing, in-house movies (charge), laundry
service, 24-hour lounge service, kiosk.

■ *Rooms* 328	*Confirm by* 6
en suite bath/shower 328	*Last dinner* 10.30
Direct dial Yes	*Parking* Ample
Room TV Yes	*Room service* 24 hours

Restaurant Chardonnay   Brighton

R **Town plan E3** East Sussex
33 Chesham Road, Kemp Town
Brighton (0273) 672733
French cooking
Credit Access, Amex, Diners, Visa
　Friendly owners and a talented chef add up to a
winning combination at this intimate, attractive
restaurant. Positive flavours and judicious
seasoning distinguish Frenchman Christian

Debu's cooking, from herby pâté and snails in puff
pastry to roast duck with pears and truite braisée
bourguignonne. Excellent sweets from a daily-
changing list. ℮

■ *Set L* £6·50	*L* 12.30–2
	D 7.30–10.45
About £45 *for two*	*Parking* Ample
Seats 34 *Parties* 34	*Closed L* Tues & Sat,
all Sun & Mon, 1 wk summer & 2 wks winter	

Courtlands Hotel   Brighton (Hove)

H **64% £D**
Town plan A2 East Sussex
19 The Drive BN3 3JE
Brighton (0273) 731055. Tlx 87574
Owner managers John & June Cutress
Credit Access, Amex, Diners, Visa
　Splendidly run by the Cutresses and Mr
Messina, their manager of 20 years, this hotel near
the seafront is popular for family holidays. Public

areas are agreeably civilised, and most bedrooms
are traditional in style. *Amenities* garden, indoor
swimming pool, solarium, whirlpool bath, keep-fit
equipment, games room, laundry service, 24-hour
lounge service, children's play area.

■ *Rooms* 57	*Confirm by* 6
en suite bath/shower 55	*Last dinner* 9.30
Direct dial Yes	*Parking* Ample
Room TV Yes	*Room service* 24 hours

Dudley Hotel   Brighton (Hove)

H **69% £C/D**
Town plan B2 East Sussex
Lansdowne Place BN3 1HQ
Brighton (0273) 736266. Tlx 87537
Credit Access, Amex, Diners, Visa
　An imposing hotel near the seafront. Public
areas, including a welcoming bar-lounge with
comfortable chesterfield seating, are generally in
need of refurbishment. Bedrooms range from

compact to commodious, some having
coordinating fabrics and smart Italian furniture.
Bathrooms offer nice toiletries but, here and
elsewhere, housekeeping could be improved.
Amenities pool table, 24-hour lounge service.

■ *Rooms* 80	*Confirm by* 6
en suite bath/shower 80	*Last dinner* 9.45
Room phone Yes	*Parking* Limited
Room TV Yes	*Room service* 24 hours

BRIGHTON

Map 7 B6
Town plan opposite

Population 153,700

Brighton is Regency squares and
terraces, the maze of art and junk
shops called the Lanes, the beach and
piers, the conferences and
entertainments, the milling crowds in
Brighton, and the quiet lawns of Hove, a
day out for Londoners, a holiday and
retirement centre, a commuter's town
and a university town. The person most
responsible for all this was George IV,
who made it the vogue and
commissioned his unique palace, the
Royal Pavilion.

Annual Events
Brighton Boat Show *May*
Brighton Festival *May*
Glyndebourne *May–Aug*
London to Brighton veteran car run *Nov*

Sights Outside Town
Arundel Castle, Petworth House,
Bluebell Railway

Information Centres
Marlborough House, Old Steine and
Sea-front opp. West Street
Telephone Brighton 23755
Weekends Brighton 26450

Fiat Dealers
Tilleys (Sussex) Ltd
100 Lewes Road
Brighton BN2 3QA
Tel. Brighton 603244
Map reference 1D

Tilleys (Sussex) Ltd
2 Church Road
Hove BN3 2FL
Tel. Brighton 738949
Map reference 2A

1 Aquarium and Dolphinarium D3
2 Booth Bird Museum *British birds in natural surroundings* B1
3 Brighton & Hove Albion F.C. A1
4 Brighton Conference & Exhibition Centre C3
5 Churchill Square C3
6 County Cricket Ground A2
7 Devil's Dyke *4 miles, Sussex beauty spot* B1
8 Information Centres C3
9 The Lanes *network of old fisherman's cottages, now world centre for antiques* C3
10 Marina E3
11 Museum & Art Gallery C/D3
12 Palace Pier D3
13 Preston Park and Preston Manor *18th c* C1
14 Race-course E1
15 Rottingdean *2¼ miles, toy museum* E3
16 Royal Pavilion *Regency exhibition, art gallery and museum* C/D3
17 Station C2
18 Sussex University *4 miles* E1
19 Theatre Royal C3
20 Volks Railway *first electric railway, on seafront* D3

THE CHIC AND VERSATILE PANDA

Panda F/I/A/T
EUROPE'S DRIVING FORCE
For your local dealers see pages 144-147

Brighton F I A T

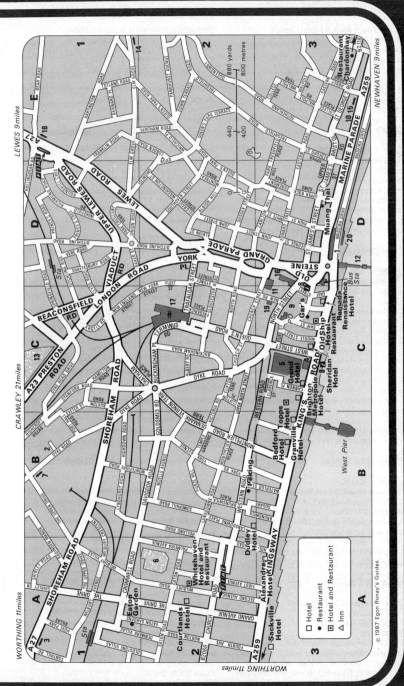

Eaton Garden   Brighton (Hove)

R ♿ **Town plan A1** East Sussex
Eaton Gardens
Brighton (0273) 738921
Manager John Derby
Credit Access, Amex, Diners, Visa
  The welcome is friendly at this popular,
traditional restaurant. Chef John Stevens is
coming up to 30 years' service, and his cooking is
classic and consistent. The choice varies from

fried dabs and salmon brioche to duckling
Oriental, veal cordon bleu and a model roast beef
with Yorkshire pudding. Delicious sweets include
a nice boozy sherry trifle. ℗

■ Set L £9, Sun £10·50	L 12.30–2
Set D £12·50	D 6.45–9.45
About £40 for two	Parking Ample
Seats 110	Parties 70
Closed D Sun, Good Fri & 25 Dec	

Gar's   Brighton

R ♿ **Town plan C3** East Sussex
19 Prince Albert Street
Brighton (0273) 21321
Chinese cooking
Credit Access, Amex, Diners, Visa
  All the food is fresh and flavoursome at the
Cheung brothers' newly refurbished little Chinese
restaurant on two floors. Five-spiced barbecued
spare ribs or plump and salty sesame prawns

could get your meal under way, with choices like
lemon chicken, crab with ginger and spring
onions or iron-plate sizzled beef to follow. The
Cantonese-style steamboat is a popular party
choice.

■ Set L & D from £8	L 12–2.30
About £32 for two	D 6–11.30
Seats 24 Parties 30	Parking Difficult
Closed 1–7 Jan	

The Grand   Brighton

H **80% £B** *E* ♿
Town plan C3 East Sussex
King's Road BN1 2FW
Brighton (0273) 21188. Tlx 877410
Credit Access, Amex, Diners, Visa
  A famous landmark on Brighton's seafront
since 1864, The Grand reopened in 1986 after
total refurbishment. With its polished marble
floors, Doric columns, finely moulded ceilings and
beautiful restored staircase, the magnificently
restored foyer cannot fail to impress. Other public
areas include an elegant lounge, handsome bar
and delightful seafront conservatory. Eight
sumptuous suites are the showpieces, while other
bedrooms are ample and comfortable, with
coordinating colour schemes and well-equipped
bathrooms. Unfortunately all this magnificence is
let down by poor standards of service and

housekeeping. *Amenities* indoor swimming pool,
sauna, solarium, whirlpool bath, keep-fit
equipment, beauty salon, laundry service, laundry
room, 24-hour lounge service.

■ Rooms 162	Confirm by arrang.
en suite bath/shower 162	Last dinner 10
Direct dial Yes	Parking Ample
Room TV Yes	Room service 24 hours

Granville Hotel   Brighton

H **65% £B/C**
Town plan B3 East Sussex
123–125 Kings Road BN1 2FA
Brighton (0273) 26302. Tlx 878149
Owner managers Audrey & David Simpson
Credit Access, Amex, Diners, Visa
  A stylish seafront hotel with a personal flavour.
Public areas are ultra-modern in a black, grey and
silver scheme. The bedrooms are dramatically

decorated in individual styles, ranging from art
deco to Japanese (complete with futon).
Bathrooms are luxurious with marble fitments,
corner baths and bathrobes. *Amenities* solarium,
in-house movies (free), 24-hour lounge service.

■ Rooms 25	Confirm by arrang.
en suite bath/shower 25	Last dinner 10.30
Direct dial Yes	Parking Difficult
Room TV Yes	Room service 24 hours

Muang Thai   Brighton

R **Town plan D3** East Sussex
77 St James' Street
Brighton (0273) 605223
Thai cooking
Credit Access, Amex, Diners, Visa .
  Enjoyable Thai cooking in a brightly decorated
Kemptown restaurant. Set menus give a good
introduction to this varied cuisine, and there's an
extensive carte ranging from satays and grated

papaya in hot and sour sauce to baked whole fish,
fried beef with black bean sauce and a spicy dish
of chicken and pork in creamy coconut. Quick-
fried vegetables are outstanding. Pleasant
service. Booking advisable.

■ Set L from £7	L 12–2
Set D from £7	D 6–11.30
About £28 for two	Parking Limited
Seats 46 Parties 24	Closed Bank Hols

Old Ship Hotel
Brighton

HR **70% £D/E**
Town plan C3 East Sussex
King's Road BN1 1NR
Brighton (0273) 29001. Tlx 877101
Manager Mr J. H. Richards
Credit Access, Amex, Diners, Visa

A seafront hotel that's always been big on courtesy and old-fashioned charm; today's staff under manager John Richards are unfailingly polite and helpful. An extensive refurbishment programme is under way, and among many improvements are natural wood furnishings – in oak, mahogany or antique pine – for many of the bedrooms together with floral bedspreads and matching curtains. Bathrooms are of a good standard, many with vanitory units. The public areas blend period charm and modern comfort:

note the panelled cocktail bar, numerous relaxing lounges and the splendid ballroom where Paganini once played. *Amenities* games room, snooker, laundry service, 24-hour lounge service.

■ *Rooms 154*	*Confirm by arrang.*
en suite bath/shower 154	*Last dinner 9.30*
Direct dial Yes	*Parking Ample*
Room TV Yes	*Room service 24 hours*

NEW ENTRY

Old Ship Hotel
Restaurant ⌒ &

Recent refurbishment in Victorian style has enhanced this handsome restaurant. Berndt Schroeter cooks capably and consistently and diners enjoy both the food and the fine sea views. His menus are based on good local produce (Dover sole from Newhaven, Sussex turkey, South Downs lamb); dishes are imaginative and appetising and sauces are particularly good. Bitey vegetables, enticing sweets – try delicious apple meringue tartlet. There's a fine wine list – note clarets, vintage ports, armagnac.
♀ Well-chosen ⊖

■ *Set L from £9*	*L 12.30–2.30,*
About £40 for two	*Sun 12.30–2*
Seats 120	*D 7–9.30, Sat 7–10*

Peking
Brighton (Hove)

R ♀ & **Town plan B2**
9 Western Road
Brighton (0273) 722090
Chinese cooking
Owner managers Messrs Liu & Man
Credit Access, Amex, Visa

The chef really excels at this bright, attractive place, certainly on a par with most of London's best Chinese restaurants. The aromatic crispy

duck is always a good bet, or you could try steamed whole fish, braised prawns Shanghai style, Szechuan pork or sliced beef with peppers in a sprightly black bean sauce. The side dishes are good too, including perfect fried rice and crisply-delicious vegetables. ♀ Well-chosen

■ *About £30 for two*	*L 12–2.15*
Seats 40	*D 6–11.30*
Closed 25 & 26 Dec	*Parking Limited*

RAMADA RENAISSANCE HOTEL ***NEW ENTRY***
Brighton

H **£A** &
Town plan C3 E. Sussex
King's Road BN1 1JA
Brighton (0273) 206700. Tlx 878555
Credit Access, Amex, Diners, Visa. **LVs**

A new luxury hotel due to open as we went to press. The sumptuous atrium lounge is the focus of the stylish day rooms. Comprehensively equipped bedrooms, all air-conditioned and

soundproofed, have first-rate bathrooms. The fourth floor of Club rooms has its own check-in and lounge. *Amenities* indoor swimming pool, sauna, gymnasium, in-house movies, laundry service, 24-hour lounge service.

■ *Rooms 204*	*Confirm by 6*
en suite bath/shower 204	*Last dinner 10.30*
Direct dial Yes	*Parking Ample*
Room TV Yes	*Room service 24 hours*

Sackville Hotel
Brighton (Hove)

H **64% £D/E**
Town plan A3 East Sussex
189 Kingsway BN3 4GU
Brighton (0273) 736292. Tlx 877830
Credit Access, Amex, Diners, Visa

A seafront hotel built about 1900, with gables, turrets and a distinctive sea-green facade. The strongest impressions of our latest visit are friendly, well-trained staff under motivated general

manager Simon Farrar; public rooms of solid Edwardian charm; much redecoration and refurbishment in the bedrooms (lots with sea views); and very good housekeeping throughout. *Amenities* laundry service.

■ *Rooms 45*	*Confirm by 6*
en suite bath/shower 45	*Last dinner 9.30*
Direct dial Yes	*Parking Ample*
Room TV Yes	*Room service Limited*

Sheridan Hotel — Brighton

H 68% £D
Town plan C3 East Sussex
64 King's Road BN1 1NA
Brighton (0273) 23221. Tlx 877659
Credit Access, Amex, Diners, Visa

New owners are refurbishing the bedrooms at this distinctive Edwardian hotel, formerly Wheeler's Sheridan. The rooms, all very well maintained, range from large and traditional, with huge double-glazed windows looking seaward, to smaller rear rooms with practical fitted units. The public areas are also receiving attention. Staff are reasonably efficient, but warm smiles are lacking. *Amenities* laundry service.

■ Rooms 57	Confirm by arrang.
en suite bath/shower 57	Last dinner 10.15
Direct dial Yes	Parking Difficult
Room TV Yes	Room service 24 hours

Topps Hotel — Brighton

HR 66% £D
Town plan B3 East Sussex
17 Regency Square BN1 2FG
Brighton (0273) 729334
Owner managers Paul & Pauline Collins
Credit Access, Amex, Diners, Visa

Paul and Pauline run this super little hotel – a conversion of two Regency houses – with an unerring sense of style. Delightful bedrooms (including five especially handsome rooms on the top floor reached by a lift) provide everything from mini-bars to aspirins. Luxurious bathrooms. No dogs. *Amenities* laundry service.

■ Rooms 12	Confirm by arrang.
en suite bath/shower 12	Last dinner 9.45
Direct dial Yes	Parking Ample
Room TV Yes	Room service 24 hours
Closed 1st 3 wks Jan	

Bottoms Restaurant ♧

English cooking
When she's wearing her chef's hat, simple but delicious dinners are Pauline's speciality down in the unpretentious basement restaurant. Beautifully light little cheese puddings and chicken pancakes in a mild curry sauce are typically appealing starters, while main courses might include Dover sole stuffed with salmon mousse or ham and mushroom-topped veal cooked in white wine. Note covers are limited so booking is essential.
♥ Well-chosen ☺

■ Set D £11·50	D only 7–9.30
About £33 for two	Seats 24 Parties 10
Closed Wed, Sun & 24 Dec–25 Jan	

Whitehaven Hotel *NEW ENTRY* — Brighton (Hove)

HR 63% £D/E ⑤
Town plan A2 East Sussex
Wilbury Road BN3 3JP
Brighton (0273) 778355
Owner managers Townend family
Credit Access, Amex, Diners, Visa

A most agreeable little hotel, peacefully yet centrally situated, and with friendly owners and staff. Relaxing is easy in the cosy lounge or bar, or outside in the walled garden. Bedrooms offer accessories both large and small, from individually controlled central heating to shower caps and shoe shines. No children under eight. No dogs. *Amenities* garden, solarium.

■ Rooms 17	Confirm by 6
en suite bath/shower 17	Last dinner 9.30, Sun 9
Direct dial Yes	Parking Ample
Room TV Yes	Room service Limited

Rolling Clock Restaurant ⑤

The rolling clock on the mantelpiece is a talking point, but the main reason for clocking in here is Lionel Roberts' cooking. His dishes do justice to excellent produce, and there's plenty of variety on menus that run from Madeira-sauced chicken livers to herby best end of lamb in puff pastry and a splendid platter of assorted seafood. Alternatively, vegetarians might go for deep-fried brie with cranberry sauce or pasta in a white wine and cream sauce. Sweets from the trolley, or savoury endings such as angels on horseback.
♥ Well-chosen ☺

■ Set L & D £8·50	L 12.30–2
About £35 for two	D 7–9.30, Sun 7–9
Seats 40	Parties 45

Crest Hotel — Bristol

H 66% £C
Town plan E1 Avon
Filton Road, Hambrook BS16 1QX
Bristol (0272) 564242. Tlx 449376 Fax 569735
Credit Access, Amex, Diners, Visa. LVs

Stylish and well equipped, this low-rise modern hotel stands in ample grounds on the A4174. Smartly furnished bedrooms offer plenty of space. Attractive, relaxing day rooms include a leisure club. *Amenities* garden, indoor swimming pool, sauna, solarium, whirlpool bath, keep-fit equipment, croquet, game fishing, games room, in-house movies (charge), laundry service, coffee shop (8.30am–9.30pm).

■ Rooms 151	Confirm by 6
en suite bath/shower 151	Last dinner 9.45
Direct dial Yes	Parking Ample
Room TV Yes	Room service 24 hours

Grand Hotel   Bristol

H **71% £D**
Town plan C2 Avon
Broad Street BS1 2EL
Bristol (0272) 291645. Tlx 449889
Credit Access, Amex, Diners, Visa. **LVs**

Situated in the quiet heart of the old city, this
fine Victorian hotel with imposing Italianate facade
successfully blends the traditional with the up-to-
date. Glittering chandeliers grace the elegant
foyer and splendid ballroom, recalling the heady
days of 1869 when the hotel first opened. By
contrast, the panelled bar-lounge with mirrored
ceiling and the nautically-themed basement bar
are smartly contemporary in style. Bedrooms vary
in size and decor. Some boast highly individual
features like half-canopied beds; others have
more modern furnishings. All offer trouser
presses, tea-makers and good bathrooms

equipped with hairdryers. Numerous conference
suites and function rooms are also available.
Amenities in-house movies (free), valeting, 24-
hour lounge service.

■ *Rooms 178*	*Confirm by 6*
en suite bath/shower 178	*Last dinner 10.15*
Direct dial Yes	*Parking Ample*
Room TV Yes	*Room service 24 hours*

Harveys   Bristol

R ♨♨ **Town plan B2** Avon
12a Denmark Street
Bristol (0272) 277665
French cooking
Manager Franco Sanfiz
Credit Access, Amex, Diners, Visa

Highly skilled service and a classical French
menu combine to admirable effect in this elegant
cellar restaurant. The long list of hors d'oeuvre is
followed by a wide choice of main dishes –
seafood, poultry, meat and game – both plain and
sauced. Good sweet and cheese trolleys.

⊳ Outstanding ⊕

■ *Set L £11·25*	*L 12–2.30*
About £52 for two	*D 7–11.15,*
Seats 120	*Sat 6.30–11.15*
Parties 50	*Parking Limited*
Closed L Sat, all Sun & Bank Hols	

⊳ is our symbol for an **outstanding** wine list.

Holiday Inn   Bristol

H **71% £B/C *E* &**
Town plan D2 Avon
Lower Castle Street BS1 3AD
Bristol (0272) 294281. Tlx 449720
Credit Access, Amex, Diners, Visa

A typical '70s high-rise hotel, located on the
inner ring road. It's a convenient, well-appointed
place, and the bedrooms, individually air-
conditioned and effectively sound-proofed, offer
excellent comfort. There's space to relax, with
desks for working, and the smart bathrooms are
provided with good-quality thick towels. The high-
ceilinged, marble-floored lobby has steps up to a
comfortable bar-lounge, down to a large
conference/function suite. Here and there the
decor is looking a little below Bristol fashion.
Amenities indoor swimming pool, sauna,
solarium, keep-fit equipment, in-house movies

(free), laundry service, coffee shop (7am–
10.30pm), 24-hour lounge service, kiosk.

■ *Rooms 284*	*Confirm by 6*
en suite bath/shower 284	*Last dinner 11*
Direct dial Yes	*Parking Ample*
Room TV Yes	*Room service 24 hours*

Howards   Bristol

R ♘ **Town plan A3** Avon
1a Avon Crescent, Hotwells
Bristol (0272) 22921
Owner managers Christopher & Gillian Howard

Sound cooking, generous portions and friendly
service continue to prove a popular formula at this
informal bistro near the Hotwells swing bridge.
Blackboard specials such as hot crab tart, mussel
and cider soup, veal with a port and Stilton sauce
supplement a regular menu of favourites such as
beef stroganoff, served with salads or lots of fresh
vegetables. Tempting sweets, too. Booking
advisable. ⊕

■ *About £34 for two*	*D only 7–11*
Seats 60	*Fri & Sat 7–11.30*
Parties 25	*Parking Ample*
Closed Sun, Mon, Bank Hols exc. Good Fri & 2	
wks Xmas	

BRISTOL

Map 4 B2
Town plan opposite

Population 401,100

The Birthplace of America–the Cabots sailed from here to discover Newfoundland in 1497. This and later voyages brought Bristol prosperity, largely in sugar, tobacco, rum and the slave trade. Architecture surviving the 1940 war damage ranges over the 13th-century Lord Mayor's Chapel, St Mary Redcliffe Church, England's oldest working theatre (Theatre-Royal–now completely renovated), and Clifton's Georgian terraces.

Annual Events
Senior Citizens' Day *21st June*
World Wine Fair and Festival *10th–19th July*
Harbour Regatta and Rally of Boats *8th–9th August*
International Balloon Fiesta *14th–16th August*
Maritime Carnival *31st August*
Bristol Flower Show *2nd–4th September*
Christmas Illuminated Water Carnival *19th–20th December*

Sights Outside City
Severn Bridge, Berkeley Castle, Wells Cathedral, Cheddar Gorge, Severn Wildfowl Trust, Castle Combe Village, Bath

Tourist Information Centre
Colston House, Colston Street
Telephone Bristol 659491

Fiat Dealers
Autotrend Ltd
724–726 Fishponds Road
Bristol BS16 3UE
Tel. Bristol 657247

Bawns Ltd
168–176 Coronation Road
Bristol BS3 1RG
Tel. Bristol 631101

1 Airport *6 miles* A3
2 Arnolfini (Arts Centre) C3
3 Ashton Court Estate and Mansion *beautiful parklands* A1
4 Blaise Castle House Folk Museum *Henbury* A1
5 National Lifeboat Museum C3
6 Bristol Cathedral *dates from 12th c* B3
7 Bristol Tapestry and Permanent Planning Exhibition D1
8 Cabot Tower *Brandon Hill, built 1897* A2
9 Central Library B3
10 Chatterton House *Chatterton's birthplace* D3
11 Christmas Steps *antique shops* C1
12 City Museum & Art Gallery *fine & applied arts* B1
13 Clifton suspension bridge A1
14 Colston Hall concert hall B2
15 Council House B2
16 Entertainment Centre B2
17 Georgian House *late 18th-c showpiece* B2
18 Harveys Wine Museum B2
19 Hippodrome B2
20 Information Centre B2
21 John Wesley Chapel *first Methodist Chapel* D1
22 Little Theatre C2
23 Lord Mayor's Chapel *13th c* B2
24 Nails and the Exchange *'pay on the nail' originated here* C2
25 Norman Arch B3
26 Observatory, Clifton Down A1
27 Red Lodge *late 16th-c showpiece* B2
28 Royal York Crescent *Regency* A2
29 St Mary Redcliffe Church *dates from 13th c* D3
30 St Nicholas Church Museum C2
31 St Peter and St Paul *R.C. Cathedral* A1
32 S.S. 'Great Britain' *first ocean-going propeller ship, launched Bristol 1843, Great Britain Dock, Gasferry Road* A3
33 Temple Meads Station E3
34 Theatre Royal *home of the Bristol Old Vic* C2
35 Zoo *including flowers and rare trees* A1

Bristol

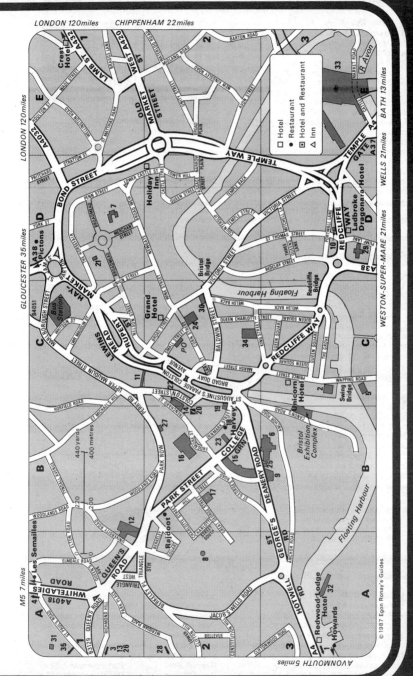

Ladbroke Dragonara Hotel   Bristol

H 75% £C **E** &
Town plan **D3** Avon
Redcliffe Way BS1 4NJ
Bristol (0272) 260041. Tlx 449240
Credit Access, Amex, Diners, Visa
   A major refurbishment programme goes on at
this tall modern hotel near Temple Meads station.
A notable feature is the choice of bold, bright
fabrics in the bedrooms, which are generously
sized, with good writing and storage space.
Bathrooms have been upgraded, too, and the
good-quality towels and toiletries are even more
luxurious in the superior Plaza rooms. The
cavernous first-floor reception area adjoins both
the all-purpose bar-lounge – a relaxing place with
fountain and indoor greenery – and extensive
conference/function facilities. The circular
restaurant, converted from an 18th-century kiln, is

very striking, but the breakfast served there is
poor. *Amenities* in-house movies (charge), coffee
shop (9am–1am), 24-hour lounge service.
■ *Rooms* 197   *Confirm by* 6
en suite bath/shower 197 *Last dinner* 10.30
Direct dial Yes   *Parking* Ample
Room TV Yes   *Room service* 24 hours

■ For a discount on next year's guide, see Offer for Answers.

Pictons Restaurant   *NEW ENTRY*   Bristol

R ⚐ Town plan **D1** Avon
46 Picton Street, Montpelier
Bristol (0272) 47312
Credit Access
   Twenty-one-year-old James West is the chef-
patron at this popular basement restaurant. His
sound, unfussy cooking is best sampled in his
monthly-changing fixed-price menus, which offer
excellent value for money. Carrot and orange

soup or minty marinated mushrooms could lead
on to poached salmon or braised pork espagnole
and to delicious puds like raspberry trifle.
Occasional theme evenings (Hungarian,
Scandinavian). ☺
■ *Set D from* £6·95   *L parties by arrang.*
About £22 *for two*   *D* 7–10.30
Seats 36 *Parties* 22 *Parking* Ample
Closed Sun, 1 wk Xmas & Aug

Rajdoot   Bristol

R Town plan **B2** Avon
83 Park Street
Bristol (0272) 28033
Indian cooking
Owner manager Mr S. D. Sharma
Credit Access, Amex, Diners, Visa
   A smart Indian restaurant, one of the first in
England to install the tandoor (clay oven).
Tandoori dishes remain a speciality, with fish,

quail and kidneys as alternatives to the usual
ingredients. Subtle curries are enhanced with
fresh herbs. The 50p cover charge includes
pickles, poppadums and hot towels.
■ *Set L* £5·50   *L* 12–2
Set D from £9·50   *D* 6.30–11.30
About £32 *for two*   *Parking* Limited
Seats 60   *Parties* 30
Closed L Sun, L Bank Hols & 25 & 26 Dec

■ Any person using our name
   to obtain free hospitality is
   a fraud. Proprietors, please
   inform the police and us.

Redwood Lodge Hotel   Bristol

H 69% £C/D
Town plan **A3** Avon
Beggar Bush Lane, Failand BS8 3TG
Bristol (0272) 393901. Tlx 444348
Credit Access, Amex, Diners, Visa
   Conferences are big business at this hotel
where guests will never run out of things to do.
Public areas are stylishly contemporary,
bedrooms comfortable. No dogs. *Amenities*

garden, indoor & outdoor swimming pools, sauna,
solarium, gymnasium, tennis, squash, badminton,
table tennis, pool table, snooker, cinema, coffee
shop (10am–10.30pm), 24-hour lounge service, in-
house movies (free).
■ *Rooms* 112   *Confirm by* arrang.
en suite bath/shower 112 *Last dinner* 9.45
Direct dial Yes   *Parking* Ample
Room TV Yes   *Room service* None

Les Semailles ★　　　　　　　　　　　　　　　**Bristol**

R ★ ♃ **Town plan A1** Avon
9 Druid Hill, Stoke Bishop
Bristol (0272) 686 456
French cooking
Credit Access, Visa

With his impeccable pedigree, including spells with Michel Guérard and Raymond Blanc, it's no surprise that Brittany-born René Gaté is a hit in this comfortable, little restaurant, which is situated in a northern suburb of Bristol. His modern, often intricate, cooking is allied to an extraordinary flair for presentation, and there's a hint of the East in some dishes, like pigeon pékinois with a sweet tomato sauce or bouillon de volaille oriental garnished with crab and sweetcorn, and made piquant with fresh coriander. Super sweets – a superlative carrot and passion fruit mousse – and excellent French farmhouse cheeses, too. There's also good-value daily-changing set lunch menus. Selective list of high-quality French wines: note Gevrey

Chambertin Cazetières (Rousseau) 1972. An efficient front-of-house team is led by René's wife Jillian. *Specialities* galette de coquilles St Jacques au poireau, sauce corail; filet d'agneau gallois aux langoustines et crème de basilic; délice de carotte et fruit de la passion. 🍷 Well-chosen ⊖
■ *Set L* from £7·80　　　L 12–2
About £48 for two　　　D 7–10.30
Seats 24 *Parties* 18　　　*Parking* Ample
Closed Sun, Mon, Bank Hols, 2 wks July, 1 wk Xmas

Unicorn Hotel　　　　　　　　　　　　　　　**Bristol**

H **66% £D** 🕎
Town plan C3 Avon
Prince Street BS1 4QF
Bristol (0272) 230333. Tlx 44315
Credit Access, Amex, Diners, Visa. **LVs**

Overlooking Narrow Quay, this friendly modern hotel makes life easy for its guests with an adjoining multi-storey car park that enables them to park on the same floor as their bedroom. The

latter are smart, neatly fitted and offer tea-makers and direct-dial telephones. Day rooms include an attractive lounge bar and the appealingly rustic Waterfront Tavern complete with terrace.
Amenities laundry service, 24-hour lounge service.
■ *Rooms* 192　　　　　*Confirm by* 6
en suite bath/shower 192　*Last dinner* 10
Direct dial Yes　　　　　*Parking* Ample
Room TV Yes　　　　　*Room service* 24 hours

■ Our inspectors are our full-time employees; they are professionally trained by us.

Quayside Hotel　　　　　　　　　　　　　　　**Brixham**

H **59% £D**
Map 3 D3 Devon
King Street TQ5 9TJ
Brixham (080 45) 55751
Owner manager Alan Robb Gibson & Family
Credit Access, Amex, Diners, Visa

Six period fishermen's cottages form this delightful hotel overlooking the harbour. The little lounge and nautically-themed bars reflect the

building's cosy charm. Some of the bedrooms are quite tiny but two are big enough for four-posters. Five rooms have been smartly refurbished and boast marble-tiled bathrooms. *Amenities* laundry service, baby listening.
■ *Rooms* 30　　　　　*Confirm by* arrang.
en suite bath/shower 30　*Last dinner* 9.30
Direct dial Yes　　　　　*Parking* Ample
Room TV Yes　　　　　*Room service* All day

Broadway Hotel　　　　　　　　　　　　　　　**Broadway**

H **60% £E**
Map 4 C1 Hereford & Worcester
The Green WR12 7AA
Broadway (0386) 852401
Manager Peggy Swinden
Credit Access, Amex, Diners, Visa

In a picturesque Cotswold village, this stone and half-timbered 16th-century hotel is both welcoming and well run. Public rooms include a

lofty, beamed and galleried lounge area, and a delightful rustic bar. Bedrooms (traditional in the main house, more modern in the garden annexe) are impeccably kept. Bathrooms are spotless. No dogs. *Amenities* garden, putting.
■ *Rooms* 24　　　　　*Confirm by* arrang.
en suite bath/shower 20　*Last dinner* 9.25
Direct dial Yes　　　　　*Parking* Ample
Room TV Yes　　　　　*Room service* All day

Broadway ▶

Collin House Hotel

Broadway

HR 65% £D/E
Map 4 C1 Hereford & Worcester
Collin Lane WR12 7PB
Broadway (0386) 858354
Owner managers John & Judith Mills
Credit Access, Visa

A Cotswold-stone house dating from the 17th century and set in eight peaceful acres. Day rooms have the charm of mullioned windows, log fires and antiques. Bedrooms, too, have fine traditional character. TVs available on request. No children under seven. No dogs.
Amenities garden, outdoor swimming pool.

■ Rooms 7	Confirm by arrang.
en suite bath/shower 6	Last dinner 9
Room phone No	Parking Ample
Room TV No	Room service All day
Closed 3 days Xmas	

Restaurant ⌕ &

English cooking
Excellent cooking by Judith Mills in a handsome period dining room. Set menus offer a sensible choice of enjoyable, tasty dishes, from chicken and leek soup to salmon cooked with vermouth and fillet steak with garlic butter. Copious carefully cooked vegetables, and some nice traditional puds (steamed syrup sponge). Roast Sunday lunch. Friendly, informal service. Interesting mature clarets on a good list.
⛳ Well-chosen ⊖

■ Set L £9·75	L Sun 12–1.30,
Set D from £11	Mon–Sat by arrang.
About £32 for two	D 7–9
Seats 24	Parties 24
Closed D Sun to non-residents, 3 days Xmas	

Dormy House

Broadway

HR 71% £C
Map 4 C1 Hereford & Worcester
Willersey Hill WR12 7LE
Broadway (0386) 852711. Tlx 338275
Manager Mr H. Pascoe
Credit Access, Amex, Diners, Visa

Ask directions when booking at this superbly run hotel at whose heart is a 17th-century farmhouse. Stone walls, exposed beams and log fires yield a cosy, mellow effect in the day rooms, and in one corner of reception there's a veritable jungle of plants and shrubs. Well-equipped bedrooms (some with private patios) are decorated and furnished with a fine feel for the hotel's character, and all have luxurious bathrooms. Excellent breakfasts. Sauna, solarium and tennis available nearby.
Amenities garden, laundry service, 24-hour lounge service, courtesy car, helipad.

■ Rooms 50	Confirm by 6
en suite bath/shower 50	Last dinner 9.30
Direct dial Yes	Parking Ample
Room TV Yes	Room service 24 hours

Dormy House Restaurant

Bearded Roger Chant is a talented chef cooking within his capabilities, sometimes with outstanding results. High-quality produce, super saucing and artistic presentation mark delicious dishes like seafood in puff pastry, rack of lamb with strawberries and breast of duck with champagne and pink peppercorns. Cheerful staff, cosy surroundings and good wines all enhance the occasion.
⛳ Well-chosen ⊖

■ Set L £9·50	L 12.30–2, Sun 12–2.30
Set D £16	D 7.30–9.30, Fri & Sat
About £60 for two	7–9.30, Sun 7.30–9
Seats 75	Parties 180
Closed L Sat & all 25 & 26 Dec	

■ We welcome complaints and bona fide recommendations on the tear-out pages for readers' comments. They are followed up by our professional team. Please also complain to the management instantly.

RECEPTION

Hunter's Lodge

Broadway

R & **Map 4 C1** Hereford & Worcester
High Street
Broadway (0386) 853247
Credit Access, Amex, Diners, Visa

Tried and trusted favourites on seasonally-changing menus please the customers at Kurt and Dotti Friedli's cottage restaurant. Sound, traditional cooking is Kurt's forte and he uses top-quality ingredients in dishes like fried scallops with chicory, rich provençale vegetable soup, pheasant pie zipped with port, and brill steamed on a bed of herbs. Simpler fare at lunchtime. ⊖

■ Set L £8	L 12.30–2
About £48 for two	D 7.30–9.45
Seats 55 Parties 35	Parking Ample
Closed D Sun, all Mon, Bank Hols (exc. Good Fri), 2 wks Feb & 2 wks Aug	

Lygon Arms   Broadway

HR 79% £A/B **E** ♿
Map 4 C1 Hereford & Worcester
High Street WR12 7DU
Broadway (0386) 852255. Tlx 338260
Manager Kirk Ritchie
Credit Access, Amex, Diners, Visa

It may be rich in history, but this renowned 600-year-old hotel also moves with the times. Modern comfort and luxury combine with fine period furnishings in the bedrooms, many of which are in two 20th-century wings warmly praised by Pevsner. There are also several sumptuous suites. Bathrooms are lavishly equipped with quality towels and toiletries. The lounges that flank the entrance hall ooze period charm with their beams, oak panelling, antiques and

crackling log fires. The Inglenook Lounge, once the kitchen of the original inn, is adorned with old cooking implements. Housekeeping and service are of high order. *Amenities* garden, tennis, valeting, laundry service, 24-hour lounge service, helipad.

■ *Rooms* 66	*Confirm by* 6
en suite bath/shower 61	*Last dinner* 9.15
Direct dial Yes	*Parking* Ample
Room TV Yes	*Room service* 24 hours

Lygon Arms Restaurant ♕

The barrel-vaulted Great Hall with minstrels' gallery is the marvellous setting for this restaurant. The seasonal menus offer much to tempt, from steamed Hebridean oysters in filo pastry with spinach and a vodka sabayon to cider-sauced turbot, braised beef in Guinness and duck quenelle with chestnut sauce and a garnish of blackberries. Low-fat and vegetarian dishes are on offer. Plentiful vegetables. Interesting cheeses and lovely traditional puds to finish. There's a well-balanced wine list. ✆

■ *Set L* £13·75	*L* 12.30–2.30
Set D £19·75	*D* 7–9.15
About £60 *for two*	*Seats* 100 *Parties* 100

■ Changes in data may occur in establishments after the Guide goes to press. Prices should be taken as indications rather than firm quotes.

Careys Manor Hotel   Brockenhurst

H 64% £C/D
Map 4 C4 Hampshire
New Forest SO42 7RH
Lymington (0590) 23551. Tlx 47442
Manager Christopher Biggin
Credit Access, Amex, Diners, Visa

Notable moments in the manor's past include its use by Charles II as a hunting lodge. It stands back from the road, and entrance is into a lofty hall with a galleried oak staircase. The lounge combines attractive contemporary and period features – note the huge brick hearth – and the bar is newly redecorated. Good-sized bedrooms,

also refurbished, are traditional in the main house (including a couple of four-poster rooms), more modern in the wing, with balconies or direct access to the garden. More bedrooms due on line November 1987.
Amenities garden, indoor swimming pool, sauna, solarium, whirlpool bath, gymnasium, putting, croquet, laundry service.

■ *Rooms* 80	*Confirm by* arrang.
en suite bath/shower 80	*Last dinner* 10
Direct dial Yes	*Parking* Ample
Room TV Yes	*Room service* 24 hours

Ladbroke Balmer Lawn Hotel   Brockenhurst

H 66% £C/D
Map 4 C4 Hampshire
Lyndhurst Road SO42 7ZB
Lymington (0590) 23116. Tlx 477649
Credit Access, Amex, Diners, Visa

A major improvement programme at this popular New Forest hotel included redesigning the bar and lounge area, and redecoration throughout. Smart bedrooms offer the usual up-

to-date accessories, with extras such as teletext in the Gold Star rooms. *Amenities* garden, indoor & outdoor swimming pools, sauna, whirlpool bath, gymnasium, tennis, squash, croquet, laundry service, 24-lounge service.

■ *Rooms* 58	*Confirm by* 6
en suite bath/shower 58	*Last dinner* 9.30
Direct dial Yes	*Parking* Ample
Room TV Yes	*Room service* 24 hours

Brockenhurst ▶

Rhinefield House Hotel *NEW ENTRY*   Brockenhurst

HR 72% £D
Map 4 C4 Hampshire
Rhinefield Road SO4 7QB
Lymington (0590) 22922
Credit Access, Amex, Diners, Visa

Take the Rhinefield turning off the A35 and approach this fine country mansion through impressive banks of rhododendrons. Much thought and money have gone into restoration, and there's a high degree of comfort and elegance throughout. Main-house rooms include the Grand Hall (modelled on the Palace of Westminster) and the Moorish Alhambra cocktail bar. A pretty orangery, where breakfast is served, links the house to a modern wing containing the

reception/lounge and spacious bedrooms with large, comfortable beds and easy chairs. Compact bathrooms. No dogs.
Amenities garden, indoor & outdoor swimming pools, tennis, sauna, whirlpool bath, keep-fit equipment, croquet, games room, laundry service, 24-hour lounge service.

■ Rooms 32	Confirm by 6
en suite bath/shower 32	Last dinner 9.30
Direct dial Yes	Parking Ample
Room TV Yes	Room service 24 hours

Rhinefield House Hotel Restaurant

French cooking
An impressive, wood-panelled dining hall where chef Paul Norman puts his personal stamp on classic French dishes, and lots of care goes into both preparation and plating. Typifying the choice are a pâté of sweetbreads, and sliced breast of duck in a wine sauce with a pastry case of duck mousse. Good fresh vegetables. Finish with a selection of pleasant sweets. ☻

■ Set D £10.50	L 12–2
About £48 for two	D 7.30–9.30
Seats 50	Parties 220

Oaksmere Country House Hotel   Brome

H 68% £E
Map 6 C2 Suffolk
Nr Eye IP23 8AJ
Eye (0379) 870326
Owner managers Bill & Mike Hasted
Credit Access, Amex, Diners, Visa

Formerly a 16th-century dower house, now a delightful hotel set in peaceful grounds which feature marvellous topiary. Public areas include a

splendid beamed bar, elegant drawing room and a Victorian conservatory with its own grape vine. Spacious, splendidly appointed bedrooms are individually furnished – one with four-poster.
Amenities garden. *Closed* 25 Dec.

■ Rooms 5	Confirm by arrang.
en suite bath/shower 4	Last dinner 10
Room phone No	Parking Ample
Room TV Yes	Room service Limited

Bromley Court Hotel   Bromley

H 67% £D/E
Map 7 B5 Kent
Bromley Hill BR1 4JD
01-464 5011. Tlx 896310
Credit Access, Amex, Diners, Visa

Follow the signs from the A21 for this extended period house at the end of a private drive. Best of the day rooms is the handsome, marble-columned cocktail bar which enjoys fine views of the lovely

garden. Neatly fitted bedrooms, in the original house and a modern wing, have tiled bathrooms.
Amenities garden, golf practice net, putting, in-house movies (free), laundry service, 24-hour lounge service.

■ Rooms 130	Confirm by arrang.
en suite bath/shower 130	Last dinner 9.45
Direct dial Yes	Parking Ample
Room TV Yes	Room service 24 hours

Peking Diner   Bromley

R ♿ Map 7 B5 Kent
71 Burnt Ash Lane
01-464 7911
Chinese cooking
Credit Access, Amex, Diners, Visa

Modern, friendly and sophisticated restaurant with the emphasis on Pekinese cooking. Chef Cheung demonstrates his skills over a lengthy repertoire, from very moreish minced pork

dumplings to scallops with a robust black bean sauce; chilli-edged shredded beef; and the ever-popular crispy duck. Much above average (even decent coffee!) Must book weekends.

■ Set D from £8	L 12–2.30
About £30 for two	D 6.30–11.30 (Fri till 12)
Seats 52 Parties 50	Parking Ample
Closed Sun, Mon, Bank Hols & 2 days Xmas	

Grafton Manor — Bromsgrove

HR 70% £C
Map 10 C4 Hereford & Worcester
Grafton Lane B61 7HA
Bromsgrove (0527) 31525
Owner managers Morris family
Credit Access, Amex, Diners, Visa

The Morris family have been lovingly restoring their glorious Elizabethan manor over a number of years. Situated near the junction of the B4091 and A38, the house is tucked away down a lane in exquisite gardens. Inside, a handsome stairway leads to a sumptuous bar/lounge with grand piano, log fire, and traditional furnishings like the coat of arms above the fireplace. The bedrooms

are individually decorated with good fabrics and stylish colour schemes. All have direct-dial phones, trouser presses, fresh fruit, magazines and teletext; most have log fires. Bathrooms are equally attractive and well equipped. No dogs. **Amenities** garden, croquet, riding, coarse fishing, laundry service.

- **Rooms** 8 — Confirm by arrang.
- en suite bath/shower 8 — Last dinner 9
- Direct dial Yes — Parking Ample
- Room TV Yes — Room service All day

Grafton Manor Restaurant

Competent cooking of good fresh ingredients by John Harris, with a major contribution from the hotel's herb garden. Start with tomato and rosemary soup, follow with dill-marinated salmon with mustard sauce or fillet of beef with parsnip mousse and tarragon and brandy sauce. Finish with steamed whisky sponge. Well-chosen

- Set L £12·75 — L 12–2
- Set D £18 — D 7–9
- About £50 for two — Seats 40

Whitehall Hotel — Broxted

HR 76% £C
Map 6 B3 Essex
Church End CM6 2BZ
Bishop's Stortford (0279) 850603
Owner managers Gerry & Marie Keane
Credit Access, Amex, Visa

Lovely grounds by the parish church provide the setting for this fine Essex hall dating from the 12th century. Gerry and Marie Keane have created an unusual and delightful country house hotel which successfully blends the old character of the house with modern furnishings and softly contemporary colour schemes. There's a small, dainty drawing room – all pinks and greys, with Heath Robinson cartoons – and a smart bar hung with pictures of Aston Martins (a passion of Gerry's). Bedrooms, six recently added with many cosseting extras, are comfortable and stylish. Friendly, personal service. Excellent breakfasts and afternoon teas. No children under five. No dogs. **Amenities** garden, outdoor swimming pool, tennis.

- **Rooms** 10 — Confirm by arrang.
- en suite bath/shower 10 — Last dinner 9.30
- Direct dial Yes — Parking Ample
- Room TV Yes — Room service All day

Whitehall Hotel Restaurant

Paula Keane continues to develop her own modern, ungimmicky style, and a meal in the lofty, beamed restaurant is something to remember. She sets great store by the quality and freshness of ingredients, as evidenced in a starter of impeccable salad leaves dressed in sherry vinegar and walnut oil, and scattered with quick-grilled slivers of pork, or a main course such as veal tournedos with watercress sauce. Exceptional praise must go to the sweets, which include English delights like plum tart and steamed fruit pudding as well as a superb chocolate ganache. There's a good selective wine list with excellent burgundies.
Specialities escalope of salmon with leeks and champagne butter sauce, grilled duck with lime sauce, white chocolate truffle cake with raspberry coulis, passion fruit délice. Well-chosen

- Set L from £12·50 — L 12–1.30
- Set D £23·50 — D 7.30–9.30
- About £58 for two — Seats 40 Parties 50
- Closed D Sun, all Mon, & Bank Hols

White Hart Hotel   Buckingham

H 58% £D
Map 5 D1 Buckinghamshire
Market Square MK18 1NL
Buckingham (0280) 815151
Credit Access, Amex, Diners, Visa

A pillared portico and white plaster facade distinguish this pleasant little town-centre hotel. A refurbishment programme is currently under way, commencing at ground-floor level with existing day rooms. Practical bedrooms with neat, usefully equipped bathrooms all have built-in unit furniture, tea-makers and remote-control TVs. *Amenities* laundry service.

■ *Rooms* 19	*Confirm by* 6
en suite bath/shower 19	*Last dinner* 9.30
Room phone Yes	*Parking* Ample
Room TV Yes	*Room service* All day

Buckland Manor   Buckland

HR 83% £B
Map 4 C1 Gloucestershire
Nr Broadway WR12 7LY
Broadway (0386) 852626
Owner managers Barry & Adrienne Berman
Credit Access, Visa

Standing in beautiful grounds on the Cheltenham side of Broadway, this tastefully converted manor house has a history spanning eight centuries. The owners have made it a haven of peace and relaxation, and both they and their staff know exactly how guests should be treated. Mullioned windows, fine oak panelling, choice antiques and open fires paint a marvellous, traditional picture in the day rooms. Luxurious bedrooms also boast antiques, along with high-quality soft furnishings, the most cosseting of carpets and all manner of extras. Bathrooms are similarly sumptuous. No children under 12. Kennels available. *Amenities* garden, outdoor swimming pool, tennis, putting, croquet, riding, stabling, laundry service.

■ *Rooms* 11	*Confirm by* arrang.
en suite bath/shower 11	*Last dinner* 8.45
Direct dial Yes	*Parking* Ample
Room TV Yes	*Room service* All day
Closed mid Jan–early Feb	

Buckland Manor Restaurant ♨ ♿

In an elegant room with baronial furnishings and marvellous views, Martyn Pearn presents an interesting menu of carefully cooked, eye-pleasing dishes. Snails with sorrel, cream and a hint of anise, quail pâté, salmon with a truffle-scented marinade and lamb with a gentle garlic sauce are typical choices. Simple sweets like crème brûlée or fruit tarts. Exceptional cellar: note the classics Ch. Palmer '71 and Ch. Beychevelle '61. ⌘ Outstanding ♀ Well-chosen ⓔ

■ *Set L* Sun only £11·25	*L* 12.30–1.45
About £55 for two	*D* 7.30–8.45
Closed mid Jan–Feb	*Seats* 32 *Parties* 20

Master Builder's House Hotel   *NEW ENTRY*   Buckler's Hard

I £F
Map 4 C4 Hampshire
Beaulieu, Brockenhurst SO42 7XB
Buckler's Hard (056 063) 253
Credit Access, Amex, Diners, Visa

Named in honour of shipbuilder Henry Adams, this extended 18th-century house has grounds reaching to the Beaulieu River. At the water's edge there's a public bar, while two other bars with beams and panelling, and a few nice old-fashioned bedrooms, are in the main building. Remaining bedrooms are in a rear extension – bright, cheerful rooms with private showers. *Amenities* garden, laundry service.

■ *Rooms* 23	*Confirm by* arrang.
en suite bath/shower 19	*Last dinner* 9.45
Direct dial Yes	*Parking* Ample
Room TV Yes	*Room service* All day

Swan   Bucklow Hill

H 59% £D
Map 10 B2 Cheshire
Nr Knutsford WA16 6RD
Bucklow Hill (0565) 830295. Tlx 666911
Credit Access, Amex, Diners, Visa

A convenient overnight stop near the M6 and M56, this much-extended old inn was once a monastery. The original building houses two beamed and flagstoned bar-lounges, plus comfortably traditional bedrooms (three with four-posters). Motel-wing rooms are comprehensively equipped and include four luxury suites with whirlpool baths. *Amenities* garden, laundry service, 24-hour lounge service.

■ *Rooms* 70	*Confirm by* 6
en suite bath/shower 70	*Last dinner* 10
Direct dial Yes	*Parking* Ample
Room TV Yes	*Room service* 24 hours

Strand Hotel · Bude

H **59% £D**
Map 2 C2 Cornwall
The Strand EX23 8RA
Bude (0288) 3222
Credit Access, Amex, Diners, Visa
  Fine views of the river Neet can be enjoyed by residents from the bright picture-windowed lounge on the third floor of this friendly modern hotel. There are also two other cosy lounge areas, and a popular, warmly decorated bar. Pleasant bedrooms with attractively coordinated colour schemes and white fitted units all have tea-makers, remote-control TVs and neat private bathrooms. *Amenities* games room.

■ *Rooms* 40	*Confirm by* 6
en suite bath/shower 40	*Last dinner* 9
Room phone Yes	*Parking* Ample
Room TV Yes	*Room service* All day

Savernake Forest Hotel · Burbage

H **60% £D/E**
Map 4 C3 Wiltshire
Nr Marlborough SN8 3AY
Marlborough (0672) 810206
Owner manager Anthony & Isabelle Sykes
Credit Access, Amex, Diners, Visa
  The Sykes take good care of their hotel, a pleasant Victorian building with chequered brickwork. A real fire warms the refurbished bar (note the local artwork for sale) and there's a comfortably furnished lounge. Bedrooms, mainly fairly plain in decor, are of a reasonable size. *Amenities* garden, coarse fishing, laundry service.

■ *Rooms* 12	*Confirm by* 6
en suite bath/shower 12	*Last dinner* 9
Room phone No	*Parking* Ample
Room TV Yes	*Room service* Limited
Closed 24 & 25 Dec	

■ We publish annually, so make sure you use the current edition. It's worth it!

Bay Tree Hotel · Burford

H **60% £D/E**
Map 4 C2 Oxfordshire
Sheep Street OX8 4LW
Burford (099 382) 3137
Owner managers Mr & Mrs P. D. King
Credit Access, Amex, Diners, Visa
  Old-world charm and a relaxed atmosphere are apparent as soon as you step inside this fine Tudor house. A sense of the past prevails in the lounges with their antiques and in the beamed bar and sun lounge. Spacious bedrooms (some in an adjoining cottage) are in traditional style. No dogs. *Amenities* garden, laundry service.

■ *Rooms* 22	*Confirm by* arrang.
en suite bath/shower 22	*Last dinner* 9.30
Direct dial Yes	*Parking* Ample
Room TV Yes	*Room service* All day
Closed 3 days Xmas	

Inn for all Seasons · Burford

I **£D/E**
Map 4 C2 Oxfordshire
The Barringtons OX8 4TN
Windrush (045 14) 324
Owner managers John & Jill Sharp
Credit Access, Amex, Diners, Visa
  Homely comforts combine with traditional appeal at this old Cotswold-stone inn on the A40. Open fires warm heavily beamed public areas like the comfortable lounge and rustic stone-flagged bar. Prettily decorated bedrooms with country views offer up-to-date accessories and modern bathrooms. No children under ten. No dogs. *Amenities* garden, clay-pigeon shooting.

■ *Rooms* 9	*Confirm by* arrang.
en suite bath/shower 9	*Last dinner* 9.30
Direct dial Yes	*Parking* Ample
Room TV Yes	*Room service* All day

Knights Farm · Burghfield

R **Map 5 D2** Berkshire
Berrys Lane, Burghfield, Nr Reading
Reading (0734) 52366
Owner manager Mr Calleja
Credit Access, Amex, Diners, Visa
  Check directions when booking at this stylish restaurant in a converted farmhouse. Emil Forde's fixed-price menus show flair and imagination, with choices like crab-filled turbot lightly sauced with red wine, and lamb fillet with an excellent calf's sweetbread mousse. Exceptional, highly selective list of the world's best wines.

🖦 Outstanding   ♟ Well-chosen   ⊝

■ *Set L* £15	*L* 12.30–1.30
Set D £20.50	*D* 7.30–9
About £55 for two	*Parking* Ample
Seats 46 *Parties* 25	*Closed* L Sat, all Sun & Mon, 2 wks Jul & 2 wks Xmas

Burley Manor Hotel   Burley

H 62% £D/E
Map 4 C4 Hampshire
Nr Ringwood BH24 4BS
Burley (042 53) 3522
Credit Access, Amex, Diners, Visa
  Public areas of this fine Victorian mansion boast
original features like stained glass and oak
carving. Comfortable bedrooms are mainly in
simple modern style, though a few have four-

posters. All have up-to-date bathrooms.
Amenities garden, outdoor swimming pool,
hairdressing, golf practice net, putting, riding,
coarse fishing, hotel boat, pool table, in-house
movies (free), laundry service, helipad.

■ *Rooms* 22	*Confirm by* arrang.
en suite bath/shower 22	*Last dinner* 10
Direct dial Yes	*Parking* Ample
Room TV Yes	*Room service* All day

■ Our inspectors never book in the
  name of Egon Ronay's Guides;
  they disclose their identity only
  after paying their bills.

Burnham Beeches Hotel   Burnham

H 65% £D
Map 5 E2 Buckinghamshire
Grove Road SL1 8DP
Burnham (062 86) 3333
Credit Access, Amex, Diners, Visa
  Ask directions when booking at this converted
hunting lodge where Gray wrote his *Elegy in a
Country Churchyard*. Bedrooms are bright and
spacious and there's a flexible foyer-lounge area

with bar. *Amenities* garden, indoor swimming
pool, sauna, solarium, whirlpool bath, keep-fit
equipment, tennis, putting, croquet, games room,
snooker, in-house movies (free), laundry service,
24-hour lounge service.

■ *Rooms* 80	*Confirm by* 6
en suite bath/shower 80	*Last dinner* 9.30
Direct dial Yes	*Parking* Ample
Room TV Yes	*Room service* 24 hours

Grovefield Hotel   Burnham

H 63% £C/D
Map 5 E2 Buckinghamshire
Taplow Common Road SL1 8LP
Burnham (062 86) 3131
Credit Access, Amex, Diners, Visa
  A welcoming hotel standing in seven acres of
grounds just outside Burnham (get directions
when booking). The brick-walled reception area is
contemporary in style and leads to a bright,

spacious bar-lounge with attractive cane
furniture. Bedrooms are of a decent size and
nicely maintained – it's good to see really well
ironed sheets. Carpeted bedrooms.
Amenities garden, laundry service.

■ *Rooms* 33	*Confirm by* arrang.
en suite bath/shower 33	*Last dinner* 10
Direct dial Yes	*Parking* Ample
Room TV Yes	*Room service* Limited

Fishes   Burnham Market

R ♀ Ꮽ Map 6 C1 Norfolk
Market Place
Fakenham (0328) 738588
Seafood
  It's seafood almost all the way at this informal
restaurant. Gillian Cape's cooking is careful but
unfussy, with fresh flavours foremost in delightful
dishes like crab soup, salmon fish-cakes or wing
of skate with black butter. Oysters, mussels and

smoked fish are other favourites. Home-made ice
cream for a lovely cool conclusion. Fine wines,
excellent dry Norfolk cider. Smoking discouraged.
♀ Well-chosen ⊖

■ *Set L* £6·45	*L* 12–2
Sun £7·45	*D* 7–9.15
About £35 for two	*Parking* Ample
Seats 42	*Closed D* Sun, all Mon
(Oct–June), 25 & 26 Dec & 3 wks Jan/Feb	

Contented Sole   Burnham-on-Crouch

R ♀ Ꮽ Map 7 C4 Essex
80 High Street
Maldon (0621) 782139
  Scrupulously fresh ingredients, simply and
reliably well prepared, sums up the appeal of this
long-established restaurant, run in charming style
by the obliging Walton family. Home-smoked trout
or rich lobster bisque might start your meal,
followed perhaps by trout with Pernod or poached

sole with vermouth sauce. Meat-eaters will enjoy
favourites like beef Stroganoff and chicken breast
with cream and Calvados. ⊖

■ *Set L* £6·50	*L* 12–2.30
About £40 for two	*D* 7–9.30
Seats 60 *Parties* 28	*Parking* Ample
Closed Sun, Mon, all Bank Hols exc. Good Fri, last	
2 wks July & 4 wks Xmas	

Keirby Hotel — Burnley

H 56% £E
Map 10 B1 Lancashire
Keirby Walk BB11 2DH
Burnley (0282) 27611. Tlx 63119
Credit Access, Amex, Diners, Visa

The town-centre location is an attraction of this mini-skyscraper hotel. Bedrooms with hessian-covered walls and fitted units are equipped with tea-makers, remote-control TVs and trouser presses; eight superior singles (with double beds) also provide teletext. The neat cocktail bar is a quiet alternative to the swinging Swiss bar. *Amenities* laundry service, 24-hour lounge service.

■ *Rooms* 49	*Confirm by* 6
en suite bath/shower 49	*Last dinner* 10
Direct dial Yes	*Parking* Ample
Room TV Yes	*Room service* 24 hours

Brookhouse Inn — Burton upon Trent

H 66% £D/E
Map 10 C3 Staffordshire
Brookside, Rolleston-on-Dove DE13 9AA
Burton-on-Trent (0283) 814188
Owner managers Bill & Deirdre Mellis
Credit Access, Amex, Diners, Visa

Between the A50 and A38, this handsome, village inn makes a charming overnight stop. A four-poster, half-tester or Victorian brass bed graces each antique-furnished bedroom; decor and fabrics are delicious and bathrooms luxurious. Downstairs is a comfortably informal bar-lounge. *Amenities* garden, laundry service.

■ *Rooms* 16	*Confirm by* 7
en suite bath/shower 16	*Last dinner* 9.45
Room phone Yes	*Parking* Ample
Room TV Yes	*Room service* All day
Closed Bank Hol weekends & 2 wks Xmas	

Riverside Inn — Burton upon Trent

H 65% £E
Map 10 C3 Staffordshire
Riverside Drive, Branston DE14 3EP
Burton-on-Trent (0283) 63117
Credit Access, Amex, Visa

Major improvements have been completed at this pleasant hotel, which stands peacefully by the river Trent on the edge of Burton. Stylish public areas include a beamed and panelled foyer, and a roomy bar with handsome furnishings and delightful river views. Bedrooms have also received a facelift and are very comfortable. Smart Italian tiling in the bathrooms. No dogs. *Amenities* garden, 24-hour lounge service.

■ *Rooms* 22	*Confirm by arrang.*
en suite bath/shower 22	*Last dinner* 9.45
Direct dial Yes	*Parking* Ample
Room TV Yes	*Room service* Limited

■ If we recommend meals in a hotel or inn, a separate entry is made for its restaurant.

Normandie Hotel — Bury

HR 62% £D/E
Map 10 B1 Greater Manchester
Elbut Lane, Birtle BL9 6UT
061-764 3869
Owner managers Moussa family
Credit Access, Amex, Diners, Visa

A steep winding lane off the B6222 leads to this agreeable little hotel with lovely views of the Pennine foothills. Many of the bedrooms have been charmingly redecorated and are now equipped with modern comforts. Day rooms include a stylish cocktail bar. *Amenities* garden, 24-hour lounge service, courtesy car.

■ *Rooms* 24	*Confirm by arrang.*
en suite bath/shower 24	*Last dinner* 9.30
Direct dial Yes	*Parking* Ample
Room TV Yes	*Room service* 24 hours
Closed 24 Dec–4 Jan	

Restaurant 🕭

Booking is advisable at this elegant restaurant which offers besides a light lunch menu and full à la carte an evening 'gourmand' menu of four carefully chosen courses. Stuart Beard's capable cooking produces excellent results, from succulent asparagus with orange hollandaise and wonderfully refreshing passion fruit sorbet to pigeon breasts in a superb kumquat and brandy sauce. A tempting selection of sweets might include Normandy pear tart. There's an excellent cheeseboard and an impressive selection of 48 Armagnacs and Cognacs. 🕭

■ *Set D* £14·50	*L* 12–2
About £50 *for two*	*D* 7–9.30
Closed L Sat, all Sun &	*Seats* 70
25 Dec–4 Jan (excl. L 25 Dec & D 31 Dec)	

Angel Hotel
Bury St Edmunds

H **71% £C/D**
Map 6 C2 Suffolk
Angel Hill IP33 1LT
Bury St Edmunds (0284) 3926. Tlx 81630
Owner manager Mrs Gough
Credit Access, Amex, Diners, Visa

Essentially a Georgian town house, but the history of this handsome hotel opposite the Abbey Gardens goes back to much earlier times, as the vaulting in the cellars shows. Friendly staff make guests feel very much at home, and relaxation is easy in the warm, inviting lounge or charming indoor patio. Mrs Gough's personal style shows in the attractive decor of the bedrooms, which vary in size but are all comfortable and well equipped, with good bathrooms. One room is preserved exactly as it was when Charles Dickens stayed to give

readings of David Copperfield (there's a long literary tradition here); another features an ornate four-poster. *Amenities* laundry service, 24-hour lounge service.

■ Rooms 36	Confirm by arrang.
en suite bath/shower 36	Last dinner 9.45
Direct dial Yes	Parking Ample
Room TV Yes	Room service 24 hours

Bradleys
Bury St Edmunds

R ♧ **Map 6 C2** Suffolk
St Andrews Street South
Bury St Edmunds (0284) 703825
Credit Visa

Guests entering this tiny but most attractive restaurant have a good view of the spotless kitchen where David Weston prepares a range of delicious dishes. His sure touch and judicious seasoning means that flavours are not masked.

Mina Weston happily serves such tasty starters as mousseline of crawfish with smoked salmon sauce, and main courses that might include rabbit ragoût. Booking is essential. ☕

■ About £45 for two	L by arrang.
Seats 18	D 7.30–11
Parties 18	Parking Difficult
Closed Sun, Mon, 2 wks July & 1 wk Xmas	

Butterfly Hotel *NEW ENTRY*
Bury St Edmunds

H **63% £E**
Map 6 C2 Suffolk
Symonds Road, Moreton Hall Estate IP32 7BW
Bury St Edmunds (0284) 60884. Tlx 818360
Credit Access, Amex, Diners, Visa

Purpose-built and brand new, this low-rise hotel stands next to the A45 on the east side of town. Bedrooms, all with tea-makers, remote-control TV/radios and functional pine furnishings, are divided

between singles with decent-sized shower cubicles and doubles/twins with both bath and shower. Day rooms include a brick-walled bar-lounge and a little conservatory lounge. No dogs. *Amenities* garden.

■ Rooms 50	Confirm by 6
en suite bath/shower 50	Last dinner 10
Direct dial Yes	Parking Ample
Room TV Yes	Room service None

Suffolk Hotel
Bury St Edmunds

H **57% £C/D**
Map 6 C2 Suffolk
38 Buttermarket IP33 1DC
Bury St Edmunds (0284) 3995
Credit Access, Amex, Diners, Visa. **LVs**

An amicable atmosphere pervades this charming old coaching inn. The spacious open foyer is welcoming and the traditional lounge, with its comfy armchairs and settees, adds a homely

touch. Dark wood and bright service make the bar a popular spot. Recent refurbishment means fewer bedrooms, but many of those that remain have been upgraded; all now boast en suite bathrooms. *Amenities* laundry service.

■ Rooms 33	Confirm by 6
en suite bath/shower 33	Last dinner 9.30
Direct dial Yes	Parking Limited
Room TV Yes	Room service Limited

Sonargaon Restaurant *NEW ENTRY*
Bushey Heath

R **Map 7 A4** Hertfordshire
55 High Road
01-950 0475
Indian cooking
Owner manager Bashir Uddin
Credit Access, Amex, Visa

Good cooking is backed up by outstandingly polite and helpful service in this smart Indian restaurant. The menu offers lots of interesting

dishes from the various regions: tandoori dishes are particularly good, and other specialities include king prawn butterfly, chicken jaipuri (in a creamy sauce with eggs and nuts) and lamb green masala (green herbs, garlic, ginger and pomegranate seeds).

■ About £25 for two	L 12–2.30
Seats 50	D 6–12
Closed 25 Dec	Parking Limited

Swainston Manor Hotel   Calbourne

H 61% £E
Map 5 D4 Isle of Wight
PO30 4HX
Newport (0983) 521121
Owner managers Mr & Mrs F. C. Woodward
Credit Access, Amex, Diners, Visa
 A lovely old manor house with spacious public rooms that include a galleried foyer-lounge, an elegant ballroom and a function room converted from a chapel. Bedrooms vary greatly in size. Decor in many parts is looking tired and housekeeping needs improving.
Amenities garden, indoor swimming pool, coarse fishing, laundry service, 24-hour lounge service.

■ Rooms 13	Confirm by arrang.
en suite bath/shower 13	Last dinner 10.30
Direct dial Yes	Parking Ample
Room TV Yes	Room service 24 hours

Danescombe Valley Hotel *NEW ENTRY*   Calstock

HR 65% £E
Map 2 C3 Cornwall
PL18 9RY
Tavistock (0822) 832414
Owner managers Martin & Anna Smith
Ask for directions on booking to find this idyllic retreat in peaceful woodlands on the Tamar estuary. The owners run the hotel without extra staff and the atmosphere is informal and extremely friendly. The bedrooms are comfortable and beautifully decorated. Public rooms include a cosy bar and a homely lounge with log fire.
Amenities garden, mooring, laundry service.

■ Rooms 5	Confirm by arrang.
en suite bath/shower 5	Last dinner 8
Room phone No	Parking Ample
Room TV No	Room service Limited

Closed mid Nov–end Mar (exc. Xmas & New Year)

Danescombe Valley Hotel Restaurant ⚘

A houseparty atmosphere prevails in this small dining room overlooking the river, and the no-choice dinner is served in one sitting. Fresh local produce features strongly in Anna Smith's competent cooking. Starter might be crisp feuilleté of prawns, followed by chicken with a mustard and green peppercorn sauce. Fabulous bread from the local baker, and a splendid selection of 18 cheeses, including ewe and local goat cheeses. Intereresting wide-ranging wine list includes Chiroubles 1986 (Duboeuf), Venegazzù 1981. ♀ Well-chosen ❂

■ Set D £15	D only 7.30 for 8
About £36 for two	Seats 12 Parties 12

Closed mid Nov–end Mar (exc. Xmas & New Year)

Frimley Hall Hotel   Camberley

H 66% £C/D
Map 5 E3 Surrey
Portsmouth Road GU15 2BG
Camberley (0276) 28321. Tlx 858446
Manager Mr M. Alamo
Credit Access, Amex, Diners, Visa
 A turn-of-the-century house with a modern bedroom extension, Frimley Hall stands in attractive gardens off the A325. The entrance hall features a splendid carved oak staircase, and there are two roomy bars. Bedrooms are quite stylish, the best being in the original house, with antiques and four-posters. *Amenities* garden, laundry service, 24-hour lounge service.

■ Rooms 66	Confirm by 6
en suite bath/shower 66	Last dinner 10
Direct dial Yes	Parking Ample
Room TV Yes	Room service 24 hours

Tithas   Camberley

R Map 5 E3 Surrey
31 High Street
Camberley (0276) 23279
Indian cooking
Owner manager Muktar Miah
Credit Access, Amex, Diners, Visa. **LVs**
 In the heart of Camberley's main shopping street, this long, narrow Indian restaurant brightened with plants and fresh flowers offers a good range of well-prepared curries, tandooris and vegetable dishes. Note, also, specialities such as garlic chicken and barbecued trout marinated in Marsala, plus the well-balanced meat or vegetarian thalis.

■ Set L £3·95	L 12–2
Set D from £12	D 6–12
About £28 for two	Parking Ample
Seats 64 Parties 60	Closed 25 & 26 Dec

Angeline   Cambridge

R Town plan B3 Cambridgeshire
8 Market Passage
Cambridge (0223) 60305
Owner manager Hilda Mayo
Credit Access, Amex, Diners, Visa
 Solidly traditional in appearance but distinctly cosmopolitan behind the scenes, this friendly restaurant above the Arts Cinema is run by English, French and Austrian owners. The new French chef still offers a simple menu of robust, enjoyable French dishes such as flavoursome fish soup served with a gentle aïoli, kidneys in Madeira sauce and tender fillet of beef with Roquefort sauce. Sweets are a high point. ❂

■ Set L £3·25, Sun £8·25	L 12–2.30
About £30 for two	D 6–11
Seats 48	Parking Difficult

Closed D Sun, Bank Hols & 3 wks Easter

CAMBRIDGE

Map 6 B3
Town plan opposite

Population 102,300

Unexcelled as a centre of learning and research, settled by the Romans as a trading bridgehead, Cambridge was a place of scholarship even before the first college, Peterhouse, was founded. Entrance to University buildings and gardens (but not up staircases without permission) is generally allowed until dusk. Ideal punting round Backs of colleges for beauty rivalling Venice and Bruges, King's College Chapel has Britain's most celebrated boys' choir.

Annual Events
Cambridge Festival of Arts *July*
Festival of Nine Carols *Christmas Eve*
May Week *first two weeks June*

Sights Outside City
Ely Cathedral, Audley End, Grantchester, Wimpole Hall, Anglesey Abbey, American Cemetery, Cromwell Museum at Huntingdon, Wicken Fen, Imperial War Museum, Duxford

Information Centre
Wheeler Street
CB2 3QD
Telephone Cambridge 322640

Fiat Dealer
Holland Fiat Centre
315–349 Mill Road,
Cambridge CB1 3DF
Tel. Cambridge 242222

1 Arts Theatre B3
2 Botanic Gardens C5
3 Church of the Holy Sepulchre *12th-c round church* B2
Colleges
4 *Clare 1326* A3
5 *Corpus Christi 1362* B3
6 *Emmanuel 1584, Wren Chapel* B/C3
7 *King's 1441 and Chapel* A3
8 *Magdalene 1542* A2
9 *Pembroke 1347, Wren Chapel* B3/4
10 *Peterhouse 1284, oldest college* B4
11 *Queen's 1448* A3/4
12 *St John's 1511 and Bridge of Sighs* A2
13 *Trinity 1546* A3
14 Fitzwilliam Museum *manuscripts, statuary, tapestry and archaeology* B4
15 Folk Museum *furniture, cooking equipment, clothes and tools* A2
16 Great St Mary's Church *University Church* B3
17 St Bene't's Church *oldest in county* B3
18 Tourist Information Centre B3
19 University Arts Faculties A4

Cambridge

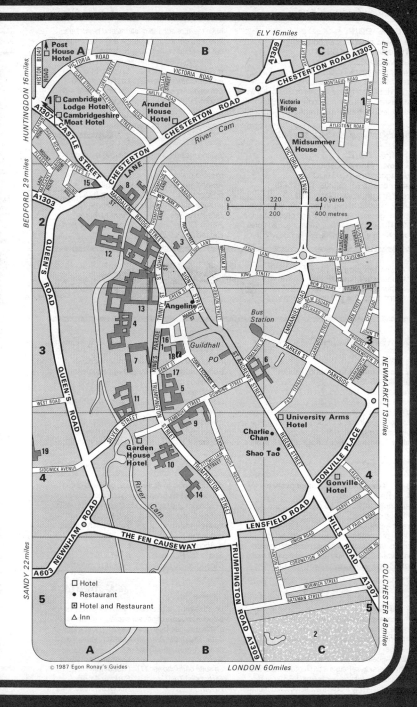

FIAT

© 1987 Egon Ronay's Guides

Arundel House Hotel
Cambridge

H 60% £E/F ♧
Town plan B1 Cambridgeshire
53 Chesterton Road CB4 3AN
Cambridge (0223) 67701
Owner manager Mr J. D. Norfolk
Credit Access, Amex, Diners, Visa
   Six Victorian terraced houses make up this well-established hotel overlooking the Cam. Bedrooms, including six in a converted stable block,

have tea-makers, radio-alarms and hairdryers.
There's a comfortable lounge and a bar that leads
out to a small walled garden. *Amenities* garden,
in-house movies, laundry service.

■ *Rooms 72*	*Confirm by 6*
en suite bath/shower 62	*Last dinner 9.30*
Direct dial Yes	*Parking Ample*
Room TV Yes	*Room service None*
Closed 25 & 26 Dec	

Cambridge Lodge Hotel
Cambridge

H 60% £D/E
Town plan A1 Cambridgeshire
Huntingdon Road CB3 0DQ
Cambridge (0223) 352833. Tlx 817438
Credit Access, Amex, Diners, Visa
   An Edwardian house on the A1307 west of
Cambridge makes a pleasant and peaceful small
hotel. The whole place has a relaxing, traditional
character epitomised in the bar-lounge with its

inviting fireside chairs. Good-sized bedrooms
have mahogany furniture and pretty floral fabrics,
plus tea-makers, hairdryers and radio-alarms.
Amenities garden, laundry service.

■ *Rooms 11*	*Confirm by 6*
en suite bath/shower 8	*Last dinner 10*
Direct dial Yes	*Parking Ample*
Room TV Yes	*Room service All day*
Closed 28 & 29 Dec	

■ Any person using our name
to obtain free hospitality is
a fraud. Proprietors, please
inform the police and us.

Cambridgeshire Moat House
Cambridge

H 63% £D
Town plan A1 Cambridgeshire
Bar Hill CB3 8EU
Crafts Hill (0954) 80555. Tlx 817141
Credit Access, Amex, Diners, Visa
A new reception area and keep-fit facilities have
updated this pleasant, modern hotel two miles
from junction 14 of the M11. Public areas include a
clubby Sportsman's Bar and agreeable first-floor

bar-lounge which overlooks the golf course.
Bedrooms are attractive and well equipped.
Amenities garden, indoor swimming pool, sauna,
tennis, squash, 18-hole golf course, pool table,
laundry service, children's playground, helipad.

■ *Rooms 100*	*Confirm by arrang.*
en suite bath/shower 100	*Last dinner 10*
Direct dial Yes	*Parking Ample*
Room TV Yes	*Room service All day*

Charlie Chan
Cambridge

R ♞ Town plan C4 Cambridgeshire
14 Regent Street
Cambridge (0223) 61763
Chinese cooking
Credit Amex
   Well-prepared dishes and friendly, helpful
service are attractions of this pleasant Chinese
restaurant. Chicken and green bean paste make a
tasty starter, with spicy prawn Szechuan style,

shredded pork in garlic sauce, beef and green
pepper in black bean sauce and chicken with
mushroom and bamboo shoots among the main
dishes. Good set menus. Try the crushed red
bean pancakes for afters. Staff are very helpful
and friendly.

■ *About £30 for two*	*L 12–2.15*
Seats 150 Parties 50	*D 6–11.15*
Closed 25–26 Dec	*Parking Limited*

Garden House Hotel
Cambridge

H 68% £C
Town plan A4 Cambridgeshire
Granta Place, Mill Lane CB2 1RT
Cambridge (0223) 63421. Tlx 81463
Manager Mr P. J. Breen
Credit Access, Amex, Diners, Visa
   The riverside setting's a big feature here, and
guests can watch the punts from the bar and
lounge or even ply a pole themselves. Most of the

practically fitted bedrooms also enjoy river views.
Good standards of housekeeping, but the decor
of this purpose-built hotel is looking just a little
dated. No dogs. *Amenities* garden, in-house
movies (free), laundry service.

■ *Rooms 117*	*Confirm by 6*
en suite bath/shower 117	*Last dinner 9.30*
Direct dial Yes	*Parking Ample*
Room TV Yes	*Room service 24 hours*

Gonville Hotel — Cambridge

H **62%** **£D/E**
Town plan C4 Cambridgeshire
Gonville Place CB1 1LY
Cambridge (0223) 66611
Manager Mrs E. Hooper
Credit Access, Amex, Visa
   In summer drinks are served in the sunny flower-filled patio of this pleasant hotel overlooking Parker's Piece. Inside, there's a

restful air-conditioned bar and a spacious, comfortably furnished lounge. Simply fitted bedrooms have tea/coffee-makers and small bathrooms. *Amenities* patio, laundry service.

■ *Rooms* 62	*Confirm by* 6
en suite bath/shower 62	*Last dinner* 9
Direct dial Yes	*Parking* Ample
Room TV Yes	*Room service* 24 hours
Closed 4 days Xmas	

Midsummer House *NEW ENTRY* — Cambridge

R ⌂ ♗ **Town Plan C1**
Cambridgeshire
Midsummer Common
Cambridge (0223) 69299
Credit Access, Amex, Diners, Visa
   An attractive Victorian house beside the river Cam. Fixed-price menus offer a short, imaginative selection of dishes such as game consommé, cod with saffron and lemon butter or braised

woodpigeon with cherries. There's a fine English cheeseboard. Thoughtful, concise wine list, spoilt by copious, pretentious tasting notes. Ask advice on parking when booking. ♗ **Well-chosen** ⊖

■ *Set L* £12·50	*L* 12–2
Set D from £16·50	*D* 7.30–10
About £50 *for two*	*Parking* Difficult
Seats 35	*Parties* 40
Closed Sun, Mon, Bank Hols & 10 days Xmas	

Post House Hotel — Cambridge

H **68%** **£C**
Town plan A1 Cambridgeshire
Lakeview Bridge Road, Impington CB4 4PH
Histon (022 023) 7000. Tlx 817123
Credit Access, Amex, Diners, Visa. LVs
   Accommodation is smart, spacious and comfortable at this well-equipped modern hotel just off the A45. Day rooms have a classic elegance with their beech panelling and pillars.

Amenities garden, indoor swimming pool, sauna, solarium, whirlpool bath, keep-fit equipment, games room, in-house movies (charge), laundry service, 24-hour lounge service, coffee shop (7am–10.30pm), children's playground.

■ *Rooms* 120	*Confirm by* 6
en suite bath/shower 120	*Last dinner* 10.30
Direct dial Yes	*Parking* Ample
Room TV Yes	*Room service* 24 hours

Shao Tao *NEW ENTRY* — Cambridge

R ♗ ♿ **Town plan C4** Cambridgeshire
72 Regent Street
Cambridge (0223) 353942
Chinese cooking
Credit Access, Amex, Diners, Visa
   Owner-chef Mr Tao shows sure skills through a tempting variety of Chinese dishes in his simple, spotless restaurant. Family favourites like steamed or fried dumplings, wun tun soup and

lemon chicken share the menu with splendid spicy dishes such as Yu-Lung duck, sautéed beef Szechuan-style and pork shreds with garlic sauce. Vegetables crisply delicious, toffee apples and bananas ditto.

■ *Set L & D from* £9·50	*L* 12–2.30
About £26 *for two*	*D* 6–11 (Sat 6–11.30)
Seats 70 *Parties* 30	*Parking* Difficult
Closed 1 wk Xmas	

University Arms Hotel — Cambridge

H **64%** **£D/E** ♿
Town plan C4 Cambridgeshire
Regent Street CB2 1AD
Cambridge (0223) 351241. Tlx 817311
Owner managers Bradford family
Credit Access, Amex, Diners, Visa
   Dating from 1891 this fine hotel has a long tradition of courteous service. The entrance hall leads to an elegant domed octagonal lounge.

Bars include Parker's Lounge with its fine view over Parker's Piece, the intimate Whisky Galore and pubby Hobson's Choice. Bedrooms are spacious and traditional. *Amenities* laundry service, 24-hour lounge service.

■ *Rooms* 115	*Confirm by* arrang.
en suite bath/shower 115	*Last dinner* 9.30
Direct dial Yes	*Parking* Ample
Room TV Yes	*Room service* 24 hours

■ Our inspectors are our full-time employees; they are professionally trained by us.

Old Rectory — Campsea Ashe

RR ⑨ ♿ **Map 6 D3** Suffolk
Nr Woodbridge
Wickham Market (0728) 746524
Credit Access, Amex, Diners, Visa

There is no menu at this delightful 17th-century house – guests discuss their requirements when booking, or give Stewart Bassett carte blanche in the knowledge that he will create a marvellous meal from fine local ingredients. Start with a drink in the recently restored Victorian conservatory, then settle down to a repast which might comprise choux buns filled with locally gathered wood mushrooms in sour cream, followed by duck en cocotte, with upside-down orange liqueur cake to follow. Wonderfully fresh fish is a speciality. Booking essential. 🍷 Well-chosen ☺

■ Set L £11·50	L by arrang.
Set D £14·50	D 7–10
About £38 for two	Parking Ample
Seats 40 Parties 20	Closed Sun to non-
	residents, all Feb & 3 days Xmas

Bedrooms £F

Rooms 8	With bath/shower 8

Pretty bedrooms (being upgraded) have comfy armchairs, tea-making facilities, TVs and telephones. No dogs.

Roman Way Hotel — Cannock

H **57% £E**
Map 10 C3 Staffordshire
Watling Street, Hatherton WS11 1SH
Cannock (054 35) 72121
Credit Access, Amex, Diners, Visa

On the A5, near junctions 11 and 12 of the M6, this modern purpose-built hotel is ideal for an overnight stop. Spacious, well-designed bedrooms in two wings offer tea-makers and neat bath or shower rooms. Day rooms, all in the main building, include a lively lounge bar, a quieter cocktail bar and a versatile function suite. Amenities garden, laundry service.

■ Rooms 24	Confirm by 9
en suite bath/shower 24	Last dinner 10
Direct dial Yes	Parking Ample
Room TV Yes	Room service None
Closed 25 Dec	

Canterbury Hotel — Canterbury

H **61% £E**
Town plan E3 Kent
71 New Dover Road CT1 3DZ
Canterbury (0227) 450551. Tlx 965809
Credit Access, Amex, Diners, Visa

A warm, relaxed atmosphere prevails in this large Victorian house, half a mile from the town centre along the New Dover Road (A2050). Visitors are welcomed in a cheerful foyer bar and may relax in a spaciously comfortable lounge. Spotlessly clean bedrooms are agreeably furnished in pine, with floral bedspreads. Private bathrooms have stylish blue Italian tiles. Dogs at discretion of management.

■ Rooms 27	Confirm by 6
en suite bath/shower 27	Last dinner 10
Direct dial Yes	Parking Ample
Room TV Yes	Room service All day

Chaucer Hotel — Canterbury

H **63% £C/D**
Town plan D3 Kent
63 Ivy Lane CT1 1TT
Canterbury (0227) 464427. Tlx 965096
Credit Access, Amex, Diners, Visa

Just an easy stroll from the cathedral, this welcoming Regency hotel makes an excellent base for a short stay. Attractively contemporary bedrooms with pretty coordinated decor and smart darkwood furnishings have tea-makers and good modern bathrooms. Day rooms include a handsome reception area and stylish bar-lounge. Amenities in-house movies (charge), laundry service, 24-hour lounge service.

■ Rooms 45	Confirm by 6
en suite bath/shower 45	Last dinner 9.30
Room phone Yes	Parking Limited
Room TV Yes	Room service All day

County Hotel — Canterbury

HR **72% £D E**
Town plan C2 Kent
High Street CT1 2RX
Canterbury (0227) 66266. Tlx 965076
Credit Access, Amex, Diners, Visa. LVs

First licensed in 1588, this fine city-centre hotel is located only five minutes' walk from the cathedral and overlooks a now pedestrianised High Street. It continues to thrive, thanks to able management and staff. A popular coffee shop with panelling and leaded windows leads from the recently refurbished foyer, while upstairs is a gracious lounge with a splendid 16th-century clock. Most bedrooms have smart mahogany units; remaining rooms are in Tudor or Georgian style and boast oak four-posters or half-testers. Accessories include remote-control TVs, tea-makers and trouser presses; lots of extras are provided in the excellent bathrooms. No dogs. Amenities valeting, laundry service, coffee shop (10.30am–11pm), 24-hour lounge service.

■ Rooms 74	Confirm by 6
en suite bath/shower 74	Last dinner 10
Direct dial Yes	Parking Ample
Room TV Yes	Room service 24 hours

Sully's Restaurant ♕

Our most recent meal here was like the curate's
egg, good in parts. Delicious home-baked bread,
spot-on vegetables and a super game terrine
were high spots, but disappointments (like a
burnt sauce with the main course) were made
worse by couldn't-care-less service. The wine list
is much improved. ♟ Well-chosen ⊖

■ Set L £9   L 12.30–2.30
Set D £12·50   D 7–10
About £46 for two   Seats 60 Parties 150

Ebury Hotel — Canterbury

H 58% £E/F
Town plan E3 Kent
65 New Dover Road CT1 3DX
Canterbury (0227) 68433
Owner managers Jane & Anthony Mason
Credit Access, Amex, Visa
A solidly comfortable Victorian hotel, where
personal service is a priority. Day rooms have a
handsome period appeal, and bedrooms are
comfortable and well appointed, with plenty of
space and practical modern furnishings.
Swimming pool and sauna planned. Excellent
breakfasts. *Amenities* garden, laundry service.
■ Rooms 15   Confirm by arrang.
en suite bath/shower 5   Last dinner 8.30
Direct dial Yes   Parking Ample
Room TV Yes   Room service All day
Closed 24 Dec–15 Jan

Falstaff Hotel *NEW ENTRY* — Canterbury

I £D/E
Town plan B1 Kent
St Dunstan's Street CT2 8AF
Canterbury (0227) 462138. Tlx 96394
Credit Access, Amex, Diners, Visa
A pilgrims' rest-house centuries ago, this
pleasantly staffed hotel was totally refurbished
two years ago. Much of its old character survives
in the residents' lounge, in the splendidly panelled
function room and in the well equipped bedrooms,
where heavy beams are the norm except for those
in a modern extension; bathrooms are stocked
with toiletries. No dogs. *Amenities* in-house
movies (free).
■ Rooms 24   Confirm by arrang.
en suite bath/shower 24 Last dinner 9.45
Direct dial Yes   Parking Ample
Room TV Yes   Room service Limited

Howfield Manor — Canterbury

HR 70% £E
Map 7 C5 Kent
Chartham Hatch CT4 7HQ
Canterbury (0227) 738294
Owner managers Clark & Janet Lawrence
Credit Access, Amex, Visa
A most hospitable welcome from Clark and
Janet Lawrence awaits you at this handsome old
manor house, set in its own secluded gardens by
the A28. The public rooms are quite captivating,
harmoniously blending elegance and intimate
comfort. The sitting room (with a blazing log fire in
winter) and library are full of fine antiques, tasteful
fabrics and good books and magazines. There's
no bar – you just help yourself to drinks from the
hallway table. Bedrooms, many recently
refurbished, are tastefully decorated and
equipped with trouser presses, hairdryers and
some thoughtful extras. Breakfasts are
noteworthy. No children under 14. No dogs.
Amenities garden, croquet.
■ Rooms 5   Confirm by arrang.
en suite bath/shower 5   Last dinner at 8
Room phone Yes   Parking Ample
Room TV No   Room service All day
Closed mid Dec–early Jan

Howfield Manor Restaurant ♟

A simple but elegant 16th-century dining room
where guests dine at two communal tables. From
a kitchen (originally a chapel) dating from 1181,
Janet Lawrence offers no-choice menus which
change nightly, starting maybe with leeks
vinaigrette, then perhaps simply cooked fresh fish
served with impeccably timed vegetables. An
excellent cheese selection and tasty pudding
follow. There's no wine list, so follow the host's
reliable suggestions. Non-residents must book
24 hours in advance. ⊖
■ Set D £13·50   D only at 8
About £36 for two   Seats 12 Parties 12
Closed mid Dec–early Jan

CANTERBURY

Map 7 C5
Town plan opposite

Population 36,290

The Metropolitan City of the English Church (since 602), where St Augustine preached (597), and Archbishop Thomas à Becket was martyred in the Cathedral (1170). Canterbury was successfully settled by the Belgae, the Romans, the Saxons and the Normans. It has been a town of pilgrim-tourists since 1008 and the Cathedral, medieval buildings and archives well repay a lingering visit. It is strong in literary association through Chaucer and Marlowe.

Sights Outside City
Bodiam Castle, Chilham, Dover Castle, Herne Bay, Leeds Castle, Lympne Castle, Reculver Towers, Rye and Winchelsea, Walmer Castle, Whitstable Castle and Grounds

Information Office
13 Longmarket
CT1 2JS
Telephone Canterbury 455490
Leisure Llne 67744

Fiat Dealer
Martin Walter Ltd
41 St George's Place
Canterbury
Kent CT1 1UR
Tel. Canterbury 66131
Map reference 3D

1 Blackfriars *13th-c Friary* C1
2 Cathedral *11th–15th c* D2
3 Christchurch Gate and Buttermarket C2
4 Conquest House C1
5 Dane John Garden *a memorial to Marlowe* C3
6 East Station B3
7 Greyfriars *first Franciscan settlement* B2
8 The Marlowe Theatre C1
9 Martyrs' Memorial *to Bloody Mary's victims* B3
10 Norman Castle *large Norman keep* B3
11 Norman Staircase *very fine roofed steps* and King's School *originally Priory hostel* D1
12 Queen Elizabeth's Guest Chamber C2
13 Roman Pavement and hypocaust C2
14 Royal Museum C2
15 St Augustine's Abbey *layered monastic remains* D2
16 St Dunstan's church *contains head of Sir Thomas More* A1
17 St George's Tower D2
18 St Martin's Church *oldest in use* E2
19 St Peter's Church *Anglo-Saxon* C2
20 St Peter's Street *typical medieval street* C2
21 St Thomas's (Eastbridge Hospital) *collection of 12th-c–17th-c buildings, beautiful Norman crypt* C2
22 Sir John Boys's House *ancient lopsided house* C1
23 The Weavers *16th-c weavers' houses* C2
24 Tower House B2
25 University and Gulbenkian Theatre A1
26 West Station B1
27 Westgate Tower *arms and armour museum* B1

Canterbury F I A T

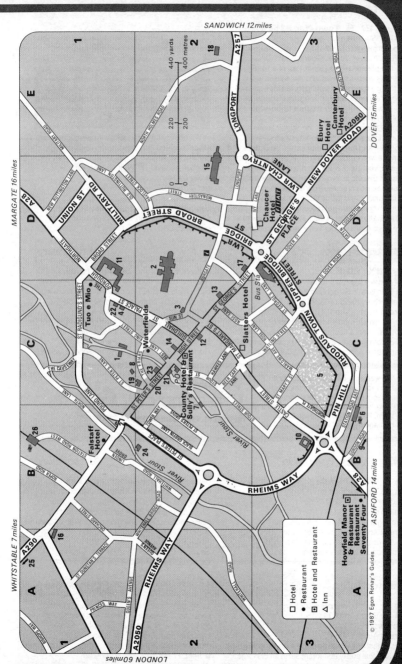

SANDWICH 12 miles

MARGATE 16 miles

WHITSTABLE 7 miles

DOVER 15 miles

ASHFORD 14 miles

LONDON 60 miles

440 yards
400 metres

□ Hotel
● Restaurant
☐ Hotel and Restaurant
△ Inn

Ebury Hotel
Canterbury Hotel
Chaucer Hotel
Slatters Hotel
County Hotel & Restaurant
Sully's Restaurant
Falstaff Hotel
Tuo e Mio
Waterfields
Howfield Manor & Restaurant
Seventy Four Restaurant

Bus Sta

RHODAUS TOWN
PIN HILL
RHEIMS WAY
River Stour

© 1987 Egon Ronay's Guides

F I A T

Restaurant Seventy Four ★   Canterbury

R ★ ♔ ♦ **Town Plan B3** Kent
74 Wincheap
Canterbury (0227) 67411
Credit Access, Amex, Diners, Visa

The panelled dining room, part of a 16th-century wine merchant's house, makes a strikingly handsome setting for Ian McAndrew's highly accomplished cooking. Masterly technique allies with great flair to produce some wonderfully subtle flavours, and tip-top ingredients combine in happy harmony. Many of the combinations are audacious and exciting: lobster with slivers of coconut and fresh raspberries; terrine of duck and tongue with herbs, tomato vinaigrette and caviar sauce; veal steak with crab mousse and crab sauce. Sweets like walnut tart with orange and Cointreau ice cream are good enough to be made compulsory, and meals end memorably with superb coffee and petits fours. Good wines. *Specialities* parfait of duck livers topped with a filo pastry shell and served with port wine sauce, tartlet of brill and baby leeks with vermouth cream sauce, sautéed fillet of lamb with scallop mousseline, white chocolate truffle torte with raspberry coulis. ♙ **Well-chosen** ℮

■ *Set L* £14	*L* 12.30–2
Set D from £22	*D* 7.30–9.30
About £56 *for two*	*Parking* Ample
Seats 34	*Parties* 34
Closed L Sat, all Sun, 2 wks Sept & Bank Hols except 25 Dec	

Slatters Hotel   Canterbury

H **58% £D/E**
Town plan C2 Kent
St Margaret's Street CT1 2TR
Canterbury (0227) 463271
Credit Access, Amex, Diners, Visa. LVs

The simple modern facade of this city-centre hotel shelters a section of the building dating from Elizabethan times. Pride of the public rooms is the handsome panelled Merchants Bar, which features a wattle-and-daub wall. Pleasant, practical bedrooms have fitted units, tea-makers and remote control TVs; most have their own well-maintained bathrooms. *Amenities* laundry service.

■ *Rooms* 32	*Confirm by arrang.*
en suite bath/shower 28	*Last dinner* 9
Direct dial Yes	*Parking* Ample
Room TV Yes	*Room service* Limited

■ We welcome complaints and bona fide recommendations on the tear-out pages for readers' comments. They are followed up by our professional team. Please also complain to the management instantly.

RECEPTION

Ristorante Tuo e Mio   Canterbury

R ♦ **Town Plan C1** Kent
16 The Borough
Canterbury (0227) 61471
Italian cooking
Managers Mr & Mrs R. P. M. Greggio
Credit Access, Amex, Diners, Visa

A small Italian restaurant with a good atmosphere and an excellent host in Signor Greggio. The regular menu includes antipasti and pasta, fish, beef, veal and chicken dishes, all competently prepared. Daily specials like liver Veneziana or skate with tomato and pimiento sauce add variety. Book for dinner. Interesting Italian wines, selected with care. ♙ **Well-chosen** ℮

■ *Set L* £7·50	*L* 12–2.30
About £40 *for two*	*D* 7–10.45
Seats 40 *Parties* 25	*Parking* Limited
Closed L Tues, all Mon, 4 days Xmas & Easter	

Waterfields   Canterbury

R ♦ ♦ **Town plan C2** Kent
5a Best Lane CT1 2JB
Canterbury (0227) 450276
Credit Access, Amex, Visa

Michael Waterfield displays sound cooking skills in this pretty restaurant set in an old forge. Dishes are generally quite straightforward – veal and herb terrine, goujons of lemon sole, salt beef with a peppercorn sauce – with one or two more elaborate offerings such as salmon and lobster coulibiac. Chocolate St Emilion and elderflower sorbet with almond flan and strawberries are typical sweets. Service is quite friendly and efficient. ℮

■ *Set L* £7·50	*L* 12–2.30
About £38 *for two*	*D* 7–10.45
Seats 60 *Parties* 20	*Parking* Limited
Closed L Mon, all Sun, Bank Hols & 1 wk Xmas	

Crest Hotel
Carlisle

H **57% £C/D**
Map 13 D4 Cumbria
Kingstown CA4 0HR
Carlisle (0228) 31201. Tlx 64201
Credit Access, Amex, Diners, Visa
　A modern low-rise hotel next to junction 44 of
the M6. Open-plan public areas are smartly
appointed and include a spacious foyer divided
from the bar by attractive arches. Businessmen

are well catered for in the functional bedrooms
with their built-in units, useful writing space, tea-
makers and trouser presses. Neat tiled
bathrooms. Sweets are provided in rooms
designated for non-smokers. *Amenities* garden.

■ *Rooms* 100	*Confirm by* 6
en suite bath/shower 100	*Last dinner* 9.45
Direct dial Yes	*Parking* Ample
Room TV Yes	*Room service* None

Ladbroke Crown & Mitre Hotel
Carlisle

H **56% £D**
Map 13 D4 Cumbria
English Street CA3 8HZ
Carlisle (0228) 25491. Tlx 64183
Credit Access, Amex, Diners, Visa. **LVs**
　Edwardian grandeur persists in the entrance
hall of this substantial city-centre hotel. The bars
and tiny lounge are more modest, and bedrooms
vary from very functional singles to some

redecorated standard rooms and four Gold Star
rooms with new furnishings and extra
accessories. *Amenities* indoor swimming pool,
whirlpool bath, in-house movies (charge), laundry
service.

■ *Rooms* 98	*Confirm by* 6
en suite bath/shower 97	*Last dinner* 9.45
Room phone Yes	*Parking* Limited
Room TV Yes	*Room service* Limited

Swallow Hilltop Hotel
Carlisle

H **56% £D**
Map 13 D4 Cumbria
London Road CA1 2PQ
Carlisle (0228) 29255. Tlx 64292
Manager Philip Sagar
Credit Access, Amex, Diners, Visa. **LVs**
　Refurbishment has raised many of the
bedrooms in this modern hotel to executive
standard. Contemporary public rooms include a

comfortable lounge near the pool.
Amenities indoor swimming pool, sauna,
solarium, whirlpool bath, keep-fit equipment, golf
practice nets, in-house movies, laundry service,
coffee shop (11am–7pm), children's play area.

■ *Rooms* 110	*Confirm by* 6
en suite bath/shower 97	*Last dinner* 9.45
Direct dial Yes	*Parking* Ample
Room TV Yes	*Room service* 24 hours

⮑ is our symbol for an **outstanding** wine list.

Carlyon Bay Hotel
Carlyon Bay

H **67% £C/D**
Map 2 B3 Cornwall
Nr St Austell PL25 3RD
Par (072 681) 2304
Credit Access, Amex, Diners, Visa
　Old-fashioned standards of service and
housekeeping go hand in hand with every modern
leisure facility at this 1930s hotel which stands
high on the cliffs surrounded by 250 acres of
lovely grounds, with splendid views across
Carlyon Bay. The hotel betrays its 30s heritage in
the spacious dimensions of public areas which
enjoy plenty of natural sunlight. Comfortably

traditional lounges enjoy fine views and there are
two smart bars plus a splendid snooker room. Airy
restful bedrooms (best ones overlook the bay)
have attractive soft furnishings and good practical
private bathrooms. *Amenities* garden, indoor &
outdoor swimming pools, sauna, solarium,
whirlpool bath, keep-fit equipment, tennis, golf
course, putting, games room, snooker, in-house
movies, laundry service, helipad.

■ *Rooms* 75	*Confirm by* arrang.
en suite bath/shower 75	*Last dinner* 9
Room phone Yes	*Parking* Ample
Room TV Yes	*Room service* 24 hours

Porth Avallen Hotel
Carlyon Bay

H **61% £E**
Map 2 B3 Cornwall
Sea Road, Nr St Austell PL25 3SG
Par (072 681) 2802
Credit Access, Amex, Diners, Visa
　Fine views of the bay are a feature of this
modernised 1930s residence perched on the
cliffs. Bedrooms vary from compact singles to
roomier doubles and twins, their furnishings from

contemporary fitted to traditional freestanding.
The panelled lounge makes a cosy retreat and the
bar looks out to sea. No dogs. *Amenities* garden,
laundry service, 24-hour lounge service.

■ *Rooms* 25	*Confirm by* arrang.
en suite bath/shower 21	*Last dinner* 8.30
Direct dial Yes	*Parking* Ample
Room TV Yes	*Room service* Limited
Closed 2 wks Xmas	

Aynsome Manor Hotel   Cartmel

H 60% £E/F
   Map 13 D6 Cumbria
Nr Grange-over-Sands LA11 6HH
Cartmel (044 854) 653
Owner managers Varley family
Credit Access, Amex, Visa
   A former manor house beautifully situated amid
unspoilt countryside. There's a welcoming
entrance hall with open fireplace and Queen Anne

chairs, and a rustic bar featuring oak tables and
wheelback chairs. Smartly appointed bedrooms
have simple carpeted bathrooms. Half-board
terms only. *Amenities* garden.

■ *Rooms* 14	*Confirm by arrang.*
en suite bath/shower 13	*Last dinner 8.15*
Direct dial Yes	*Parking Ample*
Room TV Yes	*Room service* Limited
Closed 1st 3 weeks Jan	

Uplands   Cartmel

RR ♀ **Map 13 D6** Cumbria
     Haggs Lane LA11 6HD
Cartmel (044 854) 248
Credit Access, Amex
   Tom and Diana Peter worked at Miller Howe for
12 years and John Tovey is a partner in their
attractive restaurant. The Miller Howe connection
is proudly vaunted and similar standards apply.
Raw materials are of top quality and Tom has a
sure and sympathetic touch. A set menu with
some choices might include parsnip and ginger
soup (served from a tureen at the table) and
poached fillet of salmon with a Noilly Prat,

cucumber and dill sauce. Delectable desserts
such as hot toffee date pudding. Smoking
discouraged. ♀ Well-chosen ☺

■ *Set L £9*	*L 12.30 for 1*
Set D £16	*D 7.30 for 8*
About £42 for two	*Parking* Ample
Seats 30	*Parties* 30
Closed Mon & 2 Jan–late Feb	

Bedrooms £D/E

Rooms 4	*With bath/shower* 4

For diners only there are four attractive bedrooms
with en suite facilities. No children under 12.

■ For a discount on next year's guide, see Offer for Answers.

Bond's Hotel   Castle Cary

HR 60% £F
     Map 4 B3 Somerset
Ashford Hill BA7 7JP
Castle Cary (0963) 50464
Owner managers Kevin & Yvonne Bond
Credit Access, Amex
   A warm welcome awaits at this small and
intimate hotel just off the A371. Chekhov the cat
charms visitors, who enter straight into an inviting
sitting room that doubles as a bar. The small but
delightful bedrooms, with pretty decor and
comfortable beds, have well-kept bathrooms.
Excellent breakfast. No children under eight. No
dogs. *Amenities* garden, laundry service.

■ *Rooms* 6	*Confirm by arrang.*
en suite bath/shower 6	*Last dinner* 9
Room phone No	*Parking* Ample
Room TV No	*Room service* All day

Bond's Hotel Restaurant ♀

Flair and care are vital ingredients of talented
Yvonne Bond's short, interesting menus for her
attractive little restaurant (booking necessary).
Starters may include a spinach, apple and
Cheddar strudel or cream of broccoli soup. Main
course choice ranges from casseroled pheasant
with chestnuts, beef fillet en croûte with mustard
and red wine sauce to salmon steak with
raspberry hollandaise; all served with beautifully-
cooked vegetables. Puds are most imaginative
and delicious. Last order 9.
♀ Well-chosen ☺

■ *Set D from £8·50*	*D only 7–12*
About £35 for two	*Seats* 22 *Parties* 22
Closed Sun–Tues to non-residents	

Manor House Hotel   Castle Combe

HR 72% £C
     Map 4 B2 Wiltshire
Nr Chippenham SN14 7HR
Castle Combe (0249) 782206. Tlx 449931
Credit Access, Amex, Diners, Visa
   A largely 17th-century honey-stone manor
which stands on an ancient site in England's
prettiest village. Twenty-six acres of landscaped
gardens make a beautiful setting, while inside
comfort and history intermingle. The entrance hall
boasts intricate carving dating from 1664, while a
fine 18th-century Italian frieze commemorating
Shakespeare's Falstaff decorates one of the

restful lounges. Bedrooms are well equipped, with
mini-bars and radio-intercoms; some have
splendid four-posters or testers. All have smart,
well-kept private bathrooms (one not en suite).
Amenities garden, outdoor swimming pool,
tennis, croquet, game fishing, 24-hour lounge
service, helipad.

■ *Rooms* 32	*Confirm by* 6
en suite bath/shower 31	*Last dinner 9.30*
Direct dial Yes	*Parking* Ample
Room TV Yes	*Room service* 24 hours

Restaurant

Patrick McDonald's menus provide plenty of variety and his cooking is sound and enjoyable. You might start with spinach, celeriac and carrot strudel, and continue with superb loin of lamb with mint and apricot forcemeat. Sweets are delicious. Notable selection of Spanish wines plus the outstanding Tim Knappstein wines from Australia. ℮

■ *Set L from £8·50*
Set D £18·95
About £50 for two

L 12.30–2
D 7.30–9.30
Seats 78 Parties 100

NEW ENTRY

Donington Thistle Hotel *NEW ENTRY* Castle Donington

H **73% £C/D** &
Map **11 D3** Derbyshire
East Midlands Airport DE7 2SH
Derby (0332) 850 700. Tlx 377632
Credit Access, Amex, Diners, Visa

Actually in the grounds of the East Midlands Airport, this modern low-rise hotel is an ideal stopover for air travellers. It's also handy for motorists, being close to junction 24 of the M1. Staff throughout are smart and friendly, starting with the smiling receptionists in the airy foyer. There's plenty of room to relax, both in the pleasantly rustic bar and in the splendid lounge, which features beams and many plants. Good-sized bedrooms, also with a light, airy feel, have many accessories. The buffet breakfast is not the hotel's biggest attraction.
Amenities garden, indoor swimming pool, sauna,

solarium, whirlpool bath, keep-fit equipment, in-house movies (free), laundry service, 24-hour lounge service.

■ *Rooms* 110
en suite bath/shower 110
Direct dial Yes
Room TV Yes

Confirm by 6
Last dinner 10.15
Parking Ample
Room service 24 hours

Casa Cominetti Catford

See under London

Alfonso's Cavendish

R ♀ & Map **6 C3** Suffolk
High Street, Nr Sudbury
Glemsford (0787) 280372
Italian cooking
Credit Access, Amex, Diners

Suffolk simpatico, with chianti-bottle decor, ready smiles, and capable cooking by Veronica Barricella whilst husband Alfonso looks after the customers. The pasta's home-made and

delicious, and main courses cover chicken, veal and particularly good beef. Also seafood including seasonal lobster. Whisked-to-order zabaglione is a super sweet, and the Moka coffee is excellent. ℮

■ *Set L Sun only £9·50*
About £40 for two
Seats 35 Parties 35
Closed L Mon, D Sun & L Tues–Sat exc by arrang.

L Sun 12–2
D from 7
Parking Ample

Grey Gables Cawston

RR ♀ & Map **6 C1** Norfolk
Norwich Road
Norwich (0603) 871259

Rosalind Snaith continues to win friends with her robust and simply skilful cooking at this country restaurant outside Cawston. Check directions and be sure to book as opening times may fluctuate. Fixed-price meals (three courses for lunch; five for dinner) offer ample choice. Rosalind is a fine pastrycook – try the salmon and pike mayonnaise in puff pastry, or chicken Wellington. A daily-changing three-course evening meal is offered to resident guests.

Service by James Snaith is friendly and capable. ℮
■ *Set L £7·50*
Set D £12·50
About £32 for two
Seats 25 Parties 25
Closed L Sat & 25 & 26 Dec

L Sun 12.30–2,
Mon–Fri by arrang.
D 7–9
Parking Ample

Bedrooms £F
Rooms 4 *With bath/shower 3*
Generous bedrooms are individually decorated, with period furniture and fittings. All have TVs. Carpeted bathrooms are most attractive.

HR 76% £C/D
Map 10 B4 Hereford & Worcester
Nr Kidderminster DY10 4PY
Chaddesley Corbett (0562 83) 876. Tlx 333431
Credit Access, Amex, Diners, Visa

A handsome country house seen dramatically from the A448 and approached through lovely landscaped grounds. It's the venture of Joseph and Alison Petitjean, who with their young, mainly French staff provide a pleasant welcome and willing service. Day rooms have the elegance of cornices and high ceilings, plus individual features like the pine and maple panelling in the bar. Bedrooms are furnished in solid, traditional style; housekeeping is impeccable, comfort considerable. One particularly splendid room has a four-poster; two at the top are smaller than the rest. *Amenities* garden, laundry service.

■ *Rooms* 11	*Confirm by arrang.*
en suite bath/shower 11	*Last dinner* 9.30
Direct dial Yes	*Parking* Ample
Room TV Yes	*Room service* All day
Closed 1st 2 wks Jan	

Brockencote Hall Restaurant ♛ &

French cooking
Comfort, style and quiet luxury, plus the culinary talents of Serge Demollière. Terrines are a strong point (fish and fruit with a light curry; home-cured ham with parsley and pickles) and saucing is very reliable. Hake with wild mushrooms, lamb cutlets with rosemary and sweetbreads with lobster and noodles show the range. Sweets include a true tarte tatin. A short list of good wines includes a delicious Crémant d'Alsace (Mure). ℮

■ *Set L* £10·50	*L* 12.30–2
About £50 for two	*D* 7.30–9.30
Seats 38	*Parties* 20
Closed D Sun. & 1st 2 wks Jan	

HR 81% £B/C
Map 3 D2 Devon
TQ13 8HH
Chagford (064 73) 2367
Owner managers Paul & Kay Henderson
Credit Access, Amex, Diners, Visa

Comfort, service and housekeeping are all outstanding at this superb mock-Tudor mansion, whose sylvan setting is both secluded and spectacular. Antiques blend with inviting, old-fashioned armchairs and sofas in the day rooms, which include a marvellous panelled drawing room. Log fires crackle a welcome, and fresh flower displays are a lovely feature. Bedrooms vary in size, some being very spacious and a few boasting private terraces; common to all is the owners' fine sense of style and taste, whether chintzy or cottagy in some of the smaller rooms, or grandly elegant, with heavy drapes and canopied beds. Bathrooms are luxuriously equipped. Half-board terms only.
Amenities garden, tennis, laundry service.

■ *Rooms* 14	*Confirm by arrang.*
en suite bath/shower 14	*Last dinner* 9
Direct dial Yes	*Parking* Ample
Room TV Yes	*Room service* All day

Gidleigh Park Hotel Restaurant ★ ♛ ⚘

Ponder the delights of Shaun Hill's menu over a drink in the bar before settling down to a meal in the elegant, panelled restaurant. He chooses his produce with the greatest care, and his cooking is skilled and subtle, with particularly refined sauces. Dishes that stay in the memory include noisettes of lamb with an aubergine charlotte and rosemary sauce; and apple tart with honey ice cream and caramel sauce. The wine list is magnificent, with an unequalled Californian section, exceptional 1976 and 1983 Alsace and marvellous 1978 red burgundies. Fine wines by the glass from the Cruvinet machine. No smoking. Booking essential. *Specialities* herb ravioli stuffed with chicken liver, garlic and lemon, Thai soup of chicken and coconut milk, with lemon grass, chillis and galanga, sautéed monkfish with mustard and cucumber sauce, roasted woodcock. ⊳ Outstanding ♀ Well-chosen ℮

■ *Set L* £17·50	*L* 12.30–2
Set D £25	*D* 7–9
About £80 for two	*Seats* 40

Great Tree Hotel   Chagford

H 65% £D/E
Map 3 D2 Devon
Sandy Park TO13 8JS
Chagford (064 73) 2491
Owner manager Mr & Mrs Philip Bramhall
Credit Access, Amex, Diners, Visa
　The new owners of this pleasantly situated former hunting lodge have installed direct-dial telephones but discontinued room service.

Bedrooms are traditionally furnished and bathrooms, like the rest of the hotel, are spotless. Public rooms include a large, comfortable lounge and a cosy little bar. *Amenities* garden.

■ *Rooms* 14	*Confirm by* arrang.
en suite bath/shower 14	*Last dinner* 9
Direct dial Yes	*Parking* Ample
Room TV Yes	*Room service* None
Closed 27 Dec–1 Feb	

Mill End Hotel   Chagford

HR 63% £D/E
Map 3 D2 Devon
Sandy Park TQ13 8JN
Chagford (064 73) 2282
Owner managers Mr & Mrs Craddock
Credit Access, Amex, Diners, Visa
　There's nothing run of the mill about this delightful whitewashed hotel. The Craddocks are diligent, welcoming hosts and housekeeping is immaculate. Two homely lounges – one with a bar – are cosy and relaxing. Bedrooms are traditional or modern, with sparkling bathrooms.
Amenities garden, game fishing.

■ *Rooms* 17	*Confirm by* arrang.
en suite bath/shower 15	*Last dinner* 9
Direct dial Yes	*Parking* Ample
Room TV Yes	*Room service* All day
Closed 10 days Xmas	

Mill End Hotel Restaurant �

Desserts are Hazel Craddock's speciality and surrender is sweet when the offerings include linzer torte, Drambuie bavarois or chocolate strawberry roulade. Also on the fixed-price menu might be mushrooms provençale, hot crab ramekin or cottage garden salad, with a main course choice of baked river Tamar salmon or sautéed veal kidneys with generous portions of fresh and varied vegetables. There's always an interesting vegetarian dish, too, plus a good selection of cheeses. Book for lunch.
♀ **Well-chosen** 🅔

■ *Set L* £11·25	*L* 12.30–1.30
Set D £13·50	*D* 7.30–9
About £36 *for two*	*Seats* 37
Closed 10 days Xmas	*Parties* 12

Teignworthy   Chagford

HR 65% £C
Map 3 D2 Devon
Frenchbeer TQ13 8EX
Chagford (064 73) 3355
Owner managers John & Gillian Newell
Credit Access, Visa
　A lovely sequestered setting (check directions!) for this delightful 20s hotel. Log fires crackle in the cosy bar and lounge, where guests can browse through books or play classical or jazz records. Prettily furnished bedrooms have sparkling bathrooms and enjoy magnificent views. No children under 11. No dogs. *Amenities* garden, sauna, solarium, tennis, croquet, laundry service.

■ *Rooms* 9	*Confirm by* arrang.
en suite bath/shower 9	*Last dinner* 9.30
Direct dial Yes	*Parking* Ample
Room TV Yes	*Room service* All day

Teignworthy Restaurant �

The choice on the fixed-price menu is concise but interesting; the cooking is dependable and unfussy relying on first-class produce. Start perhaps with sautéed sweetbreads with shallot and Marsala sauce and go on to roasted quail or poached sea trout with asparagus. A vegetarian main course is always available. Delicious sweets may include iced rhubarb parfait with strawberry sauce. Superb local cheeses. Fine burgundies appear on a good list (Pommard from Parent, Chassagne-Montrachet from Morey). Book, and please don't smoke in the dining room.
♀ **Well-chosen** 🅔

■ *Set D* £24·50	*L* 12.30–2 by arrang.
About £55 *for two*	*D* 7.30–9
Seats 25	*Parties* 30

♀ indicates a **well-chosen** house wine.

Bell at Charlbury   Charlbury

H 57% £D/E
Map 4 C1 Oxfordshire
Church Street OX7 3AP
Charlbury (0608) 810278
Owner manager David Jackson
Credit Access, Amex, Diners, Visa
　A huge inglenook fire warms the flagstoned bar of this welcoming hotel dating from 1700. Guests can relax in the first-floor residents' lounge that is

sometimes used for meetings. The bedrooms are prettily decorated (some in the converted stables) and homely.
Amenities garden, coarse fishing.

■ *Rooms* 14	*Confirm by* 4
en suite bath/shower 14	*Last dinner* 9.30
Room phone Yes	*Parking* Ample
Room TV Yes	*Room service* All day

The Charlecote Pheasant *NEW ENTRY*   Charlecote

H 63% £E ᵶ
Map 4 C1 Warwickshire
Nr Warwick CV35 9EN
Stratford-upon-Avon (0789) 840200. Tlx 31688
Owner managers Mr & Mrs Huterstein
Credit Access, Amex, Diners, Visa. **LVs**
   17th-century farmhouse buildings and a new
accommodation block make up this friendly hotel.
Bedrooms are decently sized, light and well

equipped (4 four-posters). There are two bars and
a lounge. *Amenities* garden, outdoor swimming
pool, sauna, solarium, keep-fit equipment, tennis,
croquet, pool table, satellite TV, laundry service,
24-hour lounge service.

■ *Rooms* 60	*Confirm by* arrang.
en suite bath/shower 60	*Last dinner* 10
Direct dial Yes	*Parking* Ample
Room TV Yes	*Room service* Limited

TraveLodge   Charnock Richard

H 58% £E
Map 10 A1 Lancashire
Mill Lane, Nr Chorley PR7 5HL
Coppull (0257) 791746. Tlx 67315
Credit Access, Amex, Diners, Visa
   A cheerful, practical stopover set back from the
northbound M6 between junctions 27 and 28 (also
accessible from the southbound carriageway).
Bedrooms – half recently refurbished – are bright,

airy and of a good size, with adequate bathrooms,
remote-control TVs and mineral trays. Reception
now incorporates a little evenings-only restaurant
next to the comfortable bar-lounge. There's also a
small conference room. *Amenities* garden.

■ *Rooms* 101	*Confirm by* 6
en suite bath/shower 101	*Last dinner* 9.30
Room phone Yes	*Parking* Ample
Room TV Yes	*Room service* None

Al San Vincenzo *NEW ENTRY*   Cheam

R ᵶ ᵶ Map 5 E3 Surrey
52 Upper Mulgrave Road
01-661 9763
Italian cooking
Credit Access, Amex, Diners, Visa
   The food in this charming little family concern is
a world away from average Italian fare, as
Vincenzo Borgonzolo seeks out top-quality
naturally produced ingredients in his cooked-to-

order dishes. The delights are varied – grilled
mushrooms with lemon juice, super seafood
casserole; fruit specialities like figs in grappa.
Wife Elaine greets and serves. Book. ☺

■ *Set L* 12.50	*L* 12–2
Set D £14·95	*D* 6.30–9.30, Sat 6–10
About £36 for two	*Parking* Ample
Seats 20 *Parties* 25	*Closed* L Sat, all Sun
(exc. Mothering Sun) & most Bank Hols	

Chedington Court   Chedington

HR 68% £C
Map 4 A4 Dorset
Beaminster DT8 3HY
Corscombe (093 589) 265
Owner managers Hilary & Philip Chapman
Credit Amex, Visa
   A log fire warms the panelled library of this
handsome mansion, and there are lovely views
from the lounges. Huge bedrooms boast some
fine period furnishings. Nice surroundings, but
lacks that real country house hotel feel. No dogs.
Amenities garden, putting, croquet, snooker,
helipad.

■ *Rooms* 10	*Confirm by* arrang.
en suite bath/shower 10	*Last dinner* 9
Room phone Yes	*Parking* Ample
Room TV Yes	*Room service* Limited
Closed mid Jan–mid Feb & 4 days Xmas	

Chedington Court
Restaurant ᵶ

Hilary Chapman's set four-course dinners
continue to please at this quietly dignified
restaurant. Good flavour combinations and fine
saucing distinguish her range of dishes. There is a
choice of classic starters like French onion tart or
avocado mousse followed by a light fish course.
The main set dish may be chicken breast with a
creamy tarragon sauce or perhaps beef fillet in
pastry. An interesting sweet course concludes a
worthy meal. Non-residents should book. Very
fine, rambling wine list. Note Volnay 1982 (Michel
Lafarge). ⊂⊃ **Outstanding** ☺

■ *Set D* £17·50	*D* only 7–9
About £44 for two	*Seats* 30 *Parties* 50
Closed 4 wks Jan–Feb & 4 days Xmas	

menu & WINE LIST 1987-8

Pontlands Park

Chelmsford

H **72% £C/D**
Map 7 B4 Essex
West Hanningford Road, Great Baddow
CM2 8HR
Chelmsford (0245) 76444. Tlx 995411
Manager David Birch
Credit Access, Amex, Diners, Visa

Fields and gardens surround this roomy hotel, a Victorian mansion with a new extension very much in keeping with the original building. Large, comfortable bedrooms in delicate pastel shades are variously furnished in cream, limed oak or mahogany, and there are two four-posters and one half-tester (king-size beds throughout). Remote-control TVs, trouser presses and writing desks are standard; bathrooms are excellent. Ground-floor rooms in the wing open directly on to the lawns. Also in the wing is a spacious lounge,

while the reception and the cosy, traditional bar are in the main house. No dogs.
Amenities garden, indoor swimming pool, sauna, solarium, whirlpool bath, laundry service.

■ *Rooms* 17	*Confirm by* 6
en suite bath/shower 17	*Last dinner* 10
Direct dial Yes	*Parking* Ample
Room TV Yes	*Room service* All day

■ We publish annually, so make sure you use the current edition. It's worth it!

Hotel de la Bere

Cheltenham

H **64% £C/D**
Map 4 C1 Gloucestershire
Southam GL52 3NH
Cheltenham (0242) 37771. Tlx 43232
Manager Mr S. John Harrison
Credit Access, Amex, Diners, Visa

Extensive leisure and conference facilities bring the world of today to this Tudor mansion. Day rooms have oak panelling and leaded windows.

Bedrooms range between old-world charm and smart modernity. *Amenities* garden, outdoor swimming pool, sauna, solarium, keep-fit equipment, tennis, squash, badminton, pitch & putt, croquet.

■ *Rooms* 49	*Confirm by* 6
en suite bath/shower 49	*Last dinner* 10
Direct dial Yes	*Parking* Ample
Room TV Yes	*Room service* 24 hours

La Ciboulette

Cheltenham

R ♵ ♿ **Map 4 C1** Gloucestershire
24 Suffolk Road
Cheltenham (0242) 573449
French cooking
Credit Access, Amex, Visa

Kevin Jenkins has built up a loyal following for fine French cooking served against a leafy backdrop of indoor plants. Moules marinière or crab with pimento and sweetcorn can lead on to

salmon braised in orange butter sauce, rack of lamb, or veal with mushrooms, cream and shallots. Tempting desserts include a huge, billowy oeuf à la neige. ☞

■ *Set L* £8·70	*L* 12.30–2
About £46 *for two*	*D* 7.30–10.30
Seats 36	*Parking* Ample
Closed Sun, Mon, Bank Hols, 1 wk Easter, 2 wks Aug & 1 wk Xmas	

☞ is our symbol for an **outstanding** wine list.

Golden Valley Thistle Hotel

Cheltenham

H **69% £C**
Map 4 C1 Gloucestershire
Gloucester Road GL51 0TS
Cheltenham (0242) 32691. Tlx 43410
Credit Access, Amex, Diners, Visa

High standards of overnight accommodation are offered at this modern hotel, near junction 11 of the M5. All bedrooms have attractive coordinated fabrics and good-quality units,

trouser presses and hairdryers; superior rooms boast extras like wall safes and three telephone extensions. Day rooms include a relaxing lounge, and bar. *Amenities* garden, putting, croquet, in-house movies (charge), 24-hour lounge service.

■ *Rooms* 97	*Confirm by* 6
en suite bath/shower 97	*Last dinner* 10
Direct dial Yes	*Parking* Ample
Room TV Yes	*Room service* 24 hours

Cheltenham ▶

The Greenway

HR 79% £B/C *E*
Map 4 C1 Gloucestershire
Shurdington GL51 5UG
Cheltenham (0242) 862352. Tlx 437216
Owner manager Julian Hook
Credit Access, Amex, Diners, Visa

Named after the pre-Roman road that runs beside the hotel, and set in lovely parkland off the A46, this splendid manor house is superbly managed. Service is exemplary and the atmosphere invites relaxation. Flowers fill the impressive dayrooms, where comfy sofas and antique furnishings happily coexist. The small clubby bar area is a quiet spot. Traditionally-furnished bedrooms in the main house are spacious and well-proportioned, with mullioned windows giving fine views. Eight new rooms in the coach-house are equally large. Carpeted

bathrooms have generous towels. Splendid breakfasts. No children under 7. No dogs. *Amenities* garden, croquet, laundry service, helipad.

■ *Rooms* 19	*Confirm by* arrang.
en suite bath/shower 19	*Last dinner* 9.30
Direct dial Yes	*Parking* Ample
Room TV Yes	*Room service* All day
Closed 28 Dec–28 Jan	

Greenway Dining Room ♨ &

This light conservatory dining room overlooking a sunken garden is a delightful spot. Stephen Whitney's style of cooking (modern on a classic base) is seen to advantage in beautifully constructed four-course dinner menus based on fine fresh produce. The lunchtime choice is simpler. Start, perhaps, with veal sweetbreads in a vegetable envelope with hazelnut butter, followed by jellied chicken bouillon. Advance to sautéed brill and calamari with tomato, garlic and coriander. Blueberry and peanut galette with blueberry coulis makes a happy ending. Imposing wine list, notable burgundies.
♟ **Well-chosen** ✆

■ *Set L* £13·50	*L* 12.30–2
Set D £22	*D* 7.30–9.30
About £60 *for two*	*Seats* 50 *Parties* 36

Closed L Sat, D Sun to non-residents, L Bank Hols & 28 Dec–28 Jan

Mayflower

R Map 4 C1 Gloucestershire
32 Clarence Street
Cheltenham (0242) 522426
Chinese cooking
Owner manager Chun F. Kong
Credit Amex, Diners. LVs

Highly enjoyable eating in a smart, relaxing setting is the successful formula at this town-centre Chinese restaurant. Start your meal with

wun tun soup, then move to sizzling beef with black beans and chilli, chicken stuffed with prawn paste, or baked crab with ginger and spring onion. Glazed fruit and fritters for dessert.

■ *Set L* £2·80	*L* 12–2
Set D £6	*D* 6–11.30 Sat 6–12
About £30 *for two*	*Parking* Limited
Seats 45	*Parties* 20

Closed L Sun & 4 days Xmas

Prestbury House Hotel

H 62% £E
Map 4 C1 Gloucestershire
The Burgage, Prestbury GL52 3DN
Cheltenham (0242) 529533
Owner manager Mr G. Gorrie
Credit Access, Visa

Comfort and traditional style are the hallmarks of this spacious Georgian town house, set back from the A46. Public rooms retain some original

features. Well-proportioned bedrooms have tea/coffee-makers, trouser presses and hairdryers. *Amenities* garden.

■ *Rooms* 10	*Confirm by* arrang.
en suite bath/shower 10	*Last dinner* 9
Direct dial Yes	*Parking* Ample
Room TV Yes .	*Room service* None

Closed Bank Hols, 4 days Easter, 2 weeks Aug, 10 days Xmas

Queen's Hotel

H 69% £C
Map 4 C1 Gloucestershire
The Promenade GL50 1NN
Cheltenham (0242) 514724. Tlx 43381
Credit Access, Amex, Diners, Visa

When the Queen's opened in 1838 it was the largest hotel in Britain. With its imposing Palladian facade it remains a fine Victorian showpiece – though constant improvements ensure fully up-to-

date standards of comfort and convenience within. Much of the original grandeur survives in the lofty and elegant public rooms, and bedrooms are all equipped to a high standard. *Amenities* garden, laundry service, 24-hour lounge service.

■ *Rooms* 77	*Confirm by* 6
en suite bath/shower 77	*Last dinner* 9.45
Room phone Yes	*Parking* Limited
Room TV Yes	*Room service* 24 hours

402

Redmond's *NEW ENTRY*

R ⛄ ♀ **Map 4 C1** Gloucestershire
12 Suffolk Road
Cheltenham (0242) 580323
Credit Access, Amex, Diners, Visa

Redmond Hayward usually works alone in his kitchen, cooking with great flair and deliberation, and his fixed-price lunches and à la carte dinners are something to relish. Starters could include smoked haddock chowder or broccoli mousse with an intense beurre blanc; main courses are exemplified by breast of corn-fed chicken with vanilla and orange zest or superlative fillet of beef with garlic, celeriac and a red wine sauce. British

cheeses are superb, sweets like ginger soufflé irresistible. The wine list is concise, carefully chosen and reasonably priced (with some interesting lesser known items). A small but stylish and very civilised restaurant, with front of house led charmingly by Redmond's wife Pippa.
♀ **Well-chosen** ☺

■ *Set L £9·50*	*L 12–2*
About £40 for two	*D 7.15–10.30*
Seats 20 Parties 12	*Parking Ample*
Closed D Sun, all Mon, 2 wks Aug/Sept	

Wyastone Hotel

H **56% £E**
Map 4 C1 Gloucestershire
Parabola Road GL50 3BG
Cheltenham (0242) 45549
Owner managers Willem & Marijke van Ommen
Credit Access, Amex, Diners, Visa

Dutch owners have brought many touches from their native land to this converted Victorian house in a quiet street. Bedrooms of varying sizes –

some in a new wing – have pretty colour schemes, and furnishings include a brass four-poster. The neat reception leads to a small cocktail bar and simple cosy lounge areas. No dogs.
Amenities garden, laundry service.

■ *Rooms 13*	*Confirm by arrang.*
en suite bath/shower 13	*Last dinner 9.00*
Direct dial Yes	*Parking Ample*
Room TV Yes	*Room service All day*

Bedford Arms Thistle Hotel

H **65% £C**
Map 5 E2 Buckinghamshire
Nr Rickmansworth WB3 6EQ
Chorleywood (092 78) 3301. Tlx 893939
Credit Access, Amex, Diners, Visa

A welcoming roadside hotel located on the outskirts of the village. Winged fireside chairs and a chintzy decor characterise the cosy lounge, and the two bars feature solid dark oak furniture.

Smartly fitted bedrooms with attractively coordinated decor offer trouser presses, hairdryers, dressing gowns and fresh fruit. Bathrooms are equally well equipped. No dogs.
Amenities garden, in-house movies (free).

■ *Rooms 10*	*Confirm by 6*
en suite bath/shower 10	*Last dinner 9.30*
Direct dial Yes	*Parking Ample*
Room TV Yes	*Room service 24 hours*

■ For a discount on next year's guide, see Offer for Answers.

Abbey Green Restaurant *NEW ENTRY*

R **Town plan B3** Cheshire
2 Abbey Green, Northgate Street
Chester (0244) 313251
Owner managers Duncan & Julia Lochhead
Credit Access. LVs

The decor is pretty, the music classical and the cooking very capable at this Edwardian-style vegetarian restaurant. A typical evening menu could include tomato and basil soup, mushroom

and cashew nut roast with a honey and mustard sauce, stir-fried vegetable medley and chocolate sherry truffle cake. Simpler lunchtime choice. There's a lovely sheltered garden for summer eating. ♀ **Well-chosen**

■ *About £25 for two*	*L 10–3.30, Sat 10–4.30,*
Seats 48 Parties 24	*Sun 12–3*
Closed D Sun, all Mon,	*D 6.30–11*
& 25 & 26 Dec	*Parking Limited*

Abbots Well Hotel

H **60% £D**
Town plan C3 Cheshire
Whitchurch Road, Christleton CH3 5QL
Chester (0244) 332121. Tlx 61561
Credit Access, Amex, Diners, Visa

Named after the nearby well that once supplied Chester with fresh water, this extended modern hotel stands east of the city on the A41. There's comfortable seating in the foyer-lounge and a

choice of two bars. Bright bedrooms (including a number of superior rooms with extra accessories) have built-in units, tea-makers and tiled private bathrooms. *Amenities* garden, laundry service, 24-hour lounge service.

■ *Rooms 128*	*Confirm by 6*
en suite bath/shower 128	*Last dinner 10*
Direct dial Yes	*Parking Ample*
Room TV Yes	*Room service 24 hours*

CHESTER

Map 10 A2
Town plan opposite

Population 117,300

Nowhere in Britain are history and architectural beauty better preserved: especially this may be seen in the Roman remains, the complete two-mile circuit of medieval walls and towers, and in the shopping Rows.
Add to this the charms of the River Dee, Canal and the Castle, the Tudor buildings, and the Cathedral. Chester was once a port, but fortunately for today's tourists the mouth of the Dee silted up in the 15th century, so that Chester's sea-trade passed to Liverpool.

Sights Outside City
Beeston Castle, Chirk Castle, Erddig, near Wrexham
Eccleston, Llangollen, Tatton Park

Tourist Information Offices
Town Hall
Telephone Chester 318356
Chester Visitor Centre
Telephone Chester 313126

Fiat Dealer
Heron, Mountview
Sealand Road, Chester CH1 4LQ
Tel. Chester 374440

1 Bishop Lloyd's House B4
2 Bus Exchange A3
3 Chester Castle and Regimental Museum B5
4 Chester Cathedral B3
5 Chester Heritage Centre B4
6 Chester Visitor Centre C4
7 Gamul House B4
8 Gateway Theatre A3
9 General Station C2
10 Grosvenor Museum B4
11 Information Centre, Town Hall B3
12 King Charles Tower B3
13 Northgate Arena B2
14 St John's Church C4
15 The Groves *for river trips* C4
16 The Rows B4
17 Toy Museum B4
18 Zoo A1

Chester FIAT

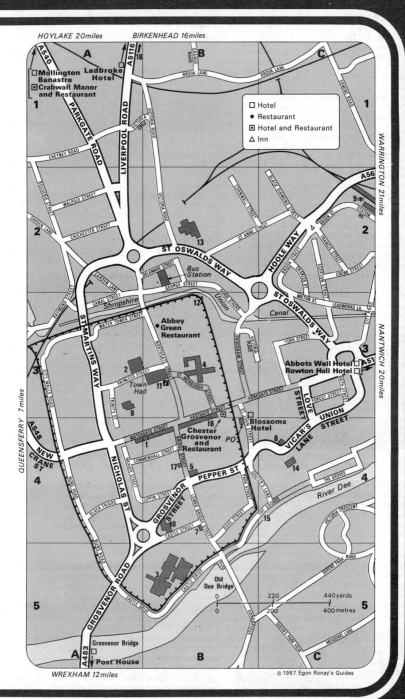

HOYLAKE 20 miles   BIRKENHEAD 16 miles

A540
A5116

A   **B**   **C**

□ Mollington
  Banastre
⊡ Crabwall Manor
  and Restaurant

Ladbroke
Hotel
18

1

GRANGE
BROOK LANE

BROOK LANE
EWING ROAD

1

PARKGATE ROAD

LIVERPOOL ROAD

CHEYNEY ROAD

VICTORIA CRES

WARRINGTON 21 miles

A56

□ Hotel
● Restaurant
⊡ Hotel and Restaurant
△ Inn

BOUVERIE STREET
WALPOLE STREET

VICTORIA ROAD

CORNWALL STREET
BLACK DIAMOND STREET

STATION
RD
9

2

GARDEN LANE
CHICHESTER STREET

ST ANNE STREET

HOOLE WAY
BROOK ST
FRANCIS STREET
CHARLES ST
EGERTON STREET
CREWE STREET

BROOK ST

2

RAYMOND STREET
GARDEN LANE

DELAMERE STREET

13

ST OSWALDS WAY

Bus
Station

MILTON ST
LEADWORKS LA.

ST OSWALDS WAY

A51

3

CANAL STREET
Shropshire

Union
12

GORSE STACKS

Canal

YORK STREET

NANTWICH 20 miles

ST MARTINS WAY

WATER TOWER STREET
CITY WALLS ROAD

GEORGE STREET

NORTHGATE STREET

FRODSHAM STREET

VICTORIA
PLACE

Abbots Well Hotel □
Rowton Hall Hotel □

QUEENSFERRY 7 miles

A548

Abbey
Green
Restaurant

2

Town
Hall
8

PRINCESS STREET
TRINITY ST

11 7
ST WERBURGH STREET

4

FOREGATE STREET

EASTGATE STREET

FOREST STREET
LOVE STREET

VICAR'S
LANE

UNION STREET

3

NEW
CRANE
ST

WATERGATE STREET

1

COMMONHALL STREET
WEAVER STREET

16

BRIDGE STREET

Blossoms
Hotel

Chester
Grosvenor
and
Restaurant

PO
6

4

NICHOLAS ST

17   5

PEPPER ST

CUPPIN STREET

GROSVENOR STREET

BLACK FRIARS

10

CASTLE STREET

7

14

SOUTH VIEW
PARK STREET

LOWER BRIDGE STREET
DUKE STREET

THE GROVES

River Dee

15

QUEENS PARK ROAD

5

3

CASTLE DRIVE

Old
Dee
Bridge

0   220   440 yards
0   200   400 metres

VICTORIA CRESCENT

QUEENS PARK VIEW

5

GROSVENOR ROAD
A483

Grosvenor Bridge
□ Post House

A   **B**   **C**

MEADOWS LANE

WREXHAM 12 miles

© 1987 Egon Ronay's Guides

Blossoms Hotel Chester

H **59%** **£C/D**
Town plan B4 Cheshire
St John Street CH1 1HL
Chester (0244) 23186. Tlx 61113
Credit Access, Amex, Diners, Visa. **LVs**

Long known as a house of hospitality, Blossoms is popular with both tourists and business visitors. Public areas range from a little lounge with button-back chairs to a cocktail bar and a public bar.

Bedrooms vary in size, decor and furnishings, all being well kept and quite comfortable. Guests have free membership of a nearby leisure centre. *Amenities* keep-fit equipment, in-house movies (charge), 24-hour lounge service.

■ *Rooms* 72	*Confirm by* 6
en suite bath/shower 72	*Last dinner* 9.30
Direct dial Yes	*Parking* Difficult
Room TV Yes	*Room service* Limited

Chester Grosvenor Chester

HR **82%** **£B/C** ***E*** &
Town Plan B4 Cheshire
Eastgate Street CH1 1LT
Chester (0244) 24024. Tlx 61240
Manager Jonathan W. Slater
Credit Access, Amex, Diners, Visa

A new leisure complex is the latest amenity offered by this opulent establishment. Superlatives are not inappropriate to describe one of the best hotels in Britain. Behind a splendid half-timbered facade the foyer features a magnificent cantilevered staircase hung with chandeliers. Most famous public room is the lounge, a study in understated elegance. Bedrooms, even the most compact, are impressive, with fine furnishings and up-to-date accessories like computerised mini-bars. Suites are sumptuous and bathrooms well equipped. No

dogs. *Amenities* sauna, solarium, whirlpool bath, keep-fit equipment, lounge service, shopping arcade.

■ *Rooms* 90	*Confirm by* 4
en suite bath/shower 90	*Last dinner* 10
Direct dial Yes	*Parking* Ample
Room TV Yes	*Room service* 24 hours
Closed 24–26 Dec	

Chester Grosvenor Restaurant ♕♕ &

Paul Reed provides imaginative and stylish menus at this hotel restaurant. Good-quality raw materials from as far afield as the Paris markets are sympathetically handled. Crisp pink linen and fine silverware grace the tables and presentation is particularly commendable. Typical offerings from the à la carte include perfectly seasoned chicken liver pâté with truffles, steamed sea bass with a delicate minted butter sauce and breast of pheasant with mangoes. Good cheeses and interesting desserts like parfait de chocolat and raspberry coulis. A wide ranging dependable wine list with some better bottles from the New World: 1977 Heitz Bella Oaks, 1982 Muscat 'Late Picked' (Brown Bros). ♀ Well-chosen ♥

■ *Set L* £10·50	*L* 12–2
Set D £17·50	*D* 7–10
About £75 *for two*	*Seats* 100
Closed 2 *days Xmas*	*Parties* 350

Crabwall Manor *NEW ENTRY* Chester

HR **75%** **£B** &
Town plan A1 Cheshire
Mollington CH1 6NE
Chester (0244) 851666. Tlx 61220
Credit Access, Amex, Diners, Visa

Set in eleven acres of grounds, two miles north of Chester on the A540, this comfortable country house hotel has recently undergone a series of major changes, including a new clock tower in keeping with the original building. The spacious residents' lounge has a galleried staircase and open fireplace and there is also a second lounge

primarily for restaurant-goers. Decor throughout is chintzy and well coordinated. Bedrooms are spacious; all have a table, armchairs, remote-control TVs, trouser presses and hairdryers. Splendid bathrooms have bidets and separate shower cubicles. No children under five. No dogs. *Amenities* garden, croquet, in-house movies (free), laundry service.

■ *Rooms* 32	*Confirm by* arrang.
en suite bath/shower 32	*Last dinner* 9.30
Direct dial Yes	*Parking* Ample
Room TV Yes	*Room service* 24 hours

Crabwall Manor Restaurant ♕ &

A spacious, split-level restaurant where you can enjoy Michael Truelove's ambitious cooking in elegant surroundings. Menus offer a well-balanced choice of dishes, changing daily according to the availability of the prime produce he requires. Flavours and saucing are excellent.

You might start with smoked salmon served with a cucumber mousse, followed perhaps by slices of beef with shallots, lightly flavoured with ginger. Enjoyable sweets and excellent coffee and petits fours to finish. 🍷

■ *Set L £12*
About £68 for two
Seats 80

L 12.30–2.15
D 7–9.30
Parties 100

Ladbroke Hotel   Chester

H 62% £C/D
Town plan A1 Cheshire
Backford Cross CH1 6PE
Chester (0244) 851551. Tlx 61552
Credit Access, Amex, Diners, Visa

A modern hotel with excellent conference facilities, located just north of the city at the junction of the A41 and A5117. A small fountain features in the foyer-lounge and there's a relaxing

bar. Comfortable bedrooms (including Gold Star rooms with extra accessories) are well equipped and have smart bathrooms. *Amenities* garden, in-house movies (charge), laundry service, 24-hour lounge service.

■ *Rooms 113*
en suite bath/shower 113
Direct dial Yes
Room TV Yes

Confirm by 6
Last dinner 10
Parking Ample
Room service Limited

Mollington Banastre Hotel   Chester

H 67% £C/D
Town plan A1 Cheshire
Parkgate Road CH1 6NN
Chester (0244) 851471. Tlx 61686
Credit Access, Amex, Visa

A much-extended Victorian mansion. Open-plan public areas are smartly up to date, and the stylish, well-equipped bedrooms in the wing are best. *Amenities* garden, indoor swimming pool,

sauna, solarium, whirlpool bath, gymnasium, beauty salon, hairdressing, tennis, squash, putting, croquet, games room, in-house movies (free), laundry service, coffee shop (11am–11pm), 24-hour lounge service, helipad.

■ *Rooms 68*
en suite bath/shower 68
Direct dial Yes
Room TV Yes

Confirm by arrang.
Last dinner 10
Parking Ample
Room service 24 hours

Post House Hotel   Chester

H 61% £C/D
Town plan A5 Cheshire
Wrexham Road CH4 9DL
Chester (0244) 680111. Tlx 61450
Credit Access, Amex, Diners, Visa

Good conference facilities and an excellent playground make this modern hotel, south of the city, well suited to both businessmen and families on holiday. Public areas include a comfortable

bar-lounge and a bar that opens on to a terrace. Bright, spacious bedrooms, with smart tiled bathrooms, offer beverage trays and mini-bars. Helpful staff. *Amenities* garden, laundry service, 24-hour lounge service, children's playground.

■ *Rooms 64*
en suite bath/shower 64
Direct dial Yes
Room TV Yes

Confirm by 6
Last dinner 9.45
Parking Ample
Room service Limited

Rowton Hall Hotel   Chester

H 59% £C/D ♿
Town plan C3 Cheshire
Whitchurch Road CH3 6AD
Chester (0244) 335262. Tlx 61172
Owner manager Mr S. D. Begbie
Credit Access, Amex, Diners, Visa

Eight acres of grounds provide the setting for this well-run hotel south of Chester, just off the A41. The panelled reception area keeps the feel of

a grand country house, and there are two lounges. A fine oak staircase climbs to bedrooms, where furnishings range from Regency style to more modern. *Amenities* garden, laundry service.

■ *Rooms 42*
en suite bath/shower 42
Direct dial Yes
Room TV Yes
Closed 24–26 Dec

Confirm by 6
Last dinner 9.30
Parking Ample
Room service All day

🍷 indicates a **well-chosen** house wine.

Chesterfield Hotel   Chesterfield

H 61% £D/E
Map 10 C2 Derbyshire
Malkin Street S41 7UA
Chesterfield (0246) 71141. Tlx 547492
Credit Access, Amex, Diners, Visa

Restyling with a 1920s theme has given a new lease of life to this Victorian station hotel. Clever use of plants, mirrors and soft lighting brings the Jazz Age to the bar, and the fine ballroom is lit by

crystal chandeliers. Pleasant bedrooms are well supplied with practical modern comforts. Suites have sitting rooms; two have whirlpool baths. *Amenities* in-house movies (free), laundry service.

■ *Rooms 61*
en suite bath/shower 61
Direct dial Yes
Room TV Yes

Confirm by arrang.
Last dinner 10
Parking Ample
Room service 24 hours

Lumley Castle Hotel   Chester-le-Street

H 68% £D
Map 15 B4 County Durham
DH3 4NX
Durham (091) 3891111. Tlx 537433
Manager Mr M. Jones
Credit Access, Amex, Diners, Visa
 The ghostly Grey Lady can't be guaranteed to
make a personal appearance, but few guests visit
this medieval hilltop castle without feeling at least
a frisson of the past. Public rooms round the
central lawned courtyard include a cosy lounge
with period furnishings, and a library bar with over
3000 volumes. Courtyard bedrooms have the

cottage appeal of beams and pretty fabrics;
bedrooms in the castle (16 new) include four
feature rooms with four-posters and antiques. All
rooms are well equipped and have excellent
private facilities. Friendly staff. No dogs.
Amenities garden, sauna, solarium, snooker,
laundry service, 24-hour lounge service.

■ *Rooms 68*	*Confirm by 6*
en suite bath/shower 68	*Last dinner 9.45*
Direct dial Yes	*Parking Ample*
Room TV Yes	*Room service 24 hours*
Closed 25 & 26 Dec & 1 Jan	

Woods   Chesterton

R ⅋ Map 5 D1 Oxfordshire
Nr Bicester
Bicester (0869) 241444
Owner managers David & Georgina Wood
Credit Access, Amex, Diners, Visa
 Top-quality ingredients, many local and some
home-grown, give the chefs a head start at this
friendly restaurant in a 250-year-old barn. Their
skills do the rest, resulting in splendid dishes like

mushroom and fennel soup, venison pie and
maize-fed chicken served with a lovely tarragon
and cream sauce. First-rate vegetables, super
sweets. ♟ Well-chosen ☺

■ *About £40 for two*	*L Sun 12–2*
Seats 45	*D 7–9.30*
Parties 45	*Parking Ample*
Closed D Sun, all Mon, L Tues-Sat exc by arrang.,	
Bank Hols & 1st wk Jan	

Chichester Lodge Hotel   Chichester

H 55% £D
Map 5 E4 West Sussex
Westhampnett PO19 4UL
Chichester (0243) 786351
Manager Roger Powell
Credit Access, Amex, Visa
 On the busy A27, this functional modern hotel
offers useful conference facilities and good
overnight accommodation. All the bedrooms have

trouser presses and tea-makers, plus practical
private bathrooms. Drinks can be taken in the
smart bar-lounge or adjacent White Swan pub.
Amenities garden, in-house movies (charge),
laundry service, 24-hour lounge service.

■ *Rooms 43*	*Confirm by 6*
en suite bath/shower 43	*Last dinner 9.30*
Direct dial Yes	*Parking Ample*
Room TV Yes	*Room service None*

Dolphin & Anchor Hotel   Chichester

H 63% £C/D
Map 5 E4 West Sussex
West Street PO19 1QE
Chichester (0243) 785121
Credit Access, Amex, Diners, Visa. **LVs**
 Originally two separate inns, this handsome
hotel enjoys a fine position opposite the cathedral.
Well-equipped bedrooms, all with good private
bathrooms, have smart units and pretty colour

schemes. Day rooms include an attractive bar-
lounge, a popular coffee shop, plus various
function rooms.
Amenities laundry service, coffee shop (10am–
10pm), 24-hour lounge service.

■ *Rooms 54*	*Confirm by 6*
en suite bath/shower 54	*Last dinner 10*
Direct dial Yes	*Parking Limited*
Room TV Yes	*Room service Limited*

Crown Inn   Chiddingfold

I £E
Map 5 E3 Surrey
Nr Godalming GU8 4TX
Wormley (042 879) 2255
Credit Access, Amex, Diners, Visa
 Nothing detracts from the old-world charm of
this delightful 13th-century timber-framed inn on
the village green. A log fire burns in the inglenook
fireplace of the beamed lounge bar. Four

bedrooms are full of character with beams,
sloping floors and antique furnishings, the others
are pleasantly modern. All have en suite
bathrooms. *Amenities* courtyard, laundry service.

■ *Rooms 8*	*Confirm by arrang.*
en suite bath/shower 8	*Last dinner 9.30*
Direct dial Yes	*Parking Ample*
Room TV Yes	*Room service All day*
Closed 2 wks Jan	

Chideock House Hotel   Chideock

HR 58% £F
Map 4 A4 Dorset
Main Street, Nr Bridport DT6 6JN
Chideock (029 789) 242
Owner managers Davies & Way families
Credit Access, Amex, Visa

Family owners create a warm and homely
atmosphere at this charming 15th-century hotel
on the A35, less than a mile from the sea. The
beamed bar and recently enlarged first-floor
lounge are both comfortably traditional, and the
neat, bright bedrooms, many with smart new
carpets, all have tea-makers.
Amenities garden, badminton.

■ Rooms 9	Confirm by arrang.
en suite bath/shower 7	Last dinner 9.30
Room phone No	Parking Ample
Room TV Yes	Room service All day

Chideock House Hotel Restaurant

Set menus and a carte provide ample choice of
tempting dishes at this attractive little restaurant
where prime ingredients are carefully prepared
and enhanced by notably successful sauces and
seasoning throughout the meal. Hot crab pot with
parmesan or mussels in white wine might be
followed by a juicy steak, rack of lamb in a piquant
red wine and onion sauce or sautéed chicken with
Pernod, cream and prawns. Good vegetables and
pleasant home-made sweets to finish. ⊖

■ Set L £8·95	L 12–2
Set D £10·50	D 7–9.30
About £35 for two	Seats 45
Closed L Mon	Parties 50

White Horse Inn   Chilgrove

R **Map 5 E3** West Sussex
High Street
East Marden (024 359) 219
Owner managers Barry & Dorothea Phillips
Credit Access, Amex, Diners, Visa

Good eating and superb drinking can be
enjoyed in the pleasant rural setting of this
wisteria-clad 18th-century inn. Barry and Dorothea
Phillips look after their guests well, and Neal
Findley does a splendid job in the kitchen,
preparing tasty dishes like roulade of smoked
salmon filled with an artichoke mousseline,
sardines in puff pastry with a provençale sauce or

meltingly tender Aylesbury duck with a rich sauce
of port wine and brandied fruit conserve. Desserts
are rather less interesting. Presentation is good,
however, and portions match country appetites.
The cellar is one of the finest in the land, with an
unequalled collection of the greatest clarets.
⊃ Outstanding ♎ Well-chosen ⊖

■ Set L £12·95	L 12.30–2
Set D £15·95	D 7–9.30
About £45 for two	Parking Ample
Seats 60	Parties 20
Closed Sun, Mon, 3 wks Feb & 1 wk Nov	

■ Our inspectors never book in the
name of Egon Ronay's Guides;
they disclose their identity only
after paying their bills.

Kings Arms Hotel   Chipping Campden

I £D/E
Map 4 C1 Gloucestershire
Market Square GL55 6AW
Evesham (0386) 840256
Credit Access, Visa

The Kings Arms is an attractive old Cotswold-
stone building on the main street. Fresh flowers fill
the homely day rooms, which include a beamed
bar and charming TV lounge. Magazines and

books are scattered around for quiet browsing,
and there's a warm, inviting feel throughout.
Bedrooms – some also with beams – offer simple,
practical comforts. *Amenities* garden.

■ Rooms 14	Confirm by arrang.
en suite bath/shower 2	Last dinner 9
Room phone No	Parking Ample
Room TV No	Room service None
Closed mid-week Jan–Feb	

Noel Arms Hotel   Chipping Campden

H 59% £E
Map 4 C1 Gloucestershire
The Square GL55 6AT
Evesham (0386) 840317
Credit Access, Visa

Steeped in history, this 14th-century coaching
inn is full of rustic charm. Exposed stone walls and
beams give character to the public rooms and a
cosy little lounge is warmed by a sunken

inglenook fireplace. Weaponry and hunting
trophies adorn the walls. Decent-sized bedrooms
are simply decorated, some with antiques
(including four-posters), others more modestly
furnished. *Amenities* bowling green.

■ Rooms 18	Confirm by 5
en suite bath/shower 18	Last dinner 9
Room phone No	Parking Ample
Room TV Yes	Room service Limited

La Madonette   Chipping Norton

R ♧ **Map 4 C1** Oxfordshire
7 Horsefair
Chipping Norton (0608) 2320
French cooking
Credit Access, Visa

Alain Ritter continues in impressive form at this lovely beamed restaurant in the heart of this Cotswold town. Since the place is generally full it's important to book. There's more than a touch of class and flair about the French dishes, and the quality and freshness of ingredients is paramount (fish from Cornwall twice a week, cheeses from Philippe Olivier). Memorable dishes range from perfectly seasoned game terrine studded with livers, fennel-perfumed sea bass crowned with puff pastry, or veal garnished with langoustine tails, showing the mouthwatering range of the menu. Finish with a light chocolate mousse on a pear purée with pear liqueur sauce. Superb service by Patti Ritter complements the fine food, as do high-quality wines at keen prices.

♀ Well-chosen ⊖

■ *About £48 for two*   *D only 7.30–9.45*
Seats 36   *Parking Ample*
*Closed Sun, Mon, Bank Hols exc. Good Fri
& 1 wk Xmas*

Highbullen Hotel   Chittlehamholt

H **60% £E**
Map 3 D2 Devon
Umberleigh EX37 9HD
Chittlehamholt (076 94) 561
Owner managers Hugh & Pam Neil

Public rooms in this fine Victorian mansion have lovely views of the surrounding parkland. Main-house bedrooms are solidly traditional, those in the outbuildings smartly modern. No children under ten. No dogs. *Amenities* garden, indoor & outdoor swimming pools, sauna, solarium, whirlpool bath, keep-fit equipment, indoor & outdoor tennis, squash, 9-hole golf course, croquet, game fishing, billiards.

■ *Rooms 35*	*Confirm by arrang.*
en suite bath/shower 35	*Last dinner 9*
Direct dial Yes	*Parking Ample*
Room TV Yes	*Room service Limited*

George Hotel   Chollerford

H **60% £D/E**
Map 15 B4 Northumberland
Nr Hexham NE46 4EW
Humshaugh (043 481) 611
Credit Access, Amex, Diners, Visa

This riverside hotel with excellent leisure facilities makes an agreeable base from which to explore the countryside. There's a choice of relaxing bars and lounges, and bedrooms are comfortable. *Amenities* garden, sauna, indoor swimming pool, solarium, whirlpool bath, keep-fit equipment, coarse & game fishing, putting green, golf driving nets, laundry service, pool table, children's play area.

■ *Rooms 54*	*Confirm by 6*
en suite bath/shower 54	*Last dinner 9.30*
Direct dial Yes	*Parking Ample*
Room TV Yes	*Room service 24 hours*

Stretton Hall Hotel   Church Stretton

H **60% £E**
Map 10 A4 Shropshire
All Stretton SY6 6HG
Church Stretton (0694) 723224
Credit Access, Amex, Diners, Visa

A sturdy 18th-century building standing in popular walking country, with Caer Caradoc on one side and Long Mynd ridge on the other. The foyer is handsomely proportioned, and there's a pleasant bar-lounge with inviting armchairs clustered round an open fire. Bedrooms are in straightforward traditional style, decently sized and all with carpeted bathrooms en suite. *Amenities* garden, laundry service.

■ *Rooms 13*	*Confirm by 6*
en suite bath/shower 13	*Last dinner 9.15*
Room phone Yes	*Parking Ample*
Room TV Yes	*Room service Limited*

Frensham Pond Hotel   Churt

H **69% £C/D**
Map 5 E3 Surrey
Nr Farnham GU10 2QB
Frensham (025 125) 3175. Tlx 858610
Owner manager Mr Michael Katzler
Credit Access, Amex, Diners, Visa

In a peaceful woodland setting on the banks of Frensham Great Pond, this is a very pleasant and very well-run hotel. The lounge is comfortably civilised, and there's a popular new attraction in the shape of a neatly-designed leisure centre. A smart coffee shop and bar overlook the pool. Seven bedrooms, convertible to private conference rooms, are in the main building, the rest in garden chalets with patios leading on to the garden. All rooms have private facilities, with good towels and toiletries. *Amenities* garden, indoor swimming pool, sauna, solarium, whirlpool bath, keep-fit equipment, squash, coarse fishing, laundry service, coffee shop (10am–10pm), 24-hour lounge service, helipad.

■ *Rooms 19*	*Confirm by arrang.*
en suite bath/shower 19	*Last dinner 9.30*
Direct dial Yes	*Parking Ample*
Room TV Yes	*Room service 24 hours*

Fleece Hotel — Cirencester

H 65% £D/E
Map 4 C2 Gloucestershire
Market Place GL7 4NZ
Cirencester (0285) 68507
Credit Access, Amex, Diners, Visa

Half-timbered Tudor and sturdy Georgian buildings link hands across the courtyard of this former coaching inn in the town centre. An open fire warms the lounge, and there are two bars, one

beamed. Individually decorated bedrooms with quality furnishings have tea-makers, trouser presses and well-equipped bathrooms (four are not en suite).

■ *Rooms* 25 — *Confirm by* 7
en suite bath/shower 21 — *Last dinner* 9.30
Direct dial Yes — *Parking* Limited
Room TV Yes — *Room service* Limited
Closed 25 & 26 Dec

Kings Head Hotel — Cirencester

H 63% £D/E &
Map 4 C2 Gloucestershire
Market Place GL7 2NR
Cirencester (0285) 3322. Tlx 43470
Manager Michael Haigh-Gannon
Credit Access, Amex, Diners, Visa

A handsome blue frontage distinguishes this 14th-century former coaching inn. Beams and stone vaulting characterise the public areas, while

bedrooms are cheerfully traditional in style. Some attention is needed to decorative standards.
Amenities games room, pool table, laundry service, 24-hour lounge service.
■ *Rooms* 70 — *Confirm by* 6
en suite bath/shower 70 — *Last dinner* 9
Direct dial Yes — *Parking* Limited
Room TV Yes — *Room service* 24 hours
Closed 27–31 Dec

Stratton House Hotel — Cirencester

H 64% £E &
Map 4 C2 Gloucestershire
Gloucester Road GL7 2LE
Cirencester (0285) 61761
Owner manager Mrs E. Manley Walker
Credit Access, Amex, Diners, Visa

A handsome Georgian wool merchant's house north-west of town on the A417 makes a friendly, appealing hotel. Comfort is the keynote here,

notably in the delightful public rooms. Well-proportioned main-house bedrooms have solid traditional furnishings, while rooms in the extensions are smaller with modern units.
Amenities garden, croquet, laundry service.
■ *Rooms* 26 — *Confirm by* 6
en suite bath/shower 22 — *Last dinner* 9.45
Room phone Yes — *Parking* Ample
Room TV Yes — *Room service* All day

⌦ is our symbol for an **outstanding** wine list.

Plough at Clanfield — Clanfield

HR 70% £D
Map 4 C2 Oxfordshire
OX8 2RB
Clanfield (036 781) 222. Tlx 449848
Credit Access, Amex, Diners, Visa

On the main road through the village, this beautifully preserved Elizabethan manor house offers a wealth of period charm and elegance in very comfortable surroundings. Notable among the day rooms is a fine lounge bar with beams, open fireplace, highly polished tables and inviting easy chairs. Good-quality fabrics and furnishings give an individual charm to bedrooms, which are equipped with trouser presses and hairdryers. There are two shower rooms, and bathrooms are

fitted with whirlpool baths. Friendly, helpful management and staff. No children under 12. No dogs. *Amenities* garden, laundry service.
■ *Rooms* 7 — *Confirm by* arrang.
en suite bath/shower 7 — *Last dinner* 9.30
Direct dial Yes — *Parking* Ample
Room TV Yes — *Room service* All day

Plough at Clanfield Restaurant ♔ &

Study the fixed-price menus in the lounge bar before sitting down to a meal in this charming low-ceilinged restaurant. Paul Barnard's carefully prepared dishes cover a tempting range, beginning with things like curried apple soup and brandade of salt cod. Next perhaps try a whole veal kidney roasted in bacon and served with a tomato tarragon sauce – or settle for pan-fried breast of chicken with a wild mushroom sauce. To follow, there's a good selection of sweets like chocolate fudge pudding, or you can opt for a savoury. Good-value clarets. ♀ **Well-chosen** ⌦
■ *Set L £9.75,* — *L 12–1.45*
Sun £10.95 — *D 7–9.30, Sat 7–10*
Set D from £17 — *Seats 45*
About £55 for two — *Parties 40*

Pines Hotel

H **67% £E**
Map 10 B1 Lancashire
Nr Chorley PR6 7ED
Preston (0772) 38551. Tlx 677584
Owner manager Mr & Mrs J. M. Duffin
Credit Access, Amex, Diners, Visa
   Pleasant gardens provide the setting for this
comfortable, much extended Victorian hotel. Best
of the bedrooms have stylish decor, a range of

extras such as hairdryers, and luxurious
bathrooms. Standard rooms are more modest. No
dogs. *Amenities* garden, solarium, squash, pool
table, laundry service, 24-hour lounge service.

■ *Rooms* 25	*Confirm by arrang.*
en suite bath/shower 25	*Last dinner* 9.30
Direct dial Yes	*Parking* Ample
Room TV Yes	*Room service* 24 hours
Closed 25 & 26 Dec	

Clearwell Castle *NEW ENTRY*

H **67% £D/E**
Map 4 B2 Gloucestershire
Royal Forest of Dean GL16 8LG
Dean (0594) 32320
Owner managers Russell-Steele family
Credit Access, Amex, Diners, Visa
   An 18th-century castle in the Gothic revival
style, set in lovely grounds complete with
peacocks. Public areas are elegant and relaxing,

with antiques, comfortable chairs and polished
wood floors, and there's a small clubby bar.
Spacious bedrooms have period furniture, pretty
fabrics and lots of extras. No dogs. *Amenities*
garden, croquet, game fishing, laundry service.

■ *Rooms* 12	*Confirm by arrang.*
en suite bath/shower 12	*Last dinner* 10
Direct dial Yes	*Parking* Ample
Room TV Yes	*Room service* All day

Kingsway Hotel

H **61% £E**
Map 11 F2 Humberside
Kingsway DN35 0AE
Cleethorpes (0472) 601122
Owner managers Mr & Mrs John Harris
Credit Access, Amex, Diners, Visa
   Friendly porterage, early-morning tea tray,
immaculate housekeeping – these are typical of
the traditional standards that apply here. The

comfortable lounges enjoy sea views, and there's
an intimate cocktail bar. Bedrooms continue to be
upgraded, and even the slightly dated ones are
spick and span. No dogs. *Amenities* garden.

■ *Rooms* 55	*Confirm by arrang.*
en suite bath/shower 49	*Last dinner* 9
Room phone Yes	*Parking* Ample
Room TV Yes	*Room service* All day
Closed 26 Dec	

Bailiffscourt

HR **75% £B/C**
Map 5 E4 West Sussex
Littlehampton BN17 5RW
Littlehampton (0903) 723511. Tlx 877870
Credit Access, Amex, Diners, Visa
   Medieval materials found throughout southern
England were used to create this 1930s replica of
a 13th-century courthouse. Set in 23 acres of
beautiful grounds, Bailiffscourt has an
atmosphere of peace and tranquillity. Furnishings
in the day rooms are simple but comfortable.
Bedrooms, superbly refurbished, combine period
features and 80s amenities: nine contain four-
posters, all offer remote-control TVs, hairdryers
and other thoughtful extras plus beautifully
appointed bathrooms. Some slightly smaller

rooms are in a separate thatched house. No
children under eight. *Amenities* garden, outdoor
swimming pool, sauna, keep-fit equipment,
tennis, croquet, games room, laundry service,
helipad.

■ *Rooms* 20	*Confirm by arrang.*
en suite bath/shower 20	*Last dinner* 9.45
Direct dial Yes	*Parking* Ample
Room TV Yes	*Room service* All day

Bailiffscourt Restaurant ♿

Oak beams, stone walls and mullion windows
provide heaps of atmosphere at this unique
restaurant. Garry Leaf produces an interesting
choice of dishes, ranging from a pastry pillow
filled with strips of calf's liver bound in a glazed
shallot sauce or a rosette of smoked pink trout
mousse with quails' eggs and herb croûtons to a
roast fillet of lamb on a bed of creamed leeks or a
poached fillet of sea bass on an orange butter
sauce. Good crisp vegetables. There's a well-
balanced list of good wines.
♥ Well-chosen ⊖

■ *Set L* £13·50	L 12.30–2
Set D £20	D 7.30–9.45, Sat 7.30–10
About £55 for two	*Seats* 45 *Parties* 35

Hall Garth   Coatham Mundeville

H **68%** **£D/E**
Map 15 B5 Co. Durham
Nr Darlington DL1 3LU
Aycliffe (0325) 313333
Owner managers E. Williamson & J. Crocker
Credit Access, Amex, Diners, Visa

Friendly owners and staff roll out the welcome
mat at this rambling hotel in a peaceful parkland
setting. Some parts date back to the 16th
century, others to Georgian and Victorian times.
The lounges have a cosy, homely appeal, with
period funishings and lots of flowers and knick-
knacks, and there's a pleasant beamed bar in the

converted stables. Accommodation is divided
between spacious, traditional rooms (some with
four-posters) in the main house and light, airy,
modern ones in the stable block.
Amenities garden, outdoor swimming pool,
sauna, solarium, tennis, 3-hole practice golf,
putting, croquet, laundry service, children's play
area.

■ *Rooms* 20	*Confirm by* arrang.
en suite bath/shower 20	*Last dinner* 9.30
Direct dial Yes	*Parking* Ample
Room TV Yes	*Room service* None
Closed 22 Dec–2 Jan	

■ For a discount on next year's guide, see Offer for Answers.

Il Giardino *NEW ENTRY*   Cobham

R ⌕ **Map 5 E3** Surrey
221 Portsmouth Road KT11 1JR
Cobham (0932) 63973
Italian cooking
Credit Access, Diners, Visa

Gabriele di Michele recently took over this very
acceptable Italian restaurant where a selection
from the hors d'oeuvre trolley starts the meal in
style, followed perhaps by chicken with

asparagus, veal escalope stuffed with dolcelatte
or monkfish with a robust sauce of onions,
tomatoes and black olives. Acceptable sweets
from the trolley (chocolate gâteau, black cherry
mousse). 🅴

■ *Set L* £7·55	*L* 12–2.15
About £45 *for two*	*D* 6.30–10.30
Seats 45	*Parking* Limited
Closed L Sat, all Mon & Bank Hols exc. Good Fri	

Ladbroke Seven Hills Hotel   Cobham

H **63%** **£B/C**
Map 5 E3 Surrey
Seven Hills Road South KT11 1EW
Cobham (0932) 64471. Tlx 929196
Credit Access, Amex, Diners, Visa

A well-equipped modern hotel in wooded
grounds near the junction of the A3 and A245. The
main public area is open-plan, with natural brick
used to attractive effect. Smart bedrooms offer

lots of extras, particularly the top-of-the-range
Plaza rooms. *Amenities* garden, indoor swimming
pool, sauna, whirlpool bath, keep-fit equipment,
tennis, squash, pool table, in-house movies
(charge), laundry service, helipad.

■ *Rooms* 139	*Confirm by* 6
en suite bath/shower 139	*Last dinner* 10
Direct dial Yes	*Parking* Ample
Room TV Yes	*Room service* Limited

Woodlands Park Hotel   Cobham

H **64%** **£D**
Map 5 E3 Surrey
Woodlands Lane, Stoke D'Abernon KT11 3QB
Oxshott (037 284) 3933. Tlx 919246
Credit Access, Amex, Diners, Visa

In a woodland setting on the Cobham-
Leatherhead road (A245), this is a splendid late-
Victorian mansion. Public rooms include a
galleried main hall and numerous function rooms.

Bedrooms are mostly fairly spacious and vary in
style, with good bath or shower rooms. Staff are
friendly and cheerful. *Amenities* garden, tennis
(summer), clay pigeon shooting, laundry service.

■ *Rooms* 33	*Confirm by* 6
en suite bath/shower 33	*Last dinner* 9.30
Direct dial Yes	*Parking* Ample
Room TV Yes	*Room service* All day
Closed 2/3 days Xmas	

Peter Langan's Restaurant *NEW ENTRY*   Coggeshall

R ♿ **Map 6 C3** Essex
4 Stoneham Street
Coggeshall (0376) 61453
Credit Access, Amex, Diners, Visa

A new Peter Langan restaurant and bar, with
the usual Langan informal chic and lots of good
paintings. Young chef Mark Bowman (ex-
Hambleton Hall) shows sound skills, and his short
menus feature some quite unusual, but

successful, flavour combinations like pear and
stilton soup or chicken with crab sauce. Crisp
vegetables, good crème brûlée (with an apricot-
flavoured variant). Concise list of decent wines.
🍷 Well-chosen 🅴

■ *Set L* £7·50	*L* 12–2.30
About £28 *for two*	*D* 7–10
Seats 56	*Parking* Ample
Parties 60	*Closed* D Sun

Coggeshall ▶

White Hart Hotel
Coggeshall

HR 68% £D/E
Map 6 C3 Essex
Market End CO6 1NH
Coggeshall (0376) 61654
Owner managers Mr & Mrs Pluck
Credit Access, Amex, Diners, Visa
   Fine timbering and a massive brick
chimneypiece in the lounge reveal the 15th-
century origins of this comfortable hotel. The bar,
too, is full of character, while attractively furnished
bedrooms offer remote-control TVs and excellent
private facilities. Super breakfasts. No dogs.
Amenities garden, laundry service.
- *Rooms* 18   *Confirm by* arrang.
- *en suite bath/shower* 18   *Last dinner* 9.30
- *Direct dial* Yes   *Parking* Ample
- *Room TV* Yes   *Room service* All day
- *Closed* Aug & 1 wk Xmas

White Hart Hotel Restaurant 🍴 &

Dine in style beneath the ancient beams of this
lovely dining room. Menus offer top-quality
produce served simply – Mersea oysters, fresh
lobsters, charcoal-grilled steaks – or sauced, as in
loin of veal with shallots, rosemary and wine.
Prettily presented vegetables are cooked with a
bite. Fairly ordinary sweets. Exceptional cellar,
notable for lovely burgundies from the best
growers, and for an unmatched choice of 90 half-
bottles. ⟣ Outstanding 🍷 Well-chosen ⊖
- *Set L* Sun only £11·75   *L* 12.30–2
- About £55 for two   *D* 7.30–9.30
- *Seats* 30   *Parties* 30
- *Closed* L Mon & Sat, D Sun to non-residents, all
  Fri, Aug & 1 wk Xmas

■ If we recommend meals in a
hotel or inn, a separate entry is
made for its restaurant.

Marks Tey Hotel
Colchester

H 57% £E
Map 6 C3 Essex
Marks Tey CO6 1DU
Colchester (0206) 210001. Tlx 987176
Credit Access, Amex, Diners, Visa
   Comfortable overnight accommodation is
provided at this modern low-rise hotel, which
stands south of Colchester on the A12. Bedrooms
are of a decent size, with restful colour schemes
and simple fitted furniture; all rooms have private
bathrooms en suite. Public areas include a
cocktail bar with a large mural depicting the city's
Roman and Saxon past. *Amenities* garden,
gymnasium, tennis, laundry service.
- *Rooms* 108   *Confirm by* 6
- *en suite bath/shower* 108   *Last dinner* 9.45
- *Direct dial* Yes   *Parking* Ample
- *Room TV* Yes   *Room service* 24 hours

Rose & Crown Hotel
Colchester

H 57% £E
Map 6 C3 Essex
East Street CO1 2TZ
Colchester (0206) 866677
Owner manager Mr J. de Andrade
Credit Access, Amex, Diners, Visa
   A half-timbered former posting house which
has changed little since it was built in the 15th
century; the public rooms, which include a cellar
bar where prisoners were once housed, still have
a wealth of ancient beams, pillars, and low
doorways. The bedrooms have a cosy and
traditional feel; most have compact shower
rooms. *Amenities* garden, laundry service.
- *Rooms* 28   *Confirm by* arrang.
- *en suite bath/shower* 19   *Last dinner* 10
- *Direct dial* Yes   *Parking* Ample
- *Room TV* Yes   *Room service* 24 hours

Speech House
Coleford

I £C/D
Map 4 B2 Gloucestershire
Forest of Dean GL16 7EL
Dean (0594) 22607
Credit Access, Amex, Diners, Visa. LVs
   The Verderers' Court still meets in this historic
former forest court house on the B4226, east of
Coleford. Open fires, reinforced by central
heating, warm the reception-lounge and bars,
which boast blackened beams and old-world
furnishings. Three principal bedrooms are
furnished with antiques including remarkable
carved four-posters; other rooms are in a more
modest, contemporary style. *Amenities* garden.
- *Rooms* 13   *Confirm by* 6
- *en suite bath/shower* 3   *Last dinner* 9
- *Room phone* Yes   *Parking* Ample
- *Room TV* Yes   *Room service* All day

Great Moreton Hall Hotel — Congleton

H **72% £C/D**
Map 10 B2 Cheshire
New Road CW12 4RY
Congleton (0260) 272340. Tlx 666537
Credit Access, Amex, Diners, Visa

Standing in 45 acres of lovely parkland and woods, this superb Gothic manor was designed by Royal architect Richard Blore and built with stone from a local quarry. The turreted frontage is most impressive, and great care has been taken to preserve the finest internal features, including vaulted archways, magnificent moulded ceilings and a grand Gothic staircase. The last leads up to the air-conditioned bedrooms, all spacious, comfortably furnished and well equipped, with mini-bars, trouser presses and bedside controls for radio and TV. Fully carpeted bathrooms are generously supplied with towels. Service does not

always match the surroundings. No children under 12. No dogs. *Amenities* garden, laundry service.

- *Rooms* 10 — *Confirm by arrang.*
- *en suite bath/shower* 10 — *Last dinner 9.30*
- *Direct dial* Yes — *Parking* Ample
- *Room TV* Yes — *Room service* All day

Coniston Sun Hotel — Coniston

H **61% £E/F**
Map 13 C5 Cumbria
LA21 8HQ
Coniston (0966) 41248
Owner managers Joan Lelong & Karen Farmer
Credit Access, Visa

Mother and daughter team run a homely, unpretentious hotel here on the edge of the village. Colourful window boxes, hanging baskets, plants and flowers brighten up the place inside and out. Prettily decorated bedrooms, many enjoying fine views, offer spacious modern bathrooms. *Amenities* garden.

- *Rooms* 11 — *Confirm by arrang.*
- *en suite bath/shower* 11 — *Last dinner 8.30*
- *Room phone* No — *Parking* Ample
- *Room TV* Yes — *Room service* All day
- *Closed* Jan & Feb

Treglos Hotel — Constantine Bay

HR **66% £D/E**
Map 2 B3 Cornwall
Nr Padstow, St Merryn PL28 8JH
Padstow (0841) 520727
Owner managers Mr & Mrs E. H. Barlow

Proper porterage and prompt, pleasant room service are pluses at this family-run hotel overlooking the bay. Five lounges and a bar provide abundant room to relax, and bedrooms are bright and modern, most having sea views. *Amenities* garden, indoor swimming pool, whirlpool bath, croquet, sea fishing, boating, board sailing, water skiing, snooker, pool table.

- *Rooms* 44 — *Confirm by arrang.*
- *en suite bath/shower* 44 — *Last dinner 9.30*
- *Direct dial* Yes — *Parking* Ample
- *Room TV* Yes — *Room service* All day
- *Closed* 8 Nov–10 Mar

Treglos Hotel Restaurant

NEW ENTRY

A roomy restaurant with many of the tables placed beside large picture windows looking across gardens to the sea. The menu has a strong emphasis on good fresh seafood, including oysters and lobsters from the hotel's own tank, and locally caught Dover sole and squid; there's also excellent locally smoked salmon. Cooking is competent, with the simple things often being the most successful. Vegetarians have their own menu. Maître d'hotel Wally Vellacott sees to it that service is very pleasant and attentive. ☺

- *Set L* £6·95 — *L* 12.30–1.30
- *Set D* £13·50 — *D* 7.45–9.30
- About £40 for two — *Seats* 120
- *Closed* 8 Nov–10 Mar

Cooden Resort Hotel — Cooden

H **63% £D/E**
Map 7 B6 East Sussex
Nr Bexhill-on-Sea TN39 4TT
Cooden (042 43) 2281. Tlx 877247
Credit Access, Amex, Diners, Visa

Converted from a 1930s row of shops, this well-run hotel stands close to both the beach and railway station. Public rooms include a pleasant lounge and cocktail bar with sea views. Bedrooms are spacious and bright. *Amenities* garden, indoor & outdoor swimming pool, sauna, solarium, whirlpool bath, keep-fit equipment, laundry service, 24-hour lounge service.

- *Rooms* 34 — *Confirm by* 6
- *en suite bath/shower* 31 — *Last dinner* 9.30
- *Direct dial* Yes — *Parking* Ample
- *Room TV* Yes — *Room service* 24 hours

Cookham ▶

Peking Inn Cookham

R 🍷 **Map 5 E2** Berkshire
High Street
Bourne End (062 85) 20900
Chinese cooking
Credit Access, Amex, Diners, Visa
    The menu at this high-street Chinese restaurant
is less extensive than many but still provides a
good regional variety. Dishes on our latest visit
were somewhat uneven: wun tun soup and

Manchurian crispy lamb with a salad of fresh and
pickled vegetables were enjoyable, Szechuan
prawns with a sticky orange-coloured sauce and
pineapple much less so. The welcome is
sometimes as cool as the decor.

■ *Set L £12*	*L 12–2.30*
Set D £12	*D 6–12*
About £35 for two	*Parking* Limited
Seats 90	*Closed 3 days Xmas*

Ipswich Moat House Copdock

H **62% £D**
 Map 6 C3 Suffolk
Nr Ipswich IP8 3JD
Copdock (047 386) 444. Tlx 987207
Credit Access, Amex, Diners, Visa
    A modern hotel standing in its own grounds by
the A12. Some of the bedrooms have been
attractively upgraded, with pleasant pastel decor,
smart lightwood units and remote-control TVs.

Older rooms have a more modest appeal. Public
areas include an open-plan entrance hall-cum-
lounge and a roomy bar. Improvements will
continue.
Amenities garden, laundry service.

■ *Rooms 45*	*Confirm by 6*
en suite bath/shower 45	*Last dinner 9.15*
Room phone Yes	*Parking Ample*
Room TV Yes	*Room service 24 hours*

Tillmouth Park Hotel Cornhill-on-Tweed

H **62% £D/E**
 Map 14 B2 Northumberland
TD12 4UU
Coldstream (0890) 2255
Credit Access, Amex, Diners, Visa
    The parkland setting is as peaceful as it is
beautiful, and nine miles of salmon fishing on the
Tweed and Till make this imposing Victorian
mansion a fisherman's paradise. Handsomely

proportioned public rooms include a lounge and
galleried hall, and there's a convivial bar. Bedrooms range from very large to small and cosy.
Mainly spacious but old-fashioned bathrooms.
Amenities garden, coarse & game fishing.

■ *Rooms 13*	*Confirm by 6*
en suite bath/shower 13	*Last dinner 9.30*
Direct dial Yes	*Parking Ample*
Room TV Yes	*Room service All day*

Corse Lawn House Hotel *NEW ENTRY* Corse Lawn

HR **68% £E** &
 Map 4 B1 Gloucestershire
Nr Gloucester GL19 4LZ
Tirley (045 278) 479
Owner managers Denis & Baba Hine
Credit Access, Amex, Diners, Visa. **LVs**
    A delightful Queen Anne-style coaching inn
which has been transformed into a peaceful hotel.
The public areas include a spacious, country-
house style foyer, with plants, newspapers and
magazines, and an elegant lounge in period
fashion. The friendly bar offers a wealth of
comfortable seating and a relaxing atmosphere.
Good-sized bedrooms are traditionally furnished
and have a wealth of homely details such as
flowers and ornaments as well as facilities like
trouser presses and hairdryers.
Amenities garden, putting, croquet, in-house
movies (free), laundry service, helipad.

■ *Rooms 10*	*Confirm by arrang.*
en suite bath/shower 10	*Last dinner 10*
Direct dial Yes	*Parking Ample*
Room TV Yes	*Room service All day*

Restaurant ★ ♕ 🍷 &

Baba Hine cooks her splendid meals with flair,
using the very best produce. Saucing and
flavours are superb, and the table d'hôte, à la
carte and vegetarian menus offer many

interesting dishes. You might start with smoked
salmon mousse or shrimps en croustade, followed
by roast woodcock, meltingly tender medallions of
veal with fresh foie gras and Noilly Prat sauce or
roast duckling in apricot sauce. Finish with one of
the mouthwatering sweets or the excellent
selection of cheeses, followed by coffee of
distinction. The wine list includes splendid clarets,
old Sauternes and cognacs. *Specialities* terrine
of sweetbreads and chicken breast with a chive
butter sauce, medallions of monkfish with a
scallop mousseline and sorrel sauce, saddle of
venison with port and cranberries, grilled
brochette of tropical fruits with brandy butter. ℮

■ *Set L from £11·50*	*L 12–2*
Set D £15·75	*D 7–10*
About £45 for two	*Seats 50 Parties 30*

Methuen Arms Hotel
Corsham

£E
I
Map 4 B2 Wiltshire
2 High Street SN13 0HB
Corsham (0249) 714867
Owner managers Long Family
Credit Access, Visa
  Refurbishment has given a facelift to this
handsome town-centre inn. The public areas have
been redecorated, and bedrooms now have

pastel decor and quality furnishings; colour TVs,
direct dial telephones and tea-makers are
standard accessories. Most also have en suite
bathrooms. *Amenities* garden, laundry service.
■ *Rooms* 24   *Confirm by* 6
en suite bath/shower 20   *Last dinner* 9.30
Direct dial Yes   *Parking* Ample
Room TV Yes   *Room service* None
Closed 1 wk Xmas

Rudloe Park Hotel
Corsham

60% £D
H
Map 4 B2 Wiltshire
Leafy Lane SN13 0PA
Bath (0225) 810555
Owner managers Ian & Marion Overend
Credit Access, Amex, Diners, Visa
  Dedicated owners take great pride in their
imposing creeper-clad Victorian house, which
stands back from the A4 at the top of Box Hill. Day

rooms are comfortably traditional, as are the
chintzy bedrooms, some with four-posters.
Thoughtful extras abound, and all rooms have
practical modern bathrooms. No children under
ten. No dogs. *Amenities* garden, croquet.
■ *Rooms* 8   *Confirm by* arrang.
en suite bath/shower 8   *Last dinner* 9.30
Direct dial Yes   *Parking* Ample
Room TV Yes   *Room service* All day

■ Any person using our name
to obtain free hospitality is
a fraud. Proprietors, please
inform the police and us.

Dove at Corton
Corton

♀ Map 4 B3 Wiltshire
R
Nr Warminster
Warminster (0985) 50378
Credit Access, Visa
  Cooing doves add to the charm of Michael and
Jane Rowse's popular village pub restaurant.
Regular dishes like honey duckling and Wylye
trout are supplemented by daily specials such as
a roast (ours was a pheasant), country casserole

or pigeon breasts flamed in brandy. Generous
portions of well-cooked vegetables, and a
tempting sweet trolley. Booking advisable. ⊖
■ *Set L* Sun only £8·50   *L* 11–2.30
About £30 for two   *D* 6–10.30
Seats 20 *Parties* 14   *Parking* Limited
Closed D Sun, all Mon (exc. Bank Hols) & 2 wks
mid Jan

Chace Crest Hotel
Coventry

64% £C/D
H
Map 10 C4 West Midlands
London Road, Willenhall CV3 4EQ
Coventry (0203) 303398. Tlx 311993
Credit Access, Amex, Diners, Visa
  A well-run half-timbered hotel south of the city
on the A423. The lofty foyer-lounge, with its fine
panelling and period furnishings, provides an
impressive entrance, and guests have a choice of

two bars. Bedrooms in a new block are neat,
practical and modern; main-house rooms are
larger and more traditional. *Amenities* garden,
pool table, laundry service, 24-hour lounge
service.
■ *Rooms* 68   *Confirm by* 6
en suite bath/shower 68   *Last dinner* 9.45
Direct dial Yes   *Parking* Ample
Room TV Yes   *Room service* All day

Crest Hotel
Coventry

65% £D &
H
Map 10 C4 West Midlands
Hinckley Road, Walsgrave CV2 2HP
Coventry (0203) 613261. Tlx 311292
Credit Access, Amex, Diners, Visa
  Pretty flower baskets hanging in the foyer and
lots of greenery about the summery, bamboo-
furnished bar-lounge typify the appeal of this hotel
on the A46. Standard bedrooms have tea-makers,

trouser presses and smart bathrooms; extra
accessories feature in the more luxurious
Executive rooms. *Amenities* garden, games
room, in-house movies (charge), laundry service,
coffee shop (9am–5pm), 24-hour lounge service.
■ *Rooms* 152   *Confirm by* 6
en suite bath/shower 152 *Last dinner* 9.45
Direct dial Yes   *Parking* Ample
Room TV Yes   *Room service* 24 hours

De Vere Hotel Coventry

H **70% £C**
Map 10 C4 West Midlands
Cathedral Square CV1 5RP
Coventry (0203) 633733. Tlx 31380
Credit Access, Amex, Diners, Visa. LVs

Friendly, helpful management and staff in a large modern hotel near the cathedral. The foyer is roomy, bright and welcoming, and beyond it there's a very stylish new bar-lounge named after, and hung with pictures of, one of Coventry's most famous cars, the Daimler. Plants abound, and a pianist plays lunchtime and evening. Day rooms generally have the edge over the bedrooms, where decor (fitted units and bright colour schemes) is looking a little dated. Housekeeping is very good, though, and rooms are of a decent size. Bathrooms are tiled. Conferences are big business, so it's not surprising that the facilities

are extensive. *Amenities* games room, in-house movies (charge), laundry service, coffee shop (7.30am–9pm), 24-hour lounge service.

■ *Rooms* 200	*Confirm by* 6
en suite bath/shower 200	*Last dinner* 11
Direct dial Yes	*Parking* Ample
Room TV Yes	*Room service* 24 hours

Hotel Leofric Coventry

H **63% £C/D**
Map 10 C4 West Midlands
Broadgate CV1 1LZ
Coventry (0203) 21371. Tlx 311193
Credit Access, Amex, Diners, Visa. LVs

Signs to West Orchard car park lead you to this modern city-centre hotel set in a shopping precinct. Both foyer and lounge bar have a bright, contemporary appeal, and there are two other

bars plus good conference facilities. Simply fitted bedrooms provide tea-makers and neat little bathrooms. *Amenities* terrace, hairdressing, laundry service, coffee shop (10.30am–5.45pm Mon–Sat), 24-hour lounge service.

■ *Rooms* 91	*Confirm by* arrang.
en suite bath/shower 91	*Last dinner* 9.45
Direct dial Yes	*Parking* Ample
Room TV Yes	*Room service* 24 hours

Novotel Coventry Coventry

H **62% £D** ᕦ
Map 10 C4 West Midlands
Wilsons Lane, Longford CV6 6HL
Coventry (0203) 365000. Tlx 31545
Credit Access, Amex, Diners, Visa. LVs

Close to junction 3 of the M6, this modern hotel offers good leisure facilities and spacious bedrooms. All the rooms have double beds and studio divans and remote control TVs. Compact

bathrooms feature bidets. The main day room is a split level lounge and bar area which overlooks the pool. *Amenities* garden, outdoor swimming pool, sauna, solarium, gymnasium, squash, pool table, childrens' play area.

■ *Rooms* 100	*Confirm by* 7
en suite bath/shower 100	*Last dinner* 11.30
Direct dial Yes	*Parking* Ample
Room TV Yes	*Room service* 24 hours

Post House Hotel Coventry

H **62% £C/D**
Map 10 C4 West Midlands
Rye Hill, Allesley CV5 9PH
Coventry (0203) 402151. Tlx 31427
Credit Access, Amex, Diners, Visa

Located just outside the city on the A45, this well-run modern hotel is only 8 miles from Birmingham's National Exhibition Centre. The foyer-lounge is smartly contemporary in appeal,

while the 70s-style bar is soon due for refurbishment. Standard bedrooms offer tea-makers, and mini-bars. Executive extras include trouser presses and hairdryers. *Amenities* garden, laundry service, 24-hour lounge service.

■ *Rooms* 190	*Confirm by* 6
en suite bath/shower 190	*Last dinner* 10
Direct dial Yes	*Parking* Ample
Room TV Yes	*Room service* 24 hours

Trinity House Hotel, Herbs Restaurant *NEW ENTRY* Coventry

R ᕦ **Map 10 C4** West Midlands
28 Lower Holyhead Road
Coventry (0203) 555654

Chef and part-owner Robert Jackson has moved vegetarian cooking into the gourmet class at this really excellent restaurant in a small city-centre hotel. His highly original menu, based on top-quality natural ingredients, includes delights like curried vegetable pâté; asparagus with hot

lemon mayonnaise; a memorable stuffed pine nut loaf; West Country hot pot – chunky vegetables in a cider and apple sauce; and a lovely peach and kiwi fruit fool. A couple of meat dishes also available. Notably capable and friendly service. No smoking. ☺

■ *About £25 for two*	*D only* 6.30–9.30
Seats 40 *Parties* 40	*Parking* Ample
Closed Sun, Bank Hols & 2 wks Xmas	

Kennel Holt Hotel — Cranbrook

HR 68% £C/D
Map 7 B5 Kent
TN17 2PT
Cranbrook (0580) 712032
Owner managers Mr & Mrs P. D. Cliff

An attractive Elizabethan manor house with Edwardian additions, standing in landscaped gardens west of Cranbrook off the A262. The sitting rooms are comfortable and inviting, and bedrooms – all with private facilities, two not en suite – boast some handsome family antiques. One has a solid mahogany four-poster. No children under six. *Amenities* garden, croquet.

- ■ *Rooms* 8
- *en suite bath/shower* 6
- *Room phone* Yes
- *Room TV* Yes
- *Closed* 1 Nov–25 Mar
- *Confirm by arrang.*
- *Last dinner* 8.30
- *Parking* Ample
- *Room service* All day

Kennel Holt Hotel Restaurant

There are just 25 covers in this charming and characterful restaurant, so booking is a must. Sue McGarry has stepped up to head chef, and her short daily set menus offer alternative starters, a soup – perhaps carrot and orange – and main courses such as fillet steak with savoury butter or excellent turbot with a delicate creamy tarragon sauce. Well-kept English and French cheeses and a selection of very tempting puddings. Generally capable cooking, but pastry can let the side down. ℮

- ■ *Set D* from £15·50
- *About £44 for two*
- *Closed* 1 Nov–25 Mar
- *D only* 7.30–8.30
- *Seats* 25

Willesley Hotel — Cranbrook

HR 60% £D/E
Map 7 B5 Kent
TN17 2LE
Cranbrook (0580) 713555
Owner manager Mr P. A. Millward
Credit Access, Amex, Diners, Visa. LVs

A characterful hotel on the junction of the A229 and B2189. The beamed bar with its open log fire is 14th century; much of the rest is Georgian. Old-fashioned comfort is the style of the relaxing lounges, while up-to-date bedrooms have tea/coffee-makers and modern bathrooms. *Amenities* garden.

- ■ *Rooms* 16
- *en suite bath/shower* 16
- *Direct dial* Yes
- *Room TV* Yes
- *Closed* 1st wk Feb
- *Confirm by arrang.*
- *Last dinner* 9.30
- *Parking* Ample
- *Room service* All day

Willesley Hotel Restaurant ♿

Plenty of choice and interest is to be found on the frequently-changing menu here. International dishes, from New Orleans risotto with mussels to stir-fried Chinese chicken, are enjoyably cooked using largely fresh ingredients. Starters might include breadcrumbed Brie puffs or melon and avocado cocktail; follow perhaps with halibut in mornay sauce or lamb cutlets with rosemary and ginger glaze. Sweets, though freshly made, are a little less interesting—profiteroles, sherry trifle and typical trolley fare. ℮

- ■ *Set L* £6·95
- *Set D* £10·50
- *About £43 for two*
- *Closed* 1st wk Feb
- *L* 12.30–2
- *D* 7–9.30
- *Seats* 48
- *Parties* 60

🍷 indicates a **well-chosen** house wine.

Crathorne Hall Hotel — Crathorne

H 73% £D/E
Map 15 C5 Cleveland
Nr Yarm, North Yorkshire TS15 0AR
Stokesley (0642) 700398. Tlx 587426
Credit Access, Amex, Diners, Visa

Standing in 15 acres of beautiful grounds above the picturesque Leven valley, Crathorne Hall is an elegant Edwardian country mansion built on the grand scale. The entrance hall with its stone-tiled floor is panelled in oak, while rich mahogany takes the eye in the roomy bar. The drawing room contains a very fine coat of arms fireplace, carved woodwork and ample inviting easy chairs and there's a smart, clubby-style bar too. Bedrooms are large, and comfortably traditional in their appointments. Plenty of seating is provided, and all rooms have well-kept private bathrooms; three of these feature splendid old tubs, while the rest

are smartly modern – many with bidets. No dogs. *Amenities* garden, snooker, laundry service, 24-hour lounge service.

- ■ *Rooms* 40
- *en suite bath/shower* 40
- *Direct dial* Yes
- *Room TV* Yes
- *Confirm by arrang.*
- *Last dinner* 10
- *Parking* Ample
- *Room service* 24 hours

George Hotel

H 65% £C/D
Map 7 B5 West Sussex
High Street RH10 1BS
Crawley (0293) 24215. Tlx 87385
Credit Access, Amex, Diners, Visa. **LVs**

Spot the George by the gallows sign that spans the high street. Parts of the hotel still evoke its 17th-century coaching origins while others are contrastingly modern. Biggest recent improvement is in the Sussex wing of bedrooms, which feature smart units and modern accessories. *Amenities* patio, in-house movies (free), laundry service, coffee shop (9am–10pm), 24-hour lounge service, transport for airport.

■ *Rooms 75*	*Confirm by 6*
en suite bath/shower 75	*Last dinner 10*
Direct dial Yes	*Parking Ample*
Room TV Yes	*Room service 24 hours*

See also under London Airports (Gatwick)

Post House Hotel

H 64% £C/D
Map 11 D4 Northamptonshire
NN6 7XR
Crick (0788) 822101. Tlx 311107
Credit Access, Amex, Diners, Visa. **LVs**

Just half-a-mile from junction 18 of the M1, this modern low-rise hotel is a favourite with business people. The lobby-lounge is roomy and relaxing, the bars cosy or convivial. Freshly decorated bedrooms have tea-makers, mini-bars and bedside controls. Mediocre breakfast. *Amenities* garden, solarium, keep-fit equipment, pool table, laundry service, coffee shop (7am–10.30pm), children's play area, helipad.

■ *Rooms 96*	*Confirm by 6*
en suite bath/shower 96	*Last dinner 10*
Direct dial Yes	*Parking Ample*
Room TV Yes	*Room service All day*

Whites ★ *NEW ENTRY*

R ★ ﯼ ᖉ Map 4 C2 Wiltshire
93 High Street
Swindon (0793) 751110
Credit Access, Amex, Visa

Two antique-furnished rooms in a 300-year-old house are the setting for some immensely enjoyable cooking from the talented and happily gimmick-free Colin White. His menus make exciting reading, and diners are not let down with dishes in which prime flavours and textures are always to the fore. Start perhaps with grilled goat's cheese salad and continue with tournedos of spring lamb served with a mint soubise and roasted shallots. Saucing is always superb, vegetables are cooked lightly and delicately, sweets are irresistible and there's a splendid cheeseboard. A concise and delightful wine list offers many bargains and gems. A la carte both sessions, plus a good-value fixed-price lunch menu. Gwen White runs the front of house with charm and authority. No cigars or pipes allowed.

Specialities veal kidneys baked in vine leaves with a sherry and grape sauce, panaché of sea fish with crab sauce, roast loin of kid with garlic, sage and an offal crépinette, exotic fruits en papillote with coconut ice cream.
♀ Well-chosen ⊖

■ *Set L £11·50*	*L 12.30–2*
About £50 for two	*D 7.30–9.30*
Seats 32 Parties 18	*Parking Ample*
Closed L Mon, all Sun & 1 wk after Xmas	

Wild Boar Hotel

H 63% £C/D
Map 13 D5 Cumbria
Nr Windermere LA23 3NF
Windermere (096 62) 5225
Manager Douglas Dale
Credit Access, Amex, Diners, Visa

This cordial country hotel stands among hills and woodland on the B5284, west of Crook. There's a warm traditional feel about day rooms like the Cockpit Bar and spacious lounge with its well-upholstered armchairs and settees. Neatly kept bedrooms offer a wealth of extras, from fresh fruit and miniature sherries to hairdryers and remote-control TVs. *Amenities* garden.

■ *Rooms 37*	*Confirm by 6*
en suite bath/shower 37	*Last dinner 8.45*
Direct dial Yes	*Parking Ample*
Room TV Yes	*Room service All day*

Crooklands Hotel
Crooklands

H **59% £D**
Map 13 D6 Cumbria
Nr Kendal LA7 7NW
Crooklands (044 87) 432
Owner managers Neil Connor & Philip J. Farmer
Credit Access, Amex, Diners, Visa

Part of this typical Lakeland building was a croft
and ale house in the 16th century, and period
charm lives on in the cosy stone-walled bars.

Bedrooms are simple, bright and attractive, and
bathrooms are provided with plenty of toiletries.
Reasonable breakfasts. *Amenities* garden, game
fishing, snooker, laundry service, coffee shop
(7.30am–10pm).

■ *Rooms* 15	*Confirm by 6*
en suite bath/shower 15	*Last dinner 9.30*
Direct dial Yes	*Parking* Ample
Room TV Yes	*Room service* All day

Crosby Lodge Hotel
Crosby-on-Eden

HR **66% £D/E**
Map 13 D4 Cumbria
High Crosby, Nr Carlisle CA6 4QZ
Crosby-on-Eden (022 873) 618
Owner managers Patricia & Michael Sedgwick
Credit Amex, Diners, Visa

Georgian with Victorian embroidery, Crosby
Lodge enjoys an attractive country setting on the
B6264. It's pleasantly informal, the tone being set
by rugs, antiques and a welcoming fire in the hall.
Bedrooms, in various styles, have decent (some
quite luxurious bathrooms). Good breakfasts.
Amenities garden, laundry service.

■ *Rooms* 11	*Confirm by* arrang.
en suite bath/shower 11	*Last dinner 8.45*
Direct dial Yes	*Parking* Ample
Room TV Yes	*Room service* All day
Closed 24 Dec–late Jan	

Crosby Lodge Hotel
Restaurant ♫

Good honest cooking by Michael Sedgwick, with
fresh ingredients, tasty sauces and man-size
portions. The à la carte menu offers basically
steaks, fish and omelettes, but the set menu
provides more variety with dishes like bean
sprouts and prawns in filo pastry, or roulade of
beef in a rich burgundy sauce. Also a trolleyful of
tempting sweets. Finer wines offer exceptional
value for money: note especially the 1966
Château Ducru Beaucaillou and the 1961 Château
Cos d'Estournel. ☺

■ *Set L* £10·25	*L* noon–1.30
Set D £15·50	*D* 7.30–8.45
About £40 for two	*Seats* 50
Closed 24 Dec–late Jan	

Bridge Hotel
Croxdale

H **58% £E**
Map 15 B4 Co. Durham
Nr Durham DH1 3SP
Durham (091) 3780524. Tlx 538156
Credit Access, Amex, Diners, Visa. **LVs**

Practical, unfussy accommodation is provided
here on the A167, three miles south of Durham.
Bedrooms, in motel-style blocks around the main
building, are neat and simple with tea-makers,

trouser presses and tiled bathrooms. In the
redecorated public area there's a bright,
comfortable cocktail lounge. *Amenities* laundry
service, 24-hour lounge service.

■ *Rooms* 46	*Confirm by 6*
en suite bath/shower 46	*Last dinner 9.45*
Direct dial Yes	*Parking* Ample
Room TV Yes	*Room service* Limited
Closed 3 days Xmas	

🍷 is our symbol for an **outstanding** wine list.

Holiday Inn
Croydon

H **71% £C** *E* ♿
Map 7 B5 Surrey
7 Altyre Road CR9 5AA
01-680 9200. Tlx 8956268
Credit Access, Amex, Diners, Visa

This modern red-brick hotel close to the centre
of Croydon offers first-class business and leisure
facilities. Wood panelling and mirrors add an extra
dimension to the spacious marble-floored foyer-
lounge, while bare brick walls and real gas lighting
create a warm and friendly atmosphere in the
Edwardian-style bar. Good-sized bedrooms with
twin double beds, practical lightwood units and
smartly tiled bathrooms have radios and
individually-controlled air conditioning. Executive
rooms offer superior bathtime extras plus trouser
press, hairdryer and drinks tray. There are also
four suites.

Amenities indoor swimming pool, sauna,
solarium, whirlpool bath, keep-fit equipment,
squash, in-house movies, laundry service, kiosk.

■ *Rooms* 214	*Confirm by 6*
en suite bath/shower 214	*Last dinner 10.30*
Direct dial Yes	*Parking* Ample
Room TV Yes	*Room service* 24 hours

Selsdon Park Hotel   Croydon

H 69% £B/C
Map 7 B5 Surrey
Addington Road, Sanderstead CR2 8YA
01-657 8811. Tlx 945003
Owner managers Sanderson family
Credit Access, Amex, Diners, Visa
  Something of an oasis this – an impressive and
historic hotel in extensive parkland with an
excellent leisure centre, and conference facilities
– only 13 miles south of central London and just
off the M25. Gracious public rooms have several
interesting architectural features including
moulded celings and dressed stone walls.

Antiques furnish the lounge bar; a second bar is
more modern. Constant refurbishment keeps
standards high here. Bedrooms are equipped
with remote-control TVs, wall safes and trouser
presses. *Amenities* garden, indoor & outdoor
swimming pools, sauna, solarium, whirlpool bath,
keep-fit equipment, tennis, squash, croquet,
riding, billiards, snooker, laundry service, 24-hour
lounge service, children's playgound, helipad.

■ Rooms 150	Confirm by arrang.
en suite bath/shower 150	Last dinner 9.30
Direct dial Yes	Parking Ample
Room TV Yes	Room service 24 hours

Tung Kum   Croydon

R ♀ **Map 7 B5** Surrey
205 High Street
01-688 0748
Chinese cooking
Owners Hung Chui & Tony Lam
Credit Access, Amex, Diners, Visa. **LVs**
  Mainly Cantonese – dishes are reliably well
prepared by chef-patron Hung Chui at this
spacious modern restaurant. Wun tun soup and

flavoursome egg roll make enjoyable starters, and
to follow there's a wide variety – from king prawns
with ginger and spring onion to crispy duck and
beef with black bean sauce and green peppers.

■ Set L £2·50	L 12–2.30
Set D from £13·50 for 2	D 5–11.15 (Sat & Sun
About £34 for two	meals 12–11.15)
Seats 100 Parties 60	Parking Limited
Closed Bank Hols	

Jeremy's at The King's Head *NEW ENTRY*   Cuckfield

R ♀ & **Map 7 B6** West Sussex
South Street
Haywards Heath (0444) 454006
Credit Access, Visa
  Imaginative cooking in cosy surroundings.
Franchisee Jeremy Ashpool is an accomplished
chef who puts a lot of care into both preparation
and presentation. After a plate of delicious
appetisers there are delights like spinach and

mushroom ravioli, steamed brill with mussels or
loin of lamb with a red wine and redcurrant sauce.
To finish, perhaps a sorbet or nice gooey toffee
pudding. 🅥

■ Set D £11·95	L 12.30–2
About £38 for two	D 7.30–10
Seats 30 Parties 24	Parking Difficult
Closed D Mon, all Sat, Sun & Bank Hol Mons,	
2 wks Aug, 4 days Xmas & 3 days Easter	

Ockenden Manor Hotel   Cuckfield

HR 71% £B/C
Map 7 B6 West Sussex
Ockenden Lane, Nr Haywards Heath
RH17 5LD
Haywards Heath (0444) 416111
Credit Access, Amex, Diners, Visa
  Seven acres of landscaped grounds, including
walled gardens, provide the setting for this fine
16th-century manor house. The entrance hall
echoes the historic exterior, with beams, oak
panelling, oil paintings and antique furniture.
These notable features are repeated in the
peaceful lounge, and there is an intimate bar.
Charming bedrooms are individually decorated
and furnished with pretty contemporary fabrics
and reproduction or antique pieces; one room
sports a splendid four-poster. Plenty of extras

including fresh fruit, home-made biscuits and
trouser presses. New owners and managers, but
many of the other staff are unchanged. No
children under seven. No dogs.
Amenities garden, laundry service.

■ Rooms 10	Confirm by 6
en suite bath/shower 10	Last dinner 9.15
Room phone Yes	Parking Ample
Room TV Yes	Room service All day

Ockenden Manor Hotel
Restaurant 🅦

Oak panelling, stained-glass mullioned windows
and smart table settings lend a civilised air to this
comfortable restaurant. You can enjoy dishes like
hot turbot soufflé with crayfish and brandy sauce,
parfait of teal breasts, vegetable terrine or roast
saddle of hare with a redcurrant and cassis
sauce. Vegetarians are well catered for, and
there's a traditional Sunday lunch. Patrician wine
list with very fine white Bordeaux.
  ⤐ Outstanding 🅥

■ Set L from £9	L 12.30–2
Set D £16·50	D 7.15–9.15,
About £60 for two	Sun 7.15–8.30
Seats 40	Parties 60

Bear & Ragged Staff   Cumnor

R **Map 5 D2** Oxfordshire
Appleton Road
Oxford (0865) 862329
Owner manager Mr H. F. Hill-Lines
Credit Access, Amex, Diners, Visa
   Time-pressed businessmen appreciate the
attentive service at this comfortable 17th-century
village inn. Elegant tables with quality crockery do
justice to an interesting menu. Russell Maddock is

proving a worthy successor to Steven Smith, and
scores with starters like bacon and wood
mushroom pancake with Cambozola cream
sauce. Main courses include fresh fish and grills,
and vegetables are perfectly cooked. ℰ

■ *About £44 for two*	*L 12–2*
Seats 40	*D 7–10*
Parties 22	*Parking Ample*
Closed L Sat & D 25 & 26 Dec	

Green End Park Hotel   Dane End

H **63% £D**
Map 6 B3 Hertfordshire
Nr Ware SG12 0NY
Dane End (092 084) 344
Owner manager Michael Charalambous
Credit Access, Amex, Diners, Visa
   Ask directions when booking at this 18th-
century manor house set in eight peaceful acres
five miles north of Ware. Chandelier-hung public

rooms are distinctly ornate in style. Comfortable,
generally spacious bedrooms offer practical bath/
shower rooms. No dogs. *Amenities* garden,
tennis, putting, croquet, laundry service, 24-hour
lounge service.

■ *Rooms 10*	*Confirm by arrang.*
en suite bath/shower 10	*Last dinner 9.30*
Direct dial Yes	*Parking Ample*
Room TV Yes	*Room service All day*

■ We welcome complaints and bona
fide recommendations on the
tear-out pages for readers' comments.
They are followed up by our professional
team. Please also complain to the
management instantly.

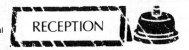

RECEPTION

Bishop's House Restaurant   Darlington

R ⌖ ♿ **Map 15 B5** Co. Durham
38 Coniscliffe Road
Darlington (0325) 286666
Credit Access, Amex, Visa
   Sound, capable cooking by Anne Lee is the
backbone of this chintzy little restaurant. Her
short fixed-price menus could include such
imaginative delights as hot spicy crab pots
topped with bananas and cheese, followed by

pork fillet served with leeks and cashew nuts on a
bed of stir-fried eggs – or the simpler option of
country pâté and plain grilled steaks. Tempting
choice of delicious sweets. ℰ

■ *Set L £9.50*	*L 12–1.30*
Set D £12.50	*D 7–9.30*
About £38 for two	*Parking Limited*
Seats 30	*Parties 20*
Closed L Sat, all Sun, 1 wk Xmas, Bank Hols	

Blackwell Grange Moat House   Darlington

H **62% £D/E**
Map 15 B5 Co. Durham
Blackwell Grange DL3 8QH
Darlington (0325) 380888. Tlx 587272
Manager Ashley Booth
Credit Access, Amex, Diners, Visa
   Wooded parkland just off the A66 surrounds
this handsome 17th-century mansion. The lofty
entrance hall with fine staircase and fireplace

recalls times past, as does the characterful
Antiquary bar. Bedrooms in both modern and
traditional styles include some impressive suites.
Amenities garden, tennis, pool table, in-house
movies (charge).

■ *Rooms 98*	*Confirm by 6*
en suite bath/shower 98	*Last dinner 9.45*
Direct dial Yes	*Parking Ample*
Room TV Yes	*Room service 24 hours*

King's Head Swallow Hotel   Darlington

H **59% £D/E**
Map 15 B5 Co. Durham
Priestgate DL1 1LW
Darlington (0325) 380222. Tlx 587112
Credit Access, Amex, Diners, Visa
   Good conference facilities and comfortable
accommodation are found behind the impressive
Victorian Gothic facade of this town-centre hotel.
Roomy bedrooms, mostly furnished with modern

units, have tea-makers, radio consoles and tiled
bathrooms. Day rooms include a choice of
lounges and two bars. Guests have free use of a
nearby leisure centre. *Amenities* laundry service,
24-hour lounge service.

■ *Rooms 86*	*Confirm by 6*
en suite bath/shower 86	*Last dinner 9.30*
Direct dial Yes	*Parking Ample*
Room TV Yes	*Room service All day*

Stakis White Horse Hotel   Darlington

H **60% £D/E**
Map 15 B5 Co. Durham
Harrowgate Hill DL1 3LD
Darlington (0325) 382121
Credit Access, Amex, Diners, Visa

Comfortable accommodation at a converted Victorian pub four miles north of town on the A167. Bedrooms, all in a modern extension, are uniform in size and style, with freestanding furniture, tea-makers and smart, up-to-date bathrooms. The traditionally furnished lounge bar is well liked by the locals, and there's a stylish cocktail bar. The hotel makes no charge for children under 14.

- *Rooms 40*
- *en suite bath/shower 40*
- *Direct dial Yes*
- *Room TV Yes*

Confirm by 6
Last dinner 10
Parking Ample
Room service Limited

- Changes in data may occur in establishments after the Guide goes to press. Prices should be taken as indications rather than firm quotes.

Bistro 33 ★ *NEW ENTRY*   Dartmouth

R ★ ⑦ **Map 3D3** Devon
33 Lower Street
Dartmouth (08043) 2882

A bistro in name, decor and atmosphere, with cheerful, friendly service and a view through to the kitchen. But there's nothing bistroish about Richard Cranfield's regularly changing menu, which reflects his bubbling enthusiasm and is always full of new ideas. Little pastry turnovers filled with chicken and sesame seeds, accompanied by a cup of mushroom consommé, make a typically imaginative starter, and equally exciting main courses include fishy specials based on the day's haul by the local boats – perhaps roast monkfish with ratatouille and new season's garlic. Sweets sustain the same high standards – try a fresh fruit tartlet filled with crème pâtissière and topped with red and white currants, or an unusual and delicious pistachio and almond loaf served with crème brûlée. *Specialities* pancake-lined vegetable and sour

cream loaf, ragout of assorted local fish in a provençale sauce with basil, mousseline of scallops and sole with saffron sauce, Beaumes de Venise ice cream with chocolate marquise and frosted grapes.

♀ Well-chosen
- *Set D from £12.75*
About £37 for two
Seats 25
Closed Sun, Mon, 24–26 Dec & 2 wks Jan–Feb

L by arrang. only
D 7–10
Parking Difficult

Carved Angel ★   Dartmouth

R ★ ⑦ **Map 3 D3** Devon
2 South Embankment
Dartmouth (080 43) 2465

A beautiful wood-carved angel surveys the scene at this light, pleasant harbourside restaurant, where Joyce Molyneux continues to delight visitors with her outstanding cooking. Local suppliers provide the finest raw materials, to which she applies a skilful blending of English and continental ideas and a great deal of care. There are some marvellous peasant dishes (oxtail with vegetables and haricot beans, chicken with red wine and pig's trotters) and fish appears in many dishes, from Provençal fish soup to turbot with lobster and prawn sauce. Venison with cherry liqueur sauce and chestnut croquettes is another fine choice, and yummy sweets vie with a select English cheeseboard. Classic wines at keen prices. Service is youthful, discreet and efficient. *Specialities* porbeagle shark with butter, lemon and parsley, pigeon pudding with mushrooms and

port, puff pastry of scallops, mussels and leeks, melon, honey and geranium leaf ice cream.
⌲ Outstanding   ♀ Well-chosen ☺
- *Set L £15*
Set D from £22
About £60 for two
Seats 40
Closed D Sun, all Mon, Bank Hols exc. Good Fri, 4 days Xmas & all Jan

L 12.30–1.45
D 7.30–9.30
Parking Limited
Parties 20

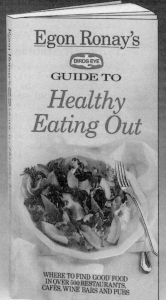

Royal Castle Hotel *NEW ENTRY* Dartmouth

£D/E
Map 3 D3 Devon
The Quay TA6 9PS
Dartmouth (080 43) 4004
Credit Access, Visa

A picture-postcard harbourside setting for this welcoming hostelry, originally four Tudor merchants' houses. Sympathetic renovation has kept interesting features like the old bell system on the stairwell, and beams, log fires and heavy carved furniture assist the traditional atmosphere. Each bedroom has its own individual appeal; several have four-posters. Well-equipped bathrooms. Decent breakfasts.

■ *Rooms* 21	*Confirm by arrang.*
en suite bath/shower 21	*Last dinner* 9.30
Direct dial Yes	*Parking* Limited
Room TV Yes	*Room service* 24 hours

Mieko's *NEW ENTRY* Deal

R **Map 7 D5** Kent
443 St Richard's Road, Gt Mongeham
Deal (0304) 367257
Japanese cooking
Credit Access, Visa

Brian and Mieko Morris run a hairdressing business by day and this attractive Japanese restaurant in the evening (it's tucked away in a housing estate, so get directions when booking). Specialities include Teppan (Charcoal-grilled meats and seafood) and Nabemono, a do-it-yourself fondue. Many other delights, too, like deep-fried tofu, quails and quails' eggs, soya bean soup, grilled trout and carp.

■ *Set D* £12	*D only* 7–11
About £45 *for two*	*Parking* Ample
Seats 42	*Parties* 42
Closed Sun, Mon & Bank Hols	

Dedham Vale Hotel Dedham

HR **72% £C/D**
Map 6 C3 Essex
Stratford Road, Nr Colchester CO7 6HW
Colchester (0206) 322273
Owner manager Gerald Milsom
Credit Access, Amex, Diners, Visa

Hand-painted murals depicting local scenes make entertaining viewing in the comfortable bar of this Edwardian country house. Next door is a cosy lounge with oil paintings hung on cheery red walls. Individually decorated bedrooms are spacious and comfortable with good easy chairs. Furniture varies from modern to traditional, with some antiques. Extras range from fresh fruit and mineral water to remote-control TV. Carpeted en suite bathrooms are stocked with good towels, face flannels and quality soaps. Service is first class. No dogs. *Amenities* garden, laundry service.

■ *Rooms* 6	*Confirm by arrang.*
en suite bath/shower 6	*Last dinner* 9.30
Direct dial Yes	*Parking* Ample
Room TV Yes	*Room service* All day

Terrace Restaurant

Toss back a glass of aquavit with your Danish herring in this summery, plant-filled restaurant – or on cooler days settle for a hot starter like pan-fried sardines or Stilton fritters with basil and tomato dip. Select your main course from the spit, cold table or grill, or enjoy a vegetarian casserole – perhaps leek, potato and mushroom. An innovation is the range of Indian specialities, including koftas, curries and a vegetarian thali. Sweets from the trolley, and a good cheeseboard.
🍷 Well-chosen ⊖

■ *Set L* £8·50	*L* 12–2
About £40 *for two*	*D* 7–9.30
Seats 100	*Parties* 100
Closed L Sat	

Maison Talbooth Dedham

HR **79% £C/D**
Map 6 C3 Essex
Stratford Road, Nr Colchester CO7 6HN
Colchester (0206) 322367. Tlx 987083
Owner manager Gerald Milsom
Credit Access, Amex, Diners, Visa

Comfort, charm and Victorian elegance in a fine country house hotel in the heart of Constable country. The setting is beautiful, and within the hotel grounds there's a fountain and sunken garden. The entrance hall opens directly on to a luxurious drawing room where guests can relax with a drink in deep-cushioned armchairs and settees. Bedrooms are all of a very good size, with attractive floral decor and thoughtful extras like fresh fruit and a drinks tray. Bathrooms are also roomy and well equipped. There's no restaurant on the premises, but breakfast is served in the rooms and other meals may be taken at the nearby Le Talbooth restaurant or Dedham Vale Hotel. No dogs. *Amenities* garden, croquet, laundry service.

■ *Rooms* 10	*Confirm by arrang.*
en suite bath/shower 10	*Last dinner* 9.30
Direct dial Yes	*Parking* Ample
Room TV Yes	*Room service* Limited

Le Talbooth ♕♕ ♿

Richard Sawyer offers a monthly changing menu in a beguiling riverside setting not far from Maison Talbooth. Good fresh produce is the basis of traditional favourites, and more innovative dishes such as terrine of eels on a parsley and red pepper sauce. Separate vegetarian menu. Outstanding friendly and attentive staff. Excellent wines at attractive prices. ♇ Well-chosen ☺
- About £60 for two   L 12–2, Sun 12–2.30
  Seats 70 Parties 24   D 7–9.30, Sun 7–9

Old Rectory Hotel   Denton

H **58% £E**
  Map 10 B2 Greater Manchester
Meadow Lane, Haughton Green M34 1GD
061-336 7516. Tlx 668615
Owner managers Challenor-Chadwick family
Credit Access
    Check directions to this pleasant family-run hotel in a quiet residential area. Fine paintings decorate the attractive panelled bar and there is a

restful first-floor lounge. Simply-furnished bedrooms have useful extras such as soda water, mini-bars and trouser presses. *Amenities* garden, laundry service.
- *Rooms 26*   *Confirm by arrang.*
  en suite bath/shower 26   *Last dinner 9.30*
  Direct dial Yes   *Parking Ample*
  Room TV Yes   *Room service None*
  Closed Bank Hols

- Changes in data may occur in establishments after the Guide goes to press. Prices should be taken as indications rather than firm quotes.

Crest Hotel   Derby

H **60% £D** ♿
  Map 10 C3 Derbyshire
Pastures Hill, Littleover DE3 7BA
Derby (0332) 514933. Tlx 377081
Credit Access, Amex, Diners, Visa
    A modernised Victorian hotel on the A5250, with a pleasant reception area and two bars. Standard bedrooms are modern with up-to-date bathrooms; executive rooms have darkwood

units, superior soft furnishings, and bathrooms equipped with extras such as good-quality bubble bath and shampoo. A converted cottage houses two attractive rustic-style suites. *Amenities* garden, whirlpool bath, 24-hour lounge service.
- *Rooms 67*   *Confirm by 6*
  en suite bath/shower 67   *Last dinner 9.45*
  Direct dial Yes   *Parking Ample*
  Room TV Yes   *Room service Limited*

International Hotel *NEW ENTRY*   Derby

H **62% £D/E**
  Map 10 C3 Derbyshire
Burton Road DE3 6AD
Derby (0332) 369321. Tlx 377759
Owner managers Flanagan family
Credit Access, Amex, Diners, Visa. **LVs**
    The owners' love of Spain is reflected in the decor of this friendly modern hotel. Day rooms are warm and cheerful, and good-sized bedrooms

(three with whirlpool baths) have trouser presses, hairdryers and mini-bars. *Amenities* satellite TV, in-house movies (free), laundry service, 24-hour lounge service.
- *Rooms 41*   *Confirm by 6*
  en suite bath/shower 41   *Last dinner 10*
  Direct dial Yes   *Parking Ample*
  Room TV Yes   *Room service All day*
  Closed 1 wk Xmas

Danum Swallow Hotel   Doncaster

H **63% £D/E**
  Map 11 D2 South Yorkshire
High Street DN1 1DN
Doncaster (0302) 342261. Tlx 547533
Credit Access, Amex, Diners, Visa. **LVs**
    A pleasant, friendly atmosphere awaits guests at this red-brick hotel in the town centre. The carpeted lobby is warm and welcoming, and there are two bars, one themed on the old Great

Northern Railway. Top-floor bedrooms with stylish pastel decor have smart pine furniture, while other rooms are furnished in mahogany. All rooms have bedside controls, TVs, hairdryers and tea-makers. *Amenities* laundry service.
- *Rooms 66*   *Confirm by 6*
  en suite bath/shower 66   *Last dinner 9.30*
  Direct dial Yes   *Parking Ample*
  Room TV Yes   *Room service 24 hours*

Doncaster ▶

Doncaster Moat House *NEW ENTRY*   Doncaster

H 71% £D &
Map 11 D2 South Yorkshire
Warmsworth DN4 9UX
Doncaster (0302) 310331. Tlx 547963
Credit Access, Amex, Diners, Visa
 Easy access from the A1(M) makes this smart
new hotel an ideal stopping place for the motorist.
The marble-floored foyer is light and welcoming,
with more than a hint of elegance, and the split-
level bar is equally appealing. Bedrooms are of a
good size, decorated and furnished to a high
standard and with the usual up-to-date
accessories of remote-control TV, trouser press,
hairdryer and tea-making facilities. Compact, tiled
bathrooms. Some of the conference/function
facilities are housed in a splendidly restored 18th-
century building in the grounds. Service is friendly
and helpful. *Amenities* garden, croquet, in-house

movies (charge), laundry service, 24-hour lounge
service.
■ *Rooms* 70   *Confirm by* 6
en suite bath/shower 70   *Last dinner* 10
Direct dial Yes   *Parking* Ample
Room TV Yes   *Room service* 24 hours
Closed 1 wk Xmas

Earl of Doncaster   Doncaster

H 58% £D/E
Map 11 D2 South Yorkshire
Bennetthorpe DN2 6AD
Doncaster (0302) 61371. Tlx 547923
Credit Access, Amex, Diners, Visa
 A general refurbishment programme is
improving this modest 1930's hotel. Day rooms
include two traditional-style bars, one doubling as
a lounge, plus several function suites. Attractively

decorated bedrooms all have tea-makers, direct-
dial telephones and neat bathrooms; smartly
fitted club rooms offer extras such as mini-bars,
hairdryers and trouser presses.
Amenities laundry service.
■ *Rooms* 53   *Confirm by* 6
en suite bath/shower 53   *Last dinner* 9.45
Direct dial Yes   *Parking* Ample
Room TV Yes   *Room service* 24 hours

George Hotel   Dorchester-on-Thames

I £D/E
Map 5 D2 Oxfordshire
High Street OX9 8HH
Oxford (0865) 340404. Tlx 83147
Credit Access, Amex, Diners, Visa
 A handsome antique carriage sets the scene
outside this charming old inn. Blackened beams
and polished brass continue the traditional appeal
in the bar and restaurant. Bedrooms, whether in

the original building or converted stable block, are
comfortably furnished and equipped with tea-
makers. Most have smart bathrooms.
Amenities garden.
■ *Rooms* 17   *Confirm by arrang.*
en suite bath/shower 15   *Last dinner* 9.45
Room phone Yes   *Parking* Ample
Room TV Yes   *Room service* Limited
Closed 1 wk Xmas

Burford Bridge Hotel   Dorking

H 70% £B/C
Map 5 E3 Surrey
Box Hill, Burford Bridge RH5 6BX
Dorking (0306) 884561. Tlx 859507
Credit Access, Amex, Diners, Visa
 Located at the foot of Box Hill, this long, low
white-fronted hotel dates back to the 18th
century. Inside, fine antique furniture and
lovely fresh flower arrangements contribute to the
traditional air of the public rooms, which radiate
from the foyer and include a spacious and
comfortable bar, and a lounge furnished with
brick-red velour seating, dominated by a brass-
canopied fireplace. Bedrooms are all of a good
size, pleasantly decorated mostly in cream and
brown shades with smart, modern darkwood
units, and feature mini-bars, armchairs and
occasional tables. All have well-equipped

bathrooms. There is a garden suite of 20 rooms
which are well heated, and two which feature four-
posters. *Amenities* garden, outdoor swimming
pool, laundry service, games room.
■ *Rooms* 48   *Confirm by* 6
en suite bath/shower 48   *Last dinner* 9.30
Direct dial Yes   *Parking* Ample
Room TV Yes   *Room service* 24 hours

■ For a discount on next year's guide, see Offer for Answers.

Punch Bowl Hotel　Dorking

H **£D**
Map 5 E3 Surrey
Reigate Road RH4 1QB
Dorking (0306) 889335
Credit Access, Amex, Diners, Visa. **LVs**
　1987 is a year of progress at this agreeable hotel built round an old stone inn. Additions include 17 new bedrooms and a conference room, and refurbishment will extend to bar, lounge,

restaurant and existing bedrooms, which are in a two-storey motel block; all rooms have remote-control TVs and quite spacious bathrooms. There are good views of Box Hill. 54% in 1987 Guide.
Amenities garden, laundry service.

■ *Rooms* 29	*Confirm by* arrang.
en suite bath/shower 29	*Last dinner 10*
Room phone Yes	*Parking* Ample
Room TV Yes	*Room service* None

White Horse Hotel　Dorking

H **62% £C/D**
Map 5 E3 Surrey
High Street RH4 1BE
Dorking (0306) 881138
Credit Access, Amex, Diners, Visa
　Situated in the town centre, this one-time coaching inn has been dispensing hospitality since 1750. Its period character is well preserved in the oak beams that are a feature in the bar and

lounge areas. Main-house bedrooms have been smartly upgraded with contemporary fabrics and furnishings to match the slightly larger garden wing rooms. *Amenities* garden, outdoor swimming pool, laundry service.

■ *Rooms* 68	*Confirm by* 6
en suite bath/shower 68	*Last dinner 9.30*
Direct dial Yes	*Parking* Ample
Room TV Yes	*Room service* Limited

Izaak Walton Hotel　Dovedale

H **59% £D/E** &
Map 10 C3 Derbyshire
Nr Ashbourne DE6 2AY
Thorpe Cloud (033 529) 555. Tlx 378406
Manager Mr A. Ricketts
Credit Access, Amex, Diners, Visa
　Izaak Walton stayed here to fish on the river Dove, and so can you. The setting is stunning, with marvellous views from the lounges. Homely

bedrooms, mostly refurbished, include five superior rooms. The dying art of shoe cleaning thrives. *Amenities* garden, putting, laundry service, coffee shop (10.30–6 summer only), 24-hour lounge service, helipad.

■ *Rooms* 33	*Confirm by* 6
en suite bath/shower 33	*Last dinner 9.45*
Direct dial Yes	*Parking* Ample
Room TV Yes	*Room service* All day

Peveril of the Peak Hotel　Dovedale

H **62% £C/D** &
Map 10 C3 Derbyshire
Nr Ashbourne DE6 2AW
Thorpe Cloud (033 529) 333
Credit Access, Amex, Diners, Visa
　A well-kept, rambling inn and a cosy, friendly base for enjoying the superb countryside. The lounge is ideal for lounging, and there are lovely views from the restaurant and modern bar. Good-

sized bedrooms, some with patios accessing the garden, offer remote-control TVs and welcoming touches like sherry and chocolates. Bathrooms are well stocked with towels and toiletries.
Amenities garden, tennis, laundry service.

■ *Rooms* 41	*Confirm by* 6
en suite bath/shower 41	*Last dinner 9.30*
Direct dial Yes	*Parking* Ample
Room TV Yes	*Room service* Limited

Dover Moat House　Dover

H **72% £D/E** *E*
Map 7 D5 Kent
Townwall Street CT16 1SZ
Dover (0304) 203270. Tlx 96458
Credit Access, Amex, Diners, Visa
　Follow the signs to the Eastern Docks to reach this modern hotel that stands close to the cross-Channel services. It's a well-maintained and efficiently run place, and the favourable first impression created by the terracotta tiles and leather seating of the comfortably furnished foyer-lounge is sustained throughout. There's a smart, pub-style cocktail bar, a large restaurant and a number of function rooms. The bedrooms are uniformly designed and surprisingly roomy, with plenty of writing space, thoughtfully organised lighting, king-size beds and a fair range of accessories, including remote-control TVs, clock-

radios and hairdryers. There's a good supply of towels and toiletries in the compact bathrooms.
Amenities indoor swimming pool, laundry service, in-house movies.

■ *Rooms* 79	*Confirm by* arrang.
en suite bath/shower 79	*Last dinner 10.15*
Direct dial Yes	*Parking* Ample
Room TV Yes	*Room service* Limited

Dover ▶

Dover Motel *NEW ENTRY* — Dover

H 60% £D ♿
Map 7 D5 Kent
Whitfield Singledge Lane CT16 3LF
Dover (0304) 821222. Tlx 965866
Credit Access, Amex, Diners, Visa
  A friendly motel just off the A2/M2. Bedrooms leading from the open-plan public area are furnished in plain, practical style and provided with trouser presses, hairdryers and bedside TV

switches. Bathrooms, too, are quite well equipped, but bigger towels would be nicer. No dogs. *Amenities* garden, laundry room, 24-hour lounge service, coffee shop (7am–11pm), in-house movies (free), courtesy coach to docks.

■ *Rooms* 67	*Confirm by* 6
en suite bath/shower 67	*Last dinner* 9.50
Direct dial Yes	*Parking* Ample
Room TV Yes	*Room service* 24 hours

White Cliffs Hotel — Dover

H 62% £D/E
Map 7 D5 Kent
Seafront CT17 9BW
Dover (0304) 203633. Tlx 965422
Manager Pamela Gibbons
Credit Access, Amex, Diners, Visa
  An enduring fixture on the Dover hotel scene, with a warm family atmosphere and outstanding housekeeping. The Victorian building is on the

seafront, handy for the Hoverport and ferry terminals, and there are sea views from the sun lounge and verandah. Central heating keeps bedrooms cosy. *Amenities* laundry service.

■ *Rooms* 56	*Confirm by* arrang.
en suite bath/shower 56	*Last dinner* 9.30
Direct dial Yes	*Parking* Ample
Room TV Yes	*Room service* 24 hours
Closed 25 & 26 Dec	

Bell Hotel — Driffield

I £E ♿
Map 15 D6 Humberside
Market Place YO25 7AP
Driffield (0377) 46661
Owner managers Mr & Mrs Riggs
Credit Access, Amex, Diners, Visa
  A former coaching inn offering a wealth of old-world charm. The spacious bar-lounge has mellow wood panelling and cheerful red upholstery;

another bar is fashioned out of the old corn exchange. Traditionally-furnished, well-kept bedrooms have bathrooms with bidets. No children under 12. No dogs. *Amenities* squash, billiards, laundry service.

■ *Rooms* 14	*Confirm by* arrang.
en suite bath/shower 14	*Last dinner* 9.30
Direct dial Yes	*Parking* Ample
Room TV Yes	*Room service* All day

Château Impney Hotel — Droitwich Spa

H 75% £C
Map 4 B1 Hereford & Worcester
WR9 0BN
Droitwich (0905) 774411. Tlx 336673
Owner manager Mr Z. Raguz
Credit Access, Amex, Diners, Visa
  Terraced gardens and abundantly stocked parkland make an attractive setting for this elegant Victorian hotel built in the style of a French château. Grandiose public rooms include an impressive entrance hall with huge chandeliers and marble pillars and a bar-lounge with a splendidly ornate ceiling. A handsome carved staircase leads to pleasantly traditional bedrooms in impeccable order, with nice touches like beautifully-ironed sheets and bowls of fresh fruit. Bedrooms in the wing are in modern style, with fitted units. All have modern bathrooms.

Courteous, well-trained staff. *Amenities* garden, sauna, gymnasium, tennis, games room, laundry service.

■ *Rooms* 66	*Confirm by* arrang.
en suite bath/shower 66	*Last dinner* 10
Direct dial Yes	*Parking* Ample
Room TV Yes	*Room service* 24 hours
Closed 25 Dec	

Raven Hotel — Droitwich Spa

H 66% £C/D
Map 4 B1 Hereford & Worcester
St Andrews Street WR9 8DU
Droitwich (0905) 772224. Tlx 336673
Manager Richard Bromwich
Credit Access, Amex, Diners, Visa. **LVs**
  A great strength of this timber-framed former manor house is the friendly, efficient service. Public areas, with carved oak panelling and

period furniture, have a mellow charm that is gradually spreading to the bedrooms as they are refurbished.
Amenities garden, laundry service, 24-hour lounge service.

■ *Rooms* 58	*Confirm by* arrang.
en suite bath/shower 58	*Last dinner* 10
Direct dial Yes	*Parking* Ample
Room TV Yes	*Room service* 24 hours

Ashwick Country House Hotel

HR 68% £E
Map 3 D2 Somerset
TA22 9QD
Dulverton (0398) 23868
Owner managers Sherwood family
The Sherwood family provide exemplary service at this peaceful Edwardian house set in six acres of sweeping lawns above the river Barle (check directions when booking). The galleried entrance hall, library-bar and spacious lounge are all most welcoming, while the bedrooms are charming. No children under eight. No dogs.
Amenities garden, croquet, in-house movies (free), laundry service.

■ *Rooms* 6	*Confirm by arrang.*
en suite bath/shower 6	*Last dinner* 8.45
Room phone Yes	*Parking* Ample
Room TV Yes	*Room service* All day

Dulverton

Ashwick Country House Hotel Restaurant

Genuine skill with fresh seasonal ingredients is evident throughout a meal enjoyed in the quiet, comfortable dining room. The chef, Miss Bramble, changes the short set dinner menus nightly, providing such delights as partridge and pheasant pâté, North Devon veal with a Calvados sauce and Torbay sole stuffed with prawn butter. Sweets include classic Bakewell pudding and fresh strawberry cheesecake. Traditional Sunday lunch. Booking advisable.

■ *Set L* £6.95	*L Mon–Sat by arrang.,*
Set D £9.75	*Sun* 12.30–1.45
About £29 *for two*	*D* 7.15–8.45
Seats 26	*Parties* 20
Closed D Sun to non-residents	

Carnarvon Arms Hotel

H 60% £D/E
Map 3 D2 Somerset
TA22 9AE
Dulverton (0398) 23302
Owner manager Mrs T. Jones
Credit Access, Amex, Diners, Visa
The rustic pantry bar at this country sporting hotel is a most convivial spot, and there are several inviting lounges. Bedrooms are neat and

Dulverton

simple, bathrooms likewise. *Amenities* garden, outdoor swimming pool, tennis, stabling, clay-pigeon shooting, game fishing, games room, snooker, laundry service, laundry room.

■ *Rooms* 27	*Confirm by arrang.*
en suite bath/shower 21	*Last dinner* 8.30
Direct dial Yes	*Parking* Ample
Room TV Most	*Room service* All day
Closed 3 wks Feb	

Luigi

See under London

Dulwich

Dun Cow Hotel

I £D/E
Map 11 D4 Warwickshire
The Green, Nr Rugby CV22 6NJ
Rugby (0788) 810233
Manager Bruno Carrouche
Credit Access, Amex, Diners, Visa
First recorded in 1560, this ancient inn conveys a strong sense of the past in its cosily beamed bars. The small lounge area is traditionally

Dunchurch

furnished, and there are some fine period pieces in the bedrooms. These are of a good size, with a homely, welcoming feel, and they all have decent private bathrooms. *Amenities* garden, laundry service.

■ *Rooms* 25	*Confirm by* 6
en suite bath/shower 25	*Last dinner* 10
Direct dial Yes	*Parking* Ample
Room TV Yes	*Room service* 24 hours

Petty France Hotel

H 63% £D
Map 4 B2 Avon
Nr Badminton GL9 1AF
Didmarton (045 423) 361
Owner managers W. J. Fraser & V. I. Minnich
Credit Access, Amex, Diners, Visa
New owners have taken over at this Georgian mansion set in attractive Cotswold countryside. No major alterations are planned for the

Dunkirk

comfortable interior, which includes a homely lounge and a relaxing foyer-cum-bar-lounge. Charming bedrooms, some in converted outbuildings, others with canopied bathrooms and a host of cosseting extras. *Amenities* garden.

■ *Rooms* 20	*Confirm by* 8
en suite bath/shower 20	*Last dinner* 9.30
Direct dial Yes	*Parking* Ample
Room TV Yes	*Room service* All day

■ We publish annually, so make sure you use the current edition. It's worth it!

Dunstable ▶

Old Palace Lodge Hotel   Dunstable

H 69% £D/E
Map 5 E1 Bedfordshire
Church Street LU5 4RP
Dunstable (0582) 62201
Credit Access, Amex, Diners, Visa
   At the edge of the Chilterns on the A505 road
from the M1, this welcoming creeper-clad hotel
makes a delightful overnight stop. Good-sized
bedrooms impress with their handsome darkwood

furniture and smart bathrooms equipped with
bidets and hairdryers. Fine oak panelling adds to
the charm of the comfortably traditional day
rooms. No dogs. *Amenities* laundry service, 24-
hour lounge service.

■ *Rooms 49*	*Confirm by arrang.*
en suite bath/shower 49	*Last dinner 9.45*
Direct dial Yes	*Parking Ample*
Room TV Yes	*Room service 24 hours*

■ Our inspectors never book in the
name of Egon Ronay's Guides;
they disclose their identity only
after paying their bills.

Luttrell Arms   Dunster

H 60% £C/D
Map 3 E1 Somerset
High Street, Nr Minehead
Dunster (0643) 821555
Managers Mr & Mrs R. A. Mann
Credit Access, Amex, Diners, Visa
   Olde worlde charm is plentiful at this hospitable
inn built around a 15th-century Gothic hall – now
the splendid first-floor lounge. The huge inglenook

fire of the former kitchen now warms the bar.
Spacious bedrooms, some with four-posters and
superior furnishings, have tea-makers and
modern bathrooms.
Amenities garden, laundry service.

■ *Rooms 25*	*Confirm by 6*
en suite bath/shower 25	*Last dinner 9.30*
Direct dial Yes	*Parking Limited*
Room TV Yes	*Room service All day*

Royal County Hotel   Durham

H 67% £C/D ♿
Map 15 B4 Co. Durham
Old Elvet DH1 3JN
Durham (0385) 66821. Tlx 538238
Manager Mr B. F. Hanley
Credit Access, Amex, Diners, Visa. **LVs**
   The Royal County, whose origins go back to the
17th century, enjoys a favoured setting near the
river, the castle and the Norman cathedral. The

foyer is bright and modern, and there's a long
lounge and a bar. Good-sized bedrooms have
remote-control TVs and well-appointed
bathrooms. *Amenities* sauna, in-house movies
(free), laundry service, 24-hour lounge service.

■ *Rooms 120*	*Confirm by 6*
en suite bath/shower 120	*Last dinner 10.15*
Direct dial Yes	*Parking Ample*
Room TV Yes	*Room service All day*

Duxford Lodge Hotel *NEW ENTRY*   Duxford

HR 66% £D
Map 6 B3 Cambridgeshire
Ickleton Road CB2 4RU
Cambridge (0223) 836444. Tlx 817438
Credit Access, Amex, Diners, Visa
   Ten minutes from the M11 (junction 10),
Duxford Lodge is a very comfortable Victorian
house standing in pleasant grounds. The
bedrooms are smart and modern in the main
house, and more functional in the stable block.
Five rooms designated de luxe are the biggest
and best equipped. Friendly but not polished
service. *Amenities* garden, laundry service.

■ *Rooms 16*	*Confirm by arrang.*
en suite bath/shower 16	*Last dinner 9.30*
Direct dial Yes	*Parking Ample*
Room TV Yes	*Room service All day*
Closed 27–29 Dec & 1 Jan	

Duxford Lodge Hotel Restaurant ♿

John Burrow is a very competent young chef with
a genuine feel for his work and a particular flair for
sauces, so a meal here is a real pleasure. Quality
produce features throughout the menus, with
typical dishes running from a refreshing game
consommé and an attractively presented smoked
salmon mousse to duck magret with an
interesting fruit sauce, Dover sole and charcoal-
grilled steak. Vegetarian dishes. Good sweets,
home-baked bread rolls. Sound wine list.
🍷 Well-chosen ⊖

■ *Set L £9.50*	*L 12–1.45*
Set D £13.50	*D 7–9.30, Sun 7–8.45*
About £38 for two	*Seats 40 Parties 40*
Closed L Sat, 27–29 Dec & 1 Jan	

New Leaf & Sinar Matahari   Ealing

See under London

Mr Underhill's   Earl Stonham

See under Stonham

Fountain House   East Bergholt

R ♐ **Map 6 C3** Suffolk
The Street
Colchester (0206) 298232
Owner managers Jim and Wendy Sarton
Credit Access, Visa
   It's all beams and rough plaster walls in this
friendly village restaurant, where Wendy's fixed-
price menus offer honest, homely fare. Carrot and
orange soup and Stilton quiche are typical

starters, while main courses could include pork
provencale, steak and kidney pie or tasty mixed
fish kebab. Enjoyable sweets. Good-value
burgundies. ♀ Well-chosen ⊖
■ *Set L £8.95*   *L 12.30–2*
Set D £10.95   *D 7.30–10*
About £30 for two   *Parking Ample*
Seats 30 Parties 36   *Closed D Sun, all Mon,*
Bank Hols exc. Good Fri & 2 weeks Jan

Lower Pitt   East Buckland

RR ♐ **Map 3 D2** Devon
Barnstaple
Filleigh (059 86) 243
Credit Access, Amex, Visa
   Although this pleasant farmhouse restaurant
with rooms is only a few miles from the A361, it is
set in the North Devon countryside and access to
it is by narrow country lanes, so seek directions
when booking. Jerome Lyons is a courteous
informal host and his wife Suzanne specialises in
home cooking of a high calibre. Vegetables, often
home grown, are a particular strength. Start,
perhaps, with local mushrooms or Devon oak-

smoked salmon, and then sample a tasty game
casserole. Desserts are delicious.
♀ Well-chosen ⊖
■ *About £34 for two*   *L by arrang.*
Seats 28   *D 7–9*
Parties 24   *Parking Ample*
Closed Sun, Mon, 1 Jan & 3 days Xmas
Bedrooms £F
Rooms 3   *With bath/shower 3*
Three double rooms, one with bath, two with
showers, accommodate restaurant guests
staying the night (half-board terms). No children.
No dogs.

King's Head Hotel *NEW ENTRY*   East Dereham

I **£F**
Map 6 C1 Norfolk
Norwich Street NR19 1AD
East Dereham (0362) 693482
Tenants Mr & Mrs R. Black
Credit Access, Amex, Diners, Visa
   First-time visitors should check the exact
location of this immaculate old inn, which lies
down a side street close to the town centre. The

bar opens on to a flower-filled patio. Bedrooms
offer standard comforts: ten, slightly larger, are in
the main building, the remainder in converted
stables. *Amenities* tennis, bowling green.
■ *Rooms 15*   *Confirm by arrang.*
en suite bath/shower 10   *Last dinner 9*
Direct dial Yes   *Parking Ample*
Room TV Yes   *Room service None*
Closed 25 & 26 Dec

Phoenix Hotel   East Dereham

H **59% £C/D**
Map 6 C1 Norfolk
Church Street NR19 1DL
Dereham (0362) 692276
Credit Access, Amex, Diners, Visa
   A red-brick 60s hotel in a quiet street close to
the market place. The residents' lounge is mainly
used for meetings, but there's ample space for
unwinding in the foyer and three cheerful bars.

Best bedrooms are six spacious rooms with
sitting areas and luxurious bathrooms; the others
are more modest, but bright and fresh, with neat,
functional bathrooms. Staff are friendly, but not
very speedy. *Amenities* laundry service.
■ *Rooms 24*   *Confirm by 6*
en suite bath/shower 24   *Last dinner 9.30*
Room phone Yes   *Parking Ample*
Room TV Yes   *Room service All day*

Evergreen   East Grinstead

R ♐ **Map 7 B5** West Sussex
192 London Road
East Grinstead (0342) 22078
Chinese cooking
Owner managers Tak Wai Liu & Tak Hing Liu
Credit Access, Amex, Diners, Visa
   Attention to detail and skilled cooking combine
in the Lius' smart Chinese restaurant. Such
favourite Peking dishes as dried scallops and

seaweed or crispy duck with pancakes are
specialities and there are also plenty of good
things from other regions. Quick-fried vegetables
are excellent and rice is perfectly cooked. Set
price meals offer value. ♀ Well-chosen
■ *Set D £11*   *L noon–2*
About £30 for two   *D 5.30–11.30*
Seats 80 Parties 50   *Parking Ample*
Closed L Sun & 5 days Xmas

Gravetye Manor

East Grinstead

HR **81% £B/C**
Map 7 B5 West Sussex
West Hoathly RH19 4LJ
Sharpthorne (0342) 810567
Owner manager Peter Herbert
Long the home of that celebrated gardener, William Robinson, this lovely manor house in superb grounds radiates tranquillity. The apparent ease with which this is achieved is largely due to the indefatigable owner, Peter Herbert, and his excellent staff. Fresh flowers in mellow public rooms with fine antiques and oils reinforce the country house atmosphere. Individually-decorated bedrooms of varying sizes are equally attractive with every comfort, including hairdryers, books and mineral water. Bathrooms boast similar considerate touches. No children under seven. No dogs.
Amenities garden, croquet, game fishing, laundry service.

■ *Rooms 14*	*Confirm by arrang.*
en suite bath/shower 14	*Last dinner 9.30*
Room phone Yes	*Parking Ample*
Room TV Yes	*Room service All day*
Closed 25 Dec	

Gravetye Manor Restaurant ★ ♛♛ ⬧

The owner's son, Leigh Stone-Herbert, is the chef de cuisine here, and his skills are matched by high-class service in the splendid panelled dining room. Typical dishes include duck consommé, succulent scallops on a bed of thyme-scented chopped tomato, and saddle of lamb stuffed with asparagus. Roast beef is a Sunday lunchtime favourite. Lovely sweets, superb cheeses. A fine cellar, with some excellent German wines in half bottles. No smoking in the restaurant (coffee served in sitting rooms). *Specialities* paupiette of smoked salmon with crème fraîche and caviar, gratin of lobster flavoured with basil on a bed of chicory, veal with calf's liver forcemeat and sauce poivrade, poached pear in puff pastry with chilled Poire William sabayon.
➥ Outstanding ♟ Well-chosen ⊟

■ *Set L £15, Sun £11·50*	*L 12.30–2*
Set D £19	*D 7.30–9.30,*
About £80 for two	*Sun 7.30–9*
Seats 50	*Parties 20*
Closed D 25 Dec	

Ladbroke Felbridge Hotel

East Grinstead

H **65% £E/F** ♿
Map 7 B5 West Sussex
London Road RH19 2BH
East Grinstead (0342) 26992. Tlx 95156
Manager B. R. Constable
Credit Access, Amex, Diners, Visa
New owners plan additional improvements to this busy hotel, which can already claim impressive leisure facilities. Bedrooms in main house are simply furnished, those in the Bahama wing more luxurious. No dogs. *Amenities* garden, indoor & outdoor swimming pools, sauna, solarium, whirlpool bath, gymnasiums, beauty salon, games room, snooker, laundry service.

■ *Rooms 54*	*Confirm by arrang.*
en suite bath/shower 54	*Last dinner 9.30*
Direct dial Yes	*Parking Ample*
Room TV Yes	*Room service Limited*

Thatchers Hotel

East Horsley

HR **65% £C/D**
Map 5 E3 Surrey
Epsom Road KT24 6BT
East Horsley (048 65) 4291. Tlx 946240
Credit Access, Amex, Diners, Visa
Just off the A246, in three acres of grounds, this attractive timbered hotel makes a relaxing place to stay. Most of the light, airy bedrooms are grouped round the pool and offer tea-makers, trouser presses and tiled bathrooms; five rooms are in a charming cottage. Day rooms include a comfortably furnished lounge-cum-bar. No dogs.
Amenities garden, outdoor swimming pool, laundry service.

■ *Rooms 29*	*Confirm by arrang.*
en suite bath/shower 29	*Last dinner 9.30*
Direct dial Yes	*Parking Ample*
Room TV Yes	*Room service All day*

Restaurant ♿

Capable, often imaginative cooking led by Jeffry Condliffe can be enjoyed in this pretty, beamed restaurant. Hot lobster mousse served with a brandy-spiked sauce and crayfish tails, pheasant poached in orange sauce, and avocado and Stilton baked in puff pastry are typical of the savoury choice, while tempting sweets might include home-made sorbets and gratin of spiced peaches and apricots. There's also an interesting selection of British farmhouse cheeses.

🍷 Well-chosen ℰ
■ *Set L £9.50*
Set D £10.50
About £45 for two

L 12.30–2
D 7.30–9.30
Seats 55 Parties 65

Bell Inn
East Langton

R ⅙ **Map 11 D4** Leicestershire
Main Street, Nr Market Harborough
East Langton (085 884) 567
French cooking
Owner managers Pascal & Eileen Trystram
Credit Access, Visa
A Frenchman and his English wife have created a charmingly Gallic atmosphere at this cosy pub restaurant. The daily-changing blackboard menu

features seafood specialities like scallops in a light curry sauce or a delicious knot of fresh salmon. We also enjoyed beautifully cooked loin of veal and a mouthwatering tournedos. Delectable desserts. Booking advised.
■ *Set L £8.50*
About £36 for two
Seats 50 Parties 25
Closed 25 Dec

L 12–2.30
D 7–11.30
Parking Ample

■ See INSPECTOR FOR A DAY

Hampton Court Brasserie *NEW ENTRY*
East Molesey

R **Map 5 E2** Surrey
3 Palace Gate Parade, Hampton Court
01-979 7891
Credit Access, Amex, Diners, Visa
White table linen and colourful pictures set the tone at this smart new brasserie. Both cooking and presentation are of a high standard. Starters include avocado and quails' eggs with hazelnut dressing and deep-fried brie with cranberry

sauce; main dishes might be roast breast of goose with juniper berry sauce or calves' liver with rosemary and bacon rolls. Delicious sweets.
🍷 Well-chosen ℰ
■ *Set L from £9.25*
About £45 for two
Seats 140 Parties 90
Closed 25 & 26 Dec

L 12–2.30
D 7–11, Fri & Sat
7–11.30, Sun 7–10.30
Parking Limited

Lantern
East Molesey

R ♙ **Map 5 E2** Surrey
20 Bridge Road
01-979 1531
French cooking
Credit Access, Amex, Diners, Visa
The reputation of this long-established restaurant rests on satisfying, unpretentious cooking of good-quality ingredients. The menu offers mostly well-known French dishes but also

some more unusual such as game mousse in pastry cases or guinea fowl with pineapple and sherry. Vegetables are carefully cooked and there are nice sweets like rich chocolate marquise. ℰ
■ *Set D from £13.85*
About £42 for two
Seats 50 Parties 32
Closed L Mon & Sat, all Sun, Bank Hols & Aug

L 12.30–2.15
D 7–10.30
Parking Limited

Vecchia Roma
East Molesey

R ♙ **Map 5 E2** Surrey
57 Bridge Road
01-979 5490
Italian cooking
Credit Access, Diners, Visa
Arches, murals and tiles bring a look of Rome to this reliable Italian restaurant, a well-run place with notably efficient service. The menu intersperses familiar favourites with less usual

dishes like veal kidneys with gin, mushrooms and mustard or lamb cutlets served Roman style with a black cherry sauce. Dishes of the day widen the choice further. ℰ
■ *Set L £9.00*
Set D £11.50
About £45 for two
Seats 75 Parties 50

L 12–2.15
D 7–11.15
Parking Difficult
Closed L Sat & 26 Dec

Kemps Country House Hotel
East Stoke

H **59% £D/E**
Map 4 B4 Dorset
Near Wareham BH20 6AL
Bindon Abbey (0929) 462563
Owner managers Michael & Valerie Kemp
Credit Access, Amex, Diners, Visa
Friendly hospitality is offered at this former rectory which stands back from the A352 and enjoys views of the Purbeck Hills. Guests can

relax in two homely lounges or a smartly-modern bar. Attractively decorated bedrooms include four in a converted coach house. All have sturdy contemporary furnishings, TVs and tea/coffee-makers. No dogs. *Amenities* garden.
■ *Rooms 9*
en suite bath/shower 8
Direct dial Yes
Room TV Yes

Confirm by arrang.
Last dinner 9.30
Parking Ample
Room service All day

Byrons
Eastbourne

R ♃ **Map 7 B6** East Sussex
6 Crown Street, Old Town BN21 1NX
Eastbourne (0323) 20171
Credit Amex, Diners, Visa

Few owners are more dedicated than Simon and Marian Scrutton, in charge of this cosy little restaurant for an unbroken 17 years. Simon always likes to feature fish from the local boats on his concise evening menu, while his meat dishes could include quail mousse, marinated free-range chicken and steak béarnaise. Mouthwatering sweets. Among the wines note the exceptional Ch. La Touche and the excellent Lebanese Ch. Musar.

🍷 **Well-chosen** ℮

■ *About £38 for two*	*L by arrang.*
Seats 24 Parties 10	*D 7.30–10*
Closed Sun & Bank Hols	*Parking Ample*

Cavendish Hotel
Eastbourne

H **73% £C**
Map 7 B6 East Sussex
Grand Parade BN21 4DH
Eastbourne (0323) 27401. Tlx 87579
Credit Access, Amex, Diners, Visa

Improvements continue here on the seafront with a brand-new games and snooker room and the addition of yet another suite to the already impressive conference facilities. The hotel is part-modern, part-Victorian and favours a style of glittering opulence in its public rooms — whether the leafy, fairy-lit foyer-lounge or the mirrored cocktail bar with twinkling 'icicle' chandeliers. Spacious, well-kept bedrooms — the best attractively refurbished with mahogany units and coordinating fabrics — offer tea-makers, radios and neatly fitted bathrooms. Many have spectacular sea views. Compact bathrooms with

shower attachments are equipped with toilet packs. The hotel is impressively staffed by uniformed personnel. *Amenities* games room, snooker, laundry service, 24-hour lounge service.

■ *Rooms 114*	*Confirm by arrang.*
en suite bath/shower 114	*Last dinner 9.30*
Direct dial Yes	*Parking Ample*
Room TV Yes	*Room service 24 hours*

Chatsworth Hotel
Eastbourne

H **62% £E**
Map 7 B6 East Sussex
Grand Parade BN21 3YR
Eastbourne (0323) 30327
Owner managers Mr & Mrs V. Benzmann
Credit Access, Visa

A traditional seafront hotel where many of the guests are regulars. The lounge and cosy bar have a quiet, gracious appeal. Best bedrooms are spacious front ones with sea views, but all are bright and fresh. *Amenities* table tennis, laundry service, 24-hour lounge service.

■ *Rooms 45*	*'Confirm by 6*
en suite bath/shower 45	*Last dinner 8*
Room phone Yes	*Parking Limited*
Room TV Yes	*Room service Limited*
Closed Jan–Feb	

🍷 indicates a **well-chosen** house wine.

Grand Hotel
Eastbourne

H **86% £B** &
Map 7 B6 East Sussex
King Edward's Parade BN21 4EQ
Eastbourne (0323) 22611. Tlx 87332
Credit Access, Amex, Diners, Visa

An aptly named Victorian hotel standing proudly behind pretty gardens and a swimming pool on the seafront. The interior is equally impressive, with a palatial lounge and restaurant. There are numerous function rooms, two bars and a shopping arcade. Bedrooms vary widely from majestic suites with balconies (some rather old-fashioned) to compact but well-designed rooms furnished to a high standard with flowing drapes and smart darkwood units. Bathrooms are all admirable. *Amenities* garden, indoor & outdoor swimming pools, sauna, solarium, whirlpool bath, gymnasium, beauty salon, hairdressing, putting,

snooker, valeting, laundry service, 24-hour lounge service, shopping arcade, children's playground.

■ *Rooms 164*	*Confirm by 7*
en suite bath/shower 164	*Last dinner 9.30*
Direct dial Yes	*Parking Ample*
Room TV Yes	*Room service 24 hours*

Queen's Hotel   Eastbourne

H **71% £C/D** &
Map 7 B6 East Sussex
Marine Parade BN21 3DY
Eastbourne (0323) 22822. Tlx 877736
Manager Mr George Barlow
Credit Access, Amex, Diners, Visa
   An imposing Victorian hotel on the seafront, near the pier. The elegant high-ceilinged lounge boasts pillars and floor-to-ceiling drapes; the restaurant is equally grand, and there are two bars. The well-equipped bedrooms are spacious, many with sea views, and are being upgraded to a pleasing standard. *Amenities* games room, snooker, laundry service, 24-hour lounge service.

■ *Rooms 108*	*Confirm by 6*
en suite bath/shower 108	*Last dinner 8.45*
Direct dial Yes	*Parking Ample*
Room TV Yes	*Room service 24 hours*

The Wish Tower   Eastbourne

H **60% £D**
Map 7 B6 East Sussex
King Edward's Parade BN21 4EB
Eastbourne (0323) 22676
Credit Access, Amex, Diners, Visa
   This seafront hotel takes its name from a local Martello Tower built to repel the Napoleonic invasion. The modern-style lounge runs the length of the Esplanade frontage. The bedrooms have been recently refurbished with coordinating fabrics and practical units, and 30 of them have been upgraded to superior standard.
Amenities laundry service, 24-hour lounge service.

■ *Rooms 67*	*Confirm by 6*
en suite bath/shower 67	*Last dinner 8.30*
Direct dial Yes	*Parking Difficult*
Room TV Yes	*Room service All day*

▭ is our symbol for an **outstanding** wine list.

Crest Hotel   Eastleigh

H **65% C/D** &
Map 5 D3 Hampshire
Leigh Road, Passfield Avenue SO5 5PG
Southampton (0703) 619700. Tlx 47606
Credit Access, Amex, Diners, Visa
   Handily situated just off the A33 and close to the airport, this modern red-brick hotel features well-equipped bedrooms and bright open public areas, such as the boldly contrasting reception area and cheerful bar. Accommodation varies from standard bedrooms to superior suites. Particularly well-planned rooms for the disabled. *Amenities* in-house movies (charge), laundry service, children's playroom.

■ *Rooms 120*	*Confirm by 6*
en suite bath/shower 120	*Last dinner 9.45*
Direct dial Yes	*Parking Ample*
Room TV Yes	*Room service 24 hours*

Whatley Manor   Easton Grey

HR **75% £C**
Map 4 B2 Wiltshire
Malmesbury SN16 0RB
Malmesbury (0666) 822888. Tlx 449380
Credit Access, Amex, Diners, Visa
   A long driveway off the B4040 between Malmesbury and Easton Grey leads to an imposing manor house with grounds running down to the Avon. Grandly-proportioned public rooms include the foyer, with its log fire, and a panelled lounge with a grand piano and leaded windows. The book-lined bar provides a more intimate atmosphere, and the range of private rooms makes it a popular venue for conferences. Bedrooms in the main house are spacious; those in converted outbuildings are more compact. All have good-quality furnishings and smart modern bathrooms. *Amenities* garden, outdoor swimming pool, sauna, solarium, whirlpool bath, keep-fit equipment, tennis, putting, croquet, game fishing, games room, snooker, laundry service, 24-hour lounge service, helipad.

■ *Rooms 25*	*Confirm by arrang.*
en suite bath/shower 25	*Last dinner 9*
Direct dial Yes	*Parking Ample*
Room TV Yes	*Room service 24 hours*

Whatley Manor Restaurant

A pretty, flower-filled dining room offers views over the garden through leaded windows. Peter Halliday's fixed-price lunch and daily-amended dinner menus offer sound, if a little uninspired, cooking. Typical starter could be melon Marsala, followed by chicken tarragon, escalope of veal, or 'Ecclesiastical Delight' (fillet of lemon sole braised in vermouth with prawns). Finish with Dutch apple flan. There's also a short vegetarian menu and a popular buffet/carvery on Sundays. ▭

■ *Set L from £8.75*	*L 12.30–1.45*
Set D £16	*D 7.30–9*
About £45 for two	*Seats 50 Parties 50*

■ If we recommend meals in a
hotel or inn, a separate entry is
made for its restaurant.

Honours Mill *NEW ENTRY*   Edenbridge

R ♨ ♀ **Map 7 B5** Kent
87 High Street
Edenbridge (0732) 866757
Credit Access, Diners, Visa
   A once derelict mill grinds stylishly back into
action as a most charming and delightful
restaurant. Neville Goodhew and Martin Radmall
are very talented chefs whose set menus show
imaginative thought, tempting at every turn.
Choose with difficulty between starters like
spinach-wrapped fish pâté served warm with a
lovely light butter sauce or a tartlet of foie gras,
sweetbreads and morels. Follow with succulent
breast of chicken with a filling of pistachio nut
mousse or noisettes of lamb accompanied by a
garlic-scented jus. Delicious desserts are usually
fruit-based, and there's a fine cheeseboard from
Androuet of Paris. Skilfully-chosen cellar: note the
very good St Aubin Blanc 'Les Dents de Chien'
1984 from Roux. Traditional Sunday lunch.
Friendly, capable service. ♀ **Well-chosen** ⊖
■ *Set L from £11·75*   *L 12.15–2*
Set D £19·75   *D 7.15–10*
About £48 for two   *Parking Ample*
Seats 38   *Parties 16*
Closed L Sat, D Sun, Mon, Bank Hols & 2 wks Jan

Three Tuns Inn   Eggleston

R ♀ **Map 15 B5** Co. Durham
Nr Barnard Castle
Teesdale (0833) 50289
English cooking
   Christine Dykes' cooking is as honest and
unpretentious as the surroundings at this cosy
little beamed restaurant. Creamy soup and game
pâté are popular starters, while main courses
include pinkly grilled lamb chops, pork chasseur
and simple rainbow trout. Puddings are a great
strength and include a good sherry trifle. The
reasonably-priced wine list includes a good 1985
Fleurie (Beaudet). Traditional Sunday lunch
served. Book a day ahead. ⊖
■ *Set L £8·25*   *L Sun only at 1*
About £25 for two   *D 7.30–9.30*
Seats 14   *Parking Ample*
Closed D Sun, all Mon & 25 Dec

La Bonne Franquette *NEW ENTRY*   Egham

R **Map 5 E2** Surrey
5 High Street
Egham (0784) 39494
French cooking
   David Smart is a dedicated, imaginative chef
who produces a sophisticated menu at this
pleasant restaurant in an old house on the high
street. Quail stuffed with sweetbreads and
spinach, and salmon in a white wine sauce with
basil and tomato are typical delights. Mouthwatering desserts include a superb assiette fraise
garnished with passion fruit and figs.   ⊖
■ *Set L £12·50*   *L noon–1.45*
Set D £20   *D 7–10*
About £58 for two   *Parking Ample*
Closed L Sat & all Bank *Seats 45 Parties 25*
Hols

Great Fosters   Egham

H **70% £D** ♿
Map 5 E2 Surrey
Stroude Road TW20 9UR
Egham (0784) 33822. Tlx 944441
Manager Mr J. E. Baumann
Credit Access, Amex, Diners, Visa
   A magnificent former hunting lodge, dating
back to 1550, Great Fosters is situated in 17 acres
of formal grounds featuring a moat and sunken
rose garden. The outstanding oak-panelled
entrance hall has an ornate plaster ceiling and a
carved Jacobean fireplace. Other public areas
include a comfortable lounge and a beamed bar
with views across the gardens. Best of the
bedrooms are eight spacious period rooms, some
with wall-hung tapestries, two with four-posters.
Other rooms have traditional oak furniture and
attractive part-tiled bathrooms. A conference

centre, with several compact single bedrooms, is
housed in a converted stable block. No dogs.
Amenities garden, outdoor swimming pool,
sauna, tennis, 24-hour lounge service.
■ *Rooms 44*   *Confirm by arrang.*
en suite bath/shower 44 *Last dinner 9.15*
Direct dial Yes   *Parking Ample*
Room TV Yes   *Room service None*

Runnymede Hotel

Egham

H **70% £C/D** *E*
Map 5 E2 Surrey
Windsor Road TW20 0AG
Egham (0784) 36171. Tlx 934900
Manager M. J. O'Dwyer
Credit Access, Amex, Diners, Visa
   Improvements continue to be made at this superbly maintained modern hotel on the banks of the Thames. The Runnymede banquet and conference room has been refurbished, and a spacious bedroom suite, with whirlpool bath, is a handsome addition. Public rooms have fine river views. The accent is on quality furnishings in light and airy surroundings. Bedrooms are pleasantly furnished and well equipped (Executive rooms in a separate wing are more stylish). Spacious well-fitted bathrooms have plenty of shelf space. *Amenities* garden, coarse fishing, in-house

movies (free), laundry service, 24-hour lounge service, helipad.

■ *Rooms* 126	*Confirm by 6*
en suite bath/shower 126	*Last dinner* 9.45
Direct dial Yes	*Parking* Ample
Room TV Yes	*Room service* 24 hours

Yardley Court Hotel

Eltham

See under London Hotels under £60

Lamb Hotel

Ely

H **59% £E**
Map 6 B2 Cambridgeshire
2 Lynn Road CB7 4EJ
Ely (0353) 3574
Credit Access, Amex, Diners, Visa
   The welcome is warm, the public rooms inviting and totally refurbished bedrooms a delight at this admirable establishment. The Fenman bar, with its ship's timbers and brass is popular, and a

similar homely charm pervades the lounge. Colour coordinated bedrooms (2 with four-posters) have modern fittings and facilities.
Amenities laundry service.

■ *Rooms* 32	*Confirm by arrang.*
en suite bath/shower 32	*Last dinner* 9.30
Direct dial Yes	*Parking* Ample
Room TV Yes	*Room service* 24 hours
Closed 25 Dec	

Post House Hotel

Epping

H **62% £C/D**
Map 7 B4 Essex
High Road, Bell Common CM16 4DG
Epping (0378) 73137 Tlx 81617
Credit Access, Amex, Diners, Visa. **LVs**
   A converted coaching inn on the B1393, offering comfortable overnight accommodation in motel blocks. Standard bedrooms have smart darkwood units, tea-makers and well-equipped

bathrooms, while Executive rooms offer, extras like hairdryers. Public areas include a comfortable foyer-lounge and an old-world bar.
Amenities garden, laundry service, 24-hour lounge service, children's playground.

■ *Rooms* 82	*Confirm by 6*
en suite bath/shower 82	*Last dinner* 10.30
Direct dial Yes	*Parking* Ample
Room TV Yes	*Room service* Limited

■ Any person using our name to obtain free hospitality is a fraud. Proprietors, please inform the police and us.

Good Earth

Esher

R **Map 5 E3** Surrey
14 High Street
Esher (0372) 62489
Chinese cooking
Owner manager Robert Cheung
Credit Access, Amex, Diners, Visa
   Best to book at this popular, pleasantly-run Chinese restaurant on the High Street. The menu ranges widely round the various regional cuisines

with enjoyable dishes like Cantonese roast duck, Peking sliced lamb, hot and sour soup from Szechuan, even Malaysian satay. Sizzling dishes include mixed seafood platter with scallops, prawns and squid.

■ *Set L* £11·75	*L* noon–2.30
Set D £11·75	*D* 6–11.30
About £40 *for two*	*Parking* Limited
Seats 68	*Closed* 24–27 Dec

Restaurant Le Pierrot — Esher

R ♃ **Map 5 E3** Surrey
63 High Street
Esher (0372) 63191
French cooking
Credit Access, Amex, Diners, Visa

Chef-patron Jean-Pierre Brichot offers an interesting variety of French dishes in this attractive little restaurant. Croustade of quails' eggs or crab mousse with cucumber could start your meal, followed perhaps by fillet steak vigneronne or sliced breast of duckling with a blackcurrant and cassis sauce. Desserts include honey and lemon pancakes, and there's a good choice of French cheeses. ℗

■ Set L £8·25	L 12.15–2.30
About £44 for two	D 7.15–10.30
Seats 50 Parties 45	Parking Difficult
Closed L Sat, all Sun, Bank Hols & 1 wk Jan	

Chase Hotel — Ettington

HR **66% £D/E**
Map 4 C1 Warwickshire
Banbury Road CV37 7NZ
Stratford-on-Avon (0789) 740000
Owner managers Mr & Mrs D. Cunliffe
Credit Access, Amex, Diners, Visa

The Cunliffes offer a warm welcome to their Victorian Gothic hotel which retains many marvellous original features. Bedrooms are delightful and have fine views; extras include home-made biscuits and tea/coffee-makers. Excellent housekeeping throughout. No children under five. Amenities garden, croquet.

■ Rooms 11	Confirm by arrang.
en suite bath/shower 11	Last dinner 9
Direct dial Yes	Parking Ample
Room TV Yes	Room service All day
Closed 24 Dec–mid Jan	

Restaurant ⌂ ♃

English cooking
A simple yet elegant restaurant in which to enjoy David Cunliffe's menus, which mix traditional with more original dishes, all cooked to a dependable high standard showing both knowledge and skill, and using best-quality ingredients. Start with suprême of pigeon salad with brandy oranges; move on to duck with grapes, pine kernels and Beaume de Venise. Delicious sweets and a first-rate choice of interesting cheeses.
♀ Well-chosen ℗

■ Set L £9·95	L 12.30–2,
Set D from £12·50	Sun 12.30–1.30
About £44 for two	D 7.30–9
Seats 65 Parties 65	Closed L Sat, D Sun to
non-residents & 24 Dec–mid Jan	

Summer Lodge — Evershot

HR **71% £C/D** ᕁ
Map 4 B4 Dorset
Summer Lane DT2 0JR
Evershot (093 583) 666
Owner managers Margaret and Nigel Corbett
Credit Access, Visa

A really special country house hotel, with the warmth of the Corbetts' hospitality one of its unique features. Their staff, too, help convey the feeling that you're staying with old friends, with a welcoming cup of tea – the first of many nice touches. Day rooms, including a sunny lounge and a room for reading or watching television, are notable for their combination of elegance and homely charm, their deep-cushioned invitations to relax and their marvellous flower arrangements. Bedrooms are very pretty and cosy, immaculately kept and attractively furnished in pine and bamboo; all have splendid carpeted bathrooms. Wonderful breakfasts. No children under 8. Amenities garden, outdoor swimming pool, tennis, croquet, games room, laundry service.

■ Rooms 12	Confirm by arrang.
en suite bath/shower 12	Last dinner 8
Direct dial Yes	Parking Ample
Room TV No	Room service All day
Closed 1 mth Dec–Jan	

Summer Lodge Restaurant ♃ ᕁ

Drinks and canapés in the lounge precede dinner, which starts promptly at 8 in the quietly elegant dining room (covers are limited so non-residents should book). Margaret Corbett's cooking is most enjoyable, and her no-choice menu offers daily-changing delights like curried vegetable soup, dressed crab and roast lamb stuffed with chopped walnuts and chestnuts. Vegetables are prepared to perfection, there's a selection of prime English cheeses and the two puds always include a fresh fruit salad. Finally, it's back to the lounge for excellent coffee with petits fours. Nigel Corbett is the perfect host.
♀ Well-chosen ℗

■ Set L £8·50	L 12.30–1.30
Set D £15	D at 8
About £40 for two	Seats 28
Closed 1 mth Dec–Jan	

New Mill *NEW ENTRY*   Eversley

R **Map 5 D2** Hampshire
New Mill Road
Eversley (0734) 732277
Credit Access, Amex, Diners, Visa

Signposted down a country lane off the A327, this atmospheric restaurant is set in a lovingly restored water mill. Cooking is capable without reaching the heights, and a varied menu runs from terrines and smoked meats to lettuce-

wrapped turbot baked in puff pastry and beef fillet with a celeriac sauce. Helpful, professional service. Good classic cellar and fine wines by the glass (Cruvinet machine).

🍷 Well-chosen ⊖
■ *Set L £13·50*   *L 12–2*
About £45 for two   *D 7–10*
Seats 80 Parties 60   *Parking Ample*
Closed L Mon & Sat, D Sun, & 1st 2 wks Jan

Evesham Hotel   Evesham

H **62% £D**
Map 4 C1 Hereford & Worcester
Cooper's Lane, Off Waterside WR11 6DA
Evesham (0386) 49111. Tlx 339342
Owner managers Jenkinson family
Credit Access, Amex, Diners, Visa

A Tudor manor house that was modernised in 1810, this friendly, family-run hotel stands in its own attractive grounds. There's an elegant yet

homely feel to the comfortably furnished lounge and bar. Well-kept bedrooms offer a long list of extras. *Amenities* garden, putting, croquet, children's play area, laundry service.
■ *Rooms 34*
en suite bath/shower 34   *Last dinner 9.30*
Room phone Yes   *Parking Ample*
Room TV Yes   *Room service All day*
Closed 25–26 Dec

■ Our inspectors are our full-
time employees; they are
professionally trained by us.

Wild Duck Inn   Ewen

I **£E**
Map 4 C2 Gloucestershire
Nr Cirencester GL7 6BY
Kemble (028 577) 364
Credit Access, Amex, Diners, Visa

Both Cirencester and Kemble are within easy reach of this rambling 16th-century inn in peaceful surroundings. Flagstones and beams are found in the Post Horn Bar, and an Elizabethan fireplace in

the cosy lounge. Bedrooms in a modern extension have functional, contemporary furnishings and smart bathrooms. Two rooms have luxurious four-posters. Excellent housekeeping by friendly staff. *Amenities* garden.
■ *Rooms 10*   *Confirm by arrang.*
en suite bath/shower 10   *Last dinner 9.45*
Direct dial Yes   *Parking Ample*
Room TV Yes   *Room service All day*

Buckerell Lodge Crest Hotel   Exeter

H **66% £C/D** ⅙
Map 3 D2 Devon
Topsham Road EX2 4SQ
Exeter (0392) 52451. Tlx 42410
Credit Access, Amex, Diners, Visa. LVs

A greatly extended and modernised Regency house, a hotel since 1882 and one of the original Crests. It's a comfortable, well-run place, with smart day rooms that give onto the garden.

Bedrooms, some beginning to look just a little tired, are standard or executive, the latter having extras like hairdryers and bathrobes. Staff are pleasant and helpful. *Amenities* garden, putting, croquet, laundry service.
■ *Rooms 54*   *Confirm by arrang.*
en suite bath/shower 54   *Last dinner 9.45*
Direct dial Yes   *Parking Ample*
Room TV Yes   *Room service 24 hours*

Rougemont Hotel   Exeter

H **62% £D/E**
Map 3 D2 Devon
Queen Street EX4 3SP
Exeter (0392) 54982. Tlx 42455
Manager David Reynolds
Credit Access, Amex, Diners, Visa. LVs

A substantial Victorian building in a prominent position opposite Central Station. The foyer and lounge are quite impressive, with classical pillars,

moulded ceilings and chandeliers. Some of the bedrooms have been stylishly modernised, and the rest would benefit from similar upgrading. *Amenities* hairdressing, laundry service, 24-hour lounge service. ⊖
■ *Rooms 68*   *Confirm by arrang.*
en suite bath/shower 68   *Last dinner 9.30*
Direct dial Yes   *Parking Difficult*
Room TV Yes   *Room service 24 hours*

White Hart Hotel   Exeter

H **60% £D/E**
Map 3 D2 Devon
South Street EX1 1EE
Exeter (0392) 79897. Tlx 42521
Owner manager Mr B. Wilkinson
Credit Access, Amex, Diners, Visa
This former coaching inn still has a warmly welcoming air. Gleaming brasses add to the charm of the beamed bars, and there are several

inviting lounges. Bedrooms in the modern extension are neat and cheerful; main-house rooms are more traditional in appeal. *Amenities* garden, laundry service, 24-hour lounge service.

■ *Rooms* 59	*Confirm by* 6
en suite bath/shower 59	*Last dinner* 9.45
Direct dial Yes	*Parking* Ample
Room TV Yes	*Room service* 24 hours
Closed 3 days Xmas	

Crown Hotel   Exford

H **62% £D/E**
Map 3 E3 Somerset
Nr Minehead TA24 7PP
Exford (064 383) 554
Owner managers John & Marjorie Millward
Credit Access, Amex, Visa
Guests can hire horses for hunting or hacking – or stable their own – at this 17th-century Exmoor hotel. Shooting and fishing can also be arranged,

so it's something of a centre for sportsmen. The whole place is comfortable and well kept, from the nice old rustic bar to the prettily and individually furnished bedrooms. *Amenities* garden, riding, stabling, laundry service.

■ *Rooms* 18	*Confirm by* 5.30
en suite bath/shower 16	*Last dinner* 9
Direct dial Yes	*Parking* Ample
Room TV Yes	*Room service* None

Imperial Hotel   Exmouth

H **60% £C/D**
Map 3 E3 Devon
The Esplanade EX8 2SW
Exmouth (0395) 274761
Credit Access, Amex, Diners, Visa. **LVs**
An excellent place to take the kids this holiday hotel set in spacious grounds looking out to sea, with both lounge and bar opening on to a terrace. Bedrooms have fitted units and tea-makers. Ten

rooms have recently been upgraded.
Amenities garden, outdoor swimming pool, sauna, solarium, tennis, games room, laundry service, 24 hour lounge service, children's play area.

■ *Rooms* 58	*Confirm by* 6
en suite bath/shower 58	*Last dinner* 9
Room phone Yes	*Parking* Ample
Room TV Yes	*Room service* All day

■ We welcome complaints and bona fide recommendations on the tear-out pages for readers' comments. They are followed up by our professional team. Please also complain to the management instantly.

Bull Hotel   Fairford

H **60% £F**
Map 4 C2 Gloucestershire
Market Place GL7 4AA
Cirencester (0285) 712535
Owner manager Mr M. Klein
Credit Access, Amex, Diners, Visa
Private fishing on the river Coln is just one of the attractions of this centuries-old Cotswold-stone inn. Low beams, panelling and two fine

fireplaces give the spacious bar a traditional air and the snug little lounge is full of character. Bedrooms are pretty, with sloping ceilings. No dogs. *Amenities* garden, game fishing, laundry service.

■ *Rooms* 21	*Confirm by* arrang.
en suite bath/shower 14	*Last dinner* 9.30
Room phone No	*Parking* Ample
Room TV Yes	*Room service* All day

Hyperion House Hotel *NEW ENTRY*   Fairford

H **62% £E**
Map 4 C2 Gloucestershire
London Street GL7 4AH
Cirencester (0285) 712349
Owner managers Peter & Gill Hands
Credit Access, Amex, Diners, Visa
Named after the 1933 Derby winner, this Cotswold stone hotel is benefiting from the enthusiasm of its friendly young owners. Over half

the bedrooms have been stylishly transformed with smart pine furnishings, contemporary prints and good quality, easy-on-the-eye fabrics. Public areas like the little stone-walled lounge are cosily traditional. *Amenities* garden, laundry service.

■ *Rooms* 20	*Confirm by* 6
en suite bath/shower 20	*Last dinner* 9.30
Direct dial Yes	*Parking* Ample
Room TV Yes	*Room service* Limited

Portledge Hotel
Fairy Cross

H **64% £D/E**
Map 2 C2 Devon
Nr Bideford EX39 5BX
Hemscross (02375) 262
Manager Mr Wragge-Morley
Credit Access, Amex, Diners, Visa
 The house dates from the 11th century, with
bits added in the 16th and 18th. Family portraits
and antiques grace the day rooms, and good solid

furnishings invest the spacious bedrooms with an
air of old-fashioned comfort; all overlook lovely
parkland. No children under five.
Amenities garden, indoor swimming pool, tennis,
croquet, private beach, games room.

■ *Rooms* 30	*Confirm by* 6
en suite bath/shower 30	*Last dinner* 8.45
Direct dial Yes	*Parking* Ample
Room TV Yes	*Room service* Limited

■ Changes in data may occur in
establishments after the Guide
goes to press. Prices should be taken
as indications rather than firm quotes.

Bay Hotel
Falmouth

H **58% £D/E**
Map 2 B4 Cornwall
Seafront TR11 4NU
Falmouth (0326) 312094
Manager Mr G. E. Fields
 Traditional seaside hotel with an ornate
Victorian facade incorporating an attractive sun
terrace (part of the enormous bar). Simply

furnished bedrooms are light and spacious, with
large carpeted bathrooms. Guests may use the
facilities of the nearby Falmouth Hotel. *Amenities*
garden, sauna, solarium, 24-hour lounge service.

■ *Rooms* 36	*Confirm by* arrang.
en suite bath/shower 36	*Last dinner* 9.30
Direct dial Yes	*Parking* Ample
Room TV Yes	*Room service* 24 hours
Closed Nov–Easter	

Falmouth Hotel
Falmouth

H **61% £C/D**
Map 2 B4 Cornwall
Castle Beach TR11 4NZ
Falmouth (0326) 312671. Tlx 45262
Manager Mr G. E. Fields
Credit Access, Amex, Diners, Visa
 Public rooms in this fine Victorian hotel offer
sweeping sea views. Refurbished bedrooms
(about half) have attractive darkwood furnishings

and chintzy fabrics; others keep their plainer
lightwood units. *Amenities* garden, outdoor
swimming pool, putting, games room, snooker,
in-house movies (free), laundry service.

■ *Rooms* 73	*Confirm by* 6
en suite bath/shower 73	*Last dinner* 9.30
Direct dial Yes	*Parking* Ample
Room TV Yes	*Room service* 24 hours
Closed Xmas	

Greenbank Hotel
Falmouth

H **67% £D/E**
Map 2 B4 Cornwall
Harbourside TR11 2SR
Falmouth (0326) 312440. Tlx 45240
Owner manager Mr Gebhard
Credit Access, Amex, Diners, Visa
 Prominently placed on the harbourside with its
own quay, a welcoming hotel with picture-
windowed public areas offering fine views.

Bedrooms are pleasant; larger rooms offer sitting
areas. *Amenities* garden, solarium, sea fishing,
hairdressing, beauty salon, 24-hour laundry
service, mooring.

■ *Rooms* 43	*Confirm by* 6
en suite bath/shower 42	*Last dinner* 9.45
Direct dial Yes	*Parking* Ample
Room TV Yes	*Room service* 24 hours
Closed 2 wks Xmas	

Pandora Inn *NEW ENTRY*
Falmouth

R **Map 2 B4** Cornwall
Restronguet Passage, Nr Mylor Bridge
Falmouth (0326) 72678
Owner managers Roger & Helen Hough
Credit Access, Visa
 Follow signs from the A39 to Mylor, then to
Restronguet, turning into Restronguet Passage.
This is a lovely whitewashed thatched pub with a
first-floor restaurant decked with fresh flowers.

Candlelit dinners feature local fish and shellfish,
also meat dishes like herby rack of lamb with
raspberry sauce. Among the sweets, a
sensational (and gigantic) lemon meringue pie.
Cold buffet only at lunchtime. Decent wines.

♥ Well-chosen ⊖

■ *About £35 for two*	*L* 12–2
Seats 48 *Parties* 10	*D* 7.30–10
Closed Sun & 26 Dec	*Parking* Ample

Red Lion Hotel *NEW ENTRY* Fareham

I £D/E
Map 5 D4 Hampshire
East Street PO16 0BP
Fareham (0329) 822640. Tlx 86204
Credit Access, Amex, Diners, Visa
 Leave the M27 at junction 11 and you'll easily find this former coaching inn, used at one time as a magistrates' court. Beams, panelling and brickwork create an old-fashioned pub feel in the

day rooms, while bedrooms combine traditional furnishings with modern accessories like trouser presses, hairdryers and remote-control TVs. Well-fitted bathrooms. No dogs. *Amenities* in-house movies (free), laundry service.

■ *Rooms 33*	*Confirm by 7*
en suite bath/shower 33	*Last dinner 10*
Direct dial Yes	*Parking Ample*
Room TV Yes	*Room service 24 hours*

Sinclairs Faringdon

R Map 4 C2 Oxfordshire
6 Market Place
Faringdon (0367) 20945
English cooking
Owner manager Anne Sawyer
Credit Access, Amex, Diners, Visa
 Sound, uncomplicated English cooking is the stock in trade of this spacious but modestly appointed town-centre restaurant. Start perhaps

with curried parsnip soup or herby sautéed mushrooms and move on to pink trout, a mixed grill, rabbit casserole or pork tenderloin in a cider cream sauce. Simple sweets include apple pie served with *real* custard. ☺

■ *About £28 for two*	*D only 7–9.30,*
Seats 34	*Fri & Sat 7–10*
Parties 26	*Parking Limited*
Closed Sun, Mon, D 25 Dec & all 26–31 Dec	

■ For a discount on next year's guide, see Offer for Answers.

Queen's Hotel *NEW ENTRY* Farnborough

H 62% £D
Map 5 E3 Hampshire
Lynchford Road GU14 6AZ
Farnborough (0252) 545051. Tlx 859637
Credit Access, Amex, Diners, Visa
 Located on the A325, a rather nice red-brick Edwardian building houses the lobby, lounge bar and coffee shop of this hotel. Here too is perhaps the pick of the accommodation, 28 lofty rooms with high ceilings, soft, soothing decor and decent darkwood furnishing. All other rooms, in modern blocks, have been refurbished to a similar standard, or are due to be by the end of 1987.

Remote-control TVs and video-recorders are installed in all rooms, with additional features in the 16 Club Rooms. There's a leisure complex and extensive conference facilities.
Amenities indoor swimming pool, sauna, solarium, whirlpool bath, keep-fit equipment, in-house movies (charge), laundry service, coffee shop (9am–11pm), 24-hour lounge service.

■ *Rooms 110*	*Confirm by 6*
en suite bath/shower 110	*Last dinner 10*
Direct dial Yes	*Parking Ample*
Room TV Yes	*Room service None*

Bishop's Table Hotel Farnham

H 60% £D/E
Map 5 E3 Surrey
27 West Street GU9 7DR
Farnham (0252) 710222
Credit Access, Amex, Diners, Visa. **LVs**
 Dating back to the 18th century, this cosy little hotel was once a training school for the clergy. Bedrooms in the main house have an individual, traditional appeal, while those in the annexe are

more modern. Day rooms include a pleasant cane-furnished lounge that overlooks the walled garden. Among recent improvements are new carpets in the corridors and new tiles in some bathrooms. *Amenities* garden.

■ *Rooms 16*	*Confirm by arrang.*
en suite bath/shower 14	*Last dinner 9.30*
Room phone Yes	*Parking Difficult*
Room TV Yes	*Room service None*

Bush Hotel Farnham

H 63% £D
Map 5 E3 Surrey
The Borough GU9 7NN
Farnham (0252) 715237. Tlx 858764
Credit Access, Amex, Diners, Visa. **LVs**
 Parts of this ivy-clad building date back to the 17th century, including beams in the bar and frescoes in the panelled lounge. Most of the bedrooms are in a modern wing, and all rooms

have remote-control TVs and up-to-date bathrooms. Club rooms get lots of extras, including trouser presses, teletext and toiletries. *Amenities* garden, laundry service, 24-hour lounge service, coffee shop (9.30am–10pm)

■ *Rooms 65*	*Confirm by 6*
en suite bath/shower 65	*Last dinner 9.30*
Direct dial Yes	*Parking Ample*
Room TV Yes	*Room service None*

Trevena House Hotel Farnham

H **60% £E**
Map 5 E3 Surrey
Alton Road GU1D 5ER
Farnham (0252) 716908
Owner manager Mr Norman Levitt
Credit Access, Amex, Diners, Visa
Five acres of grounds surround this Victorian Gothic hotel off the A31. A lofty hall is furnished with easy chairs and there is also a cosy lounge bar. Well-kept bedrooms have simple built-in units and neat and modern bath/shower rooms. No dogs. *Amenities* garden, outdoor swimming pool, tennis, laundry service.

■ *Rooms* 20	*Confirm by arrang.*
en suite bath/shower 20	*Last dinner* 9.15
Direct dial Yes	*Parking* Ample
Room TV Yes	*Room service* Limited
Closed 2 wks Xmas	

Old Parsonage Farrington-Gurney

RR ♔ ♧ **Map 4 B3** Avon
Nr Bristol BS18 5UB
Temple Cloud (0761) 52211
The charming Gofton-Watsons restored a 1680 manor house and turned it into a very civilised restaurant with rooms. Marina is a cook with great natural talent whose menus offer simple, sound delights like spinach and cottage cheese pancakes, salmon with hollandaise and grilled noisettes of lamb with a delicious mixed herb butter. Vegetables are garden-fresh, and puddings include light, crumbly coffee meringues and usually something hot like Yorkshire curd cheese tart. Traditional Sunday lunch. Concise, carefully selected wine list.
♥ Well-chosen ℮

■ *Set L* Sun £8.50	*L* 12.30–2
About £30 for two	*D* 7–9.30
Seats 26 *Parties* 12	*Parking* Ample
Closed D Sun, all Mon, Bank Hols, 1 wk Xmas & 3 wks Sept	

Bedrooms £E

Rooms 2	*With bath/shower* 0

The two bedrooms have sturdily traditional furnishings, and the bathroom and homely TV lounge are kept in sparkling order. No dogs.

String of Horses Faugh

I **£E**
Map 13 D4 Cumbria
Heads Nook, Nr Carlisle CA4 9EG
Hayton (022 870) 297
Owner managers Anne & Eric Tasker
Credit Access, Amex, Diners, Visa
Old-world charm is only one feature of this atmospheric inn. Rustic beamed bars offer a sharp contrast to flamboyant bedrooms with Hollywood-style bathrooms. *Amenities* garden, outdoor swimming pool, sauna, solarium, whirlpool bath, keep-fit equipment, in-house movies (free), pool table, laundry service.

■ *Rooms* 13	*Confirm by arrang.*
en suite bath/shower 13	*Last dinner* 10
Direct dial Yes	*Parking* Ample
Room TV Yes	*Room service* All day
Closed 25 & 26 Dec.	

■ We publish annually, so make sure you use the current edition. It's worth it!

Read's Faversham

R ♧ & **Map 7 C5** Kent
Painter's Forstal
Faversham (0795) 535344
French cooking
Credit Amex, Diners, Visa
David & Rona Pitchford converted this former village store into a most stylish and civilised restaurant decorated in salmon pink and chocolate brown. David Pitchford is a very fine chef, and his menus are so imaginative and beguiling that ordering can be quite a problem. Classic skills and modern flair are evident in superb dishes like braised marinated oxtail; fruits de mer en brioche with a dreamy Barsac-flavoured sauce; roulade of partridge with a port and redcurrant sauce and sharply dressed yet completely harmonious salad garnish. Only the sweets are not starworthy. There's a lovely wine list with some great old burgundies, notably from Leroy. Waitresses, a team of bright, knowledgeable local girls, provide excellent service.
◁ Outstanding ♥ Well-chosen ℮

■ *Set L from* £8.50	*L* 12–2
About £42 for two	*D* 7–10
Seats 36	*Parking* Ample
Closed Sun, 26 Dec & 1 Jan	

Brandshatch Place   Fawkham

HR 68% £C &
Map 7 B5 Kent DA3 8NQ
Ash Green (0474) 872239
Owner manager Mel Taylor
Credit Access, Amex, Diners, Visa
  Extensive grounds ensure peace and privacy at this extended Georgian mansion. Day rooms, particularly the bar/library, are very comfortable and bedrooms are in pleasantly uncluttered style. *Amenities* garden, indoor swimming pool, sauna, solarium, whirlpool bath, gymnasium, tennis, squash, badminton, snooker, laundry service, children's play area.

■ *Rooms* 29	*Confirm by arrang.*
en suite bath/shower 29	*Last dinner* 9.30
Direct dial Yes	*Parking* Ample
Room TV Yes	*Room service* All day
Closed 24–30 Dec	

Restaurant ♛

Colin Liddy's dishes are as attractive and elegant as the surroundings. Menus change monthly and usually include a fine, flavourful terrine such as venison and hare with beetroot and juniper. Other dishes are in modern mode, typified by marinaded fresh salmon with lime juice and basil, breast of guinea fowl filled with a mousse of cèpes served on Madeira and thyme sauce and fillet of beef with a snail tartlet and Meaux mustard. Good sweets include fruit tarts and home-made ices. English cheeses. Vegetarian menu on request. The wine list has good clarets and burgundies.
🍷 **Well-chosen** ⊖

■ *About £55 for two*	*L 12–2*
Seats 50 Parties 150	*D 7–9.30*
Closed 24–30 Dec	

Brook Hotel *NEW ENTRY*   Felixstowe

H 66% £D
Map 6 D3 Suffolk
Orwell Road 1P11 7PF
Felixstowe (0394) 278441. Tlx 987674
Credit Access, Amex, Diners, Visa
  A hotel which has recently undergone a major transformation, resulting in modern, fresh interiors with designer fabrics. Public areas include a spacious, comfortable foyer/lounge and a homely

bar. Bedrooms vary in size but all have antique-style pine furniture, hairdryers, fruit, trouser presses, remote-control TV and radio. Friendly, enthusiastic staff. No dogs. *Amenities* terrace, laundry service.

■ *Rooms* 25	*Confirm by noon*
en suite bath/shower 25	*Last dinner* 9.30
Direct dial Yes	*Parking* Ample
Room TV Yes	*Room service* 24 hours

Orwell Moat House   Felixstowe

H 70% £D/E
Map 6 D3 Suffolk
Hamilton Road IP11 7DX
Felixstowe (0394) 285511
Manager Mr N. A. Button
Credit Access, Amex, Diners, Visa
  Ornate painted ceilings and deep seating are features of the elegant day rooms at this distinctively gabled red-brick hotel. The comfortably appointed lounge is charmingly traditional in character, and there's a choice of two bars – one in light, airy garden style, the other a plush cocktail bar – plus a large banqueting suite. Roomy, attractively decorated bedrooms (including five luxurious suites) have smart cane furniture and pretty coordinated floral fabrics. Facilities include radios and direct-dial telephones, as well as good-sized modern

bathrooms (some with bidets).
Amenities garden, hairdressing, sea fishing, laundry service, 24-hour lounge service.

■ *Rooms* 58	*Confirm by arrang.*
en suite bath/shower 58	*Last dinner* 9.45
Direct dial Yes	*Parking* Ample
Room TV Yes	*Room service* 24 hours

Dormy Hotel   Ferndown

H 70% £B/C
Map 4 C4 Dorset
New Road BH22 8ES

Ferndown (0202) 872121. Tlx 418301
Manager Derek Silk
Credit Access, Amex, Diners, Visa
  With fifteen golf courses in the immediate vicinity, this carefully maintained hotel suits golfers to a tee. Opportunities for leisure are excellent and very good conference facilities add another dimension. Public rooms are attractively furnished with easy chairs and antiques and there are three bars; not surprisingly, one has a golfing theme and is aptly decorated in greens. Bedrooms – traditional in the main building, modern in the new blocks – include five suites.

Bathrooms are light and bright.
Amenities garden, indoor swimming pool, sauna, solarium, whirlpool bath, gymnasium, tennis, squash, golf practice nets, putting, games room, snooker, pool table, laundry service, coffee shop

(10am–10pm), 24-hour lounge service.

■ *Rooms* 140	*Confirm by arrang.*
en suite bath/shower 140	*Last dinner 9.30*
Direct dial Yes	*Parking Ample*
Room TV Yes	*Room service 24 hours*

Findon Manor *NEW ENTRY* Findon

HR **62% £D/E**
Map 5 E4 West Sussex
High Street BN14 0TA
Findon (090 671) 2733. Tlx 879877
Owner managers Andrew & Susan Tyrie
Credit Access, Amex, Diners, Visa

Guests are given a warm welcome at this former rectory built of brick and flint and dating back to the late 16th century. Comfortable, well-equipped bedrooms; larger rooms have four-posters, whirlpool baths and garden views. Public rooms include a cosy lounge and pubby bar.
Amenities garden, croquet, laundry service.

■ *Rooms* 9	*Confirm by arrang.*
en suite bath/shower 9	*Last dinner 9.15*
Direct dial Yes	*Parking Ample*
Room TV Yes	*Room service All day*
Closed 1 wk Xmas	

Findon Manor Restaurant &

David Colwell heads a talented team at this airy restaurant overlooking the pretty walled garden. Cooking is modern and beautifully presented, saucing is adept and sweets, though unsensational, are sound. A typical meal might start with a deliciously light feuilleté of ham and leeks, continue with tender, mushroom-topped noisettes of lamb on a minty hollandaise, and conclude with pecan pie. Carefully cooked vegetables. Full menu available in the bar when the restaurant is closed. Traditional Sunday ⊖ lunch.

■ *Set L £9*	*L 12–2*
About £36 for two	*D 7–9.15*
Seats 35	*Parties 50*
Closed L Mon & Sat, D Sun & 1 wk Xmas	

Flitwick Manor Flitwick

HR **74% £B/C** &
Map 5 E1 Bedfordshire
Church Road MK45 1AE
Flitwick (0525) 712242. Tlx 825562
Owner manager Somerset Moore
Credit Access, Amex, Diners, Visa

An avenue of tall limes leads up to this fine country house set in 50 acres of lovely grounds that include a pond and a grotto folly. Antiques and old oils grace the public rooms, which include a flagstoned entrance hall and a panelled bar. Good-sized bedrooms, boldly decorated and splendidly furnished, are provided with everything from books and magazines to hairdryers and clock radios, with a no less thoughtful range of extras in the bath/shower rooms. A new lounge and seven additional bedrooms, most with four-

posters, one a suite with its own roof garden, were due to come on line after we went to press. No dogs. *Amenities* garden, tennis, croquet, game fishing, bicycles, laundry service, helipad.

■ *Rooms* 8	*Confirm by arrang.*
en suite bath/shower 8	*Last dinner 9.30*
Direct dial Yes	*Parking Ample*
Room TV Yes	*Room service All day*
Closed 4 days Xmas	

Flitwick Manor Restaurant ⊌ &

Geoffrey Welch has recently returned to cook here, and makes a very good job of it. His menus lean heavily towards seafood, with dishes ranging from creamy mussel soup and Helford native oysters to lobster Nantua and lettuce-wrapped sea bass. Also a few meat dishes, plus choices for vegetarians. Excellent burgundies and some lovely clarets. Service is pleasant and friendly, if sometimes a little haphazard.
♀ Well-chosen ⊖

■ *Set L from £11·50*	*L 12–2*
Set D from £11·50	*D 7.30–9.30*
About £60 for two	*Seats 55 Parties 16*
Closed D Sun & 4 days Xmas	

Burlington Hotel Folkestone

H **60% £E**
Map 7 C5 Kent
Earls Avenue CT20 2HR
Folkestone (0303) 55301. Tlx 966389
Credit Access, Amex, Diners, Visa

A sturdy Victorian building near the seafront. The large lounge has a comfortable feel, and from it you can see a spectacular stained glass window over the staircase. Simply appointed bedrooms

vary in size and shape. Repainting has given them a fresh, cheerful look, but attention is needed to worn carpets and creaking floorboards. Breakfasts could also be improved.
Amenities garden, putting, laundry service.

■ *Rooms* 59	*Confirm by 6*
en suite bath/shower 59	*Last dinner 9.30*
Room phone Yes	*Parking Ample*
Room TV Yes	*Room service 24 hours*

Clifton Hotel   Folkestone

H **59%** **£D/E**
Map 7 C5 Kent
The Leas CT20 2EB
Folkestone (0303) 41231
Owner manager Peter Hail
Credit Access, Amex, Diners, Visa
   On a cliff top overlooking gardens and sea, this
hotel offers pleasant, comfortable accommoda-
tion. Bedrooms are all neatly maintained and

mostly of quite a good size. Warmly decorated
day rooms in traditional style include an inviting
bar and a bay-windowed lounge with Channel
views. *Amenities* garden, solarium, games rooms,
laundry service, 24-hour lounge service.

■ *Rooms* 58	*Confirm by 6*
en suite bath/shower 46	*Last dinner 8.45*
Direct dial Yes	*Parking* Limited
Room TV Yes	*Room service* 24 hours

Emilio's Restaurant Portofino   Folkestone

R � **Map 7 C5** Kent
124a Sandgate Road
Folkestone (0303) 55762
Italian cooking
Owner manager Mr Emilio Bevilacqua
Credit Access, Amex, Diners, Visa
   All the essentials are right at this pleasantly old-
fashioned, long-established Italian restaurant.
There are few surprises on the menu, but quality

ingredients are well prepared, and regular
favourites are supplemented by daily specials like
mussel soup and sea bass with fennel. Good
sweets include an excellent zabaglione. ℮

■ *Set L* £6·50	*L 12–2.15*
About £33 for two	*D 6–10.30, Sun 6–9.30*
Seats 55	*Parking* Difficult
Closed Mon, also Tues after Bank Hols & 25–27 Dec	

Paul's   Folkestone

R ⅋ ⅏ **Map 7 C5** Kent
2a Bouverie Road West
Folkestone (0303) 59697
Credit Access, Visa
   Chef-patron Paul Hagger's comfortable,
relaxed restaurant is a clever conversion of a
modern house. Two light, airy rooms offer ample
space for enjoying tasty dishes like hare lasagne,
sautéed lamb with lightly curried, creamy peach

chutney or lovely fresh brill poached in cream with
shrimps, prawns, sherry and smoked salmon
(cream is a favourite ingredient!). Penny Hagger
produces a trolleyload of super sweets. ℮

■ *About £32 for two*	*L 12.30–2*
Seats 44	*D 7.30–9.30*
Parties 55	*Parking* Limited
Closed Sun, Bank Hols, 2 wks Xmas, 1 wk winter & 2 wks summer	

La Tavernetta   Folkestone

R ⅋ **Map 7 C5** Kent
Leaside Ct, Clifton Gdns
Folkestone (0303) 54955
Italian cooking
Owner managers Mr R. Bocchi & Mr F. Puricelli
Credit Access, Amex, Diners, Visa
   A spacious and comfortable restaurant near the
promenade offering a friendly Italian welcome.
There is a good choice of acceptably cooked

traditional favourites such as lasagne, spaghetti
bolognese and saltimbocca, along with daily
specials which may include osso buco, pheasant
with cognac or fresh salmon. Enjoyable sweets
are crêpes suzette and zabaglione. Good coffee. ℮

■ *Set L* £6·60	*L 12.30–2.30*
About £35 for two	*D 6–10.30*
Seats 55 *Parties* 25	*Parking* Limited
Closed Sun & Bank Hols	

■ Our inspectors never book in the
   name of Egon Ronay's Guides;
   they disclose their identity only
   after paying their bills.

Fossebridge Inn *NEW ENTRY*   Fossebridge

I **£E**
Map 4 C2 Gloucestershire
Nr Cheltenham GL54 3JS
Fossebridge (028 572) 721
Owner managers Hugh & Suzanne Roberts
Credit Access, Amex, Diners, Visa. **LVs**
   A handsome creeper-covered inn standing in
extensive grounds by the river Coln. The oldest
part is the splendid 15th-century bar with its stone

walls, oak beams and inglenooks; there's also a
very homely drawing room. Bedrooms feature
good-quality freestanding furniture, fresh flowers
and ornaments, plus remote-control TVs.
Excellent breakfast. *Amenities* garden.

■ *Rooms* 9	*Confirm by 6*
en suite bath/shower 9	*Last dinner* 9.30
Direct dial Yes	*Parking* Ample
Room TV Yes	*Room service* All day

Fradley Arms Hotel *NEW ENTRY* — Fradley

I £E/F
Map 10 C3 Staffordshire
Nr Lichfield WS13 8RD
Burton-on-Trent (0283) 790186
Owner manager Mr R. K. Taylor
Credit Access, Amex, Diners, Visa

The owner and his family are friendly and enthusiastic, making their roadside inn a very pleasant spot to pause. Bedrooms are neat and comfortable, and the bathrooms are equally well kept. A small, cosy residents' lounge overlooks the garden, and there's an inviting bar with lots of beams. ***Amenities*** garden, laundry service, children's play area.

■ ***Rooms*** *6*	***Confirm by*** *7*
en suite bath/shower *6*	***Last dinner*** *10*
Direct dial *Yes*	***Parking*** *Ample*
Room TV *Yes*	***Room service*** *Limited*

Crown Hotel — Framlingham

H 59% £C/D
Map 6 D2 Suffolk
Market Hill IP13 9AN
Framlingham (0728) 723521
Credit Access, Amex, Diners, Visa. **LVs**

There's a warm, welcoming feel about this pleasant little town-centre hotel, which dates back in parts to the 16th century. Tudor wattle and daub is a feature of the comfortable bar, and the foyer-lounge has ample comfortable seating. Period or antique furnishings enhance the traditional appeal of good-sized bedrooms, all of which offer tea-makers. Smart, modern bathrooms. ***Amenities*** garden, laundry service.

■ ***Rooms*** *15*	***Confirm by*** *6*
en suite bath/shower *9*	***Last dinner*** *9.15*
Room phone *Yes*	***Parking*** *Ample*
Room TV *Yes*	***Room service*** *Limited*

Homewood Park — Freshford

HR 80% £B
Map 4 B3 Avon
Nr Bath BA3 6BB
Limpley Stoke (022 122) 3731. Tlx 444937
Owner managers Stephen & Penny Ross
Credit Access, Amex, Diners, Visa

On the A36 five miles south of Bath, this lovely country house stands in ten acres of gardens and woodland adjoining the 13th-century ruin of Hinton Priory. Stephen and Penny Ross are wonderfully caring hosts and the elegant day rooms – which include a gracefully proportioned lounge and inviting bar – are not only exquisitely furnished and decorated but filled with charming homely touches like ornaments, books and magazines. Similar attention to detail is shown in the sumptuously appointed bedrooms, which are individually decorated in supremely tasteful fashion. Luxurious bathrooms are equally well equipped. No dogs. ***Amenities*** garden, tennis, croquet.

■ ***Rooms*** *15*	***Confirm by*** *arrang.*
en suite bath/shower *15*	***Last dinner*** *9.30*
Direct dial *Yes*	***Parking*** *Ample*
Room TV *Yes*	***Room service*** *All day*
Closed *23 Dec–13 Jan*	

Homewood Park Restaurant ★ ♛ 🍷 ♿

Top-quality ingredients enhanced by superlative sauces are the backbone of Stephen Ross's imaginative menus at this handsome, two-roomed restaurant. A regular delivery of fish from Cornwall results in such delights as monkfish escalopes with mussels and wild garlic or Dover sole with smoked salmon and lemon butter sauce. Meat-lovers enjoy equally splendid choices – perhaps calf's liver terrine with pink pepper jelly followed by saddle of lamb with aubergine Madeira sauce, or stuffed veal in pastry sauced wtih mushrooms, wine and cream. Garden-fresh vegetables accompany, and tempting sweets include hot passion fruit soufflé. The worthy, carefully chosen wine list offers excellent value and some outstanding items. ***Specialities*** pot au feu of seafood in red wine, warm, spiced sweetbread salad, guinea fowl with lentils and bacon, pear and almond tart with Poire William cream.

🍷 Well-chosen

■ ***Set L*** *£16*	*L 12–1.30*
Set D *from £20*	*D 7–9.30,*
About £55 for two	*Sun 7–8.30*
Seats *50* ***Parties*** *40*	***Closed*** *24 Dec–13 Jan*

Farringford Hotel

H 57% £D/E
Map 4 C4 Isle of Wight
Bedbury Lane PO40 9PE
Isle of Wight (0983) 752500
Managers Mr & Mrs Italo Cerise
Credit Access, Amex, Diners, Visa

Lord Tennyson lived in this former mansion for many years. Now a comfortable family hotel, the public rooms and bedrooms are pleasant if relatively modest. *Amenities* garden, outdoor swimming pool, tennis, 9-hole golf course, putting, bowling green, croquet, games room, snooker, laundry service, 24-hour lounge service, children's play area.

■ *Rooms* 20	*Confirm by arrang.*
en suite bath/shower 20	*Last dinner 9.30*
Room phone Yes	*Parking* Ample
Room TV Yes	*Room service* 24 hours

Fox & Goose ★

R ★ ♀ Map 6 D2 Suffolk
Nr Eye
Fressingfield (037 986) 247
Credit Access, Amex, Diners, Visa

Rustic simplicity is just one of the charms of this appealing country restaurant dating back to the 16th century. But there's nothing unsophisticated about Adrian Clarke's superb cooking. Book, as his seasonally changing menus are sent to guests for advance ordering (although there's a limited menu for chance visitors). Imaginative dishes, consistently well prepared might include starters like langoustines provençale, calf's sweetbreads in puff pastry or quenelle of pike with a lobster and brandy sauce. Follow perhaps with turbot in a cream and mushroom sauce, fillet of pork en croûte with a Madeira and cranberry sauce, or roasted marinated venison. First-class desserts include fresh-fruit sorbets, chocolate marquise on a coffee bean sauce and hot mango soufflé. Friendly, informal service.

Specialities vegetable terrine on tomato vinaigrette, salmon with a creamy sorrel sauce, roast duckling with a rich port wine sauce, crème de menthe ice cream.
♀ Well-chosen ©

■ *Set L from* £14	*L 12–1.30*
Set D from £14	*D 7–9*
About £47 *for two*	*Parking* Ample
Seats 26	*Parties* 30
Closed Tues, also D Sun Sept–Mar & 1 wk Xmas	

■ If we recommend meals in a hotel or inn, a separate entry is made for its restaurant.

Mendip Lodge Hotel

H 61% £D/E &
Map 4 B3 Somerset
Bath Road BA11 2HP
Frome (0373) 63223. Tlx 44832
Credit Access, Amex, Diners, Visa

Standing on high ground off the A361 just outside Frome, this spotlessly kept hotel offers splendid views across the Mendips. Covered walkways connect the motel style bedrooms to the original main building, which houses a cheerful lounge and a relaxing bar. Bedrooms in the older block are particularly spacious, some opening on to the terrace. All rooms are attractively furnished, and bathrooms smart. *Amenities* garden.

■ *Rooms* 40	*Confirm by* 6
en suite bath/shower 40	*Last dinner* 9.45
Direct dial Yes	*Parking* Ample
Room TV Yes	*Room service* All day

Selwood Manor

H 64% £C/D
Map 4 B3 Somerset
BA11 3NL
Frome (0373) 63605. Tlx 444738
Owner managers John & Valerie Chorley
Credit Visa

Check directions to find this secluded, lovingly restored Jacobean manor house, where open fires warm the lounges with their period furniture and objets d'art. Appealing bedrooms show similar style and taste. Some have splendid wooded views. No children under 12. No dogs. *Amenities* garden, outdoor swimming pool, croquet, clay pigeon shooting, coarse fishing.

■ *Rooms* 6	*Confirm by arrang.*
en suite bath/shower 5	*Last dinner* 8
Room phone No	*Parking* Ample
Room TV Yes	*Room service* All day

■ Our inspectors are our full-time employees; they are professionally trained by us.

Ladbroke Hotel   Garforth

H **61% £D/E** &
Map 11 D1 West Yorkshire
Wakefield Road, Nr Leeds LS26 1LH
Leeds (0532) 866556. Tlx 556324
Credit Access, Amex, Diners, Visa
   Popular with businessmen and travellers, this 1970s hotel offers good conference facilities. A waterwheel fountain makes an attractive centrepiece for the open-plan public rooms.

Bedrooms, all with tea-makers, are in a practical modern style. *Amenities* garden, indoor swimming pool, sauna, whirl-pool bath, steam bath, keep fit equipment, pool table, in-house movies (charge), laundry service, helipad.

■ *Rooms 142*	*Confirm by 6*
en suite bath/shower 142	*Last dinner 10*
Direct dial Yes	*Parking Ample*
Room TV Yes	*Room service All day*

Springfield Hotel   Gateshead

H **63% £D/E**
Map 15 B4 Tyne & Wear
Durham Road NE9 5BT
Tyneside (091) 4774121
Credit Access, Amex, Diners, Visa
   A pretty patio garden is a popular spot in summer at this solidly built '30s hotel on the A6127. Inside, Italian marble creates a striking effect in the foyer, and there's a comfortable

lounge plus two stylish bars. Generally spacious bedrooms (street-facing ones are double-glazed) have practical fitted units, tea-makers and tiled bathrooms. *Amenities* garden, laundry service, 24-hour lounge service.

■ *Rooms 40*	*Confirm by arrang.*
en suite bath/shower 40	*Last dinner 9.30*
Direct dial Yes	*Parking Ample*
Room TV Yes	*Room service 24 hours*

Swallow Hotel Gateshead   Gateshead

H **61% £D/E**
Map 15 B4 Tyne & Wear
High West Street NE8 1PE
Tyneside (091) 477 1105
Credit Access, Amex, Diners, Visa
   A high-rise, town-centre hotel with smartly refurbished reception and lounge areas and extensive conference facilities. Bedrooms (some now of Executive standard) are designed for

practicality, with fitted units that provide ample storage and work space. *Amenities* indoor swimming pool, sauna, solarium, whirlpool bath, keep-fit equipment, laundry service, coffee shop (10.30am–10.30pm), 24-hour lounge service.

■ *Rooms 106*	*Confirm by 6*
en suite bath/shower 106	*Last dinner 10*
Direct dial Yes	*Parking Ample*
Room TV Yes	*Room service 24 hours*

Bull Hotel   Gerrards Cross

H **64% £C**
Map 5 E2 Buckinghamshire
Oxford Road SL9 7PA
Gerrards Cross (0753) 885995. Tlx 847747
Credit Access, Amex, Diners, Visa
   With the recent opening of a new 54-bedroom extension the Bull has completed its transformation from a small coaching inn on the A40 to a quite sizeable hotel with an important conference business. The new rooms – quite a way from reception – have solid modern furnishings in peach and chintz (including a couple of armchairs), and up-to-the-minute

accessories – trouser presses, hairdryers and tea-makers. Earlier rooms are due to be improved to the same executive standard. Two luxury suites are also available. There are two bars, one a cocktail bar with honey-coloured panelling with doors that open out on to a pleasant walled garden. Staff agreeable, breakfast poor. Housekeeping could be improved. *Amenities* garden, laundry service, 24-hour lounge service.

■ *Rooms 98*	*Confirm by arrang.*
en suite bath/shower 98	*Last dinner 9.30*
Direct dial Yes	*Parking Ample*
Room TV Yes	*Room service 24 hours*

Stock Hill House Hotel

Gillingham

HR 70% £D
Map 4 B3 Dorset
Wyke SP8 5NR
Gillingham (074 76) 3626
Owner managers Peter & Nita Hauser
Credit Access, Visa

Ten acres of grounds containing a lake and rare trees surround this solid Victorian house where the Hausers are most affable hosts. Public areas include a roomy hall with fine chandelier and cosy sitting area and a comfortable lounge with attractive fabrics and white marble fireplace. The bedrooms, some with open fires, have quality wallpapers and fabrics and many extras. Continuing forays to antique shops add to a growing collection of period furniture, including an ironwork four-poster which belonged to a Spanish princess. Immaculate bathrooms have modern suites. *Amenities* garden, indoor swimming pool, sauna, solarium, keep-fit equipment, croquet.

■ *Rooms* 6	*Confirm by arrang.*
en suite bath/shower 6	*Last dinner* 9
Direct dial Yes	*Parking* Ample
Room TV Yes	*Room service* All day
Closed Feb & 2 wks Nov	

Stock Hill House Restaurant ★ ♧

An elegant room and delightful table settings make for pleasing surroundings in which to enjoy Peter Hauser's dedicated and enthusiastic cooking. His short, daily-changing fixed-price menus show a classical inspiration and dishes from his native Austria are strongly featured. His skill is evidenced in deliciously distinct but subtle flavourings and seasonings. You might choose provençale fish soup as a starter, to be followed by chicken breast with scampi and cream. Sweets include some luscious Austrian confections like Schwannen Körbchen, and there's a good selection of English and Continental cheeses. Excellent wines, strong in Loires and Rhônes. *Specialities* cauliflower terrine with prawns, contrefilet d'agneau rôti aux écrevisses, grenadins de lottes au beurre de tomates.

♀ Well-chosen ℮

■ *Set L* £10	*L* 12.30–2
Set D £16	*D* 7.30–9
About £50 *for two*	*Seats* 24 *Parties* 16
Closed D Sun, Mon, 2 wks Nov & all Feb	

Combe House Hotel

Gittisham

HR 75% £D
Map 3 E2 Devon
Nr Honiton EX14 0AD
Honiton (0404) 2756
Owner managers Thérèse & John Boswell
Credit Access, Amex, Diners, Visa

The setting is peacefully pastoral while the atmosphere throughout this Elizabethan house is warm and welcoming. The stately entrance hall impresses with its Dutch-tiled fireplace, dark panelling and exotic flower arrangements. The drawing room features more fine panelling, plus moulded ceilings and ancestral portraits. There's a second, smaller lounge, and a pleasant bar in olive green. Generally spacious bedrooms are individually decorated (some with Thérèse Boswell's murals); furniture is antique or good-

quality reproduction. Bathrooms – three with shower only – are supplied with luxury toiletries. *Amenities* garden, croquet, game fishing, laundry service.

■ *Rooms* 12	*Confirm by arrang.*
en suite bath/shower 12	*Last dinner* 9.30
Direct dial Yes	*Parking* Ample
Room TV Yes	*Room service* All day
Closed mid Jan–end Feb	

Restaurant ⌣

Twin dining rooms in this period house are graced with fine moulded ceilings, chandeliers and pretty table settings. The menu offers quite a wide variety, with plenty of seasonal specialities. Some typical dishes: gravadlax of sea trout; cream cheese and spinach soufflé; roast lamb fillet with fresh mint and cream sauce; duck breast with a port and sherry sauce and a garnish of pink peppercorns; meringues with butterscotch sauce. Also a good choice of vegetarian dishes.

♀ Well-chosen ℮

■ *Set L* £11·50	*L* Sun only at 1
About £42 *for two*	*D* 7.30–9.30
Closed mid Jan–end Feb	*Seats* 56 *Parties* 30

George & Pilgrims Hotel   Glastonbury

H **60% £D/E**
Map 4 A3 Somerset
1 High Street BA6 9DP
Glastonbury (0458) 31146
Owner managers Major & Mrs Jack Richardson
Credit Access, Amex, Diners, Visa
 Lots of history and no little character in an inn
that goes back 500 years and more. Behind the
mullion-windowed, ecclesiastical frontage there's

an abundance of beams, flag-stones and sturdy
furnishings. Bedrooms in the oldest part share
this splendid old-world atmosphere, while other
rooms are rather more ordinary.
Amenities laundry service.

■ Rooms 14	Confirm by 6
en suite bath/shower 12	Last dinner 9.15
Direct dial Yes	Parking Limited
Room TV Most	Room service All day

Barretts   Glemsford

R 🛏 ⑨ **Map 6 C3** Suffolk
 31 Egremont Street, Nr Sudbury
Glemsford (0787) 281573
Credit Access, Visa
 A change of name and ownership has certainly
not meant a drop in standards at this homely
restaurant, formerly called Weeks. Nicholas
Barrett works alone in his kitchen, preparing a
variety of elegant dishes, from Blue Brie fritters
with a strawberry coulis and scampi tails on a bed
of mange-tout to grilled lamb cutlets with thyme
and fillets of turbot stuffed with leeks and
mushrooms and served with a lovely light pepper

sauce. Nice crisp vegetables, timed to perfection.
Banoffi pie makes a really scrumptious ending to
an excellent candlelit meal. Diane Barrett is a
charming, friendly host. The wine list includes
good burgundies from top growers (Dujac,
Parent, Coche-Debord). Traditional Sunday lunch.
🍷 **Well-chosen** ⊝

■ Set L Sun only £9.95	L Sun 12–2, Tues–Sat
About £50 for two	by arrang. only
Seats 18	D 7–9.30
Parties 18	Parking Ample
Closed D Sun, all Mon, Bank Hols, 4 days Xmas & 10 days Jan	

■ Any person using our name
 to obtain free hospitality is
 a fraud. Proprietors, please
 inform the police and us.

Crest Hotel   Gloucester

H **62% £D** &
Map 4 B1 Gloucestershire
Crestway, Barnwood GL4 7RX
Gloucester (0452) 613311. Tlx 437273
Credit Access, Amex, Diners, Visa
 Three miles from the city, this comfortable
modern hotel makes a useful stopover. Bright
standard bedrooms have compact bathrooms,
trouser presses, tea-makers and radio-alarms;

superior Executive rooms offer extra accessories.
Exposed brickwork features throughout, to smart
effect in the open-plan public areas.
Amenities garden, putting, laundry service,
coffee shop (9.30am–6pm), children's play areas.

■ Rooms 100	Confirm by 6
en suite bath/shower 100	Last dinner 9.45
Direct dial Yes	Parking Ample
Room TV Yes	Room service 24 hours

Hatton Court   Gloucester

HR **75% £C/D**
Map 4 B1 Gloucestershire
Upton Hill, Upton St Leonards GL4 8DE
Gloucester (0452) 617412. Tlx 449848
Credit Access, Amex, Diners, Visa
 A creeper-clad hotel, overlooking the beautiful
Severn valley, which has recently been
transformed into an extremely elegant
establishment. Complete refurbishment
throughout has resulted in public rooms with
good fabrics, period-style furniture, and a cosy
country house atmosphere; the spacious
bedrooms are to a high standard with smart
darkwood furniture, light colour schemes and
coordinating fabrics. Extras include remote-
control TV, hairdryers, trouser presses,
magazines and pot-pourri. The large, carpeted
bathrooms are equally luxurious (16 with whirlpool

bath). Enthusiastic and helpful staff. No dogs.
Amenities garden, outdoor swimming pool, in-
house movies (free), laundry service, 24-hour
lounge service.

■ Rooms 53	Confirm by 6
en suite bath/shower 53	Last dinner 10
Direct dial Yes	Parking Ample
Room TV Yes	Room service 24 hours

Mallyan Spout Hotel
Goathland

H 58% £E/F
Map 15 C5 North Yorkshire
Whitby YO22 5AN
Whitby (0947) 86206
Owner managers Peter & Judith Heslop
Credit Amex, Diners, Visa

The owners are charming and character abounds at this ivy-clad hotel named after the waterfall that flows a little way below. Carved oak furniture features in the day rooms, which include a couple of bars and a cosy lounge. Bedrooms are neat and simply appointed; one sports a splendid half-tester, two others have brass bedsteads.
Amenities garden.

■ *Rooms* 22	*Confirm by arrang.*
en suite bath/shower 18	*Last dinner 8.30*
Room phone No	*Parking Ample*
Room TV Yes	*Room service All day*

Inn on the Lake
Godalming

I £E
Map 5 E3 Surrey
GU7 1RH
Godalming (048 68) 5575
Owner managers Joy & Martin Cummings
Credit Access, Amex, Diners, Visa

There are still a few old beams in evidence from the Tudor origins of this splendid establishment, but it is predominantly Georgian with a modern extension which has views of the landscaped garden and small lake. Martin Cummings is an ebullient, enthusiastic character whose cheerfulness rubs off on all his staff, and Joy's eye for design shows in the individually styled bedrooms. Furnishings vary from room to room, and there are lots of nice touches, from scatter cushions to sewing kits, from magazines to plants. A nice feature in the seven new rooms is a mirrored wall hiding wardrobes and bathrooms (with whirlpool baths). Most rooms also have hairdryers and remote-control TVs.
Amenities garden.

■ *Rooms* 19	*Confirm by arrang.*
en suite bath/shower 16	*Last dinner 10*
Direct dial Yes	*Parking Ample*
Room TV Yes	*Room service All day*

Cormorant Hotel
Golant

H 62% £E
Map 2 C3 Cornwall
Nr Fowey PL23 1LL
Fowey (072 683) 3426
Credit Visa

Bedrooms with floor to ceiling picture windows giving panoramic views over the Fowey Estuary are the outstanding feature of this hotel, standing high above the village. Rooms are thoughtfully furnished and have well-kept modern bathrooms. Huge sofas give the lounge homely appeal, and there is also an intimate little bamboo-furnished cocktail bar. *Amenities* garden, indoor & outdoor swimming pools.

■ *Rooms* 11	*Confirm by arrang.*
en suite bath/shower 11	*Last dinner 8.45*
Direct dial Yes	*Parking Ample*
Room TV Yes	*Room service All day*

Goodwood Park Hotel *NEW ENTRY*
Goodwood

H 66% £D &
Map 5 E4 West Sussex
·Chichester PO18 0QB
Chichester (0243) 775537. Tlx 869173
Credit Access, Amex, Diners, Visa

A former inn, dating from 1786, which has been much extended and now does a thriving trade in conference delegates. While the general standard of accommodation is high, the administration and management could benefit from improvement. Bedrooms in the new wing are spacious, with smart bathrooms; those in the original building have plenty of character. *Amenities* garden, snooker, laundry service, 24-hour lounge service.

■ *Rooms* 49	*Confirm by arrang.*
en suite bath/shower 49	*Last dinner 9.30*
Direct dial Yes	*Parking Ample*
Room TV Yes	*Room service Limited*

Star & Eagle
Goudhurst

I £E
Map 7 B5 Kent
High Street TN17 1AL
Goudhurst (0580) 211512
Credit Access, Amex, Diners, Visa

Period atmosphere and charm abound in this delightful black and white timbered building. The bars have winter fires in the old brick fireplaces and there are gnarled beams everywhere. Characterful bedrooms with pretty wallpaper and fabrics and pine furniture offer radio-alarms, tea/coffee-makers and carpeted bathrooms. No dogs.
Amenities garden, in-house movies (free).

■ *Rooms* 11	*Confirm by arrang.*
en suite bath/shower 9	*Last dinner 9.15*
Room phone Yes	*Parking Ample*
Room TV Yes	*Room service None*

Barkston House

Grantham

RR   ⬥ **Map 11 E3** Lincolnshire
Barkston NG32 2NH
Loveden (0400) 50555
Owner manager Peter Cochrane
Credit Access, Amex, Diners, Visa
    Peter Cochrane, a willing and civilised host, masterminded the transformation of the Georgian farmhouse to stylish restaurant with rooms. The dining room (once the kitchen) has a rustic charm, with old farm implements on softly lit walls. Menus change frequently, and feature wonderful home-made soups (the bread and biscuits are baked on the premises too), and main courses such as

stuffed shoulder of lamb and kidney and bacon kebabs. Norfolk treacle tart is a popular pud.
♟ **Well-chosen** ☺
■ *Set L* Sun only £7·50   *L* 12–2, Sun at 1
About £40 for two   *D* 7.30–9.15
Seats 34 Parties 28   *Parking* Ample
Closed L Sat, D Sun & Mon, Bank Hols exc. Good Fri & 5 days Xmas
Bedrooms   £E/F
Rooms 2   *With bath/shower 2*
There are two large, spotlessly clean bedrooms, attractively furnished and with colour TVs and direct-dial telephones.

■ We welcome complaints and bona fide recommendations on the tear-out pages for readers' comments. They are followed up by our professional team. Please also complain to the management instantly.

RECEPTION

Michael's Nook

Grasmere

HR **79% £C**
Map 13 C5 Cumbria
Nr Ambleside LA22 9RP
Grasmere (096 65) 496. Tlx 65329
Owner manager Mr R. S. E. Gifford
Credit Amex
    A fine Victorian house with stunning views of the fells where the Giffords' care and concern for their guests continue to pay dividends. The comfortable public rooms feature antiques, paintings and porcelain, set off by elegant flower arrangements. Two superb suites, and the other spacious bedrooms, are furnished with fine antique pieces, including a Regency four-poster.

Lots of extras, such as mineral water and fruit, add to the impression of warm hospitality. Bathrooms have high-quality suites and good toiletries. Half-board only. Guests may use the leisure facilities at the nearby Wordsworth Hotel. No dogs. *Amenities* garden, laundry service.
■ *Rooms 11*   *Confirm by arrang.*
en suite bath/shower 11   *Last dinner 8*
Direct dial Yes   *Parking* Ample
Room TV Yes   *Room service* All day

Michael's Nook Restaurant ⬥

The attractive dining room provides a delightful setting for a good meal. Imaginative and unusual dishes are offered on the daily-changing menu. Starters might be paupiette of smoked salmon with spinach noodles or galantine of quail with haw jelly, followed by scallops with beetroot and dill sauce or lamb with truffle and leek coulis. Delicious sweets. Service is friendly and professional. ☺

■ *Set L* £18·50   *L* 12.30 for 1
Set D £26   *D* 7.30 for 8, Sat 7
About £65 for two   for 7.15 (9 for 9.15
Seats 26 Parties 25   Fri & Sat in summer)

Swan Hotel

Grasmere

H **65% £C/D**
Map 13 C5 Cumbria
LA22 9RF
Grasmere (096 65) 551
Credit Access, Amex, Diners, Visa
    Public rooms at this ancient coaching inn are a splendid country mix of old wing armchairs, beams and brassware, fresh flowers and roaring winter fires. Thoughtfully equipped bedrooms

(sherry on arrival, Grasmere gingerbread on the tea tray, hot water bottles) include 12 revamped rooms sporting plush fabrics and superior furnishings. Lots of extras in bathrooms too.
Amenities garden, laundry service.
■ *Rooms 36*   *Confirm by 6*
en suite bath/shower 36   *Last dinner 9*
Direct dial Yes   *Parking* Ample
Room TV Yes   *Room service* All day

Grasmere ▶

White Moss House   Grasmere

HR 68% £D/E
Map 13 C5 Cumbria
Rydal Water LA22 9SE
Grasmere (096 65) 295
Owner managers Peter & Susan Dixon

Once the property of William Wordsworth, this delightful old Lakeland house overlooking Rydal Water is today a charming hotel run by the dedicated Dixons. Antiques, comfortable armchairs, and lots of books and plants create a welcoming impression in the restful lounge, where drinks are served. Attractive bedrooms feature the odd antique and a whole host of thoughtful extras, from hairdryers and trouser presses to maps and magazines. A two-bedroomed cottage perched some 600 feet above the main house provides particularly peaceful accommodation. Half-board terms only. No children under eight. No dogs. *Amenities* garden, coarse & game fishing, laundry service.

■ *Rooms* 6   *Confirm by arrang.*
en suite bath/shower 6   *Last dinner* 8
Room phone Yes   *Parking* Ample
Room TV Yes   *Room service* All day
Closed mid Nov–mid Mar

Restaurant ★ ♧

English cooking
Peter Dixon is the talented chef at this cosy little restaurant. Using first-class ingredients, frequently enhanced by home-grown herbs, he favours a modern English style of cooking that is unpretentious and completely assured. His daily-changing five-course dinners allow for no choice except in the dessert. A typical meal gets under way with a tasty soup like lovage and leek, then moves on to a tempting fish dish such as featherlight pike soufflé. The main course could be fennel-stuffed loin of Cumbrian lamb served with apple and marjoram relish, or Westmorland beef fillet with mustard béarnaise. Delicious desserts might include Calvados-enriched bread and butter pudding or pink champagne sorbet, and there's a superb English cheeseboard. Interesting wine list with excellent Cru Bourgeois clarets (Ramage-La-Batisse '81) at keen prices. *Specialities* char, sole and salmon terrine with sorrel sauce, mallard with damson, port and claret sauce, Sussex Pond pudding.
♀ Well-chosen ⊖

■ *Set D* £16·95   *D only* 7.30 for 8
About £44 for two   *Seats* 20
Closed Sun (except Easter) & mid Nov–mid Mar

Wordsworth Hotel   Grasmere

HR 72% £C/D
Map 13 C5 Cumbria
Nr Ambleside LA22 9SW
Grasmere (096 65) 592. Tlx 65329
Managers Robin and Margaret Lees
Credit Access, Amex, Diners, Visa

A warm welcome and a relaxed atmosphere is offered at this fine 19th-century hotel. Antique furniture in the foyer sets the tone of the elegant interior. Two comfortable lounges are furnished in Victorian style and a modern conservatory overlooks attractive gardens. A smart bar sports rattan furniture. Good-sized bedrooms are individually decorated, with matching bedspreads and curtains to complement the colour scheme. Bathrooms are well equipped and have modern fittings, save one which has a fine original Victorian bath and shower. No dogs. *Amenities* garden, indoor swimming pool, sauna, solarium, games room, snooker, laundry service, 24-hour lounge service.

■ *Rooms* 35   *Confirm by arrang.*
en suite bath/shower 34   *Last dinner* 9
Direct dial Yes   *Parking* Ample
Room TV Yes   *Room service* 24 hours

Prelude Restaurant ♿

Bernard Warne's imaginative and original menu offers a good choice of nouvelle cuisine dishes. Starters might be chicken liver mousse with tarragon and brandy or pâté of salmon and sea bream with saffron and cucumber dressing; main courses could include collops of veal with morels and Marsala and breast of wild duck flamed in cider with apple. Minted white chocolate Bavarian cream may tempt among the sweets. Cold buffet lunch, except for Sunday roast. ⊖

■ *Set L* Sun only £8·50   *L* 12.30–2
Set D £16·50   *D* 7–9, Fri & Sat 7–9.30
About £44 for two   *Seats* 120 *Parties* 120

Woods   Grayshott

R ⚲ ♿ **Map 5 E3** Hampshire
Headley Road, Nr Hindhead
Hindhead (042 873) 5555
Credit Access, Amex, Diners, Visa
    No need to stand on ceremony in the
Norrgrens' infomal little place that still retains
many features of a former life as a butcher's shop.
The menu provides sufficient choice and seasonal
variation to keep the regulars happy, and we

found starters and sweets (cream of artichoke
soup, mousseline de volaille with a centre of
walnuts and roquefort, luscious Grand Marnier
soufflé) particularly good. Main-course sauces
occasionally disappoint.

■ *About £48 for two*   *D only 7–11*
Seats 30   *Parking* Limited
Closed Sun, Mon, Bank Hols exc. Good Fri
& 1 Jan

■ Changes in data may occur in
establishments after the Guide
goes to press. Prices should be taken
as indications rather than firm quotes.

Ayton Hall   Great Ayton

H **74% £C/D**
    Map 15 C5 North Yorkshire
Low Green, Nr Middlesbrough TS9 6PS
Great Ayton (0642) 723595
Owner managers Mr & Mrs M. Rhodes
Credit Access, Amex, Visa
    Melvin and Marian Rhodes have transformed a
secluded country mansion into a hotel of great
character. Bedrooms – some with four-posters –
have an almost endless inventory of extras, from
books, magazines and stationery to sherry,
sweets and fresh fruit, sewing and shoe-cleaning
kits, trouser presses and remote-control TVs.
Bathrooms are equally thoughtfully appointed –
even rubber ducks to play with in the bath! The
lounge has traditional furnishings, fine oil
paintings and a grand piano, and there's an
attractive Moroccan-style bar. No children under

11. No dogs. *Amenities* garden, tennis, croquet,
clay-pigeon shooting, in-house movies (free),
laundry service.
■ *Rooms* 6   *Confirm by arrang.*
en suite bath/shower 6   *Last dinner* 9.30
Direct dial Yes   *Parking* Ample
Room TV Yes   *Room service* All day

Pontlands Park Hotel   Great Baddow

See under Chelmsford

Saracen's Head Hotel   Great Dunmow

H **59% £C/D**
    Map 6 B3 Essex
High Street CM6 1AG
Great Dunmow (0371) 3901
Credit Access, Amex, Diners, Visa. **LVs**
    The Georgian facade of this fine town-centre
inn conceals a far earlier history. Oak beams and
panelling in the lounge-bar provide clues to its
17th-century origins. There are three suites with

original timbers, brass beds and elegant sitting
rooms. Most of the bedrooms are in modern
extensions, and offer practical comforts (remote-
control TVs, tea-makers) and good bathrooms.
Amenities laundry service.
■ *Rooms* 24   *Confirm by* 6
en suite bath/shower 24 *Last dinner* 9.30
Room phone Yes   *Parking* Ample
Room TV Yes   *Room service* All day

Starr   Great Dunmow

R **Map 6 B3** Essex
    Market Place
Great Dunmow (0371) 4321
Owner managers Mr & Mrs Brian Glyn-Jones
Credit Access, Diners, Visa
    Smithfield and Billingsgate provide many of the
prime ingredients for the imaginative menus at
this welcoming beamed dining room in a 15th-
century inn. Typical starters might include hot

lobster pot or marinated artichoke, perhaps
followed by pan-fried skate wing with capers,
spicy duck's legs or escalope of Dutch veal.
▷ Outstanding ♀ Well-chosen ℮
■ *Set L* £12.95, Sun £15   *L* 12–1.30
Set D £22, Sat £25   *D* 7–10
About £55 for two   *Parking* Difficult
Seats 60   *Parties* 16
Closed L Sat, D Sun, 3 wks Aug & 2 wks Xmas

Great Milton ▶

Le Manoir aux Quat' Saisons

Great Milton

HR 85% £A
Map 5 D2 Oxfordshire
Church Street OX9 7PD
Great Milton (084 46) 8881. Tlx 837552
Owner managers Raymond & Jenny Blanc
Credit Access, Amex, Diners, Visa

Surrounded by delightful gardens, this 15th-century manor house with tall Elizabethan chimneys and stone-mullioned windows has been superbly converted into a luxurious country house hotel. The two lounges – there's no bar – are stylish and relaxing, with deep, comfortable settees, fine fabrics and fresh flowers, while upstairs bedrooms (many of them suites) are sumptuously decorated. Elaborately draped curtains, canopied beds and abundant antique furniture, along with thoughtful touches such as a decanter of Madeira, fruit and flowers, cannot fail to please, and bathrooms are equally magnificent. Dogs in kennels only. *Amenities* garden, outdoor swimming pool, tennis, croquet, riding.

Le Manoir Restaurant
★★★ ♕♕ ⑨ ♿

French cooking
The elegant twin dining rooms, with their stylish curtains, oil paintings and pretty china, provide a charming setting in which to revel in Raymond Blanc's outstanding cooking. The à la carte menu changes three times yearly, while the tour-de-force gourmet menu varies daily; new dishes, such as the caneton rôti and an exquisite tartelette of raspberry soufflé, are only added to the wide repertoire after being perfected to exacting standards. Highlights of our meal included Raymond's famous fleur de courgette farcie and gelée de saumon sauvage à la crème aigre et caviar. Great wines at high prices: note Volnay Taillepieds (de Montille) 1971.
Specialities charlotte d'aubergines et poivrons doux aux filets mignons d'agneau de lait au romarin; caneton rôti au sirop de maïs, croque d'oignons à la coriandre; duo de millefeuille au chocolat blanc et amer à la mousse de framboises.

▬ *Rooms* 10	*Confirm by arrang.*
en suite bath/shower 10	*Last dinner* 10
Direct dial Yes	*Parking* Ample
Room TV Yes	*Room service* 24 hours
Closed 4 wks Xmas	

⌓ Outstanding ♀ Well-chosen ☺

▬ *Set L* from £18·50	*L* 12.15–2.15
Set D £38	*D* 7.15–10
About £120 for two	*Seats* 55 *Parties* 30
Closed L Tues, all Mon & 4 wks Xmas	

▬ For a discount on next year's guide, see Offer for Answers.

Old Rectory

Great Snoring

H 58% £D/E
Map 6 C1 Norfolk
Nr Fakenham NR21 0HP
Walsingham (032 872) 597
Owner managers Tooke & Scoles families
Credit Amex, Diners

Little disturbs the peace at this charming house deep in Norfolk countryside. Antique furnishings in the hall are worthy of note while the tranquil lounge offers deep armchairs and sofas. Comfortable bedrooms in traditional style include nice touches like books and fresh flowers. No dogs. *Amenities* garden.

▬ *Rooms* 7	*Confirm by arrang.*
en suite bath/shower 7	*Last dinner* 8
Direct dial Yes	*Parking* Ample
Room TV Yes	*Room service* All day
Closed 25–26 Dec	

Carlton Hotel

Great Yarmouth

H 60% £E
Map 6 D1 Norfolk
Marine Parade NR30 3JE
Great Yarmouth (0493) 855234. Tlx 975642
Credit Access, Amex, Diners, Visa. LVs

Improvements continue at this well-managed, traditional hotel on the seafront. There's comfortable new seating in the smart foyer-lounge, and the two bars have both benefited from a facelift. Bedrooms (which include a number of suites) are also undergoing refurbishment, and all offer tea-makers and radio-alarms. Simple bathrooms are well kept. *Amenities* 24-hour lounge service.

▬ *Rooms* 97	*Confirm by* 6
en suite bath/shower 67	*Last dinner* 9.30, Sun 9
Direct dial Yes	*Parking* Ample
Room TV Yes	*Room service* 24 hours

Friends Bistro *NEW ENTRY*

R ⌕ ⌖ **Map 6 D1** Norfolk
55 Deneside
Great Yarmouth (0493) 852538
Credit Access, Visa. **LVs**

A pretty little bistro with Victorian decor, softly lit and waitress-served at night. Owner Jennifer Haylett also cooks, and her weekly-changing blackboard menu, though concise, is certainly tempting: tasty spinach roulade or mushroom

pots to start; then maybe baked Italian fish, stir-fried fillet of beef with peppers and beansprouts or a quite delicious roast loin of pork dijonnaise; and a final delight like lemon tart flecked with dark chocolate. Snackier daytime choice. ℮

■ *About £26 for two*   *D 7–10*
Seats 28   *Parking Ample*
Closed Sun, Mon, Bank Hols

Seafood Restaurant
Great Yarmouth

R ⌖ **Map 6 D1** Norfolk
85 North Quay
Great Yarmouth (0493) 856009
Seafood
Owner managers Chris & Miriam Kikis
Credit Access, Amex, Diners, Visa

Order your fish grilled, poached or in batter at this popular corner restaurant and let the freshness speak for itself. Sole and sea bass,

shark and halibut, plaice and red mullet, turbot and trout all feature when available. There's also a splendid selection of shellfish. Carefully cooked vegetables and decent sweets. Good white burgundies. Booking essential. ℮
■ *About £37 for two*   *L 12–2*
Seats 40   *D 7–10.30*
Parties 40   *Parking Ample*
Closed L Sat, all Sun, Bank Hols & 1 wk Xmas

Mogul & Le Premier Cru
Greenwich

See under London & London Restaurants under £30

Morritt Arms Hotel
Greta Bridge

H **55% £E**
Map 15 B5 Co. Durham
Rokeby, Nr Barnard Castle DL12 9SE
Teesdale (0833) 27232
Owner managers John and David Mulley
Credit Access, Diners, Visa

Nothing is nicer after a hard day's fishing on the nearby Greta than to relax in front of a log fire in the bar or lounge of this splendidly traditional inn.

Simple bedrooms have tea-makers, trouser presses and TVs. Staff are friendly and warm-hearted. Good breakfasts. *Amenities* garden, coarse and game fishing, children's play area.

■ *Rooms 26*   *Confirm by arrang.*
en suite bath/shower 16   *Last dinner 8.45*
Room phone No   *Parking Ample*
Room TV Yes   *Room service All day*

Crest Hotel
Grimsby

H **57% £D/E**
Map 11 F1 Humberside
St James' Square DN31 1EP
Grimsby (0472) 59771. Tlx 527741
Credit Access, Amex, Diners, Visa

Businessmen, non-smokers and lady guests are catered for individually at this modern red-brick hotel. As well as appropriate accessories such as fashion magazines, all rooms have tea-

makers and trouser presses. The spacious foyer opens into a stylish and relaxing cocktail bar. *Amenities* sauna, solarium, laundry service, coffee shop (9.30am–5.30pm Mon–Sat).
■ *Rooms 131*   *Confirm by 6*
en suite bath/shower 131   *Last dinner 10*
Room phone Yes   *Parking Ample*
Room TV Yes   *Room service None*
Closed 10 days Xmas

Humber Royal Crest Hotel
Grimsby

H **64% £D**
Map 11 F1 Humberside
Littlecoates Road DN34 4LX
Grimsby (0472) 50295. Tlx 52776
Credit Access, Amex, Diners, Visa

Check directions when booking at this modern hotel west of town in grounds adjoining a golf course. Refurbishment of the lounge is planned; the spacious cocktail bar is more attractive. Smart

bedrooms are very well equipped, from reclining armchairs, hairdryers and trouser presses to welcome extras like fresh fruit, sweets and complimentary drinks. *Amenities* garden, whirlpool bath, laundry service.
■ *Rooms 52*   *Confirm by 6*
en suite bath/shower 52   *Last dinner 9.45*
Room phone Yes   *Parking Ample*
Room TV Yes   *Room service 24 hours*

Grimsthorpe ▶

Black Horse Inn   Grimsthorpe

IR **£D/E**
Map 11 E3 Lincolnshire
Nr Bourne PE10 0LY
Edenham (077 832) 247
Owner managers Mr & Mrs K. S. Fisher
Credit Access, Amex, Visa

The Fishers work hard for guests at their 18th century inn which possesses much character and individuality. Prettily-decorated bedrooms include thoughtful touches like books and biscuits. The bar is delightfully old-fashioned and there's a cosy TV lounge. Super breakfasts. No children under 8.
Amenities terrace.

■ *Rooms 4*	*Confirm by* arrang.
en suite bath/shower 2	*Last dinner 9.30*
Room phone No	*Parking Ample*
Room TV No	*Room service None*
Closed 1 wk Xmas	

Black Horse Inn 👑 ⏶ ♿

English cooking

Martyn Watson's traditional English cooking is well in tune with the old English inn setting. Four-course set lunches and dinners provide a good variety of tasty dishes, including several specialities: crispy Cornish fish pancakes, Stilton and herb pâté, monkfish mornay, Lincolnshire stovie potatoes, honey meringue with cream. Steak, kidney and mushroom pie is a robust favourite, and there are also plenty of lighter dishes marked for slimmers on the menu.

■ *Set L & D £12·50*	*L 12–1.45*
About £38 for two	*D 7–10.30*
Seats 22	*Parties 35*
Closed Sun, Bank Hols except Easter &	
1 wk Xmas	

■ We publish annually, so make sure you use the current edition. It's worth it!

Congham Hall   Grimston

HR **79%** **£C/D**
Map 6 B1 Norfolk
Nr King's Lynn PE32 1AH
Hillington (0485) 600250. Tlx 81508
Owner managers Christine & Trevor Forecast
Credit Access, Amex, Diners, Visa

Caring owners, the Forecasts, maintain excellent standards of housekeeping and repair at this handsome Georgian house not far from King's Lynn (follow the Grimston signs from the A148). Well-proportioned day rooms like the foyer-lounge and drawing room boast lovely period furnishings and there's a relaxing bar in summery cane. Spacious, traditionally-appointed bedrooms (many with fine country views) offer every

thoughtful comfort and all have superb modern bathrooms. The peaceful grounds include a cricket pitch. No children under 12. Dogs in kennels only. *Amenities* garden, outdoor swimming pool, whirlpool bath, tennis, croquet, laundry service, helipad.

■ *Rooms 11*	*Confirm by* arrang.
en suite bath/shower 11	*Last dinner 9.30*
Direct dial Yes	*Parking Ample*
Room TV Yes	*Room service All day*

Congham Hall Restaurant ♿

The hotel's gardens and the local markets provide much of the produce in this elegant restaurant. Enjoyable dinner dishes run from onion, apple and cider soup to ballotine of quail, sea bass en croûte and tarragon chicken. Sweets include a deliciously rich and smooth chocolate marquise. Slightly simpler lunchtime choice. Good wines on a concise list: exceptional Muscadet Domaine des Dorices 1986.

🍷 Well-chosen ⊘

■ *Set L from £8·50*	*L 12.30–2*
Set D from £27·50	*D 7.30–9.30*
About £50 for two	*Seats 34 Parties 12*
Closed L Sat & Bank Hols, D Sun to non-residents	

Maynard Arms Hotel   Grindleford

I **£E**
Map 10 C2 Derbyshire
Main Road S30 1HP
Hope Valley (0433) 30321
Owner manager Robert and Thelma Graham
Credit Access, Amex, Diners, Visa

After a pleasant walk in the Peak National Park, relax in one of the comfortable, spacious bars of this late-Victorian hotel or upstairs in the pretty

lounge with its splendid views. Attractive bedrooms, furnished in traditional style, offer tea-makers, trouser presses and carpeted modern bathrooms. Go-ahead young owners keep standards up. *Amenities* garden.

■ *Rooms 13*	*Confirm by* arrang.
en suite bath/shower 13	*Last dinner 9.30*
Direct dial Yes	*Parking Ample*
Room TV Yes	*Room service All day*

Grizedale Lodge Hotel   Grizedale

HR **57% £E/F**
Map 13 D5 Cumbria
Nr Hawkshead LA22 0QL
Hawkshead (096 66) 532
Owner managers Jack & Margaret Lamb
Credit Access, Visa

A white-painted farmhouse in a glorious
woodland setting. Simple comforts are the order
of the day – a rocking chair by the fire in winter; a
seat on the terrace when the sun shines; homely
accommodation in fresh, bright bedrooms. The
nearby theatre offers varied attractions. No dogs.
Amenities garden.

■ *Rooms* 6	*Confirm by* arrang.
en suite bath/shower 6	*Last dinner* 8.30
Room phone No	*Parking* Ample
Room TV Yes	*Room service* All day
Closed Jan	

Restaurant in the Forest ♀

Red deer trophies feature on the woodchip walls
of this simply but pleasantly styled dining room.
Margaret Lamb is well known locally, having
taught home economics at a nearby college and
broadcast two series of programmes on Border
TV. She is an expert on Lakeland cookery and her
menus often feature local produce such as
venison, trout and duck. A small choice of
interesting dishes might include watercress soup,
roast venison with spicy damson sauce and
wholefood ice cream with rum sauce. Skilful,
consistently good cooking throughout.

■ *Set D* £10·50	*D only* 7–8.30
About £30 *for two*	*Seats* 35
Closed Jan	*Parties* 36

Angel Hotel   Guildford

H **61% £C/D**
Map 5 E3 Surrey
High Street GU1 3DR
Guildford (0483) 64555
Credit Access, Amex, Diners, Visa. **LVs**

A former coaching inn with 13th-century
vaulted cellar and attractive cobbled courtyard.
The lounge features a handsome oak gallery and
there's a pleasant bar and cheeerful coffee shop.

Most bedrooms have simple fitted furniture; a few
offer freestanding pieces, even antiques.
Bathrooms have modern or slightly older units but
are all well kept. *Amenities* laundry service,
coffee shop (7am–10pm).

■ *Rooms* 27	*Confirm by* 6
en suite bath/shower 27	*Last dinner* 9.45
Direct dial Yes	*Parking* Difficult
Room TV Yes	*Room service* Limited

Rumwong   Guildford

R **Map 5 E3** Surrey
16 London Road
Guildford (0483) 36092
Thai cooking
Credit Access, Visa

Colourful parasols hang from the ceiling of this
pleasant Thai restaurant, which stands in a
parade of shops opposite the Civic Hall. The
menu lists (and carefully explains) a wide range of

excellent dishes, from hot-sour soups and
barbecued beef quenelles to spicy salads and
specialities like roast duck with pickled ginger
and cucumbers. Also one-plate rice and noodle
dishes.

■ *Set D* £12	*L* 12–2.30
About £30 *for two*	*D* 6–11
Seats 100 *Parties* 35	*Parking* Ample
Closed Mon & 1st 2 wks Aug	

University Post House Hotel *NEW ENTRY*   Guildford

H **69% £C** &
Map 5 E3 Surrey
Egerton Road GU2 5XZ
Guildford (0483) 574444. Tlx 858572
Credit Access, Amex, Diners, Visa. **LVs**

Dark wood and skilful lighting are used to
stylish effect in the public areas of this brand-new
low-rise hotel. Bedrooms, with individually-
controlled air-conditioning and neatly tiled

bathrooms, are equally attractive, and service is
good. *Amenities* garden, indoor swimming pool,
sauna, solarium, gymnasium, laundry service,
coffee shop (6.30am–11pm), 24-hour lounge
service.

■ *Rooms* 121	*Confirm by* 6
en suite bath/shower 121	*Last dinner* 10
Direct dial Yes	*Parking* Ample
Room TV Yes	*Room service* 24 hours

Tollbridge   Guist

R ♀ & **Map 6 C1** Norfolk
Nr Fakenham
Foulsham (036 284) 359
Credit Visa

The river Wensum flows past this attractive
restaurant, and one of the best dishes is
mousseline of Wensum pike. Other choices from
Bill Stark's pleasing repertoire could include
mushroom-sauced feuilleté of pheasant and rare

duck breast with a tangy lime sauce. Glynis Stark
at front of house is charming and efficient. Very
good wines – note the local Elmham Park white
1983. ♀ Well-chosen ☺

■ *Set L* £7	*L* 12–1.30
About £35 *for two*	*D* 7.30–9.15
Seats 50 *Parties* 50	*Parking* Ample
Closed Sun, Mon, 3 days Xmas, 1st 3 weeks Jan & 1st week Oct	

Horn of Plenty ★

Gulworthy

RR ★ ⚅ ♿ **Map 2 C3** Devon
Tavistock PL19 8JD
Tavistock (0822) 832528
Owner managers Patrick & Sonia Stevenson
Credit Access, Amex, Visa

The Horn of Plenty comes of age this year, and a meal overlooking the lovely Tamar valley is still an occasion to savour. Sonia Stevenson – usually the chef, always the inspiration – produces a menu of favourites old and new, from trenette with pesto and a lovely soft terrine of ham with nutmeg and green peppercorns to succulent guinea fowl with salsify and lamb in pastry with mint béarnaise. Super breads, but desserts still fall short of expectations (though the repertoire is soon to change). Charming service. Carefully constructed wine list.
Specialities roulade of Dover sole and salmon in white wine sauce, poached Tamar salmon with sorrel sauce, veal sweetbreads in brioche with two sauces. ⚌ **Well-chosen** ㊉

■ *Set L £12·50*	*L 12–2*
Set D £17·50	*D 7–9.30*
About £52 for two	*Parking Ample*
Seats 60	*Parties 60*
Closed Thurs, L Fri & all 25 & 26 Dec	

Bedrooms £C/D
Rooms 6   *With bath/shower 6*
Pine-furnished bedrooms are a real delight, with private balconies and lovely views, fresh flowers, tea-makers, and luxury toiletries in the bath/shower rooms. Superb breakfasts.

■ Our inspectors never book in the name of Egon Ronay's Guides; they disclose their identity only after paying their bills.

Hackness Grange Country Hotel

Hackness

H **69% £C**
Map 15 D6 North Yorkshire
Nr Scarborough YO13 0JW
Scarborough (0723) 82345. Tlx 527667
Manager Mark Swales
Credit Access, Amex, Diners, Visa

Extensive leisure facilities and a beautiful location make this riverside Victorian mansion a good choice. Accommodation in contemporary style is spacious; public areas pleasant and relaxing. No under fours. No dogs. *Amenities* garden, indoor swimming pool, tennis, pitch & putt, croquet, game fishing, in-house movies (free), laundry service, courtesy coach, helipad.

■ *Rooms 26*	*Confirm by arrang.*
en suite bath/shower 26	*Last dinner 9*
Direct dial Yes	*Parking Ample*
Room TV Yes	*Room service All day*

Weavers Restaurant   *NEW ENTRY*

Hadleigh

R ⚅ **Map 6 C3** Suffolk
23 High Street
Hadleigh (0473) 827247
Credit Access, Visa

Jean-Jacques Pons is a skilled, reliable chef, and dinners in his welcoming beamed restaurant provide a feast of good flavours. Start perhaps with pheasant terrine, seafood and mushroom hot pot provençale or potage St Germain and go on to a steak, cider-poached salmon or rabbit and pork pie flamed in Calvados. Tempting puddings include super-rich St Emilion au chocolat. Sound French wine list with some good half-bottles. ㊉

■ *About £30 for two*	*D only 7–9.30*
Seats 50 Parties 26	*Parking Ample*
Closed Sun & Mon	

West Lodge Park

Hadley Wood

H **65% £C/D**
Map 7 B4 Hertfordshire
Cockfosters Road, Nr Barnet EN4 0PY
01-440 8311. Tlx 24734
Manager Mr J. S. Phillips
Credit Access, Amex, Diners, Visa

Surrounded by 34 acres of landscaped grounds, this extended William IV mansion is a peaceful place to stay. Period furnishings and original oils add to the atmosphere of most public rooms. The bar is stylishly contemporary. Bedrooms, with garden views, are smart and spacious. Good bathrooms. No dogs. *Amenities* garden, putting, croquet, laundry service, helipad.

■ *Rooms 50*	*Confirm by arrang.*
en suite bath/shower 50	*Last dinner 9.30*
Direct dial Yes	*Parking Ample*
Room TV Yes	*Room service 24 hours*

La Crémaillère Hadlow

R ♨ **Map 7 B5** Kent
The Square, Nr Tonbridge
Hadlow (0732) 851489
French cooking
Credit Access, Amex, Diners, Visa
Brittany-born Michael Maillard cooks with
skilled assurance at this popular restaurant
comprising a homely dining room and a pretty
conservatory. His three-course set menus change

monthly and offer an enjoyable choice of robust
regional French dishes – perhaps cream of lettuce
soup preceding duck casserole, with classic
poached pears to finish. ♀ Well-chosen ⊖
■ *Set L* £12·50   *L* 12.30–1.30
Set D £12·50   *D* 8–9
About £35 *for two*   *Parking* Limited
Seats 31 *Parties* 20   *Closed* L Sat, all Sun,
Bank Hols, 1 wk Jan & 3 other wks annually

Holdsworth House Halifax

HR **71% £D**
Map 10 C1 West Yorkshire
Holdsworth, Nr Halifax HX2 9TG
Halifax (0422) 240024. Tlx 51574
Credit Access, Amex, Diners, Visa
A short distance from the A629 and some three
miles north of Halifax, Holdsworth House dates
back to 1633. Public rooms are elegant and
welcoming, with polished panelling, antiques
(including a grandfather clock) and fresh flower
arrangements contributing to the traditional feel.
The bar, in the older part of the hotel, is
particularly inviting, and looks out over the garden

through leaded windows. Bedrooms are in
thoughtfully designed modern extensions: they're
all of a good size, with individual decor and
furnishings, and include four stylish split-level
suites. Accessories range from remote-control
TVs and mini-bars to sewing kits and bathrobes.
Amenities garden, snooker, laundry service.
■ *Rooms* 40   *Confirm by* arrang.
en suite bath/shower 40   *Last dinner* 9.45
Direct dial Yes   *Parking* Ample
Room TV Yes   *Room service* 24 hours
Closed 1 Jan & 25 & 26 Dec

Holdsworth House Restaurant ⩊

An elegant, comfortable restaurant where chef
Eric Claveau cooks with a fine touch. There's
plenty of variety on a menu that runs from
avocado mousse and duck liver bordelaise to
grilled swordfish, chicken suprême with mango,
and fillet of beef (for two). Good sweets.
Farmhouse cheeses. Wines include an in-depth
list of fine clarets. ♀ Well-chosen ⊖
About £45 *for two*   *L* 12.30–2
Seats 50 *Parties* 100   *D* 7–10
Closed L Sat & Sun, 1 Jan & 25 & 26 Dec

Belfry Hotel Handforth

HR **71% £C/D** ⟐
Map 10 B2 Cheshire
Stanley Road, Nr Wilmslow SK9 3LD
061-437 0511. Tlx 666358
Owner managers Beech family
Credit Access, Amex, Diners, Visa. **LVs**
Situated on the A34, convenient for
Manchester, this pleasant, modern hotel has been
run by the Beech family for 25 years. Their
dedication and professionalism are noteworthy,
and staff loyalty is excellent. The whole place is
lovingly cared for, especially the decent-sized
bedrooms, which have smart mahogany furniture.
Neat, well-equipped bathrooms are immaculate.
Guests are welcomed in a marble-floored foyer

with fresh floral displays. Day rooms include a
most inviting lounge with leather-covered sofas
and armchairs and an intimate, split-level cocktail
bar. The beamed Belfry Bar, used mainly for
functions, is all that remains of the original house.
No dogs. *Amenities* garden, laundry service,
24-hour lounge service.
■ *Rooms* 90   *Confirm by* 6
en suite bath/shower 90   *Last dinner* 10
Direct dial Yes   *Parking* Ample
Room TV Yes   *Room service* 24 hours

Belfry Hotel Restaurant ⟐

Accomplished cooking is enhanced by service of
the highest standard at this hotel restaurant. The
lunchtime roast is borne on a silver trolley while
other choices include sweetbread terrine with
onion and honey confiture, scallops steamed in
leeks, pepper steak and roast duckling with
pineapple and lime. Classic wines – note the
Faiveley burgundies and a splendid Côtes-du-
Rhône (Guigal). ♀ Well-chosen ⊖
■ *Set L* £8·50   *L* 12.30–2
Set D £9·50   *D* 7–10
About £52 *for two*   *Seats* 100
Closed 26 Dec & 1 Jan   *Parties* 180

Harlow ▶

Harlow Moat House   Harlow

H 60% £D
Map 7 B4 Essex
Southern Way CM18 7BA
Harlow (0279) 22441. Tlx 81658
Credit Access, Amex, Diners, Visa
  Handily situated near junction 7 of the M11, this
modern hotel has benefited from extensive
refurbishment. Bedrooms now feature lightwood
units and smart deep-pile carpets as well as

trouser presses, tea- and coffee-makers and
remote-control TVs. All bedrooms have neat,
compact bathrooms. Spacious public areas,
including a smart foyer-lounge and a restyled bar.
Amenities garden, laundry service.

■ *Rooms 120*	*Confirm by arrang.*
en suite bath/shower 120	*Last dinner 10*
Room phone Yes	*Parking Ample*
Room TV Yes	*Room service 24 hours*

Pheasant Hotel   Harome

H 68% £E
Map 15 C6 North Yorkshire
Nr Helmsley YO6 5JG
Helmsley (0439) 71241
  Helpful staff add to the charm of this quiet
village hotel created from a smithy, a shop and
two cottages. Modern amenities blend happily
with old-world features like oak beams and a
splendid inglenook fireplace. Large, neat

bedrooms in traditional style overlook the garden
or the village pond. Half-board only. No children
under twelve. *Amenities* garden, laundry service.

■ *Rooms 12*	*Confirm by arrang.*
en suite bath/shower 12	*Last dinner 8.30*
Direct dial Yes	*Parking Ample*
Room TV Yes	*Room service Limited*
Closed Jan–Feb	

Star Inn   Harome

R Map 15 C6 North Yorkshire
Nr Helmsley
Helmsley (0439) 70397
Owner manager Tony Bowron
Credit Access, Amex, Diners, Visa
  Beamed ceilings and a country atmosphere
prevail at this pleasant pub restaurant. A large
selection of interesting starters may include
stuffed green figs or chicken bits in a barbecue

sauce. Steaks are popular: Star steak is a
marriage of beef fillet with brandy, smoked
oysters and a good cream sauce. Among other
main courses on offer are duck with mustard plus
scampi, sole or trout. Home-made meringues are
a tempting sweet. ♀ Well-chosen ©

■ *About £35 for two*	*D only 7–9.30*
Seats 36 Parties 36	*Parking Ample*
Closed Sun, Mon, 24 & 25 Dec & all Jan	

■ If we recommend meals in a
  hotel or inn, a separate entry is
  made for its restaurant.

Glen Eagle Hotel   Harpenden

H 61% £D
Map 5 E2 Hertfordshire
1 Luton Road AL5 2PX
Harpenden (058 27) 60271. Tlx 825828
Credit Access, Amex, Diners, Visa
  New owners are providing this substantial red-
brick hotel with a much needed facelift. Public
areas will be rearranged and equipped with air
conditioning, and improvements being introduced

in the bedrooms include smart modern
cherrywood units and more attractive,
coordinated fabrics. Bathrooms, too, are being
upgraded with cushioned flooring and quality
fittings. *Amenities* garden, laundry service.

■ *Rooms 51*	*Confirm by 6*
en suite bath/shower 51	*Last dinner 10*
Direct dial Yes	*Parking Ample*
Room TV Yes	*Room service 24 hours*

Harpenden Moat House Hotel   Harpenden

H 65% £C/D
Map 5 E2 Hertfordshire
Southdown Road AL5 1PE
Harpenden (058 27) 64111
Credit Access, Amex, Diners, Visa
  A listed Georgian building forms the main part
of the hotel, in which are the elegant public rooms;
they include a comfortable lounge and a glass-
ceilinged bar. Twenty-one new bedrooms have

fitted Italian furniture, queen-sized beds and
matching fabrics; the remaining bedrooms also
have a high standard of comfort. All have well-
equipped bathrooms. *Amenities* garden, laundry
·service, 24-hour lounge service.

■ *Rooms 56*	*Confirm by 6*
en suite bath/shower 56	*Last dinner 10*
Direct dial Yes	*Parking Ample*
Room TV Yes	*Room service 24 hours*

Burdekins

R **Town plan B2** North Yorkshire
21 Cheltenham Crescent
Harrogate (0423) 502610
Owner managers Tim & Kath Burdekin
Credit Access, Amex, Visa
  Traditional English dishes are a feature at the
charming Burdekins' pretty town-centre
restaurant. Their seasonally changing menus may
include hot creamed shrimps, lamb's kidneys on

puff pastry or game pie terrine preceding rack of
lamb, roast pheasant marinated in red wine or
salmon hollandaise. Lovely choice of 'proper'
puddings to finish. ♀ **Well-chosen**
■ *Set D £7·95*　　　　*D only 6.30–9.30*
About £36 for two　　*Parking Ample*
Seats 40　　　　　　*Parties 30*
Closed Sun (exc. during trade shows) & 25 & 26 Dec

♀ indicates a **well-chosen** house wine.

Crown Hotel

H **66% £C/D**
Town plan B2 North Yorkshire
Crown Place HG1 2RZ
Harrogate (0423) 67755. Tlx 57652
Credit Access, Amex, Diners, Visa
  Character and period charm are attractions of
this fine hotel with an elegant facade overlooking
the Pump Room. The spacious foyer with ornate
ceiling, the stylish Brontë Bar, and the peaceful

upstairs reading room are all pleasing, and there
are numerous function rooms. Spacious, modern
bedrooms have a good range of comforts.
Bathrooms are well kept. *Amenities* laundry
service. 24-hour lounge service.
■ *Rooms 122*　　　　*Confirm by 6*
en suite bath/shower 122　*Last dinner 9.30*
Direct dial Yes　　　*Parking Limited*
Room TV Yes　　　*Room service 24 hours*

Drum & Monkey

R **Town plan B2** North Yorkshire
5 Montpellier Gardens
Harrogate (0423) 502650
Seafood
Owner manager William Fuller
Credit Access, Visa
  Think of your favourite seafood and you'll
probably find it at this very popular restaurant.
The fish is the freshest, and the range includes

lobsters, prawns, monkfish, sole and scallops, all
carefully – and usually fairly simply – prepared.
Service is brisk, sometimes almost brusque. Be
sure to book. ☺
■ *About £34 for two*　　*L 12–2.30*
Seats 32　　　　　　*D 7–10.15*
Closed Sun & 9 days　*Parking Difficult*
Xmas

⇨ is our symbol for an **outstanding** wine list.

Granby Hotel

H **58% £C/D** ♿
Town Plan E2 North Yorkshire
Granby Road HG1 4SR
Harrogate (0423) 506151. Tlx 57423
Credit Access, Amex, Diners, Visa
  Public areas and accommodation are both very
roomy at this former spa hotel overlooking the
Stray. The entrance hall doubles as a lounge, and
both it and the bar are much in need of the

revamping that is planned. Bedrooms, also
scheduled for upgrading, are provided with tea-
making facilities and remote-control TVs.
Amenities garden, games room, snooker, in-
house movies (charge), laundry service.
■ *Rooms 93*　　　　*Confirm by 6*
en suite bath/shower 93　*Last dinner 10*
Direct dial Yes　　　*Parking Ample*
Room TV Yes　　　*Room service 24 hours*

Hospitality Inn

H **62% £D/E**
Town plan B3 North Yorkshire
West Park, Prospect Place HG1 1LB
Harrogate (0423) 64601. Tlx 57530
Credit Access, Amex, Diners, Visa
  The Hospitality Inn, originally a row of Georgian
houses, occupies a fairly central position
overlooking the Stray. Day rooms are limited to a
little foyer/reception, a restaurant and a pleasant

bar that's shared by residents and the public.
Narrowish corridors lead to decent-sized
bedrooms with military-style built-in units, easy
chairs, trouser presses and hairdryers.
Amenities in-house movies (free), laundry service.
■ *Rooms 71*　　　　*Confirm by 6*
en suite bath/shower 71　*Last dinner 9.30*
Direct dial Yes　　　*Parking Limited*
Room TV Yes　　　*Room service 24 hours*

HARROGATE

Map 15 C6
Town plan opposite

Population 67,000

The Tewit Well in Harrogate was found to have healing properties in 1571 and the town developed into a spa resort as further chalbyeate and sulphur springs were discovered. Its popularity in the Victorian era is reflected in its architecture. The Royal Baths Assembly Rooms, formerly the main hydro-therapy centre, now houses traditional Turkish baths and modern sauna and solarium facilities. As well as being a historically famous spa resort, Harrogate is now a cosmopolitan conference venue.

Annual Events
International Youth Music Festival *15th–22nd April*
Spring Flower Show *23rd–25th April*
Great Yorkshire Show *14th–16th July*
Harrogate International Festival (music and drama) *29th July–12th August*
Great Autumn Flower Show *18th–19th September*

Sights Outside Town
Fountains Abbey
Ripley Castle
Newby Hall
Knaresborough
Ripon
Pateley Bridge
Brimham Rocks

Tourist Information Office
Royal Baths Assembly Rooms
Crescent Road HG1 2RR
Telephone Harrogate 525666

Fiat Dealer
Croft & Blackburn Ltd
Leeds Road
Pannal
Harrogate HG3 1EP
Tel. Harrogate 879236

1 Art Gallery and Public Library **C3**
2 Conference Centre *incorporating a 2000-seat auditorium* **B1**
3 Exhibition Centre *six halls comprising 10,000 square metres* **B2**
4 Harrogate Theatre **B2**
5 Royal Baths Assembly Rooms *originally a hydro-therapy centre, now housing the Tourist Information Centre and Turkish baths* **B2**
6 Royal Hall *when opened in 1903, an entertainment venue for those taking the waters, now a theatre* **B2**
7 Royal Pump Room Museum *containing local historical material* **B2**
8 St John's Well **E2**
9 Sun Colonnade **A2/3**
10 Valley Gardens **A2**

Harrogate

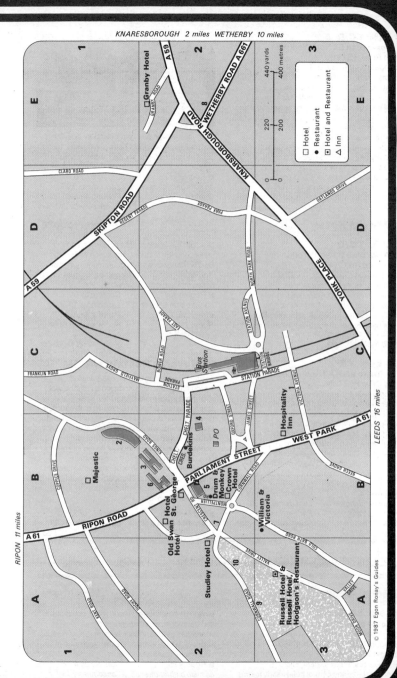

KNARESBOROUGH 2 miles WETHERBY 10 miles

KNARESBOROUGH/WETHERBY ROAD A 661

A 59

☐ Granby Hotel

GRANBY ROAD

CLARO ROAD

SKIPTON ROAD

REGENT PARADE

PARK PARADE

PARK PARADE

OAKLANDS DRIVE

YORK PLACE

A 59

A 61

EAST PARADE

NORTH PARK ROAD

STATION AVENUE

FRANKLIN ROAD

MAYFIELD GROVE

STATION PARADE

BOWER ROAD

STATION PARADE

Bus
Station

Station
BRIDGE

STATION PARADE

VICTORIA AVENUE

JAMES STREET

OXFORD STREET

CHELT PARADE

☐ Hospitality
Inn

WEST PARK

A 61

LEEDS 16 miles

☐ 4

☐ PO

Burdekins

Majestic

KINGS ROAD

CHELT

PARLIAMENT STREET

CORNWALL ROAD

BEECH GROVE

2

3

6

CHELT CRES

☐ Drum &
Monkey

☐ 5

☐ Crown
Hotel

MONTPELLIER

☐ Hotel
St. George

Old Swan
Hotel

RIPON ROAD

A 61

RIPON 11 miles

CRESCENT ROAD

William &
Victoria

COLD BATH ROAD

Studley Hotel ☐

VALLEY DRIVE

10

Russell Hotel/
Russell Hotel,
Hodgson's Restaurant

9

VALLEY DRIVE

440 yards
400 metres

220
200

☐ Hotel
● Restaurant
☑ Hotel and Restaurant
△ Inn

Majestic   Harrogate

H **72% £C/D** *E*
Town plan B1 North Yorkshire
Ripon Road HG1 2HU
Harrogate (0423) 68972. Tlx 57918
Manager Mr F. C. Flaherty
Credit Access, Amex, Diners, Visa

This turn-of-the-century hotel sits impressively in well-kept gardens, occupying one of the finest sites in Harrogate. The interior is on a grand scale, with a marble-pillared foyer, an airy lounge and a luxurious Regency Bar among the public rooms. There are comprehensive conference facilities and a recently completed leisure complex which centres around the indoor swimming pool. A fine staircase leads to spacious bedrooms, tastefully decorated in traditional style and very comfortable, all with well-equipped bathrooms. Upgraded rooms are particularly attractive, as are the suites. *Amenities* garden, indoor swimming pool, solarium, whirlpool bath, gymnasium, tennis, squash, games room, snooker, laundry service, helipad.

■ Rooms 157	Confirm by 6
en suite bath/shower 157	Last dinner 9.45
Direct dial Yes	Parking Ample
Room TV Yes	Room service 24 hours

Old Swan Hotel   Harrogate

H **68% £C/D**
Town plan B2 North Yorkshire
Swan Road HG1 2SR
Harrogate (0423) 500055. Tlx 57922
Credit Access, Amex, Diners, Visa

An imposing 18th-century building set in excessive grounds near the International Exhibition Centre. In 1926 Agatha Christie took refuge here for peace and quiet. White mouldings highlight the gracious light-blue foyer, and the striking lounge features grey suede walls. Bedrooms are pleasantly contemporary in style. *Amenities* garden, tennis, putting, croquet, in-house movies, laundry service.

■ Rooms 137	Confirm by 6
en suite bath/shower 137	Last dinner 10.30
Direct dial Yes	Parking Ample
Room TV Yes	Room service 24 hours

Russell Hotel   Harrogate

HR **64% £E**
Town plan A3 North Yorkshire
Valley Drive HG2 0JN
Harrogate (0423) 509866
Owner managers Richard & Martin Hodgson
Credit Access, Amex, Diners, Visa

A Victorian hotel of great charm and individuality. The lounge has a homely, traditional appeal, while the bar offers a more clubby atmosphere. Comfortably appointed front bedrooms enjoy splendid views over the Valley Gardens. *Amenities* garden, laundry service, 24-hour lounge service.

■ Rooms 34	Confirm by arrang.
en suite bath/shower 34	Last dinner 10.30
Direct dial Yes	Parking Limited
Room TV Yes	Room service Limited
Closed 27–30 Dec	

Hodgson's Restaurant ⌣ ⌇

Talented cooking in elegant oak-panelled surroundings. Richard Hodgson's skills are well illustrated in splendid starters like scallop and shrimp custard served in a creamy crab sauce, or herby venison drumlins poached in chicken broth. Follow perhaps with poached trout fillet in salmon mousse served with hollandaise, pot-roast pheasant in red wine sauce, or baked loin of lamb on a bed of puff pastry and mushrooms. Vegetables include delicious croquette potatoes with parsley, ham and chopped onion, and there's a scrumptious selection of sweets.
♀ Well-chosen ☺

■ Set D £14·75	D only 7–10.30
About £44 for two	Seats 75 Parties 80
Closed Sun & Mon to non-residents & 27–30 Dec	

■ For a discount on next year's guide, see Offer for Answers.

Hotel St George   Harrogate

H **65% £C/D**
Town plan B2 North Yorkshire
Ripon Road HG1 2SY
Harrogate (0423) 61431. Tlx 57995
Manager Nick Carey
Credit Access, Amex, Diners, Visa

A comfortable and central hotel handy for the Exhibition Centre and tourist sights. Good-sized bedrooms have smart modern furnishings and private bath or shower. The foyer-lounge is large and traditional, and there are two bars. *Amenities* garden, indoor swimming pool, sauna, solarium, whirlpool bath, steam room, keep-fit equipment, laundry service.

■ Rooms 85	Confirm by 6
en suite bath/shower 85	Last dinner 9.15
Direct dial Yes	Parking Ample
Room TV Yes	Room service 24 hours

Studley Hotel   Harrogate

H 66% £D
Town plan A2 North Yorkshire
28 Swan Road HG1 2SE
Harrogate (0423) 60425. Tlx 57506
Owner manager Mr G. G. Dilasser
Credit Access, Amex, Diners, Visa

Close to the lovely Valley Gardens, this conversion of a row of Victorian cottages is a hotel of considerable charm. Public rooms have a cosy, family feel. Smart darkwood furniture and chintzy fabrics team up nicely in the well equipped bedrooms. No children under 8. *Amenities* terrace, laundry service, in-house movies (free).

■ *Rooms* 39	*Confirm by arrang.*
en suite bath/shower 39	*Last dinner* 10.30
Direct dial Yes	*Parking* Ample
Room TV Yes	*Room service* 24 hours
Closed 5 days Xmas	

William & Victoria Restaurant   *NEW ENTRY*   Harrogate

R Town plan B3 North Yorkshire
6 Cold Bath Road
Harrogate (0423) 521510
Owner manager Mr Robin Straker
Credit Access

A smart, yet informal restaurant above a wine bar (same ownership), where blackboard menus offer a tempting variety of enjoyably prepared dishes. Light, fluffy terrine, served warm with butter sauce, might precede succulent medallions of beef richly sauced with burgundy – with banana caramel pie as a superb finale. Sound wines: Chablis from Bacheroy Josselin.

⟐ Well-chosen ℮

■ *About £25 for two*	*D only* 6–10
Seats 56	*Parking* Limited
Closed Sun, 1 wk Xmas & all Sept–Jan.	

■ If we recommend meals in a
hotel or inn, a separate entry is
made for its restaurant.

Mansion House at Grim's Dyke   Harrow Weald

H 64% £C/D
Map 5 E2 Middlesex
Old Redding HA3 6SH
01-954 7666. Tlx 946240
Credit Access, Amex, Diners, Visa

Sir William Gilbert lived for 20 years in this Tudor-style Victorian mansion. Gilbert and Sullivan soirées are a Sunday treat in the splendid music room. Refurbishment has enhanced the traditional appeal of public areas and several bedrooms. Main-house rooms are large and characterful; most, in a garden lodge, are pleasantly modern. *Amenities* garden, croquet.

■ *Rooms* 48	*Confirm by* 6
en suite bath/shower 48	*Last dinner* 9.30
Direct dial Yes	*Parking* Ample
Room TV Yes	*Room service* 24 hours
Closed 6 days Xmas	

Grand Hotel   Hartlepool

H 60% £D/E ⅃
Map 15 C5 Cleveland
Swainson Street TS24 8AA
Hartlepool (0429) 266345
Credit Access, Amex, Diners, Visa. **LVs**

Fine original features – including a lovely stained-glass window – marry with modern improvements at this late-Victorian hotel. The two bars and ballroom particularly impress, and there are several relaxing lounge areas. Crisp white linen and solidly traditional furniture characterise the bedrooms, and bathrooms boast splendidly old-fashioned tubs. *Amenities* 24-hour lounge service, laundry service.

■ *Rooms* 44	*Confirm by* 6
en suite bath/shower 22	*Last dinner* 10
Direct dial Yes	*Parking* Limited
Room TV Yes	*Room service* 24 hours

Pier at Harwich   Harwich

R Map 6 D3 Essex
The Quay
Harwich (0255) 503363
Seafood
Credit Access, Amex, Diners, Visa

Locally caught seafood is the star attraction at this first-floor quayside restaurant overlooking the harbour. Smoked haddock hot pot or garlicky baked mussels are typically appetising starters, while main courses range from straightforward plaice on the bone to seafood casseroled in vermouth. Steaks or steak and kidney pie for meat-eaters. ℮

■ *Set L Mon–Fri from*	*L* 12–2
£6·25, Sun £8·50	*D* 6–9.30
About £45 for two	*Parking* Ample
Seats 128	*Parties* 80
Closed D 25 Dec & all 26 Dec	

Lythe Hill Hotel   Haslemere

H 65% £C/D
Map 5 E3 Surrey
Petworth Road GU27 3BQ
Haslemere (0428) 51251. Tlx 858402
Credit Access, Amex, Diners, Visa
   A beautiful hillside setting for a fine old
timbered farmhouse and its outbuildings. Most
bedrooms are in a dated '60s style, but six are
traditional, with beams and panelling, and there

are two stylish luxury suites. The lounge is well
furnished, and there is an Italian-style covered
courtyard.
Amenities garden, sauna, tennis, croquet,
laundry service, 24-hour lounge service.

■ *Rooms* 38	*Confirm by arrang.*
en suite bath/shower 36	*Last dinner* 9.45
Direct dial Most	*Parking* Ample
Room TV Yes	*Room service* 24 hours

Morels ★   Haslemere

R ★ ☒ ⌑ **Map 5 E3** Surrey
25 Lower Street
Haslemere (0428) 51462
Credit Access, Amex, Diners, Visa
   Chef-patron Jean-Yves Morel has a lot of ideas,
and they all work. A meal in his attractive beamed
restaurant is a sustained delight, from the cheese-
filled mini-croissants to nibble with aperitifs to the
petits fours that come with coffee. Arriving in
between are superb creations like boudin of squid
with an essence of herbs and port, or chicken
studded with peppers and served with a scallop
mousse and an intensely flavoured champagne
and mushroom sauce. Vegetables are carefully
cooked and prettily presented, and you can enjoy
four delicious and dainty desserts in l'assiette du
chef. There's a fine French cheeseboard and a
good cellar with excellent burgundies. Service
runs smoothly under Jean-Yves' wife Mary-Anne.
Specialities boudin de moules au buerre d'ail,
saucisson de canard sauvage au foie gras et aux

pistaches, savarin de chevreuil aux châtaignes et
au jus, mille-feuille au chocolat et à l'orange
chinoise.
⌑ Well-chosen ☺

■ *Set L* £11	*L* 12.30–1.45
Set D Tues–Fri from £14	*D* 7–10
About £58 for two	*Parking* Difficult
Seats 45	

Closed L Sat & Tues, D Sun, all Mon, Bank Hols
exc. Good Fri, 2 wks Sept & 2 wks Feb

⌑ indicates a **well-chosen** house wine.

Shrimpton's   Haslemere

R ⌑ **Map 5 E3** Surrey
Midhurst Road
Haslemere (0428) 3539
Credit Access, Amex, Diners, Visa
   Refurbishment has doubled capacity at Beryl
Keeley's popular beamed restaurant. A varied
menu mingles the simplest of choices – grilled
sardines, pâté, trout with almonds – with more
elaborate offerings such as prawn-filled smoked

salmon and fillet steak sauced with cream, green
peppercorns and brandy. Homely sweets include
treacle tart, meringues and ices. ☺

■ *Set L* £9·50	*L* 12.30–2
Set D £16	*D* 6.30–9.45
About £36 for two	*Parking* Ample
Seats 44	*Parties* 44

Closed L Sat, all Sun, 26 Dec & 1 Jan

Woodmans Arms Auberge *NEW ENTRY*   Hastingleigh

RR ⌑ **Map 7 C5** Kent
Hassell Street, Ashford TN25 5JE
Elmsted (023 375) 250
Credit Amex
   Billy Bunter is alive and well and living in
deepest Kent. Gerald Campion, who played the
part of Bunter for many years, and his wife Susan
run a tiny restaurant in their isolated 17th-century
house. Susan's confident, imaginative home
cooking is entirely without pretension. A scallop
and artichoke soup might be followed by quails'
egg salad, fresh sea bass baked in fennel, and
home-made ice cream. There's a short, shrewdly

chosen wine list (note superb Pouilly-Fuissé
l'Arrilière 1983). Booking essential. Lunch by
arrangement only.   ⌑ Well-chosen ☺

■ *Set L* from £10·50	*L* 12.30–1
Set D £14·50	*D* 7.30 for 8,
About £38 for two	Sun 7 for 7.30
Seats 10 *Parties* 10	*Parking* Ample

Closed 1 wk May & last 2 wks Sept

Bedrooms £E/F
Rooms 3   With bath/shower 3
Bedrooms, all with TVs, are prettily rustic and very
comfortable. No smoking anywhere.

Rösers *NEW ENTRY*   Hastings

R ᛃ **Map 7 C6** East Sussex
64 Eversfield Place, St Leonards
Hastings (0424) 712218
Credit Access, Amex, Diners, Visa
   Gerald and Jenny Röser's comfortable little
restaurant on the seafront features fish and game
in season on a menu that ranges from almond and
leek soup and pike soufflé to Stilton-stuffed veal
and sole with smoked salmon. Excellent wines

with a fine selection of 1983 Chablis (Michel, Pic,
Bacheroy-Josselin). Informal cabaret is provided
by an African Grey parrot. ☺

■ *Set L* £9.50	*L 12–2*
Set D £12.50	*D 7–10*
About £50 *for two*	*Parking Ample*
Seats 40 Parties 20	*Closed* L Sat, all Sun,
& *Bank Hols* & *1st 2 wks Jan*	

Farthings Country House Hotel   Hatch Beauchamp

H **70% £D**
Map 3 E2 Somerset
Nr Taunton TA3 6SG
Hatch Beauchamp (0823) 480664
Owner managers Mr & Mrs Cooper
Credit Access, Visa
   Hatch Beauchamp is a peaceful and attractive
village with little traffic, and Farthings, a well-kept
Georgian house, is a very pleasant and relaxing
place to stay. Guests can sit by an open fire in the
comfortably furnished lounge and chat or browse
through magazines, or enjoy a drink in the inviting
little cocktail bar. Bedrooms, generally light and
spacious, are individually appointed: one pretty
bay-windowed room has a spiral staircase leading
up to its bathroom; a couple are in cottage style
with pine furniture and floral wallpaper; another
offers 'his and hers' bathrooms; a single at the top

has a private staircase, with the bathroom at the
bottom.
Amenities garden.

■ *Rooms* 6	*Confirm by* arrang.
en suite bath/shower 6	*Last dinner* 9.30
Room phone Yes	*Parking* Ample
Room TV Yes	*Room service* All day
Closed 2 wks Jan	

Comet Hotel   Hatfield

H **61% £D**
Map 7 B4 Hertfordshire
301 St Albans Road West AL10 9RH
Hatfield (070 72) 65411
Credit Access, Amex, Diners, Visa
   Named after the locally built De Havilland
Comet Racer, this 1930s hotel alongside the A1 is
a popular overnight stop with travellers and
business visitors. Good-sized bedrooms are all

neatly fitted. Tea-makers, trouser presses and
hairdryers are standard, and bathrooms, too, are
well-equipped. Day rooms include a smart bar-
lounge and the newly redecorated Mosquito Bar.
Amenities garden, laundry service.

■ *Rooms* 57	*Confirm by* 6
en suite bath/shower 54	*Last dinner* 10
Direct dial Yes	*Parking* Ample
Room TV Yes	*Room service* 24 hours

George Hotel   Hatherleigh

I **£F**
Map 3 D2 Devon
Market Street, Nr Okehampton EX20 3JN
Okehampton (0837) 810454
Owner managers Andrew & Nichola Grubb
Credit Access, Visa
   A cobbled courtyard fronts this fine old
coaching inn, where friendly owners and staff
create a homely, informal atmosphere. Blackened

beams and huge open fires characterise the cosy
bars. Solidly furnished bedrooms, three with four-
posters, are equally traditional in style.
Amenities garden, outdoor swimming pool,
croquet, pool table, laundry service.

■ *Rooms* 11	*Confirm by* arrang.
en suite bath/shower 9	*Last dinner* 9.30
Room phone No	*Parking* Ample
Room TV No	*Room service* All day

Bear Hotel *NEW ENTRY*   Havant

H **59% £D/E**
Map 5 D4 Hampshire
East Street PO9 1AA
Portsmouth (0705) 486501. Tlx 869136
Credit Access, Amex, Diners, Visa
   The street frontage of this hotel evokes
coaching days, while the rear entrance is modern,
with a new reception area; the public bar and
refurbished lounge maintain the traditional look.

Bedrooms, some redecorated in light, bright
colours, others in darker warmer shades, all have
trouser presses, hairdryers and splendidly
equipped bathrooms. *Amenities* laundry service,
in-house movies (free).

■ *Rooms* 32	*Confirm by* 6
en suite bath/shower 32	*Last dinner* 10
Direct dial Yes	*Parking* Ample
Room TV Yes	*Room service* 24 hours

Post House Hotel   Havant

H 62% £C/D
Map 5D4 Hampshire
Northney Road, Hayling Island PO11 0NQ
Hayling Island (0705) 465011. Tlx 86620
Credit Access, Amex, Diners, Visa

A fitness club has boosted the facilities of this modern hotel on Hayling Island. Overnight accommodation is neat and practical, and many rooms have been refurbished to achieve superior status. *Amenities* garden, indoor swimming pool, sauna, solarium, whirlpool bath, keep-fit equipment, laundry service, coffee shop (10am–10pm), 24-hour lounge service, children's play area, helipad.

■ *Rooms* 96	*Confirm by* 6
en suite bath/shower 96	*Last dinner* 10
Direct dial Yes	*Parking* Ample
Room TV Yes	*Room service* Limited

Fairwater Head Hotel   Hawkchurch

H 62% £D/E
Map 3 E2 Devon
Nr Axminster EX13 5TX
Hawkchurch (029 77) 349
Owner managers R. & H. Austin and J. & J. Lowe
Credit Access, Diners, Visa

A beautiful garden and fine views of the Axe Valley provide a peaceful setting here. Public rooms have been refurbished and main house bedrooms smartly upgraded to match those in the garden wing. *Amenities* garden, badminton, putting, croquet, snooker, laundry service.

■ *Rooms* 18	*Confirm by* 6
en suite bath/shower 18	*Last dinner* 8.30
Direct dial Yes	*Parking* Ample
Room TV Yes	*Room service* All day
Closed Jan & Feb	

Tudor Arms Hotel   Hawkhurst

H 64% £D/E
Map 7 C6 Kent
Rye Road TN18 5DA
Hawkhurst (058 05) 2312
Credit Access, Amex, Diners, Visa

A smart, well-maintained hotel set in attractive gardens by the A268. There's a welcoming residents' lounge with lots of chintzy comfort and a traditional feel that follows through to the bar. Bedrooms are decently sized, their furnishings a blend of period and modern; housekeeping sparkles, and accessories include tea-makers, radio-alarms and trouser presses. *Amenities* garden, tennis, children's playground.

■ *Rooms* 14	*Confirm by* arrang.
en suite bath/shower 12	*Last dinner* 9.30
Direct dial Yes	*Parking* Ample
Room TV Yes	*Room service* All day

Field Head House *NEW ENTRY*   Hawkshead

HR 67% £E
Map 13 D5 Cumbria
Outgate LA22 0PY
Hawkshead (096 66) 240. Tlx 64117
Owner managers Bob & Eeke van Gulik
Credit Amex, Diners, Visa

Follow the signs to Field Head off the B5286 to find this delightful former shooting lodge in the hills amidst lovely lakeland views. The Dutch owners, who love Cumbria, are gradually restoring the house and gardens. Wood-burning stoves warm the lounges, and the bedrooms are homely. Superb breakfasts. *Amenities* garden, croquet, laundry service, laundry room.

■ *Rooms* 8	*Confirm by* arrang.
en suite bath/shower 7	*Last dinner* 8
Room phone No	*Parking* Ample
Room TV Some	*Room service* All day

Field Head House Restaurant 🍴 ♊

Fresh local produce and an almost self-sufficient vegetable garden play important parts here. Bob van Gulik's five-course dinner menus (usually no choice; non-residents must book) feature delights like local air-dried ham, milder and more delicate than Parma, and trout gently cooked in foil and topped with buttery almond flakes. Sweets include sticky toffee pudding. A small choice of interesting cheeses. Vegetarian meals available with notice. Small carefully compiled wine list.
♊ Well-chosen 🅔

■ *Set D* £12.50	*L by* arrang.
About £32 *for two*	*D at* 8
Seats 16	*Parties* 8

Post House Hotel   Haydock

H 64% £C
Map 10 B2 Merseyside
Lodge Lane, Newton-le-Willows WA12 0JG
Wigan (0942) 717878. Tlx 677672
Credit Access, Amex, Diners, Visa

Businessmen and racegoers find this neat modern hotel conveniently close to junction 23 of the M6 and the racecourse. There's a clubby bar in which to toast the winner and an inviting foyer-lounge. Pleasant, airy bedrooms are well equipped, and have smart compact bathrooms. *Amenities* garden, in-house movies (charge), laundry service, restaurant (7am–10.30pm), 24-hour lounge service, children's playground.

■ *Rooms* 98	*Confirm by* 6
en suite bath/shower 98	*Last dinner* 10.30
Direct dial Yes	*Parking* Ample
Room TV Yes	*Room service* Limited

Bel Alp House Country Hotel *NEW ENTRY* Haytor

H **64%** **£D**
Map 3 D3 Devon
Nr Bovey Tracey TQ13 9XX
Haytor (036 46) 217
Owner managers Roger & Sarah Curnock
Credit Access, Visa
 A beautifully situated hotel where guests are
made to feel extremely welcome. Decor is
pleasing throughout, with some nice antiques in
evidence; there's an elegant, comfortable
drawing room and a homely bar. Bedrooms are
spacious and simple, with magnificent views. Two
bathrooms are Victorian, the rest stylishly
modern. *Amenities* garden, tennis, snooker.

- *Rooms 9*   *Confirm by arrang.*
en suite bath/shower 9   *Last dinner 8.30*
Direct dial Yes   *Parking Ample*
Room TV Yes   *Room service Limited*

Jade Garden *NEW ENTRY* Heaton Moor

R **Map 10 B2** Cheshire
29 Shaw Road, Stockport
061-442 0143
Chinese cooking
Credit Access, Amex, Diners, Visa
 Cantonese cooking is the speciality of this
attractive restaurant in a suburban shopping
parade. A large menu offers standard favourites
plus dishes that sound, and taste, just that little
bit different, like crispy duck with minced prawn
and mushroom sauce. Our high spot was
succulent steamed scallops with garlic and
ginger. Friendly and informal service.

- *Set L £3 50*   *L 12–2*
Set D from £7·50   *D 5.30–12 (Fri & Sat till*
About £30 for two   *2am), Sun noon–2am*
Seats 50 Parties 50   *Parking Ample*
Closed L Sat & 25 Dec

Riverside Helford

RR ⑤ **Map 2 B4** Cornwall
Nr Helston
Manaccan (032 623) 443
Owner managers Edward & Susie Darrell
 New owners have taken over this delightful
cottage restaurant at the entrance to Helford
village. The imaginative fixed-price dinner menu,
with a strong bias towards fish, offers plenty of
choice, and cooking is competent. Excellent
canapés to start, followed, perhaps, by
watercress soup, seafood tart or fish terrine. Main
courses range from deliciously fresh poached sea
bass with an excellent aioli to estoufade of lamb
with parsley noodles. Cheeses are well
presented, with homebaked biscuits, walnuts,
dried apricots and fresh fruits. Standard sweets.
- ♀ Well-chosen ☺
- *Set D £24*   *D 7.30–9.30*
About £64 for two   *Parking Ample*
Closed mid Nov–mid   *Seats 40*
Mar

Bedrooms **£C/D**
Rooms 6   *With bath/shower 6*
Six pretty rooms with pine furniture and charming
soft furnishings and all are equipped with TVs and
tea-makers. No dogs.

■ We welcome complaints and bona
fide recommendations on the
tear-out pages for readers' comments.
They are followed up by our professional
team. Please also complain to the
management instantly.

RECEPTION

Tredethy Country Hotel Helland Bridge

H **56%** **£D/E**
Map 2 B3 Cornwall
Nr Bodmin PL30 4QS
St Mabyn (020 884) 262
Owner managers A. S. & D. A. Vernoit
 Ornaments from the Far East add an exotic
touch to this friendly, largely Victorian hotel set in
beautiful wooded grounds. The spacious
entrance hall doubles as a bar-lounge, and there
is another handsomely traditional lounge. Largest,
brightest bedrooms are at the front. Half-board
only. No children under 12. No dogs.
Amenities garden, outdoor swimming pool.
- *Rooms 11*   *Confirm by arrang.*
en suite bath/shower 11 *Last dinner 8*
Room phone No   *Parking Ample*
Room TV No   *Room service All day*
Closed 2 wks Xmas

Helmsley ▶

Helmsley

Black Swan Hotel

H R **70%** **£C/D**
Map 15 C6 North Yorkshire
Market Place YO6 5BJ
Helmsley (0439) 70466
Credit Access, Amex, Diners, Visa

Facing onto the market place, this attractive hotel is built from a row of stone houses, parts of which date from Tudor times. A charming historical ambience prevails, as period features have been carefully retained in the public rooms, which include four lounges with plenty of comfortable armchairs. There's also a small but quaint bar with a fine oak dado. Individually decorated bedrooms, each one bearing the name of a Yorkshire dale, are just as thoughtfully furnished, with coordinating fabrics, smart

darkwood antique-style furniture, and compact tiled bathrooms with plenty of extras such as bathrobes and weighing scales.
Amenities garden, croquet, laundry service.

■ *Rooms* 37	*Confirm by* 6
en suite bath/shower 37	*Last dinner* 9.15
Direct dial Yes	*Parking* Ample
Room TV Yes	*Room service* All day

Black Swan Restaurant

An imaginative and creative menu offers some delightful dishes which are cooked to a high standard, with impressive saucing and first-rate presentation. Typical starters are baked avocado pear in puff pastry or vegetable lasagne; to follow try salmon coulibiac with lime sauce, turbot poached in champagne with spinach mousse or breast of duck with grapes and walnuts in claret sauce. There's also game in season. Service is professional and caring. No smoking in the dining room. ☺

■ *Set L £6.50,*	*L* 12.15–2.15
Sun £10.50	*D* 7.30–9.30
Set D £14.50	*Seats* 65
About £42 for two	*Parties* 40
Closed D 25 Dec	

Feathers Hotel

Helmsley

I **£E/F**
Map 15 C6 North Yorkshire
Market Place YO6 5BH
Helmsley (0439) 70275
Owner manager Jack Feather
Credit Access, Amex, Diners, Visa

Fifteenth-century cottage merges with 18th-century house to make a most agreeable inn. A cosy reception area leads into the welcoming

lounge bar and popular Pickwick Bar and there's a homely residents' lounge upstairs. Bedrooms are simply and modestly furnished and have tea/coffee-makers. *Amenities* garden.

■ *Rooms* 18	*Confirm by* 6
en suite bath/shower 13	*Last dinner* 9
Room phone No	*Parking* Ample
Room TV Yes	*Room service* Limited
Closed 25 & 26 Dec	

Feversham Arms Hotel

Helmsley

H **65%** **£E**
Map 15 C6 North Yorkshire
1 High Street YO6 5AG
Helmsley (0439) 70766
Owner managers Gonzalo & Rowan De Aragüés
Credit Access, Amex, Diners, Visa

The Aragüés family have run this Victorian hotel for 20 years, and the latest improvement is the enlarging of several bedrooms. Decor is restful,

and accessories include wall safes and trouser presses. All bathrooms have tubs, showers and bidets. There are two bars, one opening on to a patio. *Amenities* garden, outdoor swimming pool, tennis.

■ *Rooms* 19	*Confirm by* 4
en suite bath/shower 19	*Last dinner* 9
Direct dial Yes	*Parking* Ample
Room TV Yes	*Room service* All day

⊳ is our symbol for an **outstanding** wine list.

Casanova *NEW ENTRY*

Hemel Hempstead

R **Map 5 E2** Hertfordshire
75 Waterhouse Street
Hemel Hempstead (0442) 47482
Italian cooking
Owner manager Carlo Benigno
Credit Access, Amex, Diners, Visa

Carlo and his brother spread a happy, relaxed atmosphere through this popular Italian restaurant, and the Spanish chef produces a

range of enjoyable dishes. Various versions of veal, steak, chicken, fish and pasta. Simple starters and the usual sweets. Some excellent daily specials, and super espresso coffee.
♥ Well-chosen ☺

■ *About £40 for two*	*L* 12–2.15
Seats 52 *Parties* 50	*D* 7–11
Closed L Sat, all Sun &	*Parking* Ample
Bank Hols	

Post House Hotel   Hemel Hempstead

H **60% £C/D**
Map 5 E2 Hertfordshire
Breakspear Way HP2 4UA
Hemel Hempstead (0442) 51122. Tlx 826902
Credit Access, Amex, Diners, Visa

A two-year improvement programme includes refurbishment of 30 bedrooms at Britain's first Post House, which stands near junction 8 of the M1. Bedrooms are generally of a good size, the

best being Executive rooms with sofas, trouser presses and mini-bars. There's a comfortable bar-lounge and a bright coffee shop. Pleasant, friendly staff. *Amenities* garden, laundry service, coffee shop (10am–10.30pm).

■ *Rooms 107*	*Confirm by 6*
en suite bath/shower 107	*Last dinner 10*
Direct dial Yes	*Parking Ample*
Room TV Yes	*Room service 24 hours*

Yew Trees Hotel *NEW ENTRY*   Henley in Arden

H **72% £D**
Map 10 C4 West Midlands
154 High Street B95 5BN
Henley in Arden (05642) 4636. Tlx 334264
Owner managers Pearson family
Credit Access, Amex, Diners, Visa

An attractive and well-kept half-timbered Tudor house, parts of which date back to the thirteenth century. The neat and tidy foyer has a large open fire, and the lounge is redolent of the atmosphere of bygone days, with wooden floors, linenfold panelling and oak beams. The chairs are in a variety of styles, set off by several antique pieces and ornaments. A modern-style bar overlooks lovely landscaped gardens. The well-equipped bedrooms are large and elegantly furnished with traditional fabrics, settees and armchairs, and huge comfortable beds (one dated 1636).

Bathrooms are also good-sized, with quality toiletries. No children under eight. No dogs. *Amenities* garden, laundry service.

■ *Rooms 8*	*Confirm by arrang.*
en suite bath/shower 8	*Last dinner 9.30*
Direct dial Yes	*Parking Ample*
Room TV Yes	*Room service Limited*

Red Lion Hotel   Henley-on-Thames

H **56% £C/D**
Map 5 D2 Oxfordshire
Hart Street RG9 2AR
Henley-on-Thames (0491) 572161. Tlx 83343
Owner manager Charles Ractliff
Credit Access, Amex, Visa

Royal and famous visitors are commemorated in the names of the bedrooms in this riverside hotel. The best rooms command delightful views

of the River Thames, and all are individually decorated and have central heating, TVs and radios. Public rooms include an oak-beamed lounge, a cheerful panelled wine bar and a cocktail bar. *Amenities* laundry service.

■ *Rooms 27*	*Confirm by 6*
en suite bath/shower 20	*Last dinner 9.45*
Room phone Yes	*Parking Limited*
Room TV Yes	*Room service All day*

Green Dragon Hotel   Hereford

H **69% £D**
Map 4 A1 Hereford & Worcester
Broad Street HR4 9BG
Hereford (0432) 272506. Tlx 35491
Credit Access, Amex, Diners, Visa. LVs

An aura of elegant grandeur pervades this splendid Georgian hotel. The showcase-lined foyer leads to a spacious lounge furnished with plump-cushioned sofas and the two bars offer a

stylish and intimate atmosphere. Bedrooms vary from superior suites with lounge areas, some with four-posters, to compact singles, all furnished to a high standard with smart fabrics and furniture. *Amenities* laundry service.

■ *Rooms 88*	*Confirm by 6*
en suite bath/shower 88	*Last dinner 9.15*
Room phone Yes	*Parking Ample*
Room TV Yes	*Room service 24 hours*

Hereford Moat House   Hereford

H **61% £D/E**
Map 4 A1 Hereford & Worcester
Belmont Road HR2 7BF
Hereford (0432) 54301
Credit Access, Amex, Diners, Visa

The steeply-raked roof is a distinctive feature of this modern hotel on the A465 Abergavenny road. Bedrooms, in stark chalet-style blocks, have a uniform practicality and offer tea-makers and

radio-alarms. Day rooms include a bright comfortable bar-lounge that overlooks an ornamental pool. *Amenities* garden, laundry service, 24-hour lounge service.

■ *Rooms 32*	*Confirm by arrang.*
en suite bath/shower 32	*Last dinner 9.45*
Room phone Yes	*Parking Ample*
Room TV Yes	*Room service 24 hours*
Closed 1 wk Xmas	

L'Escargot   Herne Bay

R ♀ **Map 7 C5** Kent
22 High Street
Herne Bay (0227) 372876
French cooking
Credit Access, Amex, Diners, Visa
         Alain Bessemoulin is in sole charge of
the kitchen, while his wife Joyce provides a warm
Yorkshire welcome in the cosy dining room. The
straightforward à la carte menu offers starters like

deep-fried Camembert, garlicky snails or excellent
moules marinière to precede pepper steak, or the
day's fish special. ℮

■ Set L £6·80	L 12.30–2
Set D £7·80	D 7–10
About £34 for two	Parking Ample
Seats 36	Parties 40

Closed L Sat, Sun & Mon, also D Sun in winter,
also L Bank Hols & 2 days Xmas

The Dining Room   *NEW ENTRY*   Hersham

R̆ **Map 7 A5** Surrey
10 Queens Road, The Village Green
Walton on Thames (0932) 231686
English cooking
Credit Visa
   Old pine and pretty floral wallpaper give this
friendly, easy-going restaurant a cottagy feel. The
menu provides a tempting selection of
wholesome English dishes, from grilled sardines,

potted crab and toad-in-the-hole to steak and
kidney pie and pork with sage and cider. Plainly
cooked vegetables are plentiful, and puddings
include chocolate fudge cake with brandy sauce. ℮

■ About £32 for two	L noon–2
Seats 65	D 7–10.30
Parties 16	Parking Ample

Closed L Sat, D Sun, all Mon & Bank Hols &
2 wks Xmas

♀ indicates a **well-chosen** house wine.

Sundial   Herstmonceux

R ♀ ♿ **Map 7 B6** East Sussex
Near Hailsham
Herstmonceux (0323) 832217
French cooking
Credit Amex, Diners, Visa
   The unspoilt East Sussex countryside is the
setting for this delightful 17th-century cottage
restaurant. Giuseppe Bertoli is a highly
professional chef, who combines a classical
training with an innate flair for marrying flavours in
perfect harmony. The menu is so extensive that it
borders on the bewildering, so seek his advice
when ordering. A favourite starter is bouillabaise

with cheese and garlic croûtons, and main
courses range from thyme-flavoured Dover sole to
breast of duckling in pear sauce. Good desserts.
On an impressive wine list, exceptional clarets
include Château Lafite 1955 and Château
Margaux 1953 (magnums).
◖ Outstanding   ♀ Well-chosen ℮

■ Set L from £12·50	L 12–2.30
Set D £17·50	D 7–10
About £50 for two	Parking Ample
Seats 50	Parties 80

Closed D Sun, all Mon, Bank Hols, 3 wks Aug, 1st
wk Sept & 25 Dec–20 Jan

White Horse Inn   Hertingfordbury

H **61% £C**
Map 7 B4 Hertfordshire
Hertingfordbury Road SG14 2LB
Hertford (0992) 586791
Credit Access, Amex, Diners, Visa
   The local manor house before it became a
coaching inn, this friendly establishment stands in
attractive gardens in the village centre. The
ground floor is dominated by a spacious lounge-

bar with a central brick fireplace and velvet-clad
seating. Most of the bedrooms have darkwood
fitted furniture and all offer tea-makers, remote-
control TVs and well-equipped bathrooms.
Amenities garden, laundry service.

■ Rooms 42	Confirm by 6
en suite bath/shower 42	Last dinner 9.30
Direct dial Yes	Parking Ample
Room TV Yes	Room service All day

Park Farm Hotel   Hethersett

H **65% £E**
Map 6 C2 Norfolk
Nr Norwich NR9 3DL
Norwich (0603) 810264
Owner managers Mr & Mrs Gowing
Credit Access, Amex, Diners, Visa
   This relaxing hotel is also a working farm. The
main strength is the bedrooms which range from
smartly modern to seven superior four-poster

rooms and three with whirlpool baths. Relaxing,
comfortable public areas. Mediocre breakfast.
Amenities garden, indoor swimming pool, sauna,
solarium, putting, croquet, games room, pool
table, laundry service, helipad.

■ Rooms 22	Confirm by arrang.
en suite bath/shower 22	Last dinner 9
Direct dial Yes	Parking Ample
Room TV Yes	Room service All day

Angel Inn   Hetton

R ⚐ & **Map 15 B6** North Yorkshire
Nr Skipton
Cracoe (075 673) 263
Credit Access
In a setting that's very cosy and friendly Denis Watkins prepares four-course dinners that are a pleasure to both eye and taste buds. Choice can be difficult, as it's all very tempting: tarragon-sauced timbale of chicken and mushrooms; fish soup with garlicky croûtons; fillet of lamb with a fine red pepper sauce and multifarious vegetables; exotic fruits in a biscuit basket. On Fridays it's mainly fish. Delightfully informal service. ☺

■ *Set L* £7·75	*L Sun only 12–2*
Set D £11.95	*D 7–10*
About £33 *for two*	*Parking Ample*
Closed D Sun & some	*Seats 36*
Bank Hols	

Blue Bell at Heversham   Heversham

I **£E**
Map 13 D6 Cumbria
Princes Way, Nr Milnthorpe LA7 7EE
Milnthorpe (044 82) 2018
Credit Access, Amex, Visa
A striking black and white timbered inn alongside the A6. There's a sunny little conservatory leading to the two traditional bars, one decorated with old cock-fighting prints, and three pleasant lounges. Comfortable bedrooms, furnished in neat modern style, have tea-makers and simple bath or shower rooms. No dogs. *Amenities* garden.

■ *Rooms 27*	*Confirm by 6*
en suite bath/shower 21	*Last dinner 9*
Direct dial Yes	*Parking Ample*
Room TV Yes	*Room service All day*
Closed 25 & 26 Dec	

Beaumont Hotel   Hexham

H **58% £F**
Map 15 B4 Northumberland
Beaumont Street NE46 3LT
Hexham (0434) 602331
Owner managers Martin & Linda Owen
Credit Access, Amex, Diners, Visa
A stylish cocktail bar with velour seating is an attractive feature of Martin and Linda Owen's town-centre hotel, which overlooks the abbey grounds. There's also a spacious foyer-lounge and a popular public bar. Some of the bedrooms are in bright, simple style, while others have been upgraded with individual colour schemes. No dogs. *Amenities* laundry service.

■ *Rooms 20*	*Confirm by arrang.*
en suite bath/shower 20	*Last dinner 9.45*
Direct dial Yes	*Parking Limited*
Room TV Yes	*Room service All day*

Crest Hotel   High Wycombe

H **64% £C/D** &
Map 5 E2 Buckinghamshire
Crest Road, Handycross HP11 1TL
High Wycombe (0494) 442100. Tlx 83626
Credit Access, Amex, Diners, Visa
A spacious, mellow foyer and alcoved bar-lounge create a relaxing setting at this modern low-rise hotel at junction 4 of the M40. Attractive bedrooms have tea-makers, trouser presses, radio-alarms, and compact tiled bathrooms. Executive accommodation is very smart, with a host of thoughtful extras. No dogs. *Amenities* garden, in-house movies (charge), laundry service, coffee shop (7am–6.30pm).

■ *Rooms 108*	*Confirm by 6*
en suite bath/shower 108	*Last dinner 10.15*
Direct dial Yes	*Parking Ample*
Room TV Yes	*Room service Limited*

■ Any person using our name to obtain free hospitality is a fraud. Proprietors, please inform the police and us.

Master Brewer Motel   Hillingdon

H **58% £D/E** &
Map 5 E2 Middlesex
Western Avenue, Hillingdon Circus UB10 9BR
Uxbridge (0895) 51199
Manager Peter Walton
Credit Access, Amex, Diners, Visa
. This popular motel stands alongside the A40, about 12 miles west of London. Bedrooms are in blocks built round a garden with an ornamental pool. Most have either balconies or patios, and all have fitted units and tea-makers. The pleasant foyer-lounge has bamboo furniture, as does the cosy chocolate brown bar. *Amenities* garden, laundry service, children's playground.

■ *Rooms 106*	*Confirm by 6*
en suite bath/shower 106	*Last dinner 11*
Direct dial Yes	*Parking Ample*
Room TV Yes	*Room service Limited*

Hintlesham Hall — Hintlesham

HR 80% £C/D
Map 6 C3 Suffolk
Nr Ipswich IP8 3NS
Hintlesham (047 387) 268. Tlx 98340
Owner managers David & Ruth Watson
Credit Access, Amex, Diners, Visa

Built in 1578 but substantially altered in the 18th century, this lovely country house rejoices in wonderfully caring owners and staff. From the flagstoned hall with its exotic greenery to the mellow, pine-panelled salon and two fine lounges (one for non-smokers), all is stylish and welcoming. Refurbishment has further enhanced the appeal of spacious main-house bedrooms, which include six recent additions in mock-Tudor style; six rooms in the Queen Anne wing are more contemporary. All offer excellent accessories and superb bathrooms. Babies not frowned upon but children up to 10 are! Dogs in kennels only. *Amenities* garden, tennis, riding, games room, billiards, snooker, laundry service.

■ *Rooms 17*	*Confirm by arrang.*
en suite bath/shower 17	*Last dinner 9.30*
Direct dial Yes	*Parking Ample*
Room TV Yes	*Room service All day*
Closed 2 wks end Jan–beg Feb	

Hintlesham Hall Restaurant ♛ ♿

This handsome recently-redecorated restaurant is an admirable setting for Robert Mabey's skilful and imaginative cooking. Menus offer plenty of choice from fricassée of brill and mussels, spinach and wild mushroom tart and Sevruga caviar to roast monkfish, veal with truffles or chicken with a langoustine sauce. Round off the meal with tarte tatin or 'floating islands'. Saturday lunches by arrangement. 🍷 Well-chosen 🙂

■ *Set L £15*	*L 12–2*
Set D £25	*D 7–9.30*
About £60 for two	*Seats 70 Parties 100*
Closed L Sat, 2 wks end Jan–beg Feb	

Nuthurst Grange *NEW ENTRY* — Hockley Heath

HR 74% £C
Map 10 C4 Warwickshire
Nuthurst Grange Lane
Lapworth (056 43) 3972. Tlx 333485
Owner managers David & Darryl Randolph
Credit Access, Amex, Diners, Visa

A leafy drive just off the A34 leads to this delightful country house set in landscaped gardens and woodland. A relaxing, informal air pervades; the elegant entrance has comfortable seating and the peaceful lounge is furnished with deep-cushioned sofas, attractive lamps and coordinating curtains. Spacious bedrooms are individually designed, using pretty, top-quality fabrics and fine pieces of period furniture (one four-poster). All have a host of extras such as hairdryers, trouser presses and fruit. The carpeted bathrooms are equipped with good toiletries, bidets and telephones. Superb breakfast. *Amenities* garden, croquet, in-house movies (free), laundry service.

■ *Rooms 8*	*Confirm by arrang.*
en suite bath/shower 8	*Last dinner 9.30*
Direct dial Yes	*Parking Ample*
Room TV Yes	*Room service All day*

Nuthurst Grange Restaurant ★ 🍷

A delightfully intimate atmosphere adds to the enjoyment of David Randolph's beautifully cooked meals. The very best produce is expertly handled and artistically presented, while the saucing is superb. The frequently-changing menu features both classical and modern cuisine to maximum effect; typical starters might be veal sweetbreads sautéed in Marsala in a brioche mould or terrine of red mullet and scallop mousse; to follow breast of chicken with pistachio quenelles or fillet of veal with Stilton and chive sauce. Beautiful sweets such as a stunning banana soufflé to finish. Meticulously chosen wines with a real eye for quality: delicious Bourgogne Blanc 1985 (Aubert de Villaine). *Specialities* terrine of wild mushrooms with tarragon sauce, Arden duckling with figs, white and dark chocolate mousse in a cage of caramel threads, served with dark chocolate sauce. 🍷 Well-chosen 🙂

■ *Set L £11·50*	*L 12.30–2*
Set D £19·50	*D 7–9.30*
About £60 for two	*Seats 50*
Closed L Sun & D Sat	*Parties 20*

Alston Hall Hotel   Holbeton

H 73% £D/E
Map 3 D3 Devon
Battisborough Cross, Nr Plymouth PL8 1HN
Holbeton (075 530) 259
Credit Access, Amex, Diners, Visa
The setting is outstandingly peaceful and
beautiful for this fine Edwardian mansion between
Dartmoor and the sea. Inside, there's also plenty
to impress, starting with the oak-panelled
entrance hall with its minstrel's gallery, stained
glass and rich leather. The lounge and bar are
equally handsome, and the bedrooms (some very
large, others fairly small) certainly don't let the
side down: they are all individually decorated and
styled in a traditional way in keeping with the
house. Bathrooms are carpeted and there are lots
of extras, from iced water to hairdryers. Spotless
housekeeping is reflected in every polished

surface. Excellent personal service.
Amenities garden, outdoor swimming pool,
tennis, laundry service.

■ *Rooms 9*	*Confirm by arrang.*
en suite bath/shower 9	*Last dinner 9.30*
Direct dial Yes	*Parking Ample*
Room TV Yes	*Room service All day*

Great Danes Hotel   Hollingbourne

H 70% £C/D &
Map 7 C5 Kent
Ashford Road ME17 1RE
Maidstone (0622) 30022. Tlx 96198
Credit Access, Amex, Diners, Visa
The stylish new leisure centre is proving a
popular attraction at this extended 18th-century
country house set in parkland off the A20. Some
public areas have been stylishly refurbished –
note particularly the foyer with its marble floor and
elegant pastel furnishings. The lounge and bar are
very appealing, too, and careful thought has gone
into the styling of the bedrooms: they all offer
plenty of space and comfort and include two
suites and five de luxe rooms. *Amenities* garden,
indoor swimming pool, sauna, solarium, whirlpool
bath, keep-fit equipment, hairdressing, tennis,
pitch & putt, croquet, coarse fishing, games room,

snooker, pool table, in-house movies (free),
laundry service, coffee shop (10am–11pm), 24-
hour lounge service, kiosk, children's playground,
helipad.

■ *Rooms 126*	*Confirm by arrang.*
en suite bath/shower 126	*Last dinner 11*
Direct dial Yes	*Parking Ample*
Room TV Yes	*Room service 24 hours*

🍷 is our symbol for an **outstanding** wine list.

Poachers Arms Hotel   Hope

H 60% £E
Map 10 C2 Derbyshire
Castleton Road S30 2RD
Hope Valley (0433) 20380
Owner managers Anton & Barbara Singleton
Credit Access, Amex, Diners, Visa
There's a teddy bear in every charming
bedroom at this pleasant well-run establishment.
Presumably they approve of extras like clock

radios, tea-making facilities and TVs. Downstairs
a warm pub-like atmosphere prevails, thanks
largely to the friendly, helpful owner.
Amenities game fishing.

■ *Rooms 7*	*Confirm by arrang.*
en suite bath/shower 7	*Last dinner 9.30*
Direct dial Yes	*Parking Ample*
Room TV Yes	*Room service All day*
Closed 25 & 26 Dec	

Cottage Hotel   Hope Cove

H 57% £E
Map 3 D3 Devon
Nr Kingsbridge TQ7 3HJ
Kingsbridge (0548) 561555
Owner Managers J. K. & J. Ireland
The Ireland family offers a friendly welcome and
excellent housekeeping at this charming hotel
overlooking the cove. Public rooms are
comfortable and homely. Seven bedrooms are

fitted to luxury standard; others are more
functional, though some have balconies and sea
views. Half-board only. *Amenities* garden, games
room, laundry room.

■ *Rooms 35*	*Confirm by arrang.*
en suite bath/shower 19	*Last dinner 8.45*
Room phone Yes	*Parking Ample*
Room TV Some	*Room service Limited*
Closed 2–31 Jan	

Lantern Lodge Hotel   Hope Cove

H 59% £E
Map 3 D3 Devon
Galmpton, Nr Kingsbridge TQ7 3HE
Kingsbridge (0548) 561280
Credit Amex, Visa
  Perched on a clifftop overlooking the cove, this
peaceful hotel is an ideal holiday spot. Friendly
staff, comfortable and relaxing lounges (with
plenty of books and magazines) and well-kept

bedrooms give a favourable first impression that
lasts. No children under eight. No dogs.
Amenities garden, indoor swimming pool, sauna,
solarium, putting.

■ *Rooms 14*	*Confirm by arrang.*
en suite bath/shower 14	*Last dinner 9*
Room phone No	*Parking Ample*
Room TV Yes	*Room service All day*
Closed Dec–Feb	

Cisswood House Hotel   Horsham

HR 65% £D
Map 5 E3 West Sussex
Sandy Gate Lane, Lower Beeding RH13 6NF
Lower Beeding (040 376) 216
Owner managers Othmar & Elizabeth Illes
Credit Access, Amex, Diners, Visa
  Pleasant grounds surround this late-1920s
mansion with a comfortable lounge and a mellow,
traditional cocktail bar. Spacious bedrooms,
including two with four-posters, have drinks
fridges and carpeted bathrooms. No children
under 12. No dogs. *Amenities* garden, terrace,
sauna, croquet, laundry service.

■ *Rooms 18*	*Confirm by arrang.*
en suite bath/shower 18	*Last dinner 9.30, 10 Sat*
Direct dial Yes	*Parking Ample*
Room TV Yes	*Room service All day*
Closed 2 wks Xmas	

Cisswood House Restaurant ♈

Austrian-born Othmar Illes is responsible for the
highly professional cooking at this comfortable
restaurant overlooking lawns and garden. Prime
meat and fish feature throughout a classical
selection that typically includes game in season,
lobster Thermidor, and interesting specialities like
grilled duck breast with orange and ginger sauce.
Crisp, delicious vegetables accompany and
sweets, in true Austrian style, are richly calorific –
try a lovely light crêpe soufflé. ⊖

■ *Set L £12·50*	*L 12–2.30*
Set D £14·75	*D 7–9.30, Sat 7–10*
About £43 for two	*Seats 75*
Closed 2 wks Xmas	*Parties 82*

French Partridge   Horton

R ♛ ♈ ♿ **Map 5 D1** Northamptonshire
Nr Northampton
Northampton (0604) 870033
French cooking
  The Partridge family are approaching their
quarter century at this elegant Victorian-style
restaurant. The short set menus change monthly
and offer a choice of enjoyable French dishes –
mussels cooked in white wine with a garlic and

mushroom stuffing, entrecôte steak in a four
pepper sauce, calf's liver accompanied by a
creamy leek sauce. Irresistible sweets include
home-made ices and sorbets. Book.
♀ Well-chosen ⊖

■ *Set D £16*	*D only from 7.30*
About £39 for two	*Parking Ample*
Seats 40	*Closed Sun, Mon,*
2 wks Easter, 3 wks Jul/Aug & 2 wks Xmas	

Studley Priory Hotel   Horton-cum-Studley

H 65% £D
Map 5 D2 Oxfordshire
OX9 1AZ
Stanton St John (086 735) 203. Tlx 23152
Owner manager Mr. J. R. Parke
Credit Access, Amex, Diners, Visa
  There's a real feel of the past here, notably in
the bar, with its handsome Jacobean panelling,
and the six large bedrooms in the main part. The

rest of the bedrooms, comfortable and recently
refurbished, are in a Georgian wing. No dogs.
Amenities garden, tennis, croquet, clay-pigeon
shooting, laundry service.

■ *Rooms 19*	*Confirm by arrang.*
en suite bath/shower 19	*Last dinner 9.15*
Direct dial Yes	*Parking Ample*
Room TV Yes	*Room service Limited*
Closed 2–9 Jan	

'Quins   Houghton Bridge

R ♈ **Map 5 E4** West Sussex
Nr Amberley
Bury (079 881) 790
Credit Access, Amex, Diners, Visa
  An attractive riverside restaurant named after
the Harlequins rugby team and adorned with
rugby photographs and drawings. Marianne
Walker is a highly competent chef whose menus
feature a number of dishes from her native

Switzerland. Other choices run from asparagus
soup and mange-tout soufflé to paupiettes of sole
with salmon mousseline and duck breast with a
peach and pink peppercorn sauce. ⊖

■ *Set L £7·50*	*L 12.15–2.30*
About £38 for two	*D 7.30–9.30*
Seats 34 Parties 34	*Parking Ample*
Closed D Sun, all Mon & Tues, Bank Hols excl.	
Good Fri & Boxing Day, 1 wk Apr & 2 wks Oct	

Hove

See under Brighton

George Hotel — Huddersfield

H 60% £C/D
Map 10 C1 West Yorkshire
St George's Square HD1 1JA
Huddersfield (0484) 515444
Credit Access, Amex, Diners, Visa
    Victorian features abound in this solid hotel opposite the railway station. The lobby-cum-lounge is of handsome proportions while the guests' cocktail bar is more cosy. Locals throng the mock-Tudor public bar, where a plaque commemorates the founding of the Rugby League in 1895. Spacious bedrooms, in various styles, are well kept. *Amenities* in-house movies (charge), laundry service, 24-hour lounge service.

■ *Rooms 59*	*Confirm by 6*
en suite bath/shower 38	*Last dinner 10 (9 Sun)*
Room phone Yes	*Parking Limited*
Room TV Yes	*Room service 24 hours*

Ladbroke Hotel — Huddersfield

H 62% £C/D
Map 10 C1 West Yorkshire
Ainley Top HD3 3RH
Huddersfield (0422) 75431. Tlx 517346
Credit Access, Amex, Diners, Visa
    A handy stopover for motorists, this modern low-rise hotel stands above the town centre by junction 24 of the M62. The main public area is open-plan, with screens helping to create a little more intimacy. Bedrooms are decently sized, with simple decor and furnishings, plus remote-control TVs. Numerous extras are provided in Gold Star rooms. *Amenities* garden, in-house movies (charge), laundry service.

■ *Rooms 119*	*Confirm by 6*
en suite bath/shower 119	*Last dinner 10*
Direct dial Yes	*Parking Ample*
Room TV Yes	*Room service 24 hours*

Weavers Shed ★ — Huddersfield

R ★ ♨ & **Map 10 C1** West Yorkshire
Knowl Road, Golcar
Huddersfield (0484) 654284
English cooking
    First-class English restaurants are lamentably rare, but the Weavers Shed rates among the very best of the few. Housed in a converted 18th-century mill in the hillside village of Golcar (follow signs from the A62), the restaurant itself is an atmospheric place with exposed beams and bare stone walls. It's an agreeable setting in which to enjoy Betty Saville's superlative cooking. Her lightly seasoned sweet pepper soup is exemplary, her venison with wild mushrooms a marvellous marriage of tender medallions with lightly cooked mushrooms in a finely-balanced red wine and juniper berry sauce. Vegetables are perfectly cooked, and magnificent puddings include an unforgettable sherry trifle and mouth-watering banana toffee tart. Excellent home-made breads and English cheeses. Delightfully informal service.

Specialities rough chicken liver and pork terrine with apricot and sultana chutney, roast Norfolk duckling with Seville orange sauce, 'Old Peculiar' cake with Blue Stilton.
♀ Well-chosen ☺

■ *About £40 for two*	*L 12–1.30*
Seats 70	*D 7.30–9, Sat 7.30–9.15*
Parties 30	*Parking Ample*
Closed L Sat, D Sun, all Mon, Tues following Bank Hol Mons, 2 wks Jan & 2 wks July	

■ For a discount on next year's guide, see Offer for Answers.

Ceruttis — Hull

R Map 11 E1 Humberside
10 Nelson Street
Hull (0482) 28501
Seafood
Credit Access, Visa
    A friendly harbour-front restaurant. Seafood is the main interest here – from simple grills to unusually imaginative sauced dishes. Start perhaps with scampi brochette with fresh herbs, or smoked salmon and prawn terrine with sour cream sauce. To follow, try peppered monkfish, or halibut and avocado with hollandaise. For meat eaters there are steaks. Delicious sweets like pineapple Romanov. ♀ Well-chosen

■ *About £42 for two*	*L 12–2*
Seats 45	*D 7–9.30*
Parties 25	*Parking Ample*
Closed L Sat, all Sun, Bank Hols & 1 wk Xmas	

Crest Hotel (Humber Bridge) — Hull

H **62% £D**
Map 11 E1 Humberside
Ferriby High Road HU14 3LG
Hull (0482) 645212. Tlx 592558
Credit Access, Amex, Diners, Visa. LVs

Comfortable modern accommodation six miles from the city centre. The world's largest single-span suspension bridge provides the view from both bar and coffee shop. Bedrooms have pine fitted units, trouser presses and neatly appointed bathrooms. The executive suite features a whirlpool bath. *Amenities* garden, pool table, in-house movies (charge), laundry service, coffee shop (9am–10pm), children's playroom (wkends).

■ *Rooms* 102	*Confirm by* 6
en suite bath/shower 102	*Last dinner* 10
Direct dial Yes	*Parking* Ample
Room TV Yes	*Room service* Limited

Waterfront Hotel — Hull

H **60% £D/E**
Map 11 E1 Humberside
Dagger Lane, Old Town HU1 2LS
Hull (0482) 227222
Manager Paul Louis
Credit Access, Visa. LVs

Bare brick walls give plenty of character to the public areas of this cleverly converted Victorian warehouse overlooking Princes Dock. Pine-furnished bedrooms include two with modern four-posters. Singles under the eaves have the best views but no private bathrooms. *Amenities* solarium.

■ *Rooms* 32	*Confirm by* 6
en suite bath/shower 25	*Last dinner* 10
Room phone Yes	*Parking* Limited
Room TV Yes	*Room service* 24 hours
Closed 25 & 26 Dec	

Bear at Hungerford — Hungerford

HR **66% £D/E** &
Map 4 C2 Berkshire
Charnham Street RG17 0EL
Hungerford (0488) 82512
Credit Access, Amex, Diners, Visa

An attractive, well-maintained 13th-century inn with a colourful history – Henry VIII was a former owner and William of Orange accepted the English throne here. The reception/lounge is newly decorated in salmon pink and another, quieter lounge with classic English drawing-room decor has been created. Bedrooms now have smart co-ordinating fabrics, good furniture and lots of extras. *Amenities* laundry service.

■ *Rooms* 32	*Confirm by* 6
en suite bath/shower 32	*Last dinner* 9.30
Direct dial Yes	*Parking* Ample
Room TV Yes	*Room service* All day

Bear at Hungerford Restaurant

A comfortable environment in which to enjoy your choice from an imaginative menu. Start with mousse of Cornish scallops with leeks or aubergine terrine; follow with lamb's kidneys and wild mushrooms on rösti potatoes or lightly cured Alderton ham cooked with cider. Finish with pastry puff of raspberries. Exceptionally wide-ranging cellar with rare gems like Marqués de Murrieta (Rioja) 1960. ▭ Outstanding ▯ Well-chosen ✆

■ *Set L* £12·45	*L* 12.30–2
Set D £14·45	*D* 7.30–9.30,
About £50 for two	*Fri & Sat* 7.30–10
Seats 50	*Parties* 60
Closed 24, 25 & 26 Dec	

Hunstrete House — Hunstrete

HR **83% £B**
Map 4 B3 Avon
Chelwood, Bristol BS18 4NS
Compton Dando (076 18) 578, Tlx 449540
Owner managers Thea & John Dupays
Credit Access, Amex, Diners, Visa

The Dupays' handsome old manor house enjoys an exceptionally peaceful and picturesque setting in rolling countryside. It's very much their home, and the wealth of antiques, paintings and objets d'art is a very personal collection. Open fires warm the gracious, traditional hall, library and drawing room, and in the contrastingly contemporary bar there's a small display of modern paintings. Bedrooms, in both the main house and the Italianate courtyard, are sumptuously decorated, with plush drapes, antique or period furnishings. Bathrooms are equally well appointed. Delicious breakfasts. No children under nine. No dogs. *Amenities* garden, outdoor swimming pool, tennis, croquet, laundry service.

■ *Rooms* 21	*Confirm by* 6
en suite bath/shower 21	*Last dinner* 9.15
Direct dial Yes	*Parking* Ample
Room TV Yes	*Room service* All day

Hunstrete House Restaurant ☖

The elegant new Terrace dining room is a handsome venue for Robert Elsmore's skilful and imaginative cooking. Typical starters include such delights as galantine of trout and quenelles of chicken. Main courses have excellent sauces (but order plain if you prefer), and sweets include delicious chocolate flummery and traditional puds on Sundays. Simpler lunchtime choice. The wine list is outstanding, with fabulous burgundies, older clarets and good-value bin ends.

🥄 Outstanding ☻ Well-chosen ☺
■ Set D £26·45
About £70 for two
Seats 65

L 12.30–1.45
D 7.30–9.15
Parties 24

Brampton Hotel — Huntingdon

H 59% £E
Map 6 A2 Cambridgeshire
Brampton PE18 8NH
Huntingdon (0480) 810434
Credit Access, Amex, Diners, Visa

Standing at the A1/A604 crossroads between Huntingdon and St Neots, this former coaching inn has a friendly rural appeal – especially in its comfortable beamed bar. Identical bedrooms in a

contrastingly modern wing are bright and attractive. All have tea-makers and hairdryers, thoughtful extras like biscuits and fresh fruit, and compact bathrooms with showers. *Amenities* terrace, laundry service, 24-hour lounge service.

■ Rooms 17
en suite bath/shower 17
Room phone Yes
Room TV Yes

Confirm by 6
Last dinner 10
Parking Ample
Room service 24 hours

George Hotel — Huntingdon

H 59% £C/D
Map 6 A2 Cambridgeshire
George Street PE18 6AB
Huntingdon (0480) 432444
Credit Access, Amex, Diners, Visa. LVs

A galleried inner courtyard where a Shakespeare play is occasionally staged during the summer is an attractive feature of this welcoming town-centre hotel, which was originally

built as a posting house. Best bedrooms are on the top floor; other rooms are simpler in style. There's a comfortable foyer-lounge-cum-bar, plus several function suites. *Amenities* laundry service.

■ Rooms 24
en suite bath/shower 24
Room phone Yes
Room TV Yes

Confirm by 6
Last dinner 9.30
Parking Ample
Room service All day

Old Bridge Hotel — Huntingdon

HR 70% £C/D *E*
Map 6 A2 Cambridgeshire
1 High Street PE18 6TQ
Huntingdon (0480) 52681. Tlx 32706
Manager Raymond Waters
Credit Access, Amex, Diners, Visa

Standing in gardens by the Ouse, this handsome Georgian house has seen many recent improvements. Note in particular the Terrace lounge with its picture windows, cane furniture and climbing plants, and the impressive business centre with its four fully-equipped board rooms. The hotel's period character is epitomised in the comfortable lounge and bar, and the panelled restaurant. Bedrooms are decorated with style

and flair; bathrooms are really excellent, and all rooms offer trouser presses, hairdryers and ample writing space. Six new luxury rooms, with especially attractive decorative themes, have river views. Good breakfasts. A popular and successful hotel with affable staff. *Amenities* garden, laundry service, 24-hour lounge service.

■ Rooms 27
en suite bath/shower 27
Direct dial Yes
Room TV Yes

Confirm by 6
Last dinner 10.30
Parking Ample
Room service 24 hours

Old Bridge Hotel Restaurant 🍴 ♿

Choose the plainer items and you'll probably not be disappointed. The splendid sirloin of beef, served from a silver trolley, is a great favourite, and other choices run from oxtail soup and hot vol-au-vent filled with sweetbreads to baked kebab of monkfish, scallops and prawns. Friendly, willing service. Excellent wines include fine burgundies from the best growers.

☻ Well-chosen ☺
■ Set L £12·75
About £45 for two
Seats 60

L Sun only 12.30–2.30
D 7–10.30

Ye Olde Bell Hotel — Hurley

H 64% £C
Map 5 D2 Berkshire
High Street, Nr Maidenhead SL6 5LX
Littlewick Green (062 882) 5881. Tlx 847035
Credit Access, Amex, Diners, Visa

Built in 1135 to accommodate monks, this black-and-white inn is picture-postcard material. Entrance is through a splendid Norman porch, and the bar is all beams, brass and old-world

charm. Accommodation ranges from the antique-furnished to the stylishly modern. Housekeeping and maintenance need improvement, especially in the original part. *Amenities* garden, laundry service, 24-hour lounge service.

■ Rooms 24
en suite bath/shower 24
Direct dial Yes
Room TV Yes

Confirm by arrang.
Last dinner 9.30
Parking Ample
Room service 24 hours

Esseborne Manor
Hurstbourne Tarrant

HR 75% £C/D &
Map 4 C3 Hampshire
Nr Andover SP11 0ER
Hurstbourne Tarrant (026 476) 444
Owner manager Peter Birnie
Credit Access, Amex, Diners, Visa

A peaceful farmland setting, stylish decor and friendly personal service are key points at this Victorian country house hotel. Bedrooms – all of a good size, some really large – are individually decorated and furnished with great flair. Accessories range from remote-control TVs and portable radios to books, magazines and mending baskets. Good-sized bathrooms are well equipped, and room service extends to shoe cleaning. Antiques and quality fabrics feature in the entrance hall and lounge, and in the small,

cosy bar there's a cheerful log fire. No children under ten. No dogs. *Amenities* garden, tennis, croquet, golf practice net, laundry service.

■ Rooms 12	Confirm by arrang.
en suite bath/shower 12	Last dinner 9.30
Direct dial Yes	Parking Ample
Room TV Yes	Room service All day
Closed 2 wks Xmas	

Esseborne Manor
Restaurant   & &

Like the whole hotel, the restaurant is tasteful and attractive. Peter Birnie and Belinda Watson share the cooking on a sensibly-short but seasonally-changing menu. Dishes are interesting without being over-ambitious. Start with either a warming tomato and onion soup, cod marinated with lime and coriander or smoked pigeon breast salad followed by beef stroganoff or braised pheasant with a rich calvados-flavoured sauce. Good fresh vegetables. A super lemon sponge features among the sweets.   **Well-chosen** ♀

■ About £44 for two	L noon–2
Seats 30 Parties 20	D 7.30–9.30
Closed L Sat, all Sun, 2 wks Xmas	

♀ indicates a **well-chosen** house wine.

Fernie Lodge
Husbands Bosworth

R & Map 11 D4 Leicestershire
Berridges Lane, Nr Lutterworth
Market Harborough (0858) 880551
Credit Access, Visa

In the spacious but simply furnished dining room of this Georgian house just off the A427, fixed-price menus offer straightforward, unpretentious fare. Reliably prepared dishes range from leek soup and smoked mackerel with

cheese sauce to deep-fried fillet of plaice, hare casserole, suprême of chicken and carbonnade of beef. Carefully cooked vegetables, and tasty sweets like chocolate roulade.   **Well-chosen** ♀

■ Set L £7·75	L 12–2, Sun 12–3
Set D £11·95	D 7–10.30, Sat 7–11
About £33 for two	Parking Ample
Seats 150	Parties 150
Closed L Mon & Sat & D Sun	

♀ is our symbol for an **outstanding** wine list.

Fredericks Hotel   *NEW ENTRY*
Hythe

HR 69% £C/D
Map 7 C6 Kent
Seabrook Road CT21 5QY
Hythe (0303) 67279
Owner managers Freddie & Silvia Jones
Credit Access, Amex, Diners, Visa

There's a friendly welcome from very helpful staff at this Edwardian hotel on the A259. Sherry is offered in the informal reception area before you proceed to your luxurious and fully-equipped bedroom. Public areas include a relaxing cocktail bar and reading room/lounge. *Amenities* garden, in-house movies (free), laundry service, coffee shop (11am–11pm).

■ Rooms 9	Confirm by arrang.
en suite bath/shower 9	Last dinner 11
Direct dial Yes	Parking Ample
Room TV Yes	Room service 24 hours

Restaurant   &

An accomplished pianist provides soothing background music while you ponder the ambitious classical menu at this elegant restaurant. Dishes might include boned quail with veal forcemeat stuffing and port wine sauce, followed by halibut served with a medley of seafood and lobster sauce or chicken in cream sauce with peppers, tomato and gruyère in an aubergine shell. Freddie Jones is a skilled and experienced chef-patron but he might do better to try some simpler combinations. Desserts, however, are excellent – try the classic orange bavarois or rich chocolate and walnut mazarin.

■ Set L Sun only £10·75	L 12.30–2.30
About £45 for two	D 6.30–11
Seats 30 Parties 30	Closed D Sun & all Mon

Hythe Imperial Hotel — Hythe

H **73% £C**
Map 7 C6 Kent
Princess Parade CT21 6AE
Hythe (0303) 67441. Tlx 965082
Manager Chris Scragg
Credit Access, Amex, Diners, Visa
　Right on the seafront, this handsome Victorian hotel excels in its leisure facilities. Armchair Nigel Mansells can try their skills on the model-car racing circuit, while aspiring Rambos might opt for the assault course. It's all thirsty work, but several comfortable areas offer refreshment and relaxation (one lounge is for non-smokers). Bedrooms are gradually having their old-fashioned furniture replaced with smart modern pieces. The usual accessories are provided. No dogs. *Amenities* garden, indoor swimming pool, sauna, solarium, gymnasium, beauty salon,

hairdressing, tennis, squash, 9-hole golf course, putting, bowling green, croquet, games room, snooker, pool table, laundry service, 24-hour lounge service.

■ *Rooms* 83	*Confirm by* 6
en suite bath/shower 83	*Last dinner* 9
Direct dial Yes	*Parking* Ample
Room TV Yes	*Room service* 24 hours

Stade Court Hotel — Hythe

H **62% £E**
Map 7 C6 Kent
West Parade CT21 6DT
Hythe (0303) 68263
Manager Mr S. C. Riley
Credit Access, Amex, Diners, Visa
　The seafront location ensures fine views from the lounge and many of the bedrooms. Recent additions include a conference suite and seven new bedrooms (five non-smoking). Refurbishment continues on existing rooms. Guests may use the leisure facilities of another hotel nearby.
Amenities garden, sea fishing, games room, snooker, laundry service, 24-hour lounge service.

■ *Rooms* 40	*Confirm by* arrang.
en suite bath/shower 40	*Last dinner* 9
Direct dial Yes	*Parking* Ample
Room TV Yes	*Room service* Limited

Old Mill — Ide

R ♧ **Map 3 D2** Devon
20 High Street
Exeter (0392) 59480
Credit Access, Amex, Diners, Visa
　Once an old flour mill and bakery, this cosy beamed restaurant is now the appealing setting for Jon Cruwys' thoroughly modern and imaginative culinary skills. Typical delights might include celery soup enriched with Stilton and Chablis or marinated herrings preceding, say, fillet steak and grilled crab claws or venison with pineapple and almonds. Sweets include home-made ice creams and sorbets. ℮

■ *Set L* £5·85	*L* 12–2
Set D £10·95	*D* 7–10
About £42 for two	*Parking* Ample
Seats 36 *Parties* 6	*Closed* Sun

Box Tree Restaurant ★ — Ilkley

R ★ ☺ **Map 10 C1** West Yorkshire
Church Street
Ilkley (0943) 608484
Manager Brian Womersley
Credit Access, Amex, Diners, Visa
　Accomplished cooking, knowledgeable service and the highly individual opulence of the setting combine to make dinner here an occasion to savour. Chef-director Edward Denny's concise French menus combine classical and modern elements. Game terrine with confit d'oignons is a marvellous starter; the soupe de poissons is smooth as velvet and packed with flavour; beef and lamb are of outstanding quality, supplied by the same butcher for over 20 years; vegetables are spot on; sweets like hot apricot tart with sabayon should not be resisted. Splendid, wide-ranging cellar: note Ch. La Lagune 1966, Echezeaux (Jayer), Cabernet Sauvignon (Jordan) 1977. *Specialities* terrine de volaille et basilic au yaourt et à la ciboulette; coquilles St

Jacques à la vapeur au beurre de concombre; rondelles d'agneau avec petite garniture de légumes; fricassée de homard à l'Armagnac truffière; les choix d'entremets Maison Box Tree.
⇨ Outstanding 🍷 Well-chosen ℮

■ *About £70 for two*	*D* 7.30–9.30, Sat till 10
Seats 50	*Parties* 16
Closed Sun & Mon	*Parking* Limited

Craiglands Hotel   Ilkley

H **60% £C/D**
Map 10 C1 West Yorkshire
Cowpasture Road LS29 8RQ
Ilkley (0943) 607676
Credit Access, Amex, Diners, Visa
   An ivy-clad hotel standing in nine acres of
gardens on the edge of Ilkley Moor. Huge picture
windows make the foyer-lounge a bright, airy
place, and there's a pleasant cocktail bar.

Bedrooms are generally of a good size, with
restful, autumnal colour schemes and a warm,
comfortable feel. Some revamping would be
welcome. *Amenities* garden, tennis, games
room, snooker, laundry service.

■ *Rooms* 73	*Confirm by* arrang.
en suite bath/shower 53	*Last dinner* 9.30
Direct dial Yes	*Parking* Ample
Room TV Yes	*Room service* All day

Heybridge Moat House Hotel   Ingatestone

H **68% £D** &
Map 7 B4 Essex
Roman Road CM4 9AB
Ingatestone (0277) 355355. Tlx 995186
Manager Ermis Kyprianou
Credit Access, Amex, Diners, Visa
   A series of long, low buildings just off the A12.
Motel-style accommodation is comfortable, well-
kept and roomy, with armchairs, writing desks,

trouser presses and remote-control tele-text TVs
throughout. Outside each room is its own parking
space, and one room is specially fitted out for
disabled guests. No dogs. *Amenities* garden,
laundry service.

■ *Rooms* 22	*Confirm by* arrang.
en suite bath/shower 22	*Last dinner* 10.30
Direct dial Yes	*Parking* Ample
Room TV Yes	*Room service* 24 hours

Belstead Brook Hotel   Ipswich

H **70% £D**
Map 6 C3 Suffolk
Belstead Road IP2 9HB
Ipswich (0473) 684241. Tlx 987674
Owner manager Iain Hatfield
Credit Access, Amex, Diners, Visa
   Check directions to this country-house hotel,
which stands in a quiet garden setting only two
miles from the town centre. Much extended from
Jacobean times up to the present day, the hotel
skilfully combines old-world charm and modern
convenience. The spacious foyer, with its
glittering chandelier, and the handsome bar-
lounge offer elegant comfort. Bedrooms range
from the delightful four-poster suite in the main
house to executive rooms in a modern wing – all
rooms are well-equipped, with good carpeted
bathrooms, and some retain fine old oak

panelling. The six luxurious garden suites, with
their handsome antiques, mini-bars, teletext TVs
and whirlpool baths, are especially appealing. No
dogs. *Amenities* garden.

■ *Rooms* 33	*Confirm by* arrang.
en suite bath/shower 33	*Last dinner* 9.30
Direct dial Yes	*Parking* Ample
Room TV Yes	*Room service* 24 hours

Golden Lion Hotel   Ipswich

H **60% £E**
Map 6 C3 Suffolk
Cornhill IP1 1DP
Ipswich (0473) 56645
Credit Access, Amex, Diners, Visa. **LVs**
   The Golden Lion's been here for 600 years, and
its good accommodation and central position near
the shops keep it in demand. Bedrooms range
from traditional to modern, but all are smartly

furnished and nicely decorated, with well-
equipped bathrooms; one room has a four-poster.
There are several bars (restyling planned), and a
peaceful residents' lounge. *Amenities* in-house
movies (free), laundry service.

■ *Rooms* 23	*Confirm by* arrang.
en suite bath/shower 23	*Last dinner* 10
Room phone Yes	*Parking* Ample
Room TV Yes	*Room service* Limited

Marlborough Hotel   Ipswich

H **66% £C/D** &
Map 6 C3 Suffolk
Henley Road IP1 3SP
Ipswich (0473) 57677
Owner manager Mrs M. Gough
Credit Access, Amex, Diners, Visa
   Standing opposite Christchurch Park, this
converted Victorian house offers homely comforts
in a relaxed, traditional atmosphere. The foyer-

lounge and bar both have a warm, cosy appeal
with their soft lighting and autumnal decor. Potted
plants and sewing kits are a thoughtful touch in
the good-sized bedrooms, which have smart
furnishings. *Amenities* garden.

■ *Rooms* 22	*Confirm by* arrang.
en suite bath/shower 22	*Last dinner* 9.30
Direct dial Yes	*Parking* Ample
Room TV Yes	*Room service* 24 hours

Mortimer's *NEW ENTRY* Ipswich

R ⑼ **Map 6 C3** Suffolk
Wherry Quay
Ipswich (0473) 230225
Seafood
Credit Access, Amex, Diners, Visa
   A converted warehouse is home for this bistro-style seafood restaurant overlooking Ipswich docks. Superbly fresh ingredients form the basis of simply prepared and generously served

offerings such as pan-fried brill with béarnaise sauce, steamed salmon and skate wing with black butter and capers. There are ices or Greek yoghurt to finish. Friendly, informal service.
■ *About £30 for two*   *L 12–2*
Seats 65   *D 7–9, Mon 7–8.30*
Parties 8   *Parking Ample*
Closed L Sat & all Sun, all Bank Hols, 2 wks Xmas & 2 days Easter

Orwell House Restaurant *NEW ENTRY* Ipswich

R ⑼ **Map 6 C3** Suffolk
4 Orwell Place
Ipswich (0473) 230254
Credit Access, Amex, Diners, Visa
   A friendly welcome and sophisticated surroundings greet diners at this wood-panelled restaurant above a busy bistro. Chef-manager John Gear's menu is imaginative and ambitious. Dishes like crayfish brioche in lobster sauce,

native oysters lightly poached in white wine, rosettes of English lamb and classic boeuf en croûte are capably prepared and based on excellent ingredients. A simple dessert selection and wider-than-average vegetarian menu. ⊖
■ *About £32 for two*   *L 12–2*
Seats 40   *D 7–9.30*
Parties 32   *Parking Ample*
Closed D Sun, all Mon & Tues

Post House Hotel Ipswich

H **63% £C/D** ⅙
   Map 6 C3 Suffolk
London Road IP2 0UA
Ipswich (0473) 690313. Tlx 987150
Credit Access, Amex, Diners, Visa. **LVs**
   A stark modern exterior for this Post House on the A1214. Public rooms have been very smartly refurbished, and many of the spacious, comfortable bedrooms have been upgraded.

There are now also 12 superior executive rooms. Average housekeeping, little real personal service. *Amenities* garden, outdoor swimming pool, laundry service, coffee shop (10am–10pm), children's play area.
■ *Rooms 118*   *Confirm by 6*
en suite bath/shower 118 *Last dinner 10*
Direct dial Yes   *Parking Ample*
Room TV Yes   *Room service Limited*

King's Head Ivinghoe

R ⅙ **Map 5 E1** Buckinghamshire
Nr Leighton Buzzard
Cheddington (0296) 668388
Manager Georges de Maison
Credit Access, Amex, Diners, Visa
   Capable chef Patrick O'Keeffe offers few surprises but plenty of familiar favourites at this attractive restaurant in a 17-century posting house. Dark beams, polished oak tables and

gleaming silverware create an attractive setting in which to enjoy traditional roasts and grills – or daily specials like moules marinière, garlicky rack of lamb and crispy duckling. Good vegetables and simple, enjoyable sweets like profiteroles with hot chocolate sauce. ⊖
■ *Set L £11·75*   *L 12.30–2*
About £50 for two   *D 7.30–9.30*
Seats 55 Parties 80   *Parking Ample*

Jervaulx Hall Hotel Jervaulx

H **71% £D/E** ⅙
   Map 15 B6 North Yorkshire
Nr Masham, Ripon HG4 4PH
Bedale (0677) 60235
Owner manager John Sharp
   Standing next to the picturesque ruins of Jervaulx Abbey, set in its own sheltered grounds, this lovely 19th-century house is a haven of peace and tranquillity. Fresh flowers, and fine rugs on a gleaming polished floor, create a welcoming first impression in the entrance hall, and the comfortable, antique-filled lounge is a delightful place to relax with a drink. Spacious bedrooms, individually decorated in pastel shades and using pretty floral fabrics, are furnished in period or more contemporary style. Fresh fruit, flowers, tissues and sewing kits are among typically thoughtful extras, and carpeted bathrooms are

equally well equipped. Half-board terms only.
Amenities garden, croquet, laundry service.
■ *Rooms 8*   *Confirm by arrang.*
en suite bath/shower 8   *Last dinner 8*
Room phone No   *Parking Ample*
Room TV No   *Room service Limited*
Closed 1 Dec–1 Mar

Hungry Monk   Jevington

R **Map 7 B6** East Sussex
Nr Polegate
Polegate (032 12) 2178
Owner managers Nigel & Susan Mackenzie

A characterful restaurant where the fixed-price blackboard menu is varied and imaginative, and simple dishes are well executed and satisfying. Starter might be asparagus in puff pastry, with roast rack of lamb or superb terrine of halibut and salmon to follow. Finish with an outstanding banoffi pie. Good wines with plenty of half bottles: note Côte de Nuits Villages 1982 (Bruno Clair). Book. ♀ **Well-chosen**

■ *Set L Sun only £12*	*L Sun 12–2.30,*
Set D £12·65	*Mon–Sat by arrang.*
About £37 for two	*D 7–10.30*
Seats 40	*Parking Ample*
Parties 15	*Closed 25 & 26 Dec*

■ Our inspectors are our full-
time employees; they are
professionally trained by us.

Woolpack Hotel   Kendal

H **58% £D/E**
Map 13 D5 Cumbria
Stricklandgate LA9 4ND
Kendal (0539) 23852
Credit Access, Amex, Diners, Visa. **LVs**

Day rooms – notably the beamed bar – recall the 18th-century origins of this town-centre coaching inn. The best bedrooms are the improved ones which boast attractive soft furnishings, good carpets and brass light fittings. A modern extension houses the majority of functional bedrooms. *Amenities* in-house movies (free), laundry service, coffee shop (10am–9pm; 10am–4.30pm in winter), 24-hour lounge service.

■ *Rooms 57*	*Confirm by 6*
en suite bath/shower 57	*Last dinner 9.30*
Direct dial Yes	*Parking Ample*
Room TV Yes	*Room service 24 hours*

Restaurant Bosquet *NEW ENTRY*   Kenilworth

R ♀ **Map 10 C4** Warwickshire
97a Warwick Road
Kenilworth (0926) 52463
French cooking
Credit Amex, Visa

Bernard Lignier is a highly accomplished chef, and his menus will tempt the most blasé of palates. Some typical examples: quails' eggs in a nest of partridge mousse with a game and truffle sauce; fillet of lamb en croûte with a splendid sherry sauce; raspberry feuilleté. Friendly service led by Jane Lignier. Good clarets back to Ch. Lanessan 1961. ♀ **Well-chosen** ⊖

■ *Set D £11·50*	*D only 7–10*
About £44 for two	*Parking Ample*
Seats 26 Parties 30	*Closed Sun, Mon, Bank*
	Hols, 10 days Xmas & 3 wks July/Aug

Clarendon House Hotel   Kenilworth

H **61% £E**
Map 10 C4 Warwickshire
Old High Street CV8 1LZ
Kenilworth (0926) 57668. Tlx 311240
Owner manager Martyn Lea
Credit Access, Visa

A recently discovered 16th-century well has added to the characterful charms of this old hotel which has been renovated by enthusiastic owner Martyn Lea. Public rooms house a collection of Cromwellian armour, and traditionally furnished bedrooms vie with ten new rooms in a rear wing.

Amenities laundry service.

■ *Rooms 33*	*Confirm by arrang.*
en suite bath/shower 33	*Last dinner 9.30*
Direct dial Yes	*Parking Ample*
Room TV Yes	*Room service All day*

De Montfort Hotel   Kenilworth

H **61% £C/D**
Map 10 C4 Warwickshire
The Square CV8 1ED
Kenilworth (0926) 55944. Tlx 311012
Credit Access, Amex, Diners, Visa. **LVs**

A 1960s purpose-built hotel in the centre of town. The foyer is bright and contemporary, so too the comfortable lounge with its velour-clad settees and armchairs, and the inviting cocktail bar. Bedrooms are plain and practical; 12 executive rooms have warmer, more appealing decor. Friendly staff. *Amenities* games room, pool table, laundry service, coffee shop (10am–9pm), 24-hour lounge service.

■ *Rooms 96*	*Confirm by arrang.*
en suite bath/shower 96	*Last dinner 9.45*
Direct dial Yes	*Parking Ample*
Room TV Yes	*Room service 24 hours*

Romano's *NEW ENTRY* Kenilworth

R � **Map 10 C4** Warwickshire
60 Waverley Road
Kenilworth (0926) 57473
Italian cooking
Credit Amex, Visa

A husband and wife team runs this pleasant, unassuming Italian restaurant. Anna Goldoni cooks in sound, unpretentious style, and her menus provide ample choice, from stuffed courgettes and aubergines to lamb sweetbreads, scampi, devilled chicken, veal and steak. Ask husband Romano about daily specials. ⊖

■ *Set L £6·80*	*L 12.30–2*
Set D £11·50	*D 7.30–10.30*
About £34 for two	*Parking Limited*
Seats 26	*Parties 40*

Closed L Sat, all Sun, Bank Hols (excl. 25 Dec, 1 Jan & 1st Mon in May) & Aug

Keswick Hotel Keswick

H **62% £C/D**
Map 13 C5 Cumbria
Station Road CA12 4NQ
Keswick (076 87) 72020. Tlx 64200
Credit Access, Amex, Diners, Visa

Heavily carved mahogany antiques, willow-pattern china, old prints and stuffed birds recall the Victorian origins of this imposing hotel standing in attractive, elevated grounds.

Afternoon tea is served in the leafy conservatory and there's a pleasant bar. Mostly spacious bedrooms have good modern bathrooms. *Amenities* garden, putting, croquet, laundry service, 24-hour lounge service.

■ *Rooms 64*	*Confirm by 6*
en suite bath/shower 64	*Last dinner 8.30*
Room phone Yes	*Parking Ample*
Room TV Yes	*Room service 24 hours*

Underscar Hotel Keswick

See under Applethwaite

Kildwick Hall Kildwick

HR **69% £C/D**
Map 10 C1 North Yorkshire
Nr Keighley BD20 9AE
Crosshills (0535) 32244
Credit Access, Amex, Diners, Visa

New owners the Stothers have a programme of renovation for their splendid Jacobean manor house. The entrance hall/lounge has an inglenook fireplace, oak panelling and tapestries; bedrooms now vary in style (some have four-posters), but traditional furniture is planned throughout. They are equipped with sherry, fresh fruit, trouser presses and radio alarms. Excellent house-keeping. *Amenities* garden, laundry service.

■ *Rooms 14*	*Confirm by arrang.*
en suite bath/shower 11	*Last dinner 10*
Direct dial Yes	*Parking Ample*
Room TV Yes	*Room service 24 hours*

Candle Lite Room ♀

Oil paintings on the walls and wonderfully ornate plasterwork make for a splendid setting, while the menu is varied and imaginative. You might start with avocado and smoked chicken salad, duckling, chicken liver and veal terrine or coquille St Jacques à la sabayon d'orange, followed by roulade of chicken breast, loin of lamb with mint, honey and redcurrant sauce or escalope of wild salmon, sauce Chablis. Finish with tarte au citron. Good coffee and petits fours. Friendly and efficient service. ⊖

■ *Set L £10·50*	*L 12–2.30*
About £50 for two	*D 7.30–10*
Seats 45	*Parties 25*
Closed L Sat	

■ We welcome complaints and bona fide recommendations on the tear-out pages for readers' comments. They are followed up by our professional team. Please also complain to the management instantly.

RECEPTION

Hunt House *NEW ENTRY* Kilsby

R ♀ ♿ **Map 11 D4** Warwickshire
Main Road, Nr Rugby
Crick (0788) 823282
Credit Access, Amex, Diners, Visa

Ian Geggie gives an entertaining run-down of his wife Jan's dinner menu in this agreeable country restaurant. Her style is careful and unpretentious, with dishes ranging from feuilleté of chicken livers and mushrooms in Madeira to fillet of lamb béarnaise and boned, stuffed quail in filo pastry with a fine orange and port sauce. Tempting, well-made desserts. Mr Geggie keeps an extensive cellar – no fewer than 176 whiskies at the last count! ⊖

■ *Set D £13·50*	*D only 7.15–10,*
About £40 for two	*Sat 7.15–10.30*
Seats 40 *Parties 30*	*Parking Ample*
Closed Sun, Mon & 2 wks Xmas	

Meadow House · Kilve

HR 70% £D/E
Map 3 E1 Somerset
Nr Bridgwater TA5 1EG
Holford (027 874) 546
Owner managers David & Marion MacAuslan
Credit Access, Visa

In a rural setting near the Bristol Channel, this Georgian-style country house offers abundant peace and relaxation. It's run with care and individuality by David and Marion MacAuslan, and Marion's skills as an interior designer have produced a delightfully elegant ambience. Log fires warm the day rooms, which include a beautifully furnished lounge, a book-lined study

where drinks are served and a handsome billiards room. Bedrooms of ample, gracious proportions feature antiques, fine fabrics and numerous extras, from mineral water and a choice of teas to the latest remote-control TVs. Splendidly fitted bathrooms (one not en suite). Exemplary housekeeping. No children under nine. No dogs.
Amenities garden, croquet, billiards.

■ Rooms 5	Confirm by arrang.
en suite bath/shower 4	Last dinner 8
Room phone No	Parking Ample
Room TV Yes	Room service All day

Meadow House Restaurant 🍷

Booking is essential at this charming little restaurant overlooking the garden. Marion MacAuslan is a talented cook who uses first-class ingredients for her splendid dinners (four courses, no choice except main dish). A warm broccoli and sole salad could lead to minty lamb kebabs, then on to three-spice turkey and, finally, a delicious pear crème brûlée. Exciting wine list at keen prices – splendid Rhônes in particular.
🗢 Outstanding 🍷 Well-chosen ⊖

■ Set D £16	D only at 8
About £40 for two	Seats 12 Parties 12

Mill House Hotel · Kingham

H 66% £D/E
Map 4 C1 Oxfordshire
Nr Chipping Norton OX7 6UH
Kingham (060 871) 8188
Credit Access, Amex, Diners, Visa

A warm welcome awaits at this beautifully kept converted Cotswold-stone mill. Both flagstoned foyer and heavily beamed bar have an age-old country appeal. Smart furnishings and fresh flowers add to the charms of the lounge (a recent addition), and bright airy bedrooms (one with a four-poster) have tea-makers and excellent bathrooms. No children under five. No dogs.
Amenities garden, game fishing.

■ Rooms 20	Confirm by arrang.
en suite bath/shower 20	Last dinner 9.45
Direct dial Yes	Parking Ample
Room TV Yes	Room service All day

Butterfly Hotel *NEW ENTRY* · King's Lynn

H 63% £E
Map 6 B1 Norfolk
Beveridge Way PE30 4NB
King's Lynn (0553) 771707. Tlx 818313
Credit Access, Amex, Diners, Visa

Comfortable, practical overnight accommodation is provided at this modern, purpose-built hotel to the east of the town centre. Pine-furnished bedrooms have an attractive pastel decor and all offer tea-makers plus compact bath/shower rooms. Dried flower displays are a feature of pleasant day rooms, which include a conservatory-style lounge and informal bar. No dogs. *Amenities* garden.

■ Rooms 50	Confirm by 6
en suite bath/shower 50	Last dinner 10
Direct dial Yes	Parking Ample
Room TV Yes	Room service None

Duke's Head · King's Lynn

H 64% £C/D
Map 6 B1 Norfolk
Tuesday Market Place PE30 1JS
King's Lynn (0553) 774996. Tlx 817349
Manager Mr F. Shone
Credit Access, Amex, Diners, Visa. LVs

In a dominant position on the market place, the Duke's Head has a handsome late-17th-century facade. Inside, there's a comfortable, inviting feel to the stylish lounge and oak-clad bar. Most bedrooms now sport smart darkwood fitted furniture and well-matched colour schemes; one wing is more functional and dated. *Amenities* laundry service, coffee shop (10am–10pm).

■ Rooms 72	Confirm by 6
en suite bath/shower 72	Last dinner 9.30
Direct dial Yes	Parking Ample
Room TV Yes	Room service Limited

Buckland-Tout-Saints Hotel

Kingsbridge

HR 69% £D/E
Map 3 D3 Devon
Goveton TQ7 2DS
Kingsbridge (0548) 3055
Owner managers Shephard family
Credit Access, Amex, Diners, Visa

Dating from 1690, this handsome manor house stands in rambling gardens surrounded by the lovely countryside of South Devon. The panelled foyer-lounge sets the dignified tone for the public areas, which include a bar with inviting leather chesterfields and a quiet reading room. The first-floor bedrooms have been individually and luxuriously restyled, with flowered, striped or stippled wallpapers and well-chosen furniture of high quality. Two of these rooms are suites and another, the Buckland Room, has splendid antiques and a mahogany four-poster. Attractive bathrooms. Breakfasts are excellent. No children under 12. No dogs. *Amenities* garden, croquet, bowling green, putting.

■ *Rooms* 12	*Confirm by* arrang.
en suite bath/shower 12	*Last dinner* 9
Direct dial Yes	*Parking* Ample
Room TV Yes	*Room service* All day
Closed 2 wks Jan	

Queen Anne Restaurant

The panelled dining room is an elegant setting for the skilled, imaginative cooking of Alastair Carter. Local produce features strongly, and there's plenty to excite on the daily set menus: the most delicate scallop mousseline with a tomato and saffron sauce, breast of duck with ceps and morels, lamb in pastry with Madeira sauce, raspberry ice cream. Lovely light canapés and home-baked bread. Service is discreet and well informed. ♥ Well-chosen ℮

NEW ENTRY

■ *Set L* £14	L 12.30–1.45
Set D £17	D 7.30–9
About £46 *for two*	*Seats* 20
Closed 2 wks Jan	*Parties* 20

Ayudhya *NEW ENTRY*

Kingston-Upon-Thames

R ☖ **Map 7 A5** Surrey
14 Kingston Hill
01-549 5984
Thai cooking
Credit Access, Amex, Diners, Visa

Competent cooking and stylish surroundings are the hallmarks of this highly commendable restaurant. An all-female kitchen brigade produces a variety of dishes, from satay and soups to spicy fish cakes and green beef curry. Lot of fresh herbs, careful spicing, coconut milk in the curries. Nice Thai sweets include a lovely delicate pumpkin pie. ♥ Well-chosen

■ *About* £46 *for two*	L 12–2.30, Sun 12.30–3
Seats 85	D 6.30–11, Fri & Sat
Parties 30	6.30–11.30
Closed Mon & Bank Hols	*Parking* Limited

Penrhos Court Restaurant

Kington

R ☖ **Map 4 A1** Herefordshire
Lyonshall
Kington (0544) 230720

Set by a superb Elizabethan manor, in converted stables, Daphne Lambert's characterful restaurant features her imaginative cooking. Indulge yourself in crab salad with fresh coconut and lime followed by suprême of guinea fowl with garlic cream sauce or salmon with sorrel. Very good sweets could include ginger ice cream or apricot and Grand Marnier mousse. Traditional Sunday lunch (children under 5 free). A popular venue for medieval banquets. ♥ Well-chosen ℮

■ *Set L* £6·50	L Sun only 12.30–2
About £45 *for two*	D 7.30–10
Seats 40 *Parties* 80	*Parking* Ample
Closed D Sun, all Mon & Tues, 25 & 26 Dec & 5 Jan–end Feb	

Dundas Arms *NEW ENTRY*

Kintbury

IR £E
Map 4 C2 Berkshire
Nr Newbury DY7 6HG
Kintbury (0488) 58263
Owner managers Dalzell-Piper family
Credit Access, Amex, Diners, Visa

The Kennet and Avon Canal runs by this friendly old inn. The bar is splendidly traditional, so too the inviting lounge. Five comfortable bedrooms are in a converted stable block reached through the bar: their furnishings are solidly old-fashioned, and they all give on to a pleasant waterside terrace. No dogs. *Amenities* garden.

■ *Rooms* 5	*Confirm by* arrang.
en suite bath/shower 5	*Last dinner* 9.15
Direct dial Yes	*Parking* Ample
Room TV Yes	*Room service* None

Dundas Arms Restaurant ☖ 㔾

Mull over the menu in the bar, then move into the restaurant to enjoy the chef-patron's accomplished cooking. The freshest of ingredients are treated with respect in delightful dishes like calf's sweetbreads with carrot and Sauternes sauce, garlicky rack of lamb or monkfish with saffron and leek sauce. Super vegetables and sweets, and a magnificent wine list with great Bordeaux and burgundies at keen prices. Note the exceptional Pommards from de Montille and Mussy.
⌫ Outstanding ♥ Well-chosen ℮

■ *Set L* £9·50	L 12.30–1.30
Set D £15	D 7.30–9.15
About £45 *for two*	*Seats* 36
Closed Sun, Mon, Bank Hols & 1 wk Xmas	

Berkleys Restaurant, Piano Room   Kinver

R ⌕ **Map 10 B4** Staffordshire
High Street, Nr. Stourbridge
Kinver (0384) 873679
Credit Access, Amex, Diners, Visa
   Andrew Mortimer's smart first-floor restaurant is
situated above his popular bistro. It's a fine
setting for enjoying a meal prepared with skill
from market-fresh ingredients: salmon with
sweetcorn pancakes, hot mushroom tartlet with

quails' eggs, monkfish kebabs with saffron and
pepper rice, hazelnut-coated pork fillet with
baked apple and apricot purée. Round off with
home-made ice cream. ⊖

- *Set D £16*
- *About £42 for two*
- *Seats 36*
- *Closed Sun & Bank Hols*

D only 7–10
Parking Ample
Parties 40

Kirkby Fleetham Hall   Kirkby Fleetham

HR **76% £D**
Map 15 B5 North Yorkshire
Nr Northallerton DL7 0SU
Northallerton (0609) 748226
Owner managers David & Chris Grant
Credit Amex, Diners, Visa
   Lovely, recently relandscaped grounds with
their own lake provide a delightful setting (just a
few miles off the A1) for this sympathetically
restored manor house run with care and
enthusiasm by David and Chris Grant. The style is
charming and elegant, from the high-ceilinged
entrance hall to the various lounges with their
inviting settees, leather chesterfields, period
furniture and warming log fires. Drinks are served

informally in one of the lounges – there is no
formal bar. Spacious bedrooms are individually
furnished – some with four-posters, others with
brass beds. Spotless bathrooms – with brass taps
– are equally pretty. The hotel is in the heart of
Herriot country. No dogs. *Amenities* garden.

- *Rooms 15*
- *en suite bath/shower 15*
- *Direct dial Yes*
- *Room TV Yes*

Confirm by arrang.
Last dinner 9
Parking Ample
Room service All day

Kirkby Fleetham Hall
Restaurant 👑 ⌕

The availability of fresh produce dictates what's
on Chris Grant's daily-changing menus for this
elegant restaurant. There's always a home-made
soup – perhaps spiced apple – to start with,
followed by tempting appetisers such as herby
baked mussels, scallops with vermouth and
fennel or grapefruit and mint sorbet. Carefully
prepared main courses range from fresh salmon
baked in wine to marinated lamb steak. Delicious
sweets, too. ⊖

- *Set L £9.95*
- *Set D £16*
- *About £39 for two*

L Sun only 12.30–1.30
D 7–9.15
Seats 45 Parties 25

■ For a discount on next year's guide, see Offer for Answers.

George & Dragon   Kirkbymoorside

I **£E/F**
Map 15 C6 North Yorkshire
Market Place Y06 6AA
Kirkbymoorside (0751) 31637
Owner managers Curtis & Austin families
Credit Access, Visa
   First-rate housekeeping helps to make a stay at
this 700-year-old inn even more delightful. Rustic
charm can be sampled in the low, beamed bar,

and the lounge has a homely simplicity. Bright
bedrooms with sloping ceilings have a cosy,
unfussy character. No children under five. No
dogs. *Amenities* garden, laundry service.

- *Rooms 24*
- *en suite bath/shower 22*
- *Direct dial Yes*
- *Room TV Yes*
- *Closed 25 & 26 Dec*

Confirm by arrang.
Last dinner 9.30
Parking Ample
Room service All day

Dower House   Knaresborough

H **62% £D/E**
Map 15 C6 North Yorkshire
Bond End HG5 9AL
Harrogate (0423) 863302
Manager Derek Hickson
Credit Access, Amex, Diners, Visa
   Town-centre location; attractive gardens; good
bedrooms; friendly, helpful staff – this is the
Dower House. Some public rooms – notably the

lounge – retain period appeal. Bedrooms, whether
traditional or more modern, are comfortable and
very clean, with smart bath/shower rooms.
Amenities garden, laundry service.

- *Rooms 20*
- *en suite bath/shower 18*
- *Room phone Yes*
- *Room TV Yes*
- *Closed 25 Dec*

Confirm by arrang.
Last dinner 9
Parking Ample
Room service Limited

Schwaller's *NEW ENTRY* — Knaresborough

R ♨ **Map 15 C6** North Yorkshire
6 Bond End
Harrogate (0423) 863899
Credit Access, Visa
Order over canapés in the lounge before going upstairs to dine by candlelight in a room that's full of warmth and character. Martin Schwaller's five-course dinner menus tempt with skilfully prepared dishes like creamy little salmon parcels, coriander

chicken and fillet steak Swiss-style with gruyère, a rich wine sauce and wonderful rösti. Dessert or cheese. Caroline Schwaller is an exuberant hostess. No smoking. ♀ **Well-chosen** ⊖

■ *Set D from £12·95*   *D only 7–9.30*
About £42 for two   *Parking Difficult*
Seats 30
Closed Tues & 24 Dec–30 Jan

■ Changes in data may occur in establishments after the Guide goes to press. Prices should be taken as indications rather than firm quotes.

La Belle Epoque — Knutsford

RR 🏩 **Map 10 B2** Cheshire
60 King Street WA16 2DT
Knutsford (0565) 3060
French cooking
Owner managers Keith & Nerys Mooney
Credit Access, Amex, Diners, Visa
In a village of diverse, often eccentric, architectural styles, this Art Nouveau restaurant is among the most interesting and extravagant. Yvonne Holt's French menus show appropriate flights of fancy: how about crab-filled chicken leg with a mango and ginger coulis or snails casseroled in green chartreuse with cèpes and

hazelnuts? Terrine of duck with onion marmalade and steak with a leek, Stilton and port sauce are other typical dishes, and there's an excellent cheeseboard. Friendly, attentive service. ⊖
■ *About £51 for two*   *D only 7.15–10.15*
Seats 65 Parties 85   *Parking Ample*
Closed Sun, Bank Hols & 1st wk Jan

Bedrooms £E/F
Rooms 5   *With bath/shower 5*
Prettily-decorated bedrooms (bookable Mon–Fri) have TVs and good modern bathrooms. No children under 10. No dogs.

The Cottons Hotel *NEW ENTRY* — Knutsford

H **65% £C/D** ♿
Map 10 B2 Cheshire
Manchester Road WA16 0SU
Knutsford (0565) 50333. Tlx 669931
Credit Access, Amex, Diners, Visa
On the A50 just outside Knutsford, The Cottons is a long, two-storey building. Bedrooms are smartly up to date with many accessories. The Bourbon Street Bar evokes New Orleans, and

there's an attractive awned area serving snacks. *Amenities* terrace, indoor swimming pool, sauna, solarium, whirlpool bath, keep-fit equipment, in-house movies (free).

■ *Rooms 60*   *Confirm by arrang.*
en suite bath/shower 60   *Last dinner 9.45*
Direct dial Yes   *Parking Ample*
Room TV Yes   *Room service Limited*

■ We publish annually, so make sure you use the current edition. It's worth it!

David's Place — Knutsford

R **Map 10 B2** Cheshire
10 Princess Street
Knutsford (0565) 3356
Owner managers David & Arlette Molloy
Credit Access, Amex, Diners, Visa
The evening carte is of particular interest at this busy town-centre restaurant cheerfully presided over by David and Arlette Molloy. Prawns with peppers and lime chartreuse or curried parsnip

soup make typically piquant starters, perhaps followed by duck sauced with red wine and kumquats, juicy fillet steak or lamb with olives. Pleasant sweets. ⊖

■ *Set D £11·50*   *L 12.30–2*
About £46 for two   *D 7.15–10 (Fri & Sat*
Seats 70 Parties 40   *7.15–10.30)*
Closed Sun & Bank Hols   *Parking Ample*

Lacock ▶

Sign of the Angel   Lacock

IR £D/E
Map 4 B2 Wiltshire
6 Church Street, Nr Chippenham SN15 2LA
Lacock (024 973) 230
Owner managers Levis family
Formerly a 15th-century wool merchant's house, now a delightful and welcoming inn. Heavy beams, sloping floors, log fires and sturdy antique furniture paint a picture of traditional charm, and there's a splendid panelled lounge with TV. Bedrooms are quaint and cosy, and bathrooms well equipped and up to date. No children under 12. *Amenities* garden.

- *Rooms* 6
- *en suite bath/shower* 6
- *Direct dial* Yes
- *Room TV* No
- *Closed* 22 Dec–1 Jan

Confirm by 5
Last dinner 8
Parking Limited
Room service Limited

Sign of the Angel Restaurant ⚲

English cooking
A charmingly traditional setting, just right for the Levis family's simple, enjoyable cooking. There's no written menu but the waitress will suggest starters like lemony fennel soup, potted crab and grilled fillets of sole. To follow, there is always a daily roast – beef is the speciality. To finish, apple pie or fresh fruit salad. Milk, cream and eggs come from the family's own stock. ⊖

- *Set L* £13·50,
- *Set D* £17·50
- *About* £48 for two
- *Closed* L Sat & Bank Hols, D Sun to non-residents & all 22 Dec–1 Jan

L Mon–Fri by arrang.,
Sun at 1
D 7.30–8
Seats 40 *Parties* 20

♔ indicates a **well-chosen** house wine.

Lamorna Cove Hotel   Lamorna Cove

H 67% £C
Map 2 A4 Cornwall
Nr Penzance TR19 6XH
Penzance (0736) 731411
Owner manager Nina Schlemmer
Credit Access, Amex, Visa
In a secluded woodland setting above the cove, this delightful hotel offers colourful gardens, lovely views and perfect peace and tranquillity. There's

a choice of three relaxing lounges, also a cosy bar. Individually decorated bedrooms are light and pleasant, with modern bathrooms.
Amenities garden, outdoor swimming pool, sauna.

- *Rooms* 18
- *en suite bath/shower* 18
- *Direct dial* Yes
- *Room TV* Yes

Confirm by arrang.
Last dinner 9.30
Parking Ample
Room service All day

Post House Hotel   Lancaster

H 69% £C ⑁
Map 13 D6 Lancashire
Waterside Park, Caton Road LA1 3RA
Lancaster (0524) 65999. Tlx 65363
Credit Access, Amex, Diners, Visa
Fishing on the river Lune can be enjoyed at this modern red-brick hotel. Day rooms are pleasant; bedrooms comfortable and well planned, the best have sitting areas and river views. Friendly staff;

diligent housekeeping. *Amenities* garden, indoor swimming pool, sauna, solarium, whirlpool bath, gymnasium, clay-pigeon shooting, game fishing, in-house movies (free), coffee shop (7am–10.30pm), children's playground.

- *Rooms* 117
- *en suite bath/shower* 117
- *Direct dial* Yes
- *Room TV* Yes

Confirm by 6
Last dinner 10.30
Parking Ample
Room service 24 hours

Langdale Hotel   Langdale

H 74% £C
Map 13 C5 Cumbria
Nr Ambleside LA22 9JB
Langdale (096 67) 302. Tlx 65188
Credit Access, Amex, Diners, Visa
An extensive woodland complex in the heart of the Lake District, this up-to-date hotel offers an impressive range of leisure activities and smartly furnished accommodation. Purdeys, the main bar and restaurant area, boasts an old millstream flowing through it, and there's another smart bar and lounge in the leisure complex. Ultra-modern bedrooms – the majority are in a separate block – are equipped with drying cupboards; most have lounge areas. Bathrooms are carpeted, have modern coloured suites and all have shower units. No dogs. *Amenities* garden, indoor swimming pool, sauna, solarium, whirlpool bath, gymnasium,

squash, coarse and game fishing, games room, snooker, in-house movies (free), beauty salon, hairdressing, children's playroom, coffee shop (7.30am–10pm), laundry service.

- *Rooms* 36
- *en suite bath/shower* 36
- *Direct dial* Yes
- *Room TV* Yes

Confirm by arrang.
Last dinner 10
Parking Ample
Room service 24 hours

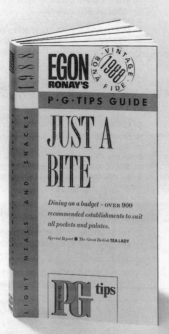

Northcote Manor Langho

HR 66% £E/F
Map 10 B1 Lancashire
Northcote Road BB6 8BE
Blackburn (0254) 40555
Owner manager Craig Bancroft
Credit Access, Amex, Diners, Visa
  Enthusiastic young staff volunteer a warm
welcome at this converted manor house off the
A59. There's an attractive oak-panelled cocktail
bar, and a homely lounge with leather chester-
fields. Spacious, prettily decorated bedrooms
have tea-makers and carpeted bathrooms.
Amenities garden, 24-hour lounge service.

■ *Rooms* 6	*Confirm by* 6
en suite bath/shower 6	*Last dinner* 9.30
Direct dial Yes	*Parking* Ample
Room TV Yes	*Room service* All day
Closed 25 & 26 Dec	

Northcote Manor Restaurant 🍴

Nigel Haworth cooks in fine modern style in this
friendly restaurant, where chandeliers and oil
paintings set an elegant tone. The menus are full
of tempting things, starting with delights like fresh
fruit timbale served on cream cheese with
avocado salad, or crab with minted cucumber
bavarois and light sorrel sauce. Main dishes range
from brill wrapped in smoked salmon and filo
pastry on a truffle butter sauce to wild duckling
marinated with passion fruit and rosemary.
Enticing sweets and a short, well-chosen wine list.

■ *Set L* £8·50	*L* 12–1.30
About £43 for two	*D* 7–9.30, Sat 7–10
Seats 50	*Parties* 90
Closed L Sat & all 25 & 26 Dec & 1 Jan	

Punch Bowl Inn Lanreath

I £F
Map 2 C3 Devon
Nr Looe PL13 2NX
Lanreath (0503) 20218
Owner managers Mr & Mrs Frith
Credit Access, Visa
  Records date this village inn at around 1620.
There's a delightful lounge bar with inglenook,
antiques, panelling and gleaming horse brasses,
and a similar public bar and children's room.
Bedrooms vary from period rooms with four-
posters to modern extension rooms. A residents'
lounge overlooks the garden.

■ *Rooms* 17	*Confirm by* arrang.
en suite bath/shower 13	*Last dinner* 9.30
Room phone No	*Parking* Ample
Room TV Yes	*Room service* Limited
Closed 2–3 days Xmas	

Swan Hotel Lavenham

H 69% £C/D
Map 6 C3 Suffolk
High Street, Nr Sudbury CO10 9QA
Lavenham (0787) 247477
Credit Access, Amex, Diners, Visa
  Splendid timbering and a cosy, mellow interior
distinguish this 14th-century hotel in the town
centre. Log fires warm the traditional lounges and
there are two bars, one with patio doors leading to
the terraced garden. Bedrooms combine a wealth
of period charm with the comforts of homely,
traditional furnishings, tea-makers plus good
modern bathrooms. *Amenities* garden, laundry
service.

■ *Rooms* 48	*Confirm by* 6
en suite bath/shower 48	*Last dinner* 9.30
Direct dial Yes	*Parking* Ample
Room TV Yes	*Room service* All day

Mallory Court Leamington Spa

HR 81% £C/D
Map 10 C4 Warwickshire
Harbury Lane, Bishop's Tachbrook CV33 9QB
Leamington Spa (0926) 30214. Tlx 317294
Owner managers Allan Holland & Jeremy Mort
Credit Access, Amex, Visa

Ten acres of landscaped grounds provide a
superb setting for this lovely country house hotel,
where a warm welcome and outstanding comfort
and elegance are the main attractions. The small
foyer area leads to a relaxing lounge, stunningly
decked out in pastel pink settees and period
furnishings, whilst the drawing room boasts
bottle-green leather chesterfields. Large
bedrooms are all highly individual, furnished with
the best fabrics, period furnishings, big
comfortable beds (including some four-posters),
as well as plants and books. Tiled and carpeted
bathrooms. No children under 12. No dogs.
Amenities garden, outdoor swimming pool,
tennis, squash, croquet, valeting, laundry service.

■ *Rooms* 10	*Confirm by* arrang.
en suite bath/shower 10	*Last dinner* 9.45
Direct dial Yes	*Parking* Ample
Room TV Yes	*Room service* All day

Mallory Court Restaurant ★ ♛♛ ♈

The two beautifully panelled and elegant dining rooms at Mallory Court provide an excellent venue in which to experience the impressive talents of chef Allan Holland. A great deal of time and care goes into every aspect of his superb menus – four-course set-price dinners and a short but varied lunchtime choice. The cooking, very much French in style, achieves an excellent combination of flavours and textures, typified by a stunning lobster terrine (of quite exceptional flavours and magnificent textures) with a light and carefully made herb mayonnaise or a perfectly seasoned creamy watercress soup of first-class consistency. Delightful sweets include chocolate terrine. *Specialities* terrine de foie gras with Sauternes jelly, fillet of lamb with basil mousseline and charlotte of aubergine, breast of duck with beetroot mousse and cassis sauce, hot raspberry soufflé.
♈ Well-chosen ⊜

■ Set L £15·75	L 12.30–1.45
Set D £27·75	*D 7.30–9.45,*
About £70 for two	*Sun 7.30–8.30*
Seats 55	*Parties 35*

Regent Hotel — Leamington Spa

H 62% £D/E
Map 10 C4 Warwickshire
The Parade CV32 4AX
Leamington Spa (0926) 27231. Tlx 311715
Manager Vernon May
Credit Access, Amex, Diners, Visa. LVs
  Dating from 1819, this historic hotel retains many original features such as beautiful stained-glass windows, a handsome staircase and elegant ceilings. Bedrooms are traditionally furnished and bathrooms are adequate. House keeping is excellent throughout.
Amenities garden, games room, laundry service, 24 hour lounge service.

■ *Rooms 80*	*Confirm by 6*
en suite bath/shower 80	*Last dinner 10.45*
Direct dial Yes	*Parking Ample*
Room TV Yes	*Room service 24 hours*

Feathers Hotel — Ledbury

H 59% £D/E
Map 4 B1 Hereford & Worcester
High Street HR8 1DS
Ledbury (0531) 2600
Credit Access, Amex, Diners
  Much traditional charm survives in this listed Elizabethan building, whose spectacular half-timbered facade is a famous town-centre landmark. Beams and period furnishings grace the pretty little lounge, and the bar has a warm, friendly appeal. Bedrooms mix old and new, with sloping floors, original beams and sturdy oak pieces complemented by up-to-date extras.
Amenities squash, laundry service.

■ *Rooms 11*	*Confirm by arrang.*
en suite bath/shower 11	*Last dinner 9.30*
Direct dial Yes	*Parking Ample*
Room TV Yes	*Room service All day*

Hope End Country House Hotel — Ledbury

HR 69% £C/D
Map 4 B1 Hereford & Worcester
Hope End HR8 1JQ
Ledbury (0531) 3613
Owner managers Mr & Mrs John Hegarty
Credit Access, Visa
  The childhood home of Elizabeth Barrett Browning is today a delightful little hotel set in 40 acres of wooded parkland and run by caring owners. Locally made furniture, woollen rugs and log fires add to the cosy charms of the two sitting rooms. Homely, pine-furnished bedrooms have tea-makers, books and thoughtfully equipped bathrooms. Half-board terms only. No children under fourteen. No dogs.
Amenities garden.

■ *Rooms 9*	*Confirm by 6*
en suite bath/shower 9	*Last dinner 8.30*
Room phone Yes	*Parking Ample*
Room TV Some	*Room service Limited*
Closed Mon & Tues & end Nov–end Feb	

Hope End Hotel Restaurant ♈

English cooking
A most attractive dining room, where accomplished chef Patricia Hegarty's short, fixed-price dinner menus change daily and offer a mouthwatering selection of dishes. Wild duck and pumpkin soup might precede beef carbonnade or venison in old ale sauce, accompanied by delicious garden-fresh vegetables. A crisp and refreshing salad follows, then superb English cheeses and lovely sweets like gooseberry and orange cream. Exquisitely chosen wines, the selection of Burgundy growers reading like a roll-call of honour.
⊃ Outstanding ♈ Well-chosen ⊜

■ *Set D £18*	*D only 7.30–8.30*
About £45 for two	*Seats 24 Parties 6*
Closed Mon & Tues & end Nov–end Feb	

LEEDS

Map 11 D1
Town plan opposite

Population 748,000

Originally Loidis, a Celtic settlement, it was given its industrial send-off by a 13th-century community of monks, who practised the crafts that made the town great–notably cloth-spinning and coal-mining but the big leap came between 1775 (population 17,000) and 1831 (population 123,000).
It has taken gargantuan efforts to eliminate the excesses of unplanned industrial and population growth, but its post-war housing and roads record and industrial mix are making Leeds a prouder city. Today it can boast as much of its University and Poly, its shopping areas, parks and new estates as it has always done of its choir, cricket, rugby league, soccer and fish and chips.
Yet it is as true today as when Henry VIII's Librarian first stated it, that 'the town stondith most by clothing'.

Information Centre
19 Wellington Street
Leeds LS1 4DE
Telephone Leeds 462453/4

Fiat Dealers
JCT 600
Spence Lane
Leeds LS12 1AG
Tel. Leeds 431843

Whitehead & Hinch Ltd
Broadgate Lane
Horsforth, Leeds LS18 4AG
Tel. Horsforth 585056

1 Adel Church *St John the Baptist 12th c* B1
2 Airport *Yeadon 8 miles* B1
3 Central Library C2
4 City Art Gallery C2
5 City Museum C2
6 City Station B/C3
7 City Varieties *'Good Old Days'* C2
8 Civil Theatre C2
9 Grand Theatre C2
10 International Pool A2
11 Kirkstall Abbey *12th c* A2
12 Kirkstall Abbey House Folk Museum A2
13 Leeds Industrial Museum A2
14 Leeds Parish Church D3
15 Leeds United F.C. *Elland Road* C3
16 Middleton Colliery Railway *1785, oldest in world* C3
17 Playhouse B1
18 Queen's Hall *Exhibitions* (Leeds Exhibition Centre) C3
19 Roman Catholic Cathedral C2
20 Roundhay Park E1
21 Rugby League and Cricket *Headingley* B1
22 Temple Newsam House *15th c and Park, home of Darnley, husband of Mary Queen of Scots; outstanding furniture collection* E2
23 University A/B1

Leeds

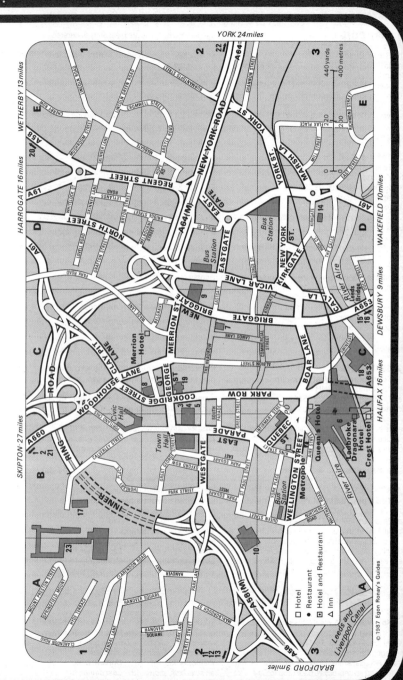

© 1987 Egon Ronay's Guides

Crest Hotel — Leeds

H 55% £C/D
Town plan B3 West Yorkshire
The Grove, Oulton LS26 8EJ
Leeds (0532) 826201. Tlx 557646. Fax 829243
Credit Access, Amex, Diners, Visa. **LVs**

Modern hotel at the junction of the A642 and A639, five miles south of the city centre. The small foyer, the bars and other public rooms are in one section, and a separate two-storey block contains the bedrooms. These are pleasantly decorated and quite thoughtfully equipped, extras including an armchair, trouser presses, mineral water and bedside radio.
Amenities garden, laundry service.

■ *Rooms 41*	*Confirm by 6*
en suite bath/shower 41	*Last dinner 9.45*
Room phone Yes	*Parking Ample*
Room TV Yes	*Room service Limited*

Ladbroke Dragonara Hotel — Leeds

H 71% £C *E* &
Town plan B3 West Yorkshire
Neville Street LS1 4BX
Leeds (0532) 442000. Tlx 557143
Manager Nigel Barfoot
Credit Access, Amex, Diners, Visa

Business people are frequent guests at this tall 1970s hotel with spacious open-plan public areas. Served by lifts, the first-floor reception – a feast of burgundy velour and mahogany, with bronzed mirrors and potted palms – doubles as a lounge, and, in the restaurant complex, the Rosewood Bar is lined with photographs of the many celebrities who have stayed here. Bedrooms with well co-ordinated decor have darkwood fitted units, trouser presses and tea-makers, and the attractive bathrooms are comprehensively equipped. Top-floor Plaza rooms have various

executive extras such as magazines, drinks and chocolates. *Amenities* in-house movies (charge), laundry service, coffee shop (11am–midnight), kiosk.

■ *Rooms 234*	*Confirm by 6*
en suite bath/shower 234	*Last dinner 10*
Direct dial Yes	*Parking Limited*
Room TV Yes	*Room service 24 hours*

Merrion Hotel — Leeds

H 65% £C/D
Town plan C1 West Yorkshire
Merrion Centre LS2 8NH
Leeds (0532) 439191. Tlx 55459
Credit Access, Amex, Diners, Visa. **LVs**

New owners plan major changes at this city-centre hotel. Leather chesterfields grace the reception area and an attractive lounge and colourful Edwardian-style cocktail bar are sited on the first floor. Compact, well-designed bedrooms give writing space and there are generous accessories. Good room service.
Amenities in-house movies (free), laundry service, coffee shop (6 days 10.30am–10.30pm).

■ *Rooms 120*	*Confirm by 6*
en suite bath/shower 120	*Last dinner 10.30*
Direct dial Yes	*Parking Ample*
Room TV Yes	*Room service 24 hours*

Metropole — Leeds

H 57% £D
Town plan B3 West Yorkshire
King Street LS1 2HQ
Leeds (0532) 450841. Tlx 557755
Credit Access, Amex, Diners, Visa

An ornate terracotta facade fronts this imposing hotel in the town centre. Public rooms have a lofty, elegant appeal, like the pillared foyer with its comfortable lounge areas and the two bars, one decorated in Victorian gas-lamp style. Good-sized bedrooms, some attractively redecorated, have mainly traditional furnishings, tea-makers and remote-control TVs.
Amenities laundry service.

■ *Rooms 113*	*Confirm by 6*
en suite bath/shower 77	*Last dinner 10*
Direct dial Yes	*Parking Limited*
Room TV Yes	*Room service Limited*

Queen's Hotel — Leeds

H 67% £C &
Town plan B3 West Yorkshire
City Square LS1 1PL
Leeds (0532) 431323. Tlx 55161
Manager Steven Maslen
Credit Access, Amex, Diners, Visa. **LVs**

Providing an impressive backdrop to City Square, this white Portland stone hotel is gradually being upgraded to a standard befitting its grandeur. An impressive foyer leads to an informal lounge and the lively Harlequin bar. Some of the spacious bedrooms have been attractively redecorated, and bathrooms are being modernised. *Amenities* laundry service.

■ *Rooms 195*	*Confirm by 6*
en suite bath/shower 181	*Last dinner 10*
Direct dial Yes	*Parking Ample*
Room TV Yes	*Room service 24 hours*

Belmont Hotel *NEW ENTRY* Leicester

H **64%** **£D/E**
Map 11 D4 Leicestershire
De Montfort Street LE1 7GR
Leicester (0533) 544773. Tlx 34619
Owner manager James Bowie
Credit Access, Amex, Diners, Visa. **LVs**

Courteous service reflects the ethos of the Bowie family, owners of this well-run hotel since 1934. Public rooms range from homely lounge and cosy lounge bar to a lively basement bar. Bedrooms have welcome touches like fresh fruit, tea-making facilities; Executive rooms have other extras. *Amenities* garden, laundry service.

- *Rooms* 61   *Confirm by* 6
en suite bath/shower 53   *Last dinner* 9.55
Direct dial Yes   *Parking* Limited
Room TV Yes   *Room service* Limited
Closed 4 days Xmas

Grand Hotel Leicester

H **66%** **£D/E**
Map 11 D4 Leicestershire
Grandy Street LE1 6ES
Leicester (0533) 555599. Tlx 342244
Manager Mr P. B. Kemp
Credit Access, Amex, Diners, Visa. **LVs**

A Victorian city-centre hotel. Recently restored, public areas include a marble-floored foyer and elegant lounge. Three pleasant bars are in different styles to appeal to everyone. Bedrooms and bathrooms are functional; refurbishment is under way. *Amenities* laundry service, coffee shop (9am–10pm), 24-hour lounge service.

- *Rooms* 93   *Confirm by* 6
en suite bath/shower 93   *Last dinner* 9.30
Direct dial Yes   *Parking* Ample
Room TV Yes   *Room service* Limited
Closed 25 & 26 Dec

Holiday Inn Leicester

H **73%** **£D** *E* &
Map 11 D4 Leicestershire
St Nicholas Circle LE1 5LX
Leicester (0533) 531161. Tlx 341281
Manager Ken Eaton
Credit Access, Amex, Diners, Visa

A roundabout is the location for this multi-storey hotel on the fringe of the city centre. The spacious foyer is tiled with stone and the lounge has recently been elegantly refurbished in tones of pastel pink. Step into the bar and you could almost be in a village 'local'. It has a thatched roof, beams, and copper-topped tables. Large comfortable bedrooms feature modern units and up-to-date fabrics and have hairdryers, trouser presses and remote-controlled TVs. Executive rooms have extras. Bathrooms are ample and well fitted. Two floors are for non-smokers.

Amenities indoor swimming pool, sauna, keep-fit equipment, in-house movies, laundry service, coffee shop (10am–10pm), 24-hour lounge service.

- *Rooms* 188   *Confirm by* 6
en suite bath/shower 188   *Last dinner* 10.15
Direct dial Yes   *Parking* Ample
Room TV Yes   *Room service* 24 hours

Ladbroke Hotel *NEW ENTRY* Leicester

H **61%** **£E**
Map 11 D4 Leicestershire
Humberstone Road LE5 3AT
Leicester (0533) 20471. Tlx 341460
Manager William McLean
Credit Access, Amex, Diners, Visa. **LVs**

Practical comforts in a friendly modern hotel near the city centre. The main bar is a popular gathering place, and there's a basement bar that appeals to the young. All bedrooms and bathrooms are neat and tidy, and superior rooms offer trouser presses, hairdryers and bathrobes. *Amenities* in-house movies (charge), laundry service, restaurant (11am–11pm).

- *Rooms* 215   *Confirm by* 6
en suite bath/shower 215   *Last dinner* 9.30
Direct dial Yes   *Parking* Limited
Room TV Yes   *Room service* None

Leicester Forest Moat House *NEW ENTRY* Leicester

H **58%** **£E**
Map 11 D4 Leicestershire
Hinckley Road, Leicester Forest East LE3 3GH
Leicester (0533) 394661
Credit Access, Amex, Diners, Visa. **LVs**

Modest accommodation for the traveller in a modern hotel just 200 yards from Leicester Forest East Services on the M1. Bedrooms are compact and practical. Day rooms include a bright, cheerful foyer and two bars, one with a lively, pubby atmosphere. The hotel is accessible from both north and south sides of the motorway. *Amenities* garden, laundry service, 24-hour lounge service.

- *Rooms* 31   *Confirm by* 6
en suite bath/shower 31   *Last dinner* 9.45
Room phone Yes   *Parking* Ample
Room TV Yes   *Room service* Limited

Post House Hotel   Leicester

H **61% £C/D**
Map 11 D4 Leicestershire
Braunstone Lane East LE3 2FW
Leicester (0533) 896688. Tlx 341009
Credit Access, Amex, Diners, Visa. LVs
   Junction 21 of the M1 is but a mile from this
1970s hotel with good conference facilities. The
tiled foyer leads to a popular lounge-bar, and
there is also a smart cocktail bar. Neat, practical

bedrooms (some family-size) offer mini-bars,
remote-control TVs and compact bathrooms.
Executive rooms have superior furnishings and
extras. *Amenities* garden, laundry service, coffee
shop (7am–10.30pm), 24-hour lounge service.

■ *Rooms* 172	*Confirm by* 6
en suite bath/shower 172	*Last dinner* 10
Direct dial Yes	*Parking* Ample
Room TV Yes	*Room service* Limited

Queens Hotel   Leicester

H **58% £D/E**
Map 11 D4 Leicestershire
Abbey Street LE1 3TE
Leicester (0533) 510666. Tlx 342434
Credit Access, Amex, Diners, Visa
   Improvements continue to be made at this city
centre hotel above a multi-storey car park.
Bedrooms have been tastefully refurbished and
now boast mini-bars in addition to trouser

presses, hairdryers, direct-dial telephones,
remote-control TVs and tea-makers. Public rooms
are light and airy. *Amenities* laundry service,
coffee shop (11am–11pm).

■ *Rooms* 73	*Confirm by* 7
en suite bath/shower 73	*Last dinner* 10.30
Direct dial Yes	*Parking* Ample
Room TV Yes	*Room service* 24 hours

Water Margin *NEW ENTRY*   Leicester

R ☺ **Map 11 D4** Leicestershire
76 High Street
Leicester (0533) 24937
Chinese cooking
Credit Access, Amex, Diners, Visa
   This long-established and justly popular
Chinese restaurant continues to draw the crowds
with an extensive and varied choice of well-
prepared dishes. Start with paper-wrapped

prawns, stuffed crab claws or flavoursome
chicken and sweetcorn soup; move on to chicken
in yellow bean sauce, or beef with oyster sauce.
There are several set menus and dim sum are a
tasty treat in the afternoons.

■ *Set L from £13 for two*	*Meals* noon–midnight
About £20 for two	*Parking* Ample
Seats 140 *Parties* 90	*Closed* 25 & 26 Dec

Greyhound Hotel   Leigh

H **57% £D/E**
Map 10 B2 Greater Manchester
Warrington Road WN7 3XQ
Leigh (0942) 671256
Credit Access, Amex, Diners, Visa
   Fronted by a refurbished pub at a roundabout
on the A580, the Greyhound is a functional
modern hotel that is popular with businessmen.
The foyer/reception is a pleasant area with

armchairs and settees; the bars are cheerful and
inviting. Accommodation in a three-storey block
comprises identical twin rooms with decent
bathrooms. Service doesn't always shine.
Amenities laundry service.

■ *Rooms* 48	*Confirm by* 6
en suite bath/shower 48	*Last dinner* 9.45
Direct dial Yes	*Parking* Ample
Room TV Yes	*Room service* None

Swan Hotel   Leighton Buzzard

HR **60% £D/E**
Map 5 E1 Bedfordshire
High Street LU7 7EA
Leighton Buzzard (0525) 372148
Owner managers Mr & Mrs E. J. Stephens
Credit Access, Amex, Diners, Visa
   Originally a coaching inn, this friendly hotel in
the town centre dates back to 1710. Public rooms
include a restful little lounge and two pleasantly
informal bars, one with handsome carved oak
counter. Brightly decorated bedrooms have
simple white units, tea-makers and up-to-date
bathrooms; there are four courtyard suites with
kitchens. *Amenities* laundry service.

■ *Rooms* 38	*Confirm by* arrang.
en suite bath/shower 38	*Last dinner* 9.30
Direct dial Yes	*Parking* Ample
Room TV Yes	*Room service* All day

Mr Swan's Restaurant &

Soft pinks create a relaxing ambience in this
attractive restaurant with smart conservatory
area. Menus offer an interesting and varied
selection of dishes, competently cooked. Eggs
Benedict and leek mousse with smoked bacon
are typical starters, and main courses ranging
from goujons of monkfish to traditional roast
pheasant are served with good fresh vegetables
or a salad. Also grills, and vegetarian dishes like
vegetable curry or butter bean pie. Enjoyable
sweets from the trolley. ☺

■ *Set L £9·75*	*L* 12–2
Set D £14·50	*D* 7–9.30
About £42 for two	*Seats* 70 *Parties* 40
Closed D 25 Dec & all 26 Dec & 1 Jan	

Chilston Park *NEW ENTRY* Lenham

H **75% £C**
Map 7 C5 Kent
Boughton Malherbe ME17 2BE
Maidstone (0622) 859803. Tlx 966154
Credit Access, Amex, Diners, Visa

Hidden in beautiful Kent countryside, this 18th-century country house was derelict for 25 years before Martin and Judith Miller bought it and brought it back to life. It's a treasure trove of antiques, Chippendale rubbing shoulders with early English oak, heavy Jacobean with delicate Oriental, and the walls are covered with oils, water colours, etchings and prints. Among the public rooms – evocatively candlelit in the evening – are the superb Marble Hall and equally magnificent Yellow Drawing Room, a library and a billiards room. From the Renaissance Hall a superb wooden staircase sweeps up to the main-house bedrooms, the largest of which boast four-posters; particularly impressive is the oak-beamed Tudor Suite. Other rooms, lacking

nothing in solid comfort, are in outbuildings. Bathrooms are luxuriously appointed.
Amenities garden, tennis, croquet, clay-pigeon shooting, hot-air ballooning, billiards, laundry service, 24-hour lounge service, helipad.

■ *Rooms* 42	*Confirm by arrang.*
en suite bath/shower 41	*Last dinner* 9.30
Direct dial Yes	*Parking* Ample
Room TV Yes	*Room service* 24 hours

Broadway Hotel Letchworth

H **57% £E**
Map 6 A3 Hertfordshire
The Broadway SG6 3NZ
Letchworth (0462) 685651
Credit Access, Amex, Diners, Visa

In the centre of Letchworth, this 60s hotel is a popular stopover for business people. On the ground floor are two bars, one a public bar with a mellow, traditional feel, the other a smart bamboo-furnished bar-lounge. Good-sized bedrooms are gradually being refurbished, with floral fabrics and smart units. Attractive modern bathrooms. All rooms have tea-makers and trouser presses.
Amenities laundry service.

■ *Rooms* 30	*Confirm by arrang.*
en suite bath/shower 30	*Last dinner* 10
Direct dial Yes	*Parking* Ample
Room TV Yes	*Room service* None

■ Our inspectors never book in the name of Egon Ronay's Guides; they disclose their identity only after paying their bills.

Fox's Earth Lewtrenchard Manor Lewdown

HR **64% £C/D**
Map 2 C2 Devon
Lewtrenchard EX20 4PN
Lewdown (056 683) 256
Owner managers Greg Shriver & Mary Ellen Keys
Credit Access, Amex, Visa

American owners are going great guns in improving this magnificent old country house, whose beautiful grounds include a lake and waterfall. Day rooms, starting with the stunning entrance hall, feature antiques and lovely panelling, some carved, some painted. Well-equipped bedrooms – new carpets in some – are individual in size, shape and decor; three have four-poster beds. No children under 12. No dogs.
Amenities garden, shooting, clay-pigeon shooting, game fishing, laundry service, helipad.

■ *Rooms* 8	*Confirm by arrang.*
en suite bath/shower 8	*Last dinner* 9.30
Direct dial Yes	*Parking* Ample
Room TV Yes	*Room service* All day

Fox's Earth Lewtrenchard Manor Restaurant

The candlelit dining room, with its mullioned windows, dark panelling and little baskets of flowers, is a most attractive setting for enjoying a meal prepared by young Martin Lyon. The emphasis is on fresh produce, and mainly straightforward cooking methods allow the ingredients to speak for themselves. Two set menus offer a tempting choice of dishes such as turbot and salmon with an orange sauce, vegetable terrine with tomato vinaigrette, or saddle of lamb with a Madeira, tarragon and cream sauce. Chocolate mousse with orange sorbet or cold pineapple soufflé and glazed fruits in a puff pastry case typify the sweets. Good wine list with splendid Gobet Beaujolais crus. ⊖

■ *Set D from* £17	*L* 12–2.30
About £50 *for two*	*D* 7.30–9.30
Seats 40 *Parties* 50	*Closed* Mon–Sat

Kenwards — Lewes

R ♧ **Map 7 B6** East Sussex
Pipe Passage, 151a High Street
Lewes (0273) 472343
Credit Access, Amex, Diners, Visa
  Old roof timbers, pine tables and a pretty little
herb garden contribute to the appeal of John
Kenward's restaurant. His enjoyable cooking
features largely local produce and there's usually
a main-course choice between two fish dishes,
one vegetarian and three meat (two game in
winter). Start perhaps with watercress soup, then
move on to leg of pork with celery and lovage
sauce. Pleasing sweets. Wine list includes a good
selection of half-bottles. ♀ **Well-chosen** ♙

■ *Set D* Tues–Fri £10·50   *L* by arrang.
About £40 for two   *D* 7.30–9.30, Sat 7–10
Seats 28   *Parking* Limited
Closed Sun, Mon & 25 & 26 Dec

Light of Bengal *NEW ENTRY* — Lewes

R **Map 7 B6** East Sussex
32 Lansdown Place
Lewes (0273) 472493
Indian cooking
Owner manager S. Rahman
Credit Access, Visa. LVs
  Above-average Indian restaurant two minutes'
walk from railway station. It's small and
comfortable, with traditional decor and speedy,
friendly staff. Tandoori dishes are the speciality,
ranging from chicken and lamb tikkas to king-size
prawns. Curries cover the heat spectrum from
mild, creamy korma to fiery phal. For a cooling
finale try delicious pistachio-studded kulfi.

■ *About £24 for two*   *L* 12–2.30
Seats 34   *D* 6–11.30
Parking Limited   *Closed* 25 & 26 Dec

■ If we recommend meals in a
hotel or inn, a separate entry is
made for its restaurant.

Shelleys Hotel — Lewes

H **66%   £C/D**
Map 7 B6 East Sussex
High Street BN7 1XS
Lewes (0273) 472361
Credit Access, Amex, Diners, Visa
  A friendly, civilised hotel, and a favourite with
visitors to nearby Glyndebourne. It's a fine period
house, with a handsome entrance hall that
features an original stone floor and an antique
desk for checking in. There's an elegant lounge,
and an attractive bar hung with oils.
Accommodation ranges from huge rooms with
four-posters to neat, compact singles.
Amenities garden, croquet, laundry service.
■ *Rooms* 21   *Confirm by arrang.*
en suite bath/shower 21   *Last dinner* 9.15
Direct dial Yes   *Parking* Ample
Room TV Yes   *Room service* 24 hours

Trumps — Lewes

R ♧ **Map 7 B6** East Sussex
19 Station Street
Lewes (0273) 473906
Credit Access, Visa
  A smart yet pleasantly informal restaurant run
by dedicated, hard-working owners, Neil and
Lesley McGown. Beautifully presented starters
from Neil's repertoire include Brie fritters with
apricot coulis, while main dishes range from the
simple (grilled sole with lemon butter) to the sinful
(mignons of beef fillet with port and cream sauce).
■ *Set L* £13·95,   *L* 12–2, Sun 12–3
Sun £8·95   *D* 7–10.30, Fri & Sat
Set D £13·95   7–11, Sun 7.30–9.30
About £40 for two   *Parking* Limited
Seats 36   *Parties* 45
Closed Wed, L Thurs & Sat, all Bank Hols, 26–30
Dec & 2 wks autumn

Ladbroke Hotel — Leyland

H **65%   £D/E** &
Map 10 A1 Lancashire
Leyland Way PR5 2JX
Leyland (0772) 422922. Tlx 677651
Credit Access, Amex, Diners, Visa
  A convenient situation next to junction 28 of the
M6 and a warm welcome (sherry on arrival) make
this modern efficiently run hotel a favourite stop-
over for business visitors and motorists.
Comfortable lounge and open-plan bar areas are
inviting. Spotless, well-equipped bedrooms (Gold
Star rooms offer extra accessories) all have
practical bathrooms. *Amenities* in-house movies
(free), 24-hour lounge service.
■ *Rooms* 93   *Confirm by arrang.*
en suite bath/shower 93   *Last dinner* 10
Direct dial Yes   *Parking* Ample
Room TV Yes   *Room service* 24 hours

George Hotel   Lichfield

H 60% £D
Map 10 C3 Staffordshire
Bird Street WS13 6PR
Lichfield (0543) 414822
Manager Mr J. A. Ewing
Credit Access, Amex, Diners, Visa
   An elegant Regency hotel in a convenient central location not far from Dr Johnson's birth place. Attractive bedrooms of varying sizes have

good-quality fitted units, tea-makers and neatly tiled bathrooms. Potted plants and smartly upholstered armchairs make the foyer-lounge an inviting spot, and there's a cosy little bar.
Amenities laundry service.

■ *Rooms* 39	*Confirm by* 6
en suite bath/shower 39	*Last dinner* 10
Direct dial Yes	*Parking* Ample
Room TV Yes	*Room service* Limited

Arundell Arms   Lifton

HR 62% £D/E
Map 2 C2 Devon
PL16 0AA
Lifton (0566) 84666
Owner manager Mrs Anne Voss-Bark
Credit Access, Amex, Diners, Visa
   This creeper-clad hotel is a great favourite with fishing and shooting enthusiasts. Refurbishment has improved public areas like the restaurant and the lounge, a restful room with comfortable armchairs and settees. Bedrooms, also revamped, favour pink decor and are furnished mainly in pine. *Amenities* garden, game fishing.

■ *Rooms* 29	*Confirm by* arrang.
en suite bath/shower 29	*Last dinner* 9
Direct dial Yes	*Parking* Ample
Room TV Yes	*Room service* All day
Closed 5 days Xmas	

Arundell Arms Restaurant

Chef Philip Burgess' short, well-chosen menu makes good use of seasonal fish and game, much of it local, in dishes like braised trout hollandaise, crab tart with Parmesan cheese, noisettes of venison wrapped in bacon with Cumberland sauce, roast pheasant (sometimes coated in breadcrumbs and served with a hot mousse of its liver and a light white wine sauce). Vegetables are good, and the ices are home-made. Devonshire clotted cream is a great temptation on the sweet trolley. ❷

■ *Set L* £8·50	*L* 12.30–2
Set D £14	*D* 7.30–9
About £45 for two	*Seats* 120
Closed 5 days Xmas	*Parties* 120

Good Friends   Limehouse

See under London

Old Lodge   Limpsfield

R Map 7 B5 Surrey
High Street
Oxted (0883) 712996
Credit Access, Amex, Diners, Visa
   Brian Clivaz and chef John Mann make a good team at this pleasant French restaurant with leaded windows, panelled walls and polished oak tables. Set menus offer a thoughtful selection of enjoyable dishes, from asparagus and mushroom

terrine and sweetly succulent scallops with samphire to calf's liver with avocado and saddle of venison with a Madeira and truffle sauce. Skilfully selected, informative wine list. ❷

■ *Set L* £15	*L* 12.30–2
Set D from £19·50	*D* 7–9
About £52 for two	*Parking* Ample
Seats 50	*Parties* 60
Closed D Sun, all Mon, Bank Hols & 2 wks Jan	

Eastgate Post House Hotel   Lincoln

H 65% £C
Map 11 E2 Lincolnshire
Eastgate LN2 1PN
Lincoln (0522) 20341. Tlx 56316
Credit Access, Amex, Diners, Visa. **LVs**
   The cathedral and city wall provide views for this well-modernised hotel in the town centre. The spacious foyer-lounge and two bars are stylishly decorated. Bedrooms are particularly good, being

comfortable and well maintained, with tea-makers, mini-bars and well equipped bathrooms. Executive rooms boast balconies.
Amenities garden, laundry service, coffee shop (10am–10pm), 24-hour lounge service.

■ *Rooms* 71	*Confirm by* 6
en suite bath/shower 71	*Last dinner* 9.45
Direct dial Yes	*Parking* Ample
Room TV Yes	*Room service* All day

■ Any person using our name to obtain free hospitality is a fraud. Proprietors, please inform the police and us.

Lincoln ▶

Moor Lodge Hotel   Lincoln

H **58% £E** ♿
Map 11 E2 Lincolnshire
Sleaford Road, Branston LN4 1HU
Lincoln (0522) 791366
Credit Access, Amex, Diners, Visa
  A friendly welcome awaits at this much-extended and modernised Edwardian house located on the B1188 south-east of the city. Recently refurbished public rooms include a

comfortable lounge and bar. Bedrooms, mostly decorated in attractive pastel shades, are simply and practically furnished. All are equipped with tea/coffee-makers. Bathrooms are neat and adequate. *Amenities* garden, laundry service.

■ *Rooms* 25	*Confirm by arrang.*
en suite bath/shower 25	*Last dinner* 9.15
Direct dial Yes	*Parking* Ample
Room TV Yes	*Room service* All day

White Hart Hotel   Lincoln

H **69% £C**
Map 11 E2 Lincolnshire
Bailgate LN1 3AR
Lincoln (0522) 26222. Tlx 56304
Credit Access, Amex, Diners, Visa. LVs
  High on the hill, between the Castle and the Cathedral, this fine old hotel has benefited from recent refurbishment of all the bedrooms to a very high standard. They are now prettily decorated

and feature quality antique furniture. Handsome tiled bathrooms are luxurious and comprehensively equipped. Public rooms include an elegant lounge, an oak-panelled bar and a glass-domed coffee shop. *Amenities* laundry service.

■ *Rooms* 48	*Confirm by* 6
en suite bath/shower 48	*Last dinner* 9.45
Direct dial Yes	*Parking* Ample
Room TV Yes	*Room service* 24 hours

The Well House   *NEW ENTRY*   Liskeard

HR **74% £D/E**
Map 2 C3 Cornwall
St Keyne PL14 4RN
Liskeard (0579) 42001
Owner manager Nicholas Wainford
Credit Access, Amex, Visa
  Turn off the B3254 three miles south of Liskeard taking the road signposted St Keyne Well. The Well House is a creeper-clad late-Victorian building standing in well-kept grounds and commanding spectacular views. Decor throughout is contemporary, with few original features apart from the beautiful tiled reception area, but the lounge is supremely comfortable and the corner bar has style. Bedrooms, several with large bay windows, are individually furnished and decorated in the modern manner, and each

has a smart bathroom, trouser press, remote-control TV and the latest telephone/clock/radio unit. *Amenities* garden, outdoor swimming pool, tennis, laundry service.

■ *Rooms* 7	*Confirm by arrang.*
en suite bath/shower 7	*Last dinner* 9.30
Direct dial Yes	*Parking* Ample
Room TV Yes	*Room service* All day

The Well House
Restaurant 🍴

In an elegant restaurant with contemporary decor and splendid views David Pope cooks in what he terms the new English style. Top-quality local produce is the basis of his dishes, and presentation is of prime importance. Concise, monthly-changing menus, separate for lunch and dinner, deal in delights like sautéed scallops with a passion fruit sauce or breast of chicken stuffed with a pistachio mousse, and best end of lamb topped with a herb and shallot crust. Sweets include a fruit salad made with not less than 15 fresh fruits. Traditional Sunday lunch. Charming service. Interesting wines, with excellent clarets: Clos du Marquis St Julien 1982.
🍷 Well-chosen 🅖

■ *Set L* £12·50	*L* 12.30–2.30
Set D £16·50	*D* 7–9.30
About £48 *for two*	*Seats* 34 *Parties* 16
Closed Mon to non-residents	

Redcoats Farmhouse Hotel   Little Wymondley

H **57% £E/F**
Map 6 A3 Hertfordshire
Redcoats Green, Nr Hitchin SG4 7JR
Stevenage (0438) 729500
Owner managers P. Butterfield & J. Gainsford
Credit Access, Amex, Diners, Visa
  Parts of this former farmhouse date back to the 15th-century. Huge open fireplaces and exposed beams set the scene. Antiques and comfortable

furniture add to the homely and welcoming feel. Good-sized traditional rooms are augmented by six pretty rooms in a converted stable block. No dogs. *Amenities* garden.

■ *Rooms* 16	*Confirm by arrang.*
en suite bath/shower 10	*Last dinner* 9
Direct dial Yes	*Parking* Ample
Room TV Yes	*Room service* Limited
Closed 24 Dec–2 Jan	

■ Our inspectors are our full-
time employees; they are
professionally trained by us.

Atlantic Tower Hotel   Liverpool

H **70% £C** *E*
Town plan B3 Merseyside
Chapel Street L3 9RE
(051) 227 4444. Tlx 627070
Credit Access, Amex, Diners, Visa. **LVs**
   The public areas are a strength of this modern
hotel, whose striking outline cleaves the Liverpool
skyline like the bows of a liner. The marble-walled
reception area and the lounge are rather smart
and stylish, and there are two bars, one themed
on a railway carriage, the other on an old sailing
ship (with extra plush!). About a third of the
bedrooms enjoy views across the Mersey; all are
above average in size, and refurbishment has
freshened them up. Hairdryers, trouser presses
and individually controlled air conditioning are
standard, and there are various extras in
Executive rooms. Very smart staff, and extensive

room service. *Amenities* hairdressing, in-house
movies (free), laundry service, 24-hour lounge
service.

■ *Rooms* 226 . *Confirm by* 6
en suite bath/shower 226 *Last dinner* 10.15
Direct dial Yes *Parking* Ample
Room TV Yes *Room service* 24 hours
Closed 25 & 26 Dec

Britannia Adelphi Hotel   Liverpool

H **69% £C**
Town plan E4 Merseyside
Ranelagh Place L3 5UL
051-709 7200. Tlx 629644
Manager Mr R. J. Pearce
Credit Access, Amex, Diners, Visa. **LVs**
   The grandeur of a bygone age has been re-
created in the colonnaded lounge of this fine
building, where chandeliers shine on marble and
glass. The foyer is equally impressive, and there's
plenty of scope for relaxation in the bars, bistro,
restaurants and discothèque. Generous
bedrooms (30 without private facilities) are

pleasantly furnished. The health and leisure
centre is particularly impressive too but alas, the
housekeeping is a sorry match for all this
splendour.
Amenities indoor swimming pool, sauna,
solarium, whirlpool bath, gymnasium,
hairdressing, squash, satellite TV, laundry service,
24-hour lounge service.

■ *Rooms* 344 *Confirm by* 6
en suite bath/shower 314 *Last dinner* 11
Direct dial Yes *Parking* Limited
Room TV Yes *Room service* 24 hours

Crest Hotel, Liverpool-City   Liverpool

H **59% £C/D**
Town plan F3 Merseyside
Lord Nelson Street L3 5QB
051-709 7050. Tlx 627954
Credit Access, Amex, Diners, Visa
   In the heart of the city right next to Lime Street
Station, this is a modern grey-brick hotel.
Bedrooms are modest but well kept, simple in
decor and furnishings, with tea-makers, radio-

alarms and trouser presses. Bathrooms have tubs
and showers but no extras. There's a smart foyer,
a first-floor bar-lounge and a traditional pub.
Amenities pool table, laundry service, 24-hour
lounge service.
■ *Rooms* 160 *Confirm by* 6
en suite bath/shower 160 *Last dinner* 9.45
Direct dial Yes *Parking* Ample
Room TV Yes *Room service* Limited

La Grande Bouffe   Liverpool

R **Town plan C4** Merseyside
48 Castle Street
051-236 3375
Credit Access, Amex, Visa. **LVs**
   A jazz pianist delights diners nightly in this
friendly basement bistro. The food's good, too,
with fresh produce the basis of enjoyable dishes
like sautéed scallops with mixed lettuces or
Madeira-sauced lamb noisettes. There's a daily

vegetarian special, and sweets include a lovely
strawberry sablé. Rhônes and burgundies offer
exceptional value for money.
♀ Well-chosen ©
■ *Set L* £6·95 *L* 12–3
Set D 6pm–7pm £7·95 *D* 6–10.30
About £37 for two *Parking* Limited
Seats 80 *Parties* 60
Closed L Sat, D Mon, all Sun & Bank Hols

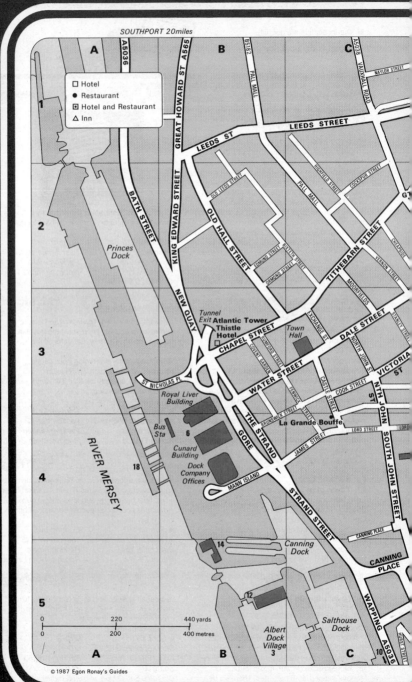

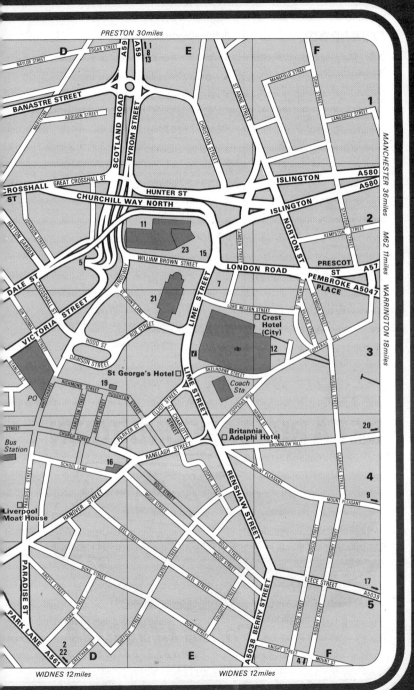

LIVERPOOL

Map 10 A2
Town plan on preceding page

Population 509,981

Since King John granted its Charter in 1207. Liverpool has taken increasing advantage of its sheltered Merseyside position to become England's leading Atlantic port and an industrial magnet, while the Arts are as vigorously pursued as football. The Royal Liverpool Philharmonic Orchestra, the Walker Art Gallery, the University's music-making, and the city's five theatres are at least as important to it as pop.

Annual Events
Grand National at Aintree
City of Liverpool Parade
Orange Day Parade *July*

Sights Outside City
Aintree, Hoylake, Chester, New Brighton, Southport

Information Office
Lime Street
Liverpool 1
Telephone 051–709 3631

Fiat Dealers
Stanley Motors Ltd
243 East Prescot Road
Liverpool L14 5NA
Tel. 051–228 9151

Crosby Park Garage Ltd
2 Coronation Road
Crosby
Liverpool L23 3BJ
Tel. 051–924 9101

Lambert Autos Ltd
Custom House
Brunswick Business Park
Liverpool L3 4BJ
Tel. 051–708 8224

1 Aintree Race-course **E1**

2 Airport **D5**

3 Albert Dock, *Shopping, business, conference centre* **B5**

4 Anglican Cathedral *20th-c Gothic, complete after 75 years* **F5**

5 Birkenhead Tunnel Entrance **D2**

6 Cunard Building, Dock Board office and Royal Liver Building *waterfront landmarks* **B4**

7 Empire Theatre **E2**

8 Everton Football Club **E1**

9 Everyman Theatre **F4**

10 Festival Gardens and Otterspool Promenade **C5**

11 Library and Museum *Hornby library has outstanding prints and first editions. Museum houses aquarium, ivories, jewellery, birds, shipping gallery* **E2**

12 Lime Street Station **E/F3**

13 Liverpool Football Club **E1**

14 Maritime Museum **B4/5**

15 Museum of Labour History **E2**

16 Neptune Theatre **D4**

17 Philharmonic Hall **F5**

18 Pier Head **A4**

19 Playhouse Theatre **D3**

20 Roman Catholic Cathedral *space-age architecture* **F4**

21 St George's Hall Former Assize Courts and Concert Hall **E3**

22 Speke Hall *Elizabethan house with beautiful gardens on the Mersey* **D5**

23 Walker Art Gallery *England's largest collection outside London* **E2**

Liverpool Moat House
Liverpool

H 69% £C/D ♿
Town plan D4 Merseyside
Paradise Street L1 8JD
051-709 0181. Tlx 627270
Credit Access, Amex, Diners, Visa
A large, modern and well-equipped hotel (formerly a Holiday Inn) near the exciting new Albert Dock development and also close to the city centre. Bedrooms, all spacious and very well kept, have solid furnishings, easy chairs, open hanging space for clothes, remote-control TVs, trouser presses and decently fitted bathrooms (actual baths rather short). Most characterful of

the public rooms is the Warehouse coffee shop and bar with flagstone floor, cast-iron beams and red-brick walls.
Amenities garden, indoor swimming pool, sauna, solarium, keep-fit equipment, in-house movies (free), laundry service, laundry room, coffee shop (11am–8.30pm), 24-hour lounge service, kiosk.

■ *Rooms 256*	*Confirm by 6*
en suite bath/shower 256	*Last dinner 10*
Direct dial Yes	*Parking Ample*
Room TV Yes	*Room service 24 hours*
Closed 4 days Xmas	

St George's Hotel
Liverpool

H 65% £C/D
Town plan E3 Merseyside
St John's Precinct, Lime Street L1 1NQ
051-709 7090. Tlx 627630
Credit Access, Amex, Diners, Visa. **LVs**
Views across Liverpool are a feature of this modern hotel, rising above the city centre. Situated opposite Lime Street railway station, it is a convenient base for sightseeing. The leafy lobby

lounge is smartly furnished in handsome darkwood, and there's a spacious and comfortable cocktail bar. Bedrooms are neat and comfortable, with stained oak fitted furniture and tea-makers. *Amenities* laundry service.

■ *Rooms 155*	*Confirm by 6*
en suite bath/shower 155	*Last dinner 10*
Direct dial Yes	*Parking Ample*
Room TV Yes	*Room service 24 hours*

■ We welcome complaints and bona fide recommendations on the tear-out pages for readers' comments. They are followed up by our professional team. Please also complain to the management instantly.

RECEPTION

Lavinia's
Loddiswell

R ♧ **Map 3 D3** Devon
Nr Kingsbridge
Kingsbridge (0548) 550306
Lavinia Davies is the splendid cook of this charming farmhouse restaurant where quality local produce is used throughout imaginative fixed-price menus. Seasonally changing fixed-price menus might include an airy cheese and watercress soufflé followed by salmon

with cucumber hollandaise or lamb en croûte. Vegetables are garden fresh and sweets simple but superb.
🍷 Well-chosen ⊖

■ *Set D £15*	*L by arrang. only*
About £50 for two	*D 7.30–9.30*
Seats 30 Parties 40	*Parking Ample*
Closed Sun, Mon, Bank Hols & Nov–Mar	

Grinkle Park Hotel
Loftus

H 67% £D/E
Map 15 C5 Cleveland
Easington, Nr Saltburn-by-the-Sea TS13 4UB
Guisborough (0287) 40515
Credit Access, Amex, Diners, Visa
Enjoying a delightful setting in 35 acres of parkland, this Victorian mansion boasts an interior where original features such as oak panelling and handsome fireplaces go hand-in-hand with 20th-

century improvements to decor and furnishings. Bedrooms, many with splendid views, are individually decorated and feature coordinating colour schemes and smart furniture.
Amenities garden, tennis, croquet, billiards.

■ *Rooms 20*	*Confirm by 6*
en suite bath/shower 20	*Last dinner 9.30*
Direct dial Yes	*Parking Ample*
Room TV Yes	*Room service All day*

Café du Commerce
London Docklands (Isle of Dogs)

See under London

Long Melford ▶

Black Lion Hotel *NEW ENTRY*　　　　　**Long Melford**

HR 68% £F
　　Map 6 C3 Suffolk
The Green CO10 9DN
Sudbury (0787) 312356
Owner managers Luke & Amelia Brady
Credit Access, Amex, Diners, Visa
　The Bradys have transformed this old coaching
inn into a thoughtfully-run hotel overlooking the
village green. The Black Lion has charming public
rooms, including a drawing room with antiques
and a russet rag-painted bar area. Spacious
individually-decorated bedrooms are well
equipped with bedside reading providing a
homely touch. *Amenities* garden, laundry service.

**Black Lion Hotel
Restaurant** ㅎ

Homely surroundings – with pine furnishings – set
the scene for food prepared from prime
ingredients. Ian Stanley's imaginative menus
include unusual combinations such as a summer
salad of lobster, asparagus and quail's eggs, and
saddle of monkfish with tomato and basil.
Desserts, such as raspberry bavarois with a
raspberry liqueur-based sabayon, are enjoyable.
Complex dishes would benefit from some
simplification. Good selection of house wines.
Booking essential Mon eves. 🍷 Well-chosen

■ Rooms 10	Confirm by arrang.
en suite bath/shower 10	Last dinner 9.30
Direct dial Yes	Parking Ample
Room TV Yes	Room service All day

■ Set L Sun only £6·50	L 12.30–2.15
About £38 for two	D 7.30–9.30
Seats 50 Parties 60	Parking Ample
Closed D Sun to non-residents & 1 wk Jan	

Bull Hotel　　　　　**Long Melford**

H 64% £C/D
　　Map 6 C3 Suffolk
Nr Sudbury CO10 9JG
Sudbury (0787) 78494
Credit Access, Amex, Diners, Visa. **LVs**
　Built for a wool merchant over 500 years ago,
this listed timbered building boasts a wealth of
period detail. Heavy black beams, flag-stoned
floors and huge inglenook fireplaces characterise

the split-level lounge, attractive writing room and
relaxing bar. Good-sized bedrooms, some
traditional in style, all have hairdryers, tea-makers
and well-equipped bathrooms.
Amenities courtyard, laundry service.

■ Rooms 27	Confirm by 6
en suite bath/shower 27	Last dinner 9.30
Direct dial Yes	Parking Ample
Room TV Yes	Room service All day

Chimneys　　　　　**Long Melford**

R ㅎ Map 6 C3 Suffolk
　　Hall Street
Sudbury (0787) 79806
Owner manager Sam Chalmers
Credit Access, Visa
　A charming beamed restaurant with genuine
period appeal. Typical dishes range from oxtail
broth with pearl barley and tiny vegetable dice to
mustard-sauced halibut, beef with shallots and a

prettily presented panaché of sweetbreads and
oyster mushrooms with a lemon cream sauce.
Interesting sweets. Good English cheeseboard.
Polished professionalism from host Mr Chalmers. ℮

■ Set L £9·50	L 12–2
About £45 for two	D 7.30–9.30
Seats 50 Parties 40	Parking Ample
Closed D Sun, all Mon & Bank Hols	

■ For a discount on next year's guide, see Offer for Answers.

Linden Hall Hotel　　　　　**Longhorsley**

H 81% £D *E*
　　Map 14 B3 Northumberland
Nr Morpeth NE65 8XF
Morpeth (0670) 516611. Tlx 538224
Credit Access, Amex, Diners, Visa
　Varied leisure facilities and a delightful setting
amid lovely gardens and parkland are major
attractions of this Georgian country mansion.
Elegant day rooms on a grand scale include a
splendid inner hall – with leather chesterfields, oil
paintings and sweeping staircase – a
sumptuously comfortable drawing room and a
stylish cocktail bar. There's also an airy
conservatory, numerous conference suites, even
a rustic pub in the grounds. Individually decorated
bedrooms offer every thoughtful extra; private
bathrooms, too, are splendidly equipped.
Amenities garden, sauna, solarium, hairdressing,

tennis, putting, croquet, clay-pigeon shooting,
games room, snooker, in-house movies (free),
laundry service, 24-hour lounge service, children's
playroom & playground, helipad.

■ Rooms 45	Confirm by 6
en suite bath/shower 45	Last dinner 10
Direct dial Yes	Parking Ample
Room TV Yes	Room service 24 hours

Bath Arms
Longleat

£E/F
Map 4 B3 Wiltshire
Horningham, Nr Warminster BA12 7LY
Maiden Bradley (098 53) 308
Owner managers Beryl & Paul Lovatt
Credit Access, Diners
   The Marquess of Bath takes a keen interest in this former Priory on his estate, even lending photographs from his private collection to adorn the walls of the main bar. There is also a rustic public bar with separate entrance. The spacious smartly refurbished bedrooms have fitted units and coordinated fabrics. *Amenities* garden, laundry service.

■ *Rooms* 5	*Confirm by* arrang.
en suite bath/shower 5	*Last dinner* 9.30
Room phone No	*Parking* Ample
Room TV Yes	*Room service* Limited

Talland Bay Hotel
Looe

HR **67% £D** &
Map 2 C3 Cornwall
Talland Bay PL13 2JB
Polperro (0503) 72667
Owner managers Major & Mrs Mayman
Credit Access, Amex, Diners, Visa
   Two features stand out among many attractions at this extended Cornish country house: the setting, in beautiful gardens with dramatic sea views, and the service, with the emphasis on old-fashioned care and courtesy. The ambience is splendidly peaceful and relaxing, and many guests return year after year. The main lounge and the little non-smokers' lounge both enjoy the views, and many of the bedrooms have cushioned window seats to make the most of the location. Bedrooms are individually decorated and furnished; the best room is panelled, with a pretty tiled fireplace and its own patio. Five rooms are in outbuildings.
Amenities garden, outdoor swimming pool, solarium, putting, croquet, games room.

■ *Rooms* 23	*Confirm by* arrang.
en suite bath/shower 21	*Last dinner* 9
Direct dial Yes	*Parking* Ample
Room TV Yes	*Room service* All day
Closed end Nov–mid Feb	

Talland Bay Hotel Restaurant &

Seafood is the appropriate main choice here, with oysters and lobsters from the tank, and crab, scallops, sole and whiting among the local catch. There are meaty options, too, and always a vegetarian main course such as mushroom and hazelnut risotto. Excellent home-made ice cream plus sweets from the trolley. Al fresco buffet lunches are a popular summer feature. ☺

■ *Set L* Sun £5·45	*L* 12.30–2
Set D £10	*D* 7.15–9
About £38 *for two*	*Seats* 55
Closed end Nov–mid Feb	

Carotel Motel
Lostwithiel

H **55% £E/F**
Map 2 C3 Cornwall
20 Castle Hill PL22 0DD
Lostwithiel (0208) 872223
Owner manager Richard Hanson
Credit Access, Amex, Diners, Visa
   A well-run motel offering a happy, welcoming atmosphere and modest comforts. Bedrooms are modern and functional including three with bunk beds for children. A pianist entertains guests on winter evenings in the relaxing bar-lounge. *Amenities* garden, outdoor swimming pool, solarium, in-house movies (free), laundry room.

■ *Rooms* 32	*Confirm by* arrang.
en suite bath/shower 32	*Last dinner* 9.30
Direct dial Yes	*Parking* Ample
Room TV Yes	*Room service* All day

Kings Head Hotel
Loughborough

H **61% £D**
Map 11 D3 Leicestershire
High Street LE11 2QL
Loughborough (0509) 233222
Credit Access, Amex, Diners, Visa
   Continued improvements are well in evidence at this solidly comfortable hotel (check directions). Smart public areas have modern sofas and Georgian-style chairs. Best bedrooms, recently refurbished, have attractive contemporary furnishings and have good accessories. Tiled bathrooms are well kept. *Amenities* games room, snooker, laundry service, 24-hour lounge service.

■ *Rooms* 86	*Confirm by* 6
en suite bath/shower 80	*Last dinner* 9.15
Direct dial Yes	*Parking* Ample
Room TV Yes	*Room service* Limited
Closed 27 & 28 Dec	

■ Changes in data may occur in establishments after the Guide goes to press. Prices should be taken as indications rather than firm quotes.

Restaurant Roger Burdell — Loughborough

R ♧ & **Map 11 D3** Leicestershire
The Manor House, Sparrow Hill
Loughborough (0509) 231813
Credit Access, Amex, Visa

A tastefully appointed manor house is the setting for Roger Burdell's very attractive restaurant. His cooking shows sound skills and a keen eye for presentation, and dishes on his set-price menus range from smoked pheasant

mousse to spiral of sole and trout with a basil sauce, sirloin steak bordelaise and a lovely iced rhubarb soufflé. Good wines, with two fine 1983 Chablis from Remon. ♀ **Well-chosen** ☺

- Set L from £8·50 — L 12.30–2
- Set D £21 — D 7.30–9.15
- About £52 for two — Parking Limited
- Seats 70 — Parties 32
- Closed L Mon, all Sun, 26 Dec & 1 Jan

■ We publish annually, so make sure you use the current edition. It's worth it!

South Lodge — Lower Beeding

HR **78% £C**
Map 5 E3 West Sussex
London Road RH13 6PS
Lower Beeding (040 376) 711. Tlx 877765
Credit Access, Amex, Diners, Visa

An impressive Victorian mansion set in 90 acres of magnificent gardens off the A281. It was built by the notable botanist and explorer Frederick Ducane Godman. Public rooms are on a grand scale, with ornate ceilings and wood panelling. The lounge boasts chandeliers and elegant seating and there is a splendid library with leather chairs and chesterfields. Bedrooms are large doubles, furnished to a high standard, and have pretty fabrics. Six bedrooms are in an even more

luxurious style and there are a few characterful beamed singles at the top of the house. Bathrooms are superb. Excellent breakfasts. *Amenities* garden, tennis, croquet, riding, clay-pigeon shooting, game fishing, laundry service, 24-hour lounge service.

- Rooms 26 — Confirm by arrang.
- en suite bath/shower 26 — Last dinner 10.30
- Direct dial Yes — Parking Ample
- Room TV Yes — Room service All day

South Lodge Restaurant ♔ &

In a grandly proportioned dining room with a splendid view of the South Downs, chef James Hayward offers thoughtful, skilled cooking of first-rate ingredients, attractively presented. The imaginative choice of dishes might include truffle and oyster mushroom soup, braised duckling with baby turnips or loin of lamb studded with garlic and juniper, carved on to aubergine and tarragon purée. Pleasing sweets and an excellent selection of English cheeses. ♀ **Well-chosen** ☺

- Set L £13·75 — L 12.30–2.30
- Set D from £22·50 — D 7.30–10.30
- About £60 for two — Seats 36 Parties 60

Lower Slaughter Manor — Lower Slaughter

H **73% £C**
Map 4 C1 Gloucestershire
GL54 2HP
Cotswold (0451) 20456. Tlx 437287
Owner managers Mr & Mrs E. T. Roby
Credit Access, Amex, Diners, Visa

Tasteful refurbishment of a 17th-century manor house has created a delightful and welcoming hotel in a lovely Cotswold village. The entrance hall has fine antique pieces, oil paintings, sofas and plenty of books; the lounges are equally pleasing, with pretty fabrics and comfortable seating. Eleven bedrooms in the main house are traditional, with period furniture and floral fabrics, while the remainder, in an adjoining coach house, are more contemporary. All are good-sized and have extras such as hairdryers, flowers and sherry. Bathrooms are carpeted and have good

toiletries. No dogs. *Amenities* garden, indoor swimming pool, sauna, tennis, laundry service, 24-hour lounge service.

- Rooms 21 — Confirm by arrang.
- en suite bath/shower 21 — Last dinner 9.30
- Direct dial Yes — Parking Ample
- Room TV Yes — Room service Limited
- Closed 4 wks Jan–Feb

Old Farmhouse Hotel   Lower Swell

I £f ♿
Map 4 C1 Gloucestershire
Stow-on-the-Wold GL54 1LF
Cotswold (0451) 30232
Owner managers Rollo & Rosemary Belsham
Credit Access, Amex, Diners, Visa
  Rollo and Rosemary are the best sort of hosts;
their friendliness, industry and lack of pretension
make this a delightful place to stay. Bedrooms,

some in converted courtyard buildings, combine
comfort with amenity. Two four-poster rooms are
very popular. There's a warm, relaxing bar and a
capacious lounge. *Amenities* garden.

■ *Rooms 13*	*Confirm by arrang.*
en suite bath/shower 11	*Last dinner 9.15*
Room phone No	*Parking Ample*
Room TV Yes	*Room service All day*
Closed 1 month Xmas	

Feathers Hotel   Ludlow

H **71% £D**
Map 10 B4 Shropshire
Bull Ring SY8 1AA
Ludlow (0584) 5261. Tlx 35637
Manager Peter Nash
Credit Access, Amex, Diners, Visa
  'A treasure of a house inside and out' is one
description given to this historic town-centre
hostelry. Certainly the magnificent Jacobean
frontage is hard to rival, and interior features
include original beams, splendid panelling, ornate
ceilings and some fine antique furniture. One of
the real gems is the carved mantelpiece in the
James I lounge. Bedrooms are stylish and very
comfortable, and several boast four-posters.
Furnishings and fabrics are of good quality, and a
long list of accessories ranges from tissues to
trouser presses, bathrobes to bidets. Super

management, friendly staff. No dogs.
Amenities laundry service, 24-hour lounge
service.

■ *Rooms 37*	*Confirm by arrang.*
en suite bath/shower 37	*Last dinner 9*
Direct dial Yes	*Parking Ample*
Room TV Yes	*Room service Limited*

Penny Anthony   Ludlow

R ♫ **Map 10 B4** Shropshire
5 Church Street
Ludlow (0584) 3282
Owner manager Penny Anthony
Credit Amex, Diners, Visa
  A variety of set menus is a feature of this
friendly restaurant which also offers capable,
enjoyable cooking. Start with crab puffs or
smoked chicken with orange sauce and follow

with salmon en croûte or lamb's kidneys
Dubonnet. Simple, pleasing sweets. Interesting
wine list with plenty of bargains, including
Château Léoville-Poyferré 1975 and Rheingau
Winkeler Auslese 1976. ♔ Well-chosen ☺

■ *Set L from £3·95*	*L 12–2*
Set D from £6·95	*D 7–10*
About £30 for two	*Parking Ample*
Seats 50	*Closed Sun*

Chiltern Hotel   Luton

H **64% £C**
Map 5 E1 Bedfordshire
Waller Avenue, Dunstable Road LU4 9RU
Luton (0582) 575911. Tlx 825048
Manager Patrick Martin
Credit Access, Amex, Diners, Visa
  Near junction 11 of the M1, this functional
modern hotel offers good overnight
accommodation. Standard rooms have tea-

makers, trouser presses and easy chairs, while
Executives provide extras like fresh fruit, dressing
gowns and remote-control TVs. There's a roomy
foyer-lounge and a comfortable cane-furnished
bar. *Amenities* laundry service.

■ *Rooms 99*	*Confirm by 6*
en suite bath/shower 99	*Last dinner 10*
Direct dial Yes	*Parking Ample*
Room TV Yes	*Room service Limited*

Crest Hotel   Luton

H **58% £C/D**
Map 5 E1 Bedfordshire
641 Dunstable Road LU4 8RQ
Luton (0582) 575955. Tlx 826283
Credit Access, Amex, Diners, Visa. **LVs**
  Located by junction 11 of the M1, the Crest is
popular with business people. Reception is on the
first floor, where there's also a lounge area and
roomy bar. Single bedrooms are fairly small, but

all rooms have well coordinated decor, tea-
makers, room to write and bedside controls for TV
and radio. Private bathrooms with showers
throughout. *Amenities* garden, games room,
laundry service.

■ *Rooms 133*	*Confirm by 6*
en suite bath/shower 133	*Last dinner 9.45*
Direct dial Yes	*Parking Ample*
Room TV Yes	*Room service None*

Leaside Hotel Luton

H **54% £E/F**
Map 5 E1 Bedfordshire
72 New Bedford Road LU3 1BT
Luton (0582) 417643
Owner managers Martin & Carole Gillies
Credit Access, Amex, Diners, Visa. LVs
   A number of original features survive in this
converted Victorian mansion, notably a handsome
oak staircase. There's a plush bar, and a club
room with a snooker table. Bedrooms are simple
and compact, with modern freestanding furniture.
Shower rooms throughout, with the exception of
one bathroom. Friendly owners and staff.
Amenities garden, snooker, laundry service.

■ Rooms 13	Confirm by arrang.
en suite bath/shower 13	Last dinner 9.30
Direct dial Yes	Parking Ample
Room TV Yes	Room service All day

Strathmore Thistle Hotel Luton

H **67% £C** &
Map 5 E1 Bedfordshire
Arndale Centre LU1 2TR
Luton (0582) 34199. Tlx 825763
Manager Tom Carr
Credit Access, Amex, Diners, Visa. LVs
   With seven floors of accommodation there is
ample choice of rooms – from simply furnished to
lavishly equipped – at this modern town-centre
hotel next to the Arndale Shopping Centre. Stylish
day rooms include an elegant, marble-floored
foyer-lounge and two appealing bars.
Amenities in-house movies (one free), laundry
service, coffee shop (11am–11pm Mon–Sat).

■ Rooms 151	Confirm by 6
en suite bath/shower 151	Last dinner 10
Direct dial Yes	Parking Ample
Room TV Yes	Room service 24 hours

■ Our inspectors never book in the
   name of Egon Ronay's Guides;
   they disclose their identity only
   after paying their bills.

Denbigh Arms Hotel *NEW ENTRY* Lutterworth

H **68% £C/D**
Map 11 D4 Leicestershire
High Street LE17 4AD
Lutterworth (045 55) 3537
Credit Access, Amex, Diners, Visa
   Originally a Georgian coaching inn, this hotel is
just one mile from the M1 (junction 20) and only
minutes from the A5 and M6. Public rooms are
light and relaxing, and the bedrooms – attractively
furnished in pine – offer ample sitting and writing
space. Good-sized bathrooms. First-class
housekeeping and good staff. No dogs.
Amenities laundry service, 24-hour lounge
service.

■ Rooms 34	Confirm by arrang.
en suite bath/shower 34	Last dinner 9.30
Direct dial Yes	Parking Ample
Room TV Yes	Room service 24 hours

Marquess of Exeter *NEW ENTRY* Lyddington

I **£E**
Map 11 E4 Leicestershire
Nr Uppingham LE15 9LR
Uppingham (0572) 822477
Credit Access, Amex, Diners, Visa
   A splendid thatched village inn dating from the
16th-century. Lots of original charm and character
survive, notably in the little low-beamed bar-
lounge area. Bedrooms are in a modern annexe
across the car park: they are light, comfortable
and quite roomy, with rattan or pine furnishings
and carpeted bathrooms. Friendly, helpful staff.
No dogs.
Amenities garden, laundry service.

■ Rooms 20	Confirm by arrang.
en suite bath/shower 20	Last dinner 9.45
Direct dial Yes	Parking Ample
Room TV Yes	Room service Limited

Alexandra Hotel Lyme Regis

H **57% £E**
Map 3 E2 Dorset
Pound Street DT7 3HZ
Lyme Regis (02974) 2010
Owner managers Mr & Mrs D. J. Haskins
Credit Access, Amex, Diners, Visa
   Dating from 1735, it's a pleasant, homely hotel
with friendly owners. The spacious, comfortable
lounge overlooks the gardens and there's also a
sun lounge and bar. Best bedrooms have fine
views; they're mostly decently-sized, with simple
decor and furniture; singles have showers only.
Amenities garden, croquet.

■ Rooms 26	Confirm by 6
en suite bath/shower 22	Last dinner 8.30
Direct dial Yes	Parking Ample
Room TV Yes	Room service All day
Closed 20 Dec–5 Feb	

Mariners Hotel   Lyme Regis

H **54% £E**
Map 3 E2 Dorset
Silver Street DT7 3HS
Lyme Regis (029 74) 2753
Credit Access, Amex, Diners, Visa
   There are splendid views of the sea and cliffs
from this 17th-century coaching inn. The little
reception area has a warm welcoming feel that
extends into the traditional lounge and cosy bar;

prints and paintings are a feature throughout.
Neat cheerful bedrooms have simple modern
furnishings, private facilities (six shower rooms)
are adequate. *Amenities* garden.

■ *Rooms* 16	*Confirm by arrang.*
en suite bath/shower 13	*Last dinner* 8.15
Direct dial Yes	*Parking* Ample
Room TV Yes	*Room service* Limited
Closed Nov–Mar	

Passford House Hotel   Lymington

H **70% £C/D**
Map 4 C4 Hampshire
Mount Pleasant Lane SO41 8LS
Lymington (0590) 682398. Tlx 47502
Owner manager Patrick Heritage
Credit Access, Amex, Visa
   A splendid leisure centre is the newest
attraction at this well-kept period house about two
miles north of Lymington. Public rooms are
comfortable and traditional, especially the oak-
panelled main lounge; the reading room has
French windows opening on to the patio, and
there's a card room and elegant bar. Most of the
bedrooms are large enough to incorporate a
sitting area, and all are equipped with remote-
control TVs, trouser presses and hairdryers.
Carpeted bathrooms are well supplied with good-
quality toiletries. *Amenities* garden, indoor &

outdoor swimming pools, sauna, solarium,
whirlpool bath, keep-fit equipment, tennis,
putting, croquet, games room, snooker, laundry
service, children's play area.

■ *Rooms* 57	*Confirm by arrang.*
en suite bath/shower 57	*Last dinner* 9
Direct dial Yes	*Parking* Ample
Room TV Yes	*Room service* All day

Provence ★ *NEW ENTRY*   Lymington

RR ★ � ♿ **Map 4 C4** Hampshire
Gordleton Mill, Silver Street, Sway
Lymington (0590) 682219
French cooking
Credit Access, Diners, Visa
   It hasn't taken Jean-Pierre and Claire Novi long
to make this charming restaurant in the New
Forest their own. The setting, on Avon Water, is
idyllic but not easily located – check directions
when booking. Jean-Pierre, a gifted chef whose
enthusiasm is soaring in this new setting,
produces memorable meals, with fish a firm
favourite. Imagine a light crisp pastry cone brimful
of juicy, perfectly tender mussels, served with a
delicate orange sauce. To follow, perhaps roast
guinea fowl on red cabbage accompanied by
perfect vegetables. Wonderful desserts.
Specialities quenelles de brochet au coulis de
homard, rouget au basilic, galette de ris de veau
au safran sur son lit d'épinard, nougat glacé à la
framboise. ♀ Well-chosen ⊖

■ *Set L* £10·50,	*L* 12.30–2
Sun £11·90	*D* 7.30–10
About £50 for two	*Parking* Ample
Seats 35	*Parties* 28
Closed D Sun, all Mon & 4 wks Jan/Feb	

Bedrooms £E

Rooms 8   *With bath/shower* 5

Six pretty cottage-style bedrooms have pine
furniture and bright co-ordinated fabrics.
Generous extras include teamakers, TVs and
sherry miniatures. No dogs.

Stanwell House Hotel   Lymington

H **61% £E**
Map 4 C4 Hampshire
High Street SO41 9AA
Lymington (0590) 77123
Owner manager Jeremy & Jane Willcock
Credit Access, Amex, Diners, Visa
   There's a friendly atmosphere at this family-run
high-street hotel, and the little lounge and bar, in
particular, are cosy and homely. Well-kept

bedrooms are divided between the main house
and a modern and more stylish two-storey
extension, where six rooms have direct access to
a pleasant paved garden. *Amenities* laundry
service.

■ *Rooms* 33	*Confirm by* 6
en suite bath/shower 30	*Last dinner* 9.30
Direct dial Yes	*Parking* Difficult
Room TV Yes	*Room service* All day

Batch Farm Country Hotel — Lympsham

H **54%** **£F**
Map 3 E1 Somerset
Nr Weston-super-Mare BS24 0EX
Edingworth (093 472) 371
Owner managers Mr & Mrs D. J. Brown
Credit Access, Visa

Families are especially welcome at this friendly whitewashed farmhouse, part of a working farm. Homely bedrooms with simple modern furnishings have panoramic views. No children under four. No dogs.
Amenities garden, coarse fishing, games room, snooker, pool table.

■ *Rooms* 8	*Confirm by* arrang.
en suite bath/shower 4	*Last dinner* 8
Room phone No	*Parking* Ample
Room TV Most	*Room service* All day
Closed end Oct–Easter	

River House *NEW ENTRY* — Lympstone

R ♔ ♧ **Map 3 E3** Devon
The Strand
Exmouth (0395) 265147
Credit Access, Amex, Visa

The views across the Exe are a delightful accompaniment to one of Shirley Wilke's super meals, and husband Michael is a charming host. Short, well-chosen menus include delights like twice-cooked cheese soufflé, and salmon with sorrel hollandaise – local fish and home-grown vegetables feature prominently. Splendid home-made ices. ♥ **Well-chosen** ⊖

■ *Set L* from £15·50	*L* 12–1.30
Set D from £15·50	*D* 7–9.30
About £35 *for two*	*Parking* Difficult
Seats 34	*Parties* 14
Closed D Sun, all Mon, Bank Hols (except Good Fri) & 25 & 27 Dec	

Crown Hotel — Lyndhurst

H **64%** **£D/E**
Map 4 C4 Hampshire
High Street SO43 7NF
Lyndhurst (042 128) 2722
Owner managers Mr & Mrs Green
Credit Access Amex, Diners, Visa

There's a nice period feel to the welcoming public rooms of this tile-hung Victorian hotel opposite the church in the main street. Bedrooms vary, the best benefiting from new carpets, tasteful coordinated fabrics and smart freestanding furniture. Other, more functional rooms, are being gradually demodernised.
Amenities garden, games room.

■ *Rooms* 43	*Confirm by* 6
en suite bath/shower 43	*Last dinner* 9.30
Direct dial Yes	*Parking* Ample
Room TV Yes	*Room service* Limited

Lyndhurst Park Hotel — Lyndhurst

H **62%** **£D/E**
Map 4 C4 Hampshire
High Street SO4 7NL
Lyndhurst (042 128) 2823. Tlx 477802
Credit Access, Amex, Diners, Visa

Manicured lawns surround this friendly, sprawling hotel in the heart of the New Forest. Bedrooms now offer trouser presses and hairdryers, and in the public rooms the accent is on restful contemporary furnishings.
Amenities garden, outdoor swimming pool, tennis, golf practice net, bicycles, games room, snooker, in-house movies (free), laundry service, 24-hour lounge service.

■ *Rooms* 59	*Confirm by* arrang.
en suite bath/shower 59	*Last dinner* 10
Direct dial Yes	*Parking* Ample
Room TV Yes	*Room service* 24 hours

Parkhill Hotel — Lyndhurst

HR **58%** **£D**
Map 4 C4 Hampshire
Beaulieu Road SO4 7FZ
Lyndhurst (042 128) 2944
Owner managers Ames Family
Credit Access, Amex, Diners, Visa

A Georgian house, attractively situated outside Lyndhurst. Best of the public rooms is the comfortably-furnished lounge. Bedrooms vary in size and style. Adequate bathrooms. Several aspects of repair and housekeeping disappointing on our last visit, and staff, though friendly, were elusive. *Amenities* garden, outdoor swimming pool, coarse fishing.

■ *Rooms* 20	*Confirm by* arrang.
en suite bath/shower 18	*Last dinner* 9
Direct dial Yes	*Parking* Ample
Room TV Yes	*Room service* Limited

Parkhill Hotel Restaurant

French windows overlook the gardens at this attractive, smoothly-run restaurant. An interesting and imaginative menu begins with appetisers like vegetable timbale with sweet red pepper sauce, and chicken-liver parfait in Madeira jelly with brioche. Follow with delights like saddle of lamb en croûte, or roast guinea fowl on a chestnut mousse with orange and cranberry sauce. Preparation is conscientious, fresh herbs are skilfully used and sauces are carefully balanced. Nondescript desserts. Good-value clarets and German wines. ♥ **Well-chosen** ⊖

■ *Set L* £8·25	*L* 12.30–2
Set D £13·25	*D* 7–9
About £50 *for two*	*Seats* 75 *Parties* 75

Tors Hotel   Lynmouth

H **57% £E**
 Map 3 D1 Devon
EX35 6NA
Lynton (0598) 53236
Owner manager Mr A. Braunton
Credit Access, Amex, Diners, Visa
   Delightfully situated in 5 acres of woodlands,
this peaceful hotel commands panoramic views.
Spacious and welcoming public rooms have

picture windows. Bedrooms are bright, several
freshly decorated. Modest public bathrooms.
Amenities garden, outdoor swimming pool,
laundry service, table tennis, pool table.

■ *Rooms 36*	*Confirm by Arrang.*
en suite bath/shower 33	*Last dinner 9*
Direct dial Yes	*Parking* Ample
Room TV Yes	*Room service* All day
Closed Nov–Easter	

Lynton Cottage Hotel   Lynton

H **60% £D/E**
 Map 3 D1 Devon
North Walk EX35 6ED
Lynton (0598) 52342
Owner manager John Jones
   Set in wooded grounds above Lynmouth Bay,
this charming hotel provides peace and friendly
personal service. It also enjoys marvellous views

from the tasteful public rooms and from nearly all
the bedrooms. These are generally quite roomy
and comfortable. Good housekeeping.
Amenities garden, laundry service.

■ *Rooms 21*	*Confirm by 6*
en suite bath/shower 15	*Last dinner 9*
Direct dial Yes	*Parking* Ample
Room TV Yes	*Room service* All day
Closed Jan	

Clifton Arms Hotel   Lytham St Anne's

H **64% £C/D**
 Map 10 A1 Lancashire
West Beach, Lytham FY8 5QJ
Lytham (0253) 739898. Tlx 677463
Credit Access, Amex, Diners, Visa
   A welcoming glass of sherry awaits arrivals at
this large, red-brick Victorian hotel near the Ribble
estuary. There's a cane-furnished cocktail bar and
also another bar which attracts younger guests.

The most spacious bedrooms face the estuary,
but all rooms are attractively furnished with
pleasing colour schemes. *Amenities* sauna,
solarium, whirlpool bath, laundry service, 24-hour
lounge service.

■ *Rooms 45*	*Confirm by arrang.*
en suite bath/shower 45	*Last dinner 9.45*
Direct dial Yes	*Parking* Ample
Room TV Yes	*Room service* 24 hours

Sutton Hall   Macclesfield

I **£D/E**
 Map 10 B2 Cheshire
Bullocks Lane, Sutton SK11 0HE
Sutton (026 05) 3211
Owner manager Robert Bradshaw
Credit Access, Amex, Visa
   Stay here and you can be sure of sleeping in a
romantically-draped four-poster bed, for all the
bedrooms are furnished in similar traditional style.

Located just off the A523, the house dates back
mainly to the 16th century, and there are plenty of
open fires, blackened beams and flagstone floors
to recall its history. *Amenities* garden, laundry
service.

■ *Rooms 10*	*Confirm by arrang.*
en suite bath/shower 10	*Last dinner 10*
Direct dial Yes	*Parking* Ample
Room TV Yes	*Room service* All day

Maiden Newton House   Maiden Newton

HR **73% £C/D**
  Map 4 B4 Dorset
Nr Dorchester DT2 0AA
Maiden Newton (0300) 20336
Owner managers Bryan & Elizabeth Ferriss
Credit Access, Amex, Diners, Visa
   Bryan and Elizabeth Ferriss take justifiable
pride in their fine Elizabethan country house, and
evident delight in sharing it with others. The
charming high-ceilinged entrance hall is filled with
fresh flowers, and antique furniture and traditional
deep-cushioned chairs and sofas provide
comfortable seating in the elegant lounge. A table
with drinks operates as a trust bar, and there is a
cosy library with TV and video. Bedrooms – four
posters, one with a half-tester – are spacious,
spotless and have thoughtful extras like trouser
presses, sewing kits and mineral water. Pretty

carpeted bathrooms are equally well equipped.
Amenities garden, game fishing, croquet, laundry
service. *Closed* Jan

■ *Rooms 6*	*Confirm by arrang.*
en suite bath/shower 6	*Last dinner 8*
Direct dial Yes	*Parking* Ample
Room TV Yes	*Room service* All day

Maiden Newton House Restaurant ⌂ ♧ ♿

The feeling of being a friend of the family is fostered by the Ferrisses in their gracious restaurant. Elizabeth's excellent menus are posted early so that guests can discuss alternatives, if necessary. A typical menu might

be devils on horseback, watercress mousse, duck with blackcurrant sauce and garden vegetables, Paris-Brest, cheeses and coffee with petits fours. Non-residents must book. ☺ Well-chosen ☺

- *Set D £15* — *D at 8*
- *About £45 for two* — *Seats 16*
- *Closed Jan* — *Parties 40*

Crest Hotel

H **66% £C** ♿
Map 5 E2 Berkshire
Manor Lane SL6 2RA
Maidenhead (0628) 23444. Tlx 847502
Credit Access, Amex, Diners, Visa

Comprehensive leisure facilities and bright, comfortable, spacious bedrooms with smart tiled bathrooms makes this modern hotel popular. Plants decorate the attractive, relaxing day rooms. *Amenities* garden, indoor swimming pool, sauna, solarium, whirlpool bath, keep-fit equipment, squash, snooker, pool table, in-house movies (charge), coffee shop (7am–11pm), 24-hour lounge service, children's playroom.

- *Rooms 189* — *Confirm by 6*
- *en suite bath/shower 189* — *Last dinner 9.45*
- *Direct dial Yes* — *Parking Ample*
- *Room TV Yes* — *Room service 24 hours*

■ If we recommend meals in a hotel or inn, a separate entry is made for its restaurant.

Fredrick's Hotel

HR **79% £B/C**
Map 5 E2 Berkshire
Shoppenhangers Road SL6 2PZ
Maidenhead (0628) 35934
Owner manager Mr F. W. Lösel
Credit Access, Amex, Diners, Visa

Housekeeping and service are beyond reproach at this civilised red-brick hotel in a peaceful residential part of Maidenhead. The splendid foyer-lounge, complete with classic busts and potted plants, creates an excellent first impression and sets the elegant tone for delightful day rooms like the lovely Winter Garden conservatory and warmly inviting bar. Smartly-decorated bedrooms are furnished in comfortable, traditional style and have mini-bars and remote-control TVs (most rooms in the wing also offer video recorders). Hairdryers and weighing scales are standard in the excellent modern bathrooms. No dogs. *Amenities* garden, in-house movies (free), laundry service, 24-hour lounge service.

- *Rooms 37* — *Confirm by arrang.*
- *en suite bath/shower 37* — *Last dinner 9.45*
- *Direct dial Yes* — *Parking Ample*
- *Room TV Yes* — *Room service 24 hours*

Fredrick's Hotel Restaurant ★ ⌂

French cooking
Owner Fredrick Lösel leads the exemplary front-of-house team at this stylishly contemporary restaurant. Prime raw materials are the guiding principle behind new chef Brian Cutler's frequently changing menus, which retain their intriguing blend of familiar favourites – baked mushrooms, roast best end of lamb with fresh herbs, Dover sole – and such exciting combinations as avocado and scallops in hot lime butter or saddle of hare with figs in a red wine and juniper berry sauce. Vegetables are notably good. Light, delicious sweets from the trolley include home-made sorbets and ice creams.
Specialities hot terrine of broccoli with shellfish on a lime sauce, smoked wild Scottish salmon on a nettle sauce, suprême of chicken with crab and grapefruit on a lobster sauce, roast boned rabbit with asparagus, tomato and mushrooms on salad with herb butter. ☺

- *Set L £18·50* — *L 12–2*
- *Set D £27·50* — *D 7–9.45*
- *About £65 for two* — *Seats 60*
- *Closed L Sat & 25–30 Dec*

Boxley House Hotel
Maidstone

H **56%** **£E**
Map 7 B5 Kent
Boxley ME14 3D7
Maidstone (0622) 692269
Owner managers Malcolm & Elizabeth Fox
Credit Access, Amex, Diners, Visa
   A modernised and extended 17th-century house set in peaceful parkland close to the M2 and M20. The Foxes care about their guests and,

although decor and furnishings don't always do justice to the period touches, the whole place is spotless. Fresh, bright bedrooms range from spacious four-poster rooms to compact singles. *Amenities* garden, outdoor swimming pool.

■ Rooms 18	Confirm by 6
en suite bath/shower 18	Last dinner 9
Direct dial Yes	Parking Ample
Room TV Yes	Room service All day

Larkfield Hotel
Maidstone

H **65%** **£D**
Map 7 B5 Kent
London Road, Larkfield ME60 6HJ
West Malling (0732) 846858. Tlx 957420
Credit Access, Amex, Diners, Visa
   A thoroughly elegant interior distinguishes this former rectory on the A20, five miles west of Maidstone. Reception, lounge and bar are positively luxurious with their attractive colour

schemes and fine furnishings, while bedrooms combine smartness with comfort. Bathrooms are first-rate with plenty of extras. *Amenities* garden, 24-hour lounge service, laundry service, in-house movies (free).

■ Rooms 52	Confirm by 6
en suite bath/shower 52	Last dinner 10
Direct dial Yes	Parking Ample
Room TV Yes	Room service 24 hours

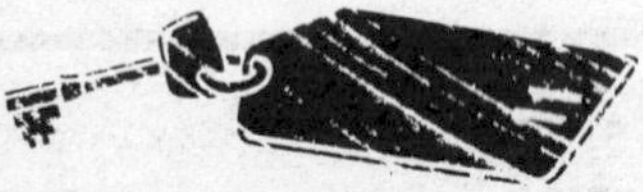

Blue Boar Hotel
Maldon

H **57%** **£D**
Map 7 C4 Essex
3 Silver Street CM9 7QE
Maldon (0621) 52681
Credit Access, Amex, Diners, Visa. LVs
   Public rooms in this former coaching inn have great period character. Part of the building, dating back to the 14th century, houses two public bars with exposed beams. Another bar, in the central

part, has a lovely exposed brick fireplace. Bedrooms in the main building are being refurbished to rival those in the annexe. *Amenities* laundry service, 24-hour lounge service.

■ Rooms 25	Confirm by 6
en suite bath/shower 25	Last dinner 9.30
Room phone Yes	Parking Ample
Room TV Yes	Room service Limited

Francine's
Maldon

R ⚘ **Map 7 C4** Essex
1a High Street
Maldon (0621) 56605
Owner managers Barry & Sue Davies
Credit Access, Visa
   Skilled cooking and a relaxed atmosphere can be enjoyed at this attractive little bistro. The menu changes each month, tempting diners with delights like pigeon breasts and bacon with

blackcurrant vinegar, fried venison with orange sauce, scallop mousse with a saffron and ginger sauce or breast of chicken stuffed with leek purée and served with wild mushrooms. Good fresh vegetables. Inspiring sweets. ℮

■ About £42 for two	D only 7.30–9.15
Seats 26 Parties 26	Parking Ample

Closed Sun, Mon, Bank Hols exc. Good Fri, 2 wks Aug & 1 wk Xmas

Old Bell Hotel
Malmesbury

H **61%** **£D**
Map 4 B2 Wiltshire
Abbey Row SN16 0BW
Malmesbury (0666) 822344
Owner managers Spengler family
Credit Access, Amex, Diners, Visa
   A characterful, wisteria-clad hotel overlooking the splendid Norman abbey. Latest improvement is a garden room that supplements the

comfortable lounge and bars. Bedrooms, most with bathrooms en suite, are gradually acquiring better-quality fabrics and furnishings; there's a splendid suite, but some rooms are very small. *Amenities* garden, teletext, laundry service.

■ Rooms 20	Confirm by arrang.
en suite bath/shower 16	Last dinner 9.30
Direct dial Yes	Parking Ample
Room TV Yes	Room service All day

Abbey Hotel   Malvern

H **62% £D**
Map 4 B1 Hereford & Worcester
Abbey Road, Great Malvern WR14 3ET
Malvern (068 45) 3325. Tlx 335008
Manager Mr R. Cave-Browne-Cave
Credit Access, Amex, Diners, Visa
  Adjoining the 11th-century Benedictine Priory,
this handsome creeper-clad hotel surrounded by
landscaped gardens enjoys lovely views towards

the Severn Valley. Day rooms include a
welcoming foyer, lounge and bar, with pretty
lamps, plants and paintings. Pleasant bedrooms
all have colour TVs, tea-makers and large, tiled
bathrooms en suite. *Amenities* garden.

■ *Rooms* 107	*Confirm by* 6
en suite bath/shower 107	*Last dinner* 8.30
Direct dial Yes	*Parking* Ample
Room TV Yes	*Room service* 24 hours

Colwall Park Hotel   Malvern

H **62% £E**
Map 4 B1 Hereford & Worcester
Colwall WR13 6QG
Colwall (0684) 40206. Tlx 335626
Owner managers Mr & Mrs B. A. R. Frost
Credit Access, Amex, Diners, Visa
  In the heart of a village at the foot of the Malvern
Hills, a turn-of-the-century hotel is run with care
and pride by the Frosts. Public rooms like the

cosy lounge and the panelled lounge bar with its
winter log fire are warmly inviting, as are the
prettily decorated bedrooms. All have good bath
or shower rooms.
Amenities garden, croquet.

■ *Rooms* 20	*Confirm by* noon
en suite bath/shower 20	*Last dinner* 9.30
Direct dial Yes	*Parking* Ample
Room TV Yes	*Room service* All day

Cottage in the Wood Hotel   Malvern

HR **66% £C/D**
Map 4 B1 Hereford & Worcester
Holywell Road, Malvern Wells WR14 4LG
Malvern (068 45) 3487
Owner manager Michael Ross
Credit Access, Amex, Visa
  The views along the Severn Valley are superb
from this Georgian dower house just south of
Great Malvern off A449. Bedrooms are spread
between the main house (traditional) and two
annexes (more modern). There's a comfortable
lounge. Good breakfasts. Friendly, if sometimes
over-relaxed, staff. No dogs. *Amenities* garden.

■ *Rooms* 20	*Confirm by* arrang.
en suite bath/shower 20	*Last dinner* 9
Direct dial Yes	*Parking* Ample
Room TV Yes	*Room service* All day
Closed 1 wk Xmas	

Cottage in the Wood Restaurant &

English cooking
The restaurant has an agreeable, airy tranquillity.
Graham Flanagan's English cooking, using the
best ingredients on seasonal menus, is excellent,
but unprofessional service can let the side down.
Among dishes much enjoyed are braised stuffed
cabbage with tomatoes and saffron rice, tender
rack of lamb with honey and almond, and
textbook profiteroles with butterscotch sauce.
Super English cheese and a fine selection of
English wines. ♀ Well-chosen ⊖

■ *Set L from* £6·50,	*L* 12.30–2
Sun £8·50	*D* 7–9
Set D £14	*Seats* 60
About £48 *for two*	*Closed* 1 wk Xmas

Croque-en-Bouche ★   Malvern

R ★ ⛺ ⏣ **Map 4 B1** Hereford &
Worcester
221 Wells Road, Malvern Wells
Malvern (068 45) 65612
French cooking
Credit Access, Visa
  Croque-en-Bouche is famed for Marion Jones's
splendid gimmick-free cooking and Robin Jones's
superlative cellar. The setting is a charming
conversion of an old bakehouse: you take drinks
and canapés in a corner drawing room, then move
to the engagingly old-fashioned little dining room
with its quaint period lighting and prettily set
tables. Marion's straightforward approach
produces a succession of delights, from fish soup
with a pungent, positive rouille and smoked trout
mousse wrapped in marinated salmon to rich,
succulent suckling pig with a leek, orange and
mushroom stuffing. The excellent salads and
herbs are largely home-grown, and both the
cheeseboard and the sweets are exceedingly

tempting. Wines include some exquisite Rhônes
and the rare Balgownie Chardonnay from
Australia. *Specialities* ceviche of monkfish and
scallops with avocado; mutton with capers and
Dijon mustard; Alpine strawberry tart with
zabaglione cream. ⌐ Outstanding ⊖

■ *Set D* £19·70	*D only* 7.30–9.15
About £50 *for two*	*Parking* Ample
Seats 22	*Parties* 10
Closed Sun, Tues & Bank Hols	

Foley Arms Hotel — Malvern

H 60% £D/E
Map 4 B1 Hereford & Worcester
14 Worcester Road, Great Malvern WR14 4QS
Malvern (068 45) 3397. Tlx 437269
Owner managers Mr & Mrs N. Ivanzov
Credit Access, Amex, Diners, Visa

Overlooking the Severn Valley, this splendid Regency inn offers well-proportioned public rooms; including a comfortable lounge, bar and foyer with elegant period furnishings and fittings. Bedrooms vary in size and style. Many have fine views. Bathrooms are tiled and carpeted. *Amenities* garden, laundry service.

■ *Rooms* 26	*Confirm by* 6
en suite bath/shower 26	*Last dinner* 9.15
Direct dial Yes	*Parking* Ample
Room TV Yes	*Room service* All day
Closed 4 days Xmas	

Mount Pleasant Hotel — Malvern

H 59% £E
Map 4 B1 Hereford & Worcester
Belle Vue Terrace, Great Malvern WR14 4PZ
Malvern (068 45) 61837
Owner managers Geoffrey & Sol Payne
Credit Access, Amex, Diners, Visa

A Georgian hotel in the centre of town overlooking the abbey. Day rooms include a spacious, comfortable bar-lounge, and a function suite. Carved oak furniture creates a traditional feel in the majority of bedrooms, all of which have compact carpeted bath or shower rooms. No children under eight. No dogs. *Amenities* garden.

■ *Rooms* 14	*Confirm by* arrang.
en suite bath/shower 14	*Last dinner* 9
Direct dial Yes	*Parking* Ample
Room TV Yes	*Room service* All day
Closed 25 & 26 Dec	

Britannia Hotel — Manchester

H 70% £B/C *E*
Town plan E3 Greater Manchester
Portland Street M1 3LA
061-228 2288. Tlx 665007
Credit Access, Amex, Diners, Visa. LVs

A converted Victorian textile warehouse with a truly dazzling foyer featuring a cantilevered staircase, gold-painted columns and chandeliers. There are three pleasant bars decorated in a similarly showy style and a comfortable lounge. Other facilities include a health and leisure centre and numerous function suites. The bedrooms are handsomely decorated, with smart darkwood units and coordinated bedspreads and curtains; fresh fruit and biscuits are a pleasing touch. The carpeted bathrooms are well-equipped. *Amenities* indoor swimming pool, sauna, solarium, whirlpool bath, gymnasium, beauty

salon, satellite TV, in-house movies (free), laundry service, coffee shop (11am–2am), 24-hour lounge service.

■ *Rooms* 362	*Confirm by* 6
en suite bath/shower 362	*Last dinner* 2am
Direct dial Yes	*Parking* Limited
Room TV Yes	*Room service* 24 hours

COPTHORNE HOTEL *NEW ENTRY* — Manchester

H £C/D ♿
Town plan A4 Greater Manchester
Clippers Quay, Salford Quays M5 3DL
061-873 7321. Tlx 669090
Credit Access, Amex, Diners, Visa

A brand-new hotel – opening as we completed research – in the redeveloped docklands, with easy parking and an agreeable waterside setting. Bedrooms are practical, comfortable and stylish, with sofa, mini-bar and well-lit dressing table/desk space. No dogs. *Amenities* indoor swimming pool, sauna, solarium, whirlpool bath, keep-fit equipment, in-house movies (charge), laundry service, 24-hour lounge service.

■ *Rooms* 166	*Confirm by* 6
en suite bath/shower 166	*Last dinner* 10.45
Direct dial Yes	*Parking* Ample
Room TV Yes	*Room service* 24 hours

Grand Hotel — Manchester

H 60% £C/D
Town Plan E3 Greater Manchester
Aytoun Street M1 3DR
(061) 236 9559. Tlx 667580
Credit Access, Amex, Diners, Visa. LVs

A solid mid-Victorian, mid-city hotel that retains some touches of grandeur, notably a fine mahogany staircase and marbled columns in the foyer. Here and there things are beginning to look a little tired, though the bedrooms, if unexciting decoratively, are comfortable. Room service can be reluctant but staff are otherwise helpful. *Amenities* solarium, snooker, laundry service, coffee shop (10am–10.30pm).

■ *Rooms* 146	*Confirm by* 6
en suite bath/shower 146	*Last dinner* 10.30
Room phone Yes	*Parking* Limited
Room TV Yes	*Room service* 24 hours

■ Our inspectors are our full-
time employees; they are
professionally trained by us.

Isola Bella Manchester

R **Town plan D3** Greater Manchester
6A Booth Street
061-236 6417
Italian cooking
Owner manager Evandro Barbieri
Credit Access, Visa

Owner Evandro Barbieri keeps things running
smoothly at this popular basement restaurant.
Cooking is sound and consistent, and the

selection runs from succulent marinated trout and
garlicky sautéed mushrooms to spaghetti
vongole, Dover sole and familiar preparations of
chicken, veal and steak. Above-average sweet
trolley. ℮

■ *About £40 for two*	*L 12.30–2.30*
Seats 70	*D 7–10.45, Sat 7–11*
Closed Sun & Bank Hols	*Parking Limited*

NOVOTEL MANCHESTER WEST *NEW ENTRY* Manchester

H **£D/E** ♿
 Town plan A4 Greater Manchester
Worsley Brow, Worsley M28 4YA
061-799 3535. Tlx 669586
Credit Access, Amex, Diners, Visa. **LVs**

On the slip road from junction 13 of the M62,
this brand new Novotel makes a practical
overnight stop. Each room has a king-size double
bed, a sofa bed and ample well-lit writing space,

plus triple glazing and central heating. Day rooms
include a piano bar. Opened as we went to press.
Amenities garden, outdoor swimming pool, in-
house movies (free), laundry service, coffee shop
(6am–12pm).

■ *Rooms 119*	*Confirm by 6*
en suite bath/shower 119	*Last dinner 12*
Direct dial Yes	*Parking Ample*
Room TV Yes	*Room service All day*

Hotel Piccadilly Manchester

HR **75%** **£B/C** *E* ♿
 Town plan D3 Greater Manchester
Piccadilly Plaza M60 1QR
061-236 8414. Tlx 668765
Credit Access, Amex, Diners, Visa. **LVs**

Public areas have been impressively restyled at
this fine modern hotel, which rises high above a
drab city-centre shopping arcade. In the
extensive and spacious public areas there's lots
of marble for floors and columns, plus good-
quality seating and, in some places, picture
windows offering city views. Smartly furnished
bedrooms are particularly well equipped, with
everything from hairdryers, trouser presses and
remote-control TVs to bathroom extensions for

radio and telephone. There are also nine suites
individually furnished, and with whirlpool baths
and bidets. Room service is comprehensive
around the clock, and staff generally are well
turned out, easy to find and helpful.
Amenities beauty salon, hairdressing, laundry
service, coffee shop (7am–11pm), 24-hour lounge
service, kiosk.

■ *Rooms 255*	*Confirm by 6*
en suite bath/shower 255	*Last dinner 11*
Direct dial Yes	*Parking Ample*
Room TV Yes	*Room service 24 hours*

Pavilion Restaurant ♛

The concise menus here are very much in the
modern idiom. While the piano is played you can
enjoy dishes like wild mushrooms and smoked
chicken salad with hot sherry vinegar, pan-fried
monkfish with a red wine and spinach sauce, or
lobster and scallops with baked rice. Smart,
attentive staff, sophisticated setting. ℮

NEW ENTRY

■ *Set L £16*	*L 12.30–2.30*
Set D £22	*D 7–10.30*
About £66 for two	*Seats 46 Parties 20*
Closed L Sat, all Sun, Bank Hols, 2 wks Aug &	
1 wk Xmas	

■ We welcome complaints and bona
fide recommendations on the
tear-out pages for readers' comments.
They are followed up by our professional
team. Please also complain to the
management instantly.

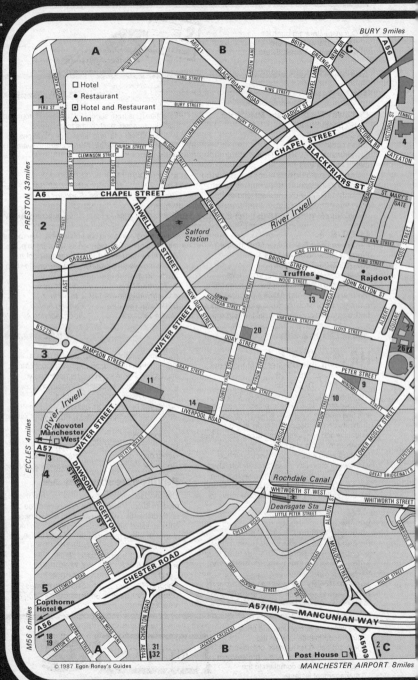

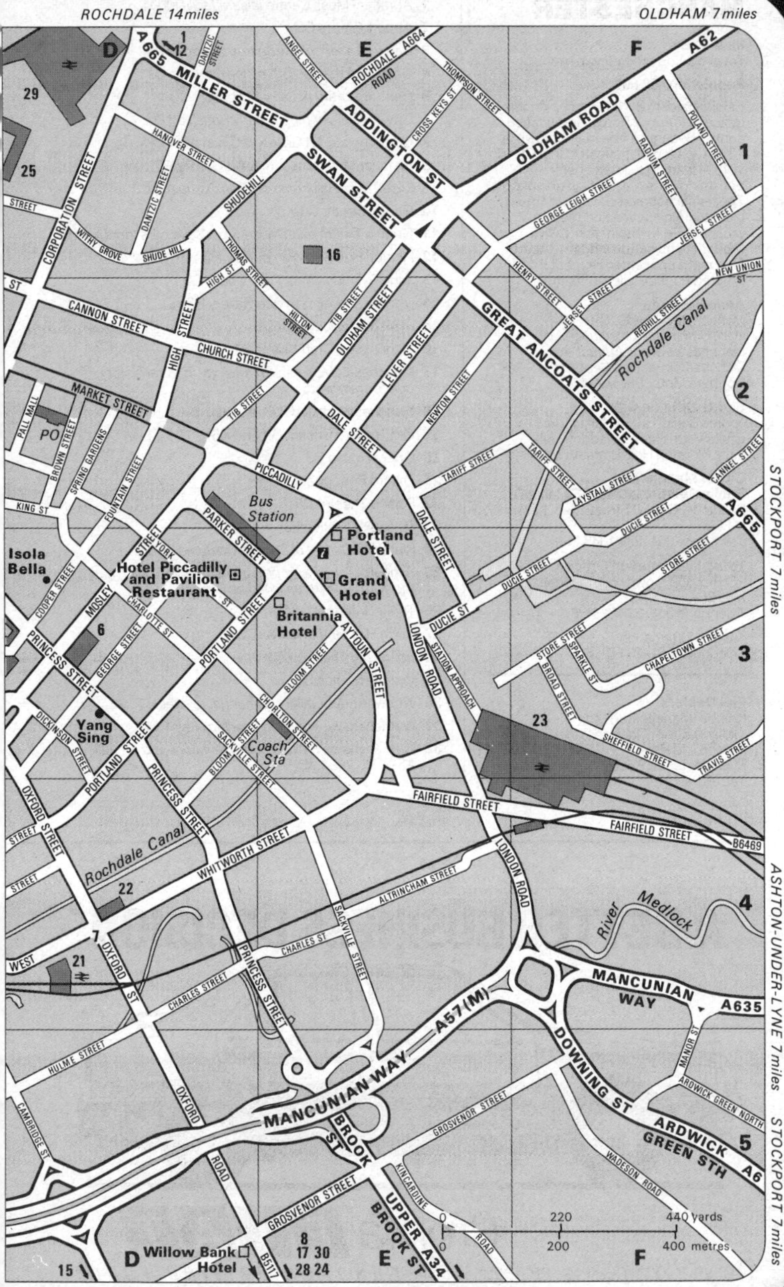

ROCHDALE 14 miles
OLDHAM 7 miles
STOCKPORT 7 miles
ASHTON-UNDER-LYNE 7 miles
STOCKPORT 7 miles
WILMSLOW 12 miles
D
E
F
1
2
3
4
5
A665 MILLER STREET
ROCHDALE ROAD A664
ANGEL STREET
THOMPSON STREET
CROSS KEYS ST
ADDINGTON ST
SWAN STREET
OLDHAM ROAD
A62
POLAND STREET
RADIUM STREET
GEORGE LEIGH STREET
JERSEY STREET
NEW UNION ST
HANOVER STREET
DANTZIC STREET
SHUDEHILL
CORPORATION STREET
WITHY GROVE
SHUDE HILL
THOMAS STREET
HIGH ST
HILTON STREET
TIB STREET
OLDHAM STREET
LEVER STREET
HENRY STREET
JERSEY STREET
REDHILL STREET
Rochdale Canal
GREAT ANCOATS STREET
CANNON STREET
CHURCH STREET
HIGH STREET
MARKET STREET
PALL MALL
PO
BROWN STREET
SPRING GARDENS
FOUNTAIN STREET
NEWTON STREET
DALE STREET
TARIFF STREET
LAYSTALL STREET
CANNEL STREET
A665
KING ST
PICCADILLY
Bus Station
PARKER STREET
Portland Hotel
Grand Hotel
Britannia Hotel
Isola Bella
Hotel Piccadilly and Pavilion Restaurant
YORK STREET
MOSLEY STREET
COOPER STREET
CHARLOTTE ST
PORTLAND STREET
AYTOUN STREET
LONDON ROAD
DALE STREET
DUCIE ST
DUCIE STREET
STORE STREET
STATION APPROACH
SPARKLE ST
BROAD STREET
CHAPELTOWN STREET
PRINCESS STREET
GEORGE STREET
BLOOM STREET
CHORLTON STREET
Yang Sing
DICKINSON STREET
PORTLAND STREET
SACKVILLE STREET
Coach Sta
23
SHEFFIELD STREET
TRAVIS STREET
OXFORD STREET
PRINCESS STREET
FAIRFIELD STREET
FAIRFIELD STREET
B6469
Rochdale Canal
WHITWORTH STREET
LONDON ROAD
22
ALTRINCHAM STREET
River Medlock
SACKVILLE STREET
WEST
21
OXFORD ST
CHARLES ST
CHARLES STREET
PRINCESS STREET
MANCUNIAN WAY
A635
A57(M)
HULME STREET
MANOR ST
DOWNING ST
ARDWICK GREEN NORTH
MANCUNIAN WAY
OXFORD ROAD
CAMBRIDGE ST
BROOK ST
GROSVENOR STREET
ARDWICK GREEN STH
A6
WADESON ROAD
GROSVENOR STREET
KINCARDINE ROAD
UPPER BROOK ST A34
0 220 440 yards
0 200 400 metres
Willow Bank Hotel
B5117
8
17 30
28 24
15
29
25
16
1
12
6
7

FIAT GUIDE TO SIGHTS

MANCHESTER

Map 10 B2
Town plan on preceding page

Population 458,600

Established 38 BC as Mancenion, the 'place of tents', a Roman fortification centre. Became a free market town in 1301. Opened Manchester Ship Canal in 1894 leading to Manchester becoming Britain's third inland seaport. The textile trade prepared it for the Industrial Revolution and the city prospered with engineering skills brought to its cotton industry. Apart from night-spot entertainment the city is noted for the Hallé Orchestra.

Annual Events
Manchester Parade *June*
Hallé Summer Proms *June–July*
Manchester Show *August*
Manchester Festival *September*
Northern Motor Show *April*

Sights Outside City
Jodrell Bank, Tatton Hall, Chatsworth House, Haddon Hall, Little Moreton Hall, Bramall Hall

**City of Manchester
Public Relations Office** St James's Buildings, Oxford Street, Manchester M1 6FL
Telephone 061–234 1343

Tourist Information Offices
PO Box 532, Town Hall, Manchester M60 2LA
Telephone 061–234 3157/8

Theatre Information
Telephone 061–234 3156

Fiat Dealers
Knibbs (Manchester) Ltd
Midland Street Garage
Ashton Old Road
Manchester M12 6LB
Tel. 061–273 4411

1 Abraham Moss Centre *leisure facilities* D1
2 Airport *8 miles* C5
3 Barton Aqueduct *swing trough bridge* A4
4 Cathedral *mainly 15th-c. fine carvings* C1
5 Central Library *houses 11 libraries* C3
6 City Art Gallery *mostly early British art* D3
7 Cornerhouse Art Gallery & Cinema D4
8 Fletcher Moss Museum & Art Gallery E5
9 Free Trade Hall *home of Hallé Orchestra* C3
10 G-Mex Centre C3/4
11 Greater Manchester Museum of Science & Industry A3
12 Heaton Hall *Georgian museum* D1
13 John Rylands Library *rare books* C3
14 Manchester Air & Space Gallery B3
15 Manchester City F.C. D5
16 Manchester Craft Village E1
17 Manchester Museum *Egyptology, natural history; coins; stamps* E5
18 Manchester United F.C. A5
19 Old Trafford Cricket Ground A5
20 Opera House B3
21 Oxford Road Station D4
22 Palace Theatre D4
23 Piccadilly Station F3
24 Platt Hall *Gallery of English Costume* E5
25 Schools Library *Europe's oldest public library; part of the 13th-c Chetham Hospital School* D1
26 Tourist Information Centre C3
27 Town Hall *Gothic revival* C3
28 University Theatre E5
29 Victoria Station D1
30 Whitworth Art Gallery *paintings; textiles* E5
31 Wythenshawe Forum *leisure facilities* A5
32 Wythenshawe Hall *Elizabethan manor and art gallery* A5

Portland Thistle Hotel

Manchester

H **76% £B/C** *E*
Town plan E3 Greater Manchester
Piccadilly Gardens M1 6DP
061-228 3400. Tlx 669157
Credit Access, Amex, Diners, Visa

A luxurious leisure centre, flexible conference facilities and elegant, comfortable surroundings are a winning combination at this impressive modern hotel in the city centre. Mirrored walls, a glittering chandelier and masses of flowers and greenery strike a sophisticated note in the spacious foyer – an excellent first impression continued in the inviting lounge and two bars. Pastel colour schemes, coordinated fabrics and freestanding darkwood furniture feature in the smart, good-sized bedrooms, which all offer trouser presses, tea-makers and hairdryers. Light, airy bathrooms are fully tiled and well equipped.

Amenities indoor swimming pool, sauna, solarium, whirlpool bath, keep-fit equipment, in-house movies (one free), laundry service, 24-hour lounge service.

■ *Rooms* 213	*Confirm by* 6
en suite bath/shower 213	*Last dinner* 10.30
Direct dial Yes	*Parking* Limited
Room TV Yes	*Room service* 24 hours

Post House Hotel

Manchester

H **60% £C**
Town plan C5 Greater Manchester
Palatine Road, Northenden M22 4FH
061-998 7090. Tlx 669248
Credit Access, Amex, Diners, Visa. **LVs**

Look out for this early Post House (now 16 years old) at junction 9 of the M63. Public areas include a popular bar-lounge and an Edwardian-themed bar. Bedrooms are gradually being refurbished – all have mini-bars and, remote-control TVs. Executive rooms offer additional extras such as hairdryers, trouser presses and extra toiletries. *Amenities* laundry service, coffee shop (10.30am–10.30pm), 24-hour lounge service.

■ *Rooms* 200	*Confirm by* 6
en suite bath/shower 200	*Last dinner* 10.30
Room phone Yes	*Parking* Ample
Room TV Yes	*Room service* 24 hours

Rajdoot

Manchester

R **Town plan C2** Greater Manchester
St James' House, South King Street
061-834 2176
Indian cooking
Credit Access, Amex, Diners, Visa

Part of a small and very popular chain offering comfort, good service and plenty to please the lover of mainstream Indian food. The menu, which doesn't change, covers an ample range, from moist, succulent tikkas and kebabs to bhunas, masalas, moghlais and other most enjoyable curries. There's also a standard spread of vegetables, sundries and sweets.

■ *Set L from* £5·50	*L* 12–2.30
Set D from £9·50	*D* 6.30–11.30
About £34 for two	*Parking* Difficult
Seats 110	
Closed L Sun & Bank Hols	

Truffles

Manchester

R ⊕ **Town plan C2** Greater Manchester
63 Bridge Street
061-832 9393
Credit Access, Amex, Diners, Visa

John Steel does the cooking in this attractive little restaurant, showing skill and care throughout a good seasonal choice. Typical dishes are paupiettes of pigeon with autumn fruits; langoustines with a garlic cream sauce in puff pastry; and loin of lamb served beautifully pink with a well-flavoured sauce paloise. Vegetables are interesting and varied. Truffles will stay open later, by arrangement, for post-theatre suppers. ⊖

■ *Set L* £7·50	*L* 12.15–2.30
About £45 for two	*D* 7–10.30
Seats 30	*Parking* Ample
Parties 12	*Closed* L Sat, all Sun &
Mon, Bank Hols, 2 weeks Aug & 1st week Jan	

Willow Bank Hotel

Manchester

H **56% £E**
Town plan D5 Greater Manchester
340 Wilmslow Road, Fallowfield M14 6AF
(061) 224 0461. Tlx 668222
Owner manager Malcolm Black
Credit Access, Amex, Diners, Visa

A modest business hotel about three miles from the city centre. In the original Victorian building are the reception, lounge and bar, the last featuring natural wood and Cumberland slate in its decor. Most of the bedrooms are in the adjacent modern part – bright, good-sized rooms with remote-control TVs and white or light pine furnishings. *Amenities* laundry service.

■ *Rooms* 124	*Confirm by* 6
en suite bath/shower 122	*Last dinner* 10.15
Direct dial Yes	*Parking* Ample
Room TV Yes	*Room service* 24 hours

Yang Sing — Manchester

R ♋ **Town plan D3** Greater Manchester
34 Princess Street
061–236 2200
Chinese cooking
Credit Access, Amex

Ask chef Harry Yueng to guide you through the vast menu of over 250 dishes that is part of the attraction of the Yueng family's immensely popular Chinese restaurant. The cuisine is mainly Cantonese, and highlights range from steamed sole with asparagus and spring onion to steak sizzled on a cast-iron plate before your very eyes. Budget eaters should opt for dim sum, with delicious prawn dumplings one among 18 choices.

- About £38 for two   D Meals noon–11
- Seats 140 Parties 200   Parking Limited
- Closed 25 Dec

- Changes in data may occur in establishments after the Guide goes to press. Prices should be taken as indications rather than firm quotes.

Excelsior Hotel — Manchester Airport

H 69% £C
Map 10 B2 Greater Manchester
Ringway Road, Wythenshawe M22 5NS
061–437 5811. Tlx 668721
Manager Edward Jones
Credit Access, Amex, Diners, Visa

Bedroom refurbishment and a leisure centre are the latest from this well-run modern hotel. Most bedrooms now sport sturdy darkwood furniture and nicer colours. Roomy public areas include a flight information screen. *Amenities* indoor swimming pool, sauna, solarium, keep-fit equipment, laundry service, coffee shop (10.30am–midnight), courtesy coach.

- Rooms 304   Confirm by 6
- en suite bath/shower 304   Last dinner 10.15
- Direct dial Yes   Parking Ample
- Room TV Yes   Room service 24 hours

Ladbroke International Hotel   *NEW ENTRY*   Manchester Airport

H 72% £C *E* &
Map 10 B2 Greater Manchester
Outwood Lane, Ringway M22 5WP
061–436 4404. Tlx 668361
Credit Access, Amex, Diners, Visa

Brand new (November '86) brick-built airport hotel on five floors. The roomy lobby (note the flight information screen) has a few easy chairs, but the main day rooms are reached by a small bridge over a stream. Bedrooms are in pleasantly simple, unfussy style, with grey-stained wooden furniture and stylish coordinated fabrics. Accessories include hairdryers, mini-bars and remote-control TVs; decent-sized bathrooms have shower fitments over the tubs. Larger plaza rooms (one whole floor) offer many little extras, from slippers to a welcoming glass of champagne. No dogs.

Amenities indoor swimming pool, sauna, solarium, whirlpool bath, keep-fit equipment, in-house movies (charge), laundry service, coffee shop (9am–midnight).

- Rooms 165   Confirm by 6
- en suite bath/shower 165   Last dinner 10.30
- Direct dial Yes   Parking Ample
- Room TV Yes   Room service 24 hours

Moss Nook — Manchester Airport

R ♨ ♋ **Map 10 B2** Greater Manchester
Ringway Road
061–437 4778
Owner managers Pauline & Derek Harrison
Credit Access, Amex, Diners, Visa

Cooking and service both shine at this intimate family-run Edwardian-style restaurant, which stands a mile from the airport on the Cheshire border. Robert Thornton displays much care and flair in his kitchen, and his sauces have really excellent flavour. Tartlet of quail and mushrooms, with exceedingly tender slices of breast of quail, is a splendid starter, and main courses run from spinach-wrapped fish with a grapefruit and orange sauce to three meats, each served with an individual sauce. Vegetables, such as crisp mange-tout, are also worthy of note, and you can wind up regally with little tastings of lots of sweets. Fine wines at highish prices.

🍷 Well-chosen ☺

- Set L from £16 50   L 12–2
- Set D from £16 50   D 7–9.30
- About £55 for two   Parking Ample
- Seats 50   Closed L Sat, all Sun & Mon, Bank Hols & 2 wks Xmas

Three Swans Hotel — Market Harborough

£E
Map 11 D4 Leicestershire
21 High Street LE16 7NJ
Market Harborough (0858) 66644
Credit Access, Amex, Diners, Visa

A magnificent wrought-iron sign, circa 1700, invites entry to this friendly town-centre hotel. Old photographs of the town evoke the past in the cosy lounge bar. A second, smaller bar is a popular 'local'. Bedrooms are bright and comfortable; two rooms have four-posters. Bathrooms, some with showers, are neat and compact. *Amenities* laundry service.

■ *Rooms 18* — *Confirm by 7*
en suite bath/shower 18 — *Last dinner 9.45*
Direct dial Yes — *Parking Ample*
Room TV Yes — *Room service All day*

Hob Green Hotel — Markington

71% £D/E
Map 15 B6 North Yorkshire
Nr Harrogate HG3 3PJ
Harrogate (0423) 770031. Tlx 57780
Credit Access, Amex, Diners, Visa

There's much to commend this lovely country house. The setting, in carefully tended grounds overlooking the Dales, is most attractive. Staff are friendly and helpful, housekeeping is exemplary and there's a relaxing atmosphere in the tastefully furnished public rooms. Principal among these is a stylish drawing room, decorated in soft spring colours, with antiques and oils giving a period charm. Fresh flowers are abundant both here and in the spacious entrance hall. There is also a sun lounge. Generous bedrooms are individually decorated with good-quality soft furnishings and fine antiques. All offer mini-bars, hairdryers,

tissues and tea-making facilities. Carpeted bathrooms have complimentary toiletries. *Amenities* garden, croquet, laundry service.
■ *Rooms 12* — *Confirm by arrang.*
en suite bath/shower 12 — *Last dinner 9.30*
Direct dial Yes — *Parking Ample*
Room TV Yes — *Room service All day*

Compleat Angler Hotel — Marlow

HR 77% £B E
Map 5 E2 Buckinghamshire
Marlow Bridge SL7 1RG
Marlow (062 84) 4444. Tlx 848644
Credit Access, Amex, Diners, Visa

A superb location on the banks of the Thames is an outstanding feature of this fine hotel, named after the masterpiece Izaak Walton wrote while staying here in 1653. One side of the building faces a tranquil stretch of water spanned by a splendid bridge, the other side overlooks a turbulent weir. An elegant, marble-floored foyer leads to welcoming day rooms like the relaxing lounge and smart bar with French windows opening on to a sunny terrace. Spacious bedrooms – many with lovely views – have an attractively coordinated decor, and bathrooms offer hairdryers and bathrobes.
Amenities garden, tennis, golf driving range, putting, coarse fishing, laundry service, 24-hour lounge service, helipad.
■ *Rooms 46* — *Confirm by arrang.*
en suite bath/shower 46 — *Last dinner 10*
Direct dial Yes — *Parking Ample*
Room TV Yes — *Room service 24 hours*

Valaisan Restaurant ♕

French cooking
Marc Legros gives the classical French repertoire some imaginative contemporary touches in this mellow and spacious oak-beamed restaurant. Pâté of quails with nicely cooked fresh artichoke is a typical starter, and main courses range from poached salmon sauced with lime and white port to saddle of rabbit with green and white noodles and a creamed garlic sauce. Efficient and pleasantly formal service. ✆

■ *Set L from £16·50,* — *L 12.30–2.30,*
Sun £22 — *Sun 12.30–3*
About £65 for two — *D 7.30–10,*
Seats 130 Parties 130 — *Sat 7.30–10.30*

■ We publish annually, so make sure you use the current edition. It's worth it!

Riber Hall   Matlock

HR **71%** **£C/D**
Map 10 C2 Derbyshire
Riber DE4 5JU
Matlock (0629) 2795
Owner manager Alex Biggin
Credit Access, Amex, Diners, Visa

A pretty walled garden and orchard provide a tranquil setting for this nicely-restored Elizabethan manor house which makes an ideal centre for exploring the Derbyshire countryside. Delightful bedrooms in converted outbuildings have nice period furniture including canopied four-posters. Exemplary housekeeping extends from impeccably ironed sheets and quantities of soft towels to a variety of thoughtful extras such as

sherry, chocolates and sewing kits. Refurbished bathrooms – five now have whirlpool baths – add an extra touch of luxury. Guests can relax in an attractive beamed lounge with a striking carved fireplace, and other public areas give an equal feeling of well-looked-after comfort. Friendly, well-managed staff. No dogs. *Amenities* garden, tennis, laundry service.

■ *Rooms* 11	*Confirm by* arrang.
en suite bath/shower 11	*Last dinner* 9.30
Direct dial Yes	*Parking* Ample
Room TV Yes	*Room service* All day

Riber Hall Restaurant

Carved English furniture, fine china, cut glass and fresh flowers make an elegant setting for a meal. Jeremy Brazelle uses only fresh produce, and his fairly straightforward approach preserves the natural flavours. Typical dishes: crab and saffron soup, fillet of lamb with a mushroom mousse and a port wine sauce; hot orange soufflé pancakes. Good-value wines. Charming, attentive service by local girls. ♀ **Well-chosen** ⊘

■ *Set L* £11	*L* 12–1.30
About £60 for two	*D* 7–9.30
Seats 30	*Parties* 34

New Bath Hotel   Matlock Bath

H **60%** **£C/D**
Map 10 C2 Derbyshire
New Bath Road DE4 3PX
Matlock (0629) 3275
Credit Access, Amex, Diners, Visa

Tucked between wooded slopes and the River Derwent, this Georgian house with modern additions offers a warm welcome. Traditional public areas include a pleasantly themed bar.

Bedrooms range in style, the most attractive being the refurbished rooms in the wing overlooking the pool. *Amenities* garden, sauna, indoor & outdoor swimming pools, solarium, keep-fit equipment, tennis, laundry service.

■ *Rooms* 55	*Confirm by* 6
en suite bath/shower 55	*Last dinner* 10
Direct dial Yes	*Parking* Ample
Room TV Yes	*Room service* All day

■ Our inspectors never book in the name of Egon Ronay's Guides; they disclose their identity only after paying their bills.

Budock Vean Hotel   Mawnan Smith

H **67%** **£C**
Map 2 B4 Cornwall
Nr Falmouth TR11 5LG
Falmouth (0326) 250288. Tlx 45266
Credit Access, Amex, Diners, Visa

New owners are injecting money and ideas into this extended 18th-century mansion, whose attractive grounds run down to the Helford River. The whole of the outside has been repainted, and changes in the public areas include a striking new pine roof for the large pool and a cavernous new lounge reclaimed from an old games room. There are other, cosier lounges, a nice cane-furnished

sun room with garden views and a stylish cocktail bar. Attention will turn next to the bedrooms, which are generally of a good size, with neat, functional bathrooms.
Amenities garden, indoor swimming pool, tennis, 9-hole golf course, sea fishing, games room, snooker, laundry service, 24-hour lounge service, mooring.

■ *Rooms* 53	*Confirm by* arrang.
en suite bath/shower 53	*Last dinner* 9.30
Direct dial Yes	*Parking* Ample
Room TV Yes	*Room service* 24 hours
Closed Jan & Feb	

Meudon Hotel — Mawnan Smith

H **69% £D**
Map 2 B4 Cornwall
Nr Falmouth TR11 5HT
Falmouth (0326) 250541. Tlx 45478
Owner managers Pilgrim family
Credit Access, Amex, Diners, Visa
   Beautifully kept grounds, designed by
Capability Brown, and sub tropical gardens lead
down to the hotel's private beach and slipway.
The outside of the building is a little faded, but
inside all is spick and span, with various members
of the Pilgrim family and their friendly staff doing
an excellent job. The classically-styled main

lounge is quite striking in pinks, greys and greens,
with wing chairs and a log fire. There are two
smaller lounges and a tiny cocktail bar.
Bedrooms, all in a modern wing, are fresh, light
and comfortable, with remote-control TVs and
neat, carpeted bathrooms. *Amenities* garden,
hairdressing, sea fishing, sailing, private beach,
stabling, laundry service.

■ *Rooms* 30	*Confirm by arrang.*
en suite bath/shower 30	*Last dinner 8.45*
Direct dial Yes	*Parking* Ample
Room TV Yes	*Room service* All day
Closed late Nov–late Feb	

Old Brew House — Mayfield

R ♧ **Map 7 B6** East Sussex
High Street
Mayfield (0435) 872342
Credit Amex, Diners, Visa
   A heavily-beamed restaurant where Sue Barnes
uses top-quality materials in her good honest
cooking. Dishes range from gazpacho Andaluz
and langoustines with ginger and garlic butter to
bream fillet provençale and chicken breast stuffed

with smoked haddock and cream cheese and
served with dill hollandaise. Excellent sweets.
Book.

■ *Set L* £6·50	*L Sat only* 12.30–1.30
Set D £8·95,	*D* 7.30–9.30
Fri & Sat £13	*Parking* Ample
About £35 for two	*Seats* 22 *Parties* 22
Closed Sun, Mon, Bank Hols & Tues following,	
2 wks Aug–Sept & 10 days Xmas	

Pink Geranium *NEW ENTRY* — Melbourn

R ♿ **Map 6 B3** Hertfordshire
Station Road, Nr Royston
Royston (0763) 60215
Owner manager Ellen Shepperson
Credit Access, Amex, Visa
   A very pleasant restaurant, pink-washed
outside, thatched on top, beamed and cottagy
within. Typical dishes run from ratatouille with
scrambled egg and Parma ham to tarragon-

sauced lamb cutlets. Excellent banoffi pie. Classic
wines include a splendid 1978 Chinon (Couly
Dutheil).
♟ Well-chosen ☺

■ *Set L* £7·25	*L* 12–2
About £49 for two	*D* 7–9
Seats 45 *Parties* 30	*Parking* Ample
Closed Sun, Mon, Bank Hols, 2 wks Aug & 1 wk	
Xmas	

King's Arms Hotel — Melksham

I **£E/F**
Map 4 B3 Wiltshire
Market Place SN12 6EX
Melksham (0225) 707272
Owner managers David & Helen Dodd
Credit Access, Amex, Diners, Visa
   Friendly owners and staff make guests very
welcome at this agreeable Bathstone inn with a
cobbled courtyard. The bar has a mellow,

traditional appeal and a handsome sideboard in
carved oak adds character to the residents'
lounge. All bedrooms are bright, cheerful and well
kept; twins and doubles have bathrooms en suite.
Amenities laundry service.

■ *Rooms* 14	*Confirm by arrang.*
en suite bath/shower 10	*Last dinner* 9
Direct dial Yes	*Parking* Ample
Room TV Yes	*Room service* Limited

Millstone Hotel *NEW ENTRY* — Mellor

I **£D/E**
Map 10 B1 Lancashire
Church Lane, Nr Blackburn BB2 7JR
Mellor (025 481) 3333. Tlx 635309
Credit Access, Amex, Diners, Visa
   The millstone is a well cared for roadside inn
just a short drive from the M6 (junction 31). The
main public area is a roomy bar and lounge with
several little alcoves for a tête-à-tête. Bedroom

decor is well coordinated, with matching fabrics
and lightwood furnishings. Tea-makers and
trouser presses are standard. Executive rooms
have extras including dressing gowns and
teletext. *Amenities* laundry service.

■ *Rooms* 16	*Confirm by* 6
en suite bath/shower 16	*Last dinner* 9.45
Direct dial Yes	*Parking* Ample
Room TV Yes	*Room service* All day

George Hotel

Melton Mowbray

H 57% £D/E
Map 11 D3 Leicestershire
High Street LE13 0TR
Melton Mowbray (0664) 62112. Tlx 341802
Owner managers Mr & Mrs C. E. Wyndham
Credit Access, Amex, Diners, Visa

The arched coaching entrance of this traditional town-centre inn makes an attractive foyer for today's guests. The thirsty are well provided for by three bars and a pleasant patio. Bedrooms, several of which have four-posters, have modern comforts including tea-makers, trouser-presses, and smart well-equipped bath or shower rooms.

■ *Rooms* 20	*Confirm by* 6
en suite bath/shower 20	*Last dinner* 10
Room phone Yes	*Parking* Limited
Room TV Yes	*Room service* All day

Harboro' Hotel

Melton Mowbray

H 57% £D/E
Map 11 D3 Leicestershire
Burton Street LE13 1AF
Melton Mowbray (0664) 60121. Tlx 858875
Credit Access, Amex, Diners, Visa

On the outskirts of town on the A606, this smart black and white inn has a warmly welcoming air. The darkly beamed and panelled bar makes a cosy spot for a drink, and residents can relax in the simple first-floor lounge. Bright, airy bedrooms – some traditional in style, others with modern furnishings – have tea-makers and compact bath or shower rooms.
Amenities laundry service.

■ *Rooms* 27	*Confirm by* arrang.
en suite bath/shower 27	*Last dinner* 10
Direct dial Yes	*Parking* Ample
Room TV Yes	*Room service* 24 hours

♀ indicates a **well-chosen** house wine.

Old Ship Hotel

Mere

I £E/F
Map 4 B3 Wiltshire
Castle Street BA12 6JE
Mere (0747) 860258
Owner manager Philip Johnson
Credit Access, Visa

This fine old town-centre inn, once the home of Sir John Coventry, MP, offers warm, comfortable accommodation, either traditionally furnished in the main house or more modern in the purpose-built block. A log fire blazes a welcome in the spacious public bar, and there's a cosy panelled bar as well as a relaxing residents' lounge.
Amenities garden.

■ *Rooms* 24	*Confirm by* arrang.
en suite bath/shower 17	*Last dinner* 9.30
Room phone No	*Parking* Ample
Room TV Yes	*Room service* All day

Manor Hotel

Meriden

H 56% £D
Map 10 C4 West Midlands
Main Road CV7 7NH
Meriden (0676) 22735. Tlx 311011
Manager John Portman
Credit Access, Amex, Diners, Visa

The location of this converted Georgian house is convenient, just three miles from the National Exhibition Centre. Bedrooms, now looking a little dated, offer practical comforts, and all have private bathrooms. Public areas include a roomy foyer-lounge and two bars. *Amenities* garden, outdoor swimming pool, games room, laundry service, 24-hour lounge service.

■ *Rooms* 32	*Confirm by* arrang.
en suite bath/shower 32	*Last dinner* 10
Direct dial Yes	*Parking* Ample
Room TV Yes	*Room service* 24 hours

Three Ways Hotel

Mickleton

H 60% £E
Map 4 C1 Gloucestershire
Nr Chipping Campden GL55 6SB
Mickleton (038 677) 429. Tlx 337497
Owner managers Keith & Jean Turner
Credit Access, Amex, Diners, Visa

Well placed for Stratford, this privately owned hotel is notable for its friendly, helpful staff. The lounge is a peaceful, homely spot, and there's a smart bar. Most bedrooms are in the extension – light rooms with modern units and tiled bathrooms. Rooms in the main house are larger. Good housekeeping, not so good breakfast. *Amenities* garden, laundry service, 24-hour lounge service.

■ *Rooms* 37	*Confirm by* arrang.
en suite bath/shower 37	*Last dinner* 9
Direct dial Yes	*Parking* Ample
Room TV Yes	*Room service* 24 hours

Fifehead Manor
Middle Wallop

HR 61% £D &
Map 4 C3 Hampshire
Nr Stockbridge SO20 8EG
Andover (0264) 781565
Owner manager Mrs Van Veelen
Credit Access, Amex, Diners, Visa

Lady Godiva and husband were early owners of
this mellow manor house where an attractive
entrance hall doubles as a bar. Main house
bedrooms have homely furnishings, and there are
some spacious modern-style rooms with excellent
bathrooms in a new wing. *Amenities* garden,
croquet, laundry service.

■ *Rooms 16*
en suite bath/shower 16
Direct dial Yes
Room TV Yes
Closed 2 wks Xmas

Confirm by 6
Last dinner 9.30
Parking Ample
Room service All day

Fifehead Manor Restaurant

The young English chef, Nicholas Ruthven-Stuart,
reveals a light touch with quality ingredients at
this tranquil restaurant. Fixed-price menus
supplement an interesting à la carte choice of
carefully prepared dishes ranging from fish and
seafood soup or cheese and walnut soufflé in
watercress sauce to local game pie, steamed brill
with onion compôte, and chicken breast with wild
mushrooms and pears. Very good sauces and
attractive presentation. Ice-cream sorbets or
perhaps coffee mousse for dessert. Note that last
orders are at 9.30. ⊖

■ *Set L £7·50*
Set D £16
About £47 for two
Closed 2 wks Xmas

L 12–2.30
D 7.30–9.30
Seats 35
Parties 40

Hotel Baltimore
Middlesbrough

H 65% £E
Map 15 C5 Cleveland
250 Marton Road TS4 2EZ
Middlesbrough (0642) 22411. Tlx 58517
Credit Access, Amex, Diners, Visa

The Baltimore is an attractive red-brick hotel
standing on the A172 just out of the town centre.
It's a friendly, well-run place, and day rooms like
the lounge and bar provide plenty of space for

relaxation. Bedrooms (largest ones are at the
front) are neat, fresh and bright, with light colour
schemes and simple white furniture.
Amenities garden, solarium, in-house movies
(free), laundry service, 24-hour lounge services.
■ *Rooms 31*
en suite bath/shower 31
Direct dial Yes
Room TV Yes

Confirm by arrang.
Last dinner 10.45
Parking Ample
Room service All day

Ladbroke Dragonara Hotel
Middlesbrough

H 63% £D
Map 15 C5 Cleveland
Fry Street TS1 1JH
Middlesbrough (0642) 232000. Tlx 58266
Credit Access, Amex, Diners, Visa

High-rise hotel in the town centre, offering a
comfortable overnight stay. Decent-sized
bedrooms have smart fitted furniture and easy-on-
the-eye colour schemes. Tea-makers and remote-

control TVs are standard, with additional
accessories in Gold Star rooms. There's a popular
public bar (music, pool table) and residents' bar
with ornamental pond. *Amenities* solarium, in-
house movies (charge), laundry service.
■ *Rooms 140*
en suite bath/shower 140
Direct dial Yes
Room TV Yes

Confirm by 6
Last dinner 10
Parking Ample
Room service Limited

Teesdale Hotel
Middleton in Teesdale

I 59% £E/F
Map 15 B5 Co. Durham
DL12 0QG
Teesdale (0833) 40264
Owner managers Dieter & Audrey Streit
Credit Visa

Dieter and Audrey Streit are the welcoming
hosts of this old coaching inn in picturesque
countryside. Spacious main-house bedrooms are

furnished in traditional style, and there are some
attractively converted cottages in the courtyard.
Bathrooms are spotless. Cosy public rooms
include a comfortable bar and lounge.
Amenities 24-hour lounge service.
■ *Rooms 18*
en suite bath/shower 11
Direct dial Yes
Room TV Yes

Confirm by arrang.
Last dinner 8.30
Parking Ample
Room service Limited

Jersey Arms
Middleton Stoney

I £E
Map 5 D1 Oxfordshire
Nr Bicester OX6 8SE
Middleton Stoney (086 989) 234
Owner manager Mr D. Livingston
Credit Access, Amex, Diners, Visa

Keen owner Mr Livingston is very proud of his
16th-century stone inn beside the busy A43. The
bars are rich in rustic charm and the six antique-

furnished bedrooms in the main building have a
homely feel. Five new rooms feature attractive
pine pieces, and there are three splendid suites.
Well-equipped modern bathrooms throughout. No
dogs. *Amenities* courtyard.
■ *Rooms 14*
en suite bath/shower 14
Direct dial Yes
Room TV Yes

Confirm by arrang.
Last dinner 9.30
Parking Ample
Room service Limited

Spread Eagle Hotel   Midhurst

H **65% £D/E**
Map 5 E3 West Sussex
South Street GU29 9NH
Midhurst (073 081) 6911. Tlx 86853
Owner managers Mr & Mrs Goodman
Credit Access, Amex, Diners, Visa
   Rich in beams, creaks and inglenooks, with a
history going back six centuries. Public areas
include the comfortable lounge bar and an

atmospheric cellar bar. The residents' lounge is
splendidly traditional, as are the older bedrooms
(some with four-posters). Bedrooms in the extension are very pleasant, too, and perhaps cosier
in winter. *Amenities* garden, laundry service.

■ Rooms 41	Confirm by arrang.
en suite bath/shower 37	Last dinner 9.15
Direct dial Yes	Parking Ample
Room TV Yes	Room service 24 hours

South Lawn Hotel   Milford-on-Sea

H **66% £D/E** &
Map 4 C4 Hampshire
Lymington Road SO41 0RF
Lymington (0590) 43911
Owner managers Ernest & Jennifer Barten
Credit Access, Visa
   A former dower house is now this hotel located
a mile from the sea. Owners the Bartens look after
things personally and maintain exemplary

standards of housekeeping. Day rooms are bright
and comfortable, and bedrooms have good
carpeted bathrooms. No children under seven. No
dogs. *Amenities* garden, laundry service.

■ Rooms 24	Confirm by arrang.
en suite bath/shower 24	Last dinner 8.30
Direct dial Yes	Parking Ample
Room TV Yes	Room service All day
Closed 1 month Xmas	

Woodford Bridge Hotel   Milton Damerel

H **68% £D/E**
Map 2 C2 Devon
Nr Holsworthy EX22 7LL
Milton Damerel (040 926) 481
Owner managers Roger & Diana Vincent
   Immaculate housekeeping puts a shine on this
thatched hotel on the river Torridge. The three
lounges with their log-burning stoves, gleaming
antiques and flowers are delightful, and there are

two rustic bars. Charming bedrooms in the main
building are complemented by luxury cottage
suites in the grounds. *Amenities* garden, indoor
swimming pool, sauna, solarium, tennis, squash,
game fishing, games room.

■ Rooms 23	Confirm by arrang.
en suite bath/shower 23	Last dinner 8.45
Direct dial Yes	Parking Ample
Room TV No	Room service All day

Old Swan Hotel   Minster Lovell

I **£D/E**
Map 4 C2 Oxfordshire
Nr Witney OX8 5RN
Witney (0993) 75614
Manager Timothy Turner
Credit Access, Amex, Diners, Visa
   Enjoying a peaceful valley setting, this ancient,
half-timbered, Cotswold-stone inn offers comfort-
able accommodation in immaculate bedrooms. All

have tea-makers, trouser presses and smart
modern bathrooms. Day rooms are rich in period
character, with low-beamed ceilings, polished
flagstones and open fires. No children under 12.
No dogs. *Amenities* garden, laundry service.

■ Rooms 10	Confirm by 6
en suite bath/shower 10	Last dinner 9.30
Direct dial Yes	Parking Ample
Room TV Yes	Room service All day

■ If we recommend meals in a
   hotel or inn, a separate entry is
   made for its restaurant.

Monk Fryston Hall   Monk Fryston

H **64% £D/E** &
Map 11 D1 North Yorkshire
Nr Leeds LS25 5DU
South Milford (0977) 682369. Tlx 556634
Manager J. M. Dodd
Credit Access, Amex, Visa
   An ancient and historic building set in beautiful
gardens alongside the A63 east of the A1. The
public rooms have retained the original style, with

dark oak panelling, oil paintings and antiques; the
lounge has comfortable seating and there's a
restful bar. The spacious bedrooms are in light
colour schemes, with traditional furniture.
Amenities garden, laundry service.

■ Rooms 29	Confirm by arrang.
en suite bath/shower 29	Last dinner 9.30
Direct dial Yes	Parking Ample
Room TV Yes	Room service 24 hours

King's Arms Inn *NEW ENTRY*

Montacute

I **£E**
Map 3 F2 Somerset
TA15 6UU
Martock (0935) 822513
Owner managers Jean & Roger Skipper
Credit Access, Visa
Old-fashioned hospitality and up-to-date comfort combine in this mellow stone inn opposite the village church. Stylish bedrooms at the front of

the inn include one with a four-poster but most of the rooms, in a converted skittles alley (part of the main building), are more standard; all have decent modern bathrooms. *Amenities* garden.

■ *Rooms* 11	*Confirm by arrang.*
en suite bath/shower 11	*Last dinner* 9
Room phone Yes	*Parking* Ample
Room TV Yes	*Room service* Limited
Closed 25 Dec	

Manor House Hotel

Moreton-in-Marsh

H **71% £D/E**
Map 4 C1 Gloucestershire
High Street GL56 0LJ
Moreton-in-Marsh (0608) 50501. Tlx 837151
Owner managers Fentum family
Credit Access, Amex, Diners, Visa
The warmest of welcomes awaits visitors to this 16th-century manor house, where the Fentums attend to one's comfort with almost passionate dedication. Behind the mellow Cotswold stone facade a long, attractive reception/lounge warmed by log fires extends the full length of the house. Guests relaxing in the simple, snug bar may enjoy views of the tranquil, lovingly tended gardens. Bedrooms in the main house are spacious and full of character; some boast four-poster beds. Bedrooms in the extension are tastefully modern, and compact. Thoughtful

touches are evident everywhere. No children under ten. No dogs. *Amenities* garden, indoor swimming pool, sauna, whirlpool-bath, tennis, putting, 24-hour lounge service, laundry service.

■ *Rooms* 38	*Confirm by arrang.*
en suite bath/shower 35	*Last dinner* 9
Direct dial Yes	*Parking* Limited
Room TV Yes	*Room service* 24 hours

Redesdale Arms Hotel *NEW ENTRY*

Moreton in Marsh

I **£E** &
Map 4 C1 Gloucestershire
High Street GL56 0AW
Moreton in Marsh (0608) 50308. Tlx 837928
Owner managers Messrs Elvis & Seedhouse
Credit Access, Amex, Visa
Hooves may no longer clatter in the courtyard, but there's still a period ring about this fine old Cotswold inn. The cosy bars feature beams and

panelling, and there's a peaceful little residents' lounge. Smart bedrooms have pretty fabrics and useful accessories like trouser presses and hairdryers. There are three suites with their own sitting areas. *Amenities* patio.

■ *Rooms* 18	*Confirm by arrang.*
en suite bath/shower 14	*Last dinner* 9.30
Direct dial Yes	*Parking* Ample
Room TV Yes	*Room service* All day

Manor House Hotel

Moretonhampstead

H **69% £C**
Map 3 D3 Devon
TQ13 8RE
Moretonhampstead (0647) 40355. Tlx 42794
Credit Access, Amex, Diners, Visa
On the B3212 out of Moretonhampstead, an imposing mock-Jacobean mansion set in 200 lovely acres. Public areas are splendid, particularly the lounge, with its panelling, ornate

fireplace and leather armchairs. Bedrooms are warm and comfortable, with well-fitted bathrooms. *Amenities* garden, tennis, squash, golf course, pitch & putt, putting, croquet, game fishing, laundry service, 24-hour lounge service.

■ *Rooms* 69	*Confirm by* 6
en suite bath/shower 69	*Last dinner* 9.30
Direct dial Yes	*Parking* Ample
Room TV Yes	*Room service* 24 hours

White Hart Hotel

Moretonhampstead

I **£E**
Map 3 D3 Devon
The Square TQ13 8NF
Moretonhampstead (0647) 40406
Owner manager Peter Morgan
Credit Access, Amex, Diners, Visa
Set in the town centre, this 300-year-old former posting house is run with great pride and professionalism. Its reassuringly solid facade

hides a reassuring solid and comfortable interior. Bedrooms, individually decorated, have well-equipped bathrooms. The place gleams with love and polish. No children under ten. *Amenities* snooker, laundry service.

■ *Rooms* 23	*Confirm by arrang.*
en suite bath/shower 23	*Last dinner* 8.30
Room phone No	*Parking* Ample
Room TV Yes	*Room service* Limited

Mottram Hall Hotel

Mottram St Andrew

H **69% £C/D**
Map 10 B2 Cheshire
Wilmslow Road, Nr Prestbury SK10 4QT
Prestbury (0625) 828135. Tlx 668181
Credit Access, Amex, Diners, Visa

Extensive grounds which include a lake surround this Georgian mansion. There is a fine bar with a moulded ceiling and a panelled lounge. Bedrooms have been attractively refurbished, and a new block contains several de luxe suites. *Amenities* garden, indoor swimming pool, sauna, solarium, whirlpool bath, keep fit equipment, tennis, squash, putting, croquet, games room, snooker, laundry service, 24-hour lounge service.

■ *Rooms* 95	*Confirm by 5*
en suite bath/shower 95	*Last dinner* 10
Direct dial Yes	*Parking Ample*
Room TV Yes	*Room service 24 hours*

Black Bull Inn Restaurant

Moulton

R **Map 15 B5** North Yorkshire
Nr Richmond
Barton (032 577) 289
Owner managers Mr & Mrs G. Pagendam
Credit Access, Amex, Diners, Visa

Customers come from near and far to eat at this popular village pub, and in the evening the old *Brighton Belle* Pullman car is a great attraction. Fish tops the bill, with a wide variety of excellent dishes spanning smoked salmon pâté, moules marinière, sole and scallops, plus lobster fresh from the tank. No evening reservations in the fish bar, otherwise must book.

♙ Well-chosen ☺

■ *Set L £7*	*L 12–2*
About £35 for two	*D 7–10.15*
Seats 90 Parties 30	*Parking Ample*
Closed L Sat, Sun & 1 wk Xmas	

■ Any person using our name to obtain free hospitality is a fraud. Proprietors, please inform the police and us.

Lobster Pot

Mousehole

H **56% £D/E**
Map 2 A4 Cornwall
Nr Penzance TR19 6QX
Penzance (0736) 731251
Owner managers Major & Mrs J. T. Kelly
Credit Amex, Visa

A splendidly run little hotel perched right on the harbour wall. The views are excellent from the public rooms, especially the glazed-in verandah by the bar. Bedrooms (some in adjacent cottages) have neat white furnishings, hairdryers, trouser presses and tea-makers. *Amenities* sea fishing.

■ *Rooms* 26	*Confirm by 6*
en suite bath/shower 23	*Last dinner 9.45*
Direct dial Yes	*Parking Difficult*
Room TV Yes	*Room service All day*
Closed early Jan to mid Mar	

Pilgrim Hotel

Much Birch

H **64% £D/E**
Map 4 A1 Hereford & Worcester
Hereford HR2 8HJ
Golden Valley (0981) 540742. Tlx 35332
Owner manager Paul Fletcher
Credit Access, Amex, Diners, Visa

A former rectory, this hotel stands in beautiful parkland, with views towards the Black Mountains. It's a comfortable, well-run place; log fires spread a cheerful glow through the public rooms. Bedrooms, mainly in a modern extension, sport plush velour furnishings and offer trouser presses. Neat carpeted bathrooms. *Amenities* garden, croquet, pitch & putt, laundry service.

■ *Rooms* 18	*Confirm by arrang.*
en suite bath/shower 18	*Last dinner 9.45*
Direct dial Yes	*Parking Ample*
Room TV Yes	*Room service All day*

Avonmouth Hotel

Mudeford

H **59% £C**
Map 4 C4 Dorset
Christchurch BH23 3NT
Bournemouth (0202) 483434
Credit Access, Amex, Diners, Visa

At the water's edge alongside Christchurch Harbour, this agreeable hotel has its own moorings and jetty. Best bedrooms are the ones with sea views and a comfortable sitting area; otherwise rooms are fairly standard, with built-in furniture, tea-makers and remote-control TVs. Picture windows in the lounge-bar make the most of the setting. *Amenities* garden, putting, games room, pool table, laundry service.

■ *Rooms* 41	*Confirm by 6*
en suite bath/shower 41	*Last dinner 9*
Direct dial Yes	*Parking Ample*
Room TV Yes	*Room service 24 hours*

Polurrian Hotel Mullion

H 57% £B ⚹
Map 2 A4 Cornwall
Helston TR12 7EN
Mullion (0326) 240421. Tlx 265871
Owner managers Francis Family
Credit Access, Amex, Diners, Visa
　First-class leisure facilities are a major
attraction of this friendly, family-run hotel with its
own private beach. The spacious, relaxing lounge
bar enjoys splendid views across the Lizard
Peninsula, too. Lofty bedrooms furnished in simple, traditonal
style offer TVs, direct-dial telephones and a

welcoming glass of sherry. Bathrooms are
adequate. *Amenities* garden, indoor & outdoor
swimming pools, sauna, solarium, whirlpool bath,
keep-fit equipment, beauty salon, tennis, squash,
badminton, putting, croquet, sea fishing, boating,
games room, snooker, pool table, in-house movies
(free), laundry service, 24-hour lounge service,
children's playground.
■ *Rooms* 42　　　　*Confirm by* arrang.
en suite bath/shower 39　*Last dinner* 9.30
Direct dial Yes　　　*Parking* Ample
Room TV Yes　　　*Room service* 24 hours
Closed Nov–Easter

Rookery Hall Nantwich

HR 85% £B
Map 10 B3 Cheshire
Worleston CW5 6DQ
Nantwich (0270) 626866
Owner managers Audrey & Peter Marks
Credit Access, Amex, Diners, Visa
　Charming owners and their smart young staff
not only provide impeccable service but make
guests feel truly welcome at this lovely château-
style mansion, set in 28 acres of gardens and
wooded parkland. Antiques, log fires and
invitingly comfortable sofas distinguish elegantly
proportioned day rooms, while attractively
refurbished bedrooms are models of style and
taste, with their rich draperies and fine
furnishings. All have thoughtful little extras,
ranging from champagne and exotic fruit to
hairdryers and bathrobes in the excellent
bathrooms. No children under ten. No dogs.
Amenities garden, tennis, putting, croquet, clay-
pigeon shooting, laundry service, helipad.
■ *Rooms* 11　　　　*Confirm by* arrang.
en suite bath/shower 11　*Last dinner* 9.15
Direct dial Yes　　　*Parking* Ample
Room TV Yes　　　*Room service* All day
Closed 4 Jan–28 Jan

Restaurant ★ ♕♕♕

A truly impressive dining room, where highly
polished panelling, a handsome moulded ceiling
and fine table settings create a suitable
background for Clive Howe's brilliant culinary
talents. His set menus contain some wonderfully
inventive ideas – like Cheshire cheese sausages
served on a creamy leek and chive sauce, rich
and buttery potted chicken liver studded with
truffles, and pinkly tender loin of lamb served on a
bed of crunchy sprouted lentils with roasted
garlic. Beautifully presented sweets include an
exquisite, tangy lemon soufflé served with
raspberry coulis, and delicious home-made
sultana bread accompanies outstanding British
cheeses. Splendid cellar, now with an exciting
Californian section (Jordan Cabernet Sauvignon
1980). *Specialities* seafood hot pot, rosettes of
veal topped with a Stilton soufflé and creamed
forest mushrooms, an envelope of salmon filled
with a mousse of scallops, apricot fritters with an
almond parfait.
⌦ Outstanding　♀ Well-chosen ☺
■ *Set L from* £12.95　　L 12.15–1.45
Set D £25　　　　D 7–9.15, Sat 7–9.45
About £65 *for two*　　Seats 55
Closed 4 Jan–28 Jan　　Parties 22

Newbus Arms Hotel Neasham

H 65% £D/E
Map 15 B5 Co. Durham
Nr Darlington DL2 1PE
Darlington (0325) 721071
Credit Access, Amex, Diners, Visa
　The country setting is pleasant and peaceful,
yet this dignified 17th-century house is quite
handy for Teesside airport and industries. Varying
sized bedrooms are handsomely furnished and

thoughtfully provided with things like tissues,
books, trouser presses and hairdryers. There's a
stylish bar and panelled lounge. Staff are friendly
enough, but not always efficient enough.
Amenities garden, laundry service.
■ *Rooms* 15　　　　*Confirm by* arrang.
en suite bath/shower 15　*Last dinner* 10
Direct dial Yes　　　*Parking* Ample
Room TV Yes　　　*Room service* Limited

Pike & Eel — Needingworth

£F
Map 6 B2 Cambridgeshire
Overcote Lane, Nr St Ives PE17 3TW
St Ives (0480) 63336
Owner managers John & Nicola Stafferton
Credit Access, Amex, Diners, Visa

Guests can arrive by boat at this popular old inn on the banks of the Ouse. Glass-cased fishing trophies decorate the spacious bar and two peaceful lounges offer traditional comfort. Simply furnished bedrooms have a cosy appeal, and bathrooms are up to date. No dogs.
Amenities garden, coarse fishing, moorings.

■ *Rooms* 10	*Confirm by arrang.*
en suite bath/shower 3	*Last dinner* 10
Room phone No	*Parking* Ample
Room TV Yes	*Room service* All day
Closed 24 & 25 Dec	

Nouveau Quiche — New Cross

See under London Restaurants under £30

Chewton Glen Hotel — New Milton

HR **87% £A/B**
Map 4 C4 Hampshire
BH25 6QS
Highcliffe (042 52) 5341. Tlx 41456
Credit Access, Amex, Diners, Visa

Parkland surrounds this magnificent country house on the edge of the New Forest. The hall has recently been redecorated and refurbished, but Persian carpets still cover the lovely wooden floors. A marble fireplace and attractive contemporary fabrics feature in the main lounge, a second has distinctive oak panelling and there's a smart bar designed by Nina Campbell. Best bedrooms (main house) are spacious, beautifully proportioned and tastefully decorated. For quiet seclusion, choose a suite in the converted coach house (each with two bathrooms) or one of the small rooms in the garden wing. Outstanding staff. No children under 7. No dogs.
Amenities garden, outdoor swimming pool, 9-hole golf course, putting, croquet, snooker, in-house movies (free), laundry service, helipad.

■ *Rooms* 44	*Confirm by arrang.*
en suite bath/shower 44	*Last dinner* 9.30
Direct dial Yes	*Parking* Ample
Room TV Yes	*Room service* 24 hours

Marryat Room ★ ♕ ♕

French cooking
Pierre Chevillard's renowned cooking is the star of the show here, with comfort, luxury, friendly service and fine wines in major supporting roles. Among the best known dishes is one created specially for Robert Morley – poached lobster served out of its shell in a citronella-flavoured sauce with a spinach mousse. Sauces are outstanding: Madeira with a hint of aniseed to accompany the excellent mille-feuille of wild mushrooms and fennel; périgourdine for fillet of beef; lobster to enhance a lovely poêlée of prawns and sweetbreads. Fresh young vegetables, good sweets, outstanding cheeses. Among the superb wines, note the splendid Sauternes, including Ch. d'Yquem '67. *Specialities* homard Robert Morley, mousseline de sandre aux langoustines, ballottine de caille au foie gras, les deux mille-feuilles gourmands.

➢ Outstanding ♥ Well-chosen ℮	
■ *Set L from* £12·50	*L* 12.30–2
Set D £27·50	*D* 7.30–9.30
About £75 for two	*Seats* 100 *Parties* 100

Robin Hood Hotel *NEW ENTRY* — Newark-on-Trent

H **58% £E**
Map 11 D3 Nottinghamshire
Lombard Street NG24 1BX
Newark (0636) 703858
Credit Access, Amex, Diners, Visa

Conference delegates and other guests are well looked after at this converted coaching inn at the corner of Lombard Street. Plush burgundy seating makes the main bar a cosy spot. Eight of the bedrooms have been tastefully refurbished with pretty fabrics and wall coverings. The rest are 60s style, clean and comfortable. Bathrooms are adequate. *Amenities* garden.

■ *Rooms* 21	*Confirm by* 6
en suite bath/shower 21	*Last dinner* 9.45
Room phone Yes	*Parking* Ample
Room TV Yes	*Room service* 24 hours
Closed 2 days Xmas	

Grange Hotel Newark-on-Trent

H **56% £F**
Map 11 D3 Nottinghamshire
73 London Road NG24 1RZ
Newark (0636) 703399
Owner managers Humphrey family
Credit Access, Visa
   There's a delightful, homely air about this
converted Victorian residence whose well-kept
day rooms include a relaxing TV lounge.

Bedrooms vary in size but all are comfortable and
attractive. Thoughtful extras include tea-makers,
radio-alarms and electric blankets. No children
under 12. No dogs. *Amenities* garden.

■ *Rooms* 8	*Confirm by arrang.*
en suite bath/shower 6	*Last dinner* 9
Room phone No	*Parking* Ample
Room TV Yes	*Room service* All day
Closed 10 days Xmas	

Chequers Hotel Newbury

H **63% £C/D**
Map 5 D2 Berkshire
Oxford Street RG13 1JB
Newbury (0635) 38000. Tlx 849205
Credit Access, Amex, Diners, Visa. LVs
   First, three houses, later a staging post for mail
coaches, now an agreeable hotel that appeals to
both business and tourist visitors. Bedrooms vary
in size, though the smallest are gradually being

eliminated; refurbished rooms have by far the
smarter furnishings, and all rooms offer remote-
control TVs. Public rooms provide ample space to
relax in comfort. *Amenities* garden, riding, clay-
pigeon shooting, laundry service.

■ *Rooms* 60	*Confirm by* 6
en suite bath/shower 60	*Last dinner* 9.30
Direct dial Yes	*Parking* Ample
Room TV Yes	*Room service* 24 hours

Elcot Park Hotel Newbury

H **69% £D/E**
Map 5 D2 Berkshire
Nr Newbury RG16 8NJ
Kintbury (0488) 58100. Tlx 846448
Credit Access, Amex, Diners, Visa
   Set in 16 acres of beautifully wooded grounds,
this 17th-century mansion commands views over
the Kennet Valley. Bedrooms in the garden annex
are sumptuously decorated while those in the

main house are full of character. Housekeeping is
impeccable throughout. The traditional lounge
and attractive cocktail bar are newly refurbished.
Amenities garden, laundry service, tennis,
croquet, helipad.

■ *Rooms* 38	*Confirm by arrang.*
en suite bath/shower 38	*Last dinner* 9.30
Direct dial Yes	*Parking* Ample
Room TV Yes	*Room service* Limited

■ Our inspectors are our full-
   time employees; they are
   professionally trained by us.

Swan Hotel Newby Bridge

H **61% £D/E**
Map 13 D6 Cumbria
LA12 8NB
Newby Bridge (0448) 31681. Tlx 65108
Credit Access, Amex, Diners, Visa
   A gleaming white-painted coaching inn on the
banks of the river Leven. Wooden timbers
characterise the reception area and lounges, and
there's a choice of two popular bars. Bedrooms

are comfortably traditional in style but have smart
modern bathrooms. *Amenities* garden, mooring,
snooker, in-house movies (free), coffee shop
(11am–9pm), kiosk, helipad.

■ *Rooms* 36	*Confirm by* 6
en suite bath/shower 36	*Last dinner* 9
Direct dial Yes	*Parking* Ample
Room TV Yes	*Room service* All day
Closed 4–13 Jan	

Solberge Hall Newby Wiske

H **69% £D/E**
Map 15 C6 North Yorkshire
Nr Northallerton DL7 9ER
Northallerton (0609) 779191
Credit Access, Amex, Diners, Visa
   A pillared portico graces this elegant early 19th-
century house set in beautiful parkland. High
ceilings lend the public rooms a vivid sense of
light and space. The billiard room boasts a full-

size antique slate table. Spacious bedrooms
combine gracious decor with modern comforts.
Excellent bathrooms have many thoughtful
extras. Friendly, efficient staff. *Amenities* garden,
billiards, laundry service.

■ *Rooms* 15	*Confirm by arrang.*
en suite bath/shower 15	*Last dinner* 9.30
Direct dial Yes	*Parking* Ample
Room TV Yes	*Room service* All day

NEWCASTLE UPON TYNE

Map 15 B4
Town plan opposite

Population 272,914

Newcastle was founded in Roman times and later became a fortress against the Scots. Its commercial influence began with the mining of coal, but today rests on engineering and other industries. The coast and hinterland of Northumberland are areas of outstanding natural beauty. The theatres, Northern Sinfonia Orchestra, and the University, provide some of the many cultural activities.

Annual Events
The Hoppings (travelling fair) *last full week in June*
Tyneside Summer Exhibition *End July–beginning August*

Sights Outside City
Hadrian's Wall, Hexham Abbey, Durham Cathedral, Alnwick, Seaton Delaval, Northumberland National Park

City Information Service
Central Library, PO Box 1DX, Princess Square
Newcastle upon Tyne NE99 1DX
Telephone Tyneside 2610691

Fiat Dealer
Benfield Motors Ltd
Railway Street
Newcastle upon Tyne
NE4 7AD
Tel. Tyneside 2732131

1 Airport **A1**
2 Bessie Surtees House *fine 17th-c timbered house* **B5**
3 Blackfriars Heritage and Interpretation Centre **A4**
4 Castle, Black Gate Museum **B5**
5 Central Library and Information Bureau **B3**
6 Central Station **A5**
7 Civic Centre *outstanding modern architecture including Carillon Tower* **B2**
8 Gosforth Park Race-course **B1**
9 Grey Monument **B3**
10 Guildhall *17th-c with Georgian facade* **B5**
11 Hancock Museum *natural history of area* **B1/2**
12 Jesmond Dene Park **C1**
13 John George Joicey Museum *history, furniture, Northumberland Fusiliers Museum* **C4**
14 Laing Art Gallery **B3**
15 Museum of Science and Engineering *exhibits of Newcastle's great engineers* **A5**
16 Newcastle Playhouse Theatre **A2**
17 Newcastle United F.C. *St James's Park* **A3**
18 Northumberland County C.C. **B1**
19 Plummer Tower *museum in rebuilt tower of old walls* **B3**
20 Quayside *open-air market on Sunday mornings* **C4/5**
21 St Nicholas's Cathedral *mainly 14th & 15th c* **B4**
22 Theatre Royal **B4**
23 Town Moor *nearly 1,000 acres of free grazing, sport and recreation* **A1**
24 Tyne Bridge **C5**
25 University and Museum of Antiquities **A2**

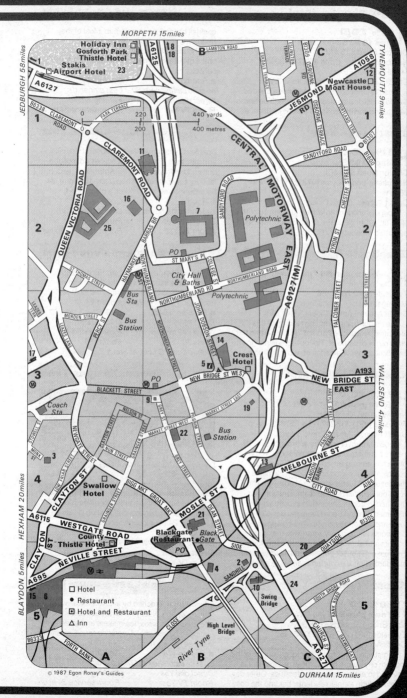

MORPETH 15 miles

JEDBURGH 58 miles

Holiday Inn
Gosforth Park
Thistle Hotel
Stakis
Airport Hotel 23

A6127
A6125
B6338 CLAREMONT ROAD
PARK TERRACE

LAMBTON ROAD

TENO...
B3109 OSBORNE RD

Newcastle
Moat House 12

TYNEMOUTH 9 miles
A105B

C

1   1

CLAREMONT ROAD

CENTRAL MOTORWAY EAST (A6127M)

SANDYFORD ROAD

JESMOND RD
OSBORNE TERRACE

CLAREMONT ROAD
11

QUEEN VICTORIA ROAD

BARRAS BR

16
25

7

Polytechnic

CHESTER STREET
BYRON ST

2   2

ST THOMAS STREET

PO

ST MARY'S PL

City Hall
& Baths

COLLEGE ST

SANDYFORD ROAD
NORTHUMBERLAND ROAD

FALCONER STREET
SHIELD STREET

HAYMARKET

Bus
Sta

NORTHUMBERLAND ST

NORTHUMBERLAND RD
Polytechnic

MORDEN STREET

Bus
Station

PERCY ST

JOHN DOBSON STREET

14
Crest
Hotel

A193
NEW BRIDGE ST

17

3   3

WALLSEND 4 miles

NORTHUMBERLAND STREET

5

NEW BRIDGE ST WEST

NEW BRIDGE ST
EAST

Coach
Sta

BLACKETT STREET

PO

9

NELSON ST

GREY ST

MARKET STREET EAST

19

HEXHAM 20 miles

STOWELL ST

CLAYTON STREET

NEWGATE STREET

NUN STREET

MARKET STREET WEST

PILGRIM STREET

Bus
Station

MELBOURNE ST

ARGYLE STREET

PANDON BANK

22

13

A188
B1305

4   4

3

Swallow
Hotel

CLAYTON ST

BIGG MKT GROAT MKT

CITY ROAD

BLAYDON 5 miles

A6115 WESTGATE ROAD

County
Thistle Hotel

GRAINGER ST

MOSLEY ST

DEAN STREET

21

Blackgate
Restaurant

Black
Gate

SIDE

20

QUAYSIDE

CLAYTON ST

A695 NEVILLE STREET

PO

4

SANDHILL

2

10
Swing
Bridge

24

SOUTH SHORE ROAD
BANK ROAD

CHURCH ST

DURHAM 15 miles

15 6

5   5

□ Hotel
• Restaurant
⊡ Hotel and Restaurant
△ Inn

CLOSE

High Level
Bridge

River Tyne

A6127

B6333

FORTH BANKS

A   B   C

© 1987 Egon Ronay's Guides

Clayton Lodge Hotel
Newcastle-under-Lyme

H **60% £C/D**
Map 10 B3 Staffordshire
Clayton Road ST5 4AF
Newcastle-under-Lyme (0782) 613093
Manager Mr F. Fuller
Credit Access, Amex, Diners, Visa. LVs
  Close to junction 15 of the M6, this extended period house is a popular stopover with business people and travellers. There's a cosy lounge, a cocktail bar and a separate pub. Most of the bedrooms are in modern wings, while those in the main house include a handsome suite with a brass bedstead. *Amenities* garden, laundry service.

■ *Rooms* 50	*Confirm by* 6.30
en suite bath/shower 50	*Last dinner* 10
Direct dial Yes	*Parking* Ample
Room TV Yes	*Room service* 24 hours

Post House Hotel
Newcastle-under-Lyme

H **61% £C/D**
Map 10 B3 Staffordshire
Clayton Road ST5 4DL
Newcastle-under-Lyme (0782) 717171 Tlx 36531
Credit Access, Amex, Diners, Visa. LVs
  A popular modern hotel near junction 15 of the M6. There's an attractive foyer-lounge, refreshed by potted greenery, and a cosy little bar. Spacious bedrooms offer functional fitted units and mini-bars. Executive rooms have darkwood units and extra accessories. *Amenities* garden, laundry service, coffee shop (7am–10.30pm), 24-hour lounge service, children's playground.

■ *Rooms* 126	*Confirm by* 6
en suite bath/shower 126	*Last dinner* 10.30
Direct dial Yes	*Parking* Ample
Room TV Yes	*Room service* Limited

Blackgate Restaurant *NEW ENTRY*
Newcastle upon Tyne

R ♿ **Town plan B5** Tyne & Wear
The Side
Tyneside (091) 261 7356
Manager Mr H. G. Seebacher
Credit Access, Amex, Diners, Visa. LVs
  The menus make tempting reading at this attractive, relaxing restaurant, and results on the plate rarely disappoint. Tip-top ingredients go into excellent dishes like parfait of wild mushrooms with chilled Madeira sauce, suprême of salmon with anisette sauce or veal steak with tomato concassé. Good wine list – note the Château Potensac 1979. ☠ Well-chosen ☣

■ *Set L from* £4·50	*L* 12–3
Set D £9.95	*D* 7.30–10.30
About £40 *for two*	*Parking* Difficult
Seats 70	*Parties* 80
Closed L Sat, D Mon, all Sun & Bank Hols	

County Thistle Hotel
Newcastle upon Tyne

H **71% £C/D**
Town plan A5 Tyne & Wear
Neville Street NE99 1AH
Tyneside (091) 232 2471. Tlx 537873
Credit Access, Amex, Diners, Visa. LVs
  Recent improvements have brought this city-centre hotel into our Grade 1 category. The whole place has an elegant, relaxing feel, and the combination of period and modern elements in the decor and furnishings succeeds well. The first-floor cocktail bar and restaurant are in dignified Victorian style, while in contrast the basement Boston Bean Company Bar is bright, lively and up-to-the-minute. Well-equipped bedrooms are also very smart with their pastel colours and attractive pine or mahogany furniture. Tea-makers, trouser presses and hairdryers are standard. Staff are courteous and very efficient;

housekeeping is first class. *Amenities* in-house movies, laundry service, coffee shop (11am–11.30pm), 24-hour lounge service.

■ *Rooms* 115	*Confirm by* arrang.
en suite bath/shower 115	*Last dinner* 10.15
Direct dial Yes	*Parking* Limited
Room TV Yes	*Room service* Limited

Crest Hotel
Newcastle-upon-Tyne

H **60% £D**
Town plan B3 Tyne & Wear
New Bridge Street NE1 8BS
Tyneside (091) 232 6191. Tlx 53467
Credit Access, Amex, Diners, Visa
  Register in the second-floor lobby-lounge of this modern city-centre hotel, whose ground floor is devoted to extensive function facilities. Other day rooms include a small residents' bar and the cosy Edward's Bar, reached by a covered walkway from reception. Neatly fitted, attractive bedrooms offer trouser presses, tea-makers and smart, well-equipped bathrooms. *Amenities* sauna, solarium, in-house movies (charge), 24-hour lounge service.

■ *Rooms* 178	*Confirm by* 6
en suite bath/shower 178	*Last dinner* 10
Direct dial Yes	*Parking* Ample
Room TV Yes	*Room service* 24 hours

Gosforth Park Thistle Hotel

Newcastle upon Tyne

H **77% £B/C E** &
Town plan A1 Tyne & Wear
High Gosforth Park NE3 5HN
Tyneside (091) 236 4111. Tlx 53655
Manager Kurt Kuen
Credit Access, Amex, Diners, Visa

Further improvements ensure that this splendid modern hotel in wooded parkland off the A1 maintains its deservedly high reputation. Conference and leisure facilities are first class, and day rooms stylish. An elegant, marble-pillared foyer-lounge and a choice of three bars provide ample space for relaxation. Attractively appointed, well-equipped bedrooms with generous storage room provide thoughtful extras like fresh flowers and magazines. Luxury suites and studios too. *Amenities* garden, indoor swimming pool, sauna, solarium, whirlpool bath,

gymnasium, beauty salon, hairdressing, squash, pool table, in-house movies, laundry service, 24-hour lounge service, children's playroom, courtesy car, helipad.

■ *Rooms* 178	*Confirm by* 6
en suite bath/shower 178	*Last dinner* 10.30
Direct dial Yes	*Parking* Ample
Room TV Yes	*Room service* 24 hours

Holiday Inn

Newcastle upon Tyne

H **75% £C E**
Town plan A1 Tyne & Wear
Great North Road, Seaton Burn NE13 6BP
Tyneside (091) 2365432. Tlx 53271
Credit Access, Amex, Diners, Visa

A modern low-rise hotel standing north of the city at the junction of the A1 and A6125. Smiling receptionists provide a friendly, efficient welcome in the marble-floored foyer, and guests will find it easy to relax in the lounge, with its central hooded fire, or in the adjoining bar that overlooks the pool. Bedrooms are of a good size, with thick carpets, light decor and neat tiled bathrooms. Trouser presses and hairdryers are standard fittings; and King Leisure rooms have more accessories and huge beds. Our breakfast was mediocre. *Amenities* garden, indoor swimming pool, sauna, solarium, whirlpool bath, keep-fit equipment,

games room, in-house movies, laundry service, coffee shop (7am–11pm), 24-hour lounge service, transport to airport.

■ *Rooms* 150	*Confirm by* 6
en suite bath/shower 150	*Last dinner* 10.30
Direct dial Yes	*Parking* Ample
Room TV Yes	*Room service* 24 hours

Newcastle Moat House

Newcastle upon Tyne

H **66% £D/E**
Town plan C1 Tyne & Wear
Coast Road, Wallsend NE28 9HP
Tyneside (091) 262 8989. Tlx 53583
Credit Access, Amex, Diners, Visa

A modern low-rise hotel located at the A1/A1058 intersection just north of the Tyne Tunnel and five miles east of the city centre. Staff are friendly, and the lobby and bars are pleasant

spots to unwind. Bedrooms are smallish but bright (thanks to floor-to-ceiling windows) and well equipped, and all have smart tiled bathrooms. *Amenities* garden, in-house movies (charge), laundry service, 24-hour lounge service.

■ *Rooms* 172	*Confirm by* arrang.
en suite bath/shower 172	*Last dinner* 9.45
Direct dial Yes	*Parking* Ample
Room TV Yes	*Room service* All day

Swallow Hotel

Newcastle upon Tyne

H **65% £D**
Town plan A4 Tyne & Wear
2 Newgate Arcade NE1 5SX
Tyneside (091) 232 5025. Tlx 538230
Credit Access, Amex, Diners, Visa

The private car park has direct access to the reception area of this well-run modern hotel in the city centre. The recently opened coffee shop is bright and attractive, and there are panoramic

views of the city from the sixth-floor lounge bar. Bedrooms are smart and generally of a good size, with neatly tiled bathrooms. *Amenities* laundry service, coffee shop (9.30am–4.30pm), 24-hour lounge service.

■ *Rooms* 94	*Confirm by* 6
en suite bath/shower 94	*Last dinner* 9.30
Direct dial Yes	*Parking* Ample
Room TV Yes	*Room service* All day

Stakis Airport Hotel · Newcastle upon Tyne

H 62% £C/D ⅖
Town plan A1 Tyne & Wear
Woolsington NE13 8DJ
Ponteland (0661) 24911. Tlx 537121
Credit Access, Amex, Diners, Visa
A modern hotel conveniently close to the airport terminal. Neat, comfortable bedrooms – many quite stylishly refitted – are all double-glazed. Accessories include tea-makers and hairdryers.

There's a spacious bar and a bright and welcoming foyer-lounge. A leisure centre was due to open autumn 1987. *Amenities* garden, in-house movies (free), laundry service, 24-hour lounge service.

■ *Rooms* 100	*Confirm by* arrang.
en suite bath/shower 100	*Last dinner* 10
Room phone Yes	*Parking* Ample
Room TV Yes	*Room service* Limited

■ We welcome complaints and bona fide recommendations on the tear-out pages for readers' comments. They are followed up by our professional team. Please also complain to the management instantly.

Newington Manor Hotel · Newington

H 55% £E/F
Map 7 C5 Kent
Callaways Lane, Nr Sittingbourne ME9 7LU
Newington (0795) 842 053
Credit Access, Amex, Diners, Visa
Oak beams, mullioned windows, sloping floors and inglenooks give this 600-year-old manor house a lot of character. Three rather basic bedrooms are in the main house, the rest in

modern chalets at the back. These are clean, bright and functional with adequate bathrooms and French windows giving direct car park access. *Amenities* garden.

■ *Rooms* 12	*Confirm by* Noon
en suite bath/shower 12	*Last dinner* 10
Room phone No	*Parking* Ample
Room TV No	*Room service* All day
Closed 26 Dec–1 Jan	

Newmarket Moat House · Newmarket

H 62% £D/E
Map 6 B2 Suffolk
Moulton Road CB8 8DY
Newmarket (0638) 667171
Manager Stephen Gross
Credit Access, Amex, Diners, Visa
This modern town-centre hotel (formerly a block of flats) has views over the heath and offers spacious accommodation, especially in the six

executive suites. Bedrooms all have tea-makers, trouser presses. The pleasant little foyer leads to a mellow bar-lounge with panelled walls and velour seating. There are also two meeting rooms. *Amenities* laundry service.

■ *Rooms* 49	*Confirm by* 6
en suite bath/shower 49	*Last dinner* 9.45
Direct dial Yes	*Parking* Ample
Room TV Yes	*Room service* 24 hours

White Hart Hotel · Newmarket

H 57% £E
Map 6 B2 Suffolk
High Street CB8 8JP
Newmarket (0638) 663051
Credit Access, Visa
This red-brick hotel dating from the 1950s enjoys a high-street location directly opposite the Jockey Club. The racing ties are emphasised in the naming of public rooms like the cosy, intimate

Rous Bar and the Guineas Restaurant. The best bedrooms have smart darkwood units, pretty pastel decor and carpeted private bathrooms, other rooms are more modestly appointed.

■ *Rooms* 21	*Confirm by* 6
en suite bath/shower 11	*Last dinner* 9
Direct dial Yes	*Parking* Ample
Room TV Yes	*Room service* Limited

Lugleys · Newport

R ⅊ **Map 5 D4** Isle of Wight
42 Lugley Street
Isle of Wight (0983) 521062
Enthusiastic chef-patronne Angela Hewitt concentrates her talents on a short interesting menu at her pretty little (just six tables) restaurant. Main courses include plaice with a seafood custard and oyster sauce, and pigeon breasts with a rich juniper glaze, while starters

could be olde English oyster stew or a mussel and bacon brioche with garlic and white wine butter. Seasonal fish and game specialities. Tempting puds too, such as light, layered chocolate mousse. ℮

■ *Set L* £8	*L by* arrang. only
About £34 *for two*	*D* 7–9.30
Seats 20 *Parties* 16	*Parking* Ample
Closed Sun, 26 Dec, 2 wks Feb & 2 wks Nov	

TraveLodge Newport Pagnell

H 57% £E &
Map 5 E1 Buckinghamshire
Linford Lane, M1 Motorway, MK16 8DS
Milton Keynes (0908) 610878. Tlx 826186
Credit Access, Amex, Diners, Visa
   Part of the Newport Pagnell service area
between junctions 14 and 15 of the M1. It's a well-
run hotel offering good overnight accommodation
in motel-style bedrooms, many with car parking

space at the front; all rooms have a drinks tray,
tea-makers and neatly fitted bathrooms, and there
are various extras in Executive rooms. Major
improvements in the day rooms include a new
bar/lounge and comfortable restaurant.

■ *Rooms* 96	*Confirm by* 6
en suite bath/shower 96	*Last dinner* 10
Direct dial Yes	*Parking* Ample
Room TV Yes	*Room service* None

Atlantic Hotel Newquay

H 58% £D/E &
Map 2 B3 Cornwall
Dane Road TR7 1EN
Newquay (0637) 872244
Owner manager Miss L. Cobley
Credit Access, Amex, Visa
   On a headland at the western end of town,
this solidly-built hotel is a friendly, relaxing place
to stay. Excellent leisure facilities make it a
family favourite. Spacious day rooms – there's
a large lounge and cheerful cocktail bar –
command fine views of the sea; bedrooms are
cheerfully modern and well-equipped. Bathrooms

are adequate.
Amenities garden, indoor & outdoor swimming
pools, sauna, solarium, whirlpool bath, keep-fit
equipment, squash, tennis, 9-hole golf course,
games room, snooker room, putting, children's
play area, laundry service, 24-hour lounge
service, in-house movies (free), coffee shop
(11am–6pm).

■ *Rooms* 86	*Confirm by* arrang.
en suite bath/shower 60	*Last dinner* 8.30
Room phone Yes	*Parking* Ample
Room TV Yes	*Room service* 24 hours

Hotel Bristol Newquay

H 64% £E
Map 2 B3 Cornwall
Narrowcliff TR7 2PQ
Newquay (0637) 875181
Owner managers Young family
Credit Access, Amex, Diners, Visa
   Friendly service gives a personal face to this
solid seafront hotel. The chintzy lounge is a
popular venue, and there are two bars and a

pleasant little writing room. Bright, spacious
bedrooms, all with spotless bathrooms, vary from
modern to traditional. *Amenities* indoor
swimming pool, sauna, solarium, games room,
billiards, in-house movies (free), laundry room.

■ *Rooms* 97	*Confirm by* arrang.
en suite bath/shower 73	*Last dinner* 9
Room phone Yes	*Parking* Limited
Room TV Yes	*Room service* 24 hours

Hotel Riviera Newquay

H 63% £D/E
Map 2 B3 Cornwall
Lusty Glaze Road TR7 3AA
Newquay (0637) 874251
Owner manager Mr Rolf
Credit Access, Amex, Visa
   A fine hotel for a family holiday, with manicured
gardens, splendid sea views and good leisure
facilities. The lounge and sun patio provide

peaceful comfort while the three bars are more
lively. Bedrooms are neat, bright and spotless.
Amenities garden, outdoor swimming pool,
sauna, hairdressing, squash, games room,
snooker, laundry room, children's playroom.

■ *Rooms* 50	*Confirm by* 6
en suite bath/shower 42	*Last dinner* 8.30
Direct dial Yes	*Parking* Ample
Room TV Yes	*Room service* 24 hours

🍃 is our symbol for an **outstanding** wine list.

Newton Park Hotel Newton Solney

H 66% £D/E
Map 10 C3 Derbyshire
Nr Burton upon Trent DE15 0SS
Burton-on-Trent (0283) 703568
Credit Access, Amex, Visa
   A creeper-covered country mansion in a
pleasant garden setting. Much use is made of
panelling in the public rooms, and there's an
eyecatching stained-glass window at the top of

the handsome staircase. Good-sized bedrooms
are being upgraded with light, attractive fabrics
and reproduction furniture. *Amenities* garden,
laundry service, 24-hour lounge service.

■ *Rooms* 27	*Confirm by* 6
en suite bath/shower 27	*Last dinner* 9
Direct dial Yes	*Parking* Ample
Room TV Yes	*Room service* Limited
Closed 3 days Xmas	

Sundial   North Cave

R ♿ ♿ **Map 11 E1** Humberside
18 Westgate
North Cave (043 02) 2537
Credit Access, Amex, Diners, Visa

Jane Marsden is the driving force behind this
pretty little village restaurant specialising in
traditional British cooking. Everything is made on
the premises, and typical tasty dishes include
salmon mousse, devilled chicken, braised oxtail

and loin of lamb, cooked on the bone with honey
and herbs. Vegetarian main dishes available, and
nice puds include syllabub made with elderflower
wine.

■ About £34 for two	L by arrang.
Seats 45 Parties 48	D 7.30–9.30
Closed Sun, Mon,	Parking Ample
Bank Hols, 2 wks Feb & 2 wks Aug	

Brookdale House *NEW ENTRY*   North Huish

HR **71% £D**
Map 3 D3 Devon
Nr South Brent TQ10 9NR
Gara Bridge (054 882) 402
Owner managers Charles & Carol Trevor-Roper
Credit Access, Visa

This handsome mid-Victorian building in pretty
wooded grounds is a haven of real country-house
hospitality. The lounge is large and extremely
comfortable, with a log fire, deep sofas and
armchairs and the latest magazines. There's also
a nice little panelled bar. Bedrooms are
individually styled and offer good modern
bathrooms plus accessories like hairdryers and
trouser presses. Excellent service and splendid
breakfasts. This is the first hotel venture for the
Trevor-Ropers, previously restaurateurs at

Knights Farm, Burghfield. No children under ten.
No dogs. *Amenities* garden, croquet.

■ Rooms 8	Confirm by arrang.
en suite bath/shower 8	Last dinner 9.30
Direct dial Yes	Parking Ample
Room TV Yes	Room service Limited
Closed Jan	

Brookdale House Restaurant ♨ ♿

An elegant candlelit restaurant, where Carol
Trevor-Roper applies a deft, delicate touch to a
wealth of local produce – beef and lamb, game,
fresh fish, splendid vegetables, farm-produced
cheeses and clotted cream. Typical dishes
include mushroom and coriander soup, duck
terrine, roast lamb with a parsnip mousse,
chocolate truffle cake. Beautifully judged list of
exceptional wines: note the Oregon Chardonnay
(Tualatin) '83 and Latricières-Chambertin (Trapet)
'78. Smokers can light up with coffee in the
lounge.

⮕ Outstanding ♀ Well-chosen ☺

■ Set D £16	D only 7–9.30
About £50 for two	Seats 24
Closed Jan	

■ For a discount on next year's guide, see Offer for Answers.

Walnut Tree Inn   North Petherton

H **64% £E/F**
Map 3 E2 Somerset
Fore Street TA6 6QA
North Petherton (0278) 662255
Owner managers Mr & Mrs Goulden
Credit Access, Amex, Diners, Visa

The Gouldens have built up a modest coaching
inn into an excellent small hotel. A well-furnished
reception area, along with a comfortable bar,

more than compensates for the lack of a separate
lounge. Bedrooms have good modern bathrooms;
extra accessories in the splendidly large
Executive rooms. Smart, efficient staff. No dogs.
Amenities garden, laundry service.

■ Rooms 20	Confirm by 6
en suite bath/shower 20	Last dinner 10
Direct dial Yes	Parking Ample
Room TV Yes	Room service All day

Stifford Moat House   North Stifford

H **61% £D**
Map 7 B4 Essex
High Road, North Stifford, Nr Grays RM16 1UE
Grays Thurrock (0375) 371451. Tlx 995126
Credit Access, Amex, Diners, Visa

A converted Georgian house set in its own
grounds just north of the Dartford Tunnel. There's
an elegant lounge overlooking the garden, a
panelled bar and a purpose-built conference

centre. Bedrooms, in two modern extensions, are
quite well fitted, and half have been recently
refurbished. No dogs. *Amenities* garden, tennis,
croquet, laundry service.

■ Rooms 64	Confirm by 6
en suite bath/shower 64	Last dinner 9.40
Direct dial Yes	Parking Ample
Room TV Yes	Room service 24 hours
Closed 25 & 26 Dec	

Springs Hotel
North Stoke

H **76% £B/C** *E* &
Map 5 D2 Oxfordshire
Wallingford Road OX9 6BE
Wallingford (0491) 36687. Tlx 849794
Credit Access, Amex, Diners, Visa

Built in mock-Tudor style in 1874 and subsequently much extended, this splendid hotel stands in peaceful grounds off the B4009, overlooking a picturesque spring-fed lake. A large open fire warms the panelled reception lounge, where elegant furnishings and a grand piano contribute to the mellow, traditional atmosphere. Handsome panelling is also a highlight of the cocktail bar and library. Sumptuous bedrooms – some with private balconies – vary in size but all offer modern comforts and excellent tiled bathrooms. Good conference facilities. *Amenities* garden, outdoor swimming pool,

sauna, keep-fit equipment, tennis, pitch & putt, croquet, bicycles, valeting, laundry service, 24-hour lounge service.

■ *Rooms* 34	*Confirm by* 6
en suite bath/shower 34	*Last dinner* 10.30
Direct dial Yes	*Parking* Ample
Room TV Yes	*Room service* 24 hours

♟ indicates a **well-chosen** house wine.

Northampton Moat House
Northampton

H **65% £D**
Map 5 D1 Northamptonshire
Silver Street NN1 2TA
Northampton (0604) 22441. Tlx 311142
Credit Access, Amex, Diners, Visa

With the refurbishment of the foyer, all parts of this tallish modern hotel have recently received attention. The neatly fitted bedrooms are light and roomy. Among the pleasant day rooms are a panelled public bar and a stylish lounge bar. *Amenities* garden, sauna, solarium, whirlpool bath, keep-fit equipment, laundry service, restaurant (7am–10pm).

■ *Rooms* 134	*Confirm by* 6
en suite bath/shower 134	*Last dinner* 10.30
Direct dial Yes	*Parking* Ample
Room TV Yes	*Room service* 24 hours
Closed 26 Dec	

Swallow Hotel *NEW ENTRY*
Northampton

H **74% £C/D** *E* &
Map 5 D1 Northamptonshire
Eagle Drive NN4 0HN
Northampton (0604) 768700. Tlx 31562
Credit Access, Amex, Diners, Visa. **LVs**

Opened in September 1986, this well-managed hotel is an excellent example of good modern design. The reception lounge is quite striking, with black seats and bright red cushions against a white background. The cocktail bar continues this high-tech theme, and there's a roomy, fully equipped leisure club. Bedrooms are particularly comfortable and stylish, with smart grey furnishings and a variety of eye-catching colour schemes. Accessories range from an iron and ironing board to soft drinks fridge, remote-control TVs and hairdryers. *Amenities* garden, indoor swimming pool, sauna, solarium, whirlpool bath,

keep-fit equipment, in-house movies (free), laundry service, coffee shop (7am–10.30pm), 24-hour lounge service.

■ *Rooms* 122	*Confirm by* Arrang.
en suite bath/shower 122	*Last dinner* 9.45
Direct dial Yes	*Parking* Ample
Room TV Yes	*Room service* 24 hours

Westone Moat House
Northampton

H **60% £D/E**
Map 5 D1 Northamptonshire
Ashley Way, Weston Favell NN3 3EA
Northampton (0604) 406262. Tlx 312587
Manager Greg Fehler
Credit Access, Amex, Diners, Visa. **LVs**

This handsome hotel stands in a quiet suburb ten minutes from the M1. An open fire banishes winter from the roomy lounge-bar. Bedrooms are mainly in unfussy modern style with standard accessories. The manager is very helpful. *Amenities* garden, sauna, solarium, keep-fit equipment, putting, croquet, laundry service.

■ *Rooms* 65	*Confirm by* arrang.
en suite bath/shower 65	*Last dinner* 9.45
Direct dial Yes	*Parking* Ample
Room TV Yes	*Room service* 24 hours
Closed 5 days Xmas	

Old Woolhouse ★

R ★ ♔ ♃ **Map 4 C2** Gloucestershire
The Square
Northleach (045 160) 366
French cooking

Real fires, beams and polished oak tables contribute to the pleasantly rustic atmosphere of this Cotswold village restaurant. There are only four tables, so booking is absolutely essential and is only accepted for two people or more. The imaginative menu is short and changes according to availability of produce, for Jacques Astic chooses only the freshest and finest ingredients on which to exercise his considerable skill. Starters might be monkfish in a crab sauce or calf's sweetbreads in cassis; main courses range from chicken in champagne sauce, pork in red wine and medallions of beef and veal in two sauces. Beautifully made sweets might include

chocolate gâteau, pear flan or a perfect prune tart. Professional service. Classic French cellar.

■ Set D £20	L by arrang. only
About £50 for two	D from 8.15
Seats 18 Parties 18	Parking Ample
Closed Sun & 1 wk Xmas	

Hartford Hall Hotel

H **60% £D/E**
Map 10 B2 Cheshire
School Lane, Hartford CW8 1PW
Northwich (0606) 75711
Credit Access, Amex, Diners, Visa. **LVs**

Carefully tended grounds with a scenic duck pond provide a delightful setting for this gabled hotel just off the A556. Old beams and stylish modern furnishings blend happily in the spacious

bar. In the generous-sized bedrooms (some with nice views) unfussy furnishings are complemented by practical facilities, and have smart bathrooms. *Amenities* garden, in-house movies (free).

■ Rooms 21	Confirm by 6
en suite bath/shower 21	Last dinner 10
Direct dial Yes	Parking Ample
Room TV Yes	Room service Limited

Green's Seafood

R ♃ **Map 6 C1** Norfolk
82 Upper St Giles Street
Norwich (0603) 623733
Seafood
Credit Access, Visa

Fishing nets and seashells set the decorative theme for Dennis Crompton's popular fish restaurant, where most of the supplies come from Lowestoft. The seafood platter is a favourite.

Other good catches include mussel soup, grilled sardines and very decent sauced dishes like poached medallions of turbot with béarnaise, provençale and mushroom sauces. Meat dishes too. Simple sweets. Service is skilful and friendly. ☺

About £40 for two	L 12–2.30
Seats 55	D 7–11
Closed L Sat, all Sun,	Parking Limited
Bank Hols & 1 wk Xmas	

Maid's Head Hotel

H **64% £D/E**
Map 6 C1 Norfolk
Tombland Nr3 1LB
Norwich (0603) 72111
Credit Access, Amex, Diners, Visa

Hospitality has flowed from this welcoming hotel opposite the cathedral for over 700 years. Two bars and an attractive covered courtyard provide ample elbow room; there are also three

comfortable lounges. Most bedrooms are practical and modern except for a few traditional ones. All offer bedside controls and neat bathrooms. *Amenities* 24-hour lounge service, in-house movies, laundry service.

■ Rooms 80	Confirm by 6
en suite bath/shower 80	Last dinner 9.45
Direct dial Yes	Parking Ample
Room TV Yes	Room service 24 hours

Marco's

R ♃ ♿ **Map 6 C1** Norfolk
17 Pottergate
Norwich (0603) 624044
Italian cooking
Credit Access, Amex, Diners, Visa

Top-notch Italian cooking in a welcoming city-centre restaurant. Marco Vessalio makes superb use of prime ingredients throughout a delicious diversity of dishes, from the good pasta

(marvellous gnocchi) to seafood, veal, chicken and rolled breast of pheasant with a splendid chestnut stuffing and a tasty port sauce. Try zabaglione semi-freddo. Charming service. ☺

■ Set L £10	L 12.30–2
About £45 for two	D 7.30–10
Seats 40 Parties 20	Parking Difficult
Closed Sun, Mon, Bank Hols & mid Aug–mid Sept	

Hotel Nelson   Norwich

H **65% £D** &
Map 6 C1 Norfolk
Prince of Wales Road NR1 1DX
Norwich (0603) 628612. Tlx 975203
Manager Peter Mackness
Credit Access, Amex, Diners, Visa
  A go-ahead modern hotel with admirable
management. Bedrooms are notably bright, and
comfortably fitted. The Executive wing provides

rooms with top-design furniture and, in most
cases, balconies. The lobby-lounge and nautic-
ally themed bar have nice river views. No dogs.
Amenities garden, sauna, keep-fit equipment,
mooring, laundry service, 24-hour lounge service.

■ *Rooms* 122	*Confirm by* arrang.
en suite bath/shower 122	*Last dinner* 9.45
Direct dial Yes	*Parking* Ample
Room TV Yes	*Room service* 24 hours

Hotel Norwich   Norwich

H **64% £D/E** &
Map 6 C1 Norfolk
121 Boundary Road NR3 2BA
Norwich (0603) 410431. Tlx 975337
Credit Access, Amex, Diners, Visa
  There's an impressive atmosphere at this
modern hotel on the ring road north-west of the
city. Old prints and maps add local colour to the
comfortable lounge and bar, which includes a

quiet corner for board games. Smart, well-
designed bedrooms have tea-makers and
practical bathrooms. No dogs. *Amenities* coffee
shop (10.30am–7pm, Sun 2–7), laundry service,
satellite TV, in-house movies (free).

■ *Rooms* 102	*Confirm by* 6
en suite bath/shower 102	*Last dinner* 9.45
Direct dial Yes	*Parking* Ample
Room TV Yes	*Room service* None

Post House Hotel   Norwich

H **63% £C/D**
Map 6 CI Norfolk
Ipswich Road NR4 6EP
Norwich (0603) 56431. Tlx 975106
Credit Access, Amex, Diners, Visa. LVs
  Good leisure facilities and spacious public
rooms typify this angular, modern hotel on the
A140. Bedrooms have mini-bars and tea-makers;
Executive rooms add trouser presses and

hairdriers. Well-equipped private bathrooms.
Amenities garden, indoor swimming pool, sauna,
solarium, whirlpool bath, keep-fit equipment,
putting, games room, laundry service, coffee shop
(10am–10.30pm), 24-hour lounge service.

■ *Rooms* 120	*Confirm by* 6
en suite bath/shower 120	*Last dinner* 9.30
Room phone Yes	*Parking* Ample
Room TV Yes	*Room service* Limited

Albany Hotel   Nottingham

H **71% £C** *E*
Map 11 D3 Nottinghamshire
St James' Street NG1 6BN
Nottingham (0602) 470131. Tlx 37211
Credit Access, Amex, Diners, Visa. LVs
  A modern high-rise hotel near the castle, and
the higher you go the more spectacular the views
over the city. Air conditioning and double glazing
keep things quiet and cosy in the bedrooms,
which provide tea-makers, remote-control TVs
and good private bathrooms. Executive rooms (on
top four floors, with best views) are superior in
decor and appointments, extras running from
magazines to mini-bars. Public areas include an
elegant marble-floored foyer with comfortable red
leather chesterfields and handsome house plants;
a stylish cocktail lounge (more plants, these
clustered round a fountain, and live music in the

evening); and a bright, lively basement bar.
Smart, helpful staff.
Amenities pool table, laundry service, 24-hour
lounge service.

■ *Rooms* 138	*Confirm by* 6
en suite bath/shower 138	*Last dinner* 11
Direct dial Yes	*Parking* Ample
Room TV Yes	*Room service* All day

Les Artistes Gourmands *NEW ENTRY*   Nottingham

R **Map 11 D3** Nottinghamshire
  61 Wollaton Road, Beeston
Nottingham (0602) 228288
French cooking
Credit Access, Amex, Diners, Visa. LVs
  Skilled cooking and an inventive menu have
built up a loyal clientele at Eddy Keon's French
restaurant, in a suburb of Nottingham just off the
A52. An imaginative menu may include scallops

with a cream and Noilly Prat sauce, conger eel
with vegetables and fillet steak with a truffle juice
sauce. Tarte tatin is a popular dessert.
♀ Well-chosen ⊝

■ *Set L from* £7·30	*L* 12–2
Set D £17·80	*D* 7–10.00
About £40 for two	*Parking* Ample
Seats 70 *Parties* 35	*Closed L* Mon & Sat,
	D Sun, all 25 & 26 Dec & 1 Jan

Novotel   Nottingham

H **62% £D/E** ♿
 Map 11 D3 Nottinghamshire
Bostock Lane, Long Eaton NG10 4EP
Nottingham (0602) 720106. Tlx 377585
Manager Mr R. Macchi
Credit Access, Amex, Diners, Visa
  A friendly welcome awaits at this well-run
modern hotel near the M1 and public rooms offer
abundant space to rev down. Spruce bedrooms

provide few frills but ample comfort. Remote-
control TVs. Bright, tiled bathrooms, separate
WCs. *Amenities* garden, outdoor swimming pool,
putting, pitch & putt, laundry service, restaurant
(6am–12pm), children's playground, helipad.
■ *Rooms 111*	*Confirm by 7*
en suite bath/shower 111	*Last dinner 12*
Direct dial Yes	*Parking Ample*
Room TV Yes	*Room service All day*

Pagoda   Nottingham

R ♨ **Map 11 D3** Nottinghamshire
 31 Greyfriar Gate
Nottingham (0602) 580745
Chinese cooking
Credit Access, Amex, Diners, Visa. **LVs**
  Staff are helpful and welcoming at this
spacious, relaxed Chinese restaurant. It's
especially popular at Sunday lunchtime, when the
choice of dim sum runs to 27 items, but the

extensive menu offers a wide selection of well-
prepared Cantonese-style dishes. Highlights of
our visit included char siu (barbecued pork in a
steamed dumpling) and tender pieces of chicken
and pork wrapped in lotus leaves.
■ *About £28 for two*	*Meals 12–11.30*
Seats 70	*Parking Limited*
Parties 90	*Closed 25 Dec*

Post House Hotel   Nottingham

H **62% £C/D**
 Map 11 D3 Nottinghamshire
Bostocks Lane, Sandiacre NG10 5NJ
Nottingham (0602) 397800. Tlx 377378
Credit Access, Amex, Diners, Visa. **LVs**
  A smooth-running modern hotel in a quiet
residential area just by the M1 (junction 25), eight
miles from Nottingham. Bedrooms are smart and
quite spacious, with tea-makers, mini-bars and

remote control TVs. The comfortably furnished
foyer-lounge overlooks an ornamental pool, and
there's a friendly, locally popular bar.
Amenities garden, laundry service, coffee shop
(10am–10.30pm), 24-hour lounge service.
■ *Rooms 107*	*Confirm by 6*
en suite bath/shower 107	*Last dinner 9.30*
Direct dial Yes	*Parking Ample*
Room TV Yes	*Room service Limited*

Royal Moat House International   Nottingham

H **71% £D** *E*
 Map 11 D3 Nottinghamshire
Wollaton Street NG1 5RH
Nottingham (0602) 414444. Tlx 37101
Credit Access, Amex, Diners, Visa
  A superb glass-roofed arcade lined with tropical
trees is a popular attraction of this impressive,
modern hotel in the city centre. The striking foyer
has a sunken lounge area with a black marble
floor and a fountain, while leading off from the
arcade are various restaurants and bars. Splendid
views over the city are a feature of the top-floor
Penthouse cocktail bar. Good-sized, very
comfortable bedrooms are air-conditioned and
have a good range of up-to-date accessories.
Executive rooms have extra luxuries; conference
facilities provide the latest technology. No dogs.
Amenities solarium, whirlpool bath, gymnasium,

hairdressing, squash, in-house movies (charge),
laundry service, coffee shop (10am–7pm).
■ *Rooms 201*	*Confirm by 6*
en suite bath/shower 201	*Last dinner 11*
Direct dial Yes	*Parking Ample*
Room TV Yes	*Room service 24 hours*
Closed 25 & 26 Dec	

Savoy Hotel   Nottingham

H **64% £D/E**
 Map 11 D3 Nottinghamshire
Mansfield Road NG5 2BT
Nottingham (0602) 602621. Tlx 377429
Credit Access, Amex, Diners, Visa
  A modern hotel on the A60, north of the city
centre. The spacious and characterful lounge
area has mahogany and mirror panelling and easy
chairs, and there are three bars. Many bedrooms

are new and the rest are recently decorated; all
have tea/coffee-makers, hairdryers and trouser
presses. Bathrooms are compact. No dogs.
Amenities laundry service, in-house movies (free).
■ *Rooms 173*	*Confirm by arrang.*
en suite bath/shower 173	*Last dinner 11*
Direct dial Yes	*Parking Ample*
Room TV Yes	*Room service 24 hours*
Closed 25 Dec	

Shôgun *NEW ENTRY*   Nottingham

R **Map 11 D3** Nottinghamshire
95 Talbot Street
Nottingham (0602) 475611
Japanese cooking
Owner manager Keiji Tomiyama
Credit Access, Amex, Diners, Visa

Chef Kato covers the whole armoury of Japanese cuisine in this neat, well-run restaurant. The menu is clearly set out, making it easier than usual to choose among the delights of tempura and teriyaki, sushi and sashimi, deep-fried seasoned chicken and meats with spicy dips. Set dinners make decisions even easier.

■ *Set L £5*	*L 12–2*
Set D from £8	*D 7–11*
About £30 for two	*Parking Limited*
Seats 50 Parties 50	*Closed L Mon, all Sun,*
25 & 26 Dec, 1 Jan & 2 wks July–Aug	

Stakis Victoria Hotel   Nottingham

H **63% £D/E**
Map 11 D3 Nottinghamshire
Milton Street NG1 3PZ
Nottingham (0602) 419561. Tlx 37401
Manager Neal Gilpin
Credit Access, Amex, Diners, Visa. **LVs**

Conveniently located next to a central shopping precinct, this red-brick hotel has a welcoming atmosphere. The foyer lounge is wood-panelled, with chesterfields and cane chairs and there is a spacious bar. Executive rooms have smart darkwood units. All bathrooms have showers and hairdryers. *Amenities* in-house movies (charge), laundry service.

■ *Rooms 167*	*Confirm by 6*
en suite bath/shower 167	*Last dinner 9.45*
Room phone Yes	*Parking Limited*
Room TV Yes	*Room service All day*

Strathdon Thistle Hotel   Nottingham

H **65% £C/D**
Map 11 D3 Nottinghamshire
Derby Road NG1 5FT
Nottingham (0602) 418501. Tlx 377185
Manager Mr Peter L. Robinson
Credit Access, Amex, Diners, Visa. **LVs**

Thoroughly stylish public and private areas at this modern hotel on the Derby side of town. The elegant foyer offers deep-cushioned comfort, and there's an American-style bar-diner, plus a cocktail bar and relaxing conservatory lounge. Smartly furnished bedrooms (all double-glazed) are well-equipped. *Amenities* in-house movies (free), laundry service.

■ *Rooms 69*	*Confirm by 6*
en suite bath/shower 69	*Last dinner 10*
Direct dial Yes	*Parking Difficult*
Room TV Yes	*Room service 24 hours*

Ten *NEW ENTRY*   Nottingham

R ⅋ **Map 11 D3** Nottinghamshire
10 Commerce Square
Nottingham (0602) 585211
Vegetarian cooking
Credit Access

Light and airy despite its basement setting, this is a pleasantly informal restaurant serving vegetarian dishes way above the ordinary. Bean and sweet pepper pâté makes an appetising prelude to main courses such as broccoli Thermidor or asparagus and cashew nut roulade. Sweets are good, too. Capable, inventive cooking by Malcolm Tandy and his team.

■ *About £26 for two*	*Meals 12–11, Mon 12–*
Seats 50	*3, Fri & Sat 12–11.30*
Parties 25	*Parking Difficult*
Closed Sun & Bank Hols (exc. Good Fri &	
L 25 Dec)	

Hambleton Hall   Oakham

HR **82% £C**
Map 11 E3 Leicestershire
Hambleton LE15 8TH
Oakham (0572) 56991. Tlx 342888
Owner managers Tim & Stefa Hart
Credit Access, Amex, Diners, Visa

With grounds leading down to Rutland Water, this Victorian mansion has a setting of complete peace and beauty. The Harts have created an intangible element of quiet attentiveness which leaves the visitor refreshed and relaxed. The public rooms display the style of Nina Campbell and the charming bar strikes a balance between opulence and a clubby atmosphere. The bedrooms are captivating, with quality fabrics and fine antiques and prints. Extra touches such as shortbread, stationery, and bathrobes in the stylish bathrooms, add to the comfort. Excellent staff. *Amenities* garden, tennis, riding, laundry service.

■ *Rooms 15*	*Confirm by arrang.*
en suite bath/shower 15	*Last dinner 9.30*
Direct dial Yes	*Parking Ample*
Room TV Yes	*Room service All day*

Hambleton Hall Restaurant ★ ♛ ♿

The attractive and mouthwatering menu of this elegant dining room raises expectations that Brian Baker's superb cooking certainly fulfils. Preparation of quality ingredients is matched by artistic presentation. As well as the à la carte, there is a daily-changing five-course set menu which combines traditional and imaginatively modern dishes. Start with a little pie of wood pigeon and wild mushrooms; for a second course, sample the red mullet with Mediterranean vegetables. Main course options might be lobster hot pot or rib of veal with morels. There's an excellent selection of French and English cheeses and delicious sweets. Magnificent cellar chosen with great flair. Note Vieux Château Certan 1964 and Château Gilette 'Crème de Tête'.
Specialities fresh Norfolk crab with a sauce of its dark meat, grilled cutlet of halibut with a bitter blood orange sauce, Hambleton's rice pudding served with exotic fruits.

Outstanding Well-chosen

■ *Set L £14·75* *L 12–2*
Set D from £29·50 *D 7–9.30*
About £70 for two *Seats 50*

Oakhill House — Oakhill

RR ♿ **Map 4 B3** Somerset
Bath Road BA3 5AQ
Oakhill (0749) 840180
Credit Access, Amex, Diners, Visa

Very much a family concern, this nice old Georgian house, with talented Ann Long in the kitchen, daughter Suzanne serving and husband Ian well cast as the genial host. Ann's daily-changing menu is short but interesting with dishes like red pepper and tomato soup, mustard-glazed game terrine and a particularly well-executed main course of salmon with a sea-food mousse, wrapped in spinach and cooked in puff pastry. Vegetables retain a marked crunch; sweets include a nice oatmeal meringue containing apples and blackcurrants.

■ *Set L £7·50, Sun £6·50* *L 12.30–1.45*
About £40 for two *D 7.30–9.30*
Seats 35 Parties 25 *Parking Ample*
Closed L Sat, D Sun, all Mon & 2–3 weeks Jan/Feb

Bedrooms £F
Rooms 3 *With bath/shower 3*
Attractive bedrooms (no children under 12; no dogs) have good traditional furnishings, smart modern bathrooms and remote-control TVs.

■ Our inspectors are our full-time employees; they are professionally trained by us.

King's Arms Restaurant — Ockley

R ♿ **Map 5 E3** Surrey
Stane Street
Dorking (0306) 711224
Credit Access, Amex, Visa

A change of chef, but Mervyn Halliday keeps the familiar favourites on the à la carte menu at this very cheerful pub restaurant, run by the Doyle family. Pan-fried sardines, chicken Kiev, rack of lamb and pepper steak are among the favourites. His special set menu (no choice) shows a more modern trend with dishes like roulade of Parma ham, cream cheese and avocado, or excellent beef fillet set on a mushroom purée, with watercress hollandaise.

■ *Set L & D from £12·50* *L 12–1.45*
About £35 for two *D 7–9.45*
Seats 40 Parties 40 *Parking Ample*
Closed D Sun & D 25 & 26 Dec

La Forêt *NEW ENTRY* — Odiham

R **Map 5 D3** Hampshire
High Street
Odiham (025 671) 2697
Owner manager Steven Houlker
Credit Access, Amex, Diners, Visa

Abundant greenery, both inside and out, justifies the name of this friendly restaurant. Candlelit set dinners start with crudités, pâtés and salami; an optional extra course may include garlicky frogs' legs, while the main dishes range from stuffed trout to tournedos en croûte. Sweets or a good cheeseboard. Nothing startling, but good honest cooking and a cheerful ambience.

■ *Set D £14·95* *D only 7–10*
About £43 for two *Parking Ample*
Seats 50 *Parties 40*
Closed Sun & 1 wk Xmas

Odiham ▶

George Hotel *NEW ENTRY*   Odiham

I £E
Map 5 D3 Hampshire
High Street RG25 1LP
Odiham (025 671) 2081. Tlx 858797
Credit Access, Amex, Diners, Visa

With new tenants this picture postcard hotel in a pretty village has been completely renovated. Two old buildings – one was the local assize court – keep many of their original features, including some unusual stonework in the residents' lounge. Beams are very much in evidence, especially in the solidly furnished bedrooms, where double glazing, central heating and plentiful hot water make for a very comfortable stay.

■ *Rooms* 10	*Confirm by arrang.*
en suite bath/shower 10	*Last dinner* 10
Direct dial Yes	*Parking* Ample
Room TV Yes	*Room service* Limited

♀ indicates a **well-chosen** house wine.

Green Man Hotel   Old Harlow

H 62% £D/E
Map 7 B4 Essex
Mulberry Green CM17 0ET
Harlow (0279) 442521. Tlx 817972
Credit Access, Amex, Diners, Visa

Public rooms are located in a 600-year-old listed building that overlooks the village green; there's a flagstoned entrance hall and two pleasant bars. Overnight accommodation in a separate block is contrastingly modern, and all rooms are equipped with tea-makers, digital clock-radios and private bathrooms. Check directions when booking.
Amenities laundry service.

■ *Rooms* 55	*Confirm by* 6
en suite bath/shower 55	*Last dinner* 10
Direct dial Yes	*Parking* Ample
Room TV Yes	*Room service* 24 hours

Salisbury ★   Old Hatfield

R ★ ⌂ ♀ ⧖ **Map 7 A4** Hertfordshire
15 The Broadway
Hatfield (070 72) 62220
Credit Access, Amex, Diners, Visa

Enjoy a pre-dinner drink in the cosy lounge, with its fire and magazines, before proceeding to the elegant dining room to sample dishes from one of Julian Waterer's short, imaginative menus. You might start with smoked beef and quail's egg salad, before going on to tender scallops, mussels and lobster with delicious crab-flavoured hollandaise sauce and a puff pastry lid, to be followed by breast of pheasant with apricots and green peppercorn sauce. There's an impressive cheeseboard and some very good sweets. Some fine wines (Château Coutet '67 and Pape-Clément '61) but highish prices. *Specialities* cucumber and prawns in a smoked salmon parcel, served with warm scallops in dill butter sauce; breast of guinea fowl in a Cointreau and green peppercorn sauce; iced raspberry parfait on a white chocolate

and pistachio nut base. ♀ Well-chosen ⊖

■ *Set L* from £10·75	*L* 12.30–2
Set D £21	*D* 7.30–9.30
About £60 for two	*Parking* Ample
Seats 60	*Parties* 30

Closed L Sat, D Sun, all Mon, Bank Hols (exc. L 25 Dec) & 1st 2 wks Jan

---

⊃ is our symbol for an **outstanding** wine list.

Ormesby Lodge Hotel   Ormesby St Margaret

H 60% £E/F
Map 6 D1 Norfolk
Decoy Road NR29 3LG
Great Yarmouth (0493) 730910
Owner managers Mr and Mrs G. Fellas
Credit Access, Amex, Diners, Visa

Situated on a peaceful village road, this solidly comfortable Victorian house is run by the welcoming Fellases. A fine period staircase leads to cosy, individually decorated bedrooms. Three new rooms have recently been added. Excellent housekeeping. No dogs. *Amenities* garden, outdoor swimming pool, laundry service.

■ *Rooms* 11	*Confirm by arrang.*
en suite bath/shower 11	*Last dinner* 10.30
Room phone Yes	*Parking* Ample
Room TV Yes	*Room service* All day
Closed 25 & 26 Dec	

Sweeney Hall Hotel — Oswestry

H **55% £E**
Map 10 A3 Shropshire
Morda SY10 9EU
Oswestry (0691) 652450
Credit Access, Visa

Eight acres of grounds in extensive parkland are the setting for this listed Georgian building just off the A483. A sense of the past is present in the lofty foyer, and there's a TV lounge and two bars, one with a Gothic vaulted ceiling. Best and biggest bedrooms are traditionally-appointed front ones; those at the back are smaller and more modern.

Amenities garden, putting, helipad.

■ *Rooms* 7 — *Confirm by* 6
en suite bath/shower 5 — *Last dinner* 9
Room phone No — *Parking* Ample
Room TV No — *Room service* Limited

Wynnstay Hotel — Oswestry

H **57% £D**
Map 10 A3 Shropshire
Church Street SY11 2SZ
Oswestry (0691) 655261
Credit Access, Amex, Diners, Visa

The wine bar is proving a popular new feature at this red-brick Georgian hotel with its own crown bowling green. The green is overlooked by a homely lounge, and there's also a roomy lounge-bar. Upgrading is planned for all bedrooms, most having already emerged light, bright and smart from revamping. Remote-control TVs.

Amenities garden, bowling green, laundry service.

■ *Rooms* 26 — *Confirm by* 6
en suite bath/shower 26 — *Last dinner* 9.30
Direct dial Yes — *Parking* Ample
Room TV Yes — *Room service* All day

■ We publish annually, so make sure you use the current edition. It's worth it!

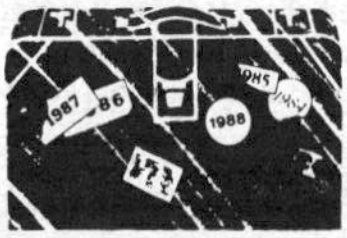

Chevin Lodge — Otley

H **65% £C/D** ♿
Map 10 C1 West Yorkshire
Yorkgate LS21 3NU
Otley (0943) 467818. Tlx 51538
Credit Access, Amex, Diners, Visa

High above Otley in 50 acres of woodland, Chevin Lodge is an unusual and distinctive hotel of pine log construction. The lounge and bar are extremely cosy, and the pine-furnished bedrooms (25 in chalets) are roomy, comfortable and well equipped – some are split level, with separate sleeping areas. *Amenities* garden, sauna, solarium, whirlpool bath, coarse & game fishing, in-house movies (free), laundry service.

■ *Rooms* 43 — *Confirm by* arrang.
en suite bath/shower 43 — *Last dinner* 9.30
Direct dial Yes — *Parking* Ample
Room TV Yes — *Room service* 24 hours

Percy Arms Hotel — Otterburn

H **60% £D/E**
Map 14 B3 Northumberland
NE19 1NR
Otterburn (0830) 20261
Owner managers M. C. & J. Shirley
Credit Access, Amex, Diners, Visa

Character and charm are much in evidence at this delightful old coaching inn on main street. It has three very comfortable old-world lounges, and a popular cosy bar. Pretty bedrooms vary in style from antique to modern. Staff are most pleasant and courteous.

Amenities garden, coarse & game fishing, games room.

■ *Rooms* 31 — *Confirm by* arrang.
en suite bath/shower 31 — *Last dinner* 8.45
Room phone Yes — *Parking* Ample
Room TV Some — *Room service* Limited

The Lodge — Ottery St Mary

R **Map 3 E2** Devon
Silver Street
Ottery St Mary (040 481) 2356
Credit Amex, Diners, Visa

Enjoy a drink in the cosy sitting room before settling down to dinner in the prettily decorated restaurant. Diane Shenton's menus are full of interest, ranging from paupiettes of salmon with sole mousseline to lamb in salt pastry with a rosemary and red wine sauce. She loves cream, and it shows in some of her dishes! Superb vegetables, delightful desserts (a couple of savouries, too).

■ *Set L* £18·50 — *L* by arrang. only
Set D £18·50 — *D* 7–9.30
About £45 for two — *Parking* Limited
Seats 20 — *Parties* 20
Closed D Sun, all Mon, Bank Hols

Talbot Hotel   Oundle

H 61% £D/E &
Map 6 A2 Northamptonshire
New Street PE8 4EA
Oundle (0832) 73621. Tlx 32364
Credit Access, Amex, Diners, Visa
  Built as a monks' hostel, then 'modernised' in the 17th century with stones from nearby Fotheringhay Castle, this ancient inn is rich in period detail. Beams and panelling, engraved glass and weaponry give plenty of character to the cosy lounge and two bars. Pleasant bedrooms (one with a four-poster) have neat fittings and good bathrooms. *Amenities* garden, laundry service, 24-hour lounge service.

■ *Rooms* 39	*Confirm by* arrang.
en suite bath/shower 39	*Last dinner* 10
Direct dial Yes	*Parking* Ample
Room TV Yes	*Room service* Limited

■ For a discount on next year's guide, see Offer for Answers.

Café Français *NEW ENTRY*   Oxford

R **Town plan C4**
  146 London Road, Headington
Oxford (0865) 62587
Owner manager Michael Sadones
Credit Access, Amex, Visa
  Old photographs line the walls of this pleasant restaurant, formerly La Salle à Manger. Set menus offer a well-balanced selection exemplified by Mediterranean fish soup, sautéed lamb's liver with winter salad and roast loin of pork sauce normande. There are good French cheeses, and apple tart rounds off the meal nicely.

♀ Well-chosen ☺

■ *Set L* from £7·45	*L* 12–2.15
Set D £10·95	*D* 7–10.30, Sat 7–11
About £34 for two	*Parking* Limited
Seats 64	*Parties* 64
Closed Sun, 2 days Xmas & 1 Jan	

Cherwell Boathouse   Oxford

R & **Town plan B1** Oxfordshire
  Bardwell Road
Oxford (0865) 52746
Owner manager Anthony Verdin
Credit Access, Amex, Diners, Visa
  As its name suggests, this is a converted boathouse on the banks of the river. Menus offer a simple choice of three starters, four main courses and a couple of sweets. Start, perhaps, with onion soup, advance to wild duck in honey, and finally push the boat out with Normandy apple pie. The wine list is a gem, with a faultless selection from impeccable sources. ⊂ Outstanding ☺

■ *Set L* £9·50	*L* 1–2.30
Set D £10·50	*D* 7.30–10
About £30 for two	*Parking* Ample
Seats 45 *Parties* 50	*Closed D* Sun & 1 wk Xmas

Restaurant Elizabeth   Oxford

R ♔ **Town plan B4** Oxfordshire
  85 St Aldates
Oxford (0865) 242230
Owner manager Antonio Lopez
Credit Access, Amex, Diners, Visa
  Antonio Lopez's intimate panelled restaurant which has run for 29 years, will soon become almost as much an Oxford institution as Christ Church College, which it faces. Chef Salvador Rodriguez sticks with a simple, classical style, letting the quality of ingredients and sound technique shine through a choice of dishes that has changed little over the years. Perennial favourites include pâté de foie de volaille, baked mussels, duck à l'orange, fillet steak with Madeira sauce and candied chestnuts in Kirsch. Typical sweets are an ever-popular crème brûlée, chocolate mousse and syllabub. A super classic cellar includes Hermitage La Chapelle 1961 and four great years of Grands Echezeaux from Domaine de la Romanee-Conti.

⊂ Outstanding ♀ Well-chosen ☺

■ *Set L* £11	*L* 12.30–2.30
About £50 for two	*D* 6.30–11, Sun 7–10.30
Seats 45 *Parties* 40	*Parking* Difficult
Closed Mon, Good Fri & 1 wk Xmas	

15 North Parade *NEW ENTRY*   Oxford

R ♧ & **Town plan B1** Oxfordshire
  15 North Parade
Oxford (0865) 513773
Credit Access, Amex, Diners, Visa. LVs
  Chef-proprietor Michael Yeadon offers his customers plenty of variety at this relaxing restaurant, where he cooks in the modern manner. Good-quality produce is capably handled in dishes like tartlet of quails' eggs, spinach and oyster mushrooms, breast of duck with a tasty chestnut sauce, and bombe Athol Brose (ours was a little too brittle). Vegetarian main course always available.

♀ Well-chosen ☺

■ *Set L* £7·50	*L* 12–2
About £40 for two	*D* 7–10.30
Seats 50	*Parking* Ample
Closed Mon, 1 Jan & last 2 wks Aug	

Ladbroke Linton Lodge Hotel   Oxford

H **65% £C**
Town plan B1 Oxfordshire
Linton Road OX2 6UJ
Oxford (0865) 53461. Tlx 837093
Credit Access, Amex, Diners, Visa
There's a busy conference trade at this friendly hotel just off Banbury Road. A small lounge with cane seating is a pleasant spot to relax, and there's an inviting bar and spacious garden.

Tasteful refurbishment has improved the bedrooms, which have remote-control TVs and neat modern bathrooms. *Amenities* garden, pool table, in-house movies (charge), laundry service, 24-hour lounge service.

■ *Rooms* 71	*Confirm by* 6
en suite bath/shower 71	*Last dinner* 9.30
Direct dial Yes	*Parking* Ample
Room TV Yes	*Room service* All day

■ Our inspectors never book in the name of Egon Ronay's Guides; they disclose their identity only after paying their bills.

Oxford Moat House   Oxford

H **60% £C/D**
Town plan A1 Oxfordshire
Wolvercote Roundabout OX2 8AL
Oxford (0865) 59933. Tlx 837925
Manager George Elliott
Credit Access, Amex, Diners, Visa
Impressive leisure facilities are the pride of this modern hotel north of the city centre. Public rooms provide plenty of space and comfort, particularly the open-plan foyer-lounge and combined bar, and there's a quieter, more intimate bar on the first floor. Bedrooms are of a good size with practical lightwood furnishings and

ample sitting and writing space. Eager-to-please staff; mediocre breakfasts from the buffet. *Amenities* garden, indoor swimming pool, sauna, solarium, whirlpool bath, keep-fit equipment, hairdressing, squash, pitch and putt, clay-pigeon shooting, games room, snooker, in-house movies (charge), laundry service, coffee shop (7am–midnight), 24-hour lounge service.

■ *Rooms* 155	*Confirm by* 6
en suite bath/shower 155	*Last dinner* 9.45
Direct dial Yes	*Parking* Ample
Room TV Yes	*Room service* Limited

Le Petit Blanc ★   Oxford

R ★ ♨ **Town plan B2** Oxfordshire
61a Banbury Road
Oxford (0865) 53540
French cooking
Credit Access, Visa
Frenchman Bruno Loubet is the culinary master at work in the kitchens of this delightful restaurant set in a splendid Victorian conservatory. His menus are full of interest and variety, with superb flavours and wonderfully delicate sauces complementing the finest of ingredients. Typical treats might include the innovative duck terrine served with a salad topped by home-made duck ham, braised brill sauced with old Madeira and celeriac or roast wood pigeon with a honey liqueur sauce and garnish of grapes and chicory. Exquisite sweets include a rich and stunning chocolate and hazelnut confection and home-made fresh fruit sorbets. Good French wines especially Ch. Simone Provence Rosé and Bandol Rouge 1982. Excellent coffee and petits fours.

Specialities borsch de pigeon gelé en terrine, court bouillon de lotte et grondin aux fleurs de safran, rognon de veau rôti pomme mousseline jus blond au persil, mille-feuille caramelisé d'agrumes. ♥ Well-chosen ⊖
■ *Set L from* £11·50	*L* 12.15–2.15
About £60 *for two*	*D* 7.15–10.15
Seats 65 *Parties* 80	*Parking* Limited
Closed L Wed, all Tues, 2 wks Xmas & 2 wks Aug/Sept

■ If we recommend meals in a hotel or inn, a separate entry is made for its restaurant.

OXFORD

Map 5 D2
Town plan opposite

Population 114,200

Despite the encroachment of industry, Oxford remains incomparable–except with Cambridge–as a centre of learning for 800 years, interrupted only by the disturbance of the Civil War siege in the 1640s. No city has more to offer the sightseer in its own architectural glories and the beauty of its surroundings–the Thames Valley, the Cotswolds and so much besides.

Annual Events
St Giles Fair *September*
Eights Week (5th week of University term)
Sheriff's Races *summer*

Sights Outside City
Blenheim Palace
Burford Village
Dorchester-on-Thames
Chipping Campden
Cogges Farm Museum
Cotswold Wild Life Park
Sulgrave Park
Waddesdon Manor

Information Centre
St Aldate's, Oxford OX1 1DY
Telephone Oxford 726871
Accommodation 726871
Guided Walking Tours 726871

Fiat Dealer
J. D. Barclay Ltd
Barclay House
Botley Road
Oxford OX2 0HQ
Tel. Oxford 722444

1 Apollo Theatre **B3**
2 Ashmolean Museum *art and archaeology treasures* **B3**
3 Bate Collection of Historical Musical Instruments **B4**
4 Botanic Garden *one of the oldest in the country* **C4**
5 Carfax Tower *viewpoint open in summer* **B4**
6 Christ Church Meadow **C5**
7 Coach Park **A4**
8 Divinity School *15th-c fine vaulted ceiling* **B3**
9 Folly Bridge **B5**
10 Martyrs' Memorial **B3**
11 Museum of History of Science **B3**
12 Museum of Oxford **B4**
13 Oxford Ice Rink **A4**
14 Oxford Information Centre **B4**
15 Oxford Story **B3**
16 Pitt Rivers Museum of Ethnology **B1/C2**
17 Playhouse **B3**
18 Sheldonian Theatre *Wren building for conferment of degrees* **B3**
19 Station **A3**
20 Town Hall **B4**
21 University Museum **B2**
22 University Parks **B/C1/2**

Oxford FIAT

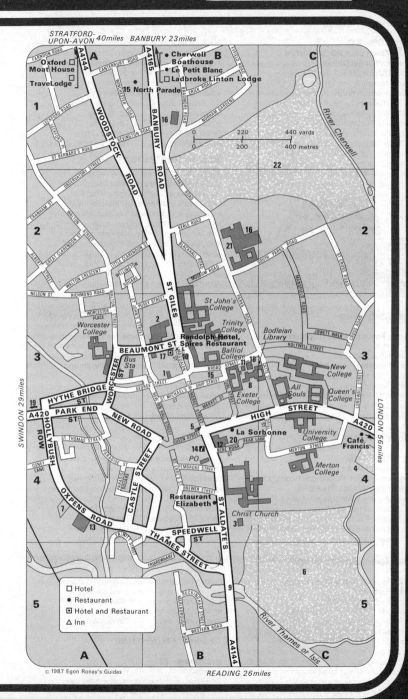

STRATFORD-UPON-AVON 40 miles   BANBURY 23 miles

Oxford Moat House
TraveLodge

● Cherwell Boathouse
□ Le Petit Blanc
□ Ladbroke Linton Lodge

15 North Parade

River Cherwell

0   220   440 yards
0   200   400 metres

22

21   16

St John's College

Worcester College

Trinity College

Bodleian Library

Randolph Hotel, Spires Restaurant

Balliol College

New College

BEAUMONT ST

Bus Sta

Exeter College

All Souls

Queen's College

HYTHE BRIDGE
PARK END
A420   ST
HOLLYBUSH ROW
NEW ROAD

La Sorbonne

HIGH   STREET   A420

University College

Café Francis

Merton College

CASTLE STREET

Restaurant Elizabeth

PO

Christ Church

OXPENS ROAD

THAMES STREET
SPEEDWELL ST

□ Hotel
● Restaurant
⊡ Hotel and Restaurant
△ Inn

READING 26 miles

SWINDON 29 miles

LONDON 56 miles

© 1987 Egon Ronay's Guides

Randolph Hotel   Oxford

HR **70% £C**
Town plan B3 Oxfordshire
Beaumont Street OX1 2LN
Oxford (0865) 247481. Tlx 83446
Credit Access, Amex, Diners, Visa. **LVs**

Situated opposite the Ashmolean Museum in
the heart of the city, this handsome Victorian
Gothic hotel offers outstanding service and
hospitality. The imposing entrance hall, manned
by helpful porters, leads to the reception area and
richly panelled club-like cocktail bar, then on to
the elegantly proportioned and beautifully
furnished lounge – a favourite spot for afternoon
tea. There is also a cheerful basement coffee
shop, plus excellent conference facilities.

Spacious bedrooms, all traditionally decorated to
a high standard, are provided with remote-control
TVs and other accessories; spotless en suite
bathrooms are also well equipped. There are two
luxurious suites. Good hearty breakfasts.
Amenities laundry service, coffee shop
(10.30am–10.30pm), 24-hour lounge service.

■ *Rooms* 109	*Confirm by* 6
en suite bath/shower 109	*Last dinner* 10
Direct dial Yes	*Parking* Limited
Room TV Yes	*Room service* 24 hours

Spires Restaurant ♔ &

A lofty, elegant restaurant overlooking the
Martyrs' Memorial. Stylish decor complements
adventurous, artistic cooking in menus that
balance new and traditional ideas: terrine of
asparagus and papaya with an avocado and lime
sauce, sole meunière, pastry-wrapped saddle of
hare with mango, lamb cutlets Reform. There's
always a vegetarian choice. Professional staff.
Good-value clarets. ℮

■ *Set L* £9	*L* 12.30–2.15
Set D £14	*D* 7–10
About £45 *for two*	*Seats* 80
Closed D 25 Dec	*Parties* 20

La Sorbonne   Oxford

R ♧ **Town plan B4** Oxfordshire
130A High Street
Oxford (0865) 241320
French cooking
Owner manager André P. Chevagnon
Credit Access, Amex, Diners, Visa

After 21 years, chef-patron André Chevagnon
remains in fine form at this comfortable restaurant
in a 17th-century building. His repertoire is

classical French, and specialities include soup au
pistou, quenelles lyonnaise and saddle of hare
sauce poivrade. Crêpes suzette and crème brûlée
are popular dessert choices. Fine clarets and
burgundies in the cellar. ℮

■ *Set L & D* £16	*L* 12–2.30
About £50 *for two*	*D* 7–11
Seats 60 *Parties* 30	*Parking* Difficult
Closed Bank Hols & 1 wk Xmas	

TraveLodge   Oxford

H **56% £D/E**
Town Plan A1 Oxfordshire
Peartree R/about, Woodstock Road OX2 8JZ
Oxford (0865) 54301. Tlx 83202
Credit Access, Amex, Diners, Visa

Children are made especially welcome at this
modern motel in a service area at the junction of
the A34 and A43. Public rooms in contemporary
style include a lounge and bar. Two-storey

accommodation blocks house spacious and well-
designed bedrooms with tiled bathrooms.
Breakfasts are served in the nearby Carvery
restaurant. *Amenities* garden, outdoor swimming
pool, laundry service.

■ *Rooms* 100	*Confirm by* 6
en suite bath/shower 100	*Last dinner* 10
Direct dial Yes	*Parking* Ample
Room TV Yes	*Room service* None

Seafood Restaurant   Padstow

RR ♧ & **Map 2 B3** Cornwall
Riverside
Padstow (0841) 532485
Seafood
Credit Access, Amex, Diners, Visa

Richard and Jill Stein run this bright and airy
quayside restaurant, complete with new
conservatory extension. Richard takes care of the
food, offering delights like aromatic bourride of
salt cod, salmon with sorrel sauce and a gratin of
monkfish, sole, prawns and scallops. Another
great favourite is a mighty platter of seafood
served on the shell. Some meat dishes, too, and

imaginative sweets lime ice cream in puff pastry
with wine-poached pears. Good drinking,
especially burgundies. ♀ Well-chosen ℮

■ *Set D* £13·95	*D only* 7.30–9.30
About £45 *for two*	*Parking* Ample
Seats 75	
Closed Sun & 13 Dec–16 Mar	

Bedrooms £F

Rooms 8	*With bath/shower* 8

Simply decorated bedrooms, all with harbour
views, have antique furnishings, TVs and good
private bathrooms.

Palace Hotel   Paignton

H 60% £C/D
Map 3 D3 Devon
Esplanade Road TQ4 6BJ
Paignton (0803) 555121
Credit Access, Amex, Diners, Visa

Families find much to offer at this grand hotel near the pier. Its strength lies in extensive leisure facilities, well-equipped contemporary bedrooms, and modern bathrooms. Pillared public areas

include an ample furnished lounge and spacious bar. *Amenities* garden, outdoor swimming pool, sauna, solarium, whirlpool bath, gymnasium, beauty salon, tennis, squash, games room, pool table, 24-hour lounge service, children's play area.

■ *Rooms* 54	*Confirm by* 6
en suite bath/shower 54	*Last dinner* 8.45
Room phone Yes	*Parking* Ample
Room TV Yes	*Room service* 24 hours

Redcliffe Hotel   Paignton

H 60% £D/E
Map 3 D3 Devon
Marine Drive TQ3 2NL
Paignton (0803) 526397
Owner managers Twigger family
Credit Access, Amex, Visa

New paint and carpets have spruced up this seaside hotel, whose architecture was inspired by an Indian palace. The main lounge affords fine

views over the bay, and a subterranean passage leads to the beach. Bedrooms are neat, practical and modern. No dogs. *Amenities* garden, outdoor swimming pool, hairdressing, putting, games room, 24-hour lounge service.

■ *Rooms* 63	*Confirm by arrang.*
en suite bath/shower 63	*Last dinner* 8.30
Direct dial Yes	*Parking* Ample
Room TV Yes	*Room service* 24 hours

Painswick Hotel   Painswick

H 67% £C/D
Map 4 B2 Gloucestershire
Kemps Lane G16 6YB
Painswick (0452) 812160. Tlx 43605
Owner manager Jacqueline Ash
Credit Access, Amex, Diners, Visa

The chief charm of this secluded former vicarage resides in the delightful mother and daughter team that runs it. It's a pleasure to

unwind in the richly panelled bar or upstairs lounge with its comfy sofas and baby grand. Comfortable bedrooms are divided between the main house and the more modern extension. *Amenities* garden, croquet, laundry service.

■ *Rooms* 15	*Confirm by arrang.*
en suite bath/shower 15	*Last dinner* 9.30
Direct dial Yes	*Parking* Ample
Room TV Yes	*Room service* All day

Copper Inn   Pangbourne

HR 66% £D
Map 5 D2 Berkshire
Church Road RG8 7AR
Pangbourne (073 57) 2244. Tlx 849041
Manager Michel Rosso
Credit Access, Amex, Diners, Visa

An agreeably civilised middle-of-town hotel, this has more than a little style behind its 19th-century coaching inn frontage. There is a modern-style foyer-lounge, a traditional main lounge and a beamed public bar with an open fire. Bedrooms, too, are in various styles, the best and brightest being those in the garden wing. No dogs. *Amenities* garden, laundry service.

■ *Rooms* 21	*Confirm by* 6
en suite bath/shower 21	*Last dinner* 9.30, Sun 9
Direct dial Yes	*Parking* Limited
Room TV Yes	*Room service* All day

Copper Inn Restaurant

The food really tastes of something in this pleasantly appointed restaurant, where capable cooking is matched by smart, attentive service. Typifying the interesting, varied choice are pastry case of Cornish mussels with saffron; a trio of game with egg noodles; and pork cutlet with garden herbs and raspberry sauce. Excellent vegetarian dishes and a selection of fine traditional British farmhouse cheeses are also available. There's a roomy lounge for enjoying a pre-prandial drink. ☺

■ *Set L from* £10·75	*L* 12.30–2
About £55 for two	*D* 7.30–9, Fri & Sat
Seats 50 *Parties* 50	7.30–10, Sun 7.30–9
Closed 25 & 26 Dec	

Ship Hotel   Parkgate

H 57% £D/E
Map 10 A2 Cheshire
The Parade, Wirral L64 6SA
051-336 3931
Credit Access, Amex, Diners, Visa

Built in the early 19th century, this black-and-white hotel overlooks the Dee Estuary and its abundant birdlife. Day rooms are fairly modest, but the bedrooms are much better: nearly all have

recently been done out in attractive pastel shades and sport solid wooden furnishings. Two club rooms are larger, with four-posters and various extras. Friendly staff. *Amenities* laundry service, coffee shop (10am–10pm summer only).

■ *Rooms* 26	*Confirm by* 6
en suite bath/shower 26	*Last dinner* 9.30
Room phone Yes	*Parking* Ample
Room TV Yes	*Room service* Limited

Cornish Arms   Pendoggett

IR £F
Map 2 B3 Cornwall
St Kew, Nr Port Isaac PL30 3HH
Bodmin (0208) 880263
Owner managers Nigel Pickstone & Margaret &
Alan Wainwright
Credit Access, Amex, Diners, Visa
   The bars of this delightful inn on the B3314
ooze atmosphere with their worn slate floor,
blackened woodwork and gleaming brass. Warm,
comfortable bedrooms have good solid Regency-
style furnishings. Excellent service. No children
under 14. *Amenities* garden.

■ *Rooms* 7	*Confirm by arrang.*
en suite bath/shower 5	*Last dinner* 8.45
Room phone No •	*Parking Ample*
Room TV No	*Room service* Limited
Closed 24–26 Dec	

Cornish Arms Restaurant

Just 30 covers (so booking's a must) in this little
beamed dining room simply furnished with plain
wooden chairs and benches. The cooking and
service are very homely, and the dishes to go for
are the plain ones like grilled sole, delicious fresh
sea trout poached in wine or one of a variety of
steaks. Fine vegetables are served in abundance,
and for pud there's fruit pie, an excellent locally
made ice cream and a treacle tart. Good service
from friendly, willing staff. Traditional lunch on
Sunday; buffet luncheon available at the bar
during the rest of the week. ☺

■ *About £30 for two*	*L Sun only* 12.30–1.45
Seats 30	*D* 7.15–8.45
Closed 25 Dec	

North Lakes Gateway Hotel *NEW ENTRY*   Penrith

H 72% £C/D ♿
Map 13 D5 Cumbria
Ullswater Road CA11 8QT
Penrith (0768) 68111. Tlx 64257
Credit Access, Amex, Diners, Visa
   High standard of accommodation in a purpose-
built hotel literally one minute from the M6
(junction 40). The design theme is a Scandinavian
hunting lodge, and natural stone and wood are
used liberally and to stylish effect in the large,
comfortable public areas, like the foyer with its
pitched pine floor, or the Stag bar with its oak
furniture. Bedrooms, situated beyond the leisure
club, are equipped with trouser presses,
hairdryers and tea-making facilities, along with
satellite TVs and videos; all have excellent
bathrooms. The 12 Executive rooms are larger,
with sitting areas and various extras.

Amenities garden, indoor swimming pool, sauna,
solarium, whirlpool bath, keep-fit equipment,
squash, in-house movies (free), laundry service.

■ *Rooms* 57	*Confirm by* 6
en suite bath/shower 57	*Last dinner* 9.45
Direct dial Yes	*Parking Ample*
Room TV Yes	*Room service* 24 hours

☞ is our symbol for an **outstanding** wine list.

Abbey Hotel   Penzance

HR 66% £D/E
Map 2 A4 Cornwall
Abbey Street TR18 4AR
Penzance (0736) 66906
Owner managers Jean & Michael Cox
   A warm welcome is provided at this delightful
little hotel, dating from 1660. A curved staircase in
the entrance hall leads to the comfortable book-
lined drawing room, filled with fresh flowers and all
manner of ornaments. Good-sized bedrooms are
individually decorated, most with antique
furniture.
Amenities garden.

■ *Rooms* 6	*Confirm by arrang.*
en suite bath/shower 4	*Last dinner* 8.30
Room phone No	*Parking Limited*
Room TV Yes	*Room service* None
Closed 2 wks Jan	

Abbey Hotel Restaurant

An attractive dining room dominated by an open
fireplace, where guests dine by soft candlelight.
The choice is limited but offers simple, well-
executed dishes such as creamy vegetable soup,
mushrooms à la grècque, tarragon chicken, and
excellent seafood gratin. Prime, fresh ingredients,
careful seasoning and subtle flavouring are all
very much in evidence here. Finish perhaps with a
treacle tart or a choice of home-made ice creams
and good strong coffee, served upstairs in the
lounge. Booking essential.

■ *Set D £11·50*	*D only* 7.30–8.30
About £33 for two	*Seats* 20
Closed 2 wks Jan	*Parties* 20

Penzance ▶

Berkeley
Penzance

R ♗ **Map 2 A4** Cornwall
Abbey Street TR18 4AW
Penzance (0736) 62541
Owner managers Ian & Denise Morris
Credit Access, Amex, Visa

English and Italian dishes form the basis of the menu at the Morris family's nostalgic '30s-style restaurant. Start with red bean and tuna salad or garlic mushrooms topped with crab then choose from Dover sole, steak and kidney pie or sirloin with Meaux mustard. Also popular are breast of chicken fried in butter with sage and tortelloni filled with meat, mortadella and herbs. Last orders 10.30 followed by dancing until 1am. ℮

■ *About £34 for two* *D only 7.30–1am*
Seats 30 Parties 30 *Parking Limited*
Closed Sun, also Mon–Wed Oct–May, Good Fri & 25 & 26 Dec

Harris's
Penzance

R ♗ **Map 2 A4** Cornwall
46 New Street
Penzance (0736) 64408
Credit Access, Amex, Diners, Visa

It is worth ferreting out this tiny restaurant in a lane off the main street. Roger Harris has a successful formula: he keeps his menu simple, cooks with considerable care and makes fine use of local fish and vegetables. His onion soup is delicious and the poached salmon meltingly tender. Well-made sweets or Stilton to follow. Light lunches except by arrangement. Booking advised. ℮

■ *About £37 for two* *L 12–1.45*
Seats 50 *D 7–10*
Parties 30 *Parking Ample*
Closed Sun, also Mon Nov–1 May, Bank Hols exc. Good Fri & Easter Mon, 1 wk April & 2 wks Nov

Higher Faugan Hotel
Penzance

H **65% £D/E**
Map 2 A4 Cornwall
Newlyn TR18 5NS
Penzance (0736) 62076
Owner managers Mr & Mrs M. Young
Credit Access, Amex, Diners, Visa

A private drive leads from the B3315 to this turn-of-the-century house, whose owners set high standards of hospitality and housekeeping. Day rooms are homely and relaxing, and bedrooms are individually decorated with simple good taste. No dogs. *Amenities* garden, outdoor swimming pool, tennis, putting, games room, snooker.

■ *Rooms 11* *Confirm by arrang.*
en suite bath/shower 11 *Last dinner 8*
Direct dial Yes *Parking Ample*
Room TV Yes *Room service All day*
Closed 28 Sept–mid Mar

■ Any person using our name to obtain free hospitality is a fraud. Proprietors, please inform the police and us.

Crest Hotel
Peterborough

H **60% £D/E** &
Map 6 A2 Cambridgeshire
Great North Road, Norman Cross PE7 3TB
Peterborough (0733) 240209. Tlx 32576
Credit Access, Amex, Diners, Visa. LVs

A low-rise modern hotel beside the A1, ideal for overnight stops. Open-plan public rooms are in a smart, contemporary style, with tall plants screening the bar. Spacious, double-glazed bedrooms, with restful brown decor, are equipped with tea-makers, trouser presses, and small shower/bathrooms. *Amenities* garden, games room, in-house movies (charge), laundry service, coffee shop (9.30am–6.30pm).

■ *Rooms 97* *Confirm by 6*
en suite bath/shower 97 *Last dinner 10*
Direct dial Yes *Parking Ample*
Room TV Yes *Room service 24 hours*

Peterborough Moat House
Peterborough

H **63% £D/E**
Map 6 A2 Cambridgeshire
Thorpe Wood PE3 6SG
Peterborough (0733) 260000. Tlx 32708
Credit Access, Amex, Diners, Visa

Business people are well catered for at this friendly modern hotel just off the ring road. The spacious lobby-lounge has plenty of comfortable chairs, and there are two bars plus an outdoor area for summer. Bedrooms are uniform in style, with low-key colour schemes, practical units, and functional bathrooms. There are also four Executive suites. *Amenities* garden, putting, laundry service, teletext.

■ *Rooms 98* *Confirm by arrang.*
en suite bath/shower 98 *Last dinner 10*
Direct dial Yes *Parking Ample*
Room TV Yes *Room service Limited*

Langrish House · Petersfield

H **63% £E**
Map 5 D3 Hampshire
Langrish
Petersfield (0730) 66941
Owner manager Miss S. M. von Kospoth
Credit Access, Amex, Diners
  Service is personal, friendly and informal at this nice old Tudor mansion set in peaceful parkland. Most of the public areas are in the basement, which leaves some of the ground floor free for accommodation. Bedrooms here and on the first floor are very roomy, those above somewhat smaller. Note the use of pretty coordinating fabrics. No dogs. *Amenities* garden.

■ *Rooms* 14	*Confirm by arrang.*
en suite bath/shower 14	*Last dinner 9.30*
Direct dial Yes	*Parking Ample*
Room TV Yes	*Room service All day*

Duck Inn · Pett Bottom

See under Bridge

Perkins Bar Bistro · Plumtree

R ⑨ & **Map 11 D3** Nottinghamshire
Station Road NG12 5NA
Plumtree (060 77) 3695
Credit Access, Amex
  Tony and Wendy Perkins run a very successful operation here in a cleverly converted railway station near Nottingham. Blackboard menus change according to season. Cooking is skilled and consistent throughout the meal from starters like sautéed chicken livers to baby squid meunière or steak à la minute béarnaise. Super saucing and fine seasoning are notable features. Good choice of sweets, and an outstanding welcome, followed by charming, efficient service are guaranteed, too. ♀ Well-chosen ℮

■ *About £27 for two*	*L 12–2 D 7–9.45*
Seats 63 Parties 20	*Parking Ample*
Closed Sun, Mon, 1 Jan & 25 & 26 Dec	

Astor Hotel · Plymouth

H **60% £D/E**
Map 2 C3 Devon
14 Elliott Street, The Hoe PL1 2PS
Plymouth (0752) 225511. Tlx 45652
Manager Mr M. A. Kelly
Credit Access, Amex, Diners, Visa
  A welcoming late-Victorian hotel near the Hoe. Chandeliers and moulded cornices grace loftily elegant public areas like the comfortable foyer-lounge and formal bar. Bedrooms are simpler, but all of good size, with practical fitted units, candlewick bedspreads and modern bath or shower rooms. No dogs. *Amenities* laundry service, 24-hour lounge service.

■ *Rooms* 56	*Confirm by 6*
en suite bath/shower 56	*Last dinner 9.30*
Direct dial Yes	*Parking Limited*
Room TV Yes	*Room service 24 hours*

Chez Nous · Plymouth

R ⑨ & **Map 2 C3** Devon
13 Frankfort Gate
Plymouth (0752) 266793
French cooking
Credit Access, Amex, Diners, Visa
  Tucked away in a shopping precinct, Chez Nous doesn't shout to the world, but seek it out, because it's a very good French restaurant. Very popular, too, for Jacques Marchal's blackboard menu (deciphered by able wife Suzanne) is packed full of interest, and the cooking lives up to it. Fresh fish is the basis of lovely dishes like fillet of brill with a coulis of red pimento; offal finds tempting varieties like ox tongue with saffron rice; duck comes with green butter rather than a fruit-based sauce; sweets include home-made ices and a superb marble gâteau with white and dark chocolate and coffee bean sauce. Post-theatre suppers available. Fine clarets: Ch. Montrose 1961 and excellent burgundies: Nuits St Georges Les Roncières (Grivot) 1982. ♀ Well-chosen ℮

■ *Set L & D £15*	*L 12.30–2*
About £50 for two	*D 7–10.30*
Seats 30 Parties 30	*Parking Limited*
Closed Sun, Mon, Bank Hols, 1st 15 days Feb & 1st 15 days Sept	

China Garden · Plymouth

R ⑨ **Map 2 C3** Devon
17 Derry's Cross
Plymouth (0752) 664472
Chinese cooking
Credit Access, Amex, Diners, Visa
  Chef Kai Ching Ng practises the traditional art of Northern Chinese cooking at this popular city centre restaurant. Good-quality raw materials are handled sympathetically in starters like fried squid, braised jumbo prawns with ginger and spring onion, and main courses such as crispy duck in wheaten pancakes, and sizzling beef and chilli. Book at weekends.

■ *Set L £4*	*L 12–2.30*
Set D £9	*D 6–11.30, Fri & Sat*
About £30 for two	*6–12, Sun 6–11*
Seats 160 Parties 80	*Parking Ample*
Closed L Sun, 25 & 26 Dec	

Copthorne Hotel   *NEW ENTRY*   Plymouth

H **70% £B** *E* &
Map 2 **C3** Devon
Armada Centre, Armada Way PL1 1AR
Plymouth (0752) 224161. Tlx 45756
Credit Access, Amex, Diners, Visa

Follow the ferry signs and they'll take you to this brand new hotel, which stands by a roundabout at Armada Way. The pleasantly designed reception is well supplied with comfortable leather seats and there's a stylish bar with marble-topped tables and Victorian prints. The main restaurant is themed on London's Burlington Arcade. Bedrooms are decorated in easy-on-the-eye russet tones, with lightwood fitted furniture providing good desk/dressing table space. Remote-control TVs, trouser presses, tea-makers and hairdryers are standard, and fully-tiled bathrooms have large mirrors and plentiful

toiletries. *Amenities* plunge pool with jet stream, keep-fit equipment, pool table, in-house movies (charge), laundry service, coffee shop (10.30am–10.30pm).

■ *Rooms* 135 — *Confirm by* 6
en suite bath/shower 135 — *Last dinner* 10.30
Direct dial Yes — *Parking* Ample
Room TV Yes — *Room service* 24 hours

Duke of Cornwall Hotel   Plymouth

H **57% £E**
Map 2 **C3** Devon
Millbay Road PL1 3LG
Plymouth (0752) 266256. Tlx 45424
Owner manager Mr McDermott-Brown
Credit Access, Amex, Diners, Visa. LVs

A fine Victorian Gothic building with a traditional atmosphere. Tartan carpets contribute to the Scottish theme in the wood-panelled Clan

Bar, and there are other bars and a lounge with plenty of easy chairs. The modestly comfortable bedrooms vary considerably. *Amenities* laundry service, 24-hour lounge service.

■ *Rooms* 67 — *Confirm by* 6
en suite bath/shower 67 — *Last dinner* 9
Room phone Yes — *Parking* Ample
Room TV Yes — *Room service* 24 hours
Closed 1 Jan, 25 & 26 Dec

Green Lanterns   Plymouth

R Map 2 **C3** Devon
31 New Street, Barbican
Plymouth (0752) 660852
English cooking
Owner managers Sally Russell & Kenneth Pappin
Credit Access, Amex, Diners, Visa

A 16th-century eating house in the old part of town. The menu befits the surroundings, offering a tasty selection of traditional English fare from

bacon-wrapped sausages and hubble-bubble (a sort of bubble and squeak with egg and cheese) to cod casserole, roast duck with marmalade-flavoured gravy and rich, robust game stew. Lots of nice puds. Less lunchtime choice. ⊖

■ *Set L* £5 — *L* 11.45–2.15
About £36 *for two* — *D* 6.30–10.45
Seats 35 *Parties* 30 — *Parking* Limited
Closed Sun, 1 Jan & 25 & 26 Dec

Holiday Inn   Plymouth

H **70% £C/D** *E* &
Map 2 **C3** Devon
Armada Way PL1 2HJ
Plymouth (0752) 662866. Tlx 45637
Credit Access, Amex, Diners, Visa

A 12-storey tower block, and of course the higher you go the better the view. Best of all is the outlook from the Penthouse Restaurant where breakfast may be taken. The foyer is large, with comfortable seating, and there's a pleasant lobby bar which has a good deal more atmosphere than the rather characterless residents' lounge. Bedrooms, simply but quite attractively decorated, offer generous-sized beds, plenty of space including a desk area and ample clothes-hanging. Hairdryers and trouser presses are standard. The fifth floor is given over to non-smoking rooms. *Amenities* indoor swimming pool,

sauna, solarium, keep-fit equipment, games room, snooker, in-house movies (two free), laundry service, coffee shop (7am–11pm), 24-hour lounge service.

■ *Rooms* 217 — *Confirm by arrang.*
en suite bath/shower 217 — *Last dinner* 11
Direct dial Yes — *Parking* Ample
Room TV Yes — *Room service* 24 hours

Mayflower Post House Hotel · Plymouth

H **67% £C/D**
Map 2 C3 Devon
Cliff Road, The Hoe PL1 3DL
Plymouth (0752) 662828. Tlx 45442
Credit Access, Amex, Diners, Visa. LVs
 Splendid views across Plymouth Sound are an outstanding feature of this ten-storey modern hotel. Day rooms like the comfortable lounge and revamped bar are bright and stylish. Much-improved bedrooms sport attractive fabrics and dark-stained unit furniture. *Amenities* terrace, outdoor swimming pool, laundry service, coffee shop (7am–9.30pm, 8pm in winter), 24-hour lounge service, children's playground.

■ *Rooms 106*	*Confirm by 6*
en suite bath/shower 106	*Last dinner 10.30*
Direct dial Yes	*Parking Ample*
Room TV Yes	*Room service Limited*

Novotel · Plymouth

H **62% £D** ⴕ
Map 2 C3 Devon
Marsh Mills Roundabout PL6 8NH
Plymouth (0752) 221422. Tlx 45711
Manager Mr P. Naneix
Credit Access, Amex, Diners, Visa
 By a roundabout on the A38, this five-year-old hotel offers practical overnight accommodation. Decent-sized bedrooms have private bathrooms with separate WCs. There's a roomy foyer-lounge (shame about the games machine) and leafy bar. *Amenities* garden, outdoor swimming pool, games room, snooker, in-house movies (free), laundry service, 24-hour lounge service.

■ *Rooms 101*	*Confirm by arrang.*
en suite bath/shower 101	*Last dinner 11.30*
Direct dial Yes	*Parking Ample*
Room TV Yes	*Room service limited*

■ For a discount on next year's guide, see Offer for Answers.

Feathers Hotel · Pocklington

I **£E**
Map 11 E1 Humberside
56 Market Place YO4 2UN
Pocklington (0759) 303155
Credit Access, Amex, Diners, Visa
 There has been an inn on this market place site since Elizabethan times, and the present occupant offers attractive, very comfortable accommodation. Main-house bedrooms are in traditional style; those in a chalet block across the car park have modern units. All have hairdryers, trouser presses, tea-makers and well-kept bathrooms. An open fire warms the large inviting lounge bar. No dogs.

■ *Rooms 12*	*Confirm by 6*
en suite bath/shower 12	*Last dinner 9.30*
Room phone Yes	*Parking Ample*
Room TV Yes	*Room service None*

Kitchen at Polperro · Polperro

R ⴑ **Map 2 C3** Cornwall
Fish Na Bridge
Polperro (0503) 72780
Credit Access, Amex, Diners, Visa
 Fixed-price menus meet most needs at this cheerful restaurant on the 'walk' into Polperro. A typical meal from chef-patron Ian Bateson might comprise Cornish smoked sausage, followed by goujons of monkfish with a crisp salad, with a lovely bread pudding to finish. There are also vegetarian and children's menus. Honest cooking with good local ingredients. ©

■ *Set L £5·45*	*L 12–2.30*
Set D £8.95	*D 6.30–10*
About £35 for two	*Parking Ample*
Closed Mon exc. Bank Hols; Sun spring & autumn	
exc. Bank Hol weekends & Sun–Thurs Nov–late	
March excl. Xmas	

■ Our inspectors are our full-time employees; they are professionally trained by us.

Pool Court ★

RR ★ ㋤㋤ **Map 10 C1** West Yorkshire
Nr Otley LS21 1EH
Arthington (0532) 842288
Owner managers Hanni & Michael Gill
Credit Access, Amex, Diners, Visa

In this elegant Georgian dining room chef
Melvin Jordan offers fine dishes like scallops and
mussels in a pastry shell, or venison on a bed of
beans with a rich game and redcurrant gravy.
Exemplary service. Superb cellar, with clarets
back to Ch. Ducru-Beaucaillou 1961.
Specialities hot sea trout and spinach strudel,
veal sweetbreads and onion Yorkshire pudding,
Lancashire duckling with pulses and tiny spinach
dumplings, rose petal ice cream.
▭ Outstanding ㋡

■ *Set D from £10* *L by arrang. only*
About £60 for two *D 7–10*
Seats 65 Parties 24 *Parking Ample*
*Closed Sun, Mon, last wk July, 1st wk Aug
& 10 days Xmas*

Bedrooms £B/C
Rooms 4 *With bath/shower 4*
If the eating is excellent, the accommodation is
outstanding. Bedrooms are individually and
sumptuously appointed, all with fine fabrics and
furnishings and innumerable cosseting extras,
plus up-to-the-minute accessories like wall safes,
drinks fridges and codable electronic door locks.
Bathrooms are no less impressive. No dogs.

Hospitality Inn, The Quay

H 70% £D *E*
Map 4 C4 Dorset
The Quay BH15 1HJ
Poole (0202) 671200. Tlx 418374
Manager Mr A. D. Marchesi
Credit Access, Amex, Diners, Visa

Standing on the quayside close to Poole's
famous pottery, this sleek, ultra-modern red-brick
hotel caters especially well for the business
visitor. Accommodation is first rate, with double
beds and sofa-beds, desks and tables standard in
all the good-sized bedrooms which are fitted with
sturdy wooden free-standing furniture. Direct-dial
telephones, trouser presses and magazines are
among the many accessories, and the well-fitted
smartly tiled bathrooms boast super-efficient
showers. Downstairs, day rooms include the pine-
panelled Anchor Bar with harbour views, a lounge

and adjoining softly lit cocktail bar.
Amenities in-house movies (free).
■ *Rooms 68* *Confirm by 6*
en suite bath/shower 68 *Last dinner 9.45*
Direct dial Yes *Parking Ample*
Room TV Yes *Room service 24 hours*

Mansion House

HR 74% £ *D/E*
Map 4 C4 Dorset
Thames Street BH15 1JN
Poole (0202) 685666. Tlx 41495
Owner managers Mr & Mrs R. Leonard
Credit Access, Amex, Diners, Visa

Few hotel bedrooms are as comprehensively
kitted out as the ones in this fine Georgian town
house, which is peacefully situated a short
distance from the quay. The list of extras includes

fresh fruit and sherry, potted plants and books,
trouser presses and hairdryers, all making for
rooms of charm and homeliness. Decor is cosy,
and bathrooms are also superbly equipped.
Notable in the public areas are a splendid
sweeping staircase, a characterful bar with
beams and brickwork and an elegant lounge with
antiques, chintz and panelling. No children under
eight. *Amenities* laundry service.
■ *Rooms 19* *Confirm by arrang.*
en suite bath/shower 19 *Last dinner 10.15*
Direct dial Yes *Parking Ample*
Room TV Yes *Room service All day*
Closed 10 days Xmas

Mansion House
Restaurant ㋤

A smart panelled restaurant where non-residents
must pay a cover charge of £3. Jackets and ties
are de rigueur, booking essential. Chef Tony
Parsons copes superbly well with a wide choice of
fairly unadventurous dishes, from delicately

sauced local seafood with dill served in a pastry case, to chicken Kiev, loin of venison or lamb's kidneys with sherry sauce. Blackcurrant bavarois is a delicious dessert. ♀ Well-chosen ©

■ *Set L from £6*
Set D from £12.95
About £50 for two
Closed L Sat & 10 days Xmas

L 12.30–2.15
D 7.30–10
Seats 80 Parties 32

Lugger Hotel   Portloe

H **58% £D/E**
Map 2 B3 Cornwall
Nr Truro TR2 5RD
Truro (0872) 501322
Owner managers Powell family
Credit Access, Amex, Diners, Visa
    Smugglers' tales seem very plausible in the beamed bar and cosy lounge of this 17th-century inn overlooking a rugged cove. Comfortable,

cottage bedrooms (larger in the annexe) have tea-makers and smartly tiled bathrooms. Half-board only. No children under 12. No dogs.
Amenities sauna, solarium, laundry service.
■ *Rooms 20*   *Confirm by 5*
en suite bath/shower 20   *Last dinner 9*
Direct dial Yes   *Parking Ample*
Room TV Yes   *Room service All day*
Closed mid Nov to early Mar

■ We welcome complaints and bona fide recommendations on the tear-out pages for readers' comments. They are followed up by our professional team. Please also complain to the management instantly.

RECEPTION

Crest Hotel   Portsmouth

H **64% £C/D** &
Map 5 D4 Hampshire
Pembroke Road, Southsea PO1 2TA
Portsmouth (0705) 827651. Tlx 827651
Credit Access, Amex, Diners, Visa
    This modern brick-built hotel is handily situated on the seafront close to the hovercraft terminal, railway station and the local maritime sights. Public rooms include a foyer lounge with plenty of

pastel-coloured sofas, and a smart coffee shop. Bedrooms vary in style. All rooms have trouser presses, tea-makers and compact tiled bathrooms. *Amenities* laundry service, games room (weekends).
■ *Rooms 165*   *Confirm by 6*
en suite bath/shower 165   *Last dinner 9.45*
Direct dial Yes   *Parking Ample*
Room TV Yes   *Room service 24 hours*

Holiday Inn   Portsmouth

H **77% £B/C** *E* &
Map 5 D4 Hampshire
North Harbour, Cosham PO6 4SH
Portsmouth (0705) 383151. Tlx 86611
Credit Access, Amex, Diners, Visa
    Constant updating and reorganization make for high standards at this smart modern hotel on the northern edge of the city. The already impressive conference facilities have been extended and the leisure centre has had a complete face-lift. Comfortable sofas are dotted about the airy foyer and there's a stylish open-plan cocktail lounge. Spacious, newly recarpeted bedrooms, all with individual heating/air conditioning controls, offer trouser presses, hairdryers and bathroom radio speakers.
Amenities garden, indoor swimming pool, sauna, solarium, whirlpool bath, gymnasium, squash,

games room, pool table, in-house movies (free), laundry service, coffee shop (7am–11pm), 24-hour lounge service, kiosk, children's playground, courtesy coach.
■ *Rooms 170*   *Confirm by 6*
en suite bath/shower 170   *Last dinner 10.45*
Direct dial Yes   *Parking Ample*
Room TV Yes   *Room service 24 hours*

Hospitality Inn   Portsmouth

H **63% £D/E**
Map 5 D4 Hampshire
South Parade, Southsea PO4 0RN
Portsmouth (0705) 731281. Tlx 86719
Credit Access, Amex, Diners, Visa
    Right opposite the esplanade, this sympathetically restored Victorian hotel combines period elegance – glittering chandeliers, ornate mouldings, mahogany panelling – with

contemporary design throughout its handsome public areas. Spacious bedrooms are mostly traditionally furnished, though some have attractive light wood units. *Amenities* laundry service, 24-hour lounge service.
■ *Rooms 115*   *Confirm by 6*
en suite bath/shower 115   *Last dinner 9.45*
Direct dial Yes   *Parking Limited*
Room TV Yes   *Room service 24 hours*

Pendragon Hotel   Portsmouth

H **59% £C/D**
Map 5 D4 Hampshire
Clarence Parade, Southsea PO5 2HY
Portsmouth (0705) 823201. Tlx 86376
Credit Access, Amex, Diners, Visa
  The views of the Solent are a pleasant feature
of this Victorian hotel. Spacious front bedrooms
take best advantage of the setting, but the
Superior and Executive rooms are mainly at the
back. The nine Executive rooms are the most
stylish, with their smart modern Italian furniture.
All rooms have private bathrooms and remote-
control TVs. Day rooms are next in line for
improvement. *Amenities* laundry service.

■ *Rooms 49*	*Confirm by 6*
en suite bath/shower 49	*Last dinner 9*
Room phone Yes	*Parking Limited*
Room TV Yes	*Room service 24 hours*

Breamish House Hotel   Powburn

HR **69% £E**
Map 15 B3 Northumberland
Nr Alnwick NE66 4LL
Powburn (066 578) 266
Owner manager Graham Taylor
  Set back off the A697 at the foot of the Cheviot
Hills, this is a peaceful hotel built in elegant
Georgian style. Antiques and ornaments grace
the inviting lounge with its marble fireplace.
Comfortable bedrooms offer many thoughtful
extras, and their smart modern bathrooms are
equally well equipped. No children under 12.
Amenities garden, croquet.

■ *Rooms 10*	*Confirm by arrang.*
en suite bath/shower 10	*Last dinner 8.30*
Room phone Yes	*Parking Ample*
Room TV Yes	*Room service Limited*
Closed Jan	

Breamish House Hotel
Restaurant ♨ ♧ ♿

English cooking
Set dinner menus show skill and imagination
throughout their five nicely balanced courses at
this welcoming dining room which is warmed by a
log fire in winter. Smoked cod's roe pâté and
cream of fennel soup might start your meal, while
guinea fowl cooked with apple, walnuts and cider,
or sea trout stuffed with lemon and watercress
typify the choice of main courses. Sweets are rich
and irresistible, and there's a roast on Sundays.
♀ Well-chosen ⊟

■ *Set L £9*	*L Sun only at 1*
Set D £15	*D 7.30 for 8*
About £39 for two	*Seats 30*
Closed Jan	

Bridge Hotel   Prestbury

I **£D/E**
Map 10 B2 Cheshire
New Road, Nr Macclesfield SK10 4DQ
Prestbury (0625) 829326
Owner managers Whiteside & Grange families
Credit Access, Amex, Diners, Visa
  A cluster of 17th-century cottages were
tastefully converted to create this delightful inn
set between the parish church and the river.
Long-serving staff maintain high standards of
service. A spacious lounge leads to the terraced
garden. Upstairs bedrooms have a cottage appeal.
No dogs. *Amenities* garden, laundry service.

■ *Rooms 6*	*Confirm by arrang.*
en suite bath/shower 6	*Last dinner 9.45*
Direct dial Yes	*Parking Ample*
Room TV Yes	*Room service All day*
Closed Good Fri	

Crest Hotel   Preston

H **63% £C/D**
Map 10 A1 Lancashire
The Ringway PR1 3AU
Preston (0772) 59411. Tlx 677147
Credit Access, Amex, Diners, Visa. **LVs**
  A modern multi-storey hotel standing in the
centre of Preston. Reception is on the first floor,
adjoining bar, lounge and restaurant; on the
ground floor is a vibrant disco-themed public bar.
Bedrooms are smallish but carefully designed,
with decent wooden units and well-coordinated
colour schemes. Lady Crest and non-smoking
rooms available. *Amenities* pool table, laundry
service, in-house movies (charge).

■ *Rooms 126*	*Confirm by 6*
en suite bath/shower 126	*Last dinner 10*
Direct dial Yes	*Parking Limited*
Room TV Yes	*Room service 24 hours*

Novotel *NEW ENTRY*   Preston

H **62% £D/E** ♿
Map 10 A1 Lancashire
Reedfield Place, Walton Summit PR5 6AB
Preston (0772) 313331. Tlx 677164
Credit Access, Amex, Diners, Visa. **LVs**
  A very modern hotel handy for the M6 and the
M61. Foyer, lounge and bar are bright and
spacious, and the restaurant overlooks the pool.
Decent-sized bedrooms contain a large double
bed, bed-settee, two chairs and ample writing
space, and bathrooms are very well fitted. Good
room service and enjoyable breakfasts.
Amenities garden, outdoor swimming pool, pool
table, laundry service, coffee shop (6am–12pm).

■ *Rooms 100*	*Confirm by 6*
en suite bath/shower 100	*Last dinner midnight*
Direct dial Yes	*Parking Ample*
Room TV Yes	*Room service All day*

Craxton Wood Hotel — Puddington

HR 69% £D/E
Map 10 A2 Cheshire
Parkgate Road, South Wirral L66 9PB
051-339 4717
Owner manager Mr M. Petranca
Credit Access, Amex, Diners, Visa. LVs

A pleasant white-painted hotel standing in 36 acres of peaceful gardens and woodland off the A540. The most noticeable thing here is the very high standard of repair and housekeeping. Bedrooms are variously furnished – all neat and harmonious. Rural views. No dogs.
Amenities garden, laundry service.

■ Rooms 14	Confirm by arrang.
en suite bath/shower 14	Last dinner 10
Room phone Yes	Parking Ample
Room TV Yes	Room service All day
Closed Sun, Bank Hols, 2 wks Aug & 1 wk Xmas	

Craxton Wood Hotel Restaurant ⌣ &

NEW ENTRY

French cooking
Mr Petranca leads a smart, efficient service team in his stylish restaurant, while Scotsman James Minnis holds the culinary reins. The French menu spans traditional and modern with dishes ranging from a pistachio-studded galantine of duck and a skilfully made mousse of carrots and broccoli to tournedos en croûte and breast of chicken with langoustines and a creamy, sherry-rich sauce. Decent sweets. Classed growth clarets offer exceptional value. ♀ Well-chosen ⊖

■ Set L £9·95	L 12.30–2
About £45 for two	D 7.30–10
Seats 80	Parties 30
Closed Sun, Bank Hols, 2 wks Aug & 1 wk Xmas	

Chequers Hotel — Pulborough

H 60% £E/F
Map 5 E3 West Sussex
Church Place RH20 1AD
Pulborough (079 82) 2486
Owner managers Searancke family
Credit Access, Amex, Diners, Visa

Set back from the A29 is this welcoming and well-run little hotel, dating from the reign of Queen Anne. Day rooms are small-scale and cosy. Pretty cottage-style bedrooms have a home-from-home appeal; they're double-glazed and well equipped. The enclosed garden is nice for a short stroll, the Downs ideal for more serious walking.
Amenities garden.

■ Rooms 9	Confirm by arrang.
en suite bath/shower 8	Last dinner 8
Room phone No	Parking Ample
Room TV Yes	Room service All day

Stane Street Hollow Restaurant — Pulborough

R ⌣ **Map 5 E3** West Sussex
Codmore Hill
Pulborough (079 82) 2819

René Kaiser's cooking in this charming Sussex stone cottage just north of Pulborough on the A29 is of the robust type you often find in his native Switzerland – utterly dependable and full of flavour. His menus change with the seasons – try anything and everything on the menu from cheese soufflé and home-smoked ham to medallions of venison with a rich, strong sauce of brandy, bacon, mushrooms and cream. Lovely vegetables, mostly home-grown, and super sweets including textbook vacherin au noisettes and Charlotte of pear with raspberry coulis. Carefully chosen wines at enticing prices – note an exceptional Gewürztraminer from Zind-Humbrecht. Anne Kaiser leads the service with a fine team of local ladies.
♀ Well-chosen ⊖

■ Set L £4·95	L 12.30–1.15
About £40 for two	D 7.30–9.15
Seats 32 Parties 20	Parking Ample
Closed L Sat & Tues, all Sun & Mon, 10 days Xmas, 2 wks end Oct & 3 wks end May	

Quorn Country Hotel — Quorn

H 74% £C/D &
Map 11 D3 Leicestershire
Charnwood House, 66 Leicester Road
LE12 8BB
Loughborough (0509) 415050
Credit Access, Amex, Diners, Visa

Old and new blend harmoniously at this fine country hotel, set in attractive grounds alongside the A6. The heart of the building is Charnwood House, dating back to the 17th century. This is now matched by a sympathetic modern extension overlooking the grounds and river Soar. Oak panelling and antiques grace the stone-floored reception hall, and the elegant lounge and bar provide deep-cushioned comfort. Light, spacious, individually-decorated bedrooms are well equipped and furnished with pretty coordinating fabrics and handsome reproduction pieces.

Bathrooms, too, are splendidly equipped, offering hairdryers – and bidets in the suites. *Amenities* garden, coarse fishing, laundry service, helipad.

■ Rooms 19	Confirm by arrang.
en suite bath/shower 19	Last dinner 10
Direct dial Yes	Parking Ample
Room TV Yes	Room service 24 hours

Post House Hotel   Reading

H 63% £C
Map 5 D2 Berkshire
500 Basingstoke Road RG2 0SL
Reading (0734) 875485. Tlx 849160
Credit Access, Amex, Diners, Visa. LVs
  Practical modern comforts in a smartly kept
hotel near junction 11 of the M4. Bedrooms are
generally of a decent size, and are well equipped.
Open hanging space, but no wardrobes. Day

rooms include a lounge and two bars, one with a
railway theme. *Amenities* indoor swimming pool,
whirlpool bath, sauna, solarium, keep-fit
equipment, laundry service, coffee shop (7am–
midnight), children's play area.
- *Rooms* 143   *Confirm* by 6
en suite bath/shower 143 *Last dinner* 10.15
Direct dial Yes   *Parking* Ample
Room TV Yes   *Room service* Limited

Ramada Hotel   Reading

H 78% £B/C *E* &
Map 5 D2 Berkshire
Oxford Road RG1 7RH
Reading (0734) 586222. Tlx 847785
Credit Access, Amex, Diners, Visa
  A sleek modern hotel notable for its excellent
conference facilities and luxurious bedrooms.
Open-plan public areas, cleverly divided by
changes in level, range from a stylish sunken
lounge to a smart mezzanine cocktail bar. There's
also a traditional tavern-style bar. Spacious
bedrooms are fitted with king-sized beds,
handsome darkwood furniture and every modern
amenity (half have in-house movies). Bathrooms
are unashamedly sumptuous, with marble
surrounds, mosaic floors, hairdryers and
fresh flowers.
Amenities indoor swimming pool, sauna,

solarium, whirlpool bath, keep-fit equipment,
beauty salon, hairdressing, laundry service,
coffee shop (7am–11.30pm), 24-hour lounge
service, kiosk.
- *Rooms* 200   *Confirm* by 6
en suite bath/shower 200 *Last dinner* 11.30
Direct dial Yes   *Parking* Limited
Room TV Yes   *Room service* 24 hours

Aubrey Park Hotel   Redbourn

H 55% £C/D
Map 5 E2 Hertfordshire
Hemel Hempstead Road AL3 7AF
Redbourn (058 285) 2105. Tlx 82195
Credit Access, Amex, Diners, Visa
  A hotel of modest pretensions standing in six
acres of grounds not far from the M1. Bedrooms
are reached by a covered corridor from the main
building, and, with parking almost adjacent, have

something of a motel character. The best are in
the new wing, but all are quite comfortable. Neat,
compact bathrooms. Plans for improvements are
afoot here. *Amenities* garden, outdoor swimming
pool, games room, laundry service.
- *Rooms* 81   *Confirm* by arrang.
en suite bath/shower 81 *Last dinner* 10
Direct dial Yes   *Parking* Ample
Room TV Yes   *Room service* All day

La Barbe   Reigate

R **Map 7 B5** Surrey
71 Bell Street
Reigate (073 72) 41966
French cooking
Owner managers Saf Tassy & Antoine Jalley
Credit Access, Amex, Diners, Visa
  Booth seating and subdued lighting bring a
touch of intimacy to this cheerful little bistro with
fixed-price menus. French flavours are well

captured in dishes like hare pâté with prunes,
lamb with a garlic and chestnut sauce, chicken
supreme in cider and calvados. Tempting sweets
include pistachio pâté with kirsch.
- *Set L* £12.50   *L* 12–2
Set D £19   *D* 7–10, Sat 7–10.30
About £38 *for two*   *Parking* Ample
Seats 55   *Parties* 30
Closed L Sat & Mon, all Sun & Bank Hols

Bridge House Hotel   Reigate

H 57% £D/E
Map 7 B5 Surrey
Reigate Hill RH2 9RP
Reigate (073 72) 46801. Tlx 268810
Credit Access, Amex, Diners, Visa
  Close to junction 8 of the M25, this modern
hotel enjoys an elevated position overlooking the
town. Most of the bright bedrooms have little
balconies to enhance the views, and all are

equipped with remote-control TVs, tea-makers
and good bathrooms (two small singles have a
shower only). Public areas include a comfortable
bar. No dogs.
Amenities laundry service.
- *Rooms* 30   *Confirm* by arrang.
en suite bath/shower 30 *Last dinner* 10.30
Direct dial Yes   *Parking* Ample
Room TV Yes   *Room service* Limited

Sitwell Arms Hotel   Renishaw

H 64% £D
Map 11 D2 Derbyshire
Nr Eckington S31 9WE
Eckington (0246) 435226. Tlx 547303
Manager Chris Odams
Credit Access, Amex, Diners, Visa

Located just off the A616, this comfortable old hotel has been considerably extended since its coaching-inn days. Smart, relaxing public areas include a well-furnished lounge and two bars. Spacious bedrooms with handsome darkwood furniture are well equipped and have excellent bath or shower rooms. *Amenities* garden, in-house movies (free), laundry service.

■ *Rooms* 32	*Confirm by arrang.*
en suite bath/shower 32	*Last dinner 9.30*
Direct dial Yes	*Parking* Ample
Room TV Yes	*Room service* 24 hours

Lichfields   Richmond

R ♀ Map 5 E2 Surrey
Lichfield Terrace, Sheen Road
01-940 5236
Credit Access, Amex

Stephen Bull's skilled cooking makes this stylish restaurant always worth visiting. Menus change frequently to reflect the choicest of market produce, offering such delights as mille-feuille of crab with orange and cardamon, salmon sauced with rhubarb, and banana mousse cake with chocolate sauce. Meticulously chosen wine list features very fine burgundies.

♀ Well-chosen ⊖

■ *Set L* £16	*L* 12.15–2
Set D £17·50	*D* 7–10.30
About £55 for two	*Parking* Limited
Seats 40	*Closed* L Sat, all Sun &

Mon, Bank Hols, 1st wk Sept & 1 wk Xmas

Caffé Mamma, Mrs Beeton, Wine & Mousaka   Richmond

See under London Restaurants under £30

Petersham Hotel   Richmond

H 62% £C/D
Map 5 E2 Surrey
Nightingale Lane, Richmond Hill TW10 6RP
01-940 7471. Tlx 928556
Manager Colin Dare
Credit Access, Amex, Diners, Visa

The best bedrooms at this striking Victorian hotel have fine river views. These largest rooms are handsomely traditional, while others are more modest. Some singles lack space. The lobby has an Italian painted ceiling, and there's a pleasant lounge and bar. Prompt porterage but a poor breakfast. No dogs. *Amenities* laundry service, 24-hour lounge service.

■ *Rooms* 56	*Confirm by arrang.*
en suite bath/shower 56	*Last dinner 9.45*
Direct dial Yes	*Parking* Ample
Room TV Yes	*Room service* All day

Richmond Gate Hotel   Richmond

H 60% £C/D
Map 5 E2 Surrey
Richmond Hill TW10 6RP
01-940 0061. Tlx 928556
Manager Nigel Mather
Credit Access, Amex, Diners, Visa

A handsome part-Georgian hotel with a comfortably traditional lounge and stylish little bar. Five spacious, well-appointed bedrooms are in the original house; remaining rooms, in a modern block, have lightwood fitted units and good accessories. Bed and breakfast only (meals may be taken at the nearby Petersham Hotel). No dogs. *Amenities* garden, laundry service.

■ *Rooms* 51	*Confirm by* 6
en suite bath/shower 51	*Last dinner* None
Direct dial Yes	*Parking* Ample
Room TV Yes	*Room service* All day

Michel's   Ripley

R ♀ Map 5 E3 Surrey
Portsmouth Road
Guildford (0483) 224777
French cooking
Credit Access, Amex, Diners, Visa

Erik Michel came into cooking after training as an artist, and the dishes he creates in his comfortable beamed restaurant (formerly Clock House) show good skills in both departments. Fresh herbs enhance many dishes, exemplified by scallops with chicory, mange-tout and coriander; cured pigeon breast on dandelion and lamb's lettuce; carrot gâteau with asparagus and chervil butter sauce; and corn-fed chicken breast with tarragon. Super sweets include malibu-banana and lime quenelles set on banana bread and surrounded by raspberry coulis, passion fruit and kiwi. Charming Karen Michel and her mother run front of house. Concise list of good wines, best in Bordeaux and Burgundy: note Ch. Dauzac Margaux 1978. ⊖

■ *Set L* £12	*L* 12.30–2
Set D £12 except Sat	*D* 7–10.30
About £50 for two	*Parking* Limited
Seats 50	*Parties* 12
Closed L Sat, D Sun, all Mon & 26 Dec	

Ripon Spa Hotel — Ripon

H 61% £E ♿
Map 15 C6 North Yorkshire
Park Street HG4 2BU
Ripon (0765) 2172. Tlx 57780
Manager G. M. Currie
Credit Access, Amex, Diners, Visa
Seven acres of grounds provide a pleasant setting for this Edwardian hotel just a short stroll from the city centre. Day rooms, all leading from the long entrance hall, are in comfortably traditional style; so, too, are the good-sized bedrooms, whose equipment includes remote-control TVs. *Amenities* garden, croquet, games room, laundry service, children's play area.

■ *Rooms* 41	*Confirm by arrang.*
en suite bath/shower 41	*Last dinner 8.45*
Direct dial Yes	*Parking* Ample
Room TV Yes	*Room service* 24 hours

Bough House — Robertsbridge

R ♟ **Map 7 B6** East Sussex
43 High Street
Robertsbridge (0580) 880440
English cooking
Credit Access, Amex, Diners, Visa
A homely black-beamed restaurant on the steep high street is the setting for Olivia Stalker's considerable culinary skills. Everything is cooked to order and her short set dinner menus feature such temptations as scampi-stuffed mousseline of sole and marinated lamb with blackcurrant sauce. Vegetables are delicious. Weekend menus more expensive (about £36 for 2). ♥

■ *Set D from £10·50*	*D 7.30–10*
About £30 for two	*Parking* Limited
Seats 20	*Parties* 26
Closed Sun, Mon, 1st 2 wks March & Oct	

Crest Hotel — Rochester

H 61% £D ♿
Map 7 B5 Kent
Rochester Airport, Maidstone Road ME5 9SF
Medway (0634) 687111. Tlx 965933
Credit Access, Amex, Diners, Visa
Located in the heart of the Medway area, this modern red-brick hotel has airy public rooms and smartly furnished bedrooms grouped around an attractive terrace and garden. Executive bedrooms feature remote-control TVs, hairdryers and bath robes. All rooms have trouser presses and tea-makers. *Amenities* garden, terrace, whirlpool bath, croquet, 24-hour lounge service, nanny & children's playroom (weekends).

■ *Rooms* 105	*Confirm by* 6
en suite bath/shower 105	*Last dinner* 9.30
Direct dial Yes	*Parking* Ample
Room TV Yes	*Room service* 24 hours

Loaves & Fishes — Rockley

R ♟ **Map 4 C2** Wiltshire
Rockley Chapel, Nr Marlborough
Marlborough (0672) 53737
Credit Access, Visa
Angela Rawson cooks while Nikki Kedge looks after customers at their friendly restaurant in a converted Victorian chapel. The set meal involves a main course – roast duck with a rich fruit stuffing, beef and venison in a winey mushroom sauce – with tasty starters like pear with Stilton dressing, and enjoyable sweets. Booking advisable. Unlicensed. ♥

■ *Set L £14*	*L Sun only 12.30–1.15*
Set D £15	*D 7.30–8.30*
About £32 for two	*Parking* Ample
Seats 28 *Parties* 28	*Closed D* Sun, all Mon,
1 Jan, 25, 26, 31 Dec & 3 wks Oct	

■ Changes in data may occur in establishments after the Guide goes to press. Prices should be taken as indications rather than firm quotes.

Rose & Crown Hotel — Romaldkirk

I £E ♿
Map 15 B5 Co. Durham
Nr Barnard Castle DL12 9EB
Teesdale (0833) 50213
Owner managers David & Jill Jackson
Credit Access, Amex, Diners, Visa
Delightful accommodation awaits at this attractive old stone inn next to the village church. The original building offers cosily traditional rooms (including three impressive suites), while those in the courtyard annexe are more modern. All have tea-makers and good bath/shower rooms. The two beamed bars are lively and convivial. *Amenities* laundry service.

■ *Rooms* 11	*Confirm by arrang.*
en suite bath/shower 11	*Last dinner* 9
Direct dial Yes	*Parking* Ample
Room TV Yes	*Room service* Limited

Old Manor House ★   Romsey

R ★ ♔ ⌕ **Map 4 C3** Hampshire
21 Palmerston Street
Romsey (0794) 517353
Credit Access, Visa

Delicious food in a charming setting – a delightfully preserved house full of atmosphere and dating from 1540. Chef Mauro Bregoli (who sometimes comes out of his kitchen to chat with diners) gathers wild mushrooms, grows his own herbs, supplies some of the game for the table and uses ingredients of outstanding quality. Duck, geese and other meats are smoked in the huge open fireplace. The menu, which changes weekly, is biased towards fish in the summer and game in the winter. Try the creamy pheasant soup (served with a croûton topped with grilled goat's cheese) or brioche with chicken mousse and lamb's sweetbreads, followed by teal with lime and honey or chicken with brandy and langoustine sauce. Finish with assiette de desserts. Splendid French and English cheeses.

Excellent wines, strong in Bordeaux (Ch. Beychevelle '66) and Alsace (two '76 Vendange Tardive). *Specialities* terrine of lobster and sweetbreads, smoked fillet of beef, smoked fillet of wild duck, sea bass grilled with thyme and fennel. ☺ Well-chosen ⊘

■ *Set L £7·95*	*L 12–2*
Set D £18	*D 7–9.30*
About £45 for two	*Parking* Limited
Seats 45 Parties 22	*Closed* D Sun, all Mon,
25–30 Dec & 3 wks Aug–Sept	

White Horse Hotel   Romsey

H **63% £C/D**
Map 4 C3 Hampshire
Market Place SO5 8ZJ
Romsey (0794) 512431
Credit Access, Amex, Diners, Visa

The facade is Georgian but there is an older history to this agreeable hotel in the town centre. The Elizabethan lounge features old beams and some fine murals. Bedrooms in the main building are stylish in decor with Italian furniture while seven in an annexe are a little more ordinary, though roomier. Refurbishment is planned for the latter, plus reception and bar areas. *Amenities* laundry service.

■ *Rooms 33*	*Confirm by 6*
en suite bath/shower 33	*Last dinner 9.45*
Room phone Yes	*Parking Ample*
Room TV Yes	*Room service All day*

■ We publish annually, so make sure you use the current edition. It's worth it!

Milburn Arms Hotel   Rosedale Abbey

I **£E/F**
Map 15 C5 North Yorkshire
Nr Pickering YO18 8RA
Lastingham (075 15) 312
Owner managers Stephen & Frances Collins
Credit Access, Visa

A homely and comfortable country inn with enthusiastic owners and lots of charm. It's also the village pub, and the beamed bar – part of it dating from the 14th century – attracts both locals and residents. The lounge has the inviting feel of a private living room. Bedrooms are equally cosy, with traditional furnishings and pretty decor. *Amenities* garden, games rooms, satellite TV.

■ *Rooms 7*	*Confirm by arrang.*
en suite bath/shower 5	*Last dinner 9*
Room phone No	*Parking Ample*
Room TV Yes	*Room service Limited*

Chase Hotel   Ross-on-Wye

H **59% £C/D**
Map 4 B1 Hereford
Gloucester Road HR9 5LH
Ross-on-Wye (0989) 63161
Owner manager Paul Rynehart
Credit Access, Amex, Diners, Visa

The setting is 11 acres of peaceful grounds, yet this characterful Victorian mansion is just a short walk from the town centre. The bar is spacious and cheerful, the lounge comfortable. Bedrooms in the main house are traditionally furnished, more functional in the wing. Friendly, helpful staff. No dogs. *Amenities* garden, laundry service, valeting, pool table.

■ *Rooms 41*	*Confirm by 6*
en suite bath/shower 41	*Last dinner 9.45*
Direct dial Yes	*Parking Ample*
Room TV Yes	*Room service 24 hours*

Pengethley Manor Hotel

H 65% £C &
Map 4 B1 Hereford & Worcester
Harewood End HR9 6LL
Harewood End (098 987) 211
Credit Access, Amex, Diners, Visa
 North of Ross-on-Wye on the A49 you'll find this splendid Georgian house in a parkland setting. The oak-panelled library makes a fine lounge and there is a cocktail bar and two handsome dining rooms. Main-house bedrooms are spacious and traditional, those in the annexe smaller and more simple. Well-equipped bathrooms. Good housekeeping. *Amenities* garden, outdoor swimming pool, snooker, laundry service.

■ Rooms 18	Confirm by arrang.
en suite bath/shower 18	Last dinner 9.30
Direct dial Yes	Parking Ample
Room TV Yes	Room service All day

Walford House Hotel

HR 62% £E &
Map 4 B1 Hereford & Worcester
Walford HR9 5RY
Ross-on-Wye (0989) 63829
Owner managers Raymond & Joyce Zarb
Credit Access, Amex, Diners, Visa
 The Zarbs give guests a warm welcome and keep them happy throughout their stay at this delightful hotel. The setting is most attractive, and the whole place has the sparkle of diligent housework. Bedrooms are furnished in solid traditional style. Antiques add ornament to the homely bar, there's a nice comfortable lounge. *Amenities* garden, croquet, game fishing, laundry service.

■ Rooms 10	Confirm by arrang.
en suite bath/shower 10	Last dinner 9.30
Direct dial Yes	Parking Ample
Room TV Yes	Room service All day

Les Cèdres ♀ &

Wye salmon, served lightly poached on a bed of fresh sorrel and cream, is one of many delights prepared expertly by Raymond Zarb in this charming restaurant, with its Welsh dresser and antiques. Other dishes range from excellent plump moules marinière to roast duck with pickled peaches, Welsh lamb and sirloin of beef. Lovely sweets and splendid cheeses including a super chèvre de Pyramide and an exemplary Reblochon. An absorbing wine list is especially good in burgundy, Rhône and Alsace. Pleasant service from young, well-trained staff. ⊖

■ Set L Sat & Sun £10·50	L 12.30–2.30
Set D £16·50	D 7–9.30
About £45 for two	Seats 30

Scafell Hotel

H 60% £D/E
Map 13 C5 Cumbria
Borrowdale CA12 5XB
Borrowdale (059 684) 208
Owner manager Mr W. Miles Jessop
 High up in Borrowdale this homely hotel is a good base for walking holidays. Two pleasant lounges provide plenty of space for relaxation and there's a cheerful bar featuring photographs of yesteryear's guests. Furniture in the bright, spick and span bedrooms ranges from antique to modern, and all have private facilities (one with shower only). *Amenities* garden.

■ Rooms 20	Confirm by 6
en suite bath/shower 20	Last dinner 9.15
Direct dial Yes	Parking Ample
Room TV Some	Room service All day
Closed early Jan–mid Feb	

Rotherham Moat House

H 73% £D/E *E* &
Map 11 D2 South Yorkshire
Moorgate Road S60 2BG
Rotherham (0709) 364902. Tlx 547810
Credit Access, Amex, Diners, Visa
 Smartly contemporary, the Rotherham Moat House stands just south of the town centre on the A618. The marble-floored foyer features a fountain, and there's a relaxing lounge bar. The other bar, the Pavilion, is attractively done out in white and green and sports a tented ceiling. Well-kept bedrooms are of a good size, with large, comfortable beds, deep-pile carpets and neat, fully tiled bathrooms. Trouser presses, hairdryers, mini-bars and beverage makers are standard equipment in all rooms. Friendly, polite management and staff. *Amenities* garden, sauna, solarium, whirlpool bath, keep-fit equipment, pool

table, in-house movies (free), laundry service, 24-hour lounge service.

■ Rooms 64	Confirm by 6
en suite bath/shower 64	Last dinner 9.45
Direct dial Yes	Parking Ample
Room TV Yes	Room service 24 hours

Tylney Hall

Rotherwick

HR 81% £C/D
Map 5 D3 Hampshire
Nr Basingstoke RG27 9AJ
Hook (025 672) 4881. Tlx 859864
Credit Access, Amex, Diners, Visa
Built at the end of the 19th century, this magnificent mansion enjoys a peaceful setting in 66 acres of beautiful grounds. Public rooms are very impressive, notably the panelled reception hall with its black-and-white chequered marble floor and the Italianate lounge, which features a lovely gilded carved oak ceiling. Another lounge has much ornate plasterwork, and there's a handsome library bar. Bedrooms are all of a generous size (six suites are enormous) and combine traditional furnishings with up-to-date accessories including remote-control TVs.

Bathrooms are equally luxurious, and some boast whirlpool baths. No dogs. *Amenities* garden, outdoor swimming pool, tennis, croquet, snooker, laundry service, 24-hour lounge service.

■ *Rooms 36*	*Confirm by 6*
en suite bath/shower 36	*Last dinner 9.30*
Direct dial Yes	*Parking Ample*
Room TV Yes	*Room service 24 hours*

Tylney Hall Restaurant ♕♕ &

The glass-domed restaurant is a sumptuous setting for the enjoyment of Stephen Hine's cuisine moderne. The emphasis is on top-quality ingredients and much care goes into both cooking and presentation; sauces show a really expert touch. Typical dishes include hot salmon and sole terrine, warm salad of duck livers and pan-fried strips of beef with a Stilton and celery sauce. There's also a roast on the dinner and Sunday lunch menus. Michael Gaud leads a skilled service team. ♀ **Well-chosen** ☺

■ *Set L from £12*	*L 12.30–2*
Set D £18	*D 7.30–9.30,*
About £68 for two	*Fri & Sat 7.30–10*
Seats 85	*Parties 100*

♀ indicates a **well-chosen** house wine.

Rothley Court

Rothley

H 68% £D
Map 11 D3 Leicestershire
Westfield Lane LE7 7LG
Leicester (0533) 374141
Credit Access, Amex, Diners, Visa
A wealth of history going back to the 13th century enriches this splendid manor house set in beautiful landscaped grounds in hunting country. Fine panelling takes the eye in the public rooms,

and there's a bright little conservatory. Bedrooms are traditional in the main house, modern in the stable block.
Amenities garden, in-house movies (free), laundry service, 24-hour lounge service.

■ *Rooms 35*	*Confirm by arrang.*
en suite bath/shower 32	*Last dinner 10*
Direct dial Yes	*Parking Ample*
Room TV Yes	*Room service 24 hours*

My Cuisine

Rottingdean

R ♧ Map 7 B6 East Sussex
1 Meadow Parade, Falmer Road
Brighton (0273) 33416
Credit Access, Amex, Diners, Visa
John Hewett sees that everything, from good bread rolls to the petit fours, is home-made at his pretty pink restaurant. His short seasonal menu is varied and interesting, with mussels in a garlic cream and Pernod sauce or quail eggs in pastry

on a bed of spinach as a preface to roast suckling pig, venison, or rack of lamb. Tempting sweets include a nutty caramel pie. Lunch by arrangement only. ☺

■ *Set D £13·95*	*L by arrang. only*
About £38 for two	*D 7–9.30, Sat 7–10*
Seats 32 Parties 32	*Parking Limited*
Closed Sun, 1 Jan, 2 days Xmas & 1 wk Mar	

Peacock Hotel

Rowsley

H 67% £D
Map 10 C2 Derbyshire
Nr Matlock DE4 2EB
Matlock (0629) 733518
Manager Mr G. M. Gillson
Credit Access, Amex, Diners, Visa
Lovely gardens reaching down to the river Derwent make this 17th-century hotel a particularly delightful spot in summer. The two

lounges with their oak furnishings and the stone walled bar are full of character. Pretty bedrooms (some with beams) offer tea-makers, hairdryers and trouser presses. Bathrooms are equally well equipped. *Amenities* garden, game fishing.

■ *Rooms 20*	*Confirm by 6*
en suite bath/shower 15	*Last dinner 9*
Direct dial Yes	*Parking Ample*
Room TV Yes	*Room service 24 hours*

Three Horse Shoes Hotel · Rugby

H **57% £D/E**
Map 11 D4 Warwickshire
Sheep Street CV21 3BX
Rugby (0788) 4585
Credit Access, Amex, Diners, Visa

The modern shopping precinct setting is in sharp contrast to this 18th-century coaching inn with its beams, oak panelling and old-world charm. Pleasant bedrooms have simple furnishings and lots of useful extras, from hairdryers and trouser presses to telephones in the bathrooms. The TV lounge doubles as a meeting room. *Amenities* in-house movies (free), laundry service, 24-hour lounge service.

■ *Rooms* 31	*Confirm by* 6
en suite bath/shower 31	*Last dinner* 10.30
Direct dial Yes	*Parking* Limited
Room TV Yes	*Room service* 24 hours

Crest Hotel · Runcorn

H **62% £C/D**
Map 10 A2 Cheshire
Wood Lane, Beechwood WA7 3HA
Runcorn (0928) 714000. Tlx 627426
Manager Mr V. Calabrese
Credit Access, Amex, Diners, Visa

Quite stylish in red brick, this modern hotel near exit 12 of the M56 has extensive self-contained conference facilities. Greenery and a fish pond are features in the lobby, and the garden theme continues in the cocktail bar. A covered walkway leads to the smart, well equipped bedrooms. *Amenities* pool table, laundry service, in-house movies (charge), helipad.

■ *Rooms* 128	*Confirm by* 6
en suite bath/shower 128	*Last dinner* 10
Direct dial Yes	*Parking* Ample
Room TV Yes	*Room service* Limited

■ Our inspectors never book in the name of Egon Ronay's Guides; they disclose their identity only after paying their bills.

Ghyll Manor · Rusper

H **71% £C/D**
Map 5 E3 West Sussex
High Street, Nr Horsham RH12 4PX
Rusper (029 384) 571. Tlx 877577
Credit Access, Amex, Diners, Visa

The lovely grounds that provide the setting for this fine half-timbered house include specimen trees, a lake and a cloistered courtyard. The leafy little bar leading out to the garden is a most pleasant spot for a quiet drink, and the library-lounge, panelled in limed oak, is particularly cosy and inviting. Bedrooms in the main house include some with attic charm, others with splendid antiques and sitting or dressing areas; there are six luxurious new suites in the converted stable block. All rooms are filled with a variety of thoughtful extras and bathrooms, too, are very well equipped. Housekeeping and service can be

a little haphazard. Very good breakfasts. *Amenities* garden, outdoor swimming pool, tennis, croquet, riding, laundry service, 24-hour lounge service.

■ *Rooms* 28	*Confirm by* 6
en suite bath/shower 28	*Last dinner* 9.30
Direct dial Yes	*Parking* Ample
Room TV Yes	*Room service* 24 hours

Biskra House Restaurant · Ryde

RR ☖ **Map 5 D4** Isle of Wight
17 St Thomas's Street
Isle of Wight (0983) 67913
Credit Access, Visa

The Solent provides an ever-changing backdrop to this small Georgian mansion. On fine days, guests may sit on a beachside patio and watch the world sail by. There are similar views from the elegant dining room, where dishes like duck terrine, steak Diane and tournedos Rossini find favour with the many regular customers. There is a good selection of fresh vegetables and the commendable sweet trolley includes a creamy strawberry shortbread. ☺

■ *Set L* £5·50	*L* 12–2
Set D £10.95	*D* 7–10.30
About £32 *for two*	*Parking* Ample
Seats 100	*Parties* 100
Closed D Sun, all Mon, D 25 Dec & all 26 Dec	

Bedrooms £E/F
Rooms 9   *With bath/shower* 9
Pretty, well-appointed bedrooms with bathrooms have mini-bars, TVs, direct-dial telephones and hairdryers. Fruit and mineral water are welcome extras. No dogs.

Hotel Ryde Castle

Ryde

H **57%** **£E**
Map 5 D4 Isle of Wight
Esplanade PO33 1JA
Ryde (0983) 63755
Owner managers Mr & Mrs K. Gibbs
Credit Access, Visa
 A striking sight on the seafront, with its crenellated battlements, this creeper-clad hotel offers notably good accommodation. Prettily

decorated bedrooms are furnished with modern white units. Downstairs, there's a cheerful bar with residents' lounge. No under sevens. *Amenities* in-house movies (free).

■ *Rooms* 17	*Confirm by* 6
en suite bath/shower 17	*Last dinner* 9.45
Direct dial Yes	*Parking* Ample
Room TV Yes	*Room service* Limited
Closed 25 & 26 Dec	

George Hotel

Rye

H **61%** **£C/D**
Map 7 C6 East Sussex
High Street TN31 7JP
Rye (0797) 222114
Credit Access, Amex, Diners, Visa
 An elegant Georgian facade hides a history of over 400 years at this smart black and white coaching inn. Oak beams and wooden settles give the bar plenty of traditional appeal and there

are two comfortable lounges plus a splendid galleried ballroom. Bedrooms of differing size and style include some de luxe rooms with smart furnishings and their own sitting areas. Neat modern bathrooms. *Amenities* laundry service.

■ *Rooms* 16	*Confirm by* 6
en suite bath/shower 16	*Last dinner* 9
Direct dial Yes	*Parking* Limited
Room TV yes	*Room service* All day

Landgate Bistro *NEW ENTRY*

Rye

R **Map 7 C6** East Sussex
5 Landgate
Rye (0797) 222829
Credit Access, Amex, Diners, Visa
 Nick Parkin and Toni Ferguson-Lees know the meaning of professionalism without pretentiousness, and their little bistro is a very agreeable evening spot. Toni produces delicious well-flavoured dishes ranging from creamy

Roquefort mousse and chicken quenelles to super scallops and turbot with a vermouth and orange sauce, garlicky noisettes of lamb and toothsome walnut and treacle tart. Excellent English cheeses. ☺

■ *About* £30 *for two*	*D only* 7–9
Seats 34 *Parties* 38	*Parking* Ample
Closed Sun, Mon, Bank Hols, 2 wks Oct, 1 wk	
Xmas & last wk June	

Mermaid Inn

Rye

H **60%** **£D/E**
Map 7 C6 East Sussex
Mermaid Street TN31 7EU
Rye (0797) 223065. Tlx 957141
Owner manager Mr M. K. Gregory
Credit Access, Amex, Diners, Visa
 With its Norman cellars, Tudor facade and smuggling connections, this highly atmospheric inn brings the past alive. Sloping floors, low

ceilings and massive timbers characterise the day rooms, while bedrooms have leaded windows and attractive antiques (including some richly carved four-posters). Friendly staff. No dogs. *Amenities* 24-hour lounge service.

■ *Rooms* 28	*Confirm by* 6
en suite bath/shower 25	*Last dinner* 9.15
Direct dial Yes	*Parking* Limited
Room TV No	*Room service* 24 hours

Saffron Hotel

Saffron Walden

HR **58%** **£E**
Map 6 B3 Essex
High Street CB10 1AY
Saffron Walden (0799) 22676
Owner managers Craddock family
Credit Access, Visa. **LVs**
 Old-world charm abounds at this high-street hotel dating back in part to the 16th-century. Open fires warm both the little foyer and traditional lounge bar. Modest bedrooms (front ones are double glazed) range from spacious to compact and characterful rooms under the eaves. Adequate bath or shower rooms. *Amenities* patio, laundry service.

■ *Rooms* 22	*Confirm by* 6
en suite bath/shower 12	*Last dinner* 9.30
Direct dial Yes	*Parking* Limited
Room TV Yes	*Room service* Limited

Saffron Hotel Restaurant ♀

Lanzarote-born chef Domingo Berriel brings a touch of Mediterranean sunshine to the lengthy menu at this cosy dining room. Try his Portuguese sardines with tartare sauce followed by, say, scampi-stuffed chicken in a curried cream sauce, or choose something more in keeping with the setting – perhaps vegetable soup, then lamb noisettes with a kidney and Madeira sauce. Excellent, varied vegetables and tempting sweets like liqueur sorbets and a rich chocolate trifle. ☺

■ *Set L & D* £12.95	*L* 12–2
About £40 *for two*	*D* 7–9.30
Seats 35	*Parties* 30
Closed L Sat, all Sun to non-residents, Bank	
Hols & 25 Dec–1 Jan	

Noke Thistle Hotel   St Albans

H 75% £C
Map 5 E2 Hertfordshire
Watford Road AL2 3DS
St Albans (0727) 54252. Tlx 893834
Credit Access, Amex, Diners, Visa

A massive refurbishment programme has been completed at this extended Victorian house near the motorway complex. Guests are greeted with a smile in the panelled reception area, beyond which is a comfortable little lounge. There are two pleasant spots for a drink, the cheerful cocktail bar and a new American-style bar/coffee shop. Bedrooms, all furnished in similar style have smart pastel decor and polished darkwood furnishings; accessories include remote-control TVs with teletext, hairdryers and trouser presses. Towelling robes are provided in the well-fitted bathrooms. Breakfast is a self-service buffet.

Amenities garden, in-house movies (free), laundry service, coffee shop (9am–9pm), 24-hour lounge service.

■ *Rooms* 57	*Confirm by* 6
en suite bath/shower 57	*Last dinner* 10
Direct dial Yes	*Parking* Ample
Room TV Yes	*Room service* 24 hours

St Michael's Manor Hotel   St Albans

H 63% £C/D
Map 5 E2 Hertfordshire
Fishpool Street AL3 4RY
St Albans (0727) 64444
Manager Mr M. Richardson
Credit Access, Amex, Diners, Visa

The history of the manor house goes back to 1512, and the present premises are a blend of architectural styles. The lofty lounge and cosy bar offer nice views of the grounds. Four of the bedrooms have four-posters. Accessories include hairdryers, trouser presses and remote-control TVs. *Amenities* garden, laundry service.

■ *Rooms* 26	*Confirm by arrang.*
en suite bath/shower 26	*Last dinner* 8.30 (Sat 9)
Room phone Yes	*Parking* Ample
Room TV Yes	*Room service* 24 hours
Closed 27–30 Dec	

Sopwell House Hotel   St Albans

H 65% £D
Map 5 E2 Hertfordshire
Cottonmill Lane AL1 2HQ
St Albans (0727) 64477
Credit Access, Amex, Diners, Visa

Bedroom refurbishment, additional bedrooms and a conference centre are included among the plans for this 18th-century mansion located off the A1081. Existing rooms are neatly kept and all have tea-makers, trouser presses and hairdryers, plus good private facilities. A new reception area makes a pleasant entrance to the fountained inner hall and splendid sunken lounge. *Amenities* garden, laundry service.

■ *Rooms* 30	*Confirm by arrang.*
en suite bath/shower 30	*Last dinner* 10
Direct dial Yes	*Parking* Ample
Room TV Yes	*Room service* 24 hours

White Hart Hotel   St Austell

I £F
Map 2 B3 Cornwall
Church Street PL25 4AT
St Austell (0726) 72100
Credit Access, Amex, Diners, Visa

In the centre of town, this old greystone hotel numbers George V and Queen Mary among past famous visitors. The comfortable foyer-lounge and two cosy bars have a pleasantly traditional appeal. Homely bedrooms (the best with attractive matching fabrics and wallpapers) all offer tea-makers. Bathrooms are adequate; some rooms have foldaway shower units.

■ *Rooms* 20	*Confirm by* 6
en suite bath/shower 7	*Last dinner* 8.30
Room phone Yes	*Parking* Difficult
Room TV Yes	*Room service* All day
Closed 2 days Xmas	

Slepe Hall Hotel   St Ives

H 63% £D/E
Map 6 B2 Cambridgeshire
Ramsey Road PE17 4RB
St Ives (0480) 63122
Owner managers Jan & Colin Stapleton
Credit Access, Amex, Diners, Visa

New owners plan few changes at this former girls' school built in 1848. Victorian style is reflected in the furnishings of the attractive public rooms. Coordinated soft furnishings and simple rattan-faced units are a feature of the good-sized bedrooms. Bathrooms are compact with modern units. *Amenities* garden, laundry service.

■ *Rooms* 14	*Confirm by arrang.*
en suite bath/shower 9	*Last dinner* 10
Room phone Yes	*Parking* Ample
Room TV Yes	*Room service* All day
Closed 25 & 26 Dec	

Boskerris Hotel — St Ives

H 57% £F
Map 2 A3 Cornwall
Carbis Bay TR26 2NQ
Penzance (0736) 795295
Owner manager Mr S. Monk
Credit Diners
  Homely comfort is a feature at Boskerris. The sunny public rooms overlooking the sea include a traditional-style lounge with adjoining bar.

Bedrooms (best ones face the sea) are neat and clean. Bathrooms are modern. *Amenities* garden, outdoor swimming pool, putting, games room, laundry service, 24-hour lounge service.

■ *Rooms* 20	*Confirm by* arrang.
en suite bath/shower 15	*Last dinner* 8
Room phone No	*Parking* Ample
Room TV Some	*Room service* All day
Closed late Oct–Easter	

Garrack Hotel — St Ives

H 61% £D/E
Map 2 A3 Cornwall
Burthallan Lane TR26 3AA
Penzance (0736) 796199
Owner managers Kilby family
Credit Access, Amex, Diners, Visa
  The warmth of this friendly hotel is epitomised in the cosy, cluttered lounge with its books, games and ornaments. Other day rooms include a

conservatory and cocktail bar. Bedrooms are old-fashioned in the main house, modern – with sea views – in the extension. *Amenities* garden, indoor swimming pool, sauna, solarium, laundry room, coffee shop (9.30am–11pm).

■ *Rooms* 21	*Confirm by* arrang.
en suite bath/shower 14	*Last dinner* 8.30
Direct dial Yes	*Parking* Ample
Room TV Yes	*Room service* Limited

Tregenna Castle Hotel — St Ives

H 65% £C/D
Map 2 A3 Cornwall
TR26 2DE
Penzance (0736) 795254. Tlx 45128
Credit Access, Amex, Diners, Visa
  Excellent leisure facilities feature at this miniature castle perched above St Ives. The grandeur of the exterior hides a slightly faded look within, though the public rooms are certainly large

and comfortable. Accommodation varies from old-fashioned standard rooms to others newly refurbished. *Amenities* garden, outdoor swimming pool, tennis, squash, badminton, golf course, putting, croquet, pool table.

■ *Rooms* 82	*Confirm by* 6
en suite bath/shower 69	*Last dinner* 8
Direct dial Yes	*Parking* Ample
Room TV Yes	*Room service* Limited

Wallett's Court *NEW ENTRY* — St Margaret's at Cliffe

HR 57% £F
Map 7 D5 Kent
West Cliffe, Dover CT15 6EW
Dover (0304) 852424
Owner managers Chris & Lea Oakley
  The Oakleys provide the warmest of welcomes at this peaceful old manor house, and guests are shown personally to their rooms. These are full of thoughtful little extras, and main-house rooms are bigger, quieter and better equipped than those in the converted barn. Breakfast is a feast. No dogs. *Amenities* garden, games room, laundry service.

■ *Rooms* 7	*Confirm by* arrang.
en suite bath/shower 7	*Last dinner* 9
Room phone No	*Parking* Ample
Room TV Some	*Room service* Limited
Closed 3 days Xmas	

Wallett's Court Restaurant 🍴

Beams, whitewashed walls and sturdy oak tables make an appropriate – almost baronial – setting for Chris Oakley's fine, unfussy cooking. Watercress soup with home-baked bread, cheese and bacon tart, turbot with asparagus in a light butter sauce, a gorgeous beef casserole – these are typical dishes, and the pleasure lasts right to the end with super sweets like strawberry bavarois or lemon tart. Mainly residents only, apart from private parties (Mon–Fri) and Saturday gourmet dinners.
🍷 Well-chosen ⊖

■ *Set D* £8, Sat £17	*L* Sun only by arrang.
About £28 for two,	*D* 7–9, Sat at 8
Sat about £40	*Seats* 30 *Parties* 30
Closed L Mon–Sat, D Sun & 3 days Xmas	

Hotel Godolphin — St Mary's

H 60% £E/F
Map 2 A2 Isles of Scilly (Cornwall)
Church Street TR21 0JR
Scillonia (0720) 22316
Owner managers Mr & Mrs C. Mumford
Credit Access, Visa
  Friendliness is a keynote at this quiet, well-kept hotel with a fine subtropical garden. The lounge has an Italian marble fireplace, and there's a

charming conservatory and a cheerful bar. Simple, modern-style bedrooms have tea-makers. Half-board terms only. No dogs. *Amenities* garden, sauna, games room.

■ *Rooms* 31	*Confirm by* arrang.
en suite bath/shower 27	*Last dinner* 8
Direct dial Yes	*Parking* Ample
Room TV Yes	*Room service* Limited
Closed mid Oct–mid Mar	

Tregarthen's Hotel St Mary's

H **60% £D**
Map 2 A2 Isles of Scilly (Cornwall)
TR21 0PP
Scillonia (0720) 22540
Credit Access, Amex, Diners, Visa
Refurbishment is brightening up this well-managed holiday hotel, which stands in terraced gardens overlooking the harbour. The main areas to benefit so far are the restaurant, now much

lighter and prettier. Most of the bedrooms, all with pleasant lightwood Scandinavian furnishings, look to sea. Half-board terms only. No dogs.
Amenities garden.

■ *Rooms* 33	*Confirm by* 7
en suite bath/shower 26	*Last dinner* 8
Direct dial Yes	*Parking* Limited
Room TV Yes	*Room service* All day
Closed 1 Nov–mid Mar	

Idle Rocks Hotel St Mawes

H **62% £D/E**
Map 2 B4 Cornwall
Tredenham Road TR2 5AN
St Mawes (0326) 270771
Owner managers Powell family
Credit Access, Amex, Diners, Visa
Lap up the sun on the long waterside terrace, or enjoy the fine harbour views from the traditional lounge bar. Most of the cosy, immaculately kept

bedrooms share the same attractive aspect, and standards of housekeeping are high. Guests may use sauna and solarium of the Lugger Hotel at Portloe. Half-board only. No children under six.

■ *Rooms* 24	*Confirm by* 5
en suite bath/shower 23	*Last dinner* 9.30
Room phone No	*Parking* Difficult
Room TV Yes	*Room service* All day
Closed end Oct–early Apr	

Rising Sun Inn St Mawes

H **62% £D/E**
Map 2 B4 Cornwall
The Square TR2 5DJ
St Mawes (0326) 270233
Owner managers Messrs. Milan & Atherley
Credit Access, Amex, Diners, Visa
New owners have improved the decor and facilities of this harbourside inn. It's a place of real charm, and the main bar and flowery terrace are

popular gathering places. Bedrooms feature stippled wallpaper in soft colours, traditional furnishings and good-quality fabrics. Both they and the bathrooms are neat, fresh and very clean. No children under nine.

■ *Rooms* 12	*Confirm by* arrang.
en suite bath/shower 9	*Last dinner* 9
Direct dial Yes	*Parking* Difficult
Room TV Yes	*Room service* All day

Hotel Tresanton St Mawes

H **69% £C**
Map 2 B4 Cornwall
Lower Castle Road TR2 5DR
St Mawes (0326) 270544
Owner managers Graham & Maureen Brockton
Credit Access, Amex, Diners, Visa
A sub-tropical garden and splendid sun terrace are pleasures of this family-run hotel. Period furniture creates an air of comfort in the drawing

room and there's a stylish cocktail bar. Bedrooms in a pretty, traditional style have nice carpeted bathrooms (seven en suite). *Amenities* garden, boating, laundry service.

■ *Rooms* 21	*Confirm by* arrang.
en suite bath/shower 7	*Last dinner* 9
Direct dial Yes	*Parking* Ample
Room TV Some	*Room service* All day
Closed Nov, Jan & Feb	

■ If we recommend meals in a hotel or inn, a separate entry is made for its restaurant.

Marine Hotel Salcombe

H **69% £B** &
Map 3 D3 Devon
Cliff Road TQ8 8JH
Salcombe (054 884) 2251. Tlx 45185
Credit Access, Amex, Diners, Visa
A waterside hotel with helpful staff and a good relaxing feel. Public areas, recently remodelled, include a stylish bar and a pleasant lounge that opens on to a wide terrace. Bedrooms, all but six

with sea views, are light and fresh, with practical modern furnishings. No dogs. *Amenities* garden, indoor swimming pool, sauna, solarium, whirlpool bath, keep-fit equipment, beauty salon, hairdressing, games room, laundry service.

■ *Rooms* 51	*Confirm by* arrang.
en suite bath/shower 51	*Last dinner* 9.30
Direct dial Yes	*Parking* Ample
Room TV Yes	*Room service* 24 hours

St Elmo Hotel — Salcombe

H **61%** **£D/E**
Map 3 D3 Devon
Sandhills Road, North Sands TQ8 8JR
Salcombe (054 884) 2233
Owner managers Janet & Tim Tremellen
Credit Access, Visa
 A family-run Edwardian hotel in an agreeable setting overlooking North Sands. Traditionally-styled day rooms – lounge and bar – offer comfort and relaxation. Simply furnished bedrooms have spotless bathrooms with good towels. *Amenities* garden, outdoor swimming pool, solarium, whirlpool bath, games room.

■ *Rooms* 25	*Confirm by arrang.*
en suite bath/shower 25	*Last dinner* 8.30
Room phone No	*Parking Ample*
Room TV Yes	*Room service All day*
Closed end Oct–Easter	

Soar Mill Cove Hotel — Salcombe

HR **63%** **£D/E**
Map 3 D3 Devon
Soar Mill Cove TQ7 3DS
Kingsbridge (0548) 561566
Owner managers Keith & Norma Makepeace
Credit Access, Visa
 A spring-water indoor swimming pool has added to the amenities of this comfortable modern hotel. Picture windows provide lovely views from the spacious lounge, and there's a nice contemporary bar. Well-equipped, mainly spacious bedrooms. *Amenities* garden, indoor & outdoor swimming pools, tennis, games room.

■ *Rooms* 14	*Confirm by arrang.*
en suite bath/shower 14	*Last dinner* 9
Direct dial Yes	*Parking Ample*
Room TV Yes	*Room service All day*
Closed 29 Dec–22 Feb	

Soar Mill Cove Hotel Restaurant

A delightful split-level restaurant overlooking the outdoor pool and sea beyond. Derek Hamlen applies sound skills to good-quality raw materials, including choice crab and lobster bought from local fishermen. Typical dishes include avocado and Stilton pâté, veal with pasta, lambs' sweetbreads with spinach, and poached salmon topped with a tangy lemon soufflé and wrapped in pastry. Enjoyable sweets like coffee and hazelnut pavlova. Lighter lunches, traditional roast for Sunday dinner. ♀ **Well-chosen** ⊖

■ *Set D £18*	*L 12.30–2.30*
About £50 for two	*D 7.30–10,*
Seats 40 Parties 40	*Sun 7.30–9.30*
Closed 29 Dec–22 Feb	

South Sands Hotel — Salcombe

H **64%** **£D/E**
Map 3 D3 Devon
South Sands TQ8 8LL
Salcombe (054 884) 3741
Owner managers Peter & Elizabeth Hey
Credit Access, Amex, Diners, Visa
 Impressive improvements, which include a new reception lounge-cum-bar, indoor leisure facilities, and refurbished bedrooms, have helped maintain the popularity of this friendly beachside hotel. There are five holiday suites.
Amenities indoor swimming pool, sauna, solarium, laundry service, in-house movies (free), coffee shop (10am–10pm).

■ *Rooms* 29	*Confirm by arrang.*
en suite bath/shower 29	*Last dinner* 9.30
Direct dial Yes	*Parking Ample*
Room TV Yes	*Room service All day*

Tides Reach Hotel — Salcombe

H **72%** **£C**
Map 3 D3 Devon
South Sands TQ8 8LJ
Salcombe (054 884) 3466
Owner manager Mr R. R. Edwards
Credit Access, Amex, Diners, Visa
 Owners and staff ensure that everything runs as smooth as silk at this superb holiday hotel. Service and housekeeping are impeccable, leisure facilities outstanding, and the setting – in a secluded sandy cove, with its own attractive gardens – especially fine. Guests can soak up the views from the lounges, or take a drink in the cocktail bar with its sea aquarium. Bedrooms (front ones balconied) are individually decorated to a high standard and have a colourful appeal. Half board only. No children under eight. *Amenities* garden, indoor swimming pool, sauna,

solarium, whirlpool bath, gymnasium, beauty salon, hairdressing, squash, mooring, board sailing, games room, snooker.

■ *Rooms* 42	*Confirm by arrang.*
en suite bath/shower 42	*Last dinner* 10
Direct dial Yes	*Parking Ample*
Room TV Yes	*Room service 24 hours*
Closed Dec–Feb	

Salisbury ▶

Rose & Crown Hotel   Salisbury

H **56% £C/D**
Map 4 C3 Harnham Road, Harnham SP2 8JQ
Salisbury (0722) 27908. Tlx 47224
Manager Dale Naug
Credit Access, Amex, Diners, Visa
A fine old half-timbered inn on the banks of the
Avon, where guests can sleep in a four-poster bed
beneath heavy oak beams or choose one of the

spacious, thoroughly modern rooms in the garden
wing. All rooms are centrally heated. The beamed
bars are full of old-world character and there's a
comfortable little lounge. *Amenities* garden,
laundry service.

■ *Rooms* 28	*Confirm by* 4
en suite bath/shower 28	*Last dinner* 9.30
Direct dial Yes	*Parking* Ample
Room TV Yes	*Room service* 24 hours

White Hart Hotel   Salisbury

H **65% £C/D**
Map 4 C3 Wiltshire
1 St John Street SP1 2SD
Salisbury (0722) 27476
Credit Access, Amex, Diners, Visa. LVs
Fronted by a fine Georgian portico, this comfortable hotel enjoys a central position near the
cathedral. The spacious, traditionally furnished
foyer-lounge, warmed by an open fire, is a popular

meeting place and there's a smart little bar. All the
good-sized bedrooms offer tea-makers, trouser-
presses and tiled bathrooms provided with
hairdryers and good thick towels. *Amenities*
garden, laundry service, 24-hour lounge service.

■ *Rooms* 68	*Confirm by* 6
en suite bath/shower 68	*Last dinner* 9.45
Direct dial Yes	*Parking* Ample
Room TV Yes	*Room service* Limited

■ Any person using our name
to obtain free hospitality is
a fraud. Proprietors, please
inform the police and us.

Swallow Trafalgar Hotel   *NEW ENTRY*   Samlesbury

H **56% £D/E**
Map 10 B1 Lancashire
Preston New Road PR5 0UL
Samlesbury (077 477) 351. Tlx 677362
Credit Access, Amex, Diners, Visa
A modern hotel and conference centre located
one mile west of the M6 (leave at junction 31).
There are two bars, one with a naval theme, and a
roomy foyer-lounge that overlooks the pool.

Bedrooms have lightwood built-in units with
writing space, plus hairdryers, trouser presses
and satellite TVs. *Amenities* garden, indoor
swimming pool, solarium, squash, in-house
movies (free), laundry service, helipad.

■ *Rooms* 80	*Confirm by* 6
en suite bath/shower 80	*Last dinner* 10
Direct dial Yes	*Parking* Ample
Room TV Yes	*Room service* 24 hours

Tickled Trout Hotel   Samlesbury

H **60% £D/E**
Map 10 B1 Lancashire
Preston New Road, Preston PR1 0UT
Samlesbury (077 477) 671. Tlx 677625
Credit Access, Amex, Diners, Visa
Halfway between London and Glasgow, this
sprawling white-painted hotel stands on a bend of
the Ribble by junction 31 of the M6. Bedrooms are
spacious and well equipped with satellite TV,

trouser presses and hair-dryers. Public rooms
include a pillared bar lounge filled with Victoriana.
Cheerful staff. New leisure centre.
Amenities garden, coarse fishing, laundry
service, in-house movies (free).

■ *Rooms* 66	*Confirm by* 6
en suite bath/shower 66	*Last dinner* 10
Direct dial Yes	*Parking* Ample
Room TV Yes	*Room service* Limited

Chimney House Hotel   Sandbach

H **61% £D/E** &
Map 10 B2 Cheshire
Congleton Road CW11 0ST
Crewe (0270) 764141. Tlx 367323
Manager Sergio Fernandez
Credit Access, Amex, Diners, Visa
A new wing of bedrooms has been added to
this half-timbered former rectory, which stands in
eight acres of grounds near junction 17 of the M6.

All the bedrooms are well equipped, and 20 have
balconies. The lobby-lounge is roomy and
comfortable, and the bar has a little conservatory
area. *Amenities* garden, sauna, solarium, putting,
in-house movies (free), laundry service.

■ *Rooms* 52	*Confirm by* 7
en suite bath/shower 52	*Last dinner* 10
Direct dial Yes	*Parking* Ample
Room TV Yes	*Room service* 24 hours

■ Our inspectors are our full-time employees; they are professionally trained by us.

Melville Hall Hotel — Sandown

H **56% £E**
Map 5 DA Isle of Wight
Melville Street PO36 9DH
Isle of Wight (0983) 406526
Owner managers Mr & Mrs K. R. Wells
Credit Access, Visa
New owners have now provided the added convenience of an all-day coffee shop at this extended Victorian house near the seafront. Day

rooms – lounge and bar – are relaxing. Bedrooms have smart units, radio-alarms and tea-makers. No dogs. *Amenities* garden, outdoor swimming pool, putting, games room, pool table, in-house movies (free), coffee shop (10.30am–12pm).

■ *Rooms* 38	*Confirm by arrang.*
en suite bath/shower 29	*Last dinner* 8.30
Direct dial Yes	*Parking* Ample
Room TV Yes	*Room service* All day

Saunton Sands Hotel — Saunton

H **65% £C/D**
Map 2 C1 Devon
Nr Braunton EX33 1LQ
Croyde (0271) 890212
Owner managers Brend family
Credit Access, Amex, Diners, Visa
Families are well catered for at this white-painted 1930s seaside hotel, which boasts abundant leisure facilities. Superb views of Saunton's golden sands are a feature of the light and spacious public rooms, which include a smart, contemporary-style cocktail bar. Major refurbishment is under way. Best bedrooms,

recently updated, have sea-facing balconies; all have neat modern furnishings and well-kept bathrooms. Many rooms are now decorated in Laura Ashley style with matching fabrics. No dogs. *Amenities* garden, indoor swimming pool, sauna, solarium, whirlpool bath, keep-fit equipment, hairdressing, tennis, squash, putting, games room, snooker, in-house movies (free), children's playroom.

■ *Rooms* 93	*Confirm by arrang.*
en suite bath/shower 93	*Last dinner* 9
Direct dial Yes	*Parking* Ample
Room TV Yes	*Room service* 24 hours

☞ is our symbol for an **outstanding** wine list.

Crown Hotel — Scarborough

H **65% £D/E**
Map 15 D6 North Yorkshire
Esplanade YO11 2AG
Scarborough (0723) 373491. Tlx 52277
Credit Access, Amex, Diners, Visa
Bedrooms and function rooms are undergoing extensive refurbishment at this 1840 Regency-style hotel. Public areas include a spacious and elegantly furnished foyer-lounge and an attractive

bar. *Amenities* garden, solarium, keep-fit equipment, hairdressing, games room, snooker, in-house movies (charge), laundry service, coffee shop (10am–7.30pm), 24-hour lounge service.

■ *Rooms* 83	*Confirm by* 6
en suite bath/shower 83	*Last dinner* 9.30
Direct dial Yes	*Parking* Limited
Room TV Yes	*Room service* 24 hours

Holbeck Hall Hotel — Scarborough

H **66% £D**
Map 15 D6 North Yorkshire
Sea Cliff Road YO11 2XX
Scarborough (0723) 374374
Owner manager Mr M. Turner
Credit Access, Amex, Diners, Visa
Built in mock Tudor style, this cliff-top hotel boasts splendid views and three acres of grounds. Public rooms include a fine baronial hall,

chandeliered restaurant and sun lounge. Individually decorated bedrooms are spacious and well equipped. *Amenities* garden, putting, laundry service, free in-house movies.

■ *Rooms* 30	*Confirm by* 6
en suite bath/shower 30	*Last dinner* 9.30
Direct dial Yes	*Parking* Ample
Room TV Yes	*Room service* 24 hours
Closed Jan–Mar	

Palm Court Hotel
Scarborough

H 57% £E
Map 15 D6 North Yorkshire
St Nicholas Cliff YO11 2ES
Scarborough (0723) 368161. Tlx 527579
Manager Philip Ward
Credit Access, Amex, Diners, Visa

Friendliness is a feature of this modern hotel close to the town centre and beach. The foyer doubles as a cosy lounge, and there's a cheerful cocktail bar. Bedrooms have simple white furnishings. No dogs. *Amenities* indoor swimming pool, sauna, solarium, keep-fit equipment, in-house movies (free), laundry service, coffee shop (9am–5pm Mon–Sat).

■ *Rooms* 50   *Confirm by arrang.*
en suite bath/shower 50   *Last dinner* 9
Direct dial Yes   *Parking* Limited
Room TV Yes   *Room service* 24 hours

Royal Hotel
Scarborough

H 72% £D
Map 15 D6 North Yorkshire
St Nicholls Street YO11 2HE
Scarborough (0723) 364333
Manager Michael Court
Credit Access, Amex, Diners, Visa

Built in the 1830s, this handsome hotel overlooking the sea still retains its Regency character. The front hall is particularly fine, with a double staircase sweeping up to classical pillared galleries, with chandeliers and antiques adding to the effect. Extensive public and function rooms offer traditional comfort. In contrast, on the lower ground floor there's a grotto-style leisure complex. Good-sized bedrooms, many with sea views, are smart and well maintained. Modern bathrooms. No dogs.
Amenities indoor swimming pool, sauna,

solarium, whirlpool bath, steam bath, keep-fit equipment, snooker, in-house movies (free), laundry service, coffee shop (9am–5pm), children's play area (summer).

■ *Rooms* 137   *Confirm by arrang.*
en suite bath/shower 137   *Last dinner* 11.30
Direct dial Yes   *Parking* Limited
Room TV Yes   *Room service* 24 hours

Sarah Brown's Wholefood Restaurant
Scarborough

R **Map 15 D6** North Yorkshire
13 Victoria Road
Scarborough (0723) 360054

High-quality wholefood and vegetarian cooking are found in this pretty restaurant with pink marbled walls. The houmus is splendidly garlicky and herby, soups are delicious, and typical main-course choice could include cashew nut and mushroom flan, vegetable moussaka and macaroni with a piquant ginger and tomato sauce. Varied selection of salads. Home-made ice cream feature among tempting sweets. Friendly waitress service. Also open 10.30am–4pm Mon–Sat for counter service.

■ *About £23 for two*   *D 7.30–10*
Seats 60 *Parties* 35   *Parking* Difficult
Closed Sun, Mon, also Tues in winter, 26 Dec & 1 Jan

NEW ENTRY

■ For a discount on next year's guide, see Offer for Answers.

Scole Inn
Scole

HR 57% £E   ⬥
Map 6 C2 Norfolk
Nr Diss IP21 4DR
Diss (0379) 740481
Owner managers Bob & Maggie Nylk
Credit Access, Amex, Diners, Visa

Oak beams, inglenook fireplaces and a finely carved staircase give plenty of character to this 17th-century inn – though public areas could do with some refurbishment. Main-house bedrooms offer period charms (three have four-posters) while annexe accommodation is compact and comfortable. Well-equipped bathrooms throughout. *Amenities* garden.

■ *Rooms* 23   *Confirm by* 6
en suite bath/shower 23   *Last dinner* 10
Direct dial Yes   *Parking* Ample
Room TV Yes   *Room service* Limited

Scole Inn Restaurant
English cooking

A handsome, beamed dining room is the setting for John Mackerel's tasty English cooking. Begin perhaps with creamy seafood soup, deep-fried Lymeswold or chicken livers in herb butter. Then perhaps, crispy Norfolk duckling, whole baby chicken, honey-roast rack of lamb, or succulent beef fillet with a red wine and garlic sauce. Fresh fish and game feature in season and there's always a choice of grills. Sweets from the trolley include a good sherry trifle. Friendly, laid-back service. ⊖

■ *Set L* £8   *L* 12–2
Set D £8   *D* 7–9.45, Sun 7–9
About £34 for two   *Seats* 50 *Parties* 70
Closed L Sat & D 25 Dec

Olde Ship Hotel *NEW ENTRY*   Seahouses

I **£F** &
Map 14 B2 Northumberland
Seahouses (0665) 720200
Owner managers Mr & Mrs A. C. Glen
   Built as a farmhouse in 1745, this delightful inn
has been in the same family ownership for over 70
years. One of the convivial bars is crammed with
nautical knick-knacks, and a comfortable upstairs
lounge looks over the harbour. The little bedrooms
are warm and cosy, with simple, homely
furnishings, tea-makers, books and magazines.
No dogs.
Amenities garden, laundry service.

■ *Rooms* 12	*Confirm by arrang.*
en suite bath/shower 9	*Last dinner* 8
Room phone No	*Parking* Ample
Room TV Yes	*Room service* None
Closed Nov 1–Apr 1	

Hog's Back Hotel   Seale

H **64% £C/D** &
Map 5 E3 Surrey
Hog's Back, Nr Farnham GU10 1EX
Runfold (025 18) 2345
Manager John Fielding
Credit Access, Amex, Diners, Visa
   Fine views from its landscaped gardens are a
feature of this handsome tile-hung hotel high on
the North Downs. A fountain and masses of
greenery adorn the smart foyer-lounge and the
stylish bar-lounge has an elegant 20s air.
Bedrooms in a modern wing have good
bathrooms. *Amenities* garden, games room, pool
table, laundry service.

■ *Rooms* 50	*Confirm by* 6
en suite bath/shower 50	*Last dinner* 9.30
Direct dial Yes	*Parking* Ample
Room TV Yes	*Room service* All day

Seaview Hotel   Seaview

H **61% £E**
Map 5 D4 Isle of Wight
High Street
Isle of Wight (0983) 612711
Owner managers Nicholas & Nicola Hayward
Credit Access, Amex, Visa
   Delightful young owners and helpful staff make
a stay at this relaxing seaside hotel a great
pleasure. Though small in scale, it provides charm
and comfort in abundance, whether in the
convivial bar (very much a local), the patio cocktail
bar or the quiet lounge. Bedrooms are cosy and
homely, with some nice period furnishings and
many useful extras. *Amenities* laundry service.

■ *Rooms* 14	*Confirm by arrang.*
en suite bath/shower 12	*Last dinner* 9.30
Room phone No	*Parking* Ample
Room TV Yes	*Room service* Limited

Pheasant Hotel   Seavington St Mary

HR **60% £D/E** &
Map 4 A4 Somerset
Nr Ilminster TA19 0QE
South Petherton (0460) 40502
Owner managers Edmondo & Jacqueline Paoloni
Credit Access, Amex, Diners, Visa
   Only 200 yards from the busy A303, but this is a
very peaceful place to stay. The main building is a
converted 17th-century farmhouse, where mellow,
relaxing day rooms and the two smallest
bedrooms are to be found. The remaining
bedrooms are across the car park (umbrellas
provided!). No dogs. *Amenities* garden.

■ *Rooms* 10	*Confirm by arrang.*
en suite bath/shower 10	*Last dinner* 9.30
Direct dial Yes	*Parking* Ample
Room TV Yes	*Room service* Limited
Closed 26 Dec–8 Jan	

Pheasant Hotel Restaurant &

Margaret Male leads a local kitchen brigade in this
smart, friendly restaurant, whose fixed-price menu
is supplemented by a long list of alternatives at
extra cost. Pâtés and pasta, devilled whitebait,
main-course meats with or without sauces, sole
and trout – there's something for everyone.
Tempting sweets like lemon or chocolate
mousse and home-made trifle to follow. Excellent
wines.
♀ Well-chosen ℮

■ *Set D* £8·95	*D only* 7.30–9.30
About £42 *for two*	*Seats* 52 *Parties* 40
Closed D Sun to non-residents, Bank Hols &	
26 Dec–8 Jan	

Brickwall Hotel   Sedlescombe

H **59% £E**
Map 7 C6 East Sussex
The Green TN33 0QA
Sedlescombe (042 487) 253
Owner manager Mr G. Pollio
Credit Access, Amex, Diners, Visa
   Set beside the village green in one of the
prettiest villages in Sussex is this Tudor mansion.
Old beams, leaded windows and open fires
provide plenty of character in the public rooms,
and there are delightful views on to the carefully
tended gardens. Nicely-maintained bedrooms are
well-equipped. *Amenities* garden, putting,
croquet, outdoor swimming pool.

■ *Rooms* 25	*Confirm by arrang.*
en suite bath/shower 25	*Last dinner* 8.45
Direct dial Yes	*Parking* Ample
Room TV Yes	*Room service* All day

Tregiffian Hotel — Sennen

H 59% £E/F
Map 2 A4 Cornwall
Nr Penzance TR19 7BE
Sennen (0736) 871408
Owner managers Mr & Mrs A. Loutit
Credit Access, Diners, Visa

A winding track leads to this characterful converted farmhouse within sight of the sea. The former kitchen, with its granite inglenook makes a cosy bar, and there are two homely lounges. Simply furnished bedrooms with compact bathrooms. Good breakfasts – with home-made muesli. *Amenities* garden, laundry service.

■ *Rooms* 11	*Confirm by* 6
en suite bath/shower 11	*Last dinner* 8.30
Room phone No	*Parking* Ample
Room TV Some	*Room service* All day
Closed Nov-Feb	

Le Chantecler — Sevenoaks

R ⅋ ⅍ Map 7 B5 Kent
43 High Street
Sevenoaks (0732) 454662
French cooking
Credit Access, Amex, Diners, Visa

'As good as any you will find in the Dordogne.' That was our inspector's verdict on the confit de canard he enjoyed at this charming restaurant. Alan Ginzler is an attentive host and his wife Gillian joins chef Nicholas Medhurst to produce essentially French provincial dishes like moules marinière and filet avec fromage, with spot-on vegetables and splendid sweets. ⊖

■ *Set L* £10·50	*L* 12–2
Set D Tues–Thurs	*D* 7.30–9.30
£11·50	*Parking* Difficult
About £45 *for two*	*Seats* 36 *Parties* 24
Closed Sun, Mon & 1 wk Xmas	

Royal Oak *NEW ENTRY* — Sevenoaks

HR 56% £E
Map 7 B5 Kent
Upper High Street TN14 5PG
Sevenoaks (0732) 451109
Owner manager Mr & Mrs M. R. Nix
Credit Access, Diners, Visa

Just opposite the entrance to Knole House stands this popular hotel with its handsome Georgian frontage. Entrance is through a little conservatory-lounge into the cosy reception area, where a warm welcome awaits. Bedrooms of various sizes combine modern fabrics and more traditional furnishings.

■ *Rooms* 21	*Confirm by* 6
en suite bath/shower 21	*Last dinner* 9.30
Direct dial Yes	*Parking* Limited
Room TV Yes	*Room service* None
Closed 3 days Xmas	

Royal Oak Restaurant

The atmosphere is pleasantly relaxing, and fixed-price menus provide a good variety of enjoyable eating. Skate with prawns and butter sauce, cheese and herb pâté, duck breast with a purée of apples and Calvados and loin of pork with lime and smoked bacon show the range. Vegetables come with a crunch, and sweets include a super bread and butter pudding. Less choice at lunchtime. A small, selective wine list with a good choice of house wines.
♟ Well-chosen ⊖

■ *Set L* £9·75	*L* 12.30–2
Set D from £12·50	*D* 7.30–9.30
About £35 *for two*	*Seats* 40
Closed L Sat & D Sun	*Parties* 26

Grosvenor Hotel — Shaftesbury

H 62% £C
Map 4 B3 Dorset
The Commons SP7 8JA
Shaftesbury (0747) 2282
Credit Access, Amex, Diners, Visa. **LVs**

Once a coaching inn, this attractive, centrally-located hotel is built round a cobbled courtyard. Next to the reception room is a smart bar hung with hunting prints. The plush upstairs lounge features a superb Victorian oak sideboard. Pastels and floral prints mix prettily in the bedrooms, many of which have been upgraded. Bathrooms offer tubs, showers and toiletries. *Amenities* laundry service.

■ *Rooms* 47	*Confirm by* 6
en suite bath/shower 41	*Last dinner* 9.30
Room phone Yes	*Parking* Ample
Room TV Yes	*Room service* All day

Royal Chase Hotel — Shaftesbury

H 61% £D/E
Map 4 B3 Dorset
Royal Chase Roundabout SP7 8DB
Shaftesbury (0747) 3355
Owner managers George & Rosemary Hunt
Credit Access, Amex, Diners, Visa

A splendid new swimming pool and steam room have come on line at this progressive hotel, where modernisation has left only the bar to reflect the building's period character. Floral fabrics feature in the bedrooms, four offer superior furnishings and extras. *Amenities* garden, indoor swimming pool, steam room, solarium, games room, in-house movies (free), coffee shop (8am–8pm).

■ *Rooms* 32	*Confirm by* 4
en suite bath/shower 30	*Last dinner* 9.45
Direct dial Yes	*Parking* Ample
Room TV Yes	*Room service* All day

Cliff Tops Hotel   Shanklin

H **61% £D**
Map 5 D4 Isle of Wight
Park Road PO37 6BB
Isle of Wight (0983) 863262
Manager Mr D. R. Beckett
Credit Access, Amex, Diners, Visa
    A smart modern hotel on the cliffs, with fine sea views from many rooms and a public lift to the beach from right outside. Day rooms are quite extensive: there's a very large lounge with lots of smart wing armchairs, a quiet reading room, a coffee shop and a couple of bars, one with a motoring theme. Bedrooms are of quite a good

size, simple in decor and furnishings, and nearly all with en suite private facilities.
Amenities garden, outdoor swimming pool, sauna, solarium, keep fit equipment, hairdressing, games room, snooker, pool table, laundry service, coffee shop (10am–6pm Apr–Oct), 24-hour lounge service.

■ *Rooms* 98	*Confirm by arrang.*
en suite bath/shower 87	*Last dinner* 8
Direct dial Yes	*Parking* Ample
Room TV Yes	*Room service* 24 hours
Closed Xmas–New Year	

Meon Valley Hotel   Shedfield

H **58% £C/D**
Map 5 D4 Hampshire
Sandy Lane SO3 2HQ
Wickham (0329) 833455. Tlx 86272
Manager Terry Hussey
Credit Access, Amex, Diners, Visa
    Bedroom refurbishment has kept up standards at this modern hotel off the A334. Comfortable day rooms are on the first floor. Poor buffet

breakfasts. *Amenities* garden, indoor swimming pool, sauna, solarium, tennis, squash, golf course, putting, croquet, snooker, pool table, children's play areas, in-house movies (free), laundry service, coffee shop (9.30am–9.30pm).

■ *Rooms* 84	*Confirm by* 6
en suite bath/shower 84	*Last dinner* 9.45
Direct dial Yes	*Parking* Ample
Room TV Yes	*Room service* None

♀ indicates a **well-chosen** house wine.

Charnwood Hotel   Sheffield

H **65% £D/E**
Map 10 C2 South Yorkshire
Sharrow Lane S11 8AA
Sheffield (0742) 589411
Owner managers Mr & Mrs C. J. King
Credit Access, Amex, Diners, Visa
    In a quiet residential area a mile from the city centre, this small hotel combines Georgian charm with up-to-date comfort. Bedrooms are

particularly appealing, with brass bedheads and well-equipped bathrooms; top-floor rooms have beamed ceilings. Day rooms include a cosy lounge with cane furnishings and potted plants. No dogs. *Amenities* laundry service.

■ *Rooms* 21	*Confirm by arrang.*
en suite bath/shower 21	*Last dinner* 10
Direct dial Yes	*Parking* Ample
Room TV Yes	*Room service* 24 hours

Grosvenor House Hotel   Sheffield

H **63% £C/D**
Map 10 C2 South Yorkshire
Charter Square S1 3EH
Sheffield (0742) 722041. Tlx 54312
Credit Access, Amex, Diners, Visa. LVs
    Direct access from a multi-storey car park is one of the advantages of this modern hotel conveniently located in the city centre. Public areas include a spacious bar and lounge. Best of

the bedrooms have been prettily refurbished. All offer mini-bars, tea-makers, remote control TVs and en suite bathrooms. *Amenities* laundry service, coffee shop (11am–10.45pm), 24-hour lounge service.

■ *Rooms* 103	*Confirm by* 6
en suite bath/shower 103	*Last dinner* 9.45
Direct dial Yes	*Parking* Ample
Room TV Yes	*Room service* 24 hours

Hallam Tower Post House Hotel   Sheffield

H **65% £C/D**
Map 10 C2 South Yorkshire
Manchester Road S10 5DX
Sheffield (0742) 670067. Tlx 547293
Credit Access, Amex, Diners, Visa
    Extensive views are a feature of this '60s tower hotel on the A57. A smart, spacious reception area opens into a split-level bar-lounge where a life-size statue of a smith in Sheffield steel

provides a focal point. Refurbishment is giving a facelift to the well-kept bedrooms. *Amenities* garden, indoor swimming pool, sauna, solarium, whirlpool bath, gymnasium, laundry service, coffee shop (10am–7pm), 24-hour lounge service.

■ *Rooms* 136	*Confirm by* 6
en suite bath/shower 136	*Last dinner* 10.15
Direct dial Yes	*Parking* Ample
Room TV Yes	*Room service* 24 hours

Hotel St George   Sheffield

H **66% £D/E**
Map 10 C2 South Yorkshire
Kenwood Road S7 1NQ
Sheffield (0742) 583811. Tlx 547030
Manager Ian Macmillan
Credit Access, Amex, Diners, Visa
Seek directions when booking at this well-designed modern hotel set in attractive grounds. Public rooms include a smart, relaxing lounge and

bar. Bedrooms are neat and practical. Friendly staff. *Amenities* garden, indoor swimming pool, sauna, solarium, whirlpool bath, gymnasium, coarse fishing, laundry service, coffee shop (10am–10pm), 24-hour lounge service.

■ *Rooms* 119	*Confirm by* 6
en suite bath/shower 119	*Last dinner* 10
Direct dial Yes	*Parking* Ample
Room TV Yes	*Room service* 24 hours

Shepperton Moat House   Shepperton

H **60% £D/E**
Map 5 E2 Middlesex
Felix Lane TW17 8NP
Walton-on-Thames (0932) 241404. Tlx 928170
Credit Access, Amex, Diners, Visa
Heathrow and the M3 are both easily accessible from this modern low-rise hotel enjoying a peaceful Thames-side position. Day rooms are comfortable and attractive, and

bedrooms provide good practical comforts. *Amenities* garden, sauna, solarium, keep-fit equipment, target golf, helipad, in-house movies (free), mooring, laundry service, children's play area, snooker, pool table, 24-hour lounge service.

■ *Rooms* 180	*Confirm by* 6
en suite bath/shower 180	*Last dinner* 10
Direct dial Yes	*Parking* Ample
Room TV Yes	*Room service* Limited

Warren Lodge Hotel   Shepperton

I **£D/E**
Map 5 E2 Middlesex
Church Square TW17 9J2
Walton-on-Thames (0932) 242972. Tlx 923981
Owner manager Douglas Gordon
Credit Access, Amex, Diners, Visa
The original part of this riverside inn is an 18th-century house, but most of the accommodation is in modern blocks. Bedrooms are fairly basic but

pleasant enough; most are provided with hairdryers, remote-control TVs and shower facilities (just 12 with baths). There's an attractive lounge bar and a riverside terrace. *Amenities* garden.

■ *Rooms* 55	*Confirm by* arrang.
en suite bath/shower 52	*Last dinner* 9.45
Direct dial Yes	*Parking* Ample
Room TV Yes	*Room service* None

Blostin's   Shepton Mallet

R ♧ **Map 4 B3** Somerset
29 Waterloo Road
Shepton Mallet (0749) 3648
Credit Access, Diners, Visa
Two blackboards in the cosy bar announce the day's offerings in this stylish little bistro. The choice is well balanced, the cooking good throughout, from sweetbreads in puff pastry and squid with white wine, shallots and tomatoes to

hake with crab sauce, beef with oyster mushrooms and honey-roasted breast of duck. To finish there are home-made ice creams and sorbets. ⊖

■ *Set L* £6·95	*L by* arrang.
Set D £9·95	*D* 7–10, Sat 7–10.30
About £30 *for two*	*Parking* Ample
Seats 30 *Parties* 25	*Closed L* Sat, all Sun, & Mon, Bank Hols exc. 25 Dec & 1st 2 wks Jan

Bowlish House Restaurant   Shepton Mallet

RR **Map 4 B3** Somerset
Wells Road
Shepton Mallet (0749) 2022
Owner managers Brian & Julia Jordan
The simple four-by-four formula (four starters, four main courses) continues to prove highly successful at Brian Jordan's handsome restaurant on the A371. A typical meal might be venison and orange pâté, followed by poached wild salmon with simple vegetables. Sweets include home-made ice creams and sorbets. Fascinating wine list presented informatively under style of wine rather than country of origin.

Lesser-known great wines include seven vintages of Chateau Musar (Lebanon), from 1966, and the seldom seen Venegazzu Black Label 1982 (Veneto). ⊃ **Outstanding** ♀ **Well-chosen** ⊖

■ *Set D* £14	*D only* 7–10.30
About £45 *for two*	*Parking* Ample
Seats 25 *Parties* 32	*Closed* 24–27 Dec

Bedrooms £F

Rooms 4	*With bath/shower* 4

Four bedrooms, with en-suite facilities, have tasteful furnishings, colour TVs and many thoughtful extras.

Eastbury Hotel *NEW ENTRY* — Sherborne

H **65% £D**
Map 4 B3 Dorset
Long Street DT9 3BY
Sherborne (0935) 813131. Tlx 46644
Owner manager David Lloyd-Jones
Credit Access, Amex, Visa

George II was on the throne when this town house was built. It's been carefully restored as a comfortably appointed hotel that combines period appeal with modern amenity. Two lounges flank the entrance hall, and there's a cosy cocktail bar too. Bedrooms are traditional, bathrooms nicely maintained. No dogs. *Amenities* garden, laundry service, in-house movies (free).

■ *Rooms 12*	*Confirm by arrang.*
en suite bath/shower 12	*Last dinner 9.30*
Direct dial Yes	*Parking Ample*
Room TV Yes	*Room service All day*

Post House Hotel — Sherborne

H **60% £C/D** ♿
Map 4 B3 Dorset
Horsecastles Lane DT9 6BB
Sherborne (0935) 813191. Tlx 46522
Credit Access, Amex, Diners, Visa

Simple modern lines for this Post House standing in its own grounds on the A30 to the west of Sherborne. Colours and fabrics are carefully coordinated in the roomy lobby-lounge and small bar. Decent-sized bedrooms with fitted units are provided with tea-makers and mini-bars; eight Executive rooms offer lots more accessories. Good bathrooms. *Amenities* garden, 24-hour lounge service, putting, children's play area.

■ *Rooms 60*	*Confirm by 6*
en suite bath/shower 60	*Last dinner 10*
Room phone Yes	*Parking Ample*
Room TV Yes	*Room service 24 hours*

■ We welcome complaints and bona fide recommendations on the tear-out pages for readers' comments. They are followed up by our professional team. Please also complain to the management instantly.

Park House Hotel — Shifnal

HR **75% £D** ♿
Map 10 B4 Shropshire
Park Street, Nr Telford TF11 9BA
Telford (0952) 460128. Tlx 35438
Credit Access, Amex, Diners, Visa

Close to the town centre, two attractive houses, one dating from 1699, the other from 1750, bridged by a block of 20 superb new bedrooms. These rooms are particularly spacious, with dressing and sitting areas, but the older rooms are also of a good size, with the same good-quality built-in units and the same accessories, including trouser presses, hairdryers, fresh fruit, and sherry in a decanter. Notable among the day

rooms are the opulently chintzy Idsall Bar and its handsomely furnished neighbour, the Chinese lounge. There's also a new leisure centre. Excellent service from pleasant staff. Good breakfasts. *Amenities* garden, indoor swimming pool, sauna, solarium, whirlpool bath, in-house movies (free), laundry service.

■ *Rooms 38*	*Confirm by arrang.*
en suite bath/shower 38	*Last dinner 10*
Direct dial Yes	*Parking Ample*
Room TV Yes	*Room service 24 hours*

Idsall Rooms ♔

The setting is comfortable and stylish, with chandeliers, elegant curtains and oak panelling. The menu starts with temptations like smoked chicken and avocado with a coconut milk and lime juice dressing, and proceeds to Dover sole, fillet steak with mushroom mousse or nuggets of pork garnished with an apricot and walnut tartlet. Friendly, effective service. ♟ Well-chosen ☺

■ *Set L £10·50*	*L 12.30–2*
Set D £15·95	*D 7.30–10*
About £50 for two	*Seats 50 Parties 50*
Closed L Sat, all Sun & Mon	

■ Changes in data may occur in establishments after the Guide goes to press. Prices should be taken as indications rather than firm quotes.

Shinfield ▶

L'Ortolan ★   Shinfield

R ★ ♔ ⚬ **Map 5 D2** Berkshire
The Old Vicarage, Church Lane
Reading (0734) 883783
French cooking
Credit Access, Visa

John Burton-Race, late of Le Petit Blanc, Oxford, is settling in well as chef-patron at this elegant restaurant in a converted mellow brick vicarage. His fixed-price menus are of a high standard and offer an ample and varied choice for each course: additional daily specialities extend the range even further. Flavours and textures harmonise beautifully, as in our galantine de pied de cochon where slices of pig's trotter had been stuffed with a mousse of guinea fowl, studded with pistachio nuts. Presentation is both careful and elaborate and sauces are a real highlight. The finely chosen wine list features interesting country wines and a few magnificent bottles such as Château Lynch Bages 1961. *Specialities* salade de queues d'écrevisses et foie gras de canard,

suprême de pigeon en robe de choux sauce madère, délice de loup de mer farçie à la mousse de homard et langoustine rôti au jus de veau, nougat glacé aux framboises et son coulis.
♀ Well-chosen

■ *Set L from £18·50*	*L 12.15–2.15*
Set D £25·50	*D 7.15–10.30*
About £80 for two	*Parking Ample*
Seats 60	*Parties 25*

Closed D Sun, all Mon, 1 Jan & 2 wks late summer

Shipdham Place   Shipdham

RR ⚬ ⚬ **Map 6 C2**
Thetford IP25 7LX
Dereham (0362) 820303

Justin and Melanie de Blank were on the point of selling Shipdham Place as we went to press, and the new owners were retaining them as consultants. It's a fine country restaurant with rooms, a former rectory with parts dating back to the early 17th century. Five-course dinners by candlelight are very pleasant affairs, with sound cooking skills evident in dishes like seafood croustade with prawn and coral sauce, lamb in puff pastry and roast beef with a vintner's butter

sauce. Nice sweets. Good English and French cheeses. ♀ Well-chosen ⊖

■ *Set D £18*	*L by arrang.*
About £46 for two	*D 7.30–9.30*
Seats 36 Parties 20	*Parking Ample*

Closed 21–27 Dec & Sun–Tues 1 Jan–19 Mar

Bedrooms   £D/E

Rooms 9	*With bath/shower 8*

Bedrooms vary in size and character, some having sloping ceilings, a couple their own lobbies. Furnishings range from antiques to more modern pine and wicker; all rooms are prettily decorated and thoughtfully equipped.

■ We publish annually, so make
sure you use the current
edition. It's worth it!

Lamb Inn   Shipton-under-Wychwood

IR **£E/F**
Map 4 C1 Oxfordshire
High Street OX7 6DQ
Shipton-under-Wychwood (0993) 830465
Owner managers Hugh & Lynne Wainwright
Credit Access, Amex, Diners, Visa

Pleasant owners extend a warm welcome to their 15th-century inn. The beamed bar is a great place to enjoy a glass of well-kept ale, and there's a cosy little lounge. Steep stairs lead to decent-sized cottage bedrooms which are immaculately kept. Splendid breakfasts. No children under 14. No dogs. *Amenities* garden.

■ *Rooms 5*	*Confirm by 6*
en suite bath/shower 5	*Last dinner 9*
Room phone No	*Parking Ample*
Room TV Yes	*Room service Limited*
Closed 1 wk Xmas	

Lamb Inn Restaurant

George Benham's fixed-price menus are full of good things, and many diners start off with the really excellent gravadlax (supplementary charge). Main courses run from local trout stuffed with spinach and fennel and partridge in puff pastry with Madeira sauce to grilled rump steak, beef stroganoff or grilled marinated lamb cutlets. Tempting puds such as treacle tart or trifle, and a fine English cheeseboard. Traditional roasts on Sunday. Good wines at reasonable prices, with lots of half-bottles. ⊖

■ *Set L £8*	*L Sun only 12.30–1.45*
Set D £12	*D 7.30–9.15*
About £34 for two	*Seats 30 Parties 30*

Closed L Mon–Sat, D Sun, 1 wk Xmas

594

Inn on the Lake — Shorne

H **62% £E**
Map 7B5 Kent
Nr Gravesend DA12 3HB
Shorne (047 482) 3333. Tlx 966356
Manager Mr R. J. Roger
Credit Access, Amex, Diners, Visa
A low-rise modern hotel in a delightful lakeside setting just off the A2. Bright day rooms include a marble-floored foyer, two relaxing bars and numerous conference suites. Practical bedrooms (best with lake views) offer trouser presses, hairdryers, tea-makers and tiled bathrooms. No dogs. *Amenities* garden, coarse fishing, 24-hour lounge service.

■ *Rooms* 78	*Confirm by* 6
en suite bath/shower 78	*Last dinner* 10
Direct dial Yes	*Parking* Ample
Room TV Yes	*Room service* 24 hours

■ Our inspectors never book in the name of Egon Ronay's Guides; they disclose their identity only after paying their bills.

Country Friends — Shrewsbury

R ♧ **Map 10 A3** Shropshire
Dorrington
Dorrington (074 373) 707
Credit Amex, Diners, Visa
In an attractive beamed restaurant, six miles south of Shrewsbury on the A49, Charles and Pauline Whittaker offer sensibly short, straightforward menus that change according to the seasons. Good-quality produce (often local) is the basis of enjoyable dishes like seafood quenelles with crab sauce and duck breast in a bacon and walnut sauce. Excellent desserts might include coffee mousse cake with a lovely bitter caramel sauce.

■ *Set L & D* £9.50	*L* 12–2
About £37 *for two*	*D* 7–9.30, Sat 7–10
Seats 45 *Parties* 45	*Parking* Ample
Closed L Mon & all Sun	

Lion Hotel — Shrewsbury

H **63% £C/D**
Map 10 A3 Shropshire
Wyle Cop SY1 1UY
Shrewsbury (0743) 53107
Credit Access, Amex, Diners, Visa. **LVs**
Original beams survive in some bedrooms of this charming former coaching inn and leaded windows are still retained in the comfortable lounge and bars. An elegant Adam ballroom and classic staircase date from Georgian times. Homely bedrooms range from standard to luxury. First-class breakfasts are a bonus. *Amenities* snooker, laundry service, 24-hour lounge service.

■ *Rooms* 59	*Confirm by* 6
en suite bath/shower 59	*Last dinner* 10
Room phone Yes	*Parking* Ample
Room TV Yes	*Room service* All day

Prince Rupert Hotel — Shrewsbury

H **60% £D**
Map 10 A3 Shropshire
Butcher Row SY1 1UG
Shrewsbury (0743) 52461. Tlx 35100
Owner manager Mr L. Morris-Jones
Credit Access, Amex, Diners, Visa
Old-world chairm blends easily with modern comforts at this 15th-century hotel. The foyer-lounge is attractively furnished with modern easy chairs. Bedrooms too are in a pleasing contemporary style, though exposed beams give extra character to some. No dogs. *Amenities* games room, pool table, snooker, laundry service, in-house movies (free).

■ *Rooms* 70	*Confirm by* 6
en suite bath/shower 70	*Last dinner* 10.15
Direct dial Yes	*Parking* Ample
Room TV Yes	*Room service* 24 hours

Belmont Hotel — Sidmouth

H **61% £C/D**
Map 3 E2 Devon
The Esplanade EX10 8RX
Sidmouth (039 55) 2555
Owner manager Mr. B. E. Fitzgerald
A delightful setting – on one side, the local cricket pitch, and straight ahead, the Esplanade and sea. This hotel, run by the same family for 67 years, is thoroughly traditional in style, and old-fashioned standards of service prevail. Public rooms enjoy good sea views; best bedrooms have period furniture and balconies. No children under 2. *Amenities* garden, 24-hour lounge service.

■ *Rooms* 50	*Confirm by arrang.*
en suite bath/shower 50	*Last dinner* 8.30
Direct dial Yes	*Parking* Ample
Room TV Yes	*Room service* All day
Closed 31 Dec–mid Feb	

Fortfield Hotel
Sidmouth

H **59% £D/E**
Map 3 E2 Devon
Station Road EX10 8NU
Sidmouth (039 55) 2403
Owner managers Mr & Mrs F. W. O. Doddrell
Credit Access, Amex, Diners, Visa
  A family-run seaside hotel whose period charms
have survived extension and modernisation.
There's a sunny lounge and a smart but

windowless bar. Some bedrooms have splendid
Victorian furniture. *Amenities* garden, indoor
swimming pool, sauna, solarium, keep-fit
equipment, putting, games room, in-house movies
(free), laundry service, 24-hour lounge service.

■ *Rooms* 52	*Confirm by* arrang.
en suite bath/shower 43	*Last dinner* 8.30
Direct dial Yes	*Parking* Ample
Room TV Yes	*Room service* 24 hours

Hotel Riviera
Sidmouth

H **64% £C/D** ♿
Map 3 E2 Devon
The Esplanade EX10 8AY
Sidmouth (039 55) 5201
Credit Amex, Diners
  Overlooking Lyme Bay, this white-painted hotel
offers a warm welcome in traditional
surroundings. Flock wallpaper and velvet seating
is the style for day rooms like the lounge and

smart Regency Bar. Refurbished bedrooms (some
with balconies and sea views) boast pretty soft
furnishings. Bathrooms are all now fully tiled.
Amenities patio, in-house movie (free), laundry
service, 24-hour lounge service.

■ *Rooms* 34	*Confirm by* arrang.
en suite bath/shower 29	*Last dinner* 9
Direct dial Yes	*Parking* Limited
Room TV Yes	*Room service* 24 hours

Victoria Hotel
Sidmouth

H **67% £C** ♿
Map 3 E2 Devon
Peak Hill EX10 8RY
Sidmouth (039 55) 2651
Manager Roy Smith
Credit Access, Amex, Diners, Visa
  Dramatic sea-views are a feature of this
imposing late-Victorian hotel. Traditionally-styled
bedrooms include some splendid balconied

suites. No dogs. *Amenities* garden, indoor &
outdoor swimming pools, sauna, solarium,
whirlpool bath, keep-fit equipment, tennis, games
room, snooker, in-house movies (free), laundry
service, 24-hour lounge service.

■ *Rooms* 61	*Confirm by* 6
en suite bath/shower 61	*Last dinner* 9
Direct dial Yes	*Parking* Ample
Room TV Yes	*Room service* 24 hours

■ Any person using our name
to obtain free hospitality is
a fraud. Proprietors, please
inform the police and us.

Romans Hotel
Silchester

H **63% £D/E**
Map 5 D3 Hampshire
Little London Road, Nr Reading RG7 2PN
Silchester (0734) 700421
Owner managers Michael & Kay Riley
Credit Access, Amex, Diners, Visa
  The house was designed by Lutyens, and it's
set in beautifully kept grounds. Oak panelling and
leaded windows characterise the public areas,

and spacious bedrooms are comfortable and
stylish. Annexe rooms are more compact.
Amenities garden, outdoor swimming pool, tennis,
putting, laundry service, 24-hour lounge service.

■ *Rooms* 25	*Confirm by* arrang.
en suite bath/shower 25	*Last dinner* 9
Direct dial Yes	*Parking* Ample
Room TV Yes	*Room service* Limited
Closed 10 days Xmas	

Simonsbath House Hotel
Simonsbath

H **63% £D/E**
Map 3 D1 Somerset
Exmoor TA24 7SH
Exford (064 383) 259
Owner managers Mike & Sue Burns
Credit Access, Amex, Diners, Visa
  Mike and Sue Burns aim to recreate the mellow
hospitality of yesteryear at their sturdy 17th-
century house in the heart of Exmoor. Log fires

warm the panelled foyer-lounge and library bar.
Bedrooms have nice touches such as fruit and
flowers, and good modern bathrooms. No children
under ten. No dogs. *Amenities* garden.

■ *Rooms* 8	*Confirm by* arrang.
en suite bath/shower 8	*Last dinner* 8.30
Direct dial Yes	*Parking* Ample
Room TV Yes	*Room service* All day
Closed 10 days Xmas	

Rankins *NEW ENTRY* Sissinghurst

R ♀ **Map 7 C5** Kent
The Street
Cranbrook (0580) 713964
Credit Access, Visa
A simple homely decor gives a cosy atmosphere
to this restaurant near the famous castle and
gardens. The set-price menu changes regularly,
using fresh produce from local farms,
imaginatively prepared. Try Hastings smokie;

ragoût of lamb with green peppercorns, orange
and honey on a croustade base; finish with
chocolate fudge pudding. Sunday lunch
♀ Well-chosen

■ Set L £9	L Sun only 12–2
Set D from £10	D 7–9
About £30 for two	Parking Ample
Seats 28 Parties 23	Closed D Sun, all
Mon, Bank Hols & 2 wks Nov	

Swynford Paddocks Six Mile Bottom

H **76% £C/D**
Map 6 B3 Cambridgeshire
Nr Newmarket CB8 0UE
Six Mile Bottom (063 870) 234
Credit Access, Amex, Diners, Visa
   Once the home of Augusta, half-sister of Lord
Byron, this elegant country mansion is set back
from the A1304 in quiet, well-tended grounds.
Portraits of the pair hang in the oak-panelled
reception hall, while the redecorated bar-lounge
features a grand piano and French windows that
provide fine views of the garden. There's also a
meeting room warmed, like others, by a glowing
log fire. Bedrooms vary in size and decor; they
have smart contemporary furniture, coordinating
fabrics and a multitude of extras including radio-
alarms, mini-bars, trouser presses and tea-
makers. Bathrooms range from fairly compact to a

sumptuous one with sunken bath, shower cubicle,
bidet and gold taps in the four-poster room.
Amenities garden, tennis, pitch & putt, croquet.

■ Rooms 15	Confirm by 6
en suite bath/shower 15	Last dinner 9.30
Direct dial Yes	Parking Ample
Room TV Yes	Room service All day

Hark To Bounty Inn *NEW ENTRY* Slaidburn

I **£F**
Map 10 B1 Lancashire
Nr Clitheroe BB7 3AQ
Slaidburn (020 06) 246
Credit Access, Amex, Diners, Visa
   Bounty was a loud-barking member of a local
pack, and this ancient village inn changed its
name in Victorian times to commemorate him.
Polished oak and burnished brass characterise

the bar-lounge, and there's a homely residents'
lounge. At the top of the inn is a characterful
family-size bedroom with sitting area; other rooms
are smaller and cosy. Amenities garden, game
fishing, laundry service.

■ Rooms 8	Confirm by arrang.
en suite bath/shower 7	Last dinner 9
Room phone No	Parking Ample
Room TV Yes	Room service All day

Holiday Inn Slough

H **76% £C E ♿**
Map 5 E2 Berkshire
Ditton Road, Langley SL3 8PT
Slough (0753) 44244. Tlx 848646
Credit Access, Amex, Diners, Visa
   Superb leisure facilities combined with
comfortable, attractive public and private areas
make this fine modern hotel an all-round winner.
An impressive marble-floored foyer leads to
various lounge areas which provide ample space
for relaxation and, like the inviting cocktail bar, are
decorated with sure taste in pleasing colour
combinations. Newer bedrooms are prettily
styled, with smart lightwood furniture; remaining
rooms are being gradually upgraded to the same
high standard. Bathrooms have hairdryers.
Amenities garden, indoor swimming pool, sauna,
solarium, whirlpool bath, gymnasium, keep-fit

equipment, hairdressing, tennis, pool table, in-
house movies, laundry service, coffee shop (7am–
11.30pm), 24-hour lounge service, children's play
area, courtesy transport.

■ Rooms 302	Confirm by 6
en suite bath/shower 302	Last dinner 11.30
Direct dial Yes	Parking Ample
Room TV Yes	Room service 24 hours

George Hotel   Solihull

H **57% £D/E**
Map 10 C4 West Midlands
The Square B91 3RF
021-704 1241
Credit Access, Amex, Diners, Visa
Guests at this modernised coaching inn can work up a gentle thirst on the bowling green before retiring to one of the various bars – either rustic and traditional or plushly contemporary in style. There's also a small foyer-lounge. Bedrooms, mostly in a modern wing with private bathrooms, offer simple, practical comforts.
Amenities garden, bowling green, laundry service, 24-hour lounge service.

■ *Rooms 46*	*Confirm by noon*
en suite bath/shower 41	*Last dinner 9.15*
Direct dial Yes	*Parking Ample*
Room TV Yes	*Room service 24 hours*

Liaison *NEW ENTRY*   Solihull

R ♤ **Map 10 C4** West Midlands
761 Old Lode Lane
021-743 3993
Credit Access, Amex, Diners, Visa
A smart restaurant in green and white and a pleasant setting for Patricia Plunkett's accomplished and imaginative cooking. Fresh seasonal produce goes into delights like asparagus gâteau with chervil butter and salmon parcels; guinea fowl with shallots; and tender lamb fillet with rosemary, forest mushrooms and Madeira. French cheeses and a tempting sweet menu. Plain dishes also available. Get directions when booking. ☺

■ *About £50 for two*	*D 7–10*
Seats 28 Parties 40	*Parking Ample*
Closed Sun, Mon, Bank Hols, 2 wks Xmas & all Aug	

Regency Hotel *NEW ENTRY*   Solihull

H **72% £D/E**
Map 10 C4 West Midlands
Stratford Road, Shirley B90 4EB
021-7456119. Tlx 334400
Manager Geoff Marshall
Credit Access, Amex, Diners, Visa
An attractive cream-painted building, this first-class hotel stands in its own grounds alongside the A34, about 7 miles from Birmingham and close to the M42. The reception area, with its plethora of potted plants, is welcoming and there's an elegant, spacious cocktail bar. The Victorian-style Pavillion Bar, the hotel's 'pub', is separated from the main building by a locked door. Generous bedrooms are tastefully furnished with free-standing units and trouser presses, hairdryers, tea-making facilities and remote-control TVs. Tiled bathrooms are well equipped if a bit small.

Amenities garden, laundry service, coffee shop (9am–noon and 2.30pm–7pm), 24-hour lounge service.

■ *Rooms 59*	*Confirm by 6*
en suite bath/shower 59	*Last dinner 10*
Direct dial Yes	*Parking Ample*
Room TV Yes	*Room service Limited*

St John's Swallow Hotel   Solihull

H **65% £D**
Map 10 C4 West Midlands
651 Warwick Road B91 1AT
021-705 6777. Tlx 339352
Credit Access, Amex, Diners, Visa
Handy for the motorway network, this smart modern hotel appeals to both business people and holidaymakers on the move. Good-sized bedrooms are equipped with irons and ironing boards, hairdryers and tea-makers. There's a quiet lounge and lively bar, and a leisure centre was due to open in October 1987.
Amenities garden, in-house movies (free), laundry service, 24-hour lounge service.

■ *Rooms 200*	*Confirm by arrang.*
en suite bath/shower 200	*Last dinner 9.45*
Direct dial Yes	*Parking Ample*
Room TV Yes	*Room service Limited*

The Lynch Country House Hotel *NEW ENTRY*   Somerton

H **69% £D/E**
Map 4 A3 Somerset
Behind Berry PA11 7PB
Somerton (0458) 72316
Owner managers Alicia & Karl Heinz Stolzenberg
Credit Access, Amex, Diners, Visa
A pleasant Georgian house standing in four acres of grounds and run in friendly style by its owners. There are two comfortable lounges and most bedrooms are spacious and attractively furnished. Bathrooms are luxurious. No children under ten. *Amenities* garden, outdoor swimming pool, solarium, croquet, laundry service.

■ *Rooms 5*	*Confirm by arrang.*
en suite bath/shower 5	*Last dinner 9.30*
Direct dial Yes	*Parking Ample*
Room TV Yes	*Room service All day*
Closed Last 2 wks Jan	

■ Our inspectors are our full-time employees; they are professionally trained by us.

Red Lion Hotel — Somerton

H 61% £E
Map 4 A3 Somerset
Broad Street TA11 7NJ
Somerton (0458) 72339
Owner managers Mr & Mrs T. J. Jacobs
Credit Access, Amex, Diners, Visa

The Jacobs team do a good job in running this popular coaching inn, which dates from the 17th century. The atmosphere throughout is warm and welcoming, with log fires and handsome panelling in the bar and restful lounge. Some of the bedrooms, too, are in fine period style, and include 4-poster beds. Well-kept private facilities. *Amenities* laundry service.

■ Rooms 15	Confirm by arrang.
en suite bath/shower 15	Last dinner 10
Direct dial Yes	Parking Ample
Room TV Yes	Room service 24 hours

White Hart Hotel — Sonning-on-Thames

H 64% £D
Map 5 D2 Berkshire
Nr Reading RG4 0UT
Reading (0734) 692277. Tlx 849031
Credit Access, Amex, Diners, Visa

Friendly, efficient staff are a major asset at this pleasant hotel in a pretty riverside setting. Beams and panelling are much in evidence in the main building, and the cottage extensions have charming Elizabethan exteriors. Bedrooms, sporting bright coordinated fabrics, offer tea-makers, hairdryers and trouser presses. We noticed the odd little lapse in maintenance. *Amenities* garden, laundry service.

■ Rooms 25	Confirm by 6
en suite bath/shower 25	Last dinner 10
Direct dial Yes	Parking Ample
Room TV Yes	Room service 24 hours

La Bonne Auberge — South Godstone

R ☖ Map 7 B5 Surrey
Tilburston Hill
South Godstone (0342) 892318
French cooking
Manager Antoine Jalley
Credit Access, Amex, Visa

An attractive Victorian house is the setting for the skilful cooking of Jean-Pierre Bonnet, whose menus are full of interest and imagination. Mussel and saffron soup, pork fillet with a sage sauce and poached scallops in a walnut and butter sauce are typical delights. Tempting sweets to finish. Good-value clarets and Beaujolais crus.
🍷 Well-chosen ⊜

■ Set L from £15·50	L 12.15–2
Set D £22	D 7–10
About £55 for two	Parking Ample
Seats 72 Parties 90	Closed D Sun, all Mon

South Marston Hotel — South Marston

H 56% £C/D
Map 4 C2 Wiltshire
Nr Swindon SN3 4SH
Swindon (0793) 827777. Tlx 444634
Credit Access, Amex, Diners, Visa

In a quiet rural setting outside Swindon, this cheerful modern hotel boasts splendid sports and leisure facilities. Attractively furnished bedrooms are located in a separate block away from the public areas. No dogs. *Amenities* garden, indoor & outdoor swimming pools, sauna, solarium, whirlpool bath, gymnasium, squash, badminton, snooker, laundry service, coffee shop (9.30am–10.30pm), children's play area.

■ Rooms 40	Confirm by arrang.
en suite bath/shower 40	Last dinner 9.45
Direct dial Yes	Parking Ample
Room TV Yes	Room service Limited

Selby Fork Hotel — South Milford

H 63% £E/F ♿
Map 11 D1 North Yorkshire
Nr Leeds LS25 5LF
South Milford (0977) 682711. Tlx 682711
Credit Access, Amex, Diners, Visa

Popular with the business community for its extensive conference facilities, this modern hotel is pleasantly situated in wooded grounds by the A1. Light spacious public areas include a bar overlooking the pool. Bedrooms vary markedly in size and decor; all are neat and tidy. *Amenities* garden, sauna, indoor swimming pool, tennis, in-house movies (charge), pitch & putt, laundry service, children's play area, helipad.

■ Rooms 109	Confirm by arrang.
en suite bath/shower 109	Last dinner 10
Direct dial Yes	Parking Ample
Room TV Yes	Room service 24 hours

Crest Hotel   South Mimms

H **60% £C/D**
Map 5 E2 Hertfordshire
Bignells Corner, Nr Potters Bar EN6 3NH
Potters Bar (0707) 43311. Tlx 299162
Credit Access, Amex, Diners, Visa
    A modern hotel on the B197, conveniently close
to junction 23 of the M25, with a bright and
welcoming foyer and bar. Good-sized functional
bedrooms with neat, compact bathrooms offer

fresh fruit, mineral water and hairdryers.
Amenities garden, indoor swimming pool, sauna,
solarium, whirlpool bath, keep-fit equipment,
snooker, pool table, laundry service, coffee shop
(9.30am–6.30pm), children's playground.
■ *Rooms* 120   *Confirm by* 6
en suite bath/shower 120   *Last dinner* 9.45
Direct dial Yes   *Parking* Ample
Room TV Yes   *Room service* All day

Swallow Hotel   South Normanton

H **71% £D** *E* &
Map 11 D3 Derbyshire
Carter Lane East DE55 2EH
Ripley (0773) 812000. Tlx 377264
Credit Access, Amex, Diners, Visa. LVs
    Popular with motorists and business people,
this modern red-brick hotel lies just off the M1
(junction 28). Bedrooms, including three adapted
for disabled guests, are comfortable and well
equipped, with ironing facilities, bedside controls
and mini-bars as standard features. Public areas
include a brick-walled and quarry-tiled lobby-
lounge, a softly lit bar and a distinctive seven-
sided restaurant, plus meeting rooms and a
leisure club. Contemporary artwork is in evidence
throughout the hotel. Unfortunately housekeeping
occasionally slips.
Amenities garden, indoor swimming pool, sauna,

solarium, whirlpool bath, gymnasium, in-house
movies (free), laundry service, coffee shop (7am–
10.30pm), 24-hour lounge service.
■ *Rooms* 123   *Confirm by* 6
en suite bath/shower 123   *Last dinner* 9.45
Direct dial Yes   *Parking* Ample
Room TV Yes   *Room service* 24 hours

■ We welcome complaints and bona
  fide recommendations on the
  tear-out pages for readers' comments.
  They are followed up by our professional
  team. Please also complain to the
  management instantly.

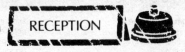

RECEPTION

South Walsham Hall Hotel   South Walsham

H **61% £E**
Map 6 D1 Norfolk
Nr Norwich NR13 6DQ
South Walsham (060 549) 378
Owner manager Alex Suss
Credit Access, Amex, Diners, Visa
    Lawns and lakes provide the setting for this
gabled red-brick mansion situated about 11 miles
outside Norwich on the B1140. A handsome
staircase dominates the roomy, traditionally-
furnished foyer, and the bar and lounge invite
relaxation. Most bedrooms are spacious and
individually furnished, with both period and

modern features, and have cool, simple colour
schemes and coordinated fabrics. There are also
seven more modern rooms in an annexe and three
luxury suites in the main house – one of which
boasts a magnificent bathroom. *Amenities* sauna,
outdoor swimming pool, solarium, keep-fit
equipment, tennis, squash, coarse fishing, riding,
pool table, badminton, kennels.
■ *Rooms* 19   *Confirm by* arrang.
en suite bath/shower 16   *Last dinner* 9.45
Room phone Yes   *Parking* Ample
Room TV Yes   *Room service* All day
Closed Jan

Ho-Ho   South Woodford

R **Map 7 B4** Essex
20 High Road
01-989 1041
Chinese cooking
Owner manager Steve Man
Credit Access, Amex, Diners, Visa
    Peking and Szechuan set dinners provide
attractive introductions to Chinese cuisine at this
smart, well-run restaurant. The rest of the menu

offers a good choice of tasty, carefully prepared
dishes, including crispy seaweed and scallops,
delicious aromatic duck with pancakes, and a
spicy hot and sour soup. Glazed toffee apples for
afters. ☻ Well-chosen
■ *Set L* £6   *L* 12–3
Set D £12   *D* 6–11.30
About £37 for two   *Parking* Ample
Seats 80 *Parties* 60   *Closed* 2 days Xmas

Dolphin Hotel   Southampton

H 59% £D
Map 5 D4 Hampshire
High Street SO9 2DS
Southampton (0703) 226178. Tlx 477735
Credit Access, Amex, Diners, Visa. LVs

There's been an inn on this site since the 13th
century, and the current one has a very
handsome Georgian facade. Ties with the sea are
shown in the nautical-style bar, and in the Spy

prints of Victorian sea lords that adorn the
splendid stairwell. Bedrooms, all with private
facilities, start at smallish singles and get larger.
Breakfast was not the high point of a recent visit.
Amenities garden, laundry service.

■ Rooms 74	Confirm by 6
en suite bath/shower 74	Last dinner 9.45
Room phone Yes	Parking Ample
Room TV Yes	Room service None

Polygon Hotel   Southampton

H 65% £C/D
Map 5 D4 Hampshire
Cumberland Place SO9 4GD
Southampton (0703) 226401. Tlx 47175
Credit Access, Amex, Diners, Visa. LVs

Impressive public rooms are a notable feature
of this 18th century hotel. Most elegant is the
drawing room, with its chandeliers mirroring
handsome furniture. A smart foyer, panelled bar

and bright coffee shop are equally fine. Bedrooms
are spacious, and some have coordinated colours
and neat units. Staff are friendly and helpful.
Amenities coffee shop (10am–10pm), laundry
service, 24-hour lounge service.

■ Rooms 119	Confirm by 6
en suite bath/shower 119	Last dinner 10
Direct dial Yes	Parking Ample
Room TV Yes	Room service 24 hours

Post House Hotel   Southampton

H 59% £C/D
Map 5 D4 Hampshire
Herbert Walker Avenue SO1 0HJ
Southampton (0703) 228081. Tlx 477368
Credit Access, Amex, Diners, Visa

Follow signs for Dock Gate 8 for easy access to
this multi-storey hotel overlooking the QE2's
berth. The foyer lounge has attractive leather-look
chesterfields; a second lounge is contemporary.

The Harbour Bar pays homage to the hotel's
location. Cheerful bedrooms have mini-bars and
tea-makers. *Amenities* garden, outdoor
swimming pool, laundry service, laundry room, 24-
hour lounge service.

■ Rooms 132	Confirm by 6
en suite bath/shower 132	Last dinner 10
Direct dial Yes	Parking Ample
Room TV Yes	Room service Limited

Southampton Park Hotel   Southampton

H 64% £D/E
Map 5 D4 Hampshire
Cumberland Place SO9 4NY
Southampton (0703) 223467. Tlx 47439
Manager Mr D. Larcombe
Credit Access, Amex, Diners, Visa

Enjoying a prime central position overlooking
Watts Park, this well-managed hotel boasts a
smartly modernised interior behind its 1930s

facade. Plush seating and a copper-canopied
fireplace impress in the foyer. Some thoughtfully
equipped bedrooms have balconies, all have
good tiled bathrooms. *Amenities* in-house movies
(free), 24-hour lounge service, laundry service.

■ Rooms 75	Confirm by 6
en suite bath/shower 75	Last dinner 11
Direct dial Yes	Parking Ample
Room TV Yes	Room service 24 hours

■ Changes in data may occur in
establishments after the Guide
goes to press. Prices should be taken
as indications rather than firm quotes.

Bold Hotel   Southport

H 54% £E/F
Map 10 A1 Merseyside
Lord Street PR9 0BE
Southport (0704) 32578
Owner managers James & Peter Moore
Credit Access, Amex, Diners, Visa

New owners James and Peter Moore have
made major improvements here, and
refurbishment of the accommodation continues.

All bedrooms have tea-makers and there's one
with a luxury sunken bath en suite. Downstairs
there's a popular public bar, a quieter cocktail bar
and an air-conditioned functions suite. *Amenities*
24-hour lounge service.

■ Rooms 25	Confirm by 5
en suite bath/shower 19	Last dinner 10
Direct dial Yes	Parking Limited
Room TV Yes	Room service 24 hours

Prince of Wales Hotel   Southport

H **65% £C/D**
Map 10 A1 Merseyside
Lord Street PR8 1JS
Southport (0704) 36688. Tlx 67415
Credit Access, Amex, Diners, Visa

Conveniently located in the town centre, and close to Royal Birkdale, this Victorian hotel is equally popular with golfers, holidaymakers and businessmen. Spacious public rooms include a lounge furnished in traditional style, two bars and two large function suites. Most bedrooms are attractively furnished with oak-effect units. Tiled bathrooms are well equipped. *Amenities* garden, in-house movies (charge), laundry service.

■ *Rooms 103*	*Confirm by 6*
en suite bath/shower 103	*Last dinner 10*
Direct dial Yes	*Parking Ample*
Room TV Yes	*Room service 24 hours*

Southsea

See under Portsmouth

Saracen's Head Hotel   Southwell

H **61% £D/E**
Map 11 D3 Nottinghamshire
Market Place NG25 0HE
Southwell (0636) 812701. Tlx 377201
Credit Access, Amex, Diners, Visa

Intimate beamed bars are in keeping with the character of this historic inn, which dates back to the 16th century. There's nothing old-fashioned about the bedroom amenities, however, which include tea-makers, trouser presses and hairdryers. Fittings are simple but of good quality and three of the bedrooms are designated for non-smokers. *Amenities* laundry service.

■ *Rooms 27*	*Confirm by 6*
en suite bath/shower 27	*Last dinner 9.45*
Direct dial Yes	*Parking Ample*
Room TV Yes	*Room service 24 hours*
Closed 27 & 28 Dec	

Crown   Southwold

IR **£E/F**
Map 6 D2 Suffolk
High Street IP18 6DP
Southwold (0502) 722275
Credit Access, Amex, Visa

A fine old inn situated in the centre of this delightful seaside town, offering a good standard of comfortable accommodation. The public rooms include a cheerful, traditional lounge and a wooden-floored bar with solid farmhouse-style furniture. There's also a cosy wood-panelled back bar with red leather seating. Bright bedrooms are simply furnished, clean and comfortable, most with bathrooms.

■ *Rooms 12*	*Confirm by arrang.*
en suite bath/shower 9	*Last dinner 9.45*
Direct dial Yes	*Parking Ample*
Room TV Yes	*Room service Limited*

Crown Restaurant &

Adjacent to the inn's main bar, this attractive little restaurant offers constantly updated short menus and a truly superb choice of wines by the glass from a Cruover machine. Chef Tim Reeson's imaginative choices might include roast monkfish with red peppercorns, steamed fillet of brill with a citronella sauce or breast of duck with a leek and Madeira coulis. To start, perhaps a fish soup or stuffed peppers; to follow a good selection of sweets (lemon syllabub, blueberry fool, chocolate mousse and homemade ices).

◇ Outstanding   ♀ Well-chosen ⊖

■ *Set L from £8*	*L 12.30–2*
Set D from £10	*D 7.30–9.45*
About £33 for two	*Seats 26 Parties 50*

Swan Hotel   Southwold

H **60% £E**
Map 6 D2 Suffolk
Market Place IP18 6EG
Southwold (0502) 722186
Credit Access, Amex, Diners, Visa

Overlooking the market place, this ivy-clad coaching inn dating back to the 17th century makes a pleasant overnight stop. Traditionally furnished bedrooms are bright and cheerful, whether in the main building or in an attractive garden complex; most have their own neat bathrooms. Public rooms include a large, panelled lounge with comfortable winged chairs, and a cosy little bar. *Amenities* garden.

■ *Rooms 53*	*Confirm by arrang.*
en suite bath/shower 36	*Last dinner 8.30*
Room phone Yes	*Parking Ample*
Room TV Yes	*Room service 24 hours*

■ We publish annually, so make sure you use the current edition. It's worth it!

Bridgefield House — Spark Bridge

HR 58% £E
Map 13 C6 Cumbria
Nr Ulverston LA12 8DA
Lowick Bridge (022 985) 239
Owner managers David & Rosemary Glister
Credit Access, Amex

Look for this sturdily built hotel above the river Crake, not far from the A5084. The Glisters are charming hosts and the atmosphere is welcoming and informal in the cosy little bar and relaxing lounge warmed by a log fire. Spacious, traditional bedrooms are equipped with hairdryers and radio-alarms. Good bathrooms.
Amenities garden, laundry service.

■ *Rooms* 5	*Confirm by arrang.*
en suite bath/shower 3	*Last dinner* 7.30
Room phone No	*Parking* Ample
Room TV No	*Room service* All day

Bridgefield House Restaurant ⑂

Fresh seasonal produce is the inspiration for Rosemary Glister's imaginative dinners at this smart, candlelit restaurant. Starters like liver pâté with a damson and bramble sauce or hot potted sea bass precede soup – perhaps curried parsnip – and a main course like roast breast of goose or lamb cutlets sauced with red wine and ginger. Creamy sweets like cinnamon and soured cream flan and a savoury follow, then it's home-made fudge and coffee in the lounge. No smoking in the dining room. Non-residents must book.

■ *Set D* £16	*D only* 7.30 for 8
About £45 for two	*Seats* 30 *Parties* 30

Old Plow Inn *NEW ENTRY* — Speen

IR £D/E
Map 5 E2 Buckinghamshire
Flowers Bottom HP17 0PZ
Hampden Row (024 028) 300
Owner managers Bill & Frances Atkins
Credit Access, Amex, Diners, Visa

The Atkins' peaceful brick-and-flint inn began life as a forge in the early 17th century. Beams and stone floor tiles give an old-fashioned, stylish charm to the bar, staffed by pleasantly efficient young staff. Delightful bedrooms are spotless, with fresh flowers, and other homely touches. No children under ten.
Amenities garden.

■ *Rooms* 3	*Confirm by* arrang.
en suite bath/shower 2	*Last dinner* 9.30
Room phone No	*Parking* Ample
Room TV No	*Room service* Limited

Atkins Restaurant ⑂

More oak beams, fresh flowers, and an open fire and crisp white linen set the scene in this spacious, comfortable restaurant for Frances Atkins' very talented cooking. Her menus, based on the freshest produce, appeal to a variety of tastes, with standards like steaks, smoked salmon and whole Dover sole with hollandaise sauce joined by daily changing delights such as asparagus and watercress mousse with prawn brochette, a warm mushroom and sweetbread salad or a trio of fowl with a spot-on rhubarb sauce. Sweets are delicious, too. ☺

■ *Set L* £12·50	*L* 12.30–2
About £50 for two	*D* 7.30–9.30
Seats 30	*Parties* 30
Closed L Sat, D Sun, all Mon & 25 Dec	

■ Our inspectors never book in the name of Egon Ronay's Guides; they disclose their identity only after paying their bills.

George & Dragon, Oak Room — Speldhurst

R **Map 7 B5** Kent
Tunbridge Wells
Langton (089 286) 3125
Credit Access, Amex, Diners, Visa

Have a drink in the bar of this mellow 13th-century inn before climbing the stairs to the charming beamed restaurant overlooking the church. Quality raw materials – often local – are used in carefully cooked dishes like grilled turbot with lobster sauce, or rump steak and oyster pie. Excellent cheeses and magnificent wines: the cellar still includes clarets from the great (now rare) 1959 vintage. ⇨ **Outstanding** ☺

■ *Set L* £9	*L* 12–3.30
Set D £16·75	*D* 7–12.30
About £48 for two	*Parking* Ample
Closed L Sat, D Sun &	*Seats* 50
all Bank Hol Mons	

■ If we recommend meals in a hotel or inn, a separate entry is made for its restaurant.

McCoy's at the Tontine   Staddle Bridge

HR 70% £C/D
Map 15 C5 North Yorkshire
Nr Northallerton DL6 3JB
East Harlsey (060 982) 671
Owner managers McCoy brothers
Credit Access, Amex, Diners, Visa

The McCoy brothers know how to cosset
guests at their delightful roadside hotel, which
has emerged fresh-as-paint after recent
refurbishment. Flowers fill every room, enhancing
the bold new floral chintzes chosen for sofas and
armchairs in the lounge and comfortably informal
1930s-style bar. Stunning wallpapers in the
bedrooms complement apple-green carpets and
handsome old furnishings. Glossy magazines,
Malvern water, a glass of sherry, and tea for
afternoon arrivals are typically thoughtful touches,
and the sparkling black-and-white private
bathrooms are equally well equipped.
Amenities garden, coarse fishing, laundry
service.

■ *Rooms* 6	*Confirm by* arrang.
en suite bath/shower 6	*Last dinner* 10
Direct dial Yes	*Parking* Ample
Room TV Yes	*Room service* All day
Closed 24–26 Dec & 1 Jan	

McCoy's Restaurant ★★ 🍸

The menus fairly sing with excitement at this most
flamboyant of restaurants, where Tom McCoy's
exquisite cooking has reached even greater
heights over the past year. The quality of
ingredients, sheer skill, and imagination are
beyond reproach, from the simplicity of fresh
tomato consommé perfumed with coriander to the
elaborate detail of superbly tender pigeon lightly
roasted with creamy baby leeks, fresh truffle and
foie gras. Crisply cooked vegetables burst with
flavour, and sweets are simply sensational – note
wickedly rich chocolate gâteau soaked through
with Tia Maria, or the colourful terrine of kiwi,
strawberry, orange and pineapple with an almond
cream filling. Wonderfully warm service. Good
classic wines include Château Beychevelle 1966
in magnums, and Eichberg Gewurztraminer 1983
(Dopff au Moulin). *Specialities* noodles,
langoustine and scallops with a tomato and herb
sauce, foie gras de canard with black cherry
sauce, mille-feuille with crème pâtisserie and
strawberries. 🍷 Well-chosen 🍷

■ *About* £60 *for two*	*L by* arrang. only
Seats 40 *Parties* 20	*D* 7–10.30
Closed Sun & Bank Hols (exc. Good Fri)	

🍷 is our symbol for an **outstanding** wine list.

Tillington Hall Hotel   Stafford

H 60% £E
Map 10 B3 Staffordshire
Eccleshall Road ST16 1JJ
Stafford (0785) 53531. Tlx 36566
Credit Access, Amex, Diners, Visa

Good conference facilities make this
whitewashed hotel near junction 14 of the M6
popular with business visitors. A smart bar-lounge
and more traditionally pubby bar provide

contrasting drinking venues. Modern wings house
bright, well-equipped bedrooms; those in the
original building are simpler, save for a luxurious
suite. *Amenities* garden, tennis, 24-hour lounge
service, laundry service.

■ *Rooms* 90	*Confirm by* 6
en suite bath/shower 90	*Last dinner* 9.45
Direct dial Yes	*Parking* Ample
Room TV Yes	*Room service* Limited

Crown Hotel *NEW ENTRY*   Stamford

I £F
Map 11 E4 Lincolnshire
All Saints Place PE9 2AG
Stamford (0780) 63136
Owner managers R. D. & E. N. McGahon
Credit Access, Amex, Diners, Visa

Dating back to 1678, the Crown stands in the
heart of town next to All Saints Church. Fresh
flowers are an attractive feature in the homely bar

and peaceful, pretty lounge, and also in the
smartly kept bedrooms, which are furnished with
a variety of modern pieces. The friendly owner is
an avid angler, and the Stamford Fly Fishers
Association meets here.

■ *Rooms* 18	*Confirm by* 7
en suite bath/shower 15	*Parking* Ample
Room phone Yes	*Room service* None
Room TV Yes	*Closed* 25 Dec

George of Stamford

Stamford

HR **71% £C/D** *E*
Map 11 E4 Lincolnshire
71 St Martin's High Street PE9 2LB
Stamford (0780) 55171. Tlx 32578
Credit Access, Amex, Diners, Visa

Jolyon Gough and his switched-on staff cope admirably and with good humour at this busy hotel, whose heart is a handsome 16th-century coaching inn. Period charm and up-to-date comfort come in equal measure, and the tone is set by a fine stone-floored entrance hall furnished with old oak travelling chests and brightened by flower displays. The comfortable lounge and the panelled bar are no less inviting, and the cobbled courtyard is a summer honeypot. Much thought has gone into the bedrooms, which are individually decorated and furnished with style

and taste; trouser presses and hairdryers are provided, and private bathrooms are generally excellent. *Amenities* garden, croquet, teletext, laundry service, coffee shop (9am–11pm).

■ *Rooms 47*	*Confirm by arrang.*
en suite bath/shower 47	*Last dinner 10*
Direct dial Yes	*Parking Ample*
Room TV Yes	*Room service 24 hours*

George of Stamford Restaurant 🍴 &

Manager Carol Bettinson
A handsome panelled dining room, very 'county' in feel, with a stone fireplace and diamond-pane windows. Chef Christopher Pitman keeps the basis of his cooking traditional, with roast beef and another joint always available, but there are many modern and imaginative touches, too, like ravioli verdi filled with smoked salmon and ricotta ravioli in a fish velouté, or quick-grilled escalopes of veal with a flavoursome cream and kümmel liqueur sauce. Excellent vegetables and good cheeses in fine condition, especially Cheddar, Stilton and Brie. High-quality wines from excellent growers: '84 Alsace Riesling (Zind Humbrecht), '79 Barbaresco (Gaja), '79 Clos St Denis (Dujac). Cheerful service.

⇨ Outstanding 🍷 Well-chosen ☺

■ *About £50 for two*	*L 12.30–2.30*
Seats 90	*D 7–10*

Harcourt Arms

Stanton Harcourt

IR **£E**
Map 5 D2 Oxfordshire
Nr Eynsham OX8 1RJ
Oxford (0865) 882192
Owner managers Mr & Mrs G. Dailey
Credit Access, Amex, Diners, Visa

Bedrooms are in pleasant cottage style at this nice old creeper-covered inn; antique country furniture complements pretty floral patterns. Ten compact rooms with modern private bathrooms are in an extension, while six with shared facilities are in a cottage across the road. One large room has a four-poster. No children under ten. No dogs. *Amenities* garden.

■ *Rooms 16*	*Confirm by arrang.*
en suite bath/shower 10	*Last dinner 9.45*
Direct dial Yes	*Parking Ample*
Room TV Yes	*Room service None*

Harcourt Arms 🍷 &

Popular demand has caused the restaurant to expand into the bar and the bar to move across the passage. The whole place has a friendly, relaxed air and you're just as welcome for a quick bowl of steaming mussels or a sandwich as you are for a slap-up meal. Prime ingredients get simple, careful treatment by George Dailey in a variety of delights, from satay, grilled prawns and splendid fish pie to liver and bacon, rack of lamb, traditional fish and chips and a selection of steaks. For pud, try treacle tart, perhaps, or delicious crème brûlée. ☺

■ *Set L & D £13·75*	*L 12–2.30*
About £35 for two	*D 6–10.30,*
Seats 100	*Sun 7–10.30*
Parties 120	*Closed 25 Dec*

Bridge Inn Restaurant

Stapleton

R 🍷 **Map 15 B5** Co. Durham
Nr Darlington DL2 2QQ
Darlington (0325) 50106
Credit Access, Amex, Diners, Visa

Be prepared to wait (but it's worth it) while owner Nicholas Young prepares his tempting menu of sound classical dishes. Local produce is often featured, vegetables are wonderfully fresh, and the seasonal choice could include salmon

quenelles, quail stuffed with prunes and walnuts, or veal stuffed with cheese, ham and sage. Lunch is a reduced choice table d'hôte. ☺

■ *Set L £7·25*	*L 12–1.45*
About £35 for two	*D 7–10*
Seats 32 Parties 32	*Parking Ample*

Closed L Sat, D Sun, all Mon & Bank Hols except Easter

Red Lion   Steeple Aston

R ⑨ **Map 5 D1** Oxfordshire
Oxford OX5 3RY
Steeple Aston (0869) 40225
Credit Access, Visa
   Margaret Mead's accomplished cooking finds a
splendid setting in this tiny pub restaurant. Pâté-
stuffed mushrooms and creamy onion soup are
popular starters, and main courses include a first-
rate pepper steak. Salmon mayonnaise is a

favourite in summer, veal with lemon the year
round. Good puds, too, like sherry-flavoured
charlotte russe. The wine list is strong in clarets.
♀ Well-chosen ⊜

■ Set D £12·70	D only 7.30–9.30
About £38 for two	Parking Limited
Seats 20	Parties 20
Closed Sun, Mon, 25 & 26 Dec & 2 wks Oct	

Roebuck Inn   Stevenage

H **59% £C/D**
Map 6 B3 Hertfordshire
Old London Road, Broadwater SG2 8DS
Stevenage (0438) 65444. Tlx 825505
Credit Access, Amex, Diners, Visa. LVs
   Dating back to the 15th-century, this much-
extended inn stands south of Stevenage on the
B197. Beams, red velour chairs and cheerful
winter fires add to the cosy, welcoming appeal of

public areas. A glass-enclosed passageway leads
to the modern bedroom block, where all the
comfortable rooms have tea-makers and private
bathrooms. *Amenities* garden, laundry service,
24-hour lounge service.

■ Rooms 54	Confirm by 6
en suite bath/shower 54	Last dinner 9.45
Direct dial Yes	Parking Ample
Room TV Yes	Room service 24 hours

Springwells Hotel   Steyning

H **58% £E**
Map 5 E4 West Sussex
9 High Street BN4 3GG
Steyning (0903) 812446
Owner manager Jeanne Heselgrave
Credit Access, Amex, Diners, Visa
   Businessmen appreciate the homely
atmosphere of this handsome little Georgian
house in the main street. There's a smart lounge

and cocktail bar in Regency style, and a
conservatory and pretty garden. Bedrooms offer
traditional comforts; two have four-posters.
Bathrooms are spotless. No dogs. *Amenities*
garden, outdoor swimming pool, sauna.

■ Rooms 10	Confirm by arrang.
en suite bath/shower 6	Last dinner None
Room phone Yes	Parking Limited
Room TV Yes	Room service Limited

Springfield Country Hotel   Stoborough

See under Wareham

Game Larder *NEW ENTRY*   Stockbridge

R ⑨ ♿ **Map 4 C3** Hampshire
New Street
Andover (0264) 810414
Credit Access, Amex, Diners, Visa
   Comfortably converted barn, with open
fireplaces and a wealth of oak beams. Charles
Donovan cooks well, using predominantly local
ingredients. Game ranges from pigeon, teal and
grouse to hare and venison; other choices could

include pike quenelles, veal escalope and the
day's roast. Carefully chosen cellar (note the very
fine Chianti Castell'in Villa 1975).
♀ Well-chosen ⊜

■ About £40 for two	L by arrang.
Seats 60	D 7–9.30
Parties 55	Parking Ample
Closed L Tues, all Sun & Mon, Bank Hols & 2 days Xmas	

Grosvenor Hotel *NEW ENTRY*   Stockbridge

H **55% £D/E**
Map 4 C3 Hampshire
High Street SO20 6EU
Andover (0264) 810606. Tlx 477677
Managers Graham & Lynda Atkins
Credit Access, Amex, Diners, Visa
   Bedrooms at this high-street coaching inn are
divided between the main building and the
converted stables, the latter reached by a glass-

walled walkway. All rooms are well equipped, and
bathrooms are liberally stocked with toiletries.
Public rooms like the bar and first-floor lounge are
traditional in style. No dogs. *Amenities* garden,
sauna, snooker, in-house movies (free).

■ Rooms 25	Confirm by 8
en suite bath/shower 25	Last dinner 10
Direct dial Yes	Parking Ample
Room TV Yes	Room service Limited

■ For a discount on next year's guide, see Offer for Answers.

Sheriff House ★ — Stockbridge

RR ★ ♛ ⚲ **Map 4 C3** Hampshire
High Street SO20 6EX
Andover (0264) 810677

A tiny restaurant run with great flair and charm by Ernest and Joan Fisher. Joan attends to the guests while Ernest busies himself in the kitchen, using only the finest ingredients in his superbly cooked, reassuringly traditional dishes. Booking is absolutely essential and this is your opportunity to discuss and approve the menu, for there'll be no choice later on. A typical meal begins with soup (perhaps a delicious avgolemono), and continues with chicken in aspic, then lobster and, finally, roast lamb. Vegetables are perfectly cooked and sweets are excellent. Second helpings offered. *Specialities* wild salmon, Dover sole with prawns, vanilla ice-cream, crêpe with apricot and pineapple flamed in rum. 🍷 Well-chosen ⊜

■ *Set D* £25 — *L by arrang. only*
About £60 for two — *D 7.30 for 8*
Seats 20 Parties 12 — *Parking Limited*

Bedrooms £D/E
Rooms 8 — *With bath/shower 3*

The eight delightfully cottagy bedrooms are spotlessly maintained and provide lots of thoughtful extras. No dogs.

Alma Lodge Hotel — Stockport

H **61% £D/E**
Map 10 B2 Greater Manchester
149 Buxton Road SK2 6EL
061-483 4431
Credit Access, Amex, Diners, Visa

South of town on the A6, this is a pleasant hotel with particularly appealing public rooms. The foyer, with its moulded ceiling and dark panelling, has a good deal of character, and there are two smart bars. Main-house and extension bedrooms (the former slightly preferable) both have attractive pastel colour schemes, and only five in the main house are without private facilities. *Amenities* laundry service.

■ *Rooms* 57 — *Confirm by* 7
en suite bath/shower 52 — *Last dinner* 9.30
Direct dial Yes — *Parking* Ample
Room TV Yes — *Room service* 24 hours

🍷 indicates a **well-chosen** house wine.

Swallow Hotel — Stockton on Tees

H **70% £C/D *E***
Map 15 C5 Cleveland
10 John Walker Square TS18 1AQ
Stockton on Tees (0642) 679721. Tlx 587895
Credit Access, Amex, Diners, Visa. LVs

Both industrial areas and some lovely countryside are within easy reach of this tall modern hotel which stands right in the centre of town, next to a multi-storey car park. Comfortable couches and good lighting make the spacious foyer an attractive place to relax in; a spiral staircase leads to the smart bar-lounge, which is equally inviting. Many of the bedrooms have been tastefully refurbished with light colour schemes, brass light fittings and co-ordinated fabrics. The rest are in a pleasant traditional style. All rooms offer remote-control TVs, hairdryers and tea-makers, and have well-equipped tiled bathrooms.

Good conference facilities. *Amenities* in-house movies (free), laundry service, coffee shop (7am–11pm), 24-hour lounge service.

■ *Rooms* 123 — *Confirm by* arrang.
en suite bath/shower 123 — *Last dinner* 10
Direct dial Yes — *Parking* Ample
Room TV Yes — *Room service* 24 hours

Belmore Hotel — Stoke Mandeville

H **61% £D/E** ♿
Map 5 D2 Buckinghamshire
Risborough Road HP22 5UT
Stoke Mandeville (029 661) 2022
Owner managers Lynda & Roy Bartman
Credit Access, Amex, Diners, Visa

Guests feel really at home at this family-run hotel on the A4010 outside the village. You can serve yourself in the cosy little bar, and then relax on one of the comfy settees. Simply-furnished, well-kept bedrooms have many useful extras. *Amenities* garden, outdoor swimming pool, solarium, keep-fit equipment.

■ *Rooms* 16 — *Confirm by* arrang.
en suite bath/shower 16 — *Last dinner* 8.45
Direct dial Yes — *Parking* Ample
Room TV Yes — *Room service* Limited
Closed 5 days Xmas

North Stafford Hotel — Stoke-on-Trent

H **63% £C**
Map 10 B3 Staffordshire
Station Road ST4 2AE
Stoke-on-Trent (0782) 48501. Tlx 36287
Credit Access, Amex, Diners, Visa. **LVs**

Popular with both tourists and business visitors, this Jacobean-style red-brick hotel stands right opposite the railway station. The local heritage is the theme of the Clayhanger Bar, and there are two other bars and an elegant lounge. Bedrooms, of a good size but otherwise unremarkable, have modern furnishings and remote-control TVs. Staff could be more professional. *Amenities* laundry service, 24-hour lounge service.

■ *Rooms* 70	*Confirm by* 6
en suite bath/shower 70	*Last dinner* 10
Room phone Yes	*Parking* Ample
Room TV Yes	*Room service* 24 hours

Chapters — Stokesley

R ⌘ **Map 15 C5 North Yorkshire**
9 Bridge Road
Stokesley (0642) 711888
Credit Access, Amex, Diners, Visa

A delightful restaurant specialising in fish dishes. A good variety of carefully prepared dishes is offered, changing daily according to availability. Typical starters could include a tuna and orange mousse or marinated dab with smoked salmon. To follow bourride (brill, prawns and monkfish) or halibut with basil sauce, perhaps. Tempting sweets are all home-made. There's a choice of meat dishes too. Service is informal and very friendly. ⊝

■ *About £28 for two*	*L Thurs only* 12.30–2.30
Seats 24	*D* 7.30–10
Parties 26	*Parking* Ample
Closed Sun, Mon & Bank Hols	

Ston Easton Park — Ston Easton

HR **88% £A**
Map 4 B3 Somerset
Nr Bath BA3 4DF
Chewton Mendip (076 121) 631
Owner managers Peter & Christine Smedley
Credit Access, Amex, Diners, Visa

Surrounded by parkland, with a stream tumbling by at the back, this magnificent Palladian mansion is an immensely civilised country house hotel. Most impressive of the superb public rooms is the salon, with its high moulded ceiling and trompe-l'oeil murals. Antiques, fresh flowers and ample easy chairs and sofas are everywhere, and there's a fine collection of books. Guests are invited 'below stairs' to see the old servants' hall, linen room and kitchens, all in full use. Bedrooms, almost all spacious, are individually decorated and very comfortably furnished, with many pieces of Hepplewhite and Chippendale (including some four-posters). Pretty bathrooms, many with marble features, offer bathrobes, face flannels and luxury toiletries. Friendly, helpful staff. No children under 12. Dogs can be kennelled by arrangement. *Amenities* garden, croquet, billiards, laundry service, helipad.

■ *Rooms* 20	*Confirm by* 6
en suite bath/shower 20	*Last dinner* 9.30
Direct dial Yes	*Parking* Ample
Room TV Yes	*Room service* All day

Ston Easton Park Restaurant ♕

High standards of cooking and service combine in comfortable, very elegant surroundings. Mark Harrington's menu tempts with delights like wholemeal pasta with cèpes, oyster mushrooms and basil, brill with banana in a light curried cream and Scottish beef fillet topped with parsnip purée. Interesting English cheeseboard, and a delicious tangerine charlotte among the sweets. There's a lovely wine list, with wonderful clarets and old Sauternes.

⊃ Outstanding ♟ Well-chosen ⊝

■ *Set L £14*	*L* 12.30–2
About £62 for two	*D* 7.30–9.30,
Seats 40 *Parties* 40	*Fri & Sat* 7.30–10

Crown Hotel — Stone

H **55% £E** &
Map 10 B3 Staffordshire
38 High Street ST15 8AS
Stone (0785) 813535
Manager Dieter Funk
Credit Access, Amex, Diners, Visa

A comfortable overnight stop is offered at this old coaching inn. Day rooms include a panelled lounge and spacious bar. A fine oak staircase leads to main-house bedrooms all equipped with trouser presses and tea-makers. Annexe rooms have stylish fitted units and shower rooms. *Amenities* bowling green.

■ *Rooms* 29	*Confirm by* 7
en suite bath/shower 29	*Last dinner* 9.30
Room phone Yes	*Parking* Ample
Room TV Yes	*Room service* Limited
Closed 25 Dec	

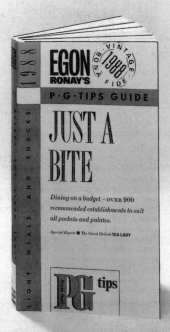

■ For a discount on next year's guide, see Offer for Answers.

Stonehouse Court Hotel — Stonehouse

H **68% £D/E** ♿
Map 4 B2 Gloucestershire
Bristol Road GL10 3RA
Stonehouse (045 382) 5155. Tlx 437244
Owner managers Mr & Mrs J. B. Smith
Credit Access, Amex, Diners, Visa

Period features abound at this stately manor house with its peaceful setting. Log fires create a warm, relaxing ambience. Bedrooms, some of palatial proportions are tastefully decorated and furnished; 16 are in an extension. No children under 11. No dogs. *Amenities* garden, croquet, putting, coarse fishing, laundry service.

■ *Rooms* 25	*Confirm by* arrang.
en suite bath/shower 25	*Last dinner* 9.30
Direct dial Yes	*Parking* Ample
Room TV Yes	*Room service* All day
Closed 2 wks Xmas	

Mr Underhill's ★ — Stonham

RR ★ ♿ **Map 6 C3** Suffolk
Stowmarket IP14 5DW
Stowmarket (0449) 711206
Credit Access, Visa

There's no choice on the set dinner menu in this warmly decorated restaurant, but you can discuss your meal with Judy Bradley when making your booking. Chris Bradley draws out some splendid flavours from the best materials, and produces lovely combinations like rib of veal with a delightful red pepper sauce. There's an excellent selection of cheeses, and sweets include a knock-out coconut parfait. The wine list shows an exceptional eye for quality and value, with particularly good burgundies and Beaujolais crus, and the choice of house wines is outstanding. *Specialities* mille-feuille of salmon with chive sauce, rack of lamb in cream and mushrooms with garlic, chocolate truffle cake with vanilla sauce.

🍷 Well-chosen

■ *Set D* from £15·45	*L* by arrang. only
About £48 for two	*D* 7.30–9
Seats 28 *Parties* 28	*Parking* Ample
Closed D Sun, all Mon & most Bank Hols	

Bedrooms £F

Rooms 1	*With bath/shower* 1

For overnight guests there's a comfortable double bedroom, with its own lounge and private facilities, in an adjacent flat.

Stratfords — Stony Stratford

R **Map 5 D1** Buckinghamshire
7 St Paul's Court, 118 High Street
Milton Keynes (0908) 566577
French cooking
Credit Access, Amex, Diners, Visa

Once the chapel of a public school, now an attractive restaurant where Michael Roberts and Linda Membride create enjoyable fixed-price meals. A tureen of soup followed perhaps by hot chicken mousse makes a splendid start, then there are appetising main courses such as pan-fried venison and monkfish with peppers and fresh pasta. Tempting sweets. 🍷 Well-chosen

■ *Set L* from £9·50	*L* 12–2
Set D from £14	*D* 7.30–10
About £44 for two	*Parking* Ample
Seats 70 *Parties* 200	*Closed* L Sat, D Sun, all Mon, 10 days Jan & 2 wks July

Abingworth Hall — Storrington

HR **70% £D/E**
Map 5 E3 West Sussex
Thakeham Road, Pulborough RH20 3EF
West Chiltington (079 83) 3636. Tlx 877835
Owner managers Philip & Pauline Bulman
Credit Access, Amex, Diners, Visa

North of Storrington on the B2139, this converted Edwardian mansion enjoys a beautiful lakeside setting. The owners are warm and welcoming, and young staff provide cheerful, attractive service. Much of the decor has a pretty, feminine touch, notably in the cocktail bar and thoughtfully equipped main-house bedrooms.

Garden wing rooms have less character, but are bright and airy, equally well kept and with the same extras. The bar is pretty, too, while the panelled lounge has a handsome, more solid appeal. No children under ten. No dogs.
Amenities garden, outdoor swimming pool, tennis, croquet, pitch & putt, laundry service.

■ *Rooms* 22   *Confirm by arrang.*
en suite bath/shower 22   *Last dinner* 9
Direct dial Yes   *Parking* Ample
Room TV Yes   *Room service* 24 hours

Restaurant 𝕨 &

The culinary skills of Peter Cannon and the decorative flair of Pauline Bulman combine in a most attractive restaurant. His cooking is modern

and disciplined, with real eye appeal complementing subtle flavours. Duck liver pâté with redcurrant and port wine sauce is a super starter, and main courses run from grilled halibut with lemon and tarragon to roast pheasant with a delicate red wine sauce and sautéed fillet of beef with brandy and peppercorns. Fresh vegetables are nicely cooked and high standards maintained in delicious desserts and fine farmhouse cheeses. Among wines to note are a well-aged Morgon (Gérard Brisson) and Rioja Faustino 1976. Cheerful service.
♀ **Well-chosen** ⊖

■ *Set D* £16·50   L 12.30–2
About £45 *for two*   D 7.15–9
Seats 50   *Parties* 50

Cottage Tandoori   Storrington

R **Map 5 E3** West Sussex
25 West Street
Storrington (090 66) 3605
Indian cooking
Credit Access, Amex, Diners, Visa
   A charming Sussex cottage, with diamond-panelled windows and high-backed booth seating, is the location for this excellent little Indian restaurant. The menu, with a wide variety of

curries, specialises in North Indian cooking, notably tandoori, masala and pasanda. The meat is good quality and the cooking exceptionally careful, from the judicious blending of spices to the perfect saffron rice. ⊖

■ *Set D from* £25 *for two*   L 12–3
About £31 *for two*   D 6–12
Seats 72   *Parking* Ample
Parties 36   *Closed* 2 days Xmas

Little Thakeham   Storrington

HR **76% £B**
Map 5 E3 West Sussex
Merrywood Lane RH20 3HE
Storrington (090 66) 4416
Owner managers Tim & Pauline Ractliff
Credit Access, Amex, Diners, Visa
   This lovely stone-built manor designed by Sir Edwin Lutyens is set in delightful gardens that are very much in keeping with the period of the house. Decor is stylish throughout. The magnificent lounge with its minstrels' gallery, huge fireplace and mullioned windows, is a joy to relax in; and there's also a splendid bar with leather armchairs and sofas. Spacious, individually decorated bedrooms offer large beds, deep armchairs and sizeable modern bathrooms. Remote-control TVs, trouser presses, hairdryers

and radio-alarms are provided, and there are nice homely touches like potpourris and mineral water. Excellent breakfasts. No dogs. *Amenities* garden, outdoor swimming pool, tennis, croquet, teletext, helipad.

■ *Rooms* 10   *Confirm by arrang.*
en suite bath/shower 10   *Last dinner* 9.15
Direct dial Yes   *Parking* Ample
Room TV Yes   *Room service* All day
Closed 2 wks Xmas

Little Thakeham Restaurant 𝕨

A massive refectory table laden with sweets stands to one side of this elegant dining room, promising good things to come. Sadly, the short, fixed-price menu is a little lacking in imagination and sparkle; fresh produce is handled simply, but textures and saucing can be disappointing. The pleasure of dining in such a beautiful house, however, helps to compensate for any shortcomings. ♀ **Well-chosen** ⊖

■ *Set L* £15   L 12.30–2
Set D £19.50   D 7.30–9.15
About £60 *for two*   *Seats* 35 *Parties* 30
Closed D Sun & 2 wks Xmas

■ Any person using our name to obtain free hospitality is a fraud. Proprietors, please inform the police and us.

Manleys ★★ Storrington

RR ★★ ♧ ♿ **Map 5 E3** West Sussex
Manleys Hill
Storrington (090 66) 2331
Credit Access, Amex, Diners, Visa

Uniform in its excellence, Karl Löderer's
cooking is all one would expect in a restaurant of
this calibre. Only the best raw materials are used
in a menu that combines old favourites with tried
and tested original dishes. No gimmicks here, but
skilfully refined combinations such as warm
raspberry vinaigrette with pigeon and poussin
salad. A typical meal might embrace Dover sole
and crab soufflé with ginger-flavoured butter
sauce, panfried guinea fowl with home-made
pasta, and a simply stunning apple tart. Fine wine
list, with good burgundies, Rhônes and German
wines. *Specialities* soufflé de sole au crabe et
beurre de gingembre, crêpe parmentière farcie
aux champignons des bois et petites légumes,
filet d'agneau rôti en infusion d'herbes et
chartreuse de légumes. ♟ Well-chosen ℮

■ *Set L* Sun only £17·25   *L* 12–2
About £62 for two   *D* 7–9, Sat 7–9.30
Seats 50 Parties 36   *Parking* Ample
Closed D Sun, all Mon, 1st 2 wks Jan, last wk
Aug & 1st wk Sept
Bedrooms £B/C
Rooms 1   *With bath/shower 1*
A luxury apartment (large bedroom, sitting room
and bath) is now available for restaurant guests
staying overnight. No children or dogs.

Talbot Hotel Stourbridge

I **£E**
Map 10 B4 West Midlands
High Street DY8 1DW
Stourbridge (0384) 394350
Manager Mr Chatterton
Credit Access, Amex, Visa. LVs

Refurbishment is complete at this fine old inn.
The foyer-lounge is smart and relaxing, with
leather chesterfields and tapestry-covered seats,
and the new lounge bar is an attractive alternative
to the jolly public bar. Good-sized pretty
bedrooms. Staff are friendly and unobtrusive.
Amenities laundry service, coffee shop (9.30am–
11pm).

■ *Rooms 25*	*Confirm by arrang.*
en suite bath/shower 25	*Last dinner 9.45*
Direct dial Yes	*Parking Limited*
Room TV Yes	*Room service None*

■ Our inspectors are our full-
time employees; they are
professionally trained by us.

Fosse Manor Hotel Stow-on-the-Wold

H **59% £D/E**
Map 4 C1 Gloucestershire
GL54 1JX
Cotswold (0451) 30354
Owner managers Mr & Mrs R. Johnston
Credit Access, Amex, Diners, Visa

This creeper-clad house in delightful gardens
on the A429 south of town has a comfortable
lounge with plenty of armchairs to draw up to the
fire and a stone-walled bar boasting a collection of
headwear. Homely bedrooms nearly all have
carpeted bathrooms. *Amenities* garden,
children's playground, laundry service.

■ *Rooms 20*	*Confirm by 5*
en suite bath/shower 16	*Last dinner 9.30*
Room phone No	*Parking Ample*
Room TV Yes	*Room service Limited*
Closed 1 wk Xmas	

Unicorn Crest Hotel Stow-on-the-Wold

H **60% £D/E**
Map 4 C1 Gloucestershire
Sheep Street GL54 1HQ
Cotswold (0451) 30257. Tlx 437186
Manager Richard Coyne
Credit Access, Amex, Diners, Visa

Sympathetic modernisation has retained the
old-world charms of this 17th-century Cotswold
stone hotel. Cosy public rooms boast exposed
beams and stonework. Narrow stairs lead to the
attractively refurbished bedrooms, now with
smart new carpets, bedspreads and darkwood
furniture. All rooms are equipped with radios and
trouser presses. Smartly tiled bathrooms.

■ *Rooms 20*	*Confirm by 6*
en suite bath/shower 20	*Last dinner 9.30*
Room phone Yes	*Parking Ample*
Room TV Yes	*Room service All day*

Wyck Hill House   Stow-on-the-Wold

HR 74% £C
Map 4 C1 Gloucestershire
Burford Road GL54 1HY
Cotswold (0451) 31936. Tlx 43611
Credit Access, Amex, Diners, Visa

Sweeping views of the Windrush valley are
enjoyed from this honey-coloured stone manor
house off the A424. Opulence is much in evidence
in day rooms like the cedar-panelled library and
the club-like bar with its leather armchairs. The
elegant drawing room has an intricate plaster
ceiling, grand piano and unusual curved doors
opening on to the lawns. A fine staircase climbs to
generally spacious bedrooms, the grandest
having a four-poster and large bay windows. All
are individually designed with luxurious curtains,
antique or period furnishings and fresh flowers.

Spotless, stylish bathrooms have bidets, robes,
quality toiletries and telephone extensions. No
children under six. Amenities garden, croquet,
laundry service, 24-hour lounge service, helipad.

■ Rooms 16	Confirm by 6
en suite bath/shower 16	Last dinner 9.30
Direct dial Yes	Parking Ample
Room TV Yes	Room service 24 hours

Wyck Hill House Restaurant ♔ ⅙

Beautiful views can be enjoyed through the bay
windows of this elegant dining room. Chef Ian
Smith offers an interesting and generally
successful menu with dishes like light, creamy
parfait of pheasant, fricassee of Cornish lobster
and turbot cooked in champagne, cream and dill.
A good list of sweets may tempt with a two-tone
soufflé of dark chocolate and vanilla. Above-
average wine list – note lovely Rully, Domaine de
la Renarde from André Delorme; lots of halves,
too. Service sometimes grudging. ℮

NEW ENTRY

■ Set L £9·50	L 12–2
Set D £15·75	D 7.30–9.30
About £52 for two	Seats 40 Parties 40

Alveston Manor   Stratford-upon-Avon

H 66% £C/D
Town plan E2 Warwickshire
Clopton Bridge CV37 7HP
Stratford-upon-Avon (0789) 204581. Tlx 31324
Credit Access, Amex, Diners, Visa. LVs

The grounds of this handsome gabled building
were reputedly used for the first performance of A
Midsummer Night's Dream. Public areas, mainly
panelled, retain a feel of the past, as do main-

house bedrooms with their quality fabrics and
splendid antique or period-style furnishings. Most
bedrooms are more modern and practical.
Amenities garden, pitch & putt, valeting, laundry
service, 24-hour lounge service.

■ Rooms 108	Confirm by 6
en suite bath/shower 108	Last dinner 9.30
Direct dial Yes	Parking Ample
Room TV Yes	Room service 24 hours

■ We welcome complaints and bona
fide recommendations on the
tear-out pages for readers' comments.
They are followed up by our professional
team. Please also complain to the
management instantly.

RECEPTION

Arden Hotel   Stratford-upon-Avon

H 59% £D/E
Town plan D3 Warwickshire
44 Waterside CV37 6BA
Stratford-upon-Avon (0789) 294949. Tlx 311726
Manager David J. Hunter
Credit Access, Amex, Diners, Visa

An enviable situation overlooking the Royal
Shakespeare Theatre and river Avon makes this a
playgoer's delight. Shakespearean prints

decorate the little foyer and there are two relaxing
lounges plus a cosy bar. Traditional bedrooms, all
with private facilities, include eight superior
rooms. Amenities garden, laundry service, 24-
hour lounge service.

■ Rooms 65	Confirm by arrang.
en suite bath/shower 65	Last dinner 10
Direct dial Yes	Parking Ample
Room TV Yes	Room service 24 hours

STRATFORD-UPON-AVON

Map 4 C1
Town plan opposite

Population 21,675

A prosperous market-town on a lovely river site, with good Tudor and Jacobean architecture, would be a fair description of Stratford-upon-Avon–if it wasn't for the Bard. It took 200 years after Shakespeare's birth for proper tribute to be paid to him in a festival staged by David Garrick. The first Theatre was not built until 1879; it was burnt down in 1926 and succeeded by the present theatre in 1932, built with large overseas subscriptions, particularly from the U.S.

Annual Events
Map Fair *12th October*
Shakespeare's Birthday Celebration *23rd April*
Shakespeare Theatre Season *from April*
Stratford Festival *July*

Sights Outside Town
Coughton Court
Ragley Hall
Charlecote
Coventry Cathedral
Packwood House
Upton House
Warwick Castle

Information Centre
Judith Shakespeare's House
1 High Street
Telephone Stratford-upon-Avon 293127

Fiat Dealer
Grays Garage Ltd
Wharf Street
Warwick CV34 4PA
Tel. Warwick 496231

1 Anne Hathaway's cottage *at Shottery* A3
2 Guild Chapel, Guildhall, Grammar School and Almshouses *exceptional medieval buildings* C3
3 Hall's Croft *fine Tudor house and walled garden, also houses Festival Club* C3
4 Harvard House *1596 home of grandfather of Harvard's founder* C2
5 Holy Trinity Church *contains Shakespeare's tomb* C3
6 Information Centre C2
7 Mary Arden's house *at Wilmcote, 3 miles. Tudor farmhouse, home of Shakespeare's mother, farming museum* B1
8 New Place *Elizabethan garden on site of Shakespeare's last home* C3
9 Picture Gallery and Museum *pictures and relics of famous actors* D3
10 Railway Station A1
11 Royal Shakespeare Theatre D3
12 Shakespeare's birthplace *architectural interest and museum of rare Shakespeariana* C1
13 Swan Theatre D3
14 Town Hall C2

STREET SMART COUNTRY CASUAL

Panda 4 X 4 FIAT
EUROPE'S DRIVING FORCE

For local dealers see pages 144-147

Stratford-upon-Avon

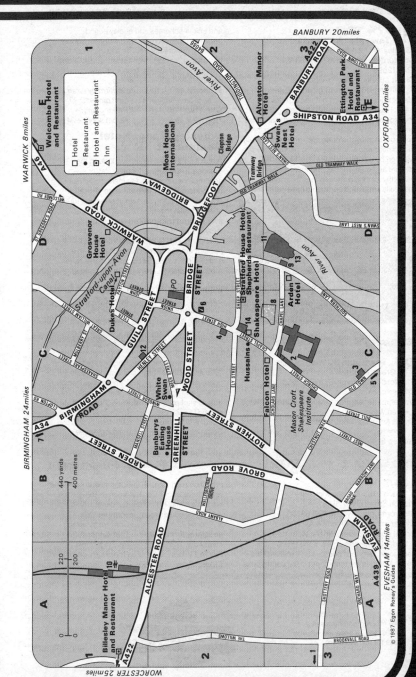

□ Hotel
● Restaurant
⊡ Hotel and Restaurant
△ Inn

© 1987 Egon Ronay's Guides

Billesley Manor — Stratford-upon-Avon

HR 77% £C/D
Town plan A1 Warwickshire
Billesley, Nr Alcester B49 6NF
Stratford-upon-Avon (0789) 763737.
Tlx 312599
Credit Access, Amex, Diners, Visa

Standing in 11 acres of grounds, Billesley Manor is just three miles outside Stratford off the A422. Recently extensively refurbished following damage by fire, this delightful gabled manor has emerged from its year-long closure looking more splendid than ever. Young staff greet guests with friendliness and efficiency in the panelled foyer, warmed by a huge open fire. The lounge is elegant and comfortable, and there's a panelled bar with a club-like atmosphere. Spacious, tastefully appointed bedrooms have pretty fabrics

and colour schemes and quality period furnishings. All rooms have hairdryers, trouser presses, remote-control TVs and excellent tiled bathrooms. No dogs. *Amenities* garden, indoor swimming pool, sauna, tennis, croquet, laundry service, 24-hour lounge service.

■ *Rooms* 41	*Confirm by arrang.*
en suite bath/shower 41	*Last dinner 9.30*
Direct dial Yes	*Parking* Ample
Room TV Yes	*Room service* 24 hours

Billesley Manor Hotel Restaurant ♔ &

A handsome dining room, overlooking the grounds, is the setting for Mark Naylor's accomplished cooking. His menus offer dishes in the modern French style using good-quality produce. Tempting starters may include turbot, sole and salmon terrine or a hot mousse of avocado and chicken filled with oyster mushrooms. Main course choices may be succulent beef fillet with green and black peppercorns or thyme-scented lamb with a garlicky leek sauce. Delicious desserts. Note Auxey Duresses (Leroy) 1976 on the sound wine list. ℮

■ *Set L* £12·50	*L 12.30–1.30,*
Set D £17	*Sun 12.30–2*
About £60 for two	*D 7.30–9.30*
Seats 48	*Parties* 80

Bunbury's *NEW ENTRY* — Stratford-upon-Avon

R ♘ **Town plan B2** Warwickshire
3 Greenhill Street
Stratford-upon-Avon (0789) 293563
English cooking
Owner managers Penny Moulds, Kate McCarthy & Keren Weller
Credit Access, Diners, Visa

Three former teachers are trying to give the public a taste of what eating in Shakespeare's time might have been like. Recipes are based on 16th- and 17th-century originals and results are good: soup made from veal, chicken, cinnamon, parsley and eggs; pork and pease pudding; rich treacle suet pudding. ♟ Well-chosen ℮

■ *Set D* £6·95	*L 12–3, Sun 12–2*
About £30 for two	*D 6–12*
Seats 42 *Parties* 42	*Parking* Ample
Closed Mon, also D Sun in winter	

Dukes Hotel *NEW ENTRY* — Stratford-upon-Avon

I £D/E
Town plan D1 Warwickshire
Payton Street CV37 6UA
Stratford-upon-Avon (0789) 69300
Owner managers Brenda & Alan Power
Credit Access, Amex, Diners, Visa

Under the personal care of the Powers, this handsome Georgian house is an excellent little hotel. Antiques are found both in the comfortable reception rooms and in the pretty bedrooms, all of which have bright tiled bathrooms. The garden adjoins a canal. No children under ten. No dogs. *Amenities* games room, laundry service.

■ *Rooms* 17	*Confirm by arrang.*
en suite bath/shower 17	*Last dinner 9.45*
Direct dial Yes	*Parking* Ample
Room TV Yes	*Room service* Limited
Closed 5 days Xmas	

■ If we recommend meals in a hotel or inn, a separate entry is made for its restaurant.

Ettington Park Hotel   Stratford-upon-Avon

HR 85% £B *E*
Town plan E3 Warwickshire
Alderminster CV37 8BS
Stratford-upon-Avon (0789) 740740.
Tlx 311825
Credit Access, Amex, Diners, Visa

Set in 40 acres of rolling countryside, parts of this splendid mansion date back to the Middle Ages, although its architectural style is pure Victorian Gothic. Entrance is through an ornate conservatory, and other magnificent day rooms include an intimate book-lined bar and a stunningly elegant drawing room with formal flower arrangements, luxurious drapes and lofty, ornate ceiling. Spacious bedrooms – all with luxury bathrooms – are in lavish traditional style and offer many cosseting extras. No children

under seven. No dogs. *Amenities* garden, indoor swimming pool, sauna, solarium, whirlpool bath, tennis, croquet, riding, shooting, clay-pigeon shooting, coarse fishing, snooker, in-house movies (free), laundry service, 24-hour lounge service, helipad.

■ Rooms 49	*Confirm by arrang.*
en suite bath/shower 49	*Last dinner 10*
Direct dial Yes	*Parking Ample*
Room TV Yes	*Room service 24 hours*

Ettington Park Hotel Restaurant ⌘⌘ &

A formal restaurant of great beauty and elegance where short, tempting menus combine French and English cooking styles. Scallops and mussels in puff pasty with a chive and champagne sauce might be followed by chicken breast stuffed with sage and onion mousse or simple Dover sole with parsley butter. Sweets are a triumph – try 'wait 'n' see', a brandy snap basket filled with a selection of delicious mouthfuls. Excellent produce, but results do not always match the promise of their surroundings. Some fine clarets on the wine list: Ch. Dauzac '78 and Ch. Palmer '66.
♀ Well-chosen ✉

■ Set L £15	L 12.30–2.30
Set D £24	D 7–10.30
About £60 for two	Seats 55 Parties 60

Falcon Hotel   Stratford-upon-Avon

H 64% £D/E &
Town plan C3 Warwickshire
Chapel Street CV37 6HA
Stratford-upon-Avon (0789) 205777. Tlx 312522
Manager Mr D. Woodhams
Credit Access, Amex, Diners, Visa

This carefully preserved 17th-century inn illustrates how well ancient and modern styles can

combine; a contemporary extension blends well with the original building. Wood-panelled and beamed bars are cosy and inviting. Bedrooms (traditional in the old part; modern in the new) are well fitted. *Amenities* garden, laundry service.

■ Rooms 73	*Confirm by 6*
en suite bath/shower 73	*Last dinner 9*
Direct dial Yes	*Parking Ample*
Room TV Yes	*Room service 24 hours*

Grosvenor House Hotel *NEW ENTRY*   Stratford-upon-Avon

H 60% £E
Town plan D1 Warwickshire
12 Warwick Road CV37 6YT
Stratford-upon-Avon (0789) 69213. Tlx 311699
Manager Maggie Gaynor
Credit Access, Amex, Diners, Visa

A comfortable hotel with a warm, welcoming feel that starts in the foyer and doesn't stop. Day rooms include a bar, two cosy lounges and a little

writing room. Bedrooms are very neat and tidy. No dogs. *Amenities* garden, sauna, solarium, whirlpool bath, gymnasium, hairdressing, beauty salon, laundry service, 24-hour lounge service.

■ Rooms 57	*Confirm by arrang.*
en suite bath/shower 52	*Last dinner 8.45*
Direct dial Yes	*Parking Ample*
Room TV Yes	*Room service 24 hours*
Closed 3 days Xmas	

Hussain's   Stratford-upon-Avon

R & **Town plan C2** Warwickshire
6a Chapel Street
Stratford-upon-Avon (0789) 67506
Indian cooking
Owner manager Noor Hussain
Credit Access, Amex, Diners, Visa

Standards of cooking, seasoning and service are high at this busy little restaurant. The menu offers a varied choice of tandoori dishes and all

manner of curries from North India and Bangladesh. The chef's specialities include lamb pasanda, chicken tikkah bhuna, and lamb korma.

■ Set L fr £20·95 for 2	L 12–2, Sun 12–2.30
Set D fr £20·95 for 2	D 5–11.30, Fri & Sat
About £28 for two	5–12, Sun 5.30–11.30
Seats 48 Parties 30	Parking Limited
Closed 25 & 26 Dec	

Moat House International

Stratford-upon-Avon

H 71% £C/D *E* &
Town plan D2 Warwickshire
Bridgefoot CV37 6YR
Stratford-upon-Avon (0789) 67511. Tlx 311127
Credit Access, Amex, Diners, Visa

A low-rise, modern hotel on the banks of the Avon, providing excellent conference facilities. There's a smart stone-flagged foyer area, and a bright and elegant bar-lounge lit by a sloping glass roof. A second, more informal bar, decked out in French-café style, is located in the hotel's shopping arcade. Bedrooms are fitted with modern black furnishings and large floral bedspreads in simple light colour schemes, and have comfortable seating, radios and mini-bars. Some rooms have been refurbished with more popular pastel fabrics. Guests may use the facilities of the adjacent leisure centre at no extra

charge. *Amenities* garden, hairdressing, coarse fishing, in-house movies (charge), laundry service, coffee shop (7.30am–10.30pm), 24-hour lounge service, shopping arcade.

■ *Rooms* 249	*Confirm by* 6
en suite bath/shower 249	*Last dinner* 11
Direct dial Yes	*Parking* Ample
Room TV Yes	*Room service* 24 hours

■ If we recommend meals in a hotel or inn, a separate entry is made for its restaurant.

Shakespeare Hotel

Stratford-upon-Avon

H 70% £C
Town plan C2
Chapel Street CV37 6ER
Stratford-upon-Avon (0789) 294771.
Tlx 311181
Credit Access, Amex, Diners, Visa

The history of the Shakespeare goes back to the 16th century, and the gables and timbers present an attractive frontage in the centre of town. A sense of the past can be felt inside, too, and the spacious lounge with beams and flagstones is amply provided with plump-cushioned armchairs and settees. There are two cosy bars, also beamed, one of them with a display of Vanity Fair cartoons. Bedrooms are decorated and furnished in keeping with the general ambience, those in the oldest part having the most character. They're roomy, housekeeping

is good and all have remote-control TVs, hairdryers and well-equipped bathrooms. Service is friendly and professional. *Amenities* garden, laundry service, 24-hour lounge service.

■ *Rooms* 70	*Confirm by* 6
en suite bath/shower 70	*Last dinner* 10
Direct dial Yes	*Parking* Limited
Room TV Yes	*Room service* 24 hours

Stratford House Hotel

Stratford-upon-Avon

HR 64% £D/E
Town plan C2 Warwickshire
Sheep Street CV37 6EF
Stratford-upon-Avon (0789) 68288
Credit Access, Amex, Diners, Visa

Just a short stroll from the river, this converted Georgian house is a quiet hotel with exemplary housekeeping and delightful staff. Antiques and fresh flowers grace the lounge, and there's a light, attractive bar. Pretty floral fabrics feature in the bedrooms, which have neat bath or shower rooms. No children under seven. No dogs. *Amenities* garden.

■ *Rooms* 10	*Confirm by* 6
en suite bath/shower 9	*Last dinner* 9.30
Direct dial Yes	*Parking* Limited
Room TV Yes	*Room service* All day
Closed 4 days Xmas	

Shepherds Restaurant ♀ &

After a spell as personal chef to Andrew Lloyd Webber, Nigel Lambert has returned to his home town as chef-partner at this light, conservatory-style restaurant. His cooking puts the emphasis on quality, with no place for pretentiousness; typical dishes run from bacon-wrapped scampi tails with garlic mayonnaise or duck pâté with green peppercorns to duckling with fresh limes, brochette of calf's liver and steak with mushrooms. Super vegetables and delicious sweets such as passion fruit mousse with creamed coconut sauce. ☺

■ *About £40 for two*	*L* 12–2
Seats 40 *Parties* 40	*D* 6–11
Closed Sun, Mon & Bank Hols	

Swans Nest   Stratford-upon-Avon

H **61% £C/D**
Town plan E3 Warwickshire
Bridgefoot CV37 7LT
Stratford (0789) 66761
Credit Access, Amex, Diners, Visa
   Overlooking the river Avon almost opposite the
Royal Shakespeare Theatre, this red-brick hotel is
a good base for visitors. The cosy, panelled bar is
popular with guests and locals alike, and there's a

comfortable lounge area. Modern bedrooms have
tea-makers, bedside controls and neat, well-
equipped bathrooms. On a winter visit, our room
was on the cold side. *Amenities* garden, laundry
service, 24-hour lounge service.
■ *Rooms 60*   *Confirm by 6*
en suite bath/shower 60   *Last dinner 9.30*
Direct dial Yes   *Parking Ample*
Room TV Yes   *Room service Limited*

■ Our inspectors never book in the
name of Egon Ronay's Guides;
they disclose their identity only
after paying their bills.

Welcombe Hotel   Stratford-upon-Avon

HR **74% £C**
Town plan E1 Warwickshire
Warwick Road CV37 0NR
Stratford-upon-Avon (0789) 295252. Tlx 31347
Manager Brian Miller
Credit Access, Amex, Diners, Visa
   Parkland, once owned by William Shakespeare,
surrounds this Jacobean-style mansion on the
A46, two miles from Stratford. Relaxing day rooms
offer many magnificent features, including Italian
chandeliers, a marvellous marble fireplace in the
lounge and a carved wooden counter in the
Trevelyan Bar. Spacious, mainhouse bedrooms
(including particularly luxurious Gallery rooms)
have some fine period furnishings, while garden
wing rooms are stylishly contemporary. All rooms
boast trouser presses and hairdryers, plus

splendidly appointed bathrooms.
Amenities garden, golf course, putting, croquet,
coarse fishing, games room, snooker, 24-hour
lounge service, laundry service, helipad.
■ *Rooms 82*   *Confirm by arrang.*
en suite bath/shower 82   *Last dinner 9.15*
Direct dial Yes   *Parking Ample*
Room TV Yes   *Room service 24 hours*
Closed 29 Dec–2 Jan

Welcombe Hotel
Restaurant 🛏 ਠ

Michael Carver is the talented chef at this elegant
restaurant, using fine, fresh ingredients
throughout a richly-varied selection of dishes.
Typical delights might include breast of quail in a
honey and armagnac dressing, oyster-filled
scallop mousse with tomato and lime sauce, veal
sauced with fennel and orange or rack of lamb
with spinach served with a burgundy jus.
Attractive sweets. Good list of burgundies and
beaujolais. ♀ Well-chosen ⊖
■ *Set L £12·50*   *L 12.15–2*
Set D £18·50   *D 6–9.15, Sun 7–9.15*
About £60 for two   *Seats 60 Parties 20*
Closed L Sun & 29 Dec–2 Jan

White Swan *NEW ENTRY*   Stratford-upon-Avon

H **62% £C/D**
Town plan C2 Warwickshire
Rother Street CV37 6NH
Stratford-upon-Avon (0789) 297022
Credit Access, Amex, Diners, Visa
   In the centre of town, this fine old hotel has
seen major improvements. Many bedrooms have
been totally refurbished, and the pastel shades
and darkwood furnishings are quite attractive.

Modern bathrooms feature throughout. Day
rooms include a beamed foyer and a lounge that
boasts some fine 16th-century wall paintings.
Friendly, helpful staff. *Amenities* laundry service,
24-hour lounge service.
■ *Rooms 35*   *Confirm by 6*
en suite bath/shower 35   *Last dinner 9*
Direct dial Yes   *Parking Limited*
Room TV Yes   *Room service Limited*

Swan at Streatley

Streatley-on-Thames

HR **69% £D/E** &
Map 5 D2 Berkshire
RG8 9HR
Goring-on-Thames (0491) 873737. Tlx 848259
Credit Access, Amex, Diners, Visa

A new leisure centre has enhanced the appeal of this old, delightful and impeccably maintained riverside inn. The traditional lounge and two smart bars open on to a terrace, while the charming barge moored alongside is a popular conference venue. Bedrooms – many balconied – are individually furnished and thoughtfully equipped. *Amenities* garden, indoor swimming pool, sauna, solarium, keep-fit equipment, games room, in-house movies (free), laundry service, 24-hour lounge service.

■ *Rooms* 26	*Confirm by* 6
en suite bath/shower 26	*Last dinner* 9.30
Direct dial Yes	*Parking* Ample
Room TV Yes	*Room service* 24 hours

Swan Hotel Restaurant ★ ♔

Dedication, care and sheer hard work earn chef Richard Sparrow his laurels at this comfortable restaurant, with its fine views, well-spaced tables and pleasing decor. Typical of his light touch are such tempting offerings as asparagus mousse wrapped in leek, served with a carrot butter sauce, chicken breast stuffed with a gently

flavoured Roquefort mousseline, and a blackcurrant torte bursting with fresh flavour. Delicious walnut bread accompanies the particularly good selection of first-class English and French cheeses, and service is relaxed, friendly and attentive. Some splendid wines – note Penfold's Grange Hermitage 1976 from Australia. *Specialities* terrine of Dover sole and shellfish with a saffron roulade, saddle of rabbit with a shallot and garlic confit and a Pommery mustard sauce, wild salmon on a warm champagne vinaigrette (with a fine dice of chives and sweet pepper), orange soufflé pancake with an almond case of sorbet on a bitter orange sauce. ♥ Well-chosen ⊖

■ *Set L from £13-50*	*L 12.30–2*
Set D from £16-95	*D 7.30–9.30*
About £60 for two	*Seats 50 Parties 25*

Bear Hotel

Street

H **60% £E**
Map 4 A3 Somerset
53 High Street BA16 0EF
Street (0458) 42021
Credit Access, Amex, Diners, Visa

Dating from the late 19th century, this attractive stone-built hotel sits pleasantly in Street's town centre. Public rooms include a comfortably traditional lounge and a pleasant bar which opens

on to the terrace and lawns. Bedrooms, some in an annexe, are furnished in attractive contemporary style with coordinated fabrics and colour schemes. All have smartly tiled bathrooms which are kept in tip-top condition. *Amenities* garden.

■ *Rooms* 15	*Confirm by* 6
en suite bath/shower 15	*Last dinner* 12
Direct dial Yes	*Parking* Ample
Room TV Yes	*Room service* Limited

Wessex Hotel

Street

H **60% £E** &
Map 4 A3 Somerset
Nr Glastonbury BA16 0EF
Street (0458) 43383
Credit Access, Amex, Diners, Visa

A modern hotel standing in the centre of a small town in King Arthur country. The foyer has some modern leather chairs for lounging, and the lounge itself doubles as a meeting room. Good-

sized bedrooms have attractive colour schemes and neat fitted units. Tea-makers and trouser presses are standard, and private facilities include separate WCs. *Amenities* laundry service, 24-hour lounge service.

■ *Rooms* 50	*Confirm by arrang.*
en suite bath/shower 50	*Last dinner* 9.30
Room phone Yes	*Parking* Ample
Room TV Yes	*Room service* 24 hours

Ram Jam Inn *NEW ENTRY*   **Stretton**

I**R** £E
Map 11 E3 Leicestershire
Great North Road, Nr Oakham LE15 7QX
Castle Bytham (078 081) 776
Credit Access, Amex, Visa

A convenient stopping-off point for travellers on the A1. Public areas are smart but informal. Bedrooms are good-sized and equipped to a high standard with pine furniture and wicker chairs for relaxation. Colour schemes are well coordinated and all rooms have remote-control TVs, clock radios, tea-makers and attractive bathrooms.
Amenities garden, coffee shop (7am–7pm). 🅮

■ *Rooms* 10	*Confirm by* arrang.
en suite bath/shower 9	*Last dinner* 11
Direct dial Yes	*Parking* Ample
Room TV Yes	*Room service* None
Closed 25 Dec	

Ram Jam Inn Restaurant &

The restaurant offers a varied selection of snacks and salads as well as more substantial dishes. You might start with a satisfying soup before moving on to freshly made fettucine with parmesan and garlic breadcrumbs, belly of pork with apple sauce, sirloin steak or barbecued chicken wings. Those with a sweet tooth can finish with a rich treacle and nut tart or fromage blanc with a purée of fresh fruits. Home-made ices are also available. Light meals and snack menu available in the bar from 7am–11pm. 🅮

■ *About £28 for two*	*Meals* 11am–11pm
Seats 50	*Parties* 90
Closed 25 Dec	

■ We publish annually, so make sure you use the current edition. It's worth it!

Bear of Rodborough   **Stroud**

H 64% £D/E
Map 4 B2 Gloucestershire
Rodborough Common GL5 5DE
Amberley (045 387) 3522. Tlx 437130
Manager Richard Kulesza
Credit Access, Amex, Diners, Visa

Major refurbishment has added to the charms of this 17th-century Cotswold inn. Two stuffed bears greet visitors in reception, and there's a sunny lounge plus two inviting bars. Accommodation ranges from upgraded older rooms to cheerfully modern ones in the extension.
Amenities garden, dinner dance (Sat in winter), 24-hour lounge service, laundry service, croquet.

■ *Rooms* 47	*Confirm by* arrang.
en suite bath/shower 47	*Last dinner* 9.15
Direct dial Yes	*Parking* Ample
Room TV Yes	*Room service* Limited

Oakes ★ *NEW ENTRY*   **Stroud**

R ★ ♙ **Map 4 B2** Gloucestershire
169 Slad Road
Stroud (045 36) 79950
Credit Access, Visa

Mullioned windows look out over the tranquil Slad valley from this comfortable restaurant in a honey-stone former college. It's a first 'own venture' for Christopher Oakes, a dedicated and very talented young chef who cooks with great self-assurance and no gimmickry – witness our triumphant main course of red mullet baked with braised onion, tomato and thyme, served on a bed of rösti with a cream sauce. Other temptations from the choice of set menus could include ragoût of seafood cooked in a white wine, cream and chervil sauce, Lancashire hot pot or steak, kidney and Guinness pie. Starters such as fish soup or sautéed chicken livers and sweets like poached pear with butterscotch or billowy cinnamon soufflé are memorable, too. Superb cheeses, exquisite petits fours. Looking after customers at

the front of house is Christopher's wife Caroline. Short, reasonably priced list of good wines.
Specialities chicken liver parfait with home-made chutney, lamb cutlets with rosemary sauce and offal tartlet; hot cinnamon soufflé with Drambuie cream. ♚ Well-chosen 🅮

■ *Set L from* £7·50	*L* 12.30–2
Set D from £14	*D* 7.30–10
About £50 for two	*Parking* Ample
Seats 30	*Parties* 25
Closed D Sun, all Mon & Jan	

The Three Lions ★ *NEW ENTRY*   Stuckton

R★ ⌕ **Map 4 C4** Hampshire
Stuckton Road, Nr Fordingbridge SP6 2HF
Fordingbridge (0425) 52489
Owner managers Karl & June Wadsack
Credit Access, Visa

Nominally a pub, but this red-brick building is
organised much more along Continental lines as a
restaurant with bar. There is an attractive
'country' atmosphere with pine furnishings, rustic-
smart decor and pretty fabrics. In the kitchen, Karl
Wadsack exercises his considerable culinary
talents; spot-on timing, beautifully clear flavours
and brilliant sauces take his dishes way above the
ordinary. Prime ingredients are sought from near
and far, for example, fish is regularly flown in from
the Seychelles. Items on the frequently-changing
menus run from delicious hot spinach and cheese
strudel on a fresh tomato sauce to plaice stuffed
with salmon mousse, beef in Guinness with
oysters, home-made bratwurst mit sauerkraut and
oeufs à la neige with raspberry sauce. Good,
interesting vegetables. There's a good selection
of English and Continental cheeses and a sound
wine list, strongest in fine Bordeaux (Ch. Léoville-
Lascases 1976 is drinking superbly now). Service
is charmingly supervised by June Wadsack. No
children under 14. ⬤ Well-chosen ☺

■ *Set L from £7·50*   *L 12.15–1.45,*
About £38 for two   *Sun 12.15–1.30*
Seats 50 Parties 20   *D 7.30–9.30*
Closed D Sun & all Mon   *Parking Ample*

Knoll House Hotel   Studland Bay

H **62% £C/D**
Map 4 C4 Dorset
Nr Swanage BH19 3AH
Studland (092 944) 251
Owner managers Ferguson family

A family-run hotel set in pleasant Dorset
countryside not far from the sea. It's a good place
for a holiday, with a relaxing atmosphere and a
long list of sports and leisure facilities. The
comfortable day rooms provide ample space for
lounging or watching TV, and children's areas
include a large adventure playground. Bedrooms
range from small singles to spacious family suites.
Staff are very friendly and helpful, with an easy
manner that fits in well with the surroundings.
High-season bookings on inclusive terms only.
Amenities garden, outdoor swimming pool,
sauna, solarium, whirlpool bath, keep-fit
equipment, tennis, 9-hole golf course, games
room, laundry room, kiosk, children's playground.

■ *Rooms 79*   *Confirm by arrang.*
en suite bath/shower 56 *Last dinner 8.15*
Direct dial Yes   *Parking Ample*
Room TV No   *Room service None*
Closed end Oct–end Mar

Peppers   Studley

R ♿ **Map 10 C4** Warwickshire
45 High Street
Studley (052 785) 3183
Indian cooking
Credit Access, Amex, Diners, Visa

Super service, friendly and very efficient, is a
trademark of this popular Indian restaurant. Flair
and care distinguish the cooking, and there's a
sure hand in charge of herbs and spices.
Specialities include suffed peppers, butter
chicken and jhinga masala (tandoori king prawns
in a delicious creamy sauce). Rice and breads are
excellent.

■ *Set L & D £16·50*   *L 12.30–2.15*
About £26 for two   *D 6.30–11.30*
Seats 48 Parties 50   *Parking Limited*
Closed L Sun & 25 & 26 Dec

Plumber Manor Restaurant   Sturminster Newton

RR ♖ ⌕ ♿ **Map 4 B4** Dorset
Hazelbury Bryan Road DT10 2AF
Sturminster Newton (0258) 72507
Credit Access, Visa

A magnificent Jacobean manor house is the
setting for this elegant restaurant where Brian
Prideaux-Brune combines classical skills with
modern ideas. Dishes range from moules
marinière, cold crab mousseline and pink-cooked
pigeon breast on plum sauce to lamb Shrewsbury,
châteaubriand béarnaise and the day's fish and
vegetarian specials. Copious fresh vegetables
and lovely sweets. ⬤ Well-chosen ☺

■ *Set D from £15*   *L by arrang. only*
About £45 for two   *D 7.30–9.30*
Seats 60 Parties 40   *Parking Ample*
Closed Mon Nov–Jan & all Feb
Bedrooms £D/E
Rooms 12   *With bath/shower 11*
Bedrooms in the main house are delightfully
traditional, while those in a converted barn are
stylishly appointed in contemporary style. All are
well equipped, but room service is limited to
continental breakfast. Amenities include
tennis and croquet. No children under 12.
No dogs.

Mill   Sudbury

H **60% £E**
Map 6 C3 Suffolk
Walnut Tree Lane CO10 6BD
Sudbury (0787) 75544
Credit Access, Amex, Diners, Visa
   A huge old cast-iron mill wheel (now behind
glass in the spacious Meadow bar) and the
nearby water meadows are reminders of the
former role of this friendly hotel. Heavy oak beams

give character to the main-house bedrooms;
those in the extension are in simple modern style.
All have private facilities, but some of the older
rooms have showers only.
Amenities coarse fishing, laundry service.

■ *Rooms* 53	*Confirm by* arrang.
en suite bath/shower 53	*Last dinner* 9.15
Direct dial Yes	*Parking* Ample
Room TV Yes	*Room service* Limited

Seaburn Hotel   Sunderland

H **59% £D/E**
Map 15 C4 Tyne & Wear
Queen's Parade SR6 8DB
Tyneside (091) 529 2041. Tlx 53168
Credit Access, Amex, Diners, Visa. **LVs**
   Standing on the seafront two miles north of
Sunderland, this 1930s hotel is a popular meeting
place for visitors and locals alike. The neat
reception area leads to the public bar and a

spacious lounge with sea views. Comfortable airy
bedrooms have practical fittings and are
equipped with tea-makers, direct dial telephones
and TVs. There are two bars and various function
rooms. *Amenities* free in-house movies.

■ *Rooms* 82	*Confirm by* 6
en suite bath/shower 82	*Last dinner* 9.30
Direct dial Yes	*Parking* Ample
Room TV Yes	*Room service* 24 hours

■ Our inspectors are our full-
   time employees; they are
   professionally trained by us.

Chez Max   Surbiton

R ⌘ **Map 5 E2** Surrey
   85 Maple Road
01-399 2365
French cooking
Credit Access, Amex, Diners, Visa
   Max Markarian is the driving force behind this
pretty, restful little restaurant, tackling an
ambitious French menu with gusto and
occasional sheer brilliance. The regularly

changing selection offers a tempting variety, from
warm duck liver mousse or salmon quenelles to
venison with juniper and pear sauce or fillet steak
with wild mushrooms. ☺

■ *Set L* £15.25	*L* 12.30–2
Set D £16.25	*D* 7.30–10.30
About £52 *for two*	*Parking* Ample
Seats 32 *Parties* 32	*Closed L* Sat, all Sun &
	Mon, Good Fri, 2 wks Aug & 24 Dec–7 Jan

Partners 23   Sutton

R ⌘ ⌖ **Map 5 F3** Surrey
   23 Stonecot Hill
01-644 7743
Credit Access, Amex, Diners, Visa
   Andrew Thomason extends a warm welcome at
this attractive little restaurant in a shopping
arcade. His partner, Tim McEntire, proffers a short
but imaginative fixed-price menu, French in style,
with starters like warm salad of roast quail vying

for attention with smoked trout mousse. Main
courses include glazed veal loin steak, and fresh
salmon with dill cream sauce. Desserts are
tempting. ☺

■ *Set L* £13.25	*L* 12.30–2
Set D £18	*D* 7.30–9.30
About £45 *for two*	*Parking* Ample
Seats 30	*Parties* 35
Closed Sun, Mon & 10 days Xmas–New Year	

Bell House Hotel   Sutton Benger

H **64% £D/E**
Map 4 B2 Wiltshire
Nr Chippenham SN15 4RH
Seagry (0249) 720401
Managers Max Geisberger & Tina Vincent
Credit Access, Amex, Diners, Visa
   Attractive gardens are a feature of this
welcoming little hotel, much extended and
modernised from its 15th-century origins. Day

rooms include the comfortable Carriage Bar,
which takes its name from the 18th-century
carriage that stands in the forecourt. Bedrooms
are smartly furnished in Regency style.
Amenities garden, laundry service.

■ *Rooms* 14	*Confirm by* 8.30
en suite bath/shower 14	*Last dinner* 10.30
Direct dial Yes	*Parking* Ample
Room TV Yes	*Room service* Limited

Moor Hall Hotel   Sutton Coldfield

H **62%** **£D/E**
Map 10 C4 West Midlands
Moor Hall Drive, Four Oaks B75 6LN
021-308 3751. Tlx 335127
Credit Access, Amex, Diners, Visa. LVs
  A handsome mansion standing in its own quiet grounds overlooking a golf course. The foyer and lounge are in spacious, traditional style, with panelling, parlour plants and antiques, while

Jake's winer/diner is modern and casual. Smartly kept bedrooms, though up-to-date in their appointments, manage to retain the period feel of the place. *Amenities* garden, sauna, steam room, solarium, gymnasium, laundry service.

■ *Rooms* 48	*Confirm by* arrang.
en suite bath/shower 48	*Last dinner* 10.30
Direct dial Yes	*Parking* Ample
Room TV Yes	*Room service* 24 hours

Penns Hall Hotel   Sutton Coldfield

HR **65%** **£C/D**
Map 10 C4 West Midlands
Penns Lane, Walmley B76 8LH
021-351 3111. Tlx 335789
Manager Colin D. Campbell
Credit Access, Amex, Diners, Visa. LVs
  Check directions to this extended 17th-century house by a picturesque lake. The foyer and lounge have been smartly refurbished, and there are two pleasant bars. Best bedrooms are those in the Connaught wing; all are neat and smart, with remote-control TVs, hairdryers and trouser presses. *Amenities* garden, coarse fishing, laundry service, 24-hour lounge service.

■ *Rooms* 115	*Confirm by* 6
en suite bath/shower 115	*Last dinner* 10
Direct dial Yes	*Parking* Ample
Room TV Yes	*Room service* 24 hours

Penns Hall Hotel Restaurant

Skilful cooking, excellent presentation and fine service from a largely Italian team. Sergio Grassi's varied à la carte menu includes a number of Italian specialities, among them some splendid pasta dishes. Main courses are accompanied by first-rate vegetables and followed by a trolley-load of hard-to-resist home-made sweets. Sunday sees a traditional lunch. The restaurant is in comfortable old-world style, with panelling, leaded windows and high-backed chairs. ⊖

■ *Set D* from £12	*L* 1–2, Sun 12.30–2
About £40 for two	*D* 7–10
Seats 120	*Parties* 600
Closed Sat & some Bank Hols	

■ For a discount on next year's guide, see Offer for Answers.

Blunsdon House Hotel   Swindon

H **70%** **£D** &
Map 4 C2 Wiltshire
Blunsdon SN2 4AD
Swindon (0793) 721701. Tlx 444491
Owner managers Clifford family
Credit Access, Amex, Diners, Visa. LVs
  A comprehensively-equipped leisure complex is the latest in a long line of improvements made by the Clifford family to their much-extended hotel set in 20 acres of grounds off the A419. Triple-glazed bedrooms range from standard, offering tea-makers, hairdryers and well-fitted bathrooms, to Executives with superior furnishings and Prestige, whose many extras include remote-control teletext TVs and bathrooms equipped with telephones and radio speakers. Five rooms have four-posters. The foyer-lounge and bars provide ample space for relaxation. No dogs.

Amenities garden, indoor swimming pool, sauna, solarium, whirlpool bath, steam bath, gymnasium, hairdressing, squash, games room, snooker, laundry service, 24-hour lounge service.

■ *Rooms* 91	*Confirm by* 6
en suite bath/shower 91	*Last dinner* 10.30
Direct dial Yes	*Parking* Ample
Room TV Yes	*Room service* 24 hours

Crest Hotel   Swindon

H **61%** **£C/D** &
Map 4 C2 Wiltshire
Oxford Road, Stratton St Margaret SN3 4TL
Swindon (0793) 822921. Tlx 444456
Credit Access, Amex, Diners, Visa
  General refurbishment has improved this modern hotel. Accommodation ranges from neat standard rooms to Lady Crest, Executive – smarter furnishings and a host of accessories –

and the new Executive Study rooms fitted out for desk work. Roomy lobby, split-level bar. Decent breakfast, but service sometimes stutters. *Amenities* pool table, in-house movies (charge), laundry service, children's playroom (weekends).

■ *Rooms* 94	*Confirm by* 6
en suite bath/shower 94	*Last dinner* 9.45
Direct dial Yes	*Parking* Ample
Room TV Yes	*Room service* Limited

Post House Hotel   Swindon

H **62% £C/D**
Map 4 C2 Wiltshire
Marlborough Road SN3 6AQ
Swindon (0793) 24601. Tlx 444464
Credit Access, Amex, Diners, Visa. LVs
 Junction 15 of the M4 is only a few miles from
this modern hotel with excellent leisure facilities.
The spacious foyer has bar and lounge areas.
Executives get superior treatment, but all rooms

have mini-bars and tea-makers.
Amenities garden, indoor swimming pool, sauna,
solarium, whirlpool bath, gymnasium, laundry
service, coffee shop (10am–10.30pm), 24-hour
lounge service, children's playground, helipad.

■ *Rooms* 104	*Confirm by* 6
en suite bath/shower 104	*Last dinner* 10
Direct dial Yes	*Parking* Ample
Room TV Yes	*Room service* 24 hours

Wiltshire Hotel   Swindon

H **63% £C/D**
Map 4 C2 Wiltshire
Fleming Way SN1 1TN
Swindon (0793) 28282. Tlx 444250
Credit Access, Amex, Diners, Visa
 Closely resembling the modern office blocks
that surround it, this purpose-built hotel in the
town centre is popular with business visitors. The
marble-floored foyer has a bright, welcoming

appeal and there is a handsome, richly panelled
bar. Up-to-date bedrooms furnished in smart,
practical style all offer tea-makers.
Amenities 24-hour lounge service, laundry
service.

■ *Rooms* 85	*Confirm by* 6
en suite bath/shower 85	*Last dinner* 10.30
Direct dial Yes	*Parking* Ample
Room TV Yes	*Room service* 24 hours

🍷 indicates a **well-chosen** house wine.

Frederick's *NEW ENTRY*   Tadworth

R 🍷 **Map 7 A5** Surrey
17 High Street
Tadworth (073 781) 2319
Credit Access, Amex, Diners, Visa
 Frederick O'Meara took over a transport cafe
and turned it into a pleasant and stylish little
restaurant. His menu changes every fortnight and
offers some unusual combinations like veal
escalope topped with smoked salmon or

pineapple with honey and peppercorns. Salmon
and mushroom strudel is a first-class starter, beef
Wellington a popular main dish. Lots of good fresh
vegetables.
🍷 Well-chosen

■ *Set L* £9·00	*L* 12.30–1.30
Set D £13·95	*D* 7.30–9.30
About £38 for two	*Parking* Ample
Seats 36	*Closed* D Sun & all Mon

Cliveden   Taplow

HR **89% £A** ***E***
Map 5 E2 Berkshire
Nr Maidenhead SL6 0JF
Burnham (062 86) 68561. Tlx 846562
Credit Access, Amex, Diners, Visa
 Exemplary service, both in the fine detail and
the grand design, makes an indelible impression
at this magnificent country house. The setting – in
400 acres of parkland beside the Thames – is
immaculate. Elegant public rooms including a
panelled hall and library and a stunningly ornate
rococo dining room where breakfast is served,
recall famous former residents like Frederick,
Prince of Wales, the Duke of Sutherland and the
Astors. Spacious bedrooms, sumptuously

furnished, combine antiques with modern
accessories. Large bathrooms are thoughtfully
equipped. *Amenities* garden, outdoor swimming
pool, sauna, keep-fit equipment, tennis, squash,
croquet, riding, coarse fishing, boating, snooker,
teletext, valeting, laundry service, 24-hour lounge
service, hotel boat, courtesy car.

■ *Rooms* 25	*Confirm by* arrang.
en suite bath/shower 25	*Last dinner* 9.30
Direct dial Yes	*Parking* Ample
Room TV Yes	*Room service* 24 hours

Cliveden Dining Room 👑👑

Wing-collared waiters couple efficiency with
warmth in this beautifully-proportioned room with
its superb views. John Webber's fixed-price
menus are full of interest without being over-
elaborate. Typical starters are a terrine of foie gras
with Sauternes or a bavarois of smoked salmon
with tomato and basil sauce. Main courses may
include scallops à la nage or noisettes of lamb in
creamy leek sauce. Excellent sweet trolley. Good
English and French cheeses. 🗢 Outstanding 🄔

■ *Set L* £26·60	*L* 12.30–2.30
Set D £35·60	*D* 7.30–9.30
About £86 for two	*Seats* 60 Parties ⸍

Langton Arms *NEW ENTRY*   Tarrant Monkton

IR £F &
Map 4 B4 Dorset
Blandford Forum DT11 8RX
Tarrant Hinton (025 889) 225
Owner manager Chris Goodinge
Credit Access, Amex, Diners, Visa

The role of this much-loved thatched village inn has expanded with the building of six splendidly appointed bedrooms. Overlooking gardens and fields, they all have spacious, well-equipped bathrooms. An excellent breakfast is served either in the rooms or in the conservatory. There are two inviting bars and a skittles alley. *Amenities* garden.

■ Rooms 6	Confirm by arrang.
en suite bath/shower 6	Last dinner 10
Direct dial Yes	Parking Ample
Room TV Yes	Room service Limited

Langtons &

A pleasantly civilised restaurant occupying the inn's converted stables. Dedicated chef Barbara Garnsworthy offers familiar favourites like jumbo prawns with garlic butter, best end of lamb and a variety of steaks, supplementing the regular menu with blackboard specials such as smoked chicken and celeriac roulade or wild salmon with dill, vermouth and cream. Delicious sweets – chocolate and walnut fudge gâteau, chestnut mousse, blackcurrant ice cream, ginger syllabub.
♟ Well-chosen ℮

■ Set L £6·25	L Sun only 12–2
About £30 for two	D 7–10
Seats 45	Parties 60
Closed 25 Dec	

Old Bakery *NEW ENTRY*   Tatsfield

R Map 7 B5 Kent
Westmore Green, Nr Westerham
Tatsfield (0959) 77605
Owner manager Joseph Boadella
Credit Access, Amex, Diners, Visa

Well-prepared, hearty fare is the attraction of this smartly rustic restaurant on the village green. Portions are generous, and favourites such as duck à l'orange, chicken Kiev and steak Diane share the menu with baked skate and scampi cooked in wine. Starters include melon with spider crab and succulent scallops in bacon. Sunday lunch is a family affair. ℮

■ Set L Tues–Fri £8·50,	L 12–2, Sun 12–2.30
Sun £7·95	D 7–9.30, Sat 7–10
Set D Mon–Fri £11·50	Parking Ample
About £45 for two	Seats 70
Closed D Sun & L Mon	Parties 80

■ See INSPECTOR FOR A DAY

Castle Hotel   Taunton

HR 80% £B/C
Map 3 E2 Somerset
Castle Green TA1 1NF
Taunton (0823) 272671. Tlx 46488
Manager David Prior
Credit Access, Amex, Diners, Visa

A fine, creeper-clad building, formerly part of a Norman fortress and now a first-class hotel. Service is of the highest order, housekeeping is exemplary and furnishings are more than equal to their magnificent setting. Splendid tapestries hang in the panelled oak room, and the bar-lounge with its beautiful fabrics and elegant chairs and sofas is the acme of sophistication. Immaculately-kept bedrooms are individually decorated with great style and taste. Garden suites have self-contained dressing rooms and bathrooms with marble vanity units, telephone extensions and radio/TV speakers. *Amenities* garden, laundry service, 24-hour lounge service.

■ Rooms 35	Confirm by arrang.
en suite bath/shower 35	Last dinner 9
Direct dial Yes	Parking Ample
Room TV Yes	Room service 24 hours

Castle Hotel Restaurant ★

The Castle prides itself on the quality of its raw materials, and head chef Gary Rhodes handles his produce with flair and respect. The newly refurbished dining room makes a handsome and elegant setting for such notably successful dishes as our beautifully tender duck breast with a rich thyme-flavoured parfait of livers in an excellent red wine and bone marrow sauce. Vegetables are cooked just so, and amongst tempting desserts shone a simple but perfect glazed apple tart highlighted by wonderfully sharp apple ice cream. No smoking. The superb wine list includes a powerful showing of fine Rhône wines (Paul Jaboulet Aîné). *Specialities* poached scallops with mussels, tomato and a julienne of garlic and ginger, fillet of John Dory with baby vegetables and saffron potatoes, best end of lamb with mint and green peppercorn sauce on a bed of lamb sauce, prune and rum ice cream.
▱ Outstanding ♟ Well-chosen ℮

■ Set L £8·50	L 12.30–2
Set D £18·50	D 7.30–9
About £62 for two	Seats 80 Parties 90

County Hotel   Taunton

H **61% £C/D**
Map 3 E2 Somerset
East Street TA1 3LT
Taunton (0823) 287651. Tlx 46484
Credit Access, Amex, Diners, Visa. **LVs**
   A handsome grey-painted Georgian facade
distinguishes this town-centre hotel. Reception is
reached through a pleasant oak-panelled lounge
or from the car park at the rear. Photographs of

Somerset cricketers line the walls of the Wyvern
Bar – a popular local meeting place. Fitted
bedrooms are mostly in simple modern style.
Amenities laundry service, 24-hour lounge
service.
■ *Rooms* 67   *Confirm by* 6
en suite bath/shower 67   *Last dinner* 9.30
Direct dial Yes   *Parking* Ample
Room TV Yes   *Room service* 24 hours

Tebay Mountain Lodge Hotel   Tebay

H **59% £D/E**
Map 13 D5 Cumbria
Tebay (West) Service Area CA10 3SB
Orton (058 74) 351
Credit Access, Amex, Diners, Visa
   Part of the service area just north of junction 38
of the M6, this neat modern hotel has open-plan
public areas that are bright and cheerful. The
identically decorated bedrooms enjoy fine views

of the Cumbrian hills. Lightwood units, duvets,
radio-alarms and tea-makers are standard, and all
have compact tiled bathrooms.
Amenities 24-hour lounge service.

■ *Rooms* 30   *Confirm by arrang.*
en suite bath/shower 30   *Last dinner* 9.30
Room phone Yes   *Parking* Ample
Room TV Yes   *Room service* 24 hours

Venn Farm Country House Hotel   Teignmouth

H **59% £E**
Map 3 E3 Devon
Higher Exeter Road TQ14 9PB
Teignmouth (062 67) 2196. Tlx 42513
Owner Managers Mr & Mrs W. Russell
Credit Access, Amex, Diners, Visa
   There's a homely, comfortable air about this
family-run hotel, which has kept many of its
Victorian farmhouse features. Views of sea or

moor are enjoyed by the cosy bedrooms, four of
which have been given a smart refit. The large,
peaceful lounge incorporates a little bar, and
there's plenty more elbow room in the pub-style
basement bar. No dogs. *Amenities* garden.
■ *Rooms* 10   *Confirm by arrang.*
en suite bath/shower 10   *Last dinner* 9
Room phone No   *Parking* Ample
Room TV Yes   *Room service* None

■ We welcome complaints and bona
   fide recommendations on the
   tear-out pages for readers' comments.
   They are followed up by our professional
   team. Please also complain to the
   management instantly.

Telford Hotel, Golf & Country Club   Telford

H **64% £D**
Map 10 B3 Shropshire
Great Hay, Sutton Hill TF7 4DT
Telford (0952) 585642. Tlx 35481
Credit Access, Amex, Diners, Visa. **LVs**
   This welcoming hotel comprises modern rustic
buildings and a converted farmhouse. Refurbish-
ment has improved the day rooms, and attention
now turns to the well-equipped bedrooms, the

largest of which are in 200-year-old Darby House.
Amenities garden, indoor swimming pool, sauna,
squash, golf course, clay-pigeon shooting, games
room, snooker, laundry service, coffee shop
(9am–10pm), children's playground.
■ *Rooms* 58   *Confirm by* 6
en suite bath/shower 58   *Last dinner* 10
Direct dial Yes   *Parking* Ample
Room TV Yes   *Room service* 24 hours

Telford Moat House   Telford

H **67% £D** &
Map 10 B3 Shropshire
Forgegate, Telford Centre TF3 4NA
Telford (0952) 506007. Tlx 35588
Credit Access, Amex, Diners, Visa
   Smart, modern and well-run, this purpose-built
hotel stands just off the M54 (leave at junction 5).
There's a light, roomy feel throughout, from the
marble-floored foyer and amply-furnished lounge

to the neatly maintained bedrooms, which all have
remote-control TVs, hairdryers and trouser
presses. *Amenities* garden, indoor swimming
pool, sauna, solarium, keep-fit equipment, laundry
service, in-house movies (charge).
■ *Rooms* 98   *Confirm by arrang.*
en suite bath/shower 98   *Last dinner* 9.30
Direct dial Yes   *Parking* Ample
Room TV Yes   *Room service* Limited

Calcot Manor   Tetbury

HR 75% £C/D ♿
Map 4 B2 Gloucestershire
Nr Beverston GL8 8YJ
Leighterton (066 689) 355
Owner managers Ball family
Credit Access, Amex, Diners, Visa

Personal attention to each guest's individual needs is the aim of the charming Ball family, who run their delightful converted farmhouse hotel on the A4135 in an unobtrusive but highly professional style. Polished wood is much in evidence as you enter the house, a welcoming log fire burns in the bar-lounge and there are plenty of inviting sofas in the comfortable drawing room. Individually furnished bedrooms – all with stylish bathrooms and a host of thoughtful extras – command sweeping country views. Faultless

housekeeping and service. No children under 12. No dogs. *Amenities* garden, outdoor swimming pool, croquet, laundry service.
■ *Rooms* 10   *Confirm by* arrang.
en suite bath/shower 10   *Last dinner* 9.30
Direct dial Yes   *Parking* Ample
Room TV Yes   *Room service* All day
Closed 1st full wk Jan

Restaurant ♛ ♿

New chef Ramon Farthing ably continues his predecessor's deft, imaginative style of cooking in this quietly elegant restaurant. His set menus offer interesting choices like hot mousse of mallard duck with grapes, fallow deer with parsnip rösti or fresh salmon and leeks in a champagne sauce. Presentation is superb, vegetables crisp, the cheeseboard excellent. Sweets might include a delicious rhubarb soufflé. Friendly service. Decent wine list with some good bottles: Ch. Gloria '76, Chianti Classico Badia a Coltibuono '78. No smoking.
■ *Set L from* £9·50   *L* 12.30–2
Set D £19·50   *D* 7.30–9.30
About £52 *for two*   *Seats* 40 *Parties* 50
Closed D Sun to non-residents & 1st wk Jan

Close at Tetbury   Tetbury

HR 68% £C/D
Map 4 B2 Gloucestershire
8 Long Street GL8 8AQ
Tetbury (0666) 52272
Credit Access, Amex, Diners, Visa

Part-16th century, part-Georgian, this former wool merchant's house abounds in old-world charm. New owners have improved service and maintenance, and comfortable bedrooms – simple well-kept bathrooms – offer many extras. Public areas include a reception with an impressive stone fireplace and a glass-domed lounge. No dogs. *Amenities* garden, laundry service.
■ *Rooms* 12   *Confirm by* arrang.
en suite bath/shower 12   *Last dinner* 9.45
Direct dial Yes   *Parking* Ample
Room TV Yes   *Room service* All day

Restaurant

NEW ENTRY

A good choice of enjoyable dishes with a modern ring is on offer at this handsome restaurant overlooking the garden. Chef Chris Amor's weekly fixed-price menus might start with sautéed duck livers with a pink peppercorn sauce or a tangy cheese and Meaux mustard soufflé, to be followed by trout with tarragon, duck in a lime sauce, or lamb with hazelnuts and Madeira. A good cellar with a fine collection of burgundies and first-growth clarets. Young staff provide excellent service.
■ *Set L* £7·95   *L* 12.30–2
Set D from £13·75   *D* 7.30–9.45
About £48 *for two*   *Parking* Ample
Seats 50   *Parties* 20

Snooty Fox Hotel   Tetbury

H 70% £D
Map 4 B2 Gloucestershire
Market Place GL8 8DD
Tetbury (0666) 52436
Credit Access, Amex, Diners, Visa

Enjoying a pleasant town-centre location opposite the old market hall, this fine Cotswold-stone hotel was built as a coaching inn during the 16th century. Today it offers high standards of comfort and hospitality. Log fires warm both the elegant residents' lounge with its luxuriously deep sofas and the stone-walled cocktail bar. Upstairs, bedrooms of varying sizes are lavishly fitted with quality fabrics and handsome furnishings. All have excellent en suite bathrooms and many thoughtful extras. No dogs. *Amenities* laundry service.

■ *Rooms* 12   *Confirm by* 6
en suite bath/shower 12   *Last dinner* 9.45
Direct dial Yes   *Parking* Difficult
Room TV Yes   *Room service* All day

Bell Hotel   Tewkesbury

H 61% £D/E
Map 4 B1 Gloucestershire
Church Street GL20 5SA
Tewkesbury (0684) 293293. Tlx 43535
Owner manager Roger Brown
Credit Access, Amex, Diners, Visa
   A handsome building with a black-and-white timbered facade, the Bell enjoys a central position by the Abbey Church and the river. There's a

warm, hospitable feel about the day rooms, which include a lounge and little panelled bar, both with beams. Bedrooms are all comfortable; there are two four-poster suites. *Amenities* garden, laundry service.

■ *Rooms 25*	*Confirm by 6*
en suite bath/shower 25	*Last dinner 9.45*
Room phone Yes	*Parking Ample*
Room TV Yes	*Room service All day*

Bredon Manor   Tewkesbury

H 67% £C/D
Map 4 B1 Gloucestershire
Bredon GL20 7EG
Tewkesbury (0684) 72293
Owner managers Mr & Mrs H. V. Whittingham
Credit Access, Amex, Diners, Visa
   An imposing mansion standing in lovely gardens by the river Avon. Day rooms are splendidly inviting and informal. Homely touches

abound both here and in the spacious, comfortable bedrooms, three of which have little dressing rooms. No children under 12. No dogs. *Amenities* garden, outdoor swimming pool, tennis, putting, croquet, coarse fishing, laundry service.

■ *Rooms 4*	*Confirm by arrang.*
en suite bath/shower 4	*Last dinner 8*
Direct dial Yes	*Parking Ample*
Room TV Yes	*Room service Limited*

Tewkesbury Park Hotel   Tewkesbury

H 61% £D/E
Map 4 B1 Gloucestershire
Lincoln Green Lane GL20 7DN
Tewkesbury (0684) 295405. Tlx 43563
Credit Access, Amex, Diners, Visa
   Excellent leisure and conference facilities are attractions of this 18th-century mansion. Bars and lounges include a charming gazebo. Best of the bedrooms are in the newer of two modern blocks.

No dogs. *Amenities* garden, indoor swimming pool, sauna, solarium, whirlpool bath, keep-fit equipment, squash, golf course, games room, snooker, coffee shop (9.30am–10.30pm), in-house movies (free), laundry service.

■ *Rooms 82*	*Confirm by 6*
en suite bath/shower 82	*Last dinner 9.30*
Direct dial Yes	*Parking Ample*
Room TV Yes	*Room service All day*

⇨ is our symbol for an **outstanding** wine list.

Old School Club *NEW ENTRY*   Teynham

R Map 7 C5 Kent
Teynham, Nr Sittingbourne
Sittingbourne (0795) 522421
Owner manager Mike Portor-Ward
Credit Access, Visa
   A pleasant little restaurant on the premises of a squash and fitness club. The interesting menu is divided between Oriental (Indonesian) and Continental (mainly Italian) dishes: among the

former you'll find things like fried cod with paw-paw leaves or a splendid beef curry, while the latter include brandy-laced pâté, trout with prawns and steak topped with dolcelatte.
♀ Well-chosen

■ *About £35 for two*	*L 12–2.30*
Seats 30	*D 7–9.30*
Parties 36	*Parking Ample*
Closed D Sun & Mon, 25 & 26 Dec & 1 Jan	

Thatchers   Thame

RR Map 5 D2 Oxfordshire
29 Lower High Street OX9 2AA
Thame (084 421) 2146
Owner manager Terry Connor
Credit Access, Diners, Visa
   Watch out for the low beams as you pass beyond the stone-flagged bar and into the cottage restaurant. Cooking is capable through a tempting French à la carte menu that ranges from pike quenelles with a rich saffron sauce to tender lamb cutlets topped with mushrooms and red pepper, served on a bed of brown noodles. Elaborate desserts feature assemblies like a trio

of sorbets in an almond biscuit. Simpler table d'hôte choice. ℮

■ *Set L & D £12.50*	*L 12–2*
About £38 for two	*D 7–10*
Seats 30	*Parking Ample*
Closed Sun & 25 & 26 Dec	

Bedrooms £E

Rooms 6	*With bath/shower 6*

One of the six bedrooms has a magnificent four-poster and a whirlpool bath. All have character, with beams, low ceilings, highly polished old furniture and open fires.

Skiffers *NEW ENTRY* — Thames Ditton

R ⑨ **Map 7 A5** Surrey
High Street
01-398 5540
Credit Access, Amex, Diners, Visa

A pleasant bistro-style restaurant, with candles, fresh flowers, decorative oars and old regatta posters. The meat (from their butcher's shop next door) is excellent and there's always a good selection of interesting vegetables. The main menu of favourites like French onion soup and seafood gratin is supplemented by daily specials such as Bombay prawns or Stilton-topped sirloin. Good Dutch apple pie for dessert. ℮

■ *About £30 for two*	*L 12–2*
Seats 60	*D 6.30–10.30*
Parties 15	*Parking Limited*
Closed Sun & Mon (exc. Bank Hol Mon when closed Tues), 1 wk Xmas & 1 wk Jan	

The Bell — Thetford

H **62% £C/D**
Map 6 C2 Norfolk
King Street IP24 2AZ
Thetford (0842) 4455. Tlx 818868
Credit Access, Amex, Diners, Visa. **LVs**

A former coaching inn overlooking the river Ouse. The beamed bar and the antique-furnished lounge have considerable character. Bedrooms provide comfort, whether beamed (seven with four-posters) in the main building or contemporary in the wing. What let the side down when we visited was the service, which lacked spark. More effort, please. *Amenities* laundry service, coffee shop (10am–10pm).

■ *Rooms 43*	*Confirm by 6*
en suite bath/shower 43	*Last dinner 9.45*
Direct dial Yes	*Parking Ample*
Room TV Yes	*Room service 24 hours*

Golden Eagle Hotel — Thornaby-on-Tees

H **58% £E/F**
Map 15 C5 Cleveland
Trenchard Avenue TS17 0DA
Stockton-on-Tees (0642) 766511. Tlx 587565
Credit Access, Visa

A town-centre hotel with the concrete-and-glass look of the 70s. The main bar is a popular meeting place, especially at lunchtime, and there are two other bars for a quieter drink. Overnight accommodation is practical and comfortable. All rooms offer remote-control teletext TVs, tea-makers and mini-bars, and luxury rooms have additional facilities. No dogs. *Amenities* in-house movies (free), laundry service.

■ *Rooms 55*	*Confirm by arrang.*
en suite bath/shower 55	*Last dinner 9.30*
Room phone Yes	*Parking Ample*
Room TV Yes	*Room service Limited*

Post House Hotel — Thornaby-on-Tees

H **63% £C/D**
Map 15 C5 Cleveland
Low Lane, By Stainton Village TS17 9LW
Middlesbrough (0642) 591213. Tlx 58428
Credit Access, Amex, Diners, Visa

The central block of this distinctive purpose-built hotel houses a large open-plan reception-cum-lounge area with plenty of seating. There are two bars: one with typical pub decor, the other more subdued, and also a cheery breakfast room/coffee shop. Spacious bedrooms have up-to-date accessories like TVs, tea-makers and mini-bars. *Amenities* garden, sauna, solarium, coffee shop (7.30am–10pm), 24-hour lounge service.

■ *Rooms 135*	*Confirm by 6*
en suite bath/shower 135	*Last dinner 10.30*
Room phone Yes	*Parking Ample*
Room TV Yes	*Room service 24 hours*

Thornbury Castle Hotel — Thornbury

HR **82% £B**
Map 4 B2 Avon
Nr Bristol BS12 1HH
Thornbury (0454) 418511. Tlx 449986
Owner manager Maurice Taylor
Credit Access, Amex, Diners, Visa

Maurice Taylor stayed at this imposing Tudor castle, fell in love with it, and bought it. He's settled in splendidly as host, and his hotel (on the northern edge of Thornbury) provides much more than the average ration of romance and luxury. Baronial public rooms with great stone fireplaces, mullioned windows and heraldic shields feature a fine and growing collection of antiques, oils and tapestries. Bedrooms, tastefully and individually decorated, range from singles to palatial suites; all offer an impressive list of accessories and cosseting comforts, and all boast splendidly appointed bathrooms. Several rooms have oriel windows that look out on to the lovely walled gardens. No children under 12. No dogs. *Amenities* garden, croquet, laundry service, helipad.

■ *Rooms* 12
en suite bath/shower 12
Direct dial Yes
Room TV Yes
Closed 1 wk Xmas

Confirm by 6
Last dinner 9.30
Parking Ample
Room service All day

Thornbury Castle Restaurant ⌣

A noble setting for Colin Hingston's consistently fine cooking, never flamboyant but always full of interest. Typical dishes include mousseline of sole set on a bed of spinach, moist flavoursome breast of chicken with a lime and hazelnut stuffing, noisettes of lamb with basil, and a waist-expanding hot butterscotch pudding. Plentiful vegetables, super British cheeses. The true collector's wine list is full of classic vintages and rarities, but still manages to offer amazing value. ➾ Outstanding ♀ Well-chosen ℮

■ *Set L* £12·50
Set D from £19·50
About £60 *for two*
Closed 1 wk Xmas

L 12.30–2
D 7.30–9.30
Seats 55
Parties 30

■ For a discount on next year's guide, see Offer for Answers.

Mamma Adele   Thornton Heath

R ♀ & **Map 7 B5** Surrey
23 Brigstock Road
01-683 2233
Italian cooking
Credit Access, Amex, Diners, Visa

An attractive, unpretentious restaurant where Kam Memon warmly welcomes guests, while his wife Adele busily prepares Italian favourites in the kitchen. Popular choices like her appetising home-made pasta, liver veneziana, various steaks and trout with almonds are supplemented by seasonal daily specialities such as artichokes and duck breast with brandy sauce. Good vegetables. ℮

■ *About* £35 *for two*
Seats 36
Parties 40
Closed L Mon & Sat,
all Sun, 1 wk Xmas & 3–4 wks July/Aug

L 12–2.30
D 7–11 (Fri &
Sat 7–11.30)
Parking Limited

River House   Thornton-le-Fylde

IR £E
Map 10 A1 Lancashire
Skippool Creek, Nr Blackpool FY5 5LF
Poulton-le-Fylde (0253) 883497
Owner managers Bill & Carole Scott
Credit Access, Amex, Visa

Overlooking the Wyre estuary four miles from Blackpool, the River House is a hotel of great charm, with delightful owners. The homely lounge and bar are ground-floor neighbours, while upstairs the traditionally styled bedrooms feature antiques and many thoughtful extras. The public bathroom boasts a Victorian hooded bath.
Amenities garden, laundry service.

■ *Rooms* 4
en suite bath/shower 1
Direct dial Yes
Room TV Yes

Confirm by arrang.
Last dinner 9.30
Parking Ample
Room service All day

River House Restaurant ♀

Order over a drink in the cosy bar, and look forward to a really splendid candlelit dinner. Bill Scott is a real enthusiast, demanding the very best ingredients and handling them with great skill and flair. His menus are full of interest, offering a wide choice that ranges from beautifully fresh salmon sashimi to soufflé suissesse, from breast of wild duck with zest of orange and green peppercorn sauce to venison served with port wine and cream. The excellence is maintained in delicious sweets like passion fruit mousse and ticky tacky – hot date and walnut sponge with caramel sauce. ℮

■ *About* £40 *for two*
Seats 45

L Mon–Sat by arrang.
Sun at 1
D 7–9.30

■ Changes in data may occur in establishments after the Guide goes to press. Prices should be taken as indications rather than firm quotes.

Wilson Arms Hotel   Threshfield

H **64% £D/E**
Map 15 B6 North Yorkshire
Grassington BD23 5EL
Skipton (0756) 752666
Owner manager Frances Cousins
Credit Access, Amex, Diners, Visa

Peace and comfort in a pleasant Wharfedale setting. This family-run hotel boasts several homely lounges with views of the garden. There are also two bars, public and colourful cocktail. Good-sized bedrooms have ample writing space, easy chairs and tea-makers. *Amenities* garden, croquet, laundry service.

■ *Rooms* 28
en suite bath/shower 28
Direct dial Yes
Room TV Yes
Closed Jan

Confirm by 6
Last dinner 9
Parking Ample
Room service All day

Thurlestone Hotel · Thurlestone

H 69% £B/C
Map 3 D3 Devon
Nr Kingsbridge TQ7 3NN
Kingsbridge (0548) 560382
Owner managers Grose family
Credit Access, Amex, Diners, Visa

The original building is now a jolly pub, and just beyond it stands the main part of this well-appointed resort hotel. The lounge provides easy relaxation in stylish surroundings, and there's a panelled cocktail bar. Bedrooms – the majority with pleasant views over the grounds and undulating farmland to the sea – are furnished with locally made ashwood pieces. There are easy chairs and writing space, and room service is excellent. *Amenities* garden, indoor & outdoor swimming pools, sauna, solarium, keep-fit equipment, whirlpool bath, beauty salon, hairdressing, tennis, squash, badminton, 9-hole golf course, putting, games room, snooker, valeting, laundry service, laundry room, 24-hour lounge service.

■ *Rooms* 68	*Confirm by* arrang.
en suite bath/shower 68	*Last dinner* 9
Direct dial Yes	*Parking* Ample
Room TV Yes	*Room service* 24 hours

Tickton Grange Hotel · Tickton

H 59% £D &
Map 11 E1 Humberside
Nr Beverley HU17 9SH
Leven (0401) 43666. Tlx 527254
Owner managers Whymant family
Credit Access, Amex, Diners, Visa

Set in 3½ acres of grounds, this handsome Georgian hotel makes a peaceful retreat. The main day room is a comfortably traditional bar-cum-lounge with French windows opening on to the lawn. Spacious, attractively decorated bedrooms are furnished with freestanding furniture and have tea-makers and radio-alarms. *Amenities* garden, laundry service.

■ *Rooms* 17	*Confirm by* arrang.
en suite bath/shower 17	*Last dinner* 9.30
Direct dial Yes	*Parking* Ample
Room TV Yes	*Room service* All day

Heskyn Mill · Tideford

R Map 2 C3 Cornwall
Nr Saltash
Landrake (075 538) 481
Owner managers Frank & Sonia Eden
Credit Amex, Visa

Old machinery provides imaginative decor for this cosy, friendly restaurant, converted from an old corn mill. Daily specials such as lamb with cranberries and satsumas supplement the regular menu of steaks, grilled sole, pork fillet with prunes and a madeira cream sauce. Start with soup, pâté, or a smoked fish platter, and try an individual rhubarb pie for afters.

■ *About £39 for two*	*L* 12–2
Seats 54	*D* 7–10
Parties 50	*Parking* Ample
Closed Sun, Mon, Bank Hols & 3 days Xmas	

Rose & Crown Hotel · Tonbridge

H 60% £C/D
Map 7 B5 Kent
125 High Street TN9 1DD
Tonbridge (0732) 357966
Credit Access, Amex, Diners, Visa. LVs

Jacobean panelling and beams feaure in the bar and restaurant of this former coaching inn. A smart lounge has loose-covered sofas and armchairs and there are several attractive function rooms. Traditional-style bedrooms in the main house contrast with modern well-fitted rooms in two new wings. Bathrooms have extras like complimentary toiletries. *Amenities* garden, laundry service, 24-hour lounge service.

■ *Rooms* 51	*Confirm by* 6
en suite bath/shower 51	*Last dinner* 10
Room phone Yes	*Parking* Ample
Room TV Yes	*Room service* Limited

Grand Hotel · Torquay

H 69% £C
Map 3 D3 Devon
Seafront TQ2 6NT
Torquay (0803) 25234. Tlx 42891
Manager Stephen Williams
Credit Access, Amex, Diners, Visa

Lots of good things on our latest visit to this Edwardian seafront hotel, and just the odd niggle. On the plus side we place diligent housekeeping, helpful porterage, well-decorated bedrooms (especially those facing the sea) and a stylish, comfortable lounge. The indoor swimming pool, full of plants, tiling and themed paintings, is one of the most attractive around. Against the good points we encountered tardy room service and a thoroughly sub-standard breakfast; let's hope they can be improved.

Amenities garden, indoor & outdoor swimming pools, sauna, solarium, whirlpool bath, keep-fit equipment, hairdressing, games room, in-house movies (free), laundry service, 24-hour lounge service.

■ *Rooms* 108	*Confirm by* arrang.
en suite bath/shower 108	*Last dinner* 9.30
Direct dial Yes	*Parking* Ample
Room TV Yes	*Room service* 24 hours

Homers Hotel

H 63% £D/E &
Map 3 D3 Devon
Warren Road TQ2 5TN
Torquay (0803) 213456
Owner managers Robert & Barbara Munro
Credit Access, Amex, Diners, Visa
  Victorian clifftop hotel with spectacular sea vistas from many rooms. New owners offer the warmest of welcomes and excellent service, and

the public areas have a comfortable, traditional feel that is most inviting. Nicely furnished bedrooms, some with little terraces. Excellent housekeeping. No children under 7. *Amenities* garden, in-house movies (free), laundry service.

■ *Rooms* 15	*Confirm by* arrang.
en suite bath/shower 15	*Last dinner* 9.30
Direct dial Yes	*Parking* Limited
Room TV Yes	*Room service* All day

Imperial Hotel

HR 84% £B *E*
Map 3 D3 Devon
Parkhill Road TQ1 2DG
Torquay (0803) 24301
Manager Harry Murray
Credit Access, Amex, Diners, Visa
  Impressively large hotel with lush gardens sloping down to the sea, and marvellous sweeping views. The foyer, decorated in the palest pink, has pillars soaring to the skylight dome, and the enormous chandeliered lounge is no less grand. All the very big sea-facing bedrooms, many with balconies, have been stylishly redecorated in pastel shades; best of all are the 14 luxurious suites. Spacious bathrooms offer numerous comforts including dressing

gowns. *Amenities* garden, indoor and outdoor swimming pools, sauna, solarium, whirlpool bath, keep-fit equipment, hairdressing, tennis, squash, snooker, in-house movies (free), laundry service, 24-hour lounge service, children's play room.

■ *Rooms* 167	*Confirm by* 6
en suite bath/shower 167	*Last dinner* 9.30
Direct dial Yes	*Parking* Ample
Room TV Yes	*Room service* 24 hours

Imperial Hotel Restaurant ♨ &

French cooking
The sea views are the best in town, and the sea-fresh fish, brought briskly from Brixham, stands out on the varied menu. Choice dishes may include a warm salad of monkfish, sole and red mullet with a fresh herb cream sauce or Torbay scallops in herb batter on spinach. There are meat dishes, too, plus a calorie-counted section for slimmers. Yves Farouz is doing great things for the cooking, now someone needs to do the same with the service. ℮

■ *Set L* £11	*L* 1–2.30
Set D £17	*D* 7.30–9.30
About £50 *for two*	*Seats* 150 *Parties* 350

NEW ENTRY

Kistor Hotel

H 59% £E
Map 3 D3 Devon
Belgrave Road TQ2 5HF
Torquay (0803) 212632
Owner Managers Mr & Mrs J. K. Hassell
Credit Access. Amex, Diners, Visa
  A friendly modern seafront hotel. Public areas, decorated in bright contemporary style, include a lounge adjoining the swimming pool. Bedrooms –

many with fine sea views – are functional and pleasantly up-to-date. Neat, well-kept bathrooms. *Amenities* garden, indoor swimming pool, sauna, solarium, whirlpool bath, keep-fit equipment, putting, croquet, laundry service.

■ *Rooms* 52	*Confirm by* arrang.
en suite bath/shower 52	*Last dinner* 8.30
Direct dial Yes	*Parking* Ample
Room TV Yes	*Room service* All day

Livermead Cliff Hotel

H 60% £E
Map 3 D3 Devon
Seafront TQ2 6RQ
Torquay (0803) 22881. Tlx 42918
Manager Mr J. F. Poat
Credit Access, Amex, Diners, Visa
  A hotel standing in a fine position at the water's edge. Picture windows in the traditional-style lounge bar give splendid sea views. Spacious

bedrooms are furnished in simple modern style. Guests may use the leisure facilities of another hotel nearby. *Amenities* garden, outdoor swimming pool, sea fishing, laundry room, 24-hour lounge service.

■ *Rooms* 64	*Confirm by* arrang.
en suite bath/shower 64	*Last dinner* 8.30
Direct dial Yes	*Parking* Ample
Room TV Yes	*Room service* All day

Livermead House Hotel — Torquay

H 64% £E
Map 3 D3 Devon
Sea Front TQ2 6QJ
Torquay (0803) 24361. Tlx 42918
Owner managers Perry family
Credit Access, Amex, Diners, Visa

A comfortable, well-run seaside hotel with excellent leisure facilities. Public rooms and most of the neat, simple bedrooms enjoy splendid sea views. *Amenities* garden, outdoor swimming pool, sauna, solarium, whirlpool bath, keep-fit equipment, hairdressing, tennis, squash, putting, sea fishing, games room, snooker, laundry room, 24-hour lounge service.

■ *Rooms 69*	*Confirm by arrang.*
en suite bath/shower 69	*Last dinner 8.30*
Direct dial Yes	*Parking Ample*
Room TV Yes	*Room service Limited*

Osborne Hotel — Torquay

H 66% £C/D
Map 3 D3 Devon
Hesketh Crescent, Meadfoot Beach TQ1 2LL
Torquay (0803) 213311. Tlx 42573
Credit Access, Amex, Diners, Visa

Major refurbishment has taken place at this handsome Regency hotel. Elegant bedrooms boast half-testers, and the six suites are particularly stylish. The main day room is a large lounge incorporating a bar and panelled library. No dogs. *Amenities* garden, outdoor swimming pool, sauna, solarium, whirlpool bath, keep-fit equipment, tennis, games room, snooker, laundry service, 24-hour lounge service.

■ *Rooms 23*	*Confirm by arrang.*
en suite bath/shower 23	*Last dinner 9.30*
Direct dial Yes	*Parking Ample*
Room TV Yes	*Room service 24 hours*

Palace Hotel — Torquay

H 68% £C
Map 3 D3 Devon
Babbacombe Road TQ1 3TG
Torquay (0803) 22271. Tlx 42606
Manager Paul Uphill   *0803 292271*
Credit Access, Amex, Diners, Visa

Roomy, comfortable and well-run, this much extended bishop's residence stands in well-kept gardens and woodland that extend down to the sea. The public rooms, all on a large scale, have a grand, period air : the foyer is a bit garish, perhaps, but the lounges and drawing rooms are rather elegant; the cocktail bar is more modern in style. Accommodation ranges from simple, spacious ordinary rooms to splendid suites with private balconies and quite lavish appointments. Bathrooms are delightfully old-fashioned. *Amenities* garden, indoor & outdoor swimming pools, sauna, beauty salon, tennis, squash, 9-hole golf course, games room, billiards, in-house movies, laundry service, nanny, children's playroom & playground, helipad.

■ *Rooms 141*	*Confirm by arrang.*
en suite bath/shower 141	*Last dinner 9.15*
Direct dial Yes	*Parking Ample*
Room TV Yes	*Room service 24 hours*

Remy's   *NEW ENTRY* — Torquay

R ⑨ **Map 3 D3** Devon
3 Croft Road
Torquay (0803) 22359
French cooking
Credit Access, Amex, Visa

There's a gentle, continental air about this comfortable little restaurant in an attractive Georgian terraced house. Remy Bopp does fine work in the kitchen, while his wife and a French waiter see to the service. Three-course dinner menus are on three price levels, and dishes run from cidery onion soup and chicken with riesling to duck foie gras, the day's fish choice and superb saddle of venison with an excellent port and cranberry sauce. Sorbets and ice creams are among the home-made sweet temptations. There's an interesting list of classic wines. Remy Bopp's previous restaurant, in Belper, appeared in the Guide for a number of years (last featured in 1985).

♥ Well-chosen ☯

■ *Set D from £9·85*	*D only 7.15–9.30*
About £32 for two	*Parking Ample*
Seats 27	
Closed Sun, Mon & Aug	

Toorak Hotel — Torquay

H 55% £E
Map 3 D3 Devon
Chestnut Avenue TQ2 5JS
Torquay (0803) 211866
Manager John Cowie
Credit Access, Visa

A busy and well-equipped seaside hotel. There's a good choice of lounges and bars, and bedrooms are bright and cheerful. In parts it's a little faded, but refurbishment plans are afoot. *Amenities* garden, outdoor swimming pool, hairdressing, tennis, croquet, games room, snooker, laundry service, 24-hour lounge service, children's playground.

■ *Rooms 41*	*Confirm by arrang.*
en suite bath/shower 38	*Last dinner 9.30*
Direct dial Yes	*Parking Ample*
Room TV Yes	*Room service 24 hours*

Old Millfloor *NEW ENTRY*   Trebarwith Strand

RR ♨ ♜ **Map 2 B2** Cornwall
Nr Tintagel
Camelford (0840) 770234
English cooking
  A steepish path leads down to this delightful
guest house, which stands in picturesque
seclusion by a millstream. The dining room is a
model of old-world charm, with leaded windows,
cottage fabrics and masses of fresh flowers.
Book, and bring your own wine to accompany
Janice Waddon-Martyn's splendid home cooking.
She uses a solid fuel Aga to produce delights like
asparagus in a creamy wine sauce, country pâté,

beef Wellington and a super bread and butter
pudding. Local lobster to order when
available. ☺
■ *Set D from £9*   *D only 7.30–9.30*
About £20 for two   *Parking Ample*
Closed Sun & 2 days   *Seats 14 Parties 14*
Xmas
Bedrooms £F
Rooms 3   *With bath/shower 0*
Three chintzy bedrooms, each with washbasin,
share a bathroom. There's a homely lounge with
lots of books and magazines. Traditional English
breakfast. No dogs.

Island Hotel   Tresco

HR **67% £C/D**
Map 2 A2 Isles of Scilly (Cornwall)
TR24 0PU
Scillonia (0720) 22883
Managers John & Wendy Pyatt
Credit Access, Visa
  No cars and no bustle, but peace and quiet
are in plentiful supply on the beautiful island of
Tresco. The Island Hotel is set in splendid
gardens at the sea's edge, with wonderful views
and its own private beach. Light, airy public
rooms include a picture-windowed lounge with
books and games, and a little bar that opens on to
a sun deck. Smartly decorated bedrooms range
from suites and large doubles to smaller singles;
all now have private facilities. A well-run hotel
where many of the guests return year after
year. No dogs.
Amenities garden, outdoor swimming pool,
bowling green, croquet, sea fishing, sailing,
boating, private beach, games room.

■ *Rooms 30*   *Confirm by arrang.*
en suite bath/shower 30 *Last dinner 8.15*
Direct dial Yes   *Parking No cars*
Room TV Yes   *Room service Limited*
Closed mid Oct–mid Mar

Island Hotel Restaurant

Sea views are a fitting backdrop to the super-
fresh fish that features here both at lunchtime and
on the six-course dinner menus. Robert Coombe's
careful preparation lets the lobsters, the crab, the
John Dory and the lemon sole keep their natural
zing, with usually just a light sauce to accompany.
There's also a good choice of plain and sauced
dishes for meat-eaters, plus a tempting sweet
selection and a first-rate cheeseboard. Good
keenly-priced wines: Ch. Potensac 1980. ☺
■ *Set D £16·50*   *L 12.30–1.30,*
About £45 for two   *Sun 1–1.45*
Seats 60   *D 7.15–8.15*
Closed mid Oct–mid Mar

Mortal Man Hotel   Troubeck

I **£E**
Map 13 D5 Cumbria
Nr Windermere LA23 1PL
Ambleside (053 94) 33193
Owner manager Mr C. J. Poulsom
  A beautifully situated 17th-century inn, ideally
placed for exploring the lakes. The small foyer
leads into a homely beamed lounge with coal fire;
copper-topped tables and antique benches

characterise the bar. Individually decorated
bedrooms are of a decent size with adjoining or
en suite bathrooms. Half-board only, no children
under five. *Amenities* garden.
■ *Rooms 13*   *Confirm by arrang.*
en suite bath/shower 8 *Last dinner 8*
Room phone No   *Parking Ample*
Room TV No   *Room service Limited*
Closed mid Nov–mid Feb

♟ indicates a **well-chosen** house wine.

Cheevers   Tunbridge Wells

R ♜ **Map 7 B5** Kent
56 High Street
Tunbridge Wells (0892) 45524
Credit Access Visa
  Chef Tim Cheevers and two partners own this
bright, simple restaurant offering modern English
cuisine. A brasserie operates at lunchtime (soup,
terrines and a good range of main dishes – meat
and fish) while the fixed-price evening meal amply

demonstrates Cheevers' skills. Refined dishes
range from a featherlight salmon mousseline to
lamb with a rosemary and hazelnut crust. Pretty
vegetables and super sweets. ♟ **Well-chosen** ☺
■ *Set D £13·95*   *L 12–2.30*
About £36 for two   *D 7–10.30*
Seats 32 Parties 32   *Parking Limited*
Closed Sun, Mon, Bank Hols, 1 wk Easter & 2 wks
Sept

☞ is our symbol for an **outstanding** wine list.

Royal Wells Inn   Tunbridge Wells

HR 60% £E
Map 7 B5 Kent
Mount Ephraim TN4 8BE
Tunbridge Wells (0892) 23414
Owner managers David & Robert Sloan
Credit Access, Amex, Diners, Visa

A double coat of arms tops this handsome whitewashed hotel, commemorating a visit by the future Queen Victoria. Guests enter straight into the popular bar-lounge with its large bay windows and inviting French-style chairs. Traditionally furnished bedrooms (two with four-posters) offer good modern bathrooms.

■ *Rooms 16* — *Confirm by arrang.*
en suite bath/shower 16 — *Last dinner 9.30*
Direct dial Yes — *Parking Ample*
Room TV Yes — *Room service Limited*
Closed 25 & 26 Dec

Royal Wells Inn Restaurant ☜

Plushly traditional surroundings for skilled, resourceful cooking in the modern idiom. The Sloan brothers' menu changes frequently and is always of interest. Starters might include chicken mousseline with Stilton, or silky-smooth watercress and scallop soup; followed perhaps by noisette of lamb in pastry with Madeira sauce, or breast of chicken with cider vinegar and Calvados. Vegetables are fresh and crisp; sweets include ices, fruit charlottes and delicious pears poached in red wine. ☺

■ *Set L from £9·50* — *L 12.30–2.30*
Set D from £9·50 — *D 7.30–9.30,*
About £42 for two — *Sat 7.30–10.30*
Seats 35 — *Parties 80*
Closed Bank Hol Mons & 25 & 26 Dec

■ Our inspectors never book in the name of Egon Ronay's Guides; they disclose their identity only after paying their bills.

Spa Hotel   Tunbridge Wells

HR 72% £C/D **E** &
Map 7 B5 Kent
Mount Ephraim TN4 8XJ
Tunbridge Wells (0892) 20331. Tlx 957188
Credit Access, Amex, Diners, Visa

Built in 1766 as a country mansion, this graciously-proportioned hotel stands in six acres of well-kept grounds. Staff are very courteous and efficient from reception and porterage through to room service. The foyer-lounge has been wood-panelled and refurbished in Victorian country house style, and there's a smart, comfortable bar with an equestrian theme. Updating also continues in the traditionally appointed bedrooms, where extras include hairdryers, remote-control TVs and bedside controls. A splendid breakfast

starts the day. *Amenities* garden, indoor swimming pool, sauna, solarium, whirlpool bath, keep-fit equipment, beauty salon, hairdressing, tennis, croquet, laundry service, children's play area.

■ *Rooms 75* — *Confirm by arrang.*
en suite bath/shower 75 — *Last dinner 9.30*
Direct dial Yes — *Parking Ample*
Room TV Yes — *Room service 24 hours*

Spa Hotel Chandelier Restaurant ♔ &

An elegant, roomy restaurant with splendid chandeliers is an excellent setting for James Donaldson's sound, enjoyable cooking. Flavoursome dishes using very fresh ingredients range from a shimmering consommé royale to sole in puff pastry and calf's liver with mango and ginger. Good crisp vegetables. Popular lunchtime specials include stuffed loin of pork, roast guinea fowl and fish pie; excellent hors d'oeuvre and sweet trolleys. Good wines, especially clarets. ☺

■ *Set L £9* — *L 12.30–2, Sun 1–2.30*
About £45 for two — *D 7–9.30*
Seats 80 — *Parties 280*

Thackeray's House ★ — Tunbridge Wells

R ★ ᗑ ⑨ **Map 7 B5** Kent
85 London Road
Tunbridge Wells (0892) 37558
Owner manager Bruce Wass
Credit Access, Visa.

A really delightful place that was once the home of the Victorian novelist William Makepeace Thackeray. Bruce Wass is the chef-patron, cooking with great care and imagination and offering diners a mouthwatering variety of good things. Hot terrine of crab and red mullet with a deep-flavoured lobster sauce is a marvellous starter, which could be followed by calf's liver and mango, mustard-sauced sirloin steak or duck breast with caramelised apple and green peppercorns. There's a good choice of lovely sweets and an excellent selection of British and Irish cheeses. Fine wines, too, including an outstanding Chénas 1985 (Fernand Charvet). Service is very professional, with just the right balance of friendliness and formality. *Specialities*

brill fricassée with spinach quenelles and a carrot and Sauternes sauce, duck breast with ginger, chocolate Armagnac loaf with coffee and walnut liqueur sauce.

♀ Well-chosen ℮
■ *Set L £10·90* *L 12.30–2.30*
Set D £18·50 *D 7.15–10*
About £50 for two *Parking Difficult*
Seats 40 *Parties 20*
Closed Sun, Mon, Bank Hols & 1 wk Xmas

Ye Olde Dog & Partridge Hotel — Tutbury

H **60% £E**
Map 10 C3 Staffordshire
High Street DE13 9LS
Burton-on-Street (0283) 813030. Tlx 347220
Manager Mr D. J. Martindale
Credit Access, Amex, Diners, Visa

Behind the attractive oak-beamed frontage there's a lot of traditional charm about this 15th-century coaching inn – the two little bars are

particularly delightful. Individually styled rooms – some in a Georgian house next door – range from smallish to spacious and airy, with four-posters. *Amenities* garden, laundry service.
■ *Rooms 18* *Confirm by arrang.*
en suite bath/shower 15 *Last dinner 9.45*
Direct dial Yes *Parking Ample*
Room TV Yes *Room service Limited*
Closed 25 & 26 Dec & 1 Jan

■ For a discount on next year's guide, see Offer for Answers.

McClements *NEW ENTRY* — Twickenham

R ⑨ **Map 7 A5** Middlesex
12 The Green
01-755 0176
French cooking
Credit Access, Amex, Diners, Visa

John McClements is an ambitious young Liverpudlian whose attention to detail is evident everywhere in this tiny but tastefully decorated restaurant on the outskirts of Twickenham.

Sophisticated starters like crab gâteau with orange and cardamom sauce lead to quite ambitious main courses such as guinea fowl with pistachio stuffing. As a delicious finale, try the plate of miniature desserts. ℮
■ *Set L £8* *Meals noon–10pm,*
About £40 for two *Sat 7pm–10.30pm*
Seats 18 Parties 12 *Parking Limited*
Closed L Sat, all Sun, 25 & 26 Dec & 2 wks Jan

Quincey's *NEW ENTRY* — Twickenham

R ♿ **Map 7 A5** Middlesex
34 Church Street
01-892 6366
Owner manager Brenda Ishani
Credit Access, Amex, Diners, Visa

Quincey's is the pride and joy of friendly owner Brenda Ishani and a cosy, informal setting for Chris Wellington's artistic and imaginative modern cooking. The menu could include

vegetables in a pastry case with tomato and peanut sauce; marinated shark or noisettes of lamb with a lovely watercress and wild mushroom sauce. End up with banana roulade.
♀ Well-chosen ℮
■ *About £35 for two* *L 12–2.30*
Seats 29 *D 7–10.30, Sat 7–11*
Parties 35 *Parking Limited*
Closed L Sat, all Sun, Bank Hols & 5 days Xmas

Horsted Place · Uckfield

HR **77% £A**
Map 7 B6 East Sussex
Little Horsted TN22 5TS
Isfield (0825) 75581. Tlx 95548
Credit Access, Amex, Diners, Visa

Rambling gardens provide a delightful setting for this gabled and turreted Victorian house just off the A26. The 90-foot Grand Gallery, hung with tapestry, dominates the interior; leading off is a tasteful drawing room and a well-stocked library with a secret door to the courtyard. A splendid hand-carved oak staircase designed by Augustus Pugin leads to two floors of sumptuous bedrooms with lovely views. Stylish furnishings are combined with thoughtful touches, and the marble bathrooms are most impressive.

Hardworking, courteous staff. No children under seven. No dogs.
Amenities garden, indoor swimming pool, tennis, croquet, valeting.

■ *Rooms* 17	*Confirm by arrang.*
en suite bath/shower 17	*Last dinner* 10
Direct dial Yes	*Parking* Ample
Room TV Yes	*Room service* All day

Horsted Place Dining Room 🍴 ♿

Chef Keith Mitchell's very capable cooking is rapidly establishing itself at this elegant restaurant. The fixed price menu is four courses, limited choice, starting maybe with a soup or salad, then a fish course – perhaps wild Scottish salmon or sole with Russian caviar. Sliced sirloin with a tarragon and tomato sauce could follow. Sweets, such as honey and saffron cream, are simple but delicious. Carefully selected wines: note St Aubin 1er cru Les Charmois 1985.
🍷 Well-chosen

■ *Set L* £15	*L* M–Sat by arrang.
Set D £25	only, Sun 12–2.30
About £65 for two	*D* 7–10.30
Seats 40	*Parties* 18

Leeming House Hotel · Ullswater

HR **75% £B/C**
Map 13 D5 Cumbria
Watermillock CA11 0JJ
Pooley Bridge (085 36) 622
Manager Christopher Curry
Credit Access, Amex, Diners, Visa

In an idyllic setting of landscaped grounds on the shore of Ullswater, this Georgian-style country house, built in 1847, retains many period features including a pillared portico and elegant entrance hall. The two traditional-style lounges offer a high degree of comfort and there is also an intimate oak-panelled bar. Three of the bedrooms have balconies and seven are in a separate cottage; they are good-sized, attractively decorated and most have mahogany furniture. All have tea/coffee-makers, plants, potpourris and magazines.

Bathrooms are equipped with good soaps and shampoos. No children under eight. No dogs.
Amenities garden, coarse fishing, laundry service.

■ *Rooms* 25	*Confirm by* 6
en suite bath/shower 23	*Last dinner* 8.45
Direct dial Yes	*Parking* Ample
Room TV No	*Room service* All day
Closed Dec–mid Mar	

Leeming House Hotel Restaurant 🍴 ♿

An elegant dining room overlooking beautiful gardens makes a memorable setting for an enjoyable meal. There are simple three-course set lunches while the evenings offer more variety with multiple-choice fixed-price menus. Starters may include Swiss cheese fritters, moving on to cassoulette of scallops and scampi tails followed by mallard duckling with blackberry and port compote. Delicious sweets. Extensive wine list.
🍷 Well-chosen

■ *Set L* from £5,	*L* 12.30–1.45
Sun £10	*D* 7.30–8.45
Set D £24.75	*Seats* 80 *Parties* 20
About £60 for two	*Closed* Dec–mid Mar

Old Church Hotel · Ullswater

HR **63% £D/E**
Map 13 D5 Cumbria
Watermillock, Nr Penrith CA11 0JN
Pooley Bridge (085 36) 204
Owner managers Kevin & Maureen Whitemore

The amiable Whitemores provide the friendliest of welcomes to their Georgian country house hotel in a beautiful setting of extensive lawns running down to Lake Ullswater. Peaceful and

comfortable day rooms and modestly furnished bedrooms have thoughtful little extras. Half-board terms only at weekends. *Amenities* garden, coarse and game fishing, boating.

■ *Rooms* 11	*Confirm by arrang.*
en suite bath/shower 7	*Last dinner* 8.15
Room phone No	*Parking* Ample
Room TV No	*Room service* All day
Closed Nov–Mar	

Restaurant ♵

Delightful views are a feature of the pleasant and relaxing dining room, with its old wooden tables and fresh flowers. The Whitemores do most of the cooking, with Kevin making tasty use of wholesome ingredients in unpretentious dishes such as roasts, scampi provençale and beef bourguignon, while Maureen prepares such old-fashioned delights as apple and raspberry crumble, a superb lemon curd and sultana steamed pud. Good, home-presented cheese comes with home-made oatcakes, apple slices and celery. Lovely patterned china. No smoking. ℮

■ Set D £15·50	D only 7.30–8.15
About £38 for two	Seats 25
Closed Nov–Easter	

Rampsbeck Hotel
Ullswater

HR 60% £E
Map 13 D5 Cumbria
Watermillock CA11 0LP
Pooley Bridge (085 36) 442
Owner managers Tom & Marion Gibb
Credit Access, Visa

14 acres of grounds on the shores of Ullswater provide an idyllic setting here, and a warm welcome is guaranteed. A spacious, well-proportioned lounge has comfortable seating, an open fire and stupendous views. Comfortable, pretty bedrooms have a fresh, light air.
Amenities garden, coarse fishing.

■ Rooms 13	Confirm by arrang.
en suite bath/shower 9	Last dinner 9
Room phone No	Parking Ample
Room TV Yes	Room service All day
Closed early Jan–mid Feb	

Restaurant ♵

A delightful pale grey and pink dining room, overlooking lawns sloping down to the lake, provides an excellent setting in which to enjoy Eamon Webster's highly imaginative and competent cooking. The monthly-changing dinner menu could include prawn and ginger egg custard with lovage rice or grilled langoustine with a herb and garlic butter, followed perhaps by turbot with rosemary juice and crayfish, or lamb in pastry with port and crème de cassis, laced with chanterelles. Equally exciting sweets. Less choice at lunchtime. ℮

■ Set D from £13	L 12–2
About £40 for two	D 7–8.30
Seats 60	Parties 20
Closed early Jan–mid Feb	

Sharrow Bay Hotel
Ullswater

HR 80% £B/C
Map 13 D5 Cumbria
Lake Ullswater, Nr Penrith CA10 2LZ
Pooley Bridge (085 36) 301
Owner managers Francis Coulson & Brian Sack

Standing on a wooded promontory at the extreme edge of Ullswater, amid 12 acres of lovely grounds, this splendid country house built of soft grey stone offers incomparable peace and tranquillity. Sumptuous furnishings, fine antiques, ornaments and fresh flower arrangements grace the luxuriously elegant lounges, where guests can enjoy a quiet drink or afternoon tea while admiring the view. Bedrooms and bathrooms are appointed in similarly delightful style and offer every imaginable cosseting extra. Apart from the main hotel, there are rooms in the Edwardian gatehouse and garden cottages, plus others further afield. Half-board only. No dogs.
Amenities garden, game fishing, laundry service.

■ Rooms 30	Confirm by arrang.
en suite bath/shower 26	Last dinner 8.45
Direct dial Yes	Parking Ample
Room TV Yes	Room service All day
Closed end Nov–4 Mar	

Restaurant ★ ♔ ♵

Johnnie Martin and his talented team continue to delight with their memorable five-course meals at this splendid restaurant. An extensive and imaginative list of starters (including delicately flavoured terrine of salmon and sole with a creamy watercress sauce) is followed by a no-choice fish course then a superb sorbet. Main courses like our supremely tender venison marinated in red wine and accompanied by a dariole of endives and mushrooms are served with a profusion of delicious vegetables, and the sweets – syllabub, orange bavarois, coconut ice cream with raspberry coulis – are an absolute must. Impeccable service. No smoking. Fine, classic wine list. *Specialities* pigeon breast and warm avocado mousse with dressed prawns, marinated saddle of hare with fresh cranberries, white chocolate cream with coffee bavarois and rum sauce. ℮

	Closed end Nov–4 Mar
■ Set L from £18·50	L 1–1.45
Set D £28·50	D 8–8.45
About £70 for two	Seats 65 Parties 10

Rising Sun Hotel   *NEW ENTRY*   Umberleigh

£E/F
Map 3 D2 North Devon
EX37 9DU
High Bickington (0769) 60447
Credit Access, Amex, Diners, Visa. LVs

Extensive rights on the river Taw make this 17th-century inn a great favourite with anglers. The smart lounge bar is festooned with fishy photographs; there's a flagstoned public bar and comfortable, stylish lounge. Bedrooms feature salmon pink decor and good-quality pine furnishings. Two rooms are in a cottage annexe. No children. *Amenities* game fishing, laundry service.

■ *Rooms 8*	*Confirm by arrang.*
en suite bath/shower 6	*Last dinner 8.30*
Direct dial Yes	*Parking Ample*
Room TV Yes	*Room service None*

Greenriggs Country House   Underbarrow

£E
Map 13 D5 Cumbria
Nr Kendal LA8 8HF
Crosthwaite (04488) 387
Owner managers Doug & Sarah Smithson

A friendly hotel in a beautiful rural setting overlooking the Lyth Valley. A narrow passage leads to a cosy bar with books, a piano and inviting armchairs. There is also a homely, traditional lounge where guests can watch TV. Bedrooms, again in period style, include some in an attractive converted stable block. *Amenities* garden, croquet, laundry service.

■ *Rooms 14*	*Confirm by 6*
en suite bath/shower 9	*Last dinner 8*
Room phone No	*Parking Ample*
Room TV No	*Room service Limited*
Closed Mon–Thurs Nov–Mar & all Jan & Feb	

Lords of the Manor Hotel   Upper Slaughter

HR **70% £C/D**
Map 4 C1 Gloucestershire
Nr Bourton-on-the-Water GL54 2JD
Cotswold (0451) 20243
Credit Access, Amex, Diners, Visa

A picturesque drive through classic Cotswold countryside brings visitors to this mellow manor house in a glorious garden setting. A corridor leads from reception to the handsome lounge with its deep sofas and open fire. Television is available in the Garden Room, and there's a plush, relaxing bar. Nearly half the bedrooms were recently refitted, using stylish designer fabrics; remaining rooms are splendidly traditional. Some areas (bathrooms, hallways, stairs) are not

particularly well kept. No dogs. *Amenities* garden, croquet, game fishing, laundry service.

■ *Rooms 15*	*Confirm by 6*
en suite bath/shower 14	*Last dinner 9.30*
Direct dial Yes	*Parking Ample*
Room TV Some	*Room service All day*
Closed 4–14 Jan	

Lords of the Manor Hotel Restaurant

Paul Hackett is the accomplished new chef at this discreetly formal restaurant. His imaginative but classically inspired dinner menus change daily, featuring first-rate seasonal produce. Start perhaps with a puff pastry case filled with perfectly cooked seafood in a light lobster sauce. Next choose a skilfully executed main dish like oven-roasted poussin on a delicately flavoured jus. Nice crisp vegetables and lovely desserts. Lunchtime menu is simpler. Friendly and efficient service. A sound wine list includes excellent clarets (Ch. Léoville-Lascases '70, Ch. Pichon-Longueville Lalande '70). ♀ Well-chosen Ⓔ

■ *Set L £8.50*	*L 12.30–2*
About £50 for two	*D 7.30–9.30*
Seats 50	*Closed 4–14 Jan*

♀ indicates a **well-chosen** house wine.

Falcon Hotel   Uppingham

H **62% £D/E**
Map 11 E4 Leicestershire
High Street East LE15 9PY
Uppingham (0572) 823535
Owner manager Mr I. T. Hackney
Credit Access, Amex, Diners, Visa

A friendly high-street hostelry dating back to the 16th century. The cobbled courtyard, where the hooves of coach-horses once clattered, is now the foyer-lounge, in comfortable country style; there are two bars, one displaying regimental plaques and badges. Excellent bedrooms vary in size and decor. *Amenities* garden, laundry service, 24-hour lounge service.

■ *Rooms 26*	*Confirm by 6*
en suite bath/shower 26	*Last dinner 9.45*
Direct dial Yes	*Parking Ample*
Room TV Yes	*Room service 24 hours*

Lake Isle · Uppingham

RR ♧ **Map 11 E4** Leicestershire
♀ 16 High Street
Uppingham (05072) 822951
Credit Access, Amex, Diners, Visa

Chef-patron David Whitfield changes the set menus daily in this charmingly rustic restaurant with rooms. Simplicity is the keynote, with careful cooking of fresh ingredients. There's usually a choice of soups – perhaps cream of mushroom with tomato and fennel – and other offerings might include goujons of seafood and grilled loin of pork with orange and Dubonnet sauce. Vegetables are good, desserts enjoyable. Wines

include an excellent range of half-bottles.
♀ Well-chosen ⊖

- Set L from £7·25   L 12.30–2
- Set D from £12·75   D 7.30–10
  About £36 for two   Parking Limited
  Seats 35   Parties 35
  Closed L Mon & D Sun

Bedrooms   £F
Rooms 8   With bath/shower 8
Overnight accommodation comprises five prettily curtained bedrooms, with neat bathrooms, TVs, trouser presses and radio alarms.

White Hart Hotel · Uttoxeter

I £E
Map 10 C3 Staffordshire
Carter Street ST14 8EU
Uttoxeter (088 93) 2437
Manager Mrs H. V. Porteous
Credit Access, Amex, Diners, Visa

An old coaching inn with a colourful history dating back to the 16th century, the well-maintained White Hart retains a welcoming

atmosphere. The split-level bar has plenty of cosy corners, and there's some splendid linenfold panelling in the function room. Bedrooms in the main building and annexe combine sturdily traditional furnishings with up-to-date features.

- Rooms 28   Confirm by arrang.
  en suite bath/shower 17   Last dinner 9.45
  Direct dial Yes   Parking Ample
  Room TV Yes   Room service Limited

- We publish annually, so make sure you use the current edition. It's worth it!

Royal Hotel · Ventnor

H 61% £D
Map 5 D4 Isle of Wight
Belgrave Road PO38 1JJ
Isle of Wight (0983) 852186
Credit Access, Amex, Diners, Visa

Pretty lawns and a long verandah front this handsome period building. Pleasant, good-sized bedrooms all have remote-control TVs, tea-makers and up-to-date bathrooms. Day rooms

include a sun lounge, a cosy beamed bar and a separate pub in the grounds. Amenities garden, outdoor swimming pool, solarium, croquet, bicycles, games room, snooker, laundry room, children's playroom & playground.

- Rooms 54   Confirm by 6
  en suite bath/shower 54   Last dinner 9
  Room phone Yes   Parking Ample
  Room TV Yes   Room service All day

Nare Hotel · Veryan

H 62% £C/D
Map 2 B3 Cornwall
Carn Beach TR2 5PF
Truro (0872) 501279
Owner manager Jonathan Richards
Credit Access, Amex, Diners, Visa

With a large, sandy beach on its doorstep, this is a popular base for family holidays. Bedrooms are spotlessly clean and solidly furnished; all but

five enjoy private facilities. There are two lounges – one a splendid suntrap – and a comfortable bar. No dogs. Amenities garden, outdoor swimming pool, sauna, solarium, gymnasium, tennis, games room, snooker, laundry service.

- Rooms 40   Confirm by arrang.
  en suite bath/shower 35   Last dinner 9.15
  Room phone No   Parking Ample
  Room TV Some   Room service Limited

- If we recommend meals in a hotel or inn, a separate entry is made for its restaurant.

Spindlewood Hotel   Wadhurst

HR **61% £D/E**
Map 7 B6 East Sussex
Wallcrouch TN5 7JG
Ticehurst (0580) 200430
Owner managers Fitzsimmons family
Credit Access, Amex, Diners, Visa

Lovely gardens, friendly owners, excellent housekeeping and a really delightful atmosphere at this late-Victorian hotel off B2099. Public rooms offer old-fashioned looks and comfort; bedrooms which vary (refurbishment is ongoing) have a fresh, bright appeal. No dogs. *Amenities* garden, tennis, laundry service.

■ *Rooms* 9	*Confirm by* arrang.
en suite bath/shower 9	*Last dinner* 9
Direct dial Yes	*Parking Ample*
Room TV Yes	*Room service* All day
Closed 4 days Xmas	

Spindlewood Hotel Restaurant

Food is a serious matter at this roomy restaurant which has the peaceful charm of a French provincial dining room. Paul Clayton's menu tempts with every item, from chestnut and brussels sprout soup to salmon and halibut roulade, pâté-stuffed chicken breast and venison with cranberries, apples and Calvados. Sauces are really special, and it's nice to see savoury Welsh rarebit, stuffed mushrooms, Scotch woodcock as well as sweet endings. English farmhouse cheeses to follow. ⊖
♗ Well-chosen

■ *Set D* £14·85	*L* 12.15–1.30
About £40 for two	*D* 7.15–9
Seats 40	*Parties* 60
Closed 4 days Xmas	

Cedar Court Hotel   *NEW ENTRY*   Wakefield

H **58% £C/D**
Map 10 C1 West Yorkshire
Denby Dale Road, Calder Grove WF4 3QZ
Wakefield (0924) 276310. Tlx 557647
Credit Access, Amex, Diners, Visa

Classical styling adds character to this modern hotel near M1 (junction 39). Open-plan public rooms include a smart lounge with sofas and glass tables. The bar is spacious and breakfasts are served in a cheerful coffee shop. Smartly-furnished bedrooms have TVs, tea-making facilities and compact, well-fitted bathrooms. *Amenities* garden, laundry service, coffee shop (7am–11pm).

■ *Rooms* 100	*Confirm by* arrang.
en suite bath/shower 100	*Last dinner* 10
Direct dial Yes	*Parking Ample*
Room TV Yes	*Room service* 24 hours

Post House Hotel   Wakefield

H **64% £C** ⅄
Map 10 C1 West Yorkshire
Queen's Drive, Ossett WF5 9BE
Ossett (0924) 276388. Tlx 55407
Credit Access, Amex, Diners, Visa

Businessmen bag most of the rooms at this popular low-rise hotel, so book early. Just off the foyer is a cheerful coffee shop, newly-decorated lounge and cocktail bar. Bedrooms are spacious; Executive rooms have double beds, seating, hairdryers and trouser presses, plus beverage facilities. All bathrooms have showers. *Amenities* garden, putting, laundry service, coffee shop (7am–11pm).

■ *Rooms* 96	*Confirm by* 6
en suite bath/shower 96	*Last dinner* 10.15
Direct dial Yes	*Parking Ample*
Room TV Yes	*Room service* 24 hours

Swallow Hotel   Wakefield

H **58% £D/E**
Map 10 C1 West Yorkshire
Queen Street WF1 1JU
Wakefield (0924) 372111. Tlx 53168
Credit Access, Amex, Diners, Visa. LVs

A net of one-way streets ensnares the unwary traveller in search of this hotel, so seek directions when booking. A popular overnight stop for businessmen, the Swallow has spacious contemporary public areas and bedrooms with modern lightwood units and coordinated soft furnishings. All have tea-making facilities and bedside controls. Well-fitted bathrooms. *Amenities* laundry service.

■ *Rooms* 64	*Confirm by* 6
en suite bath/shower 64	*Last dinner* 9.15
Direct dial Yes	*Parking Ample*
Room TV Yes	*Room service* Limited

Avisford Park Hotel   Walberton

H **66% £C/D**
Map 5 E4 West Sussex
Nr Arundel BN18 0LS
Yapton (0243) 551215. Tlx 86137
Credit Access, Amex, Visa

A much extended Georgian house set in attractive grounds and offering abundant leisure facilities. Accommodation is spacious and well equipped. Day rooms include a non-smoking lounge. *Amenities* garden, indoor & outdoor swimming pools, sauna, solarium, keep-fit equipment, tennis, squash, 9-hole golf course, croquet, games room, snooker, laundry service, 24-hour lounge service, helipad.

■ *Rooms* 94	*Confirm by* arrang.
en suite bath/shower 94	*Last dinner* 9.30
Direct dial Yes	*Parking Ample*
Room TV Yes	*Room service* 24 hours

Hadrian Hotel
Wall

£E
Map 15 B4 Northumberland
Nr Hexham NE46 4EE
Humshaugh (043 481) 232
Owner managers Mr & Mrs Mellors
Credit Access

The welcome starts in the spacious reception and lounge area of this pleasant old inn near Hadrian's Wall. Two simply furnished bars, favoured by friendly locals, add to the appeal. Homely and unpretentious bedrooms – some with fine views – offer a good degree of comfort. Sparkling bathrooms. No children under 12. *Amenities* garden.

■ *Rooms* 9	*Confirm by arrang.*
en suite bath/shower 4	*Last dinner* 9.30
Room phone No	*Parking* Ample
Room TV Some	*Room service* None

■ Any person using our name to obtain free hospitality is a fraud. Proprietors, please inform the police and us.

Brown & Boswell
Wallingford

R ⅌ **Map 5 D2** Oxfordshire
28 High Street
Wallingford (0491) 34078
Credit Access, Amex, Diners, Visa

Chef Paul Bridgewood has joined the B and B's at this friendly town centre establishment. Robert Boswell still cooks, however, and with Paul produces memorable meals. Main courses include sliced mallard breast on mango and ginger sauce, and glazed venison, with inviting starters and afters. Vegetables are a special feature and there's always a vegetarian dish. ℗

■ *Set L from £4*	*L* 12.30–2.30
Set D £16	*D* 7–10
About £40 for two	*Parking* Limited
Seats 32	*Parties* 32
Closed L Tues, all Mon, Bank Hols, 2 wks Mar & 1 wk Oct	

George Hotel
Wallingford

H **66% £D**
Map 5 D2 Oxfordshire
High Street OX10 0BS
Wallingford (0491) 36665. Tlx 847468
Manager Grant Attwater
Credit Access, Amex, Diners, Visa. **LVs**

Behind the traditional coaching-inn facade, the George is a stylish blend of period and modern features. The public bar features a splendid inglenook, and well-equipped bedrooms in the old part retain the appeal of beams and sloping floors. Bedrooms in the new wing are larger and even better equipped. *Amenities* in-house movies (free), laundry service, 24-hour lounge service.

■ *Rooms* 39	*Confirm by arrang.*
en suite bath/shower 39	*Last dinner* 10.30
Direct dial Yes	*Parking* Ample
Room TV Yes	*Room service* 24 hours

Shillingford Bridge Hotel
Wallingford

H **58% £D/E**
Map 5 D2 Oxfordshire
Ferry Road, Shillingford OX10 8LZ
Warborough (086 732) 8567. Tlx 837763
Owner manager Mr & Mrs B. J. Millsom
Credit Access, Amex, Diners, Visa

Much money has been spent on this hotel of late, and furnishings in the bar now do justice to the superb river view framed by its windows. Practical good-sized bedrooms – some in a modern annexe which are quieter. No dogs. *Amenities* garden, outdoor swimming pool, squash, coarse fishing, laundry service.

■ *Rooms* 36	*Confirm by arrang.*
en suite bath/shower 36	*Last dinner* 10
Direct dial Yes	*Parking* Ample
Room TV Yes	*Room service* All day
Closed 3 days Xmas	

Barons Court Hotel
Walsall

H **65% £E**
Map 10 C4 West Midlands
Walsall Wood WS9 9AH
Brownhills (0543) 452020. Tlx 333061
Manager Mr B. T. Garratt
Credit Access, Amex, Diners, Visa

A modern Tudor-style house, offering a first-class health hydro. Good-sized bedrooms are attractively appointed in Queen Anne style. Comfortable bars and friendly staff. *Amenities* indoor swimming pool, sauna, solarium, whirlpool bath, steam bath, keep-fit equipment, satellite TV, laundry service, 24-hour lounge service.

■ *Rooms* 76	*Confirm by arrang.*
en suite bath/shower 76	*Last dinner* 9.45
Direct dial Yes	*Parking* Ample
Room TV Yes	*Room service* All day
Closed 25 Dec	

Crest Hotel Walsall

H **65% £C/D**
Map 10 C4 West Midlands
Birmingham Road WS5 3AB
Walsall (0922) 33555. Tlx 335479
Credit Access, Amex, Diners, Visa
   A helpful manager and cheerful staff keep the
mood buoyant at this modern hotel on the A34.
Relaxing is easy in the lobby-lounge and cocktail
bar, and the basement bar is a popular venue for

live music. Housekeeping is excellent in the
decent-sized bedrooms, which have tea-makers,
trouser presses and neat, tiled bathrooms.
Amenities games room, laundry service, 24-hour
lounge service.

■ *Rooms* 101	*Confirm by* 6
en suite bath/shower 101	*Last dinner* 10
Direct dial Yes	*Parking* Ample
Room TV Yes	*Room service* Limited

Blunk's Waltham Abbey

R **Map 7 B4** Essex
20 Market Square
Lea Valley (0992) 712352
Owner manager Salvatore Urso
Credit Access, Amex, Diners, Visa
   Seafood dominates the lengthy menu of French
dishes expertly prepared by Pierre Mauroux at
this charming restaurant on the market square.
Trout meunière, sole Walewska and garlicky

snails are among favourite offerings, while meat-
eaters might opt for rack of lamb or fillet steak
with mushrooms and Gruyère. Simple sweets
include home-made ice cream.
 ♀ Well-chosen ☺

■ *Set L* £16	*L* 12.30–2.30
Set D £16	*D* 7.30–11.30
About £54 *for two*	*Parking* Ample
Seats 40	*Parties* 40

Haycock Hotel Wansford-in-England

H **69% £D**
Map 6 A2 Cambridgeshire
Nr Peterborough PE8 6JA
Stamford (0780) 782223. Tlx 32710
Manager Richard Neale
Credit Access, Amex, Diners, Visa
   In a delightful village of stone cottages, a 17th-
century coaching inn with an attractive riverside
garden. Some bedrooms are stylishly

contemporary, while others have antique
furnishings (even four-posters); all boast Italian-
tiled bathrooms. Day rooms are relatively modest,
but with a pleasant traditional appeal. *Amenities*
garden, coarse fishing, laundry service.

■ *Rooms* 25 ·	*Confirm by* 6
en suite bath/shower 25	*Last dinner* 10.15
Direct dial Yes	*Parking* Ample
Room TV Yes	*Room service* 24 hours

■ Our inspectors are our full-
time employees; they are
professionally trained by us.

Bear Hotel Wantage

H **60% £D/E**
Map 5 D2 Oxfordshire
Market Square OX12 8AB
Wantage (023 57) 66366
Credit Access, Amex, Diners, Visa
   Coaching days are called to mind by the
cobbled courtyard of this town-centre Georgian
inn. Old-style hospitality is still to be found in the
sofa-filled bar and the elegant bar-lounge with its

collection of historic letters. Bedrooms range from
smartly modern to delightfully old-fashioned; all
have tea-makers, trouser presses, radio-alarms
and spotless bath/shower rooms.
Amenities laundry service.

■ *Rooms* 33	*Confirm by* arrang.
en suite bath/shower 33	*Last dinner* 10
Direct dial Yes	*Parking* Limited
Room TV Yes	*Room service* All day

Peking Dynasty *NEW ENTRY* Wantage

R ♀ **Map 5 D2** Oxfordshire
Newbury Street
Wantage (023 57) 2517
Chinese cooking
Credit Access, Amex, Diners, Visa
   An up-market Chinese restaurant in a bijou
period building just off the market place. The
cooking is very good: spring rolls fresh, crunchy
and grease-free; deep-fried beef, nice and spicy,

served in a potato basket; curaçao-flavoured
orange slices for a final refresher. Attentive
service from the Kans and above average wines.
 ♀ Well-chosen

■ *Set meals* £13·50	*L* 12–2
About £38 *for two*	*D* 6–11.30
Seats 50 *Parties* 30	*Parking* Limited
Closed 3 days Xmas	

Harry's Java Brasserie   Wapping

See under London

Briggens House Hotel   Ware

H **70% £D**
Map 7 B4 Hertfordshire
Stanstead Road, Nr Stanstead Abbots
SG12 8LD
Roydon (027 979) 2416. Tlx 817906
Credit Access, Amex, Diners, Visa

Forty-five acres of landscaped gardens make a
fine setting for this handsome Georgian mansion.
Public rooms are on quite a grand scale: the
spacious entrance hall leads via double doors into
a lounge where salmon pink upholstery matches
the wall coverings and curtains. Next door is the
bar with its military prints. A wide, oak staircase
climbs to the main-house bedrooms, which are
individually decorated and generally roomy;
coach-house rooms tend to be smaller, though no
less attractive. Neat, compact bathrooms, ten
with whirlpool features. The hotel is showing some

signs of wear and tear. *Amenities* garden,
outdoor swimming pool, tennis, 9-hole golf course,
croquet, coarse fishing, in-house movies (free),
laundry service, courtesy transport.

■ *Rooms 58*	*Confirm by 6*
en suite bath/shower 58	*Last dinner 10*
Direct dial Yes	*Parking Ample*
Room TV Yes	*Room service 24 hours*

Priory Hotel   Wareham

HR **73% £D**
Map 4 B4 Dorset
Church Green BH20 4ND
Wareham (092 95) 51666. Tlx 41143
Owner manager John Turner
Credit Access, Amex, Diners, Visa

A secluded 16th-century priory, set in lovingly
tended gardens on the banks of the river Frome.
Here the Turners have created a haven of
elegance and tranquillity, where antiques and fine
furnishings grace the public rooms and the
bedrooms are to a similar high standard of taste
and comfort, with homely touches such as books
and flowers. All the bedrooms have spotless

private bathrooms with good-quality toiletries.
Four even more luxurious rooms in the converted
boathouse boast whirlpool baths and four-poster,
king- and queen-size beds. Superlative breakfasts
and excellent service provided by dedicated staff.
No dogs. *Amenities* garden, croquet, coarse &
game fishing, valeting, laundry service.

■ *Rooms 19*	*Confirm by arrang.*
en suite bath/shower 19	*Last dinner 10*
Direct dial Yes	*Parking Ample*
Room TV Yes	*Room service All day*

Priory Hotel Restaurant &

Manager Driss Djeebet
A cellar restaurant where Stephen West favours
local produce. Typical dishes include pigeon
breasts with capsicum and lime sauce or home-
smoked seafood with almond yoghurt for starters;
roast duckling with cointreau and shallot sauce or
sea bass with mustard sauce as a main course.
Delicious sweets and English cheeses. Good
cooking, excellent service. Traditional Sunday
lunch only. 🍷 Well-chosen 🌂

■ *Set L fr £7·50, Sun £9·95*	*L 12.30–2*
Set D £13·50, Sat £15	*D 7.30–10*
About £52 for two	*Seats 44 Parties 44*

Springfield Country Hotel   Wareham

H **58% £C/D** &
Map 4 B4 Dorset
Grange Road, Stoborough BH20 5AL
Wareham (092 95) 2177
Owner managers Alford family
Credit Access, Amex, Visa

A warm welcome is found at this delightful
family-run hotel with its relaxing lounge areas and
oak-beamed bar. Guests will find first class leisure

facilities and modern bedrooms with spotless en
suite bathrooms. No children under two.
Amenities garden, outdoor swimming pool,
solarium, tennis, riding, games room, snooker,
pool table.

■ *Rooms 29*	*Confirm by arrang.*
en suite bath/shower 29	*Last dinner 9*
Direct dial Yes	*Parking Ample*
Room TV Yes	*Room service All day*

Warminster ▶

RECEPTION

Bishopstrow House   Warminster

HR 87% £B ♿
Map 4 B3 Wiltshire
BA12 9HH
Warminster (0985) 212312. Tlx 444829
Owner manager Mr K. Schiller
Credit Access, Amex, Diners, Visa

The highest standards of housekeeping, service and maintenance are found at the Schillers' lovingly converted Georgian mansion set in delightful grounds. Antiques, oil paintings and Persian carpets grace the impressive central hall, elegant lounge and morning room, and there's a contrastingly light and leafy conservatory. Splendid bedrooms (including particularly fine courtyard rooms) are furnished in smartly contemporary or period style and offer

many extras. Many of the luxurious bathrooms have jacuzzis. No children under three.
Amenities garden, indoor & outdoor swimming pools, sauna, solarium, whirlpool baths, indoor & outdoor tennis, coarse fishing, valeting, laundry service, 24-hour lounge service, helipad.

■ Rooms 26	Confirm by 6
en suite bath/shower 26	Last dinner 9.30
Direct dial Yes	Parking Ample
Room TV Yes	Room service 24 hours

Bishopstrow House Restaurant ♕

An appealing, elegant dining room overlooking the garden – a delightful setting for generally enjoyable cooking. Fixed-price, regularly-changing menus have a pleasing bias towards both English and French provincial dishes. Starters such as poached local trout with oranges and lemons could precede fennel soup followed by rack of lamb, flavoursome guinea fowl casserole or brill with seasonal shellfish. Pleasant sweets. Precise, polite service. ℮

■ Set L £16·50	L 12.30–2
Set D from £21·50	D 7.15–9.30
About £60 for two	Seats 60 Parties 20

La Petite Cuisine Belge at Vincents *NEW ENTRY* Warminster

R ♧ Map 4 B3 Wiltshire
60 East Street
Warminster (0985) 215052
Owner managers Leslie & Anne Werrell

Belgian-born Anne Werrell offers a seasonal dinner menu that gets under way with starters such as seafood kebabs or a little casserole of snails. Main courses like guinea fowl with red wine and smoked bacon, or fillet steak with excellent

wine, cream and tarragon sauce are served with fresh, crisp vegetables. Good cooking, certainly, but just occasionally it's marred by corner-cutting. Excellent light lunches Tues–Sat. ℮

■ Set D £12·55	D 7.30–9.30
About £32 for two	Parking Difficult
Seats 26	Parties 36
Closed Sun, Good Fri, 25 & 26 Dec & 3 wks Jan	

menu & WINE LIST 1988

Lord Daresbury Hotel   Warrington

H 67% £C/D
Map 10 B2 Cheshire
Daresbury WA4 4BB
Warrington (0925) 67331. Tlx 629330
Credit Access, Amex, Diners, Visa

Stylish public areas and a smart leisure club make this modern hotel near exit 11 of the M56 a popular overnight stop. Good-sized bedrooms (including top-floor Executive rooms with extra

accessories) have decent bathrooms.
Amenities sauna, indoor swimming pool, solarium, whirlpool bath, squash, 24-hour lounge service, kiosk, snooker, gymnasium, helipad, table tennis, children's play area.

■ Rooms 139	Confirm by 6
en suite bath/shower 139	Last dinner 10.30
Direct dial Yes	Parking Ample
Room TV Yes	Room service 24 hours

Ladbroke Hotel   Warwick

H **70% £C *E* &**
Map 10 C4 Warwickshire
Stratford Road CV34 6RE
Warwick (0926) 499555. Tlx 312468
Credit Access, Amex, Diners, Visa
   The A46 Stratford road provides a convenient
link to the Midlands for this modern red-brick hotel
on the outskirts of town. It offers versatile
conference facilities and comfortable, spacious
accommodation for the night. Standard bedrooms
have lightwood units, coordinated fabrics and
smart bathrooms, while Gold Star rooms offer
superior furnishings plus a host of extras such as
trouser presses, hairdryers and bathrobes. The
open-plan foyer-lounge-cum-bar is pleasantly
contemporary in style with its strikingly patterned
sofas and bamboo chairs, masses of plants and
attractive carpeting that continues into the

bedroom wings.
Amenities garden, indoor swimming pool, games
room, pool table, in-house movies (free), helipad.
■ *Rooms* 150   Confirm by 9
en suite bath/shower 150 *Last dinner* 10
Direct dial Yes   *Parking* Ample
Room TV Yes   *Room service* 24 hours

Randolphs   Warwick

R ♧ **Map 10 C4** Warwickshire
19–21 Coten End
Warwick (0926) 491292
Credit Access, Visa
   New owners the Gordons are continuing the
high standard already set here. Iris Gordon's first-
class cooking of quality produce results in super
dishes; try potted game with port wine jelly,
followed by chicken with mousse of fresh

vegetables. Finish with iced chocolate and ginger
soufflé. Carefully chosen wine list includes
Châteauneuf du Pape Domaine du Vieux
Telegraphe 1978.
♀ Well-chosen ☺
■ *About £46 for two*   D only 7.45–9.30
Seats 30 *Parties* 30   *Parking* Limited
Closed Sun, Bank Hols, 1 wk Xmas & last 2
wks July

■ We publish annually, so make
   sure you use the current
   edition. It's worth it!

George Washington Hotel   Washington

H **69% £C/D**
Map 15 C4
Stone Cellar Road, District 12 NE37 1PH
Washington (091) 417 2626. Tlx 537143
Credit Access, Amex, Diners, Visa
   A modern low-rise hotel with superb leisure
facilities and bright, smart public areas. Good-
sized bedrooms are stylishly furnished and well-
kept. *Amenities* garden, indoor swimming pool,

sauna, solarium, whirlpool bath, keep fit
equipment, hairdressing, squash, 18-hole golf
course, pitch & putt, games room, snooker, in-
house movies (free), laundry service, coffee shop
(7am–7pm), 24-hour lounge service.
■ *Rooms* 70   Confirm by 6
en suite bath/shower 70   *Last dinner* 9
Direct dial Yes   *Parking* Ample
Room TV Yes   *Room service* 24 hours

Post House Hotel   Washington

H **62% £D**
Map 15 C4 Tyne & Wear
Emerson, District 5 NE37 1LB
Washington (091) 416 2264. Tlx 537574
Credit Access, Amex, Diners, Visa. LVs
   The situation, just off the A1(M) and close to the
A195, make this an ideal stopover for business
and casual travellers. The lounge-bar is spacious,
with plenty of comfortable seating. Bedrooms are

practically furnished with modern units. Eleven
executive rooms are to a higher standard.
Amenities garden, laundry service, coffee shop
(7am–10.30pm), 24-hour lounge service,
children's playground.
■ *Rooms* 138   Confirm by 6
en suite bath/shower 138 *Last dinner* 10
Direct dial Yes   *Parking* Ample
Room TV Yes   *Room service* 24 hours

Old Beams
Waterhouses

RR ⌂ ♦ ♿ **Map 10 C3** Staffordshire
ST10 3HW
Waterhouses (053 86) 254
Credit Access, Amex, Diners, Visa

Nigel Wallis is a dedicated, professional chef, his wife Ann a natural at front of house. Their restaurant is roomy and attractive, and the conservatory sports a grand piano and much greenery. Typical of Nigel's lovingly prepared dishes are a delicate pastry case of scampi on winter leaves and stuffed quail sitting on a nest of potatoes. Ann is responsible for desserts, and our lovely light lemon tart made a super ending.

There's an enthusiastic list of meticulously chosen wines. ⌾ Outstanding ♀ Well-chosen ☺
- **Set L** £8·95 | L 12–2
- About £48 for two | D 7–10
- Seats 50 Parties 45 | Parking Ample
- Closed Sun, Mon, Bank Hols exc. 25 & 26 Dec, 2 wks beg. Jan & 1 wk Oct

Bedrooms £D/E
Rooms 2 | With bath/shower 2
The two tastefully furnished bedrooms have remote-control TVs, and modern bathrooms with extras like bathrobes. No dogs.

Wateringbury Hotel *NEW ENTRY*
Wateringbury

H **56% £D/E** ♿
Map 7 B5 Kent
Tonbridge Road, Nr Maidstone ME18 5NS
Maidstone (0622) 812632
Credit Access, Amex, Diners, Visa. **LVs**

Splendid views of the Kent countryside are enjoyed by this well-kept hotel on the A26. Its bedrooms are furnished in modern pine, and accessories include radio-alarms, hairdryers and trouser presses. Bathrooms are well stocked with soap, shampoo and other toiletries. The cosy day rooms are augmented by a friendly pub – the King's Head. No dogs. *Amenities* garden, sauna, in-house movies (free), laundry service.
- **Rooms** 28 | Confirm by 7
- en suite bath/shower 28 | Last dinner 9.45
- Direct dial Yes | Parking Ample
- Room TV Yes | Room service Limited

Ladbroke Hotel
Watford

H **64% £C** ♿
Map 5 E2 Hertfordshire
Elton Way WD2 8HA
Watford (0923) 35881. Tlx 923422
Credit Access, Amex, Diners, Visa

A low-rise modern hotel alongside the A41, just south of junction 5 of the M1. Automatic doors lead into a spacious marble-floored foyer, on one side of which is a comfortable lounge area. Downstairs is an equally comfortable bar. Accommodation is neat and practical, Gold Star rooms having the edge in decor and accessories. Neat, compact bathrooms. *Amenities* laundry service, in-house movies (charge).
- **Rooms** 163 | Confirm by 6
- en suite bath/shower 163 | Last dinner 10
- Direct dial Yes | Parking Ample
- Room TV Yes | Room service 24 hours

Sportsman's Arms *NEW ENTRY*
Wath-in-Nidderdale

R ⌂ ♦ ♿ **Map 15 B6** North Yorkshire
Nr Pateley Bridge
Harrogate (0423) 711306
Owner manager Ray Carter
Credit Access, Amex, Diners, Visa

Drinks, crudités and orders are taken in the cosy lounge, meals are served in the very pretty dining room. Chef-patron Ray Carter's skill and imagination are demonstrated in dishes like salad of scallops and sweetbreads, trout with mustard and caper sauce, and lamb with baby beetroot and asparagus. Excellent vegetables and sweets. Good wines with some attractive burgundies (Ch. Vieilles Vignes 1983). ☺
- **Set D** £12·80 | L Sun only 12–2.30
- About £30 for two | D 7–9.30
- Seats 45 Parties 12 | Parking Ample
- Closed D Sun

Crossroads Hotel
Weedon

H **66% £D/E** ♿
Map 5 D1 Northamptonshire
High Street NW7 4PX
Weedon (0327) 40354. Tlx 312311
Owner managers Richard & Wendy Amos & Trevor Brown
Credit Access, Amex, Diners, Visa

Standing at the busy A5/A45 crossroads, this is a hotel of character, run by its long-time owners and recently extensively upgraded. In the old part, going back to 1780, are the light, leafy foyer, the restaurant with its fine collection of clocks and the cosy beamed bar with the feel of a friendly local. The majority of the bedrooms are in modern blocks (some brand new) and feature good-quality fabrics and furniture. Rooms in the original house are traditional in style, but with the same up-to-date accessories of trouser presses, mini-bars and remote-control TVs. No dogs. *Amenities* garden, tennis, in-house movies (free), laundry service, coffee shop (7am–6pm).
- **Rooms** 50 | Confirm by 6
- en suite bath/shower 48 | Last dinner 10.15
- Direct dial Yes | Parking Ample
- Room TV Yes | Room service Limited
- Closed 25 Dec

Heath Lodge Hotel   Welwyn

HR **60% £D** &
Map 7 A4 Hertfordshire
Danesbury Park Road AL6 9SL
Welwyn (043 871) 7064. Tlx 827618
Owner manager André Zayed
Credit Access, Amex, Diners, Visa

A major scheme of alterations and refurbishment is under way at this well-run hotel, which stands in ample grounds not far from the A1(M). Most of the bedrooms are in motel-style wings with their own parking bays. Furnishings are fitted, and all rooms have spotless private bathrooms. Large flower displays feature in the bright bar and lounge. *Amenities* garden.

- Rooms 32 — Confirm by 6
- en suite bath/shower 32 — Last dinner 9.30
- Direct dial Yes — Parking Ample
- Room TV Yes — Room service Limited

Heath Lodge Hotel Restaurant

French cooking
The food here is very well prepared by a French brigade under Philippe Goineau. Their talents are very evident in an imaginative range of beautifully presented dishes like warm salad of quail with a delicate ginger sauce or superb pink-roasted saddle of hare served in a beer sauce. Delicious sweets (try the assiette gourmande for a little of lots) and an outstanding cheese selection served with splendid nut breads. Crisp linen; stylish service. ☺

- Set L from £10·95, — L 12.30–2
- Sun £8·45 — D 7–9.30, Sun 7–9
- Set D from £10·95 — Seats 50
- About £45 for two — Parties 30
- Closed L Sat

Crest Hotel   Welwyn Garden City

H **59% £D/E**
Map 7 B4 Hertfordshire
Homestead Lane AL7 4LX
Welwyn Garden (070 73) 24336. Tlx 261523
Credit Access, Amex, Diners, Visa

Directions are vital to locate this unobtrusive red-brick hotel on the outskirts of town. Well-upholstered bamboo seating makes the bar-lounge a comfortable place for a drink, and there are convenient function and conference facilities. Simple, practical bedrooms (six for non-smokers) have attractive units, trouser presses and tea-makers. *Amenities* garden, in-house movies (charge), laundry service.

- Rooms 58 — Confirm by 6
- en suite bath/shower 58 — Last dinner 9.45
- Room phone Yes — Parking Ample
- Room TV Yes — Room service None

■ Our inspectors never book in the name of Egon Ronay's Guides; they disclose their identity only after paying their bills.

Hawkstone Park Hotel *NEW ENTRY*   Wem

H **60% £D/E**
Map 10 B3 Shropshire
Weston-under-Redcastle SY4 5UY
Lee Brockhurst (093 924) 611. Tlx 35793
Credit Access, Amex, Diners, Visa

Golf is chief among the many leisure activities at this friendly hotel set in 300 acres of grounds, 3 miles east of Wem. Day rooms are cosy and welcoming, and well-kept bedrooms offer tea-makers and smart bathrooms. *Amenities* garden, outdoor swimming pool, sauna, solarium, keep-fit equipment, tennis, golf courses, putting, croquet, games room, snooker, laundry service, coffee shop (12am–9.30pm), 24-hour lounge service.

- Rooms 59 — Confirm by arrang.
- en suite bath/shower 59 — Last dinner 9.30
- Direct dial Yes — Parking Ample
- Room TV Yes — Room service Limited

Woodlands   Wembley

See under London Restaurants under £30

Ladbroke International Hotel   Wembley

H **63% £B/C**
Map 5 E2 Middlesex
Empire Way HA9 8DS
01-902 8839. Tlx 24837
Credit Access, Amex, Diners, Visa. LVs

A ten-storey modern hotel next to Wembley Conference Centre. Bedrooms are light and well equipped, and Gold Star rooms get various little extras. The main open-plan public area, though quite stylish, needs some refurbishment; better is the Fultons Bar, with bentwood chairs and framed movie stills. *Amenities* in-house movies (charge), laundry service, coffee shop (11am–11pm), 24-hour lounge service.

- Rooms 305 — Confirm by 6
- en suite bath/shower 305 — Last dinner 10
- Direct dial Yes — Parking Ample
- Room TV Yes — Room service 24 hours

Wentbridge House Hotel — Wentbridge

H **62%** **£D/E**
Map 11 D1 West Yorkshire
Nr Pontefract WF8 3JJ
Pontefract (0977) 620444
Owner managers Mr & Mrs K. C. Dupuy
Credit Access, Amex, Diners, Visa
　Businessmen can enjoy peace and easy
access at this creeper-clad 18th-century hotel just
off the A1. Comfortable public rooms in traditional
style include a handsome functions suite.
Individually decorated bedrooms of various
shapes and sizes offer reassuring comforts. No
dogs. *Amenities* garden.

■ *Rooms* 20	*Confirm by arrang.*
en suite bath/shower 17	*Last dinner* 9.30
Direct dial Yes	*Parking* Ample
Room TV Yes	*Room service* All day
Closed 25 Dec	

▷ is our symbol for an **outstanding** wine list.

Red Lion Hotel — Weobley

H **59%** **£E/F**
Map 4 A1 Hereford & Worcester
Broad Street HR4 8SE
Weobley (0544) 318220
Owner manager Edward Townley-Berry
Credit Access, Amex, Visa
　One of many half-timbered buildings in the
village, this 14th-century inn has a homely,
welcoming appeal. Beams, stone flags and
gleaming copper characterise the two rustic bars,
and there's a cosy residents' lounge upstairs.
Bright, simply furnished bedrooms have tea-
makers and well-kept bath or shower rooms.
Amenities garden, bowling green.

■ *Rooms* 7	*Confirm by arrang.*
en suite bath/shower 7	*Last dinner* 9.30
Direct dial Yes	*Parking* Ample
Room TV Yes	*Room service* All day

Manor Hotel — West Bexington

H **59%** **£E**
Map 4 A4 Dorset
Near Dorchester DT2 9DP
Burton Bradstock (0308) 897785
Owner managers Richard & Jayne Childs
Credit Access, Amex, Diners, Visa
　Overlooking the sea and the famous Chesil
Bank, this ancient manor house is a delightful little
hotel with charming resident owners. The
entrance hall features some fine carved panelling,
and there's a comfortable lounge and cellar bar.
Bright, airy bedrooms have modern furnishings
and compact bath or shower rooms. No dogs.
Amenities garden, 24-hour lounge service.

■ *Rooms* 10	*Confirm by* 6
en suite bath/shower 10	*Last dinner* 9.30
Room phone No	*Parking* Ample
Room TV Yes	*Room service* Limited

West Bromwich Moat House — West Bromwich

H **59%** **£D**
Map 10 C4 West Midlands
Birmingham Road B70 6RS
021-553 6111. Tlx 336232
Credit Access, Amex, Diners, Visa
　Conveniently located for Birmingham and the
National Exhibition Centre, this modern hotel is a
popular conference venue. The lounge with its
central copper-canopied fireplace has a smart,
contemporary appeal, and there's a cosy cocktail
bar. Bedrooms, with small, spotless bathrooms,
have neat, practical units and pretty coordinating
fabrics. *Amenities* garden, in-house movies
(charge), laundry service, 24-hour lounge service.

■ *Rooms* 179	*Confirm by* 6
en suite bath/shower 179	*Last dinner* 9.45
Direct dial Yes	*Parking* Ample
Room TV Yes	*Room service* Limited

■ For a discount on next year's guide, see Offer for Answers.

Roundabout Hotel — West Chiltington

H **57%** **£D/E**
Map 5 E3 West Sussex
Monkmead Lane, Nr Pulborough RH20 2PF
West Chiltington (079 83) 3838
Manager Leon Maile
Credit Access, Amex, Diners, Visa
　Nowhere near a roundabout (the name derives
from a former iron smelter), this Tudor-style hotel
is comfortable and well kept. An attractive,
spacious lounge overlooks mature gardens.
Bedrooms are traditional, with practical
bathrooms. Five superior rooms have trouser
presses and hairdryers and there's a four-poster
in one of two cottage suites. *Amenities* garden.

■ *Rooms* 21	*Confirm by arrang.*
en suite bath/shower 21	*Last dinner* 9
Direct dial Yes	*Parking* Ample
Room TV Yes	*Room service* Limited

Onslow Arms · West Clandon

R **Map 5 E3** Surrey
Nr Guildford
Guildford (0483) 222447
Credit Access, Amex, Diners, Visa
 The cooking is both consistently reliable and
enjoyable at this large, busy restaurant in a
charming old pub, rich in character. The wide-
ranging French menu provides an interesting
choice, from garlicky fish soup with saffron to

chicken breast filled with fresh mangoes in a
cream and ginger sauce, salmon and lobster in
various guises and straightforward grills of meat
and fish. Nice sweets.   ♀ Well-chosen ☺

■ *Set L £9·95,*	*L 12.30–2.30*
Sun £11·95	*D 7.30–10*
About £56 for two	*Parking Ample*
Seats 100	*Parties 36*
Closed D Sun, all Mon & 1 wk Xmas exc. 25 Dec	

Links Country Park Hotel · West Runton

H **62% £C/D** ఉ
Map 6 C1 Norfolk
Nr Cromer NR27 9QH
West Runton (026 375) 691
Manager Mr R. M. Edwards
Credit Access, Amex, Visa
 Fine sea views and extensive grounds attract
outdoor enthusiasts to this turreted hotel. Day
rooms range from a comfortable panelled lounge

to three contrasting bars. Bedrooms are
cheerfully modern. *Amenities* garden, indoor
swimming pool, sauna, solarium, 9-hole golf
course, games room, pool table, in-house movies
(free), laundry service, 24-hour lounge service.

■ *Rooms 32*	*Confirm by arrang.*
en suite bath/shower 32	*Last dinner 9.30*
Direct dial Yes	*Parking Ample*
Room TV Yes	*Room service 24 hours*

Mirabelle Restaurant *NEW ENTRY* · West Runton

R ♿ ఉ **Map 6 C1** Norfolk
7 Station Road, Nr Cromer
West Runton (026 375) 396
Credit Access, Amex, Diners, Visa
 Hearty, enjoyable eating in a seaside village
near Cromer. Chef-patron Manfred Hollwoyer is
Austrian-born, and his international menus offer
plenty of variety. Typical choices run from seafood
vol-au-vent and veal kidneys with Madeira sauce

to pepper steak and saddle of hare with spätzli.
Finish with a cracking good crème brûlée. Long
classic wine list with some bargain half-bottles of
claret. ☺

■ *Set L from £7·50*	*L 12.30–2*
Set D from £10·50	*D 7–9.15*
About £35 for two	*Parking Ample*
Seats 45	*Closed Mon & Bank*
Hols, also D Sun (Nov–end May)	

■ If we recommend meals in a
hotel or inn, a separate entry is
made for its restaurant.

Weston Manor Hotel *NEW ENTRY* · Weston-on-the-Green

H **66% £C**
Map 5 D1 Oxfordshire
Nr Oxford OX6 8QL
Bletchington (0869) 50621. Tlx 83409
Credit Access, Amex, Diners, Visa
 Sometime a monastery and once owned by
Henry VIII, Weston Manor stands in extensive
grounds on the A43. The past comes alive as you
enter the baronial hall, and there's an oak-

panelled restaurant with a minstrel's gallery.
Bedrooms have abundant individual character.
Amenities garden, outdoor swimming pool,
tennis, squash, putting, croquet, clay-pigeon
shooting, coarse fishing, laundry service.

■ *Rooms 39*	*Confirm by arrang.*
en suite bath/shower 39	*Last dinner 9.30*
Direct dial Yes	*Parking Ample*
Room TV Yes	*Room service All day*

Grand Atlantic Hotel · Weston-super-Mare

H **64% £C/D**
Map 4 A3 Avon
Beach Road BS23 1BA
Weston-super-Mare (0934) 26543
Credit Access, Amex, Diners, Visa
 Right on the seafront, with a large garden and
leisure facilities, this imposing Victorian hotel is
ideal for family holidays. There are three bars and
a spacious foyer-lounge. Bright comfortable

bedrooms, many with seaviews, have tea-makers
and remote control TVs. *Amenities* garden,
outdoor swimming pool, tennis, games room, pool
table, laundry service, 24-hour lounge service,
children's playroom & playground.

■ *Rooms 76*	*Confirm by 6*
en suite bath/shower 76	*Last dinner 9.30*
Room phone Yes	*Parking Ample*
Room TV Yes	*Room service All day*

Hare & Hounds Hotel   Westonbirt

H 60% £D/E
Map 4 B2 Gloucestershire
Nr Tetbury GL8 8QL
Westonbirt (066 688) 233
Owner managers Jeremy & Martin Price
Credit Access, Amex, Visa

A sylvan setting is a feature of this delightful former farmhouse. Parquet floors stretch from entrance to lounge and sturdy oak furniture is favoured in public rooms and bedrooms. Recent refurbishment has enhanced the establishment's old-fashioned charm. All bedrooms now have en suite bathrooms. *Amenities* garden, tennis, squash, putting, croquet, snooker.

■ *Rooms* 26	*Confirm by* 4
en suite bath/shower 26	*Last dinner* 9 (10 Sat)
Direct dial Yes	*Parking* Ample
Room TV Yes	*Room service* All day

■ Any person using our name to obtain free hospitality is a fraud. Proprietors, please inform the police and us.

Crown Hotel   Wetheral

H 69% £D/E &
Map 13 D4 Cumbria
Nr Carlisle CA4 8ES
Carlisle (0228) 61888. Tlx 64175
Credit Access, Amex, Diners, Visa

Period character lives on at this updated coaching inn near the river Eden. Public areas include the fishing-themed public bar, popular with locals, and the smartly furnished lounge and conservatory bar. Decor is restful in the attractive well-equipped bedrooms. Executive rooms too. *Amenities* garden, sauna, in-house movies (free), games room, snooker, laundry service, squash, 24-hour lounge service.

■ *Rooms* 50	*Confirm by* arrang.
en suite bath/shower 50	*Last dinner* 9.30
Direct dial Yes	*Parking* Ample
Room TV Yes	*Room service* 24 hours

Ladbroke Hotel   Wetherby

H 65% £C/D
Map 11 D1 West Yorkshire
Leeds Road LS22 5HE
Wetherby (0937) 63881. Tlx 556428
Credit Access, Amex, Diners, Visa

Conveniently located at the junction of the A1 and A58, this modern low-rise hotel has seen recent major improvements. Most notable is the new entrance hall with its wall-length windows, central hooded fire and nicely upholstered settees and armchairs; all the day rooms are bright and cheerful. Bedrooms are practical and comfortable, the best being the Gold Star rooms. *Amenities* garden, laundry service, in-house movies.

■ *Rooms* 72	*Confirm by* 6
en suite bath/shower 72	*Last dinner* 9.45
Direct dial Yes	*Parking* Ample
Room TV Yes	*Room service* 24 hours

Maltings Hotel   Weybourne

H 57% £E
Map 6 C1 Norfolk
The Street NR25 6SY
Weybourne (026 370) 731
Owner managers Ross & Andrew Mears
Credit Access, Amex, Diners, Visa

A solid 16th-century house of Norfolk flint is at the heart of this family-run hotel just minutes from the sea. Public rooms are sturdily old-fashioned, with very few frills but definite charm. Bedroom style varies: rooms in the main house have functional modest fittings while other rooms include some delightful ones with antique furnishings in a cottage overlooking the garden.

■ *Rooms* 21	*Confirm by* 6
en suite bath/shower 17	*Last dinner* 9
Direct dial Yes	*Parking* Ample
Room TV Yes	*Room service* Limited

The Swiss Restaurant   Weybourne

R Map 6 C1 Norfolk
The Street, Holt
Weybourne (026 370) 220
Credit Access, Amex, Diners, Visa

Take a healthy appetite along to this beamed restaurant in a charming thatched cottage. Portions are king-size, and the menu takes in a fair variety of familiar Continental dishes like moules marinière, wiener schnitzel, steak au poivre and crème caramel. No great shakes gastronomically but the ambience is delightful and staff are particularly friendly and helpful. Formerly called Gasché's Swiss Restaurant. ℮

■ *Set L* £8·45	*L* 12–2
Set D from £10·15	*D* 7–9
About £50 *for two*	*Parking* Ample
Seats 65	*Closed* D Sun & all Mon

Oatlands Park Hotel | Weybridge

H **57% £D/E**
Map 5 E3 Surrey
146 Oatlands Drive KT13 9HB
Weybridge (0932) 47242. Tlx 915123
Credit Access, Amex, Diners, Visa
  A much-extended Victorian building set in parkland with a lake at the rear. The bar-lounge area features a gallery and high domed ceiling. Some of the bedrooms are very large and

traditional. Others are smaller, with a simpler look of the sixties. A major improvement plan includes bedroom refurbishment and a leisure complex.
Amenities garden, pool table, laundry service, in-house movies (free), 24-hour lounge service.

■ *Rooms 130*	*Confirm by 6*
en suite bath/shower 98	*Last dinner 9.30*
Direct dial Yes	*Parking Ample*
Room TV Yes	*Room service 24 hours*

Ship Thistle Hotel | Weybridge

H **65% £C**
Map 5 E3 Surrey
Monument Green KT13 8BQ
Weybridge (0932) 48364. Tlx 894271
Credit Access, Amex, Diners, Visa. **LVs**
  Public rooms at this agreeable hotel are in the original building, accommodation in modern extensions at the rear. There is an inviting foyer-lounge and a main bar that has been smartly

revamped in Art Deco style. Pleasantly decorated bedrooms are equipped with trouser presses, hairdryers and remote-control TVs. Good bathrooms. *Amenities* patio, in-house movies (free), laundry service, 24-hour lounge service.

■ *Rooms 39*	*Confirm by 6*
en suite bath/shower 39	*Last dinner 10.30*
Direct dial Yes	*Parking Ample*
Room TV Yes	*Room service 24 hours*

Woodhayes | Whimple

HR **74% £C/D**
Map 3 E2 Devon
Nr Exeter EX5 2TD
Whimple (0404) 822237
Owner managers John & Alison Allan
Credit Access, Amex, Diners, Visa
  In a quiet setting just off the A30, this attractive little Georgian house is charmingly run by John and Alison Allan. There are well-tended grounds, and the hotel has the intimate, inviting feel of a private house: a grandfather clock ticks a welcome in the entrance (no reception desk, just the warm hand of your host), and drinks are taken in the two elegant lounges stylishly furnished with

oil paintings and antiques. Delightful bedrooms are spacious and solidly comfortable, with good period furnishings and numerous personal touches. Bathrooms are sumptuous. Excellent breakfasts. No children under 12. No dogs.
Amenities garden, tennis, croquet, laundry service.

■ *Rooms 7*	*Confirm by 6*
en suite bath/shower 7	*Last dinner 8*
Direct dial Yes	*Parking Ample*
Room TV Yes	*Room service All day*
Closed 3 wks Jan	

Woodhayes Restaurant 🍴

Soft candlelight is reflected in highly polished darkwood furniture, making a very civilised setting for enjoying Paul Mason's modern English cooking. The menu provides three choices for each course: soup, perhaps, or warm duck salad to start, then grilled salmon or saddle of venison, with cheese or an excellent hot chocolate soufflé with orange sauce to finish. 🍷 Well-chosen 🄴

■ *Set L £16*	*L by arrang.*
Set D £17·50	*D 7.30 for 8*
About £45 for two	*Seats 20*
Closed 3 wks Jan	*Parties 20*

Inn at Whitewell | Whitewell

I **£E**
Map 10 B1 Lancashire
Forest of Bowland, Nr Clitheroe BB7 3AT
Dunsop Bridge (020 08) 222
Owner managers Bowman family
Credit Access, Amex, Diners, Visa
  Traditional comforts and a peaceful, friendly atmosphere at an ancient inn above a winding stretch of the river Hodder. There are two

characterful bars – one a popular local – and a homely residents' lounge. Most bedrooms are furnished with antique or period pieces; televisions are available on request.
Amenities garden, game fishing, pool table.

■ *Rooms 12*	*Confirm by arrang.*
en suite bath/shower 6	*Last dinner 9.30*
Room phone No	*Parking Ample*
Room TV Some	*Room service All day*

Whitwell Hall Country House Hotel

H 68% £C/D &
Map 15 C6 North Yorkshire
Nr York Y96 7JJ
Whitwell-on-the-Hill (065 381) 551
Owner managers Lt Cdr & Mrs P. F. M. Milner
Credit Access, Amex, Visa

Magnificent views are a feature of this ivy-clad hotel. Antiques and comfy chairs bring old-world charm to the foyer and lounge, contrasting with the leafy poolside bar. Bedrooms in the house have period furnishings. Coach house rooms are modern. No under-12s. *Amenities* garden, indoor swimming pool, sauna, tennis, putting, croquet, bicycles, games room, laundry service.

■ *Rooms* 20	*Confirm by arrang.*
en suite bath/shower 20	*Last dinner* 8.30
Direct dial Yes	*Parking Ample*
Room TV Yes	*Room service All day*

Old House Hotel

HR 66% £C/D
Map 5 D4 Hampshire
The Square PO17 5JG
Wickham (0329) 833049
Owner managers Richard & Annie Skipwith
Credit Access, Amex, Diners, Visa

Owners and staff provide a warm welcome at this converted Georgian house. Fresh flowers and bright rugs give style and colour to the day rooms and there are handsome period furnishings in the beamed bedrooms. No dogs. *Amenities* garden, laundry service.

■ *Rooms* 10	*Confirm by arrang.*
en suite bath/shower 8	*Last dinner* 9.30
Room phone Yes	*Parking Ample*
Room TV Yes	*Room service All day*
Closed Sat, Sun, Bank Hols, 2 wks Easter, 2 wks	
Jul–Aug & 10 days Xmas	

Old House Hotel Restaurant

French cooking
Nicholas Harman is the new chef at this elegantly rustic restaurant, whose concise French menu (four starters, four main courses) changes weekly. Steamed baby vegetables in puff pastry or smoked salmon mousse are typically light preludes to such appetising entrées as fillet steak richly sauced in red wine and grilled duck breast served with a warm herb vinaigrette. Sweets include home-made ices and sorbets. ℮

■ *About £47 for two*	*L* 12.30–1.45
Seats 45 *Parties* 14	*D* 7.30–9.30
Closed L Sat & Mon, all Sun, Bank Hols, 2 wks	
Apr, 2 wks Jul–Aug & 10 days Xmas	

♀ indicates a **well-chosen** house wine.

Brocket Arms Hotel

H 56% £E/F
Map 10 B2 Greater Manchester
Mesnes Road WN1 2DD
Wigan (0942) 46283
Owner manager W. J. Medland
Credit Access, Amex, Diners, Visa. **LVs**

The welcome is warm in this well-run red-brick hotel situated in a residential area north of town (ask for directions). The bars are local favourites, and there are good conference and banquet facilities here too. Bedrooms are simple, with sparkling bathrooms. No dogs. *Amenities* pool table, laundry service.

■ *Rooms* 27	*Confirm by arrang.*
en suite bath/shower 27	*Last dinner* 9.30
Room phone Yes	*Parking Ample*
Room TV Yes	*Room service Limited*
Closed Xmas	

Willerby Manor Hotel

HR 57% £D/E
Map 11 E1 Humberside
Well Lane HU10 6ER
Hull (0482) 652616
Owner manager Mr D. C. Baugh
Credit Access, Amex, Diners

Three acres of pleasant private grounds surround this friendly hotel less than five miles from the centre of Hull. Public areas include a comfortable bar-lounge and a wine bar. Most of the bedrooms are in an extension; they have all been refurbished in contemporary style and have modern tiled bathrooms. *Amenities* garden, laundry service, 24-hour lounge service.

■ *Rooms* 41	*Confirm by* 8
en suite bath/shower 41	*Last dinner* 9.30
Direct dial Yes	*Parking Ample*
Room TV Yes	*Room service* 24 hours

Willerby Manor Hotel Restaurant ♀ &

French cooking
Chef-patron Derek Baugh has a highly competent team around him, and their efforts bring 20,000 customers a year to this excellent French restaurant. The evening choice is the widest, and typical temptations could include mousses of chicken, pigeon and guinea fowl set on a truffle sauce, super-fresh halibut with a glazed wine sauce, or noisettes of venison with chestnut purée. Friendly Gallic service. ♀ **Well-chosen** ℮

■ *Set L* £7·50	*L* 12.30–1.45
Set D £9	*Sun* 12.30–1.30
About £40 for two	*D* 7–9.45
Seats 70 *Parties* 350	*Closed L* Sat, *D* Sun,
Bank Hol Mons & 2 days Xmas	

Home Farm Hotel — Wilmington

H 58% £D/E
Map 3 E2 Devon
Nr Honiton EX14 9JR
Wilmington (040 483) 278
Credit Access, Amex, Diners, Visa

As its name suggests, this hotel was originally a farmhouse, and the inglenook fireplace in the restaurant, and exposed stone walls in the bar give a cosy rural atmosphere. Public areas include a comfortable lounge with chintz furnishings. The cottagy feel continues in pretty bedrooms (some in a converted stable block) with well-kept en suite and public bathrooms. *Amenities* garden.

■ *Rooms 13* — *Confirm by 6*
en suite bath/shower 9 — *Last dinner 8.30*
Room phone No — *Parking Ample*
Room TV Yes — *Room service Limited*
Closed Jan & Feb

Stanneylands Hotel — Wilmslow

HR 70% £C/D ♿
Map 10 B2 Cheshire
Stanneylands Road SK9 4EY
Wilmslow (0625) 525225
Owner managers Beech family
Credit Access, Amex, Diners, Visa

Consistently good housekeeping is the hallmark of this Edwardian hotel. Standing amid fine trees the red-brick building looks solidly dependable, an impression strengthened by a warm welcome and efficient receptionist. Public areas include a comfortable, panelled lounge and a cosy bar-lounge with an open fire. There are also extensive banquet and meeting facilities. Individually-furnished bedrooms include a spacious four-poster room with an enormous period bathtub. Another room has a private sun terrace. In the purpose-built extension, rooms are large and have free-standing units. Immaculate modern bathrooms are well equipped. *Amenities* garden, laundry service, 24-hour lounge service.

■ *Rooms 33* — *Confirm by 6*
en suite bath/shower 33 — *Last dinner 10*
Direct dial Yes — *Parking Ample*
Room TV Yes — *Room service 24 hours*
Closed 1 Jan, Good Fri & 26 Dec

Restaurant ★ ♛ ♿

A club-like atmosphere prevails at this oak-panelled restaurant where smart, efficient staff serve up imaginative and consistently good food on stylish black-rimmed plates. Making a selection from Iain Donald's exciting menus is not easy. The six-course set menu offers small portions of a variety of dishes, while the market menu includes specialities like red mullet on sweet pimento cream and a casserole of lemon sole and baby langoustines flavoured with basil and vermouth. Raw materials are excellent. Delectable fruit desserts and a good selection of cheeses. Extensive wine list, strong in clarets and vintage ports. *Specialities* warm breast of partridge with oriental spices on a pillow of French salad leaves, steamed spiral of sole and salmon on a pumpkin and basil sauce, baked medallions of Welsh lamb with apricot and thyme mousse and a fondu of sweet peppers, iced maple and bourbon soufflé with exotic fruits in a crisp sesame seed biscuit. 🍷 Well-chosen ⊖

■ *Set L from £7* — *L 12.30–2*
Set D £17 — *D 7–10*
About £45 for two — *Seats 80 Parties 100*
Closed D Sun, 1 Jan, Good Fri & 26 Dec

Valley Lodge Hotel — Wilmslow

H 59% £C/D
Map 10 B2 Cheshire
Altrincham Road SK9 4LR
Wilmslow (0625) 529201. Tlx 666401
Manager Michael Schrompft
Credit Access, Amex, Diners, Visa

Leave the M56 at junction 6 for this modern hotel, which now boasts a leisure complex. Bedrooms are neat and practical. Day rooms include an open-plan bar-lounge and stylish public bar. *Amenities* garden, indoor swimming pool, sauna, steam room, solarium, whirlpool bath, gymnasium, squash, snooker, laundry service, 24-hour lounge service, courtesy coach.

■ *Rooms 105* — *Confirm by 6*
en suite bath/shower 105 — *Last dinner 10.30*
Direct dial Yes — *Parking Ample*
Room TV Yes — *Room service Limited*

The King's Head — Wimborne Minster

H 57% £C/D
Map 4 C4 Dorset
The Square BH21 1JA
Wimborne (0202) 880101
Credit Access, Amex, Diners, Visa

Soft colours and dark wood units with brass fittings in the bedrooms help to create a mellow atmosphere in this creeper-clad hotel. Once a Georgian Inn, rebuilt in the 19th century, the hotel is gradually being refurbished. Public rooms include a spacious lounge with gas log fire and wing back chairs, and simple public bar. Most bedrooms have well-kept bathrooms. *Amenities* laundry service.

■ *Rooms* 28	*Confirm by* 6
en suite bath/shower 17	*Last dinner* 9.15
Direct dial Yes	*Parking* Limited
Room TV Yes	*Room service* Limited

Holbrook House Hotel — Wincanton

H 55% £E
Map 4 B3 Somerset
Holbrook BA9 8BS
Wincanton (0963) 32377
Owner managers Mr & Mrs G. E. Taylor
Credit Access, Amex, Visa

Two miles out of town on the A371, this 17th-century house is a hotel of old-fashioned, slightly faded charms. A huge hall provides a chintzy chatting place, and there's a warm, comfortable bar. Traditional, well-kept bedrooms have tea-making facilities. *Amenities* garden, croquet, outdoor swimming pool, tennis, squash.

■ *Rooms* 19	*Confirm by* arrang.
en suite bath/shower 14	*Last dinner* 8.30
Room phone No	*Parking* Ample
Room TV No	*Room service* None
Closed 31 Dec	

Lainston House — Winchester

H 80% £B/C *E* &
Map 5 D3 Hampshire
Sparsholt SO21 2LT
Winchester (0962) 63588. Tlx 477375
Credit Access, Amex, Diners, Visa

Sixty-three acres of beautiful rolling parkland surround this splendid hotel, a graceful William and Mary manor house with many fine features. Delft tiles adorn an original fireplace in the entrance hall, and there's a handsome lounge with elegant drapes matching the covers on the sumptuous settees; the bar is notable for its lovely cedar panelling. Spacious, stylish bedrooms, most of which are in separate buildings, are attractively furnished in a variety of traditional styles; all rooms have mini-bars and most are fitted with wall safes. Well-equipped bathrooms with bidets have hand showers as well as fixed

showers over the tubs. Service, though generally friendly, is not always very polished. There are good conference facilities. *Amenities* garden, tennis, croquet, helipad, laundry service.

■ *Rooms* 32	*Confirm by* 6
en suite bath/shower 32	*Last dinner* 10
Direct dial Yes	*Parking* Ample
Room TV Yes	*Room service* 24 hours

Mr So *NEW ENTRY* — Winchester

R Map 5 D3 Hampshire
3 Jewry Street
Winchester (0962) 61234
Chinese cooking
Credit Access, Amex, Diners, Visa. LVs

In Mr So, Winchester has a Chinese restaurant to equal almost anything that London has to offer. Decor is simple but stylish, service under Wallis Leong friendly and attentive, and cooking is first class. The menu includes among its specialities Peking duck, sizzling beef, venison with celery and deep-fried quail with a subtle salt and pepper spicing. Don't miss the marvellous Singapore noodles.

■ *Set L from* £3·30	*L* 12–2.30
Set D from £7·50	*D* 6–11.30
About £30 *for two*	*Parking* Limited
Seats 40 *Parties* 40	*Closed* 2 days Xmas

Royal Hotel *NEW ENTRY* — Winchester

H 65% £D
Map 5 D3 Hampshire
St Peter Street SO23 8BS
Winchester (0962) 53468. Tlx 477071
Credit Access, Amex, Diners, Visa

Considerable effort has gone into improving this city-centre hotel. Overnight accommodation comprises 19 rooms in the original part and 40 in a new wing, all furnished in traditional style. Executive and County House rooms offer additional accessories, plus more room service. The lounge and bar have access to a pleasant walled garden. *Amenities* garden, laundry service, 24-hour lounge service.

■ *Rooms* 59	*Confirm by* 6
en suite bath/shower 59	*Last dinner* 9.30
Direct dial Yes	*Parking* Ample
Room TV Yes	*Room service* 24 hours

The Wessex   Winchester

H **69% £C**
Map 5 D3 Hampshire
Paternoster Row SO23 9LQ
Winchester (0962) 61611. Tlx 47419
Credit Access, Amex, Diners, Visa. **LVs**

A modern red-brick hotel in striking contrast to the ancient cathedral opposite. Within, different styles have been skilfully combined to give an original feel to the public areas, which include a peaceful writing lounge. Spacious executive rooms offer superb views of the cathedral. All rooms are smartly furnished and spotlessly clean. *Amenities* coffee shop (7am–10pm), laundry service.

■ *Rooms* 94	*Confirm by* 6
en suite bath/shower 94	*Last dinner* 10
Direct dial Yes	*Parking* Ample
Room TV Yes	*Room service* 24 hours

🖘 is our symbol for an **outstanding** wine list.

Langdale Chase Hotel   Windermere

H **63% £D/E**
Map 13 D5 Cumbria
LA23 1LW
Ambleside (0966) 32201
Manager Miss Hartill
Credit Access, Amex, Diners, Visa

Lakeside gardens provide an idyllic setting for this handsome Victorian mansion. The baronial entrance hall with its minstrels' gallery and fireplace is echoed by a sumptuous lounge and characterful bar. Main house bedrooms are traditional; six in a cottage are more modern. *Amenities* garden, tennis, putting, croquet, boating, laundry service, 24-hour lounge service.

■ *Rooms* 35	*Confirm by* 6
en suite bath/shower 33	*Last dinner* 8.30
Room phone Yes	*Parking* Ample
Room TV Yes	*Room service* Limited

Miller Howe Hotel   Windermere

HR **73% £C**
Map 13 D5 Cumbria
Rayrigg Road LA23 1EY
Windermere (096 62) 2536
Owner manager John Tovey
Credit Access, Amex, Diners

Panoramic views of Lake Windermere and beautiful gardens are the external delights here. Inside, the three lounges have comfortable button-back seating, antiques, decorative glassware and opulent decor. The best bedrooms are at the front, with balconies and a stunning outlook, but all rooms have stylish fabrics, good pictures, porcelain and fresh flowers. Extras include books, magazines, hairdryers, trouser presses and hi-fi systems with a choice of tapes. TV and telephone are available on request. Bathrooms (one not en suite) are smart and modern. Excellent breakfast, attentive service. Half-board only. No children under 12. *Amenities* garden.

■ *Rooms* 13	*Confirm by* 4
en suite bath/shower 12	*Last dinner* 8.30
Room phone No	*Parking* Ample
Room TV No	*Room service* All day
Closed early Dec–mid Mar	

Miller Howe Hotel Restaurant 🍴 ♧

A meal here is a theatrical performance, with dimming and raising of lights and proud parading of the goodies to be served. Head chef Robert Lyons produces a five-course feast of delights, from fennel and courgette soup and a zingy-fresh fish dish to superb roast lamb and a lovely rhubarb and ginger pie. No choice except for sweets. ♀ **Well-chosen** ℮

■ *Set D* £22	*D only* 8 for 8.30,
About £60 *for two*	*Sat* 7 & 9.30
Seats 72	*Parties* 30
Closed early Dec–mid Mar	

Roger's   Windermere

R ♧ **Map 13 D5** Cumbria
4 High Street
Windermere (096 62) 4954
Owner managers Pergl-Wilson family
Credit Access, Amex, Diners, Visa

A cosy, relaxing little restaurant, with Roger in the kitchen and Alena looking after the customers. The menu changes with the markets and offers generous helpings of tasty dishes like bean, pasta and sausage soup, langoustines wrapped in cabbage leaves and veal chop with fresh herb butter. There's an excellent selection of English cheeses. ♀ **Well-chosen** ℮

■ *About* £35 *for two*	*L by arrang. only*
Seats 24	*D* 7–9.30
Parties 20	*Parking* Difficult
Closed Sun & 2 wks Jan/Feb	

Windsor ▶

Castle Hotel

H 68% £C
Map 5 E2 Berkshire
High Street SL4 1LJ
Windsor (0753) 851011. Tlx 849220
Manager Mr A. McAinsh
Credit Access, Amex, Diners, Visa. LVs

A former posting house with a fine Georgian facade and plenty of period atmosphere. Oil paintings decorate the elegant foyer-lounge and there's a pleasant bar. Main-house bedrooms have smart darkwood furniture, annexe rooms fitted units. All have tea-makers. *Amenities* in-house movies (free), laundry service, coffee shop (7.30am–10.15pm), 24-hour lounge service.

■ *Rooms* 85	*Confirm by* 6
en suite bath/shower 85	*Last dinner* 9.45
Room phone Yes	*Parking* Ample
Room TV Yes	*Room service* All day

Oakley Court Hotel

HR 82% £C **E**
Map 5 E2 Berkshire
Windsor Road SL4 5UR
Maidenhead (0628) 74141. Tlx 849958
Credit Access, Amex, Diners, Visa

A very fine hotel standing off the A308 in mature grounds bordering the river Thames. The main building, mock-Gothic dating from 1859 and with lots of nice architectural features, houses the public rooms, which are notable for their rich panelling and opulent furnishings; the billiards room is particularly splendid. Here, too, are seven beautifully furnished bedrooms, the rest being in two modern wings; the rooms generally are of a good size – executive rooms especially so – and handsomely appointed. Remote-control TVs and trouser presses are standard, and bathrooms are well stocked with towels and toiletries. No dogs. *Amenities* garden, pitch & putt, croquet, coarse fishing, billiards, valeting, laundry service, 24-hour lounge service, helipad.

■ *Rooms* 91	*Confirm by* 6
en suite bath/shower 91	*Last dinner* 10
Direct dial Yes	*Parking* Ample
Room TV Yes	*Room service* 24 hours

Oak Leaf Room ★ ♔

A formal, ornate dining room in which to enjoy Murdo MacSween's impressive modern cooking. Using best-quality ingredients, he achieves a fine balance of flavours and impeccable textures, the saucing being particularly refined and profound in flavour. The pastry work is superb. Dinner might be a salad of smoked duck, orange and scampi, followed by fillet of beef with Stilton mousse and shallot and horseradish sauce. For simpler tastes there is a roast joint of the day. First-rate, crisp vegetables and a wide choice of attractive sweets. Fine Bordeaux and burgundies. *Specialities* terrine of pheasant, partridge and foie gras served with redcurrants in a port jelly, hot artichoke and almond soup with fresh scallops and a pastry topping, fillets of monkfish with a dill and saffron sauce served in a pastry case, quails stuffed with a tarragon mousse wrapped in Greek pastry with a light orange sauce.
🍷 Well-chosen ☺

■ *Set L* £13	*L* 12.30–2
Set D £19	*D* 7.30–10
About £70 for two	*Seats* 120 *Parties* 10

King's Arms

R ♧ **Map 3 D2** Devon
The Square
Winkleigh (083 783) 384
Credit Access, Amex, Visa

Dinner is served every evening at 8.15 in the tiny lamplit dining room of this traditional village pub. No choice on the six-course menu, but alternatives can be discussed when booking. Portions are judged so the menu courses do not intimidate. Cooking by chef Ann Rickard is light and confident, capable but not classical. Hot ham mousse, stilton and celery soup and stuffed fillet of sole might precede a lovely home-made sorbet, followed perhaps by medallions of pork with tarragon and orange sabayon to finish. ☺

■ *Set D* £16·50	*D only* 8.15
About £40 for two	*Parking* Ample
Seats 16	*Closed* Sun

Fisherman's Haunt Hotel *NEW ENTRY* Winkton

I **£F**
Map 4 C4 Dorset
Salisbury Road, Christchurch BH23 7AS
Christchurch (0202) 484071

Overlooking the river Avon, and popular with anglers, this friendly inn dates from the 17th century. Cosy day rooms include two beamed bars, one featuring an old working well, and a homely TV lounge. Bedrooms, mostly in annexes,

are bright and comfortable, with extras ranging from tea-makers and tissues to remote-control TVs. Two main-house rooms are larger and more traditional. *Amenities* garden, laundry service.

■ *Rooms* 20
en suite bath/shower 20
Direct dial Yes
Room TV Yes
Closed 25 Dec

Confirm by arrang.
Last dinner 10
Parking Ample
Room service Limited

■ Our inspectors are our full-time employees; they are professionally trained by us.

Royal Oak Inn Winsford

I **£E/F**
Map 3 D2 Somerset
Nr Minehead TA24 7JE
Winsford (064 385) 455
Owner manager Charles Steven
Credit Access, Amex, Diners, Visa

A deliciously pretty village on the edge of Exmoor National Park is the setting for this 12th-century thatched inn. Two beamed bars are full of

traditional character. Bedrooms in the original building include a luxurious suite, while the converted stables house smartly modern rooms. *Amenities* garden, coarse fishing.

■ *Rooms* 14
en suite bath/shower 14
Direct dial Yes
Room TV Yes
Closed Feb

Confirm by arrang.
Last dinner 9.30
Parking Ample
Room service Limited

Grange Hotel at Northwoods Winterbourne

H **68% £D**
Map 4 B2 Avon
Old Gloucester Road, Northwoods BS17 1RP
Winterbourne (0454) 777333. Tlx 449205
Owner manager John Cockram
Credit Access, Amex, Diners, Visa

A vast cedar dominates the gardens of this sturdy house set back from the B4427 (check directions when booking). The conservatory-style

bar has a trellised verandah, and there is a smart lounge. Stylish, well-equipped bedrooms are in a modern extension. *Amenities* garden, laundry service, 24-hour lounge service.

■ *Rooms* 32
en suite bath/shower 32
Direct dial Yes
Room TV Yes
Closed 3 days Xmas

Confirm by 7
Last dinner 10
Parking Ample
Room service 24 hours

Belfry Hotel Wishaw

H **74% £C/D** *E*
Map 10 C4 Warwickshire
Lichfield B76 9PR
Curdworth (0675) 70301. Tlx 338848
Manager René Brunet
Credit Access, Amex, Diners, Visa

Outstanding sports and leisure facilities are the main features of this hotel situated in 370 acres of parkland. The original ivy-clad building, with many beams and fine panelling, is reached via a delightful tiled conservatory. Public rooms include an attractive half-timbered night club set away from the bedrooms. Bedrooms vary in style, some traditional rooms in the old house having beams and four-posters, newer rooms having fitted units and well-equipped bathrooms. No dogs.
Amenities garden, indoor swimming pool, sauna, solarium, whirlpool bath, keep-fit equipment,

tennis, squash, golf courses, in-house movies (charge), snooker, laundry service, coffee shop (7am–10.30pm), 24-hour lounge service, children's playground, helipad.

■ *Rooms* 168
en suite bath/shower 168
Direct dial Yes
Room TV Yes

Confirm by arrang.
Last dinner 10.30
Parking Ample
Room service 24 hours

Old Vicarage   Witherslack

HR 65% £D/E
Map 13 D6 Cumbria
Nr Grange-over-Sands LA11 6RS
Witherslack (044 852) 381
Owners Burrington-Brown & Reeve families
Credit Access, Amex, Diners, Visa
  Harmony and hospitality are the keynotes at this delightful Georgian house. Sunny, rug-strewn lounges are cosy and relaxing. Well-appointed bedrooms offer many thoughtful touches, and bathrooms are immaculate. Delicious breakfasts and charming hosts. *Amenities* garden, croquet, laundry service.

■ *Rooms* 7	*Confirm by* arrang.
en suite bath/shower 7	*Last dinner* 7.30
Direct dial Yes	*Parking* Ample
Room TV Yes	*Room service* All day
Closed 5 days Xmas	

Old Vicarage Restaurant ♀

Owner-chefs take pains to procure quality produce for their set-price menus. A typical meal could start with artichoke mousseline to be followed by an interesting soup such as courgette with sherry. The main course may be pâté-stuffed breast of chicken served with copious fresh vegetables. Vegetarian main courses are provided on request. Two sweets are served (one hot, one cold), and splendid cheeses. Tea or coffee with Kendal mint cake rounds things off very satisfactorily. Impressive cellar: note Pommard Pézerolles (de Montille) 1982. ℮

■ *Set D* £16·50	*D only* 7.30 for 8
About £46 for two	*Seats* 38
Closed 5 days Xmas	*Parties* 20

Langley House Hotel   Wiveliscombe

HR 63% £D/E
Map 3 E2 Somerset
Langley Marsh TA4 2UF
Wiveliscombe (0984) 23318
Owner managers Peter & Anne Wilson
Credit Access, Amex
  In the Quantocks a mile north of Wiveliscombe, this delightful hotel stands in landscaped gardens complete with babbling brook. Guests are greeted in the entrance hall and shown up to prettily decorated bedrooms. Downstairs there's a charming morning room and comfortable lounge. No children under 7. *Amenities* garden, croquet, bicycles, laundry service.

■ *Rooms* 9	*Confirm by* 6
en suite bath/shower 8	*Last dinner* 9.30
Direct dial Yes	*Parking* Ample
Room TV Yes	*Room service* All day

Langley House Hotel Restaurant ♀ ♿

Anne Wilson is the perfect hostess, Peter the capable chef at this homely little restaurant. The set dinners, served at candlelit mahogany tables, are wholesome and unpretentious. Daily-changing menus offer appetisers like avocado and orange salad, followed perhaps by broad bean and hazelnut soup, fresh crab soufflé, and mignons of beef with rosemary and mustard. Choice only begins with the sweets, which include a platter of home-made sorbets. On Friday and Saturday there's an extra (fifth) course, hence the later start to allow the chef more time for preparation. ℮

■ *Set D* from £14·75	*D only* at 7.30,
About £40 for two	*Fri & Sat* at 8.30
Seats 20	*Parties* 22

Bedford Arms Hotel   Woburn

H 68% £C/D ♿
Map 5 E1 Bedfordshire
George Street, Nr Milton Keynes MK17 9PX
Woburn (052 525) 441. Tlx 825205
Credit Access, Amex, Diners, Visa
  Behind a fine Georgian frontage, this comfortable hotel offers efficient service in public rooms of character, and accommodation that reveals considerable thoughtfulness by the management. Nine rooms are properly equipped for the disabled, a similar number are exclusively for non-smokers, and all rooms have good accessories and well-equipped bathrooms. *Amenities* in-house movies, laundry service.

■ *Rooms* 55	*Confirm by* arrang.
en suite bath/shower 55	*Last dinner* 10.30
Direct dial Yes	*Parking* Ample
Room TV Yes	*Room service* 24 hours

Paris House   Woburn

R ♀ Map 5 E1 Bedfordshire
Woburn Park
Woburn (052 525) 692
French cooking
Credit Access, Amex, Diners, Visa
  Built for the Great Exhibition of Paris in 1878, this handsome black and white timbered house was reconstructed as a folly in Woburn Abbey Park and now provides a fine background for Peter Chandler's imaginative set menus. Recent successes have included an excellent flaky pastry case filled with smoked haddock, quail's eggs and a chive butter sauce, crispy suprême of duck with mangos and ginger sauce, and perfectly risen raspberry soufflé. Presentation is attractive, but some dishes lack flair, and service could be more polished and knowledgeable. Drink the excellent red Madiran 1983 as an alternative to the fine but pricey classic wines. First-rate selection of French cheeses.
♀ Well-chosen

■ *Set L* £13·50	*L* 12.30–2, *Sun* 12–2
Set D £18·50	*D* 7–10
About £60 for two	*Parking* Ample
Seats 38	*Parties* 16
Closed D Sun, all Mon, & 3/4 wks Feb	

Wheatsheaf Hotel
Woking

£E
Map 5 E3 Surrey
Chobham Road GU21 4AL
Woking (048 62) 73047
Credit Access, Amex, Diners, Visa
   Modest overnight accommodation is provided
by this sturdy brick-built inn just out of town and
opposite a cricket field. It has two lively bars, and
a smart reception area. Most bedrooms are

modern-style singles, but there are some larger,
traditionally furnished rooms in the original
building. All have colour TVs, radio-alarms, direct-
dial phones and tea-makers, and there are plenty
of public bathrooms.

■ *Rooms* 38	*Confirm by* arrang.
en suite bath/shower 3	*Last dinner* 10
Direct dial Yes	*Parking* Ample
Room TV Yes	*Room service* None

Seckford Hall Hotel
Woodbridge

71% £D
Map 6 D3 Suffolk
IP13 6NU
Woodbridge (0394) 385678. Tlx 987446
Owner manager Michael Bunn
Credit Access, Amex, Diners, Visa
   Clearly signposted from the A12, a fine Tudor
mansion set in beautiful parkland. Crowstep
gables and tall chimneys distinguish the mellow
red-brick facade, and the visual delights continue
inside: solid oak furnishings in the entrance hall
and sitting rooms; original linenfold panelling in
the main lounge; an abundance of beams; a
splendid minstrels' gallery in the lakeside
banqueting suite. Handsomely proportioned
bedrooms are individually styled, with pink and
green a favourite colour combination; furnishings
range from traditional (some four-posters) to

modern. Staff are friendly enough but not
particularly professional. *Amenities* garden,
coarse fishing, laundry service.

■ *Rooms* 24	*Confirm by* arrang.
en suite bath/shower 23	*Last dinner* 9.30
Direct dial Yes	*Parking* Ample
Room TV Yes	*Room service* All day
Closed 25 Dec	

Prince Regent Hotel
Woodford Bridge

57% £D/E
Map 7 B4 Essex
Manor Road IG8 8AE
01-504 7635
Credit Access, Amex, Diners, Visa
   Just a short drive from the Eastern Avenue
junction with the M11, this Georgian house in a
garden setting makes a pleasant hotel. Beyond
the classical entrance is a comfortable bar-lounge

with Regency-style furnishings. A fine staircase
leads to neat bedrooms, where guests will find a
complimentary glass of sherry, tea-makers, clock-
radios and a bath or shower en suite. No dogs.
Amenities garden, laundry service.

■ *Rooms* 10	*Confirm by* arrang.
en suite bath/shower 10	*Last dinner* 10.30
Direct dial Yes	*Parking* Ample
Room TV Yes	*Room service* 24 hours

Woodford Moat House
Woodford Green

62% £D/E
Map 7 B4 Essex
Oak Hill IG8 9NY
01-505 4511. Tlx 264428
Manager Mr G. L. Stohr
Credit Access, Amex, Diners, Visa
   The peace of Epping Forest vies with a major
road network as the setting for this purpose-built
hotel. The huge foyer, with its velour seating,

doubles as a comfortable lounge, while cane
furniture gives a smart touch to the discreetly-lit
bar. Neat bedrooms have tea-makers and remote-
control TVs. *Amenities* laundry service, 24-hour
lounge service.

■ *Rooms* 99	*Confirm by* arrang.
en suite bath/shower 99	*Last dinner* 10.15
Room phone Yes	*Parking* Ample
Room TV Yes	*Room service* 24 hours

Dower House Hotel
Woodhall Spa

62% £E
Map 11 E2 Lincolnshire
Manor Estate LN10 6PY
Woodhall Spa (0526) 52588
Owner managers Mr & Mrs Plumb
Credit Access, Amex, Diners, Visa
   The Plumbs treat strangers like family friends
and continue to improve this charming hotel on a
private estate adjoining a championship golf

course. Old-fashioned comfort rules throughout.
Spacious, traditionally furnished bedrooms boast
splendid antique wardrobes and period mirrors.
Bathrooms are neat and practical.
Amenities garden, laundry service.

■ *Rooms* 6	*Confirm by* arrang.
en suite bath/shower 6	*Last dinner* 9.30
Room phone No	*Parking* Ample
Room TV Yes	*Room service* All day

Golf Hotel Woodhall Spa

H **57% £D/E**
Map 11 E2 Lincolnshire
The Broadway LN10 6SG
Woodhall Spa (0526) 53535
Credit Access, Amex, Diners, Visa

First and foremost a golfer's hotel, with direct access to the Woodhall Spa championship course. Behind a pleasant mock-Tudor facade the place is fairly modern and functional, though the bar and restaurant have been smartly refurbished. Bedrooms are cheerfully modest, with simple bath or shower rooms, plus tea-makers and trouser presses. General Manager James Inglis runs a tidy ship. *Amenities* garden, croquet.

■ *Rooms* 51	*Confirm by arrang.*
en suite bath/shower 51	*Last dinner 9.15*
Room phone Yes	*Parking* Ample
Room TV Yes	*Room service* Limited

■ We welcome complaints and bona fide recommendations on the tear-out pages for readers' comments. They are followed up by our professional team. Please also complain to the management instantly.

RECEPTION

Bear Hotel Woodstock

H **73% £B**
Map 5 D1 Oxfordshire
Park Street OX7 1SZ
Woodstock (0993) 811511. Tlx 837921
Credit Access, Amex, Diners, Visa

Reputedly first licensed in 1232, this famous coaching inn combines old-world charm with modern comforts fairly successfully. The flag-stoned entrance hall leads into a cosy cocktail bar and a rustic, beamed public bar with open fire. Residents may also relax upstairs in a lounge brimming with antiques. Bedrooms range from the elegantly luxurious (mostly in the stable block) to the more modest (though some refurbishment has begun here). All rooms are stocked with a bewildering array of extras, from mineral water, fresh fruit and nuts, to hairdryers and some mini-bars. Bathrooms, although similarly well-

equipped, are also variable in standard. *Amenities* laundry service, 24-hour lounge service, in-house movies (free).

■ *Rooms* 45	*Confirm by* 7
en suite bath/shower 45	*Last dinner* 10.30
Direct dial Yes	*Parking* Limited
Room TV Yes	*Room service* 24 hours

Feathers Hotel Woodstock

HR **75% £C/D**
Map 5 D1 Oxfordshire
Market Street OX7 1SX
Woodstock (0993) 812291. Tlx 83138
Owner manager Gordon Campbell Gray
Credit Access, Amex, Diners, Visa

Colourful flower baskets and window boxes adorn the elegant red-brick facade of this fine, well-run 17th-century hotel in the heart of historic Woodstock. Inside, delightful public areas like the two lounges – one with an open fire, beams and splendid panelling, the other more intimate and full of old books and china – have immense appeal, while the Garden Bar (which leads to a pretty courtyard) positively oozes Victorian character and provides a popular local meeting place. Spacious, individually decorated bedrooms combine traditional grace and style with contemporary comforts, and luxuriously equipped private bathrooms have many thoughtful extras. *Amenities* garden.

■ *Rooms* 16	*Confirm by* 6
en suite bath/shower 14	*Last dinner 9.45*
Direct dial Yes	*Parking* Difficult
Room TV Yes	*Room service* All day

Feathers Hotel Restaurant ♔

Fine prints, antique furniture and immaculate tables add to the enjoyment of dining at this luxurious, formal restaurant. The concise, well-balanced menus are full of interest; a typical meal might include chicken, wild mushroom and orange consommé or marinated Scottish salmon with mustard and lime sauce followed by monkfish with raspberry vinaigrette or breast of duck with sage and apples in puff pastry. To finish, perhaps an iced pear soufflé or chocolate truffle torte. Booking essential for non-residents.
♟ Well-chosen ☺

■ *Set L* £10.50	*L* 12.30–2.15
Set D £15.50	*D* 7.30–9.45
About £50 for two	*Seats* 40 *Parties* 45

Woody Bay Hotel

H **58% £E**
Map 3 D1 Devon
Nr Parracombe EX31 4QX
Parracombe (059 83) 264
Owner managers Prue & Laurie Scott
Credit Access, Visa
No room phones, no room TVs, nothing to interfere with the peace and seclusion of this late-Victorian hotel in a spectacular setting above the bay. The bar and most of the pleasant, simply-furnished bedrooms enjoy lovely vistas. Bathrooms are spotless. No children under eight. *Amenities* garden.

■ *Rooms* 14	*Confirm by* arrang.
en suite bath/shower 9	*Last dinner* 8.30
Room phone No	*Parking* Ample
Room TV No	*Room service* None
Closed early Jan–late Feb	

Ryecroft Hotel

HR **55% £F**
Map 14 B2 Northumberland
NE71 6AB
Wooler (0668) 81459
Owner managers Pat & David McKechnie
Credit Access, Visa
Modest it may be, but this is a little gem of a hotel, and one that sparkles with the shine of good housework. The owners are immensely conscientious, and the whole place has a homely charm. The bedrooms have well-sprung mattresses and impeccably laundered sheets. A splendid breakfast. *Amenities* garden.

■ *Rooms* 11	*Confirm by* arrang.
en suite bath/shower 0	*Last dinner* 8.30
Room phone None	*Parking* Ample
Room TV No	*Room service* Limited
Closed 1st 2 weeks Nov & 1 wk Xmas	

Ryecroft Hotel Restaurant 🍴 ♿

NEW ENTRY

A simple, spotless dining room with a real home-from-home atmosphere. Pat McKechnie's obvious love of cooking results in some really enjoyable dishes, typified by our green pepper soup, smoked haddock soufflé and chicken with coriander sauce. Super sweets include strawberry syllabub. Keenly priced list of decent wines (Gewürztraminer '85 Emile Willm; Rioja Contino Gran Reserva '78).
♀ Well-chosen ⊖

■ *Set L* £5	*L* Sun only 12.30–1.30
Set D £10	*D* Tues–Sat 7–8.30
About £26 for two	*Seats* 30 *Parties* 20
Closed L Mon–Sat, *D* Sun & Mon, 1st 2 wks Nov & 1 wk Xmas	

Tankerville Arms Hotel

I **£F**
Map 14 B2 Northumberland
Cottage Road NE71 6AD
Wooler (0668) 81581
Owner managers Mr & Mrs Park & Mrs Morton
Credit Access, Visa
There's plenty to interest the visitor to this beautiful part of Northumberland, and hospitality abounds at this simple, uncluttered pub. The lounge bar is traditional. There is a TV room, and the recently redecorated bedrooms, eight of which have private facilities, are simple and unpretentious. Some rooms enjoy lovely country views. *Amenities* garden.

■ *Rooms* 15	*Confirm by* arrang.
en suite bath/shower 8	*Last dinner* 9.30
Room phone No	*Parking* Ample
Room TV Most	*Room service* Limited

Brown's Restaurant

R 🍴 🛏 ♿ **Map 4 B1** Hereford & Worcester
24 Quay Street
Worcester (0905) 26263
Credit Access, Amex, Visa
Robert Tansley presents an imaginative modern menu in his stylishly converted cornmill overlooking the Severn. Sautéed monkfish is a delicious starter, and mains could include charcoal-grilled beef, panaché of veal with raspberry vinegar and excellent roast mallard. Very good vegetables and an excellent cheeseboard. Wines include some fine Burgundies and Rhônes. ⊖

■ *Set L* £13·95, Sun £10	*L* 12.30–1.45
Set D £18·95	*D* 7.30–9.30
About £50 for two	*Parking* Ample
Seats 75	*Closed L* Sat, *D* Sun,
Bank Hols & 1 wk Xmas	

Giffard Hotel

H **64% £C/D**
Map 4 B1 Hereford & Worcester
High Street WR1 2QR
Worcester (0905) 726262. Tlx 338869
Credit Access, Amex, Diners, Visa. **LVs**
Right in the city centre, this well-run hotel presents an angular modern face that contrasts sharply with the cathedral opposite. Neat and practical bedrooms offer writing space, tea-makers and bedside controls for TV and radio. Public rooms include a cheerful coffee shop and, on the first floor, a lounge and cocktail bar. Decent breakfasts. *Amenities* snooker, laundry service, coffee shop (10am–9pm).

■ *Rooms* 104	*Confirm by* arrang.
en suite bath/shower 104	*Last dinner* 9.45
Direct dial Yes	*Parking* Ample
Room TV Yes	*Room service* 24 hours

Old Vicarage Hotel *NEW ENTRY*　　　　　　　Worfield

HR 68% £D/E
Map 10 B4 Shropshire
Bridgnorth WV15 5JZ
Worfield (074 64) 497
Owner managers Peter & Christine Iles
Credit Access, Amex, Diners, Visa
A turn-of-the-century village parsonage, now a relaxing and comfortable hotel. The owners are keen and friendly, and day rooms are inviting, but the chief strength is the bedrooms, where carefully selected Victorian and Edwardian furnishings go hand in hand with modern facilities. Excellent breakfasts. *Amenities* garden, croquet, laundry service.

■ *Rooms* 10	*Confirm by* arrang.
en suite bath/shower 10	*Last dinner* 9
Direct dial Yes	*Parking* Ample
Room TV Yes	*Room service* Limited

Old Vicarage Hotel Restaurant &
The regularly changing handwritten menu tempts with tasty dishes like vegetable soup with delicious sage and onion bread, baked halibut in oatmeal and loin of venison with spiced pears and redcurrant sauce. Good English cheeses and nice sweets such as crème brûlée or raspberry soufflé. Simpler lunchtime choice. Interesting cellar: note the excellent Jacquesson champagnes, fine early-landed cognacs, and the occasional gem like the 1962 Château Longueville Baron.
🍷 **Well-chosen** 🕲

■ *Set D* from £14	*L* 12–1.30
About £40 for two	*D* 7–9
Seats 36	*Parties* 50

■ Changes in data may occur in establishments after the Guide goes to press. Prices should be taken as indications rather than firm quotes.

Beach Hotel　　　　　　　　　　　　　　　Worthing

H 64% £E
Map 5 E4 West Sussex
Marine Parade BN11 3QJ
Worthing (0903) 34001
Manager P. G. Nash
Credit Access, Amex, Diners, Visa
Built in the 1930s, this seafront hotel just outside the town centre enjoys splendid views from its smartly decorated foyer and lounge. The best view of all is from the sun terrace, which is decked with flowering plants. Half the bedrooms benefit from a similar outlook; all are spacious and traditionally furnished. No children under eight. No dogs. *Amenities* 24-hour lounge service.

■ *Rooms* 90	*Confirm by* arrang.
en suite bath/shower 81	*Last dinner* 8.45
Direct dial Yes	*Parking* Ample
Room TV Yes	*Room service* 24 hours

Chatsworth Hotel　　　　　　　　　　　Worthing

H 59% £D/E
Map 5 E4 West Sussex
Steyne BN11 3DU
Worthing (0903) 36103. Tlx 877046
Manager John Walpole
Credit Access, Visa
Long continuity of ownership has created an atmosphere of comfort and efficiency at this handsome, seafront hotel. Recently refurbished public rooms include a traditional lounge and bar. Bedrooms are modest but comfortable. Bathrooms are spotless. *Amenities* games room, snooker, pool table, in-house movies (charge), laundry service, 24-hour lounge service.

■ *Rooms* 116	*Confirm by* 6.30
en suite bath/shower 106	*Last dinner* 8.30
Direct dial Yes	*Parking* Difficult
Room TV Yes	*Room service* 24 hours

Eardley Hotel　　　　　　　　　　　　　Worthing

H 57% £D/E
Map 5 E4 West Sussex
Marine Parade BN11 3PW
Worthing (0903) 34444. Tlx 877046
Credit Access, Visa
A traditional seafront hotel standing in a smart white stuccoed terrace. In addition to the bar – a popular local meeting place – and two bright lounges, there are function rooms aplenty. Front bedrooms overlook the well-tended garden and the sea beyond; some back rooms are quite small. *Amenities* garden, laundry service, coffee shop (10am–10pm), 24-hour lounge service, in-house movies (charge), board sailing.

■ *Rooms* 77	*Confirm by* 6
en suite bath/shower 77	*Last dinner* 9.15
Direct dial Yes	*Parking* Limited
Room TV Yes	*Room service* 24 hours

Post House Hotel　　　　　　　　　Wrotham Heath

H **74% £C _E_** &
　Map 7 B5 Kent
London Road, Nr Sevenoaks TN15 7RS
Borough Green (0732) 883311
Credit Access, Amex, Diners, Visa
　Set in attractive grounds below the North
Downs, this comfortable modern low-rise hotel is
handily situated for the local motorway network.
Interior design is well thought out and most
impressive, from the contemporary open-plan
lounge with its chic table lamps and elegant sofas
to the oak-panelled bar and delightful
conservatory. Bedrooms are all of a high
standard, spacious (no single beds) with pretty
curtains, plenty of writing space and tea/coffee-
making sets. Executive rooms boast extras like
telephone pads and trouser presses. Bathrooms
are compact but comprehensively equipped.

Amenities garden, indoor swimming pool, sauna,
solarium, whirlpool bath, gymnasium, in house
movies (charge), laundry service, 24-hour lounge
service.

■ *Rooms* 119	*Confirm by* 6
en suite bath/shower 119	*Last dinner* 11
Direct dial Yes	*Parking* Ample
Room TV Yes	*Room service* Limited

Wroxton House Hotel　　　　　　　　　Wroxton

H **62% £C/D**
　Map 7 C5 Oxfordshire
Nr Banbury OX15 6QB
Wroxton St Mary (029 573) 482
Credit Access, Amex, Diners, Visa
　There's a friendly, informal air about this
attractive thatched hotel, which stands by the
A422 on the Stratford side of Banbury.
Comfortable armchairs make for easy relaxation in
the residents' lounge (sometimes used for
meetings), and there's a pleasant, welcoming bar..
Well-equipped bedrooms are decorated in
straightforward, unfussy style. *Amenities* garden,
tennis, laundry service, 24-hour lounge service.

■ *Rooms* 15	*Confirm by* 6
en suite bath/shower 9	*Last dinner* 10
Direct dial Yes	*Parking* Ample
Room TV Yes	*Room service* 24 hours

Wife of Bath　　　　　　　　　　　　　　　Wye

R ⑬ & **Map 7 C5** Kent
　4 Upper Bridge Street
Wye (0233) 812540
Owner managers Brian Boots & Bob Johnson
Credit Access
　One of the old faithfuls, a homely restaurant
serving consistently enjoyable French country-
style dishes. Chef and part-owner Bob Johnson
offers plenty of good things on his fixed-price
menus: robust fish soup and garlicky fish tart;
lamb with a crust of anchovies and walnuts;
seasonal game; hazelnut meringue with apricot
purée; brown bread ice cream. There's a concise
list of good-quality wines. ⊖

■ *Set L & D* £14·90	*L* 12–2
About £40 *for two*	*D* 7–10
Seats 50 *Parties* 18	*Parking* Ample
Closed Sun, Mon & 1 wk Xmas	

Adlard's ★　　　　　　　　　　　Wymondham

R ★ ⑬ & **Map 6 C2** Norfolk
　16 Damgate Street
Wymondham (0953) 603533
　Two tiny rooms in a former butcher's shop
make a charmingly informal setting for the talents
of David Adlard, an outstanding exponent of
modern cuisine. Conception, execution and
presentation all shine, and marvellous sauces
feature in dishes like wild duck pâté en croûte
with turned pears and cinnamon sauce; or breast
of pheasant with a delicate yet deep-flavoured red
wine sauce. Other main course choices might be
roast rack of English lamb with a Madeira sauce,
served with a mousse of Jerusalem artichokes or
suprême of turbot with a mild Meaux mustard
sauce. Cheese or a green salad follows the main
course, and super sweets, delicious coffee and
home-made fudge round things off regally.
Excellent wines: note the Bourgogne Pinot Noir
from Michel Lafarge. David's wife Mary fronts the
house with charm and efficiency. Booking is

necessary. Smoking is discouraged. *Specialities*
warm local smoked salmon with a tart of softly
boiled quail eggs, rack of English lamb with
Madeira sauce, hazelnut and honey parfait with
praline sauce.

♀ **Well-chosen** ⊖

■ *Set D from* £15	*D only* 7.30–9
About £42 *for two*	*Parking* Ample
Seats 25	*Closed* Sun & Mon

Yattendon ▶

Royal Oak Hotel   Yattendon

IR **£D**
Map 5 D2 Berkshire
Nr Newbury RG16 0UF
Hermitage (0635) 201325
Owner managers Richard & Kate Smith
Credit Access, Amex, Visa

Richard and Kate Smith's charming old village
inn is an absolutely delightful place to stay. A log
fire and deep-cushioned sofas make the central
lounge an inviting spot, where guests can browse
in comfort through the newspapers and
magazines. The comfortable, rambling bar has a
rich, rustic appeal and offers superb bar snacks.
Antique-furnished bedrooms offer big,
comfortable beds, beautifully embroidered sheets
and many thoughtful extras. Bathrooms (all
private, three en suite) are equally well equipped.
Super breakfasts.
Amenities garden, laundry service.

■ *Rooms* 5	*Confirm by arrang.*
en suite bath/shower 3	*Last dinner* 10
Direct dial Yes	*Parking* Ample
Room TV Yes	*Room service* All day

Restaurant ★ ⊍ ♀

Richard Smith prepares his prime raw materials
with consistent skill and flair at this stylish little
restaurant. Recent delights have included a
faultless cheese soufflé sauced with wild wood

mushrooms, creamy mussel and prawn soup,
crispy duck with cherries and Armagnac, and a
rich honey and brandy ice cream with
butterscotch sauce. Good selection of British
farmhouse and French cheeses. Delicious little
savouries and excellent coffee served with super
chocolates. Intelligently chosen wines include
exciting burgundies (magnums of '81 Puligny
from Leflaive).
Specialities suprême of chicken with scallops,
oyster mushrooms and creamy curry sauce,
grilled kidneys and black pudding with green herb
mustard sauce, brioche with foie gras and wild
mushrooms.
♀ Well-chosen ⊖

■ *About £56 for two*	*L* 12.30–2
Seats 30 *Parties* 8	*D* 7.30–10
Closed D Sun & 3 wks late Jan–early Feb	

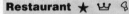

■ We publish annually, so make
sure you use the current
edition. It's worth it!

Moorland Links Hotel   Yelverton

H **64% £D/E**
Map 2 C3 Devon
Nr Plymouth PL20 6DA
Yelverton (0822) 852245. Tlx 45616
Manager Mr M. Jenkin
Credit Access, Amex, Diners, Visa

Peacefully situated on the edge of Dartmoor,
this is a popular hotel. Stylish bedrooms have
traditional furnishings, and hairdryers and trouser

presses are provided. Day rooms include split-
level bar. No dogs. *Amenities* garden, outdoor
swimming pool, tennis, laundry service, in-house
movies (free), helipad, 24-hour lounge service.

■ *Rooms* 30	*Confirm by arrang.*
en suite bath/shower 30	*Last dinner* 10
Direct dial Yes	*Parking* Ample
Room TV Yes	*Room service* 24 hours
Closed 25 Dec–1 Jan	

Little Barwick House   Yeovil

RR ♀ **Map 4 B3** Somerset
Barwick BA22 9TD
Yeovil (0935) 23902
Credit Access, Amex, Diners, Visa

Turn off the A37 opposite the Red House pub
for Barwick village and this Georgian dower
house. It's the home of Christopher and Veronica
Colley, and homeliness is one of its chief charms.
The handsome rich-red dining room enjoys
peaceful country views by day and is softly lit by
night. Veronica is a careful, enthusiastic chef, and
typical delights to be enjoyed include fish soup
with garlicky mayonnaise, whole wild duck with an

orange-zipped gravy, fillet steak plain or sauced
and a nice light syrupy treacle sponge.
♀ Well-chosen ⊖

■ *Set D* £13·60	*D only* 7–9
About £36 for two	*Parking* Ample
Seats 32 *Parties* 14	*Closed* 25 & 26 Dec

Bedrooms £D/E
Rooms 6   *With bath/shower* 6
Six rooms with TVs, cottage furnishings and lovely
views provide neat, comfortable accommodation.
Breakfasts include home-made preserves and
very good bread.

Manor Crest Hotel

H **59% £C/D**
Map 4 B3 Somerset
Hendford BA20 1TG
Yeovil (0935) 23116. Tlx 46580
Credit Access, Amex, Diners, Visa
 Near the town centre, this is a handsome
Georgian mansion with a modern extension for
accommodation. There's not really any original
character inside but high ceilings in the lounge

and bar are a reminder. Bedrooms vary in size and
shape; all have hessian-covered walls and
darkwood furniture, plus trouser presses and
radio-alarms. *Amenities* garden, laundry service,
24-hour lounge service.

■ *Rooms 42*	*Confirm by 6*
en suite bath/shower 42	*Last dinner 10*
Room phone Yes	*Parking Ample*
Room TV Yes	*Room service 24 hours*

■ Our inspectors never book in the
 name of Egon Ronay's Guides;
 they disclose their identity only
 after paying their bills.

Abbots Mews Hotel

H **56% £D/E**
Town plan B1 North Yorkshire
Marygate Lane YO3 7DE
York (0904) 34866. Tlx 57777
Owner managers Mr & Mrs Dearnley
Credit Access, Amex, Diners, Visa
 There's a cosy, relaxing feel to this modern,
family-run hotel, which stands in a quiet street a
few minutes' walk from the city centre. Some

bedrooms are in the main building, the rest in a
motel-style block across the garden. All rooms are
doubles, and decor is quite pretty. There's a little
bar-lounge and a garden lounge. No dogs.
Amenities garden, laundry service.

■ *Rooms 43*	*Confirm by 6*
en suite bath/shower 43	*Last dinner 9.30*
Direct dial Yes	*Parking Ample*
Room TV Yes	*Room service All day*

Dean Court Hotel

H **59% £C/D**
Town plan C1 North Yorkshire
Duncombe Place YO1 2EF
York (0904) 25082
Owner managers Ian & Kim Washington
Credit Access, Amex, Diners, Visa
 York Minster is the grand neighbour of this
converted Victorian house. Its lounges are homely
and traditional, and there are both a smart little

cocktail bar and a popular public. Light, bright
bedrooms have carpeted bathrooms. No dogs.
Amenities in-house movies (free), laundry service,
24-hour lounge service, coffee shop (10am–8pm).

■ *Rooms 36*	*Confirm by 6*
en suite bath/shower 36	*Last dinner 9*
Direct dial Yes	*Parking Difficult*
Room TV Yes	*Room service 24 hours*

Hill Hotel

H **59% £E**
Town plan A3 North Yorkshire
60 York Road, Acomb YO2 5LW
York (0904) 790777
Owner manager Mrs E. M. Haggan
Credit Access, Amex, Diners, Visa
 On a hilltop two miles from the city centre
stands this charming, family-run hotel with
Georgian facade. Public rooms are homely and

relaxing, the tiny bar being particularly cosy.
Bedrooms in traditional style are kept as neat as
ninepence. Two rooms have four-posters. No
dogs. *Amenities* garden, laundry service.

■ *Rooms 10*	*Confirm by arrang.*
en suite bath/shower 10	*Last dinner 8*
Direct dial Yes	*Parking Ample*
Room TV Yes	*Room service All day*
Closed 15 Dec–15 Jan	

Judges Lodging

H **69% £C/D**
Town plan B1 North Yorkshire
9 Lendal YO1 2AQ
York (0904) 38733. Tlx 57577
Owner manager Gerald Mason
Credit Amex, Diners, Visa
 Period charm and character are immediate
attractions of this splendid Georgian town house.
The entrance hall with its lofty ceiling and elegant

decor sets the scene for the rest of the house,
which has numerous delightful little lounges.
Stylish bedrooms (six with four-posters) have
many thoughtful extras. *Amenities* in-house
movies, laundry service, 24 hour lounge service.

■ *Rooms 14*	*Confirm by arrang.*
en suite bath/shower 14	*Last dinner 10.30*
Direct dial Yes	*Parking Ample*
Room TV Yes	*Room service 24 hours*

F
I
A
T

F
I
A
T

YORK

Map 15 C6
Town plan opposite

Population 99,910

A northern bastion and trading town from Roman times, in the 8th century York became a religious and learning centre, although the present university is twenty-four years old. York's medieval wealth came from wool and monasteries, its modern prosperity from the advent of the railway, chocolate factories and tourists. Architectural gems blend the Middle Ages, pre-Reformation churches and the 18th century.

Annual Events
York Races *10th–12th May, 10th & 11th June, 8th & 9th July, 16th–18th & 31st August, 1st September, 5th, 6th & 8th October*
York Early Music Festival *July*
Historic Vehicle Rally, *Knavesmine, 11th September*

Sights Outside City
Castle Howard, Fountains Abbey, Ripley Castle, Harewood House, Knaresborough, Newby Hall (Boroughbridge), Kirkham Priory

Information Centre
De Grey Rooms, Exhibition Square, York YO1 2HB
Telephone York 21756/7

1 Art Gallery *English and European* B1
2 Castle Folk Museum *unique reconstruction of period street and interiors* C3
3 Clifford's Tower *13th-c keep* C2/3
4 Guildhall and Mansion House C2
5 Impressions Gallery of Photography C2
6 Tourist Information Centre C1
7 Jorvik Viking Centre C2
8 King's Manor *home of monks and kings* B1
9 Merchant's Adventurers' Hall *timbered medieval Guild Hall* C2
10 Merchant's Taylor's Hall *14th-c tailors' livery* C1
11 Minister *chief glory of York* C1
12 Racecourse A3
13 Railriders World *model railway exhibition* B2
14 National Railway Museum *Britain's chief collection* A1/2
15 St Mary's Abbey *ruins* B1
16 Shambles *derived from 'Fleshammels' meaning 'street butchers'* C2
17 Station A/B2
18 Theatre Royal B/C1
19 Treasurer's House *mainly 17th-c valuable furniture and pictures* C1
20 University *modern architectural interest* E3
21 Waxwork Museum C2
22 York Story *exhibition of York's history and architecture* C2
23 Yorkshire Museum *archaeology, natural history* B1

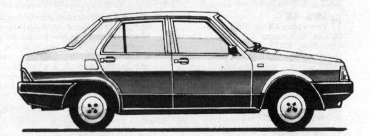

York FIAT

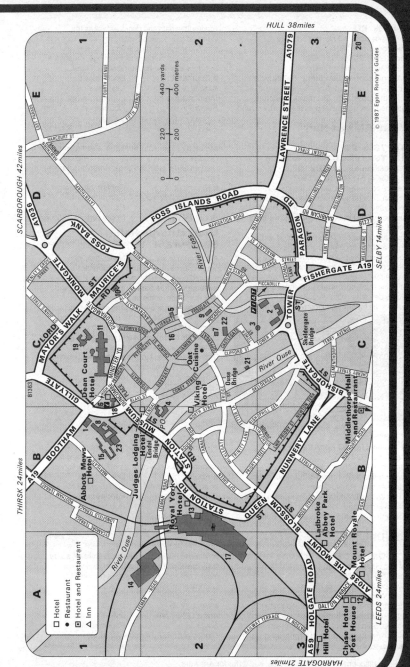

Ladbroke Abbey Park Hotel   York

H **59% £C**
Town plan A3 North Yorkshire
The Mount YO2 2BN
York (0904) 58301. Tlx 57993
Credit Access, Amex, Diners, Visa
  A good stopover just outside the city walls.
Attractively coordinated bedrooms come in two
main categories: Gold Star rooms are better
equipped, having trouser presses, hairdryers and

various little eats and drinks as well as the
standard tea-makers. Seating in the day rooms is
mostly confined to the bar and little foyer, as the
lounge is used primarily for meetings. *Amenities*
laundry service, in-house movies (charge).

■ *Rooms 84*	*Confirm by 6*
en suite bath/shower 84	*Last dinner 9.15*
Direct dial Yes	*Parking Limited*
Room TV Yes	*Room service 24 hours*

Middlethorpe Hall   York

HR **78% £B**
Town plan C3 North Yorkshire
Bishopsthorpe Road YO12 1QP
York (0904) 641241. Tlx 578802
Credit Access, Amex, Diners, Visa
  Set in 27 acres of grounds and overlooking York
racecourse, this elegant William III country house
has been very skilfully converted into a superb
hotel. Period décor, furnishings and pictures
evoke an atmosphere of great comfort and well-
being, and flower displays grace the relaxing day
rooms. The finely-proportioned lounge has inviting
deep-cushioned sofas and armchairs. A carved
oak staircase climbs to the beautifully decorated
main-house bedrooms and both these and the
equally delightful rooms in outbuildings have
period-style furniture and many thoughtful extras

and pretty ornaments. Sumptuous bathrooms.
Excellent breakfasts with plenty of choice. No
children under eight. No dogs. *Amenities* garden,
croquet, laundry service.

■ *Rooms 31*	*Confirm by arrang.*
en suite bath/shower 31	*Last dinner 9.45*
Direct dial Yes	*Parking Ample*
Room TV Yes	*Room service 24 hours*

Middlethorpe Hall Restaurant ♔

A comfortable, elegant ambience has been
created for savouring Aidan McCormack's
assured cooking in the modern style. Presentation
is attractive, ingredients are of high quality and
flavours subtle (sometimes almost elusive). A
typical menu may include pheasant and pistachio
pâté or mille feuille of wild mushrooms, plaited
salmon and turbot, best end of lamb with
mushroom cream sauce and a courgette and
tomato gâteau; finish with a feather-light
Drambuie soufflé. Jackets and ties and booking
essential. ♀ Well-chosen ⊖

■ *Set L £12*	*L 12.30–2*
Set D from £19·50	*D 7.30–9.45*
About £55 for two	*Seats 100 Parties 40*

Mount Royale Hotel   York

H **69% £D/E**
Town plan A3 North Yorkshire
The Mount YO2 2DA
York (0904) 28856. Tlx 57414
Owner managers Richard & Christine Oxtoby
Credit Access, Amex, Diners, Visa
  Two William IV houses were merged to make
this really delightful hotel, which the Oxtobys have
filled with ornaments, pictures and fine furniture.

The panelled bar is particularly cosy, and there
are two restful lounges. Comfortable bedrooms,
too, are traditionally styled. No dogs. *Amenities*
garden, outdoor swimming pool, laundry service.

■ *Rooms 17*	*Confirm by 6*
en suite bath/shower 17	*Last dinner 9.15*
Direct dial Yes	*Parking Limited*
Room TV Yes	*Room service All day*
Closed 3 wks Xmas	

Oat Cuisine *NEW ENTRY*   York

R **Town plan C2** North Yorkshire
13a High Ousegate
York (0904) 27929
Owner manager Louisa Farino
Credit Access, Amex, Visa
  Elegant and modern in black and white this city-
centre restaurant offers excellent vegetarian
cooking. Start perhaps with courgette roulade or
spinach mousseline with red pepper sauce, and

proceed to enchiladas with mozzarella, or a very
tasty cashew nut and mushroom slice with a
mushroom and sherry sauce. Super sweets.
Friendly staff. ⊖

■ *Set L £7·25*	*L 12–3*
About £25 for two	*D 7–11*
Seats 56	*Parking Difficult*
Closed Sun, 25 & 26 Dec & 1st wk Jan	

■ For a discount on next year's guide, see Offer for Answers.

Post House Hotel   York

H **63% £C**
Town plan A3 North Yorkshire
Tadcaster Road YO2 2QF
York (0904) 707921. Tlx 57798
Credit Access, Amex, Diners, Visa
  Public rooms at this modern hotel on the A1036
are built round a central lawn on which stands a
magnificent old cedar. Picture windows make
things bright and airy, and the lounge (with all-day

snack service) and bar roomy and relaxing.
Bedrooms are of a decent size and nicely
maintained; all have tea-making facilities, with
fresh milk in the mini-bars. No dogs.
Amenities garden, putting, laundry service.
■ *Rooms* 147   *Confirm by 6*
en suite bath/shower 147 Last dinner 10
Direct dial Yes   *Parking Ample*
Room TV Yes   *Room service 24 hours*

Royal York Hotel   York

H **67% £C/D** ⌕
Town plan B2 North Yorkshire
Station Road YO2 2AA
York (0904) 653681. Tlx 57912
Manager Robin MacGilchrist
Credit Access, Amex, Diners, Visa
  Refurbishment here has been elegantly done.
The main hall features pillars and a fine staircase,
and there are two bars, one in the basement.

Good-sized bedrooms include some de luxe and
executive rooms with stylish mahogany
furnishings. *Amenities* garden, keep-fit
equipment, putting, hairdressing, laundry service,
coffee shop (10am–9pm), 24-hour lounge service.
■ *Rooms* 140   *Confirm by arrang.*
en suite bath/shower 140 Last dinner 9.45
Direct dial Yes   *Parking Ample*
Room TV Yes   *Room service 24 hours*

Swallow Chase Hotel   York

H **59% £D**
Town plan A3 North Yorkshire
Tadcaster Road, Dringhouses YO2 2QQ
York (0904) 701000. Tlx 57582
Credit Access, Amex, Diners, Visa
  Practical overnight accommodation is offered
at this white-painted hotel on the A1036 just
outside the city. Bedrooms are a decent size and
furnished in traditional, unfussy style. Public areas

include a cheerful, comfortable bar. No dogs.
Amenities garden, golf practice net, laundry
service, 24-hour lounge service.

■ *Rooms 80*   *Confirm by 6*
en suite bath/shower 80   Last dinner 8.45
Room phone Yes   *Parking Ample*
Room TV Yes   *Room service 24 hours*
Closed 2 days Xmas

Viking Hotel   York

H **71% £C** *E*
Town plan C2 North Yorkshire
North Street YO1 1JF
York (0904) 59822. Tlx 57937
Credit Access, Amex, Diners, Visa. **LVs**
  A tallish modern hotel with its own moorings on
the river Ouse. The convenient central location
means that the city's main sights are within easy
walking distance. Inside, the revamped foyer
incorporates a large and comfortable lounge area.
Other public rooms all with river views include the
stylish and popular Regatta Bar on the first floor.
The leisure centre is particularly well equipped,
offering extras like a massage room and health
bar. Bedrooms in the older block have been
attractively refurbished, some in pale pastel
shades of blue, others in richer burgundy and
peach; many rooms in the newer block have

private balconies. Compact, well-fitted bathrooms
throughout. *Amenities* sauna, solarium, whirlpool
bath, gymnasium, in-house movies (charge),
laundry service.
■ *Rooms 188*   *Confirm by 6*
en suite bath/shower 188 Last dinner 10
Direct dial Yes   *Parking Limited*
Room TV Yes   *Room service 24 hours*

Satis House   Yoxford

H **63% £E**
Map 6 D2 Suffolk
Saxmundham 1P17 3EX
Yoxford (072 877) 418
Owner managers Vicki & John Bench
Credit Access, Amex, Diners, Visa
  A charming converted Georgian house run with
care and thought. Guests can relax in the bar or
lofty lounge. Spacious, characterful bedrooms

include two with splendid half-testers and giant
Edwardian bathtubs; extras range from fresh fruit
to state-of-the-art telephones. No under 14 s. No
dogs. *Amenities* garden, sauna, solarium,
whirlpool bath, keep-fit equipment.
■ *Rooms 7*   *Confirm by arrang.*
en suite bath/shower 7 Last dinner 9
Direct dial Yes   *Parking Ample*
Room TV Yes   *Room service All day*

HOTELS
RESTAURANTS
AND INNS

SCOTLAND

Ardoe House Hotel   Aberdeen

H 64% £D/E
Map 17 D4 Grampian
South Deeside Road AB1 5YP
Aberdeen (0224) 867555
Owner manager Mr McKenzie-Smith
Credit Access, Amex, Diners, Visa
    A sturdy granite mansion, set in peaceful grounds. The lobby-lounge boasts a magnificent central staircase and impressive stained glass

window. Eight small, simple bedrooms have washbasins and shower cubicles; remaining rooms vary in style but all have tea-makers, radio-alarms, trouser presses and en suite bathrooms. *Amenities* garden, game fishing.

■ *Rooms* 21	*Confirm by arrang.*
en suite bath/shower 13	*Last dinner* 9.30
Direct dial Yes	*Parking* Ample
Room TV Yes	*Room service* All day

Atlantis   Aberdeen

R **Map 17 D4** Grampian
145 Crown Street
Aberdeen (0224) 591 403
Owner manager David Edwards
Credit Access, Amex, Diners, Visa
    Ian Wilson's good seafood cooking brings visitors in shoals to this friendly basement restaurant. Oysters, mussels, garlicky crab claws and seafood terrine are popular starters, and main

courses include lobster, sole and salmon, Mediterranean prawns and pillows of turbot with a light creamed leek stuffing. One or two meaty things, but it's mainly the delights of the deep. The owner and a cheerful waitress serve. ℮

■ *About £48 for two*	*L* 12–2
Seats 35	*D* 6–10
Closed L Sat & all Sun,	*Parking* Limited
Bank Hols & 10 days Xmas	

Bucksburn Moat House   Aberdeen

H 73% £C/D
Map 17 D4 Grampian
Oldmeldrum Road, Bucksburn AB2 9LN
Aberdeen (0224) 713911. Tlx 73108
Credit Access, Amex, Diners, Visa
    A 17th-century grain mill is incorporated into the design of this modern hotel and accounts for its distinctive, somewhat esoteric building style. The foyer-lounge is smart and comfortable, with dark-tan leather chesterfields and a pleasant view of the indoor pool. There are two bars and excellent conference facilities. Spacious bedrooms with twin double beds and practical units offer radio-alarms, hairdryers, trouser presses and – a rare treat – bathroom speaker extensions for both radio and TV. The hotel stands four miles from the centre of town and two miles from the airport. *Amenities* indoor swimming pool, keep-fit

equipment, hairdressing, in-house movies, laundry service, 24-hour lounge service, courtesy coach.

■ *Rooms* 98	*Confirm by arrang.*
en suite bath/shower 98	*Last dinner* 10.30
Room phone Yes	*Parking* Ample
Room TV Yes	*Room service* 24 hours

■ Any person using our name
to obtain free hospitality is
a fraud. Proprietors, please
inform the police and us.

Caledonian Thistle Hotel   Aberdeen

H 67% £C/D
Map 17 D4 Grampian
Union Terrace AB9 1HE
Aberdeen (0224) 640233. Tlx 73758
Credit Access, Amex, Diners, Visa. LVs
    A well-run city centre hotel with a mock Regency theme throughout the smart public rooms. The well-equipped standard bedrooms have desks, comfortable chairs, darkwood

furniture and modern bathrooms and there are more luxurious executive rooms with soft colour schemes, as well as two elegant suites and compact single rooms. *Amenities* sauna, solarium, laundry service, in-house movies.

■ *Rooms* 80	*Confirm by* 6
en suite bath/shower 80	*Last dinner* 10
Direct dial Yes	*Parking* Limited
Room TV Yes	*Room service* 24 hours

Copthorne Hotel   Aberdeen

H **71% £C/D E**
Map 17 D4 Grampian
122 Huntly Street AB1 1SU
Aberdeen (0224) 630404. Tlx 739707
Credit Access, Amex, Diners, Visa. LVs

Only the facade of this building hints at its
origins as an old warehouse, so skilful was its
conversion seven years ago. The split-level
reception area and lounge has limited seating –
it's a good meeting and greeting place but not
suitable for lingering conversations. The Boodles
Bar is more roomy and there's a quiet cocktail bar
area attached to the restaurant. Spacious
bedrooms are well equipped. All have double
beds and en suite tiled bathrooms. Extras include
remote-control TVs, radio alarms, direct-dial
telephones, tea-makers, trouser presses and
hairdryers. Staff are plentiful and pleasant and

there's an atmosphere of quiet efficiency.
Amenities in-house movies (free), laundry service,
24-hour lounge service.

■ *Rooms* 67	*Confirm by arrang.*
en suite bath/shower 67	*Last dinner* 10
Direct dial Yes	*Parking* Limited
Room TV Yes	*Room service* 24 hours

Stakis Tree Tops Hotel   Aberdeen

H **62% £C**
Map 17 D4 Grampian
161 Springfield Road AB9 2QH
Aberdeen (0224) 33377. Tlx 73794
Credit Access, Amex, Diners, Visa. LVs

A well-designed leisure centre and a new wing
of bedrooms are the latest developments at this
popular hotel on the outskirts of Aberdeen. The
leafy lobby-lounge and club-like bar have a good
welcoming feel, but by comparison the first-floor
residents' lounge is rather soulless. The steak bar
has been converted into an Italian-style coffee
shop and restaurant. Smart, well-equipped

bedrooms range from singles to family rooms and
suites. Twenty rooms are designated for non-
smokers and there are five prettily appointed
Ladies' rooms. *Amenities* garden, indoor
swimming pool, sauna, solarium, whirlpool bath,
keep-fit equipment, tennis, in-house movies (free),
laundry service, coffee shop (11am–11pm), 24-
hour lounge service, children's playground.

■ *Rooms* 114.	*Confirm by* 6
en suite bath/shower 114	*Last dinner* 10.30
Direct dial Yes	*Parking* Ample
Room TV Yes	*Room service* 24 hours

Swallow Imperial Hotel   Aberdeen

H **56% £D/E**
Map 17 D4 Grampian
Stirling Street AB9 2JY
Aberdeen (0224) 589101. Tlx 73365
Credit Access, Amex, Diners, Visa. LVs

Usefully situated between station and shopping
area, this solid old stone building wins no first
prizes. But 54 Club rooms have been refurbished
to an acceptable level, with pastel decor and well-

equipped bathrooms. Other rooms, though clean,
are furnished and equipped to a lower standard.
There are two bars and limited lounge space in
the foyer. *Amenities* in-house movies (charge),
laundry service, 24-hour lounge service.

■ *Rooms* 109	*Confirm by arrang.*
en suite bath/shower 82	*Last dinner* 9.30
Direct dial Yes	*Parking* Difficult
Room TV Yes	*Room service* 24 hours

Holiday Inn   Aberdeen

H **75% £C E &**
Map 17 D4 Grampian
Riverview Drive AB2 0AZ
Aberdeen (0224) 770011. Tlx 739651
Credit Access, Amex, Diners, Visa. LVs

A well-planned hotel conveniently close to the
airport, just off the A947, yet quiet and relaxing.
Public areas include a restful lounge with
comfortable seating and a stylish cocktail bar.
Standard bedrooms are large, with good lighting
and fully tiled bathrooms; Club Europe rooms
have a higher standard of luxury, including
telephones in the bathrooms, while King Leisure
rooms have king-sized beds and a smart sitting
area. All the rooms have spyholes in the doors
and card key security locks. Friendly staff. Very
disappointing breakfast. *Amenities* indoor
swimming pool, sauna, solarium, whirlpool bath,

gymnasium, laundry service, coffee shop
(6.30am–11pm), in-house movies (free & charge),
24-hour lounge service.

■ *Rooms* 154	*Confirm by* 6
en suite bath/shower 154	*Last dinner* 10.30
Direct dial Yes	*Parking* Ample
Room TV Yes	*Room service* 24 hours

Aberdeen Airport ▶

Skean Dhu Hotel Aberdeen Airport — Aberdeen Airport

H **65% £C/D**
Map 17 D4 Grampian
Argyll Road, Dyce AB2 0DU
Aberdeen (0224) 725252. Tlx 739239
Credit Access, Amex, Diners, Visa. LVs
Glass chandeliers, marble pillars and deep settees adorn the spacious foyer-lounge and ballroom of this modern airport hotel. Decent-sized, sound-proofed bedrooms, each have a trouser-press, hairdryer and writing desk. *Amenities* garden, outdoor swimming pool, in-house movies (charge), laundry service, coffee shop (Mon–Fri 6am–11pm, Sat & Sun from 8am), 24-hour lounge service, transport for airport.

■ *Rooms* 148   *Confirm by* 6
en suite bath/shower 148   *Last dinner* 10
Direct dial Yes   *Parking* Ample
Room TV Yes   *Room service* 24 hours

Skean Dhu Hotel Dyce — Aberdeen Airport

H **61% £D/E**
Map 17 D4 Grampian
Farburn Terrace AB2 0DW
Aberdeen (0224) 723101. Tlx 73473
Credit Access, Amex, Diners, Visa. LVs
The unassuming exterior of this hotel off the A947 belies its standard of accommodation in separate blocks away from the day rooms. Well-equipped bedrooms range from spacious deluxe rooms – some attractively refurbished – with two double beds to more compact singles. *Amenities* sauna, solarium, gymnasium, squash, in-house movies, coffee shop (11am–11pm), 24-hour lounge service, airport coach, helipad.

■ *Rooms* 220   *Confirm by* 6
en suite bath/shower 220   *Last dinner* 9.45
Direct dial Yes   *Parking* Ample
Room TV Yes   *Room service* 24 hours

Summer Isles Hotel — Achiltibuie

HR **62% £D/E**
Map 16 B2 Highland
By Ullapool IV26 2YG
Achiltibuie (085 482) 282
Owner managers Mark & Geraldine Irvine
The wonderful views of the Summer Isles are a major inducement to visit this civilised, relaxing hotel. Bright, cheerful bedrooms, including some in a log-cabin annexe, offer basic comforts and no frills, and day rooms include a pleasant lounge, comfortable TV room and cosy cocktail bar. No children under eight. *Amenities* garden, game fishing, hotel boats.

■ *Rooms* 13   *Confirm by* arrang.
en suite bath/shower 12   *Last dinner* 7.30
Room phone No   *Parking* Ample
Room TV No   *Room service* None
Closed mid Oct–Easter

Summer Isles Hotel Restaurant

Dinner, which starts at 7.30 sharp, is prepared almost exclusively from local or home produce, including organically grown vegetables, herbs and fruit. The set menu offers no choices in the first three courses and begins with a soup such as fish, fennel, sorrel or carrot and tarragon, followed perhaps by mussels in white wine, scallops in saffron, or Stilton soufflé; the centrepiece could be roast duck, saddle of lamb, or loin of veal with wood mushrooms. Sweets from the trolley and a selection from the cheeseboard complete the meal. The wine list provides exceptional value. ☺

■ *Set D* £19   *D only at* 7.30
About £50 *for two*   *Seats* 28
Closed mid Oct–Easter   *Parties* 8

Tulchan Lodge — Advie

H **82% £A**
Map 16 C3 Highland
Nr Grantown-on-Spey PH26 3PW
Advie (080 75) 200. Tlx 75405
A sporting hotel par excellence, with superb shooting and eight miles of beats on the salmon-rich Spey. Non-sportsmen are also very welcome, and the vast estate and surrounding countryside provide marvellous walks and glorious scenery. Inside, all is immensely civilised, and the day rooms feature an outstanding collection of antiques, paintings and firearms. Space, fine furnishings and stylish fabrics characterise the bedrooms, and the bathrooms are equally luxurious, with handsome fittings, huge bath towels and top-quality toiletries. Splendid breakfasts are laid out in silver dishes on a sideboard in the dining room. Service and

housekeeping shine. Kennels available.
Amenities garden, tennis, shooting, game fishing, deer stalking, snooker, valeting, laundry service.

■ *Rooms* 11   *Confirm by* arrang.
en suite bath/shower 11   *Last dinner* by arrang.
Direct dial Yes   *Parking* Ample
Room TV On request   *Room service* All day
Closed Feb–mid Apr

Airth Castle Hotel · Airth

H 68% £D
Map 17 C5 Central
Nr Falkirk FK2 8JF
Falkirk (0324) 83411. Tlx 777975
Credit Access, Amex, Diners, Visa

An ancient turreted castle overlooking the
fertile Forth Valley was converted into this
luxurious hotel. Traditional appeal is offered in the
elegant lounge, the atmospheric Dungeon Bar
and the Regency restaurant. Bedrooms are
prettily decorated and thoughtfully equipped. No
dogs. *Amenities* garden, indoor swimming pool,
sauna, solarium, whirlpool bath, keep-fit
equipment, snooker, laundry service, satellite TV.

■ *Rooms* 47	*Confirm by arrang.*
en suite bath/shower 47	*Last dinner* 9.45
Direct dial Yes	*Parking* Ample
Room TV Yes	*Room service* 24 hours

Burns Byre Restaurant *NEW ENTRY* · Alloway

R ঠ Map 12 B3 Strathclyde
Mount Oliphant Farm
Alloway (0292) 43644
Credit Access, Amex, Diners, Visa. **LVs**

Robert Burns lived his teenage years at Mount
Oliphant Farm, whose cattle byre is now a
charming restaurant. Fresh produce, much of it
from the farm, is put to excellent use by chef
Craig Robertson, who offers tasty delights like
poached or oak-smoked salmon from the Doon,
pâté-stuffed pheasant and splendid medallions of
venison served with a red wine and rose-hip syrup
sauce. ℮

■ *Set L* £6·25	*L* 12–2.30
About £35 for two	*D* 7–9.30
Seats 40	*Parking* Ample
Closed Tues (exc. in summer) & 1 Jan	

Altnaharra Hotel *NEW ENTRY* · Altnaharra

H 55% £E
Map 16 B2 Highland
By Lairg Sutherland IV27 4UE
Owner managers Mr & Mrs P. Panchaud
Credit Access

Standing in beautiful, rugged country this one-
time coaching inn is now primarily a fishing hotel.
The charming owners are improving the look of
the place; the foyer boasts new carpets and some
nice reproduction furniture. Modestly appointed
bedrooms will also gradually be revamped.
There's a two-bedroom suite in an adjacent
cottage. *Amenities* garden, game fishing.

■ *Rooms* 21	*Confirm by arrang.*
en suite bath/shower 9	*Last dinner* 8.30
Room phone No	*Parking* Ample
Room TV No	*Room service* None
Closed Dec & Jan	

Lands of Loyal Hotel · Alyth

H 61% £E
Map 17 C4 Tayside
By Blairgowrie PH11 8JQ
Alyth (082 83) 3151
Owner managers Ian & Jaki Rennie
Credit Access, Amex, Visa

Ian and Jaki Rennie are relative newcomers to
the hotel business, but they are making a
splendid start in this fine Victorian mansion. Open
fires burn in all the public areas, including the
central hall with impressive glass-domed ceiling
and carved oak gallery. Bedrooms, some
traditionally furnished, some modern, are well
kept. *Amenities* garden, putting.

■ *Rooms* 14	*Confirm by arrang.*
en suite bath/shower 6	*Last dinner* 9
Direct dial Yes	*Parking* Ample
Room TV No	*Room service* All day

■ Our inspectors are our full-
time employees; they are
professionally trained by us.

Cellar Restaurant · Anstruther

R ঔ Map 17 D5 Fife
24 East Green
Anstruther (0333) 310378
Credit Access, Amex, Visa

Peter Jukes' talented cooking is developing a
justifiable reputation, so booking is essential at his
atmospheric cottage near the harbour. The
seafood is garnered from all over Scotland and
used to excellent effect in the imaginative daily
menus. Don't miss the rich crayfish bisque.
Sweets include a faultless crème brûlée. Good
wine list offering real value for money with a dozen
fine Chablis. ♀ **Well-chosen** ℮

■ *Set D from £15*	*L* 12.30–1.30
(winter £9·95)	*D* 7–9
About £40 for two	*Parking* Ample
Seats 32	*Closed* L Mon, all Sun,
Bank Hols, 1 wk May & 3 days Xmas	

Craw's Nest Hotel — Anstruther

H 59% £D/E ♿
Map 17 D5 Fife
Bankwell Road KY10 3DA
Anstruther (0333) 310691
Owner managers Clarke family
Credit Access, Amex, Diners, Visa

An unpretentious, family-run hotel, which is a much-extended manse with a busy and friendly atmosphere. The main bar is large and bright and there is an intimate cocktail bar. Practical bedrooms (19 in an extension) have darkwood units, attractively coordinated fabrics and neat bath/shower rooms. No dogs. *Amenities* garden, solarium, games room, pool table, laundry service.

■ *Rooms* 50	*Confirm by* arrang.
en suite bath/shower 50	*Last dinner* 8.45
Direct dial Yes	*Parking* Ample
Room TV Yes	*Room service* All day

■ We welcome complaints and bona fide recommendations on the tear-out pages for readers' comments. They are followed up by our professional team. Please also complain to the management instantly.

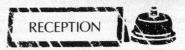

RECEPTION

Ardentinny Hotel — Ardentinny

H 59% £D/E
Map 17 B5 Strathclyde
Loch Long PA23 8TR
Ardentinny (036 981) 209
Owner managers Mr & Mrs J. Horn & Hazel Hall
Credit Access, Amex, Diners, Visa

Deer stalking can be arranged at this charming little hotel beside Loch Long. There's a homely TV lounge, and two nautical-style bars with splendid views. Simply appointed bedrooms – four with TVs – have adequate bath/shower rooms. *Amenities* garden, sea & game fishing, mooring, hotel boat, pool table.

■ *Rooms* 11	*Confirm by* 6
en suite bath/shower 11	*Last dinner* 9
Room phone No	*Parking* Ample
Room TV Some	*Room service* All day
Closed end Oct–mid Mar	

Firpark Hotel — Ardnadam

H 60% £F
Map 17 B5 Strathclyde
By Dunoon PA23 8QG
Dunoon (0369) 6506
Owner manager Pat Lamont
Credit Visa

A converted Victorian hotel overlooking the Holy Loch. It's run with cheerful efficiency and used as a base by the local sailing club, whose photographs decorate the bar. There's a nice old-world feel to the lounge, a minstrels' gallery and leather chesterfields recall the days when this was a fine private house. Variously-furnished bedrooms are well maintained. *Amenities* garden.

■ *Rooms* 6	*Confirm by* arrang.
en suite bath/shower 2	*Last dinner* 9
Room phone No	*Parking* Ample
Room TV Yes	*Room service* All day

Loch Melfort Hotel — Arduaine

HR 60% £D/E
Map 17 B5 Strathclyde
Nr Oban PA34 4XG
Kilmelford (085 22) 233
Owner managers Colin & Jane Tindal
Credit Access.

Splendid sea views are popular with yachtsmen at the Tindals' welcoming hotel between Oban and Lochgilphead. Bright, homely day rooms include an airy little lounge, cheerful bar and a new residents' lounge. Bedrooms, some in an extension, are mostly in simple modern style. *Amenities* garden, laundry service, kiosk.

■ *Rooms* 26	*Confirm by* arrang.
en suite bath/shower 23	*Last dinner* 8.30
Room phone No	*Parking* Ample
Room TV No	*Room service* Limited
Closed mid Oct–Easter	

Loch Melfort Hotel Restaurant ♀ ♿

Capable, straightforward cooking and sensibly short menus make for enjoyable meals at this light and pretty restaurant overlooking Loch Melfort. Home-made tomato soup and local jumbo prawns with mayonnaise are typical of the simple starters, while main courses might include pigeon and beef casserole or salmon, turbot and prawns in a pastry case served with Noilly Prat sauce. Tempting sweets like Dutch apple pudding or blackberry pavlova to finish. ☺
♀ Well-chosen

■ *Set D* £14·50	*L* 12.30–2
About £35 *for two*	*D* 7.15–8.30
Seats 55	

🍷 is our symbol for an **outstanding** wine list.

Arisaig House   Arisaig

HR **75% £B**
Map 17 A4 Highland
Beasdale PH39 4NR
Arisaig (068 75) 622. Tlx 777279
Owner managers Smither & Wilkinson families
Credit Access, Visa

Delightful gardens and woods that reach down
to Loch nan Uamh provide the splendid setting for
this listed 19th-century mansion. A style of
restrained elegance links the day rooms; the
gracefully-traditional drawing room has much
appeal with its open fireplace and bay windows.
The morning room and inner hall have rug-strewn
polished floors; the bar has smart, contemporary
styling. Spacious, attractive bedrooms have
period furniture, and nice touches like fresh

flowers and ornaments, as well as excellent
carpeted bathrooms. Half-board terms only. No
children under ten. No dogs. *Amenities* garden,
croquet, billiards, snooker, laundry service.
- ■ Rooms 14   Confirm by 6
- en suite bath/shower 13   Last dinner 8.30
- Direct dial Yes   Parking Ample
- Room TV Yes   Room service All day
- Closed Nov–1 wk before Easter

Arisaig House
Restaurant ☙ ♀

Polished silver and quality glassware set the tone
at this discreetly-luxurious restaurant. David
Wilkinson's fixed-price dinner menus now offer a
selection of alternative dishes. Light cheese
beignets or mussels with saffron and cream
followed by courgette and almond soup might
precede sliced duck breast and orange or
scallops with a white butter sauce, all carefully
cooked and well presented. Home-made ices to
finish. Non-smoking area. 🍷
- ■ Set D £20   L 12.30–2
- About £55 for two   D 7.30–8.30
- Seats 30   Parties 8
- Closed Nov–1 wk before Easter

■ If we recommend meals in a
hotel or inn, a separate entry is
made for its restaurant.

Auchterarder House   Auchterarder

HR **72% £B/C**
Map 17 C5 Tayside
PH3 1DZ
Auchterarder (076 46) 3646
Owner manager Ian Brown
Credit Access, Amex, Diners, Visa

Standing in 17 acres of lovely mature gardens,
this Victorian country house is a hotel of
considerable character, charm and individuality.
Ring the bell, and you'll be personally welcomed
into the handsome marble-floored entrance hall;
enjoy a drink in the billiards room with its black-
timbered vaulted ceiling, or relax in the panelled
library or the delightful conservatory. Bedrooms
are spacious, elegant and thoughtfully equipped,

and several boast fine antique wardrobes. Good
private bathrooms include one with splendid
original fittings. Efficient staff make you feel
thoroughly at home, and a good breakfast starts
the day well. No children under ten.
Amenities garden, golf practice net, croquet.
- ■ Rooms 11   Confirm by arrang.
- en suite bath/shower 11   Last dinner 10.30
- Direct dial Yes   Parking Ample
- Room TV Yes   Room service All day

Auchterarder House
Restaurant ☙ ♀ ♿

Non-residents must book to enjoy Paul Brown's
capable cooking in this handsomely furnished
room. Loch Fyne mussels, sautéed chicken livers
or tomato soup with basil could precede saddle of
hare with grapes, or maybe veal escalope with a
light yoghurt sauce. Copious medium-cooked
vegetables, well-kept cheeses, decent sweets.
On the whole, simplest choices work best.
Interesting wines include delicious Bourgogne
Rouge La Fortune (A. de Villaine). 🍷
- ■ Set L £12.50   L 12–3
- Set D from £15.50   D 7–10.30
- About £60 for two   Seats 23 Parties 50

Gleneagles Hotel

H 88% £A &
Map 17 C5 Tayside
PH3 1NF
Auchterarder (076 46) 2231. Tlx 76105
Credit Access, Amex, Diners, Visa

Built on the grand scale in 1924, this renowned hotel stands in superb countryside and boasts four championship golf courses. The leisure facilities are unrivalled, and other services include shops, a bank and a post office. Space and elegance are keynotes in the public areas, particularly the classically-pillared drawing room (afternoon teas, evening dancing) and the glittering ballroom. At the top of the hotel, the library is a peaceful hideaway for a browse or quiet drink. Well-equipped bedrooms, several with four-posters, are also generally very spacious, with fine fabrics, handsome furnishings and splendidly fitted bathrooms. Housekeeping is excellent, staff friendly and very good at their jobs. *Amenities* garden, indoor swimming pool, sauna, solarium, whirlpool bath, gymnasium, beauty salon, hairdressing, tennis, squash, golf courses, putting, pitch & putt, bowling green, croquet, clay-pigeon shooting, game fishing, snooker, in-house movies, valeting, laundry service, shopping arcade.

■ *Rooms* 254	*Confirm by* arrang.
en suite bath/shower 254	*Last dinner* 11
Direct dial Yes	*Parking* Ample
Room TV Yes	*Room service* 24 hours

Old Mansion House Hotel

HR 68% £D
Map 17 C5 Tayside
Near Dundee DD3 0QN
Auchterhouse (082 626) 366
Owner managers Nigel & Eva Bell
Credit Access, Amex, Diners, Visa

A distinguished Jacobean manor house in a lovely country setting. The flagstoned hall sets a dignified tone, and the bar-lounge and patio bar are nice spots to unwind with a dram. Bedrooms are spacious and well furnished. *Amenities* outdoor swimming pool, tennis, squash, croquet, in-house movies (free), laundry service. &

■ *Rooms* 6	*Confirm by* arrang.
en suite bath/shower 6	*Last dinner* 9.30
Room phone Yes	*Parking* Ample
Room TV Yes	*Room service* All day
Closed 25 Dec–2 Jan	

Old Mansion House Hotel Restaurant ♔

French and Scottish elements combine in the cooking at this elegant restaurant which has a fine moulded ceiling and grand Jacobean fireplace. Mussel chowder, chicken liver pâté, langoustines Lucullus and collops in the pan typify the choice. Fresh fruit features in most of the desserts. There are good burgundies on a well-selected wine list. Service is pleasant and attractive. Table d'hôte Sunday lunch. &

■ *Set L* £10·50	*L* 12–2
About £50 *for two*	*D* 7–9.30,
Seats 40 *Parties* 20	*Sun* 7–8.30
Closed 25 Dec–2 Jan	

Post House Hotel

H 62% £C/D
Map 17 C4 Highland
Aviemore Centre PH22 1PJ
Aviemore (0479) 810771
Credit Access, Amex, Diners, Visa

Day rooms are quite extensive at this smart modern hotel: on the ground floor a bar and coffee shop, upstairs a pine-ceilinged lounge and a cocktail bar. Spruced-up bedrooms (new carpets and fabrics, brass light fittings) have remote-control TVs and radios, tea-makers and tiled bathrooms. Friendly staff. *Amenities* garden, solarium, games room, laundry room, crèche, coffee shop (10am–10pm).

■ *Rooms* 103	*Confirm by* 6
en suite bath/shower 103	*Last dinner* 9.30
Direct dial Yes	*Parking* Ample
Room TV Yes	*Room service* None

Stakis Badenoch Hotel

H 58% £E
Map 17 C4 Highland
Aviemore Centre PH22 1PF
Aviemore (0479) 810261
Credit Access, Amex, Diners, Visa

Much needed refurbishment is bringing the bedrooms of this modern hotel up to the same standard as its public rooms, which include a spacious lounge with comfortable chesterfields and a smart cocktail bar. There is also a disco bar and a TV lounge frequently used for functions. No phones in the rather small rooms without private facilities. *Amenities* pool table, in-house movies (free), laundry service, 24-hour lounge service.

■ *Rooms* 81	*Confirm by* 6
en suite bath/shower 62	*Last dinner* 9.30
Direct dial Most	*Parking* Ample
Room TV Most	*Room service* 24 hours

Stakis Coylumbridge Resort Hotel   Aviemore

H **61% £C**
Map 17 C4 Highland
PH22 1QN
Aviemore (0479) 810661. Tlx 75272
Manager Mr E. R. Beach
Credit Access, Amex, Diners, Visa. **LVs**

There need never be a dull moment at this modern hotel. Those who don't head for the snow-clad hills of Aviemore can enjoy excellent leisure facilities without stirring from the hotel, or relax in the comfortable and spacious lounge-cum-lobby and bar area. Functional bedrooms cater well for family groups, with bunks and double beds in about half the rooms, all of which have en suite bathrooms. *Amenities* garden, indoor swimming pool, sauna, solarium, whirlpool bath, gymnasium, hairdressing, tennis, badminton, golf practice net, putting, shooting, games room, pool table, in-house movies (free), laundry service, coffee shop (10am–10pm), 24-hour lounge service, children's playground.

■ *Rooms 175*	*Confirm by 5*
en suite bath/shower 175	*Last dinner 9.30*
Direct dial Yes	*Parking Ample*
Room TV Yes	*Room service 24 hours*

Stakis Four Seasons Hotel   Aviemore

H **73% £C**
Map 17 C4 Highland
Aviemore Centre PH11 1PF
Aviemore (0479) 810681. Tlx 75213
Credit Access, Amex, Diners, Visa

The external facelift hides a complete and stylish transformation inside this modern high-rise hotel (formerly the Stakis Strathspey). In the lobby, blue velour-clad settees sit round glass coffee tables with stone lion bases; in the lounge-bar, where a pianist plays six nights a week, the chairs are wicker and the tables marble. A new coffee shop and leisure complex are planned. Good-sized bedrooms are fitted out with quality darkwood units and attractive ruffled curtains to match quilted bedcovers together with many modern accessories. Smart tiled bathrooms have good towels and toiletries, plus wooden loo seats

adding a touch of luxury in the bathrooms. Staff are neat and alert. *Amenities* garden, sauna, solarium, in-house movies (free), laundry service, 24-hour lounge service.

■ *Rooms 89*	*Confirm by 6*
en suite bath/shower 89	*Last dinner 9.30*
Direct dial Yes	*Parking Ample*
Room TV Yes	*Room service 24 hours*

■ We publish annually, so make
  sure you use the current
  edition. It's worth it!

Balgarth Hotel   Ayr

H **56% £E/F**
Map 12 B2 Strathclyde
8 Dunure Road, Doonfoot KA7 4HR
Alloway (0292) 42441
Credit Access, Amex, Diners, Visa
Built in sandstone towards the end of Queen Victoria's reign, this is a modestly appointed but pleasant hotel, and a convenient base for exploring Burns country. The bar, refurbished with lots of red plush, has a golfing theme, and there are two little lounges. Compact bedrooms provide straightforward comforts.
Amenities garden, laundry service, children's play area.

■ *Rooms 15*	*Confirm by arrang.*
en suite bath/shower 11	*Last dinner 10*
Room phone Yes	*Parking Ample*
Room TV Yes	*Room service All day*

Caledonian Hotel   Ayr

H **£D**
Map 12 B2 Strathclyde
Dalblair Road KA7 1UG
Ayr (0292) 269331. Tlx 776611
Credit Access, Amex, Diners, Visa. **LVs**

A modern city-centre hotel that closed temporarily in mid 1987 for refurbishment. Both the straightforward overnight accommodation and the bright public rooms were included in the programme, and a leisure centre was also in the plans. Graded at 58% in the 1987 Guide.
Amenities sauna, laundry service, 24-hour lounge service.

■ *Rooms 114*	*Confirm by 7*
en suite bath/shower 114	*Last dinner 10*
Direct dial Yes	*Parking Ample*
Room TV Yes	*Room service 24 hours*

Pickwick Hotel   Ayr

H **59% £D/E**
Map 12 B2 Strathclyde
19 Racecourse Road KA7 2TD
Ayr (0292) 260111
Manager John Murchie
Credit Visa

Neatly kept and pleasantly staffed Victorian hotel on the A719 just south of the town centre. Bedrooms all have modern units, trouser presses, drinks dispensers and remote-control TVs, plus private bath or shower rooms. The half-panelled bar is a pleasant spot for a drink, and there's a simple residents' lounge. No dogs.
Amenities garden.

■ *Rooms* 15	*Confirm by* arrang.
en suite bath/shower 15	*Last dinner* 9
Room phone Yes	*Parking* Ample
Room TV Yes	*Room service* All day

Ballachulish Hotel   Ballachulish

H **60% £E**
Map 17 B4 Highland
Argyll PA39 4JY
Ballachulish (085 52) 666
Owner managers Young family
Credit Access, Amex, Diners, Visa

Extensive refurbishment has taken place at this Victorian Gothic hotel by lochs Linnhe and Leven. Stained timber and period glasswork give the Ferry Bar a new look, and bedrooms have been attractively refurbished in pine.
Amenities garden, sea fishing, laundry service, coffee shop (all day), 24-hour lounge service.

■ *Rooms* 28	*Confirm by* 6
en suite bath/shower 28	*Last dinner* 10
Direct dial Yes	*Parking* Ample
Room TV Yes	*Room service* 24 hours
Closed mid Oct–mid March	

Tullich Lodge   Ballater

HR **70% £B**
Map 17 C4 Grampian
AB3 5SB
Ballater (0338) 55406
Owner managers Hector Macdonald & Neil Bannister
Credit Access, Amex

A wooded hillside overlooking the Dee valley is the setting for this Victorian baronial mansion. Typical of the genre (but prettier than most) it is a pink granite structure with attractively-furnished public rooms. The restful drawing room has a fine collection of antique settees and sofas, a second smaller lounge provides plenty of books and magazines, and the oak-panelled bar is cosy and convivial. Bedrooms vary in size, but all are charmingly decorated, with good antiques. Most have TVs but reception is poor. Carpeted bathrooms (two with showers only) are reasonably modern. All are private and only one is not en suite. *Amenities* garden, laundry service.

■ *Rooms* 10	*Confirm by* 5
en suite bath/shower 9	*Last dinner* 8.30
Room phone Yes	*Parking* Ample
Room TV Most	*Room service* Limited
Closed mid Dec–mid March	

Tullich Lodge Dining Room ⌑ ♧

Wild flowers on crisply clothed tables and mirror-perfect polished panelling speak of care and effort in this civilised dining room. Service by Hector Macdonald is friendly and efficient. Set menus, devoid of choice (except by payment of a supplement), include starters like smoked salmon. Soup or fish might follow, with grilled lamb cutlets or roast beef as the main course. ⊖

■ *Set L* £15	*L by* arrang. only
Set D £16	*D* 7.30–8.30
About £40 for two	*Seats* 25
Closed mid Dec–mid Mar	

Ledcreich Hotel   Balquhidder

H **60% £E**
Map 17 B5 Central
Nr Lochearnhead FK19 8PQ
Strathyre (087 74) 230
Owner managers Ms S. Bedford & Mr J. Gilhooly
Credit Access, Amex, Diners, Visa

A charming little hotel on the shore of Loch Voil. The beauty of the location is unmatched in late spring when the gardens are ablaze with azalea and rhododendron blooms. Public rooms have a homely, traditional appeal. Recent improvements provide conference facilities and four superior rooms. No dogs. *Amenities* garden, game fishing, laundry service.

■ *Rooms* 8	*Confirm by* arrang.
en suite bath/shower 6	*Last dinner* 9
Room phone No	*Parking* Ample
Room TV No	*Room service* All day

Raemoir House Hotel

H 71% £C/D ⅙
Map 17 D4 Grampian
AB3 4ED
Banchory (033 02) 4884. Tlx 73315
Owner manager Mrs Kit Sabin
Credit Access, Amex, Diners, Visa

Guests return year after year to enjoy the hospitality of Kit Sabin and her marvellous staff at this highly individual hotel. Dating back to 1750, it stands amid picturesque parkland on a 3500-acre estate at the junction of the A980 and B977. Much-loved antiques fill the whole house, and the comfortable bar even has a counter made from a Tudor four-poster; huge sash windows provide delightful views. Spacious bedrooms (including some in the historic Ha' Hoose behind the main building) feature ornately carved furnishings and bathrooms range from modern to splendidly old-

fahsioned. *Amenities* garden, sauna, keep-fit equipment, 9-hole mini-golf course, shooting, game fishing, helipad.

■ *Rooms* 22 — *Confirm by arrang.*
en suite bath/shower 22 — *Last dinner* 9
Direct dial Yes — *Parking* Ample
Room TV Yes — *Room service* All day

Tor-na-Coille Hotel

H 65% £D/E
Map 17 D4 Grampian
Inchmarlo Road AB3 4AB
Banchory (033 02) 2242
Credit Access, Amex, Diners, Visa

Housekeeping is exemplary at this solid Victorian house in attractive grounds set back from the A93. The lounge and bar are both spacious and comfortable, and roomy bedrooms

are furnished in traditional or more modern style. All have simple, carpeted bathrooms.
Amenities garden, squash, hairdressing, health clinic, game fishing, snooker, laundry service.
■ *Rooms* 23 — *Confirm by* 6
en suite bath/shower 23 — *Last dinner* 9.45
Direct dial Yes — *Parking* Ample
Room TV Yes — *Room service* Limited
Closed 3 days Xmas & 1st 2 wks Jan

Auchen Castle Hotel

H 65% £E
Map 12 C3 Dumfries & Galloway
Nr Moffat DG10 9SH
Beattock (068 33) 407. Tlx 777205
Owner managers R. L. & H. G. Beckh
Credit Access, Amex, Diners, Visa

The views are lovely from this handsome Victorian mansion, whose extensive grounds include a trout loch. A lot of improvements have recently taken place, including new carpeting in many public areas and corridors, and the stylish refurbishing of the main house bedrooms. Some of these have antique furniture, others good-

quality fitted units from a local cabinet maker. Ten rooms in the Cedar Lodge are rather more plain, with simple fitted units and showers only. The lounge is in traditional style with chintzy sofas and armchairs and the comfortable bar features some rather fine Thai furniture. Staff are friendly and helpful.
Amenities garden, game fishing.
■ *Rooms* 25 — *Confirm by arrang.*
en suite bath/shower 25 — *Last dinner* 9
Direct dial Yes — *Parking* Ample
Room TV Yes — *Room service* Limited
Closed 21 Dec–5 Jan

Dalhousie Castle Hotel

H 72% £C
Map 12 C1 Lothian
Nr Edinburgh EH19 3JB
Gorebridge (0875) 20153. Tlx 72380
Credit Access, Amex, Diners, Visa

Set in its own pleasant grounds on the banks of the Esk, this turreted sandstone castle dates back to the 13th century. Many historic features survive, including the ancient barrel-vaulted dungeons, and in the comfortable mezzanine lounge there's a mural of a medieval scene depicting the castle's past, and a lovely vaulted plaster ceiling. Bedrooms are generally of a good size with ample comforts and nice little extras like bowls of fresh fruit (tea and shortbread are offered on arrival). Furnishings are mainly solid oak, fabrics attractive but fading. There's a splendid honeymoon suite, with a circular four-

poster, in the tower wing. Neat modern bathrooms with bathrobes and generous soft towels. *Amenities* garden, games room, laundry service.
■ *Rooms* 24 — *Confirm by arrang.*
en suite bath/shower 24 — *Last dinner* 10
Direct dial Yes — *Parking* Ample
Room TV Yes — *Room service* 24 hours

Kipling's *NEW ENTRY*

R ♧ ⅙ **Map 17 C5 Central**
Milne Road
Stirling (0786) 833617
Credit Access, Amex, Visa
Local suppliers and the Glasgow markets
determine the menu at this popular picture-
windowed restaurant high above the town.
Enthusiastic chef-patron Peter Bannister (he also
takes the orders) lets good fresh flavours speak

for themselves in a tempting variety of dishes,
from venison meat balls in a delicious game sauce
to grilled crayfish tails and quail vol-au-vent
Véronique. Nice sweets, too. ☺
- *Set L* £5.50   *L* 12.30–2
About £36 for two   *D* 7–9.30
Seats 40   *Parking Ample*
*Closed Sun, Mon, Bank Hols (exc. Good Fri), 2
wks Xmas & 1st 2 wks Aug*

Royal Hotel

H **57% £D/E**
Map 17 C5 Central
Henderson Street FX9 4HG
Bridge of Allan (0786) 832284. Tlx 946240
Credit Access, Amex, Diners, Visa
A stately portico distinguishes the facade of
this white-painted hotel. Two of the three lounges
sometimes double as function rooms but there's
also a stylish bar with comfortable seating. Best

bedrooms have smart furnishings and well-fitted
bathrooms. Remaining accommodation is much
more basic. All rooms have tea/coffee-makers.
Amenities garden, laundry service, 24-hour
lounge service.
- *Rooms* 33   *Confirm by arrang.*
en suite bath/shower 24   *Last dinner 9.30*
Direct dial Yes   *Parking Ample*
Room TV Yes   *Room service 24 hours*

Bridge of Cally Hotel

HR **56% £F**
Map 17 C4 Tayside
By Blairgowrie PH10 7JJ
Bridge of Cally (025 086) 231
Owner managers Hugh & Mary Sharrock
Credit Access, Diners, Visa
In a village six miles north of Blairgowrie, this
agreeable little hotel by the river Ardle provides
peaceful, homely accommodation. Simply
furnished bedrooms (six with private bath or
shower) are neat and bright, and there's a
welcoming bar and comfortable TV lounge.
Amenities garden, game fishing.
- *Rooms* 9   *Confirm by arrang.*
en suite bath/shower 6   *Last dinner 8.30*
Room phone No   *Parking Ample*
Room TV No   *Room service Limited*
Closed Nov & 25 & 26 Dec

Bridge of Cally Hotel Restaurant ♧

Tables set with crisp white cloths and little posies
of wild flowers lend a simple charm to this modest
restaurant. Mary Sharrock uses good fresh
produce in carefully cooked, straightforward
dishes. Short, daily-changing menus offer starters
like seafood cocktail and creamed lentil soup, and
main courses like sole mornay, breast of chicken
with parsley sauce, and escalopes of pork with a
nice orange and ginger sauce. Puds are
particularly good – ranging from chocolate gâteau
to peach tart and fresh fruit pavlova. ☺
- *Set D* £10·50   *L* 12–2, Sun 12.30–1.45
About £30 for two   *D* 7–8.30
Seats 32   *Parties 35*
Closed Nov & 25 & 26 Dec

Roman Camp Hotel

HR **72% £C/D** ⅙
Map 17 C5 Central
Main Street FK17 8BG
Callander (0877) 30003
Owner managers Sami & Pat Denzler
Standing on the banks of the river Teith in 20
acres of lovely gardens, the hotel is reminiscent of
a miniature French château and makes an
excellent base from which to explore the Roman
remains which litter the surrounding countryside.
Public areas include a panelled entrance hall,
tapestry-lined lounge and impressive library with

ornate ceiling. Many of the comfortable bedrooms
have hand-painted furniture; three ground-floor
rooms have French windows and soft colour
schemes; and there are three stylish suites. All
rooms have radio-alarms, tea-makers, hairdryers
and smart modern bathrooms. *Amenities* garden.
- *Rooms* 14   *Confirm by 5*
en suite bath/shower 14   *Last dinner 9*
Direct dial Yes   *Parking Ample*
Room TV Yes   *Room service Limited*
Closed mid Nov–mid Mar

Restaurant ♧

A light and spacious restaurant where Swiss-born
Sami Denzler offers short, fixed-price menus that
embrace a range of European cuisines. The
freshest prime ingredients are carefully prepared
to produce dishes like gazpacho or avocado
ravigote, followed by beef Wellington, pot-au-feu
or medallions of venison served with spätzli.
Desserts lack inspiration – an unexceptional apple

strudel is typical – and a few traditional Scottish treats would be welcome. Good wines: note the excellent Dézaley Blanc 1ᵉʳ cru from Switzerland. Friendly service. ☺

■ Set L £8, Sun £11	L 12.15–1.30,
Set D £17	Sun 12.30–2
About £40 for two	D 7–9
Seats 40 Parties 20	Closed mid Nov–mid Mar

Riverside Inn   Canonbie

RR ♧ **Map 12 D3** Dumfries & Galloway
DG14 0UX
Canonbie (054 15) 512
Credit Access, Visa

Fresh local produce and home-grown vegetables form the basis of tasty fixed-price meals at this whitewashed inn overlooking the river Esk. There's usually a home-made soup (perhaps beef broth or Chinese mushroom) and a seafood starter such as savoury prawns in cream cheese dressing. The main course might be turbot, or partridge with brown bread sauce, and a selection of at least five vegetables could

include cabbage with pistachio nuts or carrots with coriander. Fresh fruit platter makes a fitting finale. No smoking in the restaurant. ☺

■ Set D £14·50	L by arrang. only
About £40 for two	D 7.30–8.30
Seats 30	Parking Ample
Parties 28	Closed Sun, 1 Jan,
25 Dec & 2 wks Feb	

Bedrooms £E

Rooms 6	With bath/shower 6

Light and airy bedrooms have good amenities, including en suite bathrooms and TVs. No dogs.

Nivingston House   Cleish

HR 68% £D/E
Map 17 C5 Tayside
Nr Kinross KY13 7LS
Cleish Hills (057 75) 216
Owner managers Allan & Pat Deeson
Credit Access, Amex, Diners, Visa

A delightful country setting belies the proximity of the M90 to this pleasant part-Georgian, part-Victorian house. Inside all is neat and fresh, with comfortable, civilised lounges and a plush bar. Pretty bedrooms have good modern furniture and smart, well-equipped bathrooms. *Amenities* garden, putting, croquet, laundry service.

■ Rooms 17	Confirm by arrang.
en suite bath/shower 17	Last dinner 9
Direct dial Yes	Parking Ample
Room TV Yes	Room service Limited
Closed 25 & 26 Dec	

Nivingston House Restaurant ⅏ ⅃

A comfortably and elegantly appointed restaurant, with pretty floral curtains and handsome table settings. Daily-changing menus offer plenty of choice and a cheerful blend of styles from Michael Thompson. Start perhaps with tomato and orange soup, or haddock, prawn and quail's egg terrine, then move on to loin of pork with apple and cranberry sauce or best end of lamb sauced with apricot and Madeira. Nice al dente vegetables. Finish with Scotch trifle or brandy snaps with peach ice cream. ☺

■ Set L £11·50	L 12–2
Set D £17·50	D 7–9
About £45 for two	Seats 50
Closed 26 Dec	Parties 30

Three Chimneys *NEW ENTRY*   Colbost

R ♧ **Map 16 A3** Highland
Nr Dunvegan, Isle of Skye
Glendale (047 081) 258
Credit Access, Visa

Wild flowers decorate the candlelit tables in this charming old crofter's cottage, where Shirley Spear's menus have a strong Scottish slant. She relies heavily on local produce like scallops, lobsters and the most delicious peat-smoked salmon. Many of the vegetables and soft fruits she uses are organically grown, and the lovely wholemeal bread is home-baked. Main courses run from prawn and smoked haddock pancakes

to steaks, roast pigeon and lamb hot pot with parsley dumplings. There's a good selection of cheeses, and tempting sweets like a scrumptious rhubarb oatie nut crumble. Charming waitress service supervised by Eddie Spear. Carefully chosen wine list: excellent Côtes du Ventoux (Malcolm Swan) 1985 and lovely Savigny Les Beaune (Simon Bize) 1983. ♀ Well-chosen ☺

■ Set D from £8·95	D only 7–9
About £35 for two	Parking Ample
Seats 30	Parties 35
Closed Sun Sept–May (except Bank Holiday weekends)	

Ossian's Hotel   Connel

H 53% £F
Map 17 B5 Strathclyde
North Connel PA37 1RB
Connel (063 171) 322
Owner manager Stewart & MacLean families

A small modern hotel standing in neatly kept grounds, with fine views over Loch Etive, and fishing in a little trout loch. It's a place of simple charms and the bedrooms are quite basic – no

TV, no phone, just a warm bed (electric blankets) and modest furnishings. There's a sunny lounge, a TV room and bar. *Amenities* garden, game fishing.

■ Rooms 14	Confirm by arrang.
en suite bath/shower 6	Last dinner 8
Room phone No	Parking Ample
Room TV No	Room service Limited
Closed mid Oct–Easter	

Craigdarroch Lodge Hotel — Contin

H **54% £E** ♿
Map 16 B3 Highland
Craigdarroch Drive, Nr Strathpeffer IV14 9EH
Strathpeffer (0997) 21265
Owner manager Keith Sigrist
Credit Access, Visa

In a beautiful setting at the foot of Strathconan Glen, this friendly little hotel is a popular base for fishing and walking holidays. Part of the lounge serves as a TV room, and there's a cheerful bar with pretty garden views. Simple appointed bedrooms, fairly basic bathrooms. Decent breakfasts. *Amenities* garden, tennis, croquet, game fishing, snooker, laundry service.

■ *Rooms* 19	*Confirm by* arrang.
en suite bath/shower 11	*Last dinner* 8.30
Room phone No	*Parking* Ample
Room TV No	*Room service* All day

Isle of Mull Hotel — Craignure

H **56% £D/E**
Map 17 A5 Strathclyde
Isle of Mull PA65 6BB
Craignure (068 02) 351
Manager Mr John Patrick
Credit Access, Amex, Diners, Visa

All rooms at this modern hotel enjoy the fine view across the Sound of Mull. New carpeting and easy chairs have enhanced the appeal of the foyer-lounge, and a new patio built. Bedrooms are neat and practical, with generally improved bathrooms. *Amenities* garden, in-house movies (free), games room, laundry service.

■ *Rooms* 62	*Confirm by* 7
en suite bath/shower 62	*Last dinner* 8.30
Room phone No	*Parking* Ample
Room TV Yes	*Room service* Limited
Closed end Oct–Easter	

Crinan Hotel — Crinan

HR **70% £D/E**
Map 17 B5 Strathclyde
By Lochgilphead PA31 8SR
Crinan (054 683) 261
Owner managers Nick & Frances Ryan
Credit Access, Visa

An outstanding welcome awaits guests at the Ryans' delightful hotel in a breathtakingly beautiful position on the point where the Crinan Canal meets the sea. Lovely sea views can be enjoyed from the delightful lounge, which has plenty of comfortable seating, while the outlook from the rooftop bar is positively spectacular. Residents also have their own bar, or can catch up on local gossip in the fishermen's snug. Pretty, individually decorated bedrooms – some with private balconies – have attractive pine furniture and charming bathrooms. *Amenities* garden, sea fishing, hotel boats, laundry service, coffee shop (9am–5pm).

■ *Rooms* 22	*Confirm by* 6
en suite bath/shower 22	*Last dinner* 9
Direct dial Yes	*Parking* Ample
Room TV No	*Room service* All day
Closed end Oct–17 Mar	

Lock 16 Restaurant ★ 🔔 ♿

Shellfish could not be fresher than at Nick Ryan's delightful rooftop restaurant where it receives simple but superb treatment that does full justice to flavours. The restaurant depends totally on the day's catch (it will not open if there isn't one!), which might trawl in some Jura lobsters, succulent jumbo prawns, or delicious clams to be served with a dish of seaweed. Smoked and cured fish is also very popular, with the menu featuring Arbroath smokies, sweet-cured Tarbert herring and gravad lax cured with whisky and dill. Finish with Stilton and a nice sweet.
Specialities jumbo Crinan prawns, Corryvreckan Jura lobster, Loch Craignish mussels, Isle of Islay clams.

🍷 Well-chosen 🧀

■ *Set D* £23·50	*L* 12.30–2
About £59 *for two*	*D* at 8
Seats 20	*Parties* 24
Closed L Tues, all Mon & end Oct–17 Mar	

Telford Room

A friendly restaurant with marvellous views across the sound. Susie Highnell has stepped up from assistant to head chef, and the straightforward preparation of good fresh local produce continues as before. Her five-course fixed-price menu changes daily, and a typical meal could comprise kidneys with whisky and cream, Arbroath smokies, lemon sorbet, Kintyre lamb, and Stilton or a delicious sweet.

🍷 Well-chosen 🧀

■ *Set D* £20	*D only* 7–9
About £50 *for two*	*Seats* 50
Closed end Oct–17 Mar	*Parties* 12

Seafield Arms Hotel — Cullen

H **60% £E/F**
Map 16 D3 Grampian
Seafield Street AB5 2SG
Cullen (0542) 40791
Owner managers Mr & Mrs Anderson &
Mr Corless
Credit Access, Amex, Diners, Visa
   New owners have been working hard
refurbishing this white-painted house in the village

centre. The lounge bar overlooks a paved
courtyard and is especially pleasant, with its
inviting sofas and fine carved fireplace. Brass or
cane beds are features of the well appointed
bedrooms. Hearty breakfasts and friendly service.

- *Rooms* 22
- *en suite bath/shower* 22
- *Direct dial* Yes
- *Room TV* Yes

Confirm by 6
Last dinner 9.30
Parking Ample
Room service Limited

Ostlers Close Restaurant — Cupar

R ⌕ & **Map 17 C5** Fife
Bonnygate KY15 4BU
Cupar (0334) 55574
Credit Access, Visa
   Ingredients are impressively fresh at the
Grahams' attractive little alleyway restaurant,
where husband James's short menus are very
tempting. Typical dishes include a flavourful
chicken and pheasant liver pâté, pigeon with a gin

and juniper sauce, and scallops with a delicate
tomato and basil fumet. Scrumptious sweets too.
Good, keenly priced wines.
🍷 Well-chosen ☺

- *About £36 for two*
- *Seats* 28
- *Parties* 20
- *Closed* L Mon, all Bank
Hols & 2 Jan.

L 12.15–2
D 7–9.30,
Mon by arrang.
Parking Limited

Open Arms Hotel — Dirleton

H **67% £D**
Map 12 D1 Lothian
EH39 5EG
Dirleton (062 085) 241. Tlx 727887
Manager Miss W. Campbell
Credit Access, Amex, Diners, Visa
   Everything is spotless at this warm, welcoming
hotel overlooking the village green and the ruins of
13th-century Dirleton Castle. The bedrooms are

bright with cheerful fabrics, comfortable
armchairs and fresh flowers. Day rooms include
cosy, inviting lounges and a tiny bar.
Amenities garden.

- *Rooms* 7
- *en suite bath/shower* 7
- *Direct dial* Yes
- *Room TV* Yes
- *Closed* 1 wk Jan

Confirm by arrang.
Last dinner 10
Parking Ample
Room service All day

Polmaily House Hotel — Drumnadrochit

HR **63% £D/E**
Map 16 B3 Highland
IV3 6XT
Drumnadrochit (045 62) 343
Owner managers Mr & Mrs N. Parsons
Credit Access, Visa
   A delightful country house, set in 18 acres of
beautiful grounds. Public rooms, including a
quaint reading room, have the feel of a private
home. Cottage bedrooms, though modest, are
prettily decorated and comfortable. No dogs.
Amenities garden, outdoor swimming pool,
tennis, game fishing, croquet.

- *Rooms* 9
- *en suite bath/shower* 7
- *Room phone* No
- *Room TV* No
- *Closed* mid Oct–Easter

Confirm by arrang.
Last dinner 9.30
Parking Ample
Room service All day

Polmaily House Hotel Restaurant ⌕

The menu changes daily in this quietly elegant
restaurant, where Alison Parsons heads a capable
kitchen team. Meals are varied and appealing,
ingredients generally fresh and well chosen.
Starters might include courgette and mint soup or
a tasty rabbit terrine. To follow, perhaps
medallions of veal in green ginger wine, or grilled
lamb steak with garlic purée. Tempting desserts
range from cherry meringue and strawberry
almond roulade to steamed pineapple upside-
down pudding. Scottish farm cheeses round off
the meal. Friendly, informal service. No smoking. ☺

- *About £38 for two*
- *Seats* 30
- *Closed* mid Oct–Easter

D only 7.30–9.30
Parties 50

Dryburgh Abbey Hotel — Dryburgh

H **63% £D** &
Map 12 D2 Borders
St Boswells TD6 0RQ
St Boswells (0835) 22261
Credit Access, Amex, Diners, Visa
   Set in attractive gardens, this imposing
Victorian building offers splendid views over the
river Tweed. Within, there's a cosy panelled bar
and two welcoming first-floor lounges – one with a

lovely marble fireplace and leather armchairs.
Bedrooms are homely and well kept, with
traditional furniture and candlewick bedspreads.
Amenities garden, putting, croquet, games room,
laundry service.

- *Rooms* 28
- *en suite bath/shower* 22
- *Room phone* No
- *Room TV* Yes

Confirm by arrang.
Last dinner 8.30
Parking Ample
Room service All day

Buchanan Arms Hotel

Drymen

H 61% £D
Map 17 B5 Central
Main Street G63 0BQ
Drymen (0360) 60588. Tlx 778215
Credit Access, Amex, Diners, Visa

Close to Loch Lomond, this white-painted hotel enjoys an attractive garden setting. Buchanan tartan carpets the public areas, including the spacious lounge with sun-trap extension.

Refurbishment continues in the main house to bring older rooms into line with the bright modern rooms in the new extension. *Amenities* garden, bowling green, pool table, in-house movies (free), laundry service, 24-hour lounge service.

■ *Rooms* 35	*Confirm by arrang.*
en suite bath/shower 35	*Last dinner* 9.30
Direct dial Yes	*Parking* Ample
Room TV Yes	*Room service* Limited

Muckrach Lodge Hotel

Dulnain Bridge

HR 57% £E
Map 16 C3 Highland
Nr Grantown-on-Spey PH26 3LY
Dulnain Bridge (047 985) 257
Owner managers Captain Roy & Pat Watson
Credit Access, Amex, Visa

Friendly new owners have made a good start at this former shooting lodge in beautiful Dulnain Valley. Public rooms are getting a facelift, and comfortable new settees and easy chairs are in place. Remote-control TVs and direct-dial phones are installed in the bright, fresh bedrooms; bathrooms have bigger towels and better toiletries. No dogs. *Amenities* garden.

■ *Rooms* 10	*Confirm by arrang.*
en suite bath/shower 10	*Last dinner* 9
Direct dial Yes	*Parking* Ample
Room TV Yes	*Room service* All day

Muckrach Lodge Hotel Restaurant 🍷

John Sinclair remains at the helm in the kitchen and his five-course menus are full of good things. Celery soup or curried vegetable pancakes could start things off, followed by seafood ramekins and main courses such as sole dugléré, Catalonian-style chicken, roast leg of lamb with an apricot and almond stuffing or steak balmoral. Luscious sweets (chocolate and orange soufflés, almond meringue gâteau with raspberries), then cheese and coffee. Super bar lunches. ⊖

■ *Set D* £15.20	*L by arrang. only*
About £40 for two	*D* 7.30–9
Seats 40	

Cromlix House

Dunblane

HR 82% £B
Map 17 C5 Central
Kin Buck FK15 9JT
Dunblane (0786) 822125
Credit Access, Amex, Diners, Visa

A magnificent 5000-acre estate surrounds this solid country mansion, built as a family house (with its own private chapel) in 1880. Much of the south-west part of the building remains unchanged, and period furnishings, family portraits and antiques add to the charm of flower-filled public rooms like the elegant lounge and handsome raftered library. However, carpet tiles in the halls, though durable, are not exactly elegant. Half the attractively refurbished bedrooms (which include eight suites) have sitting rooms, and splendidly restored original Victorian fittings are a feature of many of the palatial bathrooms. Some bedrooms have been refurbished with fabrics that do not quite match the sumptuous surroundings.
Amenities garden, tennis, croquet, riding, clay-pigeon shooting, coarse & game fishing, laundry service, 24-hour lounge service.

■ *Rooms* 14	*Confirm by arrang.*
en suite bath/shower 14	*Last dinner* 9.30
Direct dial Yes	*Parking* Ample
Room TV Yes	*Room service* All day

Cromlix House Restaurant ★ 👑👑 👑 ♿

Mark Salter's carefully conceived five-course menus (no-choice) are described in the drawing room over canapés before guests move in to the formal, elegant restaurant. Subtly flavoured parfait of pigeon and rabbit with Cumberland sauce might start your meal, followed by succulent crawfish tails with a lemony hollandaise, and rare beef fillet with Madeira sauce. Highlight of the meal are the exquisite sweets, including a lovely gratin of fruits served in a faultless white wine sabayon, the whole dish encased in a tuile biscuit basket. Most attentive service. Non-residents must book. Quite splendid cellar particularly fine in Bordeaux: an enthusiast's collection. *Specialities* rabbit consommé with

pigeon and herb quenelles, steamed trout with chive sauce and caviar, saddle of hare with wild mushrooms and a blueberry sauce, hot strawberry soufflé.

🥢 Outstanding ♟ Well-chosen ℮
- *Set L* £13–15 . *L by arrang.*
- *Set D* £27 *D 7–9.30*
- *About £70 for two* *Seats 30 Parties 24*

Stakis Dunblane Hydro

Dunblane

H **60%** £C/D &
Map 17 C5 Central
Perth Road FK15 0HG
Dunblane (0786) 822551. Tlx 776284
Credit Access, Amex, Diners, Visa
   Coach loads of golfers and conference delegates can be hazards for the guest in search of peace and quiet at this imposing late Victorian hotel. Best bedrooms are those in the modern

wing or main-house Executive rooms. Spacious public rooms include an attractive cocktail bar. Staff not very helpful. *Amenities* garden, outdoor swimming pool, sauna, solarium, whirlpool bath, keep-fit equipment, tennis, putting, games room.
- ■ *Rooms* 188 *Confirm by 6*
- *en suite bath/shower 188* *Last dinner 9.30*
- *Direct dial Yes* *Parking Ample*
- *Room TV Yes* *Room service 24 hours*

Angus Thistle Hotel

Dundee

H **69%** £C
Map 17 C5 Tayside
Marketgait DD1 1QN
Dundee (0382) 26874. Tlx 76456
Credit Access, Amex, Diners, Visa. **LVs**
   Right in the city centre, this friendly modern hotel is kept in an excellent state of repair. The first-floor cocktail bar has been most elegantly refurbished, and there's a comfortable lounge,

too. Attractively decorated bedrooms have good fitted units together with trouser presses, tea-makers, hairdryers and compact bathrooms. *Amenities* in-house movies (free), laundry service.
- ■ *Rooms* 58 *Confirm by 6*
- *en suite bath/shower 58* *Last dinner 10.30*
- *Direct dial Yes* *Parking Difficult*
- *Room TV Yes* *Room service All day*

Invercarse Hotel

Dundee

H **59%** £D/E
Map 17 C5 Tayside
371 Perth Road DD2 1PG
Dundee (0382) 69231. Tlx 76608
Manager Mr G. Bakes
Credit Access, Amex, Diners, Visa
   An extended Victorian building west of the city centre. The main lounge bar overlooking the garden is comfortably furnished. Best bedrooms,

in the latest extension, are fitted to a decent modern standard. Remaining rooms – 24 with shower only – vary in size and style. *Amenities* garden, in-house movies (free), laundry service, 24-hour lounge service.
- ■ *Rooms* 40 *Confirm by 6*
- *en suite bath/shower 40* *Last dinner 9.45*
- *Direct dial Yes* *Parking Ample*
- *Room TV Yes* *Room service 24 hours*

King Malcolm Thistle Hotel

Dunfermline

H **65%** £C
Map 17 C5 Fife
Queensferry Road KY11 5DS
Dunfermline (0383) 722611. Tlx 727721
Credit Access, Amex, Diners, Visa
   A well-maintained modern hotel on the outskirts of town near junction 2 of the M90. The attractively contemporary foyer doubles as a lounge, and the pastel-chic cocktail bar now

sports a stylish conservatory extension. Comfort-able, simply furnished bedrooms are well-equipped. Neat, practical bathrooms. *Amenities* in-house movies (free), laundry service.
- ■ *Rooms* 48 *Confirm by 6*
- *en suite bath/shower 48* *Last dinner 9.30*
- *Direct dial Yes* *Parking Ample*
- *Room TV Yes* *Room service 24 hours*
- *Closed 25 Dec & 1 Jan*

Stewart Hotel

Duror

H **58%** £E
Map 17 B4 Highland
Glen Duror, Appin PA38 4BW
Duror (063 174) 268
Owner manager Michael Lacy
Credit Access, Amex, Diners, Visa
   You cross a little bridge over a stream to reach this welcoming hotel situated above Loch Linnhe. The views are magnificent, and the lounge is a

comfortable spot for enjoying them. There's a convivial bar, warmed by a cheerful open fire. Bedrooms, mostly of a decent size, have solid fitted furniture; tiny but practical bathrooms. *Amenities* garden, sauna, solarium, sailing.
- ■ *Rooms* 20 *Confirm by arrang.*
- *en suite bath/shower 20* *Last dinner 9.15*
- *Room phone No* *Parking Ample*
- *Room TV Yes* *Room service Limited*

Bruce Hotel   East Kilbride

H **60% £D/E**
Map 12 B2 Strathclyde
Cornwall Street G74 1AF
East Kilbride (035 52) 29771. Tlx 778428
Credit Access, Amex, Diners, Visa. LVs
   A purpose-built hotel right in the centre of
Scotland's first new town. Double (sometimes
triple) glazing muffles traffic noise, and a waterfall
and plenty of greenery create a soothing effect in
the foyer. Vibrant colour schemes enliven the two
bars, which double as lounge areas. Bright,
attractive bedrooms have stylish modern furniture
and well-fitted bathrooms. *Amenities* laundry
service.

■ *Rooms 84*	*Confirm by 6*
en suite bath/shower 84	*Last dinner 9.45*
Room phone Yes	*Parking Ample*
Room TV Yes	*Room service 24 hours*

Stuart Hotel   East Kilbride

H **61% £E**
Map 12 B2 Strathclyde
Cornwall Way G74 1JR
East Kilbride (035 52) 21161. Tlx 778504
Credit Access, Amex, Diners, Visa. LVs
   Leather chesterfields invite lingering in the
bright, spacious public areas of this modern hotel
and the two pleasant bars are also popular. A first-
floor lounge doubles as a meeting room. Decent-
sized bedrooms with plain colour schemes have
darkwood furniture and tea-makers. There are
also 9 executive rooms. *Amenities* laundry
service, 24-hour lounge service.

■ *Rooms 39*	*Confirm by arrang.*
en suite bath/shower 39	*Last dinner 9.15*
Direct dial Yes	*Parking Ample*
Room TV Yes	*Room service 24 hours*
Closed 25 Dec & 1 Jan	

Harvesters Hotel   East Linton

H **59% £D/E**
Map 12 D1 East Lothian
Station Road EH40 3DP
East Linton (0620) 860395
Owner managers June & Alex Lannie
Credit Access, Amex, Diners, Visa
   A handsome Georgian house with cheerfully
informal staff. There are two pleasant, traditional
lounges, a rustic bar and an attractive new
conservatory, plus a nice enclosed garden for
residents. Accommodation comprises seven
rooms in a converted coach house and four in the
main house. *Amenities* garden.

■ *Rooms 11*	*Confirm by 6*
en suite bath/shower 8	*Last dinner 9*
Direct dial Yes	*Parking Ample*
Room TV Yes	*Room service None*
Closed 2 wks beg. Jan	

Marlefield Country House Hotel *NEW ENTRY*   Eckford

HR **60% £D/E**
Map 12 D2 Borders
Nr Kelso TD5 8ED
Morebattle (057 34) 561
Credit Access, Amex, Diners, Visa
   From the A698 turn off to Eckford and follow
signs to this fine old manor house. Public rooms
are beautifully proportioned but furnishing,
though comfortable, is a bit of a hotchpotch.
Clean, spacious bedrooms have large, fairly basic
bathrooms. Gradual refurbishment is planned
throughout.
Amenities garden, clay-pigeon shooting, in-house
movies (free), laundry service.

■ *Rooms 7*	*Confirm by arrang.*
en suite bath/shower 7	*Last dinner 9.30*
Direct dial Yes	*Parking Ample*
Room TV Yes	*Room service All day*

Marlefield Country House Hotel Restaurant

Stripped honey-coloured panelling gives a golden
glow to this pretty dining room – the first part of
the hotel to be refurbished since the new owners
took over – and the highly polished dark tables
are a fine foil for sparkling crystal and white china.
Swiss-born chef Rolf Müller is constrained to a
certain extent by customers' requests for prawn
cocktails and steak (very good it is too), but he
manages to include a few of his native specialities
like the excellent émincé de veau zurichoise.
Flavours are first-class. Good modest wine list,
not overpriced. ⊗

■ *Set D £12.50*	*L 12–2*
About £40 for two	*D 7–9.30*
Seats 26	*Parties 45*

Albany Hotel   Edinburgh

H **58% £C**
Town plan D1 Lothian
39 Albany Street EH1 3QY
031-556 0397. Tlx 727079
Owner manager Mrs Pauline Maridor
Credit Access, Amex, Diners, Visa
   In an early 19th-century terrace not far from the
city centre, the Albany provides modest, well-kept
accommodation. There's a traditional-style lounge
on the ground floor and a friendly bar in the
basement. A spiral staircase lit by a handsome
glass cupola leads to good-sized bedrooms with
practical modern units and neatly fitted
bathrooms. *Amenities* laundry service.

■ *Rooms 22*	*Confirm by 4.30*
en suite bath/shower 22	*Last dinner 9.30*
Room phone Yes	*Parking Difficult*
Room TV Yes	*Room service Limited*

■ Our inspectors never book in the name of Egon Ronay's Guides; they disclose their identity only after paying their bills.

Alp Horn   Edinburgh

R ♀ **Town plan C2** Lothian
167 Rose Street
031-225 4787
Swiss cooking
Owner manager Miggi Meier
Credit Access
  Robust Swiss dishes feature on the extensive menu here, and Swiss artefacts, including a huge alphorn, are part of the decor. Sausages, air-dried

beef, fondues, veal with rösti, and with spätsli (home-made noodles, unusually served crisped and brown) are all popular items, as are desserts like birchermuesli or apfelstrudel. Booking advised. ⊝

■ About £35 for two	L 12–2
Seats 65	D 6.30–10
Closed Sun, Mon, Bank	Parking Difficult
Hols, 3 wks July & 2 wks Xmas	

L'Auberge   Edinburgh

R **Town plan E3** Lothian
56 St Mary Street
031-556 5888
French cooking
Credit Access, Amex, Diners, Visa
  An elegant, sophisticated restaurant, with a high standard of service from smartly dressed waiters. Beautifully fresh seafood figures large on the menu; inventive starters include crayfish tails

and warm salad of scallops. Typical main dishes might be pheasant with honey and tarragon and rabbit with garlic and lemon. There is a particularly good selection of excellent desserts.
♀ Well-chosen ⊝

■ Set L £5·65	L 12.30–2
Set D £25	D 6.45–9.30
About £56 for two	Parking Difficult
Seats 55 Parties 30	Closed 1 Jan

Barnton Thistle Hotel   Edinburgh

H **63% £C/D**
Town plan A2 Lothian
Queensferry Road EH4 6AS
Edinburgh (031) 339 1144
Credit Access, Amex, Diners, Visa. **LVs**
  Practical modern accommodation is provided at this agreeable hotel, which stands on the A90 halfway between the city and the airport. Features common to all bedrooms are chintzy fabrics, an

easy chair and a well-lit writing area, and accessories include trouser presses, hairdryers and radio-alarms. There's a quiet lounge and a choice of bars. *Amenities* sauna, solarium, in-house movies (free).

■ Rooms 50	Confirm by 6
en suite bath/shower 50	Last dinner 10
Direct dial Yes	Parking Ample
Room TV Yes	Room service 24 hours

Braid Hills Hotel   Edinburgh

H **60% £D/E**
Town plan B5 Lothian
134 Braid Road EH10 6JD
031-447 8888. Tlx 72311
Credit Access, Amex, Diners, Visa
  Built in 1886 for golfers visiting Braid Hills course, this distinctively turreted hotel (spot it from the A702) is a pleasant place to stay. Bright bedrooms provide radio-alarms, hairdryers and

trouser presses; all have neat, carpeted bathrooms (some with shower only). Comfortable day rooms like the foyer-lounge and bar have a notably Victorian feel. *Amenities* garden, laundry service, 24-hour lounge service.

■ Rooms 68	Confirm by 6
en suite bath/shower 68	Last dinner 8.45
Direct dial Yes	Parking Ample
Room TV Yes	Room service 24 hours

Bruntsfield Hotel   Edinburgh

H **65% £C/D**
Town plan B5 Lothian
69 Bruntsfield Place EH10 4HH
031-229 1393. Tlx 727897
Manager Russell Imrie
Credit Access, Amex, Diners, Visa
  An imposing building in Scottish Baronial style, overlooking a golf course not far from the city centre. Soft pastel shades and Georgian-style

easy chairs create an elegant ambience in the foyer-lounge and cocktail bar. Good-sized bedrooms have brightly-tiled bath/shower rooms. *Amenities* garden, laundry service, coffee shop (7.30am–11pm), 24-hour lounge service.

■ Rooms 52	Confirm by 6
en suite bath/shower 52	Last dinner 11
Direct dial Yes	Parking Limited
Room TV Yes	Room service 24 hours

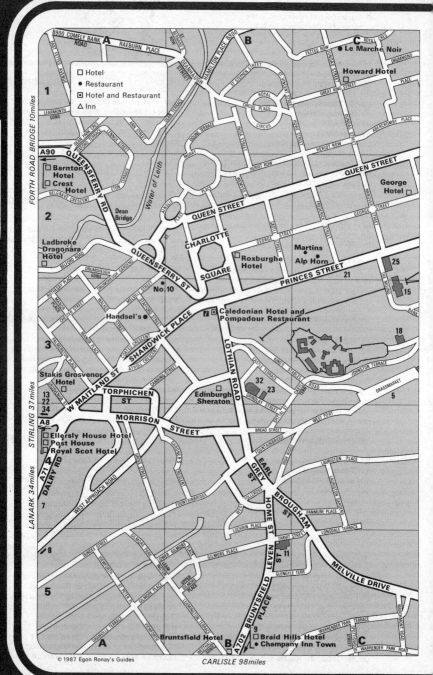

FIAT Edinburgh

Hotel
Restaurant
Hotel and Restaurant
Inn

FORTH ROAD BRIDGE 10miles

B900 COMELY BANK ROAD
RAEBURN PLACE
Le Marché Noir
Howard Hotel

A90
QUEENSFERRY RD
Barnton Hotel
Crest Hotel

Queen Street
George Hotel

Ladbroke Dragonara Hotel

Dean Bridge
Water of Leith

QUEEN STREET
CHARLOTTE SQUARE
Roxburghe Hotel
Martins
Alp Horn

QUEENSFERRY ST
No 10
PRINCES STREET 21
25
15

Handsel's
SHANDWICK PLACE
Caledonian Hotel and Pompadour Restaurant
18
1

Stakis Grosvenor Hotel
W MAITLAND ST
TORPHICHEN ST
LOTHIAN ROAD
Edinburgh Sheraton
32 23
GRASSMARKET
5

13 22 34
A8
MORRISON STREET
BREAD STREET
WEST PORT

Ellersly House Hotel
Post House
Royal Scot Hotel

A71 DALRY RD
A8
LANARK 34miles
STIRLING 37miles

WEST APPROACH ROAD
EARL GREY ST
BROUGHAM ST
HOME ST
LAURISTON PLACE

7
8

BRUNTSFIELD PLACE
LEVEN ST
11
MELVILLE DRIVE

Bruntsfield Hotel
A702
9
Braid Hills Hotel
Champany Inn Town

CARLISLE 98miles

© 1987 Egon Ronay's Guides

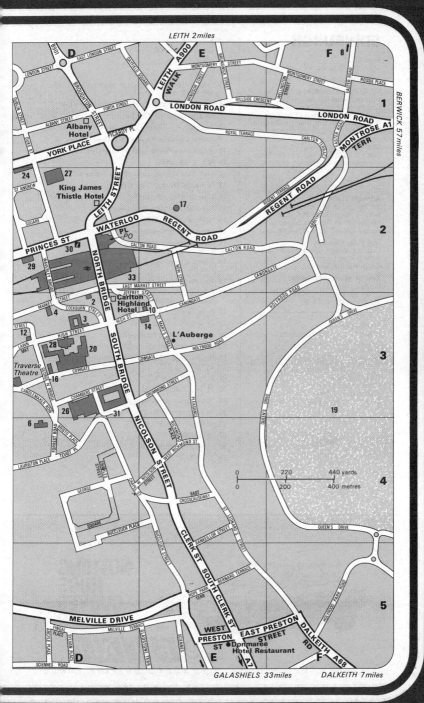

EDINBURGH

Map 12 C1
Town plan on preceding page

Population 444,741

Edinburgh was founded about a thousand years ago on the Rock which dominates the city. The narrow Old Town, with its one main street (the Royal Mile stretching from the Castle to Holyroodhouse) is the city of John Knox and Mary Queen of Scots. Its Royal Charter was granted by Robert the Bruce in 1329. The gracious New Town is a magnificent example of 18th-century town planning. Today Edinburgh is a centre of festival and pageantry, culture and conferences.

Annual Events
Edinburgh Festival *9th–30th August*
Festival Fringe *9th–30th August*
Military Tattoo *7th–29th August*
Royal Highland Show *21st–24th June*

Sights Outside City
Cramond Village, Duddingston Village, Forth Bridge, Lauriston Castle, Craigmillar Castle

Tourist Information Centre
Waverley Market
3 Princess Street EH2 2QP
Telephone 031–557 2727

Fiat Dealers
Hamilton Bros. (Edinburgh) Ltd
162 St Johns Road
Corstorphine
Edinburgh EH12 8AZ
Tel. 031–334 6248

Croall & Croall
Glenogle Road
Edinburgh EH3 5HW
Telephone 031–556 6404

1 Castle C3
2 City Art Centre D3
3 City Chambers D3
4 Festival Booking Office D3
5 Grassmarket *picturesque old buildings and antique shops* C3
6 Greyfriars Kirk *and Greyfriars Bobby statue* D4
7 Heart of Midlothian F.C. A4
8 Hibernian F.C. *Easter Road Park* F1
9 Hillend *dry ski centre open all year* B5
10 John Knox's House *1490, timber galleries* D/E3
11 King's Theatre B5
12 Lady Stair's House *1692, literary museum* D3
13 Murrayfield Rugby Ground A4
14 Museum of Childhood E3
15 National Gallery *try 'Sound Guide'* C3
16 National Library D3
17 Nelson's Monument *viewpoint* E2
18 Outlook Tower *Camera obscura and Scottish life exhibition* C3
19 Palace of Holyroodhouse and Arthur's Seat and the Park F3
20 Parliament House and Law Courts D3
21 Princes Street *shopping and gardens, bandstand, floral clock, war memorials* B3/C2/D2
22 Royal Highland Showground A3
23 Royal Lyceum Theatre B3
24 Royal Museum of Scotland D2
25 Royal Scottish Academy C2
26 Royal Scottish Museum *largest museum of science and art in U.K.* D3
27 St Andrew Square Bus Station D2
28 St Giles' Cathedral D3
29 Scott Monument *viewpoint* D2
30 Tourist Information Centre D2
31 University of Edinburgh D3
32 Usher Hall B3
33 Waverley Station D2
34 Zoo A3

Caledonian Hotel   Edinburgh

HR **78% £A/B** *E* &
Town plan B3 Lothian
Princes Street EH1 2AB
031-225 2433. Tlx 72179
Manager Dermot Fitzpatrick
Credit Access, Amex, Diners, Visa

Standing in the shadow of Castle Rock, the Caledonian is a sturdy Edwardian purpose-built hotel at the western end of Princes Street. Old-fashioned standards of service and comfort are praiseworthy, with courteous staff going out of their way to be helpful. Bedrooms are splendidly appointed, with sitting areas and high-quality furnishings and fabrics, and well-equipped

bathrooms. The pillared lounge has ample sofas and chairs, and there's a convivial bar with (in the evening) a pianist. No dogs.
Amenities hairdressing, in-house movies (free), laundry service, 24-hour lounge service, kiosk.

■ *Rooms 247*	*Confirm by 6*
en suite bath/shower 247	*Last dinner 10.30*
Direct dial Yes	*Parking Ample*
Room TV Yes	*Room service 24 hours*

Pompadour Restaurant &

Manager George Figuerola
'Legends of the Scottish Table' is the lunchtime selection in the elegant Pompadour, using the best in Scottish produce. The evening menu is modern French, with dishes like red mullet fillets with ratatouille, or rosette of beef with shallot purée and sage butter. Good home-baked bread; well-kept cheeses; tempting sweets. Note the excellent Alsace wines on a keenly priced list. ⊖

■ *Set L £11·50*	*L 12.30–2*
Set D £25	*D 7.30–10.30*
About £70 for two	*Seats 65*
Closed L Sat & Sun, 26 Dec & 2 Jan	

■ If we recommend meals in a hotel or inn, a separate entry is made for its restaurant.

Carlton Highland Hotel   Edinburgh

H **71% £B/C** *E* &
Town plan D3 Lothian
North Bridge EH1 1SD
031-556 7277. Tlx 727001
Credit Access, Amex, Diners, Visa. **LVs**

In a prime location close to Waverley Station and overlooking Princes Street, this hotel is a fine example of Scottish Baronial style. An amalgamation of the old hotel and an adjoining department store, it combines the magnificent proportions of the original building with every modern comfort. Stylish festoon blinds enhance the public areas. Bedrooms with pretty matching covers and curtains offer extras like mini-bars. Attractively decorated bathrooms have showers over the tubs. Staff are generally friendly and helpful. *Amenities* indoor swimming pool, sauna, solarium, whirlpool bath, steam bath, gymnasium,

squash, games room, snooker, pool table, in-house movies (free), laundry service, coffee shop (10am–10pm), 24-hour lounge service, crèche, nanny.

■ *Rooms 207*	*Confirm by 6*
en suite bath/shower 207	*Last dinner 10.30*
Direct dial Yes	*Parking Ample*
Room TV Yes	*Room service 24 hours*

Champany Grill   Edinburgh

R & **Town plan B5** Lothian
2 Bridge Road, Colinton EH13 0LF
031-441 2587
Credit Access, Amex, Diners, Visa

Prime Aberdeen Angus beef, chargrilled to perfection, is the star attraction at this smart little restaurant. Other main courses, also featuring first-class ingredients, range from veal and lamb to baby chicken and salmon steaks. Start perhaps

with garlicky chicken liver pâté or pickled fish. Tempting sweets, friendly and helpful service. Excellent wines include fine Beaujolais crus.
♀ Well-chosen ⊖

■ *About £50 for two*	*L 12.30–2*
Seats 40	*D 7–10*
Parties 40	*Parking Ample*
Closed Sun, 25 & 26 Dec & 1st 2 wks Jan	

Crest Hotel, Edinburgh

H 66% £C/D
Town plan A2 Lothian
Queensferry Road EH4 3HL
031-332 2442. Tlx 72541
Credit Access, Amex, Diners, Visa

A modern eight-storey hotel on the A90 with a bright foyer offering plenty of comfortable seating and a bar with '30s theme. Standard bedrooms are pleasantly decorated and there's also studio, executive, ladies' and non-smoking rooms. Small bathrooms, some with shower only. *Amenities* garden, in-house movies (charge), laundry service, coffee shop (10am–6pm), 24-hour lounge service, children's playroom.

■ *Rooms* 120	*Confirm by* 6
en suite bath/shower 120	*Last dinner* 9.45
Direct dial Yes	*Parking* Ample
Room TV Yes	*Room service* 24 hours

Donmaree Hotel Restaurant

R 😊 **Town plan E5** Lothian
21 Mayfield Gardens
031-667 3641
French cooking
Owner manager Teresa White
Credit Access, Amex, Diners, Visa

Generous portions of skilfully prepared, mainly familiar French dishes make this atmospheric Victorian hotel-restaurant a deservedly popular eating place. Onion and mussel soup is a typical tasty starter, while main courses range from straightforward grills to appetisingly sauced offerings like venison with red wine and cranberries. Tempting sweets. 🍴

■ *Set L* £6·95	*L* 12.30–2
About £50 for two	*D* 6.30–10
Seats 45	*Parking* Ample
Closed L Sat, all Sun & Bank Hols	

■ Any person using our name to obtain free hospitality is a fraud. Proprietors, please inform the police and us.

Edinburgh Sheraton

H 78% £C *E* ♿
Town plan B3 Lothian
1 Festival Square EH3 9SR
031-229 9131. Tlx 72398
Credit Access, Amex, Diners, Visa

Boasting views of city and castle, the recently-built Sheraton strikes an affluent international note with its gleaming, smooth-stone exterior and smart marble-floored foyer. Tropical plants adorn the stylishly comfortable lounge and bar areas. Elsewhere, extensive conference and banqueting suites cater for all types of function, both business and private. Spacious, air-conditioned bedrooms (including 16 suites) have pretty pastel colour schemes, functional lightwood units, good easy chairs and bedside controls. Smart bathrooms offer an abundance of towels, soaps and shelf space. No dogs. *Amenities* indoor

swimming pool, sauna, whirlpool bath, gymnasium, in-house movies (free), teletext, valeting, laundry service, 24-hour lounge service, kiosk.

■ *Rooms* 263	*Confirm by* 4
en suite bath/shower 263	*Last dinner* 10.30
Direct dial Yes	*Parking* Ample
Room TV Yes	*Room service* 24 hours

Ellersly House Hotel

H 60% £C/D
Town plan A4 Lothian
Ellersly Road EH12 6HZ
031-337 6888
Credit Access, Amex, Diners, Visa. **LVs**

An extended Edwardian house in a quiet residential setting near Murrayfield rugby ground. Improvements have been made to the day rooms, from the entrance and foyer to the lounge and cocktail bar, and attention will turn next to the accommodation. Main-house bedrooms have a traditional look, while those in the annexes are more modern. No dogs. *Amenities* garden, croquet, 24-hour lounge service.

■ *Rooms* 55	*Confirm by* 6
en suite bath/shower 55	*Last dinner* 9
Direct dial Yes	*Parking* Ample
Room TV Yes	*Room service* 24 hours

George Hotel

H **77% £B** *E*
Town plan C2 Lothian
George Street EH2 2PB
031-225 1251. Tlx 72570
Manager John Acton
Credit Access, Amex, Diners, Visa
Physical features impress at this sturdy old hotel just north of Princes Street. The lobby is particularly fine, with its marble floor, fluted columns and ornately worked ceiling; splendid, too, are the domed restaurant and the handsome bar, the latter with striking blue decor and a clan theme. Bedrooms, all with smart furnishings, provide abundant space and comfort, and bathrooms are luxuriously appointed, with excellent toiletries and generous soft towels. Reception on our latest visit was friendly and efficient, but porterage and room service were

less good, and continental breakfast definitely not up to standard. *Amenities* teletext, laundry service, 24-hour lounge service.

■ *Rooms* 195	*Confirm by* 6
en suite bath/shower 195	*Last dinner* 10
Direct dial Yes	*Parking* Limited
Room TV Yes	*Room service* 24 hours

Handsel's *NEW ENTRY*

R **Town plan A3** Lothian
22 Stafford Street
031-225 5521
Owner managers David & Tina Thomson
Credit Access, Amex, Diners, Visa
Two sumptuously decorated first-floor rooms in an elegant Georgian house. Menus are table d'hôte, with a choice at lunchtime. Meats and sauces are excellent, as in veal sweetbreads with

smoked bacon, but we found the baking variable – good oatmeal biscuits, poor petits fours. Splendid wine list, strong in Bordeaux. Pleasant, professional service. ♀ **Well-chosen** ☺

■ *Set L from* £10·50	*L* 12–2
Set D £23	*D* 7.30–10
About £60 *for two*	*Parking* Limited
Seats 28	*Parties* 30
Closed L Sat, all Sun & Bank Hols	

☞ is our symbol for an **outstanding** wine list.

Howard Hotel

H **64% £C/D**
Town plan C1
32 Great King Street EH3 6QH
031-557 3500. Tlx 727887
Credit Access, Amex, Diners, Visa. **LVs**
A fine conversion in an elegant Georgian terrace, the Howard has a real town-house feel. On the ground floor guests can relax in a quiet, lofty lounge or socialise in the smart cocktail bar;

there's also a lively basement bar. Front bedrooms are appointed in tasteful modern style, while those at the back are more traditional; all have well-fitted bathrooms and remote-control TVs. *Amenities* garden, laundry service.

■ *Rooms* 25	*Confirm by arrang.*
en suite bath/shower 25	*Last dinner* 9.30
Direct dial Yes	*Parking* Limited
Room TV Yes	*Room service* 24 hours

King James Thistle Hotel

H **71% £C** *E*
Town plan D2 Lothian
St James Centre, Leith Street EH1 3SW
031-556 0111. Tlx 727200
Credit Access, Amex, Diners, Visa
Understated luxury is the keynote here, with top-quality service to match. In a convenient location just off Princes Street, this modern hotel makes an excellent first impression with its elegant marble-floored foyer leading into a beautifully furnished wood-panelled lounge area. Plans are afoot to create a diner within the spacious American-style bar. Bedrooms with brass-inlaid darkwood units and pretty matching fabrics offer a good range of extras, including trouser presses and hairdryers. Executive guests can enjoy perks like priority parking and access to an exclusive and extremely comfortable lounge

bar. No dogs.
Amenities in-house movies (one free), laundry service.

■ *Rooms* 147	*Confirm by* 6
en suite bath/shower 147	*Last dinner* 10.25
Direct dial Yes	*Parking* Limited
Room TV Yes	*Room service* 24 hours

Ladbroke Dragonara Hotel

H **74% £B E** &
 Town plan A2 Lothian
Bells Mills, Belford Road EH4 3DG
031-332 2545. Tlx 727979
Credit Access, Amex, Diners, Visa

The setting, beside the lovely Water of Leith, is
surprisingly tranquil, as this smooth-running
modern hotel is just minutes from the city centre.
The roomy foyer-lounge has plenty of deep,
comfortable sofas, and guests with a thirst can
head for the rustic, stone-walled Granary Bar in a
converted mill building overlooking the river.
There's also an intimate cocktail bar. Decent-
sized bedrooms are pleasant and practical, with
trouser presses, hairdryers and radio-alarms. Tiled
bathrooms offer radio speakers and a good range
of toiletries. Good housekeeping, friendly staff
and easy parking are further pluses, but breakfast

is serve-yourself and mediocre.
Amenities in-house movies (charge), laundry
service, 24-hour lounge service.

■ *Rooms 146*	*Confirm by 6*
en suite bath/shower 146	*Last dinner 10.30*
Direct dial Yes	*Parking Ample*
Room TV Yes	*Room service Limited*

Le Marché Noir *NEW ENTRY*

R ⌕ & **Town plan C1** Lothian
 2/4 Eyre Place
031-558 1608
Credit Access, Visa

The atmosphere and decor are very French, the
menu ditto with the odd exotic touch. There's
good home-produced charcuterie, and fresh fish
features strongly (salmon en croûte, fillets of John
Dory and cod provençale). Meaty main dishes,

too, then tempting sweets and well-kept cheeses.
Cooking is enjoyable, service friendly. Interesting
wines at reasonable prices: Côte de Brouilly
Château Thivin 1985 is a delicious bottle.
♀ Well-chosen ℮

■ *Set L £6.50*	*L 12–2.30*
Set D from £10	*D 7–10, Sat 7–11*
About £30 for two	*Parking Limited*
Seats 45 Parties 45	*Closed Sun*

Martins

R **Town plan C2** Lothian
 70 Rose Street, North Lane
031-225 3106
Owner manager Martin Irons
Credit Access, Amex, Diners, Visa

In recognition of the current call for smaller
quantities of food, Martin Irons is offering à la
carte in place of his fixed-price 4-course meals.
Dinner might be fresh mussels in herb butter with

pasta, followed by filet en croûte. Cooking is
highly competent, with subtle use of seasonings,
and simple presentation. The extended wine list
remains praiseworthy. ♀ Well-chosen ℮

■ *About £43 for two*	*L 12–2*
Seats 28	*D 7–10,*
Parties 10	*Fri & Sat 7–10.30*
Closed L Sat, all Sun	*Parking Difficult*
& Mon & 1 week Xmas	

No 10 Restaurant

R **Town plan A3**
 10 Melville Place
031-225 8727
Credit Access, Amex, Diners, Visa

Portraits of prime ministers line the walls of this
little basement restaurant, where owner Gianni
Barbero does the hosting and Paul Subido does
the cooking. His menu offers enjoyable
international favourites running from minestrone

and fresh pasta to sole bonne femme, chicken
stuffed with pâté, veal escalope milanese and
various steaks. To finish, try nice cool zabaglione
garnished with sliced strawberries. Good-value
set lunch. ℮

■ *Set L £5*	*L 12–2.30*
About £25 for two	*D 6.30–11*
Seats 45	*Parking Limited*
Closed L Sun, also D Sun (Oct–Apr)	

Post House Hotel

H **63% £C/D** &
 Town plan A4 Lothian
Corstorphine Road EH12 6UA
Edinburgh (031 334) 0390. Tlx 727103
Credit Access, Amex, Diners, Visa. LVs

A large modern hotel on the A8, next to the
Zoological Gardens. It's also close to Murrayfield,
and the rugby theme is picked up in the Cross
Bar. Bedrooms, many of which can convert to

family rooms, have tea-makers and mini-bars, and
rooms designated superior also offer trouser
presses, hairdryers and extra toiletries. *Amenities*
garden, in-house movies (free), coffee shop
(10.30am–10.30pm), kiosk.

■ *Rooms 208*	*Confirm by 6*
en suite bath/shower 208	*Last dinner 10.30*
Direct dial Yes	*Parking Ample*
Room TV Yes	*Room service Limited*

■ Our inspectors are our full-
time employees; they are
professionally trained by us.

Roxburghe Hotel   Edinburgh

H 67% £B/C &
Town plan B2 Lothian
38 Charlotte Square EH2 4HG
031-225 3921. Tlx 727054
Manager Donald Addison
Credit Access, Amex, Diners, Visa
    Behind the fine Adam facade, traditional
standards of service and hospitality prevail. Day
rooms have a comfortable, elegant feel.

Bedrooms are generally quite roomy (singles more
compact), with freestanding furniture, tea-makers,
radio-alarms and trouser presses.
Amenities laundry service, coffee shop (7.30am–
6pm), 24-hour lounge service.

■ *Rooms* 76	*Confirm by* 6
en suite bath/shower 76	*Last dinner* 10
Direct dial Yes	*Parking* Difficult
Room TV Yes	*Room service* Limited

Royal Scot Hotel   Edinburgh

H 65% £C
Town plan A4 Lothian
111 Glasgow Road EH12 8NF
031-334 9191. Tlx 727197
Manager Mr L. Nolan
Credit Access, Amex, Diners, Visa. **LVs**
    A modern hotel on the A8, offering spacious
accommodation in double-glazed bedrooms.
Public areas include an atmospheric bar and

coffee shop. *Amenities* garden, indoor swimming
pool, sauna, solarium, whirlpool bath, keep-fit
equipment, hairdressing, golf driving range, pitch
& putt, in-house movies (charge), laundry service,
coffee shop (7.30am–11pm), courtesy transport.

■ *Rooms* 252	*Confirm by* 6
en suite bath/shower 252	*Last dinner* 10
Direct dial Yes	*Parking* Ample
Room TV Yes	*Room service* 24 hours

Stakis Grosvenor Hotel   Edinburgh

H 59% £C &
Town plan A3 Lothian
Grosvenor Street EH12 5EA
031-226 6001. Tlx 72445
Credit Access, Amex, Diners, Visa
    The Stakis Grosvenor is a conversion of several
Victorian terrace houses. The central location
makes it popular with tourists, and there are good
facilities for the business visitor. Bedrooms, where

upgrading is taking place, range from compact
singles to large family size, and all offer extras like
trouser presses, hairdryers and fresh fruit. There's
a large, relaxing lobby-lounge and a pleasant bar.

■ *Rooms* 136	*Confirm by* 6
en suite bath/shower 136	*Last dinner* 10
Direct dial Yes	*Parking* Difficult
Room TV Yes	*Room service* Limited

■ We welcome complaints and bona
fide recommendations on the
tear-out pages for readers' comments.
They are followed up by our professional
team. Please also complain to the
management instantly.

RECEPTION

Ladbroke Mercury Hotel   Ellon

H 60% £D/E
Map 16 D3 Grampian
AB4 9NP
Ellon (0358) 20666. Tlx 739200
Credit Access, Amex, Diners, Visa. **LVs**
    An unremarkable looking modern hotel on the
edge of town offering a decent standard of
accommodation to a mainly business clientele. A
small lobby leads into each bedroom, providing

useful storage space, and all rooms have fully
tiled bathrooms. The reception-lounge is large
and rather basic, and the cocktail bar with its
beige colour scheme is a more congenial spot to
unwind. *Amenities* snooker, laundry service.

■ *Rooms* 40	*Confirm by* arrang.
en suite bath/shower 40	*Last dinner* 9.30
Room phone Yes	*Parking* Ample
Room TV Yes	*Room service* 24 hours

Isle of Eriska — Eriska

HR 73% £B ⏣
Map 17 B5 Strathclyde
Ledaig, by Oban PA37 1SD
Ledaig (063 172) 371. Tlx 777040
Owner managers Mr & Mrs Buchanan-Smith
Credit Access, Amex, Diners

Cross a little bridge to the splendid Scottish Baronial Island home of Robin and Sheena Buchanan-Smith. Calm and tranquillity are all around, and the owners and their staff make sure that guests are warmly welcomed. Log fires and a liberal supply of settees and armchairs make the day rooms eminently inviting, and the bay-windowed lounge is a particularly pleasant spot. Bedrooms are large and very comfortable, with tasteful fabrics and some fine antiques. Superb housekeeping keeps everything gleaming. Half-board terms only. *Amenities* garden, tennis,

croquet, riding, coarse & game fishing, sailing, boating, board sailing, water skiing, laundry service, 24-hour lounge service.
■ *Rooms* 17 — *Confirm by* 10
en suite bath/shower 17 — *Last dinner* 8.30
Direct dial Yes — *Parking* Ample
Room TV Yes — *Room service* 24 hours
Closed Dec–20 Feb

Isle of Eriska Restaurant ꕤ ⏣ ⏣

A very civilised restaurant, with wheelback chairs set around polished antique tables. Six-course evening meals centre round a roast (with perhaps a fish alternative). Before it could come cheese aigrettes and cream of carrot and orange soup, after it nice sweets from the trolley, a savoury and cheese. Lighter lunches too, and a roast for Sunday lunch; buffet Sunday evening. Simon Burns is the head chef, with Sheena Buchanan-Smith on sweets. Carefully selected wines. ⏣
■ *Set L from* £4, — *L* 12.45–1.45
Sun £16.50 — *D* 7.30–8.30
Set D £21 — *Seats* 40
About £52 *for two* — *Parking* Ample
Closed Dec–20 Feb

Crest Hotel — Erskine

H 58% £C/D ⏣
Map 12 B1 Strathclyde
By Erskine Bridge, Nr Glasgow PA8 6AN
041-812 0123. Tlx 777713
Credit Access, Amex, Diners, Visa

A modern hotel overlooking the Clyde. Public rooms have been much improved, particularly the foyer with its new carpet, better lighting and leather armchairs. A bar and adjoining lounge are also pleasant spots to relax. Work is now in hand on corridors and bedrooms, which have attractive quilted bedcovers. *Amenities* garden, solarium, keep-fit equipment, pitch & putt, pool table, laundry service, kiosk, transport to airport.
■ *Rooms* 186 — *Confirm by* arrang.
en suite bath/shower 186 — *Last dinner* 9.45
Direct dial Yes — *Parking* Ample
Room TV Yes — *Room service* 24 hours

Ettrickshaws Hotel — Ettrickbridge

H 62% £D/E
Map 12 D2 Borders
Nr Selkirk TD7 5HW
Ettrickbridge (0750) 5229. Tlx 94013112
Owner managers Terry & Shirley Ashton
Credit Access, Amex, Diners, Visa

A substantial Victorian building standing in fine walking country by the river Ettrick. Bedrooms are comfortable and traditional, bathrooms modern. There's a cosy bar and two lounges, one reserved for non-smokers. Pleasant new owners, decent breakfasts. No children under 9. *Amenities* garden, croquet, game fishing, laundry service.
■ *Rooms* 6 — *Confirm by* 6
en suite bath/shower 5 — *Last dinner* 9.15
Direct dial Yes — *Parking* Ample
Room TV Yes — *Room service* All day
Closed mid Dec–mid Feb

■ For a discount on next year's guide, see Offer for Answers.

Hotel Cladhan — Falkirk

H 57% £E ⏣
Map 12 C1 Central
Kemper Avenue FK1 1VF
Falkirk (0324) 27421
Owner manager Mr W. L. Reid
Credit Access, Amex, Diners, Visa

Behind the stark early '70s exterior this is a warm, welcoming hotel with a conscientious owner and very pleasant staff. Half the bedrooms have been upgraded with good-quality fitted furniture; all are light and airy, with well-equipped bathrooms. Public rooms include a lounge with a bar at each end, and a new coffee shop. *Amenities* teletext, coffee shop (7am–9.20pm).
■ *Rooms* 37 — *Confirm by* arrang.
en suite bath/shower 37 — *Last dinner* 9.30
Direct dial Yes — *Parking* Ample
Room TV Yes — *Room service* None

Pierre's Falkirk

R **Map 12 C1** Central
140 Graham's Road
Falkirk (0324) 35843
French cooking
Owner manager Pierre Renjard
Credit Access, Amex, Diners, Visa

Enjoyable French dishes are reliably well prepared at this cosy little restaurant. Garlicky frog's legs, fish soup and fresh salmon pâté are among tasty starters, while main courses range from flavoursome boeuf en daube to Calvados-braised quails and various ways with steak. Crêpes and profiteroles among appealing desserts. Cheerful service. ☺

■ *Set D* 9·75   L *12–2.15*
About £44 for two   D *7–9.30*
Seats 35   *Parking Ample*
Closed L *Sat, all Sun, 25, 26 Dec & 1, 2 Jan*

Royal Hotel Forfar

H **56% £E**
Map 17 C4 Tayside
Castle Street DD8 3AE
Forfar (0307) 62691
Owner managers Brian & Alison Bonnyman
Credit Amex, Diners, Visa

A continuing programme of improvement at this tartan-carpeted hotel in the town centre is evidenced in a smart coffee shop/wine bar, a new leisure centre and a bridal suite. Bedrooms are all clean and adequate. No dogs. *Amenities* garden, indoor swimming pool, sauna, solarium, whirlpool bath, keep fit equipment, laundry service, coffee shop (10am–11pm), 24-hour lounge service.

■ *Rooms* 19   *Confirm by arrang.*
en suite bath/shower 17   *Last dinner* 9
Direct dial Yes   *Parking Ample*
Room TV Yes   *Room service* 24 hours

Factor's House Restaurant   *NEW ENTRY* Fort William

RR **Map 17 B4** Highland
Torlundy PH33 6SN
Fort William (0397) 5767
Owner manager Peter Hobbs
Credit Access, Amex, Visa

Splendid views of Ben Nevis can be enjoyed from the timber-ceilinged dining room of this former estate manager's residence. It's a delightfully civilised yet informal place, with owner Peter Hobbs – splendidly attired in kilt – directing a friendly and charming team. Blackboards display the evening's appetising selection – perhaps soup or salmon pancakes or cauliflower cheesecake followed by chargrilled steak, chicken casserole or Hebridean fish pie, with silky-rich chocolate marquise to finish. ☺

■ *Set D* £12·75   D *only 7.30–9.30*
About £35 for two   *Parking Ample*
Seats 24 *Closed* Mon & Dec–Easter

Bedrooms **£D/E**
Rooms 6   *With bath/shower* 6
For overnight guests there are six stylish, comfortable bedrooms, all with modern private facilities. Day rooms include two charming little lounges, where guests are invited to play their own choice of records on the stereo.

Inverlochy Castle Fort William

HR **91% £A**
Map 17 B4 Highland
Torlundy PH33 6SN
Fort William (0397) 2177
Owner manager Mrs Greta Hobbs
Credit Access, Visa

Built in 1863, this splendid castle in the shadow of Ben Nevis was visited ten years later by Queen Victoria, who recorded in her diaries 'I never saw a lovelier or more romantic spot'. The same holds true today for this acme of country house hotels, where antiques, fresh flowers and sumptuous furnishings fill elegant day rooms and the Great Hall boasts a fine staircase and gallery, and a lovely frescoed ceiling hung with crystal chandeliers. Spacious bedrooms are just as impressive, with their fine fabrics, dainty porcelain and many thoughtful extras. Luxurious bathrooms all have generous fluffy towels and bathrobes. No dogs. *Amenities* garden, tennis, game fishing, billiards, snooker, valeting, laundry service, 24-hour lounge service.

■ *Rooms* 16   *Confirm by arrang.*
en suite bath/shower 16   *Last dinner* 9.15
Direct dial Yes   *Parking Ample*
Room TV Yes   *Room service* 24 hours
Closed end Nov–mid Mar

Inverlochy Castle Restaurant ♔ ♔ ♔

In a setting of formal elegance youthful new chef Graham Newbould offers a menu of limited choice but ample variety, with the emphasis on local produce. Typical choices might include tartare of wild salmon with a creamy chervil dressing followed by hare consommé, with supremely tender roast beef served with braised savoy cabbage as a favourite main course. Sweets and

cheeses can be disappointing. Splendid cellar, with great Bordeaux and burgundies from the best growers. No smoking.
⊃ Outstanding   ⚲ Well-chosen

■ Set L £17·25	L 12.30–2
Set D £29·30	D 7.30–9.15
About £70 for two	Seats 40 Parties 20
Closed end Nov–mid Mar	

Ladbroke Mercury Motor Inn   Fort William

H **59% £C/D**
Map 17 B4 Highland
Achintore Road PH33 6RW
Fort William (0397) 3117. Tlx 778454
Credit Access, Amex, Diners, Visa
  Just south of Fort William on the A82, a modern hotel with splendid views of Loch Linnhe from its roomy bar-lounge. The same views are shared by half the bedrooms, which have lightwood fitted

units, pleasant autumnal decor ard smart tiled bathrooms with ample shelf space. Remote-control TVs in all rooms. *Amenities* sauna, pool table, laundry service.

■ Rooms 86	Confirm by 6
en suite bath/shower 86	Last dinner 9.30
Direct dial Yes	Parking Ample
Room TV Yes	Room service None
Closed 1 wk Xmas	

⚲ indicates a **well-chosen** house wine.

Inchbae Lodge Hotel   Garve

H **57% £F**
Map 16 B3 Highland
Inchbae IV23 2PH
Aultguish (099 75) 269
Owner manager Leslie V. Mitchell
  A former hunting lodge, this attractive, white-painted hotel nestles in a beautiful setting on the banks of the river Blackwater (about four miles from Garve on the A835). Six of the modestly-

appointed bedrooms are in the main house; six, with little shower rooms, are in a red cedar chalet. There's a warm, homely lounge and a rustic bar. *Amenities* garden, game fishing, clay-pigeon shooting.

■ Rooms 12	Confirm by arrang.
en suite bath/shower 9	Last dinner 9
Room phone No	Parking Ample
Room TV No	Room service None

Cally Palace Hotel   Gatehouse of Fleet

H **67% £C/D**
Map 13 B4 Dumfries & Galloway
DG7 2DL
Gatehouse (05574) 341
Manager Jennifer Adams
Credit Visa
  A handsome country mansion with lovely grounds. Public rooms include a marbled foyer, plush bar and sun lounge. Bedrooms have good

bathrooms and lots of extras. *Amenities* garden, outdoor swimming pool, sauna, solarium, tennis, putting, croquet, pool table, laundry service, 24-hour lounge service, children's play area.

■ Rooms 65	Confirm by arrang.
en suite bath/shower 65	Last dinner 9.30
Direct dial Yes	Parking Ample
Room TV Yes	Room service 24 hours
Closed Jan & Feb	

Murray Arms   Gatehouse of Fleet

I **£D/E**
Map 13 B4 Dumfries & Galloway
Anne Street DG7 2HY
Gatehouse (05574) 207
Manager Robin Raphael
Credit Access, Amex, Diners, Visa
  Robert Burns wrote his 'Scots Wha Hae' in this splendid red posting inn, which still retains much of its original charm. The public areas include

numerous little parlours and sitting rooms, plus cosy bars and a separate food bar. Bedrooms are simple, clean and pleasant. *Amenities* garden, tennis, 9-hole golf course, croquet, game fishing, coffee shop (noon–9.30pm).

■ Rooms 19	Confirm by 6
en suite bath/shower 17	Last dinner 8.45
Direct dial Yes	Parking Ample
Room TV Yes	Room service Limited

Macdonald Thistle Hotel   Giffnock

H **65% £C/D**
Map 12 B2 Strathclyde
Eastwood Toll G46 6RA
041-638 2225. Tlx 779138
Manager Mr J. P. F. Magennis
Credit Access, Amex, Diners, Visa
  On the A77 south of Glasgow, this is a pleasant modern hotel, well run and with high standards of repair. Comfortable bedrooms have easy chairs,

trouser presses and hairdryers, plus smartly tiled bathrooms. The colonial-themed Sundowners bar is most appealing. *Amenities* sauna, solarium, keep-fit equipment, pool table, in-house movies (free), laundry service, 24-hour lounge service.

■ Rooms 62	Confirm by 6
en suite bath/shower 62	Last dinner 9.45
Direct dial Yes	Parking Ample
Room TV Yes	Room service 24 hours

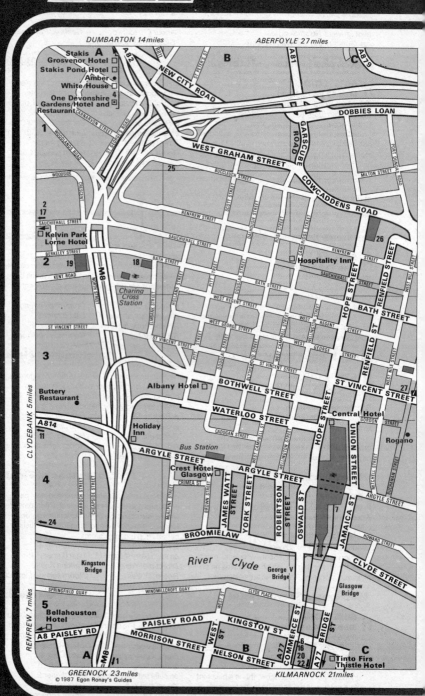

FIAT Glasgow

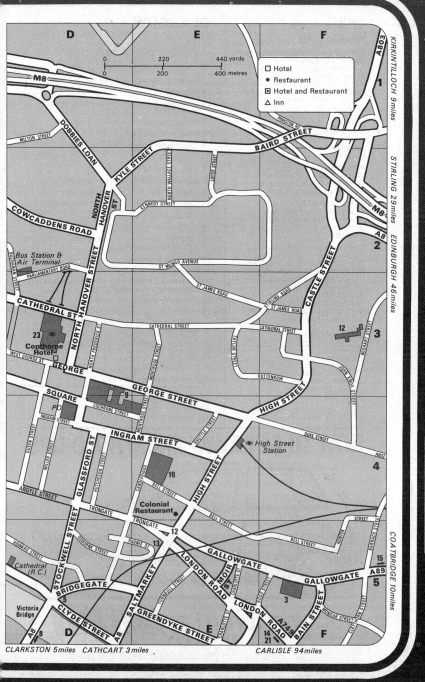

Map 12 B1
Town plan on preceding page

Population 755,429

Prime factors in Glasgow's history were the River Clyde and the Industrial Revolution (helped by the Lowland genius for shipbuilding and engineering). Glasgow is the home of Scottish Opera, Scottish Ballet and the Scottish National Orchestra. The city has a fine collection of museums, most notably that at Kelvingrove and the Burrell Gallery. Famous for learning (two universities), sport (soccer), shops, and art galleries, the city boasts over seventy parks and the Scottish Exhibition and Conference Centre.

Annual Events
Mayfest, Paisley Festival *May*
Horse Show and Country Fair *July*
Glasgow Marathon *September*

Sights Outside City
Paisley Abbey, Forth and Clyde Canal at Kirkintilloch, Clyde Muirshiel Park at Lochwinnoch, Weavers Cottage (Kilbarchan)

Tourist Information Offices
35/39 St Vincent Place, Glasgow G1 2ER. Open June–Sept Mon–Sat 9am–9pm Sun 10am–6pm. Open Oct–May Mon–Sat 9am–5pm Sun Closed Telephone 041–227 4880.
Telex 779504
Town Hall, Abbey Close, Paisley PA1 1JS. Open June–Sept Mon–Fri 9am–6pm, Sat 9am–5pm, Oct–May Mon–Fri 9am–5pm
Telephone 041–889 0711

Fiat Dealers
Peat Road Motors (Jordanhill) Ltd
120 Whittingehame Drive
Jordanhill, Glasgow GL12 0YJ
Tel. 041–357 1939

Ritchie's
393 Shields Road, Glasgow G41 1 NZ
Tel. 041–429 5611

GLASGOW

1 Airport A5
2 Art Gallery and Museum *paintings, ceramics, silver, costumes, etc.* A2
3 The Barrows *weekend street market* F5
4 Botanic Gardens A1
5 Briggait D5
6 Burrell Gallery *paintings, stained glass, tapestries, ceramics* C5
7 Central Station C4
8 Citizens' Theatre D5
9 City Chambers *fine loggia* D3
10 City Hall E4
11 Clyde Tunnel A4
12 Glasgow Cathedral *impressive Gothic* F3
13 Glasgow Cross *1626 Tolbooth Steeple* E5
14 Glasgow Green *city's oldest riverside park* F5
15 Glasgow Zoo F5
16 Haggs Castle—*children* C5
17 Hunterian Museum & Art Gallery (Glasgow University) *early books, archaeology* A2
18 King's Theatre A2
19 Mitchell Library and Theatre A2
20 Museum of Transport *comprehensive collection. Also engineering, shipbuilding* C5
21 People's Palace *local history* F5
22 Pollok House *Spanish paintings, English furniture, rare silver, in Adam building amid parkland* C5
23 Queen Street Station D3
24 Scottish Exhibition and Conference Centre A4
25 Tenement House B1
26 Theatre Royal C2
27 Tourist Information Centre C3

Currie of Shettleston
85–89 Amulree Street
Glasgow G32 7UN
Tel. 041–778 1295

Albany Hotel   Glasgow

H **75% £C** *E*
Town plan B3 Strathclyde
Bothwell Street G2 7EN
041-248 2656. Tlx 77440
Credit Access, Amex, Diners, Visa. LVs
　Popular with both tourists and the business
community, this high-rise city-centre hotel, with its
extensive conference facilities, was built in 1973.
The foyer is most impressive with a marble floor,
large leather chesterfield settees and fine prints
adorning the walls. Equally spacious and elegant
is the Albany bar, open all day, with comfortable
seating and light airy colours. There's also a pine-
panelled basement bar. The bedrooms, with
double glazing and air conditioning, are
attractively furnished in contemporary style with
white units, pine furniture, coordinated floral
fabrics and photos of the Scottish countryside. All

rooms have mini-bars, tea-makers, and fully tiled,
well-equipped bathrooms.
Amenities snooker, laundry service, 24-hour
lounge service.

■ *Rooms* 255	*Confirm by* 6
en suite bath/shower 255	*Last dinner* 11
Direct dial Yes	*Parking* Limited
Room TV Yes	*Room service* 24 hours

▷ is our symbol for an **outstanding** wine list.

Amber   Glasgow

R **Town plan A1** Strathclyde
130 Byres Road
041-339 6121
Chinese cooking
Owner manager Jimmy Tsang
Credit Access, Amex, Diners, Visa
　Cooking is of a high standard at this pleasantly
relaxed Chinese restaurant. There's a 'popular'
menu, featuring familiar dishes like sweet and

sour pork, or a choice of traditional Cantonese
specialities such as tender fillet of beef in spicy
mandarin sauce. Friendly, efficient service.

■ *Set L* £3	*L* 12–2
Set D £12	*D* 5–11.30
About £32 for two	*Thurs–Sat* 5–12
Seats 70 *Parties* 80	*Parking* Ample
Closed L Sun	

Buttery *NEW ENTRY*   Glasgow

R ⌂ ⅋ **Town plan A3** Strathclyde
652 Argyle Street
041-221 8188
Credit Access, Amex, Diners, Visa
　Seek out this converted Victorian pub for fine
food and an excellent atmosphere. The walls are
panelled, the table settings stylish, with service
sous cloche by long-aproned waitresses. Cooking
is quite skilful and sophisticated, and the modern

menu includes terrine of chicken and duck livers
with a peppered yoghurt dressing, spinach-
wrapped crayfish with apple and ginger sauce
and saddle of venison with blackcurrants and
Kirsch. ⌆ **Well-chosen** ▷

■ *Set L* £11·50	*L* 12–2.30
About £52 for two	*D* 7–10
Seats 50 *Parties* 8	*Parking* Ample
Closed L Sat, all Sun & Bank Hols	

■ Changes in data may occur in
　establishments after the Guide
　goes to press. Prices should be taken
　as indications rather than firm quotes.

Central Hotel   Glasgow

H **61% £D/E** ⅋
Town plan C3 Strathclyde
Gordon Street G1 3SF
041-221 9680. Tlx 777771
Credit Access, Amex, Diners, Visa. LVs
　The lofty foyer recalls the Victorian grandeur of
this railway hotel by Central Station. Cane seating
and modern prints give a contemporary feel to the
bar, but the lounge areas are solidly traditional.

Bedroom refurbishment is under way – all rooms
have tea-makers and trouser presses.
Amenities keep-fit equipment, in-house movies
(free), laundry service, coffee shop (9am–11pm),
24-hour lounge service.

■ *Rooms* 229	*Confirm by* 6
en suite bath/shower 170	*Last dinner* 9.30
Direct dial Yes	*Parking* Difficult
Room TV Yes	*Room service* 24 hours

The Colonial Restaurant *NEW ENTRY* Glasgow

R ⌕ **Town plan E4** Strathclyde
25 High Street
041-552 1923
Credit Access, Amex, Diners, Visa

Peter Jackson (twice in the British Culinary Olympics team) cooks in sophisticated style, combining modern Scottish and French influences and using both local sources and Paris markets for his ingredients. The menus are full of interest, with starters like terrine of crab and sole with herb yogurt sauce, poached oysters with raspberry vinaigrette. Highly imaginative main courses may include succulent chicken from the Isle of Arran garnished with wild mushrooms, pavé of beef with a Blue Lanark cheese and Sauternes sauce or escalope of brill stuffed with trout mousse on a lobster sauce. Simple but well-conceived sweets. Choose from the good-value set menus or throw caution to the wind and try Mr Jackson's 'menu surprise'. 🍷 Well-chosen ☺

■ *Set L from £5·25*   *L 12–2.30*
Set D from £16·50   *D 6–10.30*
About £48 for two   *Parking Ample*
Seats 40   *Closed L Sat, D Mon,*
all Sun, Bank Hols, last 2 wks July, 4 days Xmas & 4 days New Year

Copthorne *NEW ENTRY* Glasgow

H **63% £D/E**
Town plan D3 Strathclyde
George Square G2 1DS
041-332 6711. Tlx 778147
Credit Access, Amex, Diners, Visa

Staff are notably smart and cheerful at this former railway hotel, whose public areas give a good, quite luxurious impression. The long glassed-in verandah is a nice place to sit and watch the world hurry by. Bedrooms in the old wing (try for a front one) tend to be larger and better furnished than those in the new wing. *Amenities* in-house movies (free), laundry service, 24-hour lounge service.

■ *Rooms 140*	*Confirm by 6*
en suite bath/shower 140	*Last dinner 10*
Direct dial Yes	*Parking Difficult*
Room TV Yes	*Room service 24 hours*

■ We publish annually, so make sure you use the current edition. It's worth it!

Crest Hotel, Glasgow City Glasgow

H **65% £C/D**
Town plan B4 Strathclyde
Argyle Street G2 8LL
041-248 2355. Tlx 779652
Credit Access, Amex, Diners, Visa

The refurbishment of this modern city-centre hotel has been completed with pleasing results. Stained natural wood and brass features are used to good effect in the public rooms, and the bedrooms have smart furniture and cheerful fabrics. Trouser presses and tea-makers are standard, and Executive rooms also get hairdryers, magazines and mini-bars. *Amenities* in-house movies (charge), laundry service.

■ *Rooms 121*	*Confirm by 6*
en suite bath/shower 121	*Last dinner 10*
Direct dial Yes	*Parking Difficult*
Room TV Yes	*Room service Limited*

Holiday Inn Glasgow

H **78% £B/C** ♿
Town plan A4 Strathclyde
Argyle Street, Anderston G3 8RR
041-226 5577. Tlx 776355
Credit Access, Amex, Diners, Visa

The Anderston exit of the M8 is a convenient approach to this modern high-rise hotel, where guests will find smart, willing staff and abundant comfort. The sunken lounge has plenty of settees and armchairs round its central hooded fire, and there are two bars, one overlooking the pool. Air-conditioned bedrooms are of a good size with smart lightwood fitted units, easy chairs and attractive matching soft furnishings. All are comprehensively equipped, with trouser presses, hairdryers, mini-bars and bedside controls (even a switch for a 'do not disturb' light in the corridor). *Amenities* indoor swimming pool, sauna,

solarium, whirlpool bath, gymnasium, squash, hairdressing, in-house movies, laundry service, coffee shop (11am-11pm), 24-hour lounge service, kiosk.

■ *Rooms 296*	*Confirm by 6*
en suite bath/shower 296	*Last dinner 11*
Direct dial Yes	*Parking Ample*
Room TV Yes	*Room service 24 hours*

Hospitality Inn — Glasgow

H **70% £D/E** *E* &
Town plan C2 Strathclyde
Cambridge Street G3 7DS
041-332 3311
Credit Access, Amex, Diners, Visa. LVs

The most notable feature of this high-rise city centre hotel, Scotland's largest hotel, is the size of the bedrooms, which range from spacious studio rooms to enormous de luxe. De luxe rooms even have three-piece suites. All rooms have fitted wood units and coordinating fabrics, and are equipped with writing desks, trouser presses and hairdryers. Bathrooms are fully tiled. There's plenty of seating space, too, in the busy foyer – note the waterfall feature – and guests who feel like a drink can repair to the lively Captain's Cabin or the quieter cocktail bar. The coffee shop, with its green and white colour scheme, is fresh, bright

and cheerful. *Amenities* hairdressing, in-house movies, laundry service, coffee shop (7am–11.30pm), kiosk, 24-hour lounge service, transport to airport.

■ *Rooms 313*	*Confirm by 6*
en suite bath/shower 313	*Last dinner 11.30*
Direct dial Yes	*Parking Ample*
Room TV Yes	*Room service 24 hours*

Kelvin Park Lorne Hotel — Glasgow

H **61% £D/E**
Town plan A2 Strathclyde
923 Sauchiehall Street G3 7TE
041-334 4891
Credit Access, Amex, Diners, Visa

Situated at the western end of Sauchiehall Street, close by the M8, this pleasant modern hotel has been attractively refurbished. A bold black and white theme runs through both the conservatory style lounge and the Art Nouveau bar, which reflects the style of Charles Rennie Mackintosh. Bedrooms are bright and clean, with coordinated colours and darkwood units. *Amenities* in-house movies (free), laundry service.

■ *Rooms 80*	*Confirm by 6.30*
en suite bath/shower 80	*Last dinner 10.45*
Direct dial Yes	*Parking Ample*
Room TV Yes	*Room service 24 hours*

One Devonshire Gardens *NEW ENTRY* — Glasgow

HR **76% £B**
Town plan A1 Strathclyde
1 Devonshire Gardens G12 0UX
041-339 2001
Credit Access, Amex, Diners, Visa

Decor at this Victorian town house is both stylish and sophisticated, and it comes as no surprise to learn that the owner also runs an interior design company. The comfortable, civilised drawing room has a high, moulded ceiling, plenty of easy chairs and sofas, elegant drapes and a large artificial (but convincing) tree. Spacious bedrooms with individual colour schemes are sumptuously appointed. All feature high-quality traditional furniture (three four-posters), rich fabrics and subtle spotlighting; even

the notepads and pencils by the telephones match the colour scheme. Luxurious bathrooms (one with shower only) have drag-painted woodwork, fine toiletries and huge towels. Smart, ultra-efficient staff. *Amenities* laundry service, 24-hour lounge service.

■ *Rooms 8*	*Confirm by arrang.*
en suite bath/shower 8	*Last dinner 10.30*
Direct dial Yes	*Parking Ample*
Room TV Yes	*Room service 24 hours*

Restaurant 👑👑

Spotlit portraits adorn the dark blue walls and table settings are delightful. Chef James Kerr offers a short, imaginative, fixed-price menu that changes twice daily to include the best raw ingredients available. You might start with feuilleté of chicken livers with almonds, continue with parsnip soup, then move on to suprême of salmon with orange ginger butter sauce – all most attractively presented. Excellent service.
🍷 Well-chosen ☺

■ *Set L £12.50*	*L 12.30–2.30*
Set D £18.50	*D 7–10.30*
About £50 for two	*Seats 35 Parties 16*
Closed L Sat	

■ Our inspectors never book in the name of Egon Ronay's Guides; they disclose their identity only after paying their bills.

Rogano *NEW ENTRY*

R 🏆 **Town plan C4** Strathclyde
11 Exchange Place
041-248 4055
Credit Access, Amex, Diners, Visa

A popular restaurant with stylish 20s decor.
Fish specialities range from bouillabaisse and
steamed mousseline of cod to filo-wrapped
salmon served with a champagne and coriander
sauce. Meat entrées, too, plus interesting starters

Glasgow

like quail consommé and venison liver pâté. The
Downstairs Diner is younger, louder and more
informal, and there's also an oyster bar.

🍽 Well-chosen ⊕

■ *Set L Sat only £8.95*	*L 12–2.30*
About £52 for two	*D 7–10, Fri & Sat*
Seats 55	*7–10.30*
Closed Sun & Bank Hols	*Meals (in diner)*
Parking Difficult	*noon–midnight*

Stakis Grosvenor Hotel

Glasgow

H **72% £C**
Town plan A1 Strathclyde
Grosvenor Terrace G12 0TA
041-339 8811. Tlx 776247
Credit Access, Amex, Diners, Visa. **LVs**

Thoroughly modern behind its long, classical
facade – floodlit at night – the Stakis Grosvenor is
situated on the A82 Great Western Road. The
split-level foyer-lounge is very smart, with
panelled walls and plenty of comfortable seating,
and there are two pleasant bars. Standard
bedrooms, with decent darkwood furnishings, are
well equipped, with hairdryers, trouser presses
and remote control for the TVs, plus nice little
extras like shortbread and bowls of fresh fruit.
Rooms at the front of the building are similar in
decor but larger, with two double beds, and
bidets in the tiled bathrooms. Breakfast is self-

service for cooked and cold items.
Amenities in-house movies (free), laundry
service, 24-hour lounge service.

■ *Rooms 94*	*Confirm by arrang.*
en suite bath/shower 94	*Last dinner 10.30*
Direct dial Yes	*Parking Ample*
Room TV Yes	*Room service 24 hours*

Stakis Pond Hotel

Glasgow

H **59% £C/D**
Town plan A1 Strathclyde
2 Shelly Road, Great Western Road G12 0XP
041-334 8161. Tlx 776573
Credit Access, Amex, Diners, Visa. **LVs**

Easy to spot from the A82, this five-storey
modern hotel stands next to a boating pond.
Overnight accommodation is neat and practical,
and though the bedrooms are not large, they are

quite well equipped, with trouser presses,
hairdryers and radio-alarms. There's an attractive
pine-clad leisure complex and a choice of bars.
No dogs. *Amenities* indoor swimming pool, sauna,
solarium, keep-fit equipment, laundry service.

■ *Rooms 136*	*Confirm by 6*
en suite bath/shower 136	*Last dinner 10*
Direct dial Yes	*Parking Ample*
Room TV Yes	*Room service 24 hours*

Swallow Hotel

Glasgow

H **61% £D/E**
Town plan A5 Strathclyde
517 Paisley Road West G51 1RW
041-427 3146. Tlx 778795
Credit Access, Amex, Diners, Visa

A little west of city-centre, but with good
access, this is a modern hotel on three floors. Half
the bedrooms have been attractively refurbished
with pastel colours and brass-inlaid furniture.

Public rooms include a wicker-chaired cocktail
bar. *Amenities* indoor swimming pool, sauna,
solarium, whirlpool bath, keep-fit equipment,
laundry service, 24-hour lounge service, in-house
movies (free).

■ *Rooms 122*	*Confirm by 6*
en suite bath/shower 122	*Last dinner 9.30*
Direct dial Yes	*Parking Ample*
Room TV Yes	*Room service 24 hours*

Tinto Firs Thistle Hotel

Glasgow

H **64% £C/D**
Town plan C5 Strathclyde
470 Kilmarnock Road G43 2BB
041-637 2353. Tlx 778329
Credit Access, Amex, Diners, Visa

Two suites are included among the 27
bedrooms at this small modern hotel, which
stands on the A77 three miles south of the city
centre. All the rooms have remote-control TVs,

trouser presses and hairdryers, and there's plenty
of shelf space. Darkwood panelling and
comfortable rattan chairs feature in the lounge
and bars. *Amenities* patio, in-house movies (free),
laundry service, 24-hour lounge service.

■ *Rooms 27*	*Confirm by 6*
en suite bath/shower 27	*Last dinner 9.45*
Direct dial Yes	*Parking Ample*
Room TV Yes	*Room service 24 hours*

White House Glasgow

H **65% £C/D**
Town plan A1 Strathclyde
12 Clevedon Crescent G12 0PA
041-339 9375. Tlx 777582
Credit Access, Amex, Diners, Visa
Part of a peaceful Georgian terrace, this is a hotel with a difference. There are no public rooms apart from the entrance hall and the variously-styled bedrooms are all suites with their own

kitchens. Remote-control TVs and trouser presses are standard. Champagne for first-time guests, whisky miniatures for those returning. *Amenities* garden, in-house movies (free), laundry service, courtesy transport.

■ *Rooms* 32	*Confirm by arrang.*
en suite bath/shower 32	*Last dinner* 10
Direct dial Yes	*Parking* Limited
Room TV Yes	*Room service* 24 hours

Excelsior Hotel Glasgow Airport

H **68% £C**
Map 12 B1 Strathclyde
Abbotsinch Nr Paisley PA3 2TR
041-887 1212. Tlx 777733
Manager John Tomblin
Credit Access, Amex, Diners, Visa
Next to the airport terminal, this modern hotel is a useful stopover for travellers. The marble-floored foyer has comfortable leather seating and there's

a convivial bar. Neatly fitted bedrooms (mostly studio-style) offer tea-makers and hairdryers. Compact bathrooms. *Amenities* hairdressing, laundry service, 24-hour lounge service, courtesy car.

■ *Rooms* 290	*Confirm by* 6
en suite bath/shower 290	*Last dinner* 10.30
Direct dial Yes	*Parking* Ample
Room TV Yes	*Room service* 24 hours

Stakis Normandy Hotel Glasgow Airport

H **61% £D**
Map 12 B1 Strathclyde
Inchinnan Road, Renfrew PA4 9EJ
041-886 4100. Tlx 778897
Credit Access, Amex, Diners, Visa
The Stakis Normandy is a '60s hotel located on the A8 and very handy for the airport. The roomy reception area features a modern representation of the Bayeux Tapestry, and there are two

comfortable bars. Double-glazed bedrooms have fitted furniture, trouser presses and hairdryers, *Amenities* garden, golf driving range, in-house movies (free), laundry service, 24-hour lounge service, courtesy coach.

■ *Rooms* 142	*Confirm by* 6
en suite bath/shower 142	*Last dinner* 9.45
Direct dial Yes	*Parking* Ample
Room TV Yes	*Room service* 24 hours

■ For a discount on next year's guide, see Offer for Answers.

Blairfindy Lodge Hotel Glenlivet

H **61% £D/E**
Map 16 C3 Grampian
Ballindalloch AB3 9DJ
Glenlivet (080 73) 376
Owner managers Wilf & Dorothy Jackson
Credit Access, Visa. LVs
New owners the Jacksons are busy sprucing up this peaceful hotel, a Victorian hunting lodge that overlooks the Glenlivet distillery from its

hilltop position. Spacious day rooms include a comfortable lounge and convivial bar. Good-sized bedrooms are gradually being refurbished. *Amenities* garden, game fishing.

■ *Rooms* 7	*Confirm by arrang.*
en suite bath/shower 7	*Last dinner* 9.30
Room phone No	*Parking* Ample
Room TV No	*Room service* Limited
Closed mid Nov–mid Mar	

Balgeddie House Hotel Glenrothes

H **65% £D**
Map 17 C5 Fife
Balgeddie Way KY6 3ET
Glenrothes (0592) 742511
Owner manager Crombie Family
Credit Access, Amex, Diners, Visa
The Crombie family nurture the reassuring virtues of old-fashioned hotelkeeping at this peacefully situated hotel, with impeccable housekeeping and unfailingly pleasant service at the head. The attractive entrance hall sports a new deep carpet, the bay-windowed lounge has been stylishly redecorated, and three bars take

care of the thirsty. Bedrooms, small and very charming in the attic, roomier on the first floor, are all as neat as ninepence, with sparkling bathrooms. The breakfast is fair. The hotel is signposted from the Leslie road on the outskirts of town. *Amenities* garden, croquet, snooker, laundry service.

■ *Rooms* 18	*Confirm by arrang.*
en suite bath/shower 18	*Last dinner* 9.30
Direct dial Yes	*Parking* Ample
Room TV Yes	*Room service* All day
Closed 2 wks from 25 Dec	

Gullane ▶

Greywalls

Gullane

HR **77% £B/C**
Map 12 D1 Lothian
Muirfield EH31 2EG
Gullane (0620) 842144. Tlx 72294
Owner managers Mr & Mrs Giles Weaver
Credit Access, Amex, Visa

Originally designed by Sir Edwin Lutyens as a holiday home for a keen golfer, today's enlarged house makes an elegant hotel with a family home atmosphere. Pleasing day rooms include a panelled library where guests can relax in front of the fire, a charming sitting room and a cosy little bar. The sun room with its stylish cane furniture opens on to the Jekyll-inspired garden. Spacious bedrooms with striking individual decor and some good antiques have many comforts, from books,

fruit and flowers to remote-control TVs. Bathrooms are also thoughtfully equipped. Rooms in the modern wing are more modest.
Amenities garden, putting, croquet, tennis, laundry service.

■ *Rooms* 23	*Confirm by* arrang.
en suite bath/shower 23	*Last dinner* 9.30
Direct dial Yes	*Parking* Ample
Room TV Yes	*Room service* 24 hours
Closed Nov–mid Apr	

Greywalls Restaurant ⛺

An elegant dining room and unobtrusive service provide a pleasant ambience for Andrew Mitchell's stylish cooking. Typical of his imaginative dishes are calf's liver with an unusual apricot sauce, and the intriguing breast of duck baked in puff pastry and served with an Earl Grey tea sauce. Fresh produce is much in evidence, and tempting sweets include a delicious passion fruit cake with strawberry sauce. Good list of classic French wines. 🍷 **Well-chosen** ⊕

■ *Set L from* £8·50	*L* 12.30–2
Set D £19·50	*D* 7.30–9.30
About £55 *for two*	*Seats* 60
Closed Nov–mid Apr	*Parties* 20

La Potinière ★

Gullane

R ★ ⑨ **Map 12 D1** Lothian
Main Street
Gullane (0620) 843214

A small and pretty restaurant, decked with flowers and pictures, where the no-choice, four-course menu is served at a fixed time and a leisurely pace. Hilary Brown applies her considerable cooking skills to the very best produce the daily market has to offer, and the results are delightful. Starters might include a nicely balanced carrot and orange soup, followed perhaps by breast of chicken topped with nuts, served on a bed of apple with a cream and cider sauce. David Brown's inspired choice of the very best French wines, offered at extremely reasonable prices, rates among the finest lists in the country. There is not a single questionable bottle. Magnificent selection of wonderful clarets (Ch. Montrose 1961) and exquisite Sauternes and Barsacs (Ch. Suduiraut 1967). Book in advance, especially for Saturday. No smoking.

Specialities red pepper and orange soup, Pithiviers of leeks with fresh herb sauce, breast of turkey aux pruneaux, lemon surprise pudding.
⇨ **Outstanding** 🍷 **Well-chosen**

■ *Set L* £11·50, Sun £12	*L at* 1
Set D £17·50	*D Sat only at* 8
About £45 *for two*	*Parking* Ample
Seats 32	*Parties* 30

Closed L Sat & Wed, 1 & 2 Jan, 25 & 26 Dec, 1 wk June & all Oct

Kirklands Hotel

Hawick

H **58% £E/F**
Map 12 D3 Borders
West Stewart Place TD9 8BH
Hawick (0450) 72263
Owner manager Barrie Newland

Easy to spot from the A7, Kirklands is a converted Victorian house where old-fashioned standards of comfort and housekeeping prevail. Much of its original character remains, both in the

lofty day rooms and in the bedrooms, which are reached by a splendid staircase. Rooms are of a decent size, with traditional furnishings.
Amenities garden, keep-fit equipment.

■ *Rooms* 6	*Confirm by* 6
en suite bath/shower 3	*Last dinner* 8.30
Room phone Yes	*Parking* Ample
Room TV Yes	*Room service* All day
Closed 25 & 26 Dec & 1 Jan	

Johnstounburn House Hotel · Humbie

H **74% £B**
Map 17 C6 Lothian
EH36 5PL
Humbie (087 553) 557934
Credit Access, Amex, Diners, Visa

The tradition of hospitality dates back over 350 years at this splendid 17th-century country residence situated on the edge of the Lammermuir hills. Walled gardens, neatly clipped yew hedges and its own park provide a delightful setting that is matched by an equally attractive interior. Log fires, fine paintings and antiques grace elegant public areas like the inviting lounge. Good-sized bedrooms in the main building are individually decorated in pretty florals, with chintz curtains, stylish furniture and airy, carpeted bathrooms. The coach-house annexe houses nine larger rooms featuring extra accessories like

trouser presses, hairdryers and mini-bars, as well as more luxurious bathrooms.
Amenities garden, clay-pigeon shooting, laundry service.

■ Rooms 20	Confirm by arrang.
en suite bath/shower 20	Last dinner 8.45
Direct dial Yes	Parking Ample
Room TV Yes	Room service All day

Norton House Hotel · Ingliston

H **68% £D**
Map 12 C1 Lothian
Edinburgh EH28 8LX
031-333 1275. Tlx 727232
Credit Access, Amex, Diners, Visa

A long drive leads to this ornate Victorian mansion to the west of Edinburgh. The entrance hall is magnificent with its marble pillars and mellow oak, and the other day rooms are equally appealing. Comfortably appointed bedrooms have good-quality modern furnishings, plus trouser presses, hairdryers and tea-makers. Smart modern bathrooms. *Amenities* garden, putting, 24-hour lounge service.

■ Rooms 19	Confirm by arrang.
en suite bath/shower 19	Last dinner 9.30
Direct dial Yes	Parking Ample
Room TV Yes	Room service 24 hours

Bunchrew House Hotel *NEW ENTRY* · Inverness

H **67% £C**
Map 16 C3 Highland
Bunchrew IV3 6TA
Inverness (0463) 234917
Credit Access, Amex, Diners, Visa

This delightful 17th-century mansion stands by the Beauly Firth, with fine views of Ben Wyvis and the Black Isle. There are just six bedrooms, the best being a large and elegant four-poster room and another with a half-tester and whirlpool bath. Public areas include a panelled drawing room. Early days here, but it's a hotel of real potential. *Amenities* garden, laundry service.

■ Rooms 6	Confirm by arrang.
en suite bath/shower 6	Last dinner 9.30
Direct dial Yes	Parking Ample
Room TV Yes	Room service All day

Culloden House · Inverness

HR **76% £B/C**
Map 16 C3 Highland
Nr Culloden IV1 2NZ
Inverness (0463) 790461. Tlx 75402
Owner managers Ian & Marjory McKenzie
Credit Access, Amex, Diners, Visa

The battle of Culloden – where Bonnie Prince Charlie was defeated – took place not far from this impressive Georgian mansion set in extensive parkland, and the Prince's portrait hangs in the imposing entrance hall. Elegant day rooms, with fine furnishings and beautiful Adam-style mouldings, include a lounge redecorated in Wedgwood pink. Stylish bedrooms, reached by a handsome iron staircase, are spacious and very comfortable. Some have four-posters, others modern units; all have a comprehensive range of accessories and excellent bathrooms with a generous supply of thick towels. No children under ten. No dogs. *Amenities* garden, sauna, solarium, tennis, snooker, valeting, laundry service.

■ Rooms 20	Confirm by arrang.
en suite bath/shower 20	Last dinner 9
Direct dial Yes	Parking Ample
Room TV Yes	Room service All day

Culloden House Restaurant ♕

Scottish and modern French elements combine in the daily-changing lunch and dinner menus. Local seafood is a popular ingredient, and meat dishes could include breast of duck filled with a game mousse, loin of veal glazed with Brie, and medallion of venison in a pastry case. Soup, pâté and smoked salmon are typical starters. Capable cooking is complemented by artistic presentation

and polished service. ☺
- *Set D £23*
- *About £58 for two*
- *Seats 40*

L 12.30–2
D 7–9
Parties 22

Dunain Park Hotel — Inverness

H R **68%** **£C/D**
Map 16 C3 Highland
IV3 6JN
Inverness (0463) 230512
Owner managers Mr & Mrs E. A. Nicoll
Credit Access, Amex, Diners, Visa

A log fire glows in the drawing room of this handsome Georgian house, which stands in six secluded acres just off the A82, 2½ miles from Inverness. Quiet comfort is the keynote here. Good-sized bedrooms are furnished in sturdy traditional style, and there are two very attractive suites in the coach house. *Amenities* garden, badminton, croquet, laundry service.
- *Rooms 8*
- *en suite bath/shower 6*
- *Direct dial* Yes
- *Room TV* Yes

Confirm by arrang.
Last dinner 9
Parking Ample
Room service All day

Dunain Park Hotel Restaurant ⌘

The decor (pictures especially) may not be to everyone's taste but Ann Nicoll's cooking is undeniably sound and enjoyable. Fixed-price menus offer simple starters such as leek and potato soup, pheasant pâté and garlic mushrooms, followed by straightforward main dishes like pan-fried scallops, fillet of beef Wellington, and roast lamb with fresh garden herbs. Leave some room for a nice creamy sweet like marshmallow pudding – choose from the tempting selection displayed on the sideboard. Skilfully chosen, absorbing wine list. ☺
- *Set L £9.50*
- *Set D £17.50*
- *About £42 for two*

L 12–2
D 7–9
Seats 30 Parties 30

Kingsmills Hotel — Inverness

H **66%** **£C/D**
Map 16 C3 Highland
Culcabock Road IV2 3LP
Inverness (0463) 237166. Tlx 75566
Credit Access, Amex, Diners, Visa

Attractive in white pebbledash and grey, this late 18th-century mansion stands beside a golf course a mile from the town centre. Most of the accommodation is in the main house, but 12 fresh, bright and spacious rooms are in the garden wing. Pleasant day rooms include a comfortable lounge bar with views of the garden. *Amenities* garden, squash, pitch & putt, laundry service, 24-hour lounge service.
- *Rooms 64*
- *en suite bath/shower 60*
- *Direct dial* Yes
- *Room TV* Yes

Confirm by 6
Last dinner 9.45
Parking Ample
Room service 24 hours

Ladbroke Hotel — Inverness

H **62%** **£C/D**
Map 16 C3 Highland
Nairn Road IV2 3TR
Inverness (0463) 239666. Tlx 75377
Credit Access, Amex, Diners, Visa

A 6-storey modern hotel at the junction of A9 and A82. Refurbishment has left the bedrooms in good general order (though we met the odd maintenance lapse). Standard rooms have tea-makers and bathroom radio extensions; the better-furnished Gold Star rooms get trouser presses and hairdryers. Comfortable foyer and bar. *Amenities* in-house movies (charge), laundry service, 24-hour lounge service.
- *Rooms 118*
- *en suite bath/shower 118*
- *Direct dial* Yes
- *Room TV* Yes

Confirm by 6
Last dinner 9.30
Parking Ample
Room service 24 hours

Station Hotel — Inverness

H **65%** **£C/D** &
Map 16 C3 Highland
Academy Street IV1 1LG
Inverness (0463) 231926. Tlx 75275
Credit Access, Amex, Diners, Visa

Long-serving staff are friendly, caring and professional at this sturdy Victorian hotel. A handsome staircase sweeps up from the pillared foyer-lounge to recall earlier grandeur, and guests can enjoy a drink in the little cocktail bar or the lively modern lounge bar. Well-equipped bedrooms are pleasantly decorated and furnished. *Amenities* 24-hour lounge service.
- *Rooms 65*
- *en suite bath/shower 53*
- *Direct dial* Yes
- *Room TV* Yes
- *Closed* 10 days Xmas

Confirm by 6
Last dinner 9.15
Parking Difficult
Room service 24 hours

■ If we recommend meals in a hotel or inn, a separate entry is made for its restaurant.

Hospitality Inn Irvine

HR 69% £D/E &
Map 12 B2 Strathclyde
Roseholm, Annick Water KA11 4LD
Irvine (0294) 74272. Tlx 777097
Credit Access, Amex, Diners, Visa. **LVs**
There's a lot of style about this low, red-brick
early-80s hotel. The main day rooms have a
Moorish feel, and there's a spectacular leafy
lagoon. Good-sized bedrooms are comfortable
and very well equipped. Bathrooms are excellent.
Amenities indoor swimming pool, whirlpool bath,
hairdressing, pitch & putt, in-house movies (free),
laundry service, coffee shop (7am–11pm), 24-hour
lounge service, kiosk.

■ Rooms 128	Confirm by 6
en suite bath/shower 128	Last dinner 10
Direct dial Yes	Parking Ample
Room TV Yes	Room service 24 hours

Mirage Restaurant ♛ &
A smart, stylish setting for enjoying skilled
imaginative cooking by Bill Costley. Typical
dishes run from rich vegetable and tomato soup
and mussels in Noilly Prat to breast of duck with
pistachio stuffing garnished with a little apple
croustade or lamb fillet in a bread and mint crust.
Simple grills are also available, along with
interesting vegetarian dishes such as hot
avocado with peppered rice and a wine butter
sauce, and a temptation of sweets like hot
caramel and vanilla pudding soufflé with soft fruits
or poppy seed parfait with fresh passion fruit. ✆

■ Set L £9·95	L 12.30–2
Set D £15·50	D 7.30–10
About £45 for two	Seats 80 Parties 16

Gigha Hotel Isle of Gigha

HR 60% £E
Map 17 A6 Strathclyde
PA41 7AD
Gigha (058 35) 254
Owner managers Mr & Mrs K. L. Roebuck
Credit Access, Visa
The island's only hotel is an old slate-roofed inn
with an added wing. The setting is one of rugged
beauty and complete peace. Favourite activities
include walking, fishing and just relaxing round
the log fire in the lounge. Neat, bright bedrooms
have lovely sea views. *Amenities* garden, game
fishing, laundry room, hotel transport.

■ Rooms 9	Confirm by arrang.
en suite bath/shower 3	Last dinner 8
Room phone No	Parking Ample
Room TV No	Room service Limited
Closed end Oct–end Mar	

Gigha Hotel Restaurant
The four-course evening meal in the stone-walled
dining room includes soup and a choice of
starters – perhaps grapefruit cocktail or avocado
with a salade niçoise filling. The main course
choice is good local shellfish, including scallops
and prawns, or a meat dish, usually steak or a
roast, with fresh vegetables. Tasty sweets
such as brown bread ice cream or delicious
chocolate mousse round things off nicely.
Lunch is from a buffet. Local women take turns
with the cooking. ✆ *NEW ENTRY*

■ Set L £5·50	L Noon–2
Set D £11·50	D 7–8
About £31 for two	Seats 40
Closed end Oct–end Mar	

Isle of Raasay Hotel Isle of Raasay

H 57% £E/F &
Map 16 A3 Highland
By Kyle of Lochalsh IV40 8PB
Raasay (047 862) 222
Manager Mrs I. Nicholson
The only hotel on the lovely Isle of Raasay, a
fifteen-minute ferry trip from Skye. The lounge
takes advantage of the fine views, and there's a
pleasant pine-ceilinged bar. Spick and span
bedrooms have plain white walls, simple
furnishings and tweedy fabrics, plus bright
carpeted bathrooms. *Amenities* garden, game
fishing, laundry room, transport to ferry.

■ Rooms 12	Confirm by arrang.
en suite bath/shower 12	Last dinner 7.30
Room phone No	Parking Ample
Room TV Yes	Room service None
Closed Oct–Easter	

♀ indicates a **well-chosen** house wine.

Ednam House Hotel Kelso

H 61% £E
Map 12 D2 Borders
Bridge Street TD5 7HT
Kelso (0573) 24168
Owner manager Mr R. Alistair Brooks
Credit Visa
Fishing's the major lure at this handsome
Georgian mansion, whose grounds reach to the
banks of the Tweed. It's a pleasant place, where
most guests are regular visitors. The lounges
have a homely appeal, there are two bars and the
bedrooms are solidly traditional. *Amenities*
garden, croquet, coarse & game fishing.

■ Rooms 32	Confirm by 6
en suite bath/shower 31	Last dinner 9
Direct dial Yes	Parking Ample
Room TV Yes	Room service All day
Closed 2 wks Xmas	

Sunlaws House Hotel   Kelso

H **74% £D** &
Map 12 D2 Borders
Heiton TD5 8JZ
Roxburgh (057 35) 331. Tlx 728147
Credit Access, Amex, Diners, Visa
　Owned by the Duke and Duchess of
Roxburghe, this handsome Victorian house is
beautifully situated in 200 acres of grounds. It's
good walking country, and there's salmon and
trout fishing on the river Teviot. A log fire crackles
a winter welcome in the entrance hall, and there's
an elegant yet homely drawing room. Equally
delightful are the library bar and bright conservatory. Most of the overnight accommodation
is in the main house – individually decorated,
solidly furnished rooms – while five rooms in
the stable block are pretty, modern and just as
comfortable. Excellent housekeeping and

courteous personal service.
Amenities garden, tennis, croquet, shooting,
game fishing, laundry service, 24-hour lounge
service, helipad.

■ *Rooms* 21	*Confirm by* arrang.
en suite bath/shower 21	*Last dinner* 9.30
Direct dial Yes	*Parking* Ample
Room TV Yes	*Room service* Limited

■ Any person using our name
to obtain free hospitality is
a fraud. Proprietors, please
inform the police and us.

Kenmore Hotel   Kenmore

H **62% £D/E** &
Map 17 C5 Tayside
By Aberfeldy PH15 2NU
Kenmore (088 73) 205
Manager Mr I. H. Mackenzie
Credit Access, Amex, Visa
　Scotland's oldest inn, established in 1572,
stands in a pretty village on a lovely stretch of the
river Tay, just before it joins the loch. The hotel
owns extensive salmon fishing rights, and also
has its own parkland golf course. The charm of
the black and white facade continues in the
delightful day rooms, which include two bars and

two comfortable lounges. Well-kept bedrooms are
spacious and traditional in the main building,
smaller and more modern in the annexe. Some
main-house rooms enjoy good river views.
Excellent bathrooms with bidets. Friendly staff do
their jobs well. *Amenities* garden, golf course,
game fishing, hotel boats, laundry service,
helipad.

■ *Rooms* 38	*Confirm by* arrang.
en suite bath/shower 38	*Last dinner* 9
Direct dial Yes	*Parking* Ample
Room TV Yes	*Room service* All day
Closed Mon & Tues mid Nov–mid Feb	

Ardsheal House   Kentallen of Appin

HR **67% £C**
Map 17 B4 Highland
Argyll PA38 4BX
Duror (063 174) 227
Owner managers Jane & Bob Taylor
Credit Access, Amex, Visa
　Set amidst breathtaking scenery on the shores
of Loch Linnhe, this 18th-century house is run by
friendly proprietors. Public rooms include two
delightful lounges and an oak-panelled bar.
Handsome, exceedingly comfortable bedrooms
are individually decorated. Half-board only.
Amenities garden, tennis, snooker room.

■ *Rooms* 13	*Confirm by* 5
en suite bath/shower 13	*Last dinner* 8.30
Room phone No	*Parking* Ample
Room TV No	*Room service* None
Closed end Oct–Easter	

Ardsheal House Restaurant

Set dinners in this conservatory-style restaurant
(choice only of starters and puddings) could
include smoked pigeon breast or a well-flavoured
soup such as tomato, celery and apple or cream
mussel, followed by saddle of lamb with mustard
sauce or fillet of halibut with salmon mousseline
and wild mushroom sauce. Lovely sweets. Lighter
lunches. Good, well-balanced wine list: note
Firestone Merlot '79 among interesting Californian
wines.
♥ Well-chosen ⊖

■ About £50 for two	L 12.30–1.30
Seats 32 *Parties* 32	D 8–8.30
Closed end Oct–Easter	

Ardanaiseig

HR **73%** **£C/D**
Map 17 B5 Strathclyde
By Taynuilt PA35 1HE
Kilchrenan (086 63) 333
Credit Access, Amex, Visa

Resident directors Michael and Frieda Yeo quickly put their guests at ease in this splendid 1830s mansion, which stands in marvellous gardens and mountainous countryside by the edge of Loch Awe. An open fire glows a welcome in the flagstoned entrance hall, and the drawing room and library bar are made for relaxation. Centrally heated bedrooms, most with superb views and individual appeal, have traditional furnishings. One room has recently been nicely refurbished and recarpeted; the others would certainly look all the better for the same treatment. No children under eight. Half-board terms only. *Amenities* garden, tennis, croquet, clay-pigeon shooting, game fishing, snooker, laundry service.

■ *Rooms 14*   *Confirm by arrang.*
en suite bath/shower 14   *Last dinner 8.30*
Direct dial Yes   *Parking Ample*
Room TV Yes   *Room service All day*
Closed mid Oct–Easter

Ardanaiseig Restaurant ★

NEW ENTRY

Twenty-two-year-old Lindsay Little has quickly made his mark at this civilised restaurant, cooking with sure technique allied to a touch of imagination. His well-conceived dishes are carefully prepared and attractively presented. Local raw materials, including wild salmon, shellfish and Angus beef, are used whenever possible, and he does particularly well to get a good and varied supply of vegetables and salad items. The five-course set dinner menu may offer such tempting dishes as warm duck breast salad garnished with wild strawberries, tender beef fillet with pickled walnuts and béarnaise sauce and light, delicious strawberry mousseline. There is a light lunchtime à la carte and Sunday brunch. Service is very charming and attentive yet unobtrusive. *Specialities* poached wild salmon with tomato and basil sauce, suprême of chicken stuffed with langoustine tails and crabmeat, pan-fried fillet of beef with shallots, pimentos and a rich burgundy sauce, roast loin of lamb with a charlotte of courgettes and aubergines. ⊕

■ *Set D £23*   *L 12.30–2, Sun 10.30–2*
About £55 for two   *D 7.30–8.30*
Seats 34   *Closed mid Oct–Easter*

■ Our inspectors are our full-time employees; they are professionally trained by us.

Taychreggan Hotel

HR **66%** **£C/D**
Map 17 B5 Strathclyde
By Taynuilt PA35 1HQ
Kilchrenan (086 63) 211
Owner managers Mr & Mrs J. Taylor
Credit Access, Amex, Diners, Visa

Charm and character abound at this family-run hotel on the banks of Loch Awe, which boasts three delightful lounges (one with TV) and a homely bar opening on to a sun-trap courtyard. Bright, pretty bedrooms. Half-board only. *Amenities* garden, coarse & game fishing, boating, board sailing, laundry service.

■ *Rooms 16*   *Confirm by arrang.*
en suite bath/shower 16   *Last dinner 9*
Room phone No   *Parking Ample*
Room TV No   *Room service All day*
Closed mid Oct–Easter

Taychreggan Hotel Restaurant

Admire the view from this pretty little restaurant while choosing from a daily changing menu of Gail Struthers' capably prepared dishes featuring local produce (especially seafood). Choices range from calf's liver in red wine, or roast beef with horseradish sauce, to fresh salmon served cold with salad, or casseroled wood pigeon in port and grape sauce. For afters there are home-made sweets and a variety of mainly English and Scottish cheeses. Danish cold table at lunchtime. Good burgundies. ♀ **Well-chosen** ⊕

■ *Set L £8·50*   *L 12.30–2.15*
Set D £13·50   *D 7.30–9*
About £37 for two   *Seats 40 Parties 40*
Closed mid Oct–Easter

Kildrummy Castle Hotel   Kildrummy

HR 71% £D
Map 17 C4 Grampian
By Alford AB3 8RA
Kildrummy (033 65) 288. Tlx 94012529
Owner managers Thomas & Mary Hanna
Credit Access, Amex, Diners, Visa

The ruins of a 13th-century castle and beautifully-kept grounds provide a romantic setting for this attractive castellated country house. Hunting trophies and tapestries create a stylish impression in the entrance hall that is confirmed by the quiet library, spacious bar and charming drawing room with its chintzy seating and garden views. Carved lions guard the foot of an ornate staircase that leads to comfortable, well-appointed bedrooms including four attic

rooms in delightfully cottagy style. All offer tea-makers, fruit and flowers, and electric blankets. Modern, carpeted bathrooms with good towels. Friendly staff and good breakfasts.
Amenities garden, game fishing, billiards.

■ *Rooms* 16	*Confirm by* arrang.
en suite bath/shower 16	*Last dinner* 9
Direct dial Yes	*Parking* Ample
Room TV Yes	*Room service* All day
Closed 4 Jan–14 Mar	

Restaurant

Solidly old-fashioned furniture and vast Highland pictures provide a suitably traditional setting for satisfying, well-prepared food. Beef, game and salmon appear regularly on the menu with Cullen skink – a flavoursome smoked haddock broth – adding a taste of Scotland. A good main course choice is venison with wood mushrooms and raspberry sauce. A classic crème brûlée is one of the delights of the tempting sweet trolley. ℮

■ *Set L* £9	*L* 12.30–1.45
Set D £14·50	*D* 7–9
About £35 *for two*	*Seats* 42
Closed 4 Jan–14 Mar	*Parties* 40

NEW ENTRY

⌐ is our symbol for an **outstanding** wine list.

Killiecrankie Hotel .   Killiecrankie

H 60% £E ♿
Map 17 C4 Tayside
By Pitlochry PH16 5LG
Pitlochry (0796) 3220
Owner managers Mr & Mrs D. Hattersley Smith

The delightful owners have stamped their sunny personalities on this former dower house, which stands in attractive grounds and woodland close to the A9. The bar and sun lounge are

delightful, and pretty bedrooms, most with their own bathrooms, feature natural pine furniture built by local craftsmen. TV lounge upstairs.
Amenities garden, putting, croquet.

■ *Rooms* 12	*Confirm by* 6
en suite bath/shower 10	*Last dinner* 8.30
Room phone No	*Parking* Ample
Room TV No	*Room service* All day
Closed 12 Oct–Easter	

Montgreenan Mansion House   Kilwinning

H 74% £D/E
Map 12 A2 Strathclyde
Montgreenan Street KA13 7QZ
Kilwinning (0294) 57733. Tlx 778525
Credit Access, Amex, Diners, Visa

A handsome Regency mansion, built in 1817 and set amid 45 acres of splendid grounds. It stands at the end of a long wooded drive off the A736. The original library, now decorated in warm shades of red, makes an attractive book-lined lounge, and there's an elegant high-ceilinged bar furnished with smart leather chesterfields. The lovely light drawing room with its graceful neoclassical order, fine stucco mouldings and delightful views across the garden conveys a strong impression of gracious living. Traditionally appointed bedrooms are spacious on the first floor, more compact above. All have mini-bars.

Bathrooms – two with luxury spa baths – are mostly light and airy and of a good size. No dogs.
Amenities garden, tennis, croquet, billiards, laundry service.

■ *Rooms* 11	*Confirm by* arrang.
en suite bath/shower 11	*Last dinner* 10
Direct dial Yes	*Parking* Ample
Room TV Yes	*Room service* All day

Ballathie House
Kinclaven By Stanley

H 69% £C/D
Map 17 C5 Tayside
Perth PH1 4QN
Meikleour (025 083) 268. Tlx 777239
Credit Access, Amex, Diners, Visa
  Built in Scottish Baronial style, Ballathie House stands in peaceful grounds beside the river Tay. Some bedrooms have been decorated in luxurious period style, and all are to be upgraded.

Graceful public areas include a fine antique-furnished hall and two lounges.
Amenities garden, tennis, putting, croquet, clay-pigeon shooting, game fishing, laundry service.

■ *Rooms* 22	*Confirm by arrang.*
en suite bath/shower 22	*Last dinner 8.30*
Direct dial Yes	*Parking Ample*
Room TV Yes	*Room service All day*
Closed Feb	

The Cross
Kingussie

RR � **Map 17 C4** Highland
High Street PH21 1HX
Kingussie (054 02) 762
  There's plenty of enthusiasm for food and wine in this intimate little restaurant presided over by Tony Hadley. His wife Ruth holds the culinary reins, applying her talents to seasonal produce, much of it local. Pheasant mousse with a sweet pepper sauce, salmon with dill and garlicky Highland lamb are typical choices, and there is always a vegetarian main dish on offer. To finish, interesting cheeses and tempting sweets. Fixed-price gastronomic menu Saturday evenings only. ☺

■ *Set D* Sat only £15.50	*D only* 6.30–9.30
About £34 for two	*Parking Ample*
Seats 20	*Parties* 18
Closed Mon (& Sun in winter), 2 wks May & 3 wks Dec	

Bedrooms   £F
Rooms 3   *With bath/shower* 3
The three stylish bedrooms have smart modern showers (there's also a bathroom) and homely touches like books and magazines. There's a private lounge with TV. No smoking in restaurant or bedrooms. No dogs.

Loch Rannoch Hotel
Kinloch Rannoch

H 59% £D/E
Map 17 C4 Tayside
By Pitlochry PH16 5PS
Kinloch Rannoch (08822) 201
Credit Access, Amex, Diners, Visa
  Leisure facilities excel at this beautifully situated hotel. The bars and lounge have an agreeable hunting-lodge atmosphere and accommodation is simple and modern. Pleasant

staff with ready smiles. *Amenities* garden, indoor swimming pool, sauna, solarium, whirlpool bath, gymnasium, tennis, squash, coarse fishing, dry ski slope, marina, games room, snooker, in-house movies (free), coffee shop (8am–10pm).

■ *Rooms* 13	*Confirm by* 6
en suite bath/shower 13	*Last dinner* 10
Direct dial Yes	*Parking Ample*
Room TV Yes	*Room service All day*

Kinlochbervie Hotel
Kinlochbervie

HR 66% £D/E
Map 16 B2 Highland
By Lairg IV27 4RP
Kinlochbervie (097 182) 275
Owner managers David & Geraldine Gregory
Credit Access, Amex, Diners, Visa
  Overlooking Loch Clash and Kinlochbervie harbour, this modern hotel has spacious public rooms and attractive bedrooms. Savour the scene from the picture-windowed bar-lounge or settle in the bar or upstairs lounge. Fitted furniture, TVs and tea-makers make the spacious bedrooms comfortable. Excellent breakfasts.
Amenities laundry service.

■ *Rooms* 14	*Confirm by* 6
en suite bath/shower 14	*Last dinner 8.30*
Direct dial Yes	*Parking Ample*
Room TV Yes	*Room service All day*

Kinlochbervie Hotel Restaurant ♕

Fish is always on the menu at this modern restaurant. Try the halibut, poached in dry vermouth, perhaps, or the competently cooked fresh turbot hollandaise. The four-course set menu includes starters like smoked salmon from the hotel's own smokehouse, with a soup or sorbet to follow. If fish fails to tempt, try roast Aberdeen Angus or stroganoff. Enjoy some of the super sideboard sweets like hazelnut meringue with raspberries or chocolate boxes filled with lemon soufflé. Restricted service November–Easter. No smoking. ☺

■ *Set D* £17·95	*L by arrang. only*
About £50 for two	*D* 7.30–8.30
Seats 40	

■ We welcome complaints and bona fide recommendations on the tear-out pages for readers' comments. They are followed up by our professional team. Please also complain to the management instantly.

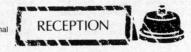

Windlestrae Hotel — Kinross

H **61% £D/E** ♿
Map 12 C1 Tayside
The Muirs KY13 7AS
Kinross (0577) 63217
Owner managers Terry & Jean Doyle
Credit Access, Amex, Diners, Visa
The pretty gardens are a major feature of this cheerfully and efficiently run hotel. A modern extension provides neat, bright, well-equipped bedrooms with good bathrooms. Main-house rooms are more homely in character but have similar facilities. There's a smart modern foyer-lounge and a two-level cocktail bar.
Amenities garden, sauna, laundry service.

■ *Rooms 18*	*Confirm by 6*
en suite bath/shower 18	*Last dinner 9.30*
Direct dial Yes	*Parking Ample*
Room TV Yes	*Room service All day*

Log Cabin Hotel — Kirkmichael

H **65% £D/E** ♿
Map 17 C4 Tayside
PH10 7NB
Strathardle (025 081) 288
Owner managers Alan Finch & Daphne Kirk
Credit Access, Amex, Diners, Visa
Set in a position of remote beauty, this sporting hotel is built from Norwegian logs. The lounge and bar are well supplied with armchairs, books and games, and the bedrooms are comfortably furnished in pine, with neat private bathrooms. Maintenance is only average. *Amenities* garden, shooting, clay-pigeon shooting, game fishing, games room, laundry service.

■ *Rooms 13*	*Confirm by arrang.*
en suite bath/shower 13	*Last dinner 9*
Room phone No	*Parking Ample*
Room TV Some	*Room service Limited*

♀ indicates a **well-chosen** house wine.

Knipoch Hotel — Knipoch

HR **75% £C**
Map 17 B5 Strathclyde
Nr Oban PA34 4QT
Kilninver (085 26) 251
Owner managers Craig family
Credit Access, Amex, Diners, Visa
In a beautifully tranquil setting by the shores of Loch Feochan, this modernised Georgian country house is owned and run by the Craig family, who clearly lavish a great deal of care and attention on it. A relaxing atmosphere pervades throughout, from the stone-tiled foyer to the sumptuous lounge, both with leather chesterfields, fine rugs and oil paintings, as well as roaring fires in winter. There's also a cosy panelled bar. Good-sized bedrooms are cheerfully decorated in bright colours and pretty floral fabrics, with inviting leather armchairs and period furniture in all rooms. No dogs.
Amenities garden, laundry service.

■ *Rooms 21*	*Confirm by arrang.*
en suite bath/shower 21	*Last dinner 9*
Direct dial Yes	*Parking Ample*
Room TV Yes	*Room service All day*
Closed Jan	

Knipoch Hotel Restaurant ᗡ ♀

With lovely views over the water, this attractive flagstone-floored restaurant offers enjoyably simple and pleasant dishes on a daily changing set-price menu. Dishes might include a subtly-flavoured tomato and thyme soup, a good, rough-textured chicken pâté or scallops with mousseline sauce, topped off with a flavoursome sweet and a choice of good cheeses. All the food is attractively presented and the service is friendly but discreet.
♀ Well-chosen ⊖

■ *Set D £23·50*	*L by arrang. only*
About £60 for two	*D 7.30–9*
Seats 44 Parties 24	*Closed Jan*

Lochalsh Hotel — Kyle of Lochalsh

H **66% £C/D**
Map 16 A3 Highland
Ferry Road IV40 8AF
Kyle (0599) 4202. Tlx 75318
Credit Access, Amex, Diners, Visa
A long, white-painted building near the terminal for the ferries that ply the narrow stretch to Skye. Bedrooms are very good, with nice solid furnishings, pretty wallpapers and attractive lighting. Remote-control TVs and hairdryers are standard. There's an open-plan lobby-lounge and bar. Friendly, willing staff. *Amenities* garden, putting, hotel boat, laundry service.

■ *Rooms 38*	*Confirm by arrang.*
en suite bath/shower 38	*Last dinner 9*
Direct dial Yes	*Parking Ample*
Room TV Yes	*Room service All day*
Closed 1 wk Xmas	

⬄ is our symbol for an **outstanding** wine list.

Cartland Bridge Hotel   Lanark

H **55% £E**
Map 12 C2 Strathclyde
ML11 9UF
Lanark (0555) 4426
Owner Managers David & Margot Laird
Credit Access, Amex, Diners, Visa
   A tree-lined drive runs from the A73 just north of Lanark to this solidly built Victorian mansion. Redecoration has perked up the public rooms, and a second, quite stylish, function room has been added. Bedrooms are generally spacious, with some nice old pieces of furniture. Well-kept bathrooms. *Amenities* garden, coarse fishing, laundry service.

■ *Rooms 15*	*Confirm by arrang.*
en suite bath/shower 0	*Last dinner 9.30*
Room phone Yes	*Parking Ample*
Room TV No	*Room service Limited*

Gleddoch House Hotel   Langbank

HR **70% £C**
Map 12 B1 Strathclyde
PA14 6YE
Langbank (047 554) 711. Tlx 779801
Manager Chris Longden
Credit Access, Amex, Diners, Visa
   An attractive, white-painted hotel, built in the 1920s by a shipbuilding magnate, and commanding fine views of the Clyde estuary. The high-ceilinged foyer with its pillars, paintings and panelling has inviting leather armchairs, and the clubby bar with its pleasant terrace and the handsome first-floor lounge have a nice relaxed atmosphere. Spacious pretty bedrooms in modern and period styles – those in the main house are more traditional – are thoughtfully equipped. All offer hairdryers, trouser presses, tea-makers and good bathrooms. Staff are an enthusiastic team. *Amenities* garden, sauna, squash, golf course, riding, snooker, pool table, laundry service.

■ *Rooms 20*	*Confirm by arrang.*
en suite bath/shower 20	*Last dinner 9.30*
Direct dial Yes	*Parking Ample*
Room TV Yes	*Room service 24 hours*

Gleddoch House Hotel Restaurant ⌣

Charles Price's knowledgeable cooking is complemented by an elegant setting. Come at lunchtime to enjoy a taste of Scotland based on local produce, while interesting and imaginative evening dishes range from a superb terrine of chicken livers and calf's sweetbreads to whisky-flavoured lobster soup, venison with a thyme and orange sauce or tender duck breast with rhubarb purée. ⬄ **Well-chosen** ⊖

■ *Set L £8·50*	*L 12.30–2*
Set D £19·50	*D 7.30–9.30*
About £57 for two	*Seats 80 Parties 120*
Closed L Sat, 1 & 2 Jan & 25 & 27 Dec	

Fernie Castle Hotel   Letham

H **63% £D/E**
Map 17 C5 Fife
Nr Cupar KY7 7RU
Letham (033 781) 381
Credit Access, Amex, Diners, Visa
   A 16th-century castle set in 30 acres of grounds off the A914. There's an attractive reception area, with some nice antiques, and two stylishly elegant lounges on the first floor. Bedrooms vary in size but all have pretty wallpapers and fabrics. Radio-alarms, trouser presses and hairdryers are standard equipment. Good modern bath/shower rooms. No dogs. *Amenities* garden, coarse fishing.

■ *Rooms 16*	*Confirm by 6*
en suite bath/shower 16	*Last dinner 9.30*
Direct dial Yes	*Parking Ample*
Room TV Yes	*Room service Limited*

Champany Inn, Chop & Ale House   Linlithgow

R **Map 12 C1** Lothian
  Champany
Philipstoun (050 683) 4352
Owner managers Clive & Anne Davidson
Credit Access, Amex, Diners, Visa
   Sharing the same premises as the starred restaurant below, but quite distinct, this hugely popular bistro serves some of the finest steak in Scotland (and beyond). Start, perhaps, with pickled fish, but save room for a succulent T-bone or chargrilled club steak. Also burgers, sausages and seafood. In summer there's a cold buffet; in winter a hot dish of the day. Simple sweets. ⬄ **Well-chosen** ⊖

■ *About £28 for two*	*L 12–2*
Seats 36	*D 6.30–10*
Closed 24 Dec–14 Jan	*Parking Ample*

Champany Inn Restaurant ★   Linlithgow

R ★ ♨ ⚜   **Map 12 C1** Lothian
Champany
Philipstoun (050 683) 4532
Credit Access, Amex, Diners, Visa
   Raw materials of consummate quality are the
main draw of this hexagonal restaurant in a 300-
year-old converted farmhouse. Clive Davidson,
who hails from South Africa and was once a
butcher, takes immense trouble over his beef,
buying it on the hoof, corn-feeding it and
butchering and hanging the meat himself.
Charcoal grilled steaks continue to steal the show
from seafood – again, grilled to superlative effect
or, less frequently, steamed and sauced. There's
even an unusual yet surprisingly successful
combination of fillet of salmon and beef. Shellfish
comes from a sea-water pool in the bar area.
Vegetables, chosen from a raw selection, are
steamed to order, and salads are crisp and fresh.
Anne Davidson is a charming hostess front of
house. An extensive cellar, carefully chosen, has

particularly impressive burgundies. Excellent
selection, too, from South Africa, Australia and
California. *Specialities* chargrilled Shetland
salmon, steak tartare, Aberdeen Angus steaks,
home-made ice cream.
  ☞ Outstanding   🍷 Well-chosen ℮
■ *Set L from £9.50*   *L 12.30–2*
About £55 for two   *D 7–10*
Seats 50 Parties 50   *Parking Ample*
Closed L Sat, all Sun & 3 wks Xmas

Lochgair Hotel   Lochgair

H **57% £F**
  Map 17 B5 Strathclyde
By Lochgilphead PA31 8SA
Minard (0546) 86333
Owner managers Craig & Susan Whale
Credit Access, Visa
   On the A83 by Loch Gair, this well-kept hotel is
a favourite with outdoor enthusiasts. Bedrooms
are simple bright and cheerful, with practical

furnishings and tea-makers; some have balconies.
There are two bars and a TV lounge. The new
owners are a charming couple who offer a
genuinely warm welcome. No dogs.
Amenities garden.
■ *Rooms 16*   *Confirm by arrang.*
en suite bath/shower 9   *Last dinner 9.30*
Room phone No   *Parking Ample*
Room TV No   *Room service Limited*

Old Manor Hotel   Lundin Links

HR **60% £E**
  Map 17 C5 Fife
Leven Road KY8 6AJ
Lundin Links (0333) 320368
Owner manager William Wallace
Credit Access, Amex, Visa
   A late Victorian sandstone manor house high
up on the A915, overlooking the golf links and the
Firth of Forth. Bedrooms are divided between the
original house (with fine views) and a modern
extension. Public rooms include a cocktail bar
with a stock of 100 malt whiskies. Decent
breakfasts. *Amenities* laundry service.
■ *Rooms 19*   *Confirm by arrang.*
en suite bath/shower 15   *Last dinner 9*
Direct dial Yes   *Parking Ample*
Room TV Yes   *Room service All day*
Closed 1 & 2 Jan

Old Manor Hotel Restaurant ৬

Enjoyable eating and super views in a pleasant,
comfortable and traditional room. Chef Albert
Trotter's daily-changing menu includes local
seafood dishes like fresh Largo Bay crab
mayonnaise or poached fillets of haddock in a
creamy asparagus sauce. Meaty options run from
chicken florentine and mustardy mignons de veau
to sirloin steak and haunch of venison. Vegetables
are fresh, and there are some very good simple
sweets such as a flavoursome home-made crème
caramel. Smaller lunch menu. ℮
■ *Set L £6.95*   *L 12.30–2*
Set D £12.50   *D 7–9, Sat 7–9.30*
About £40 for two   *Seats 50*
Closed 1 & 2 Jan   *Parties 100*

Black Bull Thistle Hotel   Milngavie

H **61% £D**
  Map 12 B1 Strathclyde
Main Street G62 6BH
041-956 2291. Tlx 778323
Credit Access, Amex, Diners, Visa
   Close proximity to Glasgow and free use of the
nearby Allander Sports Centre are attractions of
this popular town-centre hotel. There's a sunny
first-floor lounge and a choice of four bars,

including a lively, stylish wine bar. Spacious
bedrooms with smart units and floral furnishings
offer trouser presses, hairdryers, tea-makers,
mineral water and fruit. Good bathrooms.
Amenities laundry service, in-house movies (free).
■ *Rooms 28*   *Confirm by arrang.*
en suite bath/shower 28   *Last dinner 9.30*
Direct dial Yes   *Parking Limited*
Room TV Yes   *Room service 24 hours*

Ladbroke Hotel · Moffat

H **55% £D/E**
Map 12 C3 Dumfries & Galloway
Ladyknowe DG10 9EL
Moffat (0683) 20464
Credit Access, Amex, Diners, Visa

A purpose-built 1960s hotel offering practical accommodation and a cheery ambience. Simple comfortably furnished rooms feature modern fitted units and floral fabrics. Gold Star rooms, decorated to a slightly higher standard, have extras. Public rooms include a pine-panelled reception and a contemporary bar-lounge, effectively furnished in bold colours.
Amenities pool table, laundry service.

■ *Rooms* 51	*Confirm by* arrang.
en suite bath/shower 48	*Last dinner* 9
Room phone Yes	*Parking* Ample
Room TV Yes	*Room service* Limited

■ For a discount on next year's guide, see Offer for Answers.

Ord Arms Hotel *NEW ENTRY* · Muir of Ord

I **£F**
Map 16 B3 Highland
Great North Road IV6 7XR
Inverness (0463) 870286
Credit Access. LVs

The Nairns have done a lot for the decor at their mellow stone-built inn, which stands on the A862 just outside town. The foyer has been spruced up (keeping its nice antique sideboard) and the dining room and cocktail bar are quite stylish in soft pastels. Bright, pleasant bedrooms are being gradually refurbished with pretty new wallpaper and matching fabrics.
Amenities garden.

■ *Rooms* 15	*Confirm by* arrang.
en suite bath/shower 8	*Last dinner* 10
Room phone No	*Parking* Ample
Room TV Yes	*Room service* Limited

Clifton Hotel · Nairn

HR **71% £D**
Map 16 C3 Highland
Viewfield Street IV12 4HW
Nairn (0667) 53119
Owner manager Mr J. Gordon Macintyre
Credit Access, Amex, Diners, Visa

A delightful Victorian house a few minutes from the town centre and very close to the sea. Inside, paintings, sculpture and antiques create a highly individual atmosphere, and the scent of fresh flowers and potpourris wafts through all the rooms. There's an elegantly furnished lounge, a cosy TV room, and a comfortable little bar with low white marble tables. Books galore, lovely ornaments and more fine furniture lend plenty of character to the bedrooms, which are all differently styled, using pretty coordinating fabrics. Back rooms have splendid views towards the Moray Firth. Compact carpeted bathrooms are well stocked with good-quality toiletries.
Amenities garden, valeting, laundry service.

■ *Rooms* 16	*Confirm by* arrang.
en suite bath/shower 16	*Last dinner* 9.30
Room phone No	*Parking* Ample
Room TV No	*Room service* All day
Closed 1 Nov–1 Mar	

Clifton Hotel Restaurant & Green Room ⌂

Excellent eating is to be had in both the main dining room and the small and very elegant Green Room (where smoking is not allowed). Cheese mousse with tabbouleh is a typically imaginative starter, and there's always a classic French soup. Main-course delights might include salmon beurre rouge, roast stuffed quail and venison marchand de vin. Nice sweets, too, like chocolate pots and sherry trifle. Carefully selected wines.
♥ Well-chosen ⊕

■ *About £45 for two*	*L* 12.30–1.30
Seats 50 *Parties* 70	*D* 7–9.30
Closed 1 Nov–1 Mar	

Golf View Hotel · Nairn

H **59% £C/D**
Map 16 C3 Highland
Seabank Road IV12 4HD
Nairn (0667) 52301. Tlx 75134
Manager Miss M. M. Anderson
Credit Access, Amex, Diners, Visa

With the Nairn Championship course close at hand, this solid Victorian hotel is very popular with golfers. Day rooms are comfortably traditional, and bedrooms range from compact to family size.
Amenities garden, outdoor swimming pool, sauna, hairdressing, tennis, putting, games rooms, in-house movies (free), 24-hour lounge service, crèche (summer, Easter & Christmas).

■ *Rooms* 55	*Confirm by* 6
en suite bath/shower 54	*Last dinner* 9.15
Direct dial Yes	*Parking* Ample
Room TV Yes	*Room service* 24 hours

Newton Hotel   Nairn

H **65% £D/E**
Map 16 C3 Highland
IV12 4RX
Nairn (0667) 53144. Tlx 739248
Owner manager James Duncan
Credit Access, Amex, Diners, Visa
   A winding drive leads up to this stately country
house where echoes of a former era are retained
in the panelled entrance hall and grandly-

proportioned lounge. Main house bedrooms are
spacious and traditional; those in the courtyard
block more compact and modern. *Amenities*
garden, sauna, keep-fit equipment, tennis, putting,
croquet, pool table, 24-hour lounge service.

■ *Rooms* 44	*Confirm by arrang.*
en suite bath/shower 44	*Last dinner 9.15*
Direct dial Yes	*Parking* Ample
Room TV Yes	*Room service 24 hours*

■ Changes in data may occur in
  establishments after the Guide
  goes to press. Prices should be taken
  as indications rather than firm quotes.

Udny Arms Hotel   Newburgh

H **60% £E**
Map 16 D3 Grampian
Main Street AB4 0BL
Newburgh (035 86) 444. Tlx 265871
Credit Access, Amex, Visa
   A well-maintained and charming Victorian hotel
with a strong feeling of warmth and comfort.
There's a chintzy, relaxing lounge hung with
Victorian prints, and a homely cocktail bar with

Windsor chairs. The characterful bedrooms have
period furniture, tea-makers and radios;
bathrooms have tubs and showers.
Amenities garden, laundry service, coffee shop
(11am–11pm, limited in winter).

■ *Rooms* 26	*Confirm by arrang.*
en suite bath/shower 26	*Last dinner 9.30*
Room phone Yes	*Parking* Ample
Room TV Yes	*Room service 24 hours*

Bruce Hotel   Newton Stewart

H **60% £E**
Map 13 B4 Dumfries & Galloway
88 Queen Street DG8 6JL
Newton Stewart (0671) 2294
Owner managers Mr J. T. Wyllie & family
Credit Access, Amex, Diners, Visa
   Guests will receive a warm welcome from the
Wyllie family at this hotel in the town centre. The
foyer, bar and lounge are decorated in cheerful

contemporary style. Good-sized bedrooms are
simply furnished with white units and floral
curtains. *Amenities* solarium, gymnasium, in-
house movies (free), laundry service.

■ *Rooms* 18	*Confirm by arrang.*
en suite bath/shower 18	*Last dinner 8.30*
Direct dial Yes	*Parking* Ample
Room TV Yes	*Room service All day*
Closed Dec–Jan	

■ We publish annually, so make
  sure you use the current
  edition. It's worth it!

Creebridge House Hotel   Newton Stewart

H **60% £E**
Map 13 B4 Dumfries & Galloway
DG8 6NP
Newton Stewart (0671) 2121
Owner managers D. S. Oliver & family
Credit Access, Visa
   New owners have many plans for this conver-
ted farmhouse set in grounds of three acres.
Public areas are comfortable, with a mixture of

antique and modern furniture. Good-sized
bedrooms are individually decorated in traditional
style. Excellent housekeeping. *Amenities*
garden, croquet, laundry service.

■ *Rooms* 17	*Confirm by arrang.*
en suite bath/shower 17	*Last dinner 8.30*
Direct dial Yes	*Parking* Ample
Room TV Yes	*Room service All day*
Closed 23 Dec–5 Jan	

Kirroughtree Hotel

HR **75% £D**
Map 13 B4 Dumfries & Galloway
DG8 6AN
Newton Stewart (0671) 2141

Every prospect pleases at this immaculate Georgian mansion, which stands in lovely, peaceful grounds landscaped by the previous owner, Mr Velt. Decor is opulent, particularly in the lounge with its velour-clad settees and onyx-topped coffee tables, and in the twin dining rooms featuring ornate plaster ceilings. Bedroom size varies and decor is individual, but common to all rooms are the smart French-style furnishings, ample sitting areas and sparkling tiled bathrooms. Nice touches include a welcoming glass of sherry

and a selection of books. No children under ten. *Amenities* garden, putting, bowling green.
■ *Rooms* 23	*Confirm by* arrang.
en suite bath/shower 23	*Last dinner* 9.30
Direct dial Yes	*Parking* Ample
Room TV Yes	*Room service* All day
Closed early Nov–early Mar	

Kirroughtree Hotel Restaurant ♛

French cooking
Two opulent rooms, one red, the other (for non-smokers) predominantly blue. Careful cooking is highlighted by clear, honest flavours and well-balanced sauces. Typical items on the fixed-price menu (sometimes no choice) could include smoked chicken and prawn salad, delicious curried apple soup, sole in lemon butter sauce and fillet of pork with pimentos and peppercorns. Fine classic cellar, strong in Bordeaux and burgundy, with the occasional old gem from the Rhône. ♀ Well-chosen ℮

■ *Set D* £21	*D* 7–9.30
About £50 *for two*	*Seats* 52 *Parties* 30
Closed early Nov–early Mar	

Marine Hotel

H **66% £D** ⅁
Map 12 D1 Lothian
Cromwell Road EH39 4LZ
North Berwick (0620) 2406. Tlx 72550
Credit Access, Amex, Diners, Visa

Major improvements have taken place at this handsome turreted hotel overlooking a golf course. Public rooms have been redesigned (the foyer now leads directly to the pretty lounge) and

all the variously sized bedrooms have been smartly renovated. *Amenities* garden, outdoor swimming pool, sauna, solarium, squash, tennis, putting, snooker, in-house movies (free), ceefax, laundry service, 24-hour lounge service.
■ *Rooms* 83	*Confirm by* 6
en suite bath/shower 83	*Last dinner* 9.30
Direct dial Yes	*Parking* Ample
Room TV Yes	*Room service* 24 hours

Borthwick Castle

H **67% £B/C**
Map 12 D2 Lothian
By Gorebridge EH23 4QY
Gorebridge (0875) 20514
Manager Edward Cunningham
Credit Amex, Diners, Visa

Take the Borthwick road off the A7 at the village of North Middleton and you'll soon spot this twin-towered baronial keep. Built in 1430, it is one of the finest preserved Scottish castles of its type – an impregnable fortress – once the refuge of Mary Queen of Scots and the Earl of Bothwell. It retains much romance and grandeur, notably in the Great

Hall with its 40-foot Gothic arch and minstrel's gallery, and in the magnificent State Room lounge with a little private chapel. Narrow stone stairs lead on beyond the lounge to the bedrooms, whose appeal is solid and traditional and facilities almost nil (no TV, no radio, no phone, simple shower rooms). No dogs. *Amenities* garden, croquet.

■ *Rooms* 10	*Confirm by* arrang.
en suite bath/shower 10	*Last dinner* 10.30
Room phone No	*Parking* Ample
Room TV No	*Room service* None

Alexandra Hotel

H **57% £D/E**
Map 17 B5 Strathclyde
Esplanade PA34 5AA
Oban (0631) 62381
Credit Access, Amex, Diners, Visa

Pleasant sea views can be enjoyed over a drink in the modest lounges and bar of this greystone Victorian hotel overlooking the busy harbour. Bedrooms are bright and cheerful – most have

their own bathrooms, all have tea-makers, TVs and radio. *Amenities* garden, games room, in-house movies, laundry service, 24-hour lounge service, children's playground.
■ *Rooms* 56	*Confirm by* 6
en suite bath/shower 49	*Last dinner* 9
Room phone No	*Parking* Ample
Room TV Yes	*Room service* 24 hours
Closed end Oct–Easter	

Columbia Hotel *NEW ENTRY*   **Oban**

H **61% £D/E**
Map 17 B5 Strathclyde
North Pier, Corran Esplanade PA34 5PP
Oban (0631) 62183
Credit Access, Amex, Diners, Visa
 Recently reopened after refurbishment, the Columbia stands between the quayside and the town. Bedrooms vary in size and shape, but all are well equipped and most have decent darkwood furniture and smart bathrooms. Thirteen more modest rooms have showers only. Stylish day rooms include two bars, one with a cheerful nautical air. *Amenities* in-house movies (free), laundry service.

■ *Rooms* 47	*Confirm by* 6
en suite bath/shower 47	*Last dinner* 9.45
Direct dial Yes	*Parking* Limited
Room TV Yes	*Room service* Limited

■ Our inspectors never book in the name of Egon Ronay's Guides; they disclose their identity only after paying their bills.

Meldrum House Hotel   **Old Meldrum**

HR **74% £C/D**
Map 16 D3 Grampian
AB5 0AE
Old Meldrum (065 12) 2294
Manager Mr J. Giordimaina
Credit Amex, Diners. **LVs**
 A hotel since the 1940s, this magnificent greystone turreted mansion has been the seat of the Lairds of Meldrum since 1236, and the oldest part of the house – the atmospheric stone-vaulted bar – dates from that period. Fine antiques, ancestral portraits, blazing log fires, magazines and fresh flowers throughout the day rooms create an impression of relaxed and gracious family living. Spacious individually-decorated bedrooms have antique furniture (two with four-posters) and abound in homely touches, from pictures, pretty porcelain and plants to books and fruit. All have carpeted bathrooms (one not en suite, three shower rooms). *Amenities* garden, 9-hole golf course.

■ *Rooms* 11	*Confirm by* arrang.
en suite bath/shower 10	*Last dinner* 9.30
Room phone Yes	*Parking* Ample
Room TV Yes	*Room service* All day
Closed mid Dec–beginning Mar	

Meldrum House Hotel Restaurant ⌴ &

Prime local produce features in abundance on the short set menus offered at this quietly elegant restaurant. The selection changes daily and might include game terrine with Cumberland sauce, champagne-marinated herrings, venison in deliciously light puff pastry, jugged saddle of hare, and salmon hollandaise. Vegetables are good and portions are most generous, but leave room for a tempting dessert from the laden trolley. ℮

■ *Set D* £19	*D only* 7–9.30
About £50 *for two*	*Seats* 60 *Parties* 60
Closed mid Dec–beginning Mar	

■ If we recommend meals in a hotel or inn, a separate entry is made for its restaurant.

Onich Hotel *NEW ENTRY*   **Onich**

H **60% £E**
Map 17 B4 Highland
Nr Fortwilliam PH33 6RY
Onich (085 53) 214
Owner managers Iain & Ronald Young
Credit Access, Amex, Diners, Visa
 The grounds of this well-kept hotel run down to Loch Linnhe, and many of the public rooms have picture windows with marvellous views. There's also a smart paved terrace. Bedrooms are comfortable, fresh and attractive, bathrooms sparklingly clean. *Amenities* garden, solarium, whirlpool bath, putting, games room, in-house movies (free), laundry service (summer).

■ *Rooms* 27	*Confirm by* 6
en suite bath/shower 27	*Last dinner* 8.30
Direct dial Yes	*Parking* Limited
Room TV Yes	*Room service* Limited

The Peat Inn ★★   Peat Inn

RR ★★ ⚐ ⬧ **Map 17 D5** Fife
Nr Cupar
Peat Inn (033 484) 206
Credit Access, Amex, Diners, Visa

Relax in the charming bar, with its colourful
armchairs and open fire, before being seated in
this delightful restaurant, which now also offers
accommodation. Here, only the very best
ingredients will do for the wonderfully talented
David Wilson. Local produce features prominently
throughout the monthly-changing menus,
enhanced by memorably subtle, yet deep-
flavoured sauces. Recent successes have
included a beautifully presented lobster 'cake' in
a superb lobster sauce, and tender venison with a
splendidly shiny, port-enriched game sauce. Set
lunch (no choice). Smoking discouraged. Friendly,
warm-hearted service. Superb wine list
remarkable for its exquisite judgement and keen
pricing. Note the wonderful burgundies and five
top vintages of Château Pichon – Longueville

Lalande Pauillac. *Specialities* breast of pigeon in
a pastry case with wild mushrooms, Peat Inn fish
soup, loin of lamb with a lamb charlotte in a red
wine sauce with cassis, pineapple and grenadine
sorbet with fresh fruits. ➮ Outstanding ⓔ
■ *Set L* £11·50   *L at 1*
About £50 for two   *D 7–9.30*
Seats 48   *Parking Ample*
Closed Sun, Mon, Bank Hols & 2 wks Jan

Cringletie House Hotel   Peebles

H 63% £D/E
Map 12 C2 Borders
Eddleston EH45 8PL
Eddleston (072 13) 233
Owner managers Stanley & Aileen Maguire
Credit Access, Amex, Diners, Visa

An impressive building in beautiful
surroundings off the A703. Attractive public
rooms in traditional style include a comfortable

bar and splendidly furnished lounge. Bedrooms
are individually decorated. Bathrooms are
spotlessly clean. *Amenities* garden, tennis,
squash, putting, croquet.
■ *Rooms 16*
en suite bath/shower 11   *Last dinner 8.30*
Room phone No   *Parking Ample*
Room TV No   *Room service All day*
Closed Jan–Feb   *Confirm by 5*

Park Hotel   Peebles

H 64% £D/E
Map 12 C2 Borders
Innerleithen Road EH45 8BA
Peebles (0721) 20451
Credit Access, Amex, Diners, Visa

An 18th-century hotel overlooking the river
Tweed and the Cademuir hills beyond. There is a
continuing programme of improvements here,
with public areas and bedrooms gradually being

refurbished and upgraded. Newly decorated
bedrooms have stylish fabrics, good darkwood
units, comfortable easy chairs and smart
bathrooms. No dogs. *Amenities* garden, putting,
laundry service, 24-hour lounge service.
■ *Rooms 26*   *Confirm by 6*
en suite bath/shower 26   *Last dinner 10*
Room phone Yes   *Parking Ample*
Room TV Yes   *Room service 24 hours*

Peebles Hotel Hydro   Peebles

H 71% £D/E *E*
Map 12 C2 Borders
Innerleithen Road EH45 8LX
Peebles (0721) 20602. Tlx 72568
Manager Peter van Dijk
Credit Access, Amex, Diners, Visa

Perched on a hillside, this imposing Edwardian
hotel offers splendid views over the Tweed valley
and a fine choice of activities for the energetic.
The pool area with adjacent coffee shop is a great
attraction, and there's a cane-furnished sun
lounge as well as the main lounge and bar. Good-
sized bedrooms are nicely maintained and have
modern bathrooms. No dogs.
Amenities garden, indoor swimming pool, sauna,
solarium, whirlpool bath, keep-fit equipment,
hairdressing, tennis, squash, badminton, putting,
pitch & putt, croquet, riding, games room,

billiards, snooker, laundry service, laundry room,
coffee shop (12.30–10pm), 24-hour lounge
service, kiosk, crèche (July–Aug), children's
playroom & playground, helipad.
■ *Rooms 139*   *Confirm by arrang.*
en suite bath/shower 139 *Last dinner 9*
Direct dial Yes   *Parking Ample*
Room TV Yes   *Room service 24 hours*

Tontine Hotel   Peebles

H **59% £D**
Map 12 C2 Borders
High Street EH45 8AJ
Peebles (0721) 20892
Credit Access, Amex, Diners, Visa
　　Cosy, convivial public rooms – the spacious
lounge has a log fire and antique pieces – are an
attraction of this 19th-century town centre hotel.
Other public areas include a panelled bar and an

elegant dining room. Bedrooms, both those in the
main building and in the modern wing, are
modestly comfortable. All have remote-control
TVs and tea-makers. *Amenities* laundry service,
24-hour lounge service.

■ *Rooms* 37	*Confirm by* 6
en suite bath/shower 37	*Last dinner* 9.30
Room phone Yes	*Parking* Ample
Room TV Yes	*Room service* All day

Royal George Hotel   Perth

H **60% £C/D**
Map 17 C5 Tayside
Tay Street PH1 5LD
Perth (0738) 24455
Credit Access, Amex, Diners, Visa. LVs
　　Dubbed Royal after a visit by Queen Victoria in
1848, this handsome hotel has a splendid position
in the heart of Perth. The roomy lounge looks out
over the Tay, as do the best and biggest of the

bedrooms. Recent developments include
refurbishment of some public areas and
bedrooms, with plans for a new café bar.
Management and staff seem lacking in zip.
Amenities laundry service.

■ *Rooms* 43	*Confirm by* 6
en suite bath/shower 43	*Last dinner* 9.30
Direct dial Yes	*Parking* Ample
Room TV Yes	*Room service* All day

Stakis City Mills Hotel   Perth

H **59% £D**
Map 17 C5 Tayside
West Mill Street PH1 5QP
Perth (0738) 28281
Credit Access, Amex, Diners, Visa
　　The stream that flows beneath the floor of the
bar is a visible reminder that this was once a
water mill. Modern extensions house the
bedrooms, which have attractive darkwood

furniture, trouser presses, hairdryers and tea-
makers, plus neat, practical bathrooms. New day
rooms include a smart lobby-lounge and beamed
steak bar. An improving hotel with a switched-on
manager. *Amenities* garden, laundry service.

■ *Rooms* 78	*Confirm by* 6
en suite bath/shower 78	*Last dinner* 10
Direct dial Yes	*Parking* Ample
Room TV Yes	*Room service* Limited

Station Hotel   Perth

H **60% £D/E**
Map 17 C5 Tayside
Leonard Street PH2 8HE
Perth (0738) 24141. Tlx 76481
Credit Access, Amex, Diners, Visa
　　A Victorian hotel getting a new lease of life
under its go-ahead new owners. Staff are keen
and on the ball, and improvements in the day
rooms include a smart new garden bar and total

refurbishment. Bedrooms, all with remote-control
TVs, range from well-equipped 'Premier Plus'
rooms to smaller modern rooms under the eaves.
Amenities garden, keep-fit equipment, in-house
movies, laundry service.

■ *Rooms* 71	*Confirm by* 6
en suite bath/shower 51	*Last dinner* 9
Direct dial Yes	*Parking* Ample
Room TV Yes	*Room service* 24 hours

Pittodrie House Hotel   Pitcaple

HR **65% £D/E**
Map 16 D3 Grampian
Nr Inverurie AB5 9HS
Pitcaple (046 76) 444. Tlx 739935
Owner manager Theo Smith
Credit Access, Amex, Diners, Visa
　　Dating back to the 17th century, this creeper-
clad mansion enjoys a delightfully rural setting.
The lofty, antique-furnished lounge offers
splendid views, and there's a fine billiards room
and cosy bar. Antiques also feature in the
attractively decorated bedrooms. *Amenities*
garden, tennis, squash, croquet, clay-pigeon
shooting, billiards, snooker, laundry service.

■ *Rooms* 12	*Confirm by* arrang.
en suite bath/shower 8	*Last dinner* 8.45
Direct dial Yes	*Parking* Ample
Room TV Yes	*Room service* Limited

Pittodrie House Hotel Restaurant

Satisfying, straightforward dishes based on prime
local produce are enjoyably prepared at this
elegantly traditional restaurant hung with huge oil
paintings. The set menus change daily and might
include game terrine, carrot and coriander soup,
rack of lamb with Shrewsbury sauce, fillet steak
au poivre, and rainbow trout normande among the
short, nicely-balanced selection. Pleasant sweets
like honey and brandy ice cream to finish. Book for
Sunday lunch. The wine list is full of interest.
♧ Well-chosen

■ *Set L* £9·50	*L* 12.30–1.30
Set D £18·50	*D* 7.30–9
About £40 *for two*	*Seats* 45 *Parties* 40

729

Pitlochry ▶

Atholl Palace Hotel   Pitlochry

H 59% £C/D
Map 17 C4 Tayside
PH16 5LY
Pitlochry (0796) 2400. Tlx 76406
Credit Access, Amex, Diners, Visa
  The leisure facilities are excellent at this 100-year-old turreted hotel above Pitlochry. Public rooms are on the grand scale, and bedrooms with fitted units offer simple, practical accommodation.

Amenities garden, outdoor swimming pool, sauna, solarium, keep-fit equipment, tennis, putting, pitch & putt, games room, snooker, 24-hour lounge service, children's playroom, helipad.

■ *Rooms 84*	*Confirm by 6*
en suite bath/shower 84	*Last dinner 9*
Room phone Yes	*Parking Ample*
Room TV Yes	*Room service 24 hours*

Green Park Hotel   Pitlochry

H 57% £D/E ᵭ
Map 17 C4 Tayside
PH16 5JY
Pitlochry (0796) 3248
Owner managers Graham & Anne Brown
Credit Access
  Set in spacious gardens overlooking Loch Faskally, this is a pleasant Victorian house with modern bedroom extensions. Public rooms,

including a sun lounge, have a welcoming feel, and bedrooms are neat, bright and cheerful. Friendly, helpful staff. No dogs. *Amenities* garden, putting, game fishing, games room.

■ *Rooms 37*	*Confirm by 6*
en suite bath/shower 37	*Last dinner 8.30*
Direct dial Yes	*Parking Ample*
Room TV Yes	*Room service Limited*
Closed 1 Nov–end Mar	

Pitlochry Hydro Hotel   Pitlochry

H 63% £C/D ᵭ
Map 17 C4 Tayside
Knockard Road PH16 5JH
Pitlochry (0796) 2666
Credit Access, Amex, Diners, Visa
  A substantial late-Victorian hotel that's popular with group tours. Day rooms have been brought attractively up to date, and a third of the bedrooms have also been greatly improved (nice

lightwood furnishings and stylishly co-ordinated fabrics). There are similar plans for the remaining bedrooms. Service could be much improved. *Amenities* garden, tennis, croquet, putting, games room, in-house movies.

■ *Rooms 64*	*Confirm by arrang.*
en suite bath/shower 64	*Last dinner 8.30*
Room phone Yes	*Parking Ample*
Room TV Yes	*Room service Limited*

Airds Hotel   Port Appin

HR 69% £C
Map 17 B5 Strathclyde
Appin PA38 4DF
Appin (063 173) 236
Owner managers Eric & Betty Allen
  Caring hosts provide the warmest of welcomes at this lovely old ferry inn overlooking Loch Linnhe and the mountains of Morven beyond. The relaxing lounges have recently been attractively redecorated, and there's a smart bar. No phones, TVs or radios disturb the peace of comfortable bedrooms (many with enchanting views) – and all have modern bathrooms. Half board only. No children under five. *Amenities* garden.

■ *Rooms 15*	*Confirm by 4*
en suite bath/shower 15	*Last dinner 8.30*
Room phone No	*Parking Ample*
Room TV No	*Room service All day*
Closed end Nov–early Mar	

Airds Hotel Restaurant ★ ⌁

Betty Allen's four-course dinner menus change daily at this bright, airy restaurant decorated with fresh flowers. Using only the finest local produce (including superb fish and seafood), supplemented by lovely home-grown vegetables and husband Eric's excellent bread, she offers such delights as venison pâté and mousseline of scallops among starters, followed by, say,

succulent roast lamb or salmon hollandaise. To finish, tempting sweets like warm chocolate gâteau with cream, and a couple of cheeses in prime condition served with home-made oatcakes. Lunch is a light affair featuring soup, cold meats and sandwiches with still-warm bread. No smoking. Exceptional, clearly annotated wine list: sensational Barsacs and Sauternes (Ch. Coutet 1971 & Ch. d'Yquem 1967).
Specialities mousseline of scallops, fillet of trout with champagne and chive sauce, roast saddle of venison with red wine sauce and rowanberry jelly, warm chocolate gâteau.
⌑ Outstanding ⌐

■ *Set D £22*	*L 12.30–1.30*
About £50 for two	*D at 8*
Seats 46	*Parties 40*
Closed end Nov–early Mar	

Corsemalzie House Hotel · Port William

H 64% £D/E
Map 13 B4 Dumfries & Galloway
By Newton Stewart, Wigtownshire DG8 9RL
Mochrum (098 886) 254
Owner manager Peter McDougall
Credit Access, Amex, Diners, Visa

A secluded mansion set in 40 acres of beautiful wooded grounds just off the B7005 some six miles west of Wigtown. The lounge and bar are pleasant places to relax, and the bedrooms are cheerful and roomy. Good hearty breakfasts.
Amenities garden, putting, croquet, shooting, game fishing, laundry service.

■ *Rooms* 15	*Confirm by arrang.*
en suite bath/shower 15	*Last dinner 9.15*
Direct dial Yes	*Parking* Ample
Room TV Yes	*Room service* All day
Closed 25 & 26 Dec & mid Jan–Mar	

Knockinaam Lodge Hotel · Portpatrick

HR 71% £C/D
Map 13 A4 Dumfries & Galloway
Nr Stranraer DG9 9AD
Portpatrick (077 681) 471
Owner managers Marcel & Corinna Frichot
Credit Access, Amex, Diners, Visa

A wonderfully warm welcome is offered to all at this peaceful Victorian country house, beautifully situated in its own secluded valley (ask for directions). The two residents' lounges with their comfortable period furnishings have a relaxed homely feel about them, and there's an attractive bar area with wood panelling and copper-topped tables. Recently refurbished bedrooms are individually decorated; all have pretty bathrooms and many thoughtful extras. Excellent breakfasts.

Half-board only. *Amenities* garden, croquet, sea fishing, mooring, private beach, laundry service.

■ *Rooms* 10	*Confirm by arrang.*
en suite bath/shower 10	*Last dinner 9*
Direct dial Yes	*Parking* Ample
Room TV Yes	*Room service* Limited
Closed 9 Jan–Easter	

Knockinaam Lodge Hotel Restaurant ☖ ᕕ

French cooking
With splendid sea views, this delightful restaurant is a relaxing setting for Daniel Galmiche's fine cooking. Set-price dinner menus offer an imaginative choice, expertly prepared from prime ingredients and attractively presented. Dishes include monkfish and langoustines with lobster sauce, noisettes of venison with chestnut purée, and pear and apple feuilleté. Shorter lunchtime menu. Friendly service. Booking essential.
♀ Well-chosen ☻

■ *Set D £18*	*L 12–2*
About £45 for two	*D 7.30–9.30*
Seats 30	*Parties 20*
Closed 9 Jan–Easter	

Rosedale Hotel · Portree

H 52% £E
Map 16 A3 Highland
Beaumont Crescent, Isle of Skye IV51 9DB
Portree (0478) 2531
Owner manager Mr H. M. Andrew

A small, family-run hotel overlooking the sheltered harbour of Loch Portree. Created from a row of early 19th-century fishermen's houses, it makes a charming place to stay. There's a choice of two cosy bars and two modest lounges – one with TV. Bright little bedrooms (including four in a separate house) are simply furnished.
Amenities garden.

■ *Rooms* 21	*Confirm by arrang.*
en suite bath/shower 18	*Last dinner 8*
Room phone No	*Parking* Limited
Room TV No	*Room service* Limited
Closed Oct–mid May	

♀ indicates a **well-chosen** house wine.

Portsonachan Hotel · Portsonachan

I £E
Map 7 B5 Strathclyde
South Lochaweside, by Dalmally PA33 1BL
Kilchrenan (086 63) 224
Credit Access, Visa

Portsonachan means 'Port of Peace', and this large old white-painted inn by Loch Awe offers peace in plenty, plus marvellous views and a good friendly ambience. The lounges have a nice lived-in feel, and the bedrooms, whose furnishings range from antiques to functional modern, are provided with thoughtful extras. *Amenities* garden, coarse & game fishing, hotel boats.

■ *Rooms* 19	*Confirm by arrang.*
en suite bath/shower 6	*Last dinner 9*
Room phone No	*Parking* Ample
Room TV No	*Room service* None
Closed mid Nov–1 Mar (exc. 24 Dec–4 Jan)	

Carlton Hotel   Prestwick

H **61%** **£E**
Map 12 B2 Strathclyde
Ayr Road KA9 1TP
Prestwick (0292) 76811
Credit Access, Amex, Diners, Visa
   Notably high standards of repair and decoration prevail at this modern hotel on the A79. Comfortable, well-upholstered easy chairs provide relaxation in the bar, and there's a refurbished public lounge with pool table and fruit machine. Bedrooms, the majority in a wing, have smartly tiled bathrooms. *Amenities* in-house movies (free), coffee shop (11am–11pm), 24-hour lounge service.

■ Rooms 39	Confirm by 6
en suite bath/shower 39	Last dinner 10
Direct dial Yes	Parking Ample
Room TV Yes	Room service 24 hours

Baron's Craig Hotel   Rockcliffe

H **65%** **£C/D** &
Map 13 C4 Dumfries & Galloway
By Dalbeattie DG5 4QF
Rockcliffe (055 663) 225
Credit Access, Amex
   An attractive Victorian hotel set in 12 acres of grounds with lovely views across the Solway Firth. Antique furniture and a suitable period feel predominate in the public areas. Bedrooms in the extension are simple and modern; those in the main house are in traditional style and individually decorated. *Amenities* garden, golf practice net, putting, sailing, laundry service.

■ Rooms 26	Confirm by 6
en suite bath/shower 20	Last dinner 9
Direct dial Yes	Parking Ample
Room TV Yes	Room service All day
Closed mid Oct–Easter	

Rothes Glen Hotel   Rothes

H **64%** **£D**
Map 16 C3 Grampian
Nr Elgin IV33 7AH
Rothes (034 03) 254
Owner manager Donald Carmichael
Credit Access, Amex, Diners, Visa
   An impressive Victorian residence, built in Scottish Baronial style. Now fully modernised, it retains nice original touches like the stained-glass skylight over the stairwell. Antique furniture creates an elegant ambience throughout and spacious bedrooms are well equipped. *Amenities* garden, putting.

■ Rooms 16	Confirm by arrang.
en suite bath/shower 13	Last dinner 9
Direct dial Yes	Parking Ample
Room TV Yes	Room service Limited
Closed Jan	

Old Course Golf & Country Club   St Andrews

H **77%** **£B** **E** &
Map 17 D5 Fife
KY16 9SP
St Andrews (0334) 74371. Tlx 76280
Credit Access, Amex, Diners, Visa
   First and foremost a golfing hotel, with an indoor golf school, a specialist shop and a marvellous position by the Old Course. It's an impressive, if somewhat stark, modern building, and there's style and comfort in the public rooms with their polished wood, potted plants, deep carpets and generous seating. The views are splendid, and spectacular from the top-floor lounge and bar. Spacious bedrooms (sitting areas, balconies and, of course, those views) feature fine fabrics and elegant furnishings, and all have well-equipped, fully tiled bathrooms. Service on our last visit was not always up to

scratch. *Amenities* garden, indoor swimming pool, sauna, solarium, whirlpool bath, gymnasium, beauty salon, hairdressing, valeting, laundry service, helipad.

■ Rooms 140	Confirm by arrang.
en suite bath/shower 140	Last dinner 10.30
Direct dial Yes	Parking Ample
Room TV Yes	Room service 24 hours

Rufflets Hotel   St Andrews

H **65%** **£D**
Map 17 D5 Fife
Strathkinness Low Road KY16 9TX
St Andrews (0334) 72594
Manager Peter Aretz
Credit Access, Amex, Diners, Visa
   A 1920s mansion set in ten acres of landscaped gardens on the B939. Day rooms include a rather elegant bow-fronted lounge, comfortable bar and little card room. Main-house and cottage bedrooms are traditionally furnished while those in an extension have modern units. No dogs. *Amenities* garden, putting, laundry service.

■ Rooms 21	Confirm by 6
en suite bath/shower 21	Last dinner 9.15
Direct dial Yes	Parking Ample
Room TV Yes	Room service Limited
Closed mid Jan–mid Feb	

The Rusack's
St Andrews

H **77% £B**
Map 17 D5 Fife
Pilmour Links KY16 9JQ
St Andrews (0334) 74321
Manager Eric Brown
Credit Access, Amex, Diners, Visa
  1987 was the centenary year of this handsome hotel (formerly called Rusack's Marine) beside the 18th fairway of the Old Course. Inside the public areas impress with trompe-l'oeil marble columns, crystal chandeliers and book-lined 'library' decor. The roomy sun lounge commands fine views over the course, and the Champions Bar in the basement features photographs of golfing stars. Bedrooms are most attractively appointed, with good-quality darkwood furnishings. Some have sitting areas, all boast excellent tiled bathrooms. Impeccable service led by impressive manager

Eric Brown.
Amenities laundry service.
■ *Rooms 50*	*Confirm by arrang.*
en suite bath/shower 50	*Last dinner 10*
Direct dial Yes	*Parking Ample*
Room TV Yes	*Room service 24 hours*
Closed 4–11 Jan	

Four Seasons Hotel
St Fillans

HR **61% £D** &
Map 17 C5 Tayside
Nr Crieff PH6 2NF
St Fillans (076 485) 333
Owner manager Carlo Donetti
Credit Access, Amex
  A pleasant hotel with warm, caring owners. It stands by Loch Earn, and fine views are enjoyed from most of the neat, homely bedrooms. Six Scandinavian-style chalets have their own parking spaces and sitting rooms. There are two bars and an airy lounge. *Amenities* garden, game & coarse fishing, laundry service.
■ *Rooms 12*	*Confirm by arrang.*
en suite bath/shower 12	*Last dinner 9.45*
Room phone Yes	*Parking Ample*
Room TV Yes	*Room service All day*
Closed Nov–Apr	

Four Seasons Hotel
Restaurant &

Daily-changing set menus provide a fair variety of enjoyable, quite straightforward dishes. Soup, pâté and cured salmon are favourite starters, and main courses could include Loch Earn trout, cold gammon salad, chicken princesse or grilled lamb with rosemary. Copious fresh vegetables, plus a good cheeseboard and a tempting sweet trolley to finish. Excellent Italian wines: superb 1971 Chianti Classico Riserva (Valiano). Get a window table and enjoy the food, the wine *and* the Loch views. ♀ **Well-chosen** ☺
■ *Set L £8·50*	*L 12.15–2*
Set D £13·50	*D 7.15–9.45*
About £36 for two	*Parking Ample*
Seats 60	*Closed Nov–Apr*

■ Any person using our name to obtain free hospitality is a fraud. Proprietors, please inform the police and us.

Scarista House
Scarista

HR **67% £D/E**
Map 16 A2 Highland
Isle of Harris PA85 3HX
Scarista (085 985) 238
Owner managers Andrew & Alison Johnson
  Getting away from it all means just that in this former Church of Scotland manse on bleakly beautiful Harris. It's a place to come for quiet relaxation and bracing walks, and the owners are the most engaging of hosts. Bedrooms, individually furnished, have smart modern bathrooms. Splendid breakfasts. No children under 8. *Amenities* garden.
■ *Rooms 7*	*Confirm by arrang.*
en suite bath/shower 7	*Last dinner 8*
Room phone No	*Parking Ample*
Room TV No	*Room service None*
Closed end Sept–Easter	

Restaurant ♛ ♈

There are two dining rooms with polished antique tables, fresh wild flowers and attractive china. Alison Johnson uses local produce such as seafood or local lamb when she can, and her four-course, no-choice menus show considerable ingenuity with dishes like tomato granita with sweet pepper fritters, turnover of sole or pheasant with apple and rosemary. Vegetables are interesting, too, and sweets include a fabulous chocolate mousse gâteau. Vegetarian menu on request. Scrupulously selected wines with good honest burgundies: Bourgogne Rouge 'La Fortune' from de Villaine. ♀ **Well-chosen** ☺
■ *Set D £15*	*D only at 8*
About £40 for two	*Seats 20*
Closed Sun & end Sept–Easter	

Eddrachilles Hotel Scourie

H **60% £E**
Map 16 B2 Highland
Badcall Bay IV27 4TH
Scourie (0971) 2080
Owner managers Mr & Mrs A. C. M. Wood
Loch and sea fishing, walking and nature-watching are favourite pursuits at this spotlessly kept hotel overlooking beautiful Badcall Bay. Compact bedrooms, mostly with shower cubicles,

provide adequate comforts, and extended public areas include a new lobby and two roomy lounges; the sun lounge enjoys stunning views of the island-studded bay. *Amenities* garden, game & sea fishing, boating.

■ *Rooms* 11	*Confirm by* arrang.
en suite bath/shower 11	*Last dinner* 8
Room phone No	*Parking* Ample
Room TV No	*Room service* Limited

Scourie Hotel Scourie

H **62% £E**
Map 16 B2 Highland
By Lairg, Sutherland IV27 4SX
Scourie (0971) 2396
Owner managers Ian & Mary Hay
Credit Access, Diners, Visa
Trout and salmon fishing are a major attraction at this family-run hotel overlooking Scourie Bay. The hotel – once a coaching inn – conveys a

relaxed and friendly atmosphere, with cheerful tartan carpeting brightening the public areas. Simply furnished, well-kept bedrooms. *Amenities* pool table, game fishing.

■ *Rooms* 21	*Confirm by* 6
en suite bath/shower 21	*Last dinner* 8.30
Direct dial Yes	*Parking* Ample
Room TV Yes	*Room service* Limited
Closed end Oct–mid Mar	

Phillipburn House Hotel Selkirk

HR **59% £D**
Map 12 D2 Borders
Linglie Road TD7 5LS
Selkirk (0750) 20747
Owner managers Jim & Anne Hill
Credit Access, Amex, Diners, Visa
Just outside Selkirk, this delightful hotel – an imaginatively converted Georgian house – is a popular family choice. Spacious, pine-furnished bedrooms include poolside suites, a lodge and two cottages. Charming day rooms provide easy relaxation. *Amenities* garden, outdoor swimming pool, badminton, games room, snooker, laundry service, children's playground.

■ *Rooms* 16	*Confirm by* arrang.
en suite bath/shower 16	*Last dinner* 10
Direct dial Yes	*Parking* Ample
Room TV Yes	*Room service* All day

Phillipburn House Hotel Restaurant ⊲

A wide variety of menus – including set meals for vegetarians and slimmers – provides ample choice for all at this welcoming, informal restaurant. The eclectic selection ranges from local smoked salmon, pasta and gazpacho among starters to venison with apples, prunes, honey and cream, sugar-baked Cumberland ham, and lemon sole dugléré. Appealing selection of sweets like chocolate orange cream and rhubarb pie to finish. Comprehensive wine list.
♧ Well-chosen ⊖

■ *Set L* from £4·50	*L* 12–3
Set D from £12·50	*D* 6–9.30
About £42 *for two*	*Seats* 60 *Parties* 50

Skeabost House Hotel Skeabost Bridge

H **58% £D/E**
Map 16 A3 Highland
Isle of Skye IV51 9NP
Skeabost Bridge (047 032) 202
Owner managers McNab & Stuart families
Standing in 12 acres beside Loch Snizort, this family-run hotel started life as a hunting lodge. Simply furnished bedrooms ranging from old fashioned to up-to-date, include six especially

comfortable annexe rooms. The entrance hall features original pine panelling. There are three lounges, one with TV. *Amenities* garden, 9-hole golf course, putting, sea & game fishing, snooker.

■ *Rooms* 27	*Confirm by* arrang.
en suite bath/shower 18	*Last dinner* 8.30
Room phone No	*Parking* Ample
Room TV No	*Room service* 24 hours
Closed mid Oct–mid Apr	

Manor Park Hotel Skelmorlie

H **60% £D**
Map 12A Strathclyde
PA17 5HE
Wemyss Bay (0475) 520832
Owner managers Mr & Mrs C. Sebire
Fine views across the Clyde are a feature of this early-Victorian house surrounded by magnificent gardens. A log fire warms the Adams-style entrance hall, and there's a spacious lounge and

airy bar featuring a wooden relief map of the area. Bright, homely bedrooms offer tea-makers and hairdryers, and carpeted bathrooms are well-kept. Stable-block flatlets have showers only. No dogs. *Amenities* garden.

■ *Rooms* 23	*Confirm by* arrang.
en suite bath/shower 22	*Last dinner* 9
Direct dial Yes	*Parking* Ample
Room TV Yes	*Room service* All day

Kinloch Lodge | Sleat

HR 67% £C
Map 17 A4 Highland
Isle of Skye IV43 8QY
Isle Ornsay (047 13) 214
Owner managers Lord & Lady Macdonald
Credit Access, Visa

For peace, comfort, friendliness and beautiful scenery, this remote hotel is hard to beat. The drawing rooms, where drinks are served, have great charm, and bedrooms, though mostly rather small, are thoughtfully equipped. Dogs by arrangement. *Amenities* garden, shooting, coarse & game fishing.

■ *Rooms 10*	*Confirm by 4*
en suite bath/shower 8	*Last dinner 8*
Room phone No	*Parking Ample*
Room TV No	*Room service Limited*
Closed 10–28 Dec & 10 Jan–29 Feb	

Kinloch Lodge Dining Room ♔ ♛

Lady Macdonald and Peter Macpherson join forces to produce enjoyable small-choice dinners in an elegant dining room. Everything is home-made, and between the granary bread and the fudge are delights like scallops in saffron sauce, hake fillets sautéed in oatmeal, roast pheasant and haunch of venison. Hazelnut meringue cake is a typical delicious sweet. There's a long, keenly priced wine list, including some outstanding less-common wines. ☺

■ *Set D £20*	*D at 8*
About £50 for two	*Seats 30 Parties 30*
Closed L to non-residents, 10–28 Dec	
& 10 Jan–29 Feb	

Forth Bridges Moat House | South Queensferry

H 59% £C/D
Map 12 C1 Lothian
EH30 9SF
031-331 1199. Tlx 727430
Credit Access, Amex, Diners, Visa. **LVs**

A modern hotel overlooking both Forth bridges. There's a choice of two comfortable lounge bars. Bedrooms are neat and well equipped. *Amenities* garden, indoor swimming pool, sauna, solarium, whirlpool bath, keep-fit equipment, beauty salon, squash, games room, snooker, pool table, in-house movies (charge), laundry service, coffee shop (8am–7.30pm summer, 9am–5pm winter), 24-hour lounge service, crèche.

■ *Rooms 108*	*Confirm by arrang.*
en suite bath/shower 108	*Last dinner 9.45*
Direct dial Yes	*Parking Ample*
Room TV Yes	*Room service All day*

Letterfinlay Lodge Hotel | Spean Bridge

H 55% £E
Map 17 B4 Highland
PH34 4DZ
Spean Bridge (039781) 622
Owner managers Forsyth family
Credit Access, Amex, Diners, Visa

Having been here for the past 25 years, the Forsyth family certainly know a thing or two about running a hotel. The solid stone house makes a splendidly relaxed, unpretentious place for a holiday, with a lovely setting seven miles north of Spean Bridge on the banks of Loch Lochy. Picture windows make the most of the views in the spacious main lounge (a variety of pub-style games here), and there's a nice little TV room, as well as a small bar bedecked with banknotes from around the world. Bright, modestly furnished bedrooms include two with private bathrooms and three with their own showers.
Amenities garden, game fishing, mooring, games room.

■ *Rooms 15*	*Confirm by arrang.*
en suite bath/shower 5	*Last dinner 8.30*
Room phone No	*Parking Ample*
Room TV No	*Room service All day*
Closed Nov–Feb	

Chapeltoun House | Stewarton

H 74% £B/C
Map 17 B6 Strathclyde
KA3 3ED
Stewarton (0560) 82696
Owner managers Colin & Graeme McKenzie
Credit Access, Amex, Visa

There's a feeling of timelessness about this lovely turn-of-the-century mansion. In the oak-panelled hall footfalls are muffled by the thick carpet and crackling fire. Even the stag's head looks benign. An interesting feature of this room is the pargeting of the first owner's English bride. The comfortable drawing room has fine views of the 20-acre grounds and surrounding countryside, and there's also a pub-like bar. Bedrooms, individually decorated in good taste, have some nice antique furniture and plenty of extras, including sewing kits and magazines. Carpeted

bathrooms have a selection of toiletries.
Amenities garden, laundry service.

■ *Rooms 6*	*Confirm by arrang.*
en suite bath/shower 6	*Last dinner 9.30*
Room phone Yes	*Parking Ample*
Room TV Yes	*Room service All day*
Closed 25 & 26 Dec & 1st 2 wks Jan	

Stonehaven Commodore Hotel

Stonehaven

H **57% £E**
Map 17 D4 Grampian
Cowie Park AB3 2PZ
Stonehaven (0569) 62936
Manager Andy Bremner
Credit Access, Amex, Diners, Visa
   A modern hotel on the A92 offering practical accommodation and conference facilities. Antique chairs and panelling give the main bar plenty of appeal, and there is a further warmly decorated bar attached to the restaurant. Bedrooms are fitted with simple units; the best ones have attractive quilted bedcovers, trouser presses and hairdryers. *Amenities* laundry service.

■ Rooms 40	Confirm by 8
en suite bath/shower 40	Last dinner 9.45
Room phone Yes	Parking Ample
Room TV Yes	Room service 24 hours

Caberfeidh Hotel

Stornoway

H **62% £D/E**
Map 16 A2 Highland
Isle of Lewis PA87 2EU
Stornoway (0851) 2604. Tlx 75505
Manager Mr David Martin
Credit Access, Amex, Diners, Visa
   A modern low-rise hotel on the edge of town. All the bedrooms have decent-quality fitted units and smart bathrooms, plus hairdryers, trouser presses and remote-control TVs. The snug cocktail bar, the public bar and the lounge bar with its Viking ship counter are pleasant spots for a chat and a wee dram. *Amenities* garden, laundry service, 24-hour lounge service.

■ Rooms 40	Confirm by arrang.
en suite bath/shower 40	Last dinner 9.30
Direct dial Yes	Parking Ample
Room TV Yes	Room service 24 hours

■ Our inspectors are our full-time employees; they are professionally trained by us.

Creggans Inn

Strachur

H **61% £C/D** &
Map 17 B5 Strathclyde
PA27 8BX
Strachur (036 986) 279. Tlx 778425
Manager Laura Huggins
Credit Access, Amex, Diners, Visa
   A charming hotel on the banks of Loch Fyne tended with care and pride by Laura Huggins. The bars have stunning views, and a conservatory has recently been added. There are two comfortable lounges, one equipped with TV. Bedrooms are individually decorated in a cottage look, and bathrooms are bright. *Amenities* garden, sea & game fishing, games room, laundry service.

■ Rooms 22	Confirm by arrang.
en suite bath/shower 17	Last dinner 9.30
Direct dial Yes	Parking Ample
Room TV No	Room service All day

North West Castle Hotel

Stranraer

H **67% £E**
Map 13 A4 Dumfries & Galloway
Cairnryan Road DG9 8EH
Stranraer (0776) 4413. Tlx 777088
Owner managers Mr & Mrs H. C. McMillan
   The leisure facilities are a great attraction at this harbourside hotel. The foyer and lounge have a touch of luxury, and there are two bars, one overlooking the curling rink. Good-sized bedrooms are well-equipped. *Amenities* garden, indoor swimming pool, sauna, solarium, games room, snooker, pool table, in-house movies, laundry service, 24-hour lounge service, coffee shop (noon–9.30pm Oct–May), kiosk.

■ Rooms 77	Confirm by arrang.
en suite bath/shower 77	Last dinner 9.30
Direct dial Yes	Parking Ample
Room TV Yes	Room service 24 hours

Kirkhouse Inn   *NEW ENTRY*

Strathblane

I **£E**
Map 12 B1 Central
Nr Glasgow
Blanefield (0360) 70621
Credit Access, Amex, Diners, Visa
   A white-painted inn on the A81 about ten miles north of Glasgow. The public bar is popular with the locals, and there is a quieter lounge bar. Bedrooms have coordinating pastel wallcoverings and fabrics and private bathrooms, and there's also a honeymoon suite complete with four-poster. *Amenities* garden, games room, snooker, laundry service, coffee shop (7am–midnight), 24-hour lounge service.

■ Rooms 15	Confirm by arrang.
en suite bath/shower 15	Last dinner 11
Room phone Yes	Parking Ample
Room TV Yes	Room service 24 hours

Port-an-Eilean Hotel | Strathtummel

H **65% £E/F**
Map 17 C4 Tayside
By Pitlochry PH16 5RU
Tummel Bridge (08824) 233
Owner manager G. C. Hallewell

A winding drive leads down from the B8019 to this handsome stone hotel built as a Victorian sporting lodge by Loch Tummel. It's a very quiet and peaceful spot, and the large drawing room and sun lounge are just the job for relaxation. Good-sized bedrooms are bright and airy, with solid old furniture and homely little extras. *Amenities* garden, coarse & game fishing.

■ *Rooms 9*	*Confirm by 6*
en suite bath/shower 9	*Last dinner 8.45*
Room phone No	*Parking Ample*
Room TV No	*Room service None*
Closed Oct–late Apr	

Loch Maree Hotel | Talladale

I **£E**
Map 16 B3 Highland
Achnasheen IV2 2HN
Loch Maree (044 584) 288
Owner manager Kathleen Moodie

A remote but welcoming inn which enjoys sole fishing rights on Loch Maree and is run with great charm by long-standing owner Miss Moodie. There are two peaceful lounges with fireside chairs and a tiny cocktail bar. Bedrooms are modest and homely and command lovely loch views. Adequate public bathrooms. *Amenities* garden, game fishing, boating.

■ *Rooms 15*	*Confirm by 6*
en suite bath/shower 0	*Last dinner 8*
Room phone No	*Parking Ample*
Room TV No	*Room service Limited*
Closed end Oct–Easter	

Stonefield Castle Hotel | Tarbert

H **63% £D**
Map 12 A1 Strathclyde
Loch Fyne PA29 6YJ
Tarbert (088 02) 836. Tlx 776321
Credit Access, Amex, Diners, Visa

Built by the Campbells in 1837, Stonefield Castle enjoys glorious views from its wooded perch by Loch Fyne. Well-proportioned public rooms are liberally provided with leather armchairs and settees, and marvellous fresh flower arrangements are a feature throughout. The terrace that runs along the loch-facing side is a favourite spot when the weather's kind. Decent-sized bedrooms are either in the original castle (these have more character) or in the 20-year-old extension. Three bathrooms have shower only. *Amenities* garden, outdoor swimming pool, sauna, solarium, whirlpool bath, keep-fit equipment, tennis, squash, putting, riding, boating, mooring, snooker, pool table, satellite TV, laundry service, 24-hour lounge service, children's play area.

■ *Rooms 33*	*Confirm by arrang.*
en suite bath/shower 33	*Last dinner 9.45*
Direct dial Yes	*Parking Ample*
Room TV Yes	*Room service 24 hours*

West Loch Hotel Restaurant *NEW ENTRY* | Tarbert

R ♢ **Map 12 A1** Strathclyde
Loch Fyne
Tarbert (088 02) 283
Owner managers Thom family
Credit Access

Three-course dinners are served in the pleasant little restaurant of an old lochside coaching inn. Mrs Thom and her capable team produce a short selection of very tasty dishes such as creamy celeriac or parsnip and carrot soup, monkfish en croûte or pan-fried veal escalopes topped with ham and Gruyère. Scrumptious sweets or cheese, then coffee in the lounge. No smoking in dining room. Also superb bar lunches. ☻

■ *Set D £14·50*	*D only 7–8.30*
About £35 for two	*Parking Ample*
Closed Nov	

Tayvallich Inn | Tayvallich

R ♢ **Map 17 B5** Strathclyde
By Lochgilphead
Tayvallich (054 67) 282
Seafood
Credit Access, Visa

Super-fresh seafood is staple fare at John and Pat Grafton's delightfully informal harbour restaurant. Top-quality ingredients and unfussy presentation bring a touch of distinction to John's simple menus. Clams, prawns and mussels are much in evidence but tasty meat dishes are included for determined carnivores. Well-made sweets for afters. Less choice at lunchtime. ☻

■ *About £32 for two*	*L 12–2*
Seats 40	*D 7–9*
Parties 32	*Parking Ample*
Closed D Sun, Mon–Thurs Nov–Apr, 1 Jan, 25 Dec & 2 wks Jan–Feb	

Tiroran House

HR 68% £C/D
Map 17 A5 Strathclyde
Isle of Mull PA69 6ES
Tiroran (068 15) 232
Owner managers Robin & Sue Blockey

The scenery is wild and beautiful, the setting remote and utterly peaceful. Family antiques are a feature at this modernised sporting lodge, both in the civilised drawing rooms and in the bedrooms, where extras like magazines and sewing kits add a homely touch. Two rooms are in a pine annexe. No children under ten. *Amenities* garden, croquet, games room.

■ *Rooms* 9	*Confirm by* arrang.
en suite bath/shower 8	*Last dinner* 8
Room phone No	*Parking* Ample
Room TV No	*Room service* Limited
Closed early Oct–early May	

Tiroran

Tiroran House Restaurant ⌣ ♦

Two delightful dining rooms, one with antiques, the other plants and pine. Sue Blockey is a self-taught cook who produces splendidly enjoyable meals. Her four-course menus make excellent use of home-grown or local produce, and she bakes all her own bread. Starters like gravadlax or creamy cucumber soup might precede pork fillet with kumquats or rainbow trout with a mousseline of prawn and scallop coral. Delicious puds and good Scottish cheeses. Good wine list from Corney & Barrow. Note Puligny Montrachet Les Pucelles 1982 (Leflaive). ☺

■ *Set D* £18	*D only* 7.30 for 8
About £46 *for two*	*Seats* 20
Closed early Oct–May	

Tobermory Hotel *NEW ENTRY*

Tobermory

H 57% £F
Map 17 A4 Strathclyde
53 Main Street, Isle of Mull PA75 6NT
Tobermory (0688) 2091
Owner managers Michael & Christine Ratcliffe

A really delightful little place in a row of brightly coloured buildings fringing Tobermory Bay. Fresh flowers add to the charm of the neatly kept lounges, and the bedrooms, also spotless, are

provided with all sorts of thoughtful extras (but no phone or TV); most rooms look out over the bay. The hotel's yacht Sea Topaz offers cruises and nights afloat.

■ *Rooms* 15	*Confirm by* arrang.
en suite bath/shower 5	*Last dinner* 7.30
Room phone No	*Parking* Ample
Room TV No	*Room service* Limited
Closed end Oct–1 Apr	

Marine Hotel

Troon

H 64% £D
Map 12 B2 Strathclyde
Crosbie Road KA10 6HE
Troon (0292) 314444. Tlx 777595
Credit Access, Amex, Diners, Visa

A brand-new leisure centre, with swimming pool and squash courts, will add to the amenities of this splendid Edwardian hotel. The stylishly-furnished lounge-cum-bar enjoys wonderful views

over Royal Troon golf course and the Firth of Clyde beyond. Sea views are also a feature of many of the bedrooms, most of which are now prettily refurbished. *Amenities* garden, putting, games room, laundry service, helipad.

■ *Rooms* 72	*Confirm by* 6
en suite bath/shower 72	*Last dinner* 10
Direct dial Yes	*Parking* Ample
Room TV Yes	*Room service* 24 hours

Piersland House Hotel *NEW ENTRY*

Troon

H 64% £D/E
Map 12 B2 Strathclyde
Craigend Road KA10 6HD
Troon (0292) 314747
Credit Access, Amex, Diners, Visa

An attractive turn-of-the-century house set in its own grounds. The main hall features a fine staircase and galleried landing while the lounge has nice carving and stone-mullioned windows.

Bedrooms vary in size, but all have darkwood furniture, tea/coffee-makers, fresh fruit, remote-control TV and hairdryers. Bathrooms have decent fittings and toiletries. *Amenities* garden, putting, croquet, laundry service.

■ *Rooms* 15	*Confirm by* arrang.
en suite bath/shower 15	*Last dinner* arrang.
Direct dial Yes	*Parking* Ample
Room TV Yes	*Room service* All day

Sun Court Hotel

Troon

H 58% £D/E
Map 12 B2 Strathclyde
19 Crosbie Road KA10 6HF
Troon (0292) 312727
Owner managers A. & J. Breckenridge
Credit Access, Amex, Diners

Run with enthusiasm, this charming Edwardian house offers practical, spacious accommodation and a warm welcome. The traditionally furnished

cocktail bar affords views over the Royal Troon golf course, as do most of the bedrooms, which are individually decorated. *Amenities* garden, tennis, squash, real tennis, laundry service.

■ *Rooms* 20	*Confirm by* arrang.
en suite bath/shower 18	*Last dinner* 9.30
Direct dial Yes	*Parking* Ample
Room TV Yes	*Room service* All day
Closed 25 Dec	

Turnberry Hotel   Turnberry

H **81%** **£B/C**
Map 12 A3 Strathclyde
KA26 9LT
Turnberry (0655) 31000. Tlx 777779
Manager Mr C. J. Rouse
Credit Access, Amex, Diners, Visa

A world-famous hotel, overlooking the sea,
which offers marvellous sporting and leisure
facilities and sumptuous accommodation. The
elegant foyer leads on to light and airy lounges
with comfortable seating and a light pastel theme;
paintings adorn the walls and a pianist supplies
soothing music most evenings. The smart bar is
built from light wood. The spacious bedrooms are
of a high standard, with traditional furnishing and
pretty colour schemes. All have fruit, tissues and
flowers. Good-sized bathrooms have tiled marble
floors and quality toiletries. All the rooms are
spotlessly clean. Six fine suites offer an even
higher standard of luxury. Management and staff
provide superb service.

Amenities garden, indoor swimming pool, sauna,
solarium, keep-fit equipment, hairdressing, tennis,
golf courses, putting, pitch & putt, croquet, riding,
snooker, teletext, valeting, laundry service,
restaurant (8am–8pm), 24-hour lounge service,
helipad.

■ *Rooms* 130	*Confirm by* arrang.
en suite bath/shower 130	*Last dinner* 9.30
Direct dial Yes	*Parking* Ample
Room TV Yes	*Room service* 24 hours
Closed end Nov–end Feb	

Crook Inn   Tweedsmuir

H **58%** **£E**
Map 12 C2 Borders
Near Biggar ML12 6QN
Tweedsmuir (089 97) 272
Owner managers Mr & Mrs Macdowell
Credit Amex, Diners

Parts of this historic hotel on the A701 date
back to 1604. The ancient flagstoned bar boasts a
fine central fireplace; other public areas are more

modern and offer simple comfort. Bedrooms are
homely, spacious and spotlessly clean – all with
bright, carpeted bathrooms. No dogs.
Amenities garden, shooting, coarse & game fishing, games room, pool table, children's play area.

■ *Rooms* 7	*Confirm by* 6
en suite bath/shower 7	*Last dinner* 9
Room phone Yes	*Parking* Ample
Room TV No	*Room service* None

■ We welcome complaints and bona
fide recommendations on the
tear-out pages for readers' comments.
They are followed up by our professional
team. Please also complain to the
management instantly.

RECEPTION

Uig Hotel   Uig

H **59%** **£D/E** &
Map 16 A3 Highland
Isle of Skye IV51 9YE
Uig (047 042) 205
Owner managers Mrs G. Graham & David Taylor
Credit Access, Amex, Diners, Visa

Fine views and a tranquil setting are attractions
of this welcoming, family-run hotel with a lounge
bar and cheerful sun room. Main-house bedrooms

offer homely comfort; those in the attractive
garden annexe have more space and smart
shower rooms. No children under 12.
Amenities garden.

■ *Rooms* 20	*Confirm by* 6
en suite bath/shower 20	*Last dinner* 8.15
Room phone No	*Parking* Ample
Room TV Some	*Room service* All day
Closed end Sept to mid Apr	

■ Changes in data may occur in
establishments after the Guide
goes to press. Prices should be taken
as indications rather than firm quotes.

Altnaharrie Inn ★   **Ullapool**

RR ★ ♔ ♧ **Map 16 B2** Highland
IV26 2SS
Dundonnell (085 483) 230
Owner managers Fred Brown & Gunn Eriksen
Telephone to book and arrange the ten-minute
launch trip from Ullapool to this superlative
restaurant in a hauntingly beautiful setting. Gunn
Eriksen's original and exciting cooking, coupled
with her awe-inspiring dedication, results in rare
treats. The no-choice evening meal may be
hawthorn and cucumber soup, followed by
scallops in garlic butter; then saddle of lamb with
a sauce of leek, rosemary, thyme and tarragon.
Finish with Norwegian Krum kaker – biscuit filled
with cloudberries, cream and meringues and
topped with spun sugar. Selective, excellent
quality wine list. *Specialities* lobster with two
sauces, crab in parsley pasta with a sauce of
vegetable juices and a dry muscat, medallions of
roe deer in a sauce of leeks, grapes and dill,
rhubarb tart. ♀ Well-chosen ☺

■ *Set D £27·50*   *L residents only*
About £65 for two   *D at 7.45*
Seats 14 Parties 14   *Parking Ample*
Closed L to non-residents and late Oct–late Mar
Bedrooms £D
Rooms 5   *With bath/shower 5*
For overnight guests (no under-eights) there are
five immaculate bedrooms with private facilities
but only four en suite.

Ceilidh Place   **Ullapool**

I **£D/E**
Map 16 B2 Highland
West Argyle Street IV26 2TY
Ullapool (0854) 2103
Owner managers Jean & Robert Urquhart
Credit Access, Amex, Diners, Visa
Music lends enchantment to this friendly
informal inn in Wester Ross, where regular
entertainment includes folk, jazz and classical
music and even drama and poetry sessions.
Delightful bedrooms have exposed beams and
attractive soft furnishings. Breakfasts are
memorable. *Amenities* garden, laundry service,
coffee shop (8am–10pm).
■ *Rooms 15*   *Confirm by arrang.*
en suite bath/shower 8   Last dinner 9.15
Room phone Yes   Parking Ample
Room TV Yes   Room service None

■ We publish annually, so make
sure you use the current
edition. It's worth it!

Ladbroke Mercury Motor Inn   **Ullapool**

H **55% £D**
Map 16 B2 Highland
IV26 2UD
Ullapool (0854) 2314
Credit Access, Amex, Diners, Visa
Refurbishment is under way at this modern two-
storey hotel just north of town on the A835.
Bedrooms (seven suitable for families) are neat
and simple, with built-in furniture and compact
bathrooms. The bar is at one end of the spacious
foyer-lounge, where armchairs are grouped round
the central fireplace. *Amenities* garden, sauna,
putting, 24-hour lounge service.
■ *Rooms 60*   *Confirm by 6*
en suite bath/shower 60   Last dinner 8.45
Room phone Some   Parking Ample
Room TV Yes   Room service Limited
Closed Oct–end Mar

Houstoun House

Uphall

HR 70% £C/D
Map 12 C1 Lothian
EH52 6JS
Broxburn (0506) 853831. Tlx 727148
Credit Access, Amex, Diners, Visa

A 16th-century fortified tower has been sympathetically extended to form this splendid hotel. Public areas span the centuries, harmoniously blending old and new in the pleasant, contemporary foyer-lounge with floor-to-ceiling window, offering fine views of the tree-lined drive, and in the atmospheric vaulted bar with its huge log fire. The good-sized bedrooms also vary as to period, some having contemporary units and others a judicious mixture of antique

and reproduction pieces; many have four-posters. All have direct dial telephones, radio and colour TV and trouser presses. Bathrooms are modern, one with shower only. *Amenities* garden, croquet, laundry service, 24-hour lounge service (Sun–Fri).

■ *Rooms* 30	*Confirm by arrang.*
en suite bath/shower 30	*Last dinner 9.30*
Direct dial Yes	*Parking Ample*
Room TV Yes	*Room service 24 hours*
Closed 1–3 Jan	

Houstoun House Restaurant ♛

A varied and interesting menu which changes constantly. Starter might be Caribbean ratatouille, main dishes port with fruit and honey sauce or scampi with wild rice and Pernod. Good sweets and excellent cheeses. Under the change of ownership the cellar remains outstanding for its range and depth; note some lovely German wines from the best estates.

➥ Outstanding ♛ Well-chosen ℮

■ *Set L £11·50*	*L 12.30–2*
Set D £18	*D 7.30–9.30*
About £45 for two	*Seats 80*
Closed 1–3 Jan	*Parties 42*

Knockie Lodge Hotel

Whitebridge

H 65% £D
Map 17 B4 Highland IV1 2UP
Gorthleck (045 63) 276
Owner managers Ian & Brenda Milward
Credit Access, Amex, Visa

'What we sell most of here is peace and quiet,' says owner Ian Milward. A delightful hotel set in glorious scenery among lochs and hills. The lounge is splendidly relaxing. Bedrooms feature

antiques and well-chosen fabrics (Brenda's department). Books and magazines are quieter than phones and TVs. No children under 10. *Amenities* garden, game fishing.

■ *Rooms* 10	*Confirm by arrang.*
en suite bath/shower 10	*Last dinner 8.30*
Room phone No	*Parking Ample*
Room TV No	*Room service Limited*
Closed end Oct–end Apr	

Ladbroke Mercury Motor Inn

Wick

H 57% £D/E
Map 16 C2 Highland
Riverside KW1 4NL
Wick (0955) 3344
Credit Access, Amex, Diners, Visa

Modest overnight accommodation in a modern hotel down by the river that runs through the town centre. Bedrooms are in good decorative order and all have radios and tea-makers. The lounge

has plenty of seating but the revamped bar is a more attractive spot in which to relax. *Amenities* garden, laundry service, 24-hour lounge service.

■ *Rooms* 48	*Confirm by 6*
en suite bath/shower 48	*Last dinner 8.45*
Room phone Yes	*Parking Ample*
Room TV Yes	*Room service 24 hours*
Closed 10 days Xmas	

HOTELS
RESTAURANTS
AND INNS

WALES

Hotel Plas Penhelig
Aberdovey

H 62% £D/E
Map 8 B3 Gwynedd
LL35 0NA
Aberdovey (065 472) 676
Owner managers Richardson family
Credit Access, Amex, Diners, Visa

Pride of the public rooms at this welcoming hotel is a handsome panelled hall with leaded windows. There's also a pleasant drawing room and terraced bar. Fresh, bright bedrooms in a pretty, modern style have tiled bathrooms. No children under eight. No dogs. *Amenities* garden, tennis, putting, croquet, laundry service.

■ Rooms 12	Confirm by 6
en suite bath/shower 12	Last dinner 8.45
Direct dial Yes	Parking Ample
Room TV No	Room service All day
Closed 24 Dec–mid Mar	

Trefeddian Hotel
Aberdovey

H 60% £D/E
Map 8 B3 Gwynedd
LL35 0SB
Aberdovey (065 472) 213
Owner managers Cave family
Credit Access

Fine views across Cardigan bay are a feature of this friendly, family-run hotel. Bright, spacious public rooms include two lounges and a pleasant bar. Fresh, cheerful bedrooms have practical furnishings. *Amenities* garden, indoor swimming pool, solarium, tennis, badminton, putting, games room, pool table, laundry service.

■ Rooms 46	Confirm by arrang.
en suite bath/shower 46	Last dinner 8.30
Direct dial Yes	Parking Ample
Room TV Yes	Room service All day
Closed mid Nov–late Mar	

Walnut Tree Inn ★
Abergavenny

R ★ ⅋ **Map 9 D5** Gwent
Llandewi Skirrid
Abergavenny (0873) 2797

Some three miles out of Abergavenny, on the B4521 Ross-on-Wye road, is this gem of a restaurant with modest, pub-like exterior. Here, after a quarter of a century as chef-patron, Franco Taruschio still cooks with undimmed enthusiasm. Whether you squeeze into the bistro-style ante-rooms or prefer the more elegant restaurant (booking essential), you can be sure of a generous feast. Fish is the favourite main course – perhaps grilled sole or turbot with a rich mustard sauce – preceded by asparagus au gratin or maybe one of the pasta dishes. Tempting sweets include spumonia amaretto, a delicious chilled version of zabaglione. The magnificent wine list is a model of balance and discernment, with helpful, succinct tasting notes: it includes fine clarets (still some halves of Vieux Château Certan '64), mature Rhônes (Cornas '76) and a good selection of the

best Italian wines (two vintages of Sassicaia). *Specialities* scallops en croûte, calf's liver with sweet and sour onions, carré of lamb with fried garlic, rose petal ice cream.

⊳ Outstanding ♀ Well-chosen ⊖

■ About £45 for two	L 12–2.30
Seats 40	D 7–10.30
Parties 30	Parking Ample
Closed Sun, Mon, 24–26 Dec & 2 wks late Feb	

Llwynderw Hotel
Abergwesyn

HR 68% £B/C
Map 9 C4 Powys
Nr Llanwrtyd Wells LD5 4TW
Llanwrtyd Wells (059 13) 238
Owner manager Michael Yates
Credit Access, Amex

A remote 18th-century mansion in a stunning mountain setting. Guests can meet for a drink and a chat in the two comfortable lounges. Bedrooms feature antique furniture and good modern bathrooms. Half-board terms only. No children under ten. *Amenities* garden, games room, laundry service.

■ Rooms 10	Confirm by arrang.
en suite bath/shower 10	Last dinner 7.45
Room phone No	Parking Ample
Room TV No	Room service Limited
Closed Nov–mid Mar	

Llwynderw Hotel Restaurant

A huge stone fireplace dominates this charming, traditionally appointed dining room. Dinner consists of four courses and centres on delights like poached salmon trout with hollandaise, braised tongue with Madeira sauce or (more often) a well-garnished roast – maybe guinea fowl or Welsh lamb. Pâté or crêpes might start the proceedings, followed by a delicious soup such as Vichyssoise or cream of lemon. There's no choice except in the puddings – mainly straightforward fare like apple pie and crème caramel. Good ingredients and sound cooking. ⊖

■ Set D from £18	L by arrang. only
About £48 for two	D at 7.45
Seats 25	Parties 16
Closed Nov–mid Mar	

Porth Tocyn Hotel

HR **69% £D/E**
Map 8 B2 Gwynedd
Bwlch Tocyn LL53 7BU
Abersoch (075 881) 2966
Owner managers Fletcher-Brewer family
Credit Access

Refurbishment keeps standards high at this delightful family-run hotel above Cardigan Bay (check directions when booking). Day rooms are charming and inviting, while obvious care is lavished on the bright, spacious bedrooms, which feature antique furnishings and homely extras. *Amenities* garden, outdoor swimming pool, tennis.

■ *Rooms 17*	*Confirm by arrang.*
en suite bath/shower 17	*Last dinner 9.30*
Direct dial Yes	*Parking Ample*
Room TV Yes	*Room service All day*
Closed Nov–Easter exc. 10 days Xmas	

Porth Tocyn Hotel Restaurant 🖢 ᕱ

Candlelight, fresh flowers and polished parquet floors set the scene for an enjoyable meal served with charm and smiles by a young team of prettily attired waitresses. Louis Fletcher-Brewer rings the changes daily with a tempting variety of dishes, from prawn and dill mousse to poached brill florentine and lamb chops with buttermint sauce. Crisp, fresh vegetables and good sweets. Super Welsh cheeses. Informal lunches (Sunday lunch a soup and salad buffet).
🍷 **Well-chosen** ⊛

■ *Set L Sun only £8*	*L 12.30–2*
Set D £15	*D 7.30–9.30*
About £40 for two	*Seats 55*
Closed Nov–Easter exc. 10 days Xmas	

Riverside Hotel

H **57% £D/E**
Map 8 B2 Gwynedd
LL53 7HW
Abersoch (075 881) 2419
Owner managers Mr & Mrs J. C. E. Bakewell
Credit Access, Visa

A pretty spot for a pleasant holiday hotel, with the harbour just across the road and the quiet river Soch at the end of the garden. Day rooms

are neat, bright and cheerful, and bedrooms quite cosy and comfortable – the prettiest are those in the main house. No dogs. *Amenities* garden, indoor swimming pool.

■ *Rooms 14*	*Confirm by 6*
en suite bath/shower 14	*Last dinner 9*
Room phone Yes	*Parking Ample*
Room TV Yes	*Room service Limited*
Closed 1 Nov–Easter	

Conrah Country Hotel

H **62% £D**
Map 9 B4 Dyfed
Chancery SY23 4DF
Aberystwyth (0970) 617941. Tlx 35892
Owner managers John & Pat Heading
Credit Access, Amex, Diners, Visa

A peaceful country mansion with lovely views of hill and vale. Public areas include an elegant writing room. Main-house bedrooms are mostly

spacious, while adjoining motel rooms are much smaller, with tiny shower rooms. No children under three. No dogs. *Amenities* garden, indoor swimming pool, sauna, croquet.

■ *Rooms 22*	*Confirm by arrang.*
en suite bath/shower 20	*Last dinner 9.30*
Direct dial Yes	*Parking Ample*
Room TV Yes	*Room service All day*
Closed 22–31 Dec	

Mount Sorrel Hotel

H **59% £E/F**
Map 9 C6 South Glamorgan
Porthkerry Road CF6 8AY
Barry (0446) 740069
Owner managers Mr & Mrs W. Pryse Jones
Credit Access, Amex, Diners, Visa

A modern extension joins the two Victorian houses that make up this pleasant hotel on a hill in the town. Plants and rattan chairs decorate the

small tiled foyer, and there is a cosy lounge and bar. The simply furnished bedrooms are well kept; all have been refurbished. *Amenities* 24-hour lounge service.

■ *Rooms 37*	*Confirm by 6*
en suite bath/shower 37	*Last dinner 10*
Room phone Yes	*Parking Limited*
Room TV Yes	*Room service 24 hours*
Closed 3 days Xmas	

Bulkeley Arms Hotel

H **57% £E**
Map 8 C1 Gwynedd
Castle Street LL58 8AW
Beaumaris (0248) 810415
Credit Access, Amex, Diners, Visa

Purpose-built in 1834, this handsome town-centre hotel looks out across the Menai Straits to Snowdonia. Recently appointed manageress Mrs Owen takes care to keep up standards, and the

bars and lounges have been freshly painted and smartly recarpeted. Plans are in mind to upgrade bedrooms, all of which have private bath or shower rooms (three not en suite). *Amenities* garden, snooker, laundry service.

■ *Rooms 41*	*Confirm by arrang.*
en suite bath/shower 38	*Last dinner 9.30*
Direct dial Yes	*Parking Ample*
Room TV Yes	*Room service All day*

Ye Olde Bull's Head Restaurant *NEW ENTRY* Beaumaris

R 🍷 **Map 8 C1** Gwynedd
Castle Street, Anglesey LL58 8AP
Beaumaris (0248) 810329
Credit Access, Visa
  A splendid room in a rambling 16th-century
coaching inn, and a new venture for chef-partner
Keith Rothwell. Dinner is ordered downstairs in
the lounge, and the expectations aroused by the
menu are fulfilled admirably. We thoroughly

enjoyed a meal of Chinese-style stir-fried
vegetables, superb Anglesey monkfish unusually
but successfully accompanied by a cream,
brandy and peppercorn sauce, and for dessert a
lovely glazed raspberry tart.
🍷 **Well-chosen** 🍴
■ *About £38 for two* *D only 7.30–9.30*
Seats 55 Parties 45 *Parking Limited*
Closed Sun & last 2 wks Oct

Royal Goat Hotel Beddgelert

H **58% £E**
Map 8 C2 Gwynedd
LL55 4YE
Beddgelert (076 686) 224
Owner managers Mr & Mrs E. E. Roberts
Credit Access, Amex, Diners, Visa
  Improvements continue at this welcoming hotel
in spectacular Snowdonia. Bright new decor and
soft lighting have transformed the rear bedrooms,

but the best are the spacious front rooms with
splendid views. Nicest day room is the residents'
lounge, with its own bar. *Amenities* garden,
coarse & game fishing, satellite TV, laundry
service, 24-hour lounge service.
■ *Rooms 32* *Confirm by arrang.*
en suite bath/shower 32 *Last dinner 9.30*
Direct dial Yes *Parking Ample*
Room TV Yes *Room service 24 hours*

Bontddu Hall Hotel Bontddu

H **58% £D/E**
Map 8 C3 Gwynedd
Nr Dolgellau LL40 2SU
Barmouth (0341) 49661
Owner managers Mr & Mrs M. J. Ball
Credit Access, Amex, Diners, Visa
  A Victorian Gothic mansion enjoying stunning
views across the Mawddach estuary. Day rooms
have abundant character (polished panelling and

marble pillars in the hall, pine pews and stained
glass in the bar). Bedrooms include six in a chalet
block. General repair could be better. No children
under 3. *Amenities* garden, putting.
■ *Rooms 23* *Confirm by 6*
en suite bath/shower 23 *Last dinner 9.30*
Direct dial Yes *Parking Ample*
Room TV Yes *Room service All day*
Closed Jan & Feb

Tŷ Mawr Country House Hotel Brechfa

H **62% £E**
Map 9 B5 Dyfed
Nr Carmarthen SA32 7RA
Brechfa (026 789) 332
Owner managers The Flaherty Family
Credit Access, Visa
  New owners have plans to redecorate this
pleasant 16th-century house in a small village on
the river Marlais. Old beams, stone walls and tiled

floors lend their charm to the cosy bar and lounge.
Neat bedrooms provide modest comforts
including simple, spotless bathrooms.
Amenities garden, riding.
■ *Rooms 5* *Confirm by 6*
en suite bath/shower 5 *Last dinner 9.30*
Room phone No *Parking Ample*
Room TV No *Room service All day*
Closed 2 wks Feb & 2 wks Nov

■ Our inspectors never book in the
name of Egon Ronay's Guides;
they disclose their identity only
after paying their bills.

Stables Hotel Caernarfon

H **59% £E** ♿
Map 8 B2 Gwynedd
Llanwnda LL54 5SD
Llanwnda (0286) 830711
Owner managers Mr & Mrs David West
Credit Access, Amex, Visa
  Lots of horsy connections at this smartly
redecorated hotel set back from the A499. The
Victorian stable block, now the restaurant and

bar, retains characterful original features while
bedrooms, in a modern block resembling a stable,
are named after English racecourses. Bathrooms
are well equipped. *Amenities* garden, outdoor
swimming pool, laundry service.
■ *Rooms 12* *Confirm by arrang.*
en suite bath/shower 12 *Last dinner 9.45*
Direct dial Yes *Parking Ample*
Room TV Yes *Room service All day*

is our symbol for an **outstanding** wine list.

La Chaumière *NEW ENTRY* Cardiff

R ☖ **Map 9 D6** South Glamorgan
44 Cardiff Road, Llandaff
Cardiff (0222) 555319
French cooking
Credit Access, Amex, Diners
  Take the Llandaff turn off the A48 for this attractive French restaurant, where Cliff and Kay Morgan are respectively the friendly host and accomplished chef. Good-quality ingredients are the basis of very enjoyable dishes such as seafood tart with a butter sauce, breast of duck with a sharp raspberry sauce and a coffee and Tia Maria syllabub. Booking advisable.
♚ Well-chosen ⊖
■ *Set L Sun only £6·95*   *L 12–2, Sun 12–2.30*
About £35 for two   *D 7–9.30, Sat 7–10.30*
Seats 40 Parties 40   *Parking Ample*
Closed D Sun, all Mon & 1–15 Jan

Crest Hotel Cardiff

H **59% £C/D**
Town plan C2 South Glamorgan
Westgate Street CF1 1JB
Cardiff (0222) 388681
Credit Access, Amex, Diners, Visa. **LVs**
  A central hotel overlooking the castle, the river and the National Stadium. Street-level public areas include the Gatehouse Tavern, while on the first floor there's a lounge and cocktail bar.
Double-glazed bedrooms include standard, Executive and Lady Crest rooms. The suite has a whirlpool bath. *Amenities* garden, games room, in-house movies (free), laundry service, 24-hour lounge service.
■ *Rooms 160*   *Confirm by 6*
en suite bath/shower 160 *Last dinner 10*
Direct dial Yes   *Parking Ample*
Room TV Yes   *Room service 24 hours*

Holiday Inn Cardiff

H **75% £C E &**
Town plan D3 South Glamorgan
Mill Lane CF1 1EZ
Cardiff (0222) 399944. Tlx 497365
Credit Access, Amex, Diners, Visa
  Style and comfort go hand in hand at this recent and luxurious high-rise addition to Cardiff's city-centre hotel scene. Marble columns and arches divide up the open-plan public areas, which include an invitingly comfortable lounge, featuring deep sofas and armchairs and a picture window overlooking the swimming pool. Pleasantly decorated bedrooms (singles at the rear) with generous beds offer a full range of extras, from air conditioning and bedside controls to hairdryers, trouser presses and splendidly equipped bathrooms. *Amenities* indoor swimming pool, sauna, solarium, whirlpool bath,

steam bath, keep-fit equipment, squash, satellite TV, in-house movies (charge), laundry service, coffee shop (7am–10.30pm), 24-hour lounge service, kiosk.
■ *Rooms 186*   *Confirm by 6*
en suite bath/shower 186 *Last dinner 11*
Direct dial Yes   *Parking Ample*
Room TV Yes   *Room service 24 hours*

Park Hotel Cardiff

H **71% £D E**
Town plan D2 South Glamorgan
Park Place CF1 3UD
Cardiff (0222) 383471. Tlx 497195
Credit Access, Amex, Diners, Visa. **LVs**
  Located in the pedestrian zone right at the centre of Cardiff, a Victorian hotel where you can find excellent standards of service and housekeeping throughout. The small reception area and writing room have an elegant period flavour with wing chairs and leather sofas; the ground floor also houses the handsome Harlech lounge and extensive conference facilities. Top-grade bedrooms are simply enormous, and all rooms are superbly maintained, with plenty of extras such as radios, trouser presses, tea/coffee-making facilities and mineral water. The large, well-appointed bathrooms are fully tiled and

offer good toiletries and hairdryers. *Amenities* in-house movies (free), laundry service, 24-hour lounge service.
■ *Rooms 108*   *Confirm by 6*
en suite bath/shower 108 *Last dinner 11*
Direct dial Yes   *Parking Limited*
Room TV Yes   *Room service 24 hours*

CARDIFF

Map 9 D6
Town plan opposite

Population 284,400

Though it enshrines Welsh culture and history. Cardiff is both modern and cosmopolitan. Its population was less than 2,000 at the beginning of the 19th century, when its port developed with export of coal from the near-by mines. No British city is more compact in its many offerings to visitors, everything dominated by the comprehensive City Centre and the lovingly restored Castle. It is a matter of choice whether Welsh tradition, commerce or sport matter most to the visitor, though certainly the last attracts the most visitors *en masse*, especially to Cardiff Arms Park. Though Cardiff is an ideal base for touring South Wales, a short visit offers more than enough to remain within the city limits.

Annual Events
Cardiff Festival *July/August*
Festival of Music *November–December*
Horticultural Show *September*
Llandaff Festival *June*
Lord Mayor's Parade *August*
Military Tattoo *August* (every other year)

Information Office
Public Relations Officer
City Hall, Cardiff
Telephone Cardiff 822000

Wales Tourist Board
Brunel House
2 Fitzalan Road, Cardiff

Fiat Dealers
T. S. Grimshaw Ltd
329 Cowbridge Road East
Cardiff CF5 1JD
Tel. Cardiff 395322
Map reference 2A

Yapp's Garages Ltd
Fidlas Road
Llanishen
Cardiff CF4 5YW
Tel. Cardiff 751323

1 Bute Park C1/2
2 Cardiff Castle *fairy-tale magnificence bequeathed by the Bute family* C2
3 Civic Centre C1/2
4 General Station C/D3
5 Llandaff Cathedral A1
6 National Museum of Wales D1
7 National Sports Centre for Wales B1
8 New Theatre, Park Place D2
9 Queen Street Station E2
10 St David's Centre D2
11 St David's Hall D3
12 St John's Church, St John Square D2
13 Sherman Theatre D1
14 Tourist Information Office D3
15 Wales National Ice Rink D3
16 Welsh Industrial and Maritime Museum, Bute Street D3
17 Wood Street Bus Station C3

Cardiff FIAT

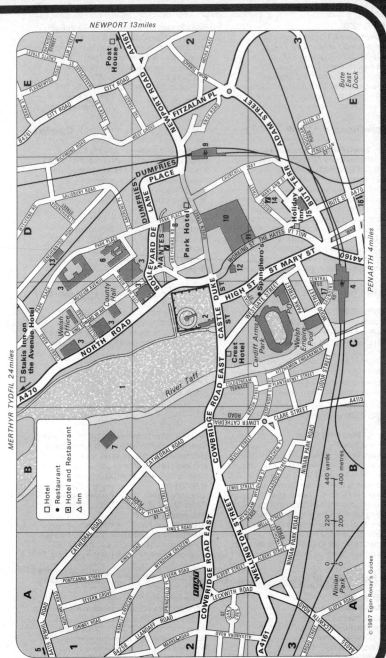

Post House Hotel   Cardiff

H **62% £D**
Town plan E1 South Glamorgan
Pentwyn Road, Pentwyn CF2 7XA
Cardiff (0222) 731212. Tlx 497633
Credit Access, Amex, Diners, Visa. LVs
   A new leisure complex and excellent
conference facilities are the big attractions here.
Located not far from junction 29 of the M4, the
hotel is bright and modern, with two stylish bars.

Bedrooms are comfortably furnished and well
equipped. *Amenities* garden, indoor swimming
pool, sauna, solarium, whirlpool bath, gymnasium,
laundry service, coffee shop (7am–10.30pm), 24-
hour lounge service, children's playroom.

■ *Rooms* 150	*Confirm by* 6
en suite bath/shower 150	*Last dinner* 10
Direct dial Yes	*Parking* Ample
Room TV Yes	*Room service* Limited

Spanghero's *NEW ENTRY*   Cardiff

R ♉ **Town Plan C3** South Glamorgan
Westgate House, Westgate Street
Cardiff (0222) 382423
Credit Access, Amex, Diners, Visa
   Chef Paul Lane leads a capable team in a
restaurant reached down a dozen steps and
through a lively bistro. The French menus,
including one for vegetarians, provide plenty of
variety, with starters like snails with forest
mushrooms or game consommé with a puff pastry
lid, and main courses ranging from the day's fresh
fish to mustard-sauced veal kidneys, steak
béarnaise and breast of duck with sweet and sour

onions. Good wines with very attractive
burgundies. The restaurant is near the National
Stadium (formerly Arms Park) and celebrates
Claude Spanghero, the legendary
French three-quarter.
♔ Well-chosen ⊖

■ *Set L* £9·75	*L* 12–2.30
Set D £14·75	*D* 7–10.30
About £45 *for two*	*Parking* Ample
Seats 50	*Parties* 70
Closed L Sat, all Sun, Bank Hol Mons & 25 & 26 Dec	

Stakis Inn on the Avenue   Cardiff

H **68% £D**
Town plan C1 South Glamorgan
Circle Way East, Llandeyrn CF3 7XF
Cardiff (0222) 732520. Tlx 497582
Credit Access, Amex, Diners, Visa
   Just off the A48, this well-equipped early-80s
hotel has seen its first major refurbishment. The
extended lounge and bar are quite plush;
generously-sized bedrooms, redecorated in bold

colours, offer ample space to relax. Smart,
youthful staff. *Amenities* garden, indoor
swimming pool, sauna, solarium, whirlpool bath,
keep-fit equipment, laundry service, 24-hour
lounge service, helipad.

■ *Rooms* 146	*Confirm by* 6
en suite bath/shower 146	*Last dinner* 10
Direct dial Yes	*Parking* Ample
Room TV Yes	*Room service* 24 hours

Rhyd-Garn-Wen   Cardigan

RR ♉ **Map 9 B4** Dyfed
SA43 3NW
Cardigan (0239) 612742
   Ask for directions when making your (essential)
reservation at this delightful Victorian house, and
look forward to the friendliest of welcomes from
Susan and Huw Jones. There are just ten places
in the dining room, where Susan offers a daily-
changing no-choice menu of five well-balanced
courses. Most of the vegetables, herbs and fruit
are home-grown in the walled garden, and other
ingredients are chosen with care from the best
local suppliers. A typical meal could start with

lettuce soup and home-baked bread; then a green
salad; roast chicken with spiced butter; Welsh
cheeses; a delicious sweet like apple chartreuse;
and finally petits fours with coffee in the lounge.
Wines include well-priced burgundies. ⊖

■ *Set D* £14	*D only* 7.30–9.30
About £35 *for two*	*Parking* Ample
Seats 10	*Closed* Oct–Easter
Bedrooms £E/F	
Rooms 3	*With bath/shower* 3

There are three comfortable double bedrooms,
one with its own bathroom, the others with
showers. No children under twelve. No dogs.

Ivy Bush Royal Hotel   Carmarthen

H **59% £D**
Map 9 B5 Dyfed
Spilman Street SA13 1LG
Carmarthen (0267) 235111. Tlx 48520
Manager Berwin Jones
Credit Access, Amex, Diners, Visa
   A modernised building on the busy A40 in the
town centre. First-floor bedrooms have recently
been improved decoratively, and all rooms have

new remote-control TVs with radios. A 1974
stained-glass window dominates in the open-plan
public area. Neither porterage nor breakfast
excelled on our last visit. *Amenities* sauna,
laundry service, 24-hour lounge service.

■ *Rooms* 80	*Confirm by* 6
en suite bath/shower 80	*Last dinner* 9
Room phone Yes	*Parking* Ample
Room TV Yes	*Room service* 24 hours

Castle View Hotel Chepstow

£E
Map 9 D6 Gwent
16 Bridge Street NP6 5EZ
Chepstow (029 12) 70349. Tlx 498280
Owner managers Mervyn & Lucia Gillett
Credit Access, Amex, Diners, Visa

The charming Gilletts run this ivy-clad inn with the minimum of fuss and formality, but are always working hard for improvements. They've recently renovated a 17th-century cottage which contains reception, residents' lounge and a splendid suite. Beams are a feature in the main house, where well-equipped bedrooms range from smallish singles to large family rooms. *Amenities* garden.

■ *Rooms* 11	*Confirm by* 6
en suite bath/shower 11	*Last dinner* 9
Direct dial Yes	*Parking* Ample
Room TV Yes	*Room service* Limited

St Pierre Hotel Chepstow

H 63% £C/D
Map 9 D6 Gwent
St Pierre Park NP6 6YA
Chepstow (02912) 5261. Tlx 497562
Credit Access, Amex, Diners, Visa

An impressive list of leisure facilities – including the two golf courses flanking the drive – is an attraction of this imposing stone mansion. Some original period features survive, such as an open fireplace in the sunken lounge area and fine panelling in one of the function rooms. The spacious cocktail bar offers stylish comfort and garden views while the public bars are more informal. Bedrooms, in various annexes and outbuildings, have fitted units and offer practical modern comforts with many extras and good bathrooms. *Amenities* garden, indoor swimming pool, sauna, whirlpool bath, tennis, squash, badminton, 18-hole golf courses, putting, croquet, bowling green, games room, snooker, pool table, in-house movies (free), laundry service, coffee shop (10am–10pm), 24-hour lounge service.

■ *Rooms* 108	*Confirm by* arrang.
en suite bath/shower 108	*Last dinner* 10
Direct dial Yes	*Parking* Ample
Room TV Yes	*Room service* 24 hours

■ If we recommend meals in a hotel or inn, a separate entry is made for its restaurant.

Hotel Seventy Degrees Colwyn Bay

H 67% £D
Map 8 C1 Clwyd
Penmaenhead, Old Colwyn LL29 9LD
Colwyn Bay (0492) 516555. Tlx 61362
Credit Access, Amex, Diners, Visa

Splendid sea views are enjoyed by this distinctive modern hotel, which sits snugly on the clifftop a short drive from the A55 expressway. Day rooms in '70s style include a lounge filled with paintings (all for sale) and two bars. Smart bedrooms, all with easy chairs, tea-makers and trouser presses, have well-equipped, carpeted bathrooms. *Amenities* in-house movies (free), laundry service, helipad.

■ *Rooms* 41	*Confirm by* 6
en suite bath/shower 41	*Last dinner* 9.30
Direct dial Yes	*Parking* Ample
Room TV Yes	*Room service* 24 hours

Sychnant Pass Hotel Conwy

HR 62% £E
Map 8 C1 Gwynedd
Sychnant Pass Road LL32 8BJ
Aberconwy (049 259) 6868. Tlx 61155
Owner managers Brian & Jean Jones
Credit Access, Amex, Diners, Visa

Wild scenery provides a spectacular setting for this friendly Edwardian hotel. A grandfather clock gives character to the all-purpose public room, while good-size bedrooms have darkwood units and smart bathrooms (two with showers only). *Amenities* garden, sauna, solarium, whirlpool bath, laundry service.

■ *Rooms* 10	*Confirm by* arrang.
en suite bath/shower 10	*Last dinner* 9.30
Direct dial Yes	*Parking* Ample
Room TV Yes	*Room service* All day
Closed Jan	

Sychnant Pass Hotel Restaurant 🍷 &

Fresh raw materials get good honest treatment at the Joneses' pretty little hotel restaurant, with its top-lit paintings on the walls and fresh flowers on the tables. Frequently changing set menus (less choice for lunch) offer simple delights such as tomato and tarragon soup, chicken breast filled with salmon pâté, baked trout filled with orange and thyme, beef simmered with horseradish and celery, roasts, grills and steaks. Finish with tipsy trifle or home-made pear cheesecake with chocolate sauce. 🍴

■ *Set L* £6·50	*L* 12–2.30
Set D £12·50	*D* 7–9.30
About £36 for two	*Seats* 50 *Parties* 20
Closed Jan & L Nov–Dec	

Coed-y-Mwstwr Hotel — Coychurch

HR 66% £D
Map 9 C6 Mid Glamorgan
Nr Bridgend CF35 6AF
Pencoed (0656) 860621
Owner managers Michael & Barbara Taylor
Credit Access, Amex, Diners, Visa

In winter a welcoming open fire burns in the lounge of this handsome Victorian mansion; in summer French windows are thrown open to the garden. Bedrooms (new wing on line for 1988) are bright and homely, with modern bathrooms. No children under 10. No dogs. *Amenities* garden, outdoor swimming pool, tennis, games room.

■ *Rooms 14*	*Confirm by arrang.*
en suite bath/shower 14	*Last dinner 10*
Direct dial Yes	*Parking Ample*
Room TV Yes	*Room service All day*
Closed 3 days Xmas	

Elliot Room ♕

Head chef Michael Griffin produces à la carte and fixed-price menus of wide appeal. English and French elements are evident in a choice that runs from sherried veal kidneys and the long-time favourite savoury chicken pancake to poached haddock, pink-cooked duck breast and beef and Guinness casserole with horseradish dumplings. Sweets from the trolley might include a delicious coffee-flavoured pavlova. Decent wine list with good burgundy showing and value-for-money Germans.
♟ Well-chosen ✆

■ *Set L from £6·95*	*L 12–2*
Set D £13·95	*D 7.30–10*
About £48 for two	*Seats 70 Parties 80*
Closed D Sun to non-residents & 3 days Xmas	

Bron Eifion Hotel — Criccieth

H 57% £E
Map 8 B2 Gwynedd
LL52 0SA
Criccieth (076 671) 2385
Owner managers Robertson family
Credit Access, Visa

Once a Victorian country residence, this friendly family-run hotel boasts a fine central hall with minstrels' gallery and lofty timbered roof; an archway leads to a small bar, and there's also a pleasant lounge. Best of the good-sized bedrooms are in traditional style. No children under three. *Amenities* garden, hairdressing, croquet, game fishing.

■ *Rooms 19*	*Confirm by arrang.*
en suite bath/shower 18	*Last dinner 9*
Direct dial Yes	*Parking Ample*
Room TV No	*Room service All day*

Bear Hotel — Crickhowell

I £F ♿
Map 9 D5 Powys
Crickhowell (0873) 810408
Owner managers Mrs Hindmarsh & Steve Sims
Credit Access, Visa

Welsh dressers and handsome antique furniture in the bar and lounge are attractive features of this fine old coaching inn on the A40. Creaking stairs and sloping landings lead to the main house bedrooms which combine tradition with modern comforts. There are more individually furnished rooms, including a de luxe suite, in a new annexe across the cobbled courtyard. *Amenities* garden, laundry service.

■ *Rooms 25*	*Confirm by 2*
en suite bath/shower 22	*Last dinner 9*
Direct dial Yes	*Parking Ample*
Room TV Yes	*Room service All day*

Gliffaes Hotel — Crickhowell

H 63% £E/F
Map 9 D5 Powys
NP8 1RH
Bwlch (0874) 730371
Owner managers Brabner family
Credit Access, Amex, Visa

An attractive hotel set in mature gardens overlooking the river Usk. There are two comfortable lounges and a simple bar. Traditionally furnished bedrooms are kept in good order. Dogs in kennels only. *Amenities* garden, tennis, golf practice net, putting, croquet, game fishing, billiards, snooker, laundry service.

■ *Rooms 19*	*Confirm by arrang.*
en suite bath/shower 18	*Last dinner 9*
Direct dial Yes	*Parking Ample*
Room TV No	*Room service Limited*
Closed 31 Dec–mid Mar	

Ynyshir Hall Hotel — Eglwysfach

H 61% £D/E
Map 8 C3 Dyfed
Nr Machynlleth Powys SY20 8TA
Glandyfi (065 474) 209
Owner managers Jane & Richard Allison
Credit Access, Amex, Diners, Visa

The Ynyshir Bird Reserve, colourful gardens and mountain views provide a peaceful and beautiful setting for this 16th-century manor house. Public areas include a nicely proportioned lounge, and a bar. Pretty floral bedrooms are well stocked with extras. Those without private baths have shower cabinets. *Amenities* garden, laundry service.

■ *Rooms 10*	*Confirm by arrang.*
en suite bath/shower 7	*Last dinner 9*
Direct dial Yes	*Parking Ample*
Room TV Yes	*Room service All day*
Closed mid Nov–Mar exc. Xmas–New Year	

Plough Inn, Hickman's Restaurant

Felingwm Uchaf

RR ♀ **Map 9 B5** Dyfed
Nantgaredig SA32 7PR
Nantgaredig (0267 88) 220
Credit Access, Amex, Diners, Visa

Take the B4310 off the A40 some seven miles east of Carmarthen to find Felingwm Uchaf. In the oak-beamed restaurant (part of the inn) you'll dine well on specialities such as hot smoked duck breast, sea bass with fennel and Pernod, steak Diane and veal zurichoise. Sweets include nice boozy gâteaux, and there's a very good, mainly French, cheeseboard. Leon and Eires Hickman are the talented chef-patrons. ♀ Well-chosen ⊖

■ About £38 for two
Seats 40
Parties 40
Closed 25 & 26 Dec

L *Mon–Sat by arrang.,*
Sun 12–2
D 7–9.30
Parking Ample

Bedrooms £E
Rooms 5 *With bath/shower* 2
A five-bedroom cottage across the road from the inn has two en suite doubles, and a family, twin and single that share two bathrooms. Pine furniture and cheerful floral curtains feature throughout. There's a panelled reception area, plus kitchen and breakfast room. No dogs.

NEW ENTRY

Fishguard Bay Hotel

Fishguard

H 60% £E/F
Map 9 A5 Dyfed
Quay Road, Goodwick SA64 0BT
Fishguard (0348) 873571. Tlx 48602
Owner manager Mr G. J. Schell
Credit Access, Amex, Diners, Visa

A rambling Victorian building standing in pleasant woodland overlooking the bay. There's an elegant panelled lounge, a TV room and various bars. Spacious Executive bedrooms in the tower are the best furnished and best equipped, the model for other rooms as they come up for improvement. *Amenities* garden, outdoor swimming pool, keep-fit equipment, snooker.

■ *Rooms* 62	*Confirm by* 7
en suite bath/shower 30	*Last dinner* 9.30
Direct dial Yes	*Parking* Ample
Room TV Some	*Room service* 24 hours

■ For a discount on next year's guide, see Offer for Answers.

Golden Pheasant Hotel

Glyn Ceiriog

H 62% £E
Map 8 D2 Clwyd
Nr Chirk LL20 7BB
Glyn Ceiriog (069 172) 281. Tlx 35664
Owner manager Jennifer Gibourg
Credit Access, Amex, Visa

Once an 18th-century inn, this comfortable hotel has plenty of old-world charm. Fine antique furniture sets the tone of the reception area and there's a heavily beamed public bar as well as the chinoiserie-style cocktail bar and elegant lounge. Prettily furnished bedrooms are all well-equipped. *Amenities* garden, riding, shooting, laundry service.

■ *Rooms* 18	*Confirm by arrang.*
en suite bath/shower 18	*Last dinner* 9.30
Room phone Yes	*Parking* Ample
Room TV Yes	*Room service* All day

Cliff Hotel

Gwbert-on-Sea

H 60% £D/E &
Map 9 B4 Dyfed
Cardigan SA43 1PP
Cardigan (0239) 613241. Tlx 48440
Credit Access, Amex, Diners, Visa

A dramatic clifftop setting and wide range of leisure activities are attractions of this popular holiday hotel. Comfortable lounges are lit by picture windows, bedrooms range from spacious and traditional to compact and modern. *Amenities* garden, outdoor swimming pool, 9-hole golf course, putting, squash, games room, snooker, pool table, game fishing.

■ *Rooms* 70	*Confirm by* 6
en suite bath/shower 70	*Last dinner* 9
Direct dial Yes	*Parking* Ample
Room TV Yes	*Room service* 24 hours
Closed Jan	

Lake Vyrnwy Hotel

Lake Vyrnwy

H 64% £F
Map 8 C3 Powys
Llanwddyn, via Oswestry, Shropshire SY10 0LY
Llanwddyn (069 173) 692. Tlx 35880
Credit Access, Amex, Diners, Visa

Enthusiastic new owners have made great strides at this popular shooting and fishing hotel. The original Victorian look has returned to the day rooms, assisted by antiques and a change of carpets and curtains. Redecorated bedrooms are now better equipped and all have baths and showers. Leisure complex planned for 1988. *Amenities* garden, tennis, shooting, game fishing, in-house movies (free), laundry service.

■ *Rooms* 30	*Confirm by arrang.*
en suite bath/shower 30	*Last dinner* 9.15
Direct dial Yes	*Parking* Ample
Room TV Yes	*Room service* All day

Court Hotel   Lamphey

H **59% £D/E**
Map 9 A5 Dyfed
Nr Pembroke SA71 5NT
Lamphey (0646) 672273. Tlx 48587
Owner managers Mr & Mrs A. W. Lain
Credit Access, Amex, Diners, Visa
A tree-lined drive leads to this handsome
Georgian mansion, where the Lain family ensure
that guests are well looked after. Day rooms are

smart and comfortable, and there's a popular
leisure complex. Bedrooms, all with modern
accessories, include four big family rooms.
Amenities garden, indoor swimming pool, sauna,
solarium, keep-fit equipment.

■ *Rooms* 23	*Confirm by* 6
en suite bath/shower 23	*Last dinner* 9.30
Direct dial Yes	*Parking* Ample
Room TV Yes	*Room service* All day

Hand Hotel   Llanarmon Dyffryn Ceiriog

I **£D/E** ♿
Map 8 D2 Clwyd
Nr Llangollen LL20 7LD
Llanarmon Dyffryn Ceiriog (069 176) 666
Owner managers Mr & Mrs T. G. Alexander
Credit Access, Amex, Diners, Visa
A picturesque drive brings visitors to this
family-run haven of peace and tranquillity at the
head of the Ceiriog Valley. The whole place is

spotless, from the cosy oak-beamed bar and little
TV room to the bright country-style bedrooms.
Amenities garden, tennis, game fishing, laundry
service.

■ *Rooms* 14	*Confirm by* arrang.
en suite bath/shower 14	*Last dinner* 9
Room phone No	*Parking* Ample
Room TV No	*Room service* All day
Closed 1 Feb–mid Mar	

Y Bistro   Llanberis

R ♧ **Map 8 B2** Gwynedd
43 High Street
Llanberis (0286) 871278
Credit Access, Amex, Visa
Imaginative four-course dinners based on prime
local produce are prepared with skill by Nerys
Roberts at this welcoming high-street restaurant.
Chunky game terrine or smoked salmon mousse
might start your meal, while main courses span

river-fresh trout, pork tenderloin with juniper
berries and gin, and roast Welsh lamb. Splendid
puddings. Lunches by arrangement only (except
during summer).

■ *Set D* £13·50	*L* 12–3 summer only
About £37 *for two*	*D* 7.30–9.30
Seats 50 *Parties* 40	*Parking* Limited
Closed Sun (exc. preceding Bank Hol Mons),	
25 & 26 Dec & 3 wks Jan	

Palé Hall   Llandderfel

H **74% £C**
Map 8 C2 Gwynedd
Nr Bala LL23 7PS
Llandderfel (067 83) 285
Owner managers Duffin family
Credit Access, Amex, Diners, Visa
A long drive leads from the B4401 to this
impressive stone mansion on the edge of
Snowdonia National Park. Built in 1870, it has
retained many original features, notably the
stained-glass skylight in the hall, some fine
panelling and parquetry, and the Italianate
painted dome in the non-smoking lounge.
Bedrooms vary in size and decor but are all
luxuriously appointed, with extras ranging from
hairdryers and trouser presses to fresh fruit and
magazines. Some rooms boast brass beds or half-
testers. Superb modern bathrooms, apart from

one splendid old one – used by Queen Victoria.
Kennels available. *Amenities* garden, sauna,
solarium, whirlpool bath, keep-fit equipment,
clay-pigeon shooting, coarse & game fishing,
laundry service.

■ *Rooms* 17	*Confirm by* arrang.
en suite bath/shower 17	*Last dinner* 9.30
Direct dial Yes	*Parking* Ample
Room TV Yes	*Room service* All day

Cawdor Arms Hotel   Llandeilo

H **67% £D/E**
Map 9 C5 Dyfed
Rhosmaen Street SA19 6EN
Llandeilo (0558) 823500
Credit Access, Amex, Diners, Visa
A handsomely refurbished Georgian hotel
offering high standards of maintenance,
housekeeping and service. Perhaps the most
notable feature is the quality of the furnishings:

plush pink sofas and fine antiques in the reception
lounge, leather chesterfields and writing desks in
the cocktail bar, many carefully chosen pieces in
the bedrooms. Two four-posters. Good bath/
shower rooms. *Amenities* laundry service.

■ *Rooms* 17	*Confirm by* arrang.
en suite bath/shower 17	*Last dinner* 9.30
Room phone Yes	*Parking* Limited
Room TV Yes	*Room service* All day

Bodysgallen Hall · Llandudno

HR 75% £B/C
Map 8 C1 Gwynedd
LL30 1RS
Llandudno (0492) 84466. Tlx 617163

Splendid grounds – even lovelier after a recent programme of restoration and replanting – provide a delightful setting for this sympathetically-restored 17th-century mansion. Oak panelling enriches the entrance hall while log fires and chintzy fabrics, fine antiques, paintings and fresh flowers distinguish the elegant day rooms; the library and bar are comfortably furnished with deep, comfortable sofas and armchairs. There is a separate, self-contained conference hall. Tastefully appointed bedrooms (including nine cottage suites) have period

furnishings and offer a host of thoughtful extras. Luxurious bathrooms boast handsome Edwardian fittings and quality toiletries. No children under 8. No dogs. *Amenities* garden, tennis, croquet, valeting, laundry service, 24-hour lounge service.

■ Rooms 28 — Confirm by 6
en suite bath/shower 28 — Last dinner 9.45
Direct dial Yes — Parking Ample
Room TV Yes — Room service 24 hours

Bodysgallen Hall Dining Room

The chef's menus are full of interest at this formal, chandelier-hung restaurant. Celery and almond soup or terrine of game with grapes and sloe gin might precede fried scallops in garlic butter followed by collops of veal with oranges and lemons, calf's sweetbreads with wine, watercress and cream or suprême of mallard with apples and calvados. Crisp vegetables. Appealing sweets such as blackcurrant and Drambuie syllabub or iced strawberry terrine. Welsh farmhouse cheeses to finish. ♀ Well-chosen

■ Set L from £7.30 — L 12.30–2
Set D £17.50 — D 7.30–9.45
About £55 for two — Seats 56 Parties 40

Empire Hotel · Llandudno

H 67% £E
Map 8 C1 Gwynedd
Church Walks LL30 2HE
Llandudno (0492) 79955. Tlx 617161
Owner managers Leonard & Elizabeth Maddocks
Credit Access, Amex, Diners, Visa

Eight luxurious bedrooms in a nearby annexe are the latest addition to the Maddocks family's lovingly updated clifftop hotel. Behind an unassuming exterior, public rooms offer plenty of interest: fine prints decorate the lounge, there's a cosy fire in the cocktail bar and Victorian chintz strikes an elegant note in the restaurant. Excellent indoor leisure facilities are an additional attraction. Bright bedrooms with stylish bathrooms offer a bewildering array of accessories, from hairdryers to wall safes. *Amenities* indoor & outdoor swimming pools, sauna, solarium, whirlpool bath, games room, satellite TV, in-house movies (free), laundry service.

■ Rooms 56 — Confirm by 6
en suite bath/shower 56 — Last dinner 9.30
Direct dial Yes — Parking Ample
Room TV Yes — Room service All day
Closed 2 wks Xmas

Lanterns Restaurant *NEW ENTRY* · Llandudno

R Map 8 C1 Gwynedd
7 Church Walks
Llandudno (0492) 77924
Credit Access, Amex, Diners, Visa

An atmosphere of easy elegance prevails at this comfortable restaurant, where cooking is handled with solo flair by Alan Hill, service by partner Adrian Rice. Seafood is an important item on the menu, and specialities include mussels with asparagus and mushrooms in a creamy wine sauce, also variations on lobster, sole and turbot. Meaty options, too – steaks, rack of lamb, duck with orange. Simple sweets.

■ About £43 for two — D only 7.15–10.15
Seats 28 — Parking Limited
Closed Sun, Mon & 26–31 Dec

St George's Hotel · Llandudno

H 64% £D/E
Map 8 C1 Gwynedd
St George's Place LL30 2GL
Llandudno (0492) 77544. Tlx 61520
Credit Access, Amex, Diners, Visa

Excellent sea views can be enjoyed from the lounge and coffee shop of this imposing Victorian hotel. Biggest and grandest of the bedrooms, on the first floor, have balconies and spacious, fully-tiled bathrooms.
Amenities sauna, solarium, whirlpool bath, keep-fit equipment, beauty salon, hairdressing, laundry service, 24-hour lounge service, coffee shop (9am–5pm).

■ Rooms 90 — Confirm by 6
en suite bath/shower 90 — Last dinner 9
Direct dial Yes — Parking Limited
Room TV Yes — Room service 24 hours

St Tudno Hotel
Llandudno

HR **69% £D/E**
Map 8 C1 Gwynedd
North Parade, The Promenade LL30 2LP
Llandudno (0492) 74411
Owner managers Mr & Mrs Martin Bland
Credit Access, Visa

Improvements continue at this stylish, well-run hotel. Soft lighting and deep, warm colours give an attractive period feel to the bar-lounge and sitting room, while individually designed bedrooms, also with nice Victorian touches, are full of thoughtful extras. Immaculate housekeeping. *Amenities* indoor swimming pool.

■ *Rooms* 21	*Confirm by* 5
en suite bath/shower 21	*Last dinner* 9.30
Direct dial Yes	*Parking* Limited
Room TV Yes	*Room service* All day
Closed 21 Dec–22 Jan	

St Tudno Hotel Restaurant

NEW ENTRY

Hand-painted wall panels, pretty table settings, comfortable seating and abundant greenery make this a delightful restaurant. The daily-changing menu – presented partly in Welsh, but with full translations – always includes fresh fish and vegetarian fare. Start perhaps with eggs Benedict, then move on to a good beefy consommé, followed by succulent fillet of pork in champagne sauce or grilled Welsh lamb coated in apple and geranium jelly. A wide choice of sweets might include a delicious, liqueur-flavoured mousse of fresh orange and pineapple. Welsh organic cheeses to finish. ⊖

■ *Set D* £14·25	*L* 12.30–2
About £40 *for two*	*D* 6.45–9.30
Seats 60	*Closed* 21 Dec–22 Jan

■ Any person using our name to obtain free hospitality is a fraud. Proprietors, please inform the police and us.

Stradey Park Hotel
Llanelli

H **58% £D/E** &
Map 9 B6 Dyfed
Furnace SA15 4HA
Llanelli (0554) 758171. Tlx 48521
Credit Access, Amex, Diners, Visa

A handsome crenellated manor house standing in a commanding hilltop position just off the B4309. Public areas, particularly the bar, could do with some refurbishment. Bedrooms, however, are mostly in a newer extension and are well designed and equipped. They offer functional built-in units and smartly tiled bathrooms. *Amenities* garden, games room, snooker, pool table, laundry service, 24-hour lounge service.

■ *Rooms* 80	*Confirm by* 6
en suite bath/shower 80	*Last dinner* 9.30
Room phone Yes	*Parking* Ample
Room TV Yes	*Room service* All day

Hand Hotel
Llangollen

H **55% £D/E**
Map 8 D2 Clwyd
Bridge Street LL20 8PL
Llangollen (0978) 860303. Tlx 61160
Credit Access, Amex, Diners, Visa

Near the town centre, this popular tourist hotel has an attractive terraced garden that stretches down to the river Dee. Public areas include a chandelier-hung foyer, comfortably-furnished lounge and lively sing-along bar. Bedrooms of varying sizes are prettily decorated and have white fitted units. Simple bath/shower rooms. *Amenities* garden, game fishing, 24-hour lounge service.

■ *Rooms* 58	*Confirm by* arrang.
en suite bath/shower 58	*Last dinner* 8.45
Room phone Yes	*Parking* Ample
Room TV Yes	*Room service* 24 hours

Royal Hotel
Llangollen

H **59% £D**
Map 8 D2 Clwyd
Bridge Street LL20 8PG
Llangollen (0978) 860202
Credit Access, Amex, Diners, Visa. **LVs**

Standing next to an ancient stone bridge that spans the river Dee, this solid little hotel makes a pleasant place to relax. A bay window in the spacious, comfortable lounge makes the most of the view, and there are two convivial bars. Most bedrooms feature lightwood fitted units and all have tea-makers plus adequate private facilities. *Amenities* game fishing, pool table, laundry service.

■ *Rooms* 33	*Confirm by* 6
en suite bath/shower 33	*Last dinner* 9
Room phone Yes	*Parking* Limited
Room TV Yes	*Room service* All day

♀ indicates a **well-chosen** house wine.

Cwrt Bleddyn Hotel *NEW ENTRY* — Llangybi

H 74% **£D**
Map 9 D6 Gwent
Nr Usk HP5 1PG
Tredunnock (0633 49) 521
Credit Access, Amex, Diners, Visa

Adjacent to the Caerleon-Usk road just outside the village, Cwrt Bleddyn is a manor house with a long and interesting history. The past has been well preserved both inside and out, with gables, 16th-century oak panelling and antique furniture among the many attractive features. Additions have been skilfully blended in, notably the splendid sun lounge with its arched glass roof. Nineteen bedrooms were added in 1986 and these are particularly spacious; some rooms feature period furniture and lovely antique four-posters or half-testers. Bathrooms throughout are roomy and well fitted. Impressive housekeeping.

No dogs.
Amenities garden, satellite TV, in-house movies (free), laundry service, 24-hour lounge service.
■ *Rooms* 30 *Confirm by arrang.*
en suite bath/shower 30 *Last dinner* 10
Direct dial Yes *Parking* Ample
Room TV Yes *Room service* 24 hours

Hawk & Buckle Inn — Llannefydd

I **£F**
Map 8 C2 Clwyd
Nr Denbigh LL16 5ED
Llannefydd (074 579) 249
Owner managers Bob & Barbara Pearson
Credit Access, Visa

Guests are provided with keys to their own side entrance, and most of the accommodation, and the residents' lounge and bar, are away from the public part of the inn. Bedrooms are compact, cheerful and thoughtfully equipped, and all but one enjoy fine views down the valley. The best room sports a four-poster bed. No children under eight. *Amenities* patio, pool table.
■ *Rooms* 10 *Confirm by arrang.*
en suite bath/shower 10 *Last dinner* 9.30
Direct dial Yes *Parking* Ample
Room TV Yes *Room service* None

▭ is our symbol for an **outstanding** wine list.

Llanrhaeadr Hall *NEW ENTRY* — Llanrhaeadr

H 65% **£D/E**
Map 8 C2 Clwyd
Nr Denbigh LL16 4NP
Llanynys (074 578) 313. Tlx 94012648
Owner managers Philip & Elaine Catlow
Credit Access, Amex, Diners, Visa

A warm welcome awaits at this handsome house dating from the 15th century and set in peaceful parkland. Antique furniture, deep carpets and delightful fabrics grace the day rooms (note also the lovely Adam-style staircase) and the bedrooms, too, are comfortably traditional. No children under eight. Dogs in kennels only. *Amenities* garden, laundry service.
■ *Rooms* 12 *Confirm by arrang.*
en suite bath/shower 12 *Last dinner* 9
Direct dial Yes *Parking* Ample
Room TV No *Room service* All day

Meadowsweet Hotel — Llanrwst

HR 60% **£F** &
Map 8 C2 Gwynedd
Station Road LL26 0DS
Llanrwst (0492) 640732
Owner managers John & Joy Evans
Credit Access, Amex, Visa

This friendly, unassuming hotel on the edge of town was originally two Victorian houses. An open fire warms the cosy bar in the homely lounge and books and board games are provided for passing the time. Bedrooms – furnished in a variety of styles – are spacious and spotless. All have smart shower rooms (there are also two well-equipped public rooms).
■ *Rooms* 10 *Confirm by arrang.*
en suite bath/shower 10 *Last dinner* 9.30
Direct dial Yes *Parking* Ample
Room TV Yes *Room service* All day

Meadowsweet Hotel Restaurant ⌘

Hardworking John Evans does all the cooking in this small, comfortable but rather subdued hotel dining room. Scallop mousse, confit of guinea fowl, monkfish provençale and sautéed lamb with orange and ginger are typical dishes, and main courses come with a miniature harvest festival of lovely fresh vegetables. Cherry pudding makes an enjoyable finish. Generally capable cooking. Super cheeses, and a magnificent cellar including splendid clarets and exceptional 1976 and 1983 Alsace.
▭ Outstanding ♟ Well-chosen ⌘
■ *Set D* £14·50 *D only* 6.30–9.30
About £55 *for two* *Parking* Ample
Seats 36

■ Our inspectors are our full-time employees; they are professionally trained by us.

Wynnstay Hotel — Machynlleth

H **57% £D/E**
Map 8 C3 Powys
Maengwyn Street SY80 8AE
Machynlleth (0654) 2941
Credit Access, Amex, Diners, Visa. **LVs**

The classic neo-Georgian frontage makes a proud sight on the main street, and at the back there's an attractive patio with outdoor tables and hanging flower baskets. Simply furnished bedrooms all now have private facilities and direct-dial telephones. The bar is a local favourite, and there's a comfortable lounge. Parking is at the rear via a narrow access – look out for the signs.

■ *Rooms* 20	*Confirm by* 6
en suite bath/shower 20	*Last dinner* 9
Direct dial Yes	*Parking* Ample
Room TV Yes	*Room service* Limited

Miskin Manor   *NEW ENTRY* — Miskin

H **71% £C/D** &
Map 9 C6 Mid Glamorgan
CF7 8ND
Llantrisant (0443) 224204
Credit Access, Amex, Diners, Visa

Just 1½ miles from junction 34 of the M4, this stone-built manor stands in 20 acres of landscaped gardens. The original house, dating back to 1092 and twice rebuilt following fires, was recently extended by the addition of a smart neo-Georgian wing. Public rooms are luxurious, with oak panelling, mullioned windows and deep armchairs. Bedrooms are vast, with sofas and breakfast and writing tables as well as remote-control TVs, radios, trouser presses and hairdryers. Bathrooms are fully tiled and carpeted. Guests have free use of the adjacent leisure centre. No dogs. *Amenities* garden, indoor

swimming pool, sauna, solarium, whirlpool bath, gymnasium, tennis, squash, badminton, snooker, laundry service, crèche.

■ *Rooms* 32	*Confirm by arrang.*
en suite bath/shower 32	*Last dinner* 9.30
Direct dial Yes	*Parking* Ample
Room TV Yes	*Room service* All day

King's Head Hotel — Monmouth

H **66% £D/E**
Map 9 D5 Gwent
Agincourt Square NP5 3DY
Monmouth (0600) 2177. Tlx 497294
Owner manager Mr K. L. Gough
Credit Access, Amex, Diners, Visa

Standing in the historic centre of the town is this former coaching inn with smart black-and-white gabled front. A plaster panel depicting the head and cypher of Charles I decorates the public bar and there's an elegant Adam fireplace in the cocktail bar-cum-lounge. Bedrooms vary in size but are all well-equipped. Good modern bathrooms. *Amenities* laundry service.

■ *Rooms* 32	*Confirm by* 6
en suite bath/shower 30	*Last dinner* 9
Direct dial Yes	*Parking* Limited
Room TV Yes	*Room service* 24 hours

Langland Court Hotel   *NEW ENTRY* — Mumbles

I **£E**
Map 9 C6 West Glamorgan
31 Langland Court Road, Langland Bay,
Swansea SA3 4TD
Swansea (0792) 361545. Tlx 498037
Owner manager Mr C. R. Birt
Credit Access, Amex, Diners, Visa

The road from Mumbles climbs steeply as it approaches this welcoming inn on the cliffs above Langland Bay. The entrance hall has impressive beams and panelling, and the bedrooms are cheerful – some with bow-windows and four-posters. *Amenities* garden.

■ *Rooms* 21	*Confirm by* 6
en suite bath/shower 20	*Last dinner* 9.30
Direct dial Yes	*Parking* Ample
Room TV Yes	*Room service* Limited
Closed 25 Dec	

Norton House Hotel   Mumbles

H **69% £E**
Map 9 C6 West Glamorgan
Norton Road, Swansea SA3 5TQ
Swansea (0792) 404891
Owner managers Mr & Mrs Rossi
Credit Access, Visa
   There's a lot of style and no little luxury about
the Rossi's 18th-century house, where
chandeliers, huge velvet drapes and period
furniture are much in evidence. The four-poster
bedrooms are particularly opulent, with deep-pile
carpets extending to the bathrooms, large sofas,
writing desks and full-length mirrors. Bedrooms in

the new wing lose in space, but not in comfort,
and those at ground level have patio doors
opening directly on to a terrace. There's a
comfortable, elegant lounge bar in the main
house, and a separate first-floor lounge in the
wing. No children under five. No dogs.
Amenities garden, laundry service.

■ *Rooms 16*	*Confirm by arrang.*
en suite bath/shower 16	*Last dinner 9.30*
Direct dial Yes	*Parking Ample*
Room TV Yes	*Room service All day*
Closed 2 wks Xmas	

Celtic Manor Hotel   Newport

H **78% £C/D**
Map 9 D6 Gwent
Coldra Woods NP6 2YA
Newport (0633) 413000
Manager Duncan Williams
Credit Access, Amex, Diners, Visa
   A swimming pool, leisure centre and further
accommodation are planned for this already
luxurious hotel. Set on a hillside near junction 24
of the M4, the house has retained much of its fine
19th-century decoration, notably the elegant
stucco mouldings in the lounge and cocktail bar.
Comfortable, elegant furnishings complement
these period touches. Below stairs there's a
cheerful rustic cellar bar, and breakfast is served
in the conservatory coffee shop under striped
awnings and leafy hanging baskets. Spacious
well-kept bedrooms (two with four-posters) have

smark darkwood units and quilted floral
bedcovers with matching curtains. No dogs.
Amenities garden, laundry service, coffee shop
(7am–11pm), 24-lounge service, helipad.

■ *Rooms 17*	*Confirm by 6*
en suite bath/shower 17	*Last dinner 10.30*
Direct dial Yes	*Parking Ample*
Room TV Yes	*Room service 24 hours*

Kings Hotel *NEW ENTRY*   Newport

H **60% £D/E**
Map 9 D6 Gwent
High Street NP9 1QU
Newport (0633) 842020. Tlx 497330
Credit Access, Amex, Diners, Visa
   Opposite the railway station and a minute from
the motorway, this 200-year-old hotel has been
extensively refurbished. The lounge is particularly
elegant and inviting, and handsome original

features include wide staircases and stained-
glass windows. Pastel decorated, oak-furnished
bedrooms have lots of up-to-date accessories.
Amenities in-house movies (free), laundry service,
24-hour lounge service.

■ *Rooms 47*	*Confirm by 6*
en suite bath/shower 47	*Last dinner 9.30*
Direct dial Yes	*Parking Limited*
Room TV Yes	*Room service 24 hours*

■ We welcome complaints and bona
fide recommendations on the
tear-out pages for readers' comments.
They are followed up by our professional
team. Please also complain to the
management instantly.

RECEPTION

Glansevern Arms   Pant Mawr

I **£F**
Map 9 C4 Powys
Nr Llangurig SY18 6SY
Llangurig (055 15) 240
Owner manager Mr W. T. O. Edwards
   Mr Edwards, owner for over 20 years, keeps
things in tip-top shape at this spendid little inn,
which stands high up on the A44 overlooking the
river Wye. Two homely bars and a residents'

lounge offer space for relaxation. Bedrooms, spick-
and-span like the rest of the inn, have a traditional
feel. All have adequate modern bath/shower
rooms. *Amenities* garden.

■ *Rooms arrang.*	*Confirm by arrang.*
en suite bath/shower 7	*Last dinner 8*
Room phone No	*Parking Ample*
Room TV Yes	*Room service Limited*
Closed 10 days Xmas	

Caprice   Penarth

R **Map 9 D6** South Glamorgan
Beach Cliff, The Esplanade
Cardiff (0222) 702424
Credit Access, Amex, Diners, Visa
 The Bristol Channel provides the view for this
long-established restaurant, whose large regular
clientele enjoy old favourites like prawn cocktail,
wiener schnitzel and chicken Maryland. Also on
the extensive menu are very good fresh fish

dishes such as sea trout with hollandaise, grilled
salmon with leek purée and John Dory with
saffron and tomato. Don't pass up the pasta or
the profiteroles. There is an extensive wine list. ⊖

■ Set L £9·95	L 12.30–2.30
Set D £12·95	D 7–11
About £45 for two	Parking Limited
Seats 76 Parties 70	Closed Bank Hols

■ For a discount on next year's guide, see Offer for Answers.

George III Hotel   Penmaenpool

I **£E/F**
Map 8 C3 Gwynedd
Nr Dolgellau LL40 1YD
Dolgellau (0341) 422525
Owner manager Gail Hall
Credit Access, Amex, Diners, Visa
 A delightful place to stay with lovely views of
Mawddach estuary. Polished brass and fishing
nets in the bar create a homely atmosphere, and

the beamed lounge boasts a copper-hooded
inglenook. Best bedrooms are in the nearby
lodge, but all are prettily appointed.
Amenities garden, coarse and game fishing.

■ Rooms 14	Confirm by 6
en suite bath/shower 7	Last dinner 8.45
Direct dial Yes	Parking Ample
Room TV Yes	Room service Limited
Closed 2 wks Xmas	

Radnorshire Arms Hotel   Presteigne

H **63% £D**
Map 9 D4 Powys
High Street LD8 2BE
Presteigne (0544) 267406
Credit Access, Amex, Diners, Visa
 Beams, panelling and sturdy antiques give
charm to the public rooms and two bedrooms of
this delightful old half-timbered inn. Other
bedrooms have stylish new furnishings, while

those in an extension are most attractive. All have
thoughtful touches such as books, flowers, and a
welcoming glass of mead, as well as tea-makers
and remote-control TVs.
Amenities garden.

■ Rooms 16	Confirm by 6
en suite bath/shower 16	Last dinner 8.30
Room phone Yes	Parking Ample
Room TV Yes	Room service None

♀ indicates a **well-chosen** house wine.

Castle Hotel   Ruthin

H **56% £E** &
Map 8 C2 Clwyd
St Peter's Square LL15 1AA
Ruthin (082 42) 2479. Tlx 617074
Owner managers Carrington-Sykes family
Credit Access, Amex, Diners, Visa
 An original 17th-century staircase leads to the
first-floor lounge of this handsome Georgian hotel,
where major refurbishment – including restoration

of the beautiful wood panelling – is under way.
Elegant front rooms overlook the town square;
rear rooms, recently repainted, await further
improvements. *Amenities* garden, laundry
service, coffee shop (8am–6pm).

■ Rooms 24	Confirm by arrang.
en suite bath/shower 24	Last dinner 9
Direct dial Yes	Parking Ample
Room TV Yes	Room service All day

Ruthin Castle   Ruthin

H **64% £E**
Map 8 C2 Clwyd
Corwen Road LL15 2NU
Ruthin (082,42) 2664. Tlx 61169
Manager Mr T. Warburton
Credit Access, Amex, Diners, Visa
 Thirty acres of grounds surround what was
originally a 13th-century Welsh fortress. Inside,
baronial halls offer old-world elegance, from the

vast lounge with its massive velvet drapes to the
octagonal oak-panelled bar. Bedrooms vary in
size but nearly all have tiled bathrooms with
showers. *Amenities* garden, game fishing,
snooker, laundry service.

■ Rooms 60	Confirm by 6
en suite bath/shower 60	Last dinner 9.30
Room phone Yes	Parking Ample
Room TV Yes	Room service All day

St Non's Hotel — St David's

H **59% £E**
Map 9 A5 Dyfed
Catherine Street SA62 6RJ
St David's (0437) 720239
Owner managers Sandy & Angela Falconer
Credit Access, Amex, Visa

Close to the majestic ruins of the Bishop's Palace, the Falconers' welcoming hotel provides a good holiday base. Visitors can mix with locals in the popular bar, or relax in the quiet lounge bar or TV room. Redecoration is bringing a floral touch to the modern-style bedrooms, which have tea-makers and spotless bathrooms.
Amenities garden, pool table, laundry service.

■ *Rooms* 20	*Confirm by arrang.*
en suite bath/shower 20	*Last dinner* 9
Direct dial Yes	*Parking* Ample
Room TV Yes	*Room service* Limited

Warpool Court Hotel — St David's

H **62% £D**
Map 9 A5 Dyfed
SA62 6BN
St David's (0437) 720300
Credit Access, Amex, Diners, Visa

A vast collection of ornamental wall tiles is a feature of this former cathedral choir school with views across St Bride's Bay. Attractive lounges and a cellar bar are complemented by pretty; well-furnished bedrooms, all with bath or shower rooms. *Amenities* garden, indoor swimming pool, tennis, croquet, pool table, in-house movies (free), laundry service.

■ *Rooms* 25	*Confirm by* 7.30
en suite bath/shower 25	*Last dinner* 9.15
Direct dial Yes	*Parking* Ample
Room TV Yes	*Room service* All day
Closed Jan–mid Feb	

Sully House — Swanbridge

RR ⌾ **Map 9 D6** South Glamorgan
Nr Penarth
Cardiff (0222) 530448
Credit Access, Diners, Visa

Paul Westmacott, owner, manager and accomplished chef, provides a fine bill of fare at this tranquil restaurant with rooms overlooking the sea. Starters range from baked mussels with herbs to duck pâté with Cumberland sauce, and main courses include pork fillet with sauerkraut and the catch of the day. The house speciality remains a diet-defying combination of beef, veal, chicken and ham on a bed of potatoes, with tomatoes and mushrooms. Vegetables are fresh and carefully cooked. Excellent clarets and burgundies. ☺

■ *Set L & D* £15	*L* 12–2
About £42 *for two*	*D* 7–10
Seats 50 *Parties* 50	*Parking* Ample
Closed L Sat, all Sun & Bank Hols	

Bedrooms £E/F

Rooms 4	*With bath/shower* 4

Attractive bedrooms, with sparkling en suite bathrooms, have fine views of Sully Island and the Bristol Channel. No dogs.

Dragon Hotel — Swansea

H **65% £C/D**
Map 9 C6 West Glamorgan
Kingsway Circle SA1 5LS
Swansea (0792) 51074. Tlx 48309
Credit Access, Amex, Diners, Visa. LVs

In the heart of the city, this modern hotel offers spacious accommodation and a public bar, popular with residents and locals alike. Other public areas include a cavernous lounge area. All bedrooms are spacious and double glazed. Standard rooms have been nicely redecorated. Best rooms have superior furnishings.
Amenities coffee shop (7am–10pm), laundry service, 24-hour lounge service.

■ *Rooms* 118	*Confirm by* 6
en suite bath/shower 118	*Last dinner* 10
Direct dial Yes	*Parking* Limited
Room TV Yes	*Room service* All day

Ladbroke Hotel — Swansea

H **66% £D/E**
Map 9 C6 West Glamorgan
Phoenix Way, Enterprise Park, Llansamlet
SA7 9EG
Swansea (0792) 790190. Tlx 48589
Credit Access, Amex, Diners, Visa

Seek out this new, low-rise, red-brick hotel by leaving the M4 at exit 44 and heading for the Enterprise Park. Open-plan public areas are pleasantly contemporary in style, with views of an artificial lake. Good-sized bedrooms are identically furnished to a high standard. *Amenities* garden, indoor swimming pool, sauna, keep-fit equipment, in-house movies, laundry service.

■ *Rooms* 114	*Confirm by* 6
en suite bath/shower 114	*Last dinner* 9.45
Direct dial Yes	*Parking* Ample
Room TV Yes	*Room service* 24 hours

Maes-y-Neuadd Hotel

HR 69% £D
Map 8 C2 Gwynedd
Nr Harlech LL47 6YA
Harlech (0766) 780200
Owner managers Slatter & Horsfall families
Credit Access, Visa

Improvements continue at this delightful hotel in a picturesque hillside setting. The screened-off lounge and adjacent bar are ideal spots to relax, and brightly decorated bedrooms feature handsome period furnishings. Two new bedrooms are in separate buildings, one a cosy house surrounded by trees. *Amenities* garden, laundry service.

■ *Rooms* 16	*Confirm by arrang.*
en suite bath/shower 15	*Last dinner 9*
Direct dial Yes	*Parking Ample*
Room TV Yes	*Room service* All day
Closed 4 Jan–4 Feb	

Maes-y-Neuadd Hotel Restaurant ♀

Traditional Welsh and modern international styles of cooking share the menu in this elegant restaurant, whose kitchen is in the capable hands of co-owner Olive Horsfall. In the former category come stuffed herrings, garlicky mussels in a wholemeal pastry tart, Welsh lamb and Monmouth pudding; in the latter, fresh pear with mustard sauce, vegetable-filled cannelloni, poached salmon with limes and pine kernels and fillet of venison in a rich red wine sauce. For Sunday lunch there's a shorter menu, featuring a roast. ᴇ

■ *Set L* £9·25	*L* Sun 12.15–2, Mon–Sat
Set D £13·75	by arrang. only
About £37 for two	*D* 7.30–11.30
Seats 36 *Parties* 65	*Closed* 4 Jan–4 Feb

Ty'n-y-Cornel Hotel

H 54% £D/E
Map 8 C3 Gwynedd
Nr Tywyn LL36 9AJ
Abergynolwyn (065 477) 282
Owner managers Mr & Mrs K. C. Thompson
Credit Access, Amex, Visa

A homely little roadside hotel with its own lake in front and mountain behind. There's a cosy little bar and a lounge that enjoys splendid picture-

window views. Bedrooms are neat and simple; bathrooms are adequate. *Amenities* garden, outdoor swimming pool, sauna, solarium, game fishing, sailing, canoeing, board sailing.

■ *Rooms* 17	*Confirm by arrang.*
en suite bath/shower 14	*Last dinner 9.30*
Direct dial Yes	*Parking Ample*
Room TV Yes	*Room service* All day
Closed Nov–Mar	

Three Cocks Hotel

HR 58% £E/F
Map 9 D5 Powys
Nr Brecon LD3 0SL
Glasbury (049 74) 215
Owner managers Mr & Mrs M. Winstone
Credit Access, Visa

A tiny 15th-century hostelry, and for a maximum of 14 residents there are three lounges, so peace and quiet are easily found. Bedrooms are sparsely equipped but charming with uneven floors and many exposed beams. Due to close temporarily end 1987 for the construction of en suite bathrooms. No dogs. *Amenities* garden.

■ *Rooms* 7	*Confirm by arrang.*
en suite bath/shower 0	*Last dinner 9*
Room phone No	*Parking Ample*
Room TV No	*Room service* All day
Closed Jan	

Three Cocks Hotel Restaurant ♀

Marie-Jeanne Winstone is a friendly, unflustered hostess, Michael a dedicated and highly skilled chef combining classical techniques with modern presentation. Our meal in the relaxed, civilised restaurant was an occasion to remember, from the hot canapé enjoyed with a drink in the lounge to delicate carrot soup, superb lamb's sweetbreads with field mushrooms and breast of duck with sesame seeds, served with first-class vegetables. Sweets include home-made sorbets. ♀ Well-chosen ᴇ

NEW ENTRY

■ *Set L* £15	*L* 12–1.30
Set D £15	*D* 7–9
About £42 for two	*Seats* 40 *Parties* 30
Closed L Sun (exc. July & Aug) & all Jan	

Beaufort Hotel

H 58% £D/E
Map 9 D6 Gwent
Chepstow NP6 6SF
Tintern (029 18) 777
Manager Chris Walters
Credit Access, Amex, Diners, Visa. LVs

Overlooking the ruins of the Cistercian abbey, this friendly hotel offers comfortable overnight accommodation in simply furnished bedrooms, all

with tea-makers and tiled bath or shower rooms. Downstairs, the lounge features a handsome fireplace, and there's a rustic beamed bar. *Amenities* garden, coarse fishing, games room, pool table, laundry service.

■ *Rooms* 24	*Confirm by* 6
en suite bath/shower 24	*Last dinner 9*
Direct dial Yes	*Parking Ample*
Room TV Yes	*Room service* Limited

Royal George Hotel

H 57% £E
Map 9 D6 Gwent
Nr Chepstow NP6 6SF
Tintern (029 18) 205
Owner managers Hollinger family
Credit Access, Amex, Visa

Situated just across the road from the Abbey, this old hotel has a tributary of the river Wye running through its prize-winning gardens. The

Tintern Abbey

public bar has characterful old beams and all but one of the bedrooms are in chalets in the garden. Redecoration and refurbishing throughout is under way. *Amenities* garden, laundry service, in-house movies (free).

■ *Rooms 15*	*Confirm by 6*
en suite bath/shower 15	*Last dinner 9.30*
Direct dial Yes	*Parking Ample*
Room TV Yes	*Room service All day*

Stone Hall

RR **Map 9 A5** Dyfed
Nr Wolf's Castle, Haverfordwest
Letterston (0348) 840212
French cooking
Credit Access, Amex, Visa

Waitresses in traditional Welsh dress serve at tables decked with wild flowers in this attractive white-painted establishment. The part of the building housing the restaurant dates back to 1400 and the flagstone floor, exposed beams and inglenook fireplace create a charming venue in which to sample competent French cooking. Rabbit pâté in aspic makes a tasty starter. To

Welsh Hook

follow, try brill with cream and chive sauce, or veal cutlets with wild mushrooms. Desserts include a praline soufflé. ♀ Well-chosen ⊖

■ *Set D from £9·20*	*L Sun 12.30–2*
About £34 for two	*D 7–10*
Seats 34 Parties 45	*Parking Ample*
Closed D Mon, 2 wks Feb & 2 wks Nov	

Bedrooms £E/F

Rooms 5	*With bath/shower 5*

Three double and two single rooms, all with en suite facilities, accommodate overnight guests in modest traditional comfort. Pleasant lounge. No dogs.

Wolfscastle Country Hotel

HR 56% £E/F
Map 9 A5 Dyfed
Nr Haverfordwest SA62 5LZ
Treffgarne (043 787) 225
Owner managers Andrew & Pauline Stirling
Credit Access, Amex, Visa

Squash coach Andrew Stirling is always willing to give guests a game at his pleasant converted Georgian house hotel just off the A40. The cosy bar has an open fire and collection of china clowns, and there is also a little upstairs lounge. Pretty, simply-furnished bedrooms have their own neat bathrooms. *Amenities* garden, tennis, squash, laundry service.

■ *Rooms 15*	*Confirm by arrang.*
en suite bath/shower 15	*Last dinner 9.15*
Direct dial Yes	*Parking Ample*
Room TV Yes	*Room service All day*

Wolf's Castle

Wolfscastle Country Hotel Restaurant

Consistency is the name of the game here, and Michael Lewis, assisted by Alex George, cooks in honest, unelaborate fashion with very successful results. Service is similarly capable and unfussy. Typifying the appetising fare served in the candlelit dining room are mushrooms with cream and paprika, duck bigarade, pepper steak, and baked salmon served with an impeccable hollandaise sauce. Vegetables are fresh and crisp; sweets are laid out in a tempting display. ⊖

About £35 for two	*L Sun only 12–2*
Seats 40	*D 7–9,*
Parties 200	*Sat 7–9.15*
Closed L Mon–Sat exc. by arrang.	

CHANNEL ISLANDS

ALDERNEY

Inchalla Hotel *NEW ENTRY* St Anne

H 62% £E &
Map 3 F4 Alderney
The Val
Alderney (048 182) 3220
Owner manager Valerie Willis
Credit Amex, Visa
  On the edge of a town of cobbled streets and colour-washed houses, Inchalla offers hospitality, easy relaxation and nice views of countryside and

sea. Light, airy bedrooms, furnished in tasteful modern style, are equipped with tea-makers and well-stocked mini-bars (a hotel bar is planned). No dogs. *Amenities* garden, sauna, solarium, whirlpool bath, laundry service.

■ *Rooms 11*	*Confirm by arrang.*
en suite bath/shower 9	*Last dinner 9*
Room phone No	*Parking Ample*
Room TV Yes	*Room service All day*

Nellie Gray's St Anne

R **Map 3 F4** Alderney
Victoria Street
Alderney (048 182) 3333
Credit Access, Amex, Diners, Visa
  A popular, well-established restaurant with pleasant chintzy decor and an attractive garden for light summer lunches. Piet Hein offers hearty portions and plenty of variety on an evening menu that includes seafood bisque, crab, lobster and

daily fish specials; ham pancakes (starter or main); chicken tandoori; and several ways with steak. Good-value drinking. ℮

■ *About £45 for two*	*L 12–2 end May–*
Seats 48	*end Sept only*
Parties 48	*D 7.30–9.30, 7.15–10*
Parking Ample	*end May–end Sept*
Closed Sun (excl. D mid July–mid Sept), also Jan–Mar	

■ Changes in data may occur in
establishments after the Guide
goes to press. Prices should be taken
as indications rather than firm quotes.

GUERNSEY

White House Hotel *NEW ENTRY* Herm Island

HR 64% £D/E
Map 3 E4
Herm (0481) 22159
Credit Access, Visa
  The only hotel on Herm, a carefree, car-free little island reached by launch from Guernsey. The White House offers a warm welcome, attentive service, pleasant bars and lounges and quiet, well-kept bedrooms, some in nearby cottages. Inclusive terms only. No dogs.
Amenities garden, outdoor swimming pool, tennis, sea fishing, mooring, coffee shop (10am–4.30pm).

■ *Rooms 32*	*Confirm by arrang.*
en suite bath/shower 32	*Last dinner 8.30*
Room phone No	*Parking No cars*
Room TV No	*Room service None*
Closed Oct–Easter	

White House Hotel Restaurant

Sound, straightforward cooking allows quality and flavours to speak for themselves in dishes like sardines with herbs and lemon, goujons of monkfish, ham and turkey pancakes and succulent grilled chicken. Excellent vegetables are kept on table warmers, and an attractive sweet trolley offers choices like fresh fruit tartlets, brandy snaps and trifle. Dinner is four courses, lunch three (also a cold buffet lunch). A carefully chosen wine list provides good drinking at keen prices. ℮

■ *Set L £6·50*	*L 12.30–1.30*
Set D £8·50	*D 7–8.30*
About £25 for two	*Seats 90*
Closed Oct–Easter	

Imperial Hotel   Pleinmont

£F
Map 3 E4 Guernsey
Torteval
Guernsey (0481) 64044
Credit Access, Visa
   Fine sandy beaches and clifftop walks are
within easy reach of this pleasant inn, a modest
place but a very friendly one. The two comfortable
residents' bars enjoy picture-window views

across the bay, and the pubby Portelet Bar is a
popular local haunt. Bright bedrooms with
functional modern furniture and tiled bath/shower
rooms. *Amenities* garden.

■ *Rooms 16*	*Confirm by arrang.*
en suite bath/shower 14	*Last dinner 9.15*
Room phone No	*Parking Ample*
Room TV Yes	*Room service All day*
Closed Nov–Mar	

St Margaret's Lodge Hotel   St Martin's

H 60% £D/E
Map 3 E4 Guernsey
Forest Road
Guernsey (0481) 35757. Tlx 4191664
Credit Access, Visa
   Seven splendid new bedrooms, with deep-pile
carpets, polished-wood furnishings and smartly
tiled bathrooms, have been created at this
cheerful white-painted hotel. Other bedrooms will

gradually be upgraded. Day rooms include a cosy
lounge and cocktail bar; a pretty poolside garden
is a pleasant spot for sipping in the sun. No dogs.
Amenities garden, outdoor swimming pool, 24-
hour lounge service.

■ *Rooms 49*	*Confirm by arrang.*
en suite bath/shower 49	*Last dinner 9.45*
Direct dial Yes	*Parking Ample*
Room TV Yes	*Room service 24 hours*

La Trelade Hotel   St Martin's

H 58% £E
Map 3 E4 Guernsey
Forest Road
Guernsey (0481) 35454
Manager Richard Cann
Credit Access, Visa
   Much modernised behind its traditional
frontage, this agreeable hotel offers a relaxing
holiday atmosphere. Public rooms include a split-

level foyer-lounge and a roomy convivial bar.
Bedrooms have neat white fitted furniture and
pretty wallpapers. Practical bathrooms.
Amenities garden, outdoor swimming pool,
putting, laundry service, 24-hour lounge service.

■ *Rooms 45*	*Confirm by arrang.*
en suite bath/shower 45	*Last dinner 9*
Direct dial Yes	*Parking Ample*
Room TV Yes	*Room service 24 hours*

Duke of Richmond Hotel   St Peter Port

H 65% £C/D
Map 3 E4 Guernsey
Cambridge Park
Guernsey (0481) 26221. Tlx 4191462
Manager Mr N. Adams
Credit Access, Amex, Diners, Visa
   The first hotel purpose built after World War II,
this white-painted establishment enjoys a hillside
position that permits sea views from some of the

superior, balconied bedrooms. All rooms are
comfortably furnished and well equipped, with
smart modern bathrooms. There are two bars and
a quiet lounge. *Amenities* outdoor swimming
pool, laundry service, 24-hour lounge service.

■ *Rooms 75*	*Confirm by arrang.*
en suite bath/shower 75	*Last dinner 9.30*
Direct dial Yes	*Parking Limited*
Room TV Yes	*Room service 24 hours*

Flying Dutchman Hotel   St Peter Port

HR 57% £D/E
Map 3 E4 Guernsey
Ruette Braye
Guernsey (0481) 23787
Owner managers Reinhard & Ulla Deutschmann
Credit Amex, Visa
   'No frills comfort' is the motto of the warm-
hearted, efficient owners of this charming hotel
about a mile out of town. The beer garden with its
old buses and carts is a kid's delight. Relaxing
lounges are kept in good order as are the modest
but comfortable bedrooms. No dogs.
Amenities garden, outdoor swimming pool.

■ *Rooms 21*	*Confirm by arrang.*
en suite bath/shower 16	*Last dinner 10*
Room phone No	*Parking Ample*
Room TV Yes	*Room service Limited*
Closed last wk Jan & all Feb	

Flying Dutchman Hotel
Restaurant ᗉ

Deliciously unpretentious cooking by Swedish-
born Ulla Deutschmann makes for a most
enjoyable meal in this relaxing, spacious and
charming restaurant with its cheerful decor. Her
culinary net embraces dishes from Sweden,
Germany and France as well as Creole
specialities. Crispy potato pancakes, venison
ragoût, pork with tasty red cabbage and a special
way with brill are among the highlights, which
culminate in husband Reinhard's blissful German
pâtisseries. Note the interesting Baden wines. ⊖

■ *Set D Sun £6.50*	*L 12–2*
About £32 for two	*D 7.30–10*
Seats 100	*Parties 100*
Closed Sun to non-residents, last wk Jan & all Feb	

La Frégate Hotel

St Peter Port

HR 65% £C/D
Map 3 E4 Guernsey
Les Côtils
Guernsey (0481) 24624
Manager G. Toffanello
Credit Access, Amex, Diners, Visa
   High standards of housekeeping and service are hallmarks of this attractive 18th-century manor house overlooking the harbour. Fine antiques grace public areas, which include a sun terrace. Sea-facing bedrooms, some with private balconies, are generally more spacious; all have modern furnishings. No children under 14. No dogs. *Amenities* garden, laundry service.

■ *Rooms 13*	*Confirm by arrang.*
en suite bath/shower 13	*Last dinner 9.30*
Direct dial Yes	*Parking Ample*
Room TV No	*Room service All day*

La Frégate Hotel Restaurant

French cooking
Fine views accompany meals enjoyed at this smart, fashionable restaurant. Local seafood is always popular – note home-smoked fish pâtés, lobster, sole and monkfish. Other choices include orange and Cointreau-sauced breast of duck and tender veal with a rich mushroom and Cognac sauce. Lovely vegetables from the hotel's own gardens, and lots of delicious sweets. Polished, professional service led by manager Gastone Toffanello. ❂

■ *Set L £7·50*	*L 12.30–1.30*
Set D £11·50	*D 7–9.30, Sun 7–9*
About £42 for two	*Seats 65 Parties 14*

■ For a discount on next year's guide, see Offer for Answers.

Le Nautique

St Peter Port

R Map 3 E4 Guernsey
Quay Steps
Guernsey (0481) 21714
French cooking
Owner manager Carlo Graziani
Credit Access, Amex, Diners, Visa
   Picture windows overlook the harbour from this popular restaurant, where owner Carlo Graziani and his staff provide charming, warm-hearted service. The menu is French with a leaning towards seafood: lobsters, langoustines, Dover sole, excellent grilled sea bass with fennel. There's also a good choice for meat-eaters, plus nice sweets like profiteroles with chocolate sauce. ❂

■ *About £40 for two*	*L 12–2*
Seats 60	*D 7–10*
Parties 28	*Parking Difficult*
Closed Sun, 25 & 26 Dec & 1st 2 wks Jan	

Da Nello's *NEW ENTRY*

St Peter Port

R Map 3 E4 Guernsey
46 Pollet Street
Guernsey (0481) 21552
Credit Access, Amex, Visa
   Nello Ciotti's pleasantly intimate restaurant is situated in a shopping street just behind the main seafront road. The menu features quite a few Italian favourites, including saltimbocca, chicken with lemon and fettuccine or spaghetti with a superlative pesto sauce. Charcoal grills are also popular, along with daily fish specials – lobster, mussels, monkfish – and seasonal game. The £4·30 set lunch is a bargain. ❂

■ *Set L £4·30*	*L 12–2*
Set D £7·90	*D 6.30–10.30*
About £30 for two	*Parking Limited*
Seats 56	*Parties 22*
Closed Feb, 26 & 27 Dec & 1 Jan	

■ We publish annually, so make sure you use the current edition. It's worth it!

Old Government House Hotel

St Peter Port

H 67% £C/D
Map 3 E4 Guernsey
Ann's Place
Guernsey (0481) 24921. Tlx 4191144
Credit Access, Amex, Diners, Visa. LVs
   A hotel since 1858, this imposing building has fine harbour views. Bedrooms – some very spacious – are furnished traditionally; day rooms include a peaceful lounge, two bars and a basement disco. Service, maintenance and breakfast all need improving. No dogs.
Amenities garden, outdoor swimming pool, solarium, hairdressing, laundry service, 24-hour lounge service.

■ *Rooms 72*	*Confirm by arrang.*
en suite bath/shower 72	*Last dinner 9.15*
Direct dial Yes	*Parking Limited*
Room TV Yes	*Room service 24 hours*

■ Our inspectors never book in the
name of Egon Ronay's Guides;
they disclose their identity only
after paying their bills.

St Pierre Park Hotel

St Peter Port

H **77% £C *E***
Map 3 E4 Guernsey
Rohais
Guernsey (0481) 28282. Tlx 4191662
Credit Access, Amex, Diners, Visa

An impressive array of sports, leisure and
conference facilities combine at this modern
luxury hotel to suit the needs of businessmen and
holiday-makers alike. Just a few miles from St
Peter Port, the hotel boasts fine grounds studded
with ornamental lakes and a grand drive which
sweeps past a small fountain to the entrance
foyer. Guests may relax and admire views of the
grounds from the spacious lounge and bar areas,
attractively decorated in Regency style. Generous
bedrooms, all with their own balconies, have
stylish contemporary darkwood fitted units and
are further enhanced by handsome soft
furnishings: coordinated curtains, bedspreads
and upholstery. All have extremely well-equipped
private bathrooms. Staff generally seem friendly

and efficient. No dogs. *Amenities* garden, indoor
swimming pool, sauna, solarium, whirlpool bath,
keep-fit equipment, beauty salon, tennis, 9-hole
golf course, croquet, games room, laundry
service, coffee shop (10am–10pm), 24-hour
lounge service, shopping arcade, children's
playground, courtesy coach.

■ *Rooms* 135	*Confirm by* arrang.
en suite bath/shower 135	*Last dinner 9.30*
Direct dial Yes	*Parking* Ample
Room TV Yes	*Room service* 24 hours

JERSEY

Water's Edge Hotel

Bouley Bay

H **70% £C**
Map 3 F4 Jersey
The Slipway, Trinity
Jersey (0534) 62777. Tlx 4191462
Manager Mr B. Oliver
Credit Access, Amex, Diners, Visa

From the comfortable lounges of this efficiently-
run holiday hotel one can, on a clear day, see the
Cherbourg Peninsula. There is a handsome,
wood-panelled bar and a formal restaurant
furnished in French style with stunning,
panoramic views. Spacious, impeccably-kept
bedrooms are mostly Regency in style, with
prettily coordinated fabrics. Guests in the best
rooms enjoy views over Bouley Bay while the rest
overlook a colourful terraced garden. All offer well-
equipped bath or shower rooms. Polite,
considerate staff follow the excellent example set

by their general manager. *Amenities* garden,
outdoor swimming pool, sauna, solarium, laundry
service, 24-hour lounge service.

■ *Rooms* 56	*Confirm by* arrang.
en suite bath/shower 56	*Last dinner 9.45*
Room phone Yes	*Parking* Limited
Room TV Yes	*Room service* 24 hours
Closed end Oct–end Mar	

Hotel de la Plage

Havre des Pas

H **67% £D/E**
Map 3 F4 Jersey
St Helier
Jersey (0534) 23474. Tlx 4192328
Credit Access, Amex, Diners, Visa

Right on the beach, this attractive holiday hotel
offers splendid sea views from the balconied front
bedrooms. Spacious public rooms include a smart
lounge with sun terrace, and two cocktail bars.

Bedrooms are traditional and comfortable, all with
spotless bathrooms. Charming staff. No dogs.
Amenities laundry service, solarium, keep-fit
equipment, games room.

■ *Rooms* 78	*Confirm by* arrang.
en suite bath/shower 78	*Last dinner 9*
Direct dial Yes	*Parking* Ample
Room TV Yes	*Room service* 24 hours
Closed end Oct–April	

Ommaroo Hotel
Havre des Pas

H 58% £D/E &
Map 3 F4 Jersey
St Helier
Jersey (0534) 23493. Tlx 4192225
Manager Mr M. Troy
Credit Access, Amex, Diners, Visa
  Behind the attractive Victorian frontage are several quiet and simply appointed lounges, one with a bar. Modest bedrooms, some with sea-facing balconies, are traditionally furnished; the majority have up-to-date en suite bathrooms.
Amenities garden, games room, laundry service, 24-hour lounge service.

■ *Rooms* 85	*Confirm by arrang.*
en suite bath/shower 74	*Last dinner* 8.30
Direct dial Yes	*Parking* Ample
Room TV Yes	*Room service* 24 hours
Closed end Oct–Apr	

Moorings Hotel
Gorey

H 64% £E
Map 3 F4 Jersey
Gorey Pier
Jersey (0534) 53633. Tlx 4192085
Credit Access, Amex, Visa
  A friendly welcome awaits visitors to this cosy, harbourside hotel below the fine Mont Orgueil Castle. Snug public rooms include an intimate panelled bar and spacious TV lounge. Bedrooms are spotlessly clean with deep-pile carpets and co-ordinated colours. Bathrooms excel with first-rate showers and splendidly thick towels. No children under eight. *Amenities* laundry service, 24 hr lounge service.

■ *Rooms* 17	*Confirm by arrang.*
en suite bath/shower 17	*Last dinner* 10.30
Direct dial Yes	*Parking* Limited
Room TV Yes	*Room service* 24 hours

Old Court House Hotel
Gorey

H 65% £E &
Map 3 F4 Jersey
Jersey (0534) 54444. Tlx 54444
Manager Mr R. Smale
Credit Access, Amex, Diners, Visa
  Built around the old courthouse, this modern-ised hotel is a short walk from the beach. Public areas include a smart cocktail bar and an aptly named Quiet Room. The best bedrooms, in the newer wing, have balconies and attractive units; others are more basic. No dogs.
Amenities garden, sauna, outdoor swimming pool, solarium, laundry service, in-house movies.

■ *Rooms* 58	*Confirm by arrang.*
en suite bath/shower 58	*Last dinner* 9
Room phone Yes	*Parking* Ample
Room TV Yes	*Room service* 24 hours
Closed mid Oct–Apr	

Sea Crest Hotel
Petit Port

HR 62% £D/E
Map 3 F4 Jersey
Nr La Corbière
Jersey (0534) 42687
Owner manager Victor Cornaglia
Credit Access, Amex, Visa
  Enjoying a pretty coastal setting, this civilised little hotel, run in friendly fashion, offers a cosy bar, a terrace and a charming sun lounge. Bright bedrooms have really comfortable beds. No children under 7. No dogs.
Amenities garden, outdoor swimming pool, laundry service, 24-hour lounge service.

■ *Rooms* 7	*Confirm by arrang.*
en suite bath/shower 7	*Last dinner* 10
Direct dial Yes	*Parking* Ample
Room TV Yes	*Room service* All day
Closed Nov–Mar	

Sea Crest Hotel Restaurant

Alfresco eating is a fair-weather attraction at this popular restaurant overlooking the bay. The menu has few surprises being a conventional compilation of French and Italian-inspired dishes – but don't be put off by this! The cooking is very sound, and tip-top ingredients – sought out by Victor at the market each morning – are used in delightful dishes like scallops meunière, veal marsala and superb châteaubriand béarnaise. Simpatico service from an Italian team. Interesting wines. 🍷 Well-chosen ☺

■ *Set L* £7·50	*L* 12.30–2
About £38 *for two*	*D* 7.30–10
Seats 50	*Parties* 50
Closed Nov–Mar	

Portelet Hotel
Portelet Bay

H 66% £C/D
Map 3 F4 Jersey
Nr St Brelade
Jersey (0534) 41204. Tlx 4192039
Credit Access, Amex, Diners, Visa
  Set high up over St Brelade's Bay, this modernised 1920s hotel offers panoramic views. Spacious public areas include a well-planned foyer, cocktail bar, ballroom and sun lounge. Many of the practically appointed bedrooms have private balconies. No dogs. *Amenities* garden, outdoor swimming pool, tennis, games room, valeting, laundry service.

■ *Rooms* 86	*Confirm by arrang.*
en suite bath/shower 86	*Last dinner* 9
Room phone Yes	*Parking* Ample
Room TV Yes	*Room service* 24 hours
Closed mid Oct–Apr	

St Aubin ▶

La Haule Manor
St Aubin

H **60% £D/E**
Map 3 F4 Jersey
La Haule
Jersey (0534) 41426
Credit Access, Amex, Visa
An 18th-century manor house in pleasant gardens overlooking a wide sandy beach. There are two comfortable lounges, a warmly-decorated cocktail bar and a function room. Many of the neat, modern bedrooms have fine sea views; they are mainly large, with many comforts including hairdryers and tea-makers. *Amenities* garden, laundry service, 24-hour lounge service.

- Rooms 20
- en suite bath/shower 14
- Room phone No
- Room TV Yes
- Closed Oct–Apr

Confirm by 6
Last dinner 8.15
Parking Ample
Room service 24 hours

Hotel La Tour
St Aubin

H **63% £F**
Map 3 F4 Jersey
High Street
Jersey (0534) 43770
Manager Mr J. Arena
Credit Access, Amex, Visa
Commanding fine sea views, this handsome Georgian house stands at the top of the High Street (check directions). There is a smart bar, a spacious lounge and quiet TV room. Well-kept bedrooms are attractively furnished; most rooms have neat private bath or shower. No dogs. *Amenities* terrace.

- Rooms 21
- en suite bath/shower 18
- Room phone No
- Room TV Yes
- Closed Nov–Mar

Confirm by arrang.
Last dinner 9.30
Parking Limited
Room service Limited

Old Court House Inn Restaurant
St Aubin's Harbour

R **Map 3 F4** Jersey
Jersey (0534) 41156
Seafood
Owner managers Jonathan & Vicky Sharp
Credit Access, Visa
Relaxed and informal, this oak-beamed restaurant is one of the island's most popular eateries. Seafood dominates both carte and daily-changing blackboard, ranging from oysters and scallops to sole, salmon and sundry smoked fish. Meaty choices include steak and simple veal dishes and there's a good selection of fresh vegetables. Simple sweets like sherry trifle. Traditional Sunday lunch. Book. ℗

- Set L Sun only £8
- About £32 for two
- Seats 56 Parties 20
- Closed 25 & 26 Dec

L 12.30–2.30
D 7.30–10.30
Parking Difficult

Atlantic Hotel
St Brelade

H **75% £C/D** *E*
Map 3 F4 Jersey
La Moye
Jersey (0534) 44101. Tlx 4192405
Manager Mario Dugini
Credit Access, Amex, Diners, Visa
A well-run modern hotel set in beautiful, peaceful landscaped gardens adjoining an 18-hole championship golf course. There is a magnificent sea view; Guernsey and Sark are visible on a clear day. Extensive refurbishment throughout the public areas has recently taken place. All the spacious and comfortable bedrooms have balconies, smart darkwood furniture and bedside controls for radio and TV. The attractive bathrooms are all equipped with hairdryers. Excellent staff and a first-class manager. Good breakfasts. No children under two. No dogs.

Amenities garden, outdoor swimming pool, tennis, in-house movies (free), 24-hour lounge service.

- Rooms 46
- en suite bath/shower 46
- Direct dial Yes
- Room TV Yes
- Closed 1 Jan–5 Mar

Confirm by arrang.
Last dinner 9.15
Parking Ample
Room service 24 hours

La Place Hotel
St Brelade

H **68% £D** &
Map 3 F4 Jersey
Route Du Coin, La Haule
Jersey (0534) 44261. Tlx 4192522
Credit Access, Amex, Diners, Visa
A 17th-century granite farmhouse is at the heart of this comfortable hotel, where an ivy-clad courtyard and cosy beamed lounge are appealing original features. The revamped bar is modern and colourful, a style echoed in many of the bedrooms, best of which have poolside patios. Inclusive terms only in July and August. *Amenities* terrace, outdoor swimming pool, sauna, laundry service, 24-hour lounge service.

- Rooms 40
- en suite bath/shower 40
- Direct dial Yes
- Room TV Yes

Confirm by arrang.
Last dinner 9.30
Parking Ample
Room service 24 hours

Hotel Château Valeuse St Brelade's Bay

H **64% £E**
Map 3 F4 Jersey
Jersey (0534) 43476
Managers Mr & Mrs C. Magris
Credit Access, Visa
Secluded from the bustle of St Brelade's Bay, this relaxing hotel is set in attractive gardens. Housekeeping is excellent throughout, from the smart public areas – including a swish cocktail bar

– through to the spotless bathrooms. Front bedrooms enjoy bay views. No children under 5. No dogs. *Amenities* garden, outdoor swimming pool, laundry service, 24-hour lounge service.

■ *Rooms* 28	*Confirm by arrang.*
en suite bath/shower 28	*Last dinner* 9
Direct dial Yes	*Parking* Ample
Room TV Yes	*Room service* 24 hours
Closed Nov–Mar	

Hotel l'Horizon St Brelade's Bay

HR **76% £B** *E*
Map 3 F4 Jersey
St Brelade
Jersey (0534) 43101. Tlx 4192281
Manager Mr J. M. H. Wileman
Credit Access, Amex, Diners, Visa
A sun terrace running the full length of this smart white hotel makes the most of the magical seafront setting. The picture-windowed bar and lounge have been attractively redecorated in soft pastels, and the handsome period-furnished drawing room is a popular choice for private meetings. Sea-facing bedrooms with generous balconies particularly impress, but all rooms have

pleasingly-coordinated fabrics and are extremely well equipped. Spacious bathrooms have shower attachments. No dogs. *Amenities* terrace, indoor swimming pool, sauna, solarium, keep fit equipment, beauty therapy, hairdressing, in-house movies (free), laundry service, 24-hour lounge service.

■ *Rooms* 104	*Confirm by* 6
en suite bath/shower 104	*Last dinner* 10.45
Direct dial Yes	*Parking* Ample
Room TV Yes	*Room service* 24 hours

Star Grill

Excellent fresh seafood features strongly on the lengthy international menu at this luxurious restaurant. Choose from garlicky bouillabaisse, locally caught lobster, Dover sole Walewska and salmon à l'hongroise. Confirmed carnivores can tuck into charcoal grills or sauced offerings like veal with wine and cream. Good wines at fair prices.

■ *Set L £10*	L 12.45–2.45
Set D £16	D 7.45–10.45
About £43 for two	*Seats* 50 *Parties* 30
Closed Mon (except Bank Hols) & Tues following Bank Hols	

■ If we recommend meals in a hotel or inn, a separate entry is made for its restaurant.

St Brelade's Bay Hotel St Brelade's Bay

H **70% £C**
Map 3 F4 Jersey
Jersey (0534) 46141
Owner manager Mr D. J. Brecknell
Credit Access, Amex, Diners, Visa
Standing in 7½ acres of terraced gardens, this fine holiday hotel offers impressive sea views and excellent leisure facilities for all the family. Public rooms are elegant and warmly welcoming, particularly the foyer-lounge with its leather chesterfields, polished parquet floor and Persian rugs. Red-stained cane chairs provide a touch of chic in the cocktail bar, and there's a stylish sun lounge. Attractive bedrooms (best are sea-facing) include 20 with smart cane furniture and marble-fitted bathrooms. No dogs.
Amenities garden, outdoor swimming pool, sauna, solarium, tennis, putting, pitch & putt,

croquet, games room, billiards, snooker, laundry service, children's playroom & playground.

■ *Rooms* 82	*Confirm by arrang.*
en suite bath/shower 82	*Last dinner* 9
Direct dial Yes	*Parking* Ample
Room TV Yes	*Room service* 24 hours
Closed Oct–Apr	

St Clement's Bay ▶

Hotel Ambassadeur   St Clement's Bay

H **66%** **£E**
Map 3 F4 Jersey
Jersey (0534) 24455
Manager Mr R. Corral
Credit Access, Amex, Diners, Visa
 Facing south, with fine views across the bay,
this efficiently managed hotel makes a
comfortable place to stay. Attractive day rooms
include a chintzy, picture-windowed lounge and

brick-walled bar. Bright, airy bedrooms with
lightwood units have bedside controls and
excellent private bathrooms. *Amenities* outdoor
swimming pool, cafe (11am–6pm).

■ *Rooms* 39	*Confirm by arrang.*
en suite bath/shower 39	*Last dinner* 9.45
Room phone Yes	*Parking* Ample
Room TV Yes	*Room service* 24 hours
Closed early Jan–early Mar	

Apollo Hotel   St Helier

H **65%** **£D/E**
Map 3 F4 Jersey
9 St Saviour's Road
Jersey (0534) 25441. Tlx 4192086
Manager Mr J. Ferreira
Credit Access, Amex, Diners, Visa
 Smartly refurbished modern hotel whose public
areas include an attractive lounge and two bars.
The new bedrooms have good bathrooms and

older rooms are being upgraded. Street-facing
rooms are noisy. No dogs. *Amenities* indoor
swimming pool, sauna, solarium, whirlpool bath,
gymnasium, games room, satellite TV, teletext, coffee shop (11–11), 24-hour lounge service.

■ *Rooms* 79	*Confirm by* 6
en suite bath/shower 79	*Last dinner* 8.45
Direct dial Yes	*Parking* Ample
Room TV Yes	*Room service* 24 hours

Beaufort Hotel   St Helier

H **59%** **£D/E**
Map 3 F4 Jersey
Green Street
Jersey (0534) 32471. Tlx 4192160
Manager Mr F. Pietrogiovanna
Credit Access, Amex, Diners, Visa
 A low-rise modern hotel just outside the town
centre. Public areas include a large open-plan
reception/lounge with a terrace and a cocktail

bar. The spacious bedrooms are well-equipped,
with hairdryers, trouser presses and tea-makers,
but standards of maintenance overall are
disappointing. No dogs. *Amenities* indoor
swimming pool, whirlpool bath, in-house movies.

■ *Rooms* 54	*Confirm by arrang.*
en suite bath/shower 54	*Last dinner* 8.45
Direct dial Yes	*Parking* Ample
Room TV Yes	*Room service* 24 hours

La Capannina   *NEW ENTRY*   St Helier

R ♿ **Map 3 F4** Jersey
65–67 Halkett Place
Jersey (0534) 34602
Italian cooking
Owner manager Mr Tino Rossi
Credit Access, Amex, Diners, Visa
 A long-established restaurant where you can
find an intimate atmosphere and sound Italian
cooking. Modern dishes such as tagliolini

Capannina – ribbons of pasta dyed with
cuttlefish ink, with cream and smoked salmon
sauce – are available as well as standard
favourites. Game in season, and daily seafood
specials. ❦

■ *Set D* £10·50 (winter)	*L* 12–2
About £40 *for two*	*D* 7–10
Seats 70 *Parties* 40	*Parking* Limited
Closed Sun, Bank Hols & 1 wk Xmas	

Grand Hotel   St Helier

HR **68%** **£B/C**
Map 3 F4 Jersey
Esplanade
Jersey (0534) 22301. Tlx 4192104
Owner managers Lapidus family
Credit Access, Amex, Diners, Visa
 The hotel where Debussy composed La Mer.
Public rooms are for the most part sombre and
traditional in character. Spacious, well-equipped
bedrooms are more contemporary in style. No
dogs. *Amenities* indoor swimming pool, sauna,
solarium, whirlpool bath, gymnasium, beauty
salon, hairdressing, snooker, in-house movies
(free), laundry service, 24-hour lounge service.

■ *Rooms* 116	*Confirm by* 6
en suite bath/shower 116	*Last dinner* 10.30
Direct dial Yes	*Parking* Limited
Room TV Yes	*Room service* 24 hours

Victoria's ♔ ♿

Manager Augusto Travaglini
Eat in style at this opulent restaurant with
Victorian-inspired decor, smart professional
service and a long international menu. The day's
specialities are a good bet in a repertoire that
ranges from soups and pâtés to grills, flambés
and sauced entrées. The choice might include a
deliciously creamy fish soup and, to follow,
medallions of milk-fed veal served in a sauce of
morels. Sound cooking extends to vegetarian
dishes like pancake of grated vegetables with
fresh tomato sauce. Good conventional sweets.
♟ Well-chosen ❦

■ *About* £40 *for two*	*L* 12.30–2.15
Seats 140 *Parties* 140	*D* 7–10.30
Closed Sun, Good Fri & Spring Bank Hol	

Pomme D'or Hotel   St Helier

H 65% £D/E ♿
Map 3 F4 Jersey
Esplanade
Jersey (0534) 78644. Tlx 4192309
Credit Access, Amex, Diners, Visa

A pleasing position opposite the harbour and a high standard of comfort are the main attractions here. The public areas are spacious, modern and well-designed; there is a bierkeller-themed bar in the basement. The bedrooms have soft colour schemes, trouser presses and spotless modern bathrooms. Maintenance is excellent throughout. No dogs. *Amenities* garden, laundry service, coffee shop (7am–10pm), 24-hour lounge service.

■ *Rooms* 151	*Confirm by* 6
en suite bath/shower 151	*Last dinner* 9
Direct dial Yes	*Parking* Limited
Room TV Yes	*Room service* 24 hours

■ Any person using our name to obtain free hospitality is a fraud. Proprietors, please inform the police and us.

Little Grove Hotel   St Lawrence

HR 71% £B
Map 3 F4 Jersey
Rue du Haut
Jersey (0534) 25321. Tlx 4192567
Credit Access, Amex, Diners, Visa

Built of local pink granite, this handsome country mansion stands in gently sloping grounds a ten-minute drive from St Helier. Fine fabrics and supremely comfortable sofas and armchairs make relaxation easy in the peaceful, elegant and finely proportioned lounges, with their exposed granite walls and stone fireplaces, and there's a smart bar, too. Pretty bedrooms (including three superior rooms with larger sitting areas) are individually decorated in excellent taste and offer welcome extras like tissues, books and flowers. The bathrooms are splendidly equipped. Delicious breakfasts. No children under 14. No dogs. *Amenities* garden, outdoor swimming pool, croquet, laundry service, 24-hour lounge service, courtesy car.

■ *Rooms* 13	*Confirm by* arrang.
en suite bath/shower 13	*Last dinner* 9.30
Direct dial Yes	*Parking* Ample
Room TV Yes	*Room service* 24 hours

Little Grove Hotel Restaurant ⛃

There's a strong French influence throughout the lengthy menu offered by Peter Marek at this chic, relaxing restaurant. Typifying his appealing and creditable range are dishes such as warm salmon and sole mousse with a light seafood sauce, king-prawn stuffed chicken breast, Scotch fillet served in a hot pepper sauce and an excellent noisette of lamb served with peppers in a Madeira sauce. Ingredients are of excellent fresh quality. Good crisp vegetables. ⚑ Well-chosen ⊖

■ *Set L* £9·80	*L* 12.30–2
Set D £17·05	*D* 7–9.30
About £48 *for two*	*Seats* 40 *Parties* 20

■ Our inspectors are our full-time employees; they are professionally trained by us.

Mermaid Hotel   St Peter

H 64% £D/E
Map 3 F4 Jersey
Airport Road
Jersey (0534) 41255. Tlx 4192249
Credit Access, Amex, Diners, Visa

Gardens and a natural lake provide attractive views for most rooms in this modern two-storey hotel near the airport. Redecoration has brightened ground-floor rooms; all are well equipped, with en suite bathrooms. The adjoining 18th-century tavern provides an atmospheric setting for drinks. *Amenities* garden, outdoor swimming pool, games room, laundry service, 24-hour lounge service.

■ *Rooms* 68	*Confirm by* arrang.
en suite bath/shower 68	*Last dinner* 9.30
Direct dial Yes	*Parking* Ample
Room TV Yes	*Room service* 24 hours

Longueville Manor Hotel
St Saviour

HR 81% £B/C
Map 3 F4 Jersey
Jersey (0534) 25501. Tlx 4192306
Owner managers Lewis & Dufty families
Credit Access, Amex, Diners, Visa

Wooded grounds with a lake and lawns make a tranquil setting for this stone-built manor house. Public areas offer plenty of comfort with deep-cushioned armchairs, nice antiques and flowing drapes. There's a bar with French windows leading to the garden, and a second, open-air bar by the pool. Many of the bedrooms have been improved and some now have small seating areas. All are furnished to a high standard with period pieces (including an 18th-century four-

poster) and fine fabrics. Remote-control TVs and radios are standard. Bathrooms are no less luxurious. Discreet and obliging staff. No children under seven. *Amenities* garden, outdoor swimming pool, in-house movies (free), teletext, valeting, laundry service, 24-hour lounge service.

■ *Rooms* 35	*Confirm by arrang.*
en suite bath/shower 35	*Last dinner* 9.30
Direct dial Yes	*Parking* Ample
Room TV Yes	*Room service* 24 hours

Restaurant ♛

There's a choice of two dining rooms here – one intimate and richly panelled, the other large, light and modern. Barry Forster cooks with care and dedication, using top-quality produce. Start perhaps with terrine of veal sweetbreads and wild mushrooms, then move on to casserole of monkfish or grilled beef with herbs and bone marrow. There's a selection of unpasteurised French and English cheeses and some pleasant sweets. Good wine list. ♟ **Well-chosen** ⊖

■ *Set L* from £10	*L* 12.30–2
Set D £15.50	*D* 7.30–9.30
About £50 for two	*Seats* 65 *Parties* 15

SARK

Aval du Creux Hotel
Sark

HR 56% £F
Map 3 E4 Sark
Sark (048 183) 2036
Owner managers Peter & Cheryl Tonks
Credit Access, Visa

A tractor takes guests from the harbour to this old stone farmhouse, which offers two relaxing lounges and a cheerful bar agleam with brassware. Main-house bedrooms are spacious, homely and old-fashioned, those in the annexe smaller and more modern. All but one have neat shower rooms. Housekeeping variable. *Amenities* garden.

■ *Rooms* 13	*Confirm by* arrang.
en suite bath/shower 12	*Last dinner* 8.30
Room phone No	*Parking* No cars
Room TV Yes	*Room service* None
Closed 1 Oct–Easter	

Restaurant ♧

Picture windows overlook the garden at this modestly appointed restaurant, noted for Cheryl Tonks' straightforward and enjoyable cooking. Seafood features prominently, with choices like local crab or grilled king prawns in herby garlic butter to start, lobster and bacon-wrapped scallops among main courses. Meaty alternatives include duckling sauced with honey and orange, or Cumberland lamb, and there's a tempting sweet trolley to finish. Peter Tonks directs service in extrovert fashion. ⊖

■ *Set D* £10	*L* 12–1.30
About £35 for two	*D* 7.30–8.30
Seats 40	*Parties* 40
Closed 1 Oct–Easter	

Hotel Petit Champ
Sark

HR 61% £F
Map 3 E4 Sark
Sark (048 183) 2046
Owner managers Mr & Mrs T. Scott
Credit Access, Amex, Diners, Visa

Charming owners and a delightfully secluded setting make this well-run hotel an ideal holiday retreat. There are three lounges for relaxing and a little bar. Spotless bedrooms (the best have balconies) are furnished in simple, traditional style. Half board only. No children under 7. No dogs. *Amenities* garden, outdoor swimming pool, hotel carriage.

■ *Rooms* 16	*Confirm by* arrang.
en suite bath/shower 13	*Last dinner* 8.15
Room phone No	*Parking* No cars
Room TV No	*Room service* Limited
Closed Oct–Apr	

Restaurant

Fixed-price menus make good use of vegetables from the hotel garden and local seafood at this cosy, informal restaurant. Deep-fried cheese soufflés, snails in puff pastry or brandy-enriched lobster soup could start your meal in splendid fashion, followed perhaps by baked conger filled with mushrooms and prawns, hot Sark lobster with hollandaise sauce or chicken breast with a creamy asparagus sauce. Tempting sweets conclude a thoroughly enjoyable meal. Non-smoking area. ⊖

■ *Set L* £6.75	*L* 12.30–1.30
Set D £9.50	*D* 8–8.15
About £25 for two	*Seats* 50 *Parties* 20
Closed Oct–Apr	

HR 60% £E/F
Map 3 E4 Sark
Via Guernsey
Sark (0481 83) 2001
Owner managers Armorgie family
Credit Amex
   A wooded valley provides a sheltered and most attractive setting for this handsome old granite hotel. Homely comfort is the order of the day, both in the day rooms and in the simple, immaculate bedrooms. Staff are cheerful and relaxed. No dogs. *Amenities* garden, outdoor swimming pool, coffee shop (10am–8.30pm).

Stocks Hotel Restaurant

Dinner in this spacious restaurant overlooking the garden is a four-course, fixed-price meal, with local crab and lobster attracting a supplementary charge. Mussels à la grecque, tagliatelle carbonara, leek and potato soup, veal fricasse and roast beef are typical choices, and main courses are served with mounds of seasonal vegetables. The sideboard beckons with a tempting selection of sweets like pineapple syllabub or delicious banoffi pie. 🕲

■ *Rooms* 24
en suite bath/shower 14
Room phone No
Room TV No
Closed Oct–Easter

Confirm by arrang.
Last dinner 8.30
Parking No cars
Room service Limited

■ *Set D* £10·50
About £28 for two
Closed Oct–Easter

D only 7.30–8.30
Seats 60
Parties 60

ISLE OF MAN

La Rosette   Ballasalla

R ⌘ **Map 13 B6** Isle of Man
Main Street
Castletown (0624) 822940
French cooking
   Bob and Rosa Phillips take good care respectively of cooking and service at this popular little restaurant just 15 minutes' drive from Douglas. There's plenty of choice on the mainly French-inspired menus, from prawn omelette with

saffron sauce to queen scallops sautéed in garlic and parsley butter, roast quails and tender beef medallions in a sweet and sour sauce. Vegetables are varied and desserts nice. Booking advisable.
♀ Well-chosen 🕲
■ *About* £49 for two
Seats 40
Parties 16
Closed L Mon, all Sun & 1st 2 wks Jan

L 12–2.30
D 7–10.30
Parking Ample

Palace Hotel   Douglas

H 58% £C/D
Map 13 B6 Isle of Man
Central Promenade
Douglas (0624) 74521. Tlx 627742
Credit Access, Amex, Diners, Visa
   Gradual improvements are planned at this 1960s seafront hotel which boasts a casino and night club. Top of the projects is a new leisure complex. Comfortable bedrooms, many with fine

views, offer mini-bars, tea-makers and functional bathrooms. There are two bright and cheerful bars, one overlooking the sea. *Amenities* outdoor swimming pool, in-house movies, laundry service, hairdressing.
■ *Rooms* 135
en suite bath/shower 135
Direct dial Yes
Room TV Yes

Confirm by arrang.
Last dinner 11.30
Parking Ample
Room service 24 hours

♀ indicates a **well-chosen** house wine.

Sefton Hotel   Douglas

H 62% £D ⌘
Map 13 B6 Isle of Man
Harris Promenade
Douglas (0624) 26011. Tlx 627519
Manager Christopher Robertshaw
Credit Access, Amex, Diners, Visa
   A Victorian seafront hotel with comfortable lounges, welcoming bars and a smart health and leisure club. Bedrooms of various sizes, some

with sea views, have pastel shades and contemporary fabrics. No dogs. *Amenities* indoor swimming pool, sauna, solarium, whirlpool bath, keep-fit equipment, laundry service, coffee shop (9.45am–1am), 24-hour lounge service.
■ *Rooms* 80
en suite bath/shower 80
Direct dial Yes
Room TV Yes

Confirm by arrang.
Last dinner 9.15
Parking Ample
Room service Limited

Grand Island Hotel *NEW ENTRY*   Ramsey

H 62% £D/E
Map 13 B5 Isle of Man
Bride Road
Ramsey (0624) 812455. Tlx 629849
Credit Access, Amex, Diners, Visa
    There are splendid sea views from this
extended Georgian house with a leafy lounge, two
bars and a well-equipped leisure centre. Decent-
sized bedrooms, good bathrooms.

Amenities garden, indoor swimming pool, sauna,
solarium, whirlpool bath, keep-fit equipment,
beauty salon, hairdressing, putting, croquet, sea
fishing, snooker, in-house movies (free), laundry
service, 24-hour lounge service, helipad.

■ *Rooms* 57	*Confirm by arrang.*
en suite bath/shower 57	*Last dinner* 10.30
Direct dial Yes	*Parking* Ample
Room TV Yes	*Room service* 24 hours

Harbour Bistro   Ramsey

R ♀ ⑤ Map 13 B5 Isle of Man
East Street
Ramsey (0624) 814182
    Locals and visitors are united in praise of Karl
Meier's friendly and unassuming bistro, where
sole, plaice, salmon and giant prawns are among
the many fishy delights. Succulent Manx queenies
are a particular speciality, cooked and sauced in a
variety of ways. Fisherman's pie is another

favourite, but if you prefer meat there are plenty of
steak, chicken and duck dishes. Hot lemon
pancakes and strawberry shortbread are popular
sweets. In summer it's advisable to book. Good-
value clarets include Ch. Gloria '70. ⊖

■ *About £30 for two*	*D only* 6.30–10.30
Seats 40 *Parties* 20	*Parking* Ample
Closed Sun, Good Fri, 24–26 Dec & 3 wks Jan	

HOTELS RESTAURANTS AND INNS

NORTHERN IRELAND

Belfast ▶

Europa Hotel Belfast

H **70% £C/D** *E*
Town plan A3 Co. Antrim
Great Victoria Street BT2 7AP
Belfast (0232) 327000. Tlx 74491
Credit Access, Amex, Diners, Visa

Formerly known as the Forum Hotel, this smart, modern, city-centre hotel offers roomy public areas and comfortable bedrooms. The first-floor public rooms include a lounge area with plenty of red velour seating and a relaxing cocktail bar. In lively contrast is the public bar, recently refurbished in an Edwardian style, where there's live music five days a week. There's also a penthouse discothèque up on the 12th floor. Good-sized bedrooms are practically furnished and provided with mini-bars, tea-makers and remote-control TVs, together with well-equipped bathrooms. There are conference and banquet

facilities. *Amenities* in-house movies (free), satellite TV, laundry service, coffee shop (7.30am–11.30pm, Sun 8am–6pm), 24-hour lounge service, kiosk.

■ *Rooms* 200	*Confirm by* 6
en suite bath/shower 200	*Last dinner* 11
Direct dial Yes	*Parking* Limited
Room TV Yes	*Room service* 24 hours

Manor House *NEW ENTRY* Belfast

R ♧ **Town plan A4** Co. Antrim
47 Donegall Pass
Belfast (0232) 238755
Chinese cooking
Credit Visa

Amiable owner Joe Wong sets great store by good cooking (his own) and good friendly service at this splendid little Chinese restaurant. The menu provides a wide variety of excellent

Cantonese fare, from spare ribs and stuffed scallops to king prawns with chilli and salt, sizzling dishes, hot pots and roast meats. Dim sum are a daytime delight and there are various set menus, including a three-course high tea.

■ *Set L & D from* £9·50	*Meals* 12–11.30
About £27 *for two*	*Parking* Ample
Seats 50 *Parties* 50	*Closed* 2 days Xmas

Mews Belfast

R **Town plan A5** Co. Antrim
3 University Street
Belfast (0232) 225137
Credit Access, Amex, Visa

Evelyn and Sam Hazlett have created a relaxed, informal atmosphere at this stylish restaurant near the university. Good, fresh ingredients are used throughout a frequently-changed menu that might feature such appetising

dishes as succulent steamed scallops with a creamed spinach sauce, pan-fried pork flamed in port and sirloin steak sauced with Meaux mustard. ℮

■ *Set L* £8·95	*L Sun only* 1–3
About £33 *for two*	*D* 6.30–12.30
Seats 48	*Parking* Ample
Closed D Sun, Easter Mon & Tues & 25 & 26 Dec	

Restaurant 44 Belfast

R **Town plan A3** Co. Antrim
44 Bedford Street
Belfast (0232) 244844
Owner manager Jenny Pearson
Credit Access, Amex, Diners, Visa. **LVs**

The decor and the staff both contribute to the cosy atmosphere in this pleasant restaurant. Tasty fresh food is the order of the day on an uncomplicated menu that runs from pâte-stuffed

mushrooms and warm chicken liver salad to scampi, salmon, sole and meat dishes, both plain and sauced. Simple sweets. ♀ **Well-chosen** ℮

■ *Set L* £11	*L* 12–3
Set D £13	*D* 6–10.30
About £38 *for two*	*Parking* Limited
Seats 50	*Parties* 50
Closed L Sat, all Sun, 1 Jan, Easter Mon & Tues, 12 & 13 July & 25 & 26 Dec	

The Strand Belfast

R **Town plan A5** Co. Antrim
Stramillis Road
Belfast (0232) 682266
Credit Access, Amex, Diners, Visa

The Turkingtons have built up a great following at their friendly bistro-style restaurant, so booking is strongly advised. The menu offers something for everyone, from seafood pancakes, artichoke hearts à la grecque and chicken nibbles with a

yoghurt mint dip to pepper steak, honeyed pork and zippy-fresh plaice in a peanut and breadcrumb coat. Good honest cooking with some imaginative touches. Note that it's now open all day.

■ *About* £25 *for two*	*Meals* noon–11
Seats 80 *Parties* 25	*Parking* Ample
Closed Sun, Easter Mon, 12 & 13 July & 25 & 26 Dec	

Wellington Park Hotel   Belfast

H **56% £C/D**
Town Plan A5 Co. Antrim
21 Malone Road BT9 6RU
Belfast (0232) 381111. Tlx 747052
Manager Mr Felix Mooney
Credit Access, Amex, Diners, Visa
   Modest accommodation in a purpose-built hotel
near Queen's University. Bedrooms, fairly basic in
style, include some with balcony sleeping areas,

and four boast whirlpool baths. There are two
bars, one housing a collection of contemporary
Irish painting and sculpture, and a popular night
club/disco. *Amenities* laundry service,
24-hour lounge service.

■ *Rooms* 54	*Confirm by* 6
en suite bath/shower 54	*Last dinner* 9.30
Direct dial Yes	*Parking* Limited
Room TV Yes	*Room service* 24 hours

■ We welcome complaints and bona
fide recommendations on the
tear-out pages for readers' comments.
They are followed up by our professional
team. Please also complain to the
management instantly.

La Mon House Hotel   Comber

H **59% £E** &
Map 18 D2 Co. Down
The Mills, 41 Gransha Road BT23 5RF
Castlereagh (023 123) 631
Owner managers I. & W. Huddleson
Credit Access, Amex, Diners, Visa
   A thriving leisure centre contributes to the
bustling atmosphere of this modern hotel set in
farmland. Good-sized but dimly lit bedrooms have

radios and tea-makers. Housekeeping could be
improved. No dogs. *Amenities* garden, indoor
swimming pool, sauna, solarium, whirlpool bath,
gymnasium, riding, laundry service, 24-hour
lounge service, kiosk, courtesy transport.

■ *Rooms* 44	*Confirm by* arrang.
en suite bath/shower 38	*Last dinner* 9
Direct dial Yes	*Parking* Ample
Room TV Yes	*Room service* 24 hours

The Old Inn   Crawfordsburn

I **£D/E**
Map 18 D2 Co. Down
15 Main Street BT19 1JH
Helons Bay (0247) 853255
Credit Access, Amex, Diners, Visa
   Well named, as this building is claimed to be
Ireland's oldest hotel. Antique furnishings are a
feature – note the 17th-century brass chandelier
in the lounge, and a door reputedly from

Canterbury Cathedral. Each bedroom has its own
appeal: some have four-posters and splendidly
old-fashioned bathrooms. Pleasant, attentive
service. *Amenities* garden.

■ *Rooms* 21	*Confirm by* 7
en suite bath/shower 21	*Last dinner* 9.30
Direct dial Yes	*Parking* Ample
Room TV Yes	*Room service* All day
Closed 2 days Xmas	

Dunadry Inn   Dunadry

I **66% £D**
Map 18 D2 Co. Antrim
BT41 2HA
Temple Patrick (084 94) 32474. Tlx 747245
Manager Mrs Hester Lusk
Credit Access, Amex, Diners, Visa
   A converted linen mill with grounds running
down to a trout river. Brick walls and pine feature
in the bedrooms, many of which open on to the

garden or courtyard. Comfortable day rooms
include a high-raftered bar/lounge with gallery. No
dogs. *Amenities* garden, game fishing, laundry
service, 24-hour lounge service.

■ *Rooms* 64	*Confirm by* 6
en suite bath/shower 64	*Last dinner* 9.45
Direct dial Yes	*Parking* Ample
Room TV Yes	*Room service* 24 hours
Closed 3/4 days Xmas	

Conway Hotel   Dunmurry

H **68% £D** &
Map 18 D2 Co. Antrim
300 Kingsway BT17 9ES
Belfast (0232) 612101. Tlx 74281
Credit Access, Amex, Diners, Visa
   The Conway is a modern hotel set back from
the A1 in attractive gardens and woodland.
Guests are greeted with a smile, and staff
throughout are cheerful and helpful. Open-plan

public areas are fresh, bright and comfortable,
and bedrooms, many recently refurbished, are
well equipped. Good bathrooms.
Amenities garden, gymnasium, squash, snooker,
in-house movies (free), 24-hour lounge service.

■ *Rooms* 78	*Confirm by* 6
en suite bath/shower 78	*Last dinner* 10.30
Direct dial Yes	*Parking* Ample
Room TV Yes	*Room service* 24 hours

BELFAST

Map 18 D2
Town plan opposite

Population 360,000

Belfast, capital of Northern Ireland, gained city status as recently as 1888. The magnificent domed City Hall, lavish Opera House and decorated facades of many banks and shops as well as the ornamented interiors of Belfast's public houses typify its Victorian character. The area stretching from the pedestrianised shopping centre (plenty of car parking) to Queen's University is theatre and cinema land, popular for eating and drinking. There are few tall buildings and wherever you are you can see the green hills which ring the city. Riverside paths follow the Lagan's course for nine miles through rose gardens and parkland.

Annual Events
Belfast Civic Festival & Lord's Mayor's Show *May*
Belfast City Marathon *May Day*
International Arts Festival *November*
International Rose Trials *July–Sept*
Circuit of Ireland International motor rally *Easter*
Opera Northern Ireland Season *Autumn*
Royal Ulster Academy Art Exhibition *Autumn*
Royal Ulster Agricultural Show *May*
Twelfth Processions *12th July*

Sights Outside City
Belfast Zoo
Carrickfergus Castle
Rowallane Gardens, Saintfield
Strangford Lough
Ulster Folk and Transport Museum near Holywood

Tourist Information Centre
River House, 48 High Street
Telephone Belfast 246609
Telex 748087

1 Belfast Cathedral **B2**
2 Belfast Civic Arts Theatre **A4**
3 Belfast Central Library **A2**
4 Belfast Central rail station **C3**
5 Bord Failte information office **A3**
6 Botanic Gardens **A/B5**
7 Botanic rail station **A4**
8 Bus station, Great Victoria Street **A3**
9 Bus station, Oxford Street **B3**
10 City Hall **A/B3**
11 Grand Opera House **A3**
12 Law Courts **B3**
13 Linenhall Library *established 1788* **A3**
14 Lyric Theatre **B5**
15 Northern Ireland Tourist Board information centre **B2**
16 Ormeau Park **C4/5**
17 Queen's University **A5**
18 Transport Museum **C2**
19 Ulster Museum *treasures from Spanish Armada* **A5**
20 Windsor Park football ground **A4**

Belfast

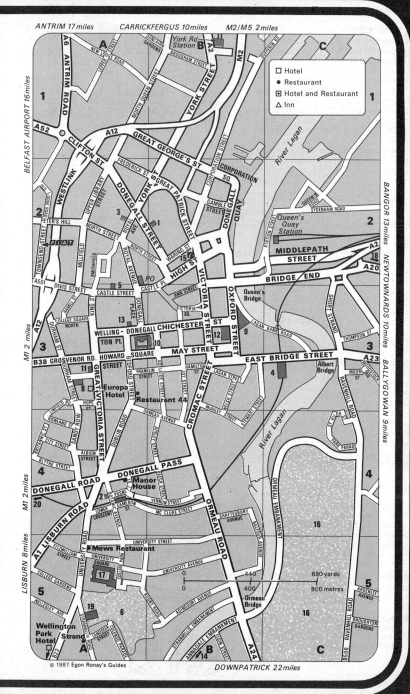

Culloden Hotel
Holywood

H 74% £C/D
Map 18 D2 Co. Down
Craigavad BT18 0EX
Holywood (023 17) 5223. Tlx 74617
Manager Mr P. J. Weston
Credit Access, Amex, Diners, Visa

Mature gardens provide a pleasant setting for this handsome 19th-century stone mansion in the Scottish baronial style. Elegant public areas boast high moulded ceilings, chandeliers and fine furnishings. A former private chapel has been transformed into a convivial bar; there is also a popular pub in the grounds. Best of the pleasing, well-kept bedrooms are in a modern extension; all have attractive modern furniture, trouser presses and other extras such as fresh fruit. New wing bath-rooms are especially luxurious. *Amenities* garden, tennis, squash, putting,

croquet, games room, snooker, in-house movies (free), laundry service, grill bar (11.30am–9.45pm), 24-hour lounge service.

■ *Rooms* 73	*Confirm by* 6
en suite bath/shower 73	*Last dinner* 9.30
Direct dial Yes	*Parking* Ample
Room TV Yes	*Room service* 24 hours
Closed 25 Dec	

Iona
Holywood

R ♀ Map 18 D2 Co. Down
27 Church Road
Holywood (023 17) 5655
French cooking

This cosy little first-floor restaurant is the setting for skilled, sophisticated cooking by Dutch chef-patron Bartjan Brave. His menus are full of interest, with dishes such as pigeon mousse with cranberries, saffron-sauced turbot and lamb fillet

with a fresh strawberry sauce. Desserts include date mousse and a nice sharp lemon sorbet. Vegetarian dishes always available. Unlicensed, but you can bring your own wine. ⊖

■ *Set D from* £15	*D only* 6.15–12.30
About £34 *for two*	*Parking* Ample
Seats 30	*Parties* 30
Closed Sun & Mon	

Schooner
Holywood

R ♀ Map 18 D2 Co. Down
30 High Street
Belfast (0232) 428880
French/English cooking
Credit Access, Visa

Raymond and Anne McClelland's pleasant town-centre restaurant offers straightforward cooking with the emphasis on seafood. Salmon, sole and scallops all feature on Raymond's

menus, though there are meaty alternatives, too. Finish with one of Anne's tempting sweets. Less choice at lunchtime. ⊖

■ *About* £46 *for two*	*L* 12.30–2,
Seats 50	*Sun* 12.30–2.30
Parties 50	*D* 7–10
Closed L Sat, D Sun,	*Parking* Ample
1 Jan, 3 days Xmas, 2 wks July	

Nick's *NEW ENTRY*
Killinchy

R ♀ Map 18 D2 Co. Down
18 Kilmood Church Road, Newtownards
Killinchy (0238) 541472
Credit Access, Diners, Visa

Check directions when booking for dinner at this charming, informal restaurant, run by enthusiastic chef-patron Nick Price. The menu, though not long, is full of good things, from tomato and basil cheesecake and lovely terrine of

pigeon to brill with sorrel hollandaise and pork fillet with chocolate and chilli sauce. Keep some space for a delicious pud like banoffi pie or squidgy chocolate log.
♀ Well-chosen

■ *About* £37 *for two*	*D only* 7.30–10
Seats 45 *Parties* 15	*Parking* Ample
Closed Sun, Mon, Bank Hols, 1 wk New Year,	
last wk Sept & 1st wk Oct	

menu & WINE LIST 1987/8

Magheramorne House Hotel   Larne

H **61% £E**   ♿
Map 18 D1 Co. Antrim
Magheramorne BT39 3HW
Larne (0574) 79444
Manager Kathryn Weir
Credit Access, Amex, Diners, Visa
  A Victorian country mansion set in 43 acres of
woodlands and meadows, with lovely views
towards Lough Larne. Well-maintained public

rooms retain much of their former elegance and
charm. Decently furnished bedrooms have smart
modern bathrooms. *Amenities* garden, games
room, in-house movies (free), laundry service, 24-
hour lounge service.

■ *Rooms* 23	*Confirm by arrang.*
en suite bath/shower 23	*Last dinner* 9.30
Direct dial Yes	*Parking* Ample
Room TV Yes	*Room service* 24 hours

■ We publish annually, so make
sure you use the current
edition. It's worth it!

Everglades Hotel   Londonderry

H **59% £E**
Map 18 C1 Co. Londonderry
Prehen Road BT47 2PA
Londonderry (0504) 44414. Tlx 748005
Credit Access, Amex, Diners, Visa
  A purpose-built mid-70s hotel by the A5, south
of Londonderry. Decent-sized bedrooms are fitted
in practical style, with fully-tiled bathrooms.
Comfortable day rooms like the lobby-lounge and

cocktail bar are in need of their planned
refurbishment. No dogs. *Amenities* garden, in-
house movies (free), laundry service, coffee shop
(11am–7pm, Sun 3pm–9.30pm).

■ *Rooms* 38	*Confirm by* 6
en suite bath/shower 38	*Last dinner* 9.45
Direct dial Yes	*Parking* Ample
Room TV Yes	*Room service* 24 hours
Closed 2 days Xmas	

Strangford Arms Hotel   Newtownards

H **58% £D**
Map 18 D2 Co. Down
92 Church Street BT23 4AL
Newtownards (0247) 814141
Owner manager Elizabeth Miller
Credit Access, Amex, Diners, Visa
  Neatly kept and well run, this Victorian hotel
with a modern extension stands towards the edge
of town. The foyer and lounge bar are pleasantly

furnished with velour seating and panelled walls.
Most of the bedrooms have attractive lightwood
fitted units and smart new bathrooms. No dogs.
Amenities in-house movies, laundry service.

■ *Rooms* 36	*Confirm by arrang.*
en suite bath/shower 36	*Last dinner* 10
Direct dial Yes	*Parking* Ample
Room TV Yes	*Room service* All day
Closed 2 days Easter, 12 July & 25 Dec	

Bayview Hotel   Portballintrae

H **60% £F**
Map 18 C1 Co. Antrim
2 Bayhead Road, Nr Bushmills BT57 8RZ
Bushmills (026 57) 31453
Owner manager Trevor Cooke
Credit Access, Visa
  Sweeping views across the bay are a major
asset at this bright and cheerful hotel located not
far from the Giant's Causeway. Both foyers offer

comfortable seating and there are two lively, well-
patronised bars. Bedrooms are attractively
furnished, bathrooms with Victorian-style brass
fittings are especially smart. *Amenities* snooker,
laundry service, 24-hour lounge service.

■ *Rooms* 16	*Confirm by arrang.*
en suite bath/shower 16	*Last dinner* 9.45
Direct dial Yes	*Parking* Ample
Room TV Yes	*Room service* 24 hours

Portaferry Hotel   Portaferry

I **£F**
Map 18 D2 Co. Down
10 The Strand BT22 1PE
Portaferry (024 72) 28231
Owner managers John & Marie Herlihy
Credit Access, Amex, Diners, Visa
  Part of a row of Georgian-fronted buildings, this
charming inn enjoys a picturesque setting over-
looking Lough Strangford. There are two bars, one

with a display of contemporary artwork (some by
regulars), and a little TV room. Bedrooms offer
straightforward comforts with few frills. Good
breakfasts. No dogs. *Amenities* mooring.

■ *Rooms* 5	*Confirm by arrang.*
en suite bath/shower 5	*Last dinner* 9
Room phone No	*Parking* Ample
Room TV No	*Room service* All day
Closed 25 Dec	

Portrush ▶

Ramore ★   Portrush

R ★ ♦ **Map 18 C1** Co. Antrim
The Harbour
Portrush (0265) 824313

Booking is essential at this attractive and very
professionally run harbourside restaurant. Part of
the charm of the place is that it's very much a
family affair, with Joy Caithness and her daughter
managing the front of house while son-in-law
George McAlpin works his magic in the kitchen.
Handling the very finest produce with great
sensitivity and flair, George is skilled at letting the
fresh flavours speak for themselves. His sauces
are masterful, his presentation superb. It perhaps
comes as a surprise to learn that this talented
artist's other great passion is motor racing! The
seafood terrine is typically eye-catching –
colourful layers of white fish and salmon, studded
with spinach and served with a fresh tomato
coulis. Move on perhaps to succulent breasts of
quail stuffed with a delicate leek mousseline and
wrapped in light puff pastry, and complete your

meal with a memorable lemon soufflé.
Specialities chicken and lobster terrine on a
lobster and champagne sauce, fillet of Irish lamb
on a bed of aubergine, strawberry timbale served
with a raspberry coulis.
♀ **Well-chosen** ☺
■ *About £38 for two*   *D only 7–10*
Seats 55 Parties 55   *Parking Ample*
Closed Sun, Mon, 25 Dec, 1 Jan & 2 wks Jan–Feb

The Barn *NEW ENTRY*   Saintfield

R ♦ **Map 18 D2** Co. Down
120 Monlough Road
Saintfield (0238) 510396
Credit Access, Diners, Visa

Be sure to ask directions when booking at this
most delightful restaurant in a converted barn.
Robbie Wright is the driving force in the kitchen,
while wife Jane provides charming, helpful
service. Raw materials are all-important, with fish
from local boats, game from Tyrone, berries from
the hedgerows and 40 types of herb from the
garden. Dishes on the monthly-changing menu
run from asparagus soup and a superb layered

smoked fish pâté to salmon-stuffed sole, roast
lamb paloise and chicken in elderberry wine
topped with Red Windsor cheese. The sweet
trolley is laden with delights, and the final fling is
home-made fudge with coffee or tea. A concise
French wine list, strongest on Bordeaux.
♀ **Well-chosen** ☺

■ *Set D £13·80*   *D only 7.30–10*
About £38 for two   *Parking Ample*
Seats 34   *Parties 40*
*Closed Sun, Mon, some Bank Hols, 10 days July,
3 days Xmas & 2 wks Feb*

The Grange   Waringstown

R ♦ **Map 18 D2** Co. Armagh
Main Street
Waringstown (0762) 881989

Antique furniture adds to the charm of this late
17th-century stone-built cottage, and the chintzy
lounges are pleasant places in which to relax with
a drink. Robert Lynn's simple menu ranges from
familiar favourites such as prawn cocktail to more
inventive dishes like spiced breast of chicken in

coconut sauce. Seasonal vegetables are carefully
cooked and there are excellent sweets. Portions
are generous and service is friendly and
thoughtful. Traditional Sunday lunch.
♀ **Well-chosen** ☺
■ *About £45 for two*   *L Sun only12.30–2.30*
Seats 45   *D 7.30–9.30*
Parties 35   *Parking Ample*
Closed D Sun, all Mon, 26 Dec & 1 wk July

HOTELS
RESTAURANTS
AND INNS

REPUBLIC OF IRELAND

Adare ▶

Mustard Seed   Adare

R   ♿   **Map 19 B5** Co. Limerick
Limerick (061) 86451
Owner manager Daniel F. Mullane
Credit Access, Visa

A pretty restaurant in a thatched cottage where modern and traditional elements blend happily throughout fixed-price dinner menus. Delicate fish mousse with mussel sauce might start your meal, followed by soup and a sorbet, then a main course like roast pigeon en croûte or rack of lamb. Irish cheeses and tempting sweets such as whiskey-rich bread and butter pudding to finish. 🍷 **Well-chosen** ©

■ *Set D from £16·95*	*D only 7–10*
About £48 for two	*Parking Ample*
Seats 28	*Parties 8*
Closed Sun, also Mon in winter, 25 Dec & Feb	

Shiro ★   *NEW ENTRY*   Ahakista

R ★ � ♿   **Map 19 A6** Co. Cork
Nr Bantry
Bantry (027) 67030
Japanese cooking
Credit Access

Japanese artist Kei Pilz and her German husband Werner are the cosmopolitan couple behind this enchanting little Japanese restaurant. It's located in an old country priest's house, idyllically set on a hillside overlooking Dunmanus Bay. Kei's delicate calligraphic work hangs on the walls, bonsai trees adorn each table – and it comes as no real surprise to discover what a true artist she is, too, in the kitchen. Superbly fresh ingredients are prepared with the lightest of touches, flavours are subtle, often surprising, and presentation is exquisite throughout every marvellous course. Start with a flower-decked tray of tempting hors d'oeuvre or a wonderfully clear fish broth garnished with fresh clams. Move on to superlative sashimi (perhaps salmon, monkfish,

tuna, squid) and featherlight tempura (crispy deep-fried seafood and vegetable morsels). Desserts like kiwi fruit and melon granité make a mouthwatering finale. All in all, a meal at Shiro is a memory to treasure. Booking essential.
Specialities sashimi, sushi, tempura, sukiyaki.

■ *Set D £20*	*D only 7–10*
About £50 for two	*Parking Ample*
Seats 14 Parties 14	*Closed Sun & Jan*

Armstrong's Barn   Annamoe

R � ♿   **Map 19 D4** Co. Wicklow
Near Glendalough
Wicklow (0404) 5194
Credit Amex, Visa

Good wholesome cooking in the relaxed ambience of a converted barn in the foothills of the Wicklow mountains. Susan Tullio's weekly changing menu provides tasty dishes ranging from chunky country pâté and spring vegetable soup to Chinese-style beef and excellent roast local lamb. To finish, perhaps syllabub or classic profiteroles. There's a carefully chosen wine list, with good Jaboulet Rhônes. ©

■ *Set L £10*	*L Sun only 1–2.30*
Set D £17·50	*D 7.30–10*
About £50 for two	*Parking Ample*
Seats 45	*Parties 50*
Closed D Sun, all Mon & Bank Hols	

Downhill Hotel   Ballina

H **65% £C/D**
Map 18 B3 Co. Mayo
Downhill Road
Ballina (096) 21033. Tlx 33796
Owner managers Brian & Ann Moylett
Credit Access, Amex, Diners, Visa

A well-run modern hotel whose attractions include a peaceful setting, a fully equipped leisure centre and extensive function facilities. The bright little residents' lounge, with views of the tumbling Brosna river, is a nice place to sit and relax, while the piano bar offers nightly entertainment. Bedrooms ranging from compact singles to spacious suites are divided between the main house and various extensions. Accessories include videos, hairdryers and tea-makers.
Amenities garden, indoor swimming pool, sauna, solarium, whirlpool bath, gymnasium, beauty salon, tennis, squash, coarse fishing, games room, snooker, in-house movies (free), laundry service, 24-hour lounge service, kiosk.

■ *Rooms 54*	*Confirm by 7*
en suite bath/shower 52	*Last dinner 9.15*
Direct dial Yes	*Parking Ample*
Room TV Yes	*Room service All day*
Closed 4 days Xmas	

Hayden's Hotel   Ballinasloe

H **62% £E**
Map 19 B4 Co. Galway
Dunloe Street
Ballinasloe (0905) 42347. Tlx 53947
Owner manager Billy O'Carroll
Credit Access, Amex, Diners, Visa
  Warm colour schemes give a cheerful feel to
the public areas of this busy family-run hotel. Best
bedrooms, furnished in contemporary style, have
modern bathrooms. Golf available nearby. No
dogs. *Amenities* garden, coarse fishing, in-house
movies (free), laundry service, coffee shop
(10am–8pm), 24-hour lounge service.

■ *Rooms* 55	*Confirm by 6*
en suite bath/shower 50	*Last dinner 9.30*
Direct dial Yes	*Parking Ample*
Room TV Yes	*Room service 24 hours*
Closed 3 days Xmas	

Ballylickey House   Ballylickey

H **61% £D/E**
Map 19 B6 Co. Cork
Bantry Bay
Bantry (027) 50071
Owner managers Mr & Mrs Graves
Credit Amex, Visa
  Rebuilding of the fire-damaged main house has
added four suites to the accommodation at this
parkland hotel. Remaining bedrooms, spacious
and simply furnished, are in rustic wooden
chalets. The all-purpose reception functions as a
bar-lounge. *Amenities* garden, outdoor
swimming pool, game fishing, laundry service.

■ *Rooms* 15	*Confirm by 6*
en suite bath/shower 15	*Last dinner 9.30*
Direct dial Yes	*Parking Ample*
Room TV Most	*Room service All day*
Closed mid Oct–Easter	

Sea View House Hotel   Ballylickey

HR **62% £E**
Map 19 B6 Co. Cork
Nr Bantry
Bantry (027) 50462
Owner manager Kathleen O'Sullivan
Credit Access, Amex, Visa
  The owner and her charming staff take
excellent care of guests in this peaceful hotel,
whose comfortably traditional main rooms enjoy
splendid views of Bantry Bay. Everywhere is spick
and span, through to the pleasantly appointed
bedrooms (some in outbuildings).
Amenities garden, laundry service.

■ *Rooms* 13	*Confirm by 6*
en suite bath/shower 13	*Last dinner 9*
Room phone Yes	*Parking Ample*
Room TV No	*Room service All day*
Closed 1 Nov–1 Apr	

Restaurant 🍴

Kathleen O'Sullivan's talented home cooking is
enjoyed in a comfortable dining room overlooking
the garden. The menu provides a nightly-
changing selection of goodies, from scallop
mousse, seafood chowder and lamb sweetbreads
in mustard cream to monkfish mornay, suprême of
salmon and roast leg of spring lamb. Good Irish
cheeses and lovely desserts like lemon syllabub.
There's a concise, well-chosen wine list: note the
Brane-Cantenac 1975 and a fine 1983
Gewürztraminer from Trimbach.
🍷 Well-chosen ⊗

■ *Set L £8*	*L Sun at 1.30, Mon–Sat*
Set D £15·50	*by arrang. only*
About £40 for two	*D 7.30–9*
Seats 35 Parties 40	*Closed 1 Nov–1 Apr*

Ballynahinch Castle   Ballynahinch

H **72% £C/D**
Map 18 A3 Co. Galway
Clifden (095) 21269. Tlx 50809
Manager John O'Connor
Credit Access, Amex, Diners, Visa
  Landscaped gardens leading down to the river
provide an idyllic setting for this handsome 17th-
century mansion. A welcoming entrance hall sets
the scene with its log fire and leather chesterfield
sofas. A popular base for game fishermen,
Ballynahinch Castle has its own fishing rights on
the river extending for some 2½ miles. Salmon and
seatrout fishing is a major attraction and guests
can weigh their catches in the convivial
fisherman's bar. Non-anglers can retreat to the
stylish cocktail bar or take refuge in the deep-
cushioned comfort of the traditional lounge or TV
lounge-cum-library. Bedrooms of varying sizes
(four with four-poster beds) have good-quality
darkwood furniture, pleasing decor, and
coordinated soft furnishings. Bathrooms are

modern in style with pretty tiling, good towels and
shower attachments. An appealing hotel with a
relaxed yet efficient atmosphere. No dogs.
Amenities garden, tennis, shooting, game
fishing, laundry service, 24-hour lounge service.

■ *Rooms* 20	*Confirm by 6*
en suite bath/shower 20	*Last dinner 9*
Direct dial Yes	*Parking Ample*
Room TV No	*Room service All day*
Closed Nov–Easter	

Gregans Castle Hotel   Ballyvaughan

HR 70% £C/D
Map 19 B4 Co. Clare
Ennis (065) 77005. Tlx 70130
Owner managers Mr & Mrs Peter Haden
Credit Visa

The Burren is a part of County Clare that is particularly rich in scenic beauty, and this handsome country house commands stunning views down the valley to Galway Bay. Peter and Moira Haden run the place with great care and pride, and recent improvements include a luxurious restyling of the restaurant and the conversion of one of the lounges into a delightful library full of interesting books and inviting armchairs. Individually furnished bedrooms are all

very comfortable, and numerous thoughtful little extras are provided. Stars of the show are three sumptuous ground-floor suites with beautifully designed bathrooms. Good service (cup of tea on arrival, bed turned down) and splendid breakfasts. No dogs. *Amenities* garden.

■ *Rooms* 17	*Confirm by* 5
en suite bath/shower 14	*Last dinner* 8
Room phone No	*Parking* Ample
Room TV No	*Room service* All day
Closed Nov–late Mar	

Gregans Castle Hotel Restaurant ♔ ♪ ♿

Moira Haden's excellent taste in fabrics and table settings is matched by Peter's sound kitchen-craft. His set menu make fine use of the best local produce in dishes like Galway Bay codling in cream and wine sauce, loin of spring Burren lamb or lobster fresh from the Aran Islands. Home-made ice cream gâteau and petits fours. Good wines; note the Guigal Rhônes.
♀ Well-chosen ☺

■ *Set D* £17	*D only* 7–8
About £48 *for two*	*Seats* 45
Closed Nov–late Mar	

■ Prices quoted for the Republic of Ireland are in Irish punts.

Chez Youen   Baltimore

R ♪ **Map 19 B6** Co. Cork
The Pier
Skibbereen (028) 20136
Seafood
Credit Amex, Diners, Visa

Brittany-bred Youen Jacob's straightforward style of cooking suits the superb seafood offered at his convivial quayside restaurant. Seasonal salmon and lobster, garlicky grilled clams and skate with black butter are typical treats. There are steaks, too, and sweets include a perfect tarte tatin. ♀ Well-chosen ☺

■ *Set L* £7·50	*L* 12.30–2.30
Set D from £14·50	*D* 6.30–10,
About £38 *for two*	6.30–12 *in summer*
Seats 45 *Parties* 60	*Parking* Ample
Closed L Mon–Sat Nov–1 Apr, also all Feb & Oct	

Hotel Dunloe Castle   Beaufort

H 72% £C
Map 19 A5 Co. Kerry
Nr Killarney
Killarney (064) 44111. Tlx 28233
Credit Access, Amex, Diners, Visa

The majestic Gap of Dunloe provides a setting of spectacular beauty for this vast modern hotel. Everything is on a grand scale, from the immense quarry-tiled foyer scattered with colourful rugs to the massive upstairs lounge which commands splendid views of the prize-winning garden. The vast function rooms, too, can accommodate hundreds, but the bar is a more intimate size. Identical bedrooms, all very light and spacious, have practical lightwood furniture, direct-dial phones, and digital radio-alarms. Bathrooms are well equipped. *Amenities* garden, indoor swimming pool, sauna, keep-fit equipment,

tennis, golf driving range, putting, riding, coarse fishing, games room, in-house movies (free), laundry service, coffee shop (11am–11pm).

■ *Rooms* 140	*Confirm by* 6
en suite bath/shower 140	*Last dinner* 9.30
Direct dial Yes	*Parking* Ample
Room TV Yes	*Room service* 24 hours
Closed end Oct–1 Apr	

Colin O'Daly's Park Restaurant · Blackrock

R ♈ **Map 19 D4** Co. Dublin
26 Main Street
Dublin (01) 886177
French cooking
Credit Access, Amex, Diners, Visa
 Lyn O'Daly is at the front of the house, while her husband Colin cooks at this stylish restaurant. Herbs and fresh produce are used to excellent effect in a short set menu of delights like crab with grapefruit and hazelnut salad, fillet of pork with fig stuffing or saucy baked hake. Good vegetables, too, and lovely desserts. ♟ Well-chosen ℮

- **Set L** £8·50 · L 12.30–2.30
Set D £20·50 · D 7–10
About £55 for two · *Parking* Ample
Seats 56 · *Parties* 40
Closed L Sat, all Sun & Mon, Bank Hols, 1 wk Easter & 3 days Xmas

Downshire House Hotel · Blessington

H **59% £D/E**
Map 19 D4 Co. Wicklow
Nass (045) 65199
Owner manager Rhoda Byrne
 Exposed stone walls catch the eye in the homely public rooms of this friendly, well-maintained Georgian house on the main street. A polished teak staircase leads to the neatly kept, pleasantly old-fashioned bedrooms, which have good modern bathrooms. Annexe rooms, accessible via the basement, are in similar style. No dogs.
Amenities garden, tennis, croquet.

- *Rooms* 25 · *Confirm by* arrang.
en suite bath/shower 25 · *Last dinner* 9.45
Direct dial Yes · *Parking* Ample
Room TV Yes · *Room service* All day
Closed 24 Dec–6 Jan

Tree of Idleness ★ · Bray

R ★ ♈ & **Map 19 D4** Co. Wicklow
Seafront
Dublin (01) 863498
Cypriot cooking
Credit Access, Diners, Visa
 Akis Courtellas and his charming wife Susan have something quite special in their friendly seafront restaurant, where the quality of local produce and the joys of Greek-Cypriot cuisine combine for some memorable meals. On an expansive menu you'll find classics like houmus, stuffed vine leaves and meat or vegetarian moussaka alongside a variety of mouthwatering original creations such as salad of duck liver and mango or superb smoked lamb, chargrilled to perfection and served with a terrific blackcurrant vinegar and wine sauce. Portions are generous, vegetables crisp and fresh, and the sweet trolley carries an impressive cargo of goodies, from Irish strawberries and exotic fruits to baklava and rich chocolate truffle cake. Excellent wines with a very

fine collection of clarets back to Ch. Cos d'Estournel '45. *Specialities* Dover Sole fillets with tarama sauce; aubergine filled with prawns, smoked salmon and monkfish topped with a cream and cheese sauce; chicken, veal and prawns in a green herb sauce.
⌦ Outstanding ℮

- **Set D** from £11 · D only 7.30–11
About £50 for two · *Parking* Ample
Seats 58 · *Parties* 30
Closed Mon, 3 wks Aug/Sept & 1 wk Xmas

- When calling a Dublin number from outside the Republic, dial 00 before the number we print, e.g. Berkeley Court is 0001 601711.

- For the rest of the Republic, dial 010-353, then the number we print less the initial zero, e.g. Park Hotel Kenmare is 010-353 64 41200.

Fitzpatrick's Shannon Shamrock Hotel · Bunratty

H **58% £C**
Map 19 B4 Co. Clare
Limerick (061) 61177. Tlx 26214
Credit Access, Amex, Diners, Visa
 A low-rise modern hotel next to Bunratty Castle and ideal for Shannon airport. Beams and stone give a rustic feel to the spacious lounge; the bar is more traditional. Simply furnished rooms have smart tiled bathrooms. No dogs.
Amenities garden, indoor swimming pool, sauna, satellite TV, in-house movies (free), laundry service, coffee shop (8am–11pm), courtesy coach.

- *Rooms* 104 · *Confirm by* 6
en suite bath/shower 104 · *Last dinner* 9.30
Direct dial Yes · *Parking* Ample
Room TV Yes · *Room service* 24 hours
Closed 25 Dec

MacCloskeys   Bunratty

R ♘ **Map 19 B4** Co. Clare
Bunratty House Mews
Limerick (061) 364082
Credit Access, Amex, Diners, Visa
 Gerry MacCloskey offers a varied and
interesting dinner menu in a characterful
restaurant in the cellars of Bunratty House (check
directions when booking). Port and Stilton soufflé,
duck and pea soup, salmon beurre blanc and
garlicky noisettes of lamb are typical of his
carefully, flairfully cooked dishes. Excellent
sauces, al dente vegetables, super sweets and a
sound, mainly French, cellar. Marie MacCloskey is
a charming hostess. ⊖

■ *Set D £20*	*D only 7–9.30*
About £53 for two	*Parking Ample*
Seats 60	*Parties 60*
Closed Sun, Mon, Bank Hols & 21 Dec–1 Feb	

Kilcoran Lodge Hotel   Cahir

See under Kilcoran

Ard-Na-Sidhe   Caragh Lake

H **68% £E**
Map 19 A5 Co. Kerry
Nr Killorglin
Tralee (066) 69105. Tlx 73833
Credit Access, Amex, Diners, Visa
 Lovely terraced gardens surround this
handsome Victorian lakeside hotel. Drinks are
served in two elegantly furnished lounges.
Handsomely appointed bedrooms, many with
splendid views, offer plenty of sitting and writing
space. Guests may use the leisure facilities of two
neighbouring hotels. *Amenities* garden, sea and
coarse fishing, laundry service.

■ *Rooms 20*	*Confirm by arrang.*
en suite bath/shower 20	*Last dinner 8.15*
Room phone No	*Parking Ample*
Room TV No	*Room service All day*
Closed mid Sept–1 May	

Caragh Lodge   Caragh Lake

H **66% £D/E**
Map 19 A5 Co. Kerry
Nr Killorglin
Caragh Lake (066) 69115
Owner managers Ines & Michael Braasch
Credit Access, Amex, Visa
 A country hotel of charm and personality set in
nine acres of beautiful gardens and parkland. The
grounds run down to Caragh Lake, where fishing,
boating and swimming facilities are available. The
whole place has the feel of a private house, and
the lounges, with their antique clocks, writing
desks, bookcases and comfortable armchairs, are
immensely inviting. Decent-sized bedrooms –
some in annexes – have pretty co-ordinated
fabrics and good bathrooms with generous
towels. Housekeeping is immaculate. Dr and Mrs
Schaper have handed over the reins to their
daughter and son-in-law. No children under ten.
No dogs. *Amenities* garden, sauna, tennis, game
fishing, rowing boats.

■ *Rooms 10*	*Confirm by 6*
en suite bath/shower 10	*Last dinner 8.30*
Room phone No	*Parking Ample*
Room TV No	*Room service All day*
Closed 15 Oct–1 Mar	

■ Our inspectors never book in the
 name of Egon Ronay's Guides;
 they disclose their identity only
 after paying their bills.

Nuremore Hotel   Carrickmacross

H **61% £D/E**
Map 18 C3 Co. Monaghan
Carrickmacross (042) 61438
Owner managers Mr & Mrs Gilhooly
Credit Access, Amex, Diners, Visa
 A modern hotel with good leisure facilities and a
delightfully peaceful setting. Public areas and
bedrooms are pleasantly furnished in
contemporary style. No dogs. *Amenities* garden,
indoor swimming pool, sauna, whirlpool bath,
squash, 9-hole golf course, putting, coarse
fishing, snooker, pool table, in-house movies
(free), laundry service.

■ *Rooms 39*	*Confirm by 6*
en suite bath/shower 39	*Last dinner 9.45*
Direct dial Yes	*Parking Ample*
Room TV Yes	*Room service 24 hours*
Closed 25 & 26 Dec	

■ Prices quoted for the Republic of Ireland are in Irish punts.

Cashel House Hotel   Cashel

HR **73% £C/D** &
Map 18 A3 Co. Galway
Cashel (095) 31001. Tlx 50812
Owner managers Dermot & Kay McEvilly
Credit Access, Amex, Diners, Visa

Splendid service – professional and efficient yet warm and considerate – is a strong point at this impeccably-kept country house. The setting, amid 35 acres of award-winning gardens at the head of Cashel Bay, is delightful. Caring owners, the McEvillys, continue to maintain high standards of traditional hospitality. Day rooms are everything one could wish for – a handsome library, a modern, roomy bar with garden views; the lounge is a haven of comfort enhanced by fresh flowers, fine antiques and paintings. Wonderfully tasteful bedrooms (including four sumptuous suites with

whirlpool baths) all have excellent decor and fabrics plus modern, well-equipped bathrooms. No children under five. *Amenities* garden, tennis, hotel boat, private beach.

■ *Rooms 32*	*Confirm by arrang.*
en suite bath/shower 32	*Last dinner 8.30*
Direct dial Yes	*Parking Ample*
Room TV Some	*Room service All day*
Closed early Nov–Mar	

Cashel House Hotel
Restaurant ☙ &

Excellent fresh seafood dominates the five-course menus offered at this elegantly traditional dining room with lovely garden views. Choices include spring nettle soup, sea urchins mayonnaise, scallops in saffron sauce, grilled lobster and poached brill with a herby hollandaise; carnivores can enjoy flavoursome roast duckling, pork en croûte or hearty Irish stew. Excellent local cheeses and appealing sweets such as rhubarb tart and lemon syllabub. Charming, warm-hearted service. ☙

■ *Set D £18·50*	*D only 7.30–8.30*
About £60 for two	*Seats 50*
Closed early Nov–Mar	

Zetland House Hotel   Cashel

H **65% £D**
Map 18 A3 Co. Galway
Clifden (095) 31111. Tlx 50853
Owner managers John & Mona Prendergast
Credit Access, Amex, Visa

Completely refurbished over recent years, this handsome Victorian house commands superb views across Cashel Bay. Day rooms include a tranquil, traditional lounge with plenty of

magazines and charming flower arrangments, and a small, modern bar. Comfortable bedrooms have antiques and ocean views. *Amenities* garden, shooting, game fishing, snooker.

■ *Rooms 19*	*Confirm by 6*
en suite bath/shower 19	*Last dinner 8.30*
Direct dial Yes	*Parking Ample*
Room TV No	*Room service All day*
Closed 15 Oct–Easter	

Cashel Palace Hotel   Cashel

HR **76% £B** Co. Tipperary
Map 19 C5
Main Street
Cashel (062) 61411. Tlx 26938
Owner manager Ray Carroll
Credit Access, Amex, Diners, Visa

Behind the elegant Queen Anne building which was once a bishop's palace are 20 acres of exquisite gardens, with peacocks, a velvet lawn and fountains playing. The gracious entrance hall has comfortable sofas, red pine panelling and Kilkenny marble fireplaces; there's a peaceful drawing room overlooking the garden and, in the cellars, a vaulted, flagstoned bar. The bedrooms,

ranging from spacious suites to smaller rooms on the top floor, are beautifully furnished with fine period pieces and coordinating fabrics. Bathrooms are well equipped and immaculate. No dogs. *Amenities* garden, riding, coarse fishing, laundry service, coffee shop (10am–10pm), 24-hour lounge service.

■ *Rooms 20*	*Confirm by 6*
en suite bath/shower 20	*Last dinner 9.30*
Direct dial Yes	*Parking Ample*
Room TV Yes	*Room service 24 hours*
Closed 25 & 26 Dec	

Four Seasons ☙

Sumptuous surroundings enhance the enjoyment of sound cooking, using good raw ingredients. You might start with smoked venison salad, followed by lobster bisque; move on to succulent baked salmon or rack of lamb. Excellent crisp vegetables as accompaniment. Finish with a delicious strawberry mille-feuille and a selection of Irish cheeses. ☙

■ *Set D £23*	*D 7–9.30*
About £60 for two	*Seats 28 Parties 50*
Closed Sun, also Thurs & Fri in winter & Xmas	

Chez Hans — Cashel

R ◁ ♿ **Map 19 C5** Co. Tipperary
Rockside
Cashel (062) 61177
Owner manager Mr & Mrs Hans Matthia
Hans Matthia cooks with a sure touch at this restaurant in a converted chapel. The quality of his seafood in particular is superb, whether you choose garlicky mussels or quenelles of sea bass to start, salmon with sorrel sauce or sole meunière

to follow. Equally tasty meat dishes include tender lamb en croûte, and there are delicious home-made ices to finish. The wine list is short and carefully chosen. ⊖

■ *About £46 for two* — *D only 7–10.30*
Seats 70 Parties 80 — *Parking Limited*
Closed Sun, Mon, Good Fri, 1 wk Xmas & 3 wks Jan

■ If we recommend meals in a hotel or inn, a separate entry is made for its restaurant.

Kilkea Castle — Castledermot

H **56% £E**
Map 19 C4 Co. Kildare
Carlow (0503) 45100. Tlx 60606
Credit Access, Amex, Diners, Visa
Surrounded by pleasant farmland, this 12th-century building is said to be the oldest inhabited castle in Ireland. Public areas include a galleried entrance hall, a beamed lounge and the stone-walled cellar bar. Bedrooms – some in converted

outbuildings – are in simple modern style and have functional bathrooms. No dogs.
Amenities garden, outdoor swimming pool, tennis, 24-hour lounge service.
■ *Rooms 52* — *Confirm by arrang.*
en suite bath/shower 52 — *Last dinner 9.30*
Direct dial Yes — *Parking Ample*
Room TV No — *Room service 24 hours*
Closed end Oct–Mar

Hotel Kilmore — Cavan

H **58% £E** ♿
Map 18 C3 Co. Cavan
Dublin Road
Cavan (049) 32288
Credit Access, Visa
A modern low-rise hotel just out of town on the Dublin road. The spacious foyer incorporates a leafy coffee shop and there's a smart split-level bar with silver-grey banquette seating. Simply-

furnished bedrooms provide basic comforts and tiled bathrooms. Four are adapted for the use of disabled guests. *Amenities* garden, in-house movies (free), coffee shop (9am–7pm), 24-hour lounge service.
■ *Rooms 39* — *Confirm by 6*
en suite bath/shower 39 — *Last dinner 9.15*
Direct dial Yes — *Parking Ample*
Room TV Yes — *Room service 24 hours*

Abbeyglen Castle Hotel — Clifden

HR **65% £D/E**
Map 18 A3 Co. Galway
Sky Road
Clifden (095) 21201. Tlx 28366
Owner manager Paul Hughes
Credit Access, Amex, Diners, Visa
Paul Hughes is the ever-genial host at this turreted modern hotel, which enjoys a setting of great beauty in a parkland valley looking out to sea. The atmosphere throughout is immensely cheerful, and singalongs are a regular evening event in the piano bar. There's no separate lounge, but settees provide comfortable seating in the foyer. Bedrooms, all of a decent size, are furnished in various styles – ranging from luxurious to fairly basic – and bathrooms have a generous supply of towels. Rooms at the front have views of the bay. No children under seven.
Amenities garden, outdoor swimming pool, sauna, solarium, tennis, 9-hole golf course, pitch & putt, snooker, in-house movies (free), laundry

service, 24-hour lounge service.
■ *Rooms 40* — *Confirm by arrang.*
en suite bath/shower 40 — *Last dinner 9*
Direct dial Yes — *Parking Ample*
Room TV Yes — *Room service 24 hours*
Closed 5 Jan–1 Mar

Restaurant

Good cooking and sunny service make this comfortable Gothic-style restaurant an excellent place for a meal. Paddy Conroy's menu is straightforward, and fresh seafood is a favourite: note Galway Bay oysters, moules marinière, grilled crayfish, salmon with dill sauce. Meat-eaters might plump for duckling à l'orange or sirloin steak. Sweets from the trolley include an excellent sherry trifle. Some window tables have sea views. ⊖
■ *Set D £14·70* — *L 12.30–2.15*
About £40 for two — *D 7.30–9*
Seats 100 — *Closed 5 Jan–1 Mar*

Hotel Ardagh | Clifden

HR **62%** **£E** ⁱ
Map 18 A3 Co. Galway
Ballyconneely Road, Ardbear Bay
Clifden (095) 21384. Tlx 28989
Owner managers Henk & Ria Berings
Credit Access, Amex, Visa

The Dutch owners give this modern hotel a lot of charm, and the setting is spectacular. Bedrooms are spacious and practical; doubles have roof-top balconies. There's a comfortable lounge and convivial bar. For breakfast, try the Dutch treat (ham, bread, fried egg, gherkins and sweet pickle). No dogs. *Amenities* snooker.

■ *Rooms* 20	*Confirm by* 6
en suite bath/shower 20	*Last dinner* 9
Direct dial Yes	*Parking* Ample
Room TV No	*Room service* All day
Closed Nov–Easter	

Hotel Ardagh Restaurant 𝄞

Resited at the front of the hotel, this restaurant offers superb views of Ardbear Bay. Daughter of the house Monique Berings remains in fine form in the kitchen, producing dinners of excellent quality. Seafood is a speciality, featuring delights like paupiettes of lemon sole with shrimp sauce or butter-baked cod cordon bleu. Outside the fishy realm there are T-bone steaks and spring lamb. Nice crisp vegetables and tempting sweets like rhubarb pie or Baileys Irish Cream cheesecake. Delightful service. Sound wine list. ☺

■ *Set D* £14·50	*D only* 7.30–9
About £38 *for two*	*Seats* 50
Closed Nov–Easter	*Parties* 30

Rock Glen Hotel | Clifden

H **61%** **£D/E**
Map 18 A3 Co. Galway
Roundstowe Road
Clifden (095) 21035
Owner managers John & Evangeline Roche
Credit Access, Amex, Diners, Visa

Hospitality, traditional comforts and immaculate housekeeping are key assets of this delightful one-time shooting lodge. The setting is as lovely as it is peaceful and the day rooms, cosy with peat fires, are splendidly relaxing. Homely bedrooms have neat, practical bathrooms. No dogs. *Amenities* garden, tennis, snooker.

■ *Rooms* 30	*Confirm by* 6
en suite bath/shower 30	*Last dinner* 9
Direct dial Yes	*Parking* Ample
Room TV No	*Room service* All day
Closed 1 Nov–15 Mar	

Clonmel Arms Hotel | Clonmel

H **62%** **£D/E**
Map 19 C5 Co. Tipperary
Sarsfield Street
Clonmel (052) 21233. Tlx 80263
Credit Access, Amex, Diners, Visa

A friendly, modern hotel behind a Georgian facade, the Clonmel Arms is a popular stopover for business people. The lounge has comfortable seating, and the bar is being enlarged and revamped. Well-equipped bedrooms of various sizes have darkwood units and some are double-glazed. *Amenities* in-house movies (free), 24-hour lounge service.

■ *Rooms* 35	*Confirm by* 6
en suite bath/shower 35	*Last dinner* 10.15
Direct dial Yes	*Parking* Ample
Room TV Yes	*Room service* 24 hours
Closed 2 days Xmas	

Ashford Castle | Cong

HR **87%** **£A** **E** ♿
Map 18 B3 Co. Mayo
Claremorris (092) 46003. Tlx 53749
Manager Rory Murphy
Credit Access, Amex, Diners, Visa

A remarkable castle, parts of which date back to the 13th century, standing in towered and turreted splendour by the edge of Lough Corrib with breathtaking views, and complete with an attractive seven-arched bridge across the river Corrib to the hotel. The impressive public rooms have panelled walls and ceilings and antique furniture. Irish airs are sung in the vaulted dungeon bar each night and guests are encouraged to join in. Many of the bedrooms have been luxuriously refurbished and the bathrooms are being newly fitted in splendid Victorian style. Service is outstanding. No dogs. *Amenities* garden, tennis, 9-hole golf course, shooting, coarse and game fishing, in-house movies (free), laundry service.

■ *Rooms* 83	*Confirm by* arrang.
en suite bath/shower 83	*Last dinner* 10.30
Direct dial Yes	*Parking* Ample
Room TV Yes	*Room service* 24 hours

Ashford Castle Restaurant ♛♛

Good cooking and outstanding service in a splendid setting of panelled walls, timbered ceiling, glittering chandeliers and marvellous views of the lake. An interesting menu offers dishes such as Clew Bay mussels in dill sauce or strudel of stilton with fresh strawberry sauce for

starters; then salmon coulibiac with lemon butter sauce, turbot fillet poached in wine sauce with prawns or brochettes of beef as a main course. Sweets include home-made ices.

♀ Well-chosen ⊖
■ *Set L £15*   *L 1–2.30*
Set D £29   *D 7–9.30*
About £85 for two   *Seats 135*

Arbutus Lodge Hotel   Cork

HR **63% £C/D**
Town plan E1 Co. Cork
Montenotte
Cork (021) 501237. Tlx 75079
Owner managers Ryan family
Credit Amex, Diners, Visa

Rare trees and shrubs dot the gardens of this handsome town house overlooking the estuary. Inside, a fine collection of contemporary Irish art adorns the walls of the cosy residents' lounge and airy bar-lounge. Bedrooms are being upgraded but remain in period style; all have mini-bars and en suite bathrooms. No dogs.
Amenities garden, croquet, laundry service, 24-hour lounge service.

■ *Rooms* 20	*Confirm by arrang.*
en suite bath/shower 20	*Last dinner* 9.30
Direct dial Yes	*Parking* Ample
Room TV Yes	*Room service* 24 hours
Closed 1 wk Xmas	

Restaurant ♀

A spacious modern restaurant with delightful views makes a pleasant setting in which to enjoy Michael Ryan's competent cooking. His ambitious menu runs from starters like hot oysters with cucumber and herbs and grilled scallops with beurre blanc to main dishes like veal kidney with mustard sauce and noisettes of venison with elderberries. Delicious desserts from the trolley might include a deliciously rich and exceedingly gooey chocolate gâteau. Good Irish cheeses and a great wine list with exceptional classics like Château Cheval Blanc '47, exquisite old Sauternes and Barsac. Friendly if rather unprofessional service.

⊂⊃ Outstanding ♀ Well-chosen ⊖
■ *Set L £14·95*   *L 1–2*
Set D £17·95   *D 7–9.30*
About £65 for two   *Seats* 60 *Parties* 100
Closed Sun & 1 wk Xmas

Crawford Gallery Café *NEW ENTRY*   Cork

R ♀ ♿ **Town plan C2** Co. Cork
Emmet Place
Cork (021) 274415

Located on the ground floor of the Crawford Art Gallery in one of Cork's finest Georgian buildings, this is a delightfully relaxed café/restaurant run by Fern Allen with lots of good advice from her famous mum Myrtle, of Ballymaloe House, Shanagarry. Lunchtime brings a selection of open sandwiches, a cold meat platter, excellent soup and a choice of at least three daily hot specials like chicken pilaff, steak and Guinness pie or delicious turbot hollandaise. Open for dinner

Wednesday, Thursday and Friday, with a slightly more elaborate menu typified by feuilleté of mussels with saffron, escalope of baby beef beurre noisette, and rhubarb almond tartlets. With the Cork Opera House next door, it's the ideal venue for a pre-theatre supper. Skilled cooking and charming, informal service. Short list of good wines.
♀ Well-chosen ⊖
■ *About £38 for two*   *L* 12.30–2.30
Seats 62   *D* 6.30–9.30
Closed D Mon, Tues &   *Parking* Ample
Sat, all Sun & Bank Hols

Imperial Hotel   Cork

H **70% £C**
Town plan D2 Co. Cork
South Mall
Cork (021) 965333. Tlx 75126
Manager Dermot Kelly
Credit Access, Amex, Diners, Visa

Behind the classical facade, much period detail survives in this early-Victorian hotel. From the lofty foyer – paved in marble and lit by a glittering chandelier – run comfortable public rooms like the conservatory-style coffee lounge and the inviting Captain's Bar with its plush upholstery and polished wood. A new grill room and open-plan piano bar will enhance the facilities. Most bedrooms are stylishly modern, with good-quality fabrics and fittings, while a few front rooms are splendidly traditional. All have smartly tiled bath/shower rooms, and three sport water beds. Good

housekeeping and friendly, helpful staff.
Amenities in-house movies (free), coffee shop (10am–10pm Mon–Sat), 24-hour lounge service.

■ *Rooms* 80	*Confirm by* 6
en suite bath/shower 80	*Last dinner* 10
Direct dial Yes	*Parking* Difficult
Room TV Yes	*Room service* 24 hours

CORK

Map 19 B6
Town plan opposite

Population 136,000

Despite its 7th-century foundation as a place of scholarship by St Fin Barre, sustained today by University College, Cork's present tranquillity belies a turbulent history from 819 (the coming of the Danes) to 1921 (the end of the Troubles). It is a place of water–the River Lee that divides into channels to give the city centre four fascinating quays, and the sea with all its harbours and resorts. It is also a hill-surrounded valley; and despite its intense Irishness, has the physical aspect of an 18th-century town in France.

Annual Events
Cork Choral Festival *Late April*
Cork Jazz Festival *October*
Cork Summer Show *June*
Grand Opera Week *May*
International Film Festival *Oct*
St Patrick's Week *14th–20th March*

Sights Outside City
Airport, Blackrock, Blarney, Cobh Harbour and Yacht Clubs, Crosshaven, Fermoy, Kinsale

Tourist Office
Grand Parade
Telephone 273251

Fiat Dealers
Grandon Car Sales Ltd
Glanmire
Cork
Tel. Cork 821874

1 Bus Office **D2**
2 Christchurch **C3**
3 Church of St Francis *Byzantine with Italian mosaics* **B/C2**
4 Crawford School of Art and Gallery **C2**
5 Fitzgerald Park and Public Museum **A2**
6 G.A.A. Athletic Grounds **E2**
7 Mardyke Walk **A2**
8 Marina **E2**
9 Opera House **C2**
10 Railway Station **E1**
11 Red Abbey *oldest ruin* **C3**
12 St Ann's Church, Shandon **C1**
13 St Fin Barre's Cathedral *Church of Ireland* **B3**
14 The Lough **B3**
15 Tourist Office **C2**
16 University College **A3**
17 University Sports Ground, Mardyke **A2**

Lee Garage (Cork) Ltd
11 South Terrace
Cork
Tel. Cork 507344
Map reference 3D

Lee Garage Ltd
Model Farm Road
Cork
Tel. Cork 42933

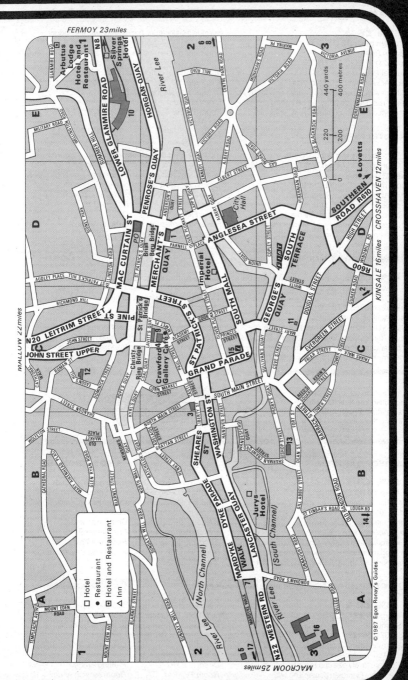

Cork

FIAT

Jurys Hotel   Cork

H 69% £B 👤
Town plan B2 Co. Cork
Western Road
Cork (021) 276622. Tlx 76073
Manager Peter Malone
Credit Access, Amex, Diners, Visa

Fifty new bedrooms and a swanky new lobby at this low-rise riverside hotel. All bedrooms provide streamlined modern comforts. A striking multi-level Pavilion includes bar, restaurants and indoor garden. Housekeeping still needs attention. *Amenities* garden, indoor/outdoor swimming pool, sauna, whirlpool bath, gymnasium, squash, laundry service, coffee shop (7am–11pm).

■ *Rooms* 200	*Confirm by arrang.*
en suite bath/shower 200	*Last dinner* 11
Direct dial Yes	*Parking* Ample
Room TV Yes	*Room service* 24 hours

Lovetts Restaurant   Cork

R ⌂ Town plan D2 Co. Cork
Churchyard Lane, off Well Road, Douglas
Cork (021) 294909
Owner manager Dermot Lovett
Credit Access, Amex, Diners, Visa

Seafood is the focus of the menu in this elegant restaurant, and Clodagh McAlinden prepares it with a sure, competent hand. Start perhaps with mousseline of turbot or mussels in garlic sauce and move on to a delicious poached trout, served plain or with a sorrel sauce. Steaks and lamb for meat-eaters, first-rate Irish cheeses and inviting sweets. There's a good choice of white burgundies and Alsace. 🍷 **Well-chosen** 🍴

■ *Set D* £16	*L* 12.30–2.15
About £60 for two	*D* 7–10
Seats 36 *Parties* 28	*Parking* Ample
Closed L Sat, all Sun & 25 Dec–7 Jan	

Silver Springs Hotel   Cork

H 60% £D/E
Town plan E1 Co. Cork
Tivoli
Cork (021) 507533. Tlx 76111
Credit Access, Amex, Diners, Visa

Just off the N25, on a hill overlooking the estuary, this modern hotel offers bright, spacious accommodation. Many of the light, simple bedrooms have fine views. Public areas include a cheerful picture-windowed lounge with cane furnishings and the hexagonal Blarney Bar. No dogs. *Amenities* garden, tennis, laundry service, 24-hour lounge service.

■ *Rooms* 72	*Confirm by* 6
en suite bath/shower 72	*Last dinner* 10
Direct dial Yes	*Parking* Ample
Room TV Yes	*Room service* 24 hours
Closed 4 days Xmas	

■ Any person using our name to obtain free hospitality is a fraud. Proprietors, please inform the police and us.

Enniscoe House   Crossmolina

H 64% £D/E
Map 18 B3 Co. Mayo
Castlehill, Nr Ballina
Ballina (096) 31112. Tlx 40855
Owner manager Susan Kellett
Credit Access, Amex, Visa

Guests will find ready warmth and relaxation at this handsome Georgian house. Antiques and family portraits adorn the living rooms, and there are solid antique furnishings and grand old beds in the large bedrooms. Extensive grounds run down to Lough Conn. *Amenities* garden, game fishing, games room, hotel boat.

■ *Rooms* 6	*Confirm by arrang.*
en suite bath/shower 5	*Last dinner* 9
Room phone No	*Parking* Ample
Room TV No	*Room service* Limited
Closed Oct–Mar	

Knockmuldowney Hotel *NEW ENTRY*   Culleenamore

H 64% £D/E
Map 18 B2 Co. Sligo
Nr Strandhill
Sligo (071) 68122
Owner managers Charles & Mary Cooper
Credit Access, Amex, Diners, Visa

There are lovely sea and mountain views from this secluded Georgian house. The two comfortable lounges have a homely, welcoming feel that extends to the traditionally appointed bedrooms. Bathrooms are neat and modern. Breakfast is a freshly prepared feast. No dogs. *Amenities* garden, laundry service.

■ *Rooms* 6	*Confirm by arrang.*
en suite bath/shower 6	*Last dinner* 9.30
Direct dial Yes	*Parking* Ample
Room TV Most	*Room service* All day
Closed early Nov–mid Mar	

Glenview Hotel   Delgany

H 61% £D
Map 19 D4 Co. Wicklow
Glen of the Downs
Dublin (01) 862896. Tlx 30638
Owner managers Patrick family
Credit Access, Amex, Visa
  A comfortable hotel standing just off the N11 on the lower slopes of Sugar Loaf mountain. Lovely views from the lounge and restaurant, and

upstairs there's a TV room. Gradual upgrading of the accommodation includes chintzy modern fabrics and more up-to-date bathrooms. No dogs.
Amenities garden, laundry service.
- *Rooms 23*   *Confirm by 6*
en suite bath/shower 23   *Last dinner 9.30*
Direct dial Yes   *Parking Ample*
Room TV Some   *Room service All day*
Closed 2 days Xmas

- Our inspectors are our full-time employees; they are professionally trained by us.

Doyle's Seafood Bar   Dingle

R ⌂ ⓖ **Map 19 A5** Co. Kerry
John Street
Dingle (066) 51174
Credit Access, Amex, Diners, Visa
  John and Stella Doyle are respectively the chatty host and super chef at their popular seafood bar. The fish is marvellously fresh and carefully prepared; dishes include crab soup, scallops with leek sauce, superb seabass and hot

poached lobster. Good wine list, strong in Chardonnays: note seven Chablis and the excellent Rosemount Estate wines from Australia. The Doyles plan to open a little town house hotel next door (March 1988). ♀ **Well-chosen** ⓔ
- *About £42 for two*   *L 12.30–2.15*
Seats 48   *D 6–9*
Parties 48   *Parking Ample*
Closed Sun, mid Nov–mid Mar

Drumlease Glebe House   Dromahair

HR 74% £D
Map 18 B2 Co. Leitrim
Co. Leitrim
Sligo (071) 64141
Owner managers Mr & Mrs Greenstein
Credit Access, Amex, Diners, Visa
  The American owners, together with their dogs Coley and Poteen, welcome guests as long-lost friends. Their home is a fine Georgian country house standing by the bubbling river Bonet in truly magnificent countryside, and the atmosphere of peace and relaxation has to be experienced to be believed. Public rooms are furnished with elegant antiques, and one room houses a collection of Irish antiques and handicrafts. A sun terrace overlooks the pool, and

there's a charming walled garden. Bedrooms are also very tasteful and comfortable, with lots of homely extras, and guests start the day with a super breakfast. No children. No dogs.
Amenities garden, outdoor swimming pool, coarse & game fishing.
- *Rooms 8*   *Confirm by arrang.*
en suite bath/shower 5   *Last dinner 8*
Room phone No   *Parking Ample*
Room TV No   *Room service Limited*
Closed Nov–Easter

Drumlease Glebe House Restaurant ⌂ ⓖ

Dinner starts at eight, with places for just 12 residents to enjoy Joan Purcell's careful, capable cooking. Tomato and peach soup or smoked trout wrapped in smoked salmon could precede rack of lamb, or maybe veal escalope with a creamy mushroom sauce. Irish farmhouse cheeses, delicious sweets, then convivial coffee in the lounge. Good younger clarets and an excellent 1985 Muscadet (Ch. du Cléray). ⓔ
- *Set D £18*   *D only, at 8*
About £50 for two   *Seats 12*
Closed Nov–Easter

NEW ENTRY

- We welcome complaints and bona fide recommendations on the tear-out pages for readers' comments. They are followed up by our professional team. Please also complain to the management instantly.

RECEPTION

DUBLIN

Map 19 D4
Town plan opposite

Population 1,003,164

Dublin (from the Erse for 'dark pool'), came into historic prominence when the Norman conquerors in England were invited to help the King of Leinster campaign against the High King of Ireland. The chapter of 'troubles' began. In 1800 the Irish Parliament was absorbed by Westminster, but in 1922 that chapter ended and Dublin is now the bustling capital of the Irish Republic.

Annual Events
Dublin Horse Show *2nd–6th August*
Dublin Millennium Celebrations *1988*
Dublin Spring Show *1st–5th May*
Gaelic Football Finals *18th September*
Hurling Finals *4th September*
St Patrick's Day Parade *17th March*

Sights Outside City
Malahide Castle, Hill Abbey of Howth, The Curragh, Bray, Enniskerry Village, Powerscourt House, Vale of Avoca, Glendalough, The Japanese Gardens, Monasterboice, Newgrange

Information Offices
14 Upper O'Connell Street
Telephone Dublin 747733
Telex 25253

Bord Failte Eireann
Baggot Street Bridge
Dublin 2
Telephone Dublin 765871

Fiat Dealers
Rialto Motors Ltd, Herberton Road
Dublin 12. Tel. Dublin 754216
Map reference 3A

Sweeney & Forte Ltd
56 Howth Road, Clontarf, Dublin 3
Tel. Dublin 332301

Tractamotors Ltd, 84 Prussia Street
Dublin 7, Tel. Dublin 791722

Autocars Ireland Ltd, Milltown Road
Dublin 6. Tel. Dublin 698577

Finglas Motors Ltd
North Road, Finglas
Dublin 11, Tel. Dublin 342977

Terenure Car Sales
Terenure Road North
Dublin 6. Tel. Dublin 902709

Tractamotors
Blanchardstown
Dublin 15. Tel. Dublin 216622

1 Abbey Theatre D1
2 Airport C1
3 Bank of Ireland *in old Parliament building* C1
4 Botanic Gardens B1
5 Castle C2
6 Christ Church Cathedral *11th-c Strongbow's tomb* C2
7 City Hall *18th-c* C2
8 Civic Museum *record of Dublin's history* C2
9 Connolly Station D1
10 Croke Park *hurling and Gaelic football* C1
11 Eblana Theatre D1
12 Four Courts *Law Courts* B1
13 Gate Theatre C1
14 Government Buildings D2
15 Heuston Station A1
16 Hugh Lane Municipal Gallery of Modern Art C1
17 Lansdowne Road Rugby Ground E3
18 Leinster House *Dail; National Library; Museum* D2
19 Mansion House *Queen Anne period* D2
20 Olympia Theatre C2
21 Pearse Station D2
22 Phoenix Park and Zoo A1
23 Pro-Cathedral C1
24 Royal Dublin Society Showgrounds E3
25 St Audoen's Church *oldest parish church* B2
26 St Michan's Church *remarkable vaults* B1
27 St Patrick's Cathedral *impressive interior, Swift's tomb* C2
28 St Stephen's Green *oasis in city's heart* C/D2
29 Tourist Information Centre C1
30 Trinity College and Library *Book of Kells* D2

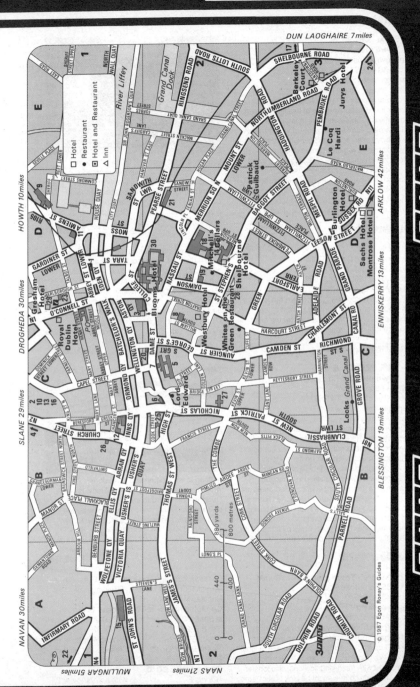

Dublin FIAT

© 1987 Egon Ronay's Guides

Berkeley Court — Dublin

H **79% £B** ***E*** ♿
Town plan E3 Co. Dublin
Lansdowne Road
Dublin (01) 601711. Tlx 30554
Manager Michael J. Governey
Credit Access, Amex, Diners, Visa

Antique and contemporary pieces mingle pleasantly in the public areas of this fine modern hotel. The vast split-level foyer lounge, with its pink marble columns, has plenty of inviting sofas, the clubby bar some fine old panelling, and beyond an extravagantly carved church rood screen is a charming little conservatory. Except for a number of luxurious suites, bedrooms are identical, with oak furniture, canopied beds with quilted covers, and smart compact bathrooms. *Amenities* indoor swimming pool, sauna, hairdressing, in-house movies (free), laundry

service, grill restaurant (7.30am–11.30pm), 24-hour lounge service, shopping arcade.

■ *Rooms 220*	*Confirm by 6*
en suite bath/shower 220	*Last dinner 10.30*
Direct dial Yes	*Parking Ample*
Room TV Yes	*Room service 24 hours*

Blooms Hotel — Dublin

H **62% £B**
Town plan C2 Co. Dublin
Anglesea Street
Dublin (01) 715622. Tlx 31688
Credit Access, Amex, Diners, Visa

A smart mirrored ceiling decorates the foyer of this modern city-centre hotel. Liveliest of the public areas (which include a cocktail bar and small lounge) is the large cheerful main bar. Decent-sized, pleasantly appointed bedrooms all have radio-alarms, trouser presses and good bathrooms (singles have showers only). No dogs. *Amenities* in-house movies (free), laundry service, 24-hour lounge service.

■ *Rooms 84*	*Confirm by 6*
en suite bath/shower 72	*Last dinner 10.15*
Direct dial Yes	*Parking Ample*
Room TV Yes	*Room service 24 hours*

Burlington Hotel — Dublin

H **74% £B/C** ***E*** ♿
Town plan D3 Co. Dublin
Upper Leeson Street
Dublin (01) 605222. Tlx 25517
Manager Mr John Glynn
Credit Access, Amex, Diners, Visa

Convenient for the city centre but away from the bustle, the Burlington is a very large modern hotel with luxurious public rooms. The chandelier-hung lobby merges into a large comfortably furnished lounge area, and there are two inviting bars, one handsomely panelled in mahogany adjacent to a domed conservatory. Bedrooms are kept in very good order; pretty, matched fabrics and brass-edged fitted units feature attractively, and bathrooms are above average. Some handsome suites have good views over the south side of the city. Breakfast on our latest visit was

nothing to write home about. No dogs. *Amenities* hairdressing, in-house movies, kiosk, laundry service, grill room (6.30am–11.30pm).

■ *Rooms 500*	*Confirm by arrang.*
en suite bath/shower 500	*Last dinner 11.30*
Direct dial Yes	*Parking Ample*
Room TV Yes	*Room service All day*

Le Coq Hardi — Dublin

RR ♛ **Town plan E3** Co. Dublin
35 Pembroke Road
Dublin (01) 689070
French cooking
Credit Access, Amex, Diners, Visa

Chef-patron John Howard cooks with flair at this elegant end-of-terrace Georgian restaurant, one of Dublin's finest. Fish, bought daily at a local market, is a popular choice, and starters include warm salad with fresh king scallops, also lobster soup. The main course might be pink fillet of lamb with tomato and tarragon, or an oven-baked free-range chicken finished with Irish whiskey. Desserts include sorbets and fresh fruit medleys. Magnificent cellar with over 30 vintages of Château Mouton-Rothschild.

Outstanding 🍷 Well-chosen

■ *Set L £13·75*	*L 12.30–2.30*
Set D £22·50	*D 7.30–11*
About £78 for two	*Parking Ample*
Seats 50 Parties 20	*Closed L Sat, all Sun,*

Bank Hols, 2 wks Aug & 2 wks Xmas

Bedrooms £C/D

Rooms 2	*With bath/shower 2*

Two luxurious bedrooms are available for overnight guests. No children or dogs.

Gresham Hotel Dublin

H 64% £B ♿
Town plan C1 Co. Dublin
O'Connell Street, Dublin 2
Dublin (01) 746881. Tlx 32473
Credit Access, Amex, Diners, Visa

In a fine Regency building on Dublin's main street, the Gresham is showing the results of major investments. Some bedrooms have been redecorated in chic, modern style; there are several antique-furnished suites with balconies and sitting areas. There's a fine marble foyer, a lively bar and a luxurious new restaurant. Friendly staff include notably courteous porters. No dogs. *Amenities* laundry service.

■ Rooms 180 — Confirm by 6
en suite bath/shower 180 — Last dinner 11.15
Direct dial Yes — Parking Ample
Room TV Yes — Room service 24 hours

Jurys Hotel Dublin

H 77% £B E ♿
Town plan E3 Co. Dublin
Pembroke Road, Ballsbridge
Dublin (01) 605000. Tlx 93723
Credit Access, Amex, Diners, Visa

The fruits of the refurbishment programme at this modern city-centre hotel can be seen immediately in the smart new glass entrance lobby. Beyond are the bustling public rooms, including the Pavilion Bar, with its waterfall and profuse greenery, the Edwardian-style Dubliners Bar and the long-hours coffee shop. The Grand Ballroom features an Irish cabaret dinner show in summer. Bedrooms are of a decent size, with quite plain modern furnishings and six-channel TVs; one floor is for non-smokers. Well-equipped bathrooms throughout. Room service is prompt and efficient. *Amenities* garden, indoor/outdoor

swimming pool, whirlpool bath, beauty salon, hairdressing, in-house movies (free), valeting, laundry service, coffee shop (6am–4.30pm, Sun till 11pm).

■ Rooms 300 — Confirm by 6
en suite bath/shower 300 — Last dinner 10.15
Direct dial Yes — Parking Ample
Room TV Yes — Room service 24 hours

Locks Dublin

R Town plan C3 Co. Dublin
1 Windsor Terrace, Portobello
Dublin (01) 752025
Owner manager Richard Douglas
Credit Access, Amex, Diners, Visa

An attractive restaurant overlooking the Grand Canal. Kevin McCarthy cooks in accomplished contemporary style and his seasonally-changing menus range from fish soup with rouille, and steak au poivre, to more elaborate dishes like smoked salmon mousse with shellfish sauce and chicken in pastry with a pungent garlic sauce. Polished service. Book. Wines include a fine Chablis from Dauvissat. ♀ Well-chosen ⊖
■ Set L £10.75 — L 12.30–2
About £56 for two — D 7.15–11
Seats 48 Parties 35 — Parking Ample
Closed L Sat, all Sun, Bank Hols & 1 wk Xmas

Mitchell's Cellars Dublin

R ♀ Town plan D2 Co. Dublin
21 Kildare Street
Dublin (01) 680367
Credit Access, Amex, Diners, Visa

Patricia Hogan's excellent bistro-style cooking draws the lunchtime crowds to this delightful basement restaurant. Her short menus change daily and offer simple treats like mushroom pâté or carrot and orange soup among starters, followed perhaps by asparagus quiche or beef burgundy with rice. All good wholesome stuff, carefully prepared and nicely presented. Super salads and bread, enjoyable desserts.
♀ Well-chosen ⊖
■ About £24 for two — L only 12.15–2.30
Seats 60 Parties 20 — Parking Limited
Closed Sun, Bank Hol weekends, 24 Dec–2 Jan & Sat (June–Sept)

Montrose Hotel Dublin

H 60% £D
Town plan D3 Co. Dublin
Stillorgan Road
Dublin (01) 693311. Tlx 91207
Credit Access, Amex, Diners, Visa

A low, modern hotel by the N11 opposite University College campus. It's popular with both business visitors and tourists, and the smart public areas include meeting and function rooms. Bedrooms, some with private balconies, have functional lightwood furnishings and six-channel colour TVs. Friendly management and staff. No dogs. *Amenities* sauna, hairdressing, coffee shop (6.30am–11pm), in-house movies (free), kiosk.
■ Rooms 200 — Confirm by 7
en suite bath/shower 200 — Last dinner 11, Sun 10
Direct dial Yes — Parking Ample
Room TV Yes — Room service All day

Patrick Guilbaud

Dublin

R ♨ **Town plan D2** Co. Dublin
46 James's Place, Lower Baggot Street
Dublin (01) 601 799
French cooking
Credit Access, Amex, Diners, Visa

Patrick Guilbaud's city-centre restaurant, with paintings on the walls and baskets of abundant greenery hanging from a high vaulted ceiling, provides relaxing surroundings in which to enjoy a sophisticated meal. The menu is comparatively short, featuring ambitious nouvelle-style dishes like scallops with cream of pepper sauce among the starters and main courses like fillet of beef with red Hermitage wine sauce or pigeon with lime mousse and beetroot sauce. Much emphasis is placed on elaborate presentation and cooking would benefit from simplification. An excellent French cheeseboard makes a good finish. Service is polished and formal. Classic French wines at high prices.

♀ Well-chosen ℮

■ Set L £12·50	L 12.30–2.45
Set D £16·50	D 7.30–10.15
About £68 for two	Parking Limited
Seats 50	Parties 60
Closed L Sat, all Sun & Bank Hols	

Royal Dublin Hotel

Dublin

H 60% £C/D
Town Plan C1 Co. Dublin
40 Upper O'Connell Street, Dublin 1
Dublin (01) 733666. Tlx 32568
Credit Access, Amex, Diners, Visa

The basement car park is a great boon for guests staying at this modern hotel in the bustling heart of the city. A programme of refurbishment is well under way, starting with bright new carpets in the corridors and a stylish revamp for the bedrooms. Day rooms include a pleasant Edwardian-style bar. No dogs.
Amenities laundry service.

■ Rooms 100	Confirm by 6
en suite bath/shower 100	Last dinner 9.30
Direct dial Yes	Parking Ample
Room TV Yes	Room service 24 hours
Closed 25–29 Dec	

■ Changes in data may occur in establishments after the Guide goes to press. Prices should be taken as indications rather than firm quotes.

Sachs Hotel

Dublin

H 59% £D
Town plan D3 Co. Dublin
19 Morehampton Road, Donnybrook
Dublin (01) 680995. Tlx 31667
Credit Access, Amex, Diners, Visa

Part of a Georgian terrace in a quiet suburb south of the city centre. The foyer incorporates a pleasant little lounge area, and there's a pub-style bar and a lively bistro. Bedrooms vary in size, style and furnishings; accessories include cable TV (English channels) and bathroom telephone extensions. Some bedroom and stair carpets have seen better days. No dogs.
Amenities bistro (10am–5pm & 6pm–11pm).

■ Rooms 20	Confirm by arrang.
en suite bath/shower 20	Last dinner 10.30
Room phone Yes	Parking Ample
Room TV Yes	Room service 24 hours

Shelbourne Hotel

Dublin

H 80% £A **E**
Town plan D2 Co. Dublin
St Stephen's Green
Dublin (01) 766471. Tlx 93653
Credit Access, Amex, Diners, Visa

Overlooking the lakes and trees of St Stephen's Green, this impressive 19th-century hotel in the city centre is luxuriously appointed throughout. Efficient staff extend a cordial welcome in the chandelier-hung foyer-lounge, and the Lord Mayor's lounge has the same elegantly Georgian air. The Horseshoes Bar is a highly popular local meeting place – its cocktail barman has been mixing drinks here for 27 years! Tastefully refurbished bedrooms offer every conceivable comfort (one even boasts a water bed), and telephones, hairdryers and bathrobes are standard fittings in the spacious bathrooms.

Amenities solarium, beauty salon, hairdressing, valeting, laundry service, coffee shop (11am–10.30pm), 24-hour lounge service, kiosk.

■ Rooms 177	Confirm by 6
en suite bath/shower 177	Last dinner 10.30
Direct dial Yes	Parking Ample
Room TV Yes	Room service 24 hours

Westbury Hotel

Dublin

H 77% £B *E*
Town plan C2 Co. Dublin
Off Grafton Street
Dublin (01) 791122. Tlx 91091
Credit Access, Amex, Diners, Visa

Luxury, style and comfort are found in abundance at this splendid modern hotel in the heart of Dublin's most fashionable shopping district. A striking stairway brings you to the open-plan foyer laid out in broad walks of cream and soft red marble and strewn with Irish hand-made rugs. Wrought-iron gates lead to the relaxing, comfortably furnished Terrace Bar; downstairs, there's a contrasting Victorian-style bar featuring carved mahogany, stained-glass windows and marble-topped tables. Elegant, spacious bedrooms (including six handsome suites) have canopied beds, writing desks and

comprehensively equipped bathrooms. No dogs. *Amenities* beauty salon, hairdressing, in-house movies (free), valeting, coffee shop (10am–11pm), kiosk, shopping arcade.

■ *Rooms* 151	*Confirm by 6*
en suite bath/shower 151	*Last dinner 10.30*
Direct dial Yes	*Parking Ample*
Room TV Yes	*Room service 24 hours*

Whites on the Green

Dublin

R ♔ ♘ Town plan C2 Co. Dublin
119 St Stephen's Green
Dublin (01) 751975
Credit Access, Amex, Diners, Visa

A fashionable restaurant of style and sophistication in a prime site on St Stephen's Green. The decor is formal but chicly modern, and service led by Frenchman Alain Bras is polished and professional. In the kitchen is Michael Clifford, whose menus are basically French, but with his own imaginative touches, as in cassolette of prawns with ginger and soya. Not everything succeeds completely, but we very much enjoyed

chicken quenelles with a walnut and apple sauce, and meltingly tender noisettes of spring lamb with an aubergine mousse. Pretty, al dente vegetables and interesting sweets. Fine wines, from a delicious Mâcon-Solutré '85 from André Depardon to splendid old clarets.
♥ **Well-chosen** ☻

■ *Set L from £10·50*	*L 12.30–2.30*
Set D £20.25	*D 7–9.45*
About £70 for two	*Parking Limited*
Seats 60	*Parties 30*
Closed L Sat, all Sun, Bank Hols & 10 days Xmas	

Dublin International Hotel

Dublin Airport

H 57% £C ♿
Map 18 D3 Co. Dublin
Collinstown
Dublin (01) 379211. Tlx 32849
Credit Access, Amex, Diners, Visa

A modern hotel in a four-acre site by the airport. Accommodation ranges from slightly dated standard rooms to others upgraded with darkwood units and pretty floral fabrics and more

luxurious Executive rooms. Spacious lobby-lounge, bar and coffee shop. No dogs. *Amenities* garden, in-house movies (free), coffee shop (6.30am–10.30pm), kiosk, transport for airport.

■ *Rooms* 195	*Confirm by 6*
en suite bath/shower 195	*Last dinner 10.15*
Direct dial Yes	*Parking Ample*
Room TV Yes	*Room service None*
Closed 25 Dec	

■ We publish annually, so make sure you use the current edition. It's worth it!

Digby's

Dun Laoghaire

R ♘ Map 19 D4 Co. Dublin
5 Windsor Terrace
Dublin (01) 804600
Credit Access, Amex, Diners, Visa

Part-owner Paul Cathcart puts his culinary skills to excellent use in this elegant restaurant overlooking the bay. You could kick off with seafood pancake, gravad trout or fresh asparagus, and proceed to salmon with sorrel,

steak with garlic butter or pigeon breasts in a port and pineapple sauce. To finish, maybe chocolate mousse or a sorbet. Sound wines, good clarets. Less choice at lunchtimes. ♥ **Well-chosen** ☻

■ *Set L £9*	*L 12.30–3*
Set D from £15·50	*D 7.30–11, Sun 7.30–10*
About £55 for two	*Parking Ample*
Seats 50 Parties 54	*Closed L Sat & Bank*
Hols, all Tues, Good Fri & 3 days Xmas	

Restaurant Mirabeau   Dun Laoghaire

R ♔♔ ⅄ **Map 19 D4** Co. Dublin
Marine Parade, Sandycove
Dublin (01) 809 873
French cooking
Owner managers Mr & Mrs Eoin Clarke
Credit Access, Amex, Diners, Visa
 The cuisine is classical French with thoughtful
modern touches in this stylishly contemporary
restaurant. Chef Michel Flamme's technique is
light and assured, resulting in fine dishes like little
pasta parcels filled with succulent lobster, prawns
and scallops; turbot steak with Meaux mustard
and a saffron sauce; and roast duck with a

delightful herb-flavoured jus. Sweets such as
strawberry feuilleté with a textbook champagne
sabayon and nougat glacé au caramel maintain
the high standard, and there's a distinguished
cheeseboard. A beautifully chosen wine list
features exceptional clarets and first-rate
burgundies.

⇨ Outstanding ♀ Well-chosen ☺

Set L from £9·50	*L 12.30–2*
Set D from £17·50	*D 7.30–10*
About £70 for two	*Parking Ample*
Seats 35	*Parties 40*
Closed L Sat, Sun & Bank Hols	

Restaurant Na Mara   Dun Laoghaire

R ♔ ⅄ **Map 19 D4** Co. Dublin
1 Harbour Road
Dublin (01) 800509
Seafood
Manager Barney Nicholson
Credit Access, Amex, Diners, Visa
 A stylish, elegant restaurant in a former railway
terminal near the quay. Its excellent seafood is
typified by dishes like salmon mousse, prawns

mornay, sole dieppoise or monkfish with a light
orange sauce. Also meat and vegetarian choices,
good al dente vegetables and pleasant sweets.
Service is agreeable and professional. ☺

■ *Set L £11·50*	*L 1–2.30*
Set D £16·50	*D 7–10.30*
About £50 for two	*Parking Ample*
Closed Sun, Mon, 1 wk	*Seats 70*
Easter & 1 wk Xmas	

Ballymascanlon Hotel   Dundalk

H **59% £E**
Map 18 D3 Co. Louth
Dundalk (042) 71124. Tlx 43735
Credit Access, Amex, Diners, Visa
 Outside town on the Carlingford road, this
extended Victorian house offers many leisure
facilities and a number of lounges and bars. Well-
maintained bedrooms are simply furnished;
bathrooms are adequate. *Amenities* garden,

indoor swimming pool, sauna, solarium, keep-fit
equipment, tennis, squash, snooker, children's
playground, in-house movies, laundry service, 24-
hour lounge service.

■ *Rooms 36*	*Confirm by arrang.*
en suite bath/shower 36	*Last dinner 9.30*
Direct dial Yes	*Parking Ample*
Room TV Yes	*Room service 24 hours*
Closed 24–26 Dec	

Dunderry Lodge Restaurant ★   Dunderry

R ★ ⅄ **Map 18 C3** Co. Meath
Robinstown, Nr Navan
Navan (046) 31671
Credit Access, Amex, Diners, Visa
 Fields surround this marvellous restaurant,
which originated as an old stone barn and cattle
byre. Stone walls hint at humble origins but tables
are elegance itself, with good-quality china and
glass. Front of house, Nicholas Healy supervises
the smooth service; his wife Catherine makes
excellent use of local produce, with plenty of fish
in the summer and game in the winter. Happy
combinations of flavours and textures are the key
to simple well-executed dishes. Start, perhaps,
with feuilleté of mussels and leeks or mushrooms
in tarragon cream; follow with goujons of plaice
with pistachio butter, roast wild duck with sauce
cassis or blanquette of mussels, monkfish and
ginger. Vegetables are cooked to perfection.
Puds may include intriguing honey and lavender
ice cream. *Specialities* terrine of two fish,

panaché of duck livers and green lentils, wild Irish
salmon with sauce verte, cassolette of lamb
sweetbreads. ♀ Well-chosen ☺

■ *Set L £9*	*L 12.30–2*
Set D £14·50	*D 7.30–9.30*
About £46 for two	*Parking Ample*
Seats 36	*Parties 25*
Closed L Sat, all Sun, Mon, Bank Hols, Easter wk	
& 20 Dec–12 Feb	

Dundrum House Hotel
Dundrum

H **66%** **£C/D**
Map 19 C5 Co. Tipperary
Nr Cashel
Cashel (062) 71116. Tlx 70255
Credit Access, Amex, Diners, Visa
Built in 1730, this handsome country manor stands in 100 acres of land including a deer park and trout river. The lounges are roomy and traditional, and stained-glass windows declare that the bar was once a private chapel. Bedrooms are tastefully furnished, with many period pieces. Good bathrooms. No dogs. *Amenities* garden, tennis, riding, game fishing, snooker.

■ *Rooms* 55	*Confirm by* 4
en suite bath/shower 55	*Last dinner* 9.30
Direct dial Yes	*Parking Ample*
Room TV No	*Room service* All day
Closed 2 days Xmas	

Seanachie
Dungarvan

R ♧ ☒ **Map 19 C5** Co. Waterford
Pulla Ring
Dungarvan (058) 46285
Credit Access, Amex
Laurann Casey's homely cooking is all part of the irresistible charm of this wonderfully atmospheric thatched pub on the N25 some five miles west of Dungarvan. Lunchtime (except Sunday) brings generous portions of tasty hot dishes from hearty soups to steaks and a tasty seafood or chicken curry pancake. Sandwiches of homebaked bread, Irish stew and delicious sweets like spicy apple pie are available throughout opening hours. Bar food only eves. Soup and sandwiches on Sunday. ℮

■ *About £24 for two*	*L* 11.30–3
Seats 76	*Parties* 76
Closed Nov–end Mar	*Parking Ample*

Dunworley Cottage
Dunworley

R ♧ **Map 19 B5** Co. Cork
Butlerstown, Bandon
Bandon (023) 40314
Credit Access, Amex, Diners, Visa
Follow signs to Butlerstown and Dunworley from the Clonakilty–Timoleague road to find Otto Kunze's restaurant, where a relaxed atmosphere enhances dedicated cooking. Otto's deft and inventive touch is evident in dishes like smoked wheat and beetroot soup, celeriac fritters and sea trout dumplings. Excellent vegetables, delicious sweets, and a good choice of Irish farmhouse cheeses. ♟ Well-chosen ℮

■ *Set L from* £7	*L* 1–3
Set D from £7	*D* 6.30–10
About £40 *for two*	*Parking Ample*
Seats 35	*Parties* 20
Closed Mon, Tues, Jan & Feb	

Blair's Cove House
Durrus

R ♧ **Map 19 A6** Co. Cork
Nr Bantry
Bantry (027) 61127
Credit Access, Diners, Amex, Visa
Belgian owners Philip and Sabine de Mey are respectively host and chef at their comfortably converted barn overlooking a picturesque cove. Sabine's cooking lacks frills but not skills; many of her dishes feature top-quality meat and fish prepared simply and deliciously over an open wood-burning fire. Start with a selection from the splendid cold buffet. The wine list has lots of interesting clarets. ♟ Well-chosen ℮

■ *Set L* £10	*L* Sun only 1–2
About £50 *for two*	*D* 7.30–9
Seats 70 *Parties* 45	*Parking Ample*
Closed D Sun, Jan & Feb, mid Oct–end Mar	

■ Our inspectors never book in the name of Egon Ronay's Guides; they disclose their identity only after paying their bills.

Old Ground Hotel
Ennis

H **66%** **£C/D**
Map 19 B4 Co. Clare
Ennis (065) 28127. Tlx 28103
Credit Access, Amex, Diners, Visa
An ivy-clad hotel of some character, the main part of the building dating from the 17th century. Check-in, by friendly, efficient staff, is at a handsome desk in the entrance hall; there are two bars – one a popular local haunt and the other a large, comfortable lounge. Bedrooms in the old house have sturdy, traditional furnishings while those in the 60s wings have smart, lightwood fitted units. *Amenities* garden, laundry service.

■ *Rooms* 60	*Confirm by* 6
en suite bath/shower 60	*Last dinner* 9
Direct dial Yes	*Parking Ample*
Room TV Yes	*Room service* 24 hours

West County Inn Hotel

Ennis

H 59% £D/E 🔥
Map 19 B4 Co. Clare
Clare Road
Ennis (065) 28421. Tlx 28294
Manager John Madden
Credit Access, Amex, Diners, Visa
   Sited on the Limerick Road, this well-run and well-maintained modern hotel has a happy atmosphere. There are several lively bars and an

attractive new conservatory lounge. Bedrooms, some refurbished with smart fitted units, have good bathrooms. No dogs. *Amenities* sauna, snooker, satellite TV, in-house movies (free), laundry service, coffee shop (7.30am–10.30pm).

■ *Rooms* 110	*Confirm by* 6
en suite bath/shower 110	*Last dinner* 9.30
Direct dial Yes	*Parking* Ample
Room TV Yes	*Room service* All day

■ If we recommend meals in a
hotel or inn, a separate entry is
made for its restaurant.

Ardilaun House Hotel

Galway

H 64% £D
Map 19 B4 Co. Galway
Taylor's Hill
Galway (091) 21433. Tlx 50013
Manager Mr McCarthy-O'Hea
Credit Access, Amex, Diners, Visa
   Much modernised over the years, this friendly Georgian hotel still has an air of period charm in its pleasant chintzy lounge. There's a smart bar,

too, and several function areas. Attractive, traditional-style bedrooms all have private baths or showers. *Amenities* garden, laundry service, 24-hour lounge service.

■ *Rooms* 93	*Confirm by* 6
en suite bath/shower 93	*Last dinner* 9.15
Direct dial Yes	*Parking* Ample
Room TV Yes	*Room service* 24 hours
Closed 1 wk Xmas	

Corrib Great Southern Hotel

Galway

H 63% £C
Map 19 B4 Co. Galway
Dublin Road
Galway (091) 55281. Tlx 50044
Credit Access, Amex, Diners, Visa
   An extensive programme of improvements is under way at this modern hotel. Half the bedrooms have been updated, four large rooms upgraded to luxury status. Public rooms include a

summery sunken lounge and a comfortable bar. Friendly staff. No dogs. *Amenities* garden, indoor swimming pool, sauna, snooker, satellite TV, in-house movies (free), laundry service.

■ *Rooms* 110	*Confirm by* 6
en suite bath/shower 110	*Last dinner* 9
Direct dial Yes	*Parking* Ample
Room TV Yes	*Room service* 24 hours
Closed 25 Dec	

Galway Ryan Hotel

Galway

H 58% £E
Map 19 B4 Co. Galway
Dublin Road
(091) 53181. Tlx 50149
Credit Access, Amex, Diners, Visa
   A mile out of the city on the road to Dublin, this modern low-rise hotel offers an overnight stop with few frills but all the basic comforts. Bedrooms are well kept and reasonably spacious, with

practical fitted furniture and neat bathrooms. Among the day rooms are a sunken lounge in bright blue and a panelled bar. No dogs. *Amenities* in-house movies.

■ *Rooms* 96	*Confirm by* 6
en suite bath/shower 96	*Last dinner* 9.15
Direct dial Yes	*Parking* Ample
Room TV Yes	*Room service* 24 hours
Closed 25 Dec	

Great Southern Hotel

Galway

H 68% £B/C
Map 19 B4 Co. Galway
Eyre Square
Galway (091) 64041. Tlx 50164
Credit Access, Amex, Diners, Visa
   A Victorian town-centre hotel where stylishly appointed public areas retain fine original features like the Connemara marble fireplace in the foyer. Bedrooms vary in size and standard but are all

quite comfortable. *Amenities* indoor swimming pool, sauna, solarium, keep-fit equipment, beauty salon, in-house movies (free), laundry service, 24-hour lounge service.

■ *Rooms* 120	*Confirm by* 6
en suite bath/shower 120	*Last dinner* 10
Direct dial Yes	*Parking* Ample
Room TV Yes	*Room service* 24 hours
Closed 3 days Xmas	

J J's Malt House

Galway

R ♀ **Map 19 B4** Co. Galway
High Street
Galway (091) 67866
Credit Access, Amex, Diners, Visa
'Simple is best' at this friendly restaurant in a converted malt house, where chef-patron John J. Coppinger is a particularly dab hand at preparing seafood. Choices of fish might include whole grilled sole, poached salmon hollandaise and scallops bonne femme, while alternatives centre around familiar ways with beef, veal and chicken. Apple pie for afters. Booking advisable, especially lunchtimes. ♀ Well-chosen ⊗

■ Set L £7·15	L 12.30–2.30
Set D £15·95	D 7–10
About £44 for two	Parking Ample
Seats 55	Parties 60
Closed Sun, Good Fri, 25 & 26 Dec	

Aherlow House Hotel

Glen of Aherlow

H **59% £E**
Map 19 B5 Co. Tipperary
Nr Tipperary
Tipperary (062) 56153
Credit Access, Amex, Diners, Visa
The setting of this former hunting lodge, in a forest overlooking the glen, is outstandingly picturesque and peaceful. Public rooms, dotted with antiques, revel in the lovely views, as do many of the bedrooms, which have traditional furnishings and colour schemes that range from pale yellow to glaring purple. Some refurbishment would be welcome, especially in the bungalow rooms. No dogs. *Amenities* terrace.

■ Rooms 10	Confirm by arrang.
en suite bath/shower 8	Last dinner 9.30
Direct dial Yes	Parking Ample
Room TV Yes	Room service All day

Ashbourne House Hotel

Glounthaune

H **60% £E** &
Map 19 B6 Co. Cork
Cork (021) 353319
Proprietors Garde family
Credit Access, Amex, Diners, Visa
An extended 19th-century mansion standing a few miles east of Cork. Period features retained in the public areas create an atmosphere of traditional elegance, and a log fire burns in the residents' lounge in winter. Bedrooms – many with lovely views over the gardens – are in neat modern style. *Amenities* garden, sauna, outdoor swimming pool, tennis, in-house movies (free), laundry service, 24-hour lounge service.

■ Rooms 27	Confirm by arrang.
en suite bath/shower 27	Last dinner 10
Direct dial Yes	Parking Ample
Room TV Yes	Room service 24 hours

Marlfield House

Gorey

HR **79% £C** &
Map 19 D5 Co. Wexford
Courtown Road
Gorey (055) 21124. Tlx 80757
Owner manager Mary Bowe
Mary Bowe and her fine young team really pamper guests at this splendid hotel, built as a dower house around 1850 and surrounded by 35 acres of secluded gardens and woodland. The impeccable Bowe style is evident throughout beautifully furnished public rooms like the sumptuous, chandelier-hung foyer, antique-filled bar-lounge and the two wonderfully comfortable lounges. Individually decorated bedrooms are equally delightful, and some have four-posters and Victorian-style brass beds. Abundant accessories range from fresh fruit and mending kits to hairdryers and trouser presses, and there are lavish toiletries in the new, improved bathrooms. Exemplary housekeeping throughout; marvellous breakfasts. No children under seven. No dogs. *Amenities* garden, sauna, tennis, croquet, laundry service.

■ Rooms 12	Confirm by 5
en suite bath/shower 12	Last dinner 9.30
Direct dial Yes	Parking Ample
Room TV Yes	Room service All day
Closed 5 days Xmas	

Marlfield House Restaurant ⌂ &

Abundant greenery, mirrored walls and garden views provide a delightfully summery background for youthful new chef John Dunn's often brilliant cooking. His short, beautifully composed menus change daily and offer such delights as warm lamb's sweetbread salad, chilled cucumber soup and superb salmon steak served atop a lovely light chive butter sauce. Excellent vegetables (many home-grown), attractively presented sweets like a beautifully light chocolate pavé, and some fine Irish cheeses from an impressive selection complete an enjoyable meal.
♀ Well-chosen ⊗

■ Set D £21·50	L 1–2.30
About £58 for two	D 7.30–9.30
Seats 60 Parties 40	Closed 5 days Xmas

King Sitric — Howth

R ⚲ ♿ **Map 19 D4** Co. Dublin
East Pier, Harbour Road
Dublin (01) 325235
Credit Access, Amex, Diners, Visa

Aidan MacManus cooks, wife Joan directs service, at this excellent harbourside seafood restaurant. Starters like moules marinière are followed by delights like lobster thermidor and turbot in a light saffron sauce. There's a couple of meat dishes, too. To follow, Irish cheeses and delicious sweets. Interesting wine list with over 20 Chablis, and Northern Rhônes from Chave and Jaboulet. 🍷 Well-chosen

■ *Set L from £9* | *L 12.30–2.30*
Set D £16·75 | *D 6.30–11*
About £60 for two | *Parking Ample*
Seats 65 Parties 65 | *Closed Sun, Bank Hols, 10 days Easter & 10 days Xmas*

Assolas Country House — Kanturk

HR 66% £C/D ♿
Map 19 B5 Co. Cork
Assolas
Kanturk (029) 50015
Owner managers Bourke family

An elegant and architecturally interesting 17th-century manor house which has been the home of the Bourke family for more than 70 years. The woodland setting, beside a river, is enchanting, and the whole place is delightfully peaceful and relaxing. The drawing room is amply furnished with deep armchairs and sofas, and guests pour their own drinks from a corner table. Comfortable traditional-style bedrooms in the main house are reached by a fine staircase and a landing that's crammed with well-stocked bookcases. There are three impressively designed bedrooms in a converted out-building. Very good breakfast, including home-baked soda bread. No dogs.
Amenities garden, croquet, tennis, coarse fishing, boating.

■ *Rooms 10* | *Confirm by 6*
en suite bath/shower 7 | *Last dinner 8.30*
Room phone No | *Parking Ample*
Room TV No | *Room service All day*
Closed end Oct–Easter

Assolas Country House Restaurant ♛ ⚲ ♿

NEW ENTRY

In a handsome period room son of the house Joe Bourke produces a daily-changing dinner menu of delights. There's a choice for each course: garlicky chicken livers or asparagus tartlet; hot or cold soup; roast or some lovely fresh fish like our baked salmon with lime and lemon beurre blanc. Pleasant desserts and well-kept Irish cheeses to finish. Good young wines include Alsace Pinot Gris Reserve 1985 from Trimbach.
🍷 Well-chosen ⊖

■ *Set D £17* | *D only 7–8.30*
About £50 for two | *Seats 24*
Closed Sun & end Oct–Easter

Park Hotel Kenmare — Kenmare

HR 88% £A ♿
Map 19 A6 Co. Kerry
Killarney (064) 41200. Tlx 73905
Owner manager Francis Brennan
Credit Access, Amex, Diners, Visa

The superlative views of the Kenmare Estuary and the mountains of West Cork from this elegant late Victorian hotel in its parkland setting are matched by the attention of Francis Brennan and his superbly trained young staff whose unobtrusive service is laced with traditional Irish warmth and charm. Impeccable taste and luxury are the keynote of the public rooms with their abundance of carefully chosen antiques and paintings. Featured in the entrance hall, with its magnificent oak staircase, is a splendidly ornate, 17th-century Italian water tank. The exceptionally comfortable and spacious bedrooms, some with four-posters and charmingly furnished lounge areas, show the same grace and style as the public areas. Half board terms only.
Amenities tennis, 9-hole golf course, croquet, laundry service.

■ *Rooms 49* | *Confirm by arrang.*
en suite bath/shower 49 | *Last dinner 8.45*
Direct dial Yes | *Parking Ample*
Room TV No | *Room service 24 hours*
Closed 1 Jan–31 Mar

Park Hotel Kenmare Restaurant ♛♛ ♿

Unforced elegance and discreetly professional service under head waiter Gerry Browne are the keynotes of this restaurant overlooking the Kenmare estuary. Matthew Darcy offers a menu ranging from the simple – grilled salmon in lemon butter sauce – to the intricate and imaginative, with dishes like hot scallop mousse with nettle sauce or lamb with sweet lavender, honey and thyme. Puddings, such as fresh fruit with a bruléed crème patissière, are a high spot. Marvellous comprehensive cellar includes fine clarets (Figeac '61) and some delicious Italian reds (Tignanello 1982).
Outstanding 🍷 Well-chosen ⊖

■ *Set L £11·50* | *L 1–2*
Set D £26·95 | *D 7–8.45*
About £85 for two | *Seats 85*
Closed 1 Jan–31 Mar

Kilcoran Lodge Hotel

Kilcoran

H **63% £E**
Map 19 C5 Co. Tipperary
Cahir
Cahir (052) 41288
Credit Access, Amex, Diners, Visa

Set in attractive gardens and parkland, this comfortable, well-run hotel has blossomed under good management. Guests are warmly welcomed in the foyer lounge which, like the rest of the hotel, has been stylishly refurbished. Bedrooms sport good-quality furnishings, clock-radios and TVs; most have modern bathrooms. *Amenities* garden, clay-pigeon shooting, game fishing, in-house movies (free), laundry service.

■ *Rooms* 24	*Confirm by arrang.*
en suite bath/shower 21	*Last dinner 9.30*
Room phone Yes	*Parking* Ample
Room TV Yes	*Room service* 24 hours

Newpark Hotel

Kilkenny

H **60% £D/E**
Map 19 C5 Co. Kilkenny
Castlecomer Road
Kilkenny (056) 22122. Tlx 80080
Manager David O'Sullivan
Credit Access, Amex, Diners, Visa

Extensive leisure and business facilities are an attraction at this modern hotel in parkland setting. Bedrooms are bright and practical; public areas stylish. No dogs. *Amenities* garden, indoor swimming pool, sauna, solarium, whirlpool bath, keep fit equipment, tennis, in-house movies (free), laundry service, coffee shop (12.30pm–11pm), 24-hour lounge service, children's playground.

■ *Rooms* 60	*Confirm by* 6
en suite bath/shower 60	*Last dinner* 10.45
Direct dial Yes	*Parking* Ample
Room TV Yes	*Room service* All day

■ Prices quoted for the Republic of Ireland are in Irish punts.

Aghadoe Heights Hotel

Killarney

H **64% £C** &
Map 19 A5 Co. Kerry
Aghadoe
Killarney (064) 31766. Tlx 73942
Manager Louis O'Hara
Credit Access, Amex, Diners, Visa

A pleasant modern hotel in well-kept grounds. Attractive public rooms include a stylish reception-lounge and a split-level bar that opens on to a sun terrace. Constant improvements maintain high standards of comfort in the pretty bedrooms. *Amenities* garden, tennis, coarse fishing, laundry service, 24-hour lounge service.

■ *Rooms* 60	*Confirm by arrang.*
en suite bath/shower 60	*Last dinner* 9
Direct dial Yes	*Parking* Ample
Room TV Yes	*Room service* 24 hours
Closed 4 wks Xmas	

Cahernane Hotel

Killarney

H **67% £C/D**
Map 19 A5 Co. Kerry
Muckross Road
Killarney (064) 31895. Tlx 73823
Credit Access, Amex, Diners, Visa

A handsome Victorian mansion with lovely mountain views. Interior features include well-proportioned public rooms and a choice of accommodation: spacious and traditional on the first floor; charming and cottage under the eaves; smart and contemporary in the extension. Above average housekeeping. *Amenities* garden, tennis, pitch & putt, game fishing, laundry service.

■ *Rooms* 52	*Confirm by* 6
en suite bath/shower 52	*Last dinner* 9.30
Direct dial Yes	*Parking* Ample
Room TV No	*Room service* All day
Closed end Oct–20 Dec & 6 Jan–Easter	

Castlerosse Hotel

Killarney

H **60% £D/E**
Map 19 A5 Co. Kerry
Killarney (064) 31144. Tlx 73910
Credit Access, Amex

A major improvement at this peaceful, rambling hotel is the redesigning in neat, contemporary style of the day rooms, which now take better advantage of the splendid lake and mountain views. Compact bedrooms, all spick and span and smartly furnished, are in motel style, each with its own parking space. Pleasant staff with sunny smiles. No dogs. *Amenities* garden, tennis, putting, game fishing.

■ *Rooms* 42	*Confirm by* 6
en suite bath/shower 42	*Last dinner* 9
Direct dial Yes	*Parking* Ample
Room TV No	*Room service* 24 hours
Closed mid Nov–mid Mar	

Hotel Europe
Killarney

HR 73% £C/D
Map 19 A5 Co. Kerry
Killorglin Road, Fossa
Killarney (064) 31900. Tlx 73913
Credit Access, Amex, Diners, Visa

Much money has been spent refurbishing and extending this efficiently-run modern hotel set in spacious grounds overlooking the mountains and lakes of Killarney. Bold, expensive fabrics are a feature of strikingly contemporary day rooms, which include a sunken lounge and a chic new cocktail bar. Streamlined bedrooms, many with balconies, have quality fitted units and luxurious marble-floored bathrooms. A new extension houses 20 mini suites. Staff, while competent, can

lack friendliness. *Amenities* garden, indoor swimming pool, sauna, solarium, keep fit equipment, riding, coarse fishing, snooker, in-house movies (free), laundry service, coffee shop (11am–4.30pm).

■ Rooms 180	Confirm by arrang.
en suite bath/shower 180	Last dinner 9.30
Direct dial Yes	Parking Ample
Room TV Yes	Room service 24 hours
Closed Nov–1 Apr	

Panorama Restaurant ♿

A spacious, comfortable restaurant with splendid scenic views where Willi Steinbeck prepares Irish specialities such as cabbage soup or whiskey-flamed fillet steak. His dishes based on local produce, including a wonderful ragoût of turbot, brill and monkfish or Dingle Bay lobster, are served with equal aplomb. Gorgeous sweets entice – try Irish Mist parfait or the excellent chocolate mousse. Serious list of wines bought directly from the best producers.
♀ **Well-chosen** ❷

■ Set D £18·50	D only 7–9.30
About £52 for two	Seats 550
Closed Nov–1 Apr	Parties 180

Gaby's
Killarney

R ♀ Map 19 A5 Co. Kerry
17 High Street
Killarney (064) 32519

The Kerry fishing fleet continues to provide the raw materials for this popular restaurant with booth seating, owned by the Maes family and deservedly renowned for its carefully prepared, beautifully fresh seafood. Scallops and oysters, salmon and sole, haddock in wine, lobster, plain

or deliciously sauced – these are typical fare from Geert Maes' menu. The indulgent can push the boat out with a hot or cold platter. Smoked fish, too, and grilled steak. Simple sweets.
♀ **Well-chosen** ❷

■ About £42 for two	L 12.30–2.30
Seats 47	D 6–10
Closed L Mon, all Sun	Parking Difficult
(exc. D Sun June–Aug) & 15 Nov–15 Mar	

Killarney Great Southern Hotel
Killarney

H 69% £B/C
Map 19 A5 Co. Kerry
Killarney (064) 31262
Credit Access, Amex, Diners, Visa

An imposing Victorian mansion with extensive conference and leisure facilities, a handsome, lofty foyer-lounge with crystal chandeliers, two further lounges and a smart modern bar. Bedrooms range from traditional in the main

building to more modern in the extension. Spacious bathrooms. *Amenities* garden, indoor swimming pool, sauna, solarium, keep-fit equipment, hairdressing, tennis, croquet, riding.

■ Rooms 180	Confirm by 6
en suite bath/shower 180	Last dinner 9.30
Direct dial Yes	Parking Ample
Room TV Yes	Room service 24 hours
Closed 2 Jan–1 Mar	

Torc Great Southern Hotel
Killarney

H 61% £D
Map 19 A5 Co. Kerry
Park Road
Killarney (064) 31611. Tlx 73807
Manager Eugene Gordon
Credit Access, Amex, Diners, Visa

The Kerry Mountains provide a backdrop for this modern low-rise hotel on the road to Cork. Cheerful day rooms and bedrooms have a

pleasantly light and airy feel. Excellent housekeeping and helpful staff (particularly courteous head porter). *Amenities* garden, indoor swimming pool, sauna, tennis, laundry service.

■ Rooms 96	Confirm by 6
en suite bath/shower 96	Last dinner 9
Direct dial Yes	Parking Ample
Room TV Some	Room service All day
Closed mid Oct–end Apr	

Court Hotel   Killiney

H **68% £C**
 Map 19 D4 Co. Dublin
Killiney Bay
Dublin (01) 851 622. Tlx 33244
Owner manager Nial Kenny
Credit Access, Amex, Diners, Visa
 A handsome Victorian building, with discreet later additions, in a lovely setting overlooking Killiney Bay. The garden at its best is a riot of colour, and there are even palm trees on this protected part of the coast. Public rooms have the appeal of cornices and moulded ceilings, and there's a sunny conservatory. The Victorian

snooker room, with four full-sized tables, is particularly splendid. Main-house bedrooms continue the period feel, while those in the extension are modern, well designed and equally comfortable. Excellent housekeeping, and charming staff.
Amenities garden, snooker, laundry service, grill room (12.15pm–11.15pm).

■ *Rooms 40*	*Confirm by arrang.*
en suite bath/shower 40	*Last dinner 10*
Direct dial Yes	*Parking Ample*
Room TV Yes	*Room service 24 hours*
Closed 25 Dec	

Fitzpatrick's Castle Hotel   Killiney

H **71% £B**
 Map 19 D4 Co. Dublin
Dublin (01) 851533. Tlx 30353
Owner manager Paddy Fitzpatrick
Credit Access, Amex, Diners, Visa
 A turreted castle built in 1741 and standing in lovely woodland overlooking Dublin Bay. Half the bedrooms have been luxuriously refurbished, with stylish fabrics setting off the excellent reproduction furniture; these rooms also have impressive modern bathrooms. Public rooms have been smartened up, too: note the elegant foyer with its Regency fireplace, French-style furnishings and resplendent suit of armour; the handsome bar, a model of plush comfort; the pastel-hued restaurant; and the zippy coffee shop with its art nouveau lighting. A much-improved hotel under well-motivated family management

and staff. No dogs. *Amenities* garden, indoor swimming pool, sauna, solarium, gymnasium, beauty salon, tennis, squash, laundry service, satellite TV, 24-hour lounge service.

■ *Rooms 100*	*Confirm by arrang.*
en suite bath/shower 100	*Last dinner 10*
Direct dial Yes	*Parking Ample*
Room TV Yes	*Room service 24 hours*

■ Prices quoted for the Republic of Ireland are in Irish punts.

Actons Hotel   Kinsale

H **62% £D**
 Map 19 B6 Co. Cork
The Pier
Cork (021) 772135. Tlx 75443
Credit Access, Amex, Diners, Visa
 A row of handsome Georgian houses standing behind well-kept gardens makes up this popular harbourside hotel. The major change here has been in the bedrooms, half of which now sport handsome darkwood reproduction furniture, pretty new curtains and smartly tiled private bathrooms. Similar improvements are planned for the rest of the accommodation, currently a little

starker and plainer. Public areas include an open-plan lounge and bar – pleasant and comfortable enough, though furnishings are looking rather tired now – and a fine new leisure club. Weaker points noted on our last visit were service (a trifle lacklustre) and breakfast (very disappointing).
Amenities garden, indoor swimming pool, sauna, solarium, snooker, in-house movies (free), laundry service.

■ *Rooms 57*	*Confirm by 6*
en suite bath/shower 55	*Last dinner 9.30*
Direct dial Yes	*Parking Ample*
Room TV Yes	*Room service 24 hours*

Blue Haven Hotel   Kinsale

I **£E**
 Map 19 B6 Co. Cork
Pearse Street
Cork (021) 772209
Owner managers Brian & Anne Cronin
Credit Access, Amex, Diners, Visa
 This attractive blue and white inn is a delightful place to drop anchor. The rustic bar with conservatory extension is a popular local

rendezvous, and there's a snug TV lounge. Cottagy bedrooms, hung with paintings by local artists, are neat and shipshape. No dogs.
Amenities garden, sea fishing, hotel boat.

■ *Rooms 10*	*Confirm by 6*
en suite bath/shower 7	*Last dinner 10*
Room phone No	*Parking Difficult*
Room TV No	*Room service All day*
Closed Jan & Feb	

Knocklofty House Hotel *NEW ENTRY* Knocklofty

H **65% £C/D** 🔥
Map 19 C5 Co. Tipperary
Nr Clonmel
Clonmel (052) 38222
Owner managers Paddy & Joyce O'Keeffe

Owners and staff provide a warm welcome at this handsome hotel, once the country seat of the Earls of Donoughmore. The parkland setting is both scenic and serene: a tree-lined drive leads to the front door, and the beautifully-tended gardens run down to the river Suir, which is well known for its salmon and trout. Outdoor pursuits are available in abundance, while those guests who list doing nothing as a favourite hobby could find no more relaxing spot than the galleried library-lounge. Bedrooms are spacious and quite stylishly decorated, lacking just a little in homeliness by being rather sparsely furnished. No dogs.
Amenities garden, indoor swimming pool, whirlpool bath, gymnasium, tennis, squash, clay-pigeon shooting, game fishing, laundry service.

■ *Rooms 14*	*Confirm by arrang.*
en suite bath/shower 14	*Last dinner 9.45*
Room phone Yes	*Parking Ample*
Room TV No	*Room service All day*

■ When calling a Dublin number from outside the Republic, dial 00 before the number we print, e.g. Berkeley Court is 0001 601711.

■ For the rest of the Republic, dial 010-353, then the number we print less the initial zero, e.g. Park Hotel Kenmare is 010-353 64 41200.

Rosleague Manor Hotel Letterfrack

HR **65% £D** 🔥
Map 18 A3 Co. Galway
Moyard (095) 41101
Owner managers Anne & Patrick Foyle
Credit Access, Visa

Paddy Foyle and his sister Anne are the warmest of hosts at this elegant Georgian manor house in a beautiful and serene setting. Day rooms, with antiques and oils, have a delightfully traditional air. Pretty bedrooms, individually decorated, feature handsome old beds and wardrobes. *Amenities* garden, sauna, tennis, game and sea fishing.

■ *Rooms 15*	*Confirm by arrang.*
en suite bath/shower 15	*Last dinner 9.30*
Direct dial Yes	*Parking Ample*
Room TV Yes	*Room service All day*
Closed 1 Nov–Easter	

Rosleague Manor Hotel Restaurant 👑 ♤

Local supplies and the hotel's kitchen gardens provide the bulk of the ingredients for Paddy Foyle's enjoyable four-course dinners. Seafood spans a good range, with crab mayonnaise, poached salmon or skate with black butter often on the menu. Sautéed lamb's liver and beef medallions with green pepper are typical meaty choices, and there are some delicious sweets (walnut liqueur syllabub, Rosleague trifle, homemade ices and a first-rate chocolate mousse). Lunches by arrangement or in the bar. ⊖

■ *Set D from £15*	*L 1–2.30*
About £50 for two	*D 8–9.30*
Seats 65	*Parties 12*
Closed 1 Nov–Easter	

Jurys Hotel Limerick

H **66% £C**
Map 19 B5 Co. Limerick
Ennis Road
Limerick (061) 55266. Tlx 28266
Manager Brendan Gallagher
Credit Access, Amex, Diners, Visa

A 1960s hotel on the banks of the Shannon, near the city centre. Polished wood and brass feature in the bar and there's a spacious foyer-lounge and versatile conference suite. Roomy bedrooms are in two-storey blocks overlooking a central garden. No dogs. *Amenities* garden, coffee shop (7am–11pm), 24-hour lounge service.

■ *Rooms 96*	*Confirm by 6*
en suite bath/shower 96	*Last dinner 11*
Direct dial Yes	*Parking Ample*
Room TV Yes	*Room service 24 hours*
Closed 25 Dec	

Limerick Inn Hotel Limerick

H **66% £C**
Map 19 B5 Co. Limerick
Ennis Road
Limerick (061) 51544. Tlx 28121
Manager John Fahey
Credit Access, Amex, Diners, Visa

The leisure centre is a major attraction at this comfortable modern hotel, offering a wide choice of pleasant, relaxing day rooms. Stylish bedrooms complete the tale. No dogs. *Amenities* garden, indoor swimming pool, sauna, solarium, whirlpool bath, gymnasium, beauty salon, tennis, putting, snooker, in-house movies (free), laundry service, coffee shop (7.30am–11pm), playground.

■ *Rooms 153*	*Confirm by 6*
en suite bath/shower 153	*Last dinner 9.45*
Direct dial Yes	*Parking Ample*
Room TV Yes	*Room service 24 hours*

New Greenhills Hotel — Limerick

H 61% £E
Map 19 B5 Co. Limerick
Ennis Road
Limerick (061) 53033. Tlx 70246
Manager Noel J. O'Mahony
Credit Access, Amex, Diners, Visa

Just outside Limerick, this modern hotel, ideal for Shannon airport, provides modest comforts. Subtle lighting, lots of natural wood, cane and wicker create a smart contemporary effect in public areas. Bedrooms have bright colour schemes and fitted units. No dogs. *Amenities* garden, in-house movies (free), laundry service.

■ *Rooms* 55
en suite bath/shower 55
Direct dial Yes
Room TV Yes
Closed 25 Dec
Confirm by 6
Last dinner 10
Parking Ample
Room service 24 hours

Two Mile Inn Hotel — Limerick

H 60% £C/D ♿
Map 19 B5 Co. Limerick
Ennis Road
Limerick (061) 53122. Tlx 70157
Owner manager Brendan Dunne
Credit Access, Amex, Diners, Visa

Practical comforts can be found in this modern red-brick hotel about three miles from Limerick. All bedrooms have good private bathrooms with plenty of thick towels. There's a leafy sunken lounge and two bars, one in pub style. Decent breakfasts, friendly staff. No dogs. *Amenities* garden, in-house movies (free), laundry service.

■ *Rooms* 125
en suite bath/shower 125
Direct dial Yes
Room TV Yes
Closed 3–4 days Xmas
Confirm by 6
Last dinner 9.30
Parking Ample
Room service All day

■ Any person using our name to obtain free hospitality is a fraud. Proprietors, please inform the police and us.

Longueville House — Mallow

HR 72% £C
Map 19 B5 Co. Cork
Longueville
Mallow (022) 47156. Tlx 75498
Owner managers Michael & Jane O'Callaghan
Credit Amex, Diners, Visa

A magnificent, elegantly proportioned country house where the O'Callaghans extend a friendly welcome. This Georgian mansion retains many original features, such as stone flags in the hall, intricate cornicing, and a handsome staircase. Public areas include a comfortable drawing room with period furnishings, a library and a Victorian conservatory. Bedrooms vary in size and are individually schemed in attractive styles with traditional furniture. All have private bathrooms (one not en suite). Children under ten by arrangement only. Dogs in kennels only. *Amenities* garden, croquet, coarse & game fishing, games room, snooker, laundry service, coffee shop (11am–6pm).

■ *Rooms* 16
en suite bath/shower 16
Room phone No
Room TV No
Closed 20 Dec–23 Mar
Confirm by 6
Last dinner 9
Parking Ample
Room service All day

Presidents' Restaurant

An elegant room, hung with portraits of Irish presidents, where you can enjoy skilled but unpretentious cooking. Starters could include baked chicken liver custard or game terrine, followed by roast Longueville lamb, salmon en croûte or fillet of pork with a lemon balm sabayon. Plentiful garden-fresh vegetables and a pleasing sweet trolley includes a good creamy cheesecake with a crunchy base. The wine list includes some excellent bargains.

■ *Set D* £20
About £55 *for two*
Seats 40 *Parties* 10
L 12.45–2
D 7–9
Closed 20 Dec–23 Mar

■ Our inspectors are our full-time employees; they are professionally trained by us.

Moyglare Manor Maynooth

HR **77%** **£B/C**
Map 19 C4 Co. Kildare
Dublin (01) 286351. Tlx 90358

Comfort and luxury combine with an appealing air of relaxed friendliness at this fine Georgian mansion standing in spacious grounds outside Maynooth. Antiques, paintings, porcelain and objets d'art fill the handsome day rooms which have high ceilings and elegant cornices. The foyer-lounge, warmed by a peat fire, is welcoming while the basement lounge bar is impressive with its huge open fireplace, flagstones and vaulted ceiling. There is also a relaxing cocktail bar. Luxurious, spacious bedrooms are individually decorated with stylish fabrics and antiques; many of the rooms have four-posters or half-testers.

Bathrooms are thoughtfully equipped, all having showers, good towels and toiletries. No children under 12. No dogs. *Amenities* garden, tennis, laundry service.

■ *Rooms* 13	*Confirm by* 6
en suite bath/shower 13	*Last dinner* 9.30
Direct dial Yes	*Parking* Ample
Room TV No	*Room service* All day
Closed Good Fri & 25 & 26 Dec	

Moyglare Manor Restaurant ⊌ &

Fruit and vegetables from the manor gardens feature in Jim Cullinan's enjoyable cooking at this elegantly-appointed restaurant. A nicely varied and skilfully-prepared choice ranges from creamy soups and light savoury mousses to succulent roasts and appetisingly sauced meat, fish and poultry dishes. Noteworthy are the temptingly displayed and delicious desserts such as lime bavarois, crème brûlées, tarts and gâteaux.

♚ **Well-chosen** ☺

■ *Set L from* £9.50	*L* 12.45–2.15
Set D from £16	*D* 7–9.45
About £60 *for two*	*Seats* 78 *Parties* 50
Closed L Sat, all Good Fri & 25 & 26 Dec	

Doon Moyard

R ♌ **Map 18 A3** Co. Galway
Nr Clifden
Moyard (095) 41139

Set in beautiful country between Clifden and Letterfrack, enjoying fine views of the Connemara Hills, this is a seafood restaurant of beguiling simplicity. Moira Stephenson offers a short menu of fishy delights like scallop soup, smoked roe pâté, crab salad and poached brill with a lovely

parsley butter sauce. Everything is beautifully fresh and of prime quality; crisp green salad is the sole accompaniment. To finish, there's a good Irish cheeseboard and a scrumptious sweet – maybe chocolate mousse. Fraser Stephenson is a most welcoming host. ☺

■ *About* £30 *for two*	*L only* 12–3
Seats 20 *Parties* 20	*Parking* Ample
Closed Wed & Oct–Easter	

Drimcong House ★ Moycullen

R ★ ⊌ ♌ & **Map 19 B4** Co. Galway
Nr Galway
Galway (091) 85115
Credit Access, Amex, Diners, Visa

The house is a handsome Queen Anne building eight miles north of Galway on the road to Oughterard and Connemara. The dining room itself is elegant and relaxing, with Marie Galvin and her young staff enhancing the pleasures of the table. And what pleasures! Gerry Galvin's cooking is genuinely original and adventurous, with brilliant saucing and judicious use of herbs. Our steamed scallops were served with a lovely refined ginger cream sauce; equally tempting starters included oysters baked in filo and a grilled goat's cheese salad. Next came a refreshing sorbet and an impressively delicate and subtle mushroom consommé, but for us the highlight of the meal was breasts of pigeon, roasted to pink perfection, served with a port sauce and accompanied by wine-braised red

cabbage and apple. Sweets are memorable, too. Carefully chosen, reasonably priced list of mainly French wines. *Specialities* onion and lovage soup, wild salmon with sweet cicely sauce, chocolate terrine with vanilla sauce and pistachios. ♚ **Well-chosen** ☺

■ *Set D from* £14.95	*L by arrang.* only
About £45 *for two*	*D* 7–10.30
Seats 50 *Parties* 50	*Parking* Ample
Closed Sun, Mon & 20 Dec–end Feb	

☞ is our symbol for an **outstanding** wine list.

■ We welcome complaints and bona fide recommendations on the tear-out pages for readers' comments. They are followed up by our professional team. Please also complain to the management instantly.

RECEPTION

Ardboyne Hotel
Navan

H **60% £E**
Map 18 C3 Co. Meath
Dublin Road
Navan (046) 23119
Credit Access, Amex, Diners, Visa
   This modern low-rise hotel stands on the Dublin road. There's a comfortably furnished foyer-lounge and a cosy bar with plush upholstered seating. Bedrooms feature smart wooden units

and pretty matching fabrics. Bathrooms have vanity units and good tiling. No dogs. *Amenities* garden, coffee shop (8am–10pm), in-house movies (free), laundry service.
■ *Rooms* 27 — *Confirm by* 6
en suite bath/shower 27 — *Last dinner* 10
Direct dial Yes — *Parking* Ample
Room TV Yes — *Room service* 24 hours
Closed 3 days Xmas

Cedar Lodge Hotel
Newbawn

H **61% £E**
Map 19 C5 Co. Wexford
Carrigbyrne, Nr New Ross
Waterford (051) 28386
Owner managers Thomas & Ailish Martin
Credit Access, Visa
   A friendly modern hotel located beneath the slopes of Carrigbyrne Forest on the N25. There's a smart lounge area and a stylish bar with dark

exposed brickwork and open fires. Good sized bedrooms (front ones with eye-catching sun blinds) have attractive contemporary fittings. *Amenities* garden, games room.
■ *Rooms* 13 — *Confirm by arrang.*
en suite bath/shower 13 — *Last dinner* 9
Room phone Yes — *Parking* Ample
Room TV Yes — *Room service* All day
Closed 3 weeks Jan

■ For a discount on next year's guide, see Offer for Answers.

Hotel Keadeen
Newbridge

H **68% £D/E** &
Map 19 C4 Co. Kildare
Ballymany
Newbridge (045) 31666. Tlx 60672
Owner managers O'Loughlin family
Credit Access, Amex, Diners, Visa
   An extended private house in spacious gardens south of Newbridge and about a mile from the Curragh racecourse. There are two bars, an

inviting lounge and self-contained function facilities. Bedrooms are bright, cheerful and generally of a good size. *Amenities* garden, in-house movies (free), laundry service.
■ *Rooms* 37 — *Confirm by* 6
en suite bath/shower 37 — *Last dinner* 10.30
Direct dial Yes — *Parking* Ample
Room TV Yes — *Room service* 24 hours
Closed 2 days Xmas

Clare Inn
Newmarket-on-Fergus

H **74% £C/D**
Map 19 B4 Co. Clare
Limerick (061) 71161. Tlx 24025
Manager Miss Mary Vaughan
Credit Access, Amex, Diners, Visa
   Staff are unfailingly friendly and courteous at this immaculate modern hotel, whose hilltop position commands spectacular views along the river Shannon. The bedrooms are a great strength – all very spacious and well lit, attractively decorated in pastels or bolder colours, and comfortably furnished. Bathrooms are also excellent. Public areas include two pleasant lounges, one a particularly bright and airy sun lounge, the other an elegantly traditional drawing room. The bar is in simpler style, with a natural stone counter. Decent breakfasts. Guests have the use of nearby Dromoland Castle's facilities,

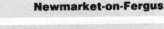

including tennis, squash, riding and game fishing. No dogs. *Amenities* garden, golf course, laundry service.
■ *Rooms* 121 — *Confirm by* 6
en suite bath/shower 121 — *Last dinner* 9
Direct dial Yes — *Parking* Ample
Room TV Yes — *Room service* 24 hours
Closed 20 Dec–1 Apr

Dromoland Castle

Newmarket-on-Fergus

H **76% £A/B**
Map 19 B4 Co. Clare
Limerick (061) 71144. Tlx 26854
Manager Patricia Barry
Credit Access, Amex, Diners, Visa

Seat of the O'Brien clan until 1963, the castle enjoys a magnificent lakeside setting amid rolling parkland. Handsomely proportioned public rooms include two picture galleries, hung with splendid family portraits; one of them doubles as a reception area. This leads to the formal lounge, the library bar and the bright and airy Terrace Room that overlooks the gardens. Bedrooms have bright coordinated wallpapers, drapes and bedcovers. Some are in the main castle, others in the older Queen Anne Court set around a flower-filled courtyard, and still others in a modern extension linking the two. No dogs.

Amenities garden, tennis, golf course, putting, croquet, coarse & game fishing, bicycles, laundry service, 24-hour lounge service, boating.

■ *Rooms* 77	*Confirm by arrang.*
en suite bath/shower 77	*Last dinner* 8.45
Direct dial Yes	*Parking* Ample
Room TV Yes	*Room service* 24 hours
Closed Nov–Apr	

Newport House

Newport

HR **63% £D/E**
Map 18 A3 Co. Mayo
Newport (098) 41222. Tlx 53740
Owner managers Kieran & Thelma Thompson
Credit Amex, Diners, Visa. LVs

On the banks of the Newport river, this creeper-clad mansion makes an elegant haven. Log fires, antiques and paintings grace the day rooms. Spacious bedrooms are traditionally furnished; most have large shower/bathrooms.
Amenities garden, croquet, sea, coarse & game fishing, games room, billiards, snooker, laundry service, 24-hour lounge service.

■ *Rooms* 20	*Confirm by arrang.*
en suite bath/shower 16	*Last dinner* 9.30
Room phone No	*Parking* Ample
Room TV No	*Room service* 24 hours
Closed end Sept–mid Mar	

Newport House Restaurant

Manager Owen Mullins

Delicious smoked salmon prepared on the premises is the favourite way to start a meal at this smart restaurant with its moulded ceiling and striking gilt mirror. Other choices on the short set menu could include chicken broth, roast stuffed loin of pork and turbot with champagne sauce. Home-grown vegetables accompany, and to finish there are nice sweets like damson tartlet. Long-serving manager Owen Mullins leads the efficient, unobtrusive service.
♀ Well-chosen ☺

■ *Set D* £19	*L* Jun–Aug only
About £50 for two	12.30–2.30
Seats 40	*D* 7.30–9.30
Closed end Sept–mid Mar	

■ When calling a Dublin number from outside the Republic, dial 00 before the number we print, e.g. Berkeley Court is 0001 601711.

■ For the rest of the Republic, dial 010-353, then the number we print less the initial zero, e.g. Park Hotel Kenmare is 010-353 64 41200.

Connemara Gateway Hotel

Oughterard

H **64% £D/E**
Map 18 B3 Co. Galway
Galway (091) 82328. Tlx 50905
Owner manager Charles Sinnott
Credit Access, Amex, Diners, Visa

Set in beautiful rugged countryside on the main route to Connemara, this modern hotel has a good deal of style and character behind its long, low facade. There's a strong local theme: note the sketches of Connemara folk in the bar, where traditional entertainment enlivens summer evenings. The residents' lounge is particularly peaceful and comfortable, and there's a pleasant sun lounge. Bedrooms are light and modern, with beds made from attractive Connemara wood. Rooms in the newer wing, including three delightful suites, feature tweedy Irish fabrics. Charles Sinnott and his charming staff are another major plus. No dogs.
Amenities garden, outdoor swimming pool, tennis, children's playground.

■ *Rooms* 62	*Confirm by* 6
en suite bath/shower 62	*Last dinner* 9
Direct dial Yes	*Parking* Ample
Room TV Yes	*Room service* All day
Closed end Nov–early Feb	

Currarevagh House

Oughterard

HR **64% £D**
Map 18 B3 Co. Galway
Galway (091) 82313
Owner managers June & Harry Hodgson
Charming hosts who make you feel like private guests, a relaxed atmosphere, good food, pristine housekeeping – you'll find them all at this Victorian mansion set in leafy gardens beside Lough Corrib. The drawing room is splendidly old-fashioned, so too the bedrooms with their handsome antiques. Bathrooms are modern. *Amenities* garden, tennis, croquet, game & coarse fishing, mooring, hotel boats.

■ *Rooms* 15	*Confirm by 3*
en suite bath/shower 14	*Last dinner 8*
Room phone No	*Parking* Ample
Room TV No	*Room service* All day
Closed early Oct–Easter	

Currarevagh House Restaurant ⚲ &

The gong sounds at 8 o'clock, and guests drift from the drawing room to sit down to June Hodgson's daily changing five-course dinner. Her cooking is staunchly traditional, with honest, unadulterated flavours foremost in dishes like kidney soup, quiche lorraine with delicious buttery pastry, salmon steaks and nostalgic roast mutton served with a proper onion sauce and home-made redcurrant jelly. Nice old-fashioned puds, too, and Irish cheeses. An attractive wine list includes Australian Shiraz Malbec and good vintage ports.
⚑ **Well-chosen** ⊖

NEW ENTRY

■ *Set D £13.50*	*D only at 8*
About £35 for two	*Seats 30*
Closed early Oct–Easter	

Sweeney's Oughterard House

Oughterard

H **59% £C/D**
Map 18 B3 Co. Galway
Galway (091) 82207
Owner managers Higgins family
Credit Access, Amex, Diners, Visa
The latest member of the Higgins family to take over Sweeney's—an attractive creeper-clad Georgian house—is a dedicated art and antiques collector. The bar and two lounges are crammed full of paintings and antiques, while period furniture also features in many of the bedrooms. Other rooms have simple lightwood units. Bathrooms are adequate. *Amenities* garden.

■ *Rooms* 20	*Confirm by* arrang.
en suite bath/shower 20	*Last dinner* 8.30
Direct dial Yes	*Parking* Ample
Room TV Some	*Room service* All day
Closed 4 days Xmas	

■ Changes in data may occur in establishments after the Guide goes to press. Prices should be taken as indications rather than firm quotes.

Parknasilla Great Southern Hotel

Parknasilla

HR **76% £A/B**
Map 19 A6 Co. Kerry
Nr Sneem
Killarney (064) 45122. Tlx 73899
Credit Access, Amex, Diners, Visa
Enjoying a spectacular setting of 300 acres of parkland overlooking Kenmare Bay, this imposing Victorian mansion combines old-fashioned standards of service and housekeeping with up-to-date leisure facilities. Day rooms, whether in traditional or modern style, are on a grand scale – note the elegant Shaw Lounge (G. B. Shaw was a regular guest), and leafy sun room. Sumptuously refurbished bedrooms offer extras like remote-control satellite TVs and generous bowls of fresh fruit, and all have chic tiled bathrooms. No dogs. *Amenities* garden, solarium, tennis, 9-hole golf course, riding, sea & game fishing, games room, snooker, laundry service, helipad.

■ *Rooms* 59	*Confirm by* 6
en suite bath/shower 59	*Last dinner* 8.30
Direct dial Yes	*Parking* Ample
Room TV Yes	*Room service* 24 hours
Closed Nov–Mar except Xmas–New Year	

Pygmalion Restaurant ♨ &

Views across the lush sub-tropical gardens accompany meals at this splendid, formal restaurant. Anthony Harvey's menus are full of interest and variety, with a blend of classical and modern French dishes. Start with garlic snails or consommé, proceed to lettuce-wrapped sole or chicken breast stuffed with grapes and cheese. Intelligent use of top-quality produce, and attractive presentation. ⊖

■ *Set L from £11*	*L* 12.30–2.30
Set D from £18	*D* 7–9
About £69 for two	*Seats 120* **Parties** 120
Closed Nov–Mar except Xmas–New Year	

Curryhills House Hotel
Prosperous

H 57% £E ♿
Map 19 C4 Co. Kildare
Nr Naas
Naas (045) 68150
Owner managers Bill & Bridie Travers
Credit Access, Amex, Diners, Visa
Converted from a red-brick Georgian farmhouse, this agreeable hotel has plenty of charm. Turf fires warm the lounges (one with TV), and homely period furniture gives a cosy, lived-in feel to the roomy bar. Bedrooms are bright and cheerful, most with simple modern units. Bathrooms are well equipped. *Amenities* garden.

■ *Rooms* 12	*Confirm by arrang.*
en suite bath/shower 12	*Last dinner* 11
Direct dial Yes	*Parking* Ample
Room TV No	*Room service* All day
Closed 1 wk Xmas	

■ We publish annually, so make sure you use the current edition. It's worth it!

Rathmullan House
Rathmullan

H 62% £D/E
Map 18 C1 Co. Donegal
Nr Letterkenny
Letterkenny (074) 58188
Owner managers Bob & Robin Wheeler
Credit Access, Amex, Diners, Visa
Relaxation and hospitality in a white-painted Georgian house on the banks of Lough Swilly. Comfortable day rooms make the most of the lovely setting. Bedrooms (some modest) vary; those at the front have the best views and the most space. No dogs. *Amenities* garden, tennis, croquet, sea-fishing.

■ *Rooms* 19	*Confirm by arrang.*
en suite bath/shower 16	*Last dinner* 8.30
Room phone No	*Parking* Ample
Room TV No	*Room service* Limited
Closed end Oct–Easter	

Tinakilly House Hotel
Rathnew

H 70% £C/D
Map 19 D4 Co. Wicklow
Wicklow (0404) 69274. Tlx 80412
Owner managers William & Bee Power
Credit Amex, Visa
Set back from the Wicklow road in seven acres of gardens, this sturdy Victorian mansion provides abundant peace and comfort, plus friendly, professional service. Pass through the portals and you'll immediately be impressed by the lofty entrance hall with handsome staircase, fine antiques and splendid floral displays. The opulence continues in the gracious furnishings and magnificent marble fireplace of the bar-lounge. Bedrooms lose little by comparison, and some have four-posters. Nice touches in all rooms include magazines, local information sheets and a welcoming glass of sherry. One bathroom retains

its grand Victorian fittings. No children under seven. No dogs. *Amenities* garden, laundry service.

■ *Rooms* 14	*Confirm by* 6
en suite bath/shower 14	*Last dinner* 9
Direct dial Yes	*Parking* Ample
Room TV Yes	*Room service* All day
Closed 3 days Xmas & all Jan	

Renvyle House Hotel
Renvyle

H 64% £E ♿
Map 18 A3 Co. Galway
Clifden (095) 43434. Tlx 50896
Owner manager Hugh Coyle
Credit Access, Amex, Diners, Visa
Amusing the family is no problem at this delightful hotel with charming owners, and an idyllic setting overlooking the sea and the Connemara mountains. Natural wood features extensively in the public areas, which include a spacious foyer with easy chairs set around peat fires, a large lounge, leafy sun lounge and boisterous bar. Bright, pretty bedrooms, all of a decent size, include several family suites. *Amenities* garden, indoor & outdoor swimming pools, sauna, solarium, gymnasium, keep-fit equipment, tennis, 9-hole golf course, putting, bowling green, croquet, riding, shooting, sea, coarse & game fishing, boating, games room, snooker, in-house movies (free), laundry service, kiosk, children's playground.

■ *Rooms* 70	*Confirm by arrang.*
en suite bath/shower 70	*Last dinner* 9
Direct dial Yes	*Parking* Ample
Room TV Some	*Room service* All day
Closed 6 Jan–mid Mar & mid Nov–mid Dec	

Coopershill

H **58% £E**
Map 18 B2 Co. Sligo
Sligo (071) 65108
Credit Amex, Visa
   At the heart of a 500-acre estate, this imposing
Georgian house commands scenic views. Elegant
public rooms are enhanced with antiques, hunting
trophies and knick-knacks. Plentiful seating gives
a homely air to the lounge. Five spacious

bedrooms, also furnished with antiques, include
two four-poster and three half-tester beds. Ask for
directions. No dogs. *Amenities* garden, coarse
fishing.

■ *Rooms 5*	*Confirm by arrang.*
en suite bath/shower 3	*Last dinner 8.30*
Room phone No	*Parking Ample*
Room TV No	*Room service Limited*
Closed end Oct–mid Mar	

Reveries   *NEW ENTRY*

R ⌣ ♃ **Map 18 B2** Co. Sligo
Sligo (071) 77371
Credit Access, Visa
   A sophisticated modern setting for the
imaginative and highly enjoyable cooking of Paula
Brennan. Her skills include a keen eye for
presentation, with dramatic use made of plain
black or white plates. Smoked trout with
horseradish jelly is a lovely starter, and main

courses include seafresh brill with a delicate dill
cream sauce and roast rack of lamb. Desserts are
delightful, and you won't find a finer Irish
cheeseboard. Friendly, well-informed service led
by Damien Brennan. ℮

■ *Set D from £14-25*	*D 7.30–10*
About £50 for two	*Parking Ample*
Seats 48	*Parties 18*
Closed Sun, 2 wks Nov & 4 days Xmas	

Casey's Cedars Hotel

H **68% £D/E**
Map 19 D5 Co. Wexford
Strand Road
Wexford (053) 32124. Tlx 80237
Owner managers Seamus & Vera Casey
Credit Amex, Diners
   Not far from the sea, this friendly hotel offers
high standards of housekeeping. Accommodation
comprises bright, airy bedrooms with pretty

fabrics, good contemporary furnishings and
stylish bathrooms. There's a relaxing lounge and a
bar with a dance floor. No dogs. *Amenities*
garden, sauna, solarium, keep-fit equipment.

■ *Rooms 34*	*Confirm by 7*
en suite bath/shower 34	*Last dinner 10*
Direct dial Yes	*Parking Ample*
Room TV Yes	*Room service All day*
Closed Jan	

Kelly's Strand Hotel

H **69% £D** ♿
Map 19 D5 Co. Wexford
Strand Road
Wexford (053) 32114. Tlx 80111
Owner manager Mrs B. Kelly
   Book in advance for this well-run hotel, where
an impressive range of sport and leisure activities
ensures a special appeal for families. A diversity
of public rooms includes the convivial Carmen
and Ivy bars and several quietly cosy lounges.
Bedrooms, some with sea views, are compact
and cheerfully decorated in contemporary style
with smartly tiled bath or shower rooms. No dogs.

Amenities garden, indoor and outdoor swimming
pools, sauna, solarium, whirlpool bath, keep-fit
equipment, beauty salon, hairdressing, tennis,
squash, badminton, croquet, bicycles, games
room, snooker, in-house movies (free), laundry
service, laundry room, crèche, children's play
area, courtesy coach.

■ *Rooms 93*	*Confirm by 4*
en suite bath/shower 93	*Last dinner 9.15*
Direct dial Yes	*Parking Ample*
Room TV Yes	*Room service 24 hours*
Closed mid Dec–mid Feb	

Sands House Hotel

H **66% £D**
Map 18 B2 Co. Donegal
Bundoran (072) 51777. Tlx 40460
Owner managers Vincent & Mary Britton
Credit Access, Amex, Diners
   The Brittons offer a friendly welcome at their
seaside hotel, where there is a continuing
programme of improvements. The comfortable
lounge has fine antiques and there is a cosy bar.

Bedrooms vary in size and style, some very large,
with antique furniture. *Amenities* garden, tennis,
9-hole golf course, croquet, sea & game fishing,
board sailing, canoeing, games room.

■ *Rooms 40*	*Confirm by 5*
en suite bath/shower 40	*Last dinner 9*
Room phone Yes	*Parking Ample*
Room TV No	*Room service All day*
Closed Oct–Easter	

■ Prices quoted for the Republic of Ireland are in Irish punts.

Ard na Greine
Schull

£E
Map 19 A6 Co. Cork
Skibbereen (028) 28181
Owner managers Frank & Rhona O'Sullivan
Credit Amex, Diners, Visa

The Fastnet Rock lighthouse provides a distant beacon to this appealing 18th-century (converted and extended) farmhouse 'twixt sea and mountains. Guests enjoy the view from the upstairs lounge, or gather round the fire in the cosy beamed bar. Cottagy-style bedrooms have tea-makers. No children under 12. No dogs.
Amenities garden.

■ Rooms 7	Confirm by 6
en suite bath/shower 7	Last dinner 8
Room phone No	Parking Ample
Room TV No	Room service Limited
Closed Oct–Easter	

Hilton Park
Scotshouse

H 64% £C
Map 18 C3 Co. Monaghan
Nr Clones
Monaghan (047) 56007
Owner managers Johnny & Lucy Madden
Credit Amex

An elegant country house set in a fine 600-acre estate, Hilton Park enjoys lovely views of woodlands, grazing cattle and a pretty lake. The place has been in the Madden family for more than 250 years, and current owners Johnny and Lucy Madden still run it very much as a private home. All the rooms have a delightfully lived-in feel; well-worn leather armchairs, fine antiques and oil paintings give plenty of character to the drawing room, and three of the bedrooms have four-poster or half-four-poster beds. Excellent breakfasts feature home-made jams and bread. No children under 12. No dogs.
Amenities garden, 9-hole golf course, croquet, shooting, coarse fishing, boating.

■ Rooms 5	Confirm by arrang.
en suite bath/shower 2	Last dinner 8
Room phone No	Parking Ample
Room TV No	Room service None
Closed Oct–Mar	

■ Our inspectors never book in the name of Egon Ronay's Guides; they disclose their identity only after paying their bills.

Ballymaloe House
Shanagarry

HR 63% £C/D
Map 19 C6 Co. Cork
Nr Midleton
Cork (021) 652531. Tlx 75208
Owner managers Mr & Mrs Allen
Credit Access, Amex, Diners, Visa

Standing in delightful sheep-grazed parkland, this rambling hotel is run with unfailing charm and efficiency by the Allen family and their staff. Day rooms are splendidly relaxing, and accommodation ranges from traditional, with antiques and huge bathrooms, to three stylishly redecorated ground-floor rooms and some pretty, more modern annexe rooms. Excellent breakfast. No dogs. *Amenities* garden, outdoor swimming pool, tennis, croquet, coarse fishing.

■ Rooms 30	Confirm by arrang.
en suite bath/shower 30	Last dinner 9.30
Direct dial Yes	Parking Ample
Room TV No	Room service All day

Ballymaloe House Restaurant ★ ♦ �

A civilised, relaxing restaurant comprising three handsome rooms filled with fine original pictures. Myrtle Allen presides over the kitchen, where prime local produce is handled with evident pride and care. Fish and seafood are among the best choices – crayfish with cream and fresh herbs, monkfish with red pepper sauce, brill stuffed with lobster – but a fine meaty alternative is braised lamb with garlic and spring onions. French peasant soup with basil is a super starter, and fruit pies and sorbets typify the simple, delicious sweets. Vegetarian main dishes available. Excellent wines with a strong showing of clarets and 1978 Rhônes.
Specialities oysters in champagne sauce, Ballycotton poached salmon hollandaise, noisettes of spring lamb with mint butter, Irish rhubarb cake.

♀ Well-chosen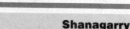

■ Set L £9.50	L at 1
Set D £19	D 7–9.30
About £53 for two	Seats 80 Parties 25
Closed 3 days Xmas	

■ If we recommend meals in a hotel or inn, a separate entry is made for its restaurant.

Shannon International Hotel — Shannon

H **61% £C** ♿
Map 19 B5 Co. Clare
Shannon Airport
Shannon (061) 61122. Tlx 24018
Credit Access, Amex, Diners, Visa

Geared to the needs of the air traveller, this modern no-frills airport hotel provides porterage from foyer to terminal and flight information on a TV screen. Bedrooms are roomy and well designed, with excellent little bathrooms. Staff go about their business briskly and amiably. No dogs. *Amenities* garden, in-house movies (free), laundry service.

■ *Rooms* 120	*Confirm by* 6
en suite bath/shower 120	*Last dinner* 8.45
Direct dial Yes	*Parking* Ample
Room TV Yes	*Room service* 24 hours
Closed 1 Nov–1 Apr	

Sligo Park Hotel — Sligo

H **55% £D/E**
Map 18 B2 Co. Sligo
Pearse Road
Sligo (071) 60291. Tlx 40397
Credit Access, Amex, Diners, Visa

A good show of flowers and shrubs surrounds the entrance to this modern low-rise hotel on the outskirts of Sligo (Dublin road). Beyond the foyer-lounge there's a roomy bar furnished with a mixture of button-back banquettes and upholstered cane. Bedrooms are bright and cheerful with simple units and neat bathrooms. *Amenities* garden, games room, in-house movies (free), laundry service, 24-hour lounge service.

■ *Rooms* 60	*Confirm by* 6
en suite bath/shower 60	*Last dinner* 9
Direct dial Yes	*Parking* Ample
Room TV Yes	*Room service* 24 hours

Bridge House Hotel — Spiddal

I **£E**
Map 19 B4 Co. Galway
Galway (091) 83118
Owner manager Michael Clancy
Credit Access, Visa

All shines like a new pin at this neatly painted pebbledash hotel. Guests can relax in the spacious foyer-lounge or upstairs TV lounge. There are also plenty of comfortable chairs in the panelled bar. Simply furnished bedrooms offer modest comforts for overnight accommodation. No dogs. *Amenities* garden, riding, laundry service, coffee shop (8am–10pm).

■ *Rooms* 14	*Confirm by* 7
en suite bath/shower 8	*Last dinner* 10
Room phone No	*Parking* Ample
Room TV No	*Room service* All day
Closed 1 wk Xmas	

■ When calling a Dublin number from outside the Republic, dial 00 before the number we print, e.g. Berkeley Court is 0001 601711.

■ For the rest of the Republic, dial 010-353, then the number we print less the initial zero, e.g. Park Hotel Kenmare is 010-353 64 41200.

Ardree Hotel — Waterford

H **61% £C/D**
Map 19 C5 Co. Waterford
Ferrybank
Waterford (051) 32111. Tlx 80684
Owner manager Anthony Breen
Credit Access, Amex, Diners, Visa

A modern hotel whose parkland setting affords views of both town and estuary. Decent-sized bedrooms (all facing the town) have functional furnishings and pretty duvets. Cheerful main bar. Extensive meeting facilities. Refurbishment would be welcome. No dogs. *Amenities* garden, tennis, in-house movies (free).

■ *Rooms* 100	*Confirm by* 7
en suite bath/shower 100	*Last dinner* 9.15
Direct dial Yes	*Parking* Ample
Room TV Yes	*Room service* 24 hours
Closed 25 Dec	

Granville Hotel   Waterford

H 69% £D
Map 19 C5 Co. Waterford
Meacher's Quay
Waterford (051) 55111. Tlx 80188
Owner managers Liam & Ann Cusack
Credit Access, Amex, Diners, Visa

A friendly welcome and good modern accommodation at this former coaching inn by the river Suir. Bedrooms have decent reproduction pieces, and are kept in tip-top repair. There's a pillared lounge and panelled bar. No dogs.
Amenities satellite TV, in-house movies (free), laundry service, grill room (10am–10.30pm).

■ *Rooms* 66	*Confirm by arrang.*
en suite bath/shower 66	*Last dinner* 9.30
Direct dial Yes	*Parking* Limited
Room TV Yes	*Room service* 24 hours
Closed 2 days Xmas	

Tower Hotel   Waterford

H 60% £D
Map 19 C5 Co. Waterford
The Mall
Waterford (051) 75801. Tlx 80699
Credit Access, Amex, Diners, Visa

On the quayside at the eastern end of town, this modern hotel provides good function facilities and modest overnight comforts. Good-sized bedrooms are furnished in plain, contemporary style and all have adequate bathrooms. Most inviting of the day rooms is a lofty, mahogany-panelled bar.
Amenities 24-hour lounge service.

■ *Rooms* 80	*Confirm by* 6
en suite bath/shower 80	*Last dinner* 10
Room phone Yes	*Parking* Ample
Room TV Yes	*Room service* 24 hours
Closed 2 days Xmas	

■ Any person using our name to obtain free hospitality is a fraud. Proprietors, please inform the police and us.

Huntsman   Waterville

RR ⚃ ⅙ **Map 19 A6** Co. Kerry
Waterville (0667) 4124
Credit Access, Amex, Diners, Visa

Owner managers Raymond and Deirdre Hunt's delightfully unpretentious restaurant, where sweeping views out to sea make the perfect accompaniment to deliciously fresh seafood, simply and lovingly prepared by Raymond to keep all its flavour. Several menus make for ample choice, from seafood bisque to sole dieppoise or salmon in white wine, as well as tempting meat dishes like noisettes of Kerry lamb and steak au poivre. There are some nice vegetables, too, like ratatouille and braised celery, and excellent brown bread. Well-kept Irish cheeses. Simple enjoyable sweets. Skilfully chosen wines. ♥

■ *Set L* £11·50	*L* 12–3
Set D £17·50	*D* 6–10
(6–7pm £10·50)	*Parking* Ample
About £48 *for two*	*Seats* 80
Closed Nov–mid Mar	*Parties* 80
Bedrooms £E/F	
Rooms 6	*With bath/shower* 6

Accommodation is available in prettily decorated twin rooms or in self-catering two-bedroom apartments which have TV. No dogs.

Waterville Lake Hotel   Waterville

H 63% £C/D
Map 19 A6 Co. Kerry
Waterville (0667) 4133. Tlx 73806
Credit Access, Amex, Diners, Visa

A long, low, modern hotel with extensive leisure facilities, a championship golf course and a secluded setting by lovely Lough Currane. Bedrooms are bright and practical, with excellent bathrooms; there are several handsome suites. Day rooms include a cheerful pine-clad bar.
Amenities garden, indoor swimming pool, sauna, solarium, whirlpool bath, tennis, golf course, riding, game fishing, snooker, laundry service.

■ *Rooms* 85	*Confirm by arrang.*
en suite bath/shower 85	*Last dinner* 10.30
Direct dial Yes	*Parking* Ample
Room TV Yes	*Room service* 24 hours
Closed 1 Nov–1 Apr	

White's Hotel

H **58% £D/E**
Map 19 D5 Co. Wexford
George Street
Wexford (053) 22311. Tlx 80630
Owner managers John & Ann Small
Credit Access, Amex, Diners, Visa
  Long-time family owners (over 200 years) maintain old world tradition of this rambling town-centre hotel. Improvements keep things

shipshape everywhere. There's a spacious fire-warmed reception and a smart bar-lounge. Bedrooms are comfortable. *Amenities* coffee shop (8am–10pm), 24-hour lounge service.

■ *Rooms* 75	*Confirm by arrang.*
en suite bath/shower 75	*Last dinner* 9.45
Direct dial Yes	*Parking* Ample
Room TV Yes	*Room service* All day
Closed Xmas	

Old Rectory

H **61% £D/E**
Map 19 D4 Co. Wicklow
Wicklow (0404) 67048
Owner managers Paul & Linda Saunders
  A warm welcome from friendly owners Paul and Linda Saunders is guaranteed at this small Georgian house located just outside Wicklow on the Dublin road. Drinks are served beside a blazing log fire in the beautifully restored lounge,

overlooking the well-tended gardens. Bedrooms are bright and airy, with antiques or neat modern units. All have private shower rooms. Dogs in kennels only. *Amenities* garden.

■ *Rooms* 5	*Confirm by* 6
en suite bath/shower 4	*Last dinner* 9
Room phone Yes	*Parking* Ample
Room TV No	*Room service* All day
Closed end Oct–Easter	

Aherne's Seafood Restaurant

R ♀ **Map 19 C6** Co. Cork
163 North Main Street
Youghal (024) 92424
Credit Access, Amex, Diners, Visa
  Tanks of oysters, mussels and lobsters await customers' inspection at the Fitzgibbon family's excellent seafood restaurant. Other fishy delights include huge prawns, superb smoked salmon and Chablis-sauced brill. Two meat dishes. Delicious

puds. Wines include a splendid Marquis de Goulaine Muscadet. No children under ten.

♀ Well-chosen ☺

■ *Set L* £8·50	*L* 12.30–2.15
About £45 *for two*	*D* 6.30–10,
Seats 60	*Sun* 6.30–9.30
Parties 60	*Parking* Ample
Closed L Sun, all Mon (except July & Aug), Good Fri & 4 days Xmas	

AN OFFER FOR ANSWERS

A DISCOUNT ON THE NEXT GUIDE

■ Readers' answers to questionnaires included in the Guide prove invaluable to us in planning future editions, either through their reactions to the contents of the current Guide, or through the tastes and inclinations indicated. Please send this tear-out page to us *after you have used the Guide for some time*, addressing the envelope to:

**Egon Ronay's Guides
2nd Floor
Greencoat House
Francis Street
London SW1P 1DH**

■ As a token of thanks for your help, we will enable respondents to obtain the 1988 Guide post free from us at a $33\frac{1}{3}$% discount off the retail price. We will send you an order form before publication, but answering the questionnaire imposes no obligation to purchase.
All answers will be treated in confidence.

**This offer closes 31 January 1988.
Open to UK residents only.**

---

1 Are You

Male? ☐   Under 21? ☐   31–45? ☐   over 65? ☐

Female? ☐   21–30? ☐   46–65? ☐

---

2 Your occupation

....

---

3 Do you have any previous editions of this Guide?

1985 ☐   1986 ☐   1987 ☐

---

4 Do you refer to this Guide

Four times a week? ☐   Once a week? ☐

Three times a week? ☐   Once a fortnight? ☐

Twice a week? ☐   Once a month? ☐

---

5 How many people, apart from yourself, are likely to consult this Guide (including those in your home and place of work)?

Male? ☐   Female? ☐

---

6 Are you likely to use the 'Bargain Break' Section?

Yes? ☐   No? ☐

---

7 Do you have our 'Just a Bite' Guide?

1985 ☐   1986 ☐   1987 ☐

8 Do you have our Pub Guide?

1985 ☐   1986 ☐   1987 ☐

9 How many times have you travelled overseas in the past year?

....

10 How many nights have you spent in hotels during the past year?

....

11 Do you occupy more than one home?

Yes ☐   No ☐

Do you own the house you live in?

Yes ☐   No ☐

12 Your car

type .... year ....

13 What is your daily newspaper?

....

14 Which of the following credit cards do you use?

Access ☐   Diners ☐

American Express ☐   Visa ☐

15 What fields would you like us to survey or what improvements do you suggest?

....

....

....

■ Please *print* your name and address here if you would like us to send you a pre-publication order form for the 1989 Hotel & Restaurant Guide.

Name ....

Address ....

....

....

Proposed Cellnet Coverage at mid 1988

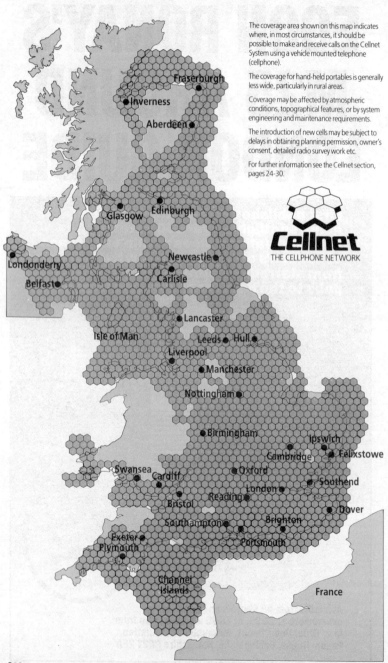

The coverage area shown on this map indicates where, in most circumstances, it should be possible to make and receive calls on the Cellnet System using a vehicle mounted telephone (cellphone).

The coverage for hand-held portables is generally less wide, particularly in rural areas.

Coverage may be affected by atmospheric conditions, topographical features, or by system engineering and maintenance requirements.

The introduction of new cells may be subject to delays in obtaining planning permission, owner's consent, detailed radio survey work etc.

For further information see the Cellnet section, pages 24-30.

Cellnet
THE CELLPHONE NETWORK

MAPS

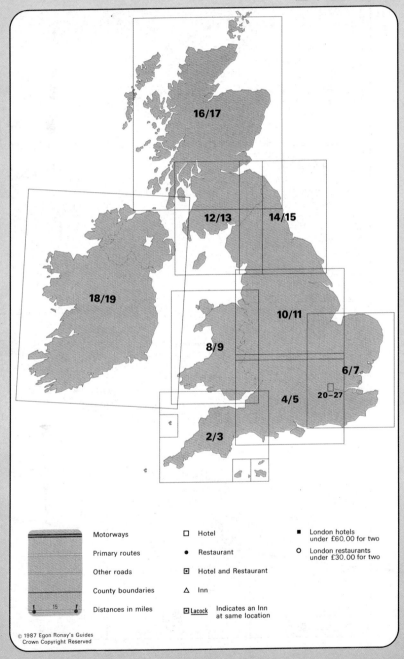

Motorways	□ Hotel	■ London hotels under £60.00 for two
Primary routes	● Restaurant	○ London restaurants under £30.00 for two
Other roads	◙ Hotel and Restaurant	
County boundaries	△ Inn	
Distances in miles	◙ <u>Lacock</u> Indicates an Inn at same location	

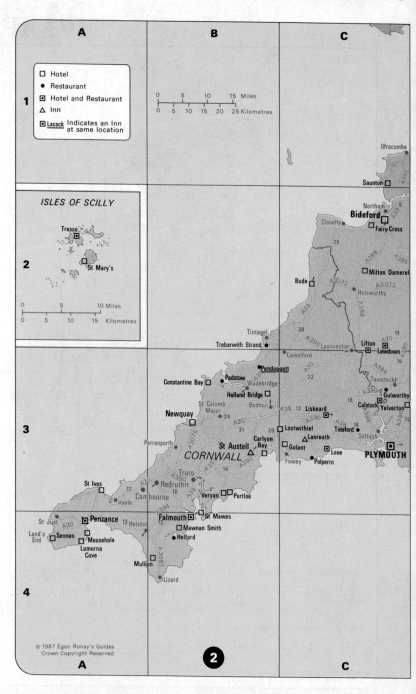

A   B   C

☐ Hotel
● Restaurant
⊡ Hotel and Restaurant
△ Inn
⊡ <u>Lacock</u> Indicates an Inn at same location

0 5 10 15 Miles
0 5 10 15 20 25 Kilometres

ISLES OF SCILLY

Tresco
St Mary's

0 5 10 Miles
0 5 10 15 Kilometres

Ilfracombe
Saunton
Northam
Bideford
Clovelly
Fairy Cross
26
Milton Damerel
Holsworthy
Bude
A3072
A3072
Tintagel
Trebarwith Strand
30
Camelford
Launceston
Lifton
Lewdown
Pendoggett
Padstow
Tavistock
Constantine Bay
Wadebridge
22
Helland Bridge
Bodmin
Gulworthy
St Columb Major
24
A38 13 Liskeard
Calstock
Yelverton
Newquay
A30
A390
18
A30
Perranporth
A3075
20 Lostwithiel
Tideford
Saltash
St Austell Carlyon Bay
Golant
△ Lanreath
CORNWALL △
Looe
PLYMOUTH
Fowey
Polperro
Truro
A390
14
31
A390
St Ives
17
Redruth 11
Cambourne
10
Veryan
Portloe
Hayle
Falmouth St Mawes
St Just
Penzance 13 Helston
Land's End
Sennen
Mawnan Smith
Mousehole
Helford
Lamorna Cove
Mullion
A3083
Lizard

© 1987 Egon Ronay's Guides
Crown Copyright Reserved

A   ❷   C

1

2

3

4

GUIDE TO HEALTHY EATING OUT

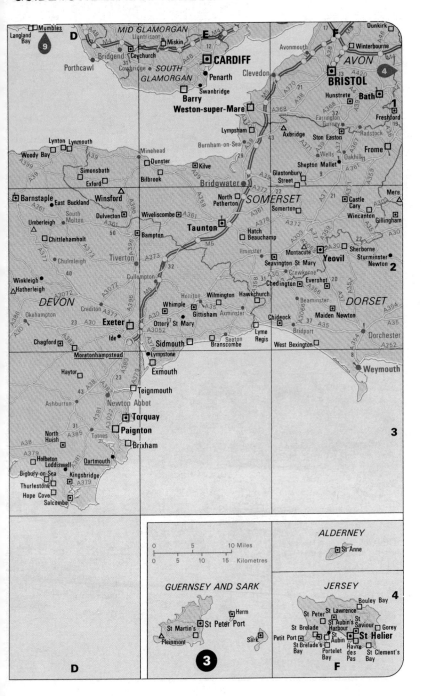

GUIDE TO THE LAKE DISTRICT AND YORKSHIRE DALES

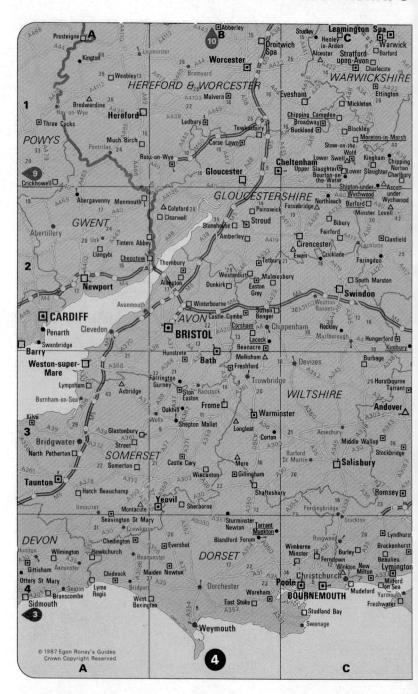

© 1987 Egon Ronay's Guides
Crown Copyright Reserved

M25 AROUND LONDON GUIDE

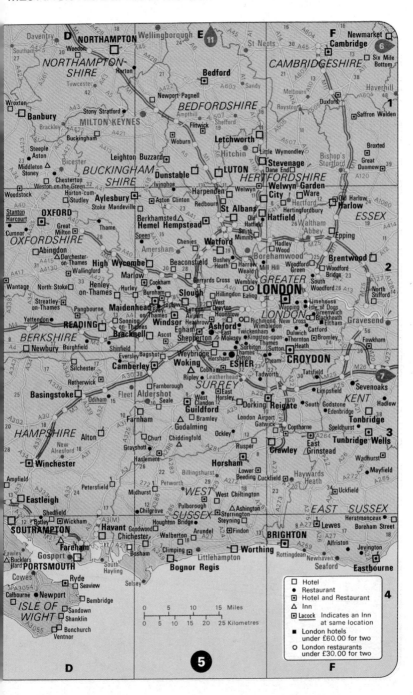

JUST A BITE GUIDE 1988

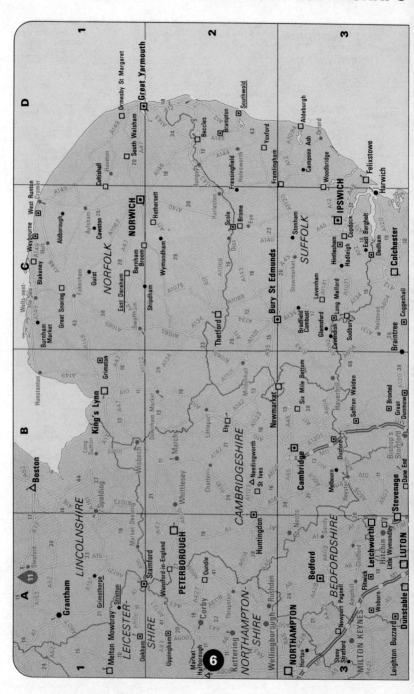

GOOD FOOD IN PUBS & BARS 1988 GUIDE

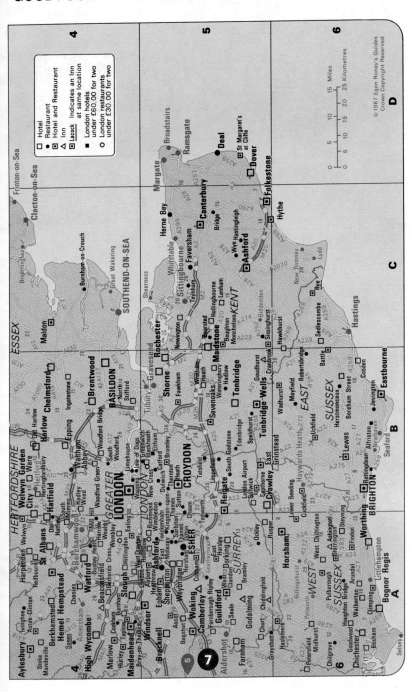

GUIDE TO HEALTHY EATING OUT

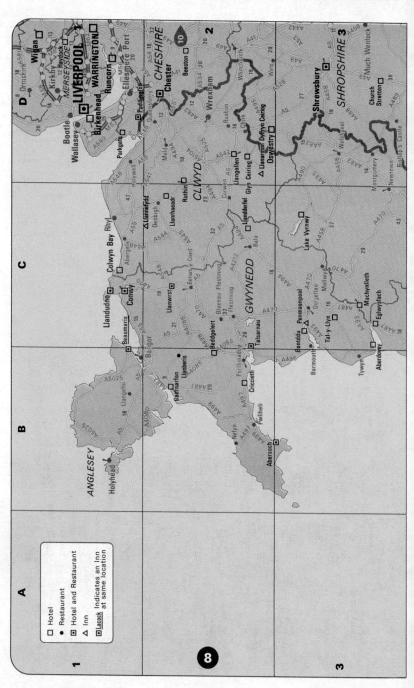

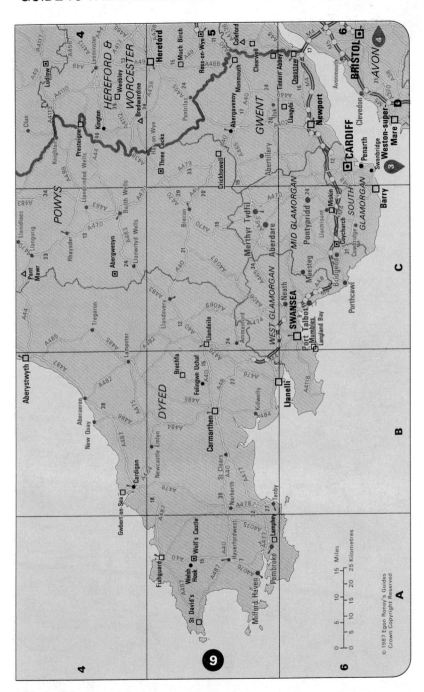

JUST A BITE GUIDE 1988

GOOD FOOD IN PUBS & BARS 1988 GUIDE

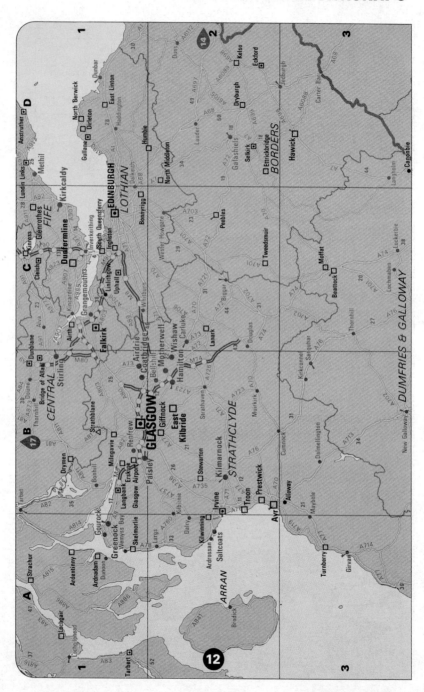

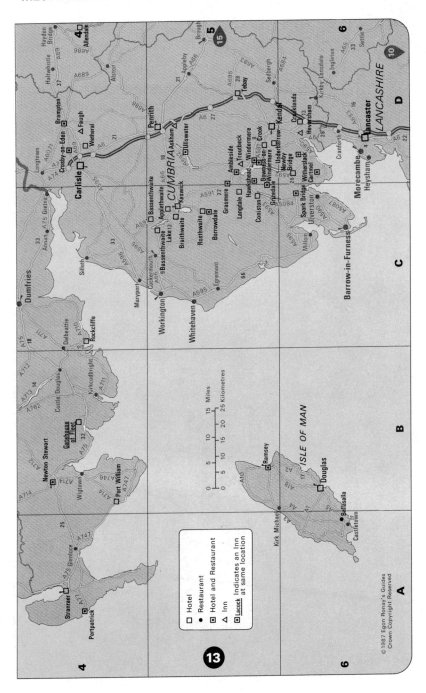

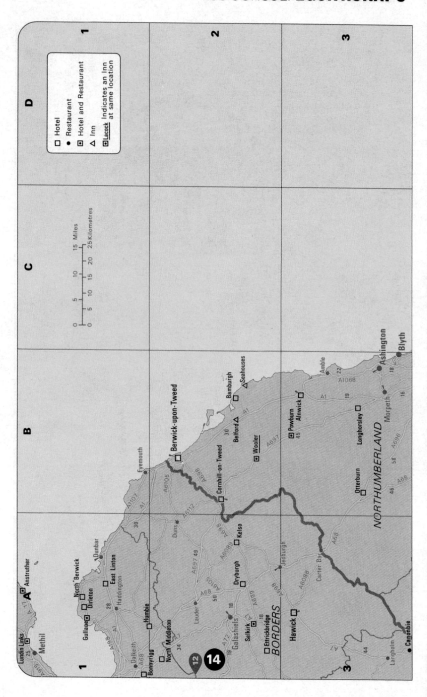

GOOD FOOD IN PUBS & BARS 1988 GUIDE

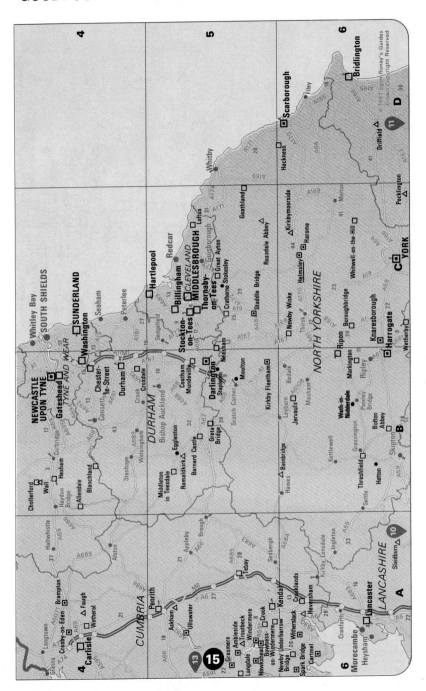

JUST A BITE GUIDE 1988

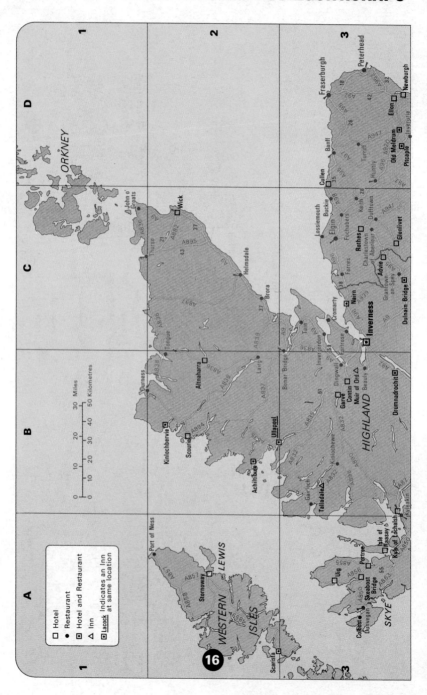

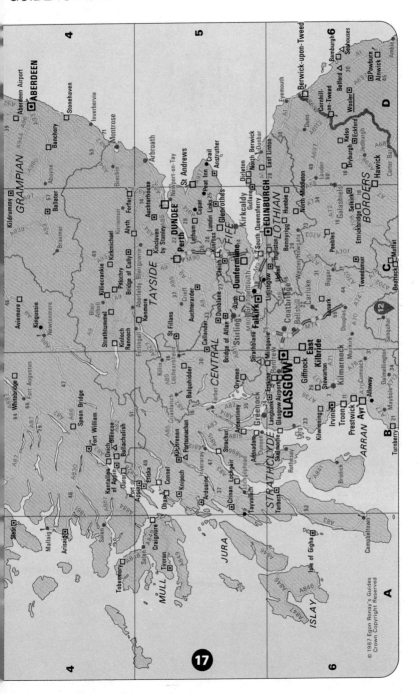

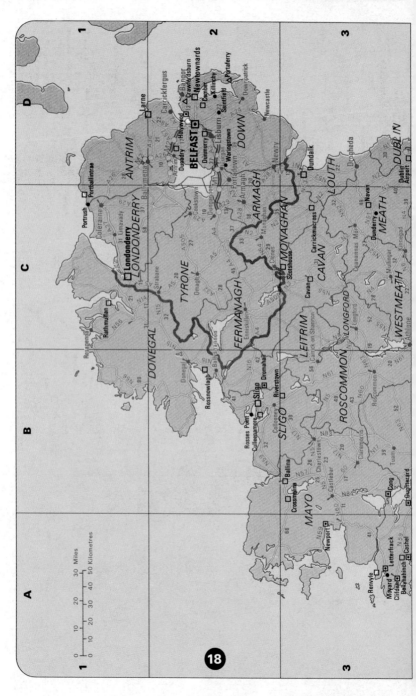

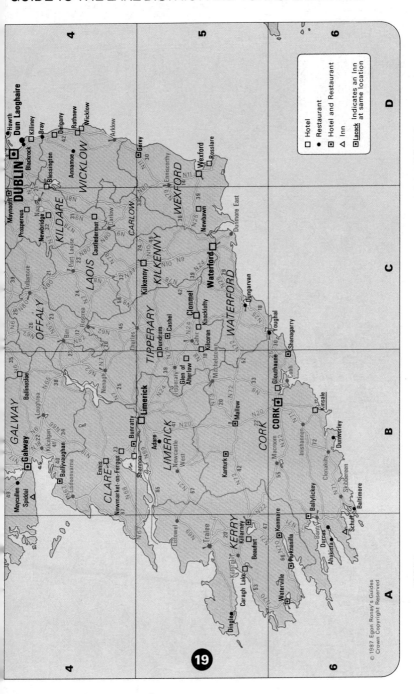

19

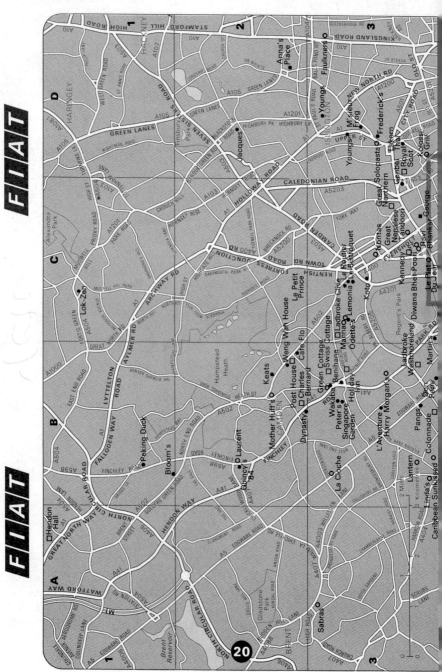

21

F I A T See pages 144-147 for list of dealers in London

Legend:
- □ Hotel
- ● Restaurant
- ⊡ Hotel and Restaurant
- ■ London hotels under £60.00 for two
- ○ London restaurants under £30.00 for two

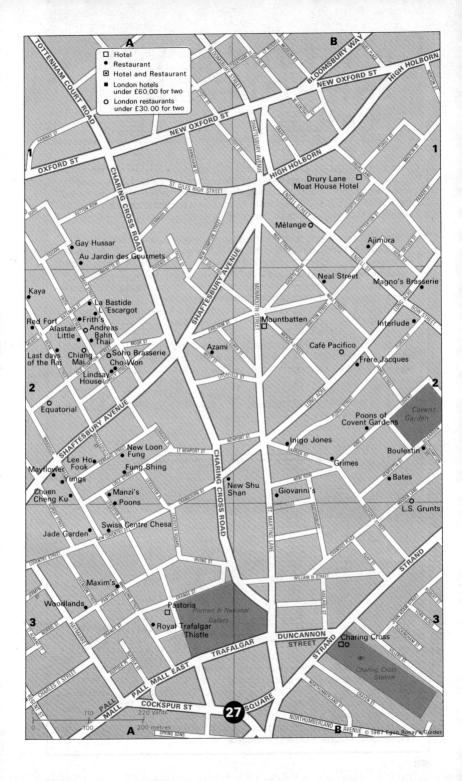

Legend

□ Hotel
● Restaurant
⊡ Hotel and Restaurant
■ London hotels under £60.00 for two
○ London restaurants under £30.00 for two

TOTTENHAM COURT ROAD

BLOOMSBURY WAY
NEW OXFORD ST
HIGH HOLBORN

OXFORD ST
CHARING CROSS ROAD
NEW OXFORD ST
SHAFTESBURY AVENUE
HIGH HOLBORN

ST GILES HIGH STREET

Drury Lane
Moat House Hotel

Mélange ○

Ajimura ●

Gay Hussar ●
Au Jardin des Gourmets ●

Neal Street ●
Magno's Brasserie ●

Kaya ●

La Bastide ●
L'Escargot ●
Frith's ●
Red Fort ●
Alastair Little ●
Andreas Bahn Thai ○

MONMOUTH STREET
SHAFTESBURY AVENUE

Mountbatten ⊡

Interlude ●

Last days of the Raj ●
Chiang Mai ●
Soho Brasserie ●
Cho-Won ●
Azami ●

Café Pacifico ○

Frère Jacques ●

Lindsay House ●

SHAFTESBURY AVENUE

LONG ACRE

Equatorial ○

Poons of Covent Gardens ●

Covent Garden

New Loon Fung ●
Lee Ho Fook ●
Fung Shing ●
Mayflower ●
Yungs ●
Chuen Cheng Ku ●
Manzi's ●
Poons ●

Inigo Jones ●

Grimes ●

Boulestin ●

Bates ●

New Shu Shan ●
Giovanni's ●

CHARING CROSS ROAD

L.S. Grunts ○

Jade Garden ●
Swiss Centre Chesa ●

ST MARTINS LANE

STRAND

Maxim's ●
Woodlands ●

Pastoria □
Portrait & National Gallery

Royal Trafalgar Thistle ●

DUNCANNON STREET

Charing Cross ⊡

STRAND

TRAFALGAR

Charing Cross Station

PALL MALL
PALL MALL EAST
COCKSPUR ST

27

SQUARE

NORTHUMBERLAND AVENUE

0 110 220 yards
0 100 200 metres
SPRING GARDENS

© 1987 Egon Ronay's Guides

CREDIT, TRAVEL AND ENTERTAINMENT CARDS

Have you ever gone into a restaurant with a wallet full of notes and still given yourself heartburn worrying if you have enough to pay the bill? Or reached for your cheque book, found you've forgotten your chequecard and then worried about whether you can afford to write the cheque in the first place? Or if the bill is more than £50, agonised about whether they'll take more than one cheque?

When you carry a credit card into the great majority of establishments you also carry peace of mind, with none of the risks of carrying a lot of cash; no fretting about whether your guest will order a fat cigar with his brandy; no reaching for the calculator before calling for a bottle of birthday bubbly; no public counting out of notes when the bill comes; none of the bother of writing a cheque. Women are increasingly playing the role of host in restaurants, and the quick, discreet means of payment by credit card eliminates embarrassment both for them and for their guests.

In hotels, too, where items like telephone calls cannot always be calculated in advance, credit cards are a boon: who wants to spend a sleepless night wondering if that last long-distance call was the one that broke the bank or drained the ready cash?

And when the credit card bill comes in, the payment is as simple and painless as the rest of the transaction.

DINERS CLUB INTERNATIONAL

Head Office Address: Diners Club House, Kingsmead, Farnborough, Hants. GU14 7SR. Tel: (0252) 516261.
Eire Address: Russell Court, St. Stephens Green, Dublin 2. Tel: (0001) 779444.
The Diners Club Card was the first card without a pre-set spending limit and is warmly accepted wherever you do business around the world. The Diners Club is the only charge or credit card to offer its members a second card free, to separate personal expenditure from business expenses, as well as lounges at international airports, including Heathrow.

ACCESS

Headquarters Address: Joint Credit Card Co. Ltd (a credit broker) 200 Priory Crescent, Southend on Sea, Essex SS2 6QQ. Tel: Southend (0702) 352211. For written details about Access cards apply at any bank displaying the Access sign or write to the above address. MasterCard and Eurocard are accepted at all Access retail and service establishments.

BARCLAYCARD

Headquarters Address: Barclaycard Centre, Northampton NN1 1SG. Tel: Northampton (0604) 21100. Holders of all VISA cards are welcome wherever they see the familiar blue, white and gold badge. Most of the best-known hotels and restaurants in the United Kingdom welcome Barclaycard.

AMERICAN EXPRESS

Around the world and around the corner, you'll find the American Express Card is warmly welcomed by leading Hotels, Restaurants, Travel Companies and Shops. As a Cardmember you have the freedom of *no pre-set spending limit,* and all the benefits and privileges the Card confers. Apply today!

Membership Application: American Express Europe Ltd, Amex House, P.O. Box 63, Edward Street, Brighton BN2 1YE. Or phone (0273) 696933.

READERS' COMMENTS

■ Please use this sheet for complaints on establishments included in the Guide or for recommending new establishments which you would like our inspectors to visit.

■ Please post to Egon Ronay's Guides, Second Floor Greencoat House, Francis Street, London SW1P 1DH.

Please use an up to date Guide. We publish annually. (1988)

Your recommendation or complaint

Name and address of establishment

Your name (block letters)

Address (block letters)

N.B. We regret that owing to the enormous volume of readers' communications received each year, we will be unable to acknowledge these forms, but they will certainly be seriously considered.

READERS' COMMENTS

■ Please use this sheet for complaints on establishments included in the Guide or for recommending new establishments which you would like our inspectors to visit.

■ Please post to Egon Ronay's Guides, Second Floor Greencoat House, Francis Street, London SW1P 1DH.

Please use an up to date Guide. We publish annually. (1988)

Your recommendation or complaint

Name and address of establishment

Your name (block letters)

Address (block letters)

N.B. We regret that owing to the enormous volume of readers' communications received each year, we will be unable to acknowledge these forms, but they will certainly be seriously considered.